THE

HISTORICAL ANTIQUITIES

OF

HERTFORDSHIRE:

WITH THE

ORIGINAL OF COUNTIES, HUNDREDS OR WAPENTAKES, BOROUGHS, CORPORATIONS, TOWNS, PARISHES, VILLAGES, AND HAMLETS;

THE

FOUNDATION AND ORIGIN OF MONASTERIES, CHURCHES, ADVOWSONS, TYTHES, RECTORIES, IMPROPRIATIONS, AND VICARAGES, IN GENERAL;

DESCRIBING THOSE OF THIS COUNTY IN PARTICULAR: AS ALSO THE SEVERAL

HONORS, MANNORS, CASTLES, SEATS AND PARKS OF THE NOBILITY AND GENTRY; AND THE SUCCESSION OF THE LORDS OF EACH MANNOR THEREIN.

ALSO

The Characters of the Abbots of St. Albans.

Faithfully collected from Public Records, Leiger Books, Ancient Manuscripts, Charters, Evidences, and other Select Authorities.

TOGETHER WITH AN

EXACT TRANSCRIPT OF DOMESDAY BOOK SO FAR AS CONCERNS THIS SHIRE, AND THE TRANSLATION THEREOF IN ENGLISH.

TO WHICH ARE ADDED,

The Epitaphs and Memorable Inscriptions in all the Parishes.

AND LIKEWISE

THE BLAZON OF THE COATS OF ARMS OF THE SEVERAL NOBLEMEN AND GENTLEMEN, PROPRIETORS IN THE SAME.

ILLUSTRATED WITH

A large Map of the County, a Prospect of Hertford, the Ichnography of St. Albans and Hitchin, and many Sculptures of the principal Edifices and Monuments.

BY

SIR HENRY CHAUNCY, KT.

SERJEANT AT LAW.

Nos Patriæ Fines et dulcia scripsimus Arva.—Virgil.

Vol. II.

LONDON:

Printed for Ben. Griffin in the Great Old Baily, Sam. Keble at the Turks-head in Fleet-street, Dan. Browne at the Black Swan and Bible without Temple Bar, Dan. Midwinter and Tho. Leigh at the Rose and Crown in St. Pauls Church-yard. MDCC.

BISHOPS STORTFORD:

REPRINTED AND PUBLISHED BY J. M. MULLINGER;

B. J. HOLDSWORTH, 18, ST. PAUL'S CHURCH YARD, LONDON.

MDCCCXXVI.

J. M. Mullinger, Printer, Bishops Stortford, Herts

THE THIRD DIVISION OF THIS COUNTY.

CONTAINING

THE HUNDREDS

OF

BRADEWATER & HITCHIN.

THE Hundreds of 𝔅𝔯𝔞𝔡𝔢𝔴𝔞𝔱𝔢𝔯 and 𝔥𝔦𝔱𝔠𝔥𝔦𝔫, Parcel of the Possessions of the Crown, make the third Division of this County; and the Sheriff hath held the Courts for these Hundreds, from time to time, with the County Court at 𝔖𝔱𝔢𝔳𝔢𝔫𝔢𝔡𝔤𝔢, and accounted yearly in the *Exchequer* for the Profits of them; the Justices of the Peace do generally hold their Privy Sessions, and keep their publick Meetings at the same Place; but their House of Correction for both these Hundreds is in 𝔥𝔦𝔱𝔠𝔥𝔦𝔫. In treating of them severally, I shall begin with the Hundred of 𝔅𝔯𝔞𝔡𝔢𝔴𝔞𝔱𝔢𝔯, for that it is next in Course, and extends from 𝔗𝔬𝔱𝔱𝔢𝔯𝔦𝔡𝔤𝔢 in the South to 𝔅𝔞𝔩𝔡𝔬𝔠𝔨 in the North, which is two and twenty Miles in Length; it is bounded on the North with the Hundred of 𝔒𝔡𝔰𝔢𝔭, on the East with the Hundreds of 𝔅𝔯𝔞𝔲𝔤𝔥𝔦𝔫𝔤 and 𝔥𝔢𝔯𝔱𝔣𝔬𝔯𝔡, on the South with 𝔐𝔦𝔡𝔡𝔩𝔢𝔰𝔢𝔵, and on the West with the Hundreds of 𝔠𝔞𝔦𝔰𝔥𝔬𝔢 and 𝔥𝔦𝔱𝔠𝔥𝔦𝔫; it is denominated from the Vill of 𝔅𝔯𝔞𝔡𝔢𝔴𝔞𝔱𝔢𝔯, and contains the following Parishes or Hamlets, which are divided between three High Constables, whereof the first has the Parishes and Hamlets of 𝔗𝔬𝔱𝔱𝔢𝔯𝔦𝔡𝔤𝔢, 𝔥𝔞𝔱𝔣𝔦𝔢𝔩𝔡, 𝔇𝔦𝔤𝔰𝔴𝔢𝔩𝔩, 𝔚𝔢𝔩𝔴𝔦𝔫𝔢, 𝔈𝔭𝔬𝔱 𝔖𝔱. 𝔓𝔢𝔱𝔢𝔯, 𝔈𝔦𝔬𝔱 𝔖𝔱. 𝔏𝔞𝔴𝔯𝔢𝔫𝔠𝔢; the second 𝔇𝔞𝔱𝔠𝔥𝔴𝔬𝔯𝔱𝔥 𝔚𝔞𝔱𝔱𝔬𝔫, 𝔖𝔞𝔠𝔬𝔪𝔟𝔢, 𝔐𝔲𝔫𝔡𝔬𝔫 𝔉𝔯𝔢𝔢𝔴𝔢𝔩𝔩, 𝔐𝔲𝔫𝔡𝔬𝔫 𝔉𝔲𝔯𝔫𝔟𝔞𝔩𝔩, 𝔕𝔬𝔴𝔢𝔫𝔭, 𝔅𝔢𝔫𝔦𝔫𝔤𝔱𝔬𝔫, 𝔚𝔞𝔩𝔨𝔢𝔯𝔫𝔢, and 𝔄𝔰𝔱𝔬𝔫; and the other High Constable has 𝔎𝔫𝔢𝔟𝔴𝔬𝔯𝔱𝔥, 𝔖𝔱𝔢𝔟𝔢𝔫𝔢𝔡𝔤𝔢, 𝔚𝔦𝔪𝔬𝔫𝔡𝔩𝔢𝔭 𝔓𝔞𝔯𝔳𝔞, 𝔚𝔦𝔪𝔬𝔫𝔡𝔩𝔢𝔭 𝔐𝔞𝔤𝔫𝔞, 𝔊𝔯𝔞𝔟𝔢𝔩𝔢𝔭, 𝔠𝔥𝔦𝔰𝔣𝔦𝔢𝔩𝔡, 𝔅𝔬𝔵, 𝔚𝔢𝔰𝔱𝔬𝔫, 𝔅𝔞𝔩𝔡𝔬𝔠𝔨, 𝔚𝔦𝔩𝔦𝔢𝔫, and 𝔏𝔢𝔱𝔠𝔥𝔴𝔬𝔯𝔱𝔥. In Pursuance to this Method, I shall begin with

2

TOTTERIDGE,

WHICH was denominated by the *Saxons* from the Situation thereof upon the Ridge of an high Hill; it seems that it was waste Ground belonging to the King's Revenue at 𝔥eathfield; for there is no Mention made of it in *Domesdei Book*, therefore King *Edgar* might convey it as a Member thereof, under the Name of 𝔥eathfield, unto the Church of Ely, which in all Probability, was the Reason it was in old time reputed Part of that Parish; and the same Church did enjoy it until the Reign of Queen *Elizabeth*, when the Bishop of Ely past it away, with the Mannor of 𝔥atfield, to Queen *Elizabeth*, in Consideration of an Annuity of 1500*l.* paid yearly out of the *Exchequer* to the Bishops of that See.

That Queen, *Anno* 32 *Regni sui*, granted it to *John Cage*, as Parcel of the Possessions of the Bishoprick of Ely, from whence it came to —— *Peacock*, from whence it descended to *Richard Peacock*, who married *Rechard*, one of the Daughters of *Michael Grigge*, Alderman of London, by whom he had Issue fourteen Children, *Richard, William, Richard, Edward, Michael,* and *Michael, Mary, Anne* married to *Reginald Williams, Rechard* married to Sir *William Wilson, Elizabeth* deceased, *Dorothy* married to —— *Walker* of London, Merchant, and three other Children; and this *Richard* the Father devised it to

Rechard his Wife and her Heirs; she surviving all her Sons, who died without Issue, sold it to Sir *Paul Whichcote*, who is the present Lord hereof.

Robert Taylor, one of the Tellers in the *Exchequer*, erected a fair House in this Vill, but being indebted to the Crown, this House was extended, and Queen *Elizabeth* sold it to *Hugh Hare*, Esq. one of the Prothonotaries in the Court of *Wards*; from whom it came to *John Hare* of London, Esq. who married *Margaret* one of the Daughters of *John Crowch* of Cornbury in this County, by whom he had Issue

Hugh, who did succeed, and was created Baron of Coleraine in the Kingdom of Ireland; he married the Lady *Elizabeth* one of the Daughters of *Edward* Earl of Manchester, by whom he had Issue, *Henry, Hugh, John, Charles,* and —— *Elizabeth* married to Sir *George Fletcher* of 𝔥utton in the Forest of Cumberland, created Baronet by Patent dated the 19th Day of *February*, 1640, 16 *Car.* II. *Susan* who died single, and *Mary* married to *Erasmus Smith* of London, Merchant. He died in 1667, leaving

Henry his Heir, who succeeded, married *Constance* the Daughter and Heir of Sir *Richard Lucy*, of Broxbourne in this County, Baronet, by whom he had Issue *Hugh;* His Arms are *Gules, two Bars Or, and a Chief indented of the same.*

Guillim's
Heraldry.

The Tythes of this Vill are paid to the Parson of 𝕳at-
fieID, who always found a Curate here; yet at the time of
making the Statute, for Relief of the Poor, and ever since,
this Vill was reputed a Parish of itself, and the Inhabitants
were wont to choose Constables, Church-wardens, and Overseers of the Poor, and made Rates which were levied by
their proper Officers for Relief of the Poor, without paying any thing to the Poor of 𝕳atfeilD, or joyning them in
any Assessment with the Town of 𝕳atfeilD; and the Church
of 𝕿otteriDge have had all parochial Rights, and never con-
tributed to the Reparation of the Church of 𝕳atfeilD; but
only to their own Church, and to the Relief of their own
Poor.

Hund. of
Brabewater
Stat. 43 Eliz.
Triu. 10 Car.I
Cro. rep. 3,
fol. 374, 395.
Rot. 222.

CURATES of 𝕮otteriDge Church.

1597	*William Stanton*	1670	*Robert Parre*
1606	*Nevill Drane*	1675	*Bowes Meeke*
1619	*Josias Morison*	1679	*George White*
1646	*William Tutty*	1685	*Robert Davison*
1661	*Winceslaus Lebanus*	1690	*Matthew Breacles.*

The Church or Chapel is situated on the Hill near the middle of the
Vill, containing the Nave or Body of the Church, covered with Tyle,
with an Erection of Wood adjoyning the West End, wherein hang three
Bells, with a short Spire of Wood.

In the Church are these Inscriptions.

D; O. M.

Johannes Hare, *armiger, Londini natus Charissima et Equestris Familia in*
Agro 𝕾uff. *ineunti Ætate in Societatem Nobilium studiosorum Legum*
hujus Regni Municipatum 𝕿empli *Interioris admissus; In provectiori in*
numerum Assessorum Domus ejusdem cooptatus fuit vir pius et prudens
Patriæ vb singulares virtutes sumem Charus Curiæ Pupillorum (vulgo
Wardorum et Liberationum) Protonotarii munere solertissime et inter-
gerrime diu per functus est rei autem familiaris erat certe satis amplæ
ampliori tamen dignissime habebatur. Quisq; cujus Domus non solum
familiaribus et amicis verum etiam cujus alii modo conditionis esset hones-
tioris inter Hospitii Cujusdam liberimi semper potuit Fide an Fama
celebrior nescias inter lites foro Domi extra lites Tranquillissime tenuit.
Talis tantusq; *vir ad omniaq; optima essent natus ad meliora moriturus* 8
Kalend. Junii *Anno Domini Jesu* 1613 *Ingenti suorum Reiq; publicæ*
Damno et Dolero obdormivit.
Vixit anno 67. MCDXXI.
Margareta *pientissima et mærentissima Conjux tam Chari heu sorti matri-*
monii superstes hoc amores et pietatis Monumentum Charissimo Marito
sibiq; et ipsorum posteris sacravit.

Under this Pew lieth interred the Body of *Richard Turner,* Esq; of this
Parish, who departed this Life the 20th of *May,* 1676. *Ætat.* 66.

Hic requiescit corpus *Annæ, Roberti, et Mariæ Raworth, filii unius qu.*
anni Infantis Charissime quam Deus Opt. max. sanctorum Infantium
amantissimus inter Parentum Lachrimas et Curas, ad se revocavit, 18 die
Junii *anno Domini* 1688.

In Memory of Mrs. *Dorothy Taylor,* late Wife of Mr. *William Taylor,*
Merchant, and Daughter of *Richard Turner,* Esq; and *Dorothy* his
Wife, of this Parish; who deceased the 7th day of *December,* 1673,
and lies interred under the two Seats adjoyning. *Ætatis* 20.

Here Youth and Vertue, Grace and Beauty met,
Rose like the morning Sun, but quickly set,
In nine months space her Nuptial Race she run,
Then God exchang'd; took her, and gave a Son,

Death soon on Earth her marriage knot unty'd
That she might live with Christ a lovely Bride;
Who will not lose one Atome of her Dust;
But (rais'd in Glory) placed with the Just.

Under the same Pews lie also interred the Body of Mrs. Susanna Turner,
Daughter of the said Richard Turner, *and* Dorothy *his Wife, who deceased the 14th of* July, 1672.   *Ætat. 15. and 10 Months.*

Now take thy Rest dear Soul in thy cold Bed,
For (tho' to Heaven thy precious Soul be fled)
Thou shalt not here as one neglected lye,
But be preserv'd by Gods most watchful Eye;
Wait but a while, that thou mayst be refin'd
And thou shalt rise and leave thy dross behind,
Grace made Thee lovely and admired by all,
And sure since Grace adorn'd thee, Glory shall.

Nigh to this place resteth in hopes of a glorious Resurrection, the Body
of *Andrew Campion*, Master of Arts, and sometime Vicar of Edles-
borough, in the County of Bucks; He died the 29th day of *January*
1677, aged 42 Years.

And also the Body of *Anne*, his beloved Wife, by whom he had Issue,
eight Sons and four Daughters. She died the 27th day of *August* 1682,
aged 39 Years.

Under this Stone lye the Bodies of four of their Children, *Andrew,
Cornelius, Elizabeth* and *Dianah*, who died soon after their Father.

Also the Body of *Robert*, their Eldest Son, who died the 13th of *September* 1691, in the 27th Year of his Age.

HEATHFIELD *or* HATFIELD.

Bede, lib. 4,
cap. 17.

WHEN *Eutyches* disturbed the Faith of the Church in
Constantinople, by his Heresie, *Theodore* Archbishop of
Canterbury desirous to preserve the English Churches from
that Contagion, called a Synod of venerable Bishops and
learned Men in this Town, which the *Saxons* term'd
Heathfield, from the Situation upon an Hill, and the
Barrenness of the Soil.

Spelm. Con.
lib. 1, fol. 164.

This Synod was held on the 15th Day of the Kalends of
October, in the tenth Year of *Egfrid*, King of the *Northumbers*, the sixth Year of *Ethelred* King of the *Mertians*,
the seventeenth Year of *Advulfe*, King of the *East Angles*,
and the seventeenth Year of *Lothaire*, King of Kent;
where *Theodore* by the Grace of God, Archbishop of the
British Isles and City of Canterbury, presided, and *Sax-
vulfe* formerly an Abbot, *Adrian* the Legate, *Putta* Bishop of Rochester, *Waldhere* Bishop of London, *Cuthbald*,
an Abbot, *John* Arch-Cantor of St. *Peter's* and Abbot of
St. *Martin's* were present.

They unanimously declared the true and orthodox
Faith, in such Manner as Christ deliver'd it to his Disciples, who saw him and heard his Words, as it is contained
in the Simbol of the Holy Fathers, and as all Saints, universal Synods, and the Quire of all the learned Men of the
Cathedral Church generally deliver'd it, and following the

Doctrine of those faithful Guides divinely inspired, they unanimously believed and professed according to the holy Fathers, in truth and propriety of Speech; confessing the Father and Son, the Trinity consubstantial in Unity, and Unity in Trinity, that is one God in three Subsistences or Persons, consubstantial, of equal Glory and Honour; and after many other Speeches to the like effect, this holy Synod added this Profession.

They received the five holy Universal Synods, one held at *Nicæa* against *Arius* and his Opinions, another at *Constantinople* against *Macedonius* and *Eudoxius*, another at *Ephesus* against *Nestorius*, another at *Calcedon* against *Eutyches* and *Nestorius*, and another at *Constantinople* against *Theodorus*, *Theodoret*, and the Epistles of *Ibas*, and their Opinions against *Cyrill*, and confirmed the Synod held at *Rome* under Pope *Martin*, in the ninth Year of the Emperor *Constantine*.

Moreover, King *Etheldred* in the same Synod, ratified and confirmed whatsoever Gifts his Brethen *Penda* and *Wolfe*, and his Sisters *Kinneburgh* and *Kineswith* had given, and by Will conferred on St. *Peter* and this Abbot, and declared his Pleasure, that their Anniversary Days shall be commemorated for the good of their and his Souls : and he gave to St. *Peter* and his Church of *Medeshamsted*, the Lands called *Bredune*, *Herpingas*, *Cedenac*, &c. and the Appurtenances, with the same Liberty as he possest them, forbidding his Successors to prejudice this Gift in any thing; and if any Person shall injure the same, he prayed that the *Anathema* of the Pope and all other Bishops, may fall upon him.

The Saxon Kings possest this Vill, until King *Edgar* bestowed it on the Monks of *Ely*, and enobled that Church with such fair Priviledges and large Revenues, that it did seem to equal any Church in *England*; and in the Reign of *William* the Conqueror, it was recorded thus in *Domesdei Book*,

Terra Abbatis de Ely.

In Bradewatre Hundred. Abbas de Ely ten. Hetfelle, pro xl Hid. se defendebat. Terra est xxx car. in Dom. xx Hid. et ibi sunt ii car. et tres adhuc possunt fieri, ibi Presbiter cum xviii Vill. et xviii Bord. habent. xx car. et adhuc v car. possunt fieri ibi xii cotar. et sex Servi, et iv Molin. de xlvii sol. et iv den. prat. x car. pastur. ad pec. Silva 2000 porc. et de consuetud. Silve et Pastur. x sol. in totis valent valet, et valuit xxv lib. T.R.E. xxx lib. Hoc Manerium jacuit et jacet in Domino Ecclesiæ Ely.

The Land of the Abbot of Ely.

The Abbot of *Ely* held *Hatfeld* in the Hundred of *Bradewater*; it was rated at forty Hides, the arable is thirty Carucates, in Demesne twenty Hides, and there are two Carucates, and now three more may be made; there is a Parson with eighteen Villains and eighteen Bordars, having twenty Carucates, and now five more may be made; there are twelve Cottagers, six Servants, and four Mills of seven and forty Shillings and four Pence Rent by the Year, Meadow ten Carucates, Common of Pas-

Hund. of
Bradewater ture for the Cattle, Wood to feed two thousand Hogs, and of the Rent of the Wood and Pasture, ten Shillings a Year. In the whole Value it is worth and was worth five and twenty Pounds a Year; in the time of King *Edward* (the Confessor,) thirty Pounds a Year. This Manner did lye and now doth lye in the Jurisdiction of the Church of Ely.

The Abbots held this Church, until such time that King *H.* I. converted this Monastery into a Bishoprick, and then the Bishops held it; among whom, *Hugh* Bishop of Ely, upon Quo Warr.
6 Edw. I.
Rol. 36, cur.
recept. Scac. a *Quo Warranto* brought before *John de Reygate*, and other Justices Itinerants at Hertford, *Anno* 6 *Edw*. I. claimed by the Grants of King *Edgar*, *Edward* the Confessor, *William* the Conqueror, *Henry* I. *Richard* I. *John*, and *Henry* III. Free-warren, Soc, Sac, Toll, Them, Infangthef, and Hamsokne, Gritbruge, and all Forfeitures inflicted upon their Tenants, in their Lands or Fees, and was eased from all Matters and Return of Writs, Prison, Gallows, and Tumbrel, Chattels of Felons, with divers large Priviledges there specified in all their Lands; and he and all his Men, were quit from the Payment of Toll through all the Kingdom of England, in buying or selling of Passage Geld, Danegeld, and of the common Forfeitures in Shires and Hundreds, and all Amercements upon all his Tenants and Men in all his Fees and Lands by the Collection of his Bailiffs, to be allowed in the Court of *Exchequer*, and of all Fines imposed upon them before the Justices Itinerants, the Chattels of Felons, Fugitives, and condemned Persons; and upon the View of the Grants these Priviledges were allowed.

Fuller's Worthies, tit.
Herts. *William*, second Son to King *Edw*. III. and *Philippa* his Wife, took his Christian Name from his Grandfather *William*, Earl of Henault, and his Sirname from this Town of Hatfield, which was the Place of his Birth, where he was born *Anno* 1335.

Holl. vol. 2,
fol. 979. When King *Henry* VIII. died, the Earl of Hertford came with divers other Lords to this Place, where King *Edward* VI. was kept and educated; they conveyed him from hence with a great Number of the Nobility and Gentry, to the *Tower* of London, in Order to his Coronation. And at the time of Queen *Mary's* Death, Queen *Elizabeth* resided in Holl. vol. 2,
fol. 1170. this Palace, from whence she was removed on Wednesday the 23d of *November*, to the *Charter-house* in London, where she lodged in the Lord *North's* House, and the great Multitude of People that met her in her Passage thither, did by their Words and Countenance, express the great Joy of the Kingdom, that she was advanced to the Crown.

Fuller's Worthies, tit.
Herts. The Bishop of Ely sold this Mannor, with those of Little Hadam and Kelshall in this County, to this Queen. *Anno* 4 *Jac*. I. a Court of Survey was held for this Mannor, where it was found, that by the Custom, there is a Leet or View of Franc-pledge held on Tuesday in the Week of *Pentecost;*

and the Lord hath, and of Right ought to have all Estrays, Goods and Chattels of Felons, Fugitives, outlaw'd Persons, Waifes, and all other Royalties; and that the Fines assessed upon the Admissions of all Copyhold and Customary Tenants are at the Will of the Lord. *Hund. of Bradewater Supervis. Manden de Hatfield, 4 Jac. I.*

The Year following, King *James* exchanged this Mannor with Sir *Robert Cecil*, Kt. for Theobalds in the Parish of Cheshunt, in this County, who was made *Anno* 38 *Eliz.* one of the Queen's principal Secretaries of State; constituted Master of the Court of *Wards Anno* 41 *Eliz.*; created Lord *Cecil* of Essingdon, in the County of Rutland, at the Tower of London, on the 3d of *May, An.* 1 *Jac.* I.; confirmed in his Office of Master of the *Wards* on the 13th of *Aug.* following; created Viscount *Cranbourn* in the County of Dorset, at Whitehall, on the 20th of *August,* 2 *Jac.* I. and was the first of that Degree that wore a Coronet. Afterward advanced to the Dignity of Earl of Salisbury the 4th of *May, Anno* 3 *Jac.* I. at Greenwich; made Lord Treasurer of England 4th of *May,* 6 *Jac.* I.; installed Knight of the most noble Order of the *Garter*, and elected Chancellor of the University of Cambridge. *Bar.* vol. 3, fol. 407. Pat. 38 Eliz. p. 11. Pat. 41 Eliz. Pat. 1 Jac. I.

The Instalment of this Earl, gives me Occasion to enquire into the Original and Cause of the Order of the *Garter.*

King *Edw.* III. engaged in War for the Recovery of his Right to the Crown of France, had great Occasion for the stoutest and most famous Soldiers of that Age, to that Purpose he restored King *Arthur's* Table at Windsor, which he exhibited with magnificent Hastitudes and general Justs, that he might draw the most brave and active Spirits to his Court; and to encourage the Design, he granted Letters of safe Conduct to all those who were desirous to try their Valour at those solemn Justs, which he appointed to he held at Windsor, on Monday next after the Feast of St. *Hillary*, in the Year 1344, that he might discover the Courage and Ability of those who were most gallant and active in the Exercise of Arms: By this Means he drew hither the prime Spirits for martial Valour, from several Parts beyond the Seas, and gained the Opportunity of engaging them on his Side in the ensuing War. *Ashmole of the Garter.*

This induced *Philip de Valois*, King of France, to practice the like Course at his Court, by which Means he prevented the Knights and valiant Men of Arms, that lived near Italy and Almania, from coming hither, and brought them to his own Court in France.

When that King had thus countermined his Design, he resolved upon a more particular and select Expedient to oblige those warlike Men, whom he thought most fit to associate to himself in a firm Bond of Friendship and Honor; to that Intent he instituted this noble Order, and gave the *Garter*,

Hund. of
Brabrwatr
which was the Signal at that fortunate Battle fought at **Cressy**, where he obtained a great Victory, about three Years after
the Erection of the round Table at **Windsor**, and made it
the chief Ensign of the Order for the Symbol of Unity and
Society, from whence that select Number was thus incorporated into a Fraternity, and are now termed Knights of the
Garter.

Stat. of the
Order.
Ashmole of
the Garter,
fol. 197.
Which Order was instituted in the 23d Year of King
Edward III. and the Queen, attended with three hundred
of the fairest Ladies, adorned with all imaginable Gallantry,
to make the Solemnity more glorious; where all the chief
Knights and Esquires appeared, that were desirous to shew
their military Prowess and Valour in all Feats of Arms, and
the publick Exercises proper for the Place and Occasion.

Ibid. 202,
203, 208, 211,
215, 220, 226.
The King did assign the *Garter, Mantle, Surcoat,* and
Hood, for the Distinction of this Order, and King *Henry*
VIII. did add the *George* and the *Collar* for the greater
Glory thereof. But I shall forbear to say more of this Or-
der, since Mr. *Ashmole* has treated so largely of it in his
learned Piece of the *Garter,* to which I refer the Reader.
But to return to this noble Lord.

He married *Elizabeth,* Daughter of *William Brooke,*
Lord *Cobham,* by whom he had Issue *William,* and *Frances*
married to *Henry* Lord *Clifford,* then Son and Heir apparent to *Francis* Earl of **Cumberland**. He erected a stately
Building in this Mannor, which is a fair Pallace, that ex-
ceeds all the Houses in this County, and two large Parkes,
one for fallow, the other for red Deer, with a Vineyard at
the Bottom of the Park; died at **Marlborough**, on Sunday
the 24th of *May, Anno Dom.* 1612, 10 *Jac.* I. and was
buried in this Parish Church.

Earl *William* succeeded, was installed Knight of the most
noble Order of the *Garter,* made *Custos Rotulorum,* and
Lord Lieutenant of the Militia in this County; he married
Katharine, the youngest Daughter of *Thomas Howard,*
Earl of **Suffolk**, by whom he had Issue seven Sons, *James*
who died young, *Charles, Robert, Philip, William, Algernon,* and *Edward;* and five Daughters, *Anne* Wife of *Algernon,* Earl of **Northumberland**, *Elizabeth* married to *William* Earl of **Devon**, *Diana,* who died single; *Katharine*
married to *Philip* Lord **Lisle**, Son and Heir apparent to
Robert Earl of **Leicester**, and *Mary* married to *William*
Lord **Chandos**.

Charles, after the Death of *James* his elder Brother, married *Jane* Daughter and Coheir to *James Maxwell,* one of
the Grooms of the Bedchamber to King *Charles* I. afterwards made Earl of **Deriton** in **Scotland**; by whom he had
Issue seven Sons, *James* who succeeded his Grandfather
Robert, Charles, William, Edward, Henry, and *George*

which six last died unmarried. He had also five Daughters, *Katharine* married to the Earl of Kenoule in Scotland, *Frances* married to Sir *William Bowyer*, Baronet, *Diana*, *Penelope*, and *Elizabeth*, which three last died young; at length *Charles* died in the Life-time of Earl *William* his Father, who also died the 3d of *December*, *Anno Dom.* 1668, and was buried in this Parish Church. *Hund. of Bradewater*

James his Grandson, inherited his Honours and Estate, married *Margaret* one of the Daughters to *John* Earl of Rutland, by whom he had Issue four Sons, *James*, *Robert* married to *Elizabeth* the Widow and Relict of *Richard Hale*, of King's Walden in this County, Esq. *William* deceased, *Charles*, and *George*, and four Daughters, *Katharine* married to Sir *George Downing*, Baronet, *Frances* married to Sir *William Hawford*, Baronet, *Mary* married to Sir *William Forester*, Kt. *Margaret* married to *John* Lord Stowel, and *Mildred* married to Sir *Uvidal Corbet*, Baronet. He died the —— day of ———— *Anno* 168—, and was buried in this Parish.

James his eldest Son succeeded, married *Frances*, one of the Daughters and Coheirs of *Simon Bennet* of Bleckington in the County of Buckingham, Esq. and *Grace* his Wife; then travelled into France, where he beheld the Splendor and Glory of that Court; from whence he proceeded to Rome, and having viewed the pleasant Country of Italy, he returned back again by France to England, where he gave large Testimonies of his Duty and Loyalty to King *James* II. When the Prince of *Orange* obtained the Crown, this Earl was committed to the *Tower* of London for High Treason, where he was confined for the Space of almost two Years; then obtained his Liberty, and died seized hereof, on the 24th Day of *October*, 1694; leaving Issue *James* his only Son and Heir, about three Years old at the time of his Death, who is the present Lord of this Mannor. His Arms are *Barry of ten, Argent and Azure, over all six Escutcheons Sable, each charged with a Lyon rampant of the first, with a Crescent for Difference.* Dale's *Exact Cat. of Nob.*

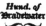

Thomas Cecil de Alternis, ━Margaretta filia et heres, Gilberti Winston, Militia.

Philippus Cecil de Alternia. ━Margaretta, filia Johan. Phelips militis.

Ricardus Sitsilt, alias Cecil, de Alternis Com. Hereford.━ Margaretta, filia Philippi Vaughan .

Philippus Cecil, de Alternis━ David Cecil, de Stamford. ━Alicia, fil. et heres Johan.
fil. et heres. │ Dickon.

Ricardus Cecil, ar.━ Alicia, fil. et heres Will. Eckington.

Maria, filia Petri Cheeke, ━Willi. Cecil, Dom. Burgley.━Mildreda, filia Antonii Cook, Mil.
ar. Ux. 1. │ Ux 2.

Thomas Cecil, ━Dorothea, fil. │ Robertus Cecil, Com. Sarisbury,━ Elizabetha, fil. Will.
Comes Exon. │ Johan. Dom. │ et Bar. de Essingdon in Com. │ Brook Dom. Cob-
│ Latimer. │ Rotul. │ ham.

William, ━Elizabetha,━Eliz. soror et │ Ricardus Ce- │ Edw. Cecil, mil. │ Will. Cecil, Com.
Comes │ fil et heres │ coheres. Ro- │ cil, Mil. nup- │ Virecom. Wim- │ Sarisb. nups. Ca-
Exon. │ Will. Com. │ berti Drury, │ sit. fil. An- │ bleton, ob. s. m. │ tharinam filia
│ Rutl. Ux. │ Mil. Ux. 2. │ tonii Cope, │ │ The. Com. Suff.
│ 1. │ │ mil. │ │ obiit 1668

William, Dom. │ Elizabeth │ David Cecil,━Elizabeth, fil. │ Carolus━ Jana, filia et hered.
Roos, ob. s. p. │ Diana │ Comes │ Joh. Com. │ Cecil. │ Com. Deriton in
in vita Patria. │ Anna. │ Exon. │ Bridgewater. │ │ Scotl. et ob. in vita
│ │ │ │ │ Patria.

Johan Ce-━Francisca, fi- │ Jacobus Cecil ━Margaretta, │ 2 Rob │ 6 Hen.
cil, Comes │ lia Johan. │ │ filia Johan. │ 3 Carol. │ 7 Georgius omnes,
Exon. │ Com. Rotel. │ │ Com. Rotel. │ 4 Will. │ ob. s. p.
│ │ │ │ 5 Edw.

Johan Cecil, │ Robertus, nupsit │ Jacobus Cecil, Com. ━Francisca, filia et │ Willi. s. p.
Com. Exon. │ Elizabetha Vtd. │ Sarisbur. ob. 24 Oc- │ heres Sim. Bennet, │ Carolus.
1680. │ Rich. Hale, Arm. │ tob. 1694. │ Arm et Graciæ │ Georgius
│ │ │ Ux. ejus.

Jacobus, modo Com. Sarisbury.

The Mannor of WOOD-HALL in HATFIELD.

SO called from the great Abundance of Wood and Tim-
ber that grew there; it was Parcel of the Possessions of
the ancient Family of the *Bassingburns,* who held it of the
Mannor of 𝕳𝖆𝖙𝖋𝖎𝖊𝖑𝖉, by the Service of half a Knight's
Fee, Suit of Court, and the yearly Rent of two Pence:
Upon an Inquisition the Jury found, that *John de Bassing-
burne* died the 5th of *Edw.* I. seized of two Messuages,
three ploughed Lands, eight Acres of Meadow, forty
Acres of Wood, besides twenty Acres of Land, twenty
Shillings Rent, in 𝕭𝖎𝖘𝖍𝖔𝖕𝖘 𝕳𝖆𝖙𝖋𝖎𝖊𝖑𝖉, for which *Beatrice* the
Wife of *William Kinneby,* brought an Assize against *Agnes*
the Wife of *John Bassingburne,* who called to Warranty
Jeoffry de Mogbrow which she held of the said *Jeoffry* to
the Value of &c. and *Jeoffry* in Mercy of &c.

John de Bassingburne was constituted Sheriff of this
County and Essex, *Anno* 32 *Edw.* I. also for the last half
of the Year 34 *Edw.* I. from whom this Mannor came to

5 Ed. 1. *Rot.*
40, cur. re-
cept. Scac.

Rot. Pip. 32
Ed. I. tit,
Herts.&Essex

John de Bassingburne, who was Sheriff of this County and *Essex Anno* 45 *Edw.* III. He also served this County in two Parliaments, one held *Anno* 46 *Edw* III. the other at Westminster, in the Year 47 *Edw.* III. This Mannor continued in this Name till it came to

John Bassingburne, who left Issue two Daughters, *Audry* married to *Thomas Gaudy*, Serjeant at Law, ——married to *Michael Hare*, Son to Sir *Nicholas Hare* of Bruspard, in the County of Suffolk, Kt. Master of the Rolls, and Clerk of the Pells in the *Exchequer*; But upon the Partition this Mannor fell to the Lot of

Audry the Wife of *Thomas Gaudy*, who was possest hereof in the time of Queen *Mary*, she levied a Fine hereof, and his Free-Warren *Anno* 3 and 4 *P.* and *M.* to the Use of the said *Thomas Gaudy* and his Heirs; but afterwards he sold it to

Sir *John Boteler*, Kt. who held it in the time of Queen *Elizabeth*, and married *Grisil* Daughter and Heir of Sir *William Roche* of Lanmer, one of the Aldermen and Lord Mayor of the City of London, *Anno* 1540, by whom he had Issue, Sir *Philip Boteler*, Sir *Henry Boteler*, *William*, *Richard*, *Nicholas*, and *Elizabeth* married to Sir *Henry Conishby* Kt. *Mary* to *Thomas Shotbolt*, *Sarah* to *Robert Colt*, *Susan* to *Julius Ferrers*, *Margaret* to *Nicholas Bristow*, and *Martha* to Sir *George Penent*, afterwards he gave this Mannor to

Sir *Henry Boteler* his second Son, who was knighted I *Jac.* I. and married *Katharine* Daughter of *Robert Waller* of Wadley, by whom he had Issue, *John*, *Henry*, *Edward*, *Ralph*, and *George*, and three Daughters, *Katharine* married to Sir *John Brown*, of Essex, *Elizabeth* to Sir *Anthony Chester* of Bucks, Baronet, and *Mary* to *John Lynn*; after the Decease of *Katharine* his Wife, he married *Alice* the Daughter of *Edward Pulter* of Bradfield, Esq. and he conveyed this Mannor to the Use of himself for Life, the Remainder to the Heirs Males of his Body.

John his eldest Son succeeded, was knighted *Anno* 1 *Jac.* I. and constituted Sheriff of this County; the same Year he married *Elizabeth*, the Daughter of Sir *George Villiers* of Brokesby in the County of Leicester, and eldest Sister to *George* Duke of Buckingham, was created Baronet by Letters Patents, dated 12 *April*, *An. Dom.* 1620, 18 *Jac.* I. advanced to the Dignity of a Baron of this Realm, by the Title of Lord *Boteler* of Bramfield, by Letters Patents, dated the 20th of *September*, 4 *Car.* I. He had Issue by *Elizabeth* his Wife six Sons, *John*, *Henry*, *Philip*, *Francis*, *John*, and *William*, all whom died without Issue; and six Daughters, *Audry* married to Sir *Francis Anderson*, Kt. afterwards to *Francis Leigh*, Lord Dunsmore,

Hund. of
Bradewater

Rot. Pip. 45
Ed. III. tit.
Herts. & Essex
Prin's Parl.
Brev. pt. 3.

Stow's Surv.
of London,
p. 582.

Rot. Pip. 1
Jac. I. tit.
Herts.

Hund. of
Bradwater

after that Earl of **Chichester**, *Helen* married to Sir *John Drake* of **Ash** in the County of **Devon**, Kt. *Jane* married to *James Ley*, Earl of **Marlborough**, Lord Treasurer of **England**, and after his Decease to —— *Ashburnham*, one of the Grooms of the Bed Chamber to King *Charles* I. *Olive* married to *Endimion Porter*, another of the Grooms of the Bed Chamber to the said King, *Mary* married to *Edward* Lord *Howard* of **Escrick**, and *Anne* married to *Mountjoy Blount* Earl of **Newport**, and Master of the Ordnance, and after him to *Thomas* Earl of **Portland**; He departed this Life at his Lodgings in St. *Martins* in the Fields, within the Liberties of **Westminster**, the 27th Day of *May*, 1637, 13 *Car*. I. was buried at **Higham Gobion**, in the County of **Bedford**, leaving

William, his only Son that survived him, who succeeded in his Barony, as also this Mannor, and dying without Issue the Barony extinguished, but this Mannor came, as I suppose, by Force of the former Settlement to

Sir *Frances Boteler* the eldest Son of *Ralph Boteler*, of **Tewyne-hall**, and *Susan* his Wife, Daughter of *Frances Saunders*, and the fourth Son of Sir *Henry Boteler:* He was a Person who had served his Majesty in **Ireland** under the Command of that great and eminent Lord *Thomas* Earl of **Strafford**, Lord Lieutenant of that Kingdom, where he had been exercised in martial Affairs, and for his good Service King *Charles* I. conferred the Honour of Knightoood upon him at **York**; on the first Day of *May*, 1642; he was a Justice of the Peace, a Deputy Lieutenant for this County, and served for the Borough of **Hertford**, in the Parliament held at **Westminster**, 1 *Jac*. II. He married *Anne* Daughter of —— *Cokaine* in the County of **Derby**, Esq. by whom he had Issue *George* who died at twelve Years of Age; and two Daughters, *Julian*, married to *Francis Shalcross* of **Diginsworth**, Esq. and *Arabella* married to *Charles Hutchinson*, in the County of **Nottingham**, Esq. and after the Decease of his first Wife, he married *Elizabeth Tudor*, Sister of *Fulk Tudor*, D.D. and Rector of **Tewine** and **Stevenedge** in this County: this Sir *Francis* died the 9th of *October*, 1690; after whose Decease this Mannor came to the Possession of

Julian Shalcross, Widow, the present Lady hereof.

He was somewhat tall in Stature, spare in Body, neat in Habit, and comely in Person, very obliging to his Lady, and most affectionate to his Children; he was grave in his Deportment, yet pleasant in his Aspect; he was very modest in his Speaking, and free from all Pride and Ostentation; he was endowed with some Competency of Learning and good Elocution: he was Master of great Reason and Understanding, and qualified with a vast Memory, and a great Presence of Mind, so that he could *ex tempore*, reduce a long Speech delivered in Confusion, under proper Heads, in good Language and excellent Method; his Manner of Delivery was very graceful, without any Affectation; he was very impartial in all his Acts of Justice, and would not be biassed by any; he was always very loyal to the King, and very zealous for the Service of the Church, which he daily frequented during his Residence in London, where he generally spent the Winter Part of the Year when Age grew upon him; he was well skilled in the Discipline of Military Affairs, and reputed an excellent Soldier; he always kept a genteel Table, treated his Neighbours with great Courtesy, assisted his Friends with much Willingness upon all Occasions, and relieved the Poor with great Cheerfulness, yet would reprimand those that commonly used the Trade of Begging.

The Mannor of PUNSBORNE

BORROWS its Name from the Situation hereof in a low Bottom, and was Parcel of the Possessions of *John Fortescue*; in the time of *Henry* VI. he was a Person of a fair Estate, for I find him enrolled *Anno* 12 *Hen*. VI. among those Gentleman who could spend 10*l. per Ann.* in this County. From him this Mannor descended to

John Fortescue, who was constituted Sheriff of this County and **Essex**, *Anno* 1481, 22 *Edw.* IV. afterwards knighted and served the Office of Sheriff again for the same Counties, in the Year 1486, 1 *Hen.* VII. He died, leaving Issue

John Fortescue, who held this Mannor 9 *Hen.* VIII. of the King, by Knight's Service; what Estate he had in it, it, the Jury knew not, but found that

Henry Fortescue was his Son, and Heir, and at full Age at the Death of his Father; but afterwards it was conveyed to the Crown, where it remained for any thing that I can find, till Queen *Elizabeth* granted it to

Sir *Henry Cock*, by the Name of 𝔓onesborne, *alias* 𝔓unesborne, *alias* 𝔓apsborne, to hold of the Queen *in Capite*, by the Service of the two hundredth Part of a Knight's Fee, and was valued by the Year in all Issues above Reprizes 12*l.* increased above the Schedule thereunto annexed 4*l.* 8*s.* 4*d.* He devised the Mannors of 𝔓unsborne, 𝔅erkhamsted 𝔓arba, 𝔅aysford, and 𝔈ssingdon to Sir *Robert Oxenbridge* and *Edward Casone*, their Executors and Assigns, to have immediately after the Death of Sir *Henry Cock*, for the Term of ten Years in Trust, that they should employ the clear Profits of the same, above all necessary Prizes, to such Person and Persons, and to such Uses as the said Sir *Henry Cock*, by his last Will and Testament in

(margin notes:)
Hund. of Braohwater

MSS. Offic. Armorum.

Inq. 9 H.VIII

Cur.Supervis. Man. de Hatfield.

Writing or Schedule, should appoint, with a Power of Revocation upon the Payment of twelve; and by another Indenture of Covenants, to stand seized for continuing all the Premisses so let in the Blood of Sir *Henry Cock*; they conveyed all the same Mannors to the Use of him the said Sir *Henry Cock* and his Wife, for the Term of their Lives, and the longer Liver of them; the Remainder to the Heirs of the Body of Sir *Henry Cock* lawfully begotten; the Remainder to Sir *Edmond Lucy*, for Term of his Life; the Remainder to Sir *Edmond*, and the Heirs Males of his Body lawfully begotten, with divers other Remainders in Tail; the Remainder to the right Heirs of Sir *Henry Cock* for ever. He died seized of this Mannor, leaving *Frances* married to Sir *Edmond Lucy*, and *Elizabeth* to *Robert West*, Son and Heir apparent to the Lord *Delaware*, and after him to Sir *Robert Oxenbridge*, who were his Daughters and Coheirs; and upon the Partition, this Mannor came to *Frances* his eldest Daughter, then married to Sir *Edmond Lucy*, by whom she had only Issue,

Elizabeth, who married Sir *John Ferrers*, Kt. one of the Gentlemen of the Privy Chamber to Queen *Elizabeth*, King *James* I. and after to King *Charles* I. whereby he became Lord hereof in Right of his Wife, and died the 17th Day of *November*, 1640.

Afterwards it was sold to *Stephen Ewre*, and *Joshua Lomax*, who granted it to *Richard Woollaston* of *Gray's Inn*, Esq.; he and *John Woollaston* his Son aliened it to

Paris Slaughter, Citizen and Factor of *Blackwell Hall* in London, who repaired and beautified the House, and died seiz'd hereof, 1698, leaving Issue *Paris*, who is his Son and Heir, and the present Lord hereof.

The Mannors of POPES and HOLBEACH

WAS Parcel of the Mannor of Essendon, and sold to *Holbeach*; after to *Pope*, from both whom it was denominated to preserve the Names and Memory of those Owners; afterwards it came to *William Stalworth*, from whom it descended to *John* his Son, who had Issue *William*; he had *John*, *Elizabeth*, and *Jane*; but *John* dying without Issue, it came to his two Sisters, *Elizabeth* and *Jane*.

Elizabeth married *Richard Hall*, by whom she had Issue *Edmond Hall*, which *Edmond* had *Elizabeth* and *Alice*.

Elizabeth married *Lawrence Woodhall*, by whom she had Issue *Foulk* and *Alice*. The other Sister married *John ap Jenkin*, who sold their Part to one *Bellamy*.

But to return to the other Moiety of this Mannor, which came to *Jane*, the younger Sister and Coheir to *John Stalworth* her Brother; she married *Charles Blount*, who had Issue *George* and *Margaret*; but *George* dying without

Issue, his Part came to his Sister *Margaret*; she married *Thomas Woodhall*, who sold this Moiety to *Foulk Woodhall*; he possest three Parts of this Mannor, joyned with *Bellamy*, who had the other fourth Part, and sold it to *William Tooke*, Esq. Auditor General of her Majesty's Court of Wards and Liveries, who had nine Sons and three Daughters. Upon his Decease, these Mannors came to

Walter Tooke, his Son and Heir, who had Issue *Ralph*, *George*, and *Thomas*; then sold his Part in the Mannor of **Essendon**, to *William* Earl of **Salisbury**, but the Mannor of **Popes** descended to

Ralph, who was his Heir, and dying without Issue, it came to

George, who married *Margery* the Daughter of *Thomas Conisby*, Esq. but having no Issue by her, he gave it to her for Life; after her Decease, it came to

Thomas the younger Brother of *George*, who held it a while, and in the Year 1664, sold it to

Stephen Ewre and *Joshua Lomax*, Esq. who aliened it the next Year to

Daniel Shutterden of **Eltham** in the County of **Kent**, Esq. who was constituted Sheriff of this County, *An.* 1689, 1 *Will. et Mariæ*. He sold it to ———— who is the present Lord hereof.

Hund. of
Bradewater

Rot. Pip.
1689. til.
Herts.

The Mannor of ASTWICK

WAS anciently Parcel of the Revenues of the *Bassingburns*; afterwards it came to the Possession of the *Hares*, and 'twas found that *Michael Hare*, Anno 4 *Jac*. I. held this Mannor late the *Bassingburns*, by free Deed of the King, as of his Mannor of **Hatfield**, by the Service of half a Knight's Fee, and the yearly Rent of 2*d*.

William Grunwild possest it about the Year 1638, sold it to

Dios, an Ironmonger in **London**. Upon his Decease it descended to

John Dios his Son and Heir, who aliened it to Sir *Henry Tulse*, Kt. one of the Aldermen and late Lord Mayor of the City of **London**; and upon his Decease, it descended to

Elizabeth Tulse his Daughter and sole Heir, who married Sir *Richard Onslow*, Baronet, who is the present Lord hereof; he has Jurisdiction of a Court Baron within this Mannor, where none can take Surrenders from any Customary Tenants of their Copyhold Lands, but by the Hands of the Lord or the Steward.

Cur. Supervis.
Man. de Hat-
field Regis et
Episcopi.

The Mannor of SYMONDS HIDE.

THIS Mannor was in the Possession of *Simon Fitz Ade*, who was Lord hereof *Anno* 1239, 23 *H*. III. He had Issue by *Fine* his Wife,

John Fitz Symon, who was knighted, received his Sir-name from his Father, and died seiz'd hereof, leaving

Hugh Fitz Symon, who inherited it, obtained the same Honor of Knighthood, enjoyed this Mannor, and at his Death left Issue

Richard Fitz Symon, who succeeded, was installed Knight of the *Garter, Anno* 24 *Edw.* III. held it some time, and died seiz'd hereof, leaving Issue

Adam Fitz Symonds, who married *Margaret,* Daughter of the Lord *Audley,* by whom he had Issue

Hugh Fitz Symonds, who succeeded his Father in this Mannor, and at the time of his Death,

Edward Fitz Symonds. who was his Son and Heir, possest it, was dubb'd a Knight. It came to

Nicholas Fitz Symonds, who was his Brother and Heir, succeeded him, but leaving only

Elizabeth, she was his Daughter and Heir, and married *William Ash,* Esq. by whom she had Issue

Elizabeth, who was her Heir, and married Sir *Thomas Brocket,* in whose Right he enjoy'd this Mannor, and in his Name it continu'd till it came to

Sir *John Brocket,* who married *Helen* Daughter and Heir of Sir *Robert Lytton* of 𝕶nebworth-place in this County, by whom he had Issue *Margaret* married to Sir *John Cutts; Anne* married to *Alexander Cave* of 𝕭agrabe; *Helen* married to *Richard Spencer,* Esq. *Elizabeth* to *George Carlton,* and *Mary* to *Thomas Read.* After the Decease of this *Helen,* he married *Elizabeth,* Daughter and Coheir to —— *Moore,* Esq. by whom he had Issue *Frances,* who married the Lord *North;* these were his Daughters and Coheirs, and this Mannor fell to the Lot of *Helen* the Wife of *Richard Spencer,* the fourth Son of Sir *John Spencer* of 𝕬lthrop in the County of 𝕹orthampton, who was knighted ; and it past from him as I shall shew in the Mannor of 𝕺ffley, to Sir *John Spencer,* the present Lord hereof.

The Mannors of *HOLDWELL* and *LUDWICK.*

'TWAS found *Anno* 4 *Jac.* I. that Sir *Humphry Wild,* Kt. held the Mannor of 𝕷udwick, with the Appurtenances, by free Deed of the Lord of the Mannor of 𝕳atfield, by the Service of the fourth Part of a Knight's Fee, to hold of the King, as of his Mannor aforesaid, rendring therefore and for the Mannor of 𝕳oldwell, 8*s.* 8*d. per An.* Suit of Court, &c.

BROCKET HALL

WAS the ancient Seat of the *Brockets,* situated upon a dry Hill in a fair Park, well wooded and greatly timber'd, enclosed with a brick Wall on the West Side of the Road, for the Length of a Mile, and plentifully water'd with the River 𝕷ea. It came to

Thomas Read, by the Marriage of *Mary* the fifth Daughter of Sir *John Brocket*, Kt. who had Issue

John, to whom this Seat descended upon the Death of his Father ; he was created Baronet by Patent dated the 16th of *March*, *Anno* 1641, and was constituted Sheriff of this County, *Anno* 1655, 7 *Car*. II. he married *Susan*, the Daughter of Sir *Thomas Stiles*, by whom he had Issue *James*, and *Mary* since married to Sir *John Bucknall* of Watford in this County, Kt. lately elected to serve for Middlesex in this present Parliament, *Anno* 1697; and this Sir *John Read* died *Anno* 1696, leaving

James his Heir, married to ——— one of the Daughters and Coheirs of ——— *Dring* of Thistleworth in the County of Middlesex; he was constituted Sheriff for this County, *An.* 1693, 5 *W. & M.* and is the present Possessor hereof.

THE Rectory in *Anno* 26 *Hen.* VIII. was valued in the King's Books, at 86*l.* 2*s. per Annum*, whereof the Earls of Salisbury, Lords of the Mannor of Hatfield, have been Patrons.

The RECTORS.

Richard Lee, D. D.   *Thomas Fuller*, D. D.

This Church is erected near the Town, in the Deanery of Hatfield, in the Diocess of Lincoln, after the Form of a Cross, with one Isle covered with Tyle and ceiled within, but the Cross is covered with Lead : There is a Gallery near the Steeple, and a fair Tower at the West End, wherein hangs a Ring of five large Bells; the Tower is covered with Lead, having a short Spire erected upon it.

There is a Chapel adjoining the North Side of the Chancel, erected by *Robert* Earl of Salisbury, in which is a fair Monument, made after this manner.

On the Ground is a Skeleton, on a black Marble Table over it is the Effigies of an Earl in white Marble, with his Treasurer's Staff in his Hand : The Table is supported by four Virgins on their Knees in white Marble, representing Fortitude, Justice, Temperance, and Prudence.

In the Chancel lies a fair Marble within the Rails that enclose the Communion Table, thus inscribed.

Here lyes the Body of Sir *Francis Boteler*, late of Wood-hall in this Parish, descended from the Right Noble House of the *Botelers*, Barons of Oversley Wem and Sudley; Knighted by King *Charles* I. at York, *May* the first 1642. His first Wife was Dame *Anne Cokaine*, of the ancient and Honourable Family of the *Cokaines*, of Ashborne of Derbyshire, where she is interred; by whom he had a Son, that died Young, and two Daughters, *Julia* and *Isabella*. He departed this Life, *October* 9th, *anno* 1690.

In the 80th Year of his Age, in hope of a joyful Resurrection.

At the North End of the Rails lies another Stone which has this Inscription.

Here lyeth Interred the Body of Dame *Elizabeth Boteler*, late Wife to Sir *Francis Boteler* of Hatfield Wood Hall in the County of Hertford, who departed this Life the 30th day of *April*, anno Dom. 168—.

Another Stone shews this Inscription.

Here lyeth the Body of *Francis Boteler*, Grandson and Heir to that Gentleman of most worthy honoured Memory, Sir *Francis Boteler*, late of Hatfield Woodhall, Kt. who departed this Life in the 18th year of his Age, the 13th day of *January*, 1602. And when God please, the Body of *Julia*, his afflicted Mother, Relict of *Francis Shallcrosse* of Digsworth in this County, Esq; one of the Daughters and Coheirs of Sir *Francis Boteler*, Kt.

Another Stone is thus Inscribed.

Fulcon Stow, *Arm. nuper summæ Cur. Parliamenti Pronotarius diuturno languescens morbo 6 Idum Aug. an. reparat. Salutis* 1602, *Ætat. suæ* 88. *Idumentum hoc mortale Humo immortalem Animam Deo Intima Charitatum, vis sera amicis commendavit et cui posuere hoc Monumentum memoriæ et Amoris ergo conjunctissimus familiaritate Consanguinis* Reginaldus Scriven *et Charissima Conjux* Elizabetha.

On the other Side of the Altar, a Stone has this Inscription.

Here lyeth the Body of Sir *Henry Godyer*, who descended of *Anne*, Aunt to the worthy Family in the County of Middlesex, with *Damara* his Wife, Daughter and Heir to *John Rumball*, Gent. who lived together in chaste Wedlock 53 Years, by whom he had Issue, seven Sons and seven Daughters, whereof two Sons *Francis, Thomas,* and four Daughters, *Anne, Judith, Ursula* and *Lucy,* survived. He deceased the 12th of ——— *Anno Dom.* 1629, in the 78th Year of his Age. She deceased the 29th day of *April, Anno Dom.* 1628, in the — Year of her Age.

Near this Stone lyeth another Marble thus Ingraved.

Hic requiescit Corpus Josephi Jordan, *Militis, qui obiit mense* Junii *die* 2d. anno Dom. 1685, *Ætat. suæ* 82 *in spe Resurrectionis.*

A Marble in the middle of the Chancel.

Depositum Richardi Lee, S. T. P. *nuper* Hatfield *Episcopalis alias Regalis cum Capella de* Cotteridge *Rectoris. Qui obiit* anno Dom. 1684. *Ætat. suæ* 73. *Hic requiescit spe Lætæ Resurrectionis.*

On another Marble on the other Side the Chancel is this Inscription.

Here lyeth Interred the Body of *John Dios*, Esq; of this Parish, who departed this Life the 2d of *March* 1677, in the 67 Year of his Age.

In the South Chancel, called Punsburne *Isle.*

Here lyes the Body of *Martha Ewre*, late the Wife of *Stephen Ewre* of Punsburne in this Parish, Gentleman, who died the 26th day of *August,* anno Dom. 1664.

Another fair Marble lyes near this Stone.

Hic requiescit Corpus Willimi Curle. *Armigeri tunc illustrissimæ Reginæ* Elizabethæ *qui potentiss. Cur. Wardorum et Libaconum* ——— *est officio summa fide et integritate fælix Liberis et Amicis vera fide christiana beatam carnis sperans Resurrectionem placid. obdormivit in Somnio* 16 *die* Aprilis, Anno Dom. 1617, *et Ætat. suæ* 78.

Near the last, another Stone shews this Inscription.

Rotamur in Urnam fracta licet lætabuntur.

Here in the hopes of a blessed Resurrection is laid up the Body of Mrs. *Elizabeth Carter*, Daughter of *William Carter* of Hatfield Woodside, Esq; and *Mary* his Wife; having finished her short Race in fourteen Years and nine Months, on the 5th. of *May*, 1652. she put off the Garment of Mortality, to assume her Palm and Robe of Glory.

  This precious Cabinet resolv'd to dust
   No more the Object of our carnal Eyes ;
  The Diamond it contain'd amongst the Just,
   Sparkles in fullest Glory above the Skies:
But when the Heavens shall meet, and Stars shall fall,
These must unite, and far out-shine them all.
    Expergiscemini et Cantate,
    Qui habitatis pulverem.

Another shews this Inscription.

Potius quæ supra nescitis horam.

Here rests in expectation of the last Trump, the Body of *William Carter*
of Hatfield Woodside, Esq; one of the Commissioners for the Peace of
this County of Hertford and Liberty of St. Albans, Counsellor at Law of
the *Middle Temple*, a Man of admirable Piety and Integrity both towards God and towards Man; he married *Mary* the Daughter of *John
Darnall* of Hertingfordbury, Esq; by whom he had divers Children;
two only survived him, viz. *William* and *Robert*. He departed this
Life to enjoy the beatifical Vision, on the 9th. of *November*, 1652.

*Novi in carne mea,
Me visurum Deum.*

This is engraved on another Stone.

Here lyeth the Body of *Robert Carter*, second Son of *William Carter*,
late of Hatfield Woodside, Esq; who departed this Life the 11th. of
April, 1664. Ætat. suæ 18.

*A fair Monument erected in the South Wall of the same Isle, with the Effi-
gies of two Women leaning on their left Elbows, with this
Inscription over them.*

Here lyes the Body of Dame *Elizabeth Brocket*, late Wife of Sir *John
Brocket* of Brocket-Hall in the County of Hertford, and formerly the
Wife of *Gabriel Fowler*, of Tilswoth in the County of Bedford, Esq;
Daughter and Coheir of *Roger Moore*, of Burcester in the County of
Oxford, Esq; the which Dame *Elizabeth* deceased the 24th. day of
June, 1612. In respective Love and Duty towards so dear a Mother,
Richard Fowler, her only Son, caused this Monument to be erected in
Memory of Her.

In Memory of Dame Agnes Saunders, *who deceased the* 20th *Day of*
October, Anno Dom. 1588.

Friend, as thou by this Monument doth pass,
And here seest what I am, read what I was;
1*Hussy* my Father was, and I his Heir,
My Husbands 2*Moore*, 3*Curson* and 4*Saunders* were;
By *Moore*, I of two Daughters was a Mother,
Whereof 5*Blount* one, 6*Brocket* espoused another :
One Daughter and sole Heir of *Cursons* Bed
I then brought forth whom I to 7*Farmer* Wed :
Of *Saunders*, Lord Chief Baron, one, no more
But only Name. I lastly hither bore ;
Where 8she, whom I enclosed in my Womb
By *Curson*, hath inclos'd me in this Tomb,
If of my Virtues then wouldst Memory see,
In her I left them who in this laid me.
Then let this sacred Act her Love set forth,
And her Religious Love declare my Worth.

1 JohnHussy
of the House
of Snapnick,
Dorsetshire.
2 Rog. Moore
of Burcester,
Esq.
3 Tho.Curson
of Waterpeny
Esq.
4 Sir Edward
Saunders, Kt.
Lord Chief
Baron.
5 Sir Michael
Blount of Ma-
ple, Durham.
6 Sir John
Brocket of
Brocket Hall
7 Sir George
Farmer of
Estoneston in
Northampton
shire.
8 Dame Mary
Farmer.

Another Monument in the same Wall, almost destroyed,
with this Inscription.

Deo Opt. Max. et Memoriæ sacrum.

Johannes Brocket, *Miles, sub hoc tumulo secundum Christi adventum ex-
pecta. Qui primo connubio junctam habuit* Helenam *unam Filiarum et
Heredum Roberti* Litton *Militis, ex qua quintas Filias suscepit* Marga-
retam *nuptam* Johanni Cuts, *Militi;* Annam, Alexandrio Cave——
Elizab. Georgio Carlton; Helenam, Ricardo Spencer; *Mariam* Thomæ Read, *Armig. et ex secunda Uxore quæ fuit relicta* Gabrielis Fowler
Armig. unicam habuit Filiam Franciscam *nuptam* Dudleo D. North
Pie Placideq; in Christo mortem obiit secundo die Octobris, *Anno Salutis restauratæ* 1598, *ætatis vero suæ plus minus sexagesimo tristissimum
sui   Desiderium Amicis Relinquens.*

DIGENSWELL.

THIS Vill is shrouded in a Bottom on the South Side of the River ᚠᛁᚾmeram, under the Hill about four Miles distant from Hatfield towards the North; it was denominated from the Springs of Water which bubble out of the Ground in this Parish; for such Springs the *Saxons* heretofore called Wells. In the time of *William* the Conqueror, *Goisfride de Manevile* and *Peter de Valongies* possest this Vill, when it was recorded, that

Domesd. Lib.
fol. 138, nu.
33.

In Bradewater Hundred.. in Micheleswelle, tenuit Torchil de Goisfrido duo hidas. Terra est octo car. et dimid. in dominio duo sunt car. et duodecim Vill. cum tribus Bordis habentibus sex car. et dimid. ibi quatuor Cotar. et duo servi et un Molin. et dimid. octo sol. et octo denar. pastura ad pec. Silva centum porc. inter totum valet quatuor lib. Isdem. tenuit tempore Regis Edwardi, qui nunc tenuit, homo Asgari Stalre fuit et vendere potuit.

Ibid. fol. 141.

In Bradewater Hundred. in Micheleswelle, tenuit Rogerus de Petro de Valongies un. hid. Terra est tres car. in Dom. est una et quinque Vill. cum tribus Bordis habent. duo car. ibi octo cotar. et dimid. Molind. de xl. denar. pratum duo bobus pastura ad pec Silva. porc. inter totum valet xxxv sol. Quando recepit vigint. sol. tempore Regis Edwardi l. sol. hanc terram tenuit Topi homo Almari et vendere potuit.

Torchil held two Hides of *Jeoffery de Manevile* in Bigswell, in the Hundred of Bradewater; the arable is eight Carucates and an half, in Demeasne are two Carucates and twelve Villains, with three Bordars, having six Carucates and an half, there are four Cottagers and two Servants, and one Mill and half a Mill of eight Shillings and eight Pence Rent; Common of Pasture for the Cattle, Wood to feed an hundred Hogs: In the whole it is worth four Pounds by the Year. The same held it in the time of King *Edward* (the Confessor) who now holds it. He was a Man (under the Protection) of *Asgar Stalri*, and might sell it.

Roger held one Hide of *Peter Valongies* in Bigswell, in the Hundred of Bradewater: The arable is three Carucates, in Demeasne is one, and five Villains, with three Bordars, having two Carucates and eight Cottagers, and half a Mill of forty Pence Rent; Meadow to feed two Oxen, Common of Pasture for the Cattle, Wood to feed fifty Hogs: In the whole it is worth five and thirty Shillings by the Year; when he received it, twenty Shillings a Year; in the time of King *Edward* (the Confessor) fifty Shillings a Year. *Topi*, a Man (under the Protection) of *Almar*, held this Land, and might sell it.

Having treated already of these great Barons, *Jeoffery de Magnavile* in the Parish of Sabridgeworth, and *Peter de Valongies* in Hertingfordbury, I shall proceed to *Lawrence* of St. Nicholas, who is the next Lord of this Mannor that I meet with, for it was found, *Anno* 6 *Edw.* I. that he had Free-warren, and one Market every Week on the Thursday in his Mannor of Dikneswell, and had there a Fair every Year, to continue for ten Days together, by the Grant of King *H.* III. and he produced his Deed, which was attested before *Henry Rigate* and others, Justices Itinerants at Hertford, upon which all these Priviledges were allowed.

Quo Warr. 6
Ed. I. Rot.
40, cur. re-
cept. Scac.

Which Mannor came afterwards to that ancient Family of the *Perients*; for in the Reign of *Richard* II. *John Perient*, Esq. possest the same; he was Penon-bearer and Squire of the Body to King *R.* II. *H.* IV. and *H.* V. and

Master of the Horse to *Joan* the second Wife of *H.* IV. and
Daughter of the King of 𝕹𝖆𝖇𝖆𝖗𝖗𝖊; therefore I think it may
be very satisfactory to discover to the Reader the Nature
and Quality of these Offices.

Hund. of
Braveware

A Penon-bearer to the King, is one who carries his Flag
or his Banner ending in a Point or Tip, wherein the Arms
of the King either in War, or at a Funeral are depainted,
which Office is equivalent with the Degree of an Esquire.

Esquires were termed in Latin *Armigeri*, because they
were Bearers of Arms, or *Scutiferi*, for that they carried
the Shield; from thence the *Goths* called them *Schilpers,*
and the *Romans*, *Scutarii*, because they bore the Shields
and Helmets of the Roman Knights at their general Musters or Triumphs, or at their high and publick Solemnities,
or were Armour-bearers to Princes, or the better Sort of the
Nobility in 𝕰𝖓𝖌𝖑𝖆𝖓𝖉. They are of as great Antiquity as the
Feudal Law; for in old time, every Knight had two of
these Esquires, who carried his Morion and his Shield; they
were inseparable Companions to him, and did wear Coats of
Mail, or Defence, to assist him, for they held certain Lands
of the Knight in Escuage, which in Latin is called *Scuta-*
gium, the Service of the Shield, in such Manner as the
Knight himself held of the King by Knight-service: From
hence these Esquires in old time were called *Servientes;*
for at 𝕭𝖆𝖗𝖍𝖆𝖒 𝕯𝖔𝖜𝖓, saith Mr. *Selden,* from *Matt. Paris,*
Æstimati inter Milites electos et Servientes strenuos et bene
armatos sexaginta millia virorum fortium. Also in the
Army at 𝕷𝖎𝖓𝖈𝖔𝖑𝖓, in the Beginning of the Reign of *H.* III.
on the King's Part; *Recensiti sunt Milites* 400 *Bachalarii,*
firmæ 250 *Servientes quoq. et Equites tot et tales affuerunt*
numeri, quod Vices Militum possent pro necessitati imulere;
and there were taken of the Barons' Part, *Milites* 400 *præ-*
ter Servientes, Equites, et Pedites, qui sub numero non ca-
debant. et interfectus est in illo conflictu Serviens quidem ex
parte Baronum omnibus ignotus. This Addition of Esquire
was in ancient time only a Name of Charge and Office, and
first crept in among other Titles of Dignity and Worship in
the Reign of *R.* II. and little Mention is made of this or the
Addition of Gentleman in ancient Deeds, till the time of
H. V. when a Statute was made 1 *Regni sui,* That in all
Cases where Process of Outlawry lyeth, the Additions of the
Estate, Degree, or Mistery of the Defendant shall be incerted.

Markham's
Decads of
Honor, tit.
Esquire.

Selden, tit.
Hon. pt. 2,
fol. 831.

Spelm. Gloss.
tit. *Armiger,*
fol. 43.

Stat. 1 H. V.
cap. 5.

The most learned in the Art or Mistery of Honour hold
now there are five Sorts of Esquires. First, Esquires of the
King's Body, who are limited to the Number of four; they
keep the Door of the King's Bed-chamber, whensoever he
shall please to go to Bed, and have Precedency of all Knights'
younger Sons. The second are the eldest Sons of Knights,
andtheir eldest Sons successively. The third, the eldest

Hund. of
Bradewater
Sons of the youngest Sons of Barons, and others of the
greater Nobility. The fourth, such to whom the King
shall grant by Letters Patents, Coat Armour, or silver Col-
lars of Ess's, and silver or white Spurs: And the fifth, such
as have eminent Place in the Commonwealth, as Justices of
the Peace, Sheriffs of Counties, &c. or bear special Office
in the King's Houshold, as Gentlemen of the Privy Chamber, Carvers, Sewers, Cup-bearers, Pentioners, Gentlemen
Ushers, Serjeants at Arms, and all that have any near or
especial Dependance on the King's royal Person, and are
not knighted.

Some add to those, two other Distinctions of Men. 1 Captains in the Wars recorded in the King's List. 2 Attendants on the Knights of the Bath, who carry their Swords,
Beautrixes, and Spurs, with which the Knights are invested
at their Creations; and *Helidorus* and most of the Greek
and Latin Historians seem to consent to it.

Markham's
*Decade of
Honor*, tit.
Esquire, fol.
62.
These Esquires are not only Companions for Knights,
but in some Cases precede and go before them; as when the
younger Sons of Earls, Viscounts, or Barons, are not knighted and have no Title but this of Esquire, for the Blood of
their Ancestors (which was enobled in such a transcendant
Manner in them) doth challenge that Prerogative; neither
is it fit or convenient (though they be truly honourable in a
much higher Nature) that they should despise this Title,
but embrace it both for the Honor and the Antiquity, for it
is the first Display of Manhood, and the true Progress to
Perfection.

This Degree of Esquire is a special Priviledge to any of
the King's ordinary and nearest Attendants; for be his
Birth gentle or base, yet if he serve in the Place of an Esquire, he is absolutely an Esquire by that Service, for 'tis
the Place which dignifies the Person, and not the Person
the Place; so if any Gentleman or Esquire shall take upon
him the Place of a Yeoman of the King's Guard, he immediately loses all his Titles of Honor, and is no more than a
Yeoman.

'Tis great Pity that some Expedient is not taken to punish those who shall abuse this Title, and give it to Men of
mean Birth or inferior Quality, as Clerks who write Commissions, Under-sheriffs or Coroners who return Juries, or
Scriveners who draw Bonds or Writings of the like Nature,
or those who shall subscribe Esquire to his unworthy Quality,
for that 'tis an Usurpation upon the Right of the King, who
has the only Power of dispencing Honor to his Subjects;
and 'tis a Dishonour to that worthy Degree.

This *Perient* was also Master of the Horse to the Queen,
who is a great Officer at Court, and of high Esteem, for he
has the Charge and Government of the Queen's Stables, and

all the Officers and Servants belonging to them. He died *Hund. of* **Bradewater**
Anno 1415, 3 *Hen.* VII. and was buried in this Church.
His Arms were *Gules, three Crescents Argent.*

Edmond Perient succeeded, lived here in the time of *H.*
VI. married *Ann* the Daughter of *Thomas Vernon,* Esq. by
whom he had Issue ———— *Joan* married to *Edward
Cressy,* Lord of the Mannor of **Wackhamsted** in **Harpen-
den**; afterwards it descended to

Thomas Perient, Esq. who was constituted Sheriff of this *Rot. Pip.* 13 H VII. tit. Essex & Herts.
County and **Essex**, *Anno* 1498, 13 *Hen.* VII. He dyed,
leaving Issue

Thomas Perient, Esq. who was also made Sheriff of this
County and **Essex**, *Anno* 1536, 27 *H.* VIII. and died leav- Ibid. 27 H. VIII.
ing *Ann* his Wife surviving, and four Daughters; *Mary,*
Wife of *George Horsey, Ann* the Wife of *Anthony Carlton,* and two others, who were his Coheirs.

Ann his Widow held this Mannor for her Life, and after
her Decease, a Fine was levied between *George Horsey* De Fin. levat. Mich. 6 Ed. VI. *Rot.* 244, cur. recept. Scac.
and *Mary* his Wife, Demandants, and *Anthony Carlton*
and *Ann* his Wife, Deforceants of the Moiety of this Mannor, and the Land in **Digswell, Welwyn, Tewing,** and **Bishops Hatfield**; to the Use of *George Horsey* and his Heirs.

Which *George* was constituted Sheriff for this County and *Rot. Pip.* 14 Eliz. tit. Essex & Herts.
Essex, *Anno* 1572, 14 *Eliz.* He had Issue

Ralph Horsey, to whom Sir *John Horsey* of **Clifton,** in Fuller's *Wor-thies,* tit. Herts. fol. 32.
the County of **Dorset,** wanting an Heir male, gave the chief
Part of his Estate, which was very considerable, and his
Father adding this Mannor to it, at the time of his Death
advised him, That if it should happen that he should have
Occasion to sell Lands, not to part with this Mannor, but
rather to make Sale of some of his Land in **Dorsetshire.**
However, this young Gentleman, ill-advised, slighted his
Father's Counsel, and sold this Mannor, which, saith my
Author, was the Reason the Rest of his Estate thrived no Ibid.
better, for shortly after, the Remainder wasted, so that he
left not one Foot of it to his Posterity: This he mentioned
to instruct others in Obedience to their Parents' lawful Commands; Nature and common Gratitude obliges Children to
pay all Duty, Respect, and Obedience to Parents, because
they were the Authors of their Lives, nourish'd them in
their Infancy, supported them in their Childhood, educated
them in their Youth, fitted them for some Employment, or
otherwise qualified them to live in some Repute in the
World, when of themselves they were in no wise capable to *Whole Duty of Man,* tit. Sund.
subsist without their Help; a Debt so great, that 'tis im-
possible Children can in any sort requite or discharge; for
no Unkindness, no Fault in the Parent can acquit the Child
from this Duty, to which God had so great a Regard, that *Jerem.* xxxv. 18, 19.
he declared *Jonadab,* the Son of *Rechab,* should not want a

Hund. of
Brabetwater

Man to stand before him for ever, because his Sons had performed the Command of their Father not to drink Wine, and kept all his Precepts, and had done according to all that he had commanded them; and God streightly commanded that *Eph.* vi. 1, 2, 3. all Children should honor their Parents; the Apostle earnestly exhorted, they should obey them in the Lord because it was right, and the first Command, with Promise that they might live well and long upon the Earth: And our Church teaches Children all this in the Catechism, *viz.* to love, honour, and succour them; a Command very contrary to the Humour of some, who now-a-days publish and deride the Infirmities of their Parents, scorn their Advice, impute their Counsel to the Effects of Dotage, and covet their Deaths that they may obtain their Possessions; nay, some impatient to stay so long, have defrauded their Fathers, opprest their Mothers, and attempted to drive them from their Habitations, that Poverty, Grief, and Sorrow might break their Hearts, and hasten their Exits: But whilst such watch for the Death of their Parents, they may untimely meet with their own; for when God has promised long Life for a Reward to dutiful Children, the Disobedient may reasonably expect the Curse of a short one, for God established a Law *Deut.* xxvii. 16. among the *Jews,* to stone rebellious Children to Death, which *Deut.* xxi. 18, 19, 20, 21. was accounted the severest Death that was then used among *Matt.* xv. 6. the *Jews:* And our blessed Saviour reprimanded those that *Mark* vii. 10, made this Law of no Effect by Tradition. But let all such 11, 12. young Men remember for these things they must come to Judgment; and though there may be a small Respite of time for Tryal of the Amendment of their Lives, yet let them not delay their Repentance, for without it, Judgment will be certain, and the longer 'tis deferred, the severer will be the Sentence; for 'tis the next Command to that by which God requires our Duty to himself.

Sir *George Perient,* a Branch of the former Family, to whom this Gentleman sold this Mannor, was constituted *Rot. Pip.* 2 Sheriff of this County, *Anno* 1604, 2 *Jac.* I. but afterwards *Jac.* 1. he conveyed it to

Richard Sidley, Esq. who was also Sheriff for this Coun- Ibid. 22 Jac.I. ty, *Anno* 1624, 22 *Jac.* I. He married *Elizabeth* Daughter of *John Dairel* of Catchill in Kent, by whom he had *William, John, Ann* married to *Anthony Madison* of the *Middle Temple,* Esq. and *Elizabeth* married to *George Tooke,* Esq. and he died leaving

William his Heir, who married *Ann* Daughter of *Henry Boteler,* Esq. by whom he had *John, Ann, Elizabeth, Susan,* and *Mary.* She died the 1st of *April, Anno* 1647. And after the Decease of his first Wife, he married *Mary* the Daughter of Sir *Robert Honiwood* of Charing in Kent. He died in *June, Anno Dom.* 1658, and was buried in this

Parish Church; but I find he sold this Mannor before his Death, to

Humphry Shalcross, Esq. Citizen and Scrivener of **London**, who was made Sheriff of this County, *Anno* 1653, 5 *Car*. II. and married *Elizabeth Katharina Kemp*, by whom he had Issue *Francis* and *Henry*, and eleven other Sons and two Daughters, and died the 25th of *August*, 1665; and she died the 15th of *February*, 1677.

Rol. Pip. 5
Car. II.

Which *Francis* was his Heir, and married *Julian* one of the Daughters and Coheirs of Sir *Francis Boteler* of **Hatfield Woodhall**, Kt. by whom he had Issue, *Francis Boteler*, and died the 26th of *February*, 1681.

Francis Boteler Shalcross, was his Heir, lived till he attained to the age of eighteen Years, and died the 13th of *January*, 1693, and was buried at **Hatfield**, upon whose Death this Mannor came to

Henry Shalcross, Brother to his Father, who is the present Lord hereof.

THIS Rectory *Anno* 26 *Hen.* VIII. was rated in the King's Books at 7*l*. 4*s*. *per Annum* whereof the Lords of this Mannor have been Patrons.

The RECTORS.
John Champney, M. A. *William Minors. William Battel.*

This Church is situated in a Bottom, near the Mannor House, upon the River **Mimeram** in the Deanery of **Hertford**, in the Diocess of **Lincoln**, is cover'd with Tyle, has a square Tower at the West End thereof, wherein are three Bells and a short Spire erected upon it, and within the Church lye some Grave Stones, which have these Inscriptions.

**Hic jacet Johannes Perient, Armiger pro corpore Regis Richardi Secundi, et Penerarius ejusdem Regis. et Armiger. Regis Henrici Quarti. et Armiger. etiam Regis Henrici Quinti et Magister Equitum Johannæ. Filiæ Regis Navarr. et Regiæ Angliæ qui obiit.
——et Johanna Uxor ejus quondam capitalis Domicilla——quæ obiit 24 Aprilis Anno Dom. 1415.**

Below the Rails in the Chancel, lyes a Grave Stone with this Inscription.

Hic jacet Johannes Perient, Armiger, Filius Johannis Perient, Armigeri qui obiit undecimo die Novembris, anno Dom. 1442. cujus Anima propitietur Deus. Amen.

On another Stone may this Inscription be read.

Here sleep two Sisters, Daughters of Sir *Alexander Cave*, Kt. *Margaret* lived and died a Virtuous Maid ; *Martha* his tenth Child, was the Wife of *John Champney*, Rector of this Church, who by her had Issue one Son and one Daughter, *Justinian* and *Mary*.

Obiit hoc per Sororum eodem pariter die, viz. 29 Jan.
Anno Epoche Christianæ. 1637.

Felices nimium Dulci queis morte Potitis
Sancta Quies Positis contigit Exuviis,
Joh. Champneis *memor Uxoris Dulcissime ejusq; Sororis Clarissime*, P. E. P. F.

In the Middle Isle another is thus Engraved.

**Hic jacet Willielmus Roberts, quondam Auditor Episcopat. de Winton et Joces Uxor ejus, qui quidem Willi. obiit die —— anno Dom. MCCCC.
——et prefata Joces obiit 27 die Febr. anno Dom. MCCCCXXXIV. quorum animabus propitietur Deus.**

Another Stone is thus Inscribed.

Hic jacet Johannes Feild et Margeria Uxor ejus qui quidem Johan. obiit 17 die mensis Junii An. Dom. 1474 et prefata Margeria obiit 27 die Decembris Anno Dom. 1485. Quorum animabus propitietur Deus. Amen.

On the North Side of the middle Isle, a Stone has these Words.

Of your Charity pray for the Soules of Robert Battyl and Joane his Wife, and William their Son; which said Robert Battyl, Died Nov. the ——— Anno Dom. 1557. of whose Souls Jesu have Mercy.
　　The aforesaid William had by Joane his Wife, four Sons and six Daughters.

In the Burying-place on the North Side of the Chancel, is a Monument erected in Marble upon the Side of the Wall.

William Sidley, the Son of *Richard Sidley*, of Digswell in the County of Hertford, Esq; died in *June, Anno Dom.* 1658, aged 63 Years, and was Interred near this Place, in the Memory of whom this Monument was erected, *Anno Dom.* 1673. His first Wife was *Anna*, the Daughter of *Henry Butler* of London, Esq ; by whom he had Issue, *Anna, Elizabeth, Susanna* and *Mary*, Co-Heirs. She departed this Life the first day of *April, Anno Dom.* 1647.
　　His second Wife was *Mary*, the Daughter of Sir *Robert Honiwood*, of Charing in Kent.

Another Marble has this Inscription.

Here lyes the Body of *Humphry Shalcross*, of Digswell in the County of Hertford, Esq; Aged Threescore and ten Years, and ten days; who departed this Life on the 25th day of *August*, in the Year of our Lord, 1665, in hopes of a glorious Resurrection.

Another Inscription upon the Marble on the Wall.

In Memory of *Elizabeth Katharina Shalcross*, Wife of *Humphry Shalcross* of Digswell, Esq ; by whom he had thirteen Sons and two Daughters, and lyeth Buried near this Place.
　　　　　　Obiit 15 Febr. 1677, *Ætat.* 72.

In Memory of *Francis Shalcross*, eldest Son of *Humphry Shalcross* of Digswell, Esq; and *Elizabeth Katharina Kemp*, his Wife. He died the 26th of *February, Anno Dom.* 1681, *Ætatis* 51.

A Tomb on the South Side of the Church Yard.

Here lyeth Interred the Body of *John Champney*, Gent. Master of Art, Rector of the Parish of Digswell, and constant Preacher of God's Word here divers Years together, who was Buried in this place according to his desire, the 9th of *September*, 1645, being aged 42 Years, and left Issue one Son and one Daughter, *viz. Justinian* and *Mary*. *In Memoriam dilectissimi Filii dicti* Johannis Champney *hoc Monumentum posuit, Pia Mater* Sarah Champney.
　　　　　　April 14th 1648.

A Coat of Arms in the North Window of the Burying-place quartered as followeth.

The First *Gules, three Crescents Argent*. The Second *Or, a Cross fleury Sable.* The Third as the Second. The Fourth as the First.

WELVES, WELWINE.

WHEN King *Etheldred* had contracted an Alliance with *Richard* Duke of Normandy, by the Marriage of *Emma* his Daughter, by whom he had Issue *Edward* the Confessor: He began to value himself much more by the Power of this Relation, and willing to relieve his People from the barbarous

Usage, and the inhuman Actions of the insulting *Danes*, redoubled his wonted Courage, and sent strict Commissions with Instructions to the Governors of all Cities, Buroughs, and Towns in his Dominions, commanding, That at a certain Hour upon the Feast of St. *Brice*, all the *Danes* should be massacred; and common Fame tells us, that this Massacre began at a little Town called 𝕎elwine in 𝕳ertfordshire, within twenty four Miles of 𝕃ondon, in the Year 1012; from which Act, 'tis said, this Vill received the Name of 𝕎elwine, because the Weal of this County (as it was then thought) was there first won; but the *Saxons* long before called this Town 𝕎elues, from the many Springs which rise in this Vill; for in old time Wells in their Language were term'd *Welues*. And it seems this Massacre was acted with much Cruelty, for several Bodies have been found buried together within a Foot or two of the Surface of the Ground, in the North End of this Town, where one of the Bodies were lately digged up, and 'twas discovered, that many others lay buried there; and an entire and firm Piece of Shoe-leather belonging to one of the Bodies was shew'd to Dr. *Towerson*, the late Rector of this Parish, a learned Man, and a credible Person, who gave me this Relation under his Hand; and 'tis recorded in *Domesdei Book*, that

In Bradewater *Hundred. in* Welge, *ten. quidam Presbiter un. hid. in elemosina de Rege. Terra. est tres car in Dominio est una, et alia potest fieri. ibi sex bord. habentes un. car. ibi duo cotar. pratum un. car. pastura ad pec. Silva* 1 *porc. Inter totum val. et valuit semper* xxxv *sol. Istemet tenuit de Rege E. in elemosina et jacet in Ecclesia ejusdem ville. De hac Elemosina invasit.* Will. Blach *homo Episcopi* Bajocensis *super Regem duodecem acras ut Hundred. testat.*

A certain Presbiter or Parson, held one Hide of the King in free Alms, in Welues, in the Hundred of Bradewater. The arable is three Carucates, in Demeasne is one, and another may be made; there are six Bordars having one Carucate; there are two Cottagers; Meadow one Carucate; Common of Pasture for the Cattle; Wood to feed fifty Hogs. In the whole, it is worth, and always was worth five and thirty Shillings a Year. He had it of King *Edward* (the Confessor) in free Alms, and it lay in the Jurisdiction of the Church of the same Vill. *William Blach*, a Man (under the Protection) of the Bishop of Bayeux, did enter upon the King and took away twelve Acres from this Church as the Hundred can witness.

By this Record 'tis observable, that the Parson held this Mannor of King *Edward* the Confessor, by free Alms, and that it was in the Jurisdiction, or did belong to the Church of this Vill; and when *William* the Conqueror seized all the Lands of England into his Hands, he granted it back again to the Parson of this Church, to hold of him, by the same Tenure, from which time they have held it.

THIS Rectory *Anno* 26 *Hen*. VIII. was rated in the King's Books at the yearly Value of 21*l. per Ann.* and the Wardens, Fellows, and Scholars of the Colledge of *All Souls* in Oxford are Patrons.

The Names of the RECTORS.

1352 26 *Edw.* III. *John de Eyland.*
1354 28 *Edw.* III. *John Vernon.*
1366 40 *Edw.* III. *John Peyland.*
1388 11 *Rich.* II. *John Pecham.*
1411 12 *Hen.* IV. *William Whyte.*
1422 1 *Hen.* VI. *Walter Wilcocks.*
1429 7 *Hen.* VI. *Edmond Thrapston.*
1460 39 *Hen.* VI. *John Rakevein.*
1473 13 *Edw.* IV. *Stephen Saunder.*
1478 18 *Edw.* IV. *William Lathell,* Bachelor of Law.
1479 19 *Edw.* IV. *John Resby,* Batchelor in Divinity.
1495 10 *Hen.* VII. *John Denby.*
1508 23 *Hen.* VII. *Thomas Tompson,* Doctor.
1541 33 *Hen.* VIII. *Thomas Cordall.*
1563 5 *Eliz. Cutlac Cordall.*
1575 17 *Eliz. George Lewis.*
1606 4 *Jac.* I. *Thomas Wiltshire.*
1651 3 *Car.* II. *Nicholas Grace,* Doctor.
1662 14 *Car.* II. *Gabriel Towerson,* Doctor in Divinity.
1697 9 *Will.* III.

These Rectors have been Lords of this Mannor, which has Jurisdiction of holding Court Leet and Baron, where are several Copiholders of Inheritance, who pay Fines upon every Change or Alteration of their Estates at the Will of the Lord.

The Mannor of MARDLEY BURY.

KING *William* the Conqueror bestowed this Mannor upon *Goisfride de Bech,* one of the *Normans,* who assisted him in that great Expedition, when he obtained the Crown of this Kingdom, for 'tis recorded in *Domesdei Book* under the Title of *Terra Goisfridi de Bech.*

In *Bradwatre Hundred.* in *Welge* ten. Rogerus de Goisfrid. ii *hid.* *Terra est septem car. in Dom. est una, et alia potest fieri, ibi sex Vill. cum quatuor bord. habent quatuor Car. et quinta potest fieri. ibi quatuor Cotar. et unus servus, et un. Molin. de octo sol. pratum. duo car. pastura ad pec. Silva* xx *porc. Inter totum val.* l *sol. Quando recepit vigint sol. Tempore Regis* Edwardi *sex lib. Hanc Terram tenuer.* Gode *et filius ejus de* Eddid. Regina. *et vendere potuerunt.*

The Land of *Goisfride de Bech. Roger* held two Hides of *Goisfride de Bech* in *Welues,* in the Hundred of *Bradwater.* The arable is seven Carucates, in Demeasne is one and another may be made. There are six Villains with four Bordars, having four Carucates, and a fifth may be made; there are four Cottagers and one Servant, and one Mill of eight Shillings Rent; Meadow two Carucates; Common of Pasture for the Cattle; Wood to feed twenty Hogs. In the whole it is worth fifty Shillings a Year, when he received it, twenty Shillings, in the time of *Edward* (the Confessor) six Pounds. *Gode* and his Son, held this Land of Queen *Editha* and might sell it.

Pat. 12 Ed. I.
M. 7, *cur re-*
cept. Scac.

This Mannor came afterwards to the Possession of *Philip de Mardley,* from whom it was denominated. In *Hilary* Term 12 *Edw.* I. he conveyed by Deed one Messuage, an hundred Acres of Land, and two Acres of Wood in the Vills of *Dachelsworth* and *Welues,* to the Use of *Robert Burnell* Bishop of *Bath* and *Wells,* to whom the King de-

livered the Broad Seal of **England**, on Tuesday the Fast of
St. *James* the Apostle, in the same Year, and caused him
to carry it with him from **Dover**, over the Sea to **France**,
and to bring it back again on Friday next after the Feast of
the Assumption of St. *Mary*, in the 17th Year of his Reign,
from **Gascoine** and **France**; but I suppose that this Conveyance made to him was only in Trust for *Philip Mardley*,
for such Conveyances in Trust were usual in those Days;
and it was reconveyed to him again, for I find that *Philip
de Mardley* gave to *William de Bernet*, Clerk, one Messuage, an hundred and forty Acres of Land, three Acres of
Wood, and twenty Pence Rent, in **Datchworth** and **Mardley**, and whatsoever he had in the same Vills, to hold to the
said *William* and his Heirs for ever, of him the said *Philip*
and his Heirs, by the Rent of a Clovegilliflower, and him
the said *William*, to be acquited of all Services, except Suit
of Court of Sir *Robert*, Son of *Thomas* in the same Vill of
Mardley.

Hund. of
Bradewater

De Banco Re-
gi, Mich. 13
Ed. 1. Herts.
Rot. 52.

Shortly after, it was in the Possession of *Bartholomew
Badlesmere*, who was summoned to Parliament among the
Barons of this Realm, from the 3d of *Edw.* II. to the 14th
of the same King; but after that, assisting *Thomas* Earl of
Lancaster, and other discontented Barons of that Age;
Margaret his Wife (Aunt and Coheir to *Thomas* the Son
of *Richard de Clare*) with *Giles de Badlesmere* his younger
Son, and all his Daughters were taken in his Castle of
Leeds, sent to the *Tower* of **London**; and he receiving a
Defeat at **Burrough-brigge** was taken there among the Rest,
and sent to **Canterbury**, to be drawn and hang'd: He was
executed at the Gallows of **Bleene**; his Head was cut off
and set upon a Pole at **Burgate**, at which time it was found,
he died seiz'd of this Mannor.

Bar. vol. 2,
fol. 58.

Giles Badlesmere was his Heir, found great Favour from
the King, obtained all his Father's Harness; and when he
came of Age, had Livery of his Lands, *Anno* 7 *Edw.* III.
He married *Elizabeth* the Daughter of *William Mounta-
cute* Earl of **Salisbury**, by whom he had no Issue, for his four
Sisters, *Maud* Wife of *John de Vere*, Earl of **Oxford**,
Elizabeth Wife of *William de Bohun*, Earl of **Northampton**,
formerly Wife of *Edmond Mortimer*, *Margaret* Wife of Sir
John Tiptoft, and *Margery*, Wife of *William* Lord *Roos*,
were his Coheirs; and upon the Partition, this Mannor came
to *Margaret* the Wife of *John Tiptoft*.

Ibid. fol. 59.

But I find no more of it till it came to the Possession of
Gertrude, Daughter of *William Blount*, Lord *Mountjoy*,
Marchioness of **Exeter**, who was attainted of High Treason
in the time of *Henry* VIII. upon which it devolved to the
Crown, but soon after, that King granted it to Sir *John
Throckmorton*, Kt. in Fee, from whom it descended to *Ni-*

De Fin. levat.
1 & 2 P. & M.
Rot. 601, cur.
recept. Scac.

Hund. of Brabdnater *cholas* his Son; he held it in the first and second Years of *Philip* and *Mary*; afterwards sold it to Sir *Rowland Lytton*, from whom it is come to Sir *William Lytton*, the right Descendant and present Lord hereof.

LOCKLEYS.

WITHIN this Vill is a fair Seat called 𝕷𝖔𝖈𝖐𝖑𝖊𝖞𝖘, from some Owner thereof, situated upon the River 𝕸𝖎𝖒𝖊𝖗𝖆𝖒, which was purchased by *Edward Wingate*, Esq. second Son of *George Wingate* of 𝕭𝖆𝖗𝖑𝖎𝖓𝖌𝖙𝖔𝖓 in the County of 𝕭𝖊𝖉𝖋𝖔𝖗𝖉, Esq. who married *Margaret* Daughter of *Peter Taverner* of 𝕳𝖊𝖝𝖙𝖔𝖓 in this County, and *Frances Docwra* his Wife, by whom he had Issue *Edward* and *Frances* married to *Eustace Needham*.

Edward was his Heir, and married *Mary* one of the Daughters and Coheirs of *Ralph Alway*, of 𝕮𝖆𝖓𝖓𝖔𝖓𝖘 in 𝕾𝖍𝖊𝖓𝖑𝖊𝖞 in this County; by whom he had Issue *Francis*, *Edward*, and three other Sons and seven Daughters: He was a Captain in the Militia, and a Justice of the Peace for this County many Years: He was a Burgess for the Borough of 𝕾𝖙. 𝕬𝖑𝖇𝖆𝖓𝖘 in the Parliament held *Anno* 16 *Car.* I. and one of the grand Commissioners of Excise for King *Charles* II. He made a fair Warren to this Seat, stocked it with a choice Breed of Rabbits, all silver haired, and planted it with great Store of excellent Walnut trees; and in the Front of his House, raised a pleasant Orchard, set with the best and rarest Fruit Trees, where several Cuts are made, through which the 𝕸𝖎𝖒𝖊𝖗𝖆𝖒 passes in several Streams, stored with fair Trouts and other Fish, for the Provision of his Table; but upon his Death, this Seat descended to *Edward* his surviving Son and Heir, a Justice of the Peace for this County, and the present Possessor hereof.

THE Church is dedicated to St. *Mary* the Virgin, and *Anno* 26 *H.* VIIl. was rated in the King's Books at the yearly Value of 21*l.* and the Wardens and Fellows of the Colledge of *All-Souls* in the University of 𝕺𝖝𝖋𝖔𝖗𝖉 are Patrons. This Church is situated near the middle of the Town, in the Deanery of 𝕳𝖊𝖗𝖙𝖋𝖔𝖗𝖉, in the Diocess of 𝕷𝖔𝖓𝖉𝖔𝖓; and contains two Isles covered with Lead, with a Chancel (adjoyning the East End, and a square Tower where was a Ring of five Bells) lately on the North Side thereof, but since has fallen down.

In the Chancel are these Inscriptions upon Grave Stones.

𝕳𝖎𝖈 jacet 𝕯𝖔𝖒𝖎𝖓𝖚𝖘, Johan. Rachvayne 𝖉𝖊 𝖁𝖎𝖑𝖑𝖊 𝖉𝖊 Welwyn ac 𝕽𝖊𝖈𝖙𝖔𝖗 𝕰𝖈𝖈𝖑𝖊𝖘𝖎æ 𝖕𝖆𝖗𝖔𝖈𝖍𝖎𝖆𝖑𝖎𝖘 𝖊𝖏𝖚𝖘𝖉𝖊𝖒 𝖁𝖎𝖑𝖑æ qui 𝖔𝖇𝖎𝖙 𝖕𝖊𝖓𝖚𝖑𝖙𝖎𝖒𝖔 𝖉𝖎𝖊 𝖒𝖊𝖓𝖘𝖎𝖘 Septembris an. 𝕯𝖔𝖒. MCCCCLXXIII.

——— 𝕸𝖆𝖌𝖗𝖎 Will. Lathel 𝖎𝖓 𝕷𝖊𝖌𝖎𝖇𝖚𝖘 𝕭𝖆𝖈𝖈𝖆𝖑𝖆𝖚𝖗𝖊𝖎 𝖓𝖚𝖕𝖊𝖗 ——— 𝖎𝖘𝖙𝖎𝖚𝖘 𝕰𝖈𝖈𝖑𝖊𝖘𝖎æ. qui obiit 𝖎𝖓 𝕱𝖊𝖘𝖙𝖔 𝕹𝖆𝖙𝖎𝖛𝖎𝖙𝖆𝖙𝖎𝖘, 𝕭𝖊𝖆𝖙æ, Mariæ, 𝖁𝖎𝖗𝖌𝖎𝖓𝖎𝖘, An. Dom. Millimo, CCCCLXXIX°.

𝕬𝖓𝖓𝖔 𝕯𝖔𝖒. Mº.CCCCLXXXXVº 𝖒𝖊𝖓𝖘. Januarij 𝖉𝖎𝖊 XX. obiit iste 𝕸𝖆𝖌𝖎𝖘𝖙𝖊𝖗 Johannes Reysby, 𝖎𝖓 𝖘𝖆𝖈𝖗𝖆 𝕿𝖍𝖊𝖔𝖑𝖔𝖌𝖎𝖆 𝕭𝖆𝖈𝖈𝖆𝖑𝖆𝖚𝖗𝖊𝖚𝖘 𝖍𝖚𝖏𝖚𝖘 𝕰𝖈𝖈𝖑𝖊𝖘𝖎æ 𝕽𝖊𝖈𝖙𝖔𝖗.

Here lyeth buried the Body of Mr. *Thomas Cordall*, sometime Parson of *Hund. of* this Church, the which departed the XXXI. day of *January* in the year *Bradewater* of our Lord God M°.DLXIII.

Georgius Lewis generosa familia natus, et hujus Ecclesiæ Rector constitutus, postquam pastorali Officio in eadem per triginta annos summa diligentia perfunctus esset, obiit 28 die Martii an. Dom. 1606. *ætatis vero suæ,* 55.

Over this Inscription is his Coat of Armes, being *a Cheveron between three Flower de Luces.*

Here lyeth *William Cordal,* Citizen and Merchant Taylor of London, and *Anne* his Wife, which *William* departed this World, the sixth day of *March* in the Year of our Lord, MCCCCCLVII———

In the Church.

In the East Window of the South Isle of the Church remains the Picture of a Man in Armour with a red Mantle over it from the arm-pits to the Knees, described in a praying posture, kneeling and stretching out his hands with this Inscription,

Johannes de Gatesden.

And not far from that in the same Window, a Coat of Arms bearing *Argent, two Barres Gules, and in it a Mullet for Distinction of a third Brother.*

What Relation he had to this Place is not known, but Dr. *Fuller* takes Notice in his Worthies, of an eminent Physician of that name, who flourished, *Anno Dom.* 1320, and *Matthew Paris* speaks of another who in all *Paris, anno* Probability may be the Person, where discoursing, whether the Order of 1245. Priesthood is debarr'd the Honour of Knighthood of the Sword, says that he finds that antiently they have been allowed it, but not without first laying aside their spiritual Cures, and applying themselves to a secular Life, and proceeds in these Words, *Dic natalis* Johan. de Gatesden *Clericum, et multis ditatum beneficiis (sed omnibus ante expectatem resignatis, quia sic oportuit) Baltheo cinxit militari.*

A fair Tomb erected in the Church Yard has this Inscription.

Here lyeth the Body of *Edward Wingate* of Lockleys, Esq; who married *Mary* one of the Daughters and Co-heirs of *Ralph Alway* of Cannons in the Parish of Shenly, Esq; and had by her five Sons and seven Daughters; he dyed the *8th* day of *August* in the year of our Lord 1685. and of his Age 79.

A REGISTER of several things belonging to the Parish Church of Welwyn. in *Anno Christi* 1541, taken out of the Register Book of that Church, as it is spelled there.

The Inventorie remembring all suche stuffe as belongyte and perteynith to the Paroche Cheurche of Welwyn, *tayn before* Thomas Cordal *Parson of the same,* Robert Bordall *and* John Culwick *Cheurchwardens, the fyrst day of* Februarie *in the yeare of our Lord God,* A. MCCCCCxlii.

Imprimis, two Chalices of Silver, to one double guylt, and the other percell gylt.

Item, a Croosse w^t Seint *Mary* and *John* w^t the foote to the same belonging of coper and gylt.

Item, ii pippis of the same metall gyltid to put upon the Crosse staffe.

Item, a croosse clothe of grene silke staynyd with the Image of the Trinite.

Item, one other croosse clothe of Latyne for every Day, an old croosse clothe of buckeram staynid and the crosse staiff.

Item, a purse of silke w^t or w^t yn ys a box of Iverie garnysshed w^t silver to bere the blissid Sacrament in visitacions to syke folke.

Item, iii Corporascasys w^t iii Corporas clothis.

Item, on box of woode within lyithe iii Lawnnys of netill clothe.

Item, on Sacrament clothe of bright violet silke for the Sacrament every day.

Item, on oulde Chousbyn of silke.

Hund. of
Bradewater

Vestiments 8.

Imprimis, on Vestiment w^t amyse and albe stoole Fannon and Parrells of Sattyne of Briggels violet or Blew colour.

Item, another Vestiment w^t the Albe stoole Fannon and parrells of branchyd dammaske broone or russet colour embrodyd w^t flowers of Venyse golde.

Item, an other Vestiment w^t the Albe stoole Fannon and parells of blew silke sparkelyd w^t. flowers or beests of venice golde callyd the Requiem Vestiment.

Item, another Vestiment w^t the Albe stole Fannon and parrells of branchyd damaske lyght grene for Sommer.

Item, on other Vestiment w^t the Albe stole Fannon and the apparells of wyght fusthian embroydyd flowers of cooper golde.

Item, on other Vestiment w^t the Albe stole Fannon and parrells of silke dark grene callyd clothe of Bawde Kyne,

Item, on other of olde velveyt tawne embrordyd with sterrys of Venice gilde w^t the Albe stolen Fannon and parrells.

Item, on Tunackyll for the decon of Broonde, silke Redde callyd clothe of Bawde kyne with the Albe stole Fannon and parrells.

Item, on other old suspendid Tunackyll for the prest w^t. an Albe stole fannon backyng the rest.

Item, ou other olde Tunnackyll lackyng all.

Item, an herse Clothe of Blew silke of sperkillyd w^t Lyons wevyd in of Venice golde.

Item, on other herse clothe of coarse blaake wullyn w^t a crosse of wyght lynyn clothe uppon it.

Books.

Item, on gret Antiphon. of Velhin. wryten and notyd. *Item*, another smaller in two parts of the gyft of *Will. Cordall* of London. Two graylls of Velhin. wryten and notyd on prewtt legent of papyr.

Item, a nother Antyphon. of Velhin. wryten, and notyd, ii Salters of Velhin wryten, iii processioners of papyr, and ii of Velhin. wryten and notyd.

Item, ii prynt Masbooks, on new, the other olde.

Item, on masbooke of Velhin. wryten, ii hymmes pryntid, and ii other of Velhin. wryten.

Item, one Lattyne baasyn and a eware, iii pykyd candlesticke w^t. a nosell, ii sensours of Lattyne, on lytle baasyn of cooper for frankynsence, one lawmpe.

Surples.

Item, one Surplesse with slevys, and other ix witout Slevys good and baad.

Item, an olde peynted clothe lyke dammaske wurke, A Vayle for lent, iiii boerds, and iiii trestills, a Basket for hollywydbred, on holywater stoop of Lattyne.

Hygh Aulter.

Imprimis, v alter clothys of lynine, on canvase clothe to cover the alter clothis, an alter clothe to hang fore the anlter of sattyne of Bryggs panyd blue and red, vi towells. ii pare of candlesticks for taappers of Lattyne, an olde payntid clothe to haug before the alter for every day, ii great stondards candelstick of Latyne, iii paxis.

Item, iiii peyntid clothis for the sepulcher, a payntyd clothe or canopye for the Sacrament, and iiii stayfs, vi Bannars clothes, ii Stremers paynted.

Saint Nicholate Aulter.

Imprimis, ii Aulter clothis halowyd on canvase clothe and ii old payntid clothis to hang afore the same Alter.

The other Aulter.

Item, One Alter clothe of Lynine, a canvase clothe and ii old payntid clothis to hang afore the same Altar.

Cooppys.

Item, ii Cooppys the on of blue velvyet w^t the parrell of Imagery embroderyd w^t Venyce golde and the body of the same w^t flowers of lyke golde.

Item, on sheyt to ley the same yn. The other Coope of grene silke callyd clothe of Bawdekyn for every day.

By this Inventory you may observe that there were three Altars in this Church, and that there was as well a Deacon as a Priest to attend in it.

The BENEFACTORS to this Church and Parish.

Anne, Wife of *Anthony Carleton*, Esq. one of the Daughters and Heirs of *Thomas Peryent*, Esq. gave a Messuage and a Rood of Ground, with the Appurtenances, lying in **Welwyn** to the Repair of this Church, and to the Relief of the Poor of this Parish; and 'tis held that the Church-house, and a Pightle called the **Anchor Pightle**, both of them lying on the East Side of the Church-yard is the same Messuage and Ground aforesaid, whereof the House is now converted into an Almshouse, and the Rent of the Pightle is now constantly disposed of to the use of the Poor.

John Baxfield of **Lawrence-Aiet** in this County Wheelwright, gave a Messuage or Tenement called **Cooks**, and three Acres and three Roods of arable Land, whereof the three Acres lying in **Letchmore-field**, and the three Roods in **Holdmore-field** in the Parish of **Caddington** in **Bedfordshire**, to the Use of the Poor in this Parish.

Josias Barners, late of **Clerkenwell** in the County of **Middlesex**, Esq. by his Will gave a Rent charge of five Pounds *per Annum*, payable to the Churchwardens and Overseers of the Poor of this Parish every Year, towards the binding out of poor Children in this Parish Apprentices, only to Trades of Manufactory.

A Person whose Name is not now known, gave to the Poor of this Parish, a Piece of Land called the **Town-piece**, abutting on the North, on the High-way, leading from this Town to **Stevenage**, and on all other Sides, upon the Lands of *Ralph Wingate*, Esq.

Hund. of **Bradewater**

Cart. dated 5 Dec. 10 Elis.

Cart. dated 9 Martii, 12 Eliz.

Test. Jos. Barners.

EYE, AIET MONTFITCHET, AIET ST. PETERS, LITTLE AIET.

THIS Vill is situated about two Miles distant from **Welwin**, towards the West, of which I find it recorded in *Domesdei Book*, under the Title of *Terra* **Bajocensis**.

In **Brachings** *Hundred, in* **Eia** *tenuit Petrus de Episc.* **Bajocensis** *dim. hid. Terra est dim. car. sed non est, ibi unum Molendinum de tribus solidis, de gurgitibus 200 Anguill. pratum dimid. car. et de fren. decem sol. Hæc terra val. vigint. sol. Quando recepit decem sol. tempore Regis Edwardi trigint. sol. Suen tenuit homo Com.* Herald. *et vendere potuit.*

The Land of the Bishop of **Bajeux**.

Peter held half an Hide in **Eye** in the Hundred of **Braughing**, of the Bishop of **Bajeux**. The arable is half a Carucate, but it is not now, there is one Mill of three Shillings Rent by the Year, two hundred Eels out of the Pool; Meadow half a Carucate, and ten Shillings Rent by the Year for Hay. This Land was worth twenty Shillings a Year, when he received it ten Shillings a Year, in the time of King *Edward* (the Confessor) thirty Shillings a Year: *Suen* a Man (under the Protection) of Earl *Harold* held it, and might sell it,

By this Record 'tis certain this was a watry Place, for here was a Mill, and a Pool which yielded two hundred Eels for Rent by the Year. From whence this Vill was denominated; for anciently *Eye* was used in the same Sense as *Ea*, which signifies a watry Place. But it seems at that time, this Vill lay in the Hundred of **Braughing**.

In the time of King *H.* II. this Vill was in the Possession of *Richard Montfitchet*, who attended King *R.* in that Expeditionmade *Anno* 6 *Regni sui* into **Normandy**, and was confirmed *Anno* 2 *Johan.* in the Forrestership of **Essex**; for

Hund. of
Bradewater

*Rot. Pip 3,
4, & 5 Johan.
tit. Essex and
Herts.*
which and the Custody of the Castle of 𝕳ertfor𝖉 he gave a hundred Marks; and was Sheriff of this County and 𝕰ssex, in the 3d, 4th, and 5th Years of King *John*, and then died leaving Issue

Richard, who was his Heir, but being within Age, the King granted the Wardship of him to *Roger de Lacy*, Constable of 𝕮hester, for a thousand Marks; but *Millicent* his Mother, *Anno* 12 *Johan.* purchased the Wardship of him again, for eleven hundred Marks. When he attained to his full Age, he joyned with the rebellious Barons against King *John*, and was so active in those Troubles, that when the Barons had got the Power into their Hands, they chose him for one of the five and twenty Governours of the Realm: He continued in Arms with the fiercest, and was taken Prisoner in the Battle fought *Anno* 1 *H.* III. at 𝕷incoln: He was in the Turnament held *Anno* 7 *H.* III. at 𝕭lith, notwithstanding the King's Prohibition, for which his Lands were siezed; but afterward he came to better Temper, made his Submission, return'd to his Allegiance, and the King received him into his Favour. He was constituted Justice of several of his Forrests *Anno* 21 *H.* III. made Sheriff of
*Rot. Pip. 26,
27, & 28 H.
III. tit. Essex
and Herts.*
this County and 𝕰ssex 26 *H.* III. for the last half of that Year, continued in the same Office for the three next succeeding Years, and for the first Half of the 30th Year of the same King; shortly after he died without Issue, and his three Sisters, *Margery* married to Sir *Hugh de Bolebet*, Kt. *Aveline* to *William de Forz*, Earl of 𝕬lbermarl, and *Philippa* to *Hugh de Playz*, were his Coheirs, among whom his Lands were divided; and from him this Vill might receive the Adjunct of *Montfitchet* to its Name, but in short time after it came to

William de Ayete, for he held this Mannor, called then by the Name of 𝕬iete 𝕸ontfitchet of the Honour of 𝕭ologne, and had View of Franc-pledge, Assize of Bread, Wine, and Ale, Gallows, Tumbrel, and Free-warren, but by what Warrant he held them, the Jury knew not; afterwards the said *William de Ayete* came and shewed the Grant
*Quo Warr. 6
Ed. 1. Rot. 14
indorso.*
of King *Henry*, that he had, and his Heirs ought to have one Fair there for ever, and it was allowed.

*Trin.1 Ed. II.
Rot. 49, cur.
recept. Scac.*
It being found in Trinity Term, *Edw.* II. that a Fine was levyed *Anno* 13 *Edw.* I. between *John de Yeland*, Plaintiff, and *Ralph* the Son of *Walter* and *Margery* his Wife, Deforceants, of the Mannor of 𝕬yete, and the Advowson of the same Church, in the County of 𝕳ertfor𝖉, *John* of 𝕷ancaster, Cousin and Heir of *Margery*, came and assign'd Errors in levying of the Fine, whereupon Judgment was given that *John de Yeland* shall recover that Moiety of the Land which was the said *Walters*; upon which *John Lancaster* entred, and that the Fine stood in Force for

these two Moieties of *Walter* and *Hugh*, and the other Moiety remained to *John Lancaster* and his Heirs. *Hund. of Bradewater*

Afterwards *Nicholas Corbet* obtained this Mannor held *in Capite* of the King, ought Suit to the County, and paid five Shillings a Year to the Sheriff's Aid; since it came to the Possession of

John Poteyn, who died seiz'd hereof, leaving Issue *John* and *Thomas*; and upon his Disoease it descended to

John who was his Heir, but since his time it has been dismembred and divided among several Persons, whereof some Part was conveyed to *Brocket*, from whom it passed to Sir *Thomas Read* by the Marriage of *Mary*, one of the Daughter and Coheirs of Sir *John Brocket*; from him it descended to Sir *John Read*, who left Issue Sir *James Read*, Baronet, the present Possessor hereof.

Another Parcel of this Land was sold to *Thomas Perient*, Esq. who left it to *Thomas Perient* his Son and Heir, from whom it descended to *Thomas* his Son and Heir, who gave for his Arms *Gules, three Crescents Argent*, and convey'd it to *Rowland Hale*, Esq. of whose Family I intend to treat in the Parish of King's Walden; from whom it came to *William Hale*, Esq. who conveyed it to *Elizabeth* his Wife, who survived him, and is the present Possessor hereof.

IN *Anno* 26 *H.* VIII. this Rectory was rated in the King's Books, at the yearly Value of 8*l.* 13*s.* 4*d.* and Sir *James Read* is the present Patron hereof.

The RECTORS.

Mr. *Bussey*
Mr. *Ivory*
Mr. *John Birch*
Mr. *Nathan Vereyard*

Mr. *Charles Horne*, present Rector, who has lately built half the Rectory House, and the Chancel.

This Church is situated upon a dry Hill, not far from the River Lea and the Mimeram; there is a short Spire erected upon the Tower, and within the Chacel some Gravestones have these Inscriptions.

Pray for the Soul of Thomas Fysh Patron of this Church, and Elizabeth his Wife, which Thomas decrased the tenth day of March, *an. Dom.* 1553. in the seventh year of the Reign of King Edward the sixth, on whose Souls God have mercy.

Hic jacet quod reliquum est Mariæ Elwes *Relictæ* Jeremiæ Elwes, *Armigeri, obiit* 4. *die* Decembris, *anno Dom.* 1667. *Ætatis suæ* 68.

Here lies the Body of *Elizabeth Horne*, Wife of *Charles Horne*, Rector of this place, who dyed in Child-bed, *Nov.* 10. 1688.

Here lyeth the Body of Mrs. *Elizabeth Birch*, Wife of Mr. *John Birch*, Rector of Spot, who departed this life the tenth day of *November*, 1669. in the 47th. year of his age, leaving two Daughters, *viz. Martha* and *Elizabeth*.

Here lyeth the Body of Mr. *John Birch*, who was Rector of this Parish 41 years, and dyed the 26th. of *July*, 1682. in the 74th year of his age.

Here lyeth the Body of Dame *Elizabeth Perient* Widow, who was the Daughter of *Richard Baron*, Esq; she was first Wife to *Richard Hare*, Esq; after to *George Rotherham*, Esq; lastly to Sir *George Perient*, Kt. She dyed the 2d. of *December*, 1655. being ninety years of age.

EYE, AIOT, ST. LAWRENCE or GREAT AIOT

STANDS among the Woods, upon an Hill about a Mile distant from Aiot St. Peter towards the West; it was Parcel of the Possessions of Earl *Harold*, who held it in the Reign of *Edward* the Confessor, and all the time of his Usurpation, but when he was slain in that fatal Battel near Hastings in Sussex, it came to *William* the Conqueror, who obtained all *Harold's* Estate with the Government of the Kingdom, and he gave a small Parcel of it to the Reeve of the Hundred, but the Residue of it to *Robert de Gernon*, a great Norman, for it is recorded in *Domesdei Book*,

Domesd. Lib.
fol.141, nu.42. *In Bradewater Hundred. in Airte, tenuit prepositus de isto Hundred. novem acras de Rege. Terra est uno bovi. valet et valuit semper novem denar. hanc terram tenuit Siward homo Aluuini de Godtone, et vendere potest.*

Ibid. fol. 137,
nu 20. *In Airte, tenuit Will. de Robert Gernon, duo hidas et dimid. Terra est sex car. In Dominio est una et alia potest fieri, ibi sex Vill. cum tribus bord. habentibus tres cor. et tertia potest fieri, ibi unus servus, prat. un. car. pastura ad pec. Silva centum porc. Inter totum valet xl sol. Quando recepit lx sol. tempore Regis Edwardi sex lib. hanc terram tenuerunt duo Teigni hom. Regis Edwardi, et vendere potuerunt; hanc invasit Will. homo Roberti super Regem si reclamat Dominum suam ad protectorem.*

The Reeve of this Hundred held nine Acres of the King in Airte, in the Hundred of Bradewater; there is arable for one Ox, it is worth, and always was worth, nine Pence a Year. *Siward* a Man (under the Protection) of *Alwine de Godtone*, held this Land and might sell it.

William held of *Robert de Gernon* two Hides and an half in Airte. The arable is six Carucates, in Demeasne is one, and another may be made; there are six Villains with three Bordars, having three Carucates, and a third may be made; there is one Servant, Meadow one Cacate, Common of Pasture for the Cattle, Wood to feed one hundred Hogs; in the whole it is worth forty Shillings a Year, when he received it sixty Shillings a Year, in the time of King *Edward* (the Confessor) six Pounds a Year. Two Thanes Men (under the Protection) of King *Edward* (the Confessor) held this Land and might sell it: *William* a Man (under the Protection) of *Robert* intruded upon the King, when he claimed his Lord again to be his Protector.

Shortly after this Mannor return'd again to the Crown, and King *H*. I. granted it to one *Radhere*.

A pleasant conceited witty Man, born of mean Parentage. Weaver's
Fun. Mon. p.
433.
Mon. Angl.
vol. 2, fol.
166, 167. When he attain'd to the Flower of his Youth, he frequented the Houses of the Nobles and Princes, but not content herewith, would often repair to Court, spent the whole Day in Sights, Banquets, Plays, and other Trifles; where by Sport and Flattery he would wheedle the Hearts of the great Lords to him, and sometimes would thrust himself into the Presence of the King, where he would be very officious to obtain his royal Favour. By these Artifices he gained this Mannor, and whatever else was fit for him to ask; when he had spent the Remainder of his Youth in this Sort, he began to reflect upon his wicked Course of Life, and to lament the Heinousness of his Sins; and that he might obtain a full

and perfect Indulgence of them, he resolved to go to the *Hund. of Bradewater*
Court of 𝕽𝖔𝖒𝖊, desiring to shew the worthy Fruit of his
Penitency, by so laborious a Journey. His Mind inspired
from Heaven, and prompt with a holy Zeal, he set forth, and
God directing his Journey, brought him safe to his desir'd
Place; where deploring all his Sins at the Tombs of the blessed
Apostles, *Peter* and *Paul*, and calling to Mind the Follies
and Ignorances of his Youth, he earnestly beseeched them,
that they would procure from the Lord the Remission of his
Sins, and promised for the Future, that he would never commit the like again, but always devoutly obey the holy Will
of God; and besought those two most famous Luminaries of
Heaven, Men of Mercy, that they would be Mediators between God and him, and he would take Care to avoid his
former Vices, and would diligently perform what he had so
solemnly promised. In the mean time, whilst he continued
there, he began to grow very weak, and his Grief and Sorrow more and more increasing, he was at length brought to
great Extremity, and fearing that God was not yet satisfi'd
for his Sins, he pour'd forth his Heart in the Sight of God
as it were Water, and dissolving the same into Tears, earnestly prayed that if his Health would permit, it might be
lawful for him to return into his Country, and that he might
build an Hospital there for the Recovery of the Poor from
Sickness, and for the Administration of Necessaries to them
so far as he might be able; and not long after, the most be-
nign and merciful Lord, who beheld the Tears of *Hezekiah*,
and answered the Importunity of *Canaan* with the Reward
of his Piety, did also favorably respect this weeping Penitent, granted him the Restoration of his Health; and when
he was perfectly recovered from his Weakness, and in short
made whole, he began his Journey for his own Country, resolving to perform the Vow which he had made. When
he had travelled some Part of the Way, and was lodged in
his Inn, he saw a Vision at Night full of Terror, yet mixt
with some Sweetness; for he beheld a living Creature having four Feet and two Wings, seated by him in an high
Place; but when he had viewed it a while, it was carried
away aloft beyond his Sight, and whilst he wonder'd at it,
he turn'd his Eyes downwards, and beheld a most horrible
Pit under him, which struck him with great Fear and Terror; for the Depth thereof render'd all Mankind very unsafe.
He, conscious to himself of his own Wickedness, thought
that he was falling into this wonderful Precipice, which Fancy did so horribly fright him, that he cryed out most vehe-
mently; to whom a certain Man immediately appeared,
shewing great Majesty in his Countenance, extraordinary
Beauty in his Face, and impour'd with imperial Authority,
assured him of Safety, and said to this Effect:—Oh Man!

What and how much Aid is ready at Hand for him, who
craves Help from God in so great Danger of Death.

When he had answered these things, and his Courage and
Strength was restored, the other proceeded:—I am *Bartholomew* the Apostle of Jesus Christ, who came to succour thee
in the time of thy Trouble, and to reveal to thee, the Secrets of the heavenly Mystery; Know ye that I by the Will
and Command of the holy Trinity, and by the common Favour and Advice of the Court of Heaven, have chosen a
Place at Smithfield in the Suburbs of London, where you
shall found a Church in my Name, and build there the
House of God, the Tabernacle of the Lamb, and the Temple
of the Holy Ghost; and Almighty God shall dwell, sancti-
fie, glorifie, and keep that House, holy, undefiled, and without Spot for ever; His Eyes shall be open, and his Ears
shall be intent upon that House Day and Night, that he
that shall ask in that Place, shall receive; he that shall seek
there, shall find; and he that shall knock, shall enter; for
every Convert and Penitent, who shall pray in that Place,
shall be heard in Heaven; He that shall seek there with a
perfect Heart, shall find Help in all his Troubles; and to
them who shall knock at the Door with an holy Desire, the
Angels assisting there, shall open the Gate of the Kingdom
of Heaven, taking and offering to God the Prayers and Desires of the Faithful; therefore let thine Hands be strengthened, and with Faith in the Lord, proceed couragiously to
build this House; neither regard thou the Charges thereof,
nor doubt any thing, only be diligent in the Work, for it
shall be my Part to provide necessary Charges to finish the
Fabrick thereof; and I will make it acceptable to God and
myself, by most evident Signs and Tokens, I will cover thee
continually under the Shadow of my Wings; and know thou,
that I have appointed thee to perform this Work, and whilst
thou shalt be diligent therein, I will discharge this Office to
God and thy Patron; having spoke these Words, the Vision
vanisht.

When he awaked, he began to call to Mind, what he had
seen in his Vision, and doubting with himself, whether it
was some fantastick Delusion or an Oracle from Heaven,
Humility and Fear did contest with each other, in the Heart
of this faithful Man, so that he was very doubtful what it
might be; and whilst his Humility incited him to live ob-
scurely, and not to aspire to such high things, Fear would
not suffer him to neglect the Commands of the Apostle, and
whilst his Thoughts were thus divided within himself; he
considered, that by Dreams many Secrets of the Divine
Will came to the Knowledge of Man, of which there were
several Instances both in the Old and New Testament; for
the holy *Daniel* by a Dream did discover from God the

Dream of the King, and the Interpretation thereof; just *Joseph*, by a Dream was warn'd that he should not fear to take *Mary* his Wife, and at the time of Persecution, to fly into *Egypt*; and when the Persecutor was dead, to return again into the Land of *Judea*: Therefore Visions in the Night do not always portend idle Fancies and vain Delusions, but sometimes discover the secret Mysteries of Heaven.

When he return'd again to *London*, he declared to his Friends with much Joy, what he had seen, and the Command he received in his Vision: and when the Barons of *London* heard it, they answered that when the King did know it, they were confident nothing would be wanting to accomplish it: And God having shewed him the Place, he took the Opportunity to disclose his Business to the King, when *Richard* Bishop of *London* was present, who favour'd his Undertaking, and he humbly implored the King, that he would be graciously pleased to give him Possession of the Place, where God had directed that he should build him an House; which Speech pleased the King, and he gave him the Place, with Authority to effect his Purpose, and whatsoever should be necessary for his Work. When all things succeeded thus prosperously with him, and he had at Hand whatsoever was necessary according to the Word of the Apostle: He built the Church with Stone, and then began the Hospital near it; which Church was founded in the Month of *March*, in the Name of our Lord Jesus Christ, in Memory of the blessed *Bartholomew* the Apostle, in the Year of the Incarnation of our Lord and Saviour, 1123, 23 *H. I.* He dedicated the same to the Honour of God and St. *Bartholomew*; and he placed therein divers black Cannons, or Cannons Regular, whom he himself govern'd about two and twenty Years, under the Title and Dignity of a Prior, according to the Rule of St. *Augustine*; and he gave this Mannor and a fair Revenue with it, for the Support and Maintenance of the Religious there: He never attain'd to the Knowledge of the liberal Arts, but was endewed with Purity of Conscience, and would vie in Devotion towards God, in Humility towards his Brethren, and in Goodwill towards his Enemies; the tryed Sincerity of his Mind, the clear Temper of his Honesty, his great Diligence in divine things, and his careful Management of earthly things were to be commended: In Entertainments he was careful and sober, in Hospitality he was a prudent Imitator, he would opportunely admit the Anguish of those in Misery, and would patiently support and competently discharge the Necessities of the Poor; in Prosperity he was never elevated, in Adversity he was very patient, and if any thing run ill with him, he would comfort himself under the Umbrage of his Patron, whom he reverenced and loved at his Heart, and under his

Hund. of Bradewater

Weav. Fun. Mon. p. 433.

Hund. of
Brabewater

Protection thought himself safe in all Dangers; he did govern his Flock with all Humility, and provided all Necessaries for them with great Diligence, and by so doing, he
gained Reverence in his Place, and Goodwill with God and
Men; he administred Joy to his Friends, Punishment to
ill Men, and Glory to Posterity: He resign'd his Soul to
God, and was buried in a fair Monument erected in that
Priory.

Quo Warr.
6 Ed. I.

Upon a *Quo Warranto*, 6 *Edw*. I. the Prior of St. *Bartholomew*, London, claimed by the Charters of *H*. II. and
H. III. to have in all their Lands, Soc, Sac, Tholl, Them,
Flemenesfrith, Hamsokene, Frethekene, Mundbrethe, Mis-
kenning, Utley Wergelthef, Breach of the Peace, Shedding
of Blood: And he also claimed to be quit from all Toll, Passage, Pontage, Stallage, Muster, Aides of the Sheriff, Shire,
and Hundred, and from all secular Works; and he also
claimed to have the View of Franc-pledge by the same
Charters, and upon the View of them, these Priviledges
were allowed.

The Monument erected to the Memory of *Radhere* in this
Priory, was renewed by *Bolton* the last Prior of that House,
who surrender'd that Monastery, *Anno Christi*, 1538, 30 *H*.
VIII. which was then valued at 575*l*. 8*s*. 4*d*. *ob*. by the Year;
but in the *Monasticon* at 653*l*. 15*s*. *ob*. *q*. and by the Dissolution of this Priory, this Mannor came to the Crown, King
H. VIII. by Grant dated the 20th of *July*, *Anno* 35 *Regni
sui*, granted it and the Advowson of this Church, to *John
Brocket*, *John Alway*, and *Nicholas Bristow*, in Fee, which
last lived to a great Age; from him it came to *Nicholas* his
Son, who had Issue *Nicholas* that did succeed him; and after his Death it came to *Nicholas* his Son, who gave it to
Robert his second Son; who had Issue *Robert* and *Nicholas*,
both whom, I suppose, died without Issue in his Life-time,
for at his Death it descended to *William* the younger Son,
who lately died leaving his Wife surviving, the present
Lady hereof.

Stephen Bourstal, in Holderness in the County of York, married the Daughter of
John Faucet.

Thomas Bourstal, married the Daughter of Herbert of Luton.

Richard Bourstal, Steward to William de For-   John Bourstal, married the Daughter of
tibus, Earl of Holderness, tempore H. III.   Sir Roger Nonall, Kt.

Thomas Bourstal, married, 1 Imbel, Daughter of Sir William Hilliard of Normanby.
2 Ann, Daughter of Jo. Holme.

Ralph Bourstal, married Alice, Daughter of John Alford, Esq.

Margaret, married   John Bourstal, married the Daugh-   Youngest Daughter married Ro-
Philip Wasnes.   ter of Robert Boynton, Esq.   bert Mapleton of Mapleton.

Nicholas Bourstal, married 1 Jane, Daughter of Sir Robert Brigham, Kt. 2 Amy, Daughter of Sir Roger Kelke, Kt.

Jane, married Ro. Staunton.	Anthony Bourstal, married St Quinton.	Daughter of Gabriel Dursaley, married W. Constable.

John Bourstal, married 1 Jane, Daughter of Sir Jo. Hotham, 2 Winifride, Daughter of John Constable. And he had Issue by his first Wife.

Robert Bourstal, married Daughter of John Gray.	John Bourstal married Joane Dalby.
Robert Bourstal, married the Daughter of Marmaduke Maines, Esq.	Simon Bourstal, alias Bristow mar. Da. and Heir of John Shatterton.
Elizabeth, sole Daughter and Heir of Robert Bourstal, married George Dakin.	John Bristow, married the Daughter and Heir of John Hewet.
Humphry Dakin, married the Daughter of Tho. Bovington.	Nicholas Bristow, married Emme, the Daughter of Barley.
Helerie Dakin, married the Daughter of ——— Constable.	Nicholas, married Margaret, Daughter of Sir John Boteler.
Richard Dakin, married the Daughter of John Belton.	Nicholas Bristow, married Eliz. the Da. of Tho. Pinder of Winchester.

Robert Bristow, married Elizabeth, Daughter of Richard Scriven.

Robert Bristow.	Nicholas Bristow.	William Bristow.

THIS Church is situated in the middle of the Parish, upon a dry Hill, in the Deanery of Hertford, in the Diocess of Lincoln, and is dedicated to St. *Lawrence, Anno 26 Henry* VIII. it was valued in the King's Books at 7*l.* 8*s.* 6*d. per Annum,* and *William Bristow,* Esq. is the present Patron hereof.

The RECTORS.

Mr. *John de Winchcombe*
Mr. *Thomas Porter*
Mr. *John Read*
Mr. *Hepburne,* a Scotchman
Mr. *George Wiltshire*

Mr. *Henry Sykes,* who rebuilt the Chancel, the Parsonage House, and repaired all the Out-houses belonging to it *An.* 1694.
Mr. *Carter,* is the present Rector.

This Church contains only the Body covered with Lead, and at the East End hereof are two Chancels; the Windows of both have been adorn'd with curious Pictures, in stained and painted Glass, beyond many other Churches; there is a Chapel that belongs to the *Bristows,* which has a curious wrought Window, in carved Stone, and is adorn'd with painted Glass, wherein are the King's Arms, and the Arms of the *Bristows.* At the West End of the Church, adjoyns a square Tower, wherein are two small Bells; it hath a short Spire erected upon it, and within the Church and Chancel, are several Grave Stones with these Inscriptions.

One fair Tomb hath this Inscription in Brass, the rest of the Brass being lost.

Quisquis eris, qui transieris, sta, perlege, plora;
Sum quod eris, eramq; quod es; pro me, precor ora.

On a fair Stone, lying in the Arch in the Passage, between the two Chancels.

——— *Dom.* Johan. de Wynchcombe *Quondam Rectoris hujus Ecclesiæ.*

A large Monument stands by the Wall without any Inscription; but the Inhabitants have a Tradition, that the two Effigies were Sir *John Barr* and his Lady.

Hund. of
Bradewater
A fair Monument in Marble, having the Pourtraiture of *Nicholas Bris-
tow*, Esq, his Wife, and six Sons, and seven Daughters.

In the North Wall.

Here lyeth the Body of *Nicholas Bristow*, Esq; in his Life time Lord of
this Manuor of *Lawrence-Apot*; who died the 19th. of *April*, *anno Dom.*
1626.   He had by his Wife *Elizabeth* Daughter of *Thomas Pinder* of
Winchester, in *Com. Hamp.* Esq; Deputy of *Portsmouth*; Issue six
Sons and seven Daughters, which *Elizabeth* at her proper Charges, in
Memory of her deceased Husbande rected this Monument.

*On the South Side of the same Chancel, a Monument is built about a
Yard high, and eight Foot long, and a Yard in breadth, which has the Effigies of a Man and a Woman in Brass.*

Hereunder lieth the Bodies of *Nicholas Bristow*, Esq; and *Emme*, his
Wife, which served the noble Princes King *Henry* the Eighth, King
Edward, Queen *Mary*, Queen *Elizabeth*, and died the day of   *anno*
15——

The Effigies of

Eight Sons.   Four Daughters.

In Brass.

On a Marble Stone in the middle of the South Chancel are these Inscriptions

Master *Thomas Porter*, Clerk, was buried, *June* the 8th 1625.
Mrs. *Agnes Porter* his Wife was buried, *Jan.* 21 1636.

Here also lieth the Body of Mrs. *Mary Marston*, sole Daughter and Heir
of the said Mr. *Porter*, Widow of Mr. *Joseph Marston* of *Blout-hall* in
Hemel-Hempsted, aged 87 years.   She died *June* the 5th and was buried
on the 8th, 1675. just fifty years after her aforesaid Father.

CHARITY.

Mr. *Ralph Skinner* of *Hitchin*, Gent. gave 5*l.* to the Poor of this Vill.

Now I shall conclude the first Part of this Hundred with
this Town, and proceed to the second Part, which contains
the Vills and Hamlets of **Datchworth, Watton, Sacombe,
Little Mundon, Great Mundon, Benington, Walkerne,**
and **Aston.**

The second Part of the third Division.

DECEWIRTH, DATCHWORTH,
THETCHWORTH.

IN old time, some of the *Saxon* Kings granted four Hides
in this Vill, by the Name of **Decewyrth**, to the Monastery
of St. *Peters* Church at **Westminster**, which Name came
from the Mansion or Dwelling-house of some Possessor
thereof, for the Syllable *Wyrth* imports as much.

Domesd. Lib.
fol. 1.
In **Bradewater** *Hundred. Archiepiscopus* Lanfrancus *in* **Baceborbe**, *et*
Anschitil *de eo tenuit unam Hidam.   Terra est duo Car. in Dom. un. Car. et
tres Vill. cum duobus Bord. habentibus un. Car. pratum dimid. Bovi, Silva
1 Porc. valet* xxx *sol. quando recepit* xx *sol. tempore Regis* Edwardi lx *sol.
hanc terram tenuit* Alnric Blac *de Abbate* **Westmonast**, *tempore Regis* Edwardi *, nec poterat eam ab. Ecclesiæ separare ut Hundret. testatur. sed pro
aliis terris homo* Stigandi. *Archiep. fuit.*
In **Baceborbe** *tenuit Abbas de* **Westmonast**. *tres Hidas, et un. Virgat.
Terra est tres Car. in Dom. duo Hide, et ibi est un. Car. et sex Vill. haben-*

les duo Car. ibi duo cotar. pratum dimid. Car. Pastura ad pec. Silva 1 *Porc. valet et valuit et* xl *sol. tempore Regis* Edwardi lx *sol. Hoc Manerium jacuit et jacet in Dom. Ecclesiæ Sancti* Petri.

Hund. of **Bradewater**

Archbishop *Lanfranc* and *Anschitil* held of him one Hide in **Baxtworth** in the Hundred of **Bradewater**. The arable is two Carucates, in Demeasne one Carucate, and three Villains with two Bordars having one Carucate, Meadow half an Oxgang, Wood to feed fifty Hogs; it is worth thirty Shillings a Year, when he received it twenty Shillings a Year, in the time of King *Edward* (the Confessor) sixty Shillings a Year. *Alwric Blac* held this Land of the Abbot of **Westminster**, in the time of King *Edward* (the Confessor) neither could he separate it from the Church, as the Hundred can witness, but there was a Man (under the Protection) of *Stigax* the Archbishop for the other Lands.

Ibid. fol. 155.

The Abbot of **Westminster** held three Hides and one Virgate, in **Datchworth**; the arable is three Carucates, in Demeasne two Hides, and there is one Carucate and six Villains having two Carucates, there are two Cottagers, Meadow half a Carucate, Common of Pasture for the Cattle, Wood to feed fifty Hogs; it is worth, and was worth, forty Shillings a Year, in the time of King *Edward* (the Confessor) sixty Shillings a Year. This Mannor did lye and now doth lye, in the Jurisdiction of the Church of St. *Peters.*

William, the Abbot of **Westminster**, held this Mannor in the fourth Year of *Richard* I. when a Fine was levied by the Assent of *William de Bockland*, who was a Tenant to the Abbot of **Westminster**, of the Vill of **Datchworth**, and the Concord or Agreement was, *That the Clerk which* Hugh *or his Heirs shall present to the said Church, before his Institution or Admission to the said Church, shall swear in the Chapter of* **Westminster***, that he shall yearly pay to the said Abbot and Convent, and to their Successors, twenty Shillings sterling.*

De Fin. levat. 4 *Rich.* I. *cur* *recept. Scac.*

John de Wanton by his Deed dated 17 *Edw.* I. granted to Sir *William de Hameldon* 200 Acres of Land and eight Acres of Meadow, with the Appurtenances in **Groveburp, Shipedon, Baronefeld, Postecroft,** and **Chirchfeld**, and all the Grove called **Baronsgrove** in **Datchesworth**, to hold of him, paying a Penny a Year Rent in lieu of all Services.

Pas. 17 Ed. I. *Rot.* 26, Herts *cur. recept. in Scac.*

Gilbert de Prochein and *Eustace* his Wife granted in free and perpetual Alms, the Church of **Datchet** with all its Appurtenances, free from all secular Services, to God and the Church of **St. Alban**, to find Ornaments for the Church of **St. Alban**, by the Hand of the Sacrist; and they levied a Fine of the Advowson of the said Church of **Datchet**, to the Abbot and his Successors for ever, in the King's Court at **Westminster**, on the Morrow of St. *John* Baptist, *Anno* 22 *H.* III. before *Robert de Leyniton, William de Colewone, Hugh Gifford, Hugh de Gatton*, and others, Justices of our Lord the King.

De Fin. levat. 22 H. III. B. R. in cur. re- cept Scac.

Helie of **Datchesworth**, and *Gilbert* her Son and Heir apparent, gave forty Acres of Land, and *Walter* of the **Oake** gave seventeen Acres of Land, and *Ivo de Birston* gave half an Acre of Land in the Vill of **Datchesworth** to the Church of **St. Alban**; all which Grants were confirmed by King *Henry* I.

Inspex. 2 H. VIII.

The Abbots of 𝔚𝔢𝔰𝔱𝔪𝔦𝔫𝔰𝔱𝔢𝔯 enjoy'd this Mannor until the fatal Year of their Dissolution, when it came to King *Henry* VIII. who chang'd this Monastery *Anno 33 Regni sui*, into a Bishoprick, but *Thomas Thirlby*, the new Bishop of this Place, dilapidating all the Patrimony thereof, the Bishoprick was dissolved, whereupon King *Edward* VI. by Patent dated 2 *April*, 4th of his Reign, granted it to *Nicholas Ridley*, then Bishop of 𝔏𝔬𝔫𝔡𝔬𝔫, and his Successors, to hold in free, pure, and perpetual Alms, paying yearly to the King one hundred Pounds, at the Feast of the Birth of our Lord; and since it is come successively to *Henry Compton*, now Lord Bishop of 𝔏𝔬𝔫𝔡𝔬𝔫, who is the [present Lord hereof, and has Jurisdiction of the Leet.

But the Court Baron of this Mannor now called 𝔇𝔞𝔱𝔠𝔥-𝔴𝔬𝔯𝔱𝔥-𝔟𝔲𝔯𝔶, was in Possession of *Richard Connet* of 𝔖𝔲𝔰-𝔰𝔢𝔵, Esq. in the time of *Henry* VII. from which *Connet* it was conveyed to one *Forster*, in whose Name it continued till it came to *Richard Forster* of 𝔖𝔱. 𝔄𝔩𝔟𝔞𝔫𝔰, Yeoman, who sold it to *John Gamon* of 𝔄𝔰𝔱𝔬𝔫, Clerk, in the time of King *James* I. from whom it descended to *Richard Gamon* his Son and Heir, who lately sold it to *William Wallis*, Esq. the present Possessor hereof.

The Mannor of THEISCOTE, or THETCHWORTH

'T IS recorded in *Domesdei Book* under the Title of *Terra Roberti de Olgi.*

Robertus de Olgi *et* Rand. Basset *de eo tenuit* 𝔗𝔥𝔢𝔦𝔰𝔠𝔞𝔱𝔢, *pro quatuor hidis se defendebat tempore Regis* Edwardi, *et modo pro duabus. Terra, est quatuor car. in Dom. sunt duo, et tres Vill, et dimid, cum li Sockman. de una hida, et quing; bord. habent ii car. ibi unus cotar. et unus servus, et un. Molin. de decem sol. prat. iii car. inter totum val.* lxx *sol. Quando recepit quatuor lib. tempore Regis Edwardi* c *sol. Hoc Manerium tenuerunt quinq. Soch. horum duo hom.* Brictrici *unum hidam et dimid. habuerunt et alii duo homines* Osulsi *filii Franc. unam hidam et dimid. et quintus homo* Edmer Attale i *hid. tenuit. Nullus eorum Antecessorum* Wigot *pertinuit, sed unus quisq; terram suam vendere potuit, horum unus terram suum emit a* W. *Rege novem unc. auri et Hom. de Hundred. testantur et postea ad* Wigot *se vertit pro protectione.*

In 𝔓𝔬𝔩𝔢𝔥𝔞𝔫𝔤𝔢𝔯 *tenuit* Martellus de Roberto Olgi *dimid hid. Terra est un. car. et ibi est cum duo cotar. et duo servis, prat. un. car. Silva* ii *porc. val. et valuit decem sol. tempore Regis* Edwardi *vigint. sol. hanc terram tenuit* Aluric Wallef *Comitis, et vendere potuit.*

The Land of *Robert de Olgi.*

Robert de Olgi and *Ralph Basset* held 𝔗𝔥𝔢𝔱𝔠𝔥𝔴𝔬𝔯𝔱𝔥 of him, it was rated for four Hides in the time of King *Edward* (the Confessor) and now for two, the arable is four Carucates, in Demeasne are two, and three Villaines and an half, with two Socmen of one Hide and five Bordars, having two Carucates, there is one Cottager, and one Servant, and one Mill of ten Shillings Rent, Meadow three Carucates. In the whole it is worth seventy Shillings a Year, when he received it four Pounds a Year; in the time of King *Edward* (the Confessor) an hundred Shillings; five Socmen held this Mannor, two of these, Men (under the Protection) of *Brictric* had one Hide and an half, and two others, Men (under the Protection) of *Osulfe* the Son of a Frenchman boin, an Hide and an half, and the fifth a Man (under the Protection) of *Edmer Attale* held one Hide, none of these but one belonged to *Wigot* the Ancestor; every one of these might sell his Land, one of these bought his Land of King *William* for nine ounces of Gold, as the Men of the Hundred can witness, and afterwards he turned himself over to *Wigot* for Protection.

Martel held half an Hide of *Robert de Olgi* in Bolehanger. The arable is one Carucate, and it is there with two Cottagers and two Servants, Meadow one Carucate, Wood to feed two Hogs; it is worth and was worth ten Shillings Rent by the Year, in the time of King *Edward* (the Confessor) twenty Shillings by the Year, *Aluric* a Man (under the Protection) of Earl *Wallef*, held this Land and might sell it.

This *Robert de Olgi* was one of those valiant *Normans* who attended Duke *William* in this famous Expedition, when he obtained the Conquest and Crown of England for which Service that King gave him four Lordships in Berkshire, seven in Buckinghamshire, three in Glocestershire, one in Bedfordshire, three in Northamptonshire, one in Warwickshire, eight and twenty in Oxfordshire, with two and forty Dwelling-houses in Oxford, and eight which then lay Waste, and thirty Acres of Meadow, adjoyning to the Wall, and a Mill valued at ten Shillings a Year, and this Mannor in this County: He was Constable of Oxford, had the Government of the whole County, and was so potent that none durst oppose him; he seized a large Meadow near the Castle of Oxford by the King's Consent, which belonged to the Monks of Abingdon, to his own Use, this exasperated them so much, that they with Tears prostrating themselves before the Altar of our Lady, prayed to God that he would vindicate this Injury; whereupon a grievous Sickness fell upon him; yet he continued Impenitent, till by a Vision in the Night, he had a perfect Representation that he saw a great many Nobles in a royal Pallace, and a beautiful Person among them, clothed in the Habit of a Woman, sitting on a glorious Throne, with two Monks of Abingdon, whom he knew, standing before her: When these Monks saw him there, they bowed to the Lady and with deep Sighs said, this is he who has taken from us that Meadow, which was the Inheritance of thy Church, for which we make this Complaint. This moved the Lady so much, that she commanded that he should be turned out of Doors, and be conveyed to that Meadow to be tormented there; immediately two young Men led him thither, and caused him to sit down, which done, divers ill-favour'd Children brought Hay on their Shoulders, and laughing said to each other, here is our dear Friend, let us play with him; then laying down their Burdens they pissed on him, and putting Fire underneath, smoaked him; others made Ropes of Hay, and threw them in his Face; others burnt his Beard, and whilst he was in this Anguish, he called out aloud, Oh! blessed Lady, have pity on me, for I am dying. His Wife lying near, being affrighted at it, said, awake Sir, for you are much troubled in your Sleep. He being thus roused up, reply'd, Yes truly, for I was among Devils; to whom she answered, The Lord preserve thee from all Harm: Then he telling his Dream, she said, God doth correct his Child whom he loveth.

'Tis reported, at her Instance he shortly after went to Abingdon, and standing there before the Altar, in the Presence of Abbot *Reginald*, the whole Covent, and divers of his Friends, he gave them Cadmeton, a Lordship of ten Pounds *per Annum*, protesting that he would never more meddle with any of their Possessions: He also gave them 100*l.* towards the new building of their Monastery; he repaired divers ruinous Churches in Oxford, and built the Bridge there: He died in the Month of *September*, and was buried at Abingdon, on the North Side of the high Altar, and his Wife was buried on his left Hand, but leaving no Issue male,

Nigel his Brother succeeded, of whom I read nothing more, but that he left Issue

Robert, who delivered up his Castle in Oxford, to Queen *Maud, Anno 6 Steph.* when she came with much Triumph from Winchester thither, and he left

Henry, who was his Heir, Constable to the King and Sheriff of Oxfordshire, from the third to the sixth Year of King *H.* II. but I do not find how long this Mannor continued in this Family, nor cannot learn what particular Part of this Vill does now bear this Name, but that sometimes the whole Vill is called Thetchworth, and sometimes Datchworth.

The RECTORY.

Anno 1347, 21 *Edw.* III. *Thomas de Lamere*, Abbot of St. Albans, and the Covent there, granted the Right of Patronage of this Church of Datchworth to the King and his Heirs, in Consideration whereof the King released to them one Pension of 5*l. per Annum*, which they paid to one of the King's Chaplaines, till he was preferred, which the King claimed from them, because his Progenitors had been Founders of the Abby.

This Advowson was afterwards granted to the Lord *Morley*, upon whose Decease it came to

Alice his Sister, who married Sir *Edward Howard*, Kt. afterwards they sold this Advowson by Deed dated the 8th of *April*, 21 *H.* VII. with the Mannor of Walkern to Sir *William Capell*, Kt. from whom it is now come to *Algernon* Earl of Essex, who is the present Patron hereof.

THIS Rectory *Anno* 26 *H.* VIII. was rated at the yearly Value of 14*l.* 3*s.* 8*d.* in the King's Books.

The RECTORS.

Mr. *Alsop*
  John *Hacket*, D.D. afterwards
    Bishop of Down and Con=
    nar in Ireland

Mr. *Charles Baggerly*
Mr. *Gale*, a Frenchman, the present Rector.

This Church is situated upon a great Hill, in the Deanery of Hertford, in the Diocess of Lincoln, and contains the Body covered with Lead, to which a Chancel covered with Tyle is annexed on the East, and a square Tower at the West End, in which is a Ring of five small indifferent Bells, the Tower is covered with Lead, and hath a small Shaft erected upon it, but I found nothing of Remark in the Church or Chancel.

WATON AT STONE.

ABOUT three Miles distant from Datchworth lies Wat-ton in a Vale, upon the River Beane or the Beneficean, it derived its Name from the Springs that abound there, which greatly augment this Stream, for *Wat* in the Saxon Lan-guage signifies a moist and watry Place. In the time of *William* the Conqueror, it was recorded that

In Bradewater Hundred in Watone tenuit Anschitillus de Archiepisc. duo hidas et dimid. Terra est sex car. in Dom. est una, et alia potest fieri, ibi tres Vill. cum Presbitero et duobus bord. habentibus duas car. et aliæ duo possunt fieri, pratum dimid. car. Silva centum porc. pastura ad pec. et duo Molendini de Septemdecim sol. valet et valuit l sol. tempore Regis Edwardi quatuor lib. De Hac terra tenuit Aluric Blac duo hid. de Abbate West-monast. non poterat separare ab Ecclesia, et Almer dimid. hid. tenuit homo ejusdam Alurici, et vendere potuit.

In Watone tenuit eisd. Abbas un. hid. Terra est duo car. in Dom. est una, et quatuor bord. habentes un. car. ibi duo botar. et un. Molin. de duobus sol. pastura ad pec. Silva centum porc. valet et valuit decem sol. tempore Re-gis Edwardi xx sol. Hæc terra jacuit in Ecclesia St. Petri.

Comes Alanus *tenuit in Watone un. hid. et dimid. Godvinus tenuit de eo. Terra est iv car. in Dom. possunt duo fieri, ibi tres bord et duo cotar. haben-tes ii car. pratum duobus bobus, pastura ad pec. valet et valuit vigint. sol. tempore Regis Edwardi trigint. sol. hanc terram tenuit Godvinus de Eccle-sia Sti. Petri, non poterat vendere, sed post mortem ejus debebat ad Ecclesiam redire ut Hundred. testatur, sed Uxor ejus cum hac terra vertit se per vim ad Eddevam pulchram et tenebat eam die qua Rex Eduuardus fuit vivus et mortuus. De hac terra sumpte sunt sexdecim acre post. adventum Regis* Will. *quas modo tenet Anschitillus de Ros sub Archiep. et tamen Comes* Alanus *acquietat eas de geldo Regis.*

Derman et Aluvardus tenuerunt de Rege Watone pro quing. hidis se defendebat. Terra est septem car. in Dom. tres hide et dimid. et ibi sunt duo car. et adhuc dimid. potest fieri, ibi decem Vill. cum quatuor bord. habentibus quatuor car. et dimid. ibi quatuor servi, et un. Molin. de tresdecim sol. et quatuor denar. pratum un. car. pastura ad pec. Silva centum porc. Inter totum valet et valuit centum sol. tempore Regis Edwardi septem lib. hanc terram tenuit Aluvinus Horne *teignus Regis Edwardi, et vendere potuit.*

Anschitill held two Hides and an half of Archbishop *Lanfranc* in Wa-tone in Bradewater Hundred The arable is six Carucates, in Demeasne is one, and another may be made, there are three Villains with the Par-son and two Bordars having two Carucates, and two others may be made, Meadow half a Carucate, Wood to feed one Hundred Hogs, Common of Pasture for the Cattle, and two Mills of seventeen Shillings Rent by the Year, it is worth and was worth, fifty Shillings by the Year; in the time of King *Edward* (the Confessor) four Pounds by the Year, *Aluric Blac* held two Hides of this Land of the Abbot of Westminster, he could not separate it from the Church, and *Almar* a Man (under the Protection) of the same *Aluric* held half an Hide and might sell it.

Domesd. Lib.
fol. 437.

48   THE HISTORICAL ANTIQUITIES

Hund. of
Bradewater

The same Abbot held one Hide in **Wattons**. The arable is two Carucates, in Demeasne is one, and four Bordars, having one Carucate, there are two Cottagers, and one Mill of four Shillings Rent, Common of Pasture for the Cattle, Wood to feed one hundred Hogs; it is worth, and was worth, ten Shillings by the Year, in the time of King *Edward* (the Confessor) twenty Shillings by the Year. This Land lies in the Jurisdiction of the Abbot of St. *Peter*.

Earl *Alan* held one Hide and an half in **Wattons**, *Godwine* held it of him The arable is four Carucates, in Demeasne two more may be made, there are three Bordars and two Cottagers having two Carucates, Meadow for two Oxen, Common of Pasture for the Cattle; it is worth and was worth twenty Shillings by the Year, in the time of King *Edward* (the Confessor) thirty Shillings by the Year: *Godwine* held this Land of the Church of St. *Peter*, he could not sell it, but after his death it ought to return to the Church, as the Hundred can witness, but his Wife turn'd over herself with the Land by force to fair *Eddera*, and she held it on the Day wherein King *Edward* (the Confessor) was alive and dead. Sixteen Acres of this Land were bought since the coming of King *William*, which *Anschitill de Ros* holds, now under the Archbishop, and yet Earl *Alan* discharged it of the King's Tax.

Derman and *Alward* two Thanes of the King held **Wattons** of the King, it was rated for five Hides, the arable is seven Carucates, in Demeasne three Hides and an half, and there are two Carucates, and now half another may be made, there are ten Villains with four Bordars having four Carucates and an half, there are four Servants, and one Mill of thirteen Shillings and four Pence Rent, Meadow one Carucate, Common of Pasture for the Cattle, Wood to feed one hundred Hogs; in the whole it is worth and was worth one hundred Shillings by the Year, in the time of King *Edward* (the Confessor) seven Pounds by the Year, *Alwine Horne* a Thane of King *Edward* (the Confessor) held this Land and might sell it.

Derman and *Alward* were two Thanes or Gentleman Retainers of King *William* the Conqueror, who did personally attend upon the King, and held these Lands of him by the Service of their Duty, and Attendance upon his Person so long as they held this Office or Place under him; but not long after, I find most of those Lands and Estates were granted to

Peter de Valoines, who held them in the time of *H. I.* and married *Albreda* Sister to *Eudo Dapifer*, Steward to that King, by whom he had Issue

Roger, who was his Heir, enjoy'd these Lands and married *Agnes*, by whom he had Issue *Peter*, *Robert*, and *Gunnora*; he obtained from *Maud* the Empress all those Lands which his Father died seiz'd of.

Peter his Heir succeeded, married *Gundred de Warren*, and by her had Issue three Daughters, *Lora* the Wife of *Alexander de Bailioll*, 2 *Christian* married to *William de Mandevile*, afterwards to *Peter de Main*, and 3 *Isabel* called by some *Elizabeth*, married to *David Comyne*, who were his Daughters and Coheirs; and upon the Partition, this Mannor of **Watton** fell to the Part of *Lora* Wife of *Alexander de Bailioll*, Brother to *John de Bailioll*, King of **Scotland**, who granted it to

Robert Aquillon who attended the King *Anno* 42 *H. III.* well fitted with Horse and Armes, to restrain the Incursions of the *Welch*; was constituted Sheriff of the County of

Surrp, *Anno* 46 *H.* III. held that Office for six Years together, then was made Governor of the Castle of Guilford; he married *Jone* Daughter of *William Ferrars,* Earl of Derby, one of the Coheirs of *Walter Marshall,* Earl of Pembrook, who died *Anno* 49 *H.* III. Shortly after he married *Margaret de Ripariis,* Countess of Debon, *Anno* 53 *Hen.* III. by whom he had Issue *Isabel,* and upon a *Quo Warranto* brought *Anno* 6 *Edw.* I. before *John Rygate* and others, Justices Itinerants at Hertford, he claimed to have Free-warren, and a Fair every Year, to continue for three Days together in his Mannors of Watton, Addington, and Pertinges, by the Grant of King *Henry* III. and upon the View thereof they were allowed; and he died the same Year, leaving

Isabel his Daughter and Heir, married, as I suppose, to *Henry le Mire,* for it was found *Anno* 6 *Edw.* I. he was Lord of Watton, and gave one Messuage, five Acres of Land, and five Acres of Wood to the Chaplain of Watton, and it was worth forty Shillings *per Annum,* but in the same King's Reign, this Mannor came to the Possession of

Eudo Pellitot, who married *Flora* the Daughter and Heir of *Philip Daubeny,* by whom he had Issue

Philip, on whom *Edw.* III. conferr'd the Honour of Knighthood: He served the King for this County in four several Parliaments, whereof two were held *Anno* 6 *Edw.* III. another 11 *Edw.* III. and another *Anno* 22 *Edw.* III. He had Issue by *Isabel* his Wife. *William* and *Katharine,* and died seiz'd of this Mannor, *Anno* 1361, 35 *Edw.* III. it descended to

William, who was his Heir, enjoyed it awhile, and dying without Issue, it came to

Katharine, who was his Sister and Heir, and married *Ralph Boteler* of Pulreback, descended from the Barons of Oversley, Wem, and Sudeley, of which Family I have found this Account.

In the Reign of *Henry* I. *Ralph Boteleir,* called *Randulphus Pincerna de Legrecestria* in Regard he bore the Office of Butler to *Robert* Earl of Mellent and Leicester, (a great Man in that time) settled himself at Oversley in the County of Warwick, where taking Advantage of the natural Ascent of the Ground near the Stream called Arrow, he built a strong Castle, and founded a Monastery for Benedictine Fryars, within a Mile of it, *Anno* 1140, 5 *Steph.* and dedicated it to the Honour of the blessed Virgin *Mary,* St. *Anne* her Mother, St. *Joseph,* St. *John* Baptist, St. *John* the Evangelist, and all Saints.

Robert his Son and Heir succeeded, and gave the Church of Theddingworth in that County to the Canons of Leicester; he left Issue

Margin notes:

Hund. of Bradewater

Rot. Pip. 46 H. III.

Quo Warr. 6 E. I Rot. 36, cur. recept. Scac.

Prin's Parl. Bree. p. 3, 43 H. V.

Register de Kenilworth, p. 144.

Bar. of Engl. vol. 1, fol. 594.

Mon. of Engl. vol. 1, fol. 474.

Ibid. vol 2, fol. 309 Register de Abby de Leic in Bib. Bodl. fol 19.

Hund. of
Bradewater

Claus. 1 H.
III. m. 19.

Pat.de eisdem
annis indors.

Plac. de Ban-
co, 4 Ed. 1.
Mich. Rot.12.
indorso.
Pat.de eisdem
annis indorso.
Claus. 12 H.
III. indorso.
Claus. 41 H.
III. indorso in
schedula.

Pat. 50 H.III.
m. 3.

Pat. 55 H.III.
m. 20.

Quo Warr.
6 Ed. 1.

Inq. 15 Ed. 1.
Inq. 18 Ed. I.

Ralph, who was his Heir, and gave the Chappel of Stock-
ton to the Cannons of Leicester; but engaging with the Barons against King *John*, his Lands were seized and given to
William de Cantilupe; at length submitting himself to his
Prince, returning to his Obedience, and paying forty Marks
for his Redemption, King *H.* III. 9 *Regni sui*, restored him
to his Estate, and he had Issue

Ralph Boteler, who was one of the Justices of Assize for
the County of Warwick, in the Years 13, 16, 21, and 25
H. III. and for the Gaol-delivery at Warwick, in the 19th,
22d, and 30th Years of *H.* III.

Ralph his Son succeeded, married *Maud* the Daughter
and Heir of *Pantulfe*, by whom that great Lordship of
Wem in the County of Salop, and divers other fair Possessions, came to this Family.   He was one of the Justices
for Gaol-delivery at Warwick, in the Years 34 and 41 *H.*
III. in which last Year, he was commanded to joyn with
Hamond le Strainge for preventing the Incursions of the
Welch in the Marches near Montgomery: He was summon'd among the Peers, *Anno* 48 *H.* III. to advise the
King, in Council held in *Midlent*, at Oxford, thence to advance against Prince *Lewellin* and his Adherents: But divers
of the Barons arming themselves against the King; he stood
so firm to the royal Interest, that the King granted the
Lordship of Kineton in the County of Warwick, Part of
the Estate, which he had formerly given to *Nicholas de Se-*
grave for his Life, upon the same Terms as *Segrave* held it,
as a Reward for his Services; and by another Grant dated
about three Days following, he granted the Inheritance to
him, but when *Segrave* redeemed his Lands, the Lordship
of Kineton was restored to him by that memorable Decree
called *Dictum de Kenilworth*, and the King gave to this
Ralph, four hundred Pounds in Lieu thereof, to be received
out of the Fines and Amercements coming into his *Exche-*
quer.   It was found upon Inquisition, that this *Ralph de*
Botiler was Lord of Wem, and held all the Mannor *in Ca-*
pite of the King, to wit, as a Baron, and did do his Suit by
his Steward to the County and Hundred, for the whole Service of a Barony: And the Mannor is fourteen Hides, besides Upton and Eiton; and he had a Park and a Warren,
but by what Warrant they knew not.   By this Inquisition,
it appears that this Barony of Wem was a Barony by Tenure, the Nature of which Baronies I have discoursed before
in Ardeley; and this *Ralph* died leaving Issue, *John*, *Gawen*,
William, *Ralph*, and *Alice*.

John and *Gawen* succeeded in their Turns, but both of
them dying without Issue, this Barony of Wem descended to

William, who succeeded, and married *Ankaret* the Neice
of *James de Adithley*: He was summon'd to Parliament in

Hund. of
Bradewater

the 23d, 24th, 25th, and 27th Years of *Edw.* I. and dying at the latter End of the last Year, left

William, who inherited the Barony of **Wem**, and married *Margaret* Daughter of *Richard* Earl of **Arundell**, by whom he had Issue *William*, and died *Anno* 18 *Edw.* III.

Inq. 18 Ed.
III.

William Boteler, who enjoyed the same Barony, and married *Elizabeth* Daughter of ——— *Handsaker*, but he dying without Issue, this Barony came to

Ralph Boteler, (the Son and Heir of Sir *Ralph Boteler* of **Pulrebatk** and **Norbury**, and *Maud* his Wife, the Daughter and Coheir of *Philip Marmion* of **Tamworth**,) was knighted, and married *Hawise* Daughter and Coheir of *Richard Gobion*, who brought the Mannor of **Gobions** to this Family; by her he had Issue *John*, who was knighted, *William*, and *Ralph*, all whom were bound to do their Service, and perform their Aid to the King, in the County of **Chester**, which was to find a Robe of the Price of 20*s.* and pay 20*s.* 8*d.* for the Mannor of **Codington**, and the Grant was attested by Sir *John de Arden*, and Sir *John de Leigh*, Kts. *William de Cotton, John de Codington, Robert* Son of *Robert de Codington, Anno* 1380, 5 *Regni Regis Edw.* III. to which were three Seals, the first containing the Coat of Armes of the *Botelers*, with the Circumscription about the Seal, *Sigillum Radulfi Boteler*, the second containing a Coat of *three Half-moons, with a bend Checque*, and this Circumscription, *Sigillum Johan. Boteler*, and the third containing a Coat of Armes with *two* ——— *and a Bend Checque* between them, and this Circumscription, *Sigillum Willielmi Boteler:* this *Ralph* dying,

Ralph his Son succeeded him, and married *Katharine*, the Daughter and Heir of Sir *Philip Pelitot*, Kt. who died seized of this Mannor of **Woodhall**, from whom it descended to *Katharine* the Wife of this *Ralph Boteler*, by whom he had Issue, *Philip, Ralph,* and *Edward.*

Philip Boteler was their Heir, succeeded them in this Mannor, was knighted, and married *Isabel* the Daughter of ——— by whom he had Issue *Philip*, and died seized of the Mannors of **Hotham, Wilkesby, Wodenderby,** and **Conningsby,** &c. and this Mannor descended with the other to

Inq. 9 H. V.
Esc. 9 H. V.

Philip Boteler, who was his Heir, and held *in Capite* the Mannor of **Pulrebatk**, by the third Part of the Moiety of the Barony of **Kilpeck**, which whole Barony was late *Hugh Kilpeck's* in the County of **Salop**, in the time of King *H.* III. He married *Elizabeth* the Daughter of *John Cokayne*, who was constituted one of the Justices in the Court of *Common-pleas, Anno* 6 *H.* IV. by whom he had Issue *Edward* and *Philip*, and after her Decease, he married ——— the Daughter of ——— *Cheiny*, and was constituted Sheriff of **Essex** and **Hertford**. *Edward* the eldest Son dying without Issue, it came to

Pat. 7 H. IV.
Origin. Jurid.

Hund. of   *Philip Boteler*, his younger Brother, who was his Heir,
Brabrwater and at that time seven Years old; he married *Elizabeth* the
Daughter of ————, by whom he had Issue *John*, and
died 3 *H.* VI.

     John Boteler was eight Years of Age at the Death of his
Father, married *Constance* the Daughter of ———— *Downhall* of Codington in the County of Northampton, by whom
he had Issue, *John, Margaret, Dorothy,* and *Katharine,*
and she died *Anno* 14—, and after her Decease, he married *Elizabeth* the Daughter of ————, who died the
28th of *October,* 1469, and *John Boteler* was his Heir; but
now I will take a View of the Mannor of Bardolfes, till it
came to this Family.

The Mannor of BARDOLFES,

DENOMINATED from the *Bardolfes,* who were Lords
hereof for many Years; whereof the first that I meet with,
was

Rot. Vascon.
22 Ed. 1. m. 8,
indorso.
Ibid. 22 Ed. 1.
m. 12.
Leland's Coll.
vol 1, fol.680.
T. Walsing.
p. 27, nu. 40.
Rot. Scac. 32
Ed. 1. m. 2.
Esc. 32 Ed. 1.
n. 64.
     Hugh Bardolfe, who was summon'd among the other
Barons and great Men, in *June,* 22 *Edw.* I. to advise the
King, touching the weighty Affairs of the Realm; and then
attended him into Gascoigne, where he had the hard Fate to
be taken Prisoner by the King of France, at the Siege of
Risunce, yet he continued in the King's Service, and was
in that Expedition which the King made into Scotland;
but died *Anno* 32 of the same King, leaving by *Isabel* his
Wife,

     Thomas his Son and Heir, at that time 22 Years of Age,
who succeeded in this Mannor; he was invested Knight of
the Bath *Anno* 34 *Edw.* I. with *Edward* Prince of Wales,
and many others, at the Feast of *Pentecost,* had an Allowance of Robes out of the King's Wardrobe, for that Ceremony; and then marched with the Prince into Scotland;

Esc. 3 Ed.III.
68.
Claus, 10 Ed.
III. m, 41
Claus. 9 Ed.
III. m. 41.
Esc. 34 Ed.
III. m. 41.
He died *Anno* 3 *Edw.* III. and was buried in the Priory at
Shelford in the County of Nottingham, leaving
     John Bardolfe his Son and Heir, then 17 Years old; he
proved his Age *Anno* 9 *Edw.* III. did his Homage, and had
Livery of his Lands. He married *Elizabeth,* Daughter and
Heir of Sir *Roger de Damory,* by that great Lady, *Eliza-
beth de Burgh* his Wife, by whom he had a fair Inheri-
Esc. 45 Ed.
III. 'm. 14.
tance; he had Issue by her *William,* and he died seized
hereof on the 3d of *August,* 45 *Edw.* III. leaving
     William Bardolfe his Heir, at that time 14 Years of Age.
Queen *Philippa,* Wife to King *Edward* III. granted the
Pat. 40 Ed.
III. p. 1.m.37.
Wardship and Marriage of him, *Anno* 40 *Edw.* III. to Sir
Michael Poynings, Kt. to the Intent that he should marry
Agnes Daughter of the said *Michael:* He proved his Age,
Claus. 45 Ed.
III. m. 14.
did his Homage *Anno* 45 *Edw.* III. and had Livery of his
Land: he was in that Expedition made into France, in the

Year following, served the King in his Wars in Ireland, *Hund. of Bradewater*
and died *Anno* 1394, 9 *R.* II. leaving

Thomas, who was 17 Years old at the Death of his Father, *Esc. 9 R. II.*
proved his Age *Anno* 13 *R.* II. did his Homage, and had *n.11, not.*
Livery of his Inheritance; he joyn'd with *Henry* Earl of
Northumberland, *Thomas* Earl *Marshal* and of Nottingham,
and *Richard Scrope*, Archbishop of York, in the Insurrection
made *Anno* 6 *H.* IV. where their Forces were routed; he
fled into Scotland, and thence into Wales; but afterwards *Bar. vol. 1,*
returning into England, engaged in Battel with the Sheriff *fol. 683.*
of Porkshire, where he was wounded, and soon after died of
his Wounds, leaving

Anne the Wife of Sir *William Clifford*, Kt. and *Joane*,
the Wife of *William Philip*, his Daughters and Coheirs,
who petition'd the King for some of the Mannors which their *Esc. 9 H. IV.*
Father had forfeited; and the King granted them after *n. 31.*
the Death of the Queen, to hold to them and the Heirs
of their Bodies; whereof *William*, *Philip*, and *Joane* his
Wife *Anno* 9 *H.* V. had Livery of their Purparty, and *Rol. Fin. 9*
they had Issue *H. V. m. 10.*

Elizabeth who married *Henry Beamont*, whom King *H.*
VI. by Patent dated the 18th Year of his Reign, advanced *Pat. 18 H.VI.*
to the Honour and Dignity of a Viscount (a Title never used *p. 2, m. 21.*
before in England) by the Name of Viscount *Beamont*, with
Precedency above all Barons of this Realm, and twenty
Markes yearly Fee out of the Revenues of the County of
Lincolne; and the same King, in Consideration of the great
Loss which he sustained by the Death of *Elizabeth* his Wife,
Daughter of *William Philip* Lord Bardolfe, and the continual Services which he had performed for him, granted to
him by another Patent dated 19 *Regni sui*, the Custody of *Pat. 19 H.VI.*
all the Castles, Mannors, and Lands, which fell by the Death *p. 3, m. 4.*
of his Wife, to *Henry* his Son and Heir, and in Case of his
Death to *William* his younger Son, with Remainder to
Joane his Daughter; and the same King farther granted by
another Patent dated 23 *H.*VI. to him and the Heirs Males of *Pat. 23 H.VI.*
his Body, Place and Precedence above all Viscounts, thence- *p. 2, m. 20.*
forth to be created, as also above the Heirs of all Earls, and
to take Place next and immediately unto Earls in all Parliaments and publick Meetings; he was summon'd to Par- *Stow's Annals*
liament from the 10th to the 38th Year of *H.* VI. when the
Duke of Pork, the Earls of Warwick and Salisbury, sent
from Calais divers Complaints to the King, among which one *Leland's Coll.*
was against him, terming him his mortal Enemy, alledging *vol. 1, fol.714.*
that he had misled the King, procured his Consent to that
Act of Parliament made against him at Coventry, had destroyed his Estate: They soon after landing in England,
fought the King at Northampton on the 10th of *July*, 38 *Esc. 38 H.VI.*
H. VI. where obtaining the Victory, this Viscount *Beamont*
was slain, with many other Persons of Note.

Hund. of
Bradewater

Henry his eldest Son being then dead, *William* his second Son succeeded, and in Right of *Elizabeth* his Mother, had the Title of Lord **Bardolfe**, with a large Inheritance: He proved his Age and his Title the same Year, that he was born at **Edenham** in the County of **Lincoln**, and baptized in that Church on the Feast-day of St. *George* the Martyr, 16 *H.* VI. whereupon he had Livery of his Lands, his Homage being respited. He married *Elizabeth* Daughter to *Richard Scrope*, Brother to the Lord *Scrope* of **Bolton**; and after her Decease, to *Joane* Daughter of *Humphry* Duke of **Buckingham**; but adhering firmly to the Lancastrian Interest, he participated (as his Ancestors had done) of the hard Fate which soon after befel that Family, for he was taken Prisoner at **Towton-field**, *Anno* 1 *Edw.* IV. and attainted in the Parliament began at **Westminster** the same Year, at which time he was seiz'd of this Mannor, among divers others, which devolved to the Crown thereby.

Catal. of Nob.
by R. B.

King *Edward* IV. by Patent dated the 25th of *July*, 7 *Regni sui*, granted this Mannor to

Pat. 7 Ed.IV.

Roger Ree, Esq. one of the Ushers to his Chamber, with several other Mannors, and the same King, by another Patent dated the 14th of *February* in the same Year, granted it to the said *Roger* and *William* his Son in Tail: *Roger* the Father was afterwards knighted, and constituted Sheriff of **Norfolke**, in the 9th and 13th Years of *Edw.* IV.

Ibid.

Rot Pip. 9 &
13 Ed. IV.
tit. Norf.

Roger the eldest Son dying without Issue, this Mannor came to *William* the second Son, who surrender'd these Patents to the King, in Consideration whereof, the King, by another Patent dated 31 *May*, 15 *Edw.* IV. 1475, granted this Mannor back again to him and his Heirs; from whom this Mannor, I suppose, was conveyed to

Pat. 15 Ed.
IV.

John Boteler, who was at that time Lord of the former Mannor called **Watton Woodhall**: He married *Dorothy* the Daughter of *Henry Belknap*, by whom he had no Issue; after her Decease, he wedded *Dorothy* the Daughter of *William Terrell*, of **Gipping**, by whom he had Issue *Philip*; and after her Decease he took to Wife *Katharine*, the Daughter of *Thomas Acton*, and was constituted Sheriff of the Counties of **Essex** and **Hertford**, *Anno* 5 *H.* VII.

Rot. Pip. 5
H. VII. tit.
Essex&Herts.

Philip Boteler was his Heir, Lord of both Mannors, and married *Elizabeth*, Daughter of *Robert Drury* of **Halsted** in the County of **Norfolk**, by whom he had Issue, *John, Thomas, William, George, Griffith, John, Thomas, Henry, Anthony, Richard, Francis, Philip, Anne* married to *Leonard Hide*, Esq. *Elizabeth* to *Henry Gill*, and afterwards to *Edward Buggin*, *Dorothy* to *Anthony Brown* of **Rutlandshire**, *Mary* to *John Harpham*, *Katharine* to *Roger Potts*, *Margaret*, and *Bridget*: He was constituted Sheriff of the Counties of **Essex** and **Hertford**, *Anno* 29 *H.* VIII. and died the 28th of *March*, in the Year of Christ 1549.

Sir *John Boteler* was his Heir, inherited these Mannors, was constituted Sheriff of the Counties of 𝔥𝔢𝔯𝔱𝔣𝔬𝔯𝔡 and 𝔈𝔰-𝔰𝔢𝔵, *Annis* 4 and 5 of *Philip* and *Mary*, and married *Gresil*, Daughter and Heir of Sir *William Roche* of 𝔩𝔞𝔫𝔪𝔢𝔯 in this County, by whom he had Issue *Philip, Henry, William, Richard, Nicholas, Elizabeth* married to Sir *Henry Conisby, Mary* to *Thomas Shotbolt, Sarah* to *Robert Colt, Susan* to *Julius Ferrers, Margaret* to *Nicholas Bristowe*, and *Martha* to Sir *George Perient*, Kt.

Hund. of Bradewater

Sir *Philip Boteler*, Kt. succeeded in these Mannors, and married *Katharine* the Daughter of Sir *Francis Knowles*, Kt. and Widow to the Lord *Gerrard* of 𝔦𝔯𝔢𝔩𝔞𝔫𝔡, by whom he had Issue *Robert, Philip, Christopher*, and *Penelope*; was constituted Sheriff of this County, 1578, 20 *Eliz.* and received the Honour of Knighthood in the same Year.

Robert his eldest Son was knighted at 𝔚𝔥𝔦𝔱𝔢𝔥𝔞𝔩𝔩, on the 30th of *March*, in the Year of our Lord, 1607, constituted Sheriff of this County, *Anno 9 Jac.* I. 1611, and married *Frances* the Daughter of Sir *Drew Drury*, by whom he had Issue *Jane:* He purchased the Mannors of 𝔖𝔞𝔠𝔬𝔪𝔟, 𝔗𝔢𝔪-𝔭𝔩𝔢 𝔆𝔥𝔢𝔩𝔰𝔦𝔫, and 𝔆𝔥𝔢𝔩𝔩𝔰 in this County, and upon his Death, *Jane* who was his Heir, enjoyed the Mannors which he purchased, but these Mannors came by Settlement to

Rot. Pip. 9 J. I. tit. Herts.

Philip Boteler, who was his Brother, and the next Heir Male of that Family: He married *Alice* one of the Daughters of *John Shotbolt* of 𝔄𝔯𝔡𝔩𝔭 in this County, Esq. by whom he had Issue *John* and *Philip*.

John Boteler was his Heir, invested Knight of the Bath 1 *Car.* I. in Order to the Coronation of that King; and constituted Sheriff of this County, *Anno* 1630, 6 *Car.* I. These Knights were denominated from their bathing at their Creation; Mr. *Camden* says in all his Reading he could find no greater Antiquity of them, than that they were in Use among the ancient *French:* and *H.* IV. King of 𝔈𝔫𝔤-𝔩𝔞𝔫𝔡, dubbed forty six Esquires, Knights of this Order in the *Tower*, on the Day of his Coronation, who washed and bathed the Night before they were knighted; and he gave to every of them green side Coats reaching to their Ankles, with strait Sleeves furr'd with Minivere, and they wore upon their left Shoulder two Cordans of white Silk, and Tassels to it hanging down; but I find that *Thomas Bardolfe*, and many others were made Knights of the Bath, *Anno* 34 *Ed.* I. with *Edward* Prince of 𝔚𝔞𝔩𝔢𝔰, as I have shewed before in this Parish; but I shall say no more of this Order, for that Sir *William Dugdale* has treated so largely of it in his Survey of 𝔚𝔞𝔯𝔴𝔦𝔠𝔨𝔰𝔥𝔦𝔯𝔢, to which I refer the Reader. This Sir *John Boteler* was a very loyal Subject to his Prince, and upon that grand Defection, *Anno* 1642, was made one of the Commissioners of Array in this County; and when

Camd. Brit. fol. 172. Seld. tit. Hon. p 820.

Hund. of
Bradewater an Army was levyed by the Influence of a predominant Party, in the Parliament then held at Westminster, under divers plausible Pretences, he supplyed the King with Money to raise Men for the Security and Preservation of the Government, and the Safety of the People, for which Act, that rebellious Party committed him to *Ely-house* in Holborn, where he was detained a long time, sequestred his Estate, made great Spoil and Havock thereof, and he died leaving Issue *Philip, John, Ralph,* ———, *Catharine* married to Sir *John Gore*, Kt. and *Elizabeth* to *Ralph Gore*, Esq. and he was buried in the Burying-place of his Ancestors adjoyning to this Parish Church.

Philip was his Heir and succeeded, he married one of the Daughters of Sir *John Langham*, Kt. one of the Aldermen of the City of London, by whom he had Issue *John, Mary* married to Sir *William Gostwicke*, of Willughton, in the County of Bedford, Kt. and Bar. *Elizabeth* to ——— *Copley*, Esq. sometime Deputy Governor of Hull, and afterwards of the Province of Maryland in America, and *Anne*; he was made one of the Knights of the Bath, *Anno* 12 *Car.* II. to attend the Coronation of that King, a Deputy Lieutenant, and one of the Justices of the Peace for this County; he died *Anno* 33 *Car.* II. and was buried here by his Ancestors.

John Boteler was his only Son, knighted 10 *Feb.* 1676, 28 *Car.* II. constituted Sheriff of this County *Anno* 1680, 32 *Car.* II. married *Elizabeth* one of the Daughters and Coheirs of Sir *Nicholas Gould* of the City of London, Kt. by whom he had *Philip* and *Elizabeth*, died *Anno Car.* II. and was buried near his Father at Watton at Stone: he constituted by his Will Sir *Richard Spencer* of Offley, Bar. and *John Boteler*, Esq. Brother to his Father Sir *Philip Boteler*, Guardians to his Son *Philip*, and *Elizabeth* his Daughter, both whom are now living, and the said *Philip* is the present Lord of these Mannors; his Armes are *Gules, a Fess counter-compony Argent and Sable, between six Crosselets of the first; Crest on a Wreath, a dexter Arm embowed in Armour Argent garnish'd, holding a Sword proper, Hilt and Pomel Gold.*

The Mannor-house of Woodhall, the ancient Seat of this knightly Family consists of a large Pile of Brick, with a fair Quadrangle in the Middle of it, seated upon a dry Hill in a pleasant Park, well wooded and greatly Timber'd, where divers christal Springs issue out of the Ground, at some Distance before the House, which run on the South Side hereof to the Beane: They do greatly adorn the Seat, and the Park, and the Hills, the Timber Trees, and these Waters render this Place so very pleasant and delicious to the Eye, that it is accounted one of the best Seats in this County.

THE PEDIGREE OF THE BOTELERS.

Botiler.

Robert Botiler.

Ralph Botiler, Baron of Overslee.

Ralph Botiler, Baron of Overslee.

Ralph Botiler, Baron of Overslee, 37 Henry III. = Maud, Daughter of William Pantulfe, Lord of Wem.

| 1 John Boteler, p 15 Edw. I. | 2 Gawen, died aged 17, s. p. 18 Edw. I. | 4 Sir Ralph Boteler of Pulretack and Norbury, Kt | Maud, eld. Da. and Coh. of Phil. Marmion, Aged 30 Years, 20th Edw. I. | Alice. | 3 William Boteler, Baron of Wem, married Ankaret, the Niece of Ja. Adithaley. |

William Boteler, Baron of Wem, 18. Edw. III married Marg. Da. of the Earl of Arundel.

Ralph Boteler of Pulreback and Norbury. = Hawise, Da. and sole Heir of Rich. Gobion, Inq. 35 Edw. I.

William Boteler, Baron of Wem, mar. Elizabeth, Da. of Handsaker.

| Katharine, Da. of Sir Phil. Pelitot, and Heiress to her Brother William, who had no Issue. | 3 Ralph Boteler, of Pulreback. | 1 Sir John Boteler, Kt. married Joan, Da. of John Argentine. | 2 William Boteler. |

John Boteler, Lord of Strange and Blackway, mar. Ankaret, Fil. and Heir of Ed. Boteler of Odington, in Com. Warw.

| Sir Philip Boteler of Wood-hall, ob. 1421, Inq. 8 H. V. | Isabel, Da. of —— | Ralph Boteler, of —— | Edward, s. p. a p. 22 Ed. III. 30 Edw. III. |

—— Cheyny, second Wife. = Philip Boteler of Woodhall = Elizabeth, Daughter of Cokain, Justicer, first Wife.

| 2 Philip Boteler, died 3 H. VI | Elizabeth. | 1 Edward Boteler, died on St. Andrew's Day, Anno 5 H. V. |

Eliz. Da. of —— 2d. Wife, ob. 28. Oct. 1465. = John Boteler. = Constance, Da of —— Downhall of Goddington in North. 1st Wife

| Dorothy, Da. of William Terril of Gipping, 2 Wife. | John Boteler, of Woodhall, ob. 1514. | Dorothy, Da. of Henry Belknap, first Wife, s. p. Katharine, Daughter of Thomas Acton, third Wife, ob. 1513. | Margaret. | Dorothy. | Katharine. |

Sir Philip Boteler of Woodhall, Kt. = Elizabeth, Daughter of Robert Drury of Halested.

| 2 Thomas. William. George. Griffith. John. Thomas. | 8 Henry. 9 Antho. 10 Rich. 11 Fran. 12 Phil. | 1 Sir John Boteler of Woodhall, Kt. | Grezil, Da. and He. of Sir William Roche of Lamer in Hertfordshire. | 1 Ann, m Leonard Hide, Esq. | 2 Elizabeth, m. Henry Gill, after his decease, Edw. Buggin. | 3 Mary, m. John Harpham. | 4 Dorothy, mar. Antho. Browne of Rutlandshire. | 5 Katharine, mar. Roger Potts. | 6 Margaret. 7 Bridget. |

| 1 Sir Philip Boteler of Woodhall, Kt. | Anne, Da. of John Conisby of North Mymms. | 2 Sir Henry Boteler of Brantfield and Hatfield Woodhall, mar. 1 Katharine, Da. of Robert Waller of Hadley. 2 Alice, Da. of Edw. Pulter of Wimundley, Com. Hertf. | 3 William. 4 Rich. 5 Nicho. | Eliz. m. Sir Henry Conisby, Kt. | Mary, m. Thomas Shotbolt. | Sarah, mar. Roger Colt. | Susan, m. Julius Ferrers. | Margaret. m. Nich. Bristow. | Martha, m. Sir George Perient. |

Sir Philip Boteler of Watton Woodhall. = Katharine, Da. of Sir Francis Knowles, Kt. and Widow to Ld. Gerrard of Ireland

| Philip Boteler. = Alice, Da. of Jo. Shotbolt. | Sir Rob. Boteler of Watton Woodhall. | Frances, Da. of Sir Drew Drury. | Christopher. | Penelope. |

Philip. Sir John Boteler, Kt. of the Bath.

Joan, sole Daughter and Heir, married John Lord Bellysia.

| Sir Philip Boteler, t. of the Bath. | Daughter of Sir John Langham, Alderman of London. | John Boteler, mar. Daughter of Sir Edward Atkins, Lord Chief Baron. | Ralph. | Catharine, married Sir John Gore, Kt. | Elizabeth, m. Ralph Gore, Esq. |

| Sir John Bote r, Kt. | Elizabeth, Da. of Sir Nicholas Gold, Kt. of London. | Mary, mar. Sir Will. Gostwick of Willughtou in Com. Bedford, Knight and Baronet. | Anne, died unmarried. | Elizabeth, mar.——Copley, Deputy Governor of Hull, afterwards of Maryland. |

Philip Boteler, Esq.   Elizabeth.

Hund. of **Brabewater**
'Tis observable that this noble Family descended from these Barons of **Kilpeck, Wem, Obersley, Sudeley,** and **Scribelby,** who were Barons by Tenure, such as I have mentioned in **Ardley,** but they who doubt whether there were any such Baronies, may be satisfied upon the View of Westmin. 2, cap. 42. the Stat. of **Westminster,** which directs that Fees shall be paid to the Earl-Marshal and Lord-Chamberlain, when every such Baron shall do his Homage to the King, whether the Baron held by whole Barony or less; and every such Baron held his Barony, Honour, Castle, or Mannor, by Grand-Serjeanty; and might grant or alien it by License Doddridge's *Treat. of Nob.* p. 69, 70, 71. from the King, and if such Grant or Alienation was made for the Continuance of the Barony in his own Name and Blood and Issue-Male; or else was made for Money or other Recompence to a Stranger, the Purchaser held and enjoy'd the Name, Stile, Title, and Dignity of a Baron to him and his Heirs, according to the Grant; but if any such Baron granted or aliened his Castle, Honour or Mannor so held *per Baroniam,* without License of the King, he forfeited it to the King, because Baronies were the Strength of the Realm, and the Kingdom would have been weakened thereby, and base Persons ennobled without desert of Vertue or Prowess, therefore they were seized into the King's Hands upon such Forfeiture, and the Dignity and Estate extinguisht in the Crown from whence it was derived: and I find that by the Grant and Alienation of these Baronies, this honourable Family lost these Honours.

THE Rectory, *Anno 26 H. VIII.* was valued in the King's Books at 19*l.* 8*s.* 6*d. per Ann.* and the Lords of this Mannor have been Patrons hereof.

The RECTORS.

Mr. *Inglesby*	John *Sawel,* D. D.
Mr. *Richard Vines.*	Mr. *Wright Burdite,*
—— *Shute,* D. D.	Mr. *William Bookey.*
Mr. *Samuel Bendy*	

This Church is situated upon the Side of an Hill, near the Town, in the Deanery of **Hertford,** in the Diocess of **Lincolne,** is covered with Lead, and a fair Chapel is erected on the North Side of the Chancel, and a fair Tower adjoins the West End of the Church, wherein is a small Ring of six untuneable Bells, and the Tower is covered with Lead, and hath a short Shaft upon it.

Within the Chancel and the Chapel are some Grave Stones which have these Inscriptions.

Hic jacent Johannes Butler, **Armiger,** et Katharina **filia** Thomæ Acton, **generosi;** Dorothæa una etiam **filiarum** Henrici Belknap, **Armigeri,** uxor Johannis Boteler, ante **dicti.** qui **quidem** Johannes obiit **undecimo die** mensis Maii, Anno Dom. **milesimo quingentesimo** et **desimo quarto,** et **dicta** Katharina **decimo octabo die** Augusti Anno Dom. **milesima quingentesima decimo tertio.**

The Effigies of a Man and his three Wives are engraved in Brass, with their several Coats of Arms.

Hic jacet Johannes Buteler Armiger, quondam Dominus de Wudehall, ac Patronus istius Ecclesiæ, qui obiit Anno Dom. milesimo ——————— Item hic jacet Elizabetha Buteler, quondam uxor predicti Johannis Buteler quæ obiit Anno Dom. milesimo quadringentesimo sexagesimo nono bicesimo octabo die mensis Octobris.

Item hic jacet Constans Buteler, quæ quidem uxor ejusdem Johannis, obiit Anno Dom. milesimo quadringentesimo.

In a Border round a Stone is this Inscription.

Ici gist Monsieur —————— Peletot Chebaler, Que morust le 14. our d. Aust L'an, de Grace Mill. CCC ———

The Pourtraicture of a Man in Brass.

I suppose this was the Stone that covered Sir *Philip Peletot*, who died in the Year of our Lord 1361.

Hic jacet *Richardus Boteler* de Stapleford in Com. Hertf. Armiger, qui obiit quinto die *Maii, Anno Dom.* 1614.

Et *Anna* uxor ejus una Filiarum *Johannis Mynn* de Hertingfordbury Armigeri, quæ obiit duodecimo, die *Octobris, Anno Dom.* 1619.

Et *Elizabetha*, unica filia eorundem *Rich.* & *Anna Rolando Graveley* de Grabeley, Arm. nupta, quæ obiit ante parentes die *Feb.* 1600. sine prole.

Icy gysent Wat. Mohinton et Jana de Gutcestri, que diur in almes Anno Christi M.D.11.

The Body of Mr. *Samuel Bendy*, the very worthy and reverend Rector of this Church for 18. years, who departed this mortal life *Apr.* the 3d. 1689.

In a Place called Welwood, lying between a Farm called Broomball in this Parish, and the Parish of Datchworth, there is a very deep Well without Water, where several Intrenchments seem to have been formerly made, and several Foundations have been digged up there, where 'tis reported that the *Danes* had a Camp, and not far from hence is a Field called Danes Field, from a great Battel which the *Danes* fought there with the *English;* and 'tis very probable that the Souldiers that were then slain, were buried at the six Hills near Stebenedge, for in those Days such Memorials as those Hills were made for the Burial of their Dead.

The Soil of this Parish is for the greatest Part Gravel, and abounds much in Wood and Timber.

CHARITIES.

Colonel *Tompson*, and Sir *William Tompson*, founded a Free-School in this Vill, and gave 14*l.* per *Annum*, whereof 10*l.* to the School, the Rest for the Repairs of the Houses, the Overplus for putting forth a poor Child Apprentice.

Mr. *Cranfield* gave 20*l.* to the Poor, and the Interest to be paid yearly among the Poor.

Mr. *Kent* gave to the Poor 20*l.* whereof the Interest to be laid out yearly in Bread.

SUEVECAMP, SAVECAMP, SACOMB.

THIS Vill was called Suevecamp from Suabis-campus, a most sweet and pleasant Field, very fertile in Corn, and wholsome for Air, where the Church is scituated upon an

Hund. of Hill, two Miles distant from 𝔚𝔞𝔱𝔱𝔬𝔫, towards the East:
𝔅𝔯𝔞𝔡𝔢𝔴𝔞𝔱𝔢𝔯 In the time of *William* the Conqueror 'tis recorded of this
Vill, under the Title of *Terra Hardvini de Scalers.*

Domesd. Lib.   *In* 𝔅𝔯𝔞𝔡𝔢𝔴𝔞𝔱𝔯𝔢 *Hundred. in* 𝔍𝔢𝔟𝔢𝔯𝔥𝔞𝔪𝔭𝔢. *tenet* Petrus de Valoines *novem*
fol.137,nu.20. *hidas un. virgat. minus: Terra est septem car. in Dom. sex hidæ, et ibi sunt
tres car. et quarta potest fieri, ibi quinq; Vill. cum sex bordis et uno Clerico, habent. tres car. ibi sex cotar. et quatuor Servi, et un. molend. de vigint.
sol. Silva, 60. porc. in totis valent. valet et valuit sex libras tempore Regis
Eduuardi octo. lib. De hoc Manerio, tenuit* Elmer *quatuor. hid. pro un.
Manerio, testante Hundredo, et* Levinus *tenuit duo hid. un. virg. minus pro
un. Manerio; hom. Comitis Heraldi, fuit et vendere potuit.*
     In Manerio quod Elmerus *tenuit fuerunt quatuor Sochi. unus eorum
dimid. hid. tenuit et vendere potuit, et alter un. virgat. tenuit, sed vendere
non potuit preter ejus licentiam Domini sui* Elmari. *Tertius et Quartus dimid. hid. habuerunt sex acras minus et vendere potuerunt: Super hos duos
habuit Rex* Edwardus *Sacam et Socam, et quisq; vicecomiti quartem partem avere inveniebat per annum vel unum denarium. Ipsi quatuor homines*
Almeri *de* Belingtone *fuerunt. In eodem Manerio quædam Fæmina tenuit
quinq; virgat. sub* Anschil de Waras, *et vendere potuit, præter unum virgat. que posuit in vadium* Almero de Belingtone *pro decem solidis, et inveniebat unam averam, et quartem partem alterius avere aut quinq; denarios.*
     Peter de Valoines *held in* 𝔍𝔢𝔟𝔢𝔯𝔥𝔞𝔪𝔭𝔢, *in the Hundred of* 𝔅𝔯𝔞𝔡𝔢𝔴𝔞𝔱𝔢𝔯,
nine Hides wanting a Virgate, the arable is seven Carucates, in Demeasne six Hides, and there are three Carucates, and a fourth may be
made, there are five Villaines with six Borders and one Clerk, having
three Carucates, there are six Cottagers, and four Servants, and one
Mill of twenty Shillings Rent by the Year, Wood to feed sixty Hogs, in
the whole Value, it is worth and was worth six Pounds by the Year, in the
time of King *Edward* (the Confessor) eight Pounds a Year. *Elmer* held
four Hides of this Mannor for one Mannor, the Hundred witnessing it;
and *Levinus* held two Hides wanting one Virgate for one Mannor: He
was a Man (under the Protection) of Earl *Herald,* and might sell it.
     In the Mannor which *Elmer* held there were four Socmen, one of them
held half an Hide, and might sell it, and another held one Virgate but
could not sell it without the leave of his Lord, *Elmer;* the third and
fourth had half an Hide wanting six Acres, and might sell it. Beside
these two, King *Edward* (the Confessor) had Sake and Soke, and every
one did find the fourth Part of an Horse by the Year, or paid one Penny
to the Sheriff. There were four Men (under the Protection) of *Almer de
Belingtone:* In the same Mannor a certain Woman held five Virgates
under *Anschil de Waras,* and might sell them, except one Virgate which
she mortgaged to *Almer de Belingtone* for ten Shillings, and she did find
an Horse, and the fourth Part of another Horse or paid five Pence.

     This *Peter de Valoines* was a great Baron in the time of
King *William* the Conqueror, and married *Albreda,* Sister
to *Eudo Dapifer,* who was Steward to King *Henry* I. by
whom he had Issue
     Robert de Valoines, who was his Heir, and married *Agnes,*
by whom he had Issue *Peter, Robert,* and *Gunnora:* he
obtained from *Maud* the Empress all those Lands and
Fees whereof his Father died seiz'd.
     Peter de Valoines succeeded him, and married *Gundred
de Warren,* by whom he had Issue three Daughters, 1 *Lora,*
who married *Alexander de Balioll,* Brother to *John* King
of Scots; 2 *Christian,* who married *William de Mandevile,*
and after his Decease *Peter de Maine;* and 3 *Elizabeth,*
who married *David Comyne:* and he died seized of the
Mannors of 𝔅𝔢𝔫𝔦𝔫𝔤𝔱𝔬𝔫, 𝔚𝔞𝔱𝔱𝔬𝔫, 𝔅𝔬𝔵, 𝔠𝔯𝔬𝔴𝔟𝔢𝔯𝔭, 𝔥𝔢𝔯𝔱𝔦𝔫𝔤-
𝔣𝔬𝔯𝔡𝔟𝔲𝔯𝔭, 𝔅𝔞𝔱𝔥𝔬𝔩, and 𝔍𝔢𝔟𝔢𝔯𝔞𝔪𝔭, in this County, and 𝔉𝔞-

kenham in Norfolke, leaving these three Daughters his Co-heirs, and upon the Partition this Mannor and Fakenham in Norfolke, fell to the Lot of

Elizabeth, the Wife of *David Comyne*, who had Issue by her

William Comyne, who was her Son and Heir, to whom this Mannor descended: He was knighted, and upon a *Quo Warranto* brought before *John de Reygate* and other Justices Itinerants at Hertford, *Anno* 6 *Edw.* I. claimed in this Mannor, which he held in Purparty of the Inheritance which was *Peter de Valoines*, Soc, Sac, Toll, Them, Infangtheof, all the Fee and Land, View of Franc-pledge, Correction of the Assize of Bread and Ale, and Tumbrel, &c. by the Grant of King *Henry* I. to *Peter de Valoines*, and the Confirmation thereof by King *Henry* II. to *Robert de Valoines*, and upon the View of the Deeds these Priviledges were then allowed; this Sir *William Comyne* married *Eufemia*, the Daughter of ———— by whom he had Issue *John*, *Edward*, and *Agnes*.

John died the the 16th of *Edw.* I. and upon his Decease this Mannor came to

Edward Comyne, who was his Brother, and married *Mary*, Daughter of ———— by whom he had Issue *Eufemia* and *Mary*, his Daughters and Coheirs, and upon his Death this Mannor fell to the Part of

Mary Comyne, who was possest of it, and married *Edmond de Pakenham*, by whom she had Issue *Thomas* and *Edmond*, who dying in their Infancy it came to

Eufemia, who was her elder Sister and Heir, and married *William de la Bech*, by whom she had Issue *Elizabeth*, and she died seized hereof *Anno* 1361, 35 *Edw.* III. leaving

Elizabeth de la Bech, who was her only Daughter and Heir, married Sir *Roger Elmerugge*, Kt. and levyed a Fine of this and the Mannors of Fakenham in Norfolke, and Asps in Suffolke, to the Use of them, the said *Roger* and *Elizabeth*, and their Heirs; and it was found *Anno* 30 *Edw.* III. that Sir *Roger Elmerugge* and his Wife, Daughter and Heir of *Eufemia de la Bech*, held this Mannor with the Advowson of the Church of the King by the Service of one Knight's Fee, and Sir *Roger* dying seized hereof, *Elizabeth* survived him, and shortly after conveyed them to

Sir *John Holt*, Kt. one of the Justices of the Common Bench, and *Alice* his Wife, and their Heirs, and Sir *John* surviving his Wife, he and five other Judges, and the King's Serjeant, at a Parliament held *Anno* 11 *Rich.* II. were attainted and banisht, whereby this Mannor was forfeited and seized into the King's Hands, and tho' he charged it with the Payment of a yearly Rent to his Son, until such time as he should be promoted to some Of-

Hund. of Bradewater

Quo Warr. 6 Ed. 1 cur. recept. Scac

Fin. 36 Ed. III. in cur. recept. Scac.

Hund. of
Braderwater

Prin's *Abr of*
Rec. in the
Tower, fol.
406.
Ex Autogr.
penesJ.G.mil.

Esc. 15 H VI.

fice, yet because it was held of the King *in Capite*, and the Grant made without License, it was given to

John Corbet, and tho' upon the Petition of Sir *Ralph Holt*, at a Parliament held 2 *H.* IV. that King restored him to his Blood, and to all his Hereditaments in the King's Possession, yet notwithstanding *John Corbet* held this Mannor during the Reign of *H.* IV. afterwards it came to the Possession of

———*Bapthorpe* who possest it till about the 15th Year of *H.* VI. when he died seiz'd hereof, leaving Issue

Ralph Babthorpe, who was knighted, and enjoyed this Mannor during the time of *Edw.* IV. had Issue *Isabel*, and died about the Beginning of the Reign of *H.* VII.

Isabel was his sole Heir, and married *William Plompton*, Esq. at the time of her Father's Decease; they had Issue *William*, held several Courts in both their Names for this Mannor during the Reign of *H.* VIII. and in the time of *Edw.* VI. he died seized hereof, and *Isabel* his Wife surviving, held it a while, and upon her Decease

William, who was his Heir, succeeded, but he being under Age at the Death of *Isabel* his Mother, a Court was held in the King's Name, *Anno* 7 *Edw.* VI. by Reason the Heir was then in Minority, afterwards this *William Plompton* held a Court for this Mannor in his own Name, and enjoy'd the Profits hereof till he sold it to

Sir *Robert Butler*, Kt. who held it during the Reign of *James* I. and dying seiz'd hereof, it descended to

Jane, who was his sole Daughter and Heir, and married *John Belasis*, Esq. they held a Court here in both their Names. This *John Belasis* was the second Son of *Thomas* Viscount Fauconbridge, who was very firm and loyal to his Prince, in the time of the late Rebellion; and when a great Army was raised against King *Charles* I. by a prevailing Party in the Parliament which began *Nov.* 3d, *Anno* 16 *Car.* I. 1640, he adhered faithfully to him, raised a compleat Regiment of foot Souldiers, when the King set up his Standard at Nottingham; fought valiantly in the Head of them, at the Battels of Kineton, Bramford, Newbury, and shewed great Courage in the Storming of Bristol; for which Services that King, by Letters Patents dated the 27th of *January*, 20th of his Reign, advanced him to the Dignity of a Baron of this Realm by the Title of Lord *Belasis* of Worlaby in the County of Lincolne, made him Lieutenant General of the Counties of York, Nottingham, Lincolne, and Derby, Governour of the City of York and the Garrison of Newark upon Trent, and Captain General of his Majesty's Guards. Afterwards King *Charles* II. made him Captain General of his Forces in Africa, and Governour of Tangier, Lord-lieutenant of the East Riding in Yorkshire,

Governour of 𝔥ull, and Captain of his Guard of Gentlemen Pensioners; but he, scrupling the Oath injoyned by
Act of Parliament made *Anno* 1672, to be taken by all such
as did then or should hereafter bear any Office under his
Majesty, resign'd his Government of 𝔗angier to the Earl of
𝔐iddleton, his Lieutenancy of the 𝔈ast 𝔕iding in Yorkshire, and Government of 𝔥ull to the Duke of 𝔐onmouth;
his Captainship of the Pensioners to his Nephew, *Thomas*
Viscount 𝔉auconbridge, and a Regiment of Foot (raised during the late Wars with the *Dutch*) to the Earl of 𝔑orth-
ampton; He had Issue by her *Henry*, made Knight of the
Bath at the Coronation of King *Charles* II. and *Mary* married to *Robert* Viscount 𝔇unbar in 𝔖cotland; but wanting
Money to defray the Charge of his Army, and to supply his
Majesty's Occasions in the time of his Exigence, sold this,
the Mannor of 𝔗emple 𝔠helsin, and 𝔚ox, otherwise called
𝔠hells, to

Sir *John Gore*, who was knighted at 𝔜ork, 1640, and
married *Catharine* the eldest Daughter of Sir *John Butler*
of 𝔚atton 𝔚oodhal in this County, Kt. of the Bath, by
whom he had Issue *John, Ralph, Charles, Anne, Catharine,*
and *Jane;* He was constituted Sheriff of this County, *An.*
6 *Car.* II. served as a Burgess in the Parliament held *An.*
1671, 23 of the same King, for the Borough of 𝔥ertford;
his Arms were *Gules, a Fesse between three Cross Cross-
lets fitched Or;* and sold this Mannor and 𝔗emple 𝔠helsin,
Anno 4 *Jac.* II. to

Sir *Thomas Rolt*, who had been President for the *East
India Company* at 𝔖urrat, was knighted at 𝔚hitehall on
the first of *October*, in the Year 1682, was constituted
Sheriff for this County, *Anno* 1696, and married *Mary*
———— by whom he had Issue *Edward* and *Constantia.*

Thıs Rectory *Anno* 26 *H.* VIII. was rated in the King's Books at the
yearly Value of 10*l* 3*s.* 4*d.* and the Lords of this Mannor are Patrons
hereof.

The RECTORS.

Mr. *John Meriton.*   Mr. *Timothy Puller*, D.D.   Mr. *John Adams.*

This Church is dedicated to the Honour of St. *Katharine*, and is si-
tuated in a fair Field upon a dry Hill, in the Deanery of 𝔅ertford, in the
Diocess of 𝔏incolne, the Church and Chancel are covered with Tile, the
Tower is erected upon the South Side of the Church, wherein are three
small Bells, and within the Church are these Inscriptions upon two
Grave Stones.

𝔥ere lyeth the 𝔅ody of John Doddington of Sacomb, 𝔊ent. who deceased a
faithful 𝔠hristian the 7th day of January, in the year of our 𝔏ord 1544.
and was 𝔥usband to Elenor Doddington whose 𝔊rabe is joyned here to
his on the right side, after whom she surbibed 7. years and 7. 𝔚eeks, and
left alibe at his departure by her his only 𝔚ife three 𝔖ons and six
𝔇aughters.

> *Cignea qui terris modulati carmina mortis;*
> *Dulce polo vitæ melos nunc usq; canunt.*

𝔒𝔣 𝔶𝔬𝔲𝔯 𝔠𝔥𝔞𝔯𝔦𝔱𝔶 𝔭𝔯𝔞𝔶 𝔣𝔬𝔯 𝔱𝔥𝔢 𝔖𝔬𝔲𝔩 𝔬𝔣 Elenor Doddington 𝔩𝔞𝔱𝔢 𝔱𝔥𝔢 𝔴𝔦𝔣𝔢 𝔬𝔣 John Doddington, 𝔊𝔢𝔫𝔱. 𝔴𝔥𝔦𝔠𝔥 Elenor 𝔡𝔢𝔠𝔢𝔞𝔰𝔢𝔡 𝔱𝔥𝔢 𝔱𝔢𝔫𝔱𝔥 𝔡𝔞𝔶 𝔬𝔣 November, 𝔦𝔫 𝔱𝔥𝔢 𝔶𝔢𝔞𝔯 𝔬𝔣 𝔬𝔲𝔯 𝔏𝔬𝔯𝔡 1550. 𝔲𝔭𝔬𝔫 𝔥𝔢𝔯 𝔖𝔬𝔲𝔩 𝔍𝔢𝔰𝔲 𝔥𝔞𝔳𝔢 𝔪𝔢𝔯𝔠𝔶.

On the North Wall of the Chancel is this Inscription.

Near this Place lyeth buried the Body of the Reverend Mr. *John Meriton*, Rector of this Parish of 𝔖𝔞𝔠𝔬𝔪𝔟 about 32 years, Aged 64. who departed this Life *December* the 20*th* 1669, much Beloved, much Lamented. He gave an 100*l.* to be laid out in Land, for the raising of 5*l. per annum* for ever, wherewith to put forth yearly some one poor Child of this Parish an A'pprentice.

Vivit post Funera Virtus.

MUNDANE PARVA, MUNDANE FREWEL.

THIS Vill lyes in a Bottom about a Mile and a Half distant from 𝔖𝔞𝔠𝔬𝔪𝔟 to the North, and the Name may be derived from the Vale, where a great Part of the Houses are shrouded under the Hill, on both Sides, from whence it may be called 𝔐𝔲𝔫𝔡𝔞𝔫𝔢, a safe Vale; for *Mund* in the Saxon Language, signifies a safe Place, and *Dane*, a Valley: in the time of *William* the Conquerour it belonged to *Walter Flandrensis*, who assumed this for his Sirname, in Regard he came from 𝔉𝔩𝔞𝔫𝔡𝔢𝔯𝔰, and was an Assistant in the Conquest of this Kingdom, to whom he gave this Mannor among others, for his good Service in that Expedition, as appears by *Domesdei Book*, where 'tis recorded under the Title of *Terra Walteri Flandrensis.*

Walter Flandrensis *tenuit* 𝔐𝔲𝔫𝔡𝔞𝔫𝔢 *pro quinque hidis et una virgat. se defendebat. Terra est octo car. in dominio tres hidæ et dimid. et ibi est una car. et adhuc duo possunt fieri, duodecem Vil. cum Presbitero, et duo Bordarii habentes quinque car. ibi duo Servi pastura ad pec. Vil. Silva ducent. porc. In totis valent. valet sex libr. Quando recepit septem libr. Tempore Regis* Edwardi *octo libr. Hoc Manerium tenuit* Leuvinus *homo Comitis* Heraldi *et vendere potuit.*

Walter Flandrensis held 𝔐𝔲𝔫𝔡𝔞𝔫𝔢. it was rated for five Hides and one Virgate. The arable is eight Carucates, in Demeasne three Hides and an half, and there is one Carucate, and now two others may be made, there are twelve Villains and a Parson, and two Bordars having five Carucates; there are two Servants, Common of Pasture for the Cattle of the Vill, Wood to feed two hundred Hogs. In the whole Value it is worth six Pounds by the Year, when he received it seven Pounds by the Year, in the time of King *Edward* (the Confessor) eight Pounds a Year: *Lewine*, a Man (under the Protection) of Earl *Herald* held this Mannor and might sell it.

Afterwards this Mannor was granted to one *Frewel*, who held it of the King *in Capite*, by the Service of one Knight's Fee and au Half, from whom it descended to

Richard Frewel, who upon a *Quo Warranto* brought against him, *Anno* 6 *Edw.* I. at 𝔥𝔢𝔯𝔱𝔣𝔬𝔯𝔡, before *John de Reygate* and others, Justices Itinerants, appeared in Court, and claimed to hold it of the King *per Baroniam*, and from these *Frewels*, this Vill received the Adjunct of *Frewel* to its Name: in the time of *Edw.* III. I find it was in the Possession of

Reginald de Grey Lord of 𝔚𝔦𝔩𝔱𝔬𝔫 upon 𝔚𝔩𝔞𝔶 in 𝔥𝔢𝔯𝔱𝔢𝔣𝔬𝔯𝔡𝔰𝔥𝔦𝔯𝔢, who was summon'd to several Parliaments, from 17 to 34 *Edw.* III. inclusive, and died upon Tuesday in *Whitson-week,* 44 *Edward* III. seized of these Mannors among divers others, leaving

Henry his Son and Heir, who did his Homage, had Livery of his Lands, and 50 *Edw.* III. was summoned to Parliament, by the Name of *Henry de Grey de Shirland,* Chevalier, and dyed on the Saturday before the Feast of Saint *George, Anno* 19 *R.* II. and it continued, as I shall shew in the next Mannor, in the same Name, until the time of *Henry* VII. when

Sir *William Say* purchased both the Mannor of 𝔏𝔦𝔱𝔱𝔩𝔢 and 𝔊𝔯𝔢𝔞𝔱 𝔐𝔲𝔫𝔡𝔞𝔫𝔢, with the Advowsons of both Churches; he had Issue two Daughters, *Elizabeth* married to *William* Lord *Mountjoy,* and *Mary* to *Henry* Earl of 𝔈𝔰𝔰𝔢𝔵, from him this Mannor passed, as the Mannor of 𝔅𝔢𝔫𝔦𝔫𝔤𝔱𝔬𝔫 did, until it came to

Michael Woodcock, Esq. who held Court Leet and Baron here, *Anno* 21 *Elizabeth.* He, by Deed dated the 4th Day of *February* following, in Consideration of Marriage with *Dorothy Woodhal,* covenanted with *William Woodhal* her Father, to stand seized of the Scite of the Mannor of 𝔏𝔦𝔱𝔱𝔩𝔢 𝔐𝔲𝔫𝔡𝔞𝔫𝔢, and all the Appurtenances to the Use of himself and his Wife for their Lives, and after their Decease, to the Use of *Michael Woodcock,* eldest Son of the said *Michael,* and the Heirs Males of his Body, and in Default of such Issue, to the Use of *John Woodcock,* second Son of *Michael* the Father, and the Heirs Males of the Body of the said *John,* and in Default of such Issue, the Remainder to the Use of the Heirs Males of the Body of *Michael Woodcock* the Father, and in Default of such Issue, to the right Heirs of *Michael Woodcock* the Father for ever; but this *Michael Woodcock* straitened for Money, mortgaged this Mannor to Sir *Peter Vanlore* for Security of the Payment of 1569*l.* and afterwards for a further Sum of Money, he absolutely passed away the Inheritance to Sir *Peter Vanlore* and his Heirs, by fine Release and other Assurances, with Warranty against himself and his Heirs.

Sir *Peter Vanlore,* by Indenture dated the 24th of *Apr.* 12 *James* I. in Consideration of Marriage had between Sir *Charles Cæsar,* Son and Heir apparent of *Julius Cæsar,* Master of the Rolls, and one of the Privy Council, and Dame *Anne,* Wife of Sir *Charles* and Daughter of Sir *Peter Vanlore,* conveyed this Mannor to the Use of Sir *Charles Cæsar,* and *Anne* his Wife, for the Life of the said *Anne,* and after her Decease, if she should leave Issue of her Body,

Hund. of
𝔅𝔯𝔞𝔡𝔢𝔴𝔞𝔱𝔢𝔯

Ex Authgr.
penes C. Cæsar, Arm.

or any Issue of such Issue then living at her Death, then to
Sir *Charles Cæsar* for his Life, and after his and her Decease, to the Use of the first Issue male, and in Default of
such Issue to the second, third, fourth, fifth, sixth, and
seventh Issue males of the Bodies of Sir *Charles* and *Anne*
to be begotten, and to the Heirs of their several Bodies, with
divers Remainders over in Tail.   Sir *Charles* was possest of
this Mannor, held several Courts for the same, but upon Information of the precedent Settlement, Sir *Peter Vanlore*
exhibited his Bill in *Chancery*, to be relieved against *Woodcock* and *Woodhal*, whereupon *Woodhal* repaid all the Money to Sir *Peter Vanlore*, and by Consent of all Parties,
this Mannor was settled and establish'd again by Act of Parliament, upon the said *Edmund Woodhal* and his Heirs, this
Edmund was Register of the Prerogative Court of Canterbury, and married *Margaret* the Daughter of *Anthony Law*
of London, Gentleman, by whom he had Issue

Edmund Woodhal, who succeeded his Father in this Lordship, had Issue *Edmund*, *John*, *Elizabeth*, and *Mary*, and
dyed seiz'd hereof.

Edmund inherited this Mannor, held it awhile, and dying
without Issue, on the 22d of *July*, 1655,

John his Brother was next Heir, deceased without Issue,
and was buried in this Parish Church the 14th of *August*,
1660.   *Elizabeth* his Sister dying also without Issue, this
Mannor came to

Mary the surviving Sister, who married —— *Thornton*,
by whom she had Issue *Mary*, and ———— who are the
Daughters and Coheirs of ——— *Thornton* and *Mary* his
Wife, and the present Possessors hereof.

The Fine upon the Admission of a Tenant to any Copyhold Land, is certain by the Custom of this Mannor, and
no more than the Value of one Year's Quit-rent.

The Lord may not by the Custom, plough or break up two
Acres of Land lying near the Church, because it was anciently granted for the Recreation of the Youth of the Parish, after Evening Service on every Lord's Day.

The Mannor of LIBURY

WAS in old time called Sutrefeld, and since Haultfotck
de alto Sito, an high Land, of which 'tis recorded in *Domesdei Book*, that

In Sutrefella *ten.* Walter *un. hid. et dimid. virgat.   Terra est duo car.
ibi est una et alia potest fieri in Dominio un. hid. et un. Vil. Silva* xv *Porc.
valet et valuit* xx *sol. tempore Regis Edw.* xxx *sol.   Hac Terra est Berewich de* Munvena.   *Torchil tenuit de Leavino non potuit vendere præter
ejus licentiam.*

In eadem tenuit iisdem Walterius ix *acr. valet et valuit semper* xii *denar.
Leavinus tenuit et vendere potuit.*

In Sutrehill *Walter Flandrensis* held one Hide and half a Virgate.
The arrable is two Carucates, there is one and another may be made, in

Demeasne one Hide and one Villain, Wood to feed fifteen Hogs, it is worth and was worth, twenty Shillings by the Year, in the time of King Edward (the Confessor) thirty Shillings: This Land is a Berewich of Mundon. Torchil held it of *Lewine*, but could not sell it, without his Licence. *Hund. of Bradewater*

The same *Walter* held in the same Berewich nine Acres, it is worth, and always was worth, twelve Pence a Year; *Lewine* held it, and might sell it.

Henry de Grey, Kt. Lord of Wilton aforementioned, was also Lord of this Mannor, and being engaged in the King's Service in the Wars of Gasconp from the Feast of St. *Peter ad Vincula, Anno 17 Edw.* II. until the Feast of St. *Mary Magdalen*, then next following, he enfeoffed *John Caldecot* Rector of Stebenedge of this Mannor, within which time his Father dyed on the Feast of *Simon* and *Jude*, so that he could not possess himself of his Inheritance, which fell to him thereby, so soon as he should have done, all which King *Edw.* III. consider'd of *Anno primo Regni sui*, and remitted a Debt to him of 152*l.* owing to the *Exchequer.*

In a Roll of a Court held for this Mannor, *An.* 17 *Edw. Fil. Edw.* 'tis recorded that ——— *Geffrey diem clausit extremum de cujus morte venit ad opus Dom. de Heriet. una Vacca et alba in fronte; pretii unius Marcæ.*———Johan. Auncel, *quer. de* Thoma Backstere *de placito transgr. plegii de prosequendo,* ——— Atheridge *et* William Jeffrey: So an Executor was sued for 2*s.* that *Adam Geffrey* owed: The Executor is summon'd, pleads *nulla bona*, Inquiry is awarded to the Tenants, who find there came to his Hands, *unum Colobium et vesturam unius ar. frumenti, prætii* xvi*d.* adjudged that he recover, and the Executor *in misericordia pro falsa detentione.*

Anno 16 *Edw.* III. the King intending a Voyage royal into France, and to take Shipping with his Army at Portsmouth, upon the first of *March*, sent his Precept to this *Henry*, to attend him there with twenty Men at Arms, and twenty Archers, but he dying the same Year, left

Reginald his Son and Heir, then thirty Years of Age, who being a Baneret upon that Expedition, which the King made into France, 19 *Edw.* III. was commanded to prepare himself and all his Retinue, to sail with him thither, upon the Feast-day of St. *Lawrence* in the same Year, and he dyed *Anno* 44 *Edw.* III. seized of the Mannors of Much Mundon, Little Mundon, Liburp, Hertfordingburp, &c. leaving

Henry his Son and Heir, then twenty eight Years of Age, who did his Homage, had Livery of his Lands, and was summoned to Parliament, held *Anno* 50 *Edw.* III. by the Name of *Henry de Grey de Shirland*, Chevalier; and dyed on Saturday next before the Feast of St. *George*, in 19 *R.* II. leaving Issue

Richard his Son and Heir, then three Years of Age, and *Margaret* a Daughter, Wife to *John* Lord *Darcy.* He was of the Retinue of *Thomas* Earl of **Dorset**, Uncle to the King, and Lieutenant of **Normandy**, in his Expedition thither; and he deceased upon Monday next preceding the Feast of the Assumption of our Lady, *Anno* 1442, leaving

Reginald his Son, then 21 Years of Age; he did his Homage the next Year, had Livery of his Lands, received the Honour of Knighthood, and had Issue

John, who was possest of this Mannor, *Anno* 14 *Edw.* IV. received the Honour of Knighthood, fought stoutly at **Black-heath**, *Anno* 11 *H.* VII. against the Cornish Men then in Rebellion, under the leading of *James* Lord **Audley**, and enjoyed this Mannor until the 12th Year of *H.* VII. in which Year, a Recognizance was enter'd upon the Court Roll of this Mannor, made by *John Grey*, Kt. and Lord of **Wilton**, and one *Matthew Langford* of **London**, Gent. to *Richard Hill*, and *John Shaw*, Citizen and Alderman of **London**, in 1000 Marks, conditioned for the Performance of Covenants, compriz'd in Indentures for the Sale of **Barron-hall** in **Essex**, and this Mannor of **Liburp**; and the Precept and the Concord for the Fine was enter'd also in the Book, wherein *John* Lord *Grey* of **Wilton**, *Edmond Grey* his Son and Heir apparent, and *Florence* his Wife, past it unto *John Breton*, Clerk, *Thomas Marrow*, *Leonard Hide*, and *Thomas Ingram;* and the Fine *pro licentia concordandi* was twenty Shillings; he was afterwards knighted, then *Edward Grey* of **Bleachley** in the County of **Bucks**, Esq. gave a Release, dated *February* 17 *Anno* 12 *Hen.* VII. by the Name of *Edward Grey*, Esq. Cozen of Sir *John Grey* Lord *Grey* of **Wilton** upon **Wpe**, *viz.* Brother of Sir *Reginald Grey*, Kt. deceased, Father of the aforesaid *John* now living, and he confirmed their Estate in **Lyburp** by it, and the 12th of *June* following, the Deed was inrolled in Chancery; this *Richard Hill* married *Elizabeth Hill*, who survived him, and held this Mannor as Part of her Jointure, and joyned with *John Gawson*, one of the six Clerks in Chancery, to pass this Mannor to

Edward Hill, Gentleman, and *Ralph Lathom*, Citizen and Goldsmith of **London**, and she passed the Reversion after her Death, by Deed dated 17 *H.* VII. and inrolled to them, the said *Edward* and *Ralph*, on the 6th of *October* in the same Year. *Robert Hill*, Citizen and Fishmonger of **London**, Merchant of the Staple at **Calice**, Son and Heir of Sir *Thomas Hill*, Kt. and Alderman, and Mayor of **London**, and of Dame *Elizabeth* his Wife, Sister and Heir unto *William Hill* and *Richard Hill* of **London**, Gent. by Indenture, sold this Mannor and several others, in the Counties of **Essex** and **Huntingdon** unto the said

Ralph Lathom, Citizen and Goldsmith of **London**, which Deed was also in the same Month inrolled in Chancery,

and *Edward Hill*, Brother of the said *Robert Hill*, having an
Annuity of eight Marks granted to him out of this Man-
nor by the Feoffees of his Father, did also alien the same
unto the said *Ralph Lathom*, and then by another Deed
dated 24th of *January*, 20 *H.* VII. remised and released
their Right to *Lathom's* Feoffees, in and to the Mannors of
Clapdom *alias* Habingfield, Lachingdon, Barnes, Lazers,
Brome, and Hide *alias* Hide-park, Baron-hall *alias*
Barne-hall in Essex, and to Lybury in Hertfordshire, which
Feoffees were *Hugh Oldham*, Bishop of Exeter, *Edmund
Carew*, Kt. *Richard Fitzlewes*, Kt. *Thomas Tirrill*, Kt.
George Roger, and *Roger Holland*, Esquires; and 21 *Hen.*
VII. levyed a Fine of the said Mannors, to *Christopher
Ursewicke*, Sir *Thomas Frowick*, Chief Justice of the *King's
Bench*, and others, who, by Deed dated the 29th of *May*,
acknowledged Lybury to be to the Use of the said *Ralph
Lathom; and* Trusts being common in those Days, *Ralph
Lathom*, 9 *H.* VIII. granted his Mannor of Lybury to *Cut-
bert Tonstal*, Clerk, and others; and he granted this Man-
nor, 5 and 6 *P.* and *M.* to the Use of his last Will and Testament, and on the 12th of *Eliz.* demised unto *Edmund
Andrews*, Gent. and *William Green*, Yeoman, who kept
several Courts and granted out several Estates, and in
17 *Eliz.* it came to

Thomas and *William*, two Sons of *Thomas Lathom.* In
19 *Eliz. Robert Lathom* of Childersly, in the County of
Cambridge, and *Dorothy* his Wife, and *William Lathom*
of South Ockendon in Essex, by Fine and Recovery passed
this Mannor to

Edmund Andrews of London, Fishmonger, and *George
Herd*, who by their Deed, declared the Use to

William Lathom, and his Heirs, who aliened it, on the
20th of *March*, 20 *Eliz.* to

Richard Brockman of St. *Bartholomew* in West Smithfield, Gent. who by his Deed dated 24th of *June*, 22 *Eliz.*
sold it unto

Rowland Berisford of London, Gent. who was a Grocer
there; and on the 5th of *December, Anno* 1608, he conveyed it to

Robert Spence, Citizen and Fishmonger of London, who
was Master of the Levant Company of Merchants, and he
devised it by his Will, dated 1616, to *Audry* his Wife, for
the Term of her Life, leaving Issue *Robert Spence*, Esq. his
only Son and Heir.

Audry Spence enjoyed this Mannor until the Year 1635,
when she died, then it came to

Robert Spence, who dwelt at Npland in Balcomb, in the
County of Sussex, was in Commission of the Peace for that
County for many Years, a Collonel in the *Militia* for the

Hund. of
Bradewater
same County, and had Issue *William* and *John*; and by Deed dated *Anno* 1647, on the Marriage of

William his Son and Heir apparent settled this Mannor on him and the Heirs males of his Body, to be begotten on the Body of *Mary* Daughter of *Samuel Short*, a Bencher of *Gray's Inn*, and for Default of such Issue, on the Heirs male of the said *William*, the Remainder to the right Heirs of him, the said *Robert Spence*. This *William Spence* was an Utter-barister of *Lincoln's Inn*, a learned Man in the Laws of this Realm, and a great Lover of Antiquity; he was a Justice of the Peace for the County of Sussex, and *Anno — Charles* II. Sheriff of the same County, but dying without Issue, this Mannor and all his other Lands came to

John Spence of South Malling in the same County, Esq. being his sole Brother and Heir; he was also an Utter-barister of *Lincoln's Inn*, well learned in the Law, and during the Life-time of his Brother *William* was constituted High Sheriff for the same County, *Anno — Charles* II. from whom it descended to *John Spence*, Esq. his Son and Heir, the present Lord thereof.

THIS Rectory in *Anno* 26 *Henry* VIII. was rated in the King's Books at the yearly Value of 15*l. per Annum*, and the Lords of this Mannor are Patrons hereof.

The RECTORS.

1658 *Richard Newton*	1659 *William Grave*
1638 *Richard Thornton*, who An.	1664 *Edward Bret*
1642, was sequestred, and	1668 *Jonathan Morris.*
died at Huntingford, 1657.	

This Church is erected upon an Hill, in the middle of this Parish, in the Deanery of Baldock, in the Diocess of Lincoln, and is covered with Lead, the Chancel with Tyle; and at the West End is a square Tower, which hath an excellent Ring of five Bells, and a Shaft upon the Tower covered with Lead.

On the North Side of the Chancel, a small Chapel is erected by the ancient Lords of this Mannor, wherein is this Inscription upon a Stone.

Here lyeth the Body of *Margaret Woodhall*, Daughter of *Anthony Law* of London, Gent. Wife of *Edmund Woodhall*, Esq; Register of the Prerogative Court of Canterbury, Lord of this Mannor of Little Munden, in the County of Hertford. She deceased the 3d day of *July* 1631. Aged 45 years.

In the two Arches, between the Chapel and the Chancel, are two old Monuments; one raised four Foot, with the Effigies of a Man and his Wife: The other raised about five Foot, with the Effigies of a Man and his Wife.

In the Chancel lyeth a Stone with this Inscription.

Here lyeth the Body of *Richard Berisford* of London, Merchant, who departed this Life the 14th day of *June*, 1643. in the 59 year of his Age. Also of *Ann Berisford*, the Wife of *Richard Berisford*, who departed this Life, the 30th of *August*, 1637, in the 42 year of her Age. They had issue three Sons, viz. *Robert*, *Rowland*, and *Samuel*, living at his Death, and two Daughters who died young.

Another Stone has this Inscription.

Here lyeth buried the Body of *Robert Berisford*, Gent. who departed this Life the 3*d* day of *January*, 1656. Aged 33. years. He was eldest Son of *Richard Berisford* of *London*. Merchant, he married *Ann*, the eldest Daughter of Sir *Thomas Nightingale*, Baronet, and had issue by her three Sons; *viz. Richard, George*, and *Robert*, and one Daughter *Ann*.

GREAT MUNDON, MUNDON FURNIVAL

IS scituated about a Mile and a half distant from *Little Mundane*, towards the North-east, and, I suppose, was denominated from the Hill on which the Church is erected; for as *Dane* signifies in the Saxon Language a Valley, as I have shewed in the last Parish, so *Don* signifies a Hill, which agrees with the Scituation of this Church: And *William* the Conqueror gave this Mannor to Earl *Alan*, for his good Services, who possest it at the time of making that general Survey, where 'tis recorded under the Title of *Terra Alani Comitis*.

In Bradewatre Hundred. Comes Alanus *tenuit Mundrne, pro septem hidis et dimid. virgat. se defendebat tempore Regis* Edwardi. *Terra est quatuor decem car. in Dominio quatuor hid. et una virgat. et ibi sunt quatuor car. ibi sexdecem Vill. cum sex bordis, habentibus decem car. ibi un. cotar. et duo servi, et un. molind. de decem sol. Silva* cl *Porc. et alteram Silvam unde ducent. Porc. pascerent de hoc Manerio* Rogerius de Mucelgros *abstulit postquam Comes* Radulphus *forisfecit ut tota Scyra testatur. In totis valent. valet sexdecem lib. Quando recepit duodecem lib. tempore Regis* Edwardi *sexdecem lib. hoc Manerium tenuit* Eddeva *pulchra.*

Domesd. Lib. fol. 137. n. 16.

Earl *Alan* held *Mundon* in *Bradewater* Hundred, it was rated for seven Hides and half a Virgate, in the time of *King Edward* (the Confessor.) The arable is fourteen Carucates, in Demeasne four Hides and one Virgate; and there are four Carucates, sixteen Villains, with six Bordars, having ten Carucates; there is one Cottager, and two Servants, and one Mill of ten Shillings Rent, Wood to feed one hundred and fifty Hogs, and *Roger de Mucelgros* took away from this Mannor another Wood (where two hundred Hogs were fed) after Earl *Ralph* had forfeited it, as the whole Shire can witness. In the whole Value it is worth sixteen Pounds by the Year, when he received it twelve Pounds, in the time of King *Edward*, sixteen Pounds. Fair *Eddeva* held this Mannor.

I have given an Account of this great Earl in the Parish of *Chesbunt*, to which I refer the Reader; for this Mannor was Parcel of the Possessions of the Earldom of *Richmond*, and continually passed with that Honour till it came to *Constance*, the Daughter and sole Heir of *Conan Alan*. She married *Jeoffry*, the fourth Son of *Henry* II. King of *England*. And after the King had retained this Earldom sometime in his own Hands, he disposed of it with the Revenue belonging to it, to *Jeoffry*, whereby he became possest hereof, and at length he sold it to

Gerrard de Furnival, from whom this Vill borrow'd the Adjunct of *Furnival*, which is annexed to its Name; he was a younger Son of *Furnival* of *Sheffield*, was at the

Hund. of
Bradewater

Siege of 𝕬con in the 𝕳oly 𝕷and, with King *Richard* I.
and at his return he married, and had Issue

Gerrard, who married *Maud*, the Daughter and Heir of
William de Luvetot, a great Baron in Nottinghamshire,
and King *John* did accept his Homage for that Barony for
400 Marks. The King employ'd him as Commissioner
with *John de Laci*, Constable of Chester, and *Jeeffry de
Nevill*, Lord-chamberlain, to treat with *Robert de Roos*,
and some others of the Barons, to reduce them to Obedience,
and he was very faithful to the King in the time of all his
Troubles which the Barons gave him, for which Cause the
King commanded him *Anno* 18th of his Reign, to reside at
his Castle of 𝕭olesober in the County of 𝕯erby, to keep
the Peace in those Parts of the Kingdom: Afterwards he
died at 𝕵erusalem, *Anno* 3 *H.* III. whereupon this Lordship
of 𝕸undon, by the King's Appointment was assigned to

Dugd. Bar.
vol.1, fol. 598.

The Lady *Nichola de Haya*, for her better Support in
the Custody of the Castle of 𝕷incoln, which she then held
for the King. She was an eminent Lady, who stoutly adhered to King *John* in the time of the Troubles which he
had with his Barons, to whom he granted *Anno* 17th of his
Reign, all the Lands which *William de Huntingfeild* had in
the County of 𝕷incoln and Town of 𝕿orkesey in the same
County, to hold during the King's Pleasure, and made her
Governess of 𝕱ramton Castle; and in the 18th Year of King
John she had the Custody of the County of 𝕷incoln; which
Office she also held 1 *H.* III. and obtained a Confirmation

Ibid.

of all the Lands which *William de Huntingfeild* had there.
She married *Gerrard de Camvill*, by whom she had Issue
Richard, and procured Livery to be made to her and her
Son of the Mannors of 𝕮herleton and 𝕳euxteruge, of which
they had been dispossest by *Hubert de Burgh*, Justice of
𝕰ngland; and was again constituted Sheriffess of the County
of 𝕷incoln *Anno* 2 *H.* III. and Governess of the City and
Castle of 𝕷incoln, having this Mannor assigned to her again
for her Support, being then in the King's Hands.

Ibid. fol. 714.

But in the time of *Edward* III. it was in the Possession
of *Reginald de Grey*, Lord of 𝕎ilton, of whom I treated
in the last Parish, to which I refer the Reader. He died
upon Tuesday in *Whitson* Week, 44 *Edw.* III. seized
(among others) of this Mannor, leaving Issue

Henry, who doing Homage had Livery of his Lands, and
died upon Saturday next before the Feast of St. *George*,
Anno 19 *Rich.* II. leaving Issue

Richard his Son and Heir, then three Years old; and
when he attained to full Age he sold it to *John Fray* and his
Heirs. This Mannor was in the Possession of Sir *William
de Say*, Kt. *Anno* 12 *H.* VII. and passed from him as the
Mannors of 𝕽oweny and 𝕭enington did, till they returned

to the Crown, where it continued till a Lease of the Demesns was granted to *William* Earl of Salisbury for three
Lives; and the Mannor, Royalties, and Demesns were sold to
    Edward Arris of London, Chirurgeon, and the Quit-rents
were granted to *Edward* Earl of Sandwich.

    Edward Arris granted the Mannor, Royalties, and Pro-
fits of Courts to

    Thomas Arris his eldest Son, Doctor in Physick, who
died seized hereof, leaving

    Edward Arris his Son and Heir, who sold it to

    Robert Hadgely, who is the present Possessor hereof.

The Priory of *ROHEINY, alias ROWENEA.*

CONAN Duke of Brittany, Earl of Richmond, and Lord *Mon. Angl.*
of the Mannor of Great Munden, about *Anno* 10 *H.*11. fol. 517.
1164, founded this Priory of Nuns, and dedicated it to the
Honor of St. *John* the Baptist, ordering that they should
live regularly, according to the Order of St. *Benedict*,
and gave Lands and Tenements to support the House and
maintain the Religious there. The Prioress and Nuns,
and their Successors, held and enjoy'd the same until *Anno*
36 *H.*VI. when they, through Negligence and Carelessness,
suffered the Church to fall, the House to decay, the Revenue thereof to be wasted, that there was not sufficient Means
left to rebuild the Church, to repair the House, to maintain
the Religious according to the Foundation thereof, and to
defray all the Charges incumbent upon them, left the House
desolate. *Agnes Selby*, the Prioress, and the Nuns, considering that *John Fray*, then Lord of the Mannor of Great
Munden, was the true Patron thereof, who had a sincere
Devotion, and pious Intent to convert all the Rents and
yearly Profits thereof in some better Manner to pious Uses
for the Souls of the Founders of the said Priory, by their
unanimous Assent and Consent, did surrender the Church
and Priory, together with all the Mannors, Lands, Tenements, Meadows, Feedings, Pastures and Woods, Rents,
Reversions, and Services, and all the Rights, Profits, and
Emoluments belonging to it: To have and to hold the same,
to *John Fray*, his Heirs and Assigns for ever.

    This *John Fray* was constituted second Baron of the 8 Feb. *Pat.*13.
Court of *Exchequer*, by Patent dated *Anno* 13 *H.*VI. and H VI. 9 Feb.
the Year following made Chief Baron thereof: Moreover, *Origin. Jurid.*
King *H.* VI. by his Charter dated at Westminster, granted fol. 63.
to him, that he might found and establish a Chantry of one vol. 1, fol.517.
Priest, to the Honour of God and the Virgin *Mary*, the
Mother of *Christ*, and St. *John Baptist* the Forerunner of
our Saviour, at the high Altar in the said Church, for the
good Estate of the King, Queen *Margaret*, Prince *Edward*,
and the said *John Fray*, whilst they lived, and for the Souls

of them and their Sons when they died: Also for the Soul of the said late Duke, Founder of the said Priory; and also for the Souls of the Donors of the said Lands, Tenements, and Possessions above specified; and of all the Faithful deceased every Day, unless reasonable Cause did interveen, to be for ever celebrated according to his Order; and when it shall be so founded, it shall be for ever called *The Chantry of St. John Baptist of* Rowenp, and shall have perpetual Succession; and that the said *John Fray*, may grant to the Chaplain of that Chantry, all the Houses, Mansions, Buildings, Lands, Tenements, and Possessions whatsoever, with all the Appurtenances belonging lately to the said Church, or Priory.

When this Priory was founded, it was valued at ten Marks by the Year; upon the Surrender of this Chantry, *Anno* 26 *H.* VIII. it was valued at 13*l.* 10*s.* 9*d. per Ann.* And the King granted it to *Henry* Earl of Essex, from whom it passed, with the Mannor of Benington, till it return'd to the Crown again.

In the time of King *Charles* I. it came to the Possession of one *Birchinghead*, who settled it upon his Wife for her Life; and she surviving him, enjoy'd the same. After her Decease, it descended to

Thomas Birchinghead their Son, who sold it to Sir *Thomas Jennor*, Kt. one of the Barons of the *Exchequer*, who settled it on *Francis Brown*, of the *Inner Temple*, Esq. upon his Marriage of *Ann* his eldest Daughter, as Part of her Portion, who is the present Possessor hereof.

THE Rectory of this Church, *Anno* 26 *H.* VIII. was valued in the King's Books at 21*l.* 19*s.* 6*d. per Ann.* whereof the Kings of this Realm have been Patrons; until King *James* II. by his Grant, dated 25 of *Feb.* 1687, the 3d of the same King, granted the Advowson hereof unto *John* Lord *Churchill* and *Thomas Docwra*, Esq. upon Trust, to present the Rector of St. Albans to the same.

The RECTORS.

John Lightfoot, D. D.	——— *Cole*, Arch-Deacon of St.
Ralph Widrington, D. D.	Albans.

This Church is situated upon an Hill in the middle of the Parish, in the Deanery of Baldock, in the Diocese of Lincoln, which contains only the Chancel covered with Tile, the Body with Lead, and a square Tower annexed to the West End hereof, wherein are five Bells, which Tower is Leaded, and has a small Spire erected upon it; but there is no Monument or other Remark herein.

BENINGTON, BENIGNTON

Norden, p. 13. STANDS upon a Hill, distant two Miles from Great Munden to the West: Some think this Town may be called Benington, from the Bounty of the Inhabitants, or from the pleasant and profitable Situation of the Place: But it may be more properly so termed from the River 𝔚ene and the Meadow there; for the Name in the Saxon Language does import as much.

Hund. of Bradewater

When *Bertulfe* was King of the *Mercians*, he often resided in his Palace here; and in the Year of Christ 850, or a little before, held a Parliament or Great Council in this Place, where the Prelates and Noblemen of 𝔐ercia did meet: And in that great Assembly, *Askill* a Monk of the Monastry of 𝔠ropland, in the Name of his Abbot *Siward*, and the Monks there, made grievous Complaints of very many Losses and Injuries lately brought on their Monastry by the neighbouring *Danes*, and other deceitful Enemies: And in Reparation thereof, King *Bertulfe* not only granted very large Mannors, but also conferred on the same Monastry, most splendid Liberties, as may be seen in his Charter, which shortly after, was solemnly confirmed in a Parliament or Council held at 𝔎ingsbury.

Spelman de Conciliis, fol. 344.

This Seat might in all Probability continue in the Crown, until it came to *Almer de Belinton*, who was a *Saxon*, and the Possessor hereof, in the time of King *Edward* (the Confessor) from whence he might receive his Name. But when *William* the Conqueror subdued this Realm, he gave this Mannor to *Peter de Valongies*, a Nobleman, who held this Vill, then called 𝔚elintone, as it appears by *Domesdei Book*; where 'tis recorded under the Title of *Terra Petri de Valongies*.

Domesd Lib fol. 144, n. 36

In 𝔚radewatre *Hund.* Petrus de Valongies *tenet* 𝔚elintone *pro decem hidis oe defendebat. Terra est undecem car. in Dominio sex hid. et dimid. et ibi sunt tres car. et duæ adhuc possunt fieri, ibi sexdecem Vill. cum Presbitero et septemdecem bord. habentes octo car. ibi un. cotar. et quinq. servi. Silva centum porc. Parcus silvatican bestiarum. In totis valent, valet duodecem lib: Quando recepit sex lib. tempore Regis Edwardi quatuor decem lib. Hoc Manerium tenuit* Almer de Belintone.

Ibid. fol. 141.

Peter de Valongies held 𝔚elintone; it was rated for ten Hides, the arrable Land is eleven Carucates (or plongh Lands,) in Demeasne six Hides and an half, and there are three Carucates, and now two more might be made; there are sixteen Villains, with a Presbyter (Priest) and seventeen Bordars having eight Carucates; there was one Cottager and five Servants, Wood to feed an hundred Hogs, a Park of Deer. In the whole Value, it is worth twelve Pounds by the Year, when he received it, six Pounds by the Year, in the time of King *Edward* (the Confessor) fourteen Pounds. *Almer de Belinton* held this Mannor.

This *Peter de Valongies* at that time had 57 Lordships, whereof 17 in this County; he married *Albreda* Sister to *Eudo Dapifer*, Steward to King *H. I.* by whom he had Issue

Ibid.

Robert de Valongies, who was his Son and Heir, obtained from *Maud* the Empress, a Confirmation of the Grant of the Mannors of 𝔈ssendon and 𝔚egesford, and the Mills at 𝔥ertford, made by King *H. I.* and all those other Lands whereof his Father died seized, and he had Issue

Peter de Valongies, who married *Gundred de Warren*, by whom he had Issue three Daughters, *Lora* married to

Hund. of
Bradewater

Alexander de Baliol, Brother to the King of *Scots*, *Christian* to *William de Mandevile*, after him to *Peter de Maine*, and *Elizabeth* to *David Comine*, who were his Coheirs. And upon the Partition, this Mannor came to *Lora*, the Wife of *Alexander de Baliol*; for upon a *Quo Warranto* brought before *John de Rygate* and others, Justices Itinerants at Hertford, *Anno* 6 *Edw*. I. *Alexander de Baliol* claimed in his Mannors of Benington, Box, and Crowberp, That he held in Purparty of the Inheritance which was *Peter de Valongies*, Soc, Sac, Toll, Them, Infangthef, &c. all the Fee and Land, View of Francpledge, Correction of the Assize of Bread, and Ale, and Tumbrel, &c. by a Grant of *H*. I. and the Confirmation of *H*. II. to *Robert de Valongies*, Brother of the said *Peter*; which Deed he there produced, and the said Liberties were thereupon allowed.

Quo Warr. 6
Ed. I. in cur.
recept. Scac.

And in another Record, in the same Year of *Edw*. I. it was found, That this *Alexander de Baliol* held this Mannor of Benintone, which was the Head of the Barony Valongues, *in Capite* of the King, by the Service of ten Knight's Fees and a Quarter of a Knight's Fee ; and he had in this Mannor, View of Francpledge, Gallowes, and Assize of Bread and Ale.

Cart. 13 Ed I.
Har. vol. 2.

This *Alexander de Baliol* conveyed this Mannor of Benington, to *John de Bensted*, *Anno* 13 *Edw*. I. And the Year following, that King confirmed the Grant hereof, with the Court Leet, and several other Priviledges conveyed to

Cart. 33 Ed. I.

him by Charter dated 33 *Edw*. I. a Market every Week to be held on the Wednesday here, and a Fair yearly on the Eve-day and Morrow after the Festivals of the Apostles

Dugd. *Chron.*
fol. 34.

Peter and *Paul*. He was constituted one of the Justices of the Court of *Common Pleas* at Westminster, in the 3d Year of *Edw*. II. and continued in that Trust till the 15th of Saint *John Baptist* following. He was employed into Scotland, upon the King's Service in the 8th and 14th of *Edw*. II. and he was summoned the same Year to Parliament among the Barons of this Realm. He was constituted one of the Commissioners to treat of Peace, *Anno* 11 *Edw*. II. betwixt the King and *Robert de Bruce* of Scotland, and sent with the Bishop of Hereford, in the 12th Year of *Edw*. II. and other eminent Persons, unto the Court of Rome,

Prin's *Parl.*
Drev. pt. 3,
p. 43.

to solicit his Holiness for the Canonization of *Thomas de Cantilupe*, sometime Bishop of Hereford.

Edward Bensted who was his Heir, was possest of this Mannor, *Anno* 7 *R*. II. had Issue *John* and *Eleanor*, and

Pip. Rot. 1 H.
IV. Decree in
Chancery,
pas. 1 H. VII.

served for this County in the Parliament held 7 *R*. II. in another held *Anno* 20 *R*. II. and in another held 1 *H*. IV. in which Year he was constituted Sheriff of the Counties of Hertford and Essex; he left Issue

John Bensted, who was his Son and Heir, received the Honour of Knighthood, and had Issue

William Bensted, who was seized of this Mannor in his *Hund. of* 𝔅𝔯𝔞𝔡𝔢𝔴𝔞𝔱𝔢𝔯 Demesn, as of Fee; he held the same of the King in Chief, by Knight's Service, and died without Heir of his Body; and *Eleanor,* who was Sister to *John* his Father, was his next Heir. His Arms were *Gules, three Barrs Gemells Or.*

Eleanor succeeded him, obtained a special and lawful Livery of this Mannor, 1 *H.*VII. entred into the same, and Morgan, lib. 3, fol. 63. being so seized, convey'd it to

Sir *William Say,* Kt. and his Heirs, who had only Issue two Daughters, *Elizabeth* married to *William* Lord *Mount-* *Rot. Pip.* 22 Ed. IV. *joy,* and *Mary* married to *Henry Bourchier,* Earl of 𝔈𝔰𝔰𝔢𝔵. In Consideration of the said Marriages, Sir *William Say* covenanted to settle an Estate in Land, to the Value of 300 Marks upon himself for Life, without Impeachment of Waste; the Remainder thereof to the said Earl and *Mary,* and to the Heirs of the Body of the said *Mary* (begotten,) the Remainder over to the said Sir *William* and his Heirs; and also farther covenanted to settle an Estate in Lands, to the yearly Value of 200 Marks, upon himself for Life, without Impeachment of Waste; the Remainder thereof to the said Lord *Mountjoy* and *Elizabeth,* and to the Heirs of the Body of the said *Elizabeth;* the Remainder to Sir *William Say* and his Heirs; and the Mannors of 𝔅𝔞𝔰𝔰, ℌ𝔬𝔡𝔡𝔢𝔰𝔡𝔬𝔫-𝔟𝔲𝔯𝔭, 𝔖𝔞𝔟𝔯𝔦𝔰𝔣𝔬𝔯𝔡, *alias* 𝔖𝔞𝔟𝔦𝔰𝔣𝔬𝔯𝔡, 𝔐𝔬𝔠𝔥𝔢 𝔐𝔬𝔫𝔡𝔬𝔫, 𝔏𝔞𝔩-𝔣𝔬𝔯𝔡, and 𝔏𝔦𝔱𝔱𝔩𝔢 𝔐𝔬𝔫𝔡𝔬𝔫, with the Advowson of the Churches of 𝔐𝔲𝔠𝔥 𝔐𝔬𝔫𝔡𝔬𝔫, 𝔏𝔞𝔩𝔣𝔬𝔯𝔡, and 𝔏𝔦𝔱𝔱𝔩𝔢 𝔐𝔬𝔫𝔡𝔬𝔫, in the *Cart.* penes Dom. Car. Cæsar. Counties of ℌ𝔢𝔯𝔱𝔣𝔬𝔯𝔡 and 𝔈𝔰𝔰𝔢𝔵; and the Mannors of 𝔅𝔢𝔡-𝔴𝔢𝔩𝔩, 𝔅𝔞𝔯𝔨𝔥𝔞𝔪𝔰𝔱𝔢𝔡, 𝔐𝔞𝔯𝔨𝔢𝔱 𝔒𝔟𝔢𝔯𝔱𝔬𝔫, ℌ𝔬𝔠𝔨𝔩𝔭, 𝔚𝔦𝔠𝔨𝔥𝔞𝔪-𝔥𝔞𝔩𝔩, and 𝔅𝔢𝔫𝔦𝔫𝔤𝔱𝔬𝔫, with the Appurtenances in the Counties of ℌ𝔢𝔯𝔱𝔣𝔬𝔯𝔡, 𝔈𝔰𝔰𝔢𝔵, and 𝔎𝔬𝔱𝔢𝔩, were settled in Sir *Thomas Frowick,* Kt. Chief Justice of the *Common Pleas,* and *Robert Turbervile,* in Trust to the Use of Sir *William Say* and his Heirs; and to the Use, and for the Performance of the said Covenants between Sir *William* and the said Earl, and the Covenants between Sir *William* and the Lord *Mountjoy.*

But this Lord *Mountjoy* having by *Elizabeth* his Wife, only one Daughter called *Gertrude,* Sir *William Say,* by *Cart.* 21 H. VII. penes Dom. Car. Cæsar. another Deed dated the 14th of *July* 21 *H.* VII. in Consideration of the said Marriages, and that neither the said *Mary* nor the said *Gertrude,* should discontinue or alien any of the Mannors, did covenant, That if the said *Gertrude* should decease without Issue of her Body, all the Mannors limited to the Lord *Mountjoy* and *Elizabeth* his Wife, and the Heirs of the Body of the said *Elizabeth,* (except the Mannor of 𝔅𝔢𝔫𝔦𝔫𝔤𝔱𝔬𝔫) should after the Decease of the Lord *Mountjoy, Gertrude,* and Sir *William Say,* remain to the Lady *Mary* and the Heirs of her Body, lawfully begotten, and for Want of such Issue, unto the Heirs of the Body of Sir *John Say,* Kt. Father of Sir *William,* the Remainder to the right Heirs of Sir *William Say* for ever. And this

Hund. of
Bradewater
Mannor of Benington, after the Decease of Sir *William*
Say, and *Gertrude*, and Want of Issue of *Gertrude*, should
go to the Lady *Mary*, and the Heirs of her Body, lawfully
begotten; and for Lack of such Issue, the Remainder
should be to the Use of the last Will of Sir *William Say*.

And if the said *Mary* should decease without Issue of
her Body, all the Mannors limited to the Earl and *Mary*,
and the Heirs of her Body, after the Decease of the Earl
and *Mary*, and Sir *William Say*, should remain to *Gertrude*, and the Heirs of her Body, the Remainder over
(except the Mannors) of Hoddesdon Bury, Much Mondon, and Little Mondon, which were purchased by the
said Sir *William*, to the right Heirs of the Body of Sir
John Say, Kt. And the Mannors of Hoddesdon Bury,
Much Mondon, and Little Mondon, after the Decease of
Sir *William Say*, and the Earl, and Lady *Mary*, and the
Lord *Mountjoy*, and *Gertrude*, and Lack of Issue of *Mary*
and *Gertrude*, should be to the Use of the last Will of Sir
William Say.

Dugd. *Bar.* 2
vol. fol. 130.
But afterwards this Earl had by *Mary* one Daughter
called *Anne*, who married Sir *William Parre*, Kt. Lord
Parre of Kendal. But the Earl adventuring to ride a
young unruly Horse at his Mannor of Base, *Anno* 31 *Hen.*
VIII. was overthrown, and by the Fall broke his Neck.

Fin. 33 H.
VIII.
Anno 38 *H.* VIII. *Crast. Animarum*, this Sir *William
Parre*, Lord *Parre* of Kendal, levyed a Fine of the said
Mannors of Base, Ferrers, Hoddesdon, Benington, Much
Mondon, Little Mondon, Weston, Argentyn, and Sa-
bridgeworth; and the Advowson of the Churches of Be-
nington, Much Mondon, and Little Mondon, and of the
free Chappel of Rowney, to the Earl of Southampton, Sir
Anthony Browne, and *Thomas Wryotesley*, who declared
by Deed the Use of the Fine to Sir *William Parre* for
Life, the Remainder to *Ann* his Wife, and of the Heirs of
her Body, lawfully to be begotten, the Remainder to the
King in Fee.

Dugd. *Bar.*
vol. 2, Stat.
34 H. VIII.

Pat. 35 H.
VIII.
In 34 *Henry* VIII. the Children of this Lady *Anne* were
bastardized by Act of Parliament; yet notwithstanding
Anno 35 *H.* VIII. this Sir *William Parre*, then Knight of
the Garter, was created Earl of Essex, by Letters Patents,
and the King granted to him the same Place and Voice in
Parliament as *Henry Bourckier* Earl of Essex had. And in
38 *Hen.* VIII. was one of those, whom the King then lying
on his Death-bed associated to his Executors, for their Assistance in Matters of Consequence. He was advanced to
Pat. 1 Ed.VI.
the Title of Marquis of Northampton, 1 *Edward* VI. and
was constituted Lord Great Chamberlain of England, in
the fourth Year of *Edward* VI. in the Place of *John* Earl
of Warwick, who surrendred that Office.

He married *Elizabeth* Daughter to *George* Lord *Cobham*, *Anno* 5 *Edw*. VI. and obtained a special Act of Parliament, for the disannulling his Marriage with the Lady *Anne Bourchier*, Daughter to *Henry* Earl of 𝔈𝔰𝔰𝔢𝔵, and also for ratifying this Marriage with *Elizabeth*, and legitimating the Children which he should have by her.

But upon the Death of King *Edw*. VI. and proclaiming the Lady *Jane Grey*, he accompanied the Duke of 𝔑𝔬𝔯𝔱𝔥𝔲𝔪𝔟𝔢𝔯𝔩𝔞𝔫𝔡 at his going out of 𝔏𝔬𝔫𝔡𝔬𝔫 with Horse and Foot, for the suppressing of those, which were raised in 𝔖𝔲𝔣𝔣𝔬𝔩𝔨, on the Behalf of Queen *Mary*, for which he was committed to the Tower of 𝔏𝔬𝔫𝔡𝔬𝔫 on the 26th of *July*, arraigned before the Duke of 𝔑𝔬𝔯𝔣𝔬𝔩𝔨, then High Steward, in the Month of *August* following, and had Judgment of Death passed upon him; But his Execution was stayed, and before the End of that Year, he was restored in Blood by Act of Parliament, but not to his Honour or Estate, and the Queen reserved this Mannor of 𝔅𝔢𝔫𝔦𝔫𝔤𝔱𝔬𝔫, and divers others of his Mannors to herself.

King *Philip* and Queen *Mary* by Letters Patents, dated at 𝔚𝔢𝔰𝔱𝔪𝔦𝔫𝔰𝔱𝔢𝔯 12th of *December*, 3 and 4 of their Reign, for good and acceptable Service done to them, by *Ann* Viscountess *Bourchier*, and Lady *Lovaine*, did grant and demise to Sir *Robert Rochester*, Kt. then Comptroller of the Queen's Household, and Sir *Edward Walgrave*, Kt. all their Lordships and Mannors of 𝔅𝔢𝔫𝔦𝔫𝔤𝔱𝔬𝔫, 𝔚𝔢𝔰𝔱𝔬𝔫, 𝔄𝔯𝔤𝔢𝔫𝔱𝔶𝔫, 𝔐𝔬𝔫𝔡𝔬𝔫 𝔐𝔞𝔤𝔫𝔞, 𝔐𝔬𝔫𝔡𝔬𝔫 𝔓𝔞𝔯𝔟𝔞, 𝔖𝔞𝔟𝔯𝔦𝔡𝔤𝔢𝔴𝔬𝔯𝔱𝔥, 𝔑𝔢𝔴𝔤𝔞𝔱𝔢-𝔰𝔱𝔯𝔢𝔢𝔱, and 𝔖𝔞𝔶𝔢𝔰-𝔭𝔞𝔯𝔨, and their Appurtenances for the Term of forty Years, if the said Sir *William Parre* then late Marquis should live so long, rendring such Rents and Services, as by the said Letters Patents were reserved.

And 2d of *June*, 18 *Eliz*. *Chideock Pawlet*, one of the Sons of *William* Marquis of 𝔚𝔦𝔫𝔠𝔥𝔢𝔰𝔱𝔢𝔯, Lord Treasurer of 𝔈𝔫𝔤𝔩𝔞𝔫𝔡, and the Lady *Frances*, then his Wife, the Widow and Relict of Sir *Edward Walgrave*, and sole Executrix of his Will, by their Deed Poll, assigned over the Remainder of the said Term of forty Years then to come, and unexpired to *Walter* Viscount 𝔥𝔢𝔯𝔢𝔣𝔬𝔯𝔡, Lord 𝔣𝔢𝔯𝔯𝔢𝔯𝔰, and 𝔠𝔥𝔞𝔯𝔱𝔩𝔢𝔶.

But after the Expiration of this Term of Years, this Mannor remained in the Crown, and Queen *Elizabeth*, considering that this late Marquis, had been deprived of his Titles through the Potency of his Adversaries; she, by her Letters Patents dated in the Tower of 𝔏𝔬𝔫𝔡𝔬𝔫, on the 13th of *January*, 1 *Regni sui*, advanced him again to the Dignity of Marquis of 𝔑𝔬𝔯𝔱𝔥𝔞𝔪𝔭𝔱𝔬𝔫, and made him one of the Lords of her Privy Council.

And on the 22d of *April* following, High Steward upon the Arraignment of *William* Lord 𝔚𝔢𝔫𝔱𝔴𝔬𝔯𝔱𝔥, late Deputy of 𝔠𝔞𝔩𝔩𝔦𝔠𝔢, in 𝔚𝔢𝔰𝔱𝔪𝔦𝔫𝔰𝔱𝔢𝔯-𝔥𝔞𝔩𝔩, upon an Indictment of Trea-

Hund. of 𝔅𝔯𝔞𝔡𝔢𝔴𝔞𝔱𝔢𝔯

Pat. 3 & 4 P. and M.

Cart 13 Eliz. penes Dom. Car. Cæsar.

Pat. 1 Eliz.

Stow's *Annals* fol. 639.

Hund. of
Brabewater

son found against him in the late Queen *Maryes* Dayes, for the Loss of **Callice**.

Queen *Elizabeth*, by her Letters Patents, dated the 10th of *November*, in the 12th Year of her Reign, granted to *Walter* Viscount **Hereford** the Reversion of this Mannor to hold in Soccage, reserving the yearly Rent of 44*l.* 4*s.* 2*d.* *ob.* And upon that Rebellion of the Earls of **Northumberland**, and **Westmoreland** in the same Year, made him Field Marshal of those Forces, then sent against them.

The Lady *Anne Bourchier* died on the 26th Day of *Jan.* in the 13th Year of Queen *Eliz.* and *Robert Savile, John Massingberd*, and *Dorothy* his Wife, *Margaret Tharold*, Widow, *Mary Hall, Thomas Horseman*, and *William Clopton*, Esq. the Heirs of Sir *William Say*, levyed a Fine in
Fin. 13 Eliz.   *October Hillarii*, in the 13th of the Queen, of this Mannor to the Use of *Walter* Viscount **Hereford**, who, by Reason of his Descent from *Cicely*, the Sister and Heir to *Henry*
Pat. 14 Eliz.   *Bourchier* Earl of **Essex**, 4th of *May*, 14 *Eliz.* was created Earl of **Essex**, and was one of the Peers, that sat upon the Tryal of the Duke of **Norfolk**, in the Year of our Lord 1572; *Anno* 15 *Eliz.* he married *Lettice*, Daughter to Sir *Francis Knolls*, Knight of the Garter, by whom he had
Dugd. Bar. 2   Issue two Sons, *Robert* and *Walter*, and two Daughters,
vol. fol. 178.   *Penelope* first married to *Robert* Lord *Rich*, and afterwards to *Charles Blunt*, Earl of **Devon**, and *Dorothy* first married to Sir *Thomas Perrot*, Kt. and afterwards to *Henry* Earl of **Northumberland**; He devised this Mannor of **Bennington** by his Will dated 18 *Eliz.* 1576, to *Lettice* his Wife for the Term of her Life, and died of a Flux, 22d of *Sept.* following, but not without Suspicion of Poyson, and was buried at **Caermarthen** in **South Wales**.

But some time after the Death of this Earl, this Lady *Lettice* his Widow and Relict, married Sir *Christopher*
Rot. Cur. 35   *Blount*, in whose Right he became possest of this Mannor,
Eliz.   and held Court Leet and Baron here *Aug.* 23, *An.* 35 *Eliz.*

But about two Years after, which was in *May*, 37 *Eliz.* this Sir *Christopher Blount* and Lady *Lettice* his Wife, and her Son *Robert* Earl of **Essex**, and others, conveyed this Mannor to *Thomas Crompton*, Esq. and to his Heirs; which *Thomas*, on the first of *July*, 37 *Eliz.* held Court Leet and Baron here; but soon after, he settled it upon *Mary* his
Ibid. 41 Eliz.   Wife for her Joynture, and on the 3d of *July*, 41 *Eliz.* a Court was held here in both their Names.

Afterwards this Mannor came to the Possession of *Rich.* Earl of **Clanrickard**, and *Frances* his Wife, the sole Daughter and Heir to Sir *Francis Walsingham*, Kt. one of the Secretaries of State to Queen *Eliz.* and Widow of *Robert* Earl of
Ibid. 1 Jac. 1.   **Essex**, who held a Court in their Names for this Mannor.

But this Mannor was conveyed, *Anno* 1614, 12 *Jac.* I. to Sir *Charles Adelmare alias Cæsar*; 29th of *April*, in the

same Year held a Court here; and soon after, Sir *Charles*
settled the same on Dame *Anne* his Wife, the Daughter of
Sir *Peter Vanlore*, Kt. and on Thursday, 4th of *April, An.*
14 *Jac.* another Court was held here, in both their Names;
he was made one of the Masters of the Court of Chancery
on the 30th of *September*, 1619, and Master of the Rolls on
the 18th of *March*, 1638, which Office he held about four
Years; and upon the Decease of *Anne* his Wife, he married *Jane* one of the Daughters of Sir *Robert Barkham*, Kt.
one of the Aldermen and Lord Mayor of the City of London;
by whom he had Issue *Julius, Henry, Charles, Edward, Charles*, and *Hugh*, but Sir *Charles* dyed of the
small Pox at Benington, on the 6th of *December*, in the
Year of our Lord 1643, and *Julius* his Son dyed *Dec.* 11th
following, and they were buried together in this Chancel.

Henry succeeded, and being within Age at the Death of
his Father, his Wardship was granted to *Jane* his Mother:
He spent some time in the Study of Logick and Philosophy
in *Jesus Colledge* in Cambridge, thence was removed to the
Inner Temple, and shortly after married *Elizabeth* the sole
Daughter and Heir of *Robert Angel* of London, Merchant,
by whom he had Issue *Julius*, who dyed in his Infancy,
Charles, and *Jane* afterwards married to Sir *Thomas Pope
Blunt* of Tittenhanger, in this County, Baronet. He served
this County faithfully, in that Healing Parliament held *An.*
1660, 12 *Car.* II. which called King *Charles* to his Crown,
was active there to suppress the Court of Wards and Liveries, and to ease the People of the Hardships and Charges
which accrew to them by the Tenures of Knight Service,
and from the Compositions which was yearly paid for Corn
and Victual; was a Justice of the Peace of the *Quorum*, and
Deputy Lieutenant for this County: He received the Honour of Knighthood on the 7th of *July*, in the same Year at
Whitehall, which he justly merited, and at the next succeeding Parliament was chosen a Member thereof for this
County (upon the Death of *Thomas* Lord Viscount Fanshaw, in the Kingdom of Ireland) but during the Sitting of
that Parliament, he unhappily fell sick of the small Pox, of
which Distemper he dyed, generally lamented of all good
People, and was buried here on the 12th Day of *January*,
1667. He was endowed with good Learning, great Parts,
a quick Apprehension, and a clear and discerning Judgment,
he was very loyal to the King, faithful to his Trust, always
ready to ease the Subjects of their Grievances, and to alle-
viate all Impositions charged upon the County, which render'd him the Darling of the People: He was very hospitable in his House, charitable to the Poor, faithful to his
Friend, Just in his Government, and a true Assertor of the
reformed Religion; he left Issue

Charles who was his Heir, spent some Years in *Katha-*

Hund. of *rine-hall*, in the University of **Cambridge**, where he com-
Bradewater menc'd Master of Arts, received the Honour of Knighthood,
on the 4th of *October*, *Anno* 1671, when that University
entertained King *Charles* II.   And in short time after married *Susanna* the Daughter and Heir of Sir *Thomas Bonfoy*
of **London**, Kt. Merchant; by whom he had Issue *Charles*
Henry, *Elizabeth*, and *Thomas;* he served this County in
two several Parliaments, one held *Anno* 30 *Car*. II. at
Westminster, and the other at the Convention held *Anno*
1 *W*. and *M*. and also for the Burough of **Hertford**, in the
Parliament held *Anno* — *Car*. II. He was a Justice of the
Peace, and of the *Quorum*, and a Deputy Lieutenant for
this County: He died seized of this Mannor, among several
others, on the 15th of *August*, *Anno* 1694.   He was very
regular in his Life, and orderly in his Family, which made
the Lives of his Servants very easie, and his House very
quiet, never repremanding a Servant oftner than once, and
if the Party offended again, he was silently discharged without Noise or Notice of his Displeasure: this created in
them an Awe and a great Observance to him; he was very
generous to all whom he employed, but seldom pardoned a
Slight to his Person, or a Contempt of his Business; he
kept a splendid House, and a bountiful Table for those that
visited him, and was very noble, yet prudent in his Entertainments; he declined all publick Imployments during the
Reigns of King *Charles* II. and King *James* his Brother,
and affected not the Roman Party nor their Proselites; he
would not contract any Friendship or Acquaintance with
any he thought scandalous, and abhorr'd those who would
purchase the Favour of their Prince with the Price of the
Rights of the People; he would not willingly quarrel with
his Neighbours, nor spair any Cost or Charge to obtain his
Point; he never made more than one false Step in his Life-
time, which was pardonable, for when he discerned the Error, he mended the Fault, but Death cut him off before he
could express it to the World, and doubtless he is happy in
the Place, to which he is gone :   And now I must proceed to

Charles his eldest Son, who succeeds him, is a Deputy
Lieutenant, a Justice of the Peace, and the present Lord
hereof; He gives *Gules, three Roses Argent on a Chief of*
the second, as many more of the Field; Crest on a Wreath,
a Dolphin embowed naiant in Water proper.

THE Rectory of **Benington** *Anno* 26 *H*.VIII. was rated in the King's
Books at 19*l. per Annum*, of which the Lords of this Mannor have been
Patrons.

RECTORS.

Henry Cæsar, D. D. Dean of **Ely**
Nathaniel Dod, who built great
  Part of the Parsonage House
  with Brick, at his own Charge,
  for the conveniency of his Successors.

Peter Fisher, D.D. who has built
  the other Part of the Parsonage
  House, made it uniform with the
  former building, adorn'd it with a
  Court Yard, and enclosed it with
  a Brick-wall before the House.

The Church is situated in the Town, near the Mannor-house, where the ruins of an old Castle is to be seen, in the Deanery of Baldock, in the Diocess of Lincolne, and contains only the Body, wherein is a fair Gallery at the West End thereof, and at the East End a Chancel, with a Chapel on the North Side, and a square Tower at the West End of the Church, both which are covered with Lead; in the Tower is a Ring of five Bells, and a short spire erected upon it.

A Marble under the Altar is thus inscribed.

Hic jacet Hugo Dod, *Generosus, a Comitatu Cestriensi ortus, erga Ecclesiam et Pauperes hujus Parochiæ amplissimus Benefactor, qui obiit cælebs sexto* Julii, 1644. Anno Ætat. 67.

Another Stone on the North Side of the Altar has this Inscription.

Exuiæ

Nathanielis Dod, S.T.P. *Rectoris hujus Ecclesiæ sub lata Resurrectionis (mediante Christo) hic reposita, qui vixit Curatus hic sub Decano Eliensi annos septem, Rector proprio jure annos* 45. *qui de novo extruxit vel reparavit Rectoriæ Ædificia pene omnia, obiit Ætat. suæ Anno* 82 Annoq; Dom. 1682.

C. S. D.

To the name and memory of
Sir *Charles Cæsar*, Kt.
Mr. of the Rolls,
Son, Heir, and Successor
To the Right Honourable
Sir *Julius Cæsar*, Knight;
Privy Counsellor to two renowned Princes
James and *Charles*.
He was
An equal Distributor of unsuspected Justice ;
Blind to the Person,
Quick-sighted to his Cause,
Just without Corruption, Merciful without Affectation.
He lived
A Pious Favourite of his God, a loyal Subject to his Prince,
A sincere Servant to his Country, a severe Master to himself,
Charitable without Ostentation,
Religious without Faction :
He Died
As strong in Faith as stout in Resolution,
Truly Penitent, humbly Patient,
Not fearing Death nor desiring it ;
Late frequent in *Hosanna's*, now fill'd with *Halelujahs*.

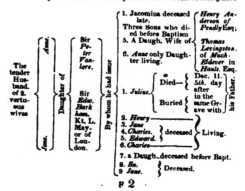

He died in the year of

Nature 53.	He died in the year of	Grace 1642.
Tuesday	————————————	Decemb. 6.

Nathaniel, David, Jonathan, Uzita, Josephus,
Simplicitate Toro, Pectore Prole Thoro.

Another Stone.

Soboles Cæsaria.

Jana *obiit* 25.	Carolus *obiit* 31mo·	Edwardus *obiit*
Jan. 1631.	Januarii 1634.	19mo· Jun. 1639.

Carolo M^{ro} Rotulorum ex Jana Parente.

Præmissi	A Daughter who	Dinah *obiit* 29.	Jana *obiit* 2^{tio}·
non Amissi.	died before *Bapt.*	Jan. 1639.	Novemb. 1642

Another Stone has this Inscription

Here lyeth the Body of the most vertuous, charitable and truly Religious Lady Dame *Jane Cæsar*, Daughter to Sir *Edward Barkham*, Kt. Lord Mayor of **London**, late Wife of Sir *Charles Cæsar*, Kt. Master of the Rolls, by whom he had nine Children, two only surviving her, *viz.* Sir *Henry Cæsar*, Kt. Lord of this Mannor, and *Charles Cæsar* of **Much Hadham**, Esq; She lived Wife to Sir *Charles Cæsar* fifteen years and remained his Widow eighteen: She died in the 60*th.* year of her age at **Much Hadham** in this County, much Honoured, much Lamented, 16. *Junii*, and was here interr'd, 27. *Junii* 1661, in hopes of a blessed Resurrection.

Sir *Charles Cæsar's*	Sir *Charles* his Coat
Coat of Armes.	with hers impaled.

Another Marble on the Right Hand.

Here lyeth the Body of a most vertuous Lady Dame *Anne Cæsar*, Wife of Sir *Charles Cæsar*, Kt. Lord of this Mannor, who as she lived, so she died most Religiously the 13th. of *June* 1625. and was buried the 15th. of the same Month and Year being 33. years and one Month old, leaving alive behind her, her first and last Child, to wit, two Daughters remaining of six Children, which she bare in less than six years, her second Child being a Son was born in **Chancery Lane, London**, and lyeth buried in St. *Dunstans* Church (in the *West*) the other three being two Sons and one Daughter lye buried by her on her left-side here in hope of the blessed Resurrection.

Cæsar's and *Vanlore's* Coat impaled.

An Encomiastick or rather Hexastick of her many Vertues,
being but touched and not fully expressed.

Unfeigned Piety, Modesty, sincere Affection,
House-Government, Patience, sweet Conversation,
Humility, Chastity, or what can be said
Ever to have been in one Woman or Maid.
Weep all in her, and more to comprehend,
If more can be, she had unto her end.

There are two ancient Monuments of the Bensteds.

In the Body of the Church.

William Clarke fourth Son of *George Clarke* exchanged his Life the 24th. day of *May*, 1591. Who was as thou art, and is as thou shalt be.

Another Stone has this.

Here lyeth the Body of *John Clarke* of this Town of **Benington**, Counsellor at Law, who married with one of the Daughters of *Robert Cole* of **Barcholt** in the County of **Suffolk**, Gent. who had issue by her one Son named *William* ; three Daughters named *Anne, Edith,* and *Elizabeth,* he died the 11th. of *June* 1604. aged——

Another Stone.

Here lyeth the Body of *Jane Parsons*, Widow of *John Parsons* sometime of Erton in the County of Southampton, Gent. and eldest Daughter of *John Norton* of Alisford in the same County, and the said *Jane* departed this Life the 13th. of *September* 1686.

Under this Stone lyeth buried the Body of *Christopher Kent*, Gent. who deceased the 15th, of *April* 1681. Aged 62 years and 6 months.

WALKERNE

HAD its Name from the moist and ousing Springs which reinforce the River of Bean or Benefician, with a Stream that driveth a Mill at the South End of the Town; for *Wall* in the Saxon Language signifies a moist or watry Place; and 'tis recorded in the time of *William* the Conqueror under the Title of *Terra Tainorum Regis.*

Derman *tenet* Walchra, *pro decem hidis se defendebat. Terra est duo-* Domesd. Lib. *decim car. in Dom. quinq; hidæ et ibi sunt duo car. et aliæ duæ possunt fieri,* fol. 142, n. 42. *ibi quatuor. decem Vill. cum Presbitero, et sex bordis habentibus octo car. ibi octo cotar. et quatuor Servi, pastura ad pec. Silva ducent. porcis, in totis valent valet decem libr. quando recepit octo libr. tempore Regis* Edwardi *sexdecim libr. Hoc Manerium tenuit* Aluuinus Horne *teignus Regis* Edwardi, *et vendere potuit.*

Derman held Walchre or Walkerne; it was rated at ten Hides, the arable is twelve Carucates, in Demeasne five Hides, and there are two Carucates and other two may be made, there are fourteen Villains with a Presbiter or Priest, and six Bordars having eight Carucates, there are eight Cottagers, and four Servants, Common for the Cattle, Wood to feed two hundred Hogs; in the whole Value it is worth ten Pounds, when he received it eight Pounds, in the time of King *Edward* (the Confessor) sixteen Pounds. *Alwine Horne* a Thane of King *Edward* held this Mannor, and might sell it.

I have spoken of this *Derman* in the Parish of Watton; he was one of the King's Thanes, and might hold this Mannor by Reason of his Office, which was a Place of Attendance on the King: But about the time of King *H.* II. it was in the Possession of *William Lanvalley*, all whose Lands were seized into the King's Hands in the Reign of Bar. vol. I. *R.* I. but upon the Payment of one hundred Marks to the fol. 633. *Rot.* King, he obtained Favour, was restored to his Estate, and 6 R. I. Essex and Herts. died *Anno* 12 *Johan.* as it seems, for then *Hawise* his Wife paid 200 Marks for his Lands.

William, who I suppose, was his Son and Heir, succeeded, for *Alan Basset, Anno* 14 *Joh.* gave to the King an hun- Rot. Pip. 14 dred Marks and an excellent Palfrey that his Daughter Joh. Essex & Herts might marry the Heir of *William de Lanvalley*, and upon Bar. vol. I. the doing of his Homage might be discharged of his Relief; fol. 633. he was very active among the rebellious Barons against the King *Anno* 17 *Joh.* but upon that general Composure made 1 *H.* III. he procured the King's Favour, and died leaving by *Hawise* his Wife

Hawise, who was his sole Daughter and Heir, then under Age, whereupon *Hubert d'Burgh*, Earl of Kent and Chief

Hund. of
Bradewater

Lel. *Coll.* vol.
2, 375.
Bar. vol. 1,
fol. 633.

Plac. Coron.
6 Ed. 1. *Rot.*
54, cur. re-
cept. in Scac.
Bar. vol. 1,
fol. 700, 933.
Rot. Fin. 8
Ed. I.
Bar. vol. 1,
fol. 221.

Claus. 6 Ed.
II.
Bar. vol. 1,
fol. 221.

Bar. vol. 2,
fol. 26.

Bar. vol. 1,
fol. 600.

Bar. vol. 2,
fol. 26.

Claus. de iis-
dem annis.

Justice of 𝔈nglan𝔡, obtained the Wardship of her, and married her to

John *d'Burgh*, his Son and Heir, who held this Mannor of 𝔚alkern𝔢 in her Right, during her Life, by whom she had Issue *John;* she died *Anno* 1249, 33 *H.* III. and after her Decease, he held her Inheritance as Tenant, by the Courtesy of the Barony of 𝔏anballe𝔭, paying one hundred Pounds for his Relief.

After his Decease, *John* their Son and Heir had Livery of this Mannor, *Anno* 3 *Edw.* I. 1275, and died seized hereof in the Year of our Lord 1280, 8 *Edw.* I. leaving Issue three Daughters who were his Coheirs; *Hawise* married to *Robert d'Grelley, Devorgil* married to *Robert Fitz Walter,* and *Margery* a Nun at ℭhickland, in the County of 𝔅e𝔡ford, and upon the Partition, this Mannor fell to the Lot of

Devorgil, the Wife of *Robert Fitz Walter*, who held it in her Right; he had Livery thereof upon the Assignment of her Purparty of the Lands of *John d'Burgh* her Father, and he surviving held it by the Courtesy of 𝔈nglan𝔡 for his Life, and obtained License of the King *Anno* 6 *Edw.* II. that *Christian,* one of the Daughters and Coheir of her Mother *Devorgil,* being then of full Age, might have this Lordship for Part of her Purparty. He had Summons to Parliament from the 23d Year of *Edw.* I. to the 19th of *Edw.* II. inclusive, when 'tis presumed that he died, for in that Year, *Ralph* his Son and Heir had Livery of his Lands.

Christian succeeded in this Mannor, married —— *Mareschal,* by whom he had Issue

William d'Mareschal, who was her Son and Heir, and upon her Death, inherited this Mannor, and had Issue *John d'Mareschal* of 𝔅engham, in the County of 𝔑orfolk𝔢, and *Hawise,* a Daughter.

John was his Heir, and was possest of this Mannor, *Anno* 10 *Edw.* II. but dying without Issue, it came to

Hawise his Sister, who at the time of his Death was fifteen Years of Age; she married *Robert* Lord 𝔐orle𝔭, who had Livery of the Lands of her Inheritance, *Anno* 10 *Edw.* II. held the Office of Marshal of 𝔗relan𝔡 by Descent, and had Issue by *Robert* her Husband, *William,* who was her Son and Heir; however *Robert d'Morley* surviving his Wife, was Tenant of this Mannor by the Courtesy of 𝔈nglan𝔡, during his Life.

After his Death, *William* who was Heir to *Hawise* his Mother, then knighted, and 30 Years of Age, held it, and doing his Homage had Livery thereof; He married *Cicely,* Daughter of the Lord 𝔅ar𝔡olf𝔢, by whom he had Issue *Thomas* and *Robert;* he was summoned to Parliament from the 38th Year of *Edw.* III. to the 2nd *Rich.* II. inclusive, and by his Will dated at 𝔥allingbur𝔭-magna in 𝔈ssex, 26

Aug. 1370, 2 *Rich.* II. bequeathed his Body to be buried in the Church of the Friars Augustines at 𝕹𝖔𝖗𝖜𝖎𝖈𝖍; and on the 30th *April* following he died seized hereof, leaving *Thomas* his Heir; but *Cicely* his Wife then surviving, she held this Mannor for her Life, bequeathed her Body by her Will dated on Thursday, the Eve of St. *Matthew* the Apostle, in the Year 1386, 10 *Rich.* II. to be buriedin the same Church where her Husband lay interred; she died on the Friday next after the Feast of St. *Andrew* the Apostle then following.

Hund. of Bradewater

Thomas being Heir to his Father, and then of full Age, was knighted, did Homage, and had Livery of his Lands; He married *Ann* Daughter of *Edward* Lord *Dispencer,* by *Elizabeth de Burghest* his first Wife, who was Widow of Sir *Hugh de Hastings,* Knight, by whom he had Sir *Thomas Morley,* Knight: He was summoned to Parliament from the 5th *Rich.* II. to the 4th *Hen.* V. and died the 24th of *September* in the same Year, seiz'd hereof.

Mon. Angl. vol. 1, fol.157.
Claus. de iisdem annis.

Upon whose Death this Mannor came to *Thomas,* the eldest Son of Sir *Robert Morley,* by *Isabel* his Wife, Daughter of the Lord *Morley,* who was his next Heir, and at that time 23 Years of Age, for Sir *Robert* dyed in his Life-time: He was Marshal of 𝕴𝖗𝖊𝖑𝖆𝖓𝖉, *Anno* 6 *Henry* V. and served that King with ten Men at Arms, and thirty Archers, in that Expedition the King then made into 𝕱𝖗𝖆𝖓𝖈𝖊; and he bore one of the Banners of Saints, which were carried at the Funeral of the King. He married *Isabel,* one of the Daughters of *Michael de la Pole,* Earl of 𝕾𝖚𝖋𝖋𝖔𝖑𝖐, by whom he had Issue *Robert,* and having been summoned to Parliament from the 5th of *Henry* VI. until the 13th of that King's Reign, dyed upon the Tuesday next after the Feast of the Conception of the Blessed Virgin, *Anno* 14 *Henry* VI. seized hereof, leaving

Bar. vol. 2, fol. 27.

Robert his Son and Heir, who was then 17 Years of Age, married *Elizabeth* Daughter of *William* Lord *Roos,* by whom he had Issue

Alianore, who was his Daughter and Heir, at that time six Months old; afterwards she married *William Lovel,* second Son to *William* Lord *Lovel* of 𝕿𝖎𝖈𝖍𝖒𝖊𝖗𝖘𝖍, and *Alice* his Wife, Sister of *William* Lord 𝕯𝖊𝖎𝖓𝖈𝖔𝖚𝖗𝖙, for which Reason he was called Lord *Morley,* and by her had Issue *Henry* and *Alice,* who married Sir *William Parker,* Knight: He dyod on the Morrow after the Feast of St. *James* the Apostle, *Anno* 16 *Edw.* IV. and *Alianore* his Wife, deceased on the 20th of *August* following, seized of this Mannor of 𝖂𝖆𝖑𝖐𝖊𝖗𝖓𝖊, leaving

Ibid. Bar. vol. 1, fol. 560. b.
Roc. 16 Ed. IV.

Henry her Son and Heir, then eleven Years of Age; He bore the Title of Lord 𝕸𝖔𝖗𝖑𝖊𝖞, had a special Livery of the Lands of her Inheritance, *Anno* 14 *H.* VII. married *Eliza-*

Hund. of
Bradwater

beth the Daughter of ————, and being sent with the Lord *Dawbeny* and others, from 𝕰𝖓𝖌𝖑𝖆𝖓𝖉 into 𝕱𝖑𝖆𝖓𝖉𝖊𝖗𝖘, in the same Year, to the Aid of *Maximilian* King of the *Romans*, against whom a Rebellion in those Parts had been raised, was unhappily slain at 𝕯𝖎𝖝𝖒𝖚𝖉𝖊 by a Gunshot, and buried at 𝕮𝖆𝖑𝖎𝖈𝖊, leaving no Issue, whereby this Mannor came to

Alice his Sister, who was then married to Sir *William Parker*, Kt. by whom he had Issue

Claus. de eod. anno indorso.

Henry, who was summoned to Parliament, by the Title of Lord 𝕸𝖔𝖗𝖑𝖊𝖞, *Anno* 21 *H.* VIII. and the said *Alice* surviving, married Sir *Edward Howard*, Kt. Both whom, by Deed dated 8th of *April*, 21 *H.* VII. sold this Mannor of 𝕸𝖆𝖑𝖐𝖊𝖗𝖓𝖊, with the Appurtenances, Leets, Courts, Liberties, and all other Lands and Tenements, Rents and Services, Profits and Commodities belonging to the same; and

Chant. penes Com. Essex.

the Advowson of the Church of 𝕿𝖍𝖆𝖙𝖈𝖍𝖜𝖔𝖗𝖙𝖍, in this County, to Sir *William Capel*, Kt. and his Heirs for ever: From whom it was past with the Mannor of 𝕳𝖆𝖉𝖍𝖆𝖒, till it came to *Arthur* late Earl of 𝕰𝖘𝖘𝖊𝖝, and *Elizabeth* his Wife, who surviving, is the present Possessor hereof.

THE Rectory *Anno* 26 *H.* VIII. was valued in the King's Books at the yearly Value of 20*l.* 1*s.* 10*d.* and Mrs *Anne Gardiner*, Widow, is Patron hereof.

The RECTORS.

Edw. How, ob. 21 *April*, 1606
John Clarke, ob. 23 *May*, 1612
George Barry, ob. 27 *July*, 1632
John Gorsuch, D.D. the Son of *Daniel Gorsuch*, of 𝕷𝖔𝖓𝖉𝖔𝖓, Merchant, who built a square Pile of Brick on the West Side of the River 𝕭𝖊𝖆𝖓; about 1632 presented his Son to it, who was Seques-

tred *Anno* 1642, for his Loyalty to King *Charles*
Simon Smeath, ob. 6 *Jan.* 1679
Sam. Gardiner, erected the Chancel, *Anno* 1685, and resigned, *Anno*——
Godfrey Gardiner, the present Rector.

This Church is dedicated to the Honour of the Virgin *Mary*, and is situated near the Vill, on the East side of the River 𝕭𝖊𝖆𝖓𝖊 in the Deanery of 𝕭𝖆𝖑𝖉𝖔𝖈𝖐, in the Diocess of 𝕷𝖎𝖓𝖈𝖔𝖑𝖓𝖊; it contains three Isles with a square Tower at the West End, wherein are five Bells, cast *Anno* 1697, and a Chancel at the East End thereof cover'd with Tile, but the Church and Tower with Lead.

In the South Wall of the Chancel is a Monument erected with the Figures of a Man and a Woman kneeling upon Cushions, and a Book before either of them, with this Inscription over their Heads.

Daniel Gorsuch Citizen and Mercer of 𝕷𝖔𝖓𝖉𝖔𝖓, in the Month of *July* 1638, caused this Tomb to be made for himself and his Wife *Alice*, by whom he had three Children, *John*, *Katharine* and *Joanna*, his age being —— years two Months —— dayes, and he died the 8th day of *October* 1638.

Over his head is his Coat of Armes, where he bears Sable, two Bends invert and three Flower d'Lucies Or.
Under him the Pourtraicture of his Son in a Scarf and Gown and his two Daughters kneeling with a Book before either of them.
Over her Head the Armes of the Halls in 𝕷𝖎𝖓𝖈𝖔𝖑𝖓𝖘𝖍𝖎𝖗𝖊, *and over both (in the top of the Monument) are the Armes of the Gorsuches.*

In the East Window of the Chancel, in the middle is the King's Armes, on the right Side the Armes of *Gorsuch*, with a Crest, a Coronet and a demy Lion; on the left Side the Armes of the Mercers Company.

In the middle of the Chancel lies a Stone with the Figures of a Man and Woman cut in Brass, with this Inscription under them.

Here rests in hopes of a joyful Resurrection the Body of *William Chapman*, Citizen and Haberdasher of *London*, and *Anne* his Wife, by whom he had six Sons and six Daughters, he departed this Life the 27th of *September* 1621. *Ætat. suæ* 71. She exchanged this life for immortality the 23d of *Apr*, 1636. *Ætat. suæ* 76.

Underneath are fixed two Brasses on the same Stone, one contains the Figures of the six Sons, the other of the six Daughters.

On the left Hand of this Stone lies another with this Inscription.

Here lieth the Body of *Henry Clerke*, Citizen and sometimes Master of the Merchant Taylors Company in *London*; he died the 8th of *October* 1660. aged 65. years, who left issue four Sons and two Daughters.

This Stone was laid at the charge of his Daughter *Johannah*, who desireth to be here interred.

A Stone lying in the Passage out of this Chancel into the Church has this Inscription.

Here lyeth the Body of *John Humberston* the Son of *Richard Humberston* late of *Walkerne-park*. who had two Wives; he had issue by them both, and departed the sixth day of *October* in the year of our Lord God 1590. His Armes *Argent three Bars sable in chief as many Egresses, Crest on a Wreath a Griffins head eras'd argent, beaked, barbed and eared sable, charged with three plates in pale.*

This Inscription is upon another Stone in the middle Isle.

Here lies the Body of *William Branfeild*, Gent. sometime Student of *Grayes-Inn*, who had two Wives, *Anne* and *Mary*, and had issue by the first six Sons and ten Daughters, and by the second five Daughters; who deceased the eighth day of *December*, *An.* 1596. being of the age of 65. years.

In the South Wall on the right Hand of the Door at the entrance into the Church, lies the Effigies of a Man in Armour, cross Legg'd with his Spurs on, a Shield in his left Hand, carved in Stone. The Inhabitants have a Tradition that he was Lord of Boxburies which anciently belonged to the Knights Templers.

A Monument erected upon a Pillar between the South Isle and the Body of the Church, where there is the Figures of a Man and a Woman having a Desk and two Books on both Sides, with the Arms of the Humberstons over the Man's Head, and a Coat over the Woman's Head quartered with the Humberstons, and this Inscription upon it.

This Monument was erected by *Mary Humberston*, Widow, in memory of her dear and loving Husband *Gyles Humberston* of this Parish in the County of *Hertford*. Gent. by whom she had seven Sons and two Daughters; he departed this Life the 15th. of *January* 1627.

'Tis not a Stone, Dear Sir, can deck your Herse,
Nor can your worth lodge in a narrow verse.
No loving Husband this engraven breadth
Is not to speak yourself, but weep your Death:
And is erected by the ingenious Trust,
Of a sad Wife in Honour of your dust.

ESTONE, ASTON.

SO called by the *Saxons*, in Regard of its Situation towards the East from some of the neighbouring Vills, and shews itself upon an Hill on the West Side of the River

Hund. of Beane or *Beneficían,* above two Miles distant from *Wal-*
Bradewater *kerne;* in the time of *William* the Conqueror it was Parcel
of the Revenue of the Bishop of *Bapeux* in *France,* for 'tis
recorded in *Domesdei Book,* that

Domesd. Lib. *Episcopus Bajocensís tenet Estone pro decem hidis se defendebat.   Terra*
fol. 124, n. 5. *est quindecim car. in dominio quatuor hídæ, et ibi quatuor car. et quinta po-*
test fieri, ibi est Presbyter, et undecim Vill. cum quinque bordis habentibus
quinque car. et alíæ quinque possunt fieri, ibi sex cotar. et quatuor servi,
pratum duo car. pastura ad pec. Silva ducent. porcis, in totis valent. valet octo
decem lib. Quando recepit quatuor decem lib. tempore Regis Edwardi vigint.
lib.   Hoc Manerium tenuerunt tres homines Stigandi Archiepiscopi, et ven-
dere potuerunt.

The Bishop of *Bapeux* held *Eston.* it was rated for ten hides. The
arrable is fifteen Carucates, in Demeasne four Hides, and there are four
Carucates and a fifth may be made, there is a Presbyter and eleven Villains, with five Bordars having five Carucates, and five other may be
made, there are six Cottagers, and four Servants, Meadow two Carucates, Common of Pasture for the Cattle, Wood to feed two hundred
Hogs; in the whole Value it is worth eighteen Pounds a Year, when he
received it fourteen Pounds, in the time of King *Edward* (the Confessor)
twenty Pounds. Three Men (under the Protection) of *Stigand* the
Archbishop, held this Mannor and might sell it.

When King *William* had secured the Crown of England
to himself, his *Normans* began to rebel, upon which he
made his Brother *Odo,* Bishop of *Bapeux,* and *William*
Fitz-Osborne, Earl of *Hereford,* Wardens of England, and
return'd into Normandy, with divers of the Nobility of
England, to reduce the People in that Country to their
former Obedience, whilst he was employed there; he had
Notice that *Odo,* Bishop of *Bapeux,* and Earl of Kent,
aspired to the Papacy, and that he had bought a Pallace at
Rome, whither he was going with a great Retinue of *Nor-*
mans, and much Treasure, but on the sudden meeting him
unexpectedly in the Isle of Wight, seiz'd on him with his
own Hands, when he could not persuade others to do it,
and took from him all his Treasure, for oppressing the
People under his Government, seducing them to leave the
Realm, robbing the Churches, and sent him Prisoner to the
Castle of Rhoan in Normandy, where he continued until
the Death of King *William*; thus this Mannor came to the
Crown.

Mon. Angl. Shortly after, *Adelia,* Queen to King *Hen.* I. gave it
vol. 1, fol. 418. with the Church, and all its Appurtenances to God, and the
blessed *Mary* the Virgin, and to the Abbot and Monks of
Reading.   And upon a *Quo Warranto* brought before *Ro-*
bert de Ufford and *Ralph de Sandwich,* the Jury did find
that it was antient Demesne, held of the King, and that the
Abbot of Reading, held it of the Gift of King *Henry,* the
Son of the Conqueror, and the Abbot shewed, that one
Adelyda, late Queen to King *Hen.* I. gave it to the same
Abbot and Monks; with Soc, Sac, Thol, Them, Infangthef,
and other Liberties, as freely as she held in Demesne of the

said *Henry* her Husband; and King *Henry* II. *Richard* I. King *John*, and *Henry* III. confirmed the Grant with divers other Liberties and Additions, that they should be quit and discharged from Shires and Hundreds, from Toll, &c. but upon the general Dissolution of Monasteries, it came to the Crown, from whence it was conveyed to Sir *John Butler* of 𝔚atton 𝔚oodhall, Knight, and continued in his Name, until it came to *John Boteler*, Esq. who is his Descendant, and the present Lord hereof.

THE Rectory, *Anno* 26 *H.* VIII. was valued in the King's Books at the yearly Value of 26*l.* 11*s.* 6*d.* and the Lords of this Mannor have been Patrons hereof.

The RECTORS.

Mr. *Craven*   Mr. *Burnap*   Mr. *James*   Mr. *Reeve*.

This Church is situated upon a Hill, in the middle of the Parish, in the Deanery of 𝔅aldock. in the Diocess of 𝔏incolne, it contains only the Body with the Chancel, and a Tower at the West End, with an admirable Ring of five Bells, all covered with Lead, and a small Shaft upon the Tower. Within the Chancel and Church are Stones which have these Inscriptions.

Here lyeth interred the Body of *Essex Reeve*, Daughter of *Richard Cooling*, Esq; and second Wife of *Samuel Reeve*, Rector of this Parish, by whom he had issue two Sons, *Samuel* and *Richard*, She departed this Life the 25*th* day of *October*, 1693. in the 24*th* year of her Age.

Here lyeth the Body of *Samuel Reeve*, Esquire, late of this Parish; who departed this Life, the 9th day of *January*, 1683.
Aged 72. Years.

This *Samuel Reeve* was sometime Alderman of the City of 𝔏ondon, and when he laid down his Cloath he was constituted Sheriff of this County, *Anno* 1671. 23 *Car.* II.

Here lyeth the Body of *Susanna*, late Wife of *Samuel Reeve* of this Parish, Rector, and Daughter of *George Nodes* of 𝔖hephalbury in this County, Esquire, She dyed in Childbed of her first Child, who was baptized *Samuel*, and lyeth buried hereunder by her,
December 27. 1685. and in the 20*th* year of her Age.

In the Church.

Here lyeth buried the Body of *John Lient*, late Servant to King *Edward* the sixth, Queen *Mary*, and Queen *Elizabeth*, who married *Mary*, the Daughter of *Thomas Saunders*, and had issue by her five Sons, and five Daughters, which *John* deceased the fourth day of *August*, in the year of our Lord God, 1592. *Ætatis suæ* 72.

Now I shall conclude the Division of this Chief Constable with this Vill, and proceed to the next, which contains the Vills and Hamlets of 𝔎nebworth, 𝔖tevenedge, 𝔚imondly 𝔓arva, 𝔚imondly 𝔐agna, 𝔊rabeley, 𝔠hibesfield, 𝔅ox, or 𝔅oxburies, 𝔚eston, 𝔅aldock, 𝔏etchworth, and 𝔚illien.

The third Part of the third Division.

CHENEPEWORDE, KNEBBE-
WORTH, KNEBWORTH.

SCITUATED upon a fair Hill, two Miles distant from
Aston to the West, you may behold Knebworth, a Vill then
called Chenepeworde in *Domesdei Book;* for in those Days,
the Letter K was not known, but exprest by Ch, and when
that Letter was used in our English, it was termed Knepe-
word, since that Knebleworth, and now by Contraction of
the Word Knebworth, derived from the Habitation or
Dwelling of some antient Possessor hereof. In the time of
William the Conqueror, it is recorded under the Title of

Terra Eudonis Filii Huberti

*Domesd. Lib.
fol. 139, n. 31.*

In Bradewater *Hundred. Eudo Dapifer, et Humphridus de eo tenet*
Chenepeworde, *pro octo hidis et un. virgat. se defendebat. Terra est duodecim car. in Dominio duo car. et aliæ duo possunt fieri. Ibi vigint. Vil. cum
duobus Militibus, et duobus Bordis habentibus octo car. ibi tres Cotarii, et
quatuor Servi. et duo Rustici et un. Molin. de duodecim sol. pratum dim.
car. Pastura ad pec. Ville, Silva mille porc. In totis valent. valet decem
libras, quando recepit centum sol. Tempore Regis* Edwardi *duodecim lib.
hoc Manerium tenuit* Aschil *Teignus Regis* Edwardi, *et ibi unus homo ejus
habuit unam hidam et unam virgatam, et vendere potuit. De consuetudine
unam averam inveniebat cum Rex in Sycra veniebat, si non quinque denar.
reddebat.*

The Land of *Eudo,* the Son of *Hubert.*

Eudo Dapifer and *Humphry* held of him Chenepeworde in the Hundred of Broadwater, it was rated for eight Hides and one Virgate. The
arrable is twelve Carucates, in Demesne two Carucates, and two others
may be made. There are twenty Villains, with two Knights, and two
Bordars having eight Carucates, there are three Cottagers, and four
Servants, and two Rusticks, and one Mill of twelve Shillings Rent by the
Year, Meadow half a Carucate, Common of Pasture for the Cattle of the
Vill, Wood to feed a thousand Hogs. In the whole Value it is worth
ten Pounds by the Year, when he received it, one hundred Shillings by
the Year, in the time of King *Edward* (the Confessor) twelve Pounds by
the Year; *Aschil,* a Thane of King *Edward* (the Confessor) held this
Mannor, and one Man of his (under his Protection) had one Hide, and
one Virgate there, and might sell it. He did find an Horse for his Service, when the King did come into the Shire, if not, he did pay five
Pence.

This *Eudo Dapifer* was the fourth Son of *Hubert de Rye,*
a wise Counsellour and trusty Servant to *William* Duke of
Normandy, of whom I have treated in the Parish of Aspe-
den, whither I refer the Reader, from whom this Mannor
passed to *William de Mandeville,* in such Manner as that did.

Robert de Hoo was the next Person whom I find was
Lord hereof; he obtained a Charter dated 20 *Edw.* I. for a
Market to be held every Week on the Friday at his Man-
nor of Knebbeworth in this County, and a Fair yearly there
on the Eve, Day, and Morrow of the Decollation of St.
John Baptist, and also for Free-warren in all his Demesne

Drawn on Stone from the Original Engravings by C.I. Tyler.

To the Right Worp.ll Sir Will.m

This Plate is humbly

Pub.d by I.M. Mullinger.

Lytton of Knebworth Place Kn.ᵗ

presented by

J. Dravenier.

Bas. Storsford, 1826.

Lands, within the Lordships of 𝕶𝖓𝖊𝖇𝖇𝖊𝖜𝖔𝖗𝖙𝖍 and 𝕭𝖆𝖗𝖕𝖊𝖉𝖊𝖓, in this County.

Hund. of
Bradewater

In the time of *Edw.* II. this Mannor was in the Possession of *Thomas de Brotherton*, who was the fifth Son to King *Edw.* I. and his second Son by Queen *Margaret*, his second Wife; he received his Sirname from 𝕭𝖗𝖔𝖙𝖍𝖊𝖗𝖙𝖔𝖓 in 𝖄𝖔𝖗𝖐𝖘𝖍𝖎𝖗𝖊, where he was born *Anno* 1300, 28 *Edw.* I. and his Mother ordered that he should be named *Thomas* at the Font, because she found speedy Ease in the time of her Extremity, when she invocated St. *Thomas* the Martyr, for the Mitigation of her Pain in Childbirth; he married *Alice* the Daughter of Sir *Roger Halys* of 𝕳𝖆𝖗𝖜𝖎𝖈𝖍, Kt. by whom he had Issue two Daughters, *Margaret* and *Alice*, who were his Heirs, he died the 12th of *Edw.* III. and was buried in the Abby of 𝕾𝖙. 𝕰𝖉𝖒𝖔𝖓𝖉𝖘-𝖇𝖚𝖗𝖞 in 𝕾𝖚𝖋𝖋𝖔𝖑𝖐.

Bar. vol. 2,
fol. 63.

Margaret, the eldest Daughter, had this Mannor upon the Partition, married *John de Segrave*, and after his Decease, Sir *Walter Manny*, Knight of the most noble Order of the Garter, who had Summons to Parliament among the Barons of this Realm, from 21 *Edw.* III. to 44 of his Reign, and died seized of this, among many other Mannors, which he held in Right of *Margaret* his Wife, on the Thursday next ensuing the Feast of St. *Hilary*, *Anno* 46 *Edw* III. leaving *Anne*, and was buried in the Monastery of the *Carthusians*, which he formed in a Place called the *Charterhouse*, without the Bars near 𝖂𝖊𝖘𝖙 𝕾𝖒𝖎𝖙𝖍𝖋𝖎𝖊𝖑𝖉, 𝕷𝖔𝖓𝖉𝖔𝖓.

Bar. vol. 2,
fol. 150.

Esc. 46 Ed.
III. n. 38.

Margaret his Widow surviving him, held this Mannor, and at the Coronation of King *R.* II. claimed the Office of Marshal of 𝕰𝖓𝖌𝖑𝖆𝖓𝖉, and prayed that she might execute it by Deputy, and have all the Fees and Profits thereof; and tho' this was not granted, because the time was so short, that her Claim could not be fully discussed, yet *Anno* 21 *R.* II. she was advanced to the Title of Duchess of 𝕹𝖔𝖗𝖋𝖔𝖑𝖐, for Life, with an Assignation of forty Marks *per Annum*, out of the Issues of that County; she died the Year following, and was buried in the Church of the Friars Minors in 𝕷𝖔𝖓𝖉𝖔𝖓, where she had made Stalls in the Quire, at her own Charges, *Anno* 1380, to the Value of 350 Marks.

Claus. 1 R. II.
m. 45.

Claus 21 R.II
23 R. II. n.22.
Rot. Parl. 21
R. II. n. 35.
T. Wals. p.
393, n. 46, &
395.
Stow's Surv.
p 341.

Anne was the Daughter and Heir of this Dutchess, and married *John de Hastings*, Earl of 𝕻𝖊𝖒𝖇𝖗𝖔𝖐𝖊, but after the Death of this Dutchess, I find

John Hotoft was possest hereof, he was an eminent Man, and served for this County in the Parliaments held 1 *H.*V. 2 *H.*V. 3 *H.*V. 5 *H.*V. 1 *H.*VI. and was constituted Sheriff of this County and 𝕰𝖘𝖘𝖊𝖝, *Anno* 7 *H.* VI. He was also Treasurer of the King's Houshold afterwards, he dyed and was buried in the Chancel of this Church, where his Monument remains at this Day.

Sir *Thomas Bourchier* shortly after obtained this Mannor; he was Son to Sir *John Bourchier*, Knight of the most noble Order of the Garter, he assisted *Henry* Earl of 𝕽𝖎𝖈𝖍𝖒𝖔𝖓𝖉, upon his March towards 𝕭𝖔𝖘𝖜𝖔𝖗𝖙𝖍-𝖋𝖎𝖊𝖑𝖉, shared in the Glory of that happy Victory, and sold this Mannor, *Anno* 7 *H.* VII. to

Robert Lytton in the County of 𝕯𝖊𝖗𝖇𝖞, Esq. who was Under Treasurer in the Court of *Exchequer*, Keeper of the great Wardrobe to King *H.* VII. and one of his Privy Council; he died seiz'd hereof, leaving Issue

William Lytton, who was his Heir, Governour of the Castle of 𝕭𝖚𝖑𝖑𝖔𝖎𝖌𝖓𝖊 in 𝕱𝖗𝖆𝖓𝖈𝖊, and constituted Sheriff for this County and 𝕰𝖘𝖘𝖊𝖝, *Anno* 2 *H.* VIII. He married *Audry* the Daughter and Heir of Sir *Philip Booth*, Kt. by whom he had Issue, *Robert*, *Rowland*, and *Dorothy*; he dyed and was buried in the Burial-place near his Father in this Parish.

Sir *Robert Lytton* succeeded, was constituted Sheriff of this County and 𝕰𝖘𝖘𝖊𝖝, *Anno* 37 *H.* VIII. he received the Honour of Knighthood, and married *Frances* the Daughter of *Anthony Cavalary*, by whom he had Issue three Daughters, *Helen* married to Sir *John Brocket*, Kt. *Elizabeth* married first to *Thomas Little*, Esq. after his Decease, to *Edward Barret*, Esq. and *Anne* married to *John Borlace*, Esq. but dying without Heir male of his Body, this Mannor came to

Sir *Rowland Lytton*, who was his Brother, and his next Heir male; constituted Sheriff of this County, *Anno* 10 *Eliz.* afterwards knighted; he married *Margaret Tate* of 𝕮𝖆𝖑𝖑𝖎𝖈𝖊, by whom he had Issue, *Mary* first married to *Thomas Harleston*, Esq. after his Decease, to *Edward Pulter*, Esq. And upon the Decease of *Margaret*, he married *Anne Carleton*, by whom he had Issue *Rowland*, and *Frances* married to Sir *Anthony Cope*, Kt.; he died the 16th of *July*, 1582, and lyes buried in this Chancel.

Sir *Rowland* succeeded his Father, was constituted Lieutenant of this County, and commanded their Forces at 𝕿𝖎𝖑𝖇𝖚𝖗𝖞 Camp, *Anno* 1588. He was also made *Custos Rotulorum*, Captain of the Band of Pensioners under Queen *Elizabeth*, Sheriff of this County, *Anno* 1594, 36 *Eliz.* and knighted, *An.* 1605, 3 *Jac.* I. He married *Anne*, one of the Daughters of *Oliver* Lord Saint *John*, Baron of 𝕭𝖑𝖊𝖙𝖘𝖔𝖊, in the County of 𝕭𝖊𝖉𝖋𝖔𝖗𝖉, (the Widow of *Robert Corbet*, Esq.) and Mother to *Elizabeth* married to Sir *Henry Wallop*, Kt. and *Anne* married to *Adulph Cary*, Esq.; this *Rowland* had Issue by her *William*, *Rowland*, *Philip*, *Anne* married to Sir *William Webb*, *Judith* to Sir *George Smith* of 𝕬𝖓𝖓𝖆𝖇𝖑𝖊𝖘, Kt.; and after his Decease, to Sir *Thomas Barring-*

ton, Knight and Baronet; *Elizabeth* to *Thomas Windham*, Esq. and *Jane* to Sir *Charles Crofts* of 𝔅𝔞𝔯𝔬𝔴𝔢𝔩 in 𝔖𝔲𝔣𝔣𝔬𝔩𝔨, Knight.

Sir *William Lytton* was his Heir, knighted, and constituted Sheriff of this County, *Anno* 1 *Car.* I. he married *Anne* the Daughter and Heir of *Stephen Slany* of 𝔑𝔬𝔯𝔱𝔬𝔫 in the County of 𝔖𝔞𝔩𝔬𝔭, Esquire, by whom he had Issue *Rowland*, *Margaret* married to *Thomas Hillersdon*, Esq. and after his Decease to Sir *Thomas Hewyt* of 𝔓𝔦𝔰𝔥𝔬𝔟𝔲𝔯𝔫, in this County, Knight and Baronet; *Dorothy* married to Sir *John Barrington* of 𝔅𝔞𝔯𝔯𝔦𝔫𝔤𝔱𝔬𝔫-𝔥𝔞𝔩𝔩, in the County of 𝔈𝔰𝔰𝔢𝔵, Baronet; *Mary* married to Sir *Edward Gostwick* of 𝔚𝔦𝔩𝔩𝔲𝔤𝔥𝔱𝔬𝔫, in the County of 𝔅𝔢𝔡𝔣𝔬𝔯𝔡, Baronet; *Jane* to Sir *Robert Boswel* in the County of 𝔎𝔢𝔫𝔱, Knight; and *Elizabeth* to *John Scrogs* of 𝔄𝔩𝔟𝔲𝔯𝔫 in this County, Esq. He was a Justice of the Peace, a Deputy Lieutenant for this County divers Years, and dyed the 14th of *Aug.* 1660.

Rowland Lytton, Esq. was knighted *Anno* 1660, served this County in the Parliament 12 King *Car.* II. called the Healing Parliament; was constituted Sheriff of this County *Anno* 14 of the same King; was a Justice of the Peace, a Deputy Lieutenant here divers Years: he married *Judith* the youngest Daugher of an East-land Merchant in 𝔏𝔬𝔫𝔡𝔬𝔫, by whom he had Issue *William, Rowland, Judith* married first to *Maurice* Abbot of 𝔉𝔲𝔩𝔪𝔢𝔯 in 𝔆𝔞𝔪𝔟𝔯𝔦𝔡𝔤𝔢𝔰𝔥𝔦𝔯𝔢, Esq. after his Decease to Sir *Nicholas Strode*, Knight, of 𝔖𝔱. 𝔍𝔬𝔥𝔫'𝔰 𝔆𝔩𝔬𝔰𝔢 in 𝔐𝔦𝔡𝔡𝔩𝔢𝔰𝔢𝔵; *Anne* married to Sir *Francis Russel* of 𝔖𝔱𝔯𝔢𝔫𝔰𝔥𝔞𝔪 in 𝔚𝔬𝔯𝔠𝔢𝔰𝔱𝔢𝔯𝔰𝔥𝔦𝔯𝔢, Baronet: and upon the Decease of the said *Judith* his Wife, he married *Rebeccah* the Daughter and Heir of *Thomas Chapman* of 𝔏𝔬𝔫𝔡𝔬𝔫, Scrivener; and the Relict of Sir *Richard Lucy* of 𝔅𝔯𝔬𝔵𝔟𝔬𝔯𝔫𝔢, Kt. and Baronet; by whom he had Issue *Rebeccah*, who married *Anthony* Viscount 𝔉𝔞𝔩𝔨𝔩𝔞𝔫𝔡 in the Kingdom of 𝔖𝔠𝔬𝔱𝔩𝔞𝔫𝔡; Sir *Rowland* died the 1st of *November*, 1674, from whom this Mannor, with others, descended to

Sir *William Lytton*, who was knighted the 6th of *May*, *Anno* 1677, 29 *Car.* II. and constituted Sheriff in this County, in the Year 1678, 30 *Car.* II. He married *Mary* Daughter of Sir *John Harrison* of 𝔅𝔞𝔩𝔩𝔰 in this County, Kt. by whom he had no Issue; After her Decease, he married *Philippa* the second Daughter of Sir *John Keyling* of 𝔖𝔬𝔲𝔱𝔥-𝔥𝔦𝔩 in the County of 𝔅𝔢𝔡𝔣𝔬𝔯𝔡, Knight, and one of the King's Serjeants at Law. He was a Justice of the Peace, a Deputy Lieutenant for this County, and the present Lord of this Mannor. He gives *Ermin, on a Chief indented Azure three Ducal Coronets Or; Crest on a Wreath, a Bitterne among Reedes proper.*

Mary d'Lytton.

Gilbert d'Lytton, Son of Mary, named in a Deed dated 1283, and 11 Edward I.

Thomas, the Son of Gilbert d'Lytton — Ivet his Wife, Da. of Thomas Son of by Deed without date. Margery d'Bayley, dated 16 Edw. II.

Robert d'Lytton, Son of Gilbert, Son of Mary d'Lytton, by Deed without date, and Fine levyed 18 Edw. I.

William d'Lytton, by Deed dated 14 Edw. I. and by Deed dated 29 Edw. I. the said William, Son of Robert, Son of Gilbert d'Lytton, in the same Deed dated 11 Edward I.

Stephen, Son of Robert d'Lytton, — Maud, his by Deed without date, and by Wife 15 Deed dated 10 Edward II. Edw. III.

Ralph, Brother of Stephen, by Deed without date.

Margery, Sister of Ralph by Deed without date.

Robert d'Lytton, Heir of his Father, by Deed dated 16 Edward II. the said Robert was Son of William, Son of Ivert d'Lytton.

William, Son of Stephen d'Lytton, by Deed dated 29 Edward III. gave Lands in Lytton.

Henry d'Lytton.

Richard d'Lytton, by Deed dated 9 Henry V. it appears he was Father of Robert Lytton, by Deed dated 11 Henry VI.

John, Son of William, Son of Stephen d'Lytton, by Deed granted to Rich. Son of Tho. Son of Richard d'Lytton, Mess. &c. Deed dated at Lytton, 33 Edw. III. and another Deed, 41 Edw. III.

Richard, Son of William d'Lytton, Deeds, 3 Edw III. 15 Edw. III 1341, 12 Edw. III 16 Edw. III. 17 Edw. III.

Henry d'Lytton.

Elizabeth, second — Robert d'Lytton, Kt. by Deed dated 11 Henry VI. the — Agnes, Daughter of John Hotoft, Widow of John Wife, Wth. Deed Queen's Recievor in the County of Derby, 27 Henry VI. Paris, Citizen and Pewterer of London, Deed dated 22 H. IV. Under Treasurer of England. dated 1 Henry 7.

Richard, Son of Richard d'Lytton, Deed 45 Edw. III.

William d'Lytton, Esq. by Deed dated 21 Henry VII. and 3 Henry VIII. — Audry, Da. and Heir of Sir Phil. Booth, Kt. of Shrubland Hall in Suffolk.

Sir Robert Lytton, Kt. of Shrubland Hall in the — Frances, Da. of County of Suff. Farmer of the Manor, 3 Edw. VI. Anthony Ca- valry.

Rowland Lytton, of Kneb- — Margaret, his first Wife, Da. — Anne, Daughter of George Carleton worth, Esq. died 16 July, of — Tate of the Town of Brightwell in Oxfordshire. 1582. of Calice.

Dorothy, married to —— Acworth.

Mary, the sole offspring of the first Wife, mar. first Thomas Barlorson, Esq., afterwards Ed- ward Pulter of Coderd.

Sir Rowland Lytton of Knebworth, Kt.

Anne, Da. of Sir Oliver St. John, Kt. Baron of Bletso.

Frances, m. to Sir Anthony Cope of Hanwel' in Com. Oxford, Kt.

Sir William Lytton, mar. Ann, Da. and Heir of Stephen Slaney of Norton in Shrop.

[2] Robert Lytton.

[3] Philip Lytton.

Helen, Da. and Coh. 1 mar to Tho. Little of Skreb- land Hall in Suff. in right of his Wife, afterwards to Edward Barret of Delftome in Aveley in the County of Essex, Esq.

Eliz. Da. and Coh. mar. John Bou- lace, Esq.

Anne, Da. and Coh.

Elizabeth, mar. Tho. Wind- ham, Esq. of —— in Norfolk.

Jane, mar Sir Charles Grofts of Bardwell in Suffolk.

Rebecca, Da. and Coh. of Sir Richard Lucy, Kt. and Baronet.

Mary, mar to Sir Ed Gostwick of Wilington, Co. Bedf. Kt. & Bar.

[4] Eliz. mar to Joh. Scrope of Albury in Com. Hertf.

[3] Jane, m. Sir The. Bo- ville, Kt.

[2] Judith, mar. Sir William Wth.

Judith, Da. and Coh. mar. Sir George Smith of Annables, after him Sir Tho. Barrington of Barrington Hall, Kt. and Bart.

Judith, Da. of Humphry Ed- warden of London, Merchant, and of Chaley in Midd- sex, Kt.

Sir Rowland — Lytton, Kt.

Will. — Phillippa, 2d. Da. of Sir

Rowland Lytton.

Rebecca, mar. to An-

[1] Margaret, mar. Tho. Hillerdon of Elnstow in the County of Bed- ford, Esq., after him Sir Thomas Henry, Kt. and Bart.

Dorothy, mar. Sir John Barrington, Kt and Bart.

[2] Anne, mar. to Sir

[1] Judith, mar. first to Maurice, Abbot

This knightly Family gives me Occasion to shew the Antiquity of their Honour, which the *Grecians* had in great Esteem before the Trojan Wars: who gave the same Title to *Nestor*, for *Homer* uses the Word ἱππότης in the same Sense as the *Latines* afterwards termed *Eques*,

Τοῖσι δὲ καὶ μετέ ειπε γερήνιον ἱππότα Νέστωρ.
Among whom thus Nestor spoke, that honour'd Knight.

The famous *Tydæus*, King of Ætolía; and *Philides* the Son of *Phileus*, attributed that Honour to themselves, the chiefest of the *Achaians* greatly coveted it, the principal of the *Grecians* much valued it, the *Chalcedonians* and the *Romans* prized it so much, that those who were rich and wealthy, bore the Title of ἱπποβαται that is *Equites*, and in other Nations were denominated from the Horse. The *Italians* termed them *Caveleiri*, the *Frenchmen*, *Chivalers*, the *Britains* in Wales, *Morgogk*, and the *Germans* called them *Ridders*, which in English signifies a Rider or Horseman; in high Dutch they are called *Ritterschaffs*, in low Dutch, *Riderschap*, and the learned *Selden* observed, that the German *Ritter* or *Ridder* wes the same with *Miles* a Gentleman; so the *Gheslagen Ridder* signifies *Eques auratus*, a Knight created by the Ceremony of a gentle Stroke, or light Touch by a naked Sword upon the Shoulder, for *Gheslaeghen* signifies *Percussus*; and though the Gentlemen in Germany write themselves at this Day in Latin *Equites*, yet no Man is called *Ritter* or *Rider* there, but such as is *Eques auratus*, actually knighted; which Epithet of *auratus* the *Romans* added to them from their Priviledge of wearing Gold upon their Swords and Spurs.

Romulus constituted them for his Life-guard and called them *Celeres*, as some say, à *Celeritate*, from their active and quick Dispatch in martial Affairs; but *Claudius Salmatius* derived it from the Greek Word Κελες, which, saith he, among the *Æolians*, signifies a Horse; and from an Horse, the ancient *Romans* derived the Title of *Eques*; hence *Livy* called them *Equites:* and when the Roman Citizens were distributed into three Degrees, *Livy* rankt them after this Order; *Senatus, Equester, Ordo,* and *Plebs*; which Order was confirmed by that remarkable Elogie, *Consensu Senatus, et Equestris Ordinis Populiq; Romani*; and though this Equestrian Order was inferior to the Degree of Senators, yet *Cicero*, *Pliny*, and others affirm, they were next in Dignity, and invested with Honours almost equivalent to them, for they were made Judges at Rome; before whom, saith *Cicero*, Causes were pleaded and argued, and they often managed the civil Affairs of the Commonwealth: *Turnebus*, in his Comment upon some Pieces of *Cicero*, applauds the Excellency and Integrity of their Judgments;

Hund. of
Bradewater and the Senators were elected from this Equestrian Order, which caused *Perseus* King of 𝕸𝖆𝖈𝖊𝖉𝖔𝖓, and after him *Severus* the Emperor, to term this Degree the Seminary or Nursery of the Senators: From hence I may parellel that Order with the Knighthood in 𝕰𝖓𝖌𝖑𝖆𝖓𝖉, who generally spring from the most ancient Families, are elected into this Order for their Birth and Estates, are plac'd between the Nobility and common People, the Judges and privy Councellors have the Honour of this Dignity, and generally the Barons are chosen out of their Rank and Quality. But afterwards *Salmatius* complained, that whenever the Censor elected a Person into the Equestrian Order, he consider'd nothing in him but the Equestrian Sense, which for the most Part will find two near a Parallel among the Knights of this Age; upon which *Andrew Tiraquell* made this Distinction between these Knights; those who were noble before their Knighthood, he termed *Milites*; but those who were ignoble he called *Equites aurati*, an Appellation which *Franciscus Philelphius* first gave them in the time of *William* the Conqueror; those Gentlemen who held Lands by Knight's Service to the yearly Value of 20*l.* were termed in *Domesdei Book, Milites, à Militia*, for that it was then held a sufficient Estate to support the Dignity of a Knight, and to maintain a Man and Horse compleatly

Dod. of Ba-
rons, p. 119. armed to serve the King in the Wars; which Service in old time was called *Regale Servitium*, because it was done to and for the King and the Realm; these Knight's Fees descended entirely to the eldest Son by Succession of Heri-

An. 7 Ed III.
296, 600.
Litt. fol. 20. tage, that he might be the better enabled to maintain the Wars against the King's Enemies or his Lords; and the Law had so great a Respect to the Dignity of Knighthood, that he was not bound by his Tenure to go in Person, as ordinary Soldiers hired or entertained by prest Mony or Wages, but might find an able Person to serve in that Expedition for him.

When the King conferred the Dignity of a Knight, he slightly struck him upon the Shoulder with a gentle Touch on the flat Side of the Sword, but in old time *Cingulo militari donati*, or as Mr. *Bracton* expresses it, *Ringæ gladiis*, because the King did not only smite him with the Sword, but invested him with Sword and Belt; neither is this Ceremony wholly lost, for the Knights of the Bath are girt with Sword and Belt, when they receive this Honour, and 'tis not unusual now a days for the Prince to bestow the Sword upon the Person whom he knighteth.

Seld. tit Hon.
pt. 2, cap. 3,
fol. 550, 551. This Degree is truly accounted with us the most ancient Title of Honour in 𝕰𝖓𝖌𝖑𝖆𝖓𝖉, and the first of a military Dignity; 'tis the Basis and Foundation of all Honours in our Nation, and hath the Addition of Batchelor from the

Name of *Buccellarii*, which signifies as much as a Soldier or military Servant, always ready for Imployment; and *Baccellarius*, as the *Frenchmen* call it, and *Baccalaureus* (made from *Buccellarius* denoting at first every Soldier,) when joyned with Chivelier, the first Degree of Knighthood: From hence it was transferr'd to the first Degree in the Universities, and to those that are *Magisterii candidati* in Trades, and to Woers that have not been married, but are *conjugii ac amoris candidati: Bachelette* is attributed to a Maid woed, as *Batchelor* to him that woes.

As the *Romans* gave to their Knights the Titles of *Splendidi* and *Illustres*, Marks of Eminence, and equivalent to that of *Nobiles*, so the Kings of this Realm have stiled our Knights, Trusty and Right Worshipful, and annexed to their Christian Name the word Sir, which cometh from the French word *Sire*, and in old French signifieth *Seignieur* or *Lord;* and the ancient Barons in ﬀrance affected rather to be called by the Name of *Sire* than Baron, as *Le Sire de Montmorencie, Le Sire de Bevien, Le Sire de Cauci*, and the like: the words Master, Lord, or Sir, were familiarly used among the *Jews* in their common Salutations and Addresses, and *Seneca* observed that where the Name of a Man occurred not in common Speech among the *Romans*, he was saluted by the Name of *Domine*, as *Domine frater* is frequent in the Epistles of *Sidonius Apollinaris* and others, or as every Batchelor of Art, Vicar, or Parson, with us were called *Domine:* but the Name *Dominus* here is used to distinguish an Attribute of Greatness, as doth our English word Lord, without Relation to an Interest of Property, or to Servitude; as the Children of *Heth* stiled *Abraham, Jacob* termed *Esau, Abigal* entitled *David*, or *Uriah* called *Joab;* and in other Countries it denotes Superiors, as King or Subjects of the greater Nobility, or Men of special Eminency, known by the Name of *Heres, Dons, Sieurs, Signiors, Signeurs, Sennores, Seniores*, and the like. Though 'tis not known when this Title of Sir was first prefixt to the Christian Name of a Knight, yet I find it very ancient, for in the time of King *Etheldred*, a Saxon Prince, this Title of Sir was annext to the Name of Sir *Odynell* of Barington, Baron of Wﬄegon, and in the Reign of *Hen*. II. to the Names of Sr. *John Curcy*, Sr. *Amoric*, Sr. *Roger Paer*, great Commanders under that King in Ireland, also of Sr. *Renaud le Fitz Oures*, Sr. *Hugh de Morvile*, Sr. *William Tracy*, and Sr. *Richard le Brut*, the four Knights that slew St. *Thomas a Becket;* and this Addition of Sir is properly attributed to the Names of all Knights Bannerets, Knights of the Bath, and Knights Batchelors, and is accounted Part of their Stile; as *Messire* is used in the same Nature among the *French*.

Hund. of Bradewater

Oppius, Pliny, Cicero, Tacitus. Seld. tit. Hon. pt. 2, cap. 3, fol. 137.

Gen. xxiii. 6, 11, 15. xxxii. 18. xxxiii. 8, 13, 14. I Sam. xxv. 24, 25, 26. II Sam. ii. 11

Brady's *Hist. of Engl.* fol. 368. Seld. tit. Hon. fol. 939.

G 2

Hund. of
Bradewater

The Stile of Madam and Lady is also given to their Wives, though the Masculine of it is Lord, which is not granted to their Husbands, and also to the Daughters of all Earles, and Dignities above them; and the like or greater Honour was attributed to that Sex in the time of the old Empire, for though the word *Domine* was used frequently in that Nation, where nothing of Honour, but Salutation, or Compellation is only exprest; and also *Adoni* and *Rabbi*, which signifies the same thing, was used among the *Jews*; yet the Word *Domine* was given to Women, for a special Mark of Honour, but by the Law of England, the Wives of Knights and Baronets, in Conveyances are only stiled Dames to distinguish them from other Ladies of greater Quality; yet if they be named Ladies in any Action, the

14 H. VI. 2
Co. 6 Report,
fol. 53.

Writ shall not abate, because they have that Title by the Curtesy of England; as it is familiar with the *French*, and among the *Italians* at this Day, but if they be named Countesses or Baronesses, the Writ shall abate.

The principal Ensignes of Knighthood were a Horse, gold Ring, Shield and Launce, Belt and Sword, guilt Spurs, gold Chain and Collar; but the later Ages have selected from these, the Belt or golden Girdle, Sword, Collar, Spurs, and Rings, which are called the Ornaments and Ensignes that belong to Knighthood, in some imperial Diploma's: And *Cassanus* saith, that a Sword shall be hung up in the Church at the Funeral of a Knight; because *Eques* and *Miles*, are the proper Attributes given to a Knight at his first Creation or Dubbing; which import some military Atchievement, and they were anciently wont to take an Oath chiefly, among all other their military Designs, to defend the Church and the Christian Religion.

Dod. of Ba-
rons, p. 130.

Though a Knight received his Dignity from a foreign Prince, yet he shall be stiled a Knight, in all leading Proceedings within England, and shall have Place and Precedency here, from the time of his Knighthood: This Degree is not only a Dignity and Honour to the Party, but also honourable and useful to the Kingdom; touching Matters of Justice in civil Affairs, as in a Writ of Right, the highest Writ in the Law, for the Trials of Titles touching Inheri-

Dyer, 79, fol.
103.

tance; for upon the Return of the Writ, *de magna Assiza elegenda*, the four Knights named in it, must appear *Gladiis cincti*; and if the Tenant shall make his Election by Battle, each Party shall choose their Champions, the Court shall award Battel, Day shall be given to the Parties, and two Knights must bring the Champions into the Lists, and if a Tenant lay an Essoin *de malo lecti*, and have a Writ out of Chancery to warrant it, four Knights shall be commanded to view him, and if they find him sick, then they shall give him Day, to the End of a Year and a Day; for these Reasons, the Kings of this Realm could heretofore compel

Men of Worth by their Prerogative, to take this Degree at *Hund. of* **Bradewater** their Pleasure, or pay a Fine; and every Lord of a Mannor ought by the common Law to have of every of his Tenants Bract., fol. 36. a reasonable Fine to make his eldest Son a Knight.

Precedency of Knights.

Some hold that if a Knight received his Honour before a Serjeant at Law was created, the Knight shall have the Dod. of Nob. Precedence, but if the Serjeant was created before the p 125, 126, Knight was dubb'd, the Serjeant shall precede; and some hold, where Knights have been Viceroys, or Ambassadors to foreign Princes, or Judges within the Realm, they may and ought to have Precedency above Men of the same Rank, after the Expiration of their Offices; and many of them stand strongly upon it, but *sub judice lis est:* However admitting it to be so, by Way of Argument, yet the Heralds deny that Priviledge to the Mayor and Aldermen of **London**, or Justice of Peace; because they had the limited Jurisdiction of Magistracy confin'd within the Compass of their own Walls: But the other were general Magistrates throughout the Realm, whose Imployment concern'd the publick Honour, Justice, and Interest of the whole Commonwealth and · Estate; therefore they more meritoriously draw from thence a greater Respect of Honour, according to the Generality of their Administration and Imployments, than an inferiour and more confined Magistracy can claim.

The Priviledge of Knights.

If a Ribaud or Man of base Birth and Condition, had Britton, 19, struck a Knight, he should by the old Law, have lost the in his Appeals Hand wherewith he offended.

Knights are excus'd from their Attendance at Leets, nei- Britton, 29, ther are they, nor their eldest Sons bound to find Pledges Stat. of Marlb. there, and their eldest Sons are allowed the Priviledge of cap. 10. wearing Hats in the *University*. Dod. of Barons, p. 138.

The King's Bailiff may not take any Demeasne Carts Mag. Char. from them. cap. 21.

Knights may keep grey Hounds, and setting Dogs, and Stat. 1 Jac. Nets to take Phesants and Partridges, though they cannot cap. 27. dispend 10l. per Annum, nor are worth 200l. Dod. of Barons, p. 146.

The Brethren and Sons born in Wedlock of every Knight, Stat. 21 H. being Clergymen, may purchase License or Dispensation, VIII. cap. 13. and keep two Parsonages or Benefices, with Cure of Souls. Dod. of Barons, p 146.

The Mannor-house of **Knebworth** consists of a large Pile of Brick, with a fair Quadrangle in the Middle of it, seated upon a dry Hill, in a fair large Park, stocked with the best Deer in the County, excellent Timber, and well wooded, and from whence you may behold a most lovely Prospect to the East.

Hund. of
Bradewater

THIS Rectory in 26 *Hen.* VIII. was valued in the King's Books at 13*l.* 1*s.* 10*d.* of which Sir *William Lytton* and his Predecessors, Lords of this Mannor of Knebworth, have been Patrons.

The Names of some RECTORS *of* Knebworth.

1606 4 *Jacobi.*   *Robert Hundleby*
1629 5 *Car.* I.   *Christopher Thornton*
1649 1 *Car.* II.   *Samuel Bentham.*

This Church was dedicated to the Honour of the Virgin *Mary*, and her Effigie remains in the Window of the Chancel. It contains only the Body with the Chancel, and a little Chapel or Burying place, built by the Family of the *Lyttons*, on the North Side of the Chancel; all which is covered with Tyle: at the West End of the Church is a small square Tower, wherein hang a Ring of five small Bells cast 1697; a short Spire covered with Lead is erected on the Tower, and within are these Monuments to be seen.

In the Body of the Chancel lies a Stone with this Inscription.

Hic jacet Dominus Simo Bache, Clericus, quondam Thesaurarius Hospitii illustrissimi Principis Domini Henrici quinti Regis Angliæ, ac Canonic. Ecclesiæ Cathedralis Sancti Pauli, London. qui obiit xix die Maii, Anno Dom. nostr. 1414.

In the upper End of the North Side of the Chancel, another Stone has this Inscription.

Here lyes interred the body of Dame *Jane Crofts*, Daughter of Sir *Rowland Lytton*, of Knebworth, in the County of Hertford, Knight, and Wife to Sir *Charles Crofts* of Bardwel, in the County of Suffolk, Knight; who departed this Life the 29*th* of *April*, 1672. Aged 70.

A Monument in the North Wall, where the Effigies of the Lady *Strode* is engraved in white Marble, with this Inscription.

Juditha
Hic juxta sita
Rolandi Lytton *Equitis Aurati ex Equestri* Lyttonorum
in hoc vico prosapia Filia,
Nicholai Strode *Equitis Aurat. ex antiquo* Strodiorum,
in Dorsettia *genere conjux,*
Binæ Prolis masculæ Familiæque Mater,
Raro bonæ mentis, Formaque Clara Contuburnio,
Mater Familias præter ætatem gravis
Domi servare nota sedet sciens domum tueri,
Eademque gratiis obsequiis moribus placidissimis,
Uni Marito semper unice studens
In sanitate composita in ægritudine constans
Modesta pudica pia (sed pauca quid multis quæror,
Tu Lector animo quicquid Uxoris proba est sac colligas huc
summa verborum redit
Nam saxa voces et maritalis dolor languent silent stupent)
Anno Conubii 3. *Ætatis* 24. *salutis reparate* cioicclxii *non mari.*
Confecto tabe decessit
Mulieris functa est Officiis bonæ adeoque sat diu vixerit nisi
conjugi et liberis
His quippe virtutis exemplar præripuit illi tristè sui desiderium reliquit
Hic mærens suprema solvit
Illa per Christum Resurrectionem fælicem expectat.

A Marble beneath it, whereon the Arms of *Strode* and *Lytton* be engraven'd: Speaks this Motto.

Sic lucent lumen
Juditha
Nicholai Strode *Equar Conjux*
Hic sita est.

On the left Side of this Stone lies another small Marble, with
this Inscription.

Juditha
Nicholai, Judithæ, *quæ Filiola Aunicola.*
Hic juxta Matrem jacet.

Between the Chancel and the Chapel stands a Monument covered
with a fair Marble, whereupon the Effigies of a Man clad in Armour
and his Wife, engraven'd in Brass. With this Inscription round the
Edge of the Stone.

Hic procerum de stirpe natum cum conjuge clara
Johanni Hotoft *iterum telluris*
Hospitii Regis qui Thesaurarius olim
Henrici sexti merito pollebat honore
Sit hic perpetua sibi post hac horida lustra
Corpora Spiritibus ———

In the Chancel Window are the Arms of *Hotolph.*

Officium Pietatis majoribus Speculum Virtutis bibentibus: Exemplar Be-
nedictionis posteris posuit —— 1408. nisi Dominus edificaverit Domum
frustra laborat.

In the Chapel a Marble tells

Rolandus Lytton, *armiger, qui insigniter arma gessit, in Bello Dux fortis,
in pace optimus Magistratus, obiit* 16 *die* Julii 1582. *Uxores habuit*
Margarettam Tate, *et* Annam Carleton, *ex prima reliquit* Mariam, *ex
altera* Rolandum *et* Franciscam.

A flat Monument in the North Wall, says

Hic jacet clarissima Fæmina Anna Lytton, *Filia* Oleveri *Baronis* Saint
John de Bletsho, *primis nuptiis juncta* Roberto Corbet *de* Moreton Corbet, *Arm. ex quo suscepit* Elizabetham *uxorem* Henrici Wallop, *Milites,
et* Annam *nuptam* Adolpho Cary, *Arm. ex altero Marito* Rolando Lytton *de* Knebworth, *Arm. reliquit Filios* Gulielmum, Rolandum, *et* Phi-
lippum; *Filias* Annam, Juditham, Elizabetham, *et* Janam, *vixit quadraginta annos nobilis venusta, pia, chara Deo et Hominibus, obiit multum
deplorata ultimo* Februarii, *anno salutis* 1601. *Pro cujus bene acta vita
Deum laudate, ut quod cum sanctis communicetis orat.*

Another Marble gives this Account.

Here lyeth interred the body of Dame *Judith Barrington*, Daughter of
Sir *Rowland Lytton* of Knebworth, in the County of Hertford, Knight;
and wife first to Sir *George Smith* of Annibals, in the same County of
Hertford, Knight; then to Sir *Thomas Barrington* of Hatfield Broad-
Oak, in the County of Essex, Knight and Baronet; who departed this
Life, upon the first day of *September,* 1657. Aged 65.

In the South Corner of the Chapel.

Here lyeth the body of Sir *William Lytton*, Knight, who dyed the 14*th*
of *August,* 1660. Aged 71. who had issue one Son, and five Daughters.

On another Marble you may read.

Here lyeth the body of *Judith*, the late Wife of *Rowland Lytton*, Esquire,
who departed this Life the 13. day of *May*, 1659. at the Age of 43
years, and left two Sons, *William*, and *Rowland*, and two Daughters
Judith, and *Anne.*

By this Marble lies another, which says,

Here lyes the body of Sir *Rowland Lytton*, Knight: He dyed the first
of *November*, 1674. Aged 59 years, who had issue two Sons and three
Daughters.

A small plain Stone shews,

Here lyes the body of the fifth Son of *Giles Strangeways*, Esquire; which
Son being nursed at Knebworth, dyed at the Age of three weeks, 26. of
April, 1646.

STEVENHAUGHT, STIGENACE, STEVENEDGE.

THIS Mannor and Vill is situated two Miles distant from Knebworth, towards the North; where the Church is erected upon an Hill, from whence, in all Probability, it might in old time be called Stevenhaught; it was Parcel of the Possessions of the Saxon Kings, until such time that *Edward* the Confessor granted it among other things, to the Abbot of Westminster, who held it in the time of King *William* the Conqueror, when it was recorded, under the Title of *Terra Alberti de* Westmonast.

Norden, p 23.

Mon. Angl.
vol. 1, fol. 61,
nu. 55.

Domesd. Lib.
fol 136, nu. 9.

In Bradewatre *Hundred Abbas de* Westmonastr. *tenet* Stigenace, *pro octo hidis se defendebat. Terra est decem car. in dominio quaturr hidæ et ibi sunt duo car ibi sexdecem Vil. cum octo Bord. habentibus septem car. et octava potest fieri, ibi quatuor servi, pastura ad pec. Silva* l *porcis; in totis valent. valet et valuit duodecim lib. tempore Regis* Edwardi, *tres decim libr. Hoc Manerium jacuit et jacet in dominio Ecclesiæ Sancti* Petri.

The Abbot of Westminster held Stigenace, in the Hundred of Bradewater. it was rated for eight Hides. The arrable is ten Carucates, in Demeasne four Hides, and there are two Carucates, there are sixteen Villains, with eight Bordars having seven Carucates, and an eighth may be made, there are four Servants, Common of Pasture for the Cattle, Wood to feed fifty Hogs; in the whole Value it is worth, and was worth, twelve Pounds by the Year, in the time of King *Edward* (the Confessor) thirteen Pounds, this Mannor did ly, and now doth ly, in the Demeasne of the Church of St. *Peter.*

But since most of the Inhabitants of this Vill have removed their Houses from the Church, about half a Mile towards the South, where they have made a fair Street, and inrich themselves by the Advantages of the great Numbers of People and Cattle that daily pass to and fro upon that Road: and by an Inquisition, it was found *Anno* 6 *Edw.* I. that this Mannor was ancient Demesne, that the Abbot held it of the Gift of King *Edward* the Confessor, and claimed here very large Liberties, by the Grant of the said King, and the Grants of *William* the Conqueror, *H.* I. and *R.* I. which upon a *Quo Warranto* were then allowed; and the Abbots thereof did continually enjoy it; until that fatal Year of the general Dissolution of the great Monasteries, when it came to the Crown.

Inq. Rot. 54,
6 Ed. I. cur.
recept. Scac.

Then King *H.* VIII. changed this Monastery into a Bishoprick, about 33 *Regni sui,* and *Thomas Thirlby* was consecrated Bishop thereof, who in short time dilapidating all the Patrimony granted to his See, the Bishoprick was dissolved, and King *Edw.* VI. by Patent dated 4 *Regni sui,* granted the Mannors of Stevenach, Ashwel, Holwel, Cadwel, and Datchworth, in this County; late belonging to the Bishoprick of Westminster, to *Nicholas Ridley,* then Bishop of London, and his Successors, to hold in free, pure, and perpetual Alms, paying yearly one hundred Pounds at the *Hund. of Bradewater* Feast of the Birth of our Lord.

When Queen *Mary* came to the Crown, she removed *Nicholas Ridley* from the Bishoprick of London, vacated the Grant of these Mannors to this Bishoprick, because it was not confirmed by the Pope's Bull, advanced *Edmund Bonner* *Cart. 1 Mar.* to it, obtained a Bull from the Pope, 3 *die Martii, Anno* 1 *Regni sui,* and by Authority thereof, granted these Mannors by a new Grant to the said *Edmund* Bishop of London, and his Successors, Bishops of London for ever; to hold in free, pure, and perpetual Alms, and paying yearly one hundred Pounds, as in the former Grant.

King *Jac.* I. by Patents dated the fifth of *April, An.* 22 *Cart. 22 J. 1.* *Regni sui,* granted to *George Mountain,* then Bishop of London, and to the Inhabitants of this Town, one Market to be held in this Vill, on Monday in every Week of the Year, and also three Fairs to be yearly held, the first on the Feast of the Ascension of our Lord, another on the Feast of St. *Swithen,* and the other on the Friday next before *Palm Sunday;* And this Mannor has continued in the several Bishops of London till it came to *Henry Compton,* the present Bishop of that See, and Brother to the late Earl of Northampton.

King *William* and Queen *Mary,* by their Charter dated at Westminster, 18th of *June,* in the fifth Year of their Reign, granted a Market to the Bishops of London, for the time being, and the Inhabitants of Stevenedge, to be held on Friday in every Week, instead of the former Market held on the Monday, and three Fairs to be held as in the former Charter; this *Henry* Bishop of London, is the present Lord hereof, and it lyes within his Liberty.

The Mannor of BROOKS

WAS doubtless derived from the Mannor of Stevenach, is Parcel of the Revenue of the *Ratcliffs,* and is now come to Sir *Ralph Ratcliff,* who is the present Lord hereof; but I refer his Family to Hitchin, because it is the Place of their Habitation.

The Mannors of CANNIX and FAIRLAND

ARE two other Mannors in this Vill, and in all Probability, were derived from the Mannor of Stevenach, they are Parcel of the Possessions of the *Lyttons,* and have passed in that Name from one to another, as the Mannor of Knebworth did, to Sir *William Lytton* the present Lord of them, and their Succession may be seen in the last Parish.

THIS Rectory *Anno* 26 *Hen.* VIII. was valued in the King's Books at 33*l.* 6*s.* 8*d.* of which *Joseph Bentham,* D. D. is the present Partron.

The Names of the RECTORS.

John Caldecote
Stephen Hellard, B. D. obiit 17
Hen. VII.
Thomas Allen
Robert Paterson
William Prat

Robert Chester, D.D.
Stafford Leventhorp
Richard Shoare
Fulke Tudor, D.D.
Joseph Bentham, D.D. the present Rector.

This Church is dedicated to the Honour of St. *Nicholas*, and is situated upon a dry Hill, in the Deanery of Hitchin. in the Diocess of London; it contains a fair Isle on either Side of the Body of the Church, with a large Chancel, having two fair Chapels, and at the West End a square Tower, wherein hang a Ring of six Bells, on which a large Spire is erected, and covered with Lead; and towards the South Side of the Communion Table, in the Chancel lyes a fair Marble with this Inscription.

In spem Resurrectionis ad vitam æternam, hic jacet Robertus Chester, (*Sacræ Theologiæ Professor,*) *et hujus Ecclesiæ Rector, qui obiit Ætatis suæ,* 67. *Redemptionis* 1664.

> *Siste Viator et Lege.*
> *Lucis Evangelica Jubax Coruscum,*
> *Spectatæ exemplar probitatis clarum,*
> *Filius Ecclesiæ verus Catholicæ,*
> *Doctrinæ Columen, Decusque Vitæ*
> *Nostræ Ætatis honos, lepos voluptas,*
> *Hic Terra Exuvias reliquit, orbi*
> *Famam, Astris animam, Viator ito.*

A Tomb erected on the South Corner of the Chancel.

Hic jacet Gulielmus Prat *Sacræ Theologiæ Baccalaureus et hujus Ecclesiæ per annos triginta prudentissimus Rector, tres habuit Filios* Johannem, Gulielmum, *et* Richardum, *totidemque Filias* Saram, Mariam, *et* Elizabetham, *ex charissima conjuge* Elizabetha; *tandem studio hujus vitæ decurso atque ætate jam ingravescente in cœlestem Patriam emigravit, anno salutis,* 1629. *Ætatis* 67.

> *Monumentum hoc amoris simul et Mæroris*
> *Perpetuum testem posuit delectissima Conjux*
> Elizabetha, *quæ juxta placidè in Christo obdormiscit.*

In the Body of the Chancel, is the Effigies of a Priest in Brass, at whose Feet is this Inscription.

Hic jacet Magister Stephanis Hilliard, Ebor. Diocesis.——Baccalaureus, quondam Rector hujus Ecclesiæ ac quam Canonicus Cathedralis,—— qui obiit——die mensis——An. milesimo, quingentesimo.——

CHARITIES.

Stephen Hellard, Rector of this Church, by Deed dated 20 *November,* 17 *Hen.* VII. gave to Sir *William Day*, Knight, *Edward Bensted,* Esquire, *Thomas Ginne, John Huckle, John Huckle* the Son, *Richard Borowel, George Newman,* alias *Wheeler, John Matthew, Richard Austyn, John Hunt, William Fletcher, Thomas Hide, John Graveley,* and *Edmond Carter,* one Croft called Glebiscroft, containing seven Acres, and one Pightle of Meadow, lying at the End of the said Croft, and the Pightle lying by Stanmer then newly built, now called *All Christian Soul House.* and a small Piece of Land lying in Churchfield, and two Pence of yearly Rent, issuing out of two Acres of Land, one lying in Kebwel-field, and the other in Sirburrough-field, to the Use of his Will; and by his Will dated the 20th of *December,* 1501, 17 *Hen.* VII. devised a Messuage with the Appurtenances newly built, lying in a Lane called Bede Lane, nigh unto Stanmer in the Parish of Stevenage, as it appears more evidently by the Feoffment made concerning the same, which Messuage he called *All Christian Soul House,* and built for the Habitation of three poor Folk without payment of any Rent, for so long as the House shall endure; and moreover willed that every one that dwelleth in it, shall say daily in the Name of the Holy Trinity; *O Thou Blessed Trinity, Father, Son, and Holy Ghost have Mercy and pity upon the Soul of Master* Stephen Hellard, *and upon all Christian Souls*, with three *Pater Nosters*, three *Ave Marins*, and one Creed; also when one of the said Houses happened to be empty, he farther willed that the Feoffees or greater number of them should provide another poor Man or Woman within four Months, and if the Feoffees shall be equal in their Votes on both Sides, then he also willed that the Rector of the Parish Church of Stebenage for the time being, should give his Voice according to his Mind on either of the Sides.

Nicholas Clerk, Gent. by Deed dated 27 *July*, 17 *Car.* II. in Consideration of 63l. sold to *Stafford Leventhorpe*, Clerk, *George Banister*, Sen. *George Banister*, Jun. *Edmond Nodes*, *Jenings Chapman*, *John Hitchin*, Sen. *John Hitchin*, Jun. *Richard Hitchin*, *Robert Heath*, Sen. *Robert Heath*, Jun. *William Heath*, *John Gynn*, *John Trigge*, Jun. and *Thomas Greene*, two Pieces of Land and Inclosure in Stebenage, one called Stonny Croft, the other Long Stockin, containing in the whole six Acres, upon Trust, that the Profits of the Premises should be employed to the Use of the most aged, impotent, and poor People, for the time being, resident in the Almshouse of Stebenage; but who gave the Consideration Money I cannot learn.

Robert Ginne, by his Will dated 1 *Jac.* I. charg'd his Dwelling-house, Lands, and Tenements with the payment of ten Bushels of Mislyne for the Relief of the poor People of the Town of Stebenage, to be yearly distributed by the Churchwardens, and six of the most substantial Inhabitants of the Town, at the Feast of Easter, or within three Days after, and in default of Payment, the Parson and Churchwardens of the Town shall enter and hold the Premises until the same shall be paid. He also gave 30s. a Year to the Parson and Churchwardens, and their Successors, to be paid out of a Messuage called the Maidenhead, for the relief of the poor Inhabitants of Stebenage, with a Clause of entry. He gave the Messuage called the Maidenhead, and all the Lands and Tenements belonging to it, unto *Richard Ginne* and his Heirs, upon Condition that he should pay to the Parson and Churchwardens of Stebenage for the time being, the Sum of 30s. a Year at the Feast of St. *Michael*, or within four Days after; the one half to be bestowed in Cloth of 12d. the Yard, for the Cloathing of poor Fatherless Children, or others most needful, the other half in Money. He also gave to *Thomas Clarke* one Tenement or Messuage situated in Stebenage, the Orchards, Lands and Tenements belonging to it, to the Heirs of his Body, with the Remainders over, upon Condition that *Thomas Clarke* shall yearly pay to the Parson and Churchwardens of Stebenage at St. *Michael*, or within four Days after, the Sum of 20s. for the Use of the poor People of Stebenage, to be distributed as aforesaid, with a Clause of entry.

George Clarke, by his Will dated the 8th of *Octo.* 3 and 4 *P.* and *M.* gave all his Tyth Corn, called Borberry Tyth, to his Son *William* in tail, upon Condition that he should pay 6l. a Year, whereof 20s. to the Poor of Sanderidge by the oversight of the Vicar, Churchwardens, and two or three of the Honest Men of that Parish, at Christmas, for ever more; and 50s. to the Poor of this Parish to be paid in the same manner, whereof 25s. in ready Money, and the other 25s. in Cloath towards the Cloathing of the poor People of this Parish, and also shall pay at Christmas unto the poor People of Bennington, the other 50s. in such manner as is appointed to the Poor of this Parish.

Thomas Chapman, Clerk, by his Will dated the 8th of *March*, 19 *Car.* II. gave and devised his Messuage or Tenement in Stebenage, and divers Lands and Tenements to *Peter Langthorne* the elder, and *Elizabeth* his Wife for ten Years, the Remainder to *Peter Langthorne* the Son in tail, with Remainders over, upon Trust that the said Messuage, Lands and Premises shall be subject to the Payment of eight Pounds a Year for ever, to buy Cloath and Bread to be distributed yearly for ever upon St. *Andrews* Day, or the Sunday following, at the Discretion of the Minister and Churchwardens, and two or three of the best Men and Inhabitants of the several Towns and Parishes of Stebenage, Ashwell, Pauls Walden, and Norton in this County, to such Persons of their several Parishes that are impotent and poor, and debilitated by their Labour, or truly necessitous by reason of Sickness, or Charge of Children, and no ways licentious or guilty of any Lewdness or Debauchery, but such as duly and constantly frequent their several Parish Churches on every Sunday, or other Days

Hund. of
Bradewater
appointed for Divine Service and Worship, and behave themselves decently and reverently all the time of Divine Service, *viz.* to such Poor in this Parish twenty Yards of Yard-wide Cloath, at **2s.** the Yard, and twenty dozen of good Wheat Bread; also the like to such poor People in the Parish of **Ashwell**; and also seven Yards of Yard-wide Cloath, at **2s.** the Yard, and six dozen of good sweet Bread to such poor People in the Parish of **St. Pauls Walden**: and also seven Yards of Yard-wide Cloath of 2*s.* the Yard, and six dozen of good sweet Bread to such poor People in the Parish of **Norton**, with a Clause of Distress.

Richard Shoare, Clerk, Rector of **Stevenage**, *George Nodes* and *Thomas Harvy*, Churchwardens of **Stevenage**. *Robert Balman*, Clerk, Vicar of **Ware**. *Robert Collup* and *John Bones*, Churchwardens of **Ware**, were impowered by a Decree to make a Lease dated 17th of *April*, 30 Car. II. to *William Cross* of all that Messuage or Tenement with the Appurtenances in **Ware**, called the **Black Swan**, for 21 Years, under the yearly Rent of 4*l.* payable to the Minister and Churchwardens of **Stevenage** and their Successors, at Michaelmas and Lady Day; and also under the yearly Rent of other 4*l.* payable to the Minister and Churchwardens of **Ware** and their Successors at Michaelmas and Lady Day by equal Portions.

The Foundation of the FREE-SCHOOL of **Stevenage**.

THOMAS Allen, Clerk, by his Will dated 24 *May*, 4 and 5 P. and M. devised all his Mannors, Messuages, Lands, Tenements and Hereditaments in the Counties of **Leicester**, **Kent**, and **Hertford**, and the City of **London**. to the Masters, Fellows, and Scholars of *Trinity Colledge* in **Cambridge**. upon several Trusts, and in particular to found three Free Grammar Schools, one at **Uttoxeter** in the County of **Stafford**, the second at **Stone** in the said County, and the third at this Town, and to pay to each of them 13*l.* 6*s.* 8*d.* per *Ann.* and also gave to four poor Men of the Town of **Stevenage** four Nobles per *Ann.* a piece.

Edward Wiltsheir, by his Deed dated 3. *Martii*, 4 *Eliz.* sold to Sir *John Boteler*, Kt. *Thomas Barrington*, Esq. *Rowland Sytton*, Esq. *John Brocket*, Esq. *Nicholas Bristow*, Esq. *Thomas Hanchet*, Esq. *Philip Boteler*, Esq. *Edward Pelitot*, Gent. *John Needham*, Gent. *Thomas Gravely*, Gent. *Nicholas Bristow* the younger, Gent. *John Batty*, Clerk, *Thomas Snagge*, *Edward Wilson* the elder, *Edward Wilson* the younger, *John Kent*, *William Clarke*, *Henry Elliot*, *John Barshawe*, Gent. *William Nodes*, Gent. *Edward Nodes*, *John Clarke*, *Thomas Clarke*, *Robert Norris* the elder, *Robert Norris* the younger, *Henry Gyn*, the elder, *Robert Gyn*, *Robert Andrew*, *John Clarke* the Son of *Thomas Clarke*, *Edward Clarke*, and *John Clarke*, the Son of *John Clarke*, and their Heirs, one Messuage or Tenement, with the Appurtenances, called the *Brotherhood House*, situated in **Stevenage**. and four Acres of Land lying in **Church Field** one Acre in **Berybachelors**, one Acre in **Bedwell Field**, one Acre in **Westal Field**, also one other Messuage or Tenement, with the Appurtenances in **Stevenage**, situated by **Berry Mead**, and one Close of Pasture containing one Acre and an half, also one Grove of Wood in **Stevenage** called the **Brotherhood Grove**, containing two Acres, to the Intent that the Premises should be employed to the Use of the School in **Stevenage** for ever; and for default of such School, then to the Use of the poor People of the Town for ever.

Edmond Nodes by Will dated 20 *Julii* 38 *Eliz.* devised one Close called **Berrymead**, with one Acre of Land, to the Use of the Free School for ever.

Robert Ginne by Will dated 1 *Jan.* 1 *Jac.* gave to the said School three Roods of arrable Land in **Church Field**.

Edward Woodward, Esq. by his Will dated 10 *Martii*, 1659, gave unto *Robert Bromhall*, Gent. Son of Sir *John Bromhall*, late of **Grapes-Inn-Lane** deceased, and his Heirs for ever, all his Messuages, Cottages, Farmes, Lands, and Tenements both Copy and Free, in the Parishes of **Great Wimondly**, **Little Wimondly**, and **Ippolits** charging the same with a Rent Charge of 12*l.* per *Ann.* payable at the Feast of St. *Michael* the Arch-Angel, the Birth of our Lord God, the Annunciation of the Blessed Virgin, and the Nativity of St. *John* Baptist, by even and equal Portions, to be distributed to the said Schools with a Clause of Distress.

It was decreed in Chancery 24 *Car.* II. in a Cause depending between *Owen Davis,* Clerk, Complainant, and the Master, Fellows, and Scholars of *Trinity Colledge* in **Cambridge,** and other Trustees, Defendants, that the Complainant and his Successors, and their Ushers should, from time to time, instruct the Petites belonging to the School, as well as the Grammar Scholars, according to the original Deeds of Purchase of the Lands and School House, and that the said Petites should have the like Priviledge of the Grammar Scholars, and be advanced to the Places in the School as their Learning should make them capable of.

Hund. of **Bradewater**

WIMUNDESLEY PARVA.

SOMEWHAT above a Mile distant from **Stebenage** towards the North West, this Vill lies in a Bottom; Of which 'tis recorded in *Domesdei Book,* under the Title of *Terra Episc. Bajocensis.*

In **Bradewatre** *Hundred. in* **Wimundesley***, tenet* Adam *de Episc.* **Bajocensis. un. hid. et un. virgat.** *Terra est un. car. et ibi est cum tribus bordis, pratum dimid. car. valet et valuit decem sol. tempore Regis* Edward *vigint sol. hanc terram tenuit* Alflet *de* Roberto *Wimare, non poterat vendere præter ejus licentiam, ut Scira testatur.*

Domesd. Lib. fol 134, n. 5

Adam held one Hide and one Virgate of the Bishop of **Bayeux** in **Wimundesley,** in the Hundred of **Bradewater.** The arrable is one Carucate, and it is now with three Bordars, Meadow half a Carucate, it is worth and was worth ten Shillings a Year, in the time of King *Edward* (the Confessor) twenty Shillings; *Alflet* held this Land without *Robert Wimare,* he could not sell it without his Licence, as the Shire can witness.

Terra Roberti de Gernon.

In **Wimundelai***, tenet* Willielmus *de* Roberto *Gernon un. hid. Terra est un. car. sed ibi non est; un. Cotar. ibi est pratum dimid. car. valet sex sol. quando recepit decem sol. tempore Regis* Edwardi *quindecim sol, hanc terram tenuit* Alflet *sub* Roberto *Wimarch die qua Rex* Edwardus *fuit vivus et mortuus, non potuit vendere præter ejus Licentiam.*

Ibid. fol 137, nu. 20.

William held of *Robert Gernon* one Hide in **Wimundeley.** The arrable is one Carucate, but now it is not there; there is one Cottager, Meadow half a Carucate; it is worth six Shillings a Year, when he received it ten Shillings a Year, in the time of King *Edward* (the Confessor) fifteen Shillings a Year, *Alflet* held this Land under *Robert de Wimarch* on the Day in which King *Edward* (the Confessor) was alive and dead, he could not sell it without his Licence.

Shortly after these Parcels were united in the Possession of *Fitzteck,* a great *Norman,* from whom they passed (as is set forth at large in the next Vill) to *Richard Argenton,* who was Lord of both Vills, and in the time of *H.* III. founded a Priory here of Cannons Regular, to be govern'd after the Order of St. *Benedict,* which they held until the time of the Suppression thereof, when it was valued to be yearly worth 37*l.* 10*s.* 6*d. ob.* but in the *Monasticon* at no more than 29*l.* 19*s.* 8*d. ob.*

Weav. Fun. *Acts & Mon.* fol. 546.

Monast. vol.1, fol. 1041.

When this Priory came to the Crown by the Dissolution, King *H.* VIII. by Deed dated 10 *Decem. Anno* 29 *Regni sui,* devised to *James Needham,* Gent. Clerk and Surveyor of the King's Works, all the Lordship and Scite, late of the Priory and Monastery of **Wymondlee,** in the County of **Hertford,** suppressed by Authority of Parliament, with all Lands, Meadows, and Pastures belonging to the Monastery and the Rectory of the Parish Church of **Wimondlee Parva,**

Cart. 29 H. VIII. penes Georgi. Needham.

and all Tythes, Oblations, Profits, Obventions, and Commodities whatsoever belonging to the Rectory, for the Term of one and twenty Years, to commence from the Feast of St. *Michael,* then last past, reserving to the King, his Heirs, and Successors, the yearly Rent of 13*l.* 7*s.* And the King did farther grant, as well the Stipend and Wages of a Chaplain to celebrate yearly divine Service, and to take the Care of the Church of 𝕬𝕡𝕞𝕠𝕟𝕕𝕝𝕖𝕖, as also all Rents, Fees, Annuities, Pensions, Portions, and Sums of Money issuing out of the Premisses, except the Rents above reserved.

This *James* was the Son of *Christopher Needham,* who was the Son of *John,* who was commonly called Black *John Needham* of 𝕹𝕖𝕖𝕕𝕙𝕒𝕞-𝕘𝕣𝕒𝕟𝕘𝕖 in the County of 𝕯𝕖𝕣𝕓𝕪, for that he was a very black Man: his Children have inherited the same Complexion, and hold it to this very Day; and for his Arms he bore *Argent, on a Bend ingreyl'd Azure, between two Buck's Heads cabosh'd Sable,* (to distinguish his Line) *an Escallop Gold; and for his Crest or Ornament of the Helme, a Buck's Head Sable attir'd Gold issuing out of a Crown or Garland.* 𝕭𝕒𝕝𝕝𝕪𝕤 Gold, anciently in the flourishing Estate of the Roman Commonwealth, was wont to be as a military Reward, bestowed on such as had valiantly enter'd into the Trench or Bulwork of the Enemy.

King *Henry* sent this *James* to 𝕭𝕦𝕝𝕝𝕠𝕚𝕘𝕟𝕖 in 𝕱𝕣𝕒𝕟𝕔𝕖, where he died in the Month of *Sept. Anno* 36 *H.*VIII. and left

John his Son and Heir, who obtained a Patent of this Mannor and Rectory from King *Henry,* to the Use of himself and his Heirs; then convey'd it to the Use of himself for Life, the Remainder to the Use of his Son *George* and his Heirs, and in the Month of *July, Anno* 34 *Eliz.* he dyed and was buried in this Chancel, where his Tomb remaineth.

George succeeded, and was possest hereof till the Month of *June, Anno* 1626, when he died at this Mannor-house, leaving Issue

Eustace, who was his Son and Heir, lived here until the Month of *May, Anno* 1658, then died and was buried in this Church.

George, who was his Heir, enjoy'd it, much improv'd it during the time he was possest thereof, and died in *July,* 1669, leaving Issue *George* his Son and Heir, and the present Possessor hereof.

This Priory has been a fair old Building with Cloysters; there was a Chappel in it consecrated since the Dissolution, almost surrounded with a Mote, is scituated upon the Side of a small Hill, incompassed with near 400 Acres of rich meadow, pasture, and arrable Land inclosed to it, with a very fair Orchard and Garden, yeilding the best Sort of Fruit. The House is supply'd from a Conduit, with sufficient Water to turn the Spit in the Kitchen upon all Occasions.

This Priory was dedicated to the blessed St. *Mary.*

The Church is a DONATIVE.

THE Proprietors hereof have continually provided Priests, and Curates, to serve the Cure at their Pleasure; it is situated in the Deanery of Hitchin, in the Diocess of Lincolne, covered with Lead, hath a square Tower at the West End, wherein hang four Bells, and in the Wall on the North Side of the upper End of the Chancel, is a Monument which has this Inscription.

James Needham, of the ancient Family of the *Needhams* in Derbyshire, came into this County of Hertford, in the Year of our Lord, 1536. He was advanced by King *Henry* the eighth, for his Services in England and France, and lyes buried in our Ladies Church in Boloigne; he had issue *John*, who had *George*, who dedicated this Monument to their Memory, *Anno* 1605.

Satius est mortis quam Natalis dies.

On the North Side lies a Stone which has this Inscription.

In hopes of the Resurrection to Eternal Life, here are laid up the remains of *George Needham*, Esquire; who dyed *June* 30th. *Anno Domini*, 1669. *Ætatis suæ* 51. His only Wife he left behind, *Barbara*, the Daughter of Sir *William Fitch* of Woodhamwater, in the County of Essex, Knight; and by her seven Children, *George*, *Barbara*, *Anne*, *Elizabeth*, *Fitch*, *James*, and *Morrice;* to whose Memory this is dedicated, by *George* his Son.

WIMUNDESLEY MAGNA.

THIS Vill borrowed its Name from some ancient Proprietor; in the time of King *Edward* the Confessor, Earl *Harold* held it, and after his Death, *William* the Conqueror seized it into his Hands, and was possest hereof at the time the general Survey was made, for it is there recorded under the Title of *Terra Regis.*

In Bradewatr Hundred. Willelmus *Rex*, tenet Wimundeslai. *pro octo hidis se defendebat. Terra est* xviii *cur. in Dominio duæ hidæ, et dimid. et ibi sunt tres car. et* xxiv *Vil. et unus Sochmannus, et quinque bord. et quinque cotar. habentes quindecim car. ibi sex Servi et un. Molin. de vigint. sol. pratum un. cur. et duo bobus, pastura ad pecud. Vil. nemus ad sepes. Hoc Manerium fuit in Dominio Ecclesiæ Sanctæ Mariæ de Cetri. sed Heraldus Comes adstulit inde ut tota Scira testatur, et apposuit in hij Manerio suo tribus annis ante mortem Regis Edwardi.*

Domesd. Lib. fol. 133, nu. 1.

Goisbertus de Balvaco tenet Wimundeslai pro tribus hidis, et un. virgat. se defendebat. Terra est quatuor car. in Dominio duo hid. et duo virgat. et dimid. et ibi sunt duo car. et tertia potest fieri, ibi quatuor Vil. cum tribus Bord. habentibus un. car. ibi quatuor cotar. et duo Servi pratum un. car. pastura ad pec. Silva decem porc. in totis valentiis, valet lx *solidis, quando recepit vigint. sol. tempore Regis* Edwardi lx *sol. Hoc Manerium tenuit Suuen homo Com Heraldi, et vendere potuit.*

Ibid. fol. 141, nu. 35.

King *William* held Wimondley in the Hundred of Broadwater, it was rated for eight Hides, the arrable is eighteen Carucates, in Demeasne two Hides and an half, and there are three Carucates and four and twenty Villains, and one Socman, and five Bordars, and five Cottagers having fifteen Carucates, there are six Servants and one Mill of twenty Shillings Rent, Meadow one Carucate, and two Oxgangs, Common of Pasture for the Cattle of the Vill, Wood for Hedges; this Mannor was in the Demeasne of the Church of St. *Mary* of Chaterir. but Earl *Harold* took it from thence, as all the Shire can witness, and laid it to his Mannor in Hij about three Years before the death of King *Edward* (the Confessor.)

Goisbert de Belvace held Wimundesley, it was rated for three Hides and one Virgate. The arrable is four Carucates, in Demeasne two Hides, and two Virgates and an half, and there are two Carucates and a

Hund. of
Brabewater
third may be made, there are four Villains, with three Bordars, having one Carucate, there are four Cottagers and two Servants, Meadow one Carucate, Common of Pasture for the Cattle, Wood to feed ten Hogs; in the whole Value it is worth sixty Shillings a Year, when be received it twenty Shillings a Year, in the time of King *Edward* (the Confessor,) sixty Shillings a Year, *Swen* a Man (under the Protection) of Earl *Harold,* held this Mannor and might sell it.

Camd. *Brit.*
tit. Herts.
fol 406.
Afterwards the King granted it to *Fitzteck,* a noble *Norman,* to hold of him by the honourable Tenure of Grand Serjeanty, that the Lords thereof should serve the Kings of **England** upon their Coronation-day with his first Cup in the Nature of his Cup-bearer, which honourable Service, certain noble Gentlemen of that Family held, until the Reign of King *H.* II. when this Name expired, and this Mannor came to

Ibid.

Reginald de Argenton, who derived his Name and Pedigree from *David de Argenton,* a *Norman* and a martial Knight, who served under King *William* the Conquerour, in the Wars, and in Remembrance of this Service, they gave for their Arms, *three Cups Argent in a Shield:* This *Reginald* demanded against the Abbess of **Elnestowe,** the Advowson of **Wimondesley,** as his Right, which belong'd to his Inheritance held in Serjeanty of the King; and *Simon de Guy,* Attorney to the Abbess, came and defended her Right, and said that *Judith* the Countess, Niece to King *William* the Conqueror, who founded the Abbey of **Alnestowe,** gave to the Church of **Alnestow** the Vill of **Hitch,** with the Church of the same Vill, and the Chappel of **Wimondesley,** which belonged to the Church of **Hitch,** by her Deed which he produced; and it was attested that she gave it in free and perpetual Alms, in which Deed the Grant and Confirmation of King *William* the Conquerour, with the Consent of King *William* his Son, was contained: He produced also the Confirmation of King *Henry* thereupon, the Confirmation of King *Henry* Father of the King, the Writings of the Bishop, who were Officials in that Diocess, the Evidence of the Archbishop, who attested that the Church of **Wimondley** was appurtenant to the Church of **Hiche,** the Evidence of the Bishop who dedicated that Church, and the Testimony of the Legate *Reginald,* said that the Church of **Wimondley** was never purtinat to the Church of **Hiche,** and that King *William* never held **Wimondley** in his Demesne, but in his time held that Land which *Alfled* had, and did present the Parson to that Church, and after her the King gave **Wimondley** as an Escheat to *Reginald* his Grandfather in Serjeanty, and thereupon he presented two Parsons to that Church, whereof the last was named *Osbert,* and upon this he brought his Suit, &c. and because the Prioress had not Entry, she put herself upon the Country, and Day was given.

Plita 7 R. I.
Rot. 22, cur.
recept. Scac.

This *Reginald* was constituted Sheriff of the Counties of Cambridge and Huntingdon, *Anno* 6 & 7 of *R.* I. but adhereing to the rebellious Barons, *Anno* 17 *Johannis* had Letters of safe Conduct to come to the King, to treat of Peace for them, wherein he effecting nothing at that time, but making his own Composition, Command was given to the Sheriff of Cambridgeshire to give him Possession of all his Land in the same County, which had been seized for that Rebellion: After his Decease

Richard de Argenton succeeded, was constituted Sheriff for the Counties of Essex and Hertford, 8 *H.* III. also Governour of the Castle of Hertford, and one of the Stewards of the King's Houshold *Anno* 11 *Edw.* III. He founded a Priory for Canons Regular, went on Pilgrimage to the Holy Land, 14 *Hen.* III. and dyed *Anno* 1246, 30 *Hen.* III. leaving Issue

Giles his Son and Heir, a Knight of great Valour, who was with the King in his Expedition made into Wales, 16 *H.* III. where he was taken Prisoner with some others in a sharp Fight with the *Welch* near Montgomery; afterwards he assisted the rebellious Barons, who took the King Prisoner in that fatal Battel of Lewis, and was elected one of those nine Counsellours who govern'd the Realm, but after the Battel of Eversham, where the Strength of those Rebels was totally vanquisht, the Lands of him, and *Reginald* his Son then with him in that Insurrection, were extended; afterwards he dyed 11 *Edw.* I. seized of this Mannor by Grand Serjeanty, to serve the King upon the Day of his Coronation with a silver Cup, leaving

Reginald Argenton his Son and Heir, at that time forty Years of Age; he did his Homage soon after his Father's Death, had Livery of all his Lands in the Counties of Cambridge, Norfolke, Suffolke, and Hertford; and having been summon'd to Parliament *Anno* 25 *Edw.* I. dyed 1 *Edw.* II. leaving

John his Son and Heir, who did his Homage, had Livery of his Land, and by *Joan* his first Wife, had Issue three Daughters, *Joan, Elizabeth,* and *Dionise,* who were Heirs to their Mother; and by *Anne* his second Wife, one Son named *John:* And dying 12th of *Edw.* II.

John was his Heir, aged six Months at the Death of his Father: this Mannor continued in this Family till the time of *Hen.* VI.

When the Name expired for Want of Issue Male; *Elizabeth Argenton,* one of the Daughters and Coheirs, but at length the entire Heretrix of her other Sister, brought this Mannor, with divers other fair Possessions, to Sir *William Alington,* Kt. whom she espoused, whose Pedigree I think proper to set forth in this Place.

VOL. II.   H

Margin notes:

Hund. of Bradewater

Rot. Pip. de iisdem annis, tit. Cambr. et Hunt. *Pat.* 17 Johan.

Rot. Pip. tit. Essex & Herts. de iisdem, an 8 H. III.

Matt. Paris, 353, 369, 718.

Rot. Vasc. 16 H. III.

Esc 11 Ed. I. Cantabr.

Rot. Fin. 11 Ed. III. n. 25.

Claus. 1 Ed. II.

Rot. Fin. 1 Ed. II.

Claus. 12 Ed. II.
Bar. vol. 2, fol. 615.

Heldebrand, who married the Daughter and Heir of *John Columbarius,* by whom he had *Alan de Alington,* who married *Maud* the Daughter of Sir *Giles Brockhil,* Kt.

Hugh, the Son of *Alan,*

Solomon de Alington,

Ralph Alington,

Herbert Alington,

Hugh de Alington,

Thomas de Alington,

William de Alington of 𝔅otesham, married *Dionise* the Daughter of *William Malet* of 𝔥orseheath, in the County of Cambridge, *Anno* 2 *H.* V.

William Alington de 𝔅otesham, in the County of Canterbury, married *Joan* the Daughter and Heir of *William Burglie.*

Sir *William Alington,* Kt. married *Elizabeth,* the Daughter and Coheir of Sir *John Argentine,* in whose Right he became possest of this Mannor.

John Alington married *Mary* Daughter of *Lawrence Cheiny* of 𝔉enditton in the County of Canterbury; and died in the time of *Edw.* IV.

Sir *William Alington* married *Elizabeth,* Daughter of *Henry Wentworth,* and after her Decease, 2 the Daughter of *Ralph Sapcoats.* He lived in the time of *Edw.* IV. and *R.* III. and left Issue by his first Wife.

Sir *Giles Alington,* Kt. who married the Daughter and Heir of *Richard Gardiner,* Lord Mayor of London.

Sir *Giles Alington,* Kt. married *Alice,* Sister and Heir of *Thomas Middleton,* and after her Decease, *Ursula,* Daughter of *Robert Drury* of 𝔥ansted in Suffolke, he had Issue by *Alice, Richard Alington,* Master of the Rolls, and others.

Robert Alington of 𝔥orseheath married *Margaret* the Daughter of *William Conisby* of 𝔑orfolke; one of the Justices of the *King's Bench,* but he dyed in the Life-time of his Father.

Giles Alington succeeded his Grandfather, and married *Margaret,* the Daughter of Sir *John Spencer,* by whom he had Issue

Giles Alington, who was knighted, and married *Dorothy* the Daughter of *Thomas* Earl of Exeter, from whom issued

William Alington, who was created Baron *Alington* of 𝔎illard, by Letters Patents, dated *Anno* 1642; he married

Elizabeth the Daughter of Sir *Lionel Talmach* of 𝔥𝔢𝔩𝔪𝔦𝔫𝔤- *Hund. of* 𝔅𝔯𝔞𝔟𝔢𝔴𝔞𝔱𝔢𝔯
𝔥𝔞𝔪 in the County of 𝔖𝔲𝔣𝔣𝔬𝔩𝔨𝔢, Baronet; by whom he had
Issue *Giles, William, Hildebrand, Argentine,* and three
Daughters, *Elizabeth* married to *Charles* Lord *Seymour* of
𝔗𝔯𝔬𝔴𝔟𝔯𝔦𝔡𝔤𝔢, *Katharine* to Sir *John Jacob,* Baronet, and
Diana who died single.

Giles Alington, Baron of 𝔎𝔦𝔩𝔩𝔞𝔯𝔡, dyed without Issue

William Alington was his Brother and Heir, succeeded
him in the Honour of 𝔎𝔦𝔩𝔩𝔞𝔯𝔡, and this Mannor, afterwards
was created Baron *Alington* of 𝔚𝔦𝔪𝔬𝔫𝔡𝔩𝔢𝔶, by Letters Patents, dated the 5th of *December,* 1682, *Anno* 35 *Car.* II.
He married *Katharine,* the Sister of *Philip* Earl of 𝔆𝔥𝔢𝔰-
𝔱𝔢𝔯𝔣𝔦𝔢𝔩𝔡, and after her Decease, *Julian* Daughter of *Baptist
Noel* Viscount 𝔆𝔞𝔪𝔟𝔡𝔢𝔫, and after her Decease, *Diana,*
Daughter of *John* Earl of 𝔅𝔢𝔡𝔣𝔬𝔯𝔡, and the Relict of Sir
Grevil Verney of 𝔆𝔬𝔪𝔭𝔱𝔬𝔫 in the County of 𝔚𝔞𝔯𝔴𝔦𝔠𝔨, Kt.
He had Issue by *Julian* his second Wife, *William* who dyed
in his Infancy, and *Julian;* and by *Diana* his last Wife, he
had *Hildebrand,* who died in his Minority, *Diana* and *Katharine,* who dyed unmarried 1693, and *Giles* Baron *Alington* of 𝔎𝔦𝔩𝔩𝔞𝔯𝔡 and 𝔚𝔦𝔪𝔬𝔫𝔡𝔩𝔢𝔶, who dyed 1691, upon whose
Death the Barony of 𝔚𝔦𝔪𝔬𝔫𝔡𝔩𝔢𝔶 expired through Want
of Heir male of the Body of the last *William* Lord *Alington,* but the Barony of 𝔎𝔦𝔩𝔩𝔞𝔯𝔡 descended to

Hildebrand Lord *Alington,* as the third Son and Heir of
William Lord *Alington* his Father, succeeded him in this
Irish Honour; but upon a Sute in *Chancery,* this Mannor
was sold upon a Decree past there to

Elizabeth Hambleton, the Widow and Relict of *James
Hambleton,* Esq. who commanded a Regiment of Foot, in
the time of King *Charles* II. in the Navy against the *Dutch,*
where he was shot in the Leg, upon which Wound he dyed.
She was one of the Daughters of Sir *John Colepeper,* a Per-
son of great Ability, and perfectly loyal to his Prince; He
was constituted Chancellour of the Exchequer, afterwards
Master of the Rolls, and sworn of the Privy Councel, to
King *Charles* I. on whose Behalf he couragiously ventured
his Life in the Battles of 𝔎𝔦𝔫𝔢𝔱𝔬𝔫, 𝔑𝔢𝔴𝔟𝔢𝔯𝔶, and divers other
sharp Encounters; for which Service he was advanced to the
Dignity of a Baron, by the Title of Baron *Colepeper* of
𝔗𝔥𝔬𝔯𝔢𝔰𝔴𝔞𝔭 in the County of 𝔏𝔦𝔫𝔠𝔬𝔩𝔫𝔢, by Patent dated at
𝔒𝔵𝔣𝔬𝔯𝔡, 21st of *October,* 1644, 20th of the same King. She
had Issue by her Husband, *James* married to *Elizabeth* the
Daughter of Sir *Robert Redding,* and *Jane* his Wife, Coun-
tess of 𝔐𝔬𝔫𝔱𝔯𝔬𝔱𝔥 in 𝔍𝔯𝔢𝔩𝔞𝔫𝔡; *George,* who commanded a
Regiment of Foot in the Service of King *William* and
Queen *Mary* in 𝔉𝔩𝔞𝔫𝔡𝔢𝔯𝔰, where he was slain in the Year
1694, and *William Hambleton:* and she is the present Lady
hereof.

H 2

Hund. of
Bradewater

THE Rectory and Vicaridge of **Wimondley** is appropriated to the perpetual Use of the Masters, Fellows, and Scholars of *Trinity Colledge* in **Cambridge**; and the Vicaridge, *Anno* 26 *H.* VIII. was valued in the King's Books at 6*l. per Ann.* whereof the Masters, Fellows, and Scholars of *Trinity Colledge*, are Patrons.

The VICAR, Mr. Ford.

This Church is erected upon low Ground in the middle of the Vill, in the Deanery of **Hitchin**, in the Diocess of **Lincolne**; the Body is covered with Lead, to which a square Tower is annexed at the West End, wherein are four small Bells, without any Spire upon it, or other Remark in the Church.

In this Vill there is a Water-mill upon the **Pirre**, from thence called **Pirral-mill**, which in the time of *William* the Conqueror, was yearly rented at twenty Shillings, as appears by *Domesdei.* Mills were of great Antiquity, for I find it recorded among the ancient Laws, that if any Man shall violently break a Water-mill, he shall be bound to repair it within thirty Dayes, and moreover to pay thirty Shillings for the Tresspass; and a little after follows, We command the same of Water-poles, which serve such Mills, and that the Water-dams shall be kept and preserved.

Spelm Gloss.
fol 416, tit.
molinum or
molendinum.

GRAVELEY, cum CHIVESFIELD.

WHEN that memorable Record of *Domesdei* was made, *William* Earl of **Ewe**, Son of *Robert de Auco*, one of the Chief Counsellours to *William* Duke of **Normandy**, before his Conquest of **England**, was possest of this Mannor of **Graveley**, for 'tis there recorded, under the Title of *Terra Willielmi de Ow.*

Domesd. Lib.
fol. 138, n. 18.

Willielmus de **Ow**, *et* Petrus *de eo ten. in* **Grabelai**, *un. virgat et dimid. Terra est dimid. car. sed non est, ibi sunt duo Vil. valet hæc terra tres sol. quando recepit quatuor sol. et consuetud. tempore Regis Edwardi, de hac terra ten.* Alesten *de* **Boscumbe**, *un. virgat. et jacebat in* **Weston**, *et* Lepsi *dimid. virgat. Sochmannus Regis Edwardi vendere poterat, et de consuetud. unum obulum Vicecom. reddebat, et de hac dimid. h. jacebant octo acræ, et una Tofta in* **Stigenace**, *quam Rex* Edwardus *dedit Sancto* Petro *de* **Weston**. *et modo ten.* Rogerus *Minister* Petri Valoinensis.

William de **Ow**, and *Peter* held of him one Virgate and an half in **Graveley**. The arrable is half a Carucate but there is not so much, there are two Villains, this Land is worth three Shillings a Year, and when he received it four Shillings a Year, and Rent in the time of King *Edward* (the Confessor,) *Alestan* of **Boscumbe**, held one Virgate of this Land, and it did lye in **Weston**, and *Lepsus* a Sochman of King *Edward* (the Confessor) half a Virgate he might sell it, and he paid an half Penny by the Year, to the Sheriff for Rent, and these eight Acres of this Moiety and one Toft did lye in **Stevenage**, which King *Edward* (the Confessor) gave to Saint *Peter* of **Westminster**, and now *Roger* a Minister of *Peter de Valongies* held it.

Norden, p.17.

Mr. *Norden* holds that this Vill was called **Graveley**, from some Reeve of the County, who might possess the same in the time of the *Saxons*, for the Name in the Saxons Language, signifies the Reeve's Land.

Anno 1088, 1 *William Rufus*, this *William* Earl of **Ewe** was one of those Lords, who assisted *Odo* Bishop of **Bayeux**, and *Robert* Earl of **Moreton** and **Cornwel**, the King's Uncles, to advance *Robert Curthose*, Duke of **Normandy**, and elder Brother of King *William Rufus*, to the Crown of **England**; but afterwards covetous of Riches, and ambitious of Honour, and having an Assurance of both, if he would promote the Interest of *William Rufus*, he deserted *Robert Curthose*, *Anno* 1093, (6 *Will. Rufus*) who was his liege Lord to whom he had sworn Fealty, and came into **England**, where he offered his Service to King *William Rufus:* but 'tis observable that those Men who will not hold to their Principle, but sell their Prince for private Gain or Preferment are not to be trusted, for they that will be false to one Master, will never be true to another; so it happen'd with this Earl *William*, for shortly after he joyned with *Robert de Molbray*, Earl of **Northumberland**, in that Conspiracy to murder *Rufus* in a Wood, and being charged with this Plot by some Person, whom he challenged to a Duel, for the Justification of his Innocency therein, and being vanquished in the Duel, his Eyes were pulled out, and his Privy-members cut off at **Saresbury**, whilst the King celebrated a great Council there on the Octaves of the Epiphany, *Anno* 1096, 9 *Will. Rufus.*

Yet *Henry* his Son succeeded him in the Earldom of **Ewe**, who joyned with the Earl of **Millent**, and others in that honourable Reception of King *H.* I. made by the Nobility of **Normandy**, when he first landed there, after he had got the Crown of **England**.

But he conspired with *Baldwin* Earl of **Flanders**, to advance *William*, Son to *Robert Curthose*, to the Crown of **England**, and the King having Notice of it, secured him at **Roan**, and kept him in Custody till he had surrender'd up all his strong Holds.

Howbeit the next Year, he made some Satisfaction for this Offence, for he attended the King in that memorable Battel at **Brennebil** near **Noyon**, where the *English* obtain'd a glorious Victory against *Lewis* King of **France**; but finding that this Mannor came to the Lords of **Thibesfield**, which was in the Possession of *Peter de Valongies*, as appears by *Domesdei Book*, where 'tis recorded under the Title of *Terra Petri de Valongies.*

In **Bradewater** *Hundred. in* **Escelbia**, *ten. Godefridus de Petro. un. hid et dimid. Terra est un. car. et ibi est cum duo Bord. et un. servo, valet.* xxx *sol. quando recepit* xx *sol. tempore Regis Edwardi*, xl *sol. de hac terra ten. Aluvinus hid. et dimid. exceptis x acris, et* i *Toft. quas ten. Aluvinus Dode homo Alurici parvi, et jacebant in* **Milga**, *non poterat vendere extra.*

Godfrey held one Hide and an half of *Peter de Valongies* in **Escelba**. in the Hundred of **Bradewater**. The arrable is one Carucate, and it is there with two Bordars and one Servant, it is worth thirty Shillings a Year, when he received it twenty Shillings a Year, in the time of King *Edward* (the Confessor) forty Shillings a Year, *Alvine* held one Hide and

Hund. of **Bradewater**

Ralph de Diceto, col. 489, n. 30.

Bar. vol. 1, fol. 136.

Domesd. Lib. fol. 141, n. 36.

Hund. of
Bradewater an half of this Land, except ten Acres and one Toft, which *Alwine Dode*, a Man (under the Protection of little *Alwric* held, and did lye in *Wilien*, he could not sell them from thence.

But in the time of *H.* III. both these Mannors were in Ral. *Hist. of the World*,
lib. 1, fol. 148. the Possession of *William de Chives*, who erected a Seat upon this Hill, and called it by his own Name, to perpetuate the Memory thereof to Posterity; for many Persons would often give their own Names, or the Names of their Ancestors to Mountains or Rivers, as to things after their Judgement freest from any Alteration, for the Names of great Kingdoms were often changed by Conquerours, and the greatest Cities burnt or demolisht.

This *William de Monte Caviso* was one of the great Captains, *Anno* 1264, 48 *H.* III. that lead the second Battalia under the Command of *Gilbert de Clara*, the second General of the Army which the Barons had then raised against King *H.* III. for by that Means he was known *Annis* 1258, and 1259, 42 and 43 *H.* III. during the Space of both which Years he served the King in the Office of Sheriff for the Counties of Hertford and Essex.

Ralph de Monte Caviso succeeded him, and did his Homage and Service to *Humphry de Bohun*, Earl of Hereford and Essex, for the Tenements which he held of him in the Vill of Chibesfield in this County, and Memmes in the County of Middlesex; and he served as Knight of the Prin's Par.
pt. 3. Shire for this County in the Parliament held *Anno* 1309, 2 *Edw.* II. which Parliament continued but a short time, for I have not seen any Statute made there.

After his Decease, this Mannor came to the Possession of *Richard de Monte Caviso*, who was a Person of great Esteem and much Value in his time, for he served this County in four several Parliaments, one held *Anno* 4 *Edw.* III. another *Anno* 5 *Edw.* III. another *Anno* 7 *Edw.* III. and another *Anno* 14 *Edw.* III.   He was also constituted Sheriff Ibid. of this County and Essex, but I suppose dyed in his Shrievalty, for that he held it no longer than the first Half of that Year.

Ibid. *Ralph de Monte Caviso* succeeded, and served this County in the Parliament held *Anno* 33 *Edw.* III. and I suppose he sold it to

Edward Barrington, who held a Court for the Mannor of Grabeley, on Monday next after the Feast of *Easter*, *Anno* 1411, 12 *H.* IV. then the Mannor of Chibesfield, came to the Possession of

Rot. cur. Ma-
nerii de Che-
visfield. *Thomas Barrington*, Esq. who held a Court there on Monday next after the Feast of *Corpus Christi*, *Anno* 1438, 16 *H.* VI. and was constituted Sheriff for the Counties of Rot. Pip. 30
H. VI. Hertford and Essex, *Anno* 1452, 30 *H.*VI. and served the King in that Office, during the whole Year.

Nicholas Barrington succeeded, was possest of both these

Mannors of 𝕮𝖍𝖎𝖇𝖊𝖘𝖋𝖎𝖊𝖑𝖉 and 𝕮𝖗𝖆𝖛𝖊𝖑𝖞, and held a Court for *Husd. of* both of them together at the Feast of *Pentecost, An.* 1492, *Braðewater* 7 *H.*VII. and the Year following he conveyed them to Sir Rot. cur. Ma-*William Pykenham, Richard Godfrey,* Esq. and others in nerii. Trust for the Benefit of himself and *Elizabeth* his Wife; by Vertue whereof the Trustees held a Court on Wednesday next before the Feast of St. *George* the Martyr, in the same Ibid. Year for the said Mannors in their Names: After the Death of this *Nicholas*

Elizabeth his Wife survived, married——— *Parker,* and for the Security of these Mannors to her own proper Use during the time of her Coverture, they were conveyed before the Marriage to *Richard Sheldon,* and other Feoffees in Trust for the Benefit of *Elizabath Parker,* and by Force of this Settlement, the Trustees held a Court on Wednesday next before the Feast of St. *Michael, Anno* 1507, 22 *H.*VII. in their Names, and upon her Death both these Ibid. Mannors descended to

Sir *Nicholas Barrington,* Knight, who conveyed them in Trust to Sir *John Greene,* Kt. and other Feoffees to such Purposes as were directed; by the Authority of which Settlement, these Feoffees held a Court on the 13th of *Jan.* 1518, 9 *H.* VIII. for both; in the mean while this Sir Ibid. *Nicholas* by Will dated 22d of *July,* 1515, disposed of them with the Mannors of 𝕷𝖊𝖙𝖈𝖍𝖜𝖔𝖗𝖙𝖍 and 𝖂𝖊𝖘𝖙𝖔𝖓, which he had given to *Thomas Leventhorpe, Thomas Peryent,* Esquires, and *Edmund Brocket,* Gent. and others, for 17 Years, to the Use of his Will, and the Residue of all his Goods unbequeathed, to Dame *Elizabeth* his Wife, except the Standerts of his Houses of 𝕮𝖍𝖎𝖘𝖋𝖎𝖊𝖑𝖉 and 𝕭𝖆𝖗𝖗𝖎𝖓𝖌𝖙𝖔𝖓-𝖍𝖆𝖑𝖑, which he willed to be left to his Heir apparent *John Barrington,* when he came to the Age of 22 Years; and it seems he dyed about the Year 1521, for in the Month of *October,* in this same Year, this Will was proved.

John Barrington, Esq. was his Son and Heir, enjoyed these Mannors, and settled them in *Thomas Peryent,* Esq. Ibid. and other Trustees, who by Force hereof, held Court here on the 4th of *November,* 1534, 25 *H.*VIII. after the Death of this *John Barrington.*

Thomas Barrington his Son and Heir succeeded: but whilst he was under Age, the Lady *Elizabeth Barrington,* who survived her Husband, was Guardian to her Son, and held Court in these Mannors in her Name on the 5th of *May,* 1546, 38 *H.*VIII. and when *Thomas* the Son attain'd Ibid. to Age, he held a Court here in his own Name, then conveyed them to

Elizabeth Barrington his Mother, who held another Court the 20th of *April,* 1555, 1 & 2 *P. & M.* in her Name, but shortly after dying, these Mannors returned again to *Thomas Barrington.*

THE PEDIGREE OF THE BARRINGTONS.

Sir Odynel Barrington, Kt. Baron of Wigon, descended from Barrington, who served Queen Emme, Wife of King Etheldred, and Mother to King Edward (the Confessor) and was subdued by King William the Conqueror.

Sir Eustace Barrington, Kt. (Son of Sir Odynel) To all Barons of Essex, sendeth Greeting——— Son of William the Conqueror granted him to hold in peace all his Lands in Hamerskine, Hatfield, Peverel, Writhncy, Ravensfield, Harting, Berking, Slyford, Cherewel, and Splow.

Sir Humphry Barrington, Kt. to whom King Stephen and Hon. Fitz Empress, granted all the above said Lands of Sir Eustace, and also all his Lands in Eldichanger; and Sir Ralph Marcy, Kt gave the Manor of Keivedon in marriage with Gealalo, his Sister.

Sir Humphry de Barrington, mar. Avele or Eau the only Daughter of Sir William, the third Son of Sir Geoffry Mandivile, Earl of Essex, who gave with her all his Lands in Sherpeshead.

There was one Sir Warren of Barrington, I know not whose Son he was, but am certain he was buried at Therliak Priory in the Forest of Hatfield.

Sir Geoffry de Mandivile, Earl of Essex, Founder of the Abby of Walden.

1 Arnulph.   2 Jeoffry.   3 William.   Alice.

Auly, or the Mandivile.

Sir Nicholas Barrington, Son and Heir of Sir Humphry, held the Offices of Woodwary and Chief Forester of Hatfield Forest, and summoned before him the Regarderers, Verderers, and Agistors, in all the Forest of Essex. He married Maud, Daughter of Sir Ralph Mortoft, Kt.

Sir Nicholas Barrington, Kt. held Tripow in Cambridgeshire, by the gift of his Father; mar. Agnes, the Da. and Heir of Sir Will. Chetwyd, Kt. and Sister to Sir Adam Chetwyd and Sir Joh. Chetwyd, Kt. both of whom died in the life-time of their Father.

2 Hugh Bar-rington.   3 George Bar-rington.   3 Humphry Bar-rington.   4 Theobald Bar-rington.   6 John Bar-rington.

Margaret, mar. to Sir James Umphrevile.   Odynel, died in his youth.

Sir Nicholas Barrington, Kt. mar Alice. Da. and Heir to Sir Rich. Belhouse, Kt. and Dame Alice his Wife, which Sir Richard gave in Marriage to the said Nicholas and Alice, 10£. of Rent in Westhal, which he had of Sir John Burgh, Son of Hobert Burgh, Earl of Kent, Chief Justice of England; and his Father, Sir Nicholas gave him the Manors of Triplow, Hatfield, Wrstel, Chigwel, Ramaldon, and also Bulinghach and Springfield.

Agatha.   John.   Philip.   Joyce.   Margaret, mar. tia Suchemor, Kt.   Margaret, mar. Sicily.

Nicholas Barrington, Esq. mar. one of the Da. and Heirs of Sir Robert Baird, Kt. who inherited Triplow, Chigwel, Balling—also Chevesfield, the Manor of Little——by the gift of Sir Robert Baird.

Roger.   Thomas.   Sir Philip Barrington, Kt. mar. Margaret, Da. of Sir William Tey, Kt.

Sir John Barrington, Kt. had the Manors of Hatfield, Chigewel, Triplow, Langeuche, Springfield, and Somerfegh in Hethingfore; and married Margaret, Daughter and Heir of Sir John Blonvile.

Humphry Bar-rington.   Thomas Bar-rington.   Philip Bar-rington.   Lettice, the first Issue, preserved a Virgin, and had 10£ Rent in Westan, for term of her Life.

Nicholas Barrington, of Raleigh, Esq. curteys Parker of Fee of Raleigh Park, married Margaret, Daughter of ——— Clovil.

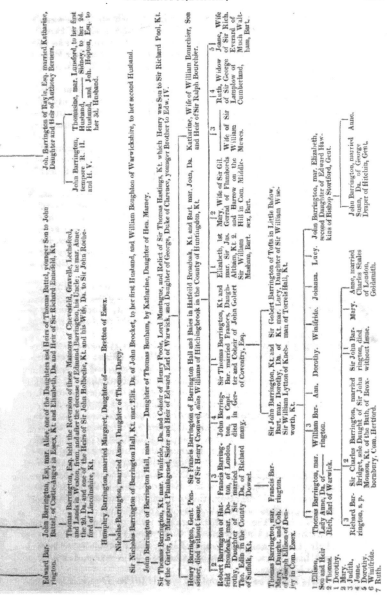

But to return to *Thomas Barrington*, whose Arms were *Argent, three Cheveronell Gules, over all a Label of three Points Azure.* He sold these Mannors to *Geo. Clerke* of 𝕭ennington in this County, Gent. who soon after this Purchase dyed, leaving Issue four Sons, *Will. Tho. Joh.* and *Geo.*

William Clerk was his Son and Heir, educated at the Inns of Court, where he improved his time in the Study of the Law, was called to the Bar, sedulous and diligent in his Profession, and had a great Reputation among the Learned; he dyed leaving Issue

George, to whom these Mannors descended by Right of Inheritance; he lived retiredly in the Country upon his Estate, enjoyed them some Years, then dyed, and left them to

William Clerk, who loved a country Life, delighted much in the Pleasure of Hawking, and would be very free, brisk and merry in all Companies; he suffered much for his Loyalty to King *Char. I.* when the factious Party was prevalent, and in the Height of those troublesome times, he rose one Evening from Supper, sat down in his Chair by the Fire, and dyed suddenly there, leaving Issue *William, Nicholas, and Francis.*

William Clerke was his Heir, possest these Mannors, and held divers Courts here; he married *Mary* the Daughter and sole Heir of *John Bagshaw* of 𝕷ondon, Merchant, by whom he had Issue four Daughters, *Elizabeth, Jane, Valeanna,* and *Frances,* and dyed.

Mary his Widow succeeded, held these Mannors for her Life, and during her time, *Elizabeth* her eldest Daughter married *George Throckmorton,* Esq. descended from that ancient Family of *Throckmorton* in 𝖂arwickshire; and after her Decease, *Jane* the second Daughter married *William Capel* of 𝕾tanton, in the County of 𝕾uffolk, Esq. who descended from Sir *Arthur Capel,* Ancestor to the Right Honourable the Earl of 𝕰ssex; *Valeanna* the third Daughter married *Thomas Story* of 𝕸oreton in the County of 𝕮ambridge, Esq. and *Frances* the youngest Daughter married Sir *Charles Neale* of 𝖂oollaston in the County of 𝕹orthampton, Kt. who were the Coheirs to these Mannors, and upon the Partition of the Estate of this *William Clerk* among these Daughters, these Mannors with the Mannor-house and Seat was allotted by Agreement to

Elizabeth the eldest Daughter, who joined with her Husband in a Conveyance of them to the Use of them for their Lives, and the longer Liver, the Remainder to him and his Heirs, by Reason whereof he became Lord of these Mannors.

His Pedigree is set out by Sir *William Dugdale* in his

Survey of 𝖂𝖆𝖗𝖜𝖎𝖈𝖐𝖘𝖍𝖎𝖗𝖊, and brought down to Sir *George*   *Hund. of*
Throckmorton of 𝕮𝖔𝖚𝖌𝖍𝖙𝖔𝖓 in the County of 𝖂𝖆𝖗𝖜𝖎𝖈𝖐,   *𝕭𝖗𝖆𝖉𝖊𝖜𝖆𝖙𝖊𝖗*
therefore I have drawn it down only from that Knight, to
this Gentleman, the last Owner of these Mannors. He
dyed at 𝕮𝖍𝖎𝖘𝖋𝖎𝖊𝖑𝖉, on the first of *October*, 1696, leaving
Issue *John, George, William, Thomas ; Mary* married to
Thomas Broomfield, Gent. *Elizabeth* married to *Gerrard*
Fitz Gerald, Doctor in Physick, *Dorothy* wedded to *John*
Hurst of 𝕳𝖆𝖇𝖊𝖗𝖎𝖑 in 𝕰𝖘𝖘𝖊𝖝, Gent. *Jane, Anne, Frances*
who dyed in her Infancy, *Katharine,* and *Monica:* He
bore *Gules, a Cheveron Argent, three Bars Gemelles Sable.*

Sir George Throckmorton of Coughton in the —Katharine, Daught. of Nich. Baron Vaux of Harwedon,
County of Warwick, Kt. died 1 Mariæ. | and Eliz. one of the Coheirs of Baron Fitzhugh.

| Sir Rob. Throckmorton, Kt. mar. Muriel, the Da. of Tho. Barou of Barkeley. | Clem. Throckmorton of Haseley. | Kenelme. | Anthony Throckmorton of Castleton, in the County of Oxford, mar. Katharine, the Da. and sole Heir of Will. Willington of Barcheston in the County of Warw. and the Relict of W. Catesby, of Lapworth in the same County, Esq. and before him of R. Kemp. | Sir Nicho. Throckmorton, Kt. | Jo. Throckmorton, Justice of Chester. | Fran. Throckmorton. |

| Jo. Throckmorton, Son and Heir died without Issue. | Thos. Throckmorton, died without Issue. | Geo. Throckmorton of Rolandwright in the County of Oxford, 1594, mar. Eliz. Da. and Heir of Rob. Gines of Colchester in Com. Essex. | Mary, Wife of Jo. Stradford. | Katharine, Wife of Rob. Acton. | Anne. | Margaret, Wife of Rob. Ansley of Brookend in the County of Oxford. | Elizabeth, Wife of Rich. Acton. | Robert, died an Infant. |

John Throckmorton of Magdalen Lavor —Dorothy, 1st. Wife, Da. of Rich. Hardy —Ursula, 2d. Wife, Rel. of Edw. Osborn of Pidin the County of Essex, Son and Heir mar. | in the County of Dorset. | dington in the County of Northampton, 1627.

| John Throckmorton died in his Infancy. | George Throckmorton of Magdalen Lavor, Son and Heir, 1665, mar. Eliz. the eldest Da. and one of the Coh of Will. Clerke of Chisfeild in Com. Hertford. | Jane, the Wife of Humphry Hide of Hurst in the County of Berks, 1662. |

1	2	1	2	3	4	6	7
John, Son and Heir mar. Mary, Widow of Humph. Foster, Gent. fourth Da. of Sir H. Chauncy, Kt.	George. 3 William. 4 Thomas.	Mary, m. to Tho. Bromfeild. Gent.	Elizabeth, m. to Edw. Fitz Gerald.	Dorothy, mar. to John Hurst of Haveril, in Essex, Gent.	Jane. 5 Anne.	Frances, died in her infancy.	Katharine. 8 Monica.

John Throckmorton beareth for his Atchievement, *four Coats quarterly,*
viz. 1. Throckmorton ; *Gules, on a Cheveron Argent three Bars Gemelles*
Sable, with a Mollette for Difference. 2. Willington ; *Or, a Saltier Vaire.*
3. Gynes; *Vaire Or and Azure, a Canton Ermin.* 4. Clerke; *Party per*
Cheveron Azure and Or, in Chief three Leopards Heads, and in base an Eagle
display'd counterchanged ; Crest on a Wreath of the Colours, a Falcon with
Wing expanded Proper, the Back, Legs, and Jesses Or.

    I. Throckmorton; *Gules, on a Cheveron Argent three Bars Gemelles*   The Arms in
Sable impaling Vaux; *Chequy Argent and Gules, on a Cheveron Azure, three*   the Hall Win-
Roses Or, seeded and barbed proper, and the Crest of Throckmorton *over*   dow at Chis-
them, being a Falcon with Wings expanded Proper, the Beak, Legs, and   feild.
Jesses Or, standing upon a Wreath of the Colours.

    II. Throckmorton; *as afore, with a Mollette impaling* Willington; *Or,*
a Saltier Vaire.

    III. Throckmorton; *differenced as before, impaling* Gynes, *Vaire Or,*
and Azure, a Canton Ermine.

    IV. Throckmorton; *with the same Difference, impaling* Hardy; *Sable,*
on a Cheveron between three Escallop shells Or, as many Dragons Heads
erazed of the first langued, Gules.

    V. Throckmorton; *with a Mollette as afore, impaling* Clerke; *Party*
per Cheveron Azure and Or, three Leopards Heads in Chief, and an Eagle
displayed in Base, all counterchanged.

Hund. of
Bradwater

Camd. *Brit.*
tit. Hantshire
fol. 272.

Near the Mannor-house, a fair Beacon might have been lately seen, which was wount by a light burning Fire, to give Notice to all the Inhabitants round about, when any Enemies were coming.

THE Church of Grabeley *cum* Chisfield, *Anno* 26 *H*.VIII. was rated in the King's Books at the yearly Value of 12*l.* 8*d.*

Record in the Priory of Wimondley, abstracted & entered in the Reg. Book of Graveley, 8 Sept. 1641, by Edm. Brocket, Minister of Graveley.

The Churches of Grabeley and Chisfield were united in the Year of our Lord 1445, 23 *H.* VI. by *William* Bishop of Lincoln, upon the Petition of *Thomas Brocket* and *Thomas Palmer,* and *Elizabeth* and *Christiana* their Wives ; by Reason the Smallness of the Revenue of each Church for the Maintenance of an Incumbent, Grabeley being then valued at eight Markes, and Chisfield at five, and that the Uncertainty of their Bounds could not be known, whence such Contentions arose between the Incumbents, that they meeting together upon Preambulation, one Parson kill'd the other, and the Churches were not distant above Half a Mile.

Yet both these Churches have been continued, and the several Patrons heretofore presented to them in their Turns, as appears by the Register in the Church of Lincolne, where 'tis recorded that

Willielmus Sely *Presbyter, presentatus per* Thomam Brocket *et* Elizabetham *uxorem ejus et* Thomam Palmer *et* Christianam *uxorem ejus ad Ecclesiam Parochialem de* Grabeley, Lincolne *Diæc. per resignationem Dom.* Thomæ London, *ultimi Rectoris ejusdem in manibus Episc. fact. et per ipsum admissam vacant, ad eundem admissus apud* London, 16 *die* Novembris, *Anno Dom.* 1439, *et Rector Institutis.*

Rogerus Megur *Clericus presentatus per* Thomam Palmer *et* Christianam *uxorem suam, et* Thomam Brocket *et* Elizabetham *uxorem ejusdem, ad Ecclesiam Parochialem de* Grabeley Lincolne, *Diæc. per Resignationem,* Will. Sely, *ultimi Rectoris ejusdem in manibus, Episc. factum, et per eum admissam vocationem ad eandum fuit admissus apud* London, 8 *Novembris, Anno Dom.* 1441. *et Rector iustitutis Canonice in eadem nulla inquisitione. Et juran Canonice Obedientia, Scriptur. fuit Archidiaconi Hun. vel ejus Official. ad inducend. eundem,* &c.

By these Entries, it seems to me that *Thomas Brocket,* in Right of *Elizabeth* his Wife, presented *William Seely,* because they are named before *Thomas Palmer,* and *Christian* his Wife, which shews it was their Turn to present, and that *Thomas Palmer,* in Right of *Christian* his Wife, presented *Roger Megur* in the next Course, for that their Names are placed before *Thomas Brocket* and *Elizabeth* his Wife, which was in those Days, the Usage in Cases of this Nature, and the like Order was not only observed here, but also between the joynt Lords of the Mannor of Albury, when they held Courts for that Mannor in their Turns, to which I refer the Reader: And the Patrons presented joyntly after this Manner in their Turns, as appears by the following Account, taken from the Register in the Church of Lincolne; and these Churches have been rated together in the King's Books, at the yearly Value of 12*l.* 8*d.* but since the Reformation every Rector read Prayers, and preached at the one Church in the Forenoon, and the other in the Afternoon, which Course was duly observed.

RECTORS of the Church of Grabeley.

| Thomas London. | 1439 *William Sely.* |

RECTORS of the Churches of Grabeley and Chibesfield; After the Union, *Anno Christi* 1445, 23 *H.* VI.

1445 *William Sely,* presented by *Thomas Brocket* and *Elizabeth* his Wife, and *Thomas Palmer* and *Christian* his wife.	1482 *John Ardesley* presented by *Edward Brocket,* Esq. to both Churches.
1448 *Roger Megur* presented by *Thomas Palmer* and *Christian* his Wife, and *Thomas Brocket* and *Elizabeth* his Wife.	*Thomas Thorley.* presented by
	1546 *Richard Bedel,* Clerk, presented by *John Brocket,* Esq. Lord of the Mannor of Alme-

shoe, to both Churches, on the Death of *Thomas Thorley*.

1555 *John Howes*, presented by

————

1572 *Benedict Quarles* presented by *John Brocket*, Esq. to the Rectory of **Grabely** cum **Chibesfield**, vacant by the Death of *John Howes*.

1596 *Benedict Quarles*, presented by Queen *Elizabeth* upon the Lapse.

1605 *John Layfield*, D.D. presented by King *James* I. by Reason

of the Minority of *John Carleton*, his Ward and Pupil.

Thomas Rooks

1613 *Edmond Brocket*
Zachary Crofton
Andrew Cater

1662 *Philip Osbaldston*, presented to both Churches by Sir *Brocket Spencer*, Baronet, vacant by Cession.

1697 *John Bower*, presented to both Churches by Sir *John Spencer*, Baronet, on the Death of *Philip Osbaldston*.

The Church of **Grabely**, is situated in a Bottom near the Vill, the Body thereof is covered with Lead, there is a fair Chancel at the East End covered with Tyle, and a square Tower is annexed to the West End thereof, in which hang four small Bells, 'tis covered with Lead, and a short Spire upon it.

In the Church lies a Stone with this Inscription engraven'd upon it.

——— *Posuit Uxori sui amoris et Officii erga* Benedictus Quarles, *quæ decessit* 4to *die* Junii, *Anno Dom.* 1687.

> *Mortalis* Winefrida *prius nunc civis* Olympi
> *Quam tibi fœlici conditione manes*
> *Peccatam mortem vicisti sub duce Christo*
> *In cœlis Christo fratre fruer e tuo.*
> *Æternum valens conjux cælosque teneto*
> *Velle mecum tecum est dei mihi velle Deus.*

RECTORS of the Church of **Chibesfield**.

John Sylesham.

1323 *John Wykins*, Parson of **Newnham**, presented by *Hugh* the Son of *Simon* to this Church, vacant by the Death of *John de Sylesham.*

Ade atte Varo

1377 *Robert Shorthale*, presented by *John de Waltero*, Teacher of **Wavesse**, and *Ralph Melchburne*, to this Church, vacant by the Resignation of *Ade atte Varo.*

1382 *Richard Wryng* presented by *Nicholas* Son of *Simon*, to the Church of **Chesfield**, vacant

by the Death of *Robert Shorthale.*

John Kilkap

1410 *Henry Trowel*, presented by *William Ash* and *John Molsey*, to the Church of **Chesfield**, vacant by the Death of *John Kilkap.*

1432 *Roger Megur*, presented by *Thomas Brocket* and *Elizabeth* his Wife, *John Molsey* and *Christian* his Wife, to this Church, by the Resignation of *Henry Trowel.*

1439 *William Sely*, presented

As for the succeeding Rectors I refer the Reader to those of **Grabely**.

On **Chibes** Hill stands an antient small Church or Chappel, with a Chancel adjoyning to the same, both which are covered with Tyles, there is a small Chappel adjoyning to the South Side of the Chancel, which belongs wholly to the Lord of **Chibesfield**, and two very small Bells hang in the Roof of the West End of the Church, whereof one is broke.

In the Chancel there is not any thing remarkable, for the Windows were defac'd in the late late time of Rebellion, *Anno* 1642, but in the North Window, there are the Figures of some Bishops, one supposed to be St. *Edmond*, in his Habit, with a Crosier in his Hand, another is thought to be St. *Thomas* of **Canterbury**, in his Archiepiscopal Habit, with his Crosier in his Hand; and at the East End thereof are the Figures of several other Bishops and holy Men now defaced.

In the Passage or Arch between the Chancel or Chapel is a Tomb raised about two Foot high, wherein some suppose that the Founder of the Church may lie; and in the Chapel did lye the Body of Sir *Francis Throck-*

Hund. of   *morton*, of **Great Coughton** in the County of **Warwick**, Bar. who dyed the
Bradewater   ——— day of *November*, 1680, which Chapel is adorned with his Banner
and Banrol, and other Ensigns belonging to his Degree; but his eldest Son
Sir *Robert* lately removed his Body from hence to the ancient Burying
Place of his Ancestors at **Coughton** in **Warwickshire**.

In the upper Window on the North Side of the Church, more Pictures
appear defaced, whereof remains a Bishop in his Habit, with a Crosier
Staff.   Near it is a Coat of Arms, *Gules, three cover Cups Argent*.

In the West Window is a Coat of Arms, *Azure ten Flower de Luces, Or*.

Each Church has alwayes two distinct Church-wardens, and the Parishoners of either Parish pay their respective Duties, and repair their
several and respective Churches to which they particularly belong; and
the Incumbent payes Duties to the Archdeacon for two distinct Livings,
because the Archdeacon did agree with the Bishop to unite them; but
the Parishoners of the several Parishes pay all Rates and Taxes to the
King and the Poor, joyntly together, and the Officers are called Officers
of **Grabeley** *cum* **Chibesfield**.

BENEFACTORS.

Mrs. *Mary Clerk*, the Widow of *William Clerk*, Esq. gave a green Car-
pet and a Damask Cloath, for the Communion Table at **Chisfield**.

Edmond Jordan of **Chisfield**, Yeoman, *Anno* 1626, by his Will gave 4*s*.
a Year unto the poor People of **Grabeley** and **Chisfield**, issuing out of au
Acre of Meadow, lying in **Span Vally Bottom**, to be paid to the Minister
and Church-wardens of the said Parishes.

BOX, BOXBURY.

WHEN *William* the Conqueror had subdued this Realm,
he gave this Mannor of **Box** to *William* Earl of **Ewe**, Son
of *Robert de Buco*, who was one of his chief Counsellours
before the time of his Conquest: for it is recorded in *Domesdei Book* under the Title of *Terra Willielmi de Ow.*

Domesd. Lib.   *In* **Box** *tenet* Petrus de Will. de Ow li hid. *et tres virgat.* Terra est
fol. 138, n. 28.   quinque car. in Dominio sunt duo et tertia potest fieri ibi duo Vill. cum quatuor bordis habentibus duo car. ibi tres cotar. et tres Servi, nemus ad sepes,
in totis valent valet 1 sol. quando recepit xxx sol. tempore Regis Edwardi lx
sol. hanc terram tenuit Aluuardus homo Alestan de Boscumbe, non potuit
vendere præter tres virgat.

Peter held of *William de Ow* two hides and three Virgates in **Box**. The
arrable is five Carucates, in Demeasne are two, and a third may be made,
there are two Villains, with four Bordars, having two Carucates, there are
three Cottagers and three Servants, Wood for Hedges; in the whole Value
it is worth fifty Shillings a Year, when he received it thirty Shillings, in
the time of King *Edward* (the Confessor) sixty Shillings, *Alward* a Man
under the Protection of *Alestan de Boscumbe* held this Land, he could not
sell above three Virgates.

This was a Vill or Parish, which was scituated between
the Parishes of **Stevenedge**, **Chibesfield**, and **Walkerne**;
there was anciently a Church to the same, which was
erected in a Field on the Hill near the Woods, now called
the Church-yard, where the Foundations may be seen; and
this Parish was called **Box** from a great Wood, which retains this Name at this Day.

This Mannor continued in this Family, as **Clothal** did,
till about the 20 *Hen*. I. when, I suppose, it came to the
Crown, where it remained until King *Hen*. III. granted it
to *William de Valence*, Earl of **Pembrook**, his half Brother;

he had Issue *John* who dyed young, *William* slain in a
Skirmish with the *Welch*, in the Life-time of his Father,
and *Aymer* Earl of 𝔓𝔢𝔪𝔟𝔯𝔬𝔬𝔨, *Anne* married to *Maurice
Fitzgerald*, next to *Hugh de Balioll* by whom she had Issue
Alexander, afterwards to *John de Sueine*, *Isabel* to *John
de* 𝔥𝔞𝔰𝔱𝔦𝔫𝔤𝔰 of 𝔅𝔢𝔯𝔤𝔞𝔟𝔢𝔫𝔫𝔭, and *Jone* to *John Comyn* of
𝔅𝔞𝔡𝔢𝔫𝔞𝔠𝔥; but *Aymer* the third Son dying without Issue,
his Sisters were his Heirs, among whom this Mannor was
allotted to *Anne* the eldest Sister, who had Issue *Alexander*,
to whom it came in Right of his Mother, for *Anno* 6 *Edw.* I.
this *Alexander de Baliol* claimed in this Mannor, which his
Mother held in Purparty of the Inheritance, which was
Peter de Valoines, by the Grant of King *Hen.* I. Soc, Sac,
Toll, Them, Infangthef, &c. and upon the View of the Deed,
and the Confirmation of King *Hen.* II. to *Robert de Valoines*, Brother to *Peter*, all the Fee and Land, View of
Franc-pledge, Correction of the Assize of Bread and Ale,
and Tumbrel, &c. in his Mannors of 𝔅𝔢𝔫𝔦𝔫𝔤𝔱𝔬𝔫, 𝔚𝔞𝔱𝔱𝔬𝔫,
𝔅𝔬𝔵, and 𝔆𝔯𝔬𝔴𝔟𝔢𝔯𝔭 were allowed.

The Master of the Knights Templers in 𝔈𝔫𝔤𝔩𝔞𝔫𝔡 claimed
by the Grant of *Hen.* III. divers very large Priviledges,
with Exemption from all secular Services, Soc, Sac, Toll,
Them, Infangeneth, Outfangeneth, Hamsocne, &c. discharged from all Affairs in all Places, and Causes, &c. from
Toll, &c. and from all secular Service and Custom, in as
ample Manner as kingly Power can grant to any religious
House, and Free-warren in 𝔇𝔦𝔫𝔢𝔰𝔩𝔢, 𝔖𝔱𝔞𝔤𝔢𝔫𝔥𝔬, 𝔓𝔯𝔢𝔰𝔱𝔬𝔫,
𝔆𝔥𝔢𝔯𝔩𝔱𝔬𝔫, 𝔚𝔞𝔩𝔡𝔢𝔫, 𝔥𝔦𝔠𝔥𝔢, 𝔆𝔥𝔢𝔩𝔢𝔰, 𝔖𝔢𝔟𝔢𝔠𝔞𝔪𝔭, and 𝔅𝔢𝔫𝔦𝔫𝔤𝔥𝔬.

These Knights Templers, and after them the Knights
Hospitallers, held this Mannor of 𝔆𝔥𝔢𝔩𝔢𝔰, so termed from a
Chil, a cold Place, till the time of the Dissolution of Monasteries, when it came to the Crown, and then King *H.*VIII.
granted this 𝔆𝔥𝔢𝔩𝔢𝔰, being the Moyety hereof, ·containing
about 410 Acres, to *John Norris*, who sometime after sold it
to Sir *Philip Boteler*, he held it of the Mannor of 𝔅𝔢𝔫𝔦𝔫𝔤𝔱𝔬𝔫 by the yearly Rent of 13*s.* 4*d.* Suit of Court and Knight's
Service, *viz.* Homage, Fealty, and Scutage, whereof the
Lord of 𝔅𝔢𝔫𝔦𝔫𝔤𝔱𝔬𝔫 pays 13*s.* to the Mannor of 𝔓𝔬𝔭𝔦𝔰𝔥𝔞𝔴,
of whom you may read in the Parish of 𝔚𝔞𝔱𝔱𝔬𝔫, and that he
dyed leaving Issue

Robert, who was possest of this Moyety in the time of
King *James*, and had Issue

Jane, his sole Daughter and Heir, to whom it came by
Right of Inheritance; she married *John Bellasis*, Esq. the
second Son of *Thomas* Viscount 𝔉𝔞𝔲𝔠𝔬𝔫𝔟𝔯𝔦𝔡𝔤𝔢, of whom you
may read in the Parish of 𝔖𝔞𝔠𝔬𝔪𝔟, and he granted it to

Sir *John Gore* of 𝔖𝔞𝔠𝔬𝔪𝔟, Kt. and to his Heirs; He enjoy'd it until the Year 1686, or thereabouts, and then he
conveyed it to *Thomas Ashby*, Merchant and Citizen in 𝔏𝔬𝔫𝔡𝔬𝔫, who is the present Possessor hereof.

Hund. of
𝔅𝔯𝔞𝔡𝔢𝔴𝔞𝔱𝔢𝔯

Quo Warr. 6
Ed. I. *Rot.* 37,
cur. recept iu
Scac.

Cur. Rot.
Man. de Ben-
ington, 4 J. I.

Hund. of
Bradewater

As to the other Moyety of this Mannor, and Tythes of Boxburp, King *H.*VIII. granted them by Letters Patents to *George Clerk* of Benington, Gent. which he held a short time, and then devised the same by his Will dated the 8th of *October,* 3 & 4 *P. & M.* to *William* his Son, and the Heirs Males of his Body lawfully begotten, and for Want of such Issue, the Remainder to his Son *Thomas,* and the Heirs Males of his Body, lawfully begotten, and for Want of such Issue, the Remainder to his Son *George,* and the Heirs Males of his Body lawfully begotten, and for Want of such Issue, the Remainder to his right Heirs for ever, under the Conditions and Payments therein limited, and appointed, that after his Decease, this Moyety should go to

William, according to the Will, and from him it passed in such Manner as the Mannors of Grabelep and Chisfeld, until it came to the Daughter and Coheirs of *William Clerk,* and upon the Division of the whole Estate among the said Coheirs, this Part of the Mannor and Tythes fell to *Jane* the second Daughter, who married *William Capell,* Esq. as I have shewed in the Parishes of Chibesfeld and Grabelep.

WESTON.

WHEN that memorable Record of *Domesdei* was made, *William* the Conqueror held a Part of this Vill, which was called Weston, in Regard of the opposite Scituation thereof to some other Towns there on the East: and he gave the other Part thereof to *William de Auco* for his good Service, for it is recorded in *Domesdei Book,* under the Title of *Terra Regis*

Domesd. Lib.
fol. 3, nu. 1.

In Dimid. Hundred. de Bij, Rex Willelmus *tenet* Weston, *pro quinque hidis se defendebat. Terra est quatuordecem car. in dominio duo hid. et duo car. sunt ibi, et sexdecem Vill. cum tribus Bord. habentibus quinque car. et adhuc quinque possunt fieri, ibi quatuor Servi, pratum septem car. Pastura ad pecud. Vill. Silva quatuor centum Porc. et tres sol. Hoc Manerium tenuit Com.* Heraldus, *et jacuit et jacet in Bij, sed Wara hujus Manerii jacuit in* Bedfordshire. *tempore Regis* Edwardi, *in Hund. de* Manchene, *et ibi est Manerium et fuit semper, et post mortem* Edwardi, *non sed acquietavit de geldo Regis.*

In the half Hundred of Bij, King *William* held Weston, it was rated for five Hides. The arrable is fourteen Carucates, in Demeasne two Hides, and two Carucates are there, and sixteen Villains with three Bordars having five Carucates, and now five others may be made, there are four Servants, Meadow seven Carucates, Common of Pasture for the Cattle of the Vill, Wood to feed four hundred Hogs, and three Shillings Rent. Earl *Harold* held this Mannor, and it did lye and doth lye in Bij, but the Ware of this Mannor lyes in Bedfordshire in the time of King *Edward* (the Confessor,) in the Hundred of Manchene; and there is a Mannor now and was always, and after the death of King *Edward* (the Confessor) but he did not discharge it from the King's Tax.

Willelmus de Ow *tenuit* Weston, *et x hidis se defendebat. Terra est xxiii car. in dominio v hidæ, et ibi sunt v car. et vi potest fieri, ibi xxxiii Vill. cum Presbyteris duobus, et uno Milite, et duo Francig. habentibus xvi car. et adhuc una potest fieri, ibi xv Bord et xii cotar et x Servi, et i molin. de x sol, pratum iii car. Pastura ad pec. Silva ccccc porc. De bosco et pas-*

tura xiii *sol. et quatuor denar. in totis valent. valet* xx *lib. quando recepit* Hund. *of* xxv *lib. tempore Regis* Edwardi xxx *lib. Hoc Manerium tenuit* Alestanus **Bradewater** *Teignus Regis* Edwardi.

William de Ow held **Weston.** it was rated for ten Hides. The arrable is twenty three Carucates, in Demeasne five Hides, and there are five Carucates, and a sixth may be made, there are thirty three Villains with two Presbyters and one Knight, and two Frenchmen born, having sixteen Carucates, and now another may be made, there are fifteen Bordars and twelve Cotars, and ten Servants, and one Mill of ten Shillings Rent by the Year, Meadow three Carucates, Common of Pasture for the Cattle, Wood to feed five hundred Hogs; of Wood and Pasture thirteen Shillings and four Pence Rent by the Year; in the whole Value it is worth twenty Pounds, in the time of King *Edward* (the Confessor) thirty Pounds. *Alestan* a Thane of King *Edward* (the Confessor) held this Mannor.

Gilbert of **Clare** was Lord of this Mannor of **Weston,** made Earl of **Pembroke,** *Anno* 1138, after which he gave this Church of **Weston,** and Lands worth ten Pounds *per Annum,* within the Precinct of this Mannor, to the Knights Templers, whereon they built a Town called **Cauoac,** since enriched by several Purchasers; divers Priviledges have been obtained from the King for them, all which were afterwards confirmed by *William Mareschal,* Earl of **Pembroke,** his hereditary Successor in his Lands and Honours. Ord *Vit.* 917.
Mon. Angl.
vol. 2; fol.
524, nu 50.

He married *Elizabeth* the Sister of *Waleran* Earl of **Mellent,** and dyed *Anno* 1148, 14 *Steph.* and was buried in the Abby of **Tynterne,** leaving Issue *Richard,* sirnamed *Strongbow,* his Son and Heir, and *Baldwin* a younger Son, who fighting stoutly for King *Stephen,* in the Battle of **Lincolne,** 6 *Steph.* was taken Prisoner. W. Gemet,
312.
Mon. Angl
vol.1, fol.725.
Ord.*Vit.* 922.

King *H.* II. 16 *Regni sui,* deprived this Earl of all his paternal Estate, *Anno* 1170, 16 *Regni sui,* upon which he invaded **Ireland** with what Forces he could get together, won **Waterford** and **Dublin,** and sent certain Messengers from thence to King *Henry, Anno* 1171, 17 *H.* II. offering to him those Cities of **Dublin** and **Waterford,** and all those Castles which he was to have there, after the Death of *Dermutius* King of **Dublin,** whose Daughter he had married; this pleased the King so well that he restored to him all the Lands in **England** and **Normandy,** which he had taken from him, and freely granted that he should enjoy all those Lands in **Ireland,** which he had with his Wife, and constituted him Constable, which was chief Governour of that Realm. This moved King *Henry* to go into **Ireland,** which he subdued wholly without any considerable Resistance, tho' the Monk of **Jorebaulx** gives another Relation hereof, that the King of **England** being much displeased that he should make this Attempt without his Consent or Knowledge, seized upon all his Patrimony here, prohibiting all further Aid, and threatning him with great Menaces, compelled him to grant him **Dublin,** and all the principle Places that he had won, and to content himself with the Dugd. *Bar.*
vol.1, fol. 208.
Jorevaulx,
1069.

Hund. of
Bradewater
Rest, and his Patrimony in England, and soon after rais-
ing an Army sailed thither himself.

When the King had obtained Ireland, he made this Earl
Justice of that Realm, and soon after he dyed untimely up-
Dugd. Bar.
vol. 1, fol. 210.
on the Nones of *April,* 1176, 22 *H.* II. and was buried in
the Chapter-house at Glocester, where this Inscription was
engraved on the Wall;—*Hic jacet* Richardus Strongbow,
Filius Gilberti *Comitis de* Pembroke.   And he left Issue

Isabel who was his Daughter and Heir, and married *Richard* Earl of Strigul, in Right of his Wife, of whom he be-
Ibid. fol. 600.
came Earl of Clare, and being thus advanced to this Honour,
he bore the royal Scepter of Gold, with the Cross on the
Head of it, at the solemn Coronation of *R.* I.   He was con-
Rot. Pip. de
iisdem annis
Lincolne.
Rot. Pip. de
iisdem annis
Sussex.
stituted Sheriff of Lincolnshire, *Anno* 2 *R.* I. and continued
in that Employment till 6 *R.* I. inclusive, in which Year he
was made Sheriff of Sussex, which Office he held during the
whole Reign of King *Richard.*   In 1 *Johannis,* that King
M Paris, 196.
R. Hoved.
450.
sent him out of Normandy into England, with *Hubert*
Archbishop of Canterbury, to keep all in Peace here till he
came over; whereupon they appointed those of the Nobility
and others, of whom they most doubted, to meet at Northampton, and to take their Oaths of Fidelity to King *John,*
and the same Year he was appointed Sheriff of Glocestershire, and again of Sussex.   He proved very loyal and faithful to that King during all the time of his Reign, and being
a Person of great Power and Prudence, he convened many
of the Earls and Barons together, and setting young *Henry*
among them, said, *Behold your King,* whereupon they appointed a Day for his Coronation; he was the chief Agent
that set the Crown upon his Head, and the Rest of the Nobility constituted him Protector during the King's Minority.
M. Paris, 289.
And he immediately raised a powerful Army, fought Prince
Lewis at Lincolne, where he utterly vanquished him, so that
he returned home to France.

Rot. Pip. de
iisdem annis
Essex & Herts.
He was constituted Sheriff for this County and Essex,
Anno 1218, 2 *H.* III. executed the Office for three Parts
of that Year, and for Half the second Year, during which
time he did many Works of Piety, among which he granted
divers Liberties and Priviledges to the Borough of Bandac
formerly given to the *Knights Templers* by his noble Ancestor *Gilbert Strongbow,* sometime Earl of Pembroke;
and also gave unto them the Mill Radewellesheded, with
two Husbandmen in that Town, and then died at Caver-
Weav. Mon.
p. 442.
sham, 1219, 3 *H.* III. and his Body was buried in the
New Temple.

This great Earl left five Sons, *William, Richard, Gilbert,*
Dugd. Bar.
vol. 1, fol. 602.
Walter, and *Anselme;* they succeeded one after another in
his Honours and Lands, all of them died without Issue;
and five Daughters, *Maud* married to *Hugh Bigot,* Earl of

Norfolk, and afterwards to *John de Waren*, Earl of Surry; Joan to *Warine de Monchensy*; *Isabel*, first to *Gilbert de Clare*, Earl of Glocester, and afterwards to *Richard* Earl of Cornwall; *Sibill* to *William de Ferrers*, Earl of Derby; and *Eve* to *William de Braheuse*.

Hund. of Bradewater

William, the eldest Son, who succeeded his Father. In 8 *H.* III. he was made Governor of the Castles of Cardigan and Carmarthen; and having married *Alianore*, the Sister of King *H.* III. he died without Issue, *Anno* 1231, 15 *H.* III. and was buried in the *New Temple*.

M. Paris, fol. 317.

Weav. Mon. p. 442.

Richard Mareschal his next Brother, returning into England about the Month of *August* following, repaired to the King then in Wales, and presenting himself to him as Heir to his deceased Brother, offered to perform his Homage, and whatsoever else could justly be required of him for that Inheritance; but the King, upon the Suggestion of *Hubert de Burgh* refused to Grant him Livery. This caused him to return into Wales, enter upon the Castle of Pembroke, with the whole Honor thereunto belonging, and to raise all the Power he could, resolving to get his Inheritance by Force if he could not obtain it otherwise; upon which the King, fearing a Disturbance, accepted his Homage and Fealty, and restored to him all his Rights.

Matt. Paris, fol. 369

But afterwards the King was so exasperated against him, that he caused his Houses and Lands to be wasted, his Castles to be besieged; and the Bishop of Winchester, who bore the great sway at that time at Court, sent Letters to *Maurice*, Chief Justice of Ireland, and other his seeming Friends there, that if they should take him when he should come into Ireland, the King would bestow all his Lands in that Realm among them, and sent them a Patent under the great Seal to that purpose, whereupon they encouraged with these fair Promises, enter'd upon his Lands and Castles there with a military Power: This Earl upon Notice of it hasted thither, raised what Force he could, laid Siege to Limerick, which yielded to him in four Days, took divers Castles, none daring to make Head against him; but those great Men endeavouring to effect by Policy what they could not obtain by Strength, desired a Truce with him; they corrupting several of his Party: in the mean time discovering that he was betray'd, then declared that he would rather die with Honour than quit the Field, put his Men in order, boldly charging into the midst of his Enemies, but some of his own Party perfidiously deserting, and others submitting to the adverse Party, till he was almost left alone, then opprest with Numbers on every side, his Horse kill'd under him, and he stab'd in the Back, was carried Prisoner to his own Castle; where he not minding his Wounds, fell into a high Fever, and through the Anguish thereof died upon the sixteenth of the Calends of *May*, and was buried according to his Desire in the Oratory of the *Friars Minors* at 𝕶𝖎𝖑𝖐𝖊𝖓𝖓𝖕, where a noble Monument was afterwards erected to his Memory.

But soon after the King seeing his Errour, removed those Aliens from his Court and Council, received to Favour all those Noblemen who had assisted this Earl, and restored his whole Inheritance to

Gilbert Mareschal his Brother, who married *Margaret* the Sister of the King of 𝖘𝖈𝖔𝖙𝖑𝖆𝖓𝖉, *Anno* 1235, 19 *Hen.* III. with whom he had above ten thousand Marks for her Portion, besides a noble Dowry in 𝖘𝖈𝖔𝖙𝖑𝖆𝖓𝖉, and after her Decease he espoused *Maud de Lanvaley*, without the King's License, for which his Lands were seized. He was at a Turnament held *Anno* 1241, 25 *Hen.* III. at 𝖂𝖆𝖗𝖊 near 𝕳𝖊𝖗𝖙𝖋𝖔𝖗𝖉, mounted upon a lusty Italian Horse with whose Qualities he being not acquainted, first curb'd him, and then gave him the Spur, the Horse furiously mounting, broke both the Reins of his Bridle, and cast him out of the Saddle ; whereupon hanging in one of the Stirrups he was so drag'd about, trodden upon, and bruised, as that he died the same Evening, the 5th of the Calends of *July*, in the Priory of 𝕳𝖊𝖗𝖙𝖋𝖔𝖗𝖉, without Issue, and the
next Day was carried to the *New Temple* in 𝕷𝖔𝖓𝖉𝖔𝖓 where he was interr'd.

The King granted Livery of this Earldom and Marshal's Office, and of all those Lands which were of the Dowry of *Margaret* his Wife, Daughter of *Robert de Quincy*, Widow of *John* Earl of 𝕷𝖎𝖓𝖈𝖔𝖑𝖓𝖊, and Constable of 𝕮𝖍𝖊𝖘𝖙𝖊𝖗 her late Husband, to *Walter* his Brother, through the Intercession of the Queen, the Bishop of 𝕯𝖚𝖗𝖍𝖆𝖒, and some other noble Persons, on the Sunday preceding the Feast of *All-Saints*, reserving to himself two of his Castles in 𝖂𝖆𝖑𝖊𝖘, 𝕮𝖆𝖗𝖉𝖎𝖌𝖆𝖓 and 𝕮𝖆𝖗𝖒𝖆𝖗𝖙𝖍𝖊𝖓, and in 27 *Hen.* III. he paid a Relief to the King for those Lands which *Hawise de Quincy*, Mother of the said *Margaret* held *in Capite* and he died, *Anno* 1246, 30 *H.* III. 8th of the Calends of *December*, at the Castle of 𝕲𝖔𝖉𝖊𝖗𝖎𝖈𝖍.

Anselme his Brother and Heir succeeded,·but shortly after died at 𝖘𝖙𝖗𝖎𝖌𝖚𝖑𝖑, upon the Nones of *December ;* He was a Youth of singular Comeliness, and great Hopes, being the last of the five Sons of the renowned *William Mareschal*, late Earl of 𝕻𝖊𝖒𝖇𝖗𝖔𝖐𝖊, of whom their Mother, as 'tis said, prophetically foretold their Deaths in this Sort, and both of them were buried at 𝕿𝖎𝖓𝖙𝖊𝖗𝖓𝖊, not far from 𝖘𝖙𝖗𝖎𝖌𝖚𝖑𝖑, among divers of their noble Ancestors.

Upon the Division of the Estate of these great Earls,

this Mannor of 𝖂𝖊𝖗𝖘𝖙𝖔𝖓 fell to the Part of *Maud* the eldest Hund. of Bradewater
Sister, who married *Hugh Bigot*, Earl of 𝕹𝖔𝖗𝖋𝖔𝖑𝖐, by whom
he had Issue, *Roger* and *Hugh*, and died *Anno* 1225, 9 Dugd. Bar. vol. 1, fol. 133.
H. III. leaving

Roger his Son and Heir, who obtained the Office and
Honour of Marshal, *Anno* 1245, 29 *H.* III. in Right of
Maud, his Mother, eldest Daughter to *Walter Mareschal,*
Earl of 𝕻𝖊𝖒𝖇𝖗𝖔𝖐𝖊; and the King solemnly gave the Marshal's Rod into her Hands, *Anno* 32 *H.* III. in Regard of
her Seniority in the Inheritance of *Walter Mareschal* her
Father, which she thereupon deliver'd unto this Earl *Roger*
her Son and Heir, whose Homage the King received for
the same, commanding the Treasurer and Barons of his
Exchequer, by his Precept, that he should thenceforth en-
joy whatsoever belonged to that Office, and to admit whom-
soever he should assign and depute to sit for him in that
Court, in Case he should be a fit Person for the same.
This *Maud* afterwards married *John de Waren,* Earl of
𝕾𝖚𝖗𝖗𝖕, died *Anno* 1248, 32 *Hen.* III. and was buried in the Mon. Angl. fol. 725.
Abbey of 𝕿𝖎𝖓𝖙𝖊𝖗𝖓𝖊 in 𝖂𝖆𝖑𝖊𝖘; her four Sons, *Roger, Hugh,*
Ralph, and *John* carrying her Body into the Quire. After
the Battle of 𝕷𝖊𝖜𝖊𝖘, where the King was taken Prisoner, Dugd. Bar. vol. 1, fol. 135.
Anno 1264, 49 *H.* III. the Barons constituted this Earl
Governor of the Castle of 𝕺𝖗𝖋𝖔𝖗𝖉 in 𝕾𝖚𝖋𝖋𝖔𝖑𝖐, and he died
Anno 1270, 54 *H.* III. without Issue. Then this Mannor
came to the Possession of

Thomas Brotherton, fifth Son to King *Edw.* I. to whom
King *Edw.* II. granted all the Honour which *Roger le Bi-* Ibid. vol. 2, fol. 63.
god, sometime Earl of 𝕹𝖔𝖗𝖋𝖔𝖑𝖐 and Marshal of 𝕰𝖓𝖌𝖑𝖆𝖓𝖉,
enjoy'd; and he died *Anno* 12 *Edw.* III. leaving Issue by
Alice his first Wife, Daughter to Sir *Roger Halys* of 𝕳𝖆𝖗𝖜𝖎𝖈𝖍, Knight, two Daughters, *Margaret* and *Alice* his
Heirs; the one married *John de Segrave,* afterwards Sir
Walter Manny, Knight of the most noble Order of the
Garter; the other to *Edward de Montacute;* both whom did
their Homage, *Anno* 23 *Edw.* III. and had Livery of all
their Lands which their Wives had in 𝕴𝖗𝖊𝖑𝖆𝖓𝖉; This *Tho-*
mas Brotherton their Father left

Mary his second Wife, the Daughter of *William* Lord
𝕽𝖔𝖔𝖘, and Widow of *William* Lord *Braose* of 𝕭𝖗𝖊𝖒𝖇𝖗𝖊,
who had an Assignment of this Mannor, among divers others,
for her Dowry: She married Sir *Ralph Cobham,* and died Esc. 36 Ed. III.
Anno 36 *Edw.* III. and upon her Death this Mannor was
assigned for the Purparty of

Margaret, then the Wife of *Walter Manny,* and she
claimed the Office of Marshal of 𝕰𝖓𝖌𝖑𝖆𝖓𝖉, and to execute
the same by her Deputy at the Coronation of *Richard* II. Claus. 1 R. 11.
with the Fees; but *Henry Percy* performed that Service,

because her Claim could not be determined in so short a
time, and she was advanced *Anno* 21 *Rich.* II. to the Title
of Dutchess of 𝔑𝔬𝔯𝔣𝔬𝔩𝔨 for Life, and had forty Marks *per
Ann.* allowed her out of the Profits of that County, but she
died the next Year, and was buried in the Church of the
Fryers Minors in 𝔏𝔬𝔫𝔡𝔬𝔫; Afterwards this Mannor came
to the Possession of

 Thomas Barrington, Esq. from whom it was conveyed in
such Form as the Mannor of 𝔠𝔥𝔦𝔰𝔣𝔦𝔢𝔩𝔡, to which I refer the
Reader, till it came to

 John Barrington, Esq. who was his lawful Descendant,
and sold it to

Weav. Mon.
p. 512. King *Henry* VIII. who in a short Space after granted it to
Sir *William Parre,* Kt. Lord *Parre* of 𝔎𝔢𝔫𝔡𝔞𝔩, who held
it till the 18th of *August, March* 1, when he was attainted
of High Treason; from which time it was conveyed by the
same Grants, with the Mannors of 𝔅𝔢𝔫𝔦𝔫𝔤𝔱𝔬𝔫, 𝔄𝔯𝔤𝔢𝔫𝔱𝔦𝔫𝔢,
𝔐𝔬𝔫𝔡𝔢𝔫 𝔓𝔞𝔯𝔟𝔞, 𝔐𝔬𝔫𝔡𝔢𝔫 𝔐𝔞𝔤𝔫𝔞, 𝔖𝔞𝔟𝔯𝔦𝔡𝔤𝔢𝔴𝔬𝔯𝔱𝔥, 𝔑𝔲𝔤𝔞𝔱𝔢
𝔖𝔱𝔯𝔢𝔢𝔱, 𝔖𝔞𝔭𝔢𝔰𝔭𝔞𝔯𝔨, and the Advowson and Right of Patronage of 𝔅𝔢𝔫𝔦𝔫𝔤𝔱𝔬𝔫, 𝔐𝔬𝔫𝔡𝔢𝔫 𝔓𝔞𝔯𝔟𝔞, 𝔐𝔬𝔫𝔡𝔢𝔫 𝔐𝔞𝔤𝔫𝔞,
until it came again to the Crown, then Queen *Elizabeth*
granted it to

 John Puckering of *Lincoln-Inn,* Esq. who was one of
the Governours there, *Anno* 18 *Eliz.* read in that Society
on the *Quadragesime,* in the Year 1577, 19 *Eliz.* was called
by Writ to the State and Degree of a Sergeant at Law,
1580, 22 *Eliz.* was made the Queen's Serjeant and received the Honour of Knighthood, 1588, 30 *Eliz.* the Custody
of the Broad Seal was committed to his Charge, 1592, 34
Eliz. and he died within four Years after, leaving

 Thomas Puckering, who was created Baronet by Patent,
dated the 25th of *Novemb.* 1612, 10 *Ja.* I. he left Issue
only one Daughter, to whom this Mannor descended, and
she dying without Issue, it came to

 Sir *Henry Newton* alias *Puckering* the Son and Heir of
the only Sister of Sir *Thomas Puckering,* who was very
loyal to King *Charles* I. and sold this Mannor to

 John Hale of 𝔖𝔱𝔞𝔤𝔢𝔫𝔥𝔬𝔢, Esq. about the Year 1654, who
was knighted at the Entertainment which Sir *Harbottle
Grimston,* Baronet, Speaker of the House of Commons,
gave to the King at his House in 𝔏𝔦𝔫𝔠𝔬𝔩𝔫𝔰-𝔍𝔫𝔫-𝔉𝔦𝔢𝔩𝔡𝔰 the
25th of *June,* 1660. He married *Rose* the Daughter of
Colonel *Beale,* by whom he had Issue *Rose,* and he died on
the 22nd of *January,* in the Year 1672, and was buried
among his Ancestors in the Chancel at 𝔎𝔦𝔫𝔤'𝔰 𝔚𝔞𝔩𝔡𝔢𝔫.

 Rose Hale was his Daughter and Heir, married to Sir
John Austen, the Son and Heir of Sir *Robert Austen* of
𝔚𝔢𝔵𝔩𝔢𝔶 in the County of 𝔎𝔢𝔫𝔱, who was created Baronet by

Patent, dated *July* 10, 1660, 12 *Car*. II. and is the present Lord hereof.

The Mannor of LANNOCK

WAS in old time Parcel of the Mannor of Weston, and *William Mareschal* Earl of Pembroke, and then Lord of that Mannor, gave this with Baudac in the time of King *Henry* I. to the *Knights Templers*; upon their Dissolution it came to

The *Knights Hospitallers*, where it continued until the Dissolution of that Order, when it came to the Crown, from whence it was granted to

John Dormer, who levied a Fine in *Michaelmas* Term, 6 *Edw*. VI. of this Mannor, Messuages, and certain Lands in Weston, to the Rectory and Advowson of the Church of Weston to the Use of himself, *John Dormer*, and his Heirs; from whom it was conveyed to

John Spurling, who afterwards sold it to

Dionise, the Daughter of *Richard Hale* of Kings Walden in this County, Esq. and the Relict of Sir *Thomas Williamson* of Lodden in the County of Norfolk, Kt. but she dying without Issue, it descended to

William Hale, Esq. who was her Nephew and Heir; and he died seized hereof, leaving Issue

Richard Hale who succeeded him, and married *Elizabeth* the Daughter of *Isaac Minnell*, Alderm n of London, by whom he had Issue *William* and *Mary;* He died the 13th of *April*, *Anno* 1689, leaving *William*, who is his Heir, within Age, and is the present Lord hereof

Fin. levat.
Mic. 6 Ed. VI.
Rot. 200, cur.
recept. Scac.

The Mannor of ARGENTINE

WAS Parcel of the Revenue of the *Argentines*, ancient Lords of the Mannor of Wimondley, from whom it borrowed this Name, and since it passed from that Family, it has been conveyed from time to time with its neighbouring Mannor of Weston, till it came to Sir *John Austen*, the present Lord hereof.

In this Town is an old Seat called Fairclough-Hall, from the Owners thereof, who have this Pedigree,

And beareth, *Or, a Lion Rampant Sable armed and langued Gules between three Flower de Luces Azure*, by the *Name of* Fairclough

Sir Lawrence Fairclough of Fairclough Hall in Com. Hertford.

Sir Richard Fairclough, Son and Heir of Sir Lawrence.

Sir Ralph Fairclough, Son and Heir of Sir Richard.

Ralph Fairclough of Fairclough Hall, Son and Heir of Sir Ralph.

Lawrence Fairclough, Son and Heir of Ralph, mar. Elizabeth the Da. of ——— an. 39 H. VI.

John Fairclough, Son and Heir died without Issue.   Ralph Fairclough, Heir to his Brother.

Lawrence Fairclough, Son and Heir of Ralph.

Thomas Fairclough, Esq. mar. Millicent, Da. and Heir of —— Bar.	Lawrence Fairclough, died without Issue.	George Fairclough, died without Issue.	John Fairclough, second Son mar. Margaret, Da. of —— Chery of Munden in Com. Hertford.

John Fairclough, Esq. mar. Anne, Da. of Tho Spencer of Cople in Com Bedford.	Thomas, died s. p.	Lawrence, died s. p.	Richard, died s. p.	Mary, Da. of ———— Beller, Dr. in Physick, 1st Wife.	Edward Fairclough of Weston, living Anno 1634.	Eliz. Da. of Web of London, 2 Wife.

Thos. Fairclough, Esq. mar. Mary, Da. of John Harvey of Thurley, in Com. Bedford, living Anno 1634.	Anne, mar. Lawrence Fairclough	Jane, mar. Edward Kent.	Miliceut, m. Andrew Bussey.	Elizabeth, m. —— Clerk, a Dean in Ireland.	Frances, married Risly.	Rose, mar. Edward Underwood.	Dorothy, Robert Underwood.	Constance, Owen Hobert.

					Susan.	Edw. Fairclough, Son and Heir aged 26 Years, Anno 1654.	Elizabeth, mar John Goodwyn.

John Fairclough, Son and Heir mar. Margaret Da.   Lytton Fairclough, second Son.
of Robert Herne of Titenham in Com. Norfolk.

Thomas, Son and Heir, mar. Anne, Da. of Arthur Pulter of Bradfeild, Esq. by whom he had no Issue ; but John the Father sold this seat to William Hale, Esq. and William his Grandson is his lineal Descendant, and Present Possessor hereof.

THE Parsonage is appropriated to the Use of this *William Hale*, who is Patron of this Church; and this Vicaridge, *Anno 26 Hen.* VIII. was valued in the King's Books at 10*l.* 6*s.* 8*d. per Annum.*

The VICARS.

24 *July* 1611 *Joh. Beesbrown,* Clerke, was buried here	*Symond Smeath* —— *Hinds*
1611 *William Andrews*	1663 *Thomas Gregory*
1626 *Richard Pooley*	1667 *John Pyke,* the present Vicar.
1648 *Thomas Marshall*	

The Church is erected about the Middle of the Parish, in the Diocess of **Baldock**, in the Bishoprick of **Lincolne**, after the Manner of a Cathedral, the Tower standing between the Church and the Chancel; In the Tower is a Ring of five Bells, with a Spire over it. In the Chancel is a fair Monument, which is made of black and mixt Marble, on the top whereof are three Coats of Arms. Under these are two naked Boys of white Marble, holding up an Earl's Coronet, and under one Boy is writ, *Vivit post;* under the other, *Funera Virtus;* down one Side the Figures of a Book, a Bill, a Coffin, and a Mattock ; down the other Side, a Death's Head, Cross-Bones, an Hour Glass, a Cross Dart, a Book, a Spade, a Mattock; underneath the Monument, a Death's Head and Sheet; and upon the Table of the Black Marble, these Lines are writ in Gold.

Epitathium Charissimi Viri Johannis Fairclough de
Fairclough-Hall, *Armigeri*
Dignus eras meliore loco meliore Sepulchro
Nolueras Titulos Grande sonare tuos
Hæc tua Laus vixisse Deo Partisque tuisque
Atque ita supremum claudere posse diem
Fælicem vitam fælicia funera ducis
Lector, cui dulce est vivere, dulce mori.

*Talis Vir iste ad omnia quæ bona essent, ortus ad meliora moriturus, cujus
constans in Domino, peritus in Fide, Amicis prestanda spectata semper
integritas in omnibus Actionibus sine acerbitate gravitas. in Eleemosi-
nis egenis conferendis prompta semper Liberalitas erga suos pa——Comi-
tati benevolentia; in omnes equitas Charu imprimis Deo grata hominibus;
Immortalem Nominis ipsius in laudem pararunt et sic plenus annis ultimo
die Decembris Anno. Salutis humanæ* 1630. *Ætatis suæ* 86. *ex hac peri-
tura ad perennem vitam (multùm deploratus) emigravit. Cum ex Charissima Selectissimaque Uxor, tam Virtute quam genere, Clarissima D.*
Anna Spencer *Filia* Thomæ Spencer *de* Cophull *in Com'* Bedf. *Armig.
filios duos undecimq; filias suscepisset Primogenitus ejus* Thomas D.
Muriam Harvey, Johannis Harvey *de* Churleigh *in Com' predict' Armig.
filiam uxorem capit, duo ex ea filios, viz.* Johannem *et* Littonam *adhuc
superstites, unamque filiam defunctam suscepit .Natu Major* Johannes D.
Margaritam Herne, Roberti Herne *de* Gebinham *in Com'* Norfol. *Gen'
filiam uxorem duxit.*

BAUDAC, BAUDOCHE, BALDOK.

GILBERT Earl of Pembroke, Lord of the Mannor of
Weston, about the 4th or 5th Year of the Reign of King
Stephen, gave to the Knights Templers a Parcel of Land
lying in the Champion within the Precincts of that Mannor, containing about 120 Acres, of the yearly Value of 10*l.*
whereon they built a Town called Baudac, and he gave ten
Marks to the Church; they improved the Town by several
Purchases, and obtained divers Priviledges from the King,
all which were afterwards confirmed by *William Mareschal,* Earl of Pembroke, his Hereditary Successor in his
Lands and Honours.

Monast. vol.2,
fol. 524, 543.
Har. vol. 1,
fol. 208.

Monast.vol. 3,
fol. 524, 530.

About the Year of our Lord 1118, certain Gentlemen
honoured with Knighthood, took upon themselves a religious Course of Life, under the Patriarch of Jerusalem,
after the Rule of Canons Regular, and began this Order;
Hugh de Paganis and *Godfrey de St. Audomare* were the
first; they were valiant Men, but so poor that both of them
had no more than one Horse to ride on; from hence the Figure
of two Men riding on one Horse was engraved on their Seal,
to put them in Mind of their primitive Poverty. *Baldwyn,*
King of Jerusalem, assigned to them a Piece of Ground
within his own Palace, on the South Part of the Temple of
our Lord, for their Habitation, to which the Canons of the
Temple added the adjacent Street, to erect Buildings necessary for their Use; the Patriarch, with the King, Nobles,
and Prelates, allowing them Lands for their Support
in Food and Rayment.

Dugd Survey
of Warwicks.
fol. 704.

They first undertook to defend Pilgrims from Spoil and
Robbery by Thieves in their Passage to and from Jerusalem, upon which their Order was ordained in the Council of
Tretas; and Pope *Honorius* gave them a white Habit,
after which their Estates greatly encreased, and they multiplied very much in the time of Pope *Eugenius;* they sewed

Crosses made of red Cloth upon the left Shoulder of their Mantles, to distinguish them from other religious Persons, and that triumphal Sign encouraged and animated them instead of a Buckler, to defend their Religion against all Infidels: They were originally called Knights Templers, from their Residence in certain Rooms adjoyning to that Temple which was built by King *Solomon.* They wore linnen Coifs on their Heads like Serjeants at Law, for their Habit; and red Caps close over them; Shirts of Mail, and Swords girded round their Bodies with broad Belts; and over these a white Cloak reaching to the Ground, with a red Cross on the left Shoulder, and they wore their Beards of a great Length.

Stow's Survey of London, fol. 483.
Jordan Briset, a wealthy and devout Man, founded in the Reign of *H.* II. an House near Smithfield, where these Knights first settled in England, from whom it was called St. *John's* of Jerusalem, and these by the Austerity of their Lives at first, obtained from a low Beginning vast Possessions; then this Order removed to Holbourn, where they remained a while; and in the time of *H.* II. built the *Temple*, and erected a Church in Fleet-street, according to the Form of the Temple of Jerusalem, dedicated to God and our blessed Lady by *Heraclius,* Patriarch of Jerusalem, *An.* 1185. Afterwards they obtained great Priviledges and vast Possessions in this Kingdom and elsewhere in Christendom; so that their Potency became a great Terrour to most Princes, which caused their Ruin; for at a general Council held at Vienna in France, in the Year 1311, under Pope *Clement* V. their whole Order was condemned, and their Possessions were seized into the King's Hands; but by a general Decree of the same Pope, dated at Vienna, the Nones of *May,* in the 7th Year of his Papacy, they were incorporated to the *Knights Hospitallers,* an Order instituted, or rather restored by one *Gerrard* a Nobleman, who visited the Sepulchre, and other holy Places about Jerusalem, out of an extraordinary Devotion, before the time of *Godfry* of Bulloign, Duke of Lorrain, when the Holy Land became famous by the Expedition of Christian Princes, and by the Assistance of divers zealous Gentlemen, who arrived there for the same Purpose, built the Hospital of St. *John* of Jerusalem, for a Relief and Harbour for the Christians, and placed a Rector or Governor to maintain good Order there: Afterwards Pope *Gelasius* II. allowed this Institution, and gave them for their Habit, a long Robe or Cloak, whereon a white Cross was fixt, containing eight Points, for an Ensign or Mark of their Purity, or of the eight Beatitudes, which they aspired by the Concession of Pope *Honorius* II. and were obliged by their Profession charitably to relieve all such as visited those holy Places; to guide them in the

Way, and to secure them against the *Arabians*, Infidels, and all other barbarous People, which Duty they did so worthily perform, by the Assistance of divers Princes, that few Conquerors have exceeded them in Worth or Valour. But after the Loss of all in 𝔓𝔞𝔩𝔢𝔰𝔱𝔦𝔫𝔢, they took from the Pagans the Isle of 𝔯𝔥𝔬𝔡𝔢𝔰, which they held above 200 Years, during which time they changed their Names, and were called Knights of 𝔯𝔥𝔬𝔡𝔢𝔰 : but when *Solyman*, the second Emperor of the *Turks*, by the Treachery of one of their own Citizens, after several Assaults made, had won that Island from them, *Charles* V. and Pope *Clement* VII. in Pity of their Loss, and for the Reward of their incomparable Valour, gave to them the Isle of 𝔪𝔞𝔩𝔱𝔞, where they have twice beaten the *Turk*, notwithstanding his Greatness, and continue there to this Day, from which Island they are now called, Knights of 𝔪𝔞𝔩𝔱𝔞.

The *Knights Templers* complained, 8 *Joh.* that the Prior of 𝔯𝔬𝔰𝔢𝔰 𝔠𝔯𝔬𝔰𝔰 took from their Men of 𝔟𝔞𝔩𝔡𝔲𝔠 37s. Rent, and other Customs granted by the Charter of the same King, upon which the Prior allowed the Stallage taken from their Men, &c. Placit. Mic h. an. 8 Joh. Rot. 12, in recept. Scac.

But not to omit the special Priviledges which they had in 𝔟𝔞𝔩𝔡𝔲𝔠, King *H.* III. *Anno* 1 *Regni sui*, granted to them and their Successors, that they should hold one Fair yearly in the Town of 𝔟𝔞𝔩𝔡𝔬𝔠𝔨, on the Feast of St. *Matthew* the Apostle, and to continue four Days following; and also one Market on Wednesday in every Week in the Year. Monast. vol.2, fol. 552.

William Marshal Earl of 𝔭𝔢𝔪𝔟𝔯𝔬𝔨𝔢, *Anno* 1201, 2 *Joh.* confirmed to the *Knights Templers* the Grant of all the Priviledges which Earl *Gilbert* his Predecessor and Ancestor had given them, among which they had Power to try by Ordale and by Battel.

Ordale came from a Saxon Word *Ordale*, which signified *Juditium magnum justum indifferens*; and the first Mention of it that I find, was at the Council of 𝔪𝔢𝔫𝔱𝔰, afterwards at the Council of 𝔗𝔯𝔶𝔢𝔯𝔰, and it was introduced into this Nation about the time of King *Ina*, and inserted into the Laws of King *Athelstan*, tho' doubtless it was in Use before that time, and was of two Sorts, by Fire and by Water.

1 By Fire, when the Party accused did bear an hot Iron in his Hand, nine Foot from the Stake to the Mark, according to the Measure of his Foot who was to come to Judgment, or else walked barefooted and blindfolded between certain Ploughshares, red hot, placed at some Distance, according to the usual Manner. This Iron was sometime of one Pound Weight, which was single *Ordalium*, sometime of three Pound Weight, which was treble *Ordalium*; and whosoever walked between the said Ploughshares without

Hund. of Hurt of his Feet, was adjudged innocent, but if his Skin
Bradewate was scorched, he was forthwith condemn'd as guilty of the
Trespass whereof he was accused, according to the Propor-
tion and Quantity of the Burning.

The fiery Manner of Purgation belonged only to Noblemen and Women, and such as were free-born, and the Proceedings were after this Manner.

THE Accusation was lawfully made, and three Days spent
in Fasting and Prayer, the Men who were to be tryed, were
brought to the Church, and the Priest clad in all his holy
Vestures, saving his Vestment, took the Iron laid before
the Altar with a Pair of Tongs, and singing the Hymn of
the three Children in Latin, *Benedicite omnia opera, &c.*
O all ye Works of God the Lord, &c. carried it solemnly to
the Fire, (where it was cast upon the Coals, and lay from the
Beginning of the Benediction to the last Collect) saying these
Words in Latin, over the Place where the Fire was kindled,
whereby this Purgation was to be made, *Benedic Domine
Deus, &c.* Bless thou O Lord this Place, that it may be to
us Health, Holiness, Chastity, Virtue, Victory, Pureness,
Humility, Goodness, Gentleness, and Fulness of the Law,
Obedience to God the Father, the Son, and the Holy Ghost:
This Blessing be upon this Place and all that dwell therein.

Then followed the Blessing of the Fire.

Domine Deus Pater Omnipotens, &c. Lord God, Father
Almighty, Light everlasting, hear us, since thou art the
Maker of all Lights; Bless O Lord this Light that is al-
ready sanctifyed in thy Sight, which hast lightened all Men
that come into the World, to the End, that by the same
Light we may be lightened with the shining of thy Bright-
ness. As thou didst lighten *Moses*, so now illuminate our
Hearts and our Senses, that we may come to everlasting
Life through Christ our Lord.

This ended, the Priest said the *Pater Noster*, after that,
these Words in Latin, *Salvum fac, &c.* O Lord save thy
Servant, &c. Send him Help from thy holy Place, &c. Defend him out of Sion, &c. The Lord hear, &c. The Lord be
with you, &c.

The Prayer.

Benedic Domine, &c. Bless we beseech thee, O Lord holy
Father, everlasting God, through the Invocation of thy most
holy Name, by the coming of thy Son, and the Gift of the
Holy Ghost, and to the Manifestation of thy true Judgment,
that this Kind of Mettal being hallowed, and all fraudulent
Practices of the Devil utterly removed, the manifest Truth
of thy Judgment may be revealed by the same Lord Jesus,
&c.

This done, the Iron was laid into the Fire, sprinkled with *Hund. of* *Bradewater* holy Water, and whilst it heated, the Priest said Mass, and did as Order required.

The Office of the Mass.

Justus es Domine, &c. Just art thou, O Lord, and righteous are thy Judgments, O deal with thy Servants according to thy great Mercy: Blessed are the unspotted in the Way.

The Prayer.

Absolve quæsimus Domine, &c. Pardon, we beseech thee, O Lord, the Sins of thy Servants, that being loosed from the Bond of their Iniquities, which they have contracted through their Infirmities, they may be cleared by thy preventing Justice according as they have deserved, and obtain a manifest Declaration of the Truth by Christ our Lord.

Then follows the Lesson taken out of *Leviticus*, Chap. xix. Ver. 10—14, beginning Ver. 10. *I am the Lord your God, &c.* The second Lesson taken out of the *Ephesians*, Chap. iv. Ver. 23—28.

Then followed these Responses.

Be favourable, O Lord, unto our Sins, lest the Heathen should say, Where is their God?

Help us, O Lord God of our Salvation, and deliver us, O Lord, for the Honour of thy Name.

Allelujah! God is a just Judge, strong and patient, he will not be angry for ever.

The Gospel is taken out of St. *Mark*, Ch. x Ver. 17—21.

Then the Priest called the Men to be purged; and abjured them after this Form.

Adjuro vos per Patrem, &c. I adjure you, by the Father, the Son, and the holy Ghost, and by the Christian Religion which ye profess, by the only begotten Son of God, the holy Trinity, the sacred Gospels, and all the holy Relicks which are in this Church, and by that Baptism wherewith the Priest did regenerate you, that you do in no Wise presume to communicate, or draw nigh to this Altar, if you have either committed, or consented to or do know who has committed this Fact.

If they say nothing, nor own any thing of it, then they make their Offerings, and the Priest proceedeth and saith,

Grant, O Lord, that the Intercession may reconcile these our Oblations to thy merciful Acceptance, and that thy gracious Indulgence, which thro' our Unworthiness we cannot hope for, we may obtain by their Prayers, through our Lord Jesus Christ.

Hund. of
Bradewater

The Preface.

O Everlasting God, who dost not only pardon Sins, but also justifie Sinners, who doth not only release the Punishment of the Guilty, but dost likewise highly and greatly reward them; We do most humbly beseech thee of thy Goodness, that thou wouldest not in this Trial judge these thy Servants of their former Offences, but that thou wouldest be pleased to manifest the Truth of this Accusation to the Spectators, that the People may therefore extol thy holy Name, and believe thee to be the only Giver of Life, as well in this World as in the World to come, through Christ our Lord.

The Benediction before the Trial

God of whom it is written, that thou art righteous, and that thy Judgments are true, deal with these thy Servants according to thy great Mercy, that they be not judged for their former Sins, but in this Trial, according as they have deserved, they may through thy preventing Benediction, obtain a Judgment of the Truth.

Thou who art just, and a Lover of Justice, in whose Prescence is all Equity, grant that here in the Sight of thy People, the Enquiry after thy Truth, by the deceitful Contrivance of wicked Persons, may not be obscured. *Amen.*

We beseech thee favourably to receive our most humble Petitions, and mercifully to vouchsafe these thy Servants the Pardon of all their Sins past, and if they are guilty, let the Fulness of thy Benediction manifest the Truth of their Offence. *Amen.*

Then the Priest permits them to receive the Sacrament, and saith,

The Body and Blood of our Lord Jesus Christ be unto you for your Purgation this Day.

Just is the Lord, and loveth Righteousness, his Countenance doth behold the thing that is right.

After they have received the Sacrament, the Priest saith,

Grant, O Lord God, that we having now received thy holy Gift, may through this Partaking of this Sacrament, be henceforth purged from our Offences, and that in these thy Servants it may be of Force to declare the Sentence of Truth, through Christ our Lord.

Then follows *Kirielison*, the Litany, and certain Psalms, and after them the Priest proceeds, saying, *Oremus*, Let us pray, &c.

Deus qui per Ignem, &c. O God, who in shewing great Tokens by Fire, didst deliver Abraham thy Servant, from the burning of the *Chaldees*, whilst others perished; O God, who suffer'd the Bush to burn in the Sight of *Moses*, and yet not to consume; O God, who delivered the three Children from bodily Harm in the Furnace of the *Chaldees*, while divers were consumed; O God, who by Fire, didst wrap the People of *Sodom* in their Destruction, and yet savedst *Lot* and his Daughters from Peril; O God, who, by the shining of thy Brightness at the coming of the holy Ghost in Likeness of Fire, didst separate the Faithful from such as believed not; shew unto us in the Trial of this our Wickedness, the Power of the same Spirit, &c. and by the Heat of this Fire discern the faithful from the unfaithful, that the guilty, whose Cause is now in Trial, by touching thereof, may tremble and fear, and his Hand be burned, or being innocent, that he may remain in Safety, &c. O God, from whom no Secrets are hidden, let thy Goodness answer to our Faith, and grant that whosoever in this Purgation shall touch and bear this Iron, may either be tryed as innocent, or revealed as an Offendor, &c.

After this the Priest sprinkled the Iron with Holy Water saying

The blessing of God the Father, the Son, and the Holy Ghost, be upon this Iron to the Revelation of the just Judgment of God.

Then the Person accused bore it by the length of nine Foot; that done, his Hand was wrapped and sealed up for the space of three Days; after this if any corruption or raw Flesh appeared where the Iron touched it, he was condemned as Guilty: if it was whole and sound, he gave Thanks to God.

WATER ORDALE

Was appointed for Husbandmen and Villains; and was of two Sorts, either by hot Water, or cold Water. 1. Trial by hot Water, where the Person accused was required to put his Hand up to the Wrist into a Vessel of scalding Water, or his Arm up to the Elbow in a Chaldron of seething Water, from whence if he withdrew his Hand or his Arm without any Manner of Damage, he was adjudged Innocent; but if his Hand or Arm was scalded, he was then held guilty, and punisht for it. 2 Trial by cold Water was when the Party thought Guilty, was tumbled into some Pond or huge Vessel of cold Water, where if he continued for a Season without strugling for Life, he was presently acquitted as guiltless of the Fact whereof he was accused; but if he began once to plunge and labour for Breath immediately upon his falling into Liquor, he was condemn'd as guilty of the Crime, and receiv'd his Punishment for it.

The Form of the Trial by Water was after this Manner.

When the Mass was done, the Priest shall make Holy Water, go to the Place where the Men are to be tried, and shall give of the Holy Water to them to drink, then he shall conjure the Water wherein they are to be put.

The Exorcism of the Water.

O God, who by the Substance of Water did assert thy Judgments by destroying thousands of People in the great Flood, and didst spare *Noah* thy Servant and his Family: Thou, O God, who didst drown the Armies of the *Egyptians* in the *Red Sea*, and at the same time didst lead the Children of *Israel* through the Sea without Fear; vouchsafe we beseech thee to pour down the Virtue of thy Blessing upon these Waters, and to manifest a new and wonderful Sign, that they may receive the Innocent according to their Nature, upon whose Trial we are to put them into the Waves and carry them down into the Deep; but repel and throw from them those, who are guilty of this Crime, nor suffer that Body to enter therein, which being void of the Weight of Goodness, is puft up with the vain Air of Iniquity, and that as they want the Weight of Virtue, they may not have the Weight of their natural Substance, in these Waters, through our Lord.

Another Form of Exorcism of the Water.

I adjure thee, O Creature of Water, in the Name of God the Father Almighty, who created thee in the Beginning, and charged thee to minister to Human Necessities, who also commanded that thou shouldest be separated from the Waters that were above; I adjure thee by the ineffable Name of Jesus Christ, Son of the living God, under whose Feet the Sea and the divided Element yielded itself to be trod upon : who also willed himself to be baptized in the same Element of Water; I adjure thee also by the Holy Ghost, who descended upon our Lord in his Baptism; I adjure thee by the sacred Name of the individual Godhead, at whose Will the Element of Water was divided, and the People of *Israel* passed over on dry Land, and which the Prophet *Elisha* did invoke, causing the Iron to swim thereby, when it was parted from the Handle of the Ax, that in no wise ye do receive these Men if they are any ways Guilty of this Fact whereof they are accused, either in Deed, or by Consent, or Knowledge thereof, but cause them to swim upon thee, and that no Imposture of the Enemy may effect any thing whereby it may be concealed; but we charge thee being adjured in the Name of Christ. that thou be obedient to us through his Name, whom every

Creature does serve, whom Cherubim and Seraphim do *Hund. of* Bradewater
praise, saying, Holy, Holy, Holy, Lord God of Hosts, who
reigneth for ever and ever. *Amen.*

A third Form of adjuring the cold Water.

I adjure thee, O Creature of Water, in the Name of
God the Father, the Son, and the Holy Ghost, and by the
dreadful Day of Judgment, by the twelve Apostles, and the
seventy two Disciples, by the twelve Prophets, and the
four and twenty Elders, who do perpetually praise the Lord,
and by the hundred and forty four thousand which follow
the Lamb, and by all the Troops of Holy Angels, Archan-
gels, Thrones, Principalities and Powers, Cherubim and
Seraphim, and by all the thousands of Holy Martyrs, Virgins, and Confessors: I adjure thee by the Blood of our
Lord Jesus Christ, and by the four Gospels and Evangelists, by the seventy two Books of the old and new Testament, and by all the Holy Writers and Teachers of them :
I adjure thee by the holy Catholick Church, by the Communion of Saints and their Resurrection, that thou dost become exorcised Water, adjured and fortified against that
Enemy of Man the Devil, and against the Man, who being
seduced by him, hath committed this Fact, whereof we do
now make this Enquiry, that by no Means, thou dost receive him, or suffer him to sink down in thee, but that thou
do reject and put him from thee, nor suffer that Body to
enter in, which is void and empty of Goodness, but that as
it doth want the Weight of Virtue, so it may want the
Weight of its natural Substance in thee; and that thou after
the Manner of Water, receive those that are innocent of the
alledged Crime, and draw them down into the Deep
without any Hurt or Harm, through Christ our Lord.

After these Conjurations of the Water, the Men who were
supposed to be guilty, putting off all their Garments, kissed
the holy Gospel and the Cross, and the Priest sprinkling
holy Water upon them all, and their Thumbs and their Toes
tied together, were one after the other cast into the Water.
Those who sunk, were judged innocent, but those who
swam were deemed guilty; and all those who were present,
were required to be fasting.

In the time of King *Athelstan,* a Law was made for the
regulating of the Proceedings upon these Tryals by Fire
and Water, after this Manner.

Concerning Ordale, we command in the Name of God, *Anglecta.*
and by the Precepts of our Archbishops and Bishops, that *Angla. Brit.* lib. 2, cap. 8.
no Man enter into the Church after the Fire is brought in, Inter Leges Athelstani,ca.
wherewith the Judgement is to be made hot, except the 30.
Priest, and he who is to undergo the Trial; and let there be

Hund. of Bradewater measured nine Foot from the Stake unto the Mark, according to the Measure of his Foot, who is to come to Judgment.

And if the Trial be by Water, let it be made hot till it boil in a Vessel of Iron, Brass, Lead, or Clay; and if it be single, let his Hand be put therein, after a Stone or Stock, up to his Wrest; but if the Accusation be threefold, then to his Elbow. And when the Judgement shall be prepared, let two Men be brought in on each Side, to make Experiment, that it be as hot as is before exprest.

Let as many come in on each Side the Judgment along the Church; and let them be fasting and abstain from their Wives that Night, and the Priest shall sprinkle holy Water on them, and give them the Text of the holy Gospel to kiss, as also the Sign of the Cross. And no Man shall make the Fire any longer than whilst the Benediction beginneth; but shall cast the Iron upon the Coals unto the last Collect. Afterwards it shall be put upon the —— without any more Words, then that they pray earnestly to God, that he will vouchsafe to manifest the Truth therein. Then shall the Person accused drink holy Water, and his Hand, wherewith he shall carry the Judgement, shall be sprinkled therewith, and so let him go, the nine Foot measured, being distinguished by three and three.

At the first Mark next to the Stake, he shall set his right Foot, and at the second his left Foot, and thence he shall remove his right Foot unto the third Mark, where he shall throw down the Iron, and hasten to the holy Altar; which done, his Hand shall be sealed up, and the third Day after viewed whether it be clean or unclean, where it was so sealed. And he who shall transgress these Laws, let the Ordale Judgment or Tryal be done upon him, that he pay 120 Shillings for a Fine or Mulct.

I find other Laws made touching Ordale, which the Reader may see recorded in the same King's Reign, and 'tis said that *Emma*, Mother to King *Edward* the Confessor, did undergo this Kind of fiery Trial, and that *Richard Haiward* suffered in the time of *H.* II. by the Judgement of Water; and it was used until the time of King *H.* III. who abolish'd *Origin. Jurid.* fol. 87. it *Anno* 3 *Regni sui*, as appears by a Record set forth by Sir *William Dugdale* at large, in his *Origines Juridiciales*, to which I refer the Reader.

TRIAL BY BATTEL.

THESE Trials by Combat or Battel and by Ordalé, came to us from the *Lombards*, who coming out of Scandia overran Europe, and 'tis thought that it was instituted by *Frotho* III. King of Denmark, at the time of the Birth of Christ, for he ordained that every Controversy should be determined by the Sword, and it continued in Holsatia until the time of

Christian, the third King of Denmark, who began his Reign,
1585. And in Appeals, was after this Manner.

A the Appellee with his left Hand took *B* the Appellant
by his right Hand, and laid his own right Hand upon a Book,
and said,

Here you this, you Man, that call yourself *B*, that I Man
who call myself *A*, such a Day and such a Year, did not
kill *C* your Father, as you surmised, neither am I guilty of
that Felony, So help me God: And kissing the Book saith,
This will I defend against you by my Body, as this Court
will award.

Then *B* the Appellant with his left Hand, takes *A* the
Appellee by his right Hand, and laying his own right Hand
upon the Book, saith,

Here you this, you Man who call yourself *A*, that you
furiously in such a Day and such a Year, did kill *C* my
Father, So help me God: And kissing the Book saith,
This will I justify against you by my Body, as this Court
will award.

Then the Court appoints them a Day to make their Combat, and the Appellee puts in Pledges to the Court to perform the Battel, and to defend himself; the Plaintiff puts
in Pledges to deraign the Battle at the Day assigned; the
Appellant shall go at Liberty, but the Appellee shall be kept
in Prison at Ease, and have sufficient Meat and Drink.

The Marshal apparels the Appellant and Appellee, both
alike at their own Costs, the Night before the Combat is
appointed to be fought, that they may be in the Field the
next Morning, ready to perform the Combat by the rising
of the Sun; the Apellee's Head shall be poled, but not the
Appellant's, and the Marshal brings them attired into the
Field ready to perform the Battel before the Justices, who
causeth Proclamation to be made when they be set, and the
Appellant and the Appellee brought within the Lists, ready
to atchieve the Combat.

That none but the two Combatants shall be so hardy to
stir, or make any Noise whatsoever he shall see and hear,
whereby the Battle may be disturbed; and whosoever shall
do any thing contrary to the Proclamation, shall be im-
prisoned for a Year and a Day.

When the Appellant and the Appellee are ready to join
Battel, or in Battel, if the Appellant will confess his Ap-
peal to be false, 'tis a sufficient Vanquishment, for by this
Acknowledgement, he shall be adjudged to be overcome in
the Field, and barred of his Appeal for ever; but if the
Appellee confess himself in the Field to be vanquished, he
shall be presently hanged. They fought with Weapons of
K 2

small Length, bareheaded, having their Hands and Feet
bare, with two Staves of one Length horned at both Ends,
and either of them have a Scutcheon four cornered, without
any Iron, for that one may not hurt the other with the Iron;
and if the Appellee can defend himself, until the Stars may
be seen in the Firmament, then he shall go quit from the
Appellant.

It seems by Mr. *Glanvil*, that Tryal by Duel or Combat
was much used for Tryal of Right before King *H*. II. instituted or revived the Way of Tryal by Grand Assize in
Favour of Life; however this Tryal by Battel was not, nor
yet is repealed in 𝔈𝔫𝔤𝔩𝔞𝔫𝔡.

In a Writ of Right, wherein *Chevin* demanded certain
Lands against *Paramour*, *Termino Trin*. 13 *Eliz*. the Te-
nant chose Tryal by Battel, for whom *George Thorn* was
Champion, and the Demandant elected *Henry Nailer*, a
Dyer, 13 Eliz.
40. fencing Master for his Champion, and the Champions were
mainprize, and sworn to perform the Battel at 𝔗𝔬𝔱𝔥𝔦𝔩 Fields
in 𝔚𝔢𝔰𝔱𝔪𝔦𝔫𝔰𝔱𝔢𝔯, on *Monday* next after the Morrow of the
Holy Trinity, which was the first Day of the *Utas* of the
Term, and the same Day was given to the Parties, at which
Day and Place a List was made in an even and plain Ground;
their Squadrant, that is to say every Square consisted of
sixty Foot East, West, North and South, and the Place or
Court for the Justices of the *Common Bench* was made
without; and upon the Lists furnish with the same Cloath,
which belonged to their Court in *Westminster-hall*, and a
Bar was made there for the Serjeants at Law; and about
the tenth Hour of the same Day, *Dyer*, *Weston*, and *Har-
per*, Justices of the Court of *Common Pleas*, (*Welshe* only
absent by Rëason of Sickness) appeared in their scarlet
Robes, with their Appurtenances and their Coiffs, also the
Serjeants in their Scarlet Robes; then Proclamations were
solemnly made with three *O yes*, &c. that done, the Demandant was first solemnly demanded, and did not appear,
whereupon the Mainprize of the Champion was demanded
to bring forth the Champion of the Demandant, who came
to the Place apparalled with red Sandells, upon his Back
Armour, bare legged from the Knee downward, bare headed, and bare Arms to the Elbows, being brought in by the
Hand of a Knight, Sir *Jerome Bowes*, who carried a red Baston of an Ell long, tipped with Horn, and a Yeoman; the
Target made of double Leather; they were brought in at
the North Side of the Lists, went about the Sides, and then
came towards the Bar before the Justices, with three solemn
Congies, and was made to stand there on the South Side of
the Place, being the right Side of the Court; after that the
other Champion was brought in like Manner at the South
Side of the Lists, with like Congies by the Hand of Sir

Henry Cherry, Kt. and was placed on the North Side of *Hund. of* *Bradwater.* the Bar, and two Serjeants being of Council of each Party in the Midst between them; this done, the Demandant was solemnly called again, and appeared not, but made Default; Serjeant *Barham* for the Tenant, prayed the Court to record the Nonsuit, *Quod factum fuit.* Then *Dyer*, Chief Justice, reciting the Writ and Count, and Issue join'd upon the Battel, and the Oath of the Champion to perform it, and the Prefixion of the Day and Place, gave Judgment against the Demandant, and that the Tenant should have the Land to him and his Heirs for ever.

And the Demandant and his Pledges, *de prosequendo in Misericordia Reginæ*, then solemn Proclamation was made, that the Champions and all other present there, who were above four thousand Persons by Estimation, might depart in the Peace of God and the Queen. *Et sic fecerunt magno clamore, vivat Regina*; and upon another Writ of Right Claxton against Lilburne, Cook, Rep. 3, 522. in **Durham**, *Termino Michaelis, Anno* 14 *Car.* I. the Tenant waged Battel, which was accepted, and at the Day to be performed, Exception was taken to it, and what became of it afterwards I know not; but whoever would read more of those Tryals by Battel, may read *Bracton, lib.* 3. *cap.* 18. *Breton, cap.* of Appeals, and *Dugd. Origines Juridiciales*, from *fol.* 75 to 86.

Richard Earl of **Strigull**, who married *Isabel* the sole Daughter and Heir of *Richard Strongbow*, Earl of **Pem-** *Bar.* vol. 1, fol. 602. **brook**, gave divers Liberties and Priviledges to the Borough of **Baudac**, (formerly granted to the Knights Templers, by his noble Ancestor *Gilbert Strongbow*, sometime Earl of **Pembrook**) and gave unto them the Mill of **Radewellesheved**, with two Husbandmen in that Town.

King *Hen.* III. 1 *Regni sui*, granted to the Knights *Mon. Angl* vol.2, fol.552. Templers, and their Successors for ever, that they should have a Fair yearly in the Town of **Baldock**, on the Feast of St. *Matthew* the Apostle, and four Days following, also one Market to be held on Wednesday in every Week of the Year, in the new Borough.

The Master of the Knights Templers in **England**, claimed by the Grant of *H.* III. very large Liberties, with Exemption from all secular Service, Soc, Sac, Toll, Them, Infangeneth, Outfangeneth, Hamsocne, Discharge in all things, in all Places and Causes, &c. from Toll, and all secular Service and Custom, in as large a Manner as any kingly Power can grant to any religious House, and Fair and Market. Also the Correction of the Assize of Bread, Wine, and Ale, Tumbrel, Pillory, View of Franc-pledge, &c. and they were allowed.

King *H.*VII. 7 *Regni sui*, granted to *John Kendal* Prior

Hund. of
Bradewater

of the Hospital of St. *John* of 𝔍erusalem, in 𝔈ngland, and his Fraternity and their Successors, a Market to be held on Wednesday in every Week of the Year, in this Town, free from all Tolls, Taxes, Tallages, Piccage, Stallage, or other Charge whatsoever, to them that shall sell any Wares or Merchandize; And also two Fairs there every Year, one on the Vigils and Feast of St. *Matthew* the Apostle, and for one Day then next ensuing; and the other Fair on the Eve and Feast of St. *James* the Apostle, and one Day next after, with Power to receive Tolls, Taxes, Tallages, Stallages, Piccage, and other Charges or Profits of Merchandizes, and other things saleable there.

But upon the Dissolution of Monasteries in the time of *Hen.* VIII. this Mannor of 𝔚aldock came into the King's Hands; afterwards it was conveyed to *Thomas Rivet* of 𝔏ondon, Mercer, and his Heirs, who in the eighth Year of Queen *Elizabeth*, surrendered up his Patent to the Queen, and in Consideration thereof, she granted to the said *Thomas Rivet* and his Heirs, a Market on the Saturday throughout the Year in this Town, for Beasts and other things, and Wares to be bought and sold there, and also three several Fairs to be held yearly in this Town, whereof the first to be on the Feast of St. *James* the Apostle, and the Day following the same, the second on the Feast of St. *Andrew* the Apostle, and the Day following, and the third on the Feast of St. *Matthew* the Apostle, and the Day following, with a Grant of all Stallage, Piccage, Tolls, Taxes, customary and other Profits of the same Markets and Fairs, with a Pypowder-court, and all the Profits thereunto belonging.

This *Thomas Rivet* had Issue *Thomas*, who was his Son and Heir, and succeeded him in this Mannor, and after he had enjoyed it sometime, sold it to the Lady *Anne Windesor* and *James Jeeve*, and *Katharine* his Wife, and their Heirs.

The Lady *Windesor*, by Deed dated the 23d of *January*, 1605, conveyed her Moiety of it to *John Hurst*, who fined for Sheriff of 𝔏ondon, he dyed leaving Issue *John, William*, and *Edward*; upon his Death, this Moyety came to

John, who was his first Son, to whom *James Jeeve*, and *Katharine* his Wife, by Deed dated 29th *January*, 1613, sold their Moyety, whereby he came possest of the whole; he married *Mary* Daughter of *Miles March* of 𝔚adenham in the Isle of 𝔈ly in 𝔠ambridgeshire, Esq. by whom he had Issue *John, William, Humberston* married to *Love* Daughter of ———, *Isaac* married to *Anne*, Daughter of *John King* of 𝔖udbury, Draper, *Thomas* married to *Mary* Daughter of *John Read*, Alderman of the City of 𝔑orwich; *Mary* married to *William Layer* of 𝔖hepered in the County of 𝔠ambridge, Esq. *Anne* married to *Jonathan Waller* of 𝔄shbel in this County, Gentleman, and *Elizabeth* married to *John Pamplin* of **Hadenham** in the Isle of **Ely**, Esq. upon his Decease,

John his eldest Son succeeded, married the Daughter of *William Plomer* of **Radwel** in this County, Esq. and after her Decease, *Constance* the eldest Daughter of *Thomas Hawes* of **Hertford**, Gent. but dying about the Year 1684, without Issue, this Mannor came to

William his Brother and next Heir, who married the youngest Daughter of *Henry Chauncy* of **Ardley** in this County, Esq. by whom he had *William, John, Humberston; Mary* married to *James*, only Son of *James Bets* of **Bis** in the County of **Norfolk**, Gent. *Anne, Elizabeth* married to —— —— the only Son of —— *Bowker*, Rector of one of the Parish Churches of **Icklingham** in the County of **Suffolk**, and *Jane*, whereof *William* and *Humberstone* dyed in his Life-time; and he deceased on the 30th of *Dec.* 1699, leaving *John* his Heir, who gave for his Arms *Argent, a Star of sixteen Points, Gules; Crest on a Wreath, a Grove of Wood Proper;* and he sold this Mannor to

Pierce Clever, Esq. who is the present Lord hereof, and gives for his Arms, *Or, three Bars Vert on a Canton Argent, a Fesse between as many Mascles Sable.*

To this Mannor belongs Court Leet and Baron, and 'tis the Custom when the Steward appears at any Court, the Bell tolls, and the Tenants immediately attend the Court, do their Suit and Service at Dinner, whither every Baker and Victualler sendeth a Loaf of Bread, and a Flaggon of Ale or Beer, that the Steward and Jury may examine the Measures of their Pots, weigh their Bread, and taste whether their Bread, Ale, and Beer, be wholsom for Man's Body.

THIS Rectory *Anno* 26 *H.* VIII. was rated in the King's Books at the yearly Value of 10*l.* 8*s.* 6*d.* and the King is the Patron.

The RECTORS.

1550 *Henry Howe*	1614 *Josiah Bird*
1558 *Robert Little*	1667 *Richard Worthley*
1561 *Augustine Lawry*	1680 *Richard Fyson*, M. A.
1600 *Richard Price*	

The Church is a fair Pile of Building, erected within the Town by the Knights Templers about the beginning of the Reign of King *Stephen;* is situated about the middle of the Town, in the Deanery of **Baldock**, in the Diocess of **Lincolne**. The Church and three Chancels are large, covered with Lead, to which a goodly Tower is annexed, in which is a large Ring of six excellent Bells, the greatest very ancient; it was baptiz'd in the time that the Romish Religion was exercised here, which Custom is still continued among the Papists to this Day, where a Bell was lately baptiz'd at **Beletree** in **Italy**, after this Manner.

The Bell was placed at the lower End of the Church, hanging upon two Gudjeons covered with rich Velvet of a Violet colour, and the Bell itself with a Robe of the same. Two Theatres were built on each Side of it for the Musicians, and an Ampitheatre for the Ladies who desired to see the Ceremony. The Pillars and Walls of the Church were curi-

Hund. of   ously adorn'd with Sheets of Silk and Pictures; an Altar was erected
Bradetrater near the Bell, very neatly set forth; a white Sattin Robe was laid upon
it, in order to cover the Bell, so soon as it was baptiz'd; and a great
fair Garland of choice Flowers stood by it, to be plac'd upon it: There
was also a Roman Ritual, a Censor, and a Vessel of Holy Water; and
rich Velvet Chairs were set round the Altar for the Priests appointed to
perform the Ceremony: And a Throne was erected by it, magnificently
hung, for the Godfather and Godmother of the Bell.

About ten of the Clock in the Forenoon the Company came, and having taken their several Places, the Priests began their Function; the
Bishop of **Beletrer** being at that time very sick, another was deputed for
that Purpose, and his Chair was placed upon the Steps of the High Altar:
He sang the first Psalm, which was continued by the Musick, and when
all the Psalms were ended, the Bishop bless'd the Holy Water, that it
might afterwards sanctify the Bell. This Benediction was very long, but
when it was finish'd the Bishop and Priests dipt Spunges in it, with which
they rub'd the Bell within and without, from the Crown to the Skirts thereof,
repeating in the mean while, divers Prayers full of Heavenly Blessings,
to purify, sanctify, and consecrate the Bell; *Ut hoc Tintinnabulum,* said
they, *cœlesti benedictione perfundere, purificare, sanctificare, et consecrare,
digneris.* That thou wouldst be pleased to rinse, purify, sanctify, and
consecrate this Bell with thy heavenly Benediction. The Bell being thus
wash'd, they dryed it with clean Napkins, and the Bishop taking the
Viol of Holy Oyl (which were those they blest on Ascension Day for the
whole Year following) he anointed the Cross of Metal fixed on the Crown
of the Bell, in order to make the Devil flee at the Sound of it, *Ut hoc au-
dientes Tintinnabulum tremiscant, et fugiant ante Crucis in eo depictum vex-
illum.* That hearing this Bell they may tremble, and flee before the
Banner of the Cross design'd upon it. Then he made seven other Crosses
with the Oyl on the outside, and four more on the inside of the Bell; this
done he caused the Godfather and the Godmother to draw near, and demanded of them in *Italian* whether they were the Persons that presented this Bell to be consecrated? they answered, they did. He proceeded, and ask'd whether the Founder was paid, and satisfy'd for the
Metal and Workmanship of the Bell? They answered, Yea. Then he
demanded whether they believed all that the Catholick, Apostolick Roman Church believes concerning the Holiness and Virtue of Bells? The
answer was, Yea. Lastly, he demanded of them, what Name they desired should be put upon the Bell? The Lady answer'd, *MARY.* Then
the Bishop took two great Silk Ribons, which had been fastened to the
Gudjeons of the Bell, and gave each of them one in their Hands, and
pronounced with a loud intelligible Voice the Words of Consecration, *Con-
secretur, et Sanctificetur, Sigistud in nomine Patris, Filii et Spiritus Sancti,
Amen.* Let this Sign be consecrated, and sanctified, in the Name of the
Father, Son, and Holy Ghost, Amen. Then turning himself to the People, he said, the Name of this Bell is *MARY;* after that he took the Censor,
and censeth it round about on the outside, then put the Censor under the
Bell, full of sacred Fumes, repeating all the while Prayers, and Invoca-
tions, that it might be fill'd with the Holy Spirit, saying, *Tu hoc Tintinnabulum Spiritus, Sancti rore perfundere, ut ante sonitum illius semper
fugiat Bonorum Inimicus:* Do thou besprinkle this Bell with the Dew
of thy Holy Spirit, that the Enemies of all Good, may always fly at the
Sound thereof. The Office was carried on with a great many Psalms,
which the Bishop and Priests repeated, the Musick playing all the while;
then the Bishop covered the Bell with a white Robe of a Convert, and
with a loud Voice read the Gospel of *Martha* and *Mary.* The whole solemnity thus ended, the Bishop gave his Benediction to the People, and
the Godfather and Godmother great Presents to the Priests. See the
whole form of Baptizing Bells in the Roman Ritual at large.

In the North Chancel is this Inscription upon a Gravestone.

Margaretta Bennet *Matri suæ piissimæ.*
Quæ obiit in Domino, Mense Novembris,
Anno Dom. 1587. Robertus Bennet *Episcopus*
Hereford *pietatis nomine posuit.*

Here is an Ancient Monument which has this Inscription.

Farewell my Frendys, the trw abideth no man,
I am departed hens, and so sal ye
But in this pasage the best Song I can
Is Requiem æternam, now Jesu grant it me
When I habe ended all myn adbersity,
Grant me in Baradys to hau a mansion
That shedst thy bloud for my redemption.

Prey for the Sowlys of William Crane, Jone and Margaret his Wyffes ——— which William dyed ——— 1483 —— on whos.

Orate pro ——— Wilielmi Vynter, generosi, et Margarete consortis suæ, qui quidem Wilielmus obijt 2 Junii. 1416. et Margareta ob——— Octob. 1411. eorum animabus, parentum, amicorum, Benefactorum suorum Deus omnipotens pro sua magna misericordia propitietur, Amen.

This French Epitaph was Engraved upon the Monument of one of the *Argentons.*

Reignald d'Argentein ci gist
Que cest Chappel feire fist;
Fut Chabalier Sainct Mariæ
Chescini pardon pour l'alme prie,

Englished.

Regnald de Argentyne, here is laid,
That cause this Chapel to be made :
He was a Knight of St. *Mary* the Virgin
Therefore prey pardon for his sin.

Within this Church are three Arches made in the Wall, whereof two in the South, and the other in the North Wall, where the Inhabitants have a Tradition, that three Knights Templers were buried in Stone Troughs or Coffers, and the two Coffins in the South Wall happening to be opened in the Year 1691, there was a fair Skelleton of a Man lying in either Coffin, whereof one of them had Hair on his Head.

A high Gravestone in the Churchyard has this Inscription.

Josias Bird lies Buried here,
Who taught this Parish three and fifty year,
Aged he was, as I have heard some say,
He was Eighty eight before he past away,
And died in the year
When 1 and sixes three made up the Quere,

CHARITIES.

John Parker of Radwel, Esq. gave an Annuity of 10*l. per Ann.* ont of all his Estate in Radwel, to find twenty six Two-penny Loaves for twenty six poor People in this Town every Sunday in the Year. The Bread to stand upon his Gravestone in the Chancel of this Church.

John Winne gave 1100*0l.* to build six Alms-houses, and purchase Land to raise an Annuity of 40*s.* a piece for every poor Person settled in those Houses.

Several Persons whose Names I cannot learn gave about eleven Pounds *per Ann.* issuing out of some Houses and Lands in Baldock, Offley, Weston, Clothal, and Willien, towards the Repair of this Church.

Several Persons whose Names I know not, gave the yearly Value of 30*l.* for repairing of the Church and the payment of fifteenths, and defraying of Charges of the Parish.

John Yardly gave five Acres of Land in the Parish of Willien, the Rent to be disposed among the poor and indigent Persons in this Parish.

E Relat. Ed.
Lawndry,
Gent

LECEWORTHE, LETCHWORTH.

THIS Vill derived its Name from the Seat of some ancient Possessor hereof; and King *William* the Conqueror gave it to *Robert Gernon,* a great *Norman,* who assisted

Hund. of Bradewater　him in that famous Battle at **Lewes,** where he obtained the Crown of this Realm, for 'tis recorded in *Domesdei Book* under the Title of *Terra Roberti Gernon.*

Domesd. Lib. fol. 138, n. 28.　Willielmus *tenet de* Roberto Gernon **Lecewort,** *pro decem hid. se defendebat. Terra est septem car. in Dom. sunt duo, et novem Vill. cum Presbitero habente quinq; car. ibi duo Soch. de un. hida et dimid. et quatuor car. et unus Servus, pratum dimid. car. pastura ad pec. Silva cent. porc. in totio valent valet sex lib. quando recepit septem lib. tempore Regis* Edwardi *octo lib. Hoc Manerium tenuit* Godvinus de Souberiæ *Teignus Regis* Edwardi, *et vendere potuit, et ibi tres Soch. homines ejus duo hidæ et tres virgat. habuerunt, et vendere potuerunt.*

　　William held **Lecewort** of *Robert Gernon,* it was rated for ten Hides. The arrable is seven Carucates, in Demeasne are two, and nine Villains with the Presbiter or Parson having five Carucates, there are two Sochmen of one Hide and an half, and four Carucates and one Servant, Meadow half a Carucate, Common of Pasture for the Cattle, Wood to feed an hundred Hogs; in the whole Value it is worth six Pounds by the Year, when he received it seven Pounds, in the time of King *Edward* (the Confessor) eight Pounds; *Godvine de Souberiæ* a Thane of King *Edward* (the Confessor) held this Mannor and might sell it, and there are three Sochmen (under his Protection), have two Hides, and three Virgates, and may sell them.

Inspex. 2 H. VIII.　　Shortly after this Mannor was conveyed to *William de Montfitchet,* who with *Rohais* his Wife, and *William* their Son, in the Reign of King *Hen.* I. gave this Church of **Leechworth** with all its Appurtenances, and twelve Acres of Land in this Vill, to the Monastery of **St. Alban.**

　　William the Son succeeded his Father in this Mannor, and married *Margaret* Daughter to *Gilbert Fitz Richard* of **Clare,** by whom he had Issue

Lib. rub. sub. tit Essex. Bar. vol. 1, fol. 438.　*Gilbert,* who was his Heir, and upon the Assessment for that Aid made for the Marriage of the King's Daughter, *Anno* 12 *Hen.* II. certified that he had eight and forty Knights' Fees, and a fifth Part *de Veteri Feoffamento,* and he dyed leaving Issue

Ibid. fol. 439.　*Richard,* who succeeded him, and attended the King in his Expedition into **Normandy,** *Anno* 6 *Rich.* I. and King *John* granted to him, *Anno* 2 *Regni sui,* a Confirmation of the Forrestership of **Essex,** and the Custody of the Castle of **Hertford,** for both which he gave a hundred Marks; he was constitued Sheriff of **Essex** and **Hertford,** 3 *Johannis,* and bore that Office three Years, and dyed *Anno* 5 *Joh.* leaving by *Milicent* his Wife

　　Richard, who was his Heir, but being within Age at the Death of his Father, the Wardship was granted to *Roger de Lacy,* Constable of **Chester,** for one thousand Marks, but this *Roger* dying, *Milicent,* the Mother of the Heir, surviving, bought the Wardship for eleven hundred Pounds; when this Heir arrived to his full Age, he joyned with the rebellious Barons of that time, and was so active on their Behalf, that they made him one of the five and twenty

6 Ed. I. Rot. 39, cur. recept. Scac.　Governors of the Realm; he gave his Mannor to the Knights Templers, and their Successors, and the Master of that Order held this Mannor, *Anno* 6 *Edw.* I. by the

Hund. of
Bradewater

Service of half a Knight's Fee of the Baronage of **Montfitchet**, and was wont to be gildable with the County until
the Knights Templers obtained the Discharge thereof.

At length these Knights Templers sold this Mannor to
Thomas Barrington, Esq. who was constituted Sheriff for
the Counties of **Hertford** and **Essex**, *Anno* 1452, 30 *H.* VI.
and this Mannor passed by the same Persons as **Chisfield**,
did, till it came to *Thomas Barrington*, who sold it to
William Hanchet, and *Bridget* his Wife, from whom it
descended to

John Hauchet, who was his Son and Heir, and granted
it to *Thomas Snagge*, to whom he levyed a Fine of this Mannor and Lands in **Lechworth**, **Wipleen**, and **Wimondslen**,
for the Use of the said *Thomas Snagge*, from him it came to

Fin. Mich 1
Ed. VI. Rol.
46, cur. re-
cept. Scac.

William Snagge, from whom it descended to

Thomas Snagge his Son, who married *Elizabeth* Daughter to *Calton* of **Walden** in **Essex**, he was elected for the
Autumn Reader, *An.* 16 *Eliz.* for *Grays-Inn* was double
Reader *Anno* 22 *Eliz.* Was elected one of the Treasurers
of that Society, in *February* following he received a writ
to be Serjeant at Law, returnable in *Michaelmas* following,
was advanced by Patent, dated 32 *Eliz.* to be the Queen's
Serjeant; from whom it descended to

William Snagge, who was his Heir, succeeded him and
gave for his Arms, *Argent, three Pheons Sable; Crest on
a Wreath, a Demy Roebuck Ermin, attired and unguled
Or.* He sold this Mannor to

Sir *Rowland Lytton*, from whom it is lineally descended
to Sir *William Lytton* the present Lord hereof.

T HIS Rectory *Anno* 26 *Hen.* VIII. was rated in the King's Books, at
the yearly Value of 11*l.* 1*s.* 10*d.* and Sir *William Lytton*, the Lord of this
Mannor, is Patron hereof.

The RECTORS.

Mr. *Witsey.*   Mr. *Ralph Battel.*

This Church is erected in the Middle of the Vill, in the Deanery of
Hitchin, in the Diocess of **London**; 'tis small and hath nothing of Remark in it.

WELEI, WILLIEN.

I N the time of *William* the Conqueror, 'tis recorded in
Domesdei Book, under the Title of *Terra Regis.*

*In Dimidio Hundred. de **Tit**, Rex* Willielmus *tenet **Welei**, pro duobus
hidis se defendebat. Terra est septem car. in dominio una hida, et ibi sunt
duo car. et octo Vill. cum quinque Bord. habentibus quatuor car. et quinta
potest fieri, ibi duo Cotarii, et quatuor Servi, Pastura ad pecud. Ville. Silva
trecent Porc: Hoc Manerium tenuit Comes Heraldus, et jacet in **Tit**, ubi
jacuit tempore Regis Edwardi.*
*In **Welei** tenet unus Sochmannus unam hidam. Terra est duo Car. et ibi
sunt duo Vill. cum duobus Bord. et novem Cotariis, pratum dimid Car.
Pastura ad Pecud. Ville, nemus ad sepes, huic Terræ adjacet Silva ad quinquaginta Porc. quam invasit* Osmundus *de Valle **Badonis**, super Regem*

Domesd. Lib.
fol. 133, n. 1.

Hund. of Bradewater Willielmum, *et jacuit in Soca de* 𝕳𝕚𝕥, *tempore Regis* Edwardi, *ut Scyra testatur, valet et valuit hæc Terra vigint. sol. tempore Regis* Edwardi *trigint. sol. Hanc Terram tenuit* Godvinus *Homo Comitis* Heraldi, *et vendere potuit.*

Hanc posuit Petrus *Vice-comes in* 𝕳𝕚𝕥, *ad firmam, quæ non fuit ibi tempore Regis* Edwardi, *neque consuetudinem ibi reddidit.*

Quam Terram dederat Ilbertus *cuidam suo Militi dum erat Vicecomes, pro qua Terra reclamat* Gaufridus de Bech *misericordiam Regis.*

In 𝖂ilei *tenet unus Sochmannus dimid. hid. Terra est un. car. et ibi est cum un. Cotar. Nemus ad sepes valet decem sol. quando recepit quinque sol. tempore Regis* Edwardi *sexdecim sol. Hanc Terram tenuit* Edmundus *homo Comiti* Heraldi, *et vendere potuit, Soca remansit in* 𝕳𝕚𝕥, *unam averam invenit.*

In 𝕭radewatre *Hund. in* 𝖂ilie *tenuit* Goisfridus de 𝕭ech, *quinque hid. et unam virgatam. Terra est novem Car. in dominio duo hid. et ibi sunt duo Car. et aliæ duo possunt fieri, ibi decem Villi cum uno Milite, et quatuor Bord. habentes quinque Car. Pratum dimid. Car. Pastura ad pec. Nemus ad sepes inter totum valet, decem lib. et quatuordecim sol. quando recepit quatuor lib. tempore Regis* Edwardi, *duodecim lib. Hoc Manerium tenuit* Leuric Huscarl, *Com.* Leuvini, *et vendere potuit, et ibi unus Sochmannus homo* Elmari de Beningtone *dimid. hid. habuit et vendere potuit, et una Vidua. dimid. hid. habuit decem acras minus non potuit vendere præter licentiam* Goduine de Laceworde.

King *William* held 𝖂ilei in the half Hundred of 𝕳𝕚𝕥, it was rated for two Hides. The arrable is seven Carucates, in Demeasne one Hide, and there are two Carucates, and eight Villains with five Bordars, having four Carucates, and a fifth may be made, there are two Cottagers, and four Servants, Common of Pasture for the Cattle of the Vill, Wood to feed three hundred Hogs; Earl *Harold* held this Mannor, and it lyes in 𝕳𝕚𝕥, where it lay in the time of King *Edward* (the Confessor).

One Sochman held one Hide in 𝖂ilei. The arrable is two Carucates; and there are there two Villains, with two Bordars, and nine Cottagers, Meadow half a Carucate, Common of Pasture for the Cattle of the Vill, Wood for Hedges, a Wood lyes to this Land to feed fifty Hogs, which *Osmond* of the Vale of 𝕭aton, got by a Sleight of King *William*, and it did lye in the Soke of 𝕳𝕚𝕥, in the time of King *Edward* (the Confessor) as the Shire can witness; this Land is worth and was worth twenty Shillings a Year, in the time of King *Edward* (the Confessor) thirty Shillings. *Godwin* a Man (under the Protection) of Earl *Harold*, held this Land and might sell it.

Peter the Sheriff set this in 𝕳𝕚𝕥 to Farme, which was not there in the time of King *Edward* (the Confessor) nor paid any Rent there.

Which Land *Ilbert* gave to a certain Knight, whilst he was Sheriff, for which Land *Godfrey de Bech* did obtain Judgment.

One Sochman held half an Hide of Land in 𝖂ilie. The arrable is one Carucate, and it is now there with one Cottager, Wood for Hedges, it is worth ten Shillings a Year, when he received it five Shillings, in the time of King *Edward* (the Confessor) sixteen Shillings; *Edmund* a Man (under the Protection) of Earl *Harold* held this Land and might sell it. The Soke remained in 𝕳𝕚𝕥, he found one Horse.

Goisfride de Bech held five Hides and one Virgate in 𝖂ilie, in 𝕭rade= water Hundred. The arrable is nine Carucates, in Demeasne two Hides, and there are two Carucates, and two others may be made, there are ten Villains, with one Knight, and four Bordars having five Carucates, Meadow half a Carucate, Common of Pasture for the Cattle, Wood for Hedges ; in the whole it is worth ten Pounds and fourteen Shillings a Year, when he received it four Pounds, in the time of King *Edward* (the Confessor) twelve Pounds; *Leuric Huscarle* a Tenant of Earl *Lewin* held this Mannor and might sell it, and one Sochman a Man (under the Protection) of *Elmar de Belinton*, had half a Hide there and might sell it, and a Widow had half a Hide there, wanting ten Acres, she might not sell it, without the License of *Godwin de Laceworde.*

At that time it appears by this Record, that a great Part of this Vill lay in the Hundred of 𝕳𝕚𝕥, but about the time of King *H. II.* I find that *Ralph Punchardon* was Lord of this Mannor, for in those Dayes *Gilbert de Tany*, a great Baron, did demise and grant to the Church of 𝕾t. 𝕬lban and the Monks of the same Place, all his Land which he had in the Vill of 𝖂illie, to wit, one Virgate and an half to be holden of him and his Heirs at Fee-farme, paying 12*d*. *per Annum*, at the Octaves of Easter, for all Services which did belong to him and his Heirs, saving the Service due to the Lord of the Soil, to wit, the eighth Part of a Knight's Fee, which the said Monks did freely discharge; before this Agreement was made the Monks gave to this *Gilbert* two Marks of Silver, and four Shillings to *Walter* his Son and Heir, in the Presence of *William* Priest of 𝕹ortune, *Joiley* the Priest of 𝕹ewham, *Robert* the Priest, *Gervase* the Priest of 𝖀pgrave, *Ralph de Punchard, William de Craward, Alan* Clerk to the Sheriff, *William* the Son of *Robert de Terefel, Luke* of 𝕹ortune, *Balderick Litlingtone, William de Punchard, Utrede, Richard Barate, Godwine,* Esq. *Ely Alvered* of 𝕽ichmereswortl, *John Revel, William Faber, Bernard de Shepheard, Roger de Litlingtone, Gaufride de Shephale, Adam* the Reeve, *William* the Reeve, *Hamor* of 𝕾hatesburp, *John* of 𝕾taunford, *Henry Theotonic, Ralph Mansel,* and *Richard* the Hostler.

Walter Tany granted and confirmed to God and the Church of 𝕾t. 𝕬lban, the Agreement made between the said Monks and *Gilbert* his Father, of one Virgate and an half of Land in 𝖂illie, which his Father held in this Vill, and as the said Monks held it now of him and his Heirs, freely from all Services which belonged to him and his Heirs, paying yearly 12*d*. at the Octaves of Easter, saving the Service due to the Lord of the Soil, which was the eighth Part of a Knight's Fee, which the Monks freely discharged; and this Grant was made for the Health of his Soúl, and for the Health of the Souls of his Father and Mother, and all his Parents, and his Friends, in the Presence of *Ralph de Widen, William de Sisseverne, Richard de Newport, William* the Chaplain of 𝕹ortune, *Alexander* the Youth, *Roger* the Son of *Race, Ralph Panchester, William* the Clerk, *William de Therfield, Warme* his Brother, *Hugh Long,* and mony others.

Ralph Punchardon being Lord of this Mannor, confirmed this Agreement made between *Gilbert Tany,* and the Monks of 𝕾t. 𝕬lbans, one Virgate of Land and an Half in the Vill of 𝖂illie, held of his Fee, saving his Service in all things, to wit, the eighth Part of a Knight's Fee, which they freely paid in Money; the Witnesses to this Confirmation were *Richard de Crokesle, Geoffry de Gorham, Ralph de Wyden, Alexander de Thurold, Geoffry de Childwick, Geoffry* the Son of *William de Redburne, William de Sisseverne, Robert* the Son of *Hamon, Ade* the Son of *Amfride, Robert* the Porter, *Alom de Chaler, Roger Orbech, Reginald* the Son of *Adeliz.*

Geoffry the Son of *Ralph Punchardon*, succeeded his Father in 𝔚𝔦𝔩𝔩𝔦𝔢, he had Issue

William, who succeeded upon his Father's Death, and confirm'd the Grant which *Simon* Abbot of 𝔖t. 𝔄𝔩𝔟𝔞𝔫𝔰, and the Monks there, made to *Alan* Clerk, of 𝔏𝔢𝔱𝔠𝔥𝔴𝔬𝔯𝔱𝔥, and his Heirs, of one Virgate and an Half of Land in the Vill of 𝔚𝔦𝔩𝔩𝔦𝔢, of the Fee of *Gilbert de Tany*, to hold of them by Right of Inheritance, paying five Shillings to the Cellerer, at the four usual Terms of the Year, saving the Service due to the King and the Lord of the Soil, which the same *Alan* shall pay; the Witnesses were *Richard de Crochesle, Ralph de Midon, Philip de Cimitray, Robert* the Porter, and *Richard* the Dispensor.

And this *Geoffry*, in the time of *Edw.* I. granted to the venerable Father *Roger*, Abbot of 𝔖t. 𝔄𝔩𝔟𝔞𝔫𝔰, and his Covent, all the Right and Claim which he had, or in any Manner might have, in a certain Tenement, which the Abbot of 𝔖t. 𝔄𝔩𝔟𝔞𝔫𝔰 held of him in the Vill of 𝔚𝔦𝔩𝔩𝔦𝔢, with the Lands, Rents, Homages, Fealty, Releases, Escheates, Aides, Wardes, and other Gifts and Profits to the same Tenement emerging; which Deed was executed in the Presence of *Robert de Gravele, John Gyle, William de la Moore, Roger de Punchardon, Walter de Grevile, Walter de Linlie, Geoffry Punchardon* of 𝔏𝔢𝔱𝔠𝔥𝔴𝔬𝔯𝔱𝔥, *Wygan de la Mare. William de Norreis* of 𝔖t. 𝔄𝔩𝔟𝔞𝔫, *Philip de Belver* of 𝔖t. 𝔄𝔩𝔟𝔞𝔫, *Robert de la Sale*, and many others.

But I find that this Mannor, in the time of *R.* II. was in the Possession of *Henry Frowick* who resided here, and married *Anne* the sole Daughter and Heir of Sir *Robert Knolls* of 𝔑𝔬𝔯𝔱𝔥𝔪𝔭𝔪𝔢𝔰 in this County, by whom he had Issue *Thomas, Isabel* married to *Thomas Bedlow*, and *Elizabeth* married to *John Conisby*.

Thomas succeeded his Father, and dying without Issue, his Sisters were his Coheirs, and, I guess, upon the Partition, this Mannor might come to *Isabel*, and that *Thomas Bedlow* her Husband might sell it to

John Thorogood, who died seized hereof, leaving only *Anne* his Daughter and Heir, to whom it descended, she married Sir *Thomas Cheiny*, Kt. who enjoy'd it some time, and then he and his Wife conveyed it to

John Cock and his Heirs, who afterwards demised it to *John Needham* for a Term of Years, but before the Term was expired, he, by Deed dated the 8th of *May*, Anno 5 *Eliz.* granted all his Interest and Term of Years in this Mannor of 𝔚𝔯𝔞𝔭𝔢𝔰, with all other his Lands, Tenements, and Hereditaments in the Vill and Fields of 𝔚𝔦𝔩𝔩𝔢𝔫, (which Mannor of 𝔚𝔯𝔞𝔭𝔢𝔰 was also *John Cock's*, Esq. and before him *John Thurgood's*) to

Thomas Rivet of 𝔠𝔥𝔦𝔭𝔫𝔞𝔪 in the County of 𝔠𝔞𝔪𝔟𝔯𝔦𝔡𝔤𝔢, Esq. who, I suppose, sold it to *Edward Wilson*, from whom it came by lineal Descent, to ——— *Wilson* the last Owner hereof.

THE Rectory in *Anno* 26 *Hen.* VIII. was valued in the King's Books at the Rate of 5*l. ob. per An.* and ——— *Ward*, Clerk, is Patron hereof.

The RECTORS.
Mr. *Fleetwood.*   Mr. *Way.*   Mr. *Ward.*

The Church is erected in the Middle of the Vill, in the Deanery of 𝔅𝔞𝔩𝔡𝔬𝔠𝔨. in the Diocess of 𝔏𝔦𝔫𝔠𝔬𝔩𝔫; it is covered with Lead; there is a square Tower, wherein are four Bells, with a short Spire upon it, and these Inscriptions are upon the Gravestones in the Chancel and Church.

𝔥𝔦𝔠 𝔧𝔞𝔠𝔢𝔱 𝔇𝔬𝔪𝔦𝔫𝔲𝔰 Richardus Golden quondam ——— 𝔐𝔢𝔫𝔰𝔦𝔰 𝔒𝔠𝔱𝔬𝔟𝔯𝔦𝔰, Anno Domini, 1417.

P. M. S.
Sub hoc Marmore jacet
Exiguum illud quod mortale fuit
Richardi Way Theologiæ Baccalaurei,
Qui, dum omnia flagrarent civili bello
Obstrepera et inter arma leges silerent,
Subditus Regis et Ecclesiæ filius.
Fidelis erat utriusqu; infortunii Comes.
Terras Astræa tandem revisens nostras,
Tam suos quam Ecclesiæ filios
A propriis laribus diu exules
In propriam quemque sedem restituit:
Atque hos inter Pastor 𝔚𝔦𝔩𝔩𝔦𝔢𝔫𝔰𝔦𝔰
Ejusdem hic et Ecclesiæ patronus,
Sedecem annorum exilium passus,
Viduam et polantem revisit gregem,
Tam Officio quam Beneficio restauratus
Possessionem obtinuit antiquam:
Sed hujus vitæ Lubricæ ærumnis
——— quibus frui videbatur,
Ne bis fortunæ fieret ludibrium,
Migravit lubens in certiorem,
Obiit, 23 Apr. Ann. Dom. 1673. *Ætatis suæ* 62.

P. M. S.
Alicia Way *nata* 𝔅𝔢𝔡𝔣𝔬𝔯𝔡𝔦𝔞 *uxor* Rici. Way, *istius Ecclesiæ Vicarii, simile Patroni, filia* Gulielmi Abbis, *generosi, natu secunda nec tamen ulli secunda erat enim erga Deum relegiosa, Parentes morigera,* ——— *et liberorum amans. Talis vitæ ratio Sex parvidos reliquit rum filios tres* Richardum, Thomam, Gulielmum, *totidemque filias,* Aliciam, Mariam, *et* Katharinam *in Cunabulis. Denata est vicessimo secundo die* Novembris, *Anno Ætatis* 33. *Salutis Reparatæ* 1622. *per quam expectat hic resurrectionem fœlicem.*

Monumentum hoc qualecunque
Richardus Way
Uxori plurimùm desideratæ
posuit superstes.

Μόνῳ τῷ Θεῷ δόξα
Hic jacet Johannes Chapman, *Theologiæ Baccalaureus, Collegii Sanctæ et individuæ Trinitatis* 𝔠𝔞𝔫𝔱𝔞𝔟𝔯 *inter seniores quondam Socius, et istius Ecclesiæ Vicarius, qui obiit* 27 *die* Decembris, Anno Domini 1624.
Ætatis suæ 74.

Who in Profession of the Deity,
Worshipt one God in Blessed Trinity;
Adorn'd his Age with comly Gravity,
Supported Friends with true Fidelity.
In Peace, and Truth, and Love, detesting Pride,
He was a Monument before he died.

Talis erat mortis ratio moderatio vitæ,
Dulce sit ut tecum vivere dulce mori.

Underneath.

And likewise *Anne* his Wife, who died upon *Ascention* Day, 1683.

A double Surgeon She; She oft restor'd to Health
The pined Wretch, as oft the Poor to Wealth.

A Monument in the Wall.

Hic jacet Edvardus Lacon, *Arm. de Domo de* Willis *in Com.* Salopiæ, *qui obiit,* A. D. 1625. *Ætat. suæ* 80.

Et Joanna *Uxor ejus, aliquando uxor* Edwardi Wilson, *Arm. Domini istius Manerii, Fæminæ spectatæ virtutis, Modestiæ, Prudentiæ, Gratiæ, et Naturæ donis adornata Liberos; quos suscepet in timore Dom. educavit pie, et religiose vixit. Morbum doloris ætate ingravescente summa patientia, et constanti fide sustinuit: animam Deo redidit, pieque in* Christo *obdormivit* 13 *die mensis* Aug. *A. D.* 1624.
Ætatis suæ 79.

A Monument in the Wall.

Hic jacet Matheus Thorley, *quondam Vicarius istius Ecclesiæ, qui obiit vicessimo nono die* Decembris 1634.
Quatuor haud denos Chapman *quos duplicat annos
Serius aut Citius metam properamus ad unam.*

Mors mihi lucrum.

P. M. S.

Thomas Wilsonus, *Arm.*
Hartfordiensis *Patriâ,* Londini *natus,
Parentum optimorum filius optimus,
Nec eorum virtutum minùs quam facultatum hæres.
  Qui in Hospitio* Grejano *dum adhuc juvenis
Patriæ potius quam sibi leges asserere didicit:
Postmodum provectior factus in latifundiis suis propri*
Apud Hartfordienses *suos consedit.*
Ubi
*Pietate in Deum Christiana,
Cum Charitate in egenos conjuga,
Vitæ Scantimoniâ singulari,
Spectata in omnes probitate,
Summaq; in rebus agendis prudentia,
Temperantia constanter immutabili,
Priscis illustribus comparandus extitit.*
Idem,
*Semper idem ejusdem Pietatis Vitutis
Cultor perennis Servus consevit:
Postquam enim annos fecisset uno minus octoginta,
Annorum satur, et presens pertæsus sæculum,
Plaudè migravit hinc animumque Deo redidit,
Triste relinquens posteris sui desiderium*
*Cui dum superstes erat Christianis spes vita fuit
Jam defuncto* Christi   *resurgendi fit* ὑπόρασις
*Hac igitur fide fretus hac spe regemus
Tandem denascitur cum renascendi plerophoriâ.*
*Interim in Sancto vestibulo
Primitias dormientium* Christum *dum reducem
Cum fratribus suis candidatos opperitur.*
Ἀμὴν κ̀ ἔρχ^υ κυριε Ἰησῦ
Obiit Ann. { *Salutis* 1656.——— } *in Festo St.* Joh.
          { *Ætatis suæ supradicto* } *Evan.*

Et Lucia *uxor ejus* Antonii Jenkensoni *filia, Reginæ* Elizabethæ *apud Exteros tum Christianos tum Barbaros per annos vigint. sex legalis.*

Having now ended Broadwater Hundred, I shall proceed to the neighbouring Hundred of Hitchin, which is the second Part of the third Division of this County.

THE HUNDRED

OF

HIZ, NOW HITCHIN·

IS the second Part of the third Division of this County, was denominated from the Town of 𝔥𝔦𝔷, since changed its Name with that Town to 𝔥𝔦𝔱𝔠𝔥𝔦𝔫, and was Parcel of the Revenue of the Crown: The Sheriffs of this County, have collected the Profits thereof for the Use of the King, and the Justices of Peace have usually held their private Sessions and publick Meetings for this Hundred at the Town of 𝔥𝔦𝔷: Most of the Hundred is Champion, and bounded on the North and West with the County of 𝔅𝔢𝔡𝔣𝔬𝔯𝔡, on the East and South, with the Hundreds of 𝔅𝔯𝔬𝔞𝔡𝔴𝔞𝔱𝔢𝔯 and 𝔠𝔞𝔦𝔰𝔥𝔬, and contains these Parishes or Hamlets, which are divided between two High Constables, whereof one has for his Division, the several Towns and Hamlets of 𝔥𝔦𝔱𝔠𝔥𝔦𝔫, 𝔐𝔦𝔫𝔰𝔡𝔢𝔫, 𝔓𝔯𝔢𝔰𝔱𝔬𝔫, 𝔇𝔦𝔫𝔢𝔰𝔩𝔢𝔶, 𝔥𝔦𝔭𝔭𝔬𝔩𝔦𝔱𝔰, 𝔦𝔠𝔨𝔩𝔢𝔣𝔬𝔯𝔡, 𝔖𝔱. 𝔗𝔥𝔬𝔪𝔞𝔰 𝔠𝔥𝔞𝔭𝔭𝔢𝔩, and 𝔓𝔦𝔯𝔱𝔬𝔫; and the other High Constable has 𝔒𝔣𝔣𝔢𝔩𝔶, 𝔩𝔦𝔩𝔩𝔶, 𝔎𝔦𝔫𝔤'𝔰-𝔴𝔞𝔩𝔡𝔢𝔫, 𝔖𝔱𝔞𝔤𝔢𝔫𝔥𝔬𝔢, and 𝔎𝔦𝔪𝔢𝔱𝔬𝔫; after which Order I shall treat of all these Parishes and Hamlets.

Hund. of Hitchin.

HIZ, HITCH, HITCHIN.

THIS Town was Parcel of the Possessions of the Mertian Kings, which may be the Reason why this Mannor extends into the Parish of 𝔒𝔣𝔣𝔢𝔩𝔢𝔶, where the magnificent *Offa* sometimes held his Court, and at last ended his Life: It was called 𝔥𝔦𝔷, from the Name of the River that passes through it; and doubtless was a Place of some Remark, when King *Alfred* divided this County into Hundreds; for at that time, this Hundred was denominated from this Town, which remained then in the Possession of the Saxon Kings, and continued in the Crown until King *Edward* the Confessor gave it with 𝔒𝔣𝔩𝔞𝔶, 𝔚𝔞𝔩𝔡𝔢𝔫𝔶, 𝔚𝔦𝔪𝔬𝔫𝔡𝔢𝔰𝔩𝔞𝔶, 𝔚𝔞𝔢𝔩𝔢𝔶, 𝔚𝔞𝔟𝔢𝔡𝔢𝔫𝔢, 𝔇𝔢𝔫𝔢𝔰𝔩𝔞𝔶, 𝔥𝔢𝔰𝔪𝔢𝔯𝔢, 𝔥𝔢𝔤𝔢𝔰𝔱𝔞𝔫𝔢𝔰𝔱𝔬𝔫, and 𝔈𝔶𝔢, all in this County, to Earl *Harold*, who held and enjoyed them so long as he lived; but when he was slain at 𝔅𝔞𝔱𝔱𝔩𝔢, nine Miles from 𝔥𝔞𝔰𝔱𝔦𝔫𝔤𝔰 in 𝔖𝔲𝔰𝔰𝔢𝔵, they came to King *Wil-*

Matt. Paris, de Vita Offæ.

Bar. of Engl. vol. 1, fol. 21.

Hund. of
Hitchin.

liam the Conqueror, who reserved this Mannor in the Crown, for 'tis recorded in *Domesdei Book* under the Title of

Terra Regis.

Domesd. Lib.
fol. 132.

In Dimidio Hundred. de Hit. *Rex* Willielmus *tenet* Hit *pro quinq; hidis se defendebat. Terra est* xxxiv *car. in Dominio una hida, et ibi sunt sex car. et* xli *Villani cum septem decem Bord. habentibus viginti carucat. et* viii *adhuc possunt fieri, ibi* xxii *cotar. et Servi, et* iv *Molini de* liii *sol. et* iv *denar. pratum quatuor car. pastura ad pec. Ville. Silva* cccccc *porc. Hoc Manerium tenuit Com.* Heraldus. *de his* v *Hid jacent duo in Monasterio hujus Ville. Terra est* iv *car in Dominio* i *Hida et dimid, et ibi est* i *car. et alia potest fieri, et ibi* iv *Vill. habentes* ii *car. et* vii *cotar. pratum* ii *boris, pastura ad pec. hæ* ii *hidæ sex lib. quando recepit* xl *sol. tempore Regis* Edwardi iv *lib. Hoc Manerium tenuit Comes* Heraldus.

Rex Willielmus *tenet* Wabcrne *pro tribus virgat. sedefen debat. Terra est* ii *car. et* vi *bobus, et ibi sunt cum* vi *Villis. Silva* vi *porc, hanc terram tenuit Comes* Heraldus *in* Hit. *suo Manerio et ibi modo jacet.*

Rex Willielmus *tenet* Cerlctone *pro* i *virgat. se defendebat. Terra est* i *car. et ibi est cum* ii *cotar. et* i *Molin. de* xx *denar. Valet et valuit semper* x *sol. hanc terram ten.* ii *Soch. de Com.* Heraldo, *et vendere potuerunt absq; licentia ejus. Soca fuit semper in* Hit. Ilbertus *quando fuit Vicecomes apposuit in* Hit.

Inter totum reddit Hit *cum suis pertinentibus per annum centum et sex lib. arsas, et pensatas, et decem lib. ad numerum. Quando recepit* Petrus *Vicecomes qt.* xx *lib. et sex tempore Regis* Edwardi lx *lib. de* Hit. *et de Soch. ibidem pertin.* xl *lib. ad numerum.*

The Land of the King.

King *William* held Hit in the half Hundred of Hit. it was rated for five Hides. The arrable is four and thirty Carucates, in Demeasne one Hide, and there are six Carucates and one and forty Villains, with seventeen Bordars, having twenty Carucates and now eight more may be made, there are two and twenty Cottagers, and twelve Servants, and four Mills of three and fifty Shillings and four Pence Rent, Meadow four Carucates, Common of Pasture for the Cattle of the Vill, Wood to feed six hundred Hogs; Earl *Harold* held this Mannor: Of these five Hides, two lye in the Monastery of this Vill, the arrable is four Carucates, in Demeasne one Hide and an half, and there is one Carucate, and another may be made, and there are four Villains having two Carucates, and seven Cottagers, there are Meadow to feed two Oxen, Common of Pasture for the Cattle; these two Hides are worth six Pounds by the Year, when he received it forty Shillings, in the time of King *Edward* (the Confessor) four Pounds. Earl *Harold* held this Mannor.

King *William* held Wabedene, it was rated for three Virgates. The arrable is two Carucates and six Oxgangs, and they are there with six Villains, Wood to feed forty Hogs. Earl *Harold* held this Land in his Mannor in Hit, and there it now lyeth.

King *William* held Cerlstone; it was rated for one Virgate. The arrable is one Carucate, and it is there with two Cottagers, and one Mill of twenty Pence Rent; it is worth, and always was worth, ten Shillings by the Year. Two Sochmen held this Land of Earl *Harold* by the Year, and might sell it without his leave. The Soke was always in Hit. When *Ilbert* was Sheriff he laid it in Hit.

Among all the Rent, Hit, with the Appurtenances, was worth an hundred and six Pounds by the Year, burnt and weighed, and ten Pounds numbred: When *Peter* the Sheriff received it, he held it for as much as six and twenty Pounds of Hit, in the time of King *Edward* (the Confessor) sixty Pounds by the Year, and of the Soke there belong to it forty Pounds number'd.

Inq. 6 R. III.
Rot. 1, cur.
recept. Scac.
Bar. vol. 1,
fol. 523.

This Mannor was ancient Demesne of the King; and *William Rufus* gave it to *Bernard de Baliol*, whom that King had made Baron of Bitwell in Northumberland. He was sent with *Robert de Bruce*, in the third Year of King *Stephen*, unto *David* King of Scotland, then advanced with

his Army to the Banks of **Tefe**, to persuade his Retreat; *Hund. of*
Hitchin.
but not prevailing, he raised all the Power he could make,
to oppose him, and at length shared in the Honour of that
glorious Victory, which the English obtained by the exemplary Valour of *William* Earl of **Albemarle**, and other
valiant Men of those Parts near **North Alberton**, in that
memorable Battle fought upon the 11th of the Calends of
September, called the Battle of the *Standard:* But after *Bar.* vol. 1,
fol. 523.
this Engagement for King *Stephen*, the Earls of **Glocester**
and **Chester**, General of that Army raised on the Behalf
of *Maud* the Empress, *Anno* 1142, 7 *Steph.* took the King
and him Prisoners: He with the Consent of *Ingelram* his
Son gave Lands of the yearly Value of 15*l.* lying in
Werelee, a Member of **Hitchin**, and King *Stephen* con- Ibid.
firmed the Grant; but it seems this *Ingelram* died without
Issue in the Life-time of his Father, for upon the Death of
his Father

Eustace de Baliol succeeded; He gave one hundred
Pounds for a License to marry the Widow of *Robert Fitzpiers*, and had Issue

Hugh de Baliol, of whom 'twas certified that he held the
Barony of **Bitwell** of the King, by the Service of five
Knights' Fees, and to find thirty Soldiers for the Guard of
Newcastle upon **Tine**, and held this Lordship of **Hiche**, *in
Capite* of the King, as an Augmentation of his Barony by
the Service of two Knights' Fees; He had a fair Estate,
for upon levying the Scutage of **Wales**, *Anno* 13 *Joh.* he
answered for thirty Knights' Fees, and in the 17th Year of
the same King he was in great Favour with him: He was
also very serviceable to King *Henry* III. who in the fourth
Year of his Reign gave him the Lordship of **Meere** for his
better Support.

John de Baliol his Son and Heir paid *Anno* 13 *H.* III.
one hundred and fifty Pounds for his Relief for the thirty
Knights' Fees which he then held: He married *Dervor-
guill*, one of the three Daughters and Heirs to *Alan* of
Galway, (a great Baron in **Scotland**,) by *Margaret* the
eldest Sister of *John Scot*, the last Earl of **Chester**, and one
of the Heirs of *David*, sometime Earl of **Huntindon**, by
Reason whereof he was seized of **Galway** in **Scotland**, and
had in her Right an Assignment of the Mannor **Thorkesey**
in the County of **Lincoln**, the Fee-farm of **Gernemuth** in
Norfolk, and **Ludlingland** in **Suffolk**, until the King should
make them a reasonable Exchange of other Lands in Satisfaction of her Part of the Earldom of **Chester**: He stoutly
assisted that King against the rebellious Barons in that
great Defeat given to them at **Northampton**, *Anno* 48 *H.*
III. but fighting again soon after, on the Behalf of the
King at **Lewes**, was taken Prisoner with the King in that

*Hund. of
Hitchin.* fatal Battel, but it seems he made his Escape soon afterwards: For *Monford*, Earl of **Leicester**, having there got the King into his Custody, and made all **England** subject to him, excepting the utmost Parts of the North, which opposed his usurped Power: At the Instigation of the King of *Scots*, and this valiant Lord *John de Balioll*, and by the Assistance of the other northern Barons, he raised a great Force, and redeemed the King: At length he died, *Anno* 53 *H*. III. seized of this Mannor, leaving

Hugh his Son and Heir, 28 Years old, who then doing Homage, had Livery of his Land: But *Devorguill* his Wife surviving, this Mannor of **Hiche**, with several other Lordships, were assigned to

Devorguill for her Dower, who held it *Anno* 6 *Edw*. I. of the King *in Capite*, by the Service of one Knights' Fee and an Half, and it was then valued at 40*l. per Annum ;* after her Decease, this Mannor descended to

Alexander de Balioll the second Son of *John, Hugh* his elder Brother being dead ; he held it in Gross, at length dying without Issue *Anno* 7 *Edw*. I.

John de Balioll succeeded him, and married *Isabel,* the Daughter of *John de Warren*, Earl of **Surry**, was one of the chief Competitors for the Crown of **Scotland**, *An*. 19 *Edw*. I. and the Decision being, by the joynt Consent of all, referr'd to the King of **England**, the Right was adjudged to this *John*, who thereupon obtained the Kingdom of **Scotland**; and his Barony and Estate, with the Dignity, devolved to the Crown of **England**, where, I believe this Mannor continued until the 14th Year of King *R*. II. when it was then called in the Record **Hychen**, and valued at 100*l. per Annum ;* and that King granted it to

Edmund de Langeley the fifth Son of *Edw*. III. and Earl of **Cambridge**, in Part of Satisfaction of 1000*l, per Annum* promised to him upon his Advancement to the Dukedom of **York**, to which Dignity he was promoted 9 *R*. II. when the King girted him with the Sword, and put a Cap on his Head with a Circle of Gold, at **Hoselow-Lodge** in **Tibdale**. He was constituted Lieutenant of **England**, *Anno* 18 *R*. II. whilst the King was in **Ireland**, and during that time called a Parliament in **London**. Afterwards he was made Lieutenant again of this Realm, *Anno* 20 *R*. II. and died the first of *August,* 3 *H*. IV. seized of this, (among many other Mannors) then called by the Name of **Hychen**, and left

Edward Earl of **Rutland** his Son and Heir, then thirty Years of Age: He was created by Patent, dated 25 *Febr*. 13 *R*. II. Earl of **Rutland**, to hold that Title no longer than his Father's Life ; but having treated of this Duke before in the Parish of **Anstp**, and shewed that he was restored to the Dutchy of **York**, married *Philippa* one of the Daughters and Coheirs of *John* Lord *Mohun*, died valiantly in that

*Har. of Engl.
vol. 2, fol. 155,*

*Pat. 9 R. II.
n. 26.
T Wals. fol.
386, n. 30.*

*Pat. 20 R. II.
P. 1. M. 28.
Esc. 3 H. IV.
n 35.
Holl. fol. 520,
n. 30.*

*Cart. 13 R. II.
n. 5.
Bar. of Engl.
vol. 2, fol. 156.*

famous Battel of **Agincourt**, without Issue; that *Richard* his Nephew, Son to *Richard* Earl of **Cambridge** his younger Brother was his next Heir, succeeded him, married *Ciceley* Daughter to *Ralph Nevill* Earl of **Westmorland**, was slain at **Wakefield**; that *Edward* Duke of **York**, his second Son, was his Heir, and obtained the Crown from King *H*.VI. I shall refer the Reader thither, and proceed: That this King · *Edw*. IV. by Letters Patents dated 1 *Regni sui*, granted to his most dear Mother *Cicilie*, Dutchess of **York**, the Mannor of **Lechlade**, with the Appurtenances in the County of **Glocester**, the Mannor and Lordships of **Hitchen, Ansten, Standon**, and **Popes-hall** in this County, and the Mannor of **Fodringay** in the County of **Northampton**, for the Term of her Life. She enjoy'd the Profits of all these Mannors until the 11 *Hen*. VII. 1496, when she died, and they reverted to the Crown, where this Mannor has remained to this Day, several Queens of **England** having since that time successively enjoyed it, as Parcel of their Jointures.

This Mannor hath Jurisdiction of Court Leet and Baron; it extends into several other Parishes near adjoyning, and the Courts have been usually held every Year after the Feast of St. *Michael* the Archangel, where two Constables have been yearly chosen for the Town, and two for the Forrein; two Headboroughs for **Bancroft** Ward, two others for **Bridge** Ward, and two others for **Tylehouse-street** Ward; also two Leather-sellers, two Ale-tasters, a Bell-man, and an Heyward, have been yearly elected there.

The Inhabitants within this Leet have, time out of Mind, yearly paid to the Lord of this Mannor, at every Court Leet, the Sum of 40*s*. for a common Fine, whereof the Inhabitants within **Hitchin Portman** pay 12*s*. within **Hitchin Forrein**, 12*s*. within the Hamlet of **Langley**, 7*s*. within **Offley**, 4*s*. within **Minch-hill**, 2*s*. and **Wandon-end**, 8*s*. which common Fine in some Places, is called *Capitagium*, in other Places, *Certum Letæ*, and is a certain Sum of Money, which the Resiants and Inhabitants have, by Custom paid to the Lord at the Leet, in Regard that his Predecessor had purchased the same to discharge them from their Attendance at the Sheriff's Turn, which was a great Ease to them; or in Respect that the Lord of the Leet was obliged to claim his Liberty at his own Costs and Charges, whensoever the Justices in *Eire* should come: and the Lords of this Mannor have allowed the Steward 60*s*. yearly for his Fee, the Bailiff 100*s*. for his Fee, and 100*s*. more for the Dinner of the Steward, Jurors, and Homagers.

The Fines upon Admissions to Copihold Estates are certain, by the Custom, *viz*. the Moyety of a Year's Quitrent for the Admission either upon Descent, Alienation, or other Change, or upon a License to Demise.

The King, in Consideration of 266*l*. granted *An*. 6 *Jac*. I.

Hund. of
Hitchin.
all the Wood, Timber-trees growing, or which shall hereafter grow, upon any of the Copihold Lands within this Mannor, to certain Trustees, for the Benefit and Use of the
Copiholders within this Lordship.

The Mannor of the Rectory of HICHE.

Mon. Angl.
vol. 1, fol.360.
KING *William Rufus* gave the Church of St. *Andrews*
of Hiche, with the Chappels, one Virgate of Land worth
40*l. per Annum*, the Tythes, and all the Liberties thereunto
belonging to the Church of St. Mary de Helenestow, and
the Nuns there; afterwards King *H.* II. confirm'd the Gift,
and the Abbess of Elnestowe claimed at Hertford, before
John de Reygate and others, Justices Itinerants, in a *Quo*

Inq. 6 Ed 1.
Rot. 6, cur.
recept. Scac.
Warranto brought *Anno 6 Edw.* I. by the Grant of *H.* III.
Soc, Sac, Toll, Them, Infangthef, and Discharge from all
Aides, Gelds, Danegelds, Assizes, Hidages, Murders, Pleas,
and from all Actions, Plaints, Scutages, Ward-peny, and
upon View of the Grant, they were allowed; and whilst they
were possest hereof, this Church was rebuilt, and dedicated
to the Honour of the Virgin *Mary*, the particular Saint of
their Monastery; but when the fatal Year of their Dissolution happened, this Rectory came to the Crown, and King
Henry VIII. bestowed it upon his own Foundation, dedicated it to the *Holy Trinity* in Cambridge, to hold of the
King in free Socage, as of his Mannor of East Greenwich in
Kent; and the Master, Fellows, and Scholars of the same
Colledge, are the present Possessors hereof.

The Mannor of MOREMEAD

LIES, like the last Mannor, promiscuously among the
Lands within the Mannor of Hitchin, from whence, doubtless both these Mannors were at the first derived; most of
the Lands belonging to them are freehold, and Sir *Ralph
Ratcliffe* is the present Possessor hereof.

The Priory of WHITE CARMELITES.

Weav. Acta
and Mon. fol.
596,
IN this Town *John Blomvill, Adam Rouse*, and *John Cobham* founded a Priory of *White Carmelites* of the Order of
St. *Benedict*, dedicated it to the Honor of our alone Saviour
and the blessed Virgin, and King *Edward* confirmed the
Grant: These Friars held this House until the 9th of *May*,

Mon Angl.
vol. 1, fol.
1041.
Anno 21 *H.* VIII. when they surrender'd it into the Hands
of that King; it was then valued at no more than 4*l.* 9*s.* 4*d.*
King *H.*VIII. suppress this Fraternity of the *Carmelites*, and granted by Patent dated 22d *July*, 38 *H.*VIII. the

Cur. Aug.
Scite of the House to *Edmund Watson* and *Henry Herd-
son* in Fee, who conveyed it to

Ralph Radcliffe, the Son of *Thomas Radcliffe*, descended
from a younger Brother, sprung from Radcliffe Tower,
others say, from Ordhall in Lancashire, and married *Eliza-*

beth the Daughter of ——— *Marshall*, in this Town, Gentleman; by whom he had Issue three Sons, *Ralph, Jeremy, Edward*, and *Elizabeth* Wife to *William Fryar* of 𝔖𝔱𝔢𝔳𝔢𝔫𝔱𝔞𝔤𝔢; He lived here above the Space of twenty three Years, and laid the Foundation of an Estate; then died *An.* 1559, 1 *Eliz.* leaving the Care of his Children during their Minority to the Government of his Wife, who survived him, and afterwards married *Thomas Norton*, Gent. from whom the *Nortons* of 𝔒𝔣𝔣𝔩𝔢𝔭 descend.

Ralph Ratcliffe was his Heir, a Member of the *Inner Temple*, where he improved his time in the Study of the Common Law; was Reader there in Autumn, *Anno* 1541, 33 *Eliz.* double Reader to that Society in the *Quadragesimes*, 1600, 42 *Eliz.* and Treasurer of that House the Year following; also one of the Justices of the Peace for this County: He married *Elizabeth* the Relict of *William Wilcocks*, Esq. and Daughter of *John Edelphe*, by whom he had six Children, all whom died in his Life-time, and *Elizabeth* his Wife deceased *Anno* 1597, 39 *Eliz.* He lived a Widower about the Space of twenty four Years, during which time, he greatly augmented his Estate by the Practice of the Law, departed this Life in *January*, *Anno* 1621, 19 *Jac.* I. and leaving no Issue,

Edward, one of his Brother's Sons, was his Heir, and married *Anne* one of the Daughters of Sir *Robert Chester* of 𝔕𝔬𝔭𝔰𝔱𝔬𝔫, in this County, Kt. who was a vertuous and religious Woman, a wise and indulgent Wife, courteous and obliging to her Neighbours, knowing and skilful in Chirurgery, always ready to help the lame and indigent, bountiful and charitable to the Poor; kept her Family in great Order, govern'd it with much Discretion, and died about the Year 1656, to the great Grief of all that knew her; and he deceased on the fifth Day of *October*, 1660, being at that time about seventy Years of Age.

Ralph Ratcliffe, the Son of *Ralph*, the youngest Son of Sir *Edward Ratcliffe*, was his Heir, and married *Anne Pigot*, one of the Daughters of *John Pigot* of 𝔄𝔟𝔦𝔫𝔤𝔱𝔬𝔫 in the County of 𝔒𝔞𝔪𝔟𝔯𝔦𝔡𝔤𝔢, Esq. and *Frances* his Wife, by whom he had Issue *Edward*; this *Ralph* was knighted on the 18th of *February*, *Anno* 1667, by King *Charles* II. After the Decease of *Anne*, he married *Sarah* the Daughter of ——— ———, and after her Death, *Elizabeth* the Daughter of Sir *John Musters* of 𝔏𝔬𝔫𝔡𝔬𝔫, Kt. and Widow of Sir *Richard Spencer* of 𝔒𝔣𝔣𝔩𝔢𝔭, Bar. He is the present Possessor hereof, and gives, *Argent, two Bends engrail'd Sable.*

The Priory of *NEWBIGGING*.

THERE was another small Priory founded in this Town, called 𝔑𝔢𝔴𝔟𝔦𝔤𝔤𝔦𝔫𝔤, of the Order of St. *Benedict*, valued at

Hund. of
Hitchin.

Weav. Mon.
fol. 546.
Mon. Angl.
fol. 1041.

the Suppression to be worth 15*l*. 1*s*. 11*d*. but in the Catalogue at the End of the *Monasticon*, no more than 13*l*. 16*s*. and since the Dissolution, King *H*.VIII. by Charter, dated the first of *August*, 36 *Regni sui*, granted the Scite of this Priory to

John Coke and his Heirs; In the time of *Edw*. VI. it was conveyed to

Thomas Parrys, to hold of the King, by the yearly Rent of 1*l*. 11*d*. and these Lands have been since granted to divers Persons, among whom Mr. *Joseph Kemp*, Master of Arts, and Schoolmaster in this Town, purchased some Part of them, and did convert the House into a School in the Year 1655, and devised it among several other Lands in Hitchin, to charitable Uses.

This Town is situated in a Vale at the Foot of a great Hill in the Champion Country, which secures it from the cold Easterly Winds, is water'd with a small River termed the Hiz, and contains three Wards, Bancroft Ward, Bridge Ward, and Tyle-house-street Ward, is reputed the second Town in this County for the Number of Streets, Houses, and the Multitude of Inhabitants; heretofore it has been accounted famous for the Staple Commodities of this Kingdom; and divers Merchants of the Staple of Calice have resided here; therefore I think it may be some Satisfaction to the Reader to shew what these Merchants were

A Merchant was a Person who transported the Merchandize, Ware, or Goods of his own Country, over the Seas, into a foreign Country; where he sold them by wholesale, for ready Money, or exchanged or bought other Commodities there, and imported them to his Warehouse in his own Country.

Staple signified a City or Town, whither the Merchants of England, by Order or Command, carried their Wooll, Woollfells, Cloaths, Lead, Tin, and such like Commodities of this Land for Sale by the Great; and in the Saxon Language signified the Stay or Hold of a thing, because the Place is certain and settled; in the French 'tis called *Estape*, which signifies *Forum Vinarium*; because the French Merchants meet the English Merchants at those Places, where they brought their Commodities to trade and traffick with them, which consisted chiefly in Wines; and Dr. *Cowell* thinks this the truer, because these Words are written in French in the Mirrour of the World, *A* Calais *y avoit Estape de la laine*, &c. which is the Staple of Wool at Calais.

Mag. Chart.
cap. 9.
Stat. 9 H. III.
cap. 1.

In ancient time, when Staple Towns and Cities were appointed in foreign Parts, Merchants carried away the Trade of Wooll, Leather, and Woollfells hence into those Countries, where those Staples were held, which much inriched those People with our native Commodities, and impoverish- ed our own; for which Reason divers Laws were made to encourage Merchant Aliens to reside and keep their Markets here: But when these Laws obtained not that Effect which was designed, King *Edward* appointed that the Staple for English Wooll, Leather, Woollfell, and Lead, should be held for **England** at **Newcastle** upon **Tine, York, Lincoln, Norwich, Westminster, Canterbury, Chichester, Winchester, Exeter,** and **Bristol;** for **Wales** at **Caermarthen;** and for **Ireland** at **Dublin, Waterford, Corke,** and **Drogheda,** and not elsewhere; that in every Staple Town, there should be a Mayor and two Constables; the Mayor should be yearly chosen, as well by the Aliens as Denizens.   The Mayor and Constables had Power to keep the Peace, to arrest Offenders for Debt, Trespass, or Contract, to imprison and punish them according to the Law of the Staple, and had a Prison for that Purpose.   The Mayor was also authorized to take Recognizances for Debt in the Presence of one of the Constables, and had a Seal to seal every Obligation upon such Recognizance, and after Default of Payment, the Mayor could imprison the Debtor, arrest his Goods, and sell them for the Satisfaction of the Creditors; but if the Debtor could not be found within the Staple, the Mayor return'd the Obligation into *Chancery*, whence issued out a Writ against the Debtor, his Lands, Goods, and Chattels, returnable there, and Execution was awarded thereupon as the Statute Merchant directed.   In every Staple there were Correctors appointed, to record Bargains between Buyers and Sellers, and a certain Number of Porters, Packers, Winders, and other Labourers of Wooll and Merchandize; and all Officers of the Staple were duly Sworn before the Mayor, to execute their several Offices.

When any Merchandize was to be exported, it was first brought to the Staple, weighed by the Standard, and every Sack or Sarplet of Wooll was sealed under the Seal of the Mayor, who took an Oath of all Merchants that transported Merchandize, that they held no Staple thereof beyond the Seas: these Mayors and Constables had only Conusance of Debts, Covenants, Contracts, and all other Pleas touching Merchandizes, and the Surety thereof between known Merchants.

The Staple was removed from **Calais** to the Towns named for **England** in the Statute of the Staple, 27 *Edw*. III. by the Statute made *Anno* 14 *R*. II. and Recognizances taken before the Mayor of the Staple at **Calais,** were made effectual in **England,** *Anno* 10 *H*. VI. and the Merchants that resided here conveyed their Commodities to the Staple at **Calais,** and were sworn before the Mayor and Constables there, to maintain the Laws and Usages of the Staple,

Hund. of **Hitchin.**

14 Ed. III. Parl. 2, cap. 2. 25 Ed. III. *Stat* 4, 2. *Stat.* 27 Ed. III.

Stat. 36 Ed. III. cap. 7.

Stat. 14 R. II. cap. 1.

Stat. 10 H. VI. cap. 1.

which might be the Reason why these Merchants styled themselves, *Mercatores Stapulæ Villæ Calisiæ.*

For the better Incouragement of Trade in this Town, the Inhabitants have used to hold a Market here every *Tuesday* in the Week by Prescription free from the Payment of Toll for any Sort of Corn or Grain sold here: also three Fairs every Year, one on *Easter Tuesday*, another on *Whitsun Tuesday*, and another on the 13th of *October*, for the Sale of all Manner of Cattle, Corn, Grain, and other Merchandize, paying Piccage and Stallage of the Markets and Fairs, to the Lord of the Mannor of Hitchin.

THIS Vicaridge, *Anno* 26 *H.* VIII. was valued in the King's Books at 35*l.* 6*s.* 8*d.* whereof the Master and Fellows of *Trinity Colledge* in Cambridge are Patrons.

A Catalogue of the Names of the VICARS of Hitchin.

J. Sperehawke, obiit 1474	*Will. Lyndall*, D. D. 1636
James Hert, B. D. 1498	Mr. *King*
William Clophill	Mr. *Thomas Kidner*
Mr. *Chambers*, M. A.	Mr. *Johnson*, M. A.
Alured Birthie, 1562	Mr. *William Gibs*, M. A.
John Hudleston, 1603	Mr. *Francis Bragge*, B. D.
Stephen Peirce, D. D. 1620	

This Church is situated near the Middle of the Town, 'tis a fair Building, containing in length one hundred and fifty-three Foot, in breadth sixty-seven Foot, with three fair Chancels, and a square Tower about twenty one Foot diameter, in which hang a deep Ring of six Bells, cast in the Year 1689, with a short Shaft or Spire erected upon the Tower; which Church was anciently dedicated to the Honour of St. *Andrew*; but as the Church of St. *Mary's the Less* in Hertford, upon the rebuilding thereof, was dedicated *de novo* to St. *John*; so this Church, upon the like Occasion, was dedicated again to the Virgin *Mary*.

In the Middle Chancel lyes a Stone with this Inscription.

3 *August* 1654.
Senam suam hic depositum
Exuit
Magni Nominis
Josephus Kempe.
Qui
Omnes Terras suas Ædes ac Redditus in Hitchin *ad valorem Librarum plus mille in Egenorum istius Oppidi Liberorum in bonis Literis et Artibus ingenuis provectionem nec non Viduarum sustentationem pie consecravit et inperpetuum munificè donavit.*
Ne pereat Populus populires condidit Olim
Egypti Joseph *noster at ille suas*
Cujus Opes ditant inopes tenet Ossa Sepulchrum
Atqui Animam Omnipotens Angliæ *nomen habet*
Hoc Mnemosynum
Anna
Relicta ejus Observantissima
Lachrymis posuit
1655.

On the North Side of the same Chancel, lies a Marble with this Inscription.

Depositum Viri Omni memoria Dignissimi Thomæ Kidneri *Collegii* Magd. *Academiæ,* Oxon. *in Artibus Magistri hujus Ecclesiæ quondam Vicarii.*
Ἐκεῖνος ἦν ὁ λύχνος ὁ καιόμενος κ̀ φαίνων.

Drawn on Stone from the Original Engravings by O.E.Tyler.

To The Reverend Mᵣ.
Bachelor of Divinity &.

This Draught is hum

Pubᵈ by I.M.Mull:

HITCHIN.

Francis Bragge,
Minister of Hitchin.

ly presented by
    J. Drapentier.
or Bps: Stortford.

In Higham Galvin Agro Bedfordiensi omnes quas habuit Terras ad An- `Hund. of`
nualem Redditum 24 Librarum Scholæ Libræ hujus Oppidi Testamento `Hitchin.`
donavit; Quibus decem Egenorum Liberos per Scholarchas ibidem eruden-
dos liberè in perpetuum curavit.

> *Kidnerum quæris! Terras has ipse reliquit*
> *Sedibus Ethereis jam sibi parta Domus*
> *Sint nihili terrenat ibi modo morte parûris*
> *Christum sic docuit sic obiitque pie*
> *Ultimo die Augusti.*
> **1676.**
> *Imitand. Posteris.*

Another Stone has this Inscription.

Fælicem expectans Resurrectionem sub hoc Marmore requiescit in Dominio
Corpus Mri. Roberti Lucas Senioris obiit vicessimo septimo die Jannarii,
Ann. Domini 1678. Ætatis suæ 69. Æmulandum hic dum vixit.

> *Pietatis, et Justitiæ,*
> *Honestatis et Industriæ,*
> *Charitatis et Beneficentiæ,*
> *Se præbuit Exemplum Vicinio.*

A large Stone there has these Words engraven'd upon it.

Hic jacent ——————— quondam Mercatoris Stapulæ Villæ Calesiæ, qui
obiit 19 die mensis Aprilis, Ann. Dom. 1452. et pro anima Aliciæ Uxoris
ejus, quæ obiit die —— mensis, 1400.——

Another Marble there says,

Hic jacet Jacobus Hert, in Theologia Baccalaureus, ac Vicarius hujus
Ecclesiæ, qui obiit, 23 Jan. 1498.

Here lyes a Marble, which sets forth these Words,

Orate pro anima Johannis Sperehawke, hic jacentis quondam Doctoris
Theologiæ ac Canonici Ecclesiæ Cathedralis Wellon' et nuper istius
Ecclesiæ Vicarii, qui obiit undecimo die mensis, Semptembris, Ann. Dom.
MCCCCLXXIV.

In the North Chancel, you may view a Stone which says,

Gulielmus Clophill, et Petronella Uxor ejus, qui quidem Gulielmus nuper
Vicarius hujus Ecclesiæ ——

Another Marble tells you,

Hic jacet Johanna quondam Uxor Johannis Flexman, quæ obiit ——

Another Stone has this,

Here lieth *Stephen Fox*, Gentleman, and *Mary* his Wife, which *Stephen*
deceased 7 *Aug.* in the Year of our Lord God, 1582. and *Mary* 25 day
of *Jan.* 1581.

In the South Chancel there is a Monument raised from the Ground
from which the Brasses and Arms are taken away, but the Inhabitants
there do believe, that it was the Monument of *Sir John Sturgeon*, Kt.
who lived in the Reign of *Richard* III. was Sheriff of this County, and a
Man of great Account at that time.

In the South Chancel a Monument erected in the Wall, at the
East End thereof, speaks thus,

Here lieth the Body of *Ralph Ratcliffe*, Gentleman, whose Wife was
Elizabeth, Daughter of ——— *Marshall*, Gentleman, by whom he had
three Sons, *Ralph*, *Jeremy*, and *Edward*, whom having left to the care
of his Wife, (who was afterwards married to *Thomas Norton*, Gent. from
whom the *Nortons* of Offley descended.) He departed this life in the
40th year of his Age, in the Reign of *Henry* VIII. He came out of
Lancashire, where his Ancestors were antiently seated ; one of whom
was *Richard Radcliffe* of Radcliffe Tower, who lived there in the
Reign of *Edward* III. having three Sons, from the eldest of which did

descend the Right Honourable *Robert* (first) Earl of **Sussex**, of that Family; from the youngest, Sir *John Radcliffe* **Woodhall**. This *Ralph Radcliffe* was Son of a younger Brother, and who by Grant of *Henry* VIII. to whom the *White-Friers* of **Hitchin** surrendered their Priory, had the same confirmed to him, which he enjoyed fourteen years, and was then here interred in the year 1559. leaving this and the rest of his Estate to descend to *Ralph* his eldest Son.

In the second Column.

Here lie the Bodies of *Ralph Radcliffe*, Esq; and *Elizabeth* his Wife, the Relict of *William Wilcocks*, Esq; by whom he had six Children, but all of them short lived. He was Counsellor at Law, a Bencher of the *Inner-Temple*, and a double Reader of that Society, as also for many years a Justice of the Peace of the County, where he survived his Wife twenty four years, who died in 1597. and lived all that time Unmarried, in the enjoyment of a plentiful Estate, with that of a good Conscience, fraught with an humble submission to God, and void of Offence to his Neighbours; hereby being fitted for another World, he departed this life in the threescore and eighteenth year of his Age, and was buried upon the 4th day of *January* in the year 1621. having left his Estate, which he had very much improved, to *Edw. Radcliffe* Esq; his Nephew, whom he had adopted his Son, and lived to see married to *Anne* one of the Daughters of Sir *Robert Chester*, six months before his death.

In the third Column.

Here lie the Bodies of Sir *Edward Radcliffe*, Kt. (sworn Servant and Physitian to King *James*) and of Dame *Martha* his Wife, Daughter to *Eliz.* the Wife of his elder Brother *Ralph Radcliffe*, Esq; and one of the Sisters and Coheirs of *John Wilcocks*, Esq; by whom he had the Mannors of **Hampton** and **Coclescomb** in the County of **Kent**, but which was more Dear to him an hopeful Issue, *viz.* three Sons, *Edward, Jeremy,* and *Ralph,* and two Daughters, *Martha* and *Elizabeth,* whom having carefully and religiously Educated, he departed this life, aged 78, in hopes of a better, and was buried the 27th of *September,* in the year 1631. his Wife surviving him about 4 years, was upon the 2d of *March* 1636. decently Interred near him, they both leaving their Lands to *Edward* their eldest Son, and him to the Blessing and Providence of God, in whose Service they both lived, and in whose Fear they both died.

In the fourth Column.

Here lie the Bodies of *Edward Radcliffe*, Esq; (Son and Heir of Sir *Edw. Radcliffe*, Kt. and Nephew and Heir of *Ralph Radcliffe*, Esq;) and of *Anne* his Wife, one of the Daughters of Sir *Robert Chester* of **Royston**, Kt. who not having Issue of their own, did both agree upon an Intermarriage betwixt *Ralph Radcliffe* his Nephew and Heir, Son of *Ralph Radcliffe* his Brother, and *Anne Pigot* one of the Daughters of *Frances* her Sister, Wife of *John Pigot* of **Abbington Pigot** in the County of **Cambridg**, Esq; thus being agreed to unite their Bloods, they settled the Part greatest of their Estate in Trust for them, which Marriage he only lived to see Solemnized, and having survived his Wife four years, departed this life the 5th of *October,* being near 70 years of Age, in the year 1660. In their life time they were very industrious to improve the good and the interest of their Friends, having made the Poor of **Hitchin** no less, by the greatness of their Charity, and all others by the eminent Examples of their Piety.

Memoria conservanda et Inhumationis magis Decore Causa posuit hoc Monumentum et suffossam Cameram Rad. Radcliffe, *Miles,* A. D. 1675.

On a Monument raised are these Words.

Hic jacent Thomas Abbot **De** Hitchin, **Merceras, et** Johanna **Uxor** ejus. qui **quidem** Johannes, **obiit ultimo die** Januarii, **Anno Dom.** 1481. qui multa dona contulit huic Ecclesiæ et Fraternitati Natibitatis Beatæ Mariæ Virginis ejusdem Ecclesiæ.

Ḩic jacet Thomas Abbot, ——— qui quidem Thomas erat Filius Thomæ Abbot, sen. et predictus Thomas, obiit 16 Maii, 1498. et dicta die mensis ———1400———

In the Church a fair Stone tells yon,

M. S.

Mortuo quietem ne invideatis posteri
Hic subtus requiescit Corpus Edwardi Docwra hujus Villa in Domo dicta fraternitatis incolæ ; qui filius fuit natu minimus Thomæ Docwra, senioris de Ḩutterȳdge. armigeri, ob Justitiam, Pietatem, Hospitalitatem, inter cæteros in hoc tractu prænobilis.
Fuit Edwardo huic in ætatis flore corpus agile et vegetum, Statura justa, Vultus alacer, Animus fortis, Sermo promptus, Ingenium benignum, Judicium acre, juxta et experientia in rebus iis singulis quæ vitæ hujus vel usum, vel ornatum spectant. Citra avaritiæ sordida suspicione parcus, pro fortunarum suarum modulo vitam egit splendidam frugi hominum amicus, amicorum amantissimus. Ætate Paulo provectus aliquantum factus obesior, ingenti dolore calculi, diu multumque conflictus et tandem oppressus, placidum nihilominus vita exitum consectus est, pieque in Christo obdormivit die decimo octavo Junii, Anno Dom. 1610. Ætatis suæ 57. prolam masculam reliquit nullam, Filias tres.
Et te, Lector, tua sors manet, memento, et vade.

Another Marble shews this Inscription.

D. O. M.

Proxime hunc Lapidem conditi cinere
jacent
Johannis Skynner, *Generos.*
Qui hujusce loci municeps
Ultra 70 annos superfuit
Equibus 30 totus
Munerii Custodis (vulgò Stuartum vocant)
Provinciam tenuit
In Urbe Norbicensi natus
Parentibus in re honesta et splendida
Homo accerrimo Judicio et summa Fide
Juris Præsertim municipalis consultissimus
Gratiæque per viciniam concilianda studiocissimus
Juxta cubant
Mariæ dulcissimæ conjugis reliquiæ
par egregium
Quod sanctimoniam concordiam, Charitatem mutuam ad Annum usque 6um · supra 50um · una coluit,
Liberos 7. Filios 2. Filas 5 ex se genuit.
Uterque nunc fato functus.
Ille 16 Decembris, ⎫ ⎰ 1660.
Illa 6 Junii, ⎭ *Anno Dom.* ⎱ 1651.
⎰ *Sui* 91.
Ætat. ⎱ *Suæ* 82.
Felicis Resurrectionis præmia expectant.

Other Inscriptions.

Ḩic jacent Johannis Parmontor, qui obiit Vigilia Ḩatibitatis 143—. Et Margeria Ǔror ejus.———
Orate pro animabus Richardi Edmunds, fabri istius Villæ; et Johannis Web; et Margaretta Ǔroris eorun: quidem Richardus obiit primo die Octobris, Anno 1472. Quorum animabus propitietur Ḍeus.

In the Middle Isle.

Ḩic jacet Johannes Pulter, Ḍraper; qui obiit Februarius——— 1421. 9 *H.* V.

Another Inscription.

Hic jacet Johannes Ilom, Filius Thomæ Ilom, Aldermanni London, qui quidem Johannes obiit 1480.

Of the Earth I was formed, and to the Earth I am returned.

Here lyeth John Wisebeard, and Ellin his Wife, which John dyed 9. April, 1486. and Ellin dyed the 4. day of the same month and year.

Here lyeth William Pulter, Esq: late of Hitchin, who deceased the 20. of March, in the fifth year of Henry VI.

Pray ye all for Charity.

Here lyeth William Pulter, Esq: late of Hitchin, who dyed the 23. May, 1549. and in the third year of Edward VI.

On a Stone Monument raised is this Inscription.

Here lyeth John Pulter, Esq: late of Hitchin, who deceased the 20 day of June, 1485.

On another Stone.

Hic jacent corpora Nicol. Mattock, Mercatoris Stapulæ Villæ Callesiæ ac Civis Espisen. Civitatis London, ac bona et laudabilitis generosæ; Elizabethæ Uxoris suæ, qui quidem Nicholas obiit ——— die mensis ——— Anno 1400. Et dicto Elizabetha obiit sexto die Septembris 1485.
And over the Arms is this Motto.
Semper Colitemus.———

In the North Chancel.

To the Pious Memory of *Ralph Skinner*, Gent. who died *June* 17 1697. in the 90. year of his Age. He was for many years a public Blessing, not only to his Parish but the Neighbourhood. So truly Good that the most Censorious could spy out no occasion for Detraction: His Charity so Great, Publick and Private, and so well plac'd, that he was indeed the Patron of the Poor; The Widow and the Fatherless were his Wife and Children, for whom in his Life so at his Death, he made a Bountiful Provision. In the Communion of the Church of England, he lived sincerely up to his Profession and deserv'd the Character of a true Primitive Christian, and as such he dyed in Modest, Humble Hope, and longing Expectation of Eternal Bliss, through the Merits of *Jesus.*
Oh Saviour may we live and die like him!

Another Monument near it.

Here under lyeth the Body of *Frances,* Wife of *Ralph Skinner Byde,* Esq; Daughter of *George Nodes* of Shephal-bury, Esq; and *Elizabeth* his Wife, she departed this Life in the 33 Year of her Age, the 24. of *April, Anno Dom.* 1697.

At the Foot of their Monument lyes a fair Black Marble Grave Stone under which the Body of the said Frances Skinner *lyeth.*

A Catalogue of the BENEFACTORS to the Church and Poor of Hitchin.

1591 *William Warren,* Yeoman, gave 20*l.* per *Ann.* for ever, issuing out of an House in Cylehouse-street, to the Poor.

1600 *Elizabeth Radcliffe,* the Wife of *Ralph Radcliffe,* Esq. gave Money to purchase four Acres of Land for the Relief of the Poor.

1618 *Thomas Whitamore,* Yeoman, gave by his Will 20*l.* with which his Executors by the consent of the Inhabitants of this Town, purchased four Acres of Land near Walsworth, for the Use of the Poor for ever.

1625 *Edward Radcliffe,* Esq. Son and Heir of Sir *Edward Radcliffe,* Kt. gave an House in Cylehouse-street, to the Poor for ever.

1635 *James Huckle,* Esq. born in this Town, gave his House and Lands in Wingfield in the County of Berks, to the Poor of this Town for ever.

1639 *John Mattock* of Coventry, Esq. gave two Closes of Pasture towards the Education of Children at the Free-School, for ever.

1653 *William Giver*, Gentleman, gave 4*l*. yearly for ever, to put forth a poor Child of this Town an Apprentice every Year to some Trade.

1655 *Joseph Kempe*, Master of Arts, and Schoolmaster of this Town, gave all his Houses, Lands, and Revenues in Hitchin, towards the Education of six poor Children in the Free-School, the putting out four poor Children Apprentices every Year, and the Relief of ten poor Widows.

James Carter of London, Bricklayer, born in this Town, gave the Rent of two Tenements in Hounsditch for the Term of a Lease now expired.

1660 *Edward Radcliffe*, Esq. gave 20*l*. towards finishing of the Free-School, and 20*l*. more to purchase Lands to augment the Revenues thereof.

1660 Sir *Thomas Byde*, Kt. gave the two Stone Dials on the South Side of the Church: And in *Anno* 1670, gave the Ground whereon the eight Almes-houses are built.

Thomas Honylove of London, Haberdasher, built the Wall of the Free-School next to the Street.

1668 *John Skynner*, Gentleman, gave by his Will 300*l*. to build Almes-houses, 300*l*. to purchase Lands for a Revenue to the same, 100*l*. to put out poor Children Apprentices, 100*l*. to purchase Lands for the educating poor Children in the Free-School, and also an Orchard near the Churchyard; and upon his Death, this Inscription was fixt over the Gate of the Alms-houses.

Deo et Pauperibus
Ædificia hæc dicat sacratque
Johannes Skynner, Generosus
Nihil habuit quod Dei causâ non dedisset
Testamentum condidit verè pium:
Trecentas Libras in fundum erogandas
Pro perpetuâ harum Ædium dote;
Et
Pomarium cæmiterio affine annualis
Quadraginta solidorum reditus;
Centum Libros hujus Oppidi Ludo Literario
Erudiendis Egenorum Liberis
Et centum Libras denis pueris.
Apud artific. elocandis; et
Decem Libras ad Exequias inter inopes
Distribuendas;
Legata hæc omnia pia mente dedit
Charitatem vel Marmor ipsum
Loquitur.
1674.

Juxta hæc requiescit in Dominio Johannes Skynner, Generosus; vir eruditione spectabilis, moribus honestis, ac per omnia laudandus Legis Communis scientia non modo peritissimus sed et ejusdem usu et praxi longo tempore exercitatissimus cujus in Clientum causas defendendo, industria quanta fuit. quanta integritas, quanta fides, it qui ejus usi sunt patrocinio optime prædicare possunt, et illius fama nunquam moritura tam remotos quam proximos percrebuit, inter quos officium Seneschalli annos supra viginti fungebatur discretè, pacificè: Ac etiam inter Socios Hospitii Furnivacensis, adeo probatus ut communi omnium suffragia successive seniorem Thesaurarium principalem conscripserint.

Prope et hanc tabulam inhumatur Gratia uxor ejus, Pudicitiâ, Pietate, Humilitate decora, ex qua genuit duas filias Muriam, Elizabetham, Elizabetha hic subjacet. Maria, Thomæ Byde, Equiti aurato, nupta superest.

Obiit hic vicessimo die Martii 1668
Illa: vicessimo tertio Octobris 1681.

1673 *William Chambers*, Tanner, gave two Tenements in Back-street to the Poor of this Town for ever.

1676 *Thomas Kidner*, Master of Arts, and late Vicar of this Town, gave all his Lands in Bedfordshire, purchased of *Nicholas Crouch*, to the Free-School in Hitchin for ever, for the teaching ten poor Children there.

Oliver Clement gave one Annuity or Rent Charge of 6*l.* 13*s.* 4*d. per An.* to the Vicar of Hitchin, and to his Successors for ever, out of certain Houses in the Parish of St. Nicholas, London.

1678 Mr. *Robert Lucas*, by his Will, gave the brass Branch now hanging in the middle Isle of this Church, to the Use of the Inhabitants of this Town for ever.

Plate given to the Church.

Alice Pigot the Widow of *Thomas Pigot*, Esq. gave one Communion Cup with a Cover.

1625 Mr. *Thomas Weale* gave one Plate.

Anne Chapman, the Widow of *John Chapman*, late Rector of the Parish Church of Millpan in this County, gave one other Piece of Plate.

1635 *Dorothy Hill*, Widow, gave a silver Bason to receive the Offerings given at every Communion.

Mr. *Ralph Skinner*, Gent. in his Life-time, repaired the Free-school in Hitchin, and the Dwelling-house belonging to it, which I am informed cost about 200*l.* and he gave as much more in Portions towards the Maintenance of his poor Relations, and the Relief of the Poor of this Town; And at the time of his Death, he gave by his Will 200*l.* to purchase Lands for the Maintenance of the Vicar of this Parish Church and his Successors; 400*l.* more for the building of eight Alms-houses for the Habitation of poor old impotent People of Hitchin, and 400*l.* more to purchase Lands for their Maintenance in those Houses, 60*l.* more to bind forth ten poor Children of Hitchin, Apprentices to some Trade, whereby they may gain a Livelihood; 20*l.* to the Poor of Hitchin, and 5*l.* a piece to the Poor of the several Towns of Shillington and Clifton in the County of Bedford, and of Norton and Riot St. Lawrence in this County.

MENLESDENE, PRESTON, and DENSLEY,
are Hamlets within the Parish of Hitchin.

R*EX* Willielmus *tenet* Menlesdene *pro quatuor hidis se defendebat. Terra est octo Car. in Dominio duo hide et duo virgat. et dimid. et ibi sunt tres car. Presbiter cum octavis Vill. et duobus cotariis habentibus tres car. et adhuc duæ possunt fieri, ibi sex servi pratum un. car. pastura ad pecud. Ville Silva trigint. porc. hoc Manerium jacuit et jacet in* Hit, *Haroldus Comes tenuit.*

Deneslai.

Rex Willielmus *ten.* Deneslai *pro septem hidis se defendebat. Terra est vigint. car. in Dominio tres hidæ et dimid. et ibi sunt tres car. et xix Vill. habentes octo car. et novem adhuc possunt fieri, ibi septem cotar. et sex servi' et una Francigena elemosinar. Regis ibi duo molin' de xvi sol. pratum un. car. pastura ad pecud. Ville. Silva ccc porc. in totis valent. reddit per annum quatuordecim lib. arsas et pensatus et quinque .ib. ad numerum.*

Similiter tempore Regis Edwardi, *quando Petrus Vicecomes recepit, hoc Manerium tenuerunt duo Sochm. pro duobus Maneriis de Com'* Heraldo *tempore Regis* Edwardi, *et vendere potuerunt. tamen duas averas et duas in warda unus quisque inveniebat in* Hit, *sed per vim et injuste, ut Hund. testatur. Hæc duos Manerios tenuit* Ilbertus *pro uno Manerio, et inde fuit seisitus per breve Regis quamdiu Vicecomes fuit ut Scyra testatur postquam vero dimisit Vicecomitatum* Petrus de Valongies *et* Radulfus Tailgebosch *abstulerunt ab eo Manerio et posuerunt in* Hit, *propter quod nolebat invenire averam Vicecomiti* Goisbertus de Bech *successor* Ilberti *reclamat pro hoc Manerio misericordiam Regis.*

Menlesdene now Minsden.

King *William* held Menlesdene, it was rated for four Hides. The arable is eight Carucates, in Demean two Hides and two Virgates and an Half, and there are three Carucates, a Presbyter or Parson, with eight Villaines and two Cottagers having three Carucates, and now two more may be made, there are six Servants, Meadow one Carucate, Common of Pasture for the Cattle of the Vill, Wood to feed thirty Hogs. This Mannor did lie and doth lie in Hit. Earl *Harold* held it.

TEMPLE I

Drawn on Stone from the Original Engraving by C.L. Tyler.

To the Right Worp. *S* *Edwin Sadler,*

This Draught is

Pub. *by J.W.Hullinger.*

of Temple Dinsley, Barronet.

humbly presented by

J. Drapentier.

Bps: Stortford, 1626.

Beneslei now Temple Dinsley.

King *William* held **Beneslei**, it was rated for seven Hides. The arable is twenty Carucates, in Demeasne three Hides and an Half, and there are three Carucates, and nineteen Villaines having eight Carucates, and nine more may be now made, there are seven Bordars, and seven Cottagers, and six Servants, and one Frenchwoman born an Almswoman of the King; there are two Mills of sixteen Shillings Rent by the Year, Meadow one Carucate, common of Pasture for the Cattle of the Vill, Wood to feed 300 Hogs; in the whole Value it yielded by the Year fourteen Pounds burnt and weighed, and five Pounds told.

Likewise in the time of King *Edward* (the Confessor) when *Peter* the Sheriff received it, two Socmen held this Mannor for two Mannors of Earl *Harold*, in the time of King *Edward* (the Confessor) and might sell them, notwithstanding either of them did find two Horses and two Horse trappings in **Vit**, but by Force and unjustly, as the Hundred can witness. *Ilbert* held these two Mannors for one Mannor, and was thereof seized by the King's Writ, so long as he was Sheriff, as the Shire can witness; but after he demised the Sheriffdom, *Peter de Valongies* and *Ralph Tailgebosch* took it from this Mannor and laid it to **Vit**; for that he would not find an Horse for the Sheriff; *Goisbert de Bech* Successor to *Ilbert* did obtain again Judgment of the King for this Mannor.

Barnard Baliol, Son of *Guy de Baliol*, Lord of the Mannor of **Hitchin** gave to the Knights Templers, Land worth 15*l. per annum*, called **Wedelee**, a Member of **Hitchin**, and the rough and plain Fields, with the Grove called **Flubios**, which Gift was made in the Capital of **Rome**, where Pope *Eugenius* was present, on the Octaves of Easter, and at **Paris** where the King of **France** the Archbishop of **Sceaber**, **Bardell**, **Rothomage**, **Drascumb**, and 130 Knights Templers clothed in their white Vestments, were present; and *Everard de Bretvill*, *Theodore Waleran*, *Baldwin Calder*, and divers others, were Witnesses, and King *Stephen* did confirm the Grant.

John de Baliol purchased the Mannor of **Menlesdene** of *Wiat de Bodicot*; but when he obtained the Crown of **Scotland**, and levied War against King *Edward* the first, that King seized it into his own Hands, and granted it to *Roger le Strainge* for his Life; afterwards to *Robert de Kendall*, and *Margaret* his Wife for her Life, and to the Heirs of their Bodies, upon which Presentment, Sir *Edward de Kendall*, Kt. Son and Heir of *Robert*, was impleaded, who said, the Mannor of **Mendlesden** was a certain Hamlet of **Hitchin**, and in the Parish, but the Jury found it was in Gross by itself, as was supposed by the Presentment, and not Parcel of the Mannor of **Hitchen**, nor at any time was, and that the Mannor of **Mendlesham** was worth 13 Marks by the Year, and the Arable 473 Marks, and Judgment was given for the King.

The Master of the Knights Templers in **England** claimed by the Grant of *Henry* III. in all their Lands, divers large Priviledges, with Exemption from all secular Services, Soc, Sac, Toll, Them, Infangeneth, Utfangthef, Hamsocne, &c. and Discharge from all Business in all Places, &c. and Causes &c. and from all Toll and Custom, &c. in as

Margin notes:

Hund. of **Hitchin**.

Mon. Angl. vol. 2, fol 523.

Hill. 39 Ed. III. Rot. 28, cur. recept. in Scac.

Quo Warr. 6 Ed. I. Rot 37, cur. recept. in Scac.

ample a Manner as kingly Power can grant to any religious House, and also Free-warren in 𝕯insle, &c.

The Prior of 𝖂imondley, held the Scite of the Castle of 𝕯inesle, and gave the yearly Rent of 10s. for the same.

An Agreement was made between the Knights Templers, and the Abbess and Nuns of 𝕰lnestow, by the Assent and Free-will of their Chapters, that the Nuns of 𝕰lnestow, should find a Chaplain, who should reside at 𝕯inesle, and celebrate Mass on Sundays, Wednesdays, and Fridays in every Week in the Mornings, and Vespers in the Afternoons, unless it should happen that a Festival should fall in the Week, then that should be accounted one of the three Days; and the Chaplain or Minister of 𝕳itchin, shall make Oath to the Brethren, for the Performances of these Duties: And the Knights Templers shall pay to the Nuns, with all Integrity, all the Tythes of Corn issuing out of all the Lands, which they plough in 𝕳itchin, of whom the Church of 𝕳itchin, or the Church belonging to it was used to have received Tythes, and also of all the Ground newly broken up and sowed.

In *Anno* 21 *Edw.* III. 'twas found, that the Prior of the Hospital of St. *Johns* of 𝕵erusalem, in 𝕰ngland, held the Mannor of 𝕿emple 𝕯insley with the Appurtenances, which lately was the Templers, in free, pure, and perpetual Alms, of the Heirs late of the Lords of 𝕳itchin, 𝕯insley, 𝕱urnibal, and 𝕶ing's 𝖂alden, by finding yearly two Chaplains to celebrate divine Service in the Chapel of this Mannor for ever, for the Souls of the Feoffees of the Templers for all secular Services.

The Knights Hospitallers held these Mannors until the fatal Year of the Dissolution of Monasteries, when it came to King *Henry* VIII. who by Letters Patents dated at 𝖂estminster, the 13th of *March*, 33 *Regni sui*, in Consideration of 843*l.* 2*s.* 6*d.* granted to Sir *Ralph Sadlier*, Kt. one of the Principal Secretaries of State, the Mannors of 𝕿emple 𝕯insley and 𝕿emple 𝕮helsin, and all their Rights, Members, and Appurtenances, lately belonging to the dissolved Priory of St. *Johns* of 𝕵erusalem, and all the Messuages, Mills, Buildings, Gardenings, Knight's Fees, Wards, Marriages, Escheats, Reliefs, Heriots, Fairs, Markets, Tolls, Customs, Warrens, Rent-Charges, Rentseck, Annuities, Fee-Farms, Waters, Fishings, Piscaries, Court-Leets, Profits of Courts, View of Franc-Pledge, Fines, Amerciaments, Assize and Assay of Bread, Wine, and Ale, Goods and Chattels, Waifs, Estreats, &c. and all other Rights and Profits, in as full, large, and ample Manner, as the last Prior and his Brethren, or any of their Predecessors enjoyed them, to have and to hold of the King *in Capite*, by the Service of the twentieth Part of a Knight's Fee, rendring yearly to the King 4*l.* 9*s.* 4*d.* at the

Feast of St. *Michael* the Archangel, in Lieu of all Services. Which Sir *Ralph Sadlier* by Indenture Tripartite, dated the 25th of *October*, in the 12th Year of Queen *Elizabeth*, did covenant to convey this Mannor to Trustees for the use of himself for his Life, without Impeachment of Waste, the Remainder to the Use of *Edward Sadlier* and *Anne* his then Wife, (the Daughter and Heir of Sir *Rich. Leigh*) and to the Heirs of *Edward*, on the Body of the said *Anne*, lawfully to be begotten, and for Want of such Issue to the Use of the said Sir *Ralph Sadlier* for ever.

'Twas found by Inquisition taken at **Hertford**, on Saturday the 2nd of *December*, *Anno* 35 *Eliz.* that *Edward Sadlier*, Esq. died seized of the Remainder of this Mannor on the 4th of *April*, in the 26th Year of Queen *Elizabeth* and left *Anne* his Wife surviving by whom he had Issue, *Leigh*, *Richard*, *Edward*, and *Thomas* and died in the Lifetime of his Father, afterwards Sir *Ralph Sadlier*, Kt. died seized hereof in the 29th Year of the Queen, after whose Death, *Anne* entered into the Premises, held it for her Life, and upon her Death, the Remainder thereof descended to

Leigh Sadlier, who married *Elizabeth*, Daughter of —— *Paschall* of **Preston** in the County of **Essex**, by whom he had Issue *Thomas Sadlier*, and one Daughter, *Anne* married to *Edward Aston*, Esq. Brother of *Walter* Lord *Aston:* He died on the fifth Day of *June*, *Anno* 30 *Eliz.* seized of this and the Mannor of **Aspley** in the County of **Bedford**, leaving

Thomas his Son and Heir, five Years old on the 6th of *April*, *Anno* 35 *Eliz.* He married *Frances* Daughter of *Francis Berry* of **Bickering Park** in the County of **Bedford**, by whom he had Issue *Thomas* who died in his Infancy, *Edwin*, *Ralph* who died unmarried, *Leigh*, *Edward* who deceased without Issue, *William* married *Sarah* Daughter to *Jasper Symonds*, Minister of **Dabentry** in the County of **Northampton**, *Richard* and *Robert*, both whom died without Issue, and five Daughters, *Elizabeth*, *Frances*, *Anne*, *Jane*, and *Sarah*.

Edwyn Sadlier was the Heir, created Baronet by Letters Patents dated the 3d of *December*, *Anno* 1663, 13 *Car.* II. He married *Elizabeth* the eldest Daughter of Sir *Walter Walker*, Kt. Doctor of the Civil Law, by whom he had Issue *Walter*, *Ralph*, both whom died in their Childhood, and *Edwyn*; also two Daughters, *Mary* and *Elizabeth*.

Sir *Edwyn Sadlier* succeeded, and married *Mary* Daughter and Coheir of *John Lorymer*, Citizen, and an Apothecary of **London**, who fined for Alderman of that City, and the Relict of *William Croane*, Doctor in Physick: His Arms are, *Or, a Lyon Rampand per Fesse Azure and Gules; Crest on a Wreath a demi Lyon rampant Azure crowned Or*; Motto, *Servire Deo sapere*.

M 2

THE PEDIGREE OF THE SADLIERS.

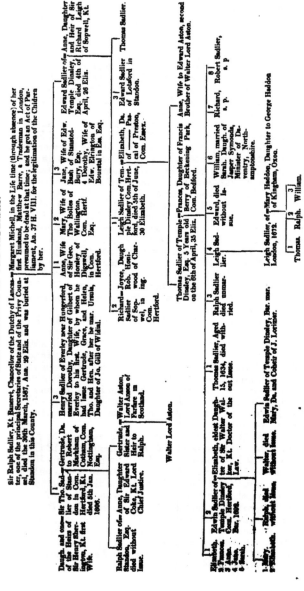

HIPPOLITS, *vulgarly called* EPPALETS, *or* PALLETS.

THE Church of this Vill was dedicated to a supposed Saint called St. *Hippolits,* from whom this Vill received its Name, who was a good Tamer of Colts, an excellent Horse-leach, and so devoutly honour'd for these Qualities after his Death, that all Passengers that passed that Way on Horseback, thought themselves bound to bring their Steeds to the high Altar in this Church, where this holy Horseman was shrined, and a Priest continually attended to bestow such Fragments of *Hippolits'* Miracles upon their untamed Colts, and old wanton and forworn Jades, as he had in Store, and did avail so much the more or less, as the Passengers were bountiful or hard handed; but he that was niggardly of his Coin, had but a cold and counterfeit Cure. The Horses were brought out of the North Street, through the North Gate, and the North Door of the Church, which was boarded on Purpose to bring up the Horses to the Altar, since which time, the Church has always been boarded. This Vill is situated a Mile distant from Hitchin towards the South.

The Mannor of MAYDECROFT or MAYDENCROFT

IN the time of *Edw.* III. was Parcel of the Possessions of Sir *Robert Nevill* of Hornby, Kt. from whom it came to

Sir *Thomas Nevill,* who had Issue only *Margaret* his Daughter and Heir. She married *Thomas Beaufort,* the youngest Son to *John of Gaunt,* Duke of Lancaster, by *Katharine Swineford,* his third Wife, and he did his Homage, *Anno* 1 *H.* V. and had Livery of her Lands of Inheritance. He commanded the Rereward of the English Army in the Battle of Agincourt, and was made Lieutenant of Normandy the 28th of *February,* 3 *H.* V. created Duke of Exeter in the Parliament held at London about the Feast of St. *Lucy* for his Life, 18th of *November,* 4 *H.* V. having only a Grant of 1000*l. per Annum,* out of the *Exchequer,* and 40*l. per Annum* more payable from the City of Exeter; and he died seized hereof on the 27th of *December, Anno* 5 *H.* VI. among divers others, at his Mannor-house of Greenwich, and was buried at St. Edmundsbury, leaving

John Earl of Somerset his Nephew, (Son of *John* Earl of Somerset his Brother) his next Heir, at that time twenty four Years of Age.

But I have read nothing more of this Mannor until it came to the Possession of *Ralph Radcliffe,* whom I have spoken of in the Parish of Hitchin, from whom by meer

Assignment, it came to Sir *Ralph Radcliffe*, the present Lord hereof.

This Mannor has Jurisdiction of Court Leet and Baron, and extendeth itself within the Mannor and Parish of 𝔥𝔦𝔱𝔠𝔥𝔦𝔫; the Fines of the Copiholds upon every Alienation, Descent, or Change, are at the Will of the Lord, and no Tenant may fell and carry away any Timber growing upon any of the Copyhold Lands, without License of the Lord of the Mannor.

The Mannor of ALMESHOE.

THE Bishop of 𝔅𝔞𝔶𝔢𝔲𝔵, who was Uncle to *William* the Conqueror, was Lord of this Mannor in those Days, for 'tis recorded in *Domesdei Book*, under the Title of *Terra Epi. Bajocensis*.

In 𝔄𝔩𝔪𝔢𝔰𝔥𝔬𝔲 *tenet* Adam *de Ep.* Bajocensis *unam hidam. Terra est un. car. et ibi est cum tribus Bord. Silva 60 Porc. valet vigint. sol. quando recepit decem sol. tempore Regis* Edwardi *trigint. sol. hanc terram tenuit Edmundus homo Com.* Heraldi *et vendere potuit.*

The Land of the Bishop of 𝔅𝔞𝔶𝔢𝔲𝔵.

Adam held of the Bishop of 𝔅𝔞𝔶𝔢𝔲𝔵 one Hide in 𝔄𝔩𝔪𝔢𝔰𝔥𝔬𝔲. The arrable is one Carucate, and it is there with three Bordars, Wood to feed sixty Hogs; it is worthy twenty Shillings a Year, when he received it ten Shillings, in the time of King *Edward* (the Confessor) thirty Shillings. *Edmond* a Man under the Protection of Earl *Harold*, held this Land and might sell it.

This Mannor came to the Possession of *Simon Fitz Ade*, who upon the Day of his Marriage endowed *Fyne* his Wife, *ad Ostium Ecclesiæ, Anno* 1241, 25 *H.* III. with this Mannor, the capital Messuage, and all the Lands belonging to it, together with the Advowson of the Church of 𝔊𝔯𝔞𝔟𝔢𝔩𝔢𝔢, and the Service of *Ralph de Gravelee*, and all his Lands in 𝔐𝔦𝔫𝔩𝔢𝔰𝔡𝔢𝔫, in the Parish of 𝔥𝔦𝔱𝔠𝔥, with the Rents and Services, &c. and all he had in 𝔏𝔞𝔫𝔤𝔩𝔢𝔢, 𝔈𝔰𝔱𝔢𝔟𝔢𝔫𝔞𝔠𝔥, 𝔒𝔣𝔣𝔢𝔩𝔢𝔶, 𝔚𝔶𝔩𝔦𝔢, and 𝔏𝔢𝔱𝔠𝔥𝔴𝔬𝔯𝔱𝔥, with all the Demeasn, Rents, and Services, &c. which Deed was attested by twelve Witnesses, who were present at the Marriage, whereof seven were Knights; and of the other five, one was *William* of 𝔥𝔞𝔱𝔣𝔦𝔢𝔩𝔡, and another was *Roger de Wylie*.

This *Simon Fitz Ade* had Issue Sir *John Fitz Symon*, who received his Sirname from his Father, and upon his Death, he left Issue, *Hugh Fitz Symon*, who also received the Honour of Knighthood, and left Issue Sir *Richard Fitz Symon*, who was installed a Knight of the most noble Order of the Garter; and after he had been possest sometime, he died seized hereof, leaving Issue

Adam Fitz Symons, who had Issue *Hugh Fitz Symons*, who left *Edward* and *Nicholas.*

Edward was knighted, afterwards died without Issue, then it came to

Nicholas Fitz Symon his Brother, and next Heir, who had Issue two Daughters, whereof one had only one Son, who died without Issue, whereupon this Mannor came to

Elizabeth, the Grandaughter of the said *Nicholas* by his other Daughter; She married *Thomas Brocket*, Esq. in the time of *H.* VI. who, in Right of his Wife, became Lord of this Mannor; and since it has continued in his Name for divers Generations, which I forbear to mention, for that they are set forth in his Pedigree, which you may read under the Name of the Mannor of Symondshide in the Parish of Hatfield, and it has always passed with the Mannor of Symondshide, through the same Hands, until it came to Sir *John Spencer*, who is the present Lord hereof.

The Lord of this Mannor granted to the Prior and Convent of our blessed Lady next Hertford, a Portion of Tythes out of Parcel of the Demeans of this Mannor, before the Council of Lateran, which was held *Anno* 1215, when the Laity were restrained from giving of their Tythes to any religious Houses, and retaining them in their own Hands, which before that time was usual; but since all these are now become due of common Right to the Minister of the Parish where they arise, excepting Tythes formerly given to some religious Houses, and the Custom of tithing in particular Towns and Places; and these are the Lands that are now exempted from the Payment of Tythes at this Day.

Thomas the Prior of the House of our blessed Lady next Hertford, and the Convent there, *Anno* 1535, 26 *H.*VIII. by Deed indented and executed under their common Seal, *viz.* a Lady with an Infant in her Arms, demised to *Edward Brocket*, Esq. all their Tythes of Corn, Grain, Hay, Wood, Wooll, and Lamb, arising within the Parishes of Hitchin, Minsden, Langley, and Hippolits, for forty and one Years; which Lease coming to *Edward Brocket* of Bradfield, his Son, as Administrator to the Goods and Chattels of his Father, assign'd over the said Term, *Anno* 4 *Eliz.* to *John Brocket* of Brocket-hall, Esq. then Lord of this Mannor.

The Priory at Hertford was dissolved, *Anno* 27 *H.*VIII. and all their Mannors, Lands, Tythes, and Portions of Tythes, were, by Act of Parliament, given to the King and to his Heirs and Successors for ever.

The King, by Letters Patents under the Great Seal of England, *Anno* 29 *H.*VIII. granted unto *Anthony Denny*, Esq. and *Joan* his Wife, and the Heirs of *Anthony*, the Priory at Hertford, together with divers other Mannors and Lands; and among them, the Tythes issuing out of this Mannor, late belonging to the dissolved Monastery, to hold of the King and his Heirs *in Capite*.

Henry Denny and *Edward Denny* of Waltham, Esq. *An.* 11 *Eliz.* sold these Tythes in Hitchin, Minsden, Langley, and Hippolits, to Sir *John Brocket* of Brocket-hall, Kt. and his Heirs for ever, who died *Anno* 40 *Eliz.* After his Death, it was found by Inquisition, that Sir *John Broc-*

Hurd. of Hitchin.

ket was seized of these Tythes in **Almesbor**, in Fee, and the same were held *in Capite*, and they passed to Sir *Richard Spencer*, who married *Hellen* one of the Daughters and Co-heirs of the said Sir *John Brocket*, and upon the Death of Sir *Richard Spencer*, the like Office was found; and that *John Spencer* was his Son and Heir, who was created Baronet by Patent dated *Anno* 1626, 1 *Car.* I. and married the Daughter of Sir *Richard Anderson* of **Penly** in this County, Kt. he levied a Fine *Anno* 5 *Car.* I. of the Mannor of **Almesbou**, these Tythes and two Messuages at **Popters-end**, with the Lands belonging to them; and obtained a License to alien to Sir *John Boteler* and *Brocket Spencer*, Esq. the two Messuages, Lands, and the Tythes of Corn, Hay, and Wood, arising in 400 Acres of Land, 40 Acres of Pasture, and 140 Acres of Wood, in **Hippolites**, **Almeshouburp**, **Hitchin**, **Wimondley Magna**, **Wimondley Parva**, and **Preston**, which were holden of the King *in Capite*; but Sir *John* dying without Issue,

Sir *Brocket* was his Brother and Heir, from whom they came to Sir *Richard*, from him to Sir *John* the present Owner hereof.

THIS Vicaridge, *Anno* 26 *H.*VIII. was rated at the yearly Value of 5*l.* *per Annum;* The Parsonage is appropriated to the perpetual Use of the Master and Fellows of *Trinity Colledge* in **Cambridge**, who are the Patrons hereof.

VICARS.

Mr. *Wilford*   Mr. *Wharton*   Mr. *Alyn*
Mr. *Henry Sykes*   Mr. *Gregory*   Mr. *Ford.*

The Church is erected near the Vill, in the Deanery of **Hitchin**, in the Diocess of **Lincoln**. where there is a square Steeple, in which are three small Bells, and this Inscription upon a Gravestone in the Chancel.

Here lieth buried the Body of *Alice Hughes*, late Wife of *Rice Hughes*, Citizen and Haberdasher in **London**, by whom he had Issue, one Son and two Daughters all deceased, and lie buried likewise in this Church, at the Chancel Door, she being the Daughter of *Thomas Kybeworth* an ancient Dweller in this Parish, she dyed the 13th of *August*, 1594, being of the Age of 29 Years.

> Her Body and Bones the Ground doth possess,
> Her Soul to Heaven is gone for redress:
> Who living in Life, did die unto Sin,
> And dying by Death, to live did begin.

ICKLETON, or ICKLEFORD.

THIS Vill, I suppose, was waste Ground in the time of *William* the Conqueror, for there is no Mention of it in *Domesdei Book*, and I believe it was then comprehended under the Name of **Periton**, for without the Addition of this Vill I cannot find so much Land in **Periton**, as is continued under that Name in *Domesdei*, but when this Ground was improved and became a Parish, it was termed **Ickleton** or Ickleford, from the old Roman Way called Icknal, and the Ford which crosses the River there. *Hund. of Hitchin.*

This Mannor was anciently Parcel of the Revenue of the *Argentines*, of whose Family I have treated in the Parish of Great Wimondley, to which Parish I refer the Reader. But this Name expiring through want of Issue Male, about the Reign of *Hen.* VI. it was conveyed to the Crown, where probably it remained till King *Rich.* III. by Letters Patents dated the 4th of *March*, 2 *Regni sui*, granted the Mannors of Lawnardwyke, Ikylford, and Periton in this County, and Lands in Arlessey in the County of Bedford, (which had been Sir *Roger Towcot's*, Kt.) to Sir *William Meering*, to have and to hold to him, and the Heirs Males of his Body, who, I suppose, married *Agnes*, Heir of *Henry Gloucester* of Carcolston, by whom he had Issue

John Meering, who espoused *Katharine*, one of the Sisters and Coheirs of Sir *John Hercy* of Grove, by whom he had *Francis*, *Thomas*, and *John*.

Then it came to the *Dearmans*, an ancient Name in this County, in which Family it remained till about the Year 1580, when *Thomas Auncel* of the County of Northampton purchased it, and since that time the Owners hereof have born the Name of *Thomas* for four or five Generations to this Day, *Thomas Auncel* being the present Possessor hereof; was constituted High Sheriff of this County *Anno* 1698, he has Jurisdiction of Court Leet and Baron, all the Tenants being Freeholders.

The Mannor of ROMERICK.

THIS was Parcel of the Possession of the Church of Ramsey, and *Anno* 8 *H.* III. that King made an Agreement at Newcastle upon Tyne, between *Aldwin* the Abbot, and *Reinald de Argentuem*, concerning the Mills of Ickles-ford, and the Land of the Fee of the Abbot and *Reinald*, to wit, that *Reinald* shall hold the Mill and Lands, and one Part seated in the Fee of *Reinald*, so long as he shall live, and after his Death, the Abbot shall resume the Mill and Land in his Demeasne, with all the Encrease which *Reinald* shall make upon it, and *Gundrit* shall hold the Mill of the Abbot, as he held it of *Reinald*, and if *Reinald* shall die in England, he shall be buried in the said Abby, and for this Agreement, *Reinald* shall give to the Abbot every Year, ten Shillings, and the same King confirmed these Gifts and Grants to *Simon*, then Abbot of Ramsey, and the Convent of the same Place. *Mon. Angl* vol. 1, fol. 231.

Which Abbots held it till the Dissolution of their Church, when it came to the Crown; where this Mannor remained till the time of King *James* I. who *Anno* 5 *Regni sui*, granted the Court Leet and View of Franc-pledge, of all the Tenants belonging to this Mannor to the Master, Fellows, and Scholars of St. *John's* Colledge in Cambridge, who are the present Lords hereof.

THE Rectory of this Parish Church, with the Church of Pirton, *An.* 26 *H.* VIII. was valued together in the King's Books at 8*l. per An.* whereof *William Deane,* Esq. is Patron.

VICARS.

Mr. *Rotheram*   Mr. *William Goodwin.*

This Church is situated in the Middle of the Vill, which is in the Deanery of Hitchin in the Diocess of Hertford: The Church is small, covered with Lead, having a low square Towe without Battlements, at the West End thereof, covered also with Lead, where hangs a Ring of five Bells with a short Spire about four Foot long.

ST. THOMAS CHAPPEL

Is a small Hamlet scituated about two Miles distant from Ickleford Church, severed from any Part of this County about Half a Mile, by the Interposition of the Parishes of Henlow and Stanton in the County of Bedford; and, I suppose, was wast Ground in the time of *William* the Conqueror, for there is no Mention of it in *Domesdei Book,* and might then belong to some Mannor in this County, for that Cause made Part hereof, as I have observed some other Hamlets have been, as Collshill, &c. and it was denominated from the Chappel, which was dedicated to St. *Thomas a Becket;* but after it came to be improved, it was granted to the Monastery of Chicksand in Bedfordshire, and the Abbots enjoy'd it, until the time of their Dissolution, when it came to the Crown, from whence it was conveyed to the Earl of Kent, in Exchange for the Mannor of Steppingly in the County of Bedford; from whom it came by mean Conveyance, to *Gray Longuerville,* Esq. who is a Branch of that noble Family, and the present Possessor hereof.

In this Hamlet is a pretty Chappel, now converted into a Barn, and has no Relation to religious Offices, more than that the Rector of Meppershal, time out of Mind, beyond the Memory of Man, have read the second Service there upon Ascention Day, after he has performed the first Service, at the Parish Church of Meppershal.

PIRITON, or PIRTON.

KING *William* the Conqueror gave this Vill, then called Pirit on from one *Peri,* an ancient Saxon Possessor hereof, to *Ralph de Limesie,* a great Man in those Days, as is apparent by the Possessions which he had in divers Counties of England, set forth in *Domesdei Book,* among which it is recorded under this Title of *Terra Radulfi Limesie.*

Radulfus de Limesy *tenet* Peritone *pro decem hid. se defendebat. Terra est vigint. Car. in Dominio duo hidæ et ibi sunt sex car. ibi vigint. quatuor Vil. cum Presbitero et vigint novem Burd. habentes duodecem car. et adhuc duo possunt fieri, ibi unus Miles Anglicus, et unus Sochmannus, cum quatuor cotar. ibi quatuor Molin. de* lxxiii *sol. et* iv *denar. in Terra Anglici et Soch. id est ab duabus hid manent un Vil. et octo cotar. pratum decem car. ibi decem Servi pastura ad pec. Vil. silva quingent. porc. de Pastura et silva decem sol. in totis valent vigint. lib. quando recepit vigint. duo lib. tempore Regis Edwardi vigint. quinque lib. Hoc Manerium tenuit* Stigandus, *Archiep. et ibi fuerunt duo Sochmanni, et adhucibi sunt, non potuerunt vendere. Hic de super est dimid. Hundred de* Pij.

Ralph de Limesy held Pirton, it was rated for ten Hides. The arable is twenty Carucates, in Demeasne two Hides, and there are six Carucates there are four and twenty Villains, with a Presbyter or Priest, and nine and twenty Borders, having twelve Carucates, and now two more may be made, there is one Knight, an Englishman born, and one Sochman with four Cottagers, there are four Mills of seventy three Shillings and four Pence Rent in the Land of the Englishman and the Sochman, that is one Villain and eight Cottagers remained of two Hides, Meadow ten Acres, there are ten Servants, Common of Pasture for the Cattel of the Vill, Wood to feed five hundred Hogs, of Pasture and Wood ten Shillings Rent; in the whole Value it is worth twenty Pound a Year, when he received it twenty two Pounds, in the time of King *Edward* (the Confessor) twenty five Pounds. *Stigand* the Archbishop held this Mannor, and there were two Sochmen and now they are there, they could not sell. Moreover this is in the Half Hundred of 𝔇𝔦𝔷.

This *Ralph de Limesy* founded a Church in this Vill, to which he gave two Parts of his Tythes, issuing out of one of his chief Seats, called 𝔚𝔬𝔩𝔟𝔢𝔯𝔩𝔦𝔢, scituated on the North Part of 𝔖𝔬𝔩𝔦𝔥𝔲𝔩 Parish in 𝔚𝔞𝔯𝔴𝔦𝔠𝔨𝔰𝔥𝔦𝔯𝔢, from which Place he derived the Title of his Barony.

But afterwards this *Ralph*, having a great Respect to the Abby of 𝔖𝔱. 𝔄𝔩𝔟𝔞𝔫𝔰, gave the Tythes of this Church of 𝔓𝔦𝔯𝔦𝔱𝔬𝔫, and the Church of 𝔥𝔢𝔯𝔱𝔣𝔬𝔯𝔡, which he also built and endowed with divers Lands and Tithes, to that Monastery. *Bar.* vol. 1, fol. 414. *Antiq of War.*

Alan, who was his Son and Heir, succeeded him, and gave to the Monks at 𝔥𝔢𝔯𝔱𝔣𝔬𝔯𝔡, the Church of 𝔦𝔠𝔥𝔢𝔫𝔱𝔬𝔫𝔢, in the County of 𝔚𝔞𝔯𝔴𝔦𝔠𝔨, he had Issue *Gerrard* who was his Son and Heir.

Which *Gerrard* married *Amy* the Daughter of *Horne-lade de Bidun*, by whom he had Issue *John*, and *Basilia* who married *Hugh de Odingsels*, Grandson to *Hugh de Odingsels* a *Fleming*, and *Alianore* who married *David de Linsey* a *Scot*; and he gave to those Monks at 𝔥𝔢𝔯𝔱𝔣𝔬𝔯𝔡, half a Yard Land in 𝔓𝔦𝔯𝔦𝔱𝔬𝔫, and a Croft called 𝔊𝔯𝔞𝔰𝔰𝔠𝔯𝔬𝔣𝔱 in 𝔦𝔠𝔥𝔢𝔱𝔬𝔫𝔢, and two Yard Land in 𝔥𝔦𝔠𝔨𝔩𝔢𝔣𝔬𝔯𝔡, to pray for the Health of his Soul, and the Souls of *Amy* his Wife, and *John* his Son.

This *John* had Issue *Hugh*, who died in the Life-time of his Father without Issue, and afterwards this Mannor and Barony of 𝔏𝔦𝔪𝔢𝔰𝔶 came to *Basilia* and *Alianore*, the Sisters and Coheirs of *John de Limesy*, by Reason hereof they were on the 12th Year of King *John*, divided between the said *Basilia* and *Alianore;* and the said *Hugh Odingsells*, and *Basilia* his Wife, paid a Fine of five hundred Marks to the King, for Livery of the Moyety of those Lands by Inheritance, pertaining to her upon the Death of her Brother, *John de Limesy*, lying in the Counties of 𝔥𝔢𝔯𝔱𝔣𝔬𝔯𝔡, 𝔒𝔵𝔣𝔬𝔯𝔡, 𝔚𝔬𝔯𝔠𝔢𝔰𝔱𝔢𝔯, 𝔖𝔲𝔣𝔣𝔬𝔩𝔨, and 𝔚𝔞𝔯𝔴𝔦𝔠𝔨, and for the Security of the Payment thereof, *Hugh* and *William*, two of his Sons became bound; which *John de Limesis* dyed 9 *Rich.* I. whereupon *Alice* his Widow married *Walter* Earl of 𝔚𝔞𝔯𝔴𝔦𝔠𝔨. *Mon. Angl. Antiq. of War.* fol. 229.

This *Hugh de Odingsels* was a Knight, and a Man of Ibid.

Hund. of
Hitchin.

great Note in his time, for in 5 of *Hen.* III. he attended
the King in Person to the Siege of 𝔚𝔦𝔱𝔥𝔞𝔪 Castle in the
County of 𝔏𝔦𝔫𝔠𝔬𝔩𝔫𝔢, with considerable Forces, for which
he had a Warrant to levy Escuage upon all his Tenants,
that held of him by Military Service, he died *Anno 23 H.*
III. whereupon *Gerrard* his Son, had Livery of the Lands
that were of the Inheritance of *Basilia* his Mother, and
held of the King *in capite*, doing then his Homage, and
giving Security to the Sheriff of the County for the Payment of fifty Pounds for his Relief.

Antiq. of War.
fol. 239.

This *Gerrard Anno 26 Hen.* III. being a Kt. gave a
Fine of fifty Marks, to be freed from Attendance upon the
King into 𝔊𝔞𝔰𝔠𝔬𝔦𝔤𝔫 towards the Payment whereof, he had
Power to levy Escuage upon all the Knights' Fees held of
him; he had Summons with many other, and great Men to
be at 𝔒𝔵𝔣𝔬𝔯𝔡, in *Midlent. Anno* 48 *Hen* III. sufficiently
furnish'd with Horse and Arms, to give the King Advice
there, and assist him against *Lewellin* Prince of 𝔚𝔞𝔩𝔢𝔰,
and his Adherents then in Rebellion.

But the other Moyety of this Estate of *John de Limesy,*
came to *Alianore* his younger Sister, who had married *Da-*
vid de Limesy.

Rot. Fin. 6
H. III.
Bar. vol 1,
fol. 796.

In 6 *H.* III. *Alexander* King of 𝔖𝔠𝔬𝔱𝔩𝔞𝔫𝔡, gave 200*l.*
for the Wardship and Marriage of the Heirs of *David de*
Limesy, and for all the Lands of their Inheritance, which
were the Lands of *John de Limesy* his Kinsman, and lay
in the Counties of 𝔈𝔰𝔰𝔢𝔵, 𝔥𝔢𝔯𝔱𝔣𝔬𝔯𝔡, 𝔒𝔵𝔣𝔬𝔯𝔡, 𝔚𝔞𝔯𝔴𝔦𝔠𝔨,
𝔏𝔢𝔦𝔠𝔢𝔰𝔱𝔢𝔯, 𝔑𝔬𝔯𝔣𝔬𝔩𝔨, and 𝔖𝔲𝔣𝔣𝔬𝔩𝔨.

Claus. 25 H.
III. m. 9.

To whom another *David* succeeded, he died *Anno 25 H.*
III. leaving

Gerrard his Brother and Heir, who doing his Homage
had Livery of his Lands, but departed this Life without

Rot. Pip. 33
H III Nor-
thampton.
Bar vol. 1,
fol. 769, 556.

Issue, *Anno 33 H.* III. whereupon
Henry de Pinkney who had married *Alice,* his Sister
and Heir, and paying fifty Pounds for his Relief, for her

Esc. 38 H III.
m. 3.

Moyety of the Barony of *Limesy,* had Livery thereof, he
died *Anno 38 H.* III. leaving

Henry his Son and Heir, 26 Years of Age, who performing his Fealty, and paying one hundred Pounds for his
Relief, had Lands, he was commanded to fit himself with

Claus. 42 H.
III. indorso.
m. 11.

his Horse and Arms *Anno 42 H.* III. to attend the King
at 𝔠𝔥𝔢𝔰𝔱𝔢𝔯, upon *Monday* preceding the Feast of St. *John*
Baptist to restrain the *Welch* in their Hostilities. But
shortly after this Moyety of the Mannor came to the Possession of *William de Odingsels,* and *Gerrard Odingsels*
dying seized of the other Moyety of this Mannor, *Anno* 50
H. III. his Heir not then of full Age, the Custody of him
and his Lands, then held of the King *in Capite,* were
granted to *Edmund,* (sirnamed *Crouchback*) the King's Son.

The next Year *Hugh Odingsels* accomplisht his full Age,

for then he did his Homage and had Livery of his Land, and I find that soon after that this Mannor was held of the Barony of **Hulberly**, whereof *Hugh Odingsels* held his own Moyety, and *William de Odingsels* held the other Moyety thereof, by the Service of two Knight's Fees; the whole Mannor was then valued at 80*l. per Annum*, and they paid to the Sheriff for the View of Franc-pledge 5*s.* they claimed to have Gallows, Tumbrel, and Correction of the Assize of Bread, and Ale; *Hugh* died seiz'd hereof, *Anno* 33 *Edw.* I. leaving

Hund. of **Hitchin.**

Antiq. of War. fol. 229.

Quo Warr. 6 *E.* I.

Esc. 33 E. 1.

John his Son and Heir, then 28 Years of Age, who being one of those that assisted the Earls of **Warwick** and **Lancaster**, in the Murder of *Piers de Gavestone, Anno* 7 *Edw.* II. had the King's Pardon for that Fact, in 9 *Edw.* II. He was made a Knight, and died the 10th of *Edward* III. leaving Issue,

Pat. 7 E. II.

John his Son and Heir, then 24 Years of Age, who was also a Knight, *Anno* 25 *Edw.* III. but for divers Felonies and Seditions, was shortly after outlawed; whereupon his Lands were seized into the King's Hands, and extended; he married *Amy* the Daughter of *Roger Corbet*, and he dyed *Anno* 27 *Edw.* III. leaving

John his Son and Heir, sixteen Years of Age, who *An.* 31 *Edw.* III. gave a Fine to the King of 200 Marks, for License to marry whom he pleased, so he continued in his due Allegiance, at which time he did his Homage and had Livery of his Lands; he was knighted *Anno* 32 *Edw.* III. he dyed 4 *R.* II. leaving

John his Son and Heir, 15 Years of Age, who did his Homage, had Livery of his Lands, *Anno* 9 *R.* II. also the Honour of Knighthood, and dyed *Anno* 5 *H.* IV. leaving

Edward his Son and Heir, then in Minority, who accomplisht his full Age, *Anno* 3 *H.* V. was knighted *Anno* 6 *H.* V. and much honour'd with several Imployments of Note; he married *Margaret* Daughter to *John Cokaine* of **Burphatley**, in the County of **Bedford**, by whom he had *Gerrard; Anno* 6 *Edw.* IV. dyed leaving

Esc. 6 E. IV.

Gerrard his Son, 35 Years of Age, who had Issue by *Margaret* his Wife, *Edward*; and died about the 8th Year of *H.* VII. leaving

Edward within Age, who accomplishing his full Age, *Anno* 9 *H.* VII. had then Livery of his Lands; he was a Justice of the Peace for the County of **Warwick**, from 17 *H.* VII. till the time of his Death, and married *Anne* the Daughter of *Richard Verney* of **Compton Merdat** in the County of **Warwick**, Esq. by whom he had Issue *Edmund*.

Pat. 9 H. VII. Ibid.

Esc. de eodem anno.

But afterwards one Moyety of this Mannor came to the Possession of *Samuel Marow* of **Berkswel** in the County of **Warwick**, who married *Margaret* the Daughter of Sir *John Littleton* of **Frankley** in the County of **Worcester**, Kt. by whom he had Issue *Edward;* he died in the Month of *August,* 1610, seized of this Moyety, leaving

Edward his Son and Heir, of full Age, who had Livery thereof, received the Honour of Knighthood, and married *Ursula* the Daughter of *Richard Fines,* Lord Say and Seal, but *Anno* 1611, 8 *Jac.* I. he sold this Mannor of Pirton *alias* Perton to

Thomas Docwra of Putteridge in this County, Esq. from whom it is descended to *Thomas Dowcra,* Esq. his Grandson; who is the present Possessor hereof.

The other Moyety of this Mannor, was for Distinction, called Pirton Dodingsels, and conveyed to the Provost of Eaton Colledge, who let the same by several Leases for Years, to the *Hammonds,* and since to *Matthew Lacy,* who is the present Possessor hereof. The Fines of both Mannors are at the Will of the Lord.

The Mannor of the Rectory of PIRTON.

RALPH de Limesie devised this Mannor out of the former, for he was Lord of both, and gave it to the Priory of Hertford; those Priors held it from that time to the Dissolution of their Monastery, when it came to the Crown, and in Process of time, this Mannor and the Mannor of Dodingsel, which passed with it, came to Sir *John Davy,* who sold it to —— *Poultney,* who conveyed it to —— *White,* who devised it to his Sons for the Payment of his Debts, and they sold it to *William Deane* the Son of Sir *Anthony Deane,* who is the present Possessor hereof.

THIS Vicaridge with the Rectory of Ickleford, *Anno* 26 *Hen.* VIII. was rated in the King's Books, at the yearly Value of eight Pounds, whereof *William Deane* is Patron.

The VICARS.
William Denn.   *William Goodwin.*

· The Church is erected in the Vill, which is in the Deanery of Hitchin in the Diocese of Lincolne, and is cover'd with Lead, having a fair Tower standing between the Chancel and the Church; wherein hang a Ring of five Bells, with a small Spire upon the Tower.

Within the Church is a Monument which has this Inscription.

Blessed are the Dead which dye in the Lord.
Jane the Relict of *Thomas Docwra,* Esq. and formerly the Wife of *Thomas,* the sole Son of Sir *Gabriel Pointes,* Kt. and one of the Daughters and Coheirs of Sir *William Periam,* Kt. Lord Chief Baron of the Exchequer, was in the service of God truly and zealously Religions, to his Ministers Liberal, to the Poor Charitable, and having Lived 25 years a Widow, in a contemplative and retired course of Life, she changed her mortal habitation for an Heavenly, the 15th of *March,* 1645. *Ætat.* 73.

Now I shall close this Part of the half Hundred of Hitchin, with this Vill of Perton, and proceed to the other Part, which contains the Parishes and Hamlets of Offley, Lilley, King's Walden, Stagenhoe, and Kimpton.

OFFLEY.

THIS Vill received its Appellation from *Offa*, that great King of the *Mertians*, who was the Lord hereof, resided often here, and in this Place resigned his Soul to the Disposal of God; this Parish derived its Name from him, for in the Saxon Language it signifies the Land of *Offa;* after his Decease, the Crown, with his Possessions, came to his Son King *Egfrid*, who imitated his Father in his Judgment and Mercy, after him it continued in the Crown till it came to Earl *Harold*, who enjoyed it in the time of King *Edward* the Confessor, and after this Earl's Death, it came to King *William* the Conqueror, who held it when that memorable Survey was made, for it is recorded in *Domesdei Book*, that

Matt. Paris de Vita Offa. secun. fol. 32.

Rex Williel. tenet *Offelei* pro duobus hid. se defendebat. Terra est novem car quinque Soch. tenuerunt tempore Regis Edwardi, et modo tenet de Rege Williel. ibi sunt octo car. et nona potest fieri, ibi duo Vill. et septemdecim Bord. et tres cotar. et tres Servi, pratum un. car. pastura ad pecud. Silva centum et vigint. porc. Nemus ad sepes, inter totum valet et valuit semper quatuor lib. et quatuor sol. Istimet tenuerunt de Com. Haroldo et dare et vendere potuit Soca vero jacuit semper in *Hit*, et duo averas et duo imcardos invenerunt.

Domesd. Lib. fol. 132, nu. 1

In eadem Villa tenet Edwardus de Pirton, tres virgat. Terra est duo car. ibi est dimid. et una et dimid. potest fieri, ibi est un. Vill. et nemus ad sepes valet quinque sol. quando recepit sex sol. et octo denar. tempore Regis Edwardi decem sol.

De hac terra dimid. Hidam tenet. Alvin homo Stigan Archiepiscopi, et unus homo Com. Haroldi, Abo nomine un. virgat. habuit isti et dare et vendere terram suam potuerunt Soca remansit in *Hit*.

King *William* held *Offley;* it was rated for two Hides; The arable is nine Carucates, five Sochmen held it in the time of King *Edward* (the Confessor) and now they hold it of King *William;* there are eight Carucates, and a ninth may be made; there are two Villains, and seventeen Bordars, and three Cottagers, and three Servants, Meadow one Carucate, Common of Pasture for the Cattle, Wood to feed one hundred and twenty Hogs, Wood for the Hedges; In the whole it is worth, and alwas was worth, four Pounds and four Shillings a Year: These held it of Earl *Harold*, and might give or sell it, but the Soke lay always in *Hit*, and they found two Horses, and two Horse Trappings or Furniture.

Edward de Perton held three Virgates in the same Vill. The arable is two Carucates; there is half a one, and one and a half may be made; there is one Villain, and Wood for Hedges; it is worth five Shillings a Year, when he received it six Shillings and eight Pence a Year, in the time of King *Edward* (the Confessor) ten Shillings.

Alwin, a Man (under the Protection) of *Stigan* the Archbishop, held half an Hide of this Land; and a Man (under the Protection) of Earl *Harold*, by Name *Abo*, had one Virgate: These might both give or sell their Land. The Soke remains in *Hit*.

Not long after the Conquest, this Mannor came to that noble and ancient Family of St. *Legiers*, who were Lords hereof for many Descents, till it came to *John* St. *Legiers*, who had Issue only *Isabel* who was his Daughter and Heir, and having no Son to preserve the Memory of his Name, the Addition of St. *Legiers* was added to the Name of this Mannor, and upon his Death this *Isabel* succeeded him:

She married Sir *Thomas Hoo* Kt. and *Anno* 16 *Edw.* III. they levied a Fine of the Mannors of Offley and Cokernhoo, and had Issue

Sir *William Hoo* of Laton-hoo in the County of Bedford, Kt. he and Dame *Eleanor* his Wife, *anno* 3 *R.* II. levied a Fine of the Mannors of Offley and Cokernhoo, and had Issue.

Sir *Thomas Hoo*, Esq. who married *Elizabeth Eckingham:* They entailed divers Mannors in Sussex of great Value, by Deed dated *Anno* 6 *H.* V. upon the Heirs of their Bodies, with Remainders over, &c. and they had Issue

Sir *Thomas Hoo* Kt. who was created Lord Hoo and Hastings, by King *H.* VI. *Anno* 26 *Regni sui,* and was installed a Knight of the Garter, he married the Daughter of the Lord *Welles,* who with other Persons of Honour, Trustees of his Estate, kept a Court Baron at Offley for
this Mannor, *anno* 31st of the same King, but this Lord Hoo had only Issue four Daughters; the eldest married Sir *Godfry Bullen,* Ancestor to Queen *Elizabeth,* and by his Will dated *Anno* 33 *H.* VI. gave Pensions to some of his Servants, issuing out of these Mannors of Offley, Cokernhoo.

Thomas Hoo, Esq. (for his Christian Name is so mentioned in the Will of his Brother, Sir *Thomas Hoo* and *Hastings,* dated the 12th of *February* 23 *H.* VI.) was Lord
of these Mannors, and held a Court here, *Anno* 30 *H.* VI. as appears by the Style of the Court.

Sir *William Bullen,* Kt. of the Bath, Son of Sir *Godfry Bullen* by his Wife, Daughter of the Lord Hoo, was Lord of the Mannor of Offley, *Anno* 3 *H.* VII. and held a Court for these Mannors in the same Year. This Sir *William Bullen* and Sir *James* St. *Legier* married the two Daughters and Coheirs of *Thomas Butler,* Earl of Wiltshire and Ormond. Then this Mannor was conveyed to
Richard Farmer, Esq. Merchant of the Staple, who held a Court here, *Anno* 18 *H.* VIII.

Afterwards it came to the same King in the 34th Year of his Reign, who held Courts here in his Name: but King *Edward* VI. granted the Mannor of St. *Legiers* in Offley, by Charter dated 17 *Nov. Anno* 4 *Regni sui,* to

Richard Farmer, Esq. who died in the Year following seized hereof, leaving Issue

John Farmer, who was his Heir, and of full Age, for he obtained Livery hereof the same Year, and some suppose him Ancestor to Sir *George Farmer* of Northamptonshire, Kt. They sold these Mannors to that honourable Knight

Sir *John Spencer* of Althorp, in the County of Northampton, who married *Catharine* Daughter of Sir *Thomas Kitson* of Hengrave in the County of Suffolk, Kt. by whom

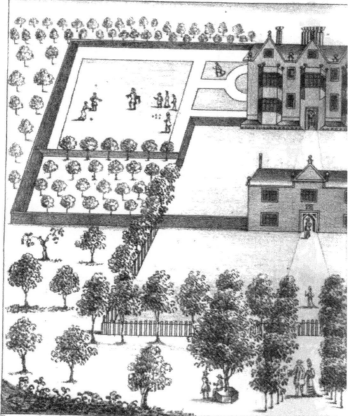

Drawn on Stone from the Original Engravings by O.L. Tyler

To the Right Worshipfull S.ʳ John

This Plate is humbly

Pub.ᵈ by J.M. Mullinger.

Spencer of Offley Place, Baronett.

presented by

J. Drapentier.

Bps. Stortford. 1826.

he had Issue, 1 *John*, who was knighted, and married *Mary*, Daughter and sole Heir of Sir *Robert Catline*, Kt. 2 *Thomas*, who married the Daughter of *Henry Cheek*. 3 Sir *William Spencer* of Yarnton, who married *Margaret*, Daughter of Sir *Francis Bowyer*. 4. Sir *Richard Spencer*, who married *Helen*, Daughter and one of the Heirs apparent of Sir *John Brocket* of Brocket Hall in this County: And this Sir *John Spencer* gave this Mannor of *St. Legiers* in Offley to

Sir *Richard Spencer*, his youngest Son, who had Issue by *Helen* his Wife, two Sons, *John* and *Brocket*, and three Daughters, one married to Sir *William Colepepper* of Alesford in Kent. 2 *Elizabeth*, married to Sir *John Boteler* of Watton Woodhall in this County, Knight of the Bath. 3 *Alice* married to Sir *John Jennings* of St. Albans, in this County, Knight of the Bath. And this *John* obtained from that King a Patent, dated *Anno* 1626, 1 *Car.* I. to be a Baronet. He married the Daughter of Sir *Richard Anderson*, by whom he had only Issue *Alice*, who married Sir *James Altham* of Markeshall in Essex, but dying without Issue Male of his Body, the Honour extinguish'd and these Mannors came to

Brocket Spencer, his Brother and next Heir, he married *Susan* the Daughter of Sir *Nicholas Cary* of Bedington, in the County of Surrey; he had a Patent dated *Sept.* 26, *Anno* 1642, 18 *Car.* I. to be a Baronet, and died seized hereof on the 3rd of *July*, 1668, leaving Issue Sir *Richard*, *John*, *William*, *Robert*, *Charles*, and *Thomas*, and four Daughters, *Elizabeth* married to Sir *Humphry Gore* of Gilston in this County, Kt. *Susan* married to *Abraham Nelson*, Gentleman, *Anne* married to *Robert Meredith*, Esq. Son to Sir *William Meredith* of Leedes in Kent, Bart. Master in *Chancery*, and *Alice* who is unmarried.

Sir *Richard* succeeded in this Lordship, and married *Elizabeth* Daughter of Sir *John Musters* of London, Kt. by whom he had Issue, *John*, and died seized hereof leaving Sir *John* an Infant, who is his Son and Heir and the present Lord hereof: His Arms are, *Quarterly Argent and Gules, in the second and third a Fret Or, over all a bend Sable charged with three Escallops of the first, with a Molette for Difference Fretty Or, on a Bend Sable three Flower de Liz of the first, Crescent.*

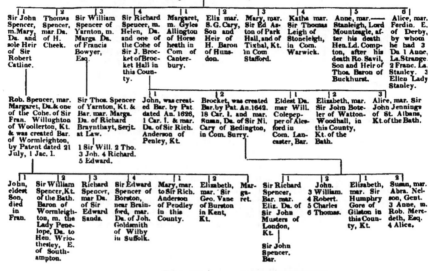

Sir John Spencer of Althorp in Com. Northampton, Kt. mar. Katharine, Daughter of Sir Thomas Kitson of Hengrave in Com. Suffolk, Kt.

1 Sir John Spencer, m.Mary, Da. and sole Heir of Sir Robert Catline.

2 Thomas Spencer, mar Da. of H. Cheek.

3 Sir William Spencer of Yarnton, m. Marga. Da. of Francis Bowyer, Esq.

4 Sir Richard Spencer, m. Helen, Da. and one of the Cohe of Sir J. Brocket of Brocket Hall in this County.

1 Margaret, m. Gyles Allington of Horse heath in Com. of Canterbury.

2 Eliz mar. S.G. Cary, Son and Heir of H. Baron of Hunsdon.

3 Mary, mar. Sir Ed Aston of Park Hall, and of Tixthal, Kt. in Com Stafford.

4 Katha mar. Sir Thomas Leigh of Stoneleigh, in Com. Warwick.

5 Anne, mar.—— Stanleigh, Lord Mounteagle, after his death Hen.Ld. Compton, after his death Ro. Savil, Son and Heir of Thos. Baron of Buckhurst.

6 Alice, mar. Ferdin. E. of Derby, by whom he had 3 Da. 1 Anne, La.Strange 2 Franc. La. Stanley. 3 Ellen Lady Stanley.

Rob. Spencer, mar. Margaret, Da. & one of the Cohe. of Sir Fran. Willughton of Woollerton, Kt. & was created Bar. of Wormleighton, by Patent dated 21 July, 1 Jac. 1.

Sir Thos. Spencer of Yarnton, Kt. & Bar. mar. Marga. Da. of Richard Braynthayt, Serjt. at Law.

1 Sir Will. 2 Tho. 3 Joh. 4 Richard. 5 Edward.

1 John, was created Bar. by Pat dated An. 1626, 1 Car. I. & mar. Da. of Sir Rich. Anderson of Penley, Kt.

2 Brocket, was created Bar. by Pat. An.1642. 18 Car. I. and mar. Susan, Da. of Sir Ni. Cary of Bedington, in Com. Surry.

1 Eldest Da. mar Will. Colepeper of Alesford in Com. Lancaster, Bar.

2 Elizabeth, mar. Sir John Boteler of Watton-Woodhall, in this County, Kt. of the Bath.

3 Alice, mar. Sir John Jennings of St. Albans, Kt. of the Bath.

1 John, eldest Son, died in Fran.

2 Sir William Spencer, Kt. of the Cohe. of the Bath Baron of Wormleighton, m. the Lady Penelope, Da. to Hen. Wriothesley, E. of Southampton.

3 Richard Spencer, mar Da. of Sir Edward Sands.

4 Sir Edward Spencer of Borston, near Brainford, mar. Da. of Joh. Goldsmith of Wilby in Suffolk.

1 Mary, mar. to Sir Rich. Anderson of Pendley in this County.

2 Elizabeth, mar. Sir Geo. Vane of Burston in Kent, Kt.

Margaret.

1 Sir Richard Spencer, Bar. mar. Eliz. Da. of Sir John Musters of London, Kt.

Sir John Spencer, Bar.

2 John. 3 William. 4 Robert. 5 Charles 6 Thomas.

1 Elizabeth, mar. Sir Humphry Gore of Gilston in this County, Kt.

2 Susan, mar. Abra. Nelson, Gent. 3 Anne, m. Rob. Meredeth, Esq. 4 Alice.

The Mannor of PODERICH.

IN the time of the *Saxons*, this Mannor was Part of the Revenues of the Crown, but at the time of the Conquest, King *William* gave it to *William de Owe*, who was a faithful Counsellor to him, for I find it recorded in *Domesdei* Book, under the Title of *Terra Willielmi de Owe*.

In Offley tenuit Willielmus de Mara *octo hidas, et octo acras de* Willielmus de Owe. *Terra est sexdecim car. in Dominio sunt quatuor, et sex decem* Vill. *cum Presbitero, et tres Milites habentes novem car. et tres adhuc possunt fieri, ibi octo Bord. et quatuor cotar. et octo Servi, pastura ad pec. Ville. Silva duodecem porc. in totis valent. valet novem lib. quando recepit octo lib. tempore Regis* Edwardi, *quindecim lib. Hoc Manerium tenuit* Alestan de Boscumbe, Teignus Regis *Edwardi.*

William de Mara, held eight Hides and eight Acres of *William de Owe* in Offley. The arable is sixteen Acres, in Demeasne are four, and sixteen Villains, with a Priest or a Parson, and three Knights, having nine Carucates, and three more may now be made; there are eight Bordars, and four Cottagers, and eight Servants; Common of Pasture for the Cattle of the Vill, Wood to feed twelve Hogs; in the whole Value, it is worth nine Pounds by the Year, when he received it eight Pounds, in the time of King *Edward* (the Confessor) sixteen Pounds: *Alestan* of Boscombe a Thane of King *Edward* (the Confessor) held this Mannor.

I have treated of this *William de Owe*, in the Parish of Grabely, to which I refer the Reader.

Henry, his eldest Son, enjoy'd his Honour and Estate, and married —— Daughter of *William* Lord of Solléi, eldest Son to the Earl of Blois by whom he had Issue four

Sons, and one Daughter, and died *Anno* 1139, 4 *Steph.*
leaving Issue

John, who was his Son and Heir, who upon the Aid for
marrying the King's Daughter, *Anno* 12 *H.* II. certifi'd
that he had fifty six Knight's Fees, and that his Father
had sixty in the Rape of ꟾ𝔥𝔞𝔰𝔱𝔦𝔫𝔤𝔰, for which he paid 44*l.*
6*s.* 8*d. Anno* 14 *H.* II. and had also sixty Fees of his own
Demeasn of ancient Feofment in the time of *Hen.* I.   He
married *Alice* Daughter of *William de Albini,* Earl of
𝔄𝔯𝔲𝔫𝔡𝔢𝔩, and died *Anno* 1170, 17 *H.* II. leaving Issue

Henry, who paid 62*l.* 10*s.* for levying the Scutage,
Anno 6 *R.* I. upon the King's Redemption, and died, leaving only Issue

Alice, who married *Robert de Usendon,* by whom she
had Issue *William,* but she surviving her Husband, after
his Death forfeited her Honour and Estate to the Crown,
whereupon King *Henry* gave it to

Prince *Edward* his Son, who disposed of it to

Henry of 𝔄𝔩𝔪𝔞𝔦𝔫𝔢, Son to *Richard* Earl of 𝔆𝔬𝔯𝔫𝔴𝔞𝔩𝔩.
In Process of time this Mannor came to the Family of
the *Darrels,* and it was found *Anno* 30 *H.* VI. that *Elizabeth Darrel* held this Mannor of 𝔓𝔬𝔡𝔢𝔯𝔦𝔠𝔥𝔟𝔲𝔯𝔦𝔢 by the yearly Rent of one Pound of Pepper, and one Pound of Cummin, and that the Lord of this Mannor, *Anno* 24 *Edw.* IV.
had not paid the said Rent for six Years then last past.

In the 9th Year of *H.* VII. one *Darrel* held it, and
shortly after it came to the Possession of *Joan Darrell,*
Widow, who held it by Fealty, and one Pound of Pepper,
and another of Cummin, and died seiz'd thereof, whereupon it descended to

Sir *Edward Darrell,* Kt. who was her Son and Heir.

John Docwra, Esq. purchased this Mannor, he married
Anne Daughter of *Thomas St. George* of 𝔊𝔢𝔬𝔯𝔤𝔢 ꟾ𝔞𝔱𝔩𝔢𝔶,
by *Alice,* Sister of Sir *Thomas Rotherham,* Kt. by whom
he had Issue, *Thomas, Humphry, Frances* married to *Thomas Cheiny,* of 𝔅𝔯𝔞𝔪𝔥𝔞𝔫𝔤𝔢𝔯, after her Decease to *A. Docwra, Catharine* to *Thomas Potkin* of 𝔎𝔢𝔫𝔱, and *Anne,* to
Darnell, of 𝔏𝔦𝔫𝔠𝔬𝔩𝔫𝔰𝔥𝔦𝔯𝔢.

Thomas Docwra was his Heir, married *Mildred Hales,*
of 𝔎𝔢𝔫𝔱, Sister of *John Hales,* of 𝔆𝔬𝔟𝔢𝔫𝔱𝔯𝔶, by whom he
had Issue *Thomas, Ralph, John, Edward, Frances,* married to *Peter Taverner,* Esq. *Helen* to *Jasper Horsey,* Esq.
who was constituted Sheriff for this County, *Anno* 22 *Eliz.*

Thomas the eldest Son succeeded, and married *Helen*
Daughter of *George Horsey* of 𝔇𝔦𝔤𝔢𝔫𝔰𝔴𝔢𝔩𝔩 in this County,
Esq. by whom he had Issue,

Thomas Docrwa, who married *Jane,* one of the Daughters and Coheirs of Sir *William Periam,* Kt. who was
made Lord Chief Baron of the *Exchequer, April* 26, 1 *Jac.*
I. on whom he begat, *Periam, Henry, Jane* married to

——— *Powell*, Esq. *Anne* to *Humphry Walcote* of ꝯꝯꝛal-
cote in the County of ꙅalop, Esq. *Elizabeth* to *James Beverley*, Esq. and *Mary*. He was constituted Sheriff for this
County, *Anno* 1605, 3 *Ja.* I.

Periam was his Heir, married *Martha* Daughter of *Oliver* Lord *St. John* of ꙅletꙅhoe, in the County of ꙅedforꙅ,
by whom he had Issue, *Thomas, Saint John, John, Peter,
Lancelot, Henry, Margaret, Elizabeth, Martha, Dorothy,*
and *Jane*.

Thomas the eldest Son, married *Margaret* Daughter of
Robert Cherey, Relict of *Thomas Docwra*, by whom he had
Issue, one Daughter married to Sir *Peter Warburton* of
Cheꙅhire, Bar. He served as a Burgess for the Borough
of ꙅt. Albanꙅ, *Anno* 1 *Jac.* II. is the present Lord hereof,
and gives, *Sable, a Cheveron ingrail'd Argent between three
Plates, each charged with a Pale Gules.*

Peter Docwra of Kendal.

Robert Docwra of Kirby Kendal in Westmorland, mar. Sibil, Daugh. of Sir Thomas
Leybourne, Kt.

Roger Docwra, younger Son of Peter, mar.
Eliz. Daugh. of Edw. Brocket of Brocket
Hall in Yorkshire.

Thomas Docwra, mar. Katharine, Sister to Sir Henry
Thyrkil, Kt.

James Doc-
wra of Ire-
land.

Reignold Docwra, Son and Heir of Roger,
mar. Da. of Reignold Docwra of Hitchin
Bradkirk,

Robert Docwra, mar Janet, Daugh. of Sir
John Lamplo of Northumberland, Kt.

Richard Docwra, mar. Alice, D. of Thomas
Green of Gresingham.

Walter Doc-
wra, Son &
Heir of Rob.
mar. Janet,
Da. of Roger
Salkeld.

Sir Lance-
lot, Kt. of
the
Rhodes.

Thomas.
John.
Miles.

Margaret.
Katharine.

Thomas, Lord
Prior of St.
John's, 1508.

James, mar Katharine,
Da. of John Haspedine
of Murden and Chester-
ford in Cambridgeshire.

John Docwra, Son and Heir of James,
mar. Anne, Da. of St. George.

Eliz. mar. Tho. Chicheley of Wimple, who had
Issue Clement, who had Issue Tho. Father of Sir
Thomas Chichley.

Katharine, mar.
to Tho. Pot-
kin.

Humphry
Docwra.

Thomas Docwra, Son and
Heir of Joh. mar. Mil-
dred, Da. of Hales, died
1602.

Anne, mar.
to Darnel

Frances mar. to Tho.
Cheiny, after to
A——— Docwra.

2
Ralph.
3 John.
4 Edward.

1
Thomas, Son and Heir of Thomas, mar.
Helen, Daughter of George Horsy.

Frances, eldest Da.
of Pet. Tavener,
Esq.

Helen, 2d. mar.
Jasp. Horsey,
Esq.

Thomas, Son and Heir, mar. Jane, one of the
Da. and Coheirs of Sir Will. Periam, Kt. Ld.
Ch. Ba. of the Exchequer, died 6 May, 1620.

Henry Doc-
wra.

Periam, Son and Heir of Tho. mar.
Martha, Da. of Oliver, Lord St.
John of Bletso.

Jane.
Anne.
Elizabeth.
Mary.

2
St. John.
mar.——

3
John.

Thomas, eldest Son and Heir of Periam, m.
Margaret, Daughter of Cherry ———

Da. and Heir of Tho. mar. Sir Peter
Warburton of Cheshire, Bart.

4
Peter
5 Lancelot.
6 Henry.

Margaret.
2 Elizabeth.
3 Martha.
4 Dorothy.
5 Jane.

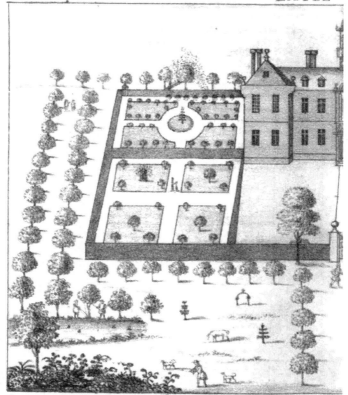

Drawn in Stone from the Original Engravings by O.E.Tyler.

To Richard

This Draught is

Pub.ᵈ by I.M.Mullinger

Helder Esq.

presented by
J. Drapentier.

Bps Stortford. 1826.

The Mannor of *LITTLE OFFLEY*

WAS held of *William* the Conqueror, for I find it recorded in *Domesdei Book*, under the Title of *Terra Regis.*

*In altera Offley tenet unus Sochmannus unum hidam. Terra est duo car.
ibi est una et alia potest fieri, ibi unus Vill. et unum Bord. et un. cotar.
Nemus ad sepes valet et valuit semper vigint. sex sol. octo denar.*

*Iisdem qui nunc Tenens ten. tempore Regis Edwardi de Com. Haroldo, et
vendere potuit Soca ramansit in Hii, averam et inwardus reddidit. Hic
Sochmannus et quinque superiores de Offlei. Apposuit Ilbertus de Hertford
in Hii.*

A Sochman held one Hide in the other *Offlei.* The arable is two Carucates, there is one and another may be made; there is one Villain, one
Bordar, and one Cottager, Wood for Hedges; it is worth, and always
was worth, six and twenty Shillings and eight Pence by the Year.

The same Tenants who are now, held it in the time of King *Edward*
(the Confessor) of Earl *Harold*, and might sell it: The Soke remained in
Hii. This Sochman and five of the Chief of *Offley*, found an Horse and
Furniture. *Ilbert* of Hertford laid it to Hii.

This was a Hamlet which consisted of divers Houses, as
is evident by the Marks of ancient Foundations, often digg'd
up there, and did belong to the Parish of Offley, but
since these Houses came to the Possession of one Person, they have been reduced to one House, which was held
by Knights' Service, until the taking away of the Court of
Wards and Liveries: It is scituated on the great Ledge of
Hills, which crosses the Northerly Part of this County,
called by some the Alps of England, and bounded on the
North by that famous Roman Road, called Icknall, which
in this Place divides this County from Bedfordshire, the
Height of these Hills turn all the Waters that fall on the
Southern Part, to the River Lea, which leads to the
Thames, but the Waters that fall on the Northern Side to
the River Ouse, which empties itself into the Sea at Lyn
in Norfolk.

This Seat in the time of *H.* VIII. was in the Crown, E. Relatione
Richardi Hel-
and about *Anno* 3 *P. & M.* was granted to *Richard Spicer,* der, Arm.
alias *Helder* and his Heirs, from whom it descended to *Thomas Spicer* alias *Helder,* who was his Son and Heir, and
from him it past to his eldest Son *Richard,* who succeeded him; Upon his Decease, it descended to *William* who was his Heir, and had Issue *Richard,* who
succeeded him; from whom it came to *William* his Son,
who had Issue, *Richard Spicer* alias *Helder,* the present
Owner hereof; and long before this Estate was in the Crown,
the same was held by long Leases in the *Helder's* from the
time of *H.* VI.

The most ancient Seat of the ancestors of these *Helder's*
was at Lilley, and were Owners of the principal Part of Ibid.

Hund. of
Hitchin.

the Estate at 𝕷𝔦𝔩𝔩𝔢𝔭, that now belongs to *Thomas Halpeny*, Esq. whose Father purchased the same of one *Robert Spicer* alias *Helder*, a Branch of the same Family.

E Relatione
RichardiHel-
der, Arm.

William Spicer alias *Helder*, last mentioned, married *Sarah*, one of the Daughters of *Matthew Denis* of 𝕶𝔢𝔪𝔭-𝔰𝔱𝔬𝔫 in the County of 𝕭𝔢𝔡𝔣𝔬𝔯𝔡, Gentleman, elder Brother to *William Denis*, Citizen, and Alderman of 𝕷𝔬𝔫𝔡𝔬𝔫, from whom she had a great Part of her Fortune.

Ibid.

By her he left four Sons and three Daughters, *Richard, William, Denis*, and *Matthew, Katharine, Sarah*, and *Anne.*

Ibid.

Richard married *Mary*, the eldest Daughter of *John Hinde* of the Parish of *St. Andrews* 𝕳𝔬𝔩𝔟𝔬𝔲𝔯𝔫, in the County of 𝕸𝔦𝔡𝔡𝔩𝔢𝔰𝔢𝔯, Brewer, by whom he had Issue a Son, *William*, and gives, *Sable, a Fesse embattelled between three Lions Rampant Or; Crest on a Wreath, on an Helmet a Castle Argent.*

The Mannor of WELLS.

I N the time of *William* the Conqueror, this Mannor was Parcel of the Revenues of the Crown, for 'tis recorded in *Domesdei Book*, under the title of *Terra Regis*.

In 𝖀𝖆𝖊𝖑𝖑𝖊, *tenet unus Sochmannus unam hidam. Terra est quinque car. In Dominio est una. et duo possunt fieri, ibi quatuor Bord. habentes unam car. et alia potest fieri, pastura ad pec. Ville. Nemus ad sepes, inter totum valet vigint. sex sol et octo denar. quando Petrus recepit quadragint. Sol. tempore Regis* Edwardi *sexagint. sol. hanc terram tenuit ;* Leveva de Com. Heraldo, *et vendere potuit.* Ilbertus *apposuit in* 𝕷𝖎𝖓𝖑𝖊𝖎𝖆 *suo Manerio, dum erat Vicecomes post quam Vicecomitatum perdidit* Petrus de Valongies *et* Radulphus Tailgebosch *tulerunt ab eo et posuerunt in* 𝕳𝖎𝖙, *ut tota Scyra testatur, que non jacuit ibi tempore Regis* Edwardi *nec aliquam consuetudinem reddidit.*

One Sochman held one Hide in 𝖀𝖆𝖊𝖑𝖑. The Arable is five Carucates, in Demeasne is one, and two may be made, there are four Bordars having one Carucate, and another may be made; Common of Pasture for the Cattle of the Vill, Wood for Hedges; in the whole it is worth twenty six Shillings and eight Pence a Year, when *Peter* received it forty Shillings, in the time of King *Edward* (the Confessor) sixty Shillings ; *Leveva* held this Land of Earl *Harold*, and might sell it. *Ilbert* laid it to his Mannor in 𝕷𝖎𝖓𝖑𝖊𝖕 when he was Sheriff ; after he lost the Shrivalty *Peter de Valongies* and *Ralph Tailgebosch* took it away from him and laid it to 𝕳𝖎𝖙, as the whole Shire can witness, that it did not lye there in the time of King *Edward* (the Confessor) nor paid any Rent.

Bar. vol. 1,
fol. 192, 193.

This Mannor was denominated from the Springs that arise out of an adjacent Hill, from whence it is supplied with Water, by leaden Pipes, from a Conduit contiguous to the Spring Head.

But in Process of time it came to the Possession of *John* Earl of 𝕺𝔯𝔣𝔬𝔯𝔡, who was possest hereof in the time of *Edw.* III. He was in several Expeditions in 𝕾𝔠𝔬𝔱𝔩𝔞𝔫𝔡, 𝔉𝔯𝔞𝔫𝔠𝔢, and 𝔉𝔩𝔞𝔫𝔡𝔢𝔯𝔰. He married *Maud*, one of the Sisters and Coheirs of *Giles de Badlesmere* a great Baron in 𝕶𝔢𝔫𝔱, and Widow of *Robert Fitz Pain*, by whom he had Issue

Thomas de Vere of Age, *Aubrey*, and two Daughters, *Margaret* married to *Henry* Lord *Beamont*, and after to Sir *John Devereux*, and *Isabel* first married to Sir *John Courtney*, Grandfather to *Hugh* the fifth Earl of **Devon**, of that Family, and after to Sir *Oliver Denham*, Kt. and he died, leaving Sir *Thomas de Vere*, Kt. his Heir, but *Maud* the Mother then surviving had for her Purparty of the Inheritance descended to her by the Death of *Giles de Badlesmere* this Mannor of **Wells** among divers others: and shortly after it was sold to

Bar. vol. 1, fol. 193. *Bar.* vol. 2, fol. 60, 196.

Thomas of **Woodstock**, Earl of **Buckingham**, and Duke of **Glocester**, who married *Alianore*, one of the Daughters and Coheirs of *Humphry de Bohun*, late Earl of **Hereford** and **Essex**. He obtained the Custody of all those Castles, Mannors, and Lands in **England** and **Wales**, *Anno* 3 *R.* II. which were allotted to her upon the Partition made between her and *Mary* her Sister, the other Daughter of *Humphry de Bohun*, Earl of **Hereford** and **Essex**. He founded a Colledge in the Parochial Church of **Plessy**, in **Essex**, *anno* 17 *R.* II. consisting of nine Priests, two Clerks, and two Choristers, and endowed the same with nine Acres of Land in **Plessy**, and the Advowson of that Church, the Mannors of **Bokinfield**, and **Whitstaple** in the County of **Kent**, and this Mannor of **Welles**, and the Mannor of **Wernestone** in **Essex**, but upon the Dissolution this Mannor came to

Bar. vol. 2, fol. 171.

Henry VIII. from whence it was conveyed to Sir *John Gates*, who was attainted of Treason in the time of *P. & M.* of whom I have treated in the Parish of **Cheshunt**: Upon his Attainder it return'd again to the Crown, from whence it was granted to Sir *Henry Gates* and Dame *Lucy* his Wife, and their Heirs, reserving the yearly Rent of 9*l.* 2*s.* 1*d.* which is still paid to *Katharine* the Queen Dowager, being Parcel of the Fee-Farm Rents that were settled for her Dowry.

Sir *Henry Gates* and Dame *Lucy* his Wife, granted it to *Richard Spicer* alias *Helder*, and his Heirs, who disposed thereof to *William Crawley* who sold the same to *Wells* who had Issue one Daughter, his Heir, married to *Henry Dolderne*, since which it has been divided, and one Part of it is now come to the Possession of Sir *Ralph Ratcliffe*, another Part remains in the Possession of *Richard Helder*, Esq. and the Mannor House and chiefest Part of it to Mr. *Henry Dolderne* the present Owner, Great Grandfather to Mr. *Wells.*

This Mannor-house is scituated in a very dry and warm Place, under the Brow of an Hill, in a most pleasant and healthful Air, and at all times much more dry and clean than any other Place in this Parish of **Offley**, it is much im-

proved by good Husbandry, and neatly adorned with Walks
which shews the Ingenuity of the Owner. and the Delight
that he takes in his Habitation

The Rectory of OFFLEY.

THE Church of Offley, anciently dedicated to the blessed *Mary Magdalen*, was appropriated by that Name, and
annexed to the *Chauntrey* of Chalgrave in the County of
Bedford, which Sir *Nigell Loring* directed by his Will, dated about the Beginning of *H.* IV's Reign, should be founded, and made *Robert Braybroke* then Bishop of London,
his Executor : But the Bishop living a short time after him
could not accomplish it in his Life-time, but made his Will,
and appointed Sir *Gerrard Braybroke*, Kt. *Edmund Camden*, Esq. *Roger Albrighton*, Clerk, and *John Wicke*, Clerk,
his Executors, and devised, That his said Executors should
found such a Chauntry to celebrate divine Service, in the
Parish Church of Chalgrave, for the Souls of Sir *Nigel Lorain*, his Parents and Friends, and the said Bishop *Braybroke*, and for the Souls of all the Faithful departed.

Pursuant to the said Will, these Executors the 10th
Year of *H.* IV. obtained a License of the said King to
found a Chauntrey accordingly, and endowed the same in
these Words, *viz.*

Sciant presentes et futuri ; Quod nos Gerardus Braybroke, *Miles,* Edmundus Hamden, *Armiger,* Rogerus Albrighton, *Clericus, et* Johannes
Wyke, *Clericus, Executores, Testamenti Recolendæ Memoriæ* Roberti
Braybroke, *quondam Episcopi* London *de Licencia Spirituali Metuendis-
simi Domini nostri* Henrici *Regis* Angliæ *post conquestum quarti prout per
ipsius domini nostri Regis Literas inde confectas plenius patet nobis gratiose
concessa Dedimus Concessimus et hac presenti carta nostra Confirmavimus
Dilectis nobis* Richardo Parthemener *Magistro ac* Thome Nongell *et*
Willielmo Brown *Capellanis Cantarie perpetue in Ecclesia Parochial' de*
Chalgrave, *pro animabus* Nigelli Loryng *Militis, ac* Roberti Braybrok,
quondam Episcopi London, *predicti et omnium fidelium defunctorum per nos
factæ fundatæ et stabilitæ prout in literis nostris inde confect' plenius con-
tinetur unum Mesuag. cum pertinent. in* Chalgrave *vocat* Old Orchard *ac*
Advocationem Ecclesiæ de Offeley *in Com.* Hertford *habend. et tenend.
eisdem Magistro et Capellanis et Successioribus suis pro Dotatione Cantarie
predictæ ac sustentatione Magistri et Capellanorum hujusmodi inperpetuum.
In cujus Rei Testimonium Sigilla nostra presentibus apposuimus. Dat.* Lon=
don, *vicessimo septimo die mensis* Marcii, *Anno Regni Regis* Henrici *quarti
post conquestum, Angl. Decimo.*

Which was afterwards confirmed on the 2nd of *August,
Anno* 1411, by the apostolical Letters of *John*, then Bishop of
Rome, to *Thomas*, then Archbishop of Canterbury, his Dele-
gate, directed: and was also confirmed the Year following
by *Philip* Bishop of Lincoln then within his Diocess.

This Chauntrey at last had the Fate of other Religious
Houses, to be dissolved about the 1st of *Edw.* VI. At
which time, one *Thomas Shele*, and Sir *William Rote* his
Co-fellow, had long before let a Lease of the said Parsonage
to one *John Friday* for the Term of 44 Years, which was

injoyed accordingly, and some time after the Expiration thereof, Queen *Elizabeth* by her Letters Patent, in the 32nd Year of her Reign, granted the same to *Richard Spencer* Esq. and *Edward Adams* and their Heirs, who sold it to *George Gravely*, who had one Daughter *Lettice* his only Child and Heir. She married *Luke Norton*, and by Reason thereof the Impropriation of the Parsonage of **Offley**, came into the Family of the *Nortons*, and from *Luke* it descended to *Gravely Norton* his Son and Heir, who disposed of the greatest Part of the Tithes and Glebe belonging to the said Impropriation to several Persons, but the Residue thereof descended to *Luke Norton* his Son and Heir, who conveyed it to *William Angel*, Gent. and his Heirs; and by this Division of the Parsonage, the greatest Part of the Parishioners have purchased the Tythes of their several Lands to themselves in Fee.

During all the time of the *Graveley's* and *Norton's*, the Right of Presentation to the Vicaridge was in them, and Mr. *Gravely Norton* presented Mr. *Willows* the last Incumbent.

Ex Informat Richard Helder, Arm.

There are two Mannors more within this Parish; the one called, the Mannor of **Offley** *alias* **Westbury**, and the other **Hallbury**, of which having but an imperfect Account I purposely omit.

THIS Vicaridge *Anno* 26 *H.* VIII. was rated in the King's Books at the yearly Value of 9*l.* and pays about 6*s.* 8*d.* a Year for Tenths.

The VICARS.

Anno 17 *E.* I. *William*, Vicar of **Offley**
Anno 31 *E.* III. *Laurence*, Vicar of **Offley**
Anno 25 *Eliz. Roger Henley*
1603 1 *J. I. Oliver Perkins*
1606 4 *J. I. Fulk Roberts*
1607 5 *J. I. Will. Sherlock*
1614 *William Chauntrell*
1617 *Thomas Reed*
1654 *Richart Swift*
1657 *William Carter*

1657 *Edward Warren*
1657 *John Baker*
1658 *Philip Osbaldeston*
1661 *Richard Willows*, the last Incumbent, who was barbarously murdered as he was coming home from **Hitchin** to **Offley**, by whose Death this Vicaridge is now void. He was a Man of a very sober, pious, and inoffensive Life, and continued Minister for the space of 37 Years.

The Church is erected near the Mannor House of **Offley St. Legers**, in the Deanery of **Hitchin**, in the Diocess of **Lincoln**; The Chancel and Church are covered with Lead, having a square Tower at the West End thereof, where is a Ring of six Bells: In the Chancel are these Inscriptions.

Here lieth Interred the Body of Sir *Brocket Spencer*, Baronet, Son to Sir *Richard Spencer* of **Offley**, who having four Sons and four Daughters by *Susanna*, Daughter to Sir *Nicholas Carew*, of **Bedington** in the County of **Surry**, deceased, *July* 3 in the 63d year of his Age, in the Year of our Lord, 1668.

Here lieth John Samuel, Elizabeth and Joan **his Wives, which** John **deceased the 23th of February, in the year of our Lord 1529. on whose Souls** Jesu **have mercy**, Amen. With their several Effigies above the Inscription.

In the North Window is the Effigies of a Bishop with a Crosier in his Hand.

LINDLEY *alias* LILLY HOO.

IN the time of *William* the Conqueror, that King gave
this Mannor to *Goisfride de Bech* for his good Service at
the Battle of 𝕳astings, for 'tis recorded in *Domesdei Book*,
under the Title of *Terra Goisfridi d'Bech.*

*Domesd. Lib.
fol. 140, nu. 4.*

In Dimidio Hundred. de 𝕳it ipse Goisfridus *tenet* 𝕷inley *pro quinq; hidis
se defendebat. Terra est novem car. in Dominio duo hid. et ibi sunt tres
car. ibi novemdecem Villi. cum Presbit. habentes quinque; car. et sexta potest fieri, ibi sex bord. et quatuor cotar, et sex Servi, pastura ad pecud.
Silva sex porc. in totis valent. valet et valuit centum sol. tempore Regis
Edwardi, septem lib. hoc Manerium tenuit* Leveva *de Comit.* Haroldo *et ibi
unus Sochmannus homo* Haroldi, *de ead. terra tres virgut. et dimid. habuit
et vendere potuit, et unam aver. in* 𝕳it *redidit vel tres denar. et unum
obolum.*

Goisfride de Bech held 𝕷inley, in the half Hundred of 𝕳it. It was
rated for five Hides. The arable is nine Carucates, in Demeasne two
Hides, and there are three Carucates; there are nineteen Villains with
a Presbiter or Priest having five Carucates, and a sixth may be made,
there are six Bordars, and four Cottagers, and six Servants, Common of
Pasture for the Cattle, Wood to feed six Hogs, in the whole Value it is
worth and was worth one hundred Shillings by the Year, in the time of
King *Edward* (the Confessor) seven Pounds. *Leveva* held this Mannor of
Earl *Harold*, and there is one Sochman, a Man (under the Protection) of
Earl *Harold*, he had three Virgates and an half of the same Land, and
might sell it, and he found one Horse in 𝕳it, or paid three Pence Half-
penny.

This Vill received the Addition of 𝕳oo to its Name from
that ancient Family of the *Hoos*, who in old time were Possessors hereof, and in the Reign of *Edw.* I. *Robert d'Hoo*,
whose chief Seat was at 𝕳oo, in the County of 𝕭edford,
was Lord of this Mannor; but having treated of this Family in the Parishes of 𝕶nebworth and 𝕺ffley, and intending
to say more of them in 𝕻auls 𝕸alden, I shall refer the
Reader thither, and conclude this Name with *Thomas Hoo*,
who sold it in the time of *H.* VII. to

*Ex stemate
penes D'Vaux
Har. of Engl.
vol.3, fol.304.*

Nicholas d'Vaux, who descended from *Robert d'Vaux*,
a great Man in the North of this Realm in the Dayes of
King *Stephen* and *H.* II. but *William d'Vaux*, the chief
Branch of that Family in the time of those sharp Contests
between the Houses of 𝕻ork and 𝕷ancaster, lost all for his
Fidelity to King *H.* VI. but at length *Henry* Earl of 𝕽ich-
mond obtaining the Crown, *Nicholas* his Son and Heir had
Restitution thereof, which caused him to fight stoutly for

*Polydor Vir-
gil, p 573.
Bar. of Engl.
Stow's Annals*

that King in the Battle of 𝕾toke (near 𝕹ewark) against *John*
Earl of 𝕷incoln and his Adherents in Arms, 2 *H.* VII. on
the Behalf of *Lambert Simnel* (a counterfeit Son to *George*
Duke of 𝕮larence,) for which good Service King *Henry*
conferred on him the Honour of Knighthood, and 17 *H.*
VII. he wore a Gown of purple Velvet at that great Solemnity of Prince *Arthur's* Marriage, adorn'd with Pieces of

Gold so thick and massy, that it was valued at a thousand Hund. of Hittchin.
Pounds beside the Silk and Furs, also a Collar of SS's
weighing eight hundred Pounds in Nobles. He was one Holl. fol. 817, 849.
of the Embassadors who were then sent into *France* to
confirm the Articles of Peace between King *Henry* and Stow's *Annals*
the *French*, and shortly after grew in that great Esteem
at Court, that on the 27th of *April*, 15 *H*. VIII. he
was advanced to the Dignity of a Baron of this Realm, Ex stemate. Bar. vol. 3, fol. 304.
and the Solemnity of his Creation was performed at the
King's Royal Pallace of Bridwel in the Suburbs of London: He married first *Elizabeth* Daughter and Heir to
Henry Lord *Fitzhugh*, Widow of Sir *William Parre*, Kt.
by whom he left Issue three Daughters, *Katharine* married to Sir *George Throckmorton* of Coughton in *Com.*
Warwickshire, Kt. *Anne* to Sir *Thomas Strainge* of Huns-
ton, in *Com.* Norfolk, Kt. and *Alice* to Sir *Edward Sapcote*
of Elton in the County of Huntingdon, Kt. after her Decease he married *Anne* Daughter of *Thomas Green* of
Greens Norton in the County of Northampton, Esq. by
whom he had Issue two Sons, *Thomas* and *William*, and
three Daughters, *Margaret* married to *Francis Pultney*
of Misterton in the County of Leicester, Esq. *Maud* to
Sir *John Farmer* of Eston, near Toucester, in the County
of Northampton, Kt. and *Bridget* to *Maurice Welch* of
Sudbury in the County of Glocester, Esq. he died the third
of *July* following.

Thomas was his Son and Heir, and one of those who at- Stow's *Annals*
tended Cardinal *Wolsey Anno* 19 *Henry* VIII. when he went
Embassador in great State beyond the Sea to make Peace
between the Emperor, King *Henry* of England and King
Francis of France. He took his Place on the 19th of *January*
22 *H*. VIII. among the Peers in Parliament, waited on the
King to Calais on the 24 *H*. VIII. and thence to Boloine;
was one of the Knights of the Bath made at the Coronation
of Queen *Anne* of *Bullen*, on the 25th Year of *H*. VIII.
also Captain of the Isle of Jersey, and surrendred that Bar. vol. 3, fol. 305.
Trust *Anno* 28 *H*. VIII. He married *Elizabeth* Daugh-
ter and Heir to Sir *Thomas Cheny* of Irtlingburgh in the
County of Northampton, Kt. by whom he had Issue two
Sons, *William* and *Nicholas*, and two Daughters, *Anne* married to *Reginald Bray* Brother to *Edmond* Lord *Bray* of
Eton, in the County of Bedford, and *Maud* who died unmarried: He by the Name of Sir *Thomas Vaux*, Lord
Harrowdon, by Deed dated 8th of *Feb.* 2 *P. & M.* sold Cart. 2 and 3 P. & M. penes Tho. Docwra.
this Mannor of Lindley, alias Lilley, with the Advowson of
the Church to *Thomas Docwra* of Temple Dinsley, in this
County, Esq. from whom it descended to *Thomas Docwra*,
Esq. the present Possessor hereof.

Hund. of
Hitchin. THIS Rectory was rated *Anno* 26 *H*. VIII. in the King's Books at the
yearly Value of 19*l*. 8*s*. 6*d*. *per Annum*, and the Lords of this Mannor are
Patrons.

The RECTORS.

Mr. *Potter*.   Mr. *Sherlock*.   Mr. *Beverley*.   Mr. *Stone*.

This Church is situated in the Vill, which is in the Deanery of Hitchin,
in the Diocess of Lincoln, and I suppose is dedicated to our Saviour, by
the Effigies of our Saviour; 'tis small, with an erection of Timber at the
West End thereof, wherein are three Bells, and is cover'd with Lead.

A Monument on the North Side of the Chancel.

M. S.

Beati mortui qui in Dom. moriuntur.

Here under lieth the Body of *Thomas Docwra* the elder, Esq; Lord of
this Town, and Patron of this Church, descended of the ancient Family
of the *Docwra's* of Docwra-hall in Kendal in the County of Westmoreland, Nephew and Heir unto the Right Honourable Sir *Thomas Docwra*,
Lord Grand Prior of the Knights of St. *Johns* of Jerusalem: He had to
Wife *Mildred Hales* of an antient Family in Kent, a grave and vertuous Matron with whom he lived 52 years, having been Justice of the
Peace forty years, and high Sheriff of the Shire, *Anno* 23 *Eliz*. Beloved and reverenced of all for his Gravity, Wisdom, Piety, Justice
and Hospitality. He died in his House at Putteridge, by him built, in
the 84th year of his Age, *Anno Dom*. 1602.

Leaving four Sons and two Daughters.

Thomas Docwra his eldest Son, by his Study in the University, Inns of
Court, and France, attain'd unto good knowledge and experience;
his first Wife was *Helen* Daughter of *George Horsey*, Esq; and of his
Wife the Daughter of the Right Honourable Sir *Ralph Sadlier*, Kt. by
whom he left only one Daughter, married to Sir *Henry Pakenham*, Kt.
his second was *Jane* one of the Daughters and Heirs of Sir . *William
Periam*, Kt. Lord Chief Baron of the *Exchequer*, with whom he lived
two and twenty years, and left issue *Periam*, and *Henry*; *Anne, Elizabeth, Jane* and *Mary*. He was Justice of the Peace and High Sheriff
for this County, *an*. 3 *Jac*. He was not ambitious of Honours or Titles,
but contenting himself with his Estate, whereof he lived plentifully,
was worthily esteemed for his Wisdom, Judgment, Moderation and
Liberal House-keeping. in the 92d. year of his age, he did Meekly
and Christianly render his Soul unto God at Putteridge aforesaid, 6th.
Martii an. Dom. 1620. and was here interred.

A Prevention of Forgetfulness.

Coats of Arms.		Coats of Arms.
Docwra, Green.	This is the Tomb of him who gave content,	*Docw. Haspedine*
Docw. Docwra.	By shunning that to which the most are bent.	*Docw St. George.*
Docw. Brocket.	He did not stoop to vain ambitious lure,	*Docw. Hales*
	But deem'd his own more happy and more sure:	*Docw. Periam.*
	And thus my due and last farewel I take,	*Docw. St. John.*
	Bound to protect his State and Children for his sake.	

Here lye the Bodies of *Thomas Docwra*, late of Putteridge, Esq; Lord of
this Town, and Patron of this Church, and *Mildred* his Wife, who
lived together in much Happiness fifty two years. They had at the
time of their deaths four Sons and two Daughters living, *Thomas,
Ralph, John, Edward*, and two Daughters *Frances* and *Ellen: Mildred*
above the age of 70 died *October* the 18th. 1596. *Thomas* above the
age of 83. died *July* the 14th. 1602.

Hic jacet Christopherus Middylton qui obiit 27. die Mensis Augusti, Anno
Dom. 1467. Cujus animæ propitietur Deus.

Hic situs est
Pientissimus Daniel Houghton,
Filius Daniel Houghton *de* Chroington *in agro* Bucks,
Et Franciscæ Carter *de* Lilly *in Com*. Hertford,
Ortus Majoribus pietate per longam
Annorum seriem insignibus
Scholæ Eton *alumnus*

Ubi sub Dom. Buncle *linguis orientalibus*
imbutus
Dein Coll. Magdal. **Oxon.**
Sub auspitiis R. Doct. Goodwin *in albinos Demies*
Cooptatus sab tutelâ D. Theophili Gale *multum*
per septennium in Philosophia
Profecit
Laudem **Lillii** *Præceptoris munere indefessâ dilligentiâ*
Defunctus est
Ab incunabilis sanctitatem spiravit conscientia ad officia.
sua attentissimus
Semestria ante obitum gaudio ineffabili et omnagenis spiritus
S. Fructibus exinde mirum in modum auctis repletus
Natus 15 Octobris Anno Dom 1636.
Denatus Aprilis 29. An. Dom. 1672
Cælebs migrans ad Cælestes nuptias
Celherandas Ætatis suæ 35.

WALDENEY *or* WALDEN REGIS.

Norden, p. 26.

SOME hold that this Vill was denominted from *Salvis Silvestris,* the woody Dean, but others rather believe, that it was so named from the Springs where the Head of the **Marran** or **Mimeram** did rise, for the Syllable *Wal* in the Saxon Language signifies as much: In the time of King *Edward* the Confessor, Earl *Harold* was Lord hereof and died seiz'd of this Mannor; upon his Death it came to King *William* the Conqueror, who annexed it to the Crown, from which it might receive the Adjunct of **King's Wal-den,** to distinguish it from the other **Walden,** and 'tis recorded in *Domesdei Book,* That

In Dimidio Hundred. de **Hij,** *Rex* Willielmus *tenet* **Walduenei** *pro duobus hidis se defendebat. Terra est vigint. car. in Dominio duo virgat. et ibi sunt duo car. Presbiter cum tredecim* Vill. *et quatuor Bordis habentibus sex car. et adhuc duo possunt fieri, ibi duo cotar. et quatuor servi, pratum dimid. car. Pastura ad pec. Vill. Silva quatuor cent. porc. in totis valent. valet et valuit octo lib. tempore Regis* Edwardi *decim* lib. *hoc Manerium tenuit* Leveva *de Comit.* Haroldo, *et vendere potuit absq; ejus licentia. In servitio Regis inven. unam averam et inwardam, sed injuste et per vim, ut Scyra testatur. De his duobus hidis tenuit quidam Vidua femina* Asgari *un. hid. de Rege pro un. Manerio, et habet ibi un. car, et septemdecim Vill. cum septem Bord. habent. sex car. et tres possunt fieri ibi quinque cotar. et pratum dimid. car. Silva quatuor centum porc. pastura ad pecud. Ville, in totis valent. valet et valuit quatuor lib. temp. Regis* Edwardi *octo lib. eadem femina tenuit hoc Manerium tempore Regis* Edwardi *de Com.* Haroldo, *et potuit vendere absq; ejus licentia et injuste per vim inveniebat unam averam et inward. in servitio Regis, ut Scyra testatur hæc duo Manneria apposuit* Ilbertus *in* **Hij** *quando erat Vicecomes testante Hundred.*

King *William* held **Walden** in the half Hundred of **Hij.** It was rated for two Hides, the arable is twenty Carucates, in Demeasne two Virgates, and there are two Carucates, a Presbiter or Priest with thirteen Villains, and four Bordars, having six Carucates, and now two others may be made; there are two Cottagers, and four Servants, Meadow half a Carucate, Common of Pasture for the Cattle of the Vill, Wood to feed four hundred Hogs; in the whole Value, it is worth and was worth eight Pounds a Year, in the time of King *Edward* (the Confessor) ten Pounds. *Leveva* held this Mannor of Earl *Harold,* and might sell it without his leave. He found one Horse and Furniture in the King's Service, but unjustly and by force, as the Shire can witness. A certain Woman the Widow of *Asgar* held one of these two Hides of the King for one Mannor,

Hund. of *Hitchin.* and she hath there one Carucate, and seventeen Villains, with seven Bordars, having six Carucates, and three others may be made, there are five Cottagers, and Meadow half a Carucate, Wood to feed four hundred Hogs, Common of Pasture for the Cattle of the Vill; in the whole Value it is worth and was worth four Pounds a Year, in the time of King *Edward* (the Confessor) eight Pounds: The same Woman held this Mannor in the time of King *Edward* (the Confessor) of Earl *Harold*, and she might sell it without his leave, and he did find unjustly one Horse and Furniture by force in the King's Service, as the Shire can witness. *Ilbert* laid these two Mannors to *Mk?* when he was Sheriff, witness the Hundred.

King *Henry* I. granted this Mannor to *Peter de Valoines*, to whom he was very generous, of whom I have treated in *Hertingfordbury*: From that Family it might probably come to the *Nevils*, for it was found *Anno* 6 *Edw.*

Placit. Coron. Herts. 6 E. I. Rot. 48, cur. recept. Scac. I. that *Walter de Nevil* held this Vill of the Honour of *Valoynes* by the Service of one Knight's Fee, and he paid yearly to the Sheriff for the View of Franc-pledge half a Mark.

Mon. Angl. vol. 2, fol. 819. *Walter de Nevil* and *Alan Hayrun*, Patrons of this Church, gave it to the Canons of the Order of *Semplingham* at *Norton*, in the County of *York*, for ever: but the Mannor in short time after was granted to —— *Dokesworth*, who died seiz'd hereof *An.* 11 *Edw.* III.

In Process of time it came to the Possession of *Thomas* Lord *Burgh*, who died seiz'd hereof *Anno* 4 *Edw.* VI. leaving Issue *William* Lord *Burgh*, who was his Son and Heir, of full Age at the time of his Father's Death, and sued out his Livery the same Year.

Rot. in Canc. King *H.* VIII. granted the Rectory Church and Advowson of the Vicaridge of *King's Walden*, late Parcels of the Possessions of the late Priory of *Malton* to Sir *Ralph Sadlier*, Kt. and his Heirs.

Richard Hale, Citizen and Grocer of *London*, in the time of Queen *Elizabeth* purchased this Mannor, married *Mary* Daughter and Heir of —— *Lambert*, erected and endowed a Free-School at *Hertford*, and did many Acts of Charity, and died seiz'd hereof, leaving Issue *William* and *Richard.*

William succeeded his Father, and married *Rose* the Daughter of Sir *George Bond*, Kt. was Lord Mayor of *London, An.*1588, by whom he had Issue *William, Rowland, Barnard, John*, and divers other Sons and Daughters: he was constituted Sheriff of this County *Anno* 1621 19 *Jac.* I. and died seiz'd hereof 17 *Aug.* 1634, leaving Issue.

William, who was his Heir, but I presume he died on the 21st of *July, An.* 1641 without Issue, for it came to

Rowland, who succeeded his Brother, and married *Elizabeth* Daughter to Sir *Henry Garway*, Kt. by whom he had Issue *William:* He was constituted Sheriff for this County, *Anno* 23 *Car.* I. 1647, and died on the seventh Day of *April,* 1669.

Upon his Death, this Mannor came to *William*, who served twice in Parliament for this County, where he so gained the Hearts of the People, that if he was named in an Election for Parliament for this County, the Free-holders would choose him contrary to his Inclination; he desiring to be excused in Regard of his Health: He was endowed with excellent Parts, great Integrity, and general Learning; he was a good Philospher, a great Historian, and used an excellent Stile in writing, was firm to the establish'd Religion in the Church of 𝔈𝔫𝔤𝔩𝔞𝔫𝔡; a kind Husband, a provident Father, prudent in his House, and very faithful and stedfast to the Interest of his Country; he built a Chappel or Burying-place for his Family, adjoyning to the Chancel, and died seiz'd of this Mannor, leaving Issue *Richard, Rowland, William, John, Hierome, Henry, Barnard, Thomas,* and *Mary* married to *John Plomer* of 𝔅𝔩𝔞𝔨𝔢𝔰𝔴𝔞𝔯𝔢 in this County, Esq. *Katharine* and *Elizabeth* both unmarried.

Richard succeeded, and married *Elizabeth* the Daughter of *Isaac Mennel*, Alderman of 𝔏𝔬𝔫𝔡𝔬𝔫, by whom he had Issue *William* and *Mary*, he died the 13th Day of *Apr.* 1689, and *William* who was his Heir, is now the present Lord hereof.

THIS Church is a Donative, and the Rectory is appropriated to the Use of the Lord of this Mannor, who is Patron of this Church, and hath given 10*l. per Annum* to maintain a Minister to officiate here.

The VICARS.
Mr. *Smeath.*　　Mr. *Sherlock.*　　Mr. *Mott.*

The Church is erected near the Mannor-house, in the Deanery of 𝔥𝔦𝔱𝔠𝔥𝔦𝔫. in the Diocess of 𝔏𝔦𝔫𝔠𝔬𝔩𝔫. with a Chappel annexed to the same, at the West End thereof a square Tower adjoyns to the Church, wherein are six Bells, and within the Chancel and Church there are Monuments and Grave Stones which shew these Inscriptions.

A Stone under the Altar.

Here lyeth the Body of *William Hale*, Esq; Son and Heir of *Richard Hale*, Esq; who departed this life the 27. of *August*, 1634. and in the 66*th*. year of his age.
Let him rest in peace.

Here lyeth the Body of *Rose*, the Daughter of Sir *George Bond*, Kt. and Wife of *William Hale*, Esq; who departed this life the 31*th*. day of *July, anno Dom.* 1648. in the 75*th*. year of her age.
Let her rest in peace.

Here lyeth the Body of *William Hale*, the Son and Heir of *William Hale* Esq; who departed this Life the 21*th*. of *July, anno Dom.* 1641. being the 44*th*. year of his age.
Let him rest in peace.

Here lyeth the Body of *Rowland Hale*, Esq; one of the Sons of *William Hale*, and *Rose*, his Wife, he died the seventh day of *April*, 1669. in the 64*th* year of his age.
Let him rest in peace.

Here lyeth the Body of *Elizabeth Hale*, Widow, Daughter of Sir *Henry Garway*, Kt. and Relict of *Rowland Hale*, Esq; She died the 9th. of *January*, 1678. in the 70th. year of her age.

At the Foot of the Altar.

Here lies the Body of Sir *John Hale*, Kt. who was the seventh Son and eleventh Child of *William Hale*, Esq; and *Rose* his Wife, he died the 22*th.* day of *January, anno Dom.* 1672. and in the 79*th.* of his age.

Here lieth the Body of *Sibil* late Wife of *Robert Barbor*, Gent. who had issue two Sons and two Daughters, she was Daughter to *William Shepheard* of **Great Koletwright** in the County of **Oxon**, Esq; and the Sister of *Timothy Shepheard*, who was buried here. She deceased the 24*th.* day of *May, Anno Dom.* 1614.

On the South Side of the Chancel.

Deo Uni Trino Opt. Max. Gloria.

Timotheo Sheppard *filiæ Quatuor-genito*, Gulielmo Sheppard *de* **Koletwright**, in *Com.* **Oxon**, *Armigeri; Juveni optimæ indolis et perquam bono; Qui die Mensis Aprilis* 29. Anno Dom. 1613 *Ætat. suæ* 29. *in Dom. placidè obdormivit;* Tho. Sheppard *et* Johannes Ferrar *fratres ejus et Executores hoc Exile sui grandis amoris posuerunt Monumentum.*
De reliquis dici quæ possunt optima, de te
Dicere quisq; potest, credere quisq; potest.

On the South Side of a Chapel built by Colonel *Hale* on the North Side of the Chancel.

Gulielmus Hale
Natus ex Rolando Hale, *Armigero,*
Et Elizabetha *ejus Uxore,*
Denatus 25. *die* Maii *Anno Salutis* 1688
Ætat. suæ 56,
In hoc quod ipse posuit, sacello,
Reconditorio, si Deus voluerit
Sibi et sui futuro
Heic juxta primus quiescit

Heic juxta requiescit
Richardus Hale, *Armiger,*
Qui ingenio et Comitate morum,
Ut Patrem Optimum expressit,
Ita fato heic nimis properato!
Intra anni spatium, quo Pater sublatus est,
Et ipse eodem concessit
Duxerat Uxorem Elizabetham
Filiam et heredem Isaaci Mennel
De **Mennel Langley** *Comitatu* **Barbiensi***:*
Quæ hoc illi Monumentum
Pio affectu et modesto apparatu posuit
Obiit 13. *die* Aprilis *anno salutis* 1689. *et Ætat. suæ* 30.

STAGENHOE.

THIS Hamlet belongs to the Parish of **Paul's Walden**, but lies in this half Hundred of **Hitchin**, where it is charged with all parliamentary and extraordinary Taxes. In the time of *William* the Conqueror, it was Parcel of the Possessions of *Ralph* the Brother of *Ilgerius*, for it was then recorded in *Domesdei Book*, that

Ranulfus *frater* Ilgerii, *et* Willielmus *de eo tenet in* **Staghou**, *unam hidam. Terra est tres carucat. in Dominio est una, et sex Villani habentes aliam, et tertia potest fieri, ibi duo cotarii, Silva vigint. porc. Hæc Terra valet quinquagint. sol. quando recepit vigint. sol tempore Regis* Edwardi *quatuor lib. Hoc Manerium tenuit,* Turburnus *homo Regis* Edwardi, *et vendere potuit.*

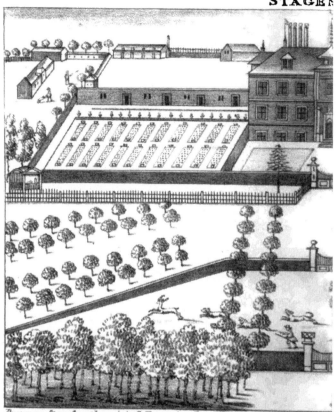

Drawn on Stone from the original Engravings by G.T.Tyler.

To the Right Worp.^{ll}

This Draught is humbly

Pub.^d by I.M. Mullinger.

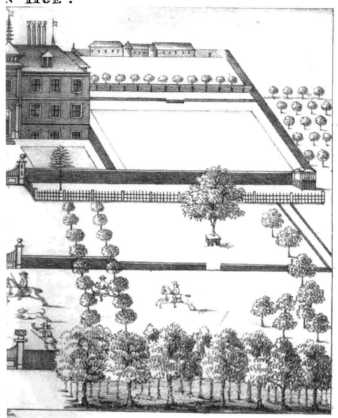

Sir John Austen Bar^t

presented by

J. Drapentier.

Bps Storßord.

Hund. of
Hitchin.

Ralph, the Brother of *Ilger*, and *William* held of him one Hide in Stagnehou. The arable is three Carucates, in Demeasne is one, and six Villains having another Carucate, and a third may be made; there are two Cottagers, Wood to feed twenty Hogs. This Land is worth fifty Shillings by the Year, when he received it twenty Shillings a Year, in the time of King *Edward* (the Confessor) four Pounds. *Turnbern*, a Man (under the Protection) of King *Edward*, held this Mannor and might sell it.

From the Conquest, to the time of *Edw*. III. I find not as yet any Account of this Mannor, but in all Probability, it was Parcel of the Possessions of a Family sirnamed *de Verdun*, who were Lords of several Mannors in the Counties of Norfolk and Suffolk; one of that Sirname, *viz. Wydo de Verdun*, being possest of the Mannors of Brisingham and Reydun in Norfolk, in or before the time of *H*. III. whose Successor *John de Verdun* was possest of them in the ninth Year of King *Edw*. I. and was then in Ward to the Earl Marshal.

Inq pro Hund. 1 Norf. penes Camer. Scac.

Sir *John de Verdun*, Kt. I suppose succeeded him, by the Calculation of the time, who levied a Fine *Anno* 12 *Edw*. III. between himself and *Maud* his Wife, Quer. and Master *Alan de Hotham*, Deforceant, of the Mannors of Saxlingham and Moulton, and the Advowsons of the Churches in Norfolk, and other Mannors in Suffolk, who settled them to the Use of himself, and his Wife, and to his Heirs.

- There was likewise one *Thomas de Verdune* who lived at the same time, and died in the one and twentieth Year of the same King's Reign, but what Mannors he died seized of, is not to our Purpose to mention. After this a Fine was levied of this Mannor, *An*. 24 *Edw*. III. and that of Chedeburge in Suffolk, between *Edmund de Verdune*, and *Jane* his Wife, Plaintiffs, and *John de Verdune*, Deforceant; in which *John* granted them to *Edmond* and *Joan* in Tail, with the Services of divers Tenants of these Mannors herein particularly named; in which Family it continued till *Margaret* the Daughter and Heir of Sir *John Verdun*, Kt. and Widow of *Hugh Bradshaw*, brought it with other Mannors to the *Pilkingtons*, a Family of good Account, sirnamed *de Pilkington* in Lancashire; for though this Mannor is not particularly named, yet there was a Fine levied of a Part of the Inheritance of the Family of *Verdun*, in the first Year of King *Hen*. IV. *viz*. the Mannors of Brisingham in the County of Norfolk, and Bricklesworth in the County of Northampton, between Sir *John Pilkington*, Kt. and *Margaret* his Wife, Plaintiffs, *Robert de Veere de Lobenham* and *John Weston*, Deforceants, wherein they settled them on Sir *John* and *Margaret*, and the Heirs Males of *Margaret*, with Remainders to their right Heirs, which Settlement would not have been made, if those Mannors had not

Pedes fin. ejus. annis. Esc. 21 Ed. III. p. 2 & 36, ejusd. p.

Fines diver. Com. 1 H. IV n. 21.

been the Inheritance of the Wife, and 𝔅𝔯𝔦𝔰𝔦𝔫𝔤𝔥𝔞𝔪 Mannor,
and this had the same Owners as abovesaid.

These *Pilkingtons* were possest of a great Estate in 𝕷𝖆𝖓𝖈𝖆𝖘𝖍𝖎𝖗𝖊, as by the Escheat Rolls in the *Tower* may be seen,
and by this following Record, amongst many others, which
I have seen, being a Grant of Free-warren to this very Sir
John Pilkington, Kt. (in all his Mannors in 𝕷𝖆𝖓𝖈𝖆𝖘𝖍𝖎𝖗𝖊,
wherein at least twenty are named) Grandson and Heir to
Roger de Pilkington, who had a Grant of that Liberty in
them *An.* 19 *Edw.* I. The Family of the *Pilkingtons* I have
incerted, by which the Reader may plainly perceive the Reason of levying the Fines which I shall hereafter quote.

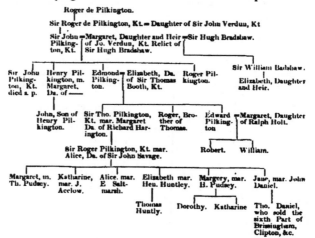

Roger de Pilkington.

Sir Roger de Pilkington, Kt. ⚭ Daughter of Sir John Verdun, Kt

Fines Com.
Herts 1 H. IV.
    A Fine was levied of this Mannor of 𝕾𝖙𝖆𝖌𝖊𝖓𝖍𝖔𝖊, *Anno* 1
H. IV. between *John* Son of *Henry de Pilkington,* Plain-
tiff, and *J. de Pilkington* and *Margaret* his Wife, Deforc.

Diver. Fin
Com. Herts.6
H. VI. lig. 1,
n. 96.
This *Margaret* lived *Anno* 6 *Hen.* VI. was then possest of
this Mannor, for in that Year, she levied a Fine of the
Mannors of 𝔅𝔯𝔦𝔠𝔨𝔩𝔢𝔰𝔴𝔬𝔯𝔱𝔥 in the County of 𝕹𝖔𝖗𝖙𝖍𝖆𝖒𝖕𝖔𝖓,
and 𝔅𝔯𝔦𝔰𝔦𝔫𝔤𝔥𝔞𝔪 in 𝕹𝖔𝖗𝖋𝖔𝖑𝖐, between *Ralph Briche* and
others, Plaintiffs, and *Margaret* the Widow of Sir *John
Pilkington,* Deforceant, whereby those Mannors were settled on Trustees for the Life of *Margaret;* the Remainder
to Sir *John Pilkington,* Kt. her Son, the Remainder to *Edmond Pilkington* in Tail, the Remainder to *Robert,* the
Remainder to *Elizabeth,* Daughter and Heir of Sir *William Bradshaw* her first Husband's Son and Heir: This
Margaret lived to a great Age, for she was living till al-

most the 29th of *H.* VI. in which Year there is an Inquisition found after her Death, but her Husband died *An.* 6 *H.* VI. as appears by the Inquisition after his Death, which was not found till the 15th of that King.

Sir *John Pilkington* the Son, was admitted one of the Chamberlains of the *Exchequer,* the 14th of *April,* 17 *Edw.* IV. but the Mannor of 𝔖tagenhoe, was settled on the Descendants of *Edmond,* for another Fine was levied *Anno* 38 *H.*VI. between *Ralph Lever* and *Nicholas Noble,* Plaintiffs, and *William Harrington,* Kt. and *Elizabeth* his Wife, *Thomas Pilkington,* Esq. and *Margaret* his Wife, and *Arthur Pilkington,* Deforceants of the Mannor and Advowson of 𝔅risingham in 𝔑orfolk, 𝔖tansted in 𝔖uffolk, 𝔒lypston Church and Chantery: This Mannor of 𝔖tagenhoe, and divers great Parcels of Land here particularly named in this County, wherein they settled them upon these Trustees, quit of the Heirs of *Elizabeth,* who regranted them to *Thomas Pilkington* in Tail; Remainder to *Roger Pilkington,* Brother of *Thomas,* Remainder to *Arthur Pilkington,* Remainder to *William Harrington* in Tail, Remainder to *John Pilkington,* Son of *Robert Pilkington,* Esq. which *Thomas Pilkington* was afterwards knighted, and took Part with the House of 𝔜ork, in the Wars of those times, which created great Trouble to him in the time of *H.*VII. for he was one of those great Men in 𝔏ancashire, who joyned with the Earl of 𝔏incoln, Earl of 𝔎ildare, Lord 𝔏obell, Sir *Thomas Broughton,* and others, on the Behalf of *Lambert Simnel,* the counterfeit *Plantagenet;* and fighting on his Side at the Battle of 𝔖toke near 𝔑ewark, *Anno Dom.* 1487, was there slain; whereupon all his Lands were forfeited to the Crown, being a vast Estate in 𝔏ancashire, and other Counties, and this Mannor among the Rest, was seized into the King's Hands. Shortly after, that King, *Anno* 4 *Regni sui.* granted this Mannor and divers other Mannors and Lands in 𝔎ent, of this Sir *Thomas Pilkington's* to *George* Lord *Strainge,* Son of *Thomas* Earl of 𝔇arby; he or his Son sold it to *Richard Godfry* of ———— in this County, Esq. in which Family, it continued for two or three Generations, till *Godfry* sold it to *Richard Hale* of 𝔎ing's 𝔚alden, Esq. from whom it came to *William,* who had divers Children, but it seems gave this Mannor to

John Hale, who was his seventh Son, and eleventh Child by *Rose* his Wife, was knighted at Sir *Harbottle Grimsion's* House in 𝔏incoln's 𝔍nn 𝔉ields, then Speaker of the House of Commons, *Anno* 1660, and constituted Sheriff for this County, *Anno* 1663, 15 *Car.* II. He married *Rose,* one of the Daughters of ———— *Bale* of 𝔖addington in the County of 𝔏eicester; was a Person of great Judgment, and good Understanding, delighted in Husbandry, was very kind

Hund. of
Hittchin.

to his Tenants, and would often please himself with the Conversation of the most intelligent Men in the Affairs of the Country: He built the Mannor-house about the Year 1650, and left Issue only

Rose, who was his Daughter and Heir, married Sir *John Austen* of 𝕭exley in the County of 𝕶ent, Son and Heir of Sir *Robert Austen*, who was created Baronèt by Letters Patents dated the 10th of *July*, 1660, 12 *Car.* II. He served in two Parliaments for the Town of ——— in the County of 𝕶ent, one held *Anno* 7 *W.* III, the other 9 *W.* III. He gives *Or, a Cheveron Gules between three Bears' Paws erected and erazed Sable*, and is the present Lord hereof.

William Austen of Herendon in ⟶ Elizabeth, Daughter of Sir
Tenterden in East Kent.   Edward Hale.

Margaret, first Wife, Daughter of ⟵Sir Robert Austin of⟶ Anne, second Wife, Daughter of
William Williamson of Loudon,   Bexley in Kent.   Thomas Nun of Otteridge in
Vinter.   Bersted in Kent.

Sir John Austen of Hall-place in Bexley in Kent, ⟶ Rose, Daughter and sole Heir of Sir
and Stagenhoe in Hertfordshire, in right of his   John Hale, of Stagenhoe, Kt. died in
Wife, obiit Ann. 1698.   May, 1695.

Edward   Robert Austen of Hall-place⟶ Elizabeth, Daughter and Coheir of   Elizabeth.
Austen.   in Bexley, Esq. Son and Heir,   G. Stowel of Cotherston in Somer-   Rose.
     living 1699.   setshire, second Son of Sir Jo.   Anne.
                  Stowel, Kt.

Rose.   Elizabeth

KAMINTON, *or* KIMPTON.

THIS Vill was called by the old *Saxons*, 𝕶imeton, from a Brook called 𝕶ime, which rises near this Place, but in *Domesdei Book* it is writ 𝕶aminton, for it is thus recorded there under the Title of *Terra Episcopi* 𝕭ajocensis.

Domesd. Lib.
fol. 134, nu. 5.

In dimidio Hundred. de 𝕳ij. Radulphus tenet de Episcopo 𝕶amintone pro quatuor hidis se defendebat. Terra est decem car. in Dominio sunt duo, et tertia potest fieri, ibi duo Francig. et duodecim Vill. cum duobus Bordis habentibus septem car. ibi tres cotar. et quinq; Servi, pratum sex bobus, Silva octingint. porc. et unum Molin. de octo sol. in totis valent. valet et valuit duodecim lib. tempore Regis Edwardi quindecim lib. Hoc Manerium tenuit Alveva mater Comitis Morcari.

Ralph held 𝕶amintone of the Bishop of 𝕭ayeux, in the half Hundred of 𝕳ij; it was rated for four Hides. The arable is ten Carucates, in Demeasne are two, and a third may be made; there are two Frenchmen born, and twelve Villains, with two Bordars having seven Carucates, there are three Cottagers, and five Servants, Meadow for six Oxen, Wood to feed eight hundred Hogs, and one Mill of eight Shillings Rent by the Year; in the whole Value it is worth, and was worth, twelve Pounds by the Year; in the time of King *Edward* (the Confessor) fifteen Pounds. *Alveva* the Mother of Earl *Morcar* held this Mannor.

I have treated of this Bishop in the Parish of 𝕮lothall; but I find there were three Mannors in this Vill, 1 𝕭uckinhanger, 2 𝕭arkbury and 𝕷egats, 3 𝕭ibpsworth

The Mannor of KIMETON.

IN old time was termed 𝕭uckinhanger, from some Owner hereof, who having no Issue Male, might so call it to preserve the Memory of his own Name to Posterity; afterward it came to the Lord *Mordant*, in whose Name and Family it continued for divers Generations, until such time that it was sold to *Thomas Hoo*, Esq. and *William Hoo*, Gent. who was Son and Heir apparent to the said *Thomas*, both whom, on the 22nd of *September, Anno* 38 *Eliz.* held a Court for this Mannor. *William* had Issue *William Hoo*, who succeeded him, and held a Court here on the 26th of *September, Anno* 3 *Car.* I. He was constituted Sheriff of this County, *Anno* 5 *Car.* I. and died seized hereof the 14th of *March, An.* 1636, *Susan* his Wife surviving him, by whom he left Issue *Thomas* and *Elizabeth*.

Shortly after *Thomas* died, and this Mannor came to *Elizabeth*, who was his Sister and next Heir: She married Sir *Jonathan Keate*, Bart. who held a Court Baron here, *Anno* 1657, and is now the present Lord hereof.

The Mannor of PARKBURY and LEGATS

WAS so denominated from one *Legat*, who was Lord hereof; but since it became Parcel of the Possessions of the *Knightons*, and afterwards of the *Ferrers*, whose Daughter and Heir married *Thomas Fanshaw*, Esq. of all which Families I have treated in the Parish of 𝕭epford. This *Thomas Fanshaw* and *Katharine* his Wife, held a Court Baron here on the fifth of *April*, 1649, but shortly after conveyed it to the Lady *Amy Mordant*, who married *Basset Cole*, and held two Courts for this Mannor, one on the first of *Apr.* 1656, and the other on the first of *June*, 1658, but soon after it was sold to Sir *Jonathan Keate*, Bar. who called a Court in his Name on the seventh of *April*, 1665, and is the present Lord hereof.

The Mannor of BYBBYSWORTH HALL

WAS Parcel of the Possessions of that ancient Family of *Bibbysworth*, from whence it was denominated, for I find Sir *Walter Bibbysworth* held it in the time of *H.* III. died seized hereof, *Anno* — *Edw.* I. and was buried before the Altar of the blessed *Peter* in the Church of 𝕭unmotv.

It continued in this Name till the third Year of *H.*VII. when it expired in a Daughter and Heir, who had Issue, *Richard Barley;* at length it was sold to *Robert Barley*, a Kinsman and Tenant to *William Wiseman*, both which

Hund. of
Pitchin.

Robert and *William*, by Indenture dated the 26th of *May*, 1659, sold it to Sir *Jonathan Keat*, Bar. who is the present Lord hereof.

THIS Vicaridge was rated, *Anno 26 Hen.* VIII. in the King's Books at 12*l. per Annum*, and Sir *Jonathan Keate* is Patron hereof.

John Millet, VICAR.

This Church is erected in the Deanery of Pitchin in the Diocess of Lincoln, in the Middle of the Hill, and consists of the Body and one Isle, with a Chapel erected on the North Side of the Church, which is cover'd with Lead, and a square Tower adjoyns the West End of the Church, wherein hang a small Ring of six Bells, with a Spire upon it, about fifteen Foot high, which hath a Weather Cock, and a Crown of Thorns under it.

In this Church are two ancient Monuments, one raised half a Yard above the Ground, the other a Yard, in which it is believed that two of the *Bibbysworths* lye interred; and there is a Grave Stone which has the Name of *Margaret Bibbysworth* inscribed upon it.

Here I conclude this Hundred with this Parish, and proceed to the fourth Division of this County, which is the Hundred of Caisbor.

THE

FOURTH

DIVISION OF THIS COUNTY

————

CONTAINS the Hundred of **Albaneston**, so termed heretofore from the Town of **St. Albans**, but now called **Caisho** from **Caisho**, the ancient Seat of *Cassibelan*, King of the *Cassians:* since it became Parcel of the Possessions of the late Monastery of **St. Albans**. It was made a Liberty by the Grant of *Edward* IV. and upon the Dissolution of that Church, it rested in the Crown, and remained there until such time that King *James* I. by Letters Patents dated the 7th of *April, Anno* 9 *Regni sui,* granted the whole Liberty of the late Monastery of **St. Albans** in the County of **Hertford**, with all and every the Appurtenances, to *William Whitmore*, Esq. and *John Eldred*, and their Heirs, who conveyed it in the same Year to *Robert* Earl of **Salisbury**, from whom it is lineally descended to *James* Earl of **Salisbury**, the present Lord hereof.

Within this Liberty stood the great City of **Verolam**, where *Cassibelan* kept his Court, and was afterwards made a Free-city of the *Romans,* but since destroyed, so that nothing now remains thereof, more than the Foundation of the Walls, with the Marks of the Ditches that enclosed about four hundred and fifty Acres of Ground; which shewed the Extent of the City, and also the Borough of **St. Albans**, which was built out of the Ruins of it, and is scituated within this Liberty.

'Tis bounded on the North and East with the Hundreds of **Hitchin** and **Broadwater**, on the South with **Middlesex**, and on the West with the Hundred of **Dacorum**: The Town and Borough of **St. Albans** is the chief Place where the Justices of the Peace hold the general Sessions, and act the publick Business, as well for the Liberty as the Borough: It contains these Parishes and Hamlets, which are divided between three high Constables; whereof one has in his Division, **Abbots Langley**, **Barret**, **Rickmersworth**, **Watford**, **Caisho**, **Aldenham**, **Edlestree**, (near **Sulloniaca**, heretofore a Roman City, but now an uninhabitable Place) **Chipping Bernet**, **East Bernet**, **Northaw**, and **Ridge**; another high Constable hath **St. Stephens**, **Park Ward**, **Sleep**, and

Hund. of Caishoe. Smalford, Tittenhanger, St. Michaels, Windridge Ward, Redburne, and Sandridge; and the third high Constable hath Paul's Walden, Codicote, Brantfield, Shephale, Hexton, Norton, and Newnham: But before I enter upon this Liberty, I shall take Notice of the ancient decayed City of Verolam, and the Borough of St. Alban, which is a Liberty of itself within the Liberty of St. Alban, exempted from it by the King's Grant, for that it gives them Justices of the Peace and Officers of their own, chosen out of themselves; and then I shall proceed to the other Parishes and Hamlets after the Manner I have prescribed.

VEROLAMIUM, VERULAMIUM.

Brady's Hist. of Engl. fol 9. WAS a great and populous City, when *Julius Cæsar,* Emperor of the *Romans,* invaded the *Britains,* and the Place where *Cassibelan,* Prince of the *Cassians,* and the most great and potent of the Kings of this Island kept his Court, which was the Reason they chose him their General by common Consent; but *Cæsar* knowing their Design, forthwith marched on the South Side of the Thames, with his Army, towards the Frontiers of his Country, which was *Camd. Brit. tit. Suthery, fol. 295, 296.* divided from the maritime Cities by that River, to a Place now called Coway Stakes, near Oatland in Surrey, distant from the Sea about eighty Miles; where some Prisoners and Fugitives showed him that the River was forda- *Ram's Antiq. of Brit fol. 197.* ble, but the Passage proving difficult, because the Bank itself was fenced with sharp Stakes of the Thickness of a Man's Thigh, cover'd over with Lead and Water, that they could not be discern'd and driven deep into the Bottom of the River, that they were unmoveable, and as the Watermen there now say, do remain to this Day; and he perceiving great Forces of the Enemy in good Order, ready to receive him on the other Side of the River, first commanded his Horse through the Water, then sent his Legions after them, who waded through the River with great Speed and Resolution, (their Heads only appearing above Water) then both Horse and Foot charged the Enemy with such Violence, that they forsook the Bank and fled.

Brady's Hist. of Engl. fol. 10. *Cassibelan* despairing of Victory, dismist his Forces, and the *Cassians* by their Ambassadors yielded themselves to *Cæsar,* from whom he understood that Verolam, where *Cassibelan* usually resided, was not far off, strengthened and surrounded with Woods and Marshes, well filled with Men and Cattle, for the *Britains* called intricate Woods, compass about with a mud Wall and a Ditch, a Town whither they were wont to resort, for the avoiding the incursion of their Enemies.

Cæsar marched with his Legions thither, and though he found the Place notably fortified by Nature and Art, yet he assaulted it in two Places: The *Britains* defended it for some time, but when they were not able to withstand the Force and Power of the *Romans*, they fled out at another Part of the City, where the *Romans* took many Prisoners, put great Numbers of them to the Sword in the View of the Rest, and seized great Store of Cattle for the present Support and Provision of their Army.

This City was scituated on the gentle Descent or Side of the Western Hill facing the East, fenced about with very strong Walls, a double Rampire, deep Trenches toward the South, and water'd with a Brook on the East Part, which in old time made a great Meere or standing Pool: *Tacitus* called it 𝔚𝔢𝔯𝔲𝔩𝔞𝔪𝔦𝔲𝔪; *Ptolomy*, 𝔚𝔯𝔬𝔫𝔞𝔪𝔦𝔲𝔪 and 𝔚𝔢𝔯𝔬𝔩𝔞𝔪𝔦𝔲𝔪, so denominated from the River 𝔚𝔢𝔯; and *Humphrey Lhuid* makes it as if it was 𝔚𝔢𝔯𝔲𝔩𝔥𝔞𝔪, a Church upon the 𝔚𝔢𝔯: When the Inhabitants hereof had lived sometime under the Government of the *Romans*, divers of them became excellent Soldiers, and did notable Service for them; in Consideration whereof, the *Romans* granted to them the Priviledges of Roman Citizens, and made the Town a Free-city: In the time of *Nero* it was accounted à *Municipium*, so that *Ninius* in his Catalogue of Cities, calls it 𝔠𝔞𝔢𝔯 𝔐𝔲𝔫𝔦𝔠𝔦𝔭𝔦𝔲𝔪, which makes it probable, this was the very 𝔠𝔞𝔢𝔯 𝔐𝔲𝔫𝔦𝔠𝔦𝔭𝔦𝔲𝔪 which *Hubert Coltzius* found in an old Inscription. These *Municipia*, saith *Cambden*, were Towns endowed with the Rights of Roman Citizens; this Name came *a muneribus Capiendis*, of having publick Offices and Charges in the Commonwealth, as I have shewed before in treating of the Town of 𝔥𝔢𝔯𝔱𝔣𝔬𝔯𝔡.

Whilst *Suetonius Paulinus*, Lieutenant of 𝔅𝔯𝔦𝔱𝔞𝔦𝔫, and one of the most famous military Men of his Age, was busied in the Conquest of 𝔐𝔬𝔫𝔞, (the Isle of 𝔄𝔫𝔤𝔩𝔢𝔰𝔢𝔭,) *Bunduica* or *Boaditia*, Queen of the *Icenians*, incited by the deep Love she bore to her Country, and exasperated by the bitter Hatred she had to the *Romans*, took the Opportunity to raise a bloody and mortal War upon them; brought a great Army hither, and rased and destroyed this City, because the Inhabitants were very true and faithful to the *Romans*; therefore they hanged some, burned others, and crucify'd others, using all the Cruelty and inhumane Outrage that a giddy Rabble, elevated with Success, could think of: They took no Prisoners to preserve for Ransom or Exchange, according to the Law of War; but cut in Pieces both *Romans* and their Allies, to the Number of seventy thousand, or, as *Dio* saith, eighty thousand: They stripped naked the noblest and honestest of their Matrons, hanged them, cut off their Breasts, and sowed them to their

Hund. of Caishoe.

Brady's Hist. of Engl. fol. 10.

Camd. Brit. tit. Herts. fol. 408.

Polyolbion, fol. 254.

Brady's Hist. of Engl. fol. 19.

Hund. of
Caistor.
Mouths, that they might seem to eat their own Flesh; all
which they did, whilst they sacrificed and carowsed in the
Temple of Andatt, their Goddess of Victory.

Tacitus, Ann.
4, cap. 34,
fol. 252.
During the time these things were acting, *Suetonius* returned from Mona with the fourteenth Legion, the Standard Bearers of the twentieth, and about ten thousand of
the Auxiliaries, resolved to fight them, and forthwith chose
a Place with a narrow Entrance, a thick Wood for Defence
behind him, a wide Plain before him, and prepared for
Battle: the Legionaries were drawn up in close Order, and
encompast them with the light-armed Horsemen, who always fought first, and moved as Occasion offer'd. In the
meantime, the *Britains*, ranged abroad in great Companies
and Brigades, triumphing, and supposing no Force could
resist them; in Confidence whereof, they brought their
Ral. Hist. of
the World,
lib. 2, pt. 1,
sect. 3, fol. 253
Wives, and plac'd them in Wagons about the utmost Parts
of the Plain, to View the Slaughter of the *Romans*, and to
be Witnesses of their expected Victory: *Boaditia* commanding in Chief, mounts her Chariot with her two Daughters, after the usual Manner of the ancient *Britains*, who
were wont to fight in Chariots against the *Romans*, armed
like the *Ægyptians*, with sharp and broad Hooks on both
Sides, like the Mower's Scythe, and encouraging her Army
with a Speech, used many Arguments to animate her
Soldiers, who were a rude and undisciplin'd Multitude,
consisting of 230,000 fighting Men, and perswading
them to pursue their Enemies, as Dogs and Wolves chase
fearful Hares and Foxes; she let lose a live Hare out of
her Lap, at which the *Britains* shouted, apprehending the
speedy Course of the Hare through the Army was ominous,
and presag'd the Flight of the *Romans: Suetonius* on the
other Side, exhorted his Soldiers not to be frightened with
the great Numbers of their Enemies, but to fall on boldly,
and keeping close together, to continue the fight, which
could not be long after they should break their Front, for
the rest were but an irregular unweildy Multitude. At the
first, the *Britains* surrounded their Enemies, throwing Darts
where they saw Advantage, and oftentimes, by the Fierce-
ness of their Horses, and Rufflings of their Wheels, they
brake their Ranks, and crowding themselves in among the
Troops of Horse, they leapt out of their Chariots, and fought
on Foot; in the mean time the Drivers withdrew from the
Battle, and so plac'd themselves, that if their Masters were
opprest in Fight, or out numbred, they might readily return
to them, when they had perform'd the Duties of Horsemen
in their nimble motion, and of Footmen in keeping their
Ground; and they were so expert by Use in managing their
Horses, that they could stop or turn them on a Speed,
down a steep Hill, and could run along on the Pole of the

Hund. of
Caishoe.

Chariot, stand firm 'upon the Yoke, and return speedily into it. But the Legions kept the Streight as a Place of Defence, whilst the *Britains* spent their Darts, then marching into the Plain, where the Auxiliaries and Horsemen made Way, they marshall'd the Body of their Army in the Form of an irresistible Wedge, which enter'd, broke, and dissipated the Party that opposed them, the Rest fled but could not easily escape, by Reason of their own Wagons which were placed about the Plain; they spared none, and the dead Bodies of Men and Women were intermixt together, on Heaps with the dead Carcasses of Horses: 'Tis said there were eighty thousand *Britains* slain in this Fight, and four hundred *Romans* killed, and as many wounded. *Boaditia, Tacitus* saith, poisoned herself; but *Dio* reported she died of Sickness, when the *Britains* had prepared for another Battle.

After the *Romans* had subdued this Isle, and made the *Britains* subject to their Government, by the great Prudence and Wisdom of *Agricola*, who was a Terrour to them that opposed him, and a Patron to those who were obedient to their Magistrates: He assisted and encouraged the People to build Houses, Temples, and Courts of Justice: Taught the Sons of Noblemen the Roman Eloquence, and by Degrees brought their Gowns and Habits in Request with the *Britains*. He taught the Gentry the liberal Arts, and the Common People the Advantages of Trade and Traffick among themselves; which made the Government acceptable, and Order and Civility very delightful to them: Then the Breaches of this City were repaired and it began to flourish again; for it grew exceeding populous, and the Inhabitants very rich: Then the ancient Coins of Money were stamped here, Money became very plentiful, and the *Britains* lived at great Ease and Quiet till the Year of Christ 303, when the innocent and harmless Christians, throughout the Empire, suffered under a most horrid and dreadful Persecution, because they would not worship the Roman Gods according to the Command of *Dioclesian*.

Barnabas and *Saul* assembled themselves about the Year of the World 4046, at Antioch, where they preached the Gospel to the People, and their Disciples were first denominated Christians, because they profess the Name of Christ, and all the Articles of their Faith were afterwards comprised in the three Creeds, called the *Apostles'*, the *Athanasian*, and the *Nicene* Creed, confirmed by the four first General Councils observed by the primitive Christians, and are now practis'd in the Church of England, without any Addition, Diminution, or Alteration, as is manifest by the same Creeds, which makes it the same Church that our Saviour Christ instituted, and the Scriptures now warrant. But whosoever

Brady's *Hist.*
of *Engl.* fol. 7.

Bede, lib. 1,
cap. 7, fol. 31,
Brady's *Hist.*
fol. 32.

Acts of the
Apostles, xi.
v. 26.

Hund. of
Caishoe.
shall add to these Articles of Faith,' and force new Doc-
trines upon their Proselites, do erect a new Church, and
may reasonably dread the Anathema of St. *Paul*, who de-
Galat. i. 8, 9.
clared, *Though we or an Angel from Heaven, preach any
other Gospel, than that which we have preached, let him*
2 Tim. iii. 16.
2 Peter i. 21.
Rom. ii. 2.
be accursed ; for all Faith is founded upon divine Authority; and there is now no divine Authority but the Scriptures
which were given by the Inspiration of God, and delivered
by holy Men, as they were moved by the Holy Ghost, which
was the Reason that neither the Jewish Church, (to whom
Council of
Laodicea,
Can. 60.
Usher de Pri-
mords, p. 15.
the Oracles of God were committed) nor the Christian Church
would allow the Apocriphal Books, because they were wrote
after the time that Prophecy and divine Inspiration ceased ;
neither is it rational to believe that our blessed Saviour will
know them at the Day of Judgment, who separate from his
Church, and communicate with others who prefer their own
extemporary Notions before that sacred Prayer which he
composed for the Use of his Disciples, and glory in their
rude Addresses to God, which could never proceed from
his Spirit, for they are fraughted with Nonsense, which
none will dare to charge upon the Wisdom of God.   This
was the Cause that Liturgies were first ordained, that we
Matt. vi. 9.
Luke xi. 1, 2.
might worship God in Order, in Decency, in Humility, and
in Righteousness: To this Purpose St. *James*, whom the
Apostles ordained the first Bishop of 𝕵erusalem, composed
a Liturgy for that Church, from whence he was called *Jacobus Liturgus;* St. *Clement* his Constitution; St. *Basil*
and St. *Chrysostome* their Liturgies in the Greek Church;
St. *Ambrose* and St. *Augustine* their Hymn of *Te Deum ;*
the Apostles, St. *Athanasius*, and the Fathers in the Council of 𝕹ice, those sacred Confessions of the Christian Faith,
and excellent Compendiums of the holy Gospel, from whence
the Liturgy of the Church of 𝕰ngland was compiled, by
Men famous for the Excellency of their Lives, and the Glory of their Martyrdom ; which Compilers were so cautious
of Offence, that they would not admit any thing in it which
might give Occasion to the inquisitive Presbyter, or the
most industrious Wits of the Roman Party to raise a Doubt,
or scarce a Scruple in a wise Spirit, so that they joyn'd with
us in Devotion about ten or eleven Years after the Decease
of Queen *Mary*, till the temporal Interest of their Church
widen'd the Schism, and then they charged it only with Im-
perfection or Want of something which they thought convenient to be inserted in it; and these Compilers shew'd a
prophetick Spirit, to compose every Word therein at that
time, proper to the present Language used in this Age.
'Tis reported when the Apostles were sent abroad to propo-
gate the Gospel, some of them, or others who lived in the
next succeeding Age, might bring the Christian Religion

hither. Some hold, when *Philip* one of the twelve Apostles came to ﬀrance, where he converted divers Pagans, hearing there of the *Britains*, sent *Joseph* of Arimathea, with *Josephus* his Son, and eleven more of his Disciples hither, who, with great Zeal and undaunted Courage, preached the true and lively Faith of Christ: And when King *Arviragus* consider'd the Difficulties that attended their long and dangerous Journey from the Holy Land, beheld their civil Behaviour and innocent Lives, and observed their Sanctity and the Severities of their Religion, he gave them a certain Island in the West Part of his Dominions for their Habitation, called Abalon, containing twelve Hides of Land, where they built a Church, which was made of wreathen Wands, and set a Place apart for the Burial of their Servants: These holy Men were devoted to a religious Solitude, confined themselves to the Number of twelve, lived there after the Manner of Christ and his Apostles, and by their Preaching converted a great Number of the *Britains*, who became Christians.

Upon this Ground the Ambassadors of the Kings of England, claimed Precedency of the Ambassadors of the Kings of ﬀrance, Spain, and Scotland, in several Councils held in Europe; one at Pisa, *Anno* 1409, another at Constance in the Year 1414, another at Siena, *Anno* 1424, and especially at Basil, *Anno* 1434, where the Point of Precedency was strongly debated, and the Ambassadors from ﬀrance insisting much upon the Dignity and Magnitude of that Kingdom, said, 'Twas not reasonable that England should enjoy equal Priviledges with ﬀrance; but the Ambassadors for England insisting upon the Honour of the Church, declared that the Christian Faith was first received in England, affirming, that *Joseph* of Arimathea came with others, in the 15th Year after the Assumption of the Virgin *Mary*, and converted a great Part of the People to the Faith of Christ, and in short time after the Passion of Pope *Eluthe-rius*, reduced the whole Kingdom entirely to the Faith; but ﬀrance received not the Christian Religion till the time of *Dionisius*, by whose Ministery it was converted, and by Reason thereof, the Kings of this Land ought to have the Right of Precedency, for that they did far transcend all other Kings in Worth and Honour, so much as Christians were more excellent than Pagans.

But to return to these religious Men; when they died, King *Lucius* confirmed the Grant of this Island to *Phagian* and *Diruvian*, and their Successors, who baptized him, his Nobles, and People, at the holy Font; and limited their Company to the same Number, until St. *Patrick* came, and taught them the Order of a monastick Life, and became their first Abbot; after whom *Benignus, Columkilla,* and *Gildas*

Hund. of *Caishoe.*

Conc. Constan *Sess. 30.* *Usher de* *Primo Eccl.* *Brit. p. 22.*

Cressy's Chur. *Hist. of Brit.* *fol. 26.*

Alphonsus *Garsius Advoc* *for the Right* *of Spain.*

Godolph. Abr. *of Eccl. Laws,* *Introd. p. 7.*

Hund. of
Caishae.
lived most religiously here with these Brethren: Then *Da-vid*, Archbishop of 𝔐enebía, now called 𝔖t. 𝔇abíd, came hither, and adjoyned another small Chappel, after the Form of a Chancel, on the East End of the Church, and consecrated it to the Honour of the Virgin *Mary ;* to whose Memory he built an Altar in this Place, and erected a Pyramid without, on the North Side, and a Pair of Stairs within the Pyramid, and the Chappels were divided by a Line or Step, where the holy *Joseph*, and many pious Men are said to lie buried, according to some Antiquaries.

Still. *Antiq.*
of the Bril.
Church, fol. 6,
45.
But others hold, that this Story was a mere Invention of the Monks of 𝔊lassenburp, to advance the Reputation of their Monastery; and that St. *James* the Son of *Zebedee*, another of the Apostles, taught the Christian Religion in 𝔅rítaín, about the time of *Claudius Tiberius Cæsar:* Others Ibid. attribute this great Work to *Simon Zelotes ;* and others affirm, That St. *Paul* came from 𝔖paín to the British Islands, and planted this Religion in the time that the *Romans* govern'd here, and have proved it by several Passages from *Gildas, Eusebius, Theodoret,* St. *Jerome, Clement Romanus,* and others; but be it whomsoever you will that brought it hither, 'tis certain it came from some of the Eastern Churches; for when *Augustine* the Monk came hither, he found a great Number of Christians here, but to his great Ibid. 356,357,
358, 359. Grief, they observed the Usages and Customs of the Eastern Churches.

The religious Men who first brought it hither, resided together with the Bishop in his House, where they lived under his Government after the Manner of Christ and his Apostles, and the People resorting to them, worshipped God with great Zeal and Fervency of Spirit, and the Bishop continually sent them abroad to preach the Gospel to the People; and they lived upon the free Offerings which those Christians sent to the Bishop, from the several Places of their Devotions ; and the Bishop allowed to every Clerk his Dividend out of the same for his Maintenance ; and they were seldom seen abroad by Reason of their continual Residence with the Bishop, which caused the People to flock about a Clergyman whensoever they espied him, and to beg Council of
Antioch, cap.
103, 104.
Syn. Rom.
cap. 5. his Benisons with all Reverence, which he would grant, either by signing them with the Cross, or by recommending them to God in his Prayers; and their great Zeal and religious Deportment, raised in the People the greater Earnestness of Attention when they preached. And after the Number of these religious Men grew too great for the Bishop's Family, Monasteries, so termed from the Greek Word Μὸνος, were erected for their Habitation ; and these were made Schools or Nurseries at the first for these religious Men, before Universities were founded.

But when some Christians that lived remote from them, could not upon all Occasions repair to them by Reason of the Distance of their Habitations, the great and wealthy Men erected Churches, Chapels, and Oratories in the Country Villages, after the Form of Building used in those Days, by publick Contributions of well affected Converts; and they were supplied by such Ministers whom the Evangelical Bishops sent to officiate there; then the Founders of those Oratories provided them Houses for their Habitation, and gave them Offerings for the Provision of their Families.

But when these Priests were driven from their Habitations, because they would not sacrifice to the Roman Gods in the time of *Dioclesian,* their Churches and Oratories were burnt, and the Christians fled to remote and obscure Places to preserve their Lives; at that time a Christian Preacher, called by some *Amphibalus,* flying from Caerleon in Wales to the East of this Island, that he might avoid the Persecution, came to the House of *Alban,* an eminent Citizen of Verolam, who received him there, and observing for some time the strict and holy Life of his Guest, and his continual Perseverance therein, accompanied with a fervent Zeal and hearty Devotion, it made a great Impression upon his Heart, and raised an ardent Desire in him to discourse and know the Reasons of the Severity of his Life, and the Ground of his Religion; thus he gave the Priest Opportunity to make him sensible of the Blindness of Idolatry, and the Danger that attended the Worship of false Gods; then he gladly learnt the Knowledge of the true God, and was convinced that Jesus Christ was the Son of God and the Saviour of the World; by this Means he made *Alban* a true Convert and a perfect Christian.

When the Judge of the City was informed that this Clerk (for so he was then stiled) lodged in *Alban's* House, he sent some Soldiers to conveen him before him, but *Alban* having Notice of it, privately sent him away, and clothing himself in his Habit, personated his Guest, and offered himself to the Soldiers, who bound and brought him to the Pagan Judge, at the time whilst he was sacrificing unto Devils at his Altar; upon his Sight of *Alban,* he was moved with great Rage because he had conveyed his Guest away, and offered himself a Prisoner in his Stead to the Soldiers; therefore commanded to bring him before the Images of the Devils, saying, Because thou hadst rather hide and convey away a Rebel, than deliver him to the Officers, if thou shalt refuse to worship these Gods, thou shalt suffer the same Punishment which he should have done; But the holy *Alban* who had betray'd himself to the Persecutors, being armed with spiritual Warfare, slighted the Threats and Menaces of the Judge, and openly declared he would not obey his

Bede, lib. 1, cap. 1, 7, fol. 31, 32, 33, 34, 35.

Hund. of
Caistor.
Commands; then said the Judge, what is your Family or
Kindred? *Alban* answered, That is nothing to thee from
what Stock I descend; but if thou desirest to know my Religion? I am a Christian, and apply myself to the Profession
of that Religion. The Judge demanding his Name, he answered, My Parents called me *Alban*, and I adore and worship the true and living God, who created all the World.
The Judge moved with Anger, said, If thou wilt enjoy the
Happiness of this present Life, delay not to sacrifice to these
mighty Gods? *Alban* replied, These Sacrifices which you
offer to Devils, can neither help them that sacrifice to them,
nor yet answer the Prayers and Desires of their Supplicants;
but whosoever shall offer Sacrifices to these Images, shall
receive the eternal Pains of Hell for their Reward: These
and the like Words moved the Judge to great Wrath, so
that he commanded the Tormentors to whip the holy Confessor of God, fancying that Stripes might overcome the
Constancy of his Heart, when Words would not prevail;
but he conquer'd their Cruelty by his Patience, and rejoyced that he had the Honour to suffer for the Lord's Sake,
till rather their Weariness than their Pitty made them de-
sist; At length the Judge finding this Punishment would
not prevail, commanded that his Head should be sever'd
from his Body.

Bede, ibid.
Many People going to a Hill called 𝕭olmshurst, the
Place appointed for his Execution, were stop'd at a Bridge
which crost the River, because the Passage being streight
admitted few to go on Breast; so that *Alban* following the
Multitude, could not pass over before the Evening, and
covetous of a Crown of Martyrdom, came to the Stream,
where lifting up his Eyes to Heaven, prayed that the Water
might part, that the Crowd of People might pass through
the River on dry Ground, whereupon, 'tis said, the Water
immediately stop'd, and the Multitude walked over like the
Child renof *Israel* through the River of 𝕵ordan. The sight
of this Miracle made so great an Impression upon the Heart
of the Executioner, that he refused to perform his Office,
choosing rather to die for him, than to offer any Violence
to him; whereupon another was substituted in his Place,
and he condemned to suffer the same Punishment for his
Contempt and Disobedience.

Bede, ibid.
Alban deck'd with divers Flowers, and his Face adorn'd
with a natural Comliness, came to the Top of the Hill, distant about two hundred Paces from the River; and being
thirsty desired some Water, and upon his Prayer my Author
adds, that a Spring of Water immediately gushed out of the
Earth at his Feet, to the Amazement of all that saw it:
Then the Head of the most constant Martyr was parted from
his Body, and he received a Crown of immortal Life on the

20th day of *June*, in the Year 293. At the same Instant, the Eyes of the Executioner drop'd out of the Sockets and fell to the Ground with the Head of the Martyr; soon after, the Convert Executioner appointed to perform this bloody Part upon *Alban*, was executed in the same Manner for refusing to act this Office, after whom *Aaron* and *Julius*, two other Citizens of *Verolam*, suffered Martyrdom with them.

The Citizens of *Verolam* engraved the Martyrdom of *Alban* on a Marble Stone, and inscribed the same upon their Walls, to reproach the Martyrs and terrify the Christians; till such time that the Blood of Martyrs conquered the Cruelty of Tyrants: Afterwards Christianity was restored again, and established by *Constantine* the Great, who was the first Christian Emperor, Son of *Constantius* King of *Britain*, who secured the Christian Religion, and would not suffer any Person to die for it in his Dominions; He deceased, was buried at *York*, and *Constantine* his Son was proclaimed Emperor the sixth Day of *August*, in the Year of Christ 306.

He raised here an Army of forty thousand Foot, and eight thousand Horse, against *Maxentius*, who opposed him at *Rome*, committed the civil Administration of *Britain* to *Pacatianus* Vicar to the Pretorian Prefect of *Gallia*, declared himself a Christian in the Head of his Army, which certainly he would never have done had not Christianity at that time been profest in *Britain*.

He in his March towards *Italy* beat back the Barbarians, who would have passed the *Rhine* to enter into his Territories, won the Affections of all his Subjects, attack'd the Tyrant *Maxentius*, who had exercised his Cruelties at *Rome*, seiz'd upon all the Cities that opposed his Passage, defeated the Troops of *Maxentius* three several times, and meeting him with a great Army near *Rome*, totally routed him, and *Maxentius* was destroyed in his Flight, by the Fall of a Bridge, as he endeavoured to make his Escape over it. *Constantine* told *Eusebius* that in his March he saw in the Heavens a Cross of Light with this Inscription, *Hoc signo vinces, By this Signe you shall overcome your Enemies.* After that Jesus appeared unto him in his Sleep, and commanded him to make a Standard in the Form of a Cross, which he did in Obedience to this Revelation; and after his Victory, he placed his Standards among his Trophies in the Midst of the City of *Rome*, with this Inscription; *By this Salutary Signe, which is the Marke of the true Power, I have delivered your City, from the Yoke of Tyranny, and establish'd your Senate and People in their ancient Splendor.*

After *Constantine* had settled the Affairs of *Rome*, he

VOL. II.   P

Side notes:

Hund. of Caishoe.

Camd. Brit. tit. Herts. fol. 410.

Sam's Antiq. of Brit. fol. 313
Camd. Brit. tit Herts. fol. 41.
Lloyd, Bp. of St Amph's Church Gov. in Brit. p. 49.
Du Pin's Eccl. Hist. vol. 2, fol. 11.

Brady's Hist. of Engl. fol 33

Du Pin's Eccl. Hist. vol. 2, fol. 11.

Ibid. fol. 12.

Hund. of
Caishoe.

celebrated the Nuptials of his Sister with the Emperor
Licinius at **Millan**, then the two Emperors publish'd their
first Edict in Favour of the Christians, by which they
granted Liberty of Conscience to all their Subjects, and at
their going thence, they allowed the Christians by another
Edict, the publick Exercise of their Religion, and commanded those Places should be restored to them, where
they were wont to serve God.

Shortly after a great Breach arose between the two Emperors. War was proclaimed in the Year 314, and they
fought a great Battle at **Panonia,** where the Army of *Licinius* was defeated, after that another in **Thracia**, where
the Advantage proving equal on both Sides, the Emperors
concluded a Peace for that time; but this did not hinder
Constantine from promoting the Affairs of the Christians;
for upon the Complaint of the *Donatists,* he called a Coun-

Brady's Hist.
of Engl. fol.
33.

cil at **Arles** in the Year 314, where *Ebonius,* Bishop of
York, *Restitutus* Bishop of **London,** and *Adelphus* Bishop
Camolodunum or **Maldon,** *Sacerdos* a Priest, and *Armin-
ius* a Deacon were present, and brought thence the Cannons of this Council into **Britain,** that they might be observed here; in which Council 'twas ordain'd that

Du Pin's Eccl.
Hist. vol. 2,
fol. 12.

Masters should manumise their Slaves, that were within
the Church, in the Presence of the Bishop and the People.
The People should observe the Sunday, and no Person be
allowed to travel on that Day, and all Men should be permitted to devise Goods by their Will to the Church. Dur-

Ibid.

ing all this while, *Licinius* Emperor of the East, publish'd
Edicts against the Christians, persecuted them, and demolish'd their Churches ,upon which *Constantine* declared War
against him *Anno* 324, conquer'd him near **Adrianople** and
Chalcedon; then besieged him in **Nicomedia,** whither he retired after his Defeat. *Licinius* unable to maintain the
Siege surrender'd and lay himself at the Feet of *Constantine,* who sent him to **Thessalonica,** where shortly after he
was put to Death under Pretence, that he design'd to stir
up Sedition; then *Constantine* repeal'd all the Edicts that
Licinius had made against the Christians, releas'd those
who had been condemned to the Mines, recall'd them who
had been banish'd, restored those who had been deprived
of their Honours or Estates upon the Account of Religion,

Eusebius.
Spelm. Coun-
cils, p. 37 to
47.
Seld. Hist. of
Tythes, cap 8.
sect. 3, cap. 9,
11, 12.

return'd the Goods of the Martyrs, which had been confis-
cated, to their Heirs, rebuilt the Christian Churches, and
restored their Burial Places to them. Then he demolish'd
the Pagan Idols and Temples, and suppress'd Idolatry
throughout the Roman Empire: After that he erected divers stately Churches for the publick Worship of God in
several Places and by his great Magnificence and pious
Example, other Christian Kings, Princes, Nobles, and Men

of Fair Estates (in his Reign and in succeeding Ages) at their proper Cost and Charges, built convenient Churches, Chapels, and Oratories, as well in all Christian Realms, as in this Island, within their several Lordships, near their Mansion Houses, for the most Part where they with their Families and Tenants might conveniently worship God, receive the Sacrament, and enjoy all publick Ordinances for the better Edification and Salvation of their Souls: Hence three Sorts of Churches were instituted. Hund. of Caishoe. Sam's Antiq. of Brit. fol. 19.

I. Cathedrals, denominated from the Bishop's Chair or See, where the Bishop or Superintendant over the Diocess resided, as the Dean and Chapter do to this Day.

II. Convents or Monasteries, which were derived from the Communities of religious Men and Women in the primitive Church, who lived after the Manner of the Apostles, with the Believers of both Sexes, that they might be the better instructed in the Faith and Duties of Christianity, and enabled to provide for their Poor, live charitably together, and continue to practice all religious Duties: Monasteries were of three kinds.

The first consisted of Clerks and Monks who professed some Order of Religion; shaved their Heads like St. *Paul* at Cencrea, and lived under a Vow. These were the Schools and Universities of those times, wherein Men were qualified for the several Offices in Religion, as the Monastery of Bangor, where *Bede* tells us, above two thousand Persons resided together in seven Colledges; of which none had less than three hundred Monks: and *William* of Malmsbury who writ about 400 Years after *Bede*, seems to confirm it, where he saith, We see so many half ruin'd Walls, so many Windings of Porticos, so great an Heap of Ruins, as you shall scarce meet with else-where. Guil. Malmsb. lib. 1, in Angl. p. 9, l. 3.

Another Sort consisted of Men and Women, who lived like the religious Women that followed and accompanied the blessed Apostles in one Society, and travelled together for the Advantage of their Improvement in an holy Life; from those Women these Monasteries were deriv'd, and govern'd only by devout Women, so ordain'd by the Founders, in respect of the great Honour they had for the Virgin *Mary*, whom *Jesus* upon the Cross recommended to St. *John* the Evangelist: These Governesses had as well Monks as Nuns in their Monasteries, and Jurisdictions over both Men and Women, and those Men who improved themselves in Learning, and the Abbess thought qualify'd for Orders, she recommended to the Bishop, who ordained them, yet they remained still under her Government, and officiated as Chaplains, until she pleased to send them forth upon the Work of the Ministry. *Ebba* Abbess of Cloudesburgh, St. *Bridget* Abbess of Kildare in Ireland, the Abbess of Re- Lloyd's Chur. Gov. p. 170. Bede's Hist. 4, 25. War. Descript Hibern. 1, 2.

P 2

Hund. of
Caishoe.

Bede, 4, 23,
P. 320, 322,
3, 25.
pandun in England, and others, had several Monks under
their Charge; particularly *Hilda*, great Grandchild to King
Edwine Abbess of Streanshalchnow Whitby, famous for her
Learning, Piety, and excellent Government in the time of
the *Saxons*; when *Bede* said, She held her Subjects so
strictly to the reading of the Scripture and the Performance
of the Works of Righteousness, that many of them were fit
to be Churchmen, and to serve at the Altar; so that afterwards, saith he, we saw five Bishops who came out of her
Monastery, and *Tatfrith* a sixth was elected, but died before
he could be ordained. She was a profest Adversary to all
the Rights of Rome, especially clerical Censure: And we
read, she appear'd with her Clergy in the Synod held at her
Monastery *Anno* 664, for the deciding of that great Controversie about the right time of holding *Easter*, and maintain'd the Argument on the Part of *Coleman*, a *Scotchman*,
Bishop of Holyhead, who held the Quartodeciman Way,
according to the Asian Tradition on the Behalf of the *Scotch*,
Bede, cap. 4,
25.
Sam's *Antiq.*
of *Brit.* fol.
541.
against *Wilfride* an *Englishman*, who maintained the Custom of the Romish Church in the Behalf of the *English*;
and 'tis reported the like Government is continued at this
Day in the Abby of Fountrault, scituated three Leagues
from Saumur in France, near the Confines of Tourain, where
the Monks are obliged by solemn Vow of Obedience to the
Nuns, make Profession between the Hands of the Lady Abbess, and are very observant to her Commands in all things:
The Novices declaim, dispute, and perform all publick Exercises before her and the Nuns, in a very great Hall, divided in the Middle by a curious guilded Iron Grate, the
one Half assign'd to the Nuns, the other to the Fathers who
maintain the Disputations: 'Tis said that most of those
Nuns very well understand both Latin and Philosophy; and
my Author likewise adds, that he heard some of them dispute very prettily upon some metaphisical Points; and that
they had conceived a Design of establishing the Study of
the liberal Arts amongst themselves, declaring they would
give the World a sensible Demonstration, that it is a great
Piece of Injustice done to their Sex not to suffer them to
study, that they may keep them the more in Subjection
and Ignorance. Among the Abbesses of this Monastery,
fifteen have been Princesses, whereof five of the House
of Burbon; for their Habit they are cloathed in White,
and wear a black Veil over it, and in the Quire a great
black Cloke or Mantle. The Monks wear a black Cassock
and a Hood, and in the Church they put on a black Cloke
or Mantle. This Order contains about threescore Abbies
of Nuns, all whom own Fontrault for their Mother, and
depend on it. The Abbess is General of the Order, visits
those Monasteries, sends them Directors and Confessors,

and recalls them at her Pleasure. Though I do not prefer, *Hund. of Caishoe.*
yet it does not become any Person to contemn the Government of this Sex, nor my Author to redicule that of this
Monastery, when God constituted *Deborah*, the Wife of
Lapidoth, a Judge over Israel, *Huldah* the Wife of *Shallum*, a Prophetess to King *Josiah Hilkiah* the High Priest, *Judges iv. 4. 2 Kings xxii. 14.*
and their other Officers; delivered the *Jews* by the Hand of
Jael and *Judith*, and ordained Women, Governesses, not
only over Men in private Families, but also constituted them
Sovereign Queens over the People in many Kingdoms: *Eudochia* and *Theodora* govern'd the Roman Empire; *Semiramis*, Scythia; the Queen of Sheba, Arabia Fælix; *Boaditia*, the Icænians; *Richard* I. and *Henry* V. constituted
their Mothers Regents of this Realm, whilst they remain'd
in France; Queen *Mary* and *Elizabeth* held this Crown
during their Lives; and five Abbesses made Laws and signed the Acts of Counsel in the great Counsel at Berancelb
in Kent.

A third Sort consisted of religious Women, govern'd by
an Abbess or Prioress, according to the Constitution of their
Order: These were excellent Nurseries for the Education
of young Virgins in the Practice of Piety, and all other necessary Accomplishments fit for Gentlewomen, as working,
singing by Notes, dancing, and playing upon Instruments
of Musick; this Form of Government much resembled that
used now in Colledges in our Universities, where the Abbess
or Prioress, represented the Master, the Nuns, the Fellows;
the Novices and Boarders, the Scholars and Pensioners;
and these holy Virgins were totally freed from the Cares of
this World, accommodated with all the Helps convenient
for a religious Life, and attended with all Officers and Servants necessary for their Society; but in those Days no Religious were restrained by Vows from Matrimony, for the
Apostle declared, *That Marriage was honourable in all*, *Heb. xiii. 4.*
and gave an hard Character on that Doctrine that forbad it, *1 Tim iv. 3.*
because God and Nature had created Desires in them for
the Pleasures of a nuptial Life, establishing thereby the Continuance of Mankind to the End of the World; and since
that time divers of the holy Apostles and devout Men of
the primitive times, and several Bishops, Priests, Deacons,
and other religious Persons of both Sexes in after Ages,
changed the Condition of their Lives when they could contain no longer, and followed the Advice of the Apostle *rather to marry than burn:* Neither were any of these religious bound by Vows of Inclosure from their natural Liberty, *1 Cor. vii. 9.*
which God granted and ordained for their Health and the
Pleasure of their Lives; for they did not think to merit thereby at God's Hands, yet kept their Chastity inviolate; and *Spotsw. of the Church of Scotl. fol. 12.*
the Boudage of Vowes with the Opinion of Merit and Per-

fection were things unknown to the holy Women of those
primitive times, till the Votarists of these later Ages transported with such Delusions, confined themselves (like Birds
in Cages) to melancholly Cells, where, instead of serving
God with merry and cheerful Hearts, as becomes all good
Christians, some of these poor Souls have been most grievi-
ously afflicted and tormented with the sad and dismal
Thoughts of their Confinement, because it excluded them
from the Enjoyment of their choicest Friends, and they were
buried there alive, without the least Hopes of seeing them
again, but must be forgotten of them for evermore; which
often moves them to curse the Parents or Persons that decoyed them thither with fair Speeches to save their Portions,
or to gain their Fortunes to themselves, and forced them to
make that unreasonable Vow, which can never be reversed,
but has often given great Occasion of Sin, for 'tis natural
for all young People, especially those who are confin'd, to
desire Liberty, and I could give sad Instances, where young
Virgins have severely repented the taking of these Vows,
and have been immured between two Walls, for attempting their Escape from their Cloisters.

Seld. Hist. of
Tythes, cap.6,
sect. 3.
Prin's Plea
for Advow.
p. 9.
Doddridge of
Advow. p 5.
Du Pin's
Church Hist.
vol. 2, fol. 13.

III. Parochial Churches, which were erected in Villages,
for the reading divine Service, administring the Sacrament,
and performing the holy Ordinances to the People, dwelling
within a certain Piece of Ground, near adjacent to it.

When Churches were thus erected, *Constantine* endeavoured to quiet all Sects and Schismes in the Church; to
that Purpose he summon'd a General Council consisting of
the Eastern and Western Bishops called from all Parts of
the Roman Empire in the City of 𝕹𝖎𝖈𝖊 in 𝕭𝖎𝖙𝖍𝖎𝖓𝖎𝖆, about

Ibid. fol. 450.

the Month of *July*, in the Year 325, where divers Canons
and the Nicene Creed were made, the Council happily ended the 25th of *August* following, when *Constantine* gave
the Bishops a noble Entertainment, exhorting them to Unity,
and sent them loaded home with Presents: and notwith-

Ibid. fol. 13.

standing the great Care he took of the Christian Affair, I
have read that he deferr'd his Baptisme to the time of his
Death, as some think because that Sacrament might thoroughly expiate his Sins, that he might so appear innocent
before God, and when he fell sick, he had the Imposition of
the Bishop's Hands to make him a Catechumen, and *Eusebius* baptized him at 𝕳𝖊𝖑𝖊𝖓𝖔𝖕𝖎𝖑𝖎𝖘, a little before his Death,
which was in the Year 337.

Brady's Hist.
of Engl. fol.
34.

This *Constantine* assign'd over the Government of
𝕱𝖗𝖆𝖓𝖈𝖊, 𝕾𝖕𝖆𝖎𝖓, and 𝕭𝖗𝖎𝖙𝖆𝖎𝖓, to *Constantine* his eldest Son,
who enjoyed it three Years, then was murder'd by the Contrivance of his Brother *Constans*, who usurped this Part of
the Empire, but before he was fully possest hereof, *Maxentius* destroyed him, and seized the greatest Part of the Em-

pire; whereupon his Brother *Constantius* invaded him, routed him from Place to Place, till deserted by all, he slew himself.

Constantius thus obtaining the Government of Britain, deputed *Martinus* under the Pretorian Prefect, whose Fortune it was to be slain; he favoured the Arian Heresie, which made a great Disturbance in Britain, and called four hundred Bishops of the Western Church, whereof three came from Britain to Arminum to maintain the wicked Opinions of the Arians, but the British Bishops being very poor and necessitous, accepted the Allowance of Diet from the Emperor which the other refused; he died of a Fever in *October*, 362 and made *Julian* his Successor by his Will; after him *Jovian* succeeded, both whose reigns were short. Then *Valantinian* was chosen Emperor, and about *Anno* 364, (which was in his time) the *Picts* and *Scots*, with the *Francs* and *Saxons*, invaded Britain, killed *Nectaridius* the Admiral of the Sea Coast, and surprized *Buchobaudes* the General of the Land Forces by a Stratagem; harassed, destroyed, and ruined almost all Britain with Fire and Sword; he sent *Theodosius* a Man of known Valour and Experience, with an Army of stout young Men to relieve therewith Britain, where he divided his Army into several Bodies, and took the Enemy as they roved up and down in Parties to pillage and plunder; recover'd from them the Prisoners and Spoil which they had taken, and restored it to the right Owner; but the *Huns*, *Goths*, *Vandals*, and other barbarous People invaded the Empire, and most of the Soldiers being transported out of *Britain* for the Defence of Rome, the *Scots* and *Picts* took that Advantage to spoil and wast this Country again; but the Roman Empire unable to afford the *Britains* any further Assistance, they by Degrees laid aside their Laws, and fell from them, took Arms and used all the proper Ways they could imagine to free and deliver themselves from the Danger of their barbarous Neighbours; and during this great Distraction and Confusion, *Agricola* a Disciple to *Pelagius* a Monk of Bangor in Flintshire, set up here the Pelagian Heresie, and the sounder Part of the Christians disliking his Opinion, but not able to confute him, beg'd Assistance from the Churches in France, who sent *German* Bishop of Auxerre, and *Lupas* Bishop of Troyes; they, by their assiduous preaching in Churches, Fields, and Streets, confirmed many in the Faith, and regained others: Shortly after a Sinod or Council was held in this City of Verolam, *Anno* 429, which was then famous for Religion, where these Bishops confuted the chiefest of the Hereticks in a publick Disputation, which almost extinguish'd that Heresie, and gaining thereby a great Reputation among the *Britains* to themselves, especially *German*, to whose Memory many

Camd. Brit.
tit. Herts. fol.
410.

Hund. of Caisboe. Churches in this Island have since been dedicated, among which a Chapel here lately bore his Name, where he usually preached in publick, and it remained near the ruin'd Walls of this decayed City, till of late Days, when it was converted into a Barn, and put to prophane Use: This *German* commanded the Sepulchre of St. *Alban* to be opened, and deposited in it several Reliques of Saints, that whom one Heaven had received should be lodged in one Sepulchre together.

Not long after the *English Saxons* won this City, and termed it 𝔚atlingcester from the famous Road called 𝔚atlingstreet, which passeth through it, yet it did not totally lose its old Name, for when *Uthur*, the *Britain* sirnamed *Pendagron* for his serpentine Wisdom, recovered it again by a long and sore Siege, about the Year 498; it was then called 𝔙erlamcester; He reigned 18 Years, and upon his Death the *Saxons* obtained the Possession of it again.

Cave's Church Gov. p. 2511. Pope *Gregory* sent *Augustine* the Monk, in the Year 596, to convert the Pagans here, where he found a considerable Church among the *Britains*, which had seven Bishops, who had seven Churches, one at 𝔥ereford, another at 𝔗abansis or 𝔏andaff, another at 𝔏hanpavan-𝔙aux, another at 𝔅angor, another at 𝔈lbiensis, or 𝔖t. 𝔄saph, another at 𝔚orcester 𝔐organensis, supposed by *Hovedon* to be 𝔠hester, but by Archbishop *Usher* to be 𝔠aer 𝔠uby or 𝔥olyhead in the Isle of 𝔄nglesy, all which were under the Superintendancy of a Metropolitan, whose Archiepiscopal See had been formerly at 𝔠arleon upon 𝔘ske in 𝔐onmouthshire, but some Years before the Arrival of *Augustine* had been translated to 𝔐enevia; and besides the Episcopal Sees the *Britains* had at that time Colledges, or Semenaries, and great Numbers of Christian Monks in them, especially at 𝔅angor, as I have shewed before. He converted *Ethelbert* King of 𝔎ent, and the greatest Part of his People to the Faith, whom he baptized in the Church of St *Martin* at 𝔠anterbury, on the Day of *Pentecost* in the Year 597, then he went to 𝔄rles where *Etherius*, Archbishop of that City, by the Command of *Gregory*, ordained him the Archbishop of the *English*; upon his Return to 𝔈ngland the King and People received him with all Imaginable Joy and Solemnity suitable to his Quality: The King gave him the Royal City of 𝔠anterbury for an Episcopal See, and his Pallace for a Cathedral Church to be dedicated to Christ: Then he consulted with *Gregory* by Messengers, and Questions, what form of Government he should impose on the Church, which he had lately established among the *English Saxons*; *Gregory* advised him to act in the Church according as St. *Paul* directed *Timothy* in his Epistle, where he endeavoured to teach him how to behave himself in the House of God: order'd how he should di-

Hund. of
Caishoe.

vide every thing that came to the Altar, declaring that the
Clergy ought to possess nothing apart from the Rest of the
Church, which by God's Grace is lately brought to the
Faith, but to imitate the Conversion used by the Fathers
in the Beginning of the Church, when no Man owned
any thing which he possest, but all things were in
common among them; that secondly, If any of the Clergy
could not contain, he ought to marry; and that thirdly,
He should carefully choose whatsoever Custome of Mass or
Service he could find in the Roman, Gallick or any other
Church most pleasing to God, and introduce into the
English Church whatsoever he could collect from any
Churches of honest Institution, for things were not to
be loved for the Places, but the Places for the good things
in them, therefore he should choose whatsoever was pious,
religious and right out of every Church, and infuse them
by Practice into the Minds of the English; the rest
are Trifles and therefore I omit them, then *Gregory* gave
him the Honour of a Pall, which signified the Fulness of
Power, in the Year of Christ, 601, but this did not make
him an Archbishop, for Sir *H. Spelman*, saith that the Title of Archbishop was never given by *Gregory* to *Agus-
tine*, for it is scarce so old in the Western Church; but
Isidore the Disciple of *Gregory*, and one that understood
the Language of that Age very Well, saith *Augustine*
could not properly call his Successors, Archbishops, for
that Title belonged only to them who had Power over
Metropolitans as well as other Bishops, and *Mabilon* and
others observe, that it was not commonly used for a Metropolitan before the ninth Age.

Spelm Coun.
p. 124.
Mabil. l. 2,
cap. 2, n. 13.

Augustine called a Council at **Ac** or **Oak** in **Worcester-
shire**, that he might be near the British Bishops and Clergy
then residing in **Wales**, whom he summon'd thither; when
he demanded from them Obedience to the Bishop of **Rome**,
and the Reception of the Roman Ceremonies into the
British Church; the *Britains* stifly opposed it, for that
they could not lay aside their ancient Customs, without the
Consent and free Leave of their whole Nation, and thereupon desired that another Synod might be called, because
their Number was small. This agreed, seven British
Bishops, and many learned Men, went thither from their
famous Monastery, called **Bancornaburg**, over which Abbot
Dinoth presided, in their Way an holy and wise Man, who
lived like an Anchorite, advised them that if *Augustine*
should rise up to them when they came near him, he
was the Servant of God, and they ought to hear him; but
if he should sit still, and shew no Respect when they were
more in Number, then he is proud, and comes not from
God, and in such a Case ought not to be regarded.

Hund. of
Catshoe.

They appeared before *Augustine*, and observing he sat still in his Chair without shewing any Courtesie or Respect to them, they were very angry, and discoursing among themselves, said, If he will not now rise up unto us, how much more will he contemn us when we are subject to him. Then *Augustine*, renewing the old Controversie, exhorted them earnestly to embrace the Rites and Usages of the Church of 𝕽𝖔𝖒𝖊; but they were so fixed to their own Traditions and Customs, that they would not exchange them without the Leave and License of their own Church; and Abbot *Dinoth* plainly told him, they owed no more to him whom they called Pope of 𝕽𝖔𝖒𝖊, and would be stiled Father of Fathers, than Obedience of Love and brotherly Assistance, which was due to every Godly Christian; for they were under the Government of the Bishop of 𝕮𝖆𝖊𝖗𝖑𝖊𝖔𝖓 upon 𝖀𝖘𝖐𝖊, who under God was to oversee and guide them; and that they could no more change the Rites and Usages of their Church without his Leave, than *Augustine* could alter the Customs of the Romish Church without the License of his Bishop. Then *Augustine* desired their Conformity only in three things, 1 In the Observation of *Easter*. 2 In the Administration of Baptism. 3 In their Assistance by Preaching to the *English Saxons*. But when he could not obtain their Compliance with him in these things, he threatned them, that if they would not accept Peace with his Brethren, they should receive War from their Enemies, and because they would not preach the Way of Life to the English People they should suffer by their Hands the Punishment of Death.

Sam's Antiq.
of Brit. fol.
512.

But *Augustine* behaved himself very uncharitably towards the poor *Britains*, when he depriv'd them suddenly of the old Customs and Ceremonies of their Church, and imposed new upon them, contrary to the Directions of his great Master *Gregory*, who advised him to proceed with more Moderation in the Affairs of the Church, for there were different Customs in several Churches, and he ought not to impose the Roman Rites themselves every where, but wisely to consider the Custom of the Place, the Circumstance of Time, and the Constitution of Believers; for he said, things were not to be valued for the Sake of the Place, but the Places for the good things in them: However, *Augustine* depriv'd the Archbishop of 𝕮𝖆𝖊𝖗𝖑𝖊𝖔𝖓, and the other British Bishops of their several Provinces, which they and their Predecessors had enjoy'd from the time of King *Lucius*, almost 400 Years, without Crime or the Sentence of the Synod; and procured *Edilfrid*, King of the Northumbrians, and other Saxon Princes, to raise a great Army against tne innocent Christians, and expos'd their naked Priests, standing apart on a Place of Advantage, because they came thither to pray for the Success of their Hand. of Caisbor. Army, slew 1200 of them, and routed their whole Army. But observe the Justice of God: when this bloody King was hastning home in Triumph, to destroy the Remains of this famous Monastery, three British Princes, the Revengers of God's Wrath, routed the Northumbrian King with his whole Army, reeking in the Blood of those poor Innocents, killed ten thousand and threescore of them, and put the wounded King with some others to Flight; from whence 'tis manifest, that the British Church at that time acknowledged no Subjection, either to the Roman Bishop or any other foreign Patriarch; neither had it Communion with the Roman Church, but was subject from the Days of *Eleutherius* to a Metropolitan of its own, the Archbishop of 𝕮𝖆𝖊𝖗𝖑𝖊𝖔𝖓, who, as 'tis reported, acknowledged no Superior in Dignity, but under God governed the Church and People committed to his Charge without any other Sharer in his Authority; and they received their Customs from the Eastern and Asiatick Churches.

This *Augustine*, saith *Copgrave*, was very tall by Stature, his Face lovely, but withal majestical: The Wonders and Cures he perform'd among the People, 'tis said, were many: He always walked on Foot, and most commonly visited his Provinces barefooted; and the Skin on his Knees was grown hard and insensible, through continual kneeling. 'Tis rerorted that he was a learned, pious Man, an Imitator of primitive Holiness, frequent in Watchings, Fastings, Prayers, and Alms; zealous in propagating the Church of his Age, and of the Roman Religion; earnest in rooting out Paganism; diligent in repairing and building Churches; extraordinary famous for working Miracles, and from hence perhaps his Mind might be puft up through human Frailty, with the Greatness of his Miracles, which caused St. *Gregory* to admonish him for it. He was the first Introducer of Roman Monks and other Rites and Ceremonies: but is much censur'd for the Massacre of the Priests of 𝕭𝖆𝖓𝖌𝖔𝖗, and not without Cause, if it was true, as 'tis reported, that he excited King *Edilfrid* to that horrid Slaughter; but now I shall return to the City of 𝖁𝖊𝖗𝖔𝖑𝖆𝖒, which was govern'd by *Offa* King of the *Mercians*, in the Year of Christ 796, in whose Reign *Humbert* Archbishop of 𝕷𝖎𝖙𝖈𝖍𝖋𝖎𝖊𝖑𝖉, lately made the Metropolitan See, and *Unwora* Bishop of 𝕯𝖔𝖗𝖈𝖍𝖊𝖘𝖙𝖊𝖗, holy and wise Men, and the chief of the King's Matt. Paris de Vita Offa, 2, fol. 23. Council, advised him to marry *Ælfleda* his third Daughter, to Prince *Albert* King of the *East Angles*, a Prince of great Learning, very charitable, delighted in good Works, wise in Council, merciful in Judgment, and sober in Speech, whom the Poet thus describes.

> Albertus *Juvenis fuerat Rex, Fortis ad Arma,*
> *Pace Pius, Pulcher Corpore, Mente Sagax.*

Hund. of
Catsboc.

These Qualifications encouraged *Offa* to propose the Match, the King valued the Offer as a great Honour, which incited him to make his Address at *Offa's* Court, where he found a noble Reception; but Queen *Drida* fell with Anger, and full of Wrath, grieving that the Prince should be so acceptable to the King and his People; and inraged that her wicked Arguments could not prevail to send this Daughter beyond the Seas, to be disposed of at her Pleasure: She curs'd the Bishops who were the Authors of it, and vented her poison'd Malice against King *Albert*.

Offa, ignorant of these things, never suspecting her Malice, verily believed, she was well pleased with it, till such time that the King advising with her, how and when these things shall be accomplisht? She unexpectedly answered; Behold God hath this Day delivered thy Enemy into thy Hand, if thou be wise, to be murdered, who conceals his Treason against thee, (as 'tis reported) desiring whilst he is young and eloquent, to supplant thee, now an old Man, of thy Kingdom; and moreover to vindicate the Wrong which he and many others have suffered, (as he boasts) whose Kingdom and Possessions thou hast unjustly spoiled; with more Words to the same Effect.

This much disturbed the King in his Mind, but he giving no Credit to her, with great Indignation answered; Thou speakest like one of the foolish Women; Be gon from me, be gon; I abhor so villanous an Act, which done, would be a Blot to me and my Successors for ever, and the Sin would return upon my Family with great Revenge; with these Words the angry King left her, detesting such great Wickedness in a Woman.

But when his troubled Thoughts were somewhat allayed, and these things concealed, both the Kings sat down at Table to Dinner, where they eat and drank together with Pleasure: and when their Appetites were satisfied, they rejoyc'd all Day with great Mirth, in Timbrels, Drums, Harps, Songs, and Dances.

Whilst the malicious Queen retaining her wicked Purposes in her Mind, commanded a Chamber to be richly furnisht with Tapestry and Silk Hangings, after a princely Manner, wherein King *Albert* might take his Repose at Night; and caused the King's Couch to be prepar'd, garnish'd with most noble Trimming, beset on every Side with Curtains, directing withal a deep Ditch to be made under the Chamber to effect her wicked Purposes.

But the Queen dissembling her villanous Design, with a serene Countenance, enter'd the Palace, that she might make as well King *Offa* as King *Albert* merry, and joking with him whilst he suspected no Ill, said, Son, I am come with an earnest Expectation to see my Daughter married to thee in my Chamber, that your future Loves may be renew'd with most pleasing Discourses; and under this Disguise, she invited King *Albert*, who, poor Prince, not dreaming of any ill Contrivance against him, immediately arose, and followed the Queen to her Chamber, whilst King *Offa* staid behind, not mistrusting the least Mischief: King *Albert* being gone with the Queen, all the Soldiers who follow'd at their Heels were shut out; and when he expected the young Princess, the Queen said, She's called, sit down my Son till she comes; and when he had sat sometime in a memorable Seat, set forth with delicate Furniture, longing for the delightsome Company of the Princess, the innocent King drop'd suddenly through a Trap-door into a deep Ditch made under the Chamber, where he was strangled by the Executioner, whom the Queen had hid there, and she and her wicked Instruments immediately smother'd him with the Boulsters, Cloaths, and Curtains, so that none could hear him cry: Thus this elegant young King and Martyr *Albert* was innocently destroyed without Offence, and immediately received a Crown of Glory.

When the most beautiful *Ælfled* heard these things, she abhorred the Villany and detestable Wickedness of her Mother, bewailed the Loss of the unfortunate King, and slighting all the Pomp and Vanity of this World, took upon her a religious Habit, that she might follow the Steps of her Martyr: Whilst the Queen, glorying in her Cruelty, caused the Head of Prince *Albert* to be sever'd from his Body, because it seemed that he breathed, and the Body was ignobly buried by the Executioner.

After this wicked Act was known to the Soldiers of the blessed King and Martyr, they feared the like Fate would fall upon themselves, but the Queen counterfeiting a great Passion of Grief, threw herself upon her Bed, feigning she was sick at Heart, confin'd herself to her Chamber. When King *Offa* learnt the Truth hereof, his Heart was overcome with Grief, and he lamenting the villanous Act with a vehement Passion, shut himself up in his inner Chamber, refusing Meat and Drink almost for three Days, drowning his Soul in Tears, afflicting his Heart with Lamentations and Fasting, and cursing the Wickedness of his Wife; banisht her from his Bed, and inclosed her in a private Place, where she might bewail her Sins all the Days of her Life; And when she had lived some Years in the Place assign'd for her Confinement, she was rob'd of all her Silver and Gold, and drown'd in a deep Well; in the mean While *Humbert*, Archbishop of 𝔏𝔦𝔱𝔠𝔥𝔣𝔦𝔢𝔩𝔡, solemnly buried the Body of King *Albert* at his Church of 𝔏𝔦𝔱𝔠𝔥𝔣𝔦𝔢𝔩𝔡, where all the Deacons and Clerks performed his Obsequies.

But when King *Offa* had received some Comfort from all the holy Bishops, who were well satisfied in his Innocence

touching this Murther; he under Pretence that he was the
next Heir, wisely consolidated the Kingdom of the *East
Angles* to his own.

But whilst he was thus busied with careful Thoughts, how
he might expiate the the treacherous and base Murther of
King *Albert*, he thought as he slept one Night upon his
Couch, in the City of Bath, that an Angel appear'd to him
from Heaven, and admonish'd him that he should search
for *Alban*, the holy Saint of God, and the Protomartyr of
the *English* and *Britains*, and should lay up his Reliques
in a Chest: And studying how he might perform this divine
Command, he imparted it to *Ceolwolfe* and *Unwan*, his
Suffragan Bishops, who explain'd the same unto him; then
the Archbishop taking the Suffragan Bishops, and a great
Number of People with him, met the King on the Day
appointed at Verolam, where he beheld the Beams of a
Light to shine after the Manner of a great Torch, darting
from Heaven upon the Place of his Sepulchre; which
Miracle all the People beholding, rejoyced, and were fully
satisfied with the Truth of the Vision; then King *Offa*
caused the Reliques of this holy Man to be taken up in the
Month of *August*, 793, and put in a Shrine adorned with
Gold and precious Stones: and in the same Month he held
a Parliamentary Counsel at Verolam, where Archbishop
Humbert, his Suffragans, and all his chief Governours of
Cities, diligently and effectually treated together of select-
ing a Convent of Monks, building a Monastery, and endowing it with great and royal Priviledges, in the Place where
he found the Reliques of this Protomartyr, which he consecrated with his own Blood; and relying upon the wholsome Advice of his great Lords, presently took a painful
and costly Journey to Rome, where *Adrian* the Bishop understanding the Reason of his coming thither, received this
penitent Prince with the like Compassion and Joy as the
Father did the Prodigal.

But others hold, that *Matthew Paris*, and the other
Monks of St. Albans, invented these fabulous Stories to
blind the World, and induce the People of future Ages to
believe the Innocency of this wicked King, because he was
their Founder, and by such Artifices they were wont to encrease their Benefactions, and the Revenue of their Church,
when 'tis evident by divers Circumstances, that King *Offa*
decoyed him into his Dominions, under the specious Pretence of marrying his Daughter to him, that he might take
off his Head and seize the Kingdom of the *East Angles*,
which he claimed as his Right by Inheritance; and to expiate this foul Murther he went to Rome, where he humbly
implored that Bishop's Pardon.

When *Offa* had confest all his Sins, and manifested his

Penitency to the World; his Holiness imposed this Penance upon him, that the blessed *Albert* should be canonized for a Saint at his Charge, and that he should build the Cathedral at Hereford, and dedicate it to him; and moreover that he should forthwith erect a fair Monastery to the Memory of the blessed *Alban*, in the Place where he suffered Martyrdom; this done, he gave him Absolution, dismist him with his Benediction: And the King returning safe to England, he called another parliamentary Counsel at this City of Verolam, by the Advice of his Bishops and Nobles, and the unanimous Consent and Goodwill of his People, and proceeded to the building of the Monastery, which he dedicated to St. *Alban*, and gave large Revenues to it, that great Hospitality might be kept there, because the Highway called Watling-street lay near, through which Men continually travelled to and from London to the North and back again; and he accounting it a pious thing to erect a House where Travellers might be freely entertained, built one near the Monastery, which he honoured with divers Priviledges and Immunities; and confirm'd the famous Alms called *Peter-Pence*, toward the maintaining of a Saxon School at Rome, which was a Penny of every House or Family, payable yearly at the Feast of St. *Peter ad Vincula*, which is the first of *August*.

About the Year 792, *Charles* the Great, King of France, sent the Decrees of the second Counsel of Nice, which he imposed upon the *English Saxons*, which contain many things, which *Hovedon* says, were inconvenient, nay quite contrary to the true Faith, especially the worshipping of Images, which the Church of God doth absolutely hate. Against which Book *Albinus* wrote an Epistle, excellently well strengthened with the Authority of the holy Scripture, and presented it with the Book in the Name of the Princes and Bishops of this Land unto the said *Charles* King of France.

Afterwards this City of Verolam was sackt and destroy'd by the continual Wars which happened among the *Saxons* in the time of the Heptarchy, who were ambitious to enlarge their Dominions out of the neighbouring Territories, and the Depredations made here; and King *Ethelwolph*, his Nobility and Clergy, apprehending that these Calamities and Miseries were inflicted upon them for their Sins, considered what Atonement they might make to pacify the Wrath of God, whereupon the King call'd another great Council or Parliament at Winchester in the Year 855, where King *Ethelwolph* granted the Tythe of the Profits of all Lands free from all Burthens, Taxes, and Exactions whatsoever to the Church, which Grant was past by the Consent of that Council, and signed by *Beorred* King of Mercia, and

Hund. of Caishoe.

Matt. Paris de Vita Offæ, 2, fol. 29, 30.

Prin's Collect. of Parl. pt. 1, p. 7; Spelm. Coun. 314.

Sam's Brit. Antiq. fol. 558. Brady's Hist. of Engl. fol. 109.

Hundred *Caishoe.*

Brady's Hist. *fol 112.*

Edmund King of the *East Angles*, both then Subjects and Tributaries to *Ethelwolph*, and all the Archbishops, Bishops, and secular States of 𝕰ngland; which being done, King *Ethelwolph* offer'd it upon the Altar of St. *Peter* the Apostle in the Cathedral Church of 𝖂inchester, and the Bishops caused it to be publish'd in every Church of their several Dioceses or Parishes. This is the first publick Act that (I find) imposed the Payment of Tythes; but doubtless they were paid before this Grant by some Persons in divers Places,

Sam's Brit. *Antiq fol. 569* *570, 576.*

for a Law was made by King *Ina*, who began his Reign, *Anno* 689, that the Portion or Dues of the Church shall be paid by the Feast of St. *Martin*, and he that shall not pay them by that time, shall be punish'd 40*s*. and moreover shall pay the Dues twelve times over; and by the same King, another Law was made, that every one shall pay his Church Dues at that Place where he resided in the Midst of Winter.

ST. ALBANS.

Camd. Brit. *tit. Herts. fol.* *401.*

WHEN 𝖁erulam was almost destroyed by the Wars of the *Saxons*, *Offa* the most mighty King of the *Mercians*, *An. Christi*, 793 and 38 *Regni sui*, built on the other Side of the River on a Hill over against it, in a Place called 𝕳olmehurst, where the Remains of St. *Alban's* Bones were said to be found, a goodly and large Monastery to the Memory of that Saint; and in this Church he laid those Bones under a Marble Stone, with an Inscription upon it to this Effect.

MS. ex Bibl. *Rob. Cotton,* *Milit.* *Weav. Fun.* *Mon. fol. 554.*

Here lyeth interred the Body of St. Alban, *a Citizen of old* 𝖁erulam, *of whom this Town took Denomination, and from the Ruins of which City this Town did arise; He was the first Martyr of* England, *and suffered his Martyrdom the 17th. day of* June, *in the year of Man's Redemption* 293.

Inspex. 3 H. *VIII.* *Mon. Angl.* *vol.1, fol. 177.*

This King studying how to enrich this Monastery with fair Possessions for the Maintenance of an hundred black Monks, called a parliamentary Council at 𝕮elcyth, *Anno* 793, 33 *Regni sui*, and in the Presence, and by the Advice and Consent of King *Ceolyolf*, *Egfrid* Son of *Offa*, King *Cenyolf*, King *Beornulf*, King *Ludec*, King *Yilaf*, King *Egbright*, King *Beortulf*, King *Bukred*, and King *Alfred*; also *Higberd*, and *Ayleheard*, Archbishops; and *Keolyolf*, *Vayonan*, *Ceolumudyng*, *Ealheard*, *Delfhum*, *Heaberch*, *Keneaherd*, *Headored*, *Benefer*, *Keneyalh*, *Yarumud*, *Yilhum*, and *Imberd*, Bishops; also Duke *Brordan*, Duke *Duma*, Duke *Erne*, Duke *Yicga*, Duke *Ayemud*, Duke *Euberch*, Duke *Harberch*, Duke *Ceolyard*, and Duke *Ceolmund* gave to the Lord Jesus Christ, and to St. *Alban* the Martyr, thirty-four Mansions at 𝕽ageshoo, six Mansions at 𝕳enhamsted, and ten Mansions at 𝕾tanemere, with the Corn Fields, Meadows, Feedings, Woods, and all things belonging to those Places, in Hope of present Prosperity and future Happiness; and by the great Name of Almighty God, and his terrible Judgment, he adjured, that no King, Bishop, or other Person should hereafter dare to change, take away, or diminish any of these Gifts, which he had dedicated to God and his holy Martyr, nor presumeto molest either the Church or the Woods belonging to it; but that it should be free from all Tribute and Taxes; and desired that his Successors would as freely aid, defend, and take Care of this Church as he has done, that they may enjoy the Blessing and Protection of the holy Martyr for ever; and if any shall evilly intreat it, that he shall be deprived of the Blessing of the holy Martyr, and be accountable for the same before the Tribunal of Christ; and he did constitute *Pilcoea* the Presbyter, so named in the Record, but others call him *Willigod,* the first Abbot, to whom he committed the Care of this Church, the Government of the Monks, and the Management of the Revenues of this House; and he did command in the Name of God, and adjure, that the Monks and all others there should live reverently and regularly under him, according to the Order of St. *Benedict;* and that continual Intercessions should be made for the Souls of himself and Friends at Canonical Hours in the Church; and then did confirm this Gift with the Sign of the Cross.

The affixing of Crosses to all publick Instruments, and other original Charters, was the Manner of Signature in these Days, for *Ingulphus* says, the ancient English Charters to the time of *Edward* the Confessor, were attested by Witnesses, who set their Names with Golden Crosses or other Marks before them. But *Edward* the Confessor, who was bred up in Normandy, where Seals were usually fixed to Deeds, brought that Custom with him into this Nation, for that it was more conspicuous and distinguishable than that of Crosses; but others hold sealing of Deeds and Charters much more ancient; for the Charter of King *Edwine,* Brother of King *Edgar,* dated 956, made of the Land call'd Jecclea in the Isle of Ely, was not only sealed with his own Seal, as appears by these Words, *Ego* Edwinus *Gratia Dei totius* Britaniæ, *Telluris Rex meum Donum proprio Sigillo confirmavi;* but also the Bishop of Winchester affixt his Seal to it, *Ego* Elfewinus Winton *Ecclesiæ Divinus Speculator proprium Sigillum impressi:* The Charter by which King *Offa* gave the *Peter*-pence doth yet remain under Seal; and King *Cnut* used Seals; but Seals were commonly used in the time of *William* the Conqueror, for Mr. *Twyne* affirms he saw a Charter of that King sealed on the left Side of the Parchment; and a pendant Seal was fixed to the Charter of *Battle Abby,* printed by Mr. *Selden;* the Great Seal was put to the Charter of *H.* I. granted to *Anselme* on

Side notes:
Hund. of Caishoe.

Matt. Paris *de Vita Offæ,* 2, fol. 30. Matt. Paris *de Vitis Abbat.* fol. 35.

Phil. of Kent, fol. 360. Ingulp. *Chron* MS. in Bibl. A.T.C.

Still. *Antiq. of Brit. Church,* fol. 19.

Hund. of
Caisboe.
the left Side of the Parchment, and the Charter which *H.*
II. granted to the Abby of 𝔊lassenbury had a Seal of
green Wax hanging to it by a String of red and white
Silk. King *R.* 1. sealed with a Seal of two Lions, and
King *John* in Right of 𝔄cquittaine bore three Lions, and
used a Seal with three Lions, and all the modern Kings
have followed him: But I have read that *William* Earl of
𝔚aren, *Anno* 2 *H.* II. sealed with the Figure of a Chevalier on Horseback; his *Caparizons, Tabard, and Sheild
being all Cheque,* the paternal Coat of his Family; and
Richard Cursor of 𝔠rox-hall in 𝔇erbyshire, in the Reign
of King *John,* was pourtray'd in a standing Posture in a
Window, *cloathed with a Surcoat, surmounted with a
Bend, charged with a Martlet.* And Seals were so sacred
in former Days, that being lost they were usually decry'd
by the Owners, who were wont in such Intervals to seal
with the Seal of the Bishop of the Diocess, or next adjacent Abbot, all Deeds or Instruments of public or private
Interest.

Inspex. 2 H.
VIII.
Mon. Angl.
fol. 177.
About two Years after, the same King by his Charter
dated at 𝔅eoran-ford, *Anno* 795, and *Regni sui* 35, with
the Consent of *Egfrid* his Son, and in the Presence of
Lughberth, Archbishop, *Ceolumf, Heccored,* and *Bunona,*
Bishops, and *Ashmind, Beonunam,* and *Munimund,* Abbots,
and also Duke *Brordan,* Duke *Bynnan,* Duke *Elstuum,*
Duke *Alimund,* Duke *Vigberti,* Duke *Ethelmund,* Duke
Edgar, Duke *Heharbert,* Duke *Ealhumud,* Duke *Cuthbert,* Duke *Eadbyrth,* and Duke *Tulfheard,* gave twelve
Mansions at 𝔈twinxistaune, and three Mansions at 𝔖eelf-
dune or 𝔅almingeot, whereof three of those Mansions were
called 𝔥uanaburne, 𝔥eortmere, 𝔥tenealabert; also ten
Mansions called 𝔥hintaublaun or 𝔣emitum, with the
Wood called 𝔥orofwood, and five Mansions at 𝔏igtune,
which *Ashmund* the Abbot had given to the King upon
his Reconciliation; and he did also grant that this Church
and all the Possession thereof should from thenceforth be
always free, and quit from all Tributes and Taxes, and
from the Repair of Bridges, Castles, and making of Trenches
against the Enemy; and that the Abbot and Monks and all
their Churches shall be free from Episcopal Jurisdiction; and
that Part of the Punishment which shall hereafter be inflicted upon any Persons for Theft, Fornication, or the like
Offence within their Liberty, which shall belong to the
King, shall be always given to this Monastery.

And the same King by another Charter gave to God
and this Church, the Mannors of 𝔚iteslep, 𝔅erethon,
𝔅irkmeresworth, 𝔅achesworth, 𝔠rosselep, 𝔐ichelfeild,
𝔅urkenbel, 𝔚atford, 𝔅isserie, 𝔚endele, 𝔥elvenham,
𝔥pret, 𝔅enefeld, 𝔥edentone, 𝔐ildentone, and two other
Vills, called 𝔅yrstone and 𝔚incelfeld.

Pope *Adrian* the first granted by his Bull, that the Abbot or Monk whom he should appoint Archdeacon, should have Pontifical Jurisdiction over the Priests and Laymen of all the Possessions belonging to this Church; and that no Archbishop, Bishop, or Legate, save the Pope himself, should intromit herein; and also that the Abbot shall collect and receive through all the Province of Hertford, all the Rent and Imposition called *Romscot* or *Peter*-pence.; when no King, Archbishop, Bishop, Abbot, Prior, or other Person in the Kingdom, had the like Exemption.

The Bishops of Rome called Charters of Grants, Bulls Παρὰ τὴν Βυλὴν, *à Concilio*, of Council: for that anciently a golden Bull, Broach, or Ornament round and hollow within, was usually fastened about the Necks of young Children, and to all their Pictures, signifying that their tender, unbridled Age ought to be govern'd by the grave Counsel of others of more Maturity in Years; and they were confirmed with leaden Seals, which had on one Side the Impression of the Name of the Pope, and on the other Side the Head of St. *Paul* on the right Side of the Cross, and of St. *Peter* on the left; which was done to the Church in Regard of Honour, not Preeminence, for though St. *Peter* be Head of the Apostolick Order, yet the Church will have them to be of an undistinct Excellence.

In the Space of five Years, this King erected divers Houses for the necessary Habitation and Use of all Officers and Servants that belonged to this Monastery, which, in Process of time, did encrease to a Town, and was called by the Name of this Saint; and when he had almost completed all his Buildings, and settled all the Officers and Government of this Monastery, he died (as many believe) in the Vill of Offelp in this County, and his Body was buried royally in a Chappel in a Vill scituated upon the Ouse near Bedford, where to the great Shame of the Monks of this House, they suffered it to remain till the Water washt away the Body with the Banks of the River.

Matt. Paris
de Vita Offæ,
2, fol. 32.

Eyfrid his Son succeeded, who resembled his Father in Judgment and Mercy, and *Anno Christi* 796, and 1 *Regni sui*, did not only confirm all the gracious Concessions and noble Gifts of his Father to this Monastery, but farther granted to it five Mannors in a Place called Hynesfeld, with their antient Bordars, together with the Mannors of Sanderuge, and Thitrefeld; and the same Year, this Abbot *Willegod*, commended much for the good Government of this Church, but greatly opprest with Sorrow for the Death of King *Offa*, whom he exceedingly loved, and the great Ingratitude of the Monks, who had not removed his Body to the Monastery, but suffered the Water to destroy it, pined away, till at length he died, and was buried in a Place unknown to this Day.

Matt. Paris de
Vitis Abbat.
fol 36.

Hund. of
Caistor.

Matt. Paris de
Vitis Abbat.
fol. 37.

II. *Edric,* who was near related in Blood to King *Offa* and King *Egfrid,* by both whom he was well-beloved, was in the same Year elected and advanced to the pastoral Seat, without Delay or Difference among them, according to the Desire of King *Offa,* who, whilst he lived, often and earnestly advised them that they should never choose an Abbot out of any other Church; he was supported by the King's Aid, which enabled him to govern well, tho' the most potent Men greatly opposed him, and murmured at the Munificence of King *Offa,* which they called Prodigality, and endeavoured to possess King *Egfrid* that the Generosity of his Father to this Church, had in a great Measure lessened the Revenues of the Crown, and thereby charged the royal Dignity.

Ibid.

III. When this good Abbot died, *Vulsig* or *Ulsin* did succeed him: He issued from the royal Family, yet was soon elated with Pride; he wore silk Vestments, rid a hunting, eat and drank sumptuously, and always preferred the Goodwill of Princes before his Duty to God; he would often invite many noble Women to his Table, where he would exceed the Bounds of Modesty, which drew upon himself a Scandal, that did reflect upon the Honesty of his Brethren, though there was no Cause for it: When his good Name was lost, Charity grew cold, and the Devotion of many dwindled away: He wasted the Revenues of the Church, sold the Vestments and Furniture which *Offa* had given, and could not be recovered again; he often married his Kinswomen to Lords, gave them great Fortunes, and sumptuous Apparel, all which possest his Convent against him, and in the Reign of King *Edward* he died, 'tis said by Poyson, under the Hatred and Curse of the Convent: Then the most grave and powerful Men there, sued all his Relations for their Goods which they had gotten, and recovering them, many of his Kindred became poor through Want.

Ibid. fol. 38.

IV. *Vulnoth* was created Abbot in the time of King *Ethelstan,* and in two or three Years reformed the Errors of his Predecessors; he caused the holy Semi-seculars to live after one and the same Manner in one House, that they might be free from the Suspition of ill Report, restrain'd their wandring abroad, appointed the times and Places for their Silence, sleeping, eating, drinking, and praying, regulating their Dyet and eating of Flesh; and commanded that they should daily hear Morning Prayer in the great Church, and perform their Duty there.

Ibid.

Whilst this Abbot govern'd this Church, the *Danes* raged in this Isle in a hostile Manner, and came to the Tomb of St. *Alban,* where they hearing the Fame of the Protomartyr, took away his broken Bones, carried them into their Country, and there reverently laid them in a precious Cof-

fin made for that Purpose in a certain religious House of
Black Monks; that as in **England**, so in **Denmark**, they
might be worshipped: But when this Abbot had governed
this Church about the Space of eleven Years, he ended this
Life most happily.

V. *Eadfrith* from a Prior, was elected Abbot, and govern'd here in the Reign of *Edmond* the Just: He issued
from the Saxon Nobility, was neat and large in Body, but
vain and contemptible in Deeds; he delighted much in riot-
ing and Idleness, was frequent in his Chamber, seldom in
the Cloyster, not worthy to appear in the Quire; he was
careful to preserve the Goods of the Church, but slow to purchase, and was a Pastor that gave ill Example to his Flock.

In his time *Ulpho* the Prior of St. *Alban*, a Man of great
Holiness, by his Permission, built a famous Chappel to the
Honour of St. *German*, a venerable Bishop of worthy Memory; and another Chappel was built by his Licence, where
Ulpho a *Dane*, a Relation of the Abbot's, a Monk of the
Cloyster, and a Man of great Sanctity, had for a long time
like an Hermit, tilled Gardens, and was indefatigable in setting Herbs and Pulse, and admirable in abstaining from
Wine, and so remarkable for his Holiness, that many Bishops
and grave Men came to him, that by Confession they might
be worthy to be absolved from their Sins, and be recommended to God by his Prayers; and after his Death he was reverently laid among the Abbots for his great Virtues.

The Death of this good Man caused the Abbot to reflect
so severely upon his own Condition, that he laid aside all
State, and resign'd up the Burden and Honour of his pastoral Life, with his Staff; he retired himself to a small
House near the Chappel, where the Hermit dwelt, bewailing his former Sins, betook himself to a solitary Life, and by
this great Change from his Pallace to his Cell, made himself
a Companion and Coheir of the former Hermit, following
the Steps of his Holiness; by Reason hereof, the Abbot-
ship became void, and continued vacant for the Space of a
Year, and during that time, a Division arising among them,
touching the Election of a new Abbot, the Goods of the
Church were imbezzlled, and there was a great Distraction
in the Monastery on every Side, for the Prior with his Fa-
vourites was averse to the greater Part of the Convent in
their Election, till at length by Mediation of the neighbouring Bishops, the Difference was composed, and the Monks
chose an Abbot by their unanimous Consent.

VI. *Ulsin* or *Ulsig* was a pious Man, and of good Life,
famous in all spiritual and secular Affairs, and govern'd here
in the Reign of King *Etheldred*, surnamed the Most Pious,
An. Christi 950, from whom he obtained a Confirmation of
all the former Grants to this Monastery; and also procur'd

Hund. of
Caishoe.
a new Grant of a Market in this Town, where he built divers Houses at his own Costs and Charges, for the Conveniency of all those who were disposed to live here, and by
the Addition of these Houses, this Town became a Borough:
Then he built the Church, dedicated to St. *Peter*, in the
North Part, the Church of St. *Stephen* in the South Part,
and the Church of St. *Michael* in the West Part, as well
for the Ornament and Profit of the Borough, as the Health
of his Soul; He honoured *Eadfrith*, the late Abbot, and
then an Hermit, giving him great Reverence for his strict
and holy Life, and at his Death performed the Solemnities
of his Funeral, buried him among the Abbots, and greatly
loved the Church wherein he lived; and for the great Reverence of St. *German*, and the Saint of God, he often celebrated Mass there, built another Chappel near it to the Honour of St. *Mary Magdalen;* and he, holy Man, and full of
Days, did happily go from hence to God.

Matt. Paris,
fol. 40.
Weav. Mon.
Camd. Brit.
tit. Herts. fol.
411.
VII. *Alfric* was the next Abbot, who for a great Sum
of Money, the precious Cup wherein the Body of our
Lord was kept, and divers other great Gifts, purchased
of King *Edgar*, a large and deep Fishpool, which lay
between old Verulam and this Town, and belonged to the
Castle of Kingsbury, a stately Pallace scituated at the
North West End of the Town, where the King often re-
creating himself, passed by Boat to and fro within the Pool,
according to the Order of the Noblemen and Gentlemen of

Norden, p. 10.
Rome, who usually made fair Fishponds about their Houses
to recreate themselves, and those with exceeding Cost, as
Marcus Varro related of the wonderful large and costly
Fishpond of *Hortensius, Hircius,* and *Lucullus;* and these
Citizens of Verulam took their Pattern for this great Pond
from these and such other princely *Romans,* who coming
afterwards to the Kings of this Land, they often recreated
themselves herein, accompanied commonly with no small
Troops of their Nobles, therefore the Boats were provided
of large Hull, furnished with Cable and Anchor, that they
might at the King's Pleasure, be moored in any Part of the
Pool, which might cause the Use of so large Anchors as
have been found there, and by Reason hereof, the King's
Officers and Fishers so frequently resorted to this Monastery, that they were a great Burden and Charge to the Abbot and Monks, which thing induced this Abbot to purchase
the same, and to drain the Water out of it, that no more
Fish might remain there, so this Grievance was removed ;
but the Bounds and Banks hereof may yet be seen near
the Street now called Fishpool-street.

Matt. Paris,
fol. 40.
Weav. fol.
557.
VIII. *Ældred* succeeded next in the Government of
this Church, in the Reign of King *Edgar,* he searched for
the ancient Vaults under Ground at Verulam, and found

several Ways and Passages, which were strongly and arti- Hund. of Caishoe.
ficially arched over-head, where Men were wont in antient
time to make Vaults, hollow Places and Substructions under Camd. fol. 411.
Ground for Receipts or Receptacles for keeping of their
Wives, Children, Money, and Goods secret, to avoid Vio-
lence and Rapine in time of Hostility or Rebellion; these Coke, Inst. 3, fol. 203.
Kind of Buildings they had from the old *Germans*, who
used to build Vaults under the Earth, for where the Enemy was wont to come he destroyed all upon and above
Ground, but such things as were hid in a Cave, either they
were unknown, or at least they deceived them in that they
were forc'd to find them out.

He stop'd them up *Anno* 960, for that they were lurk-
ing Holes of Whores and Thieves, and level'd all the
Ditches of the City, and certain Dens, into which Malefactors used to fly, as Places of Refuge; and near unto
the Bank they found Planks of Oak, with Nails driven
into them, cemented with Stone and Pitch, and the Tackle
and Furniture of Ships, as Anchors half eaten with Rust,
and Oars of Furre; but the whole Tiles and Stones which
he found fit for building he laid aside, with an Intent to
have raised a new Church out of the Ruins of the old, but
that Death hindred him.

IX. *Eadmer* his Successor proceeded with the Work Matt. Paris, fol. 41. Weav. fol. 551. Camd fol. 411.
that *Ælfric* had begun, and his Pioneers overthrew the
Foundation of a Pallace in the Middle of the old City; and
in the hollow Place of a Wall, as it was in a little Closet,
Books were found cover'd with oaken Boards and silk
Strings fix'd to them, whereof one contained the Life of
St. *Alban*, written in the British Tongue, the rest the
Ceremonies of the Heathen; and when they delv'd into
the Ground, they found old Tables of Stone, Tiles, Pillars,
Pitchers, Pots of Earth, and Vessels of Glass, containing
the Ashes of the Dead, &c. And out of the Remains of
Verulam, *Eadmer* built a-new the greatest Part of his
Church and Monastery, with an Intent to have finish'd the
whole, but Death disappointed him.

About the time of this Abbot, *Anno* 10 9, *Spelman*
thinks a Council was held at **Eanham** of all the great and
wise Men, at the Instance of *Ælfage*, Archbishop of **Canterbury**, and *Wulstan*, Archbishop of **York**, where it was
decreed among other things, that Priests should not marry,
it being the Custom then for them to have two or three
Wives; that none should be sold out of their Country, especially to Pagans; and that Widows should remain single
for twelve Months after their Husband's Death.

X. *Leofric*, Son of the Earl of **Kent**, a Man of comly Spelm. Conc. fol. 511. Brady's Hist. of Engl. fol. 126.
Stature and beautiful Aspect, was elected Abbot: whilst
he was a Secular, he exchanged his paternal Estate for a

Hund. of
Caishoe.

Celestial, for he gave his temporal Inheritance to his younger Brother, whom he entirely loved, and took upon him a religious Habit. He was very charitable to the Poor, and strengthened by Friends and noble Relations, represt the rebellious, and with a strong Hand defended the Possessions of the Church; but his great Merits advanced him to the Archbishoprick of Canterbury, and he departed with the Benediction of his Brethren, leaving his Monastery very rich; afterwards died *Anno* 1046.

Matt. Paris,
fol. 43.

XI. *Alfric* his younger Brother, a learned Man, and equal to him in Shape and Mind, succeeded: He gloried in the Works of his Brother, and was a Teacher and a Pastor to the People, without Fault in his Life, eloquent in his Speech, wary in his Counsel, bountiful to Strangers, pious to his Brethren, austeer to the Refractory, frugal to the Poor,

Lib, Mr. Cox.

very compassionate to the Afflicted; and being admonish'd in a Vision, compiled the Life and Death of St. *Alban*. Whilst he was a Secular, he was Chancellor to King *Etheldred*, and perswaded him to renew the Charters, and confirm the Gifts of his Predecessors, and bestow an Onyx Stone on this Church: He bought of the same King the royal Mannor of Kingsbury, with the Parks and Woods belonging to it, excepting one small Fortress near the Monastery, which the King would not suffer to be demolish'd, that the Marks of his royal House might not be forgotten. He also purchas'd Oxonage and Adulfinton for 1000 Marks; Northon, Upton, Wecces, and Wartham for 50 Pounds, which he gave to this Church, and the Land of *Tiwas*, which was then mortgaged for ten Pounds to *Leofsigo* and his Fellows; to the Intent, that if the Monks alone shall pay the Money, that then they should have the Land, if not, *Leofsigo* and his Partners should have their respective Shares, for their several Lives, and after their Deceases it should return to the Monks.

Matt. Paris,
fol. 45.

XII. *Leofstan*, who was of the Family of King *Edward* the Confessor, and Counsellor to him, and Queen *Editha* his Wife; was advanced to the Government of this Monastery, and prevailed with the King to confirm the Grant of this Mannor of Stodham, which *Oswalph* and *Adelitha* his Wife had made to this Church, and the Grant of the Mannors of Redburn, Langley, Greenburrow, and Thwancton, with all the Rents, Gifts, and Ornaments which *Egelwine* the Black, and *Wincelfled* his Wife had given to this Monastery.

This Abbot caused the thick and shady Woods near the

Camd. Brit.
fol. 415.
Matt. Paris,
fol. 45.

Edge of the Chiltern by Watling-street, to be stock'd up, the rugged Plains to be levelled, Bridges to be built, the uneven Ways to be made plain and safe for Passage; and gave to a certain Knight call'd *Thurnoth* and his two Soldiers, *Waldef* and *Thurman*, the Mannor of 𝕱lamstet, *Hund. of* *Caishoc.* for which *Thurnoth* gave him presently five Ounces of Gold, and a fair Palfrey, upon Condition, that *Thurnoth* with his two Soldiers and their Fellows, should keep all Passengers, who should travel thro' that western Road safe from the Harm of Thieves and Beasts, who greatly infested those Parts, and if any Traveller should suffer by them, that they should answer the Damage; and if any publick War should happen in the Kingdom, then they should use all their Diligence and Power to preserve the Safety of this Church; and they did perform the same until King *William* conquer'd this Island, when he took this Mannor from them because they would not bear the Yoke of the *Normans*; and gave it to *Roger de Thoni*, who will'd that Right should be done to St. *Alban*, and the same Service should be strictly performed. He gave certain Ornaments to the Church, and died soon after the Death of King *Edward* the Confessor.

XIII. *Frederic* sprung from the antient *Saxons*, related to *Canutus*, King of the *Danes*, and his next Heir by lineal *Matt. Paris* *Vita Freder.* *fol. 46.* Descent, was elected Abbot of this Church in the Reign of King *Harold*, who rashly usurped the Crown contrary to his Oath, and was slain at the Battle near 𝕳astings, before he had reigned the Space of a Year; and when King *William* prevail'd against him, he marched to 𝕶allingfort, and crossing the River there rested his Army awhile, then came to 𝕭erkhamstet in this County, in order to go forward to 𝕷ondon, but was forced to make some Stay there, for that this Abbot had caused the Timber Trees, growing near that Road, which belonged to his Church, to be fell'd and laid across the Way that he could not pass with his Forces, by which Means this Abbot preserv'd this Monastery from Spoil; whereupon King *William* sent for him, and demanded why so much Wood was fell'd about him more than in other Places? To which *Frederic* answer'd, I have done what I ought, for if all the spiritual Persons thro' this Land had used their Endeavours to have hindred thee as they should and might have done, it would not have been in your Power to have come thus far; then King *William* reply'd, Is the Spirituality of 𝕰nglant of such Power? If I may live and enjoy what I have got, I will make their Power less; whereupon this courageous Abbot summon'd all the great Lords and Nobles of 𝕰nglant together, and consulting them how they might free themselves from the Slavery of the Norman Yoke, repair'd to the Conqueror at 𝕭erkhamstet, where after great Debate of Matters, in the Presence of Archbishop *Lanfranc*, the King doubted the Result hereof, and fearing that if he should not comply with them, he should lose the Kingdom with Shame, which

ı

...

Hund. of
Caishoe.

he had got with the Effusion of so much Blood, condescended so far to them for his own Security, that he laid his Hand upon the holy Gospel, and swore upon all the Reliques of St. *Alban's* Church before this Abbot, who administered the Oath, that he would observe and keep inviolably the good and approved antient Laws of the Kingdom, which the holy and devout Kings of 𝔈𝔫𝔤𝔩𝔞𝔫𝔡 his Predecessors, especially King *Edward,* had ordained and appointed; which done, they submitted themselves to his Governance, and swore Fealty to him, who with many fair Words, received them immediately into his Protection, and the People departed with great Joy to their Habitations; but the bold Answers which this Abbot gave the King, so offended him, that he deprived this Church of the Mannors of 𝔑𝔢𝔡𝔟𝔲𝔯𝔫𝔢, and all the Lands and Revenues belonging to it, which lay between 𝔅𝔢𝔯𝔫𝔢𝔱 and 𝔏𝔬𝔫𝔡𝔬𝔫-𝔰𝔱𝔬𝔫𝔢; whereupon this Abbot called a Chapter of his Brethren, shew'd to them their approaching Dangers, and to avoid the present Storm, he went to 𝔈𝔩𝔭, where he desisted not from his Contrivances against the Conqueror, until he ended his Days there in great Grief of Mind; And when King *William* heard of his Death, he seized this Church into his Hands, destroy'd the Woods, and impoverished the People: and had not *Lanfranc* the Archbishop interposed, he had destroy'd the Monastery, but at length he prevail'd that *Paul* his Kinsman, whom he brought with him into 𝔈𝔫𝔤𝔩𝔞𝔫𝔡, should be chosen Abbot. 'Tis recorded in *Domesdei Book* under the Title of

Terra Abbatis 𝔖𝔞𝔫𝔠𝔱. 𝔄𝔩𝔟𝔞𝔫𝔦

Domesd Lib.
fol. 135.

Vil 𝔖𝔞𝔫𝔠𝔱. 𝔄𝔩𝔟𝔞𝔫𝔦 pro decem hidis se defendebat. Terra est xvi *car. in Dom. tres hid. et ibi sunt duo car. et tertia potest fieri. Ibi,* iv *Francig. et* xvi *Villi. cum* xiii *bord. habentibus* xiii *car. Ibi* xl *Burgenses, de Theloneo et de aliis reditibus Vill. undecim lib. et quatuor decem sol. per ann. et tres molend. de* xl *sol. pratum* ii *car. Silva mill. porc. et septem sol. in totis valent val.* xx *lib. quando recepit* xii *lib. tempore Regis* Edwardi xxiv *lib. in eadem Villa sunt adhuc* xii *cotar et unus parcus, ibi est bestiarum silvaticarum et unum vivarium piscium predicti Burgenses dimid. hid. habent.*

The Vill of St. 𝔄𝔩𝔟𝔞𝔫 was rated for ten Hides, the arable is sixteen Carucates, in Demeasne three Hides, and there are two Carucates and a third may be made, there are four Frenchmen born, and sixteen Villains, with thirteen Bordars, having thirteen Carucates, there are forty six Burgesses, of Toll and other Rent of the Vill, eleven Pounds and fourteen Shillings by the Year, and three Mills of forty Shillings Rent by the Year, Meadow two Carucates, Wood to feed a thousand Hogs in pannage time, and seven Shillings Rent; in the whole Value it is worth twenty Pounds by the Year, when he received it twelve Pounds, in the time of King *Edward* (the Confessor) four and twenty Pounds; in the same Vill there are now twelve Cottagers, and there is one Park of Deer, and one Vivary of fishing, the aforesaid Burgesses had half an Hide.

Spelm. Coun.
vol. 2, fol. 7
Brady's Hist.
fol. 215

In the Year of our Lord 1075, a Counsel was held at 𝔏𝔬𝔫𝔡𝔬𝔫, where Archbishop *Lanfranc* presided, in which it was decreed, that no Bishop or Abbot or any of the Clergy, should give Judgment touching the Life of any Man or Loss

of Member, nor by their Authority should countenance any
that should do it, according to the Council of Elberis; and
the eleventh of Toledo; and at another Council held the
Year following at Winchester it was decreed that no Cannon should marry; and that Priests who lived in Buroughs
and Villages that had Wives should not put them away:
but if they had none, they were prohibited to take any; and
Bishops were to take Care that they did not ordain married
Men either Deacons or Priests.

XIV. This *Paul* was preferred to the Government of
this Church, *Anno* 1077, 11 *Willielmi Conquest.* & 4 *Ca-
lend Julii*, who rebuilt it and all the other Structures (but
the Bake-house and the Pastry) out of the Stones, Tyles,
and wooden Materials of the City of Verulam, which his
Predecessors had reserved. He was a religious and learned
Man, rigid and prudent in the Observance of the religious
Order, and by Degrees reformed the Rule of the Monastery;
so as this Church was like a School of Religion and Discipline, for he had brought hither the Customs of *Lanfranc*,
and the written Statutes approved by the Pope; commanded the Observance of them, which made this Church glorious,
and the Fame thereof flew to the Roman Court, and the
remotest Kingdoms, and did happily draw the Hearts of
many Prelates and Lords to this Monastery. This Abbot
recover'd the Mannors of Tiwa, Apsa, and Cnicumbe, with
the most pleasant Wood of Eiwood, which this Church enjoy'd in the Reign of King *Edward*, but in the time of
Trouble, was constrain'd to mortgage it; for in the Life-
time of Abbot *Frederick, Odo* the Bishop of Baïeux, and
Earl of Kent had the Mannor of Tiwa and Apsa now Aps-
bury with Epwood in their Demeasne; and *Remigius* Bishop
of Lincolne had Cnicum, which they held until the Mannors
with the Wood were restored.

This Abbot, in the Space of eleven Years, finished this
Church with many other Buildings, by the Help of *Lanfranc*, who 'tis said gave an hundred Marks to the same;
he recovered what *Ailwin* the Black, and *Ailfled* his Wife
had given to this Church in the Vill of Redburn, and a
Place called Childwick, of their Gift, which had been fraudu-
lently alienated from them; and was so called because it
was given for the Sustenance of the younger Monks with
Milk. There was also another Place for Cows, which was
anciently called Child Langley for the same Reason, which
Abbot *Paul* could never recover.

He obtained the Grant of two Hides of Land in Scepe-
hal, which *Asketill de Ros* formerly held of *Lanfranc*, and
since of this Church, and three Virgates of Land in Potton
which *R. Flandrensis* held, one Carucate of Land called
Letinge, the Land of Talinton with the Appurtenances, the

Hund. of
Caishoe.

Spelm fol. 13.

Matt. Paris de
Vita Pauli
fol. 49.

Matt. Paris,
fol. 50.

Ibid.

Land of three Houses, where one *Smith* now liveth, with three Gardens in Glaston, and a Carucate of Land in the same Vill, the Mannor of Penereth, which Abbot *Richard* gave since to the Monks of Maring, the Churches of St. *Benet*, and the Churches of *All-saints* in Cambridge, with the Tithes and all things belonging to many Churches in London; one Church in Stamford, and eleven Acres of Land in that Town, and the Church of Glaston with one Carucate of Land, and the Tithes belonging to it.

He also obtained the Grant of the Tithes of Cundell, Ringeton, Riomges, Bretheham, Herlage, Themilford, Clifton, Punteflege, Gertheham, Brunfelld, Reedlage, and two Parts of the Tith of Sedington and Bocton, all the Tith of Trumpington, two Parts of Macerly; and two Parts of the Tiths of Essendon, Betford, and Hertfordensbiri in this County.

This Abbot erected a Cell of Monks at Wallingford, and appointed that the Order used in this Church should be observed there; he perswaded *Robert de Moubrai* Earl of the Northumbers, to place Monks of this Church in the Cell of Thinemue; *Robert de Todenei* to give the Cell of Belber; *Robert de Limesi* the Cell of Hertford, and *William de Valoins* and *William* his Son the Cell of Binham to this Church; and *Robert*, a Knight, to give two Parts of the Tiths of his Demesne in the Vill of Hatfield, to purchase Books, and a Library necessary for this Church; he caused several choice Books to be writ at his Charge; and gave a silver Bason to contain burning Wax continually before the great Altar, three Candlesticks covered with Gold and Silver of rare Work, to stand before the same Altar, with wax Lights, two silver Candlesticks of admirable Work and excellently gilded, to be carried before the Martyr, upon the chief Festivals, with wax Lights: He also ordain'd a pitcht Lanthorn with a Candle in the Quire, to be carried about in the Night, that he might stir up the idle and drowsy People, and appointed a greater Lanthorn, to be born before those who were guilty of greater Offences; made a Prison for the Stubborn, and rebuilt the Tower for a Bell: But when this Abbot had governed this Church sixteen Years and four Months, he died the third of the Ides of *November*, *Anno Christi* 1093, *quinto Regis* Willielmi *secundi*. After whose Death this Church was vacant four Years, during which time King *William* held this Monastery in his own Hands, and did miserably impoverish it, felling the Woods and extorting Money from the Monks; but when the Contest in the Convent between the *Normans*, who were now encreased there, and the *English* who were old and lessen'd in Number, was quieted, they agreed to choose *Richard* for their Abbot.

Hund. of
Caishoe.

XV. This *Richard* took upon him the pastoral Care *Anno* 1097, 10 *Will.* II. He descended from a noble Family of the *Normans*, was supported by the Assistance of his Parents and Friends, and by the Favour of *Will.* II. and *Henry* I. obtained many Honours and Possessions; for by his great Eloquence, wherein he exceeded all the Abbots of 𝕰𝖓𝖌𝖑𝖆𝖓𝖉, he perswaded King *H.* I. to confirm the Cell and the Church of St. *Mary* of 𝖂𝖎𝖒𝖔𝖓𝖉𝖑𝖞, with the Appurtenances which *Richard Argentine* had given, and the Cell of 𝖍𝖊𝖆𝖙𝖍𝖋𝖊𝖑𝖉, with the Church of 𝕸𝖎𝖑𝖊𝖇𝖗𝖔𝖈, and all things belonging to them; also the Mannor of 𝕿𝖎𝖓𝖌𝖍𝖚𝖗𝖘𝖙, and the Church with all the Tyths belonging to it; the Town of 𝖂𝖎𝖇𝖆𝖑𝖉𝖊𝖘𝖙𝖚𝖉𝖊, and thirty Shillings' worth of Land in the Town of 𝖂𝖆𝖗𝖊𝖓𝖌𝖊𝖋𝖔𝖗𝖉, the Mannor of 𝕰𝖆𝖘𝖙𝖜𝖆𝖑𝖊 in 𝕽𝖊𝖓𝖙, which *Nigel de Alban* gave, and to grant the Mannor of 𝕭𝖎𝖘𝖘𝖔𝖕𝖊𝖘𝖈𝖔𝖙𝖊, and confirm the Mannor of 𝕭𝖗𝖊𝖓𝖙𝖊𝖋𝖊𝖑𝖉, which *Hardwine de Scalers* and *Odelphi* his Wife had given to St. *Alban*.

King *Henry* I. by his Charter dated at 𝖂𝖊𝖘𝖙𝖒𝖎𝖓𝖘𝖙𝖊𝖗 granted and confirmed to God and this Church, all their Cells of 𝕿𝖞𝖓𝖊𝖒𝖚𝖊, 𝕭𝖎𝖓𝖍𝖆𝖒, 𝖂𝖕𝖒𝖔𝖓𝖉𝖊𝖘𝖍𝖆𝖒, 𝕭𝖊𝖗𝖓𝖊𝖍𝖊𝖗, 𝖂𝖆𝖑𝖕𝖓𝖌𝖋𝖔𝖗𝖉, 𝕳𝖊𝖗𝖙𝖋𝖔𝖗𝖉, 𝕳𝖆𝖙𝖍𝖋𝖊𝖑𝖉, and 𝕭𝖊𝖑𝖑𝖔𝖑𝖔𝖈𝖔, this Town of 𝕾𝖙. 𝕬𝖑𝖇𝖆𝖓, with the Market and Liberty; the Town of 𝖂𝖆𝖙𝖋𝖔𝖗𝖉, with the Market, 𝕽𝖎𝖓𝖘𝖇𝖊𝖗𝖗𝖞, 𝖂𝖊𝖘𝖙𝖜𝖎𝖈, 𝕽𝖊𝖉-𝖇𝖚𝖗𝖓𝖊, 𝕾𝖆𝖓𝖉𝖗𝖚𝖈𝖍, 𝕭𝖗𝖎𝖉𝖊𝖑𝖑𝖊, 𝕿𝖎𝖉𝖊𝖍𝖆𝖓𝖌𝖆𝖒, with the Wood of 𝕹𝖔𝖗𝖙𝖍𝖆𝖜, which *Peter de Valoines* held for his Life, 𝕭𝖊𝖗-𝖓𝖊𝖙, with the Wood of 𝕾𝖔𝖚𝖙𝖍𝖆𝖜, 𝕭𝖔𝖗𝖊𝖍𝖆𝖒, 𝕳𝖚𝖘𝖊𝖍𝖊𝖔𝖌, and the Park with all the Soke, 𝕷𝖆𝖓𝖌𝖑𝖊𝖕, 𝕮𝖆𝖎𝖘𝖍𝖔𝖊, 𝕽𝖎𝖈𝖐𝖒𝖆𝖗𝖊𝖘-𝖜𝖔𝖗𝖙𝖍, 𝕾𝖊𝖗𝖊𝖙𝖍, 𝕲𝖗𝖊𝖊𝖓𝖘𝖇𝖚𝖗𝖕, 𝖂𝖕𝖓𝖊𝖘𝖑𝖆𝖜, 𝕾𝖎𝖕𝖊𝖙𝖔𝖓, and 𝕳𝖔𝖗-𝖜𝖔𝖔𝖉, with the Forest and Chase, 𝕰𝖘𝖙𝖔𝖓, 𝕭𝖎𝖘𝖍𝖔𝖕𝖊𝖘𝖈𝖔𝖙𝖊, 𝕳𝖊𝖈𝖘𝖙𝖆𝖓𝖊𝖘𝖙𝖊𝖗, 𝕹𝖔𝖗𝖙𝖔𝖓, 𝕹𝖊𝖜𝖍𝖆𝖒, 𝕮𝖚𝖉𝖎𝖈𝖔𝖙𝖊, 𝖂𝖆𝖑𝖉𝖊𝖓, and 𝕭𝖗𝖆𝖉𝖜𝖆, with the Churches and other things belonging to them; and he also granted the Churches of 𝕰𝖉𝖊𝖑𝖋𝖎𝖓𝖌𝖊𝖙𝖍 and 𝕾𝖙. 𝕾𝖙𝖊𝖕𝖍𝖊𝖓𝖘, with their Chappels, 𝕷𝖎𝖓𝖙𝖔𝖓, 𝕳𝖔𝖕𝖙𝖔𝖓𝖊, and 𝕻𝖔𝖙𝖊𝖘𝖌𝖗𝖆𝖇𝖊, with all the Mannors, Lands, and Tythes to maintain their Kitchin; the Churches of 𝖂𝖆𝖑𝖉𝖊𝖓 and 𝕬𝖕𝖚𝖑𝖙𝖔𝖓 in 𝕻𝖔𝖗𝖐𝖘𝖍𝖎𝖗𝖊, and 𝖂𝖆𝖙𝖋𝖔𝖗𝖉 to entertain Strangers, and the Churches of 𝕿𝖍𝖎𝖗𝖊𝖋𝖊𝖑𝖉, 𝕽𝖊𝖉𝖇𝖚𝖗𝖓, 𝖂𝖕𝖓𝖊𝖘𝖍𝖆𝖜, and 𝕷𝖆𝖓𝖌𝖑𝖊𝖕 to cloath their Monks; the Lands of 𝕮𝖔𝖒𝖇𝖊𝖘 and 𝕲𝖗𝖊𝖊𝖓𝖘𝖙𝖚𝖉𝖊 in 𝕾𝖚𝖘𝖘𝖊𝖗, 𝕸𝖎𝖉𝖉𝖑𝖊𝖙𝖔𝖓 in 𝕭𝖚𝖈𝖐𝖎𝖓𝖌𝖍𝖆𝖒𝖘𝖍𝖎𝖗𝖊, and 𝕾𝖓𝖎𝖈𝖙𝖔𝖓𝖊 in 𝕭𝖊𝖉𝖋𝖔𝖗𝖉𝖘𝖍𝖎𝖗𝖊, and 𝕿𝖍𝖔𝖗𝖕𝖊 in 𝕻𝖔𝖗𝖐𝖘𝖍𝖎𝖗𝖊, with the Church and all the Appurtenances, and the Lands of the Knights who held the Demesne of the Abby, to defend all Scutages and foreign Services; and the Mannors of 𝕮𝖗𝖔-𝖈𝖍𝖊𝖘𝖑𝖊𝖕,* 𝕸𝖚𝖈𝖈𝖑𝖊𝖋𝖊𝖎𝖑𝖉,† 𝕾𝖊𝖗𝖊𝖙, 𝕭𝖆𝖈𝖍𝖊𝖘𝖜𝖔𝖗𝖙𝖍, 𝕭𝖗𝖚𝖙𝖊𝖜𝖊𝖑, 𝕻𝖞𝖓𝖊𝖋𝖊𝖑𝖉, 𝕸𝖚𝖗𝖊𝖉𝖊𝖓𝖊, 𝕮𝖍𝖎𝖑𝖉𝖜𝖎𝖈𝖍,‡ 𝕳𝖎𝖉𝖊 of 𝕷𝖆𝖓𝖌𝖑𝖊𝖕, 𝕾𝖎𝖘-𝖘𝖊𝖛𝖊𝖗𝖓𝖊, the Land of *Alexander* Son of *Turold*, 𝕭𝖚𝖝𝖙𝖔𝖓𝖊, 𝖂𝖎𝖓𝖉𝖗𝖎𝖓𝖌𝖊, *William de Northum,* *Hammond* the Verderar, the Hide of 𝕳𝖆𝖗𝖕𝖊𝖘𝖋𝖊𝖑𝖉, the Land of *Richard de Reimes*,

* Croxley Green.
† Miccleford Green.
‡ Khildwick, near St. Michael.

Robert de Talbois, John de Walden in **Walden,** and in **Thiteburst** the Land of *Hugh de Thiteburst,* the Vale of **Thebruge,** *Hugh de Bradwa, Helie, Peter de Chambre, William de Hahat, William de Wiche,* and *Nicholas* his Son, and *Ralph de Helpesfeld,* with all things belonging to them, with Soke and Sake, ou Stroude and Stream, ou Mude, Feld, Toll and Them, and Gribruche, Hamsoche, Murdre, Forestall, Danegeld, Infangenetheof and Out-fangenetheof, Flemenefremth, Blodewite, Wrec, that they may have upon all their Lands, and are upon their Tenants, in as large a Manner as the King's Officer might have them to his Use, and that no Person should intromit.

The same King, by another Charter dated at **Winches-ter,** granted and confirmed to this Abbot and his Church, all the Inquisitions which *Adam* the Monk, the Cellarer of the Abby, hath purchased of *Eli de Sumer,* the Church of *All-saints* in **Sudbury,** with the Chappel of **Weledon,** and and all the Land of **Middleton,** which is of the Fee of the Earl of **Glocester,** with all other their Appurtenances ; one Messuage in **Bigrabe,** and five hundred Acres of Land, and the Church of the same Vill of the Gift of *William de We-don ;* the Church of **Wilenge,** with all the Appurtenances, and nine Acres of Land, and one Messuage of the Gift of *William de Montfitchet,* and *Rohais* his Wife, and *William* their Son; the Church of **Lechetworth,** with all things be-longing to it, and twelve Acres of Land in the same Vill, and all their Part of the Church of **Waudelington** belonging to their Fee; and sixty Acres of Land in the same Vill, of the Gift of *William* the Son of *Robert de Waulington,* and all his Part of the Church of **Waudelington ;** and four and twenty Acres of Land in the same Vill, of the Gift of *Eustace de Chauz;* twenty Acres in **Waudelington,** of the Gift of *Thurston* the Archer, and all his Land in **Bernet ;** and six Acres of Land in **Waudelington,** of the Gift of *Julian* and *Hamond* her second Husband ; six Acres in the same Vill, of the Gift of *Ralph* and *Herbert* his Son; sixty Acres of Land in the same Vill of the Gift of *Eudo ;* twenty Acres of *Walter de Gravely ;* five Acres of Poll Measure, and ten or eight Foot in **Aiselle,** of the Gift of *Ade* the Son of *Humphry* and *Alum Wisthard* and *Odelina* his Mother; and all the Land inclosed by the Ditch, within the Bounds in **Woolwinwich,** of the Gift of *Allen de Winter,* and *Christian* his Wife, and *Simon* their Son; half an Hide in **Bishopescote,** of the Gift of *Richard de Bircherolls,* and of *Clare;* the old Mill of **Stapleford,** with the Place where it is scituated and the Pool adjoyning, and all the Marsh on either Side of the Water unto the Ditch which the Monks made; and sixty Acres of Land, of the Gift of *Agnes Fai* and *Ralph* her Son; seventy and six Acres of arable Land,

with one Marsh in 𝔖epehale, of the Gift of *Wimer de Ardes* and *Alice* his Wife, and all their Land lying between
the Highway which leads to 𝔥ertforð, and divided from
𝔖epehale, of the Gift of *Robert de Talbois* and *Ralph* his
Son; four hundred and one and thirty Acres of Land in
𝕿itehurst, of the Gift of *William* the Son of *Racon;* half
an Hide in 𝔊ravestone, one Acre in 𝔚atforð, of the Gift
of *Simon Talbois;* half a Virgate of *Ralph* of 𝔓uncharðon,
another half in 𝔇achesworth, of the Gift of *Ivo de Berstone;*
forty Acres of Land, one of Meadow, and one House in
𝔚ochemesteð, seven and twenty Acres in the same Vill, of
the Gift of *Godfry de Tiwing;* and sixty Acres in 𝕿iwing,
all the Land at 𝔄bsa, which lies between the Water at
𝔠olne, and the plough'd Ground called the 𝔥orsepole,
which *Alexander* the Son of *Turold,* before all the Court

at 𝔖t. 𝔄lbans, did release, with one Croft, which lies before the House of *Serlong* at 𝔄bsa,* of the Gift of *Ade* the
Son of *Ralph Buchmite* and *Ade* his Wife; and all the
Land which lies between the Lands of St. *Alban de Cam-
vera,* and the Lands of St. *Bartholomew,* which is of the
Fee of *William de Raunes,* near the Wood of 𝔄lðenham;
forty Acres of Land of *Helie* in 𝔇achesworth and *Gilbert*
her Son and Heir; seventeen Acres of Land in the Vill of
𝔇achesworth, of the Gift of *Walter* of the 𝔒ak; a Portion
of Land of 𝔠umbliton, which in Length is twelve Perches,
and in one Place six in Breadth, and in other Places three;
four or five Perches, of the Gift of *Richard Talbot* of
his Land in 𝔚penge, and at least twenty Foot in Breadth,
and as much in Length, to make the Pool to the Mill at
𝔊aston, to hold quit of all Customs and Services for the
Use of the Monks Kitchin, and that none shall presume to
convert them to any other Use.

The King also granted to this Abbot and his Church a
Fair to be held every Year within this Town of 𝔖t. 𝔄lban,
to continue for the Space of eight Days next before the
Nativity of St. *John* the Baptist, and also Free-Warren in
all the Lands within five Miles of 𝔖t. 𝔄lbans, that belonged to this Church, and that his Tenants should be discharged from the Payment of all Tolls.

This Abbot also obtained the Restoration of one Virgate,
half an Hide of Land in 𝔠uðicote, half an Hide of Land in
𝔚eðburn, and the Vill of 𝔖tanmeere, and all things belonging to them, which had been taken away by Force; and
he gave to *Geoffery Mapeham* the Land of 𝔐eriðene in
Exchange for the Land of 𝔅raðway, according to the
Deed of Agreement made by King *Henry.*

This Abbot bought of the same King twenty Shillings
worth of Land in 𝔅issopescote for one hundred fat Oxen,
and obtained for this Church a Saltpit at 𝔜icam, with the

Hund. of
Caishoe,
Salter and Land, one Hide of Land in 𝔐𝔢𝔦𝔫𝔡𝔩𝔢𝔱𝔬𝔫 with
the Tyth of the Church of that Vill, and the Hermitage of
𝔐𝔬𝔬𝔯𝔦, which was *Ralphs* the Hermites, with the Church-
es, Tyth, and many other things.

In *Anno* 1115, 15 *H.* I. this Church was dedicated by
Archbishop *Rodulf, Jeoffery, Richard* of 𝕷𝔬𝔫𝔡𝔬𝔫, *Ralph* of
𝔇𝔲𝔯𝔥𝔞𝔪, *Robert* of 𝕷𝔦𝔫𝔠𝔬𝔩𝔫, *Roger* of 𝔖𝔞𝔯𝔲𝔪, Bishops, and
many Abbots, King *Hen.* I. Queen *Maud,* and many Earls,
Barons, and great and famous Persons, Archdeacons, Deans,
Presbiters, and Guardians of Churches, whereof the Number is not known for Multitude, on the fifth of the Calends
of *January,* where the greatest Part, as well banqueting in
the Pallace, as worshipping in the Church, eating and re-
joycing in the Court of St. *Albans,* did honourably continue
till the Epiphany, to the Praise of the blessed Protomartyr
Alban; and when he had govern'd this Church one and
twenty Years, he died the 17th of the Calends of *June, An.*
1119, 19 *H.* I. and was buried in the Chappel which he had
built near the Church, dedicated to St. *Cuthbert.*

Matt. Paris *de*
l'itis Abbat.
fol. 56.
XVI. *Jeoffery* was a Person born of the noble Progeny
of the *Normans,* endowed with moral Honesty and divine
Knowledge, elected by all the Monks, with the Assent of
King *Henry,* and took upon him the Government of this
Church; he gave to the Sacrist of this Monastery the Church
of St. *Mary* of 𝔕𝔦𝔠𝔨𝔪𝔢𝔯𝔢𝔰𝔴𝔬𝔯𝔱𝔥 and the Appurtenances, and
the Church of St. *Peter* in this Town to the Infirmary, for
Medicines for the Sick; he founded the Hospital of St.
Julian, by the Advice and Consent of the Convent; called
together divers poor People, and assign'd to them the Tyth
of the Rent of the Town of 𝔖𝔱. 𝔄𝔩𝔟𝔞𝔫, which was 60*s.* also
30*s.* which *Peter* of 𝔖𝔭𝔯𝔢𝔱 received of *Redings* of 𝔖𝔭𝔯𝔢𝔱,
all the Tyth Corn of the Lordship of 𝔥𝔞𝔪𝔰𝔱𝔲𝔡𝔢, all the
Tyth of the Lordship of 𝕶𝔦𝔫𝔤𝔰𝔟𝔢𝔯𝔯𝔭, and two Parts of the
Tyth Corn of St. *Michaels* and St. *Stephens,* except that
which the Chaplain of the Leapers had; two Parts of the
Tyth-corn of the Lordship of 𝔈𝔰𝔱𝔬𝔫, two Parts of the Tyth-
Corn of the Lordship of 𝔚𝔯𝔞𝔱𝔢𝔴𝔦𝔠𝔨, two Parts of the Tyth-
corn of the Lordship of *Roger de Limes* in 𝔚𝔯𝔞𝔱𝔢𝔴𝔦𝔠𝔨, two
Parts of the Tyth-corn of *Richard d'How,* two Parts of the
Tyth-corn of the Lordship of *William* Son of *Anketill* of
𝔆𝔲𝔡𝔦𝔠𝔬𝔱𝔢, the tenth Part of the Corn of the Lordship of
𝔖𝔱𝔯𝔞𝔱𝔩𝔢, the half Part of the Tyth of *Stephen de Lege* of his
Lordship of 𝔥𝔞𝔫𝔢𝔩𝔬𝔴, two Parts of the Tyth of *Roger de
Chandes* of his Lordship of 𝔖𝔦𝔟𝔢𝔩𝔢𝔰𝔥𝔬, and two Parts of the
Tyth of *Simon de Bellocampo* of his Lordship of 𝔖𝔱𝔞𝔪𝔣𝔬𝔯𝔡,

Ibid. fol. 58.
This Abbot built a large and noble Hall with a double
Roof to entertain Strangers honourably, near to which he
built a fair Bed-chamber, which they usually called the
Queen's Bed-chamber, because it was assign'd to her Use,

besides it was not lawful for any other Woman to lodge in *Hund. of* *Caishoe.* the Monastery: He built another House like the Hall, with a Chappel towards the East, where was the Infirmary; in which and the Chappel, he commanded Silence to be strictly observed, and the sick Men to be called every Day to a Table in the Refectory by a Bell; also he commanded another Hall to be built by the same Workmen, conformable to the former at **West Wicam**, for his Friend and Kinsman, who had been bountiful to this Church.

He did also erect a small Nunnery at **Sopwell** for a select Matt. Paris, fol. 58. Number of Virgins, with a Church-yard which he caused to be dedicated; and ordained that none but those of the same Nunnery should be buried there.

Anno 1143, 8 *Steph.* when *Henry* Duke of **Normandy** *Mon. Angl.* vol. 1, fol. 119, 203. had received the Honour of Knighthood from *David* King of *Scots*, and came into **England** with the Countenance of many of the great Men here, Earl *Jeoffery de Magnavile*, an expert Soldier, adhereing to the King for a time, was charged through Envy by some of the Prince's Nobility, for complying with the King's Enemies; and at a Council call'd at this Town, he was seized by the King's Command, and committed to safe Custody; and tho' many of his Friends interceded for him, alledging that those Accusations were not true, yet they could not obtain his Liberty, till he had rendred up the Tower of **London**, with his Castles of **Walden** and **Plesby** into the King's Hands.

This Abbot gave many rich Ornaments to this Monastery, with a Chalice and Cover of massy pure Gold, which afterwards he sent to Pope *Celestine* II. that he might appease or mitigate the Covetousness of his Holiness, who would have impropriated the Mannor of——————. When he had governed this Church twenty six Years and some Months, he died on the fifth of the Calends of *March*, *An.* 1146, 11 *Steph.* and was buried in this Church, with this Inscription upon his Stone.

> *Abbas* Galfridus *Papa, cui fuit ipse modestus*
> *Hic jacet innocuus, prudens, pius atque modestus.*

XVII. *Ralph*, who was Chaplain and Treasurer to the Ibid. fol. 64. MS. Mr. Cox. Bishop of **Lincoln**, by his Means was made a Monk, and in the Reign of King *Stephen*, advanced to be Abbot of this Church, in whose time Queen *Maud* gave the Mannors of **Berwick** and **Lilleburne** to this Monastery.

King *Stephen*, by his Charter, confirmed to this Abbot and the Monks, all their Customs and Lands, and granted that this Church should be free from all Tribute, and the Reparation of Castles, and making of Trenches against the Enemy, and granted to them Toll and Them, &c. and exempted them from episcopal Jurisdiction.

Hund. of
Caishor.

Matt. Paris,
fol. 64.

This Abbot built the Chambers of the Abbots adjoyning
to the Church with solid Work, covered the Roof with
shingled Oak, and gave divers rich Coats and Vestments
for the Orders of his Church, which he govern'd between
four and five Years; then a grievous Sickness seiz'd him,
which was incurable, and seeing the Monastery would be
destitute of a Rector, he recommended *Robert de Gorham*
the Prior, and all the Monks unanimously desired him to
take that Province upon him, and after that Election, the
old Abbot lived some small time, and then died *Anno* 1151,
16 *Steph.*

Ibid. fol. 66.

XVIII. This *Robert* was Nephew to Abbot *Geoffery*,
and took upon him the Abbot of a Monk beyond the Seas;
but obtaining Leave there to see his Friends in 𝔈nglan𝔡,
came to this Monastery, where he was received with great
Respect, and when he saw the Glory of their Discipline, he
desired that they would admit him into their Monastery;
and upon Letters dimissory from his own Monastery, and the
Request of his Uncle *Jeoffery*, then Abbot, he was admitted
a Monk and a Brother of this Church; sometime after he was
made Secretary, in which Office he decently cover'd the
greater Part of this Church with Lead; from thence he was
advanced to be Prior, and when he had held that Office near
two Years, the Place of Abbot falling *Anno* 1151, 16 *Steph.*
he was preferr'd to the pastoral Staff, and prevailed with
King *Stephen* to give him a Promise that he would demolish

MS. Mr Cox.

the Castle of 𝔎inesbury, for that Thieves lurked there, and
were troublesome and very vexatious to the Abby.

Matt. Paris,
fol. 66, 70.

In his time *Nicholas*, Son to *Robert Breakspeare*, born
in a Village near this Place call'd 𝔄bbots 𝔏angley, a Youth
in Age and comly in Body, but an easy Clerk, addrest
himself to the Abbot, and humbly beg'd the religious Habit; when he was examin'd and found insufficient, the
Abbot gave him this civil Answer, wait my Son a while,
and fit thyself at School, that thou mayest be qualified for
the Cloath which thou desirest: He modestly taking this
Answer for a Denial, went away, and reflecting upon his
own Neglect and and Loss of time at School, set forth immediately for 𝔓aris, where he improved his time with
great Diligence at School, and by the Advantage of his quick
and natural Parts soon recovered his lost time, became a
great Proficient in all sorts of Learning, and far exceeded
all his Schoolfellows, so that he was removed to 𝔖t. 𝔎ufus,
a Place not much distant from 𝔙alentia, where he was
made a Regular, and in short time was advanc'd by his
great merits to be Abbot there, from whence he was sent
on a Messuage to 𝔎ome on the Behalf of his Monastery,
and by this Means gained the Opportunity of shewing his
Parts and Learning; and by the Performance of his Busi-

Hund. of
Caishoe.

ness he obtain'd a great Opinion in Pope *Eugenius*, who
said, it was great Pity that so much Learning should be
buried in a little Hole, and thinking him fit to serve the
Church in a higher Station, chose him Bishop of Alba near
Rome; not long after, his Holiness having great Occasion
to send two prudent and learned Men, to convert the People of Norway from Paganisme to the Christian Religion,
thought him a fit Person for that great Work, and sent
him thither with another, where he managed his Part ad-
mirably well, and upon his Return, declaring the Success he
obtain'd, with great Gravity and Eloquence, the Pope advanced him to be a Cardinal, in which Office, he gain'd
much Credit and Reputation among the whole Conclave of
Cardinals, insomuch that when the Chair became vacant,
they chose him Pope of Rome for his great Worth and
Merit, by the Name of *Adrian* the fourth.

Matt. Paris,
fol. 70.

When the News of the Promotion of this Pope reach'd
this Monastery, this Abbot rejoyced much, and resolved to
make a Journey to Rome to confirm the antient Priviledges of this Church; and acquainting King *Henry* II.
with his Intentions, he employ'd him upon an Embassage
thither, and gave him Letters under his Royal Seal,
humbly and devoutly requesting his Holiness, that he
would be pleased to extend his Favour to him, as well in the
Business of this Church, as in his own Affairs: This Abbot
then set forth and came to Beneventum, where he found
the Pope, who received him with a serene Countenance
and a joyful Heart, and treating him with more than usual
Honour, the Abbot presented his Holiness with Gold and
Silver of no small Weight, and other precious Gifts of
great Value, also three Mitres and Sandals of admirable
Work, which the Lady *Christian*, Prioress of Margate,
had diligently made; the Pope viewed the Mitres and
Sandals, and commended greatly his Devotion and Courtesie; but merrily said, I refuse thy Gifts, because thou
once denied me shelter under the Wings of your Religious
House when I craved your Charity, and beg'd the Monastic Habit; to which this Abbot readily answer'd, my
Lord, it was not in our Power to receive you when the
Will of God oppos'd it, whose great Wisdom had design'd
you to serve him in a higher Station; then the Pope ap-
plauding his witty and ingenious Answer, added, dear
Abbot, ask boldly what thou desirest, for nothing shall be
wanting to the blessed *Alban;* then the Abbot incouraged
by the Leave of the Pope, disposed of all those Gifts of
Silver and Gold (valued at two hundred Marks) to the
Cardinals and Servants of the Pope, with pleasant Speeches
and Repertees: He gave many pretty Trifles which he had
got at London and Paris among them, and by this Means

R 2

Hund. of
Caishoe.
obtained so great Favour of the *Romans*, that his Name
was extol'd to the Skies; but one Day whilst the Pope
and the Abbot were familiarly and secretly talking together, the Abbot intimated, Tears trickling down his Cheeks,
the great and intolerable Oppressions which the Church
suffered under the Bishop of Lincolne; and the Pope pity-
ing him for the same, granted this great Priviledge, that
this Church henceforth should be so free from the Subjection of any Bishop, as well in the Body of the Monastery
as in their Cells and Vills, that no Bishop (except the
Roman Bishop) should intermeddle there.

Matt. Paris,
fol. 72.
When this Abbot had dispatchd his Business, and receiv'd the Apostolic Benediction, he returned to England,
where within few Days after a National Synod was call'd
at London, and the Abbot produced his Letters from the
Pope, and shew'd the Priviledges which he had granted,
and the Presents which he had sent to this Monastery.

King *Hen.* II. granted and confirm'd to God and this
Church, all their Cells, Lands and Possessions, *viz.* Tyne-
meto, Dynham, Wimundesham, Bernether, Wallingford,
Hertford, Heathfield, and Belloloco, with the Churches,
Lands and Homages, Rents, and all things belonging to
them, the Vill of St. Albans, with the Market and all the
Liberty, the Vill of Watford with the Market, Kinseberry,
Westwick, Sanderidge, Redburne, Brydelle and Tyde-
hangam, with the Wood of Northaw, which *Peter de Va-*
loines sometime held; Bernet, with the Wood of Southaw,
Borham, Huseheog, and the Park with all the Soke,
Langley, Caishoe, Rickmaresworth, Sereth, Grenesbury,
Wynseslaw, Sppetumam, and Horwood, with the Forest
and Chase, Estume, Bishopscote, Heastanester, Nortune,
Newham, Caldecot, Walden, and Bradewate, with the
Churches, Lands, Woods, Homagers, Rents, Mills, Mea-
dows, Feedings, and all things belonging to them.

Also for the Sustentation of the Kitchin of the Hospital,
the Churches of Luiton, Hoctune and Portesgrabe, with all
Lands, Homagers, and Tythes whatsoever, the Churches
of Walden, and Appleton in the County of York, and the
Church of Watford for the Entertainment of Strangers;
and the Churches of Thyrefeld, Redburne and Wyneslaw,
with their Chappels, and of Langley, to cloath their Monks;
and the Churches of Coulfingeth and St. Stephens, with
their Chapels, to sustain the Kitchen of their Monks; and
the Lands of Cumbes and Greensted in Sussex, and of
Middleton in Buckinghamshire, of Snicton in Bedfordshire, and Thorpe in Yorkshire, with the Church, and
Norton with their Appurtenances, also the Lands of the
Knights who held the Demeasne of the Abbot, to defend
all Scutages and all other Foreign Services; also Croches-

lep, 𝕸inclefelð, Serret, 𝕯achesworth, 𝕭rutestwel, 𝕻ine-
felð, 𝕸uriðene, 𝕮hilðwick, the Hide of 𝕷angley, 𝕾isse-
berne, the Land of *Alexander* the Son of *Turold*, 𝕭urtone,
𝖂imrinch, the Land of *William de Northum*, the Land of
Hugh Derrarius, the Hide of 𝕳arpesfelð, the Land of
Richard de Rennes, the Land of *Robert Talboyes*, also the
Lands of all the Free Tenants, *John de Weld* in 𝖂alð
and in 𝕿iteburst, the Land of *Hugh de Titeburst*, of *Vei-
lis de Theyburge*, *Hugh de Bradwere*, *Helie*, *Peter de
Chambre*, *William de Hahate*, *William de Wich*, *Nicholas*
his Son, and *Ralph* of 𝕳elpesfelð, and all their Appurtenances, with Soke and Sake, ou Strode and Stream, ou
Wude and Feld, Toll, and Them, and Gribuche, and
Hamsochne, Murdre, Forestald, Danegeld, Infangenetheof, Outfangenetheof, Flemenfreneth, Bloudwite, Wrec
upon all their Tenements wheresoever, in as full and ample
manner as the King's Minister ought to have for his Use,
and the King will not that any *French* or *English* shall intromit in any thing upon their Lands or their Tenements,
unless they themselves and their own Ministers desire them
for their Use, to whom they have committed the Care
hereof, because the King hath given them to God and this
Church of St. *Alban*, for the Redemption of his Soul and
his Parents, with all the Liberties and Free Customs
which Kingly Power hath or can Grant to any Church;
and the King prohibited upon Forfeiture, that not any one
shall presume in any manner to break them; also the King
prohibited that neither Munscher, Steward, Baker, Chamberlain, Porter, Custos or Reeve, shall enter into their
Lands or Houses, without their Leave or Assent, in his time
or his Successors, by the means of any Prince or Justice
whatsoever.

King *Hen.* II. by several Charters confirm'd to this Matt. Paris,
fol. 75.
Church the Grants of all the Mannors, Lands, Tenements,
Priviledges, Liberties and Immunities, which any of his
royal Predecessors had heretofore made, yet the Bishop
of 𝕷incolne and his Chapter incited many powerful Men
to the Prejudice of this Church, and at length raised the
King's Anger against the Abbot and Monks hereof, whereupon *Hugh* Bishop of 𝕯urham interposed, and being an
eloquent and noble Man, amicably ended the Difference;
from that time the Bishop of 𝕷incolne dared not to attempt
again, to bring this Monastery under his Subjection
whilst Pope *Adrian* lived, but when he died and *Alexander*
III. succeeded, the new Priviledges which Pope *Adrian*
had granted were disputed again, till *Anno* 1178, 24 *Hen.*
II. when that Pope confirm'd them.

About twenty Years after, new Commotions and Quar- Ibid. fol 80.
rells were raised again between this Monastery and the

Hund. of
Caistoe.

Matt. Paris,
fol. 90.

Church of **Lincolne**; but *Clement* III. quieted them and confirmed again all the Priviledges granted to this Church.

This Abbot procur'd the Church of **Luton**, to be annexed to this Monastery; and when he had nobly govern'd this Church fifteen Years, and four Months, and some Days, he died on the tenth of the Calends of *November*, *Anno* 1166, 12 *Hen.* II. and was buried at the Feet of Abbot *Paul* in this Monastery.

Ibid. fol. 91.

XIX. *Simon*, a learned and moral Man, born in **England**, and educated in this Monastery, succeeded; was very diligent, to support and augment the Order, caused many Books to be written for the Use of the Convent; and began to gather a Treasury of Gold, Silver, and precious Jewels; and a most noble Bier or Coffin; at his Instance, the Bishop of **Durham** dedicated the Chapel of St. *Cuthbert*, which was near the Cloister of St. *Albans*, to the Honour of the same Saint and St. *John Baptist*.

Ibid. fol. 92.

This Abbot gave a great golden Chalice of most pure Gold, adorn'd with precious Gems, and beautified with delicate Works of curious Flowers to this Church; and a little Cup worthy of great Admiration, of pure and shining Gold, with incomparable Gems of divers Kinds, neatly annexed to it, in which the Work did exceed the Substance, to lay up the Eucharist; to set upon the great Altar of the Martyr; and King *Henry* sent another noble and precious Cup, in which the Body of Christ might be contained; this Abbot gave three other small Chalices of Gold to this Church, and a noble Cross golden Plate, with a golden Jewel, plac'd in the middle of it; and when he had govern'd this Church about fifteen Years, he died *Anno* 1188, *ultimo* H. II.

Ibid fol. 56,
57.

XX. *Garine* was born at **Cambridge**, and the Year before he took upon him the Monastic Habit, his Fame was great, and his Name was celebrated, for the Reverence of his honest Life; He was excellently well learned, and fair in Body, for which Reasons he was received into this Monastery; in short time after he was made Prior, and thence promoted to the pastoral Staff by the unanimous Consent of all the Convent, except *William Martel* the Sacrist, who then aspir'd to the same Dignity; soon after *Matthew* his Brother was elected Prior, who built the School in this Borough, which at that time was very famous, greatly flourisht, very profitable, and had more Scholars in it than any School in **England**, and he prefer'd his Nephew Mr. *Garinus* to be Master there, who govern'd it many Years.

Ibid.
fol. 56, 57.

This Abbot obtained a Grant from King *Richard* I. that no Prior of any Cell, that belong'd to this Monastery, should be made Collector of Tenths, or Subsidies, or of any other Tax, or Duty whatsoever; and he and his Con-

vent gave to the sick Women of St. *Mary de Prato*, the
Place wherein their Church was built, the Shops on either
Side the public Street, with the Way in the End of the
arable Feild and Meadow of 𝕶ingsburp; and for their
Sustenance, all the Procurations, which were wont, or
should after that time, be given, at the Decease of the Ab-
bots, also the Procuration of King *Offa*, King *Henry*, and
Pope *Adrian*, with Meat and Drink assigned at the same
Procurations for ever; and until they should fall they
should receive of the Cellerer four Loaves of Bread, and
one for Sopwell, and the same Measure of Beer, and a
Mess of Meat of the Cook, and the first and last Loaf of
Bread from the Oven of the Court; and they shall quietly
grind every Week the Chief of their Dichmuln, and their
Mault, at the Maultmuln of the Abby, and every of them
shall have an old Coat of a Monk every Year; and one
Frock, to the Number of thirteen, and three Pence every
Year, out of the Toll of St. *Alban;* and the Chaplain that
shall serve at the Chapel of St. *Mary de Prato*, shall
have one Loaf of Bread, and one Measure of Beer, and
one Mess of the Cook; and the Chaplain and the Clerk
shall have one Mark of the Church of 𝕶alden every Year,
and half a Mark of the Church of 𝕹ewham; they moreover granted to the sick Women, that they should have the
Tyth of the Lordship of 𝕷uton and a little Barn there,
where their Tyth should be laid, and the Servant that shall
gather this Tyth shall eat with the Family, with many
other things too long to relate, and when this Abbot had
govern'd this Church eleven Years, eight Months and
eight Days, he full of Years died the third of the Calends
of *May, Ann.* 1195, 6 *R.* I.

XXI. *John de Cella*, a Person born of mean Parents,
not far from a Street called 𝕾to(ham, but of great Piety
and a Lover of the Order and Discipline of the Cloyster;
in his Youth he was a diligent Frequenter of the Schools at
𝕻aris, and became a Companion for the Masters there,
and when he took upon him the religious Habit, he daily
increased in Vertue, and by Reason thereof was chosen
Prior of 𝕮allyngford, where he behaved himself so well
in that Office, that his Merits induced the Convent to advance him to the Government of this Church; but after the
Manner of Schollars, ignorant of the Care of the Family,
he devoted himself wholly to Study, Contemplation, and
continual Devotion, and quitted himself of the Trouble of
Martha, choosing the better Part like *Mary ;* for he carefully observed the Commands of his Master, as the most
worthy thing, and committed the Reins of the Government
of the outward things to the Lord *Reimund* his Prior,
(who who was a Person of great Council, Prudence, and

Hund. of
Caisboe.

Matt. Paris,
fol. 95, 96, 97..

Ibid. fol. 103.

Hund. of Caishoe. Religion), and to the Lord *Roger de Parco* his Cellerer, (who was very provident and circumspect in secular Affairs), that being eased of the Charge of those worldly things he might be at Leisure more freely to contemplate and pray; and by the Advice and Assistance of those two Brethren, and with the Encouragement of an hundred Marks laid up by his Predecessor, design'd for the Work of the Church, he pull'd down the Wall of the Front of the Church to the Ground, with the old Roof, and indissolvable Cement; after that the old Refectory and Dormitory, and built a new and fair Refectory, where he rejoiced with his Brethren, then a most noble Dormitory; and the Convent spared their Wine for fifteen Years towards the building of these two Houses.

Brady's Hist. of Engl. fol. 467. In the time of this Abbot, King *John* sent his Precept to all Sheriffs of England, that they should cause four lawful Men with the Reeve of every Vill, which they kept in their own Hands, to meet at this Town of St. Albans, that by those and their other Ministers, he might enquire and be informed, what Damage every Bishop had sustain'd? what had been taken from? and what was due to them? and the same Year confirmed all the Grants of his Predecessors to this Church.

Matt. Paris, fol. 239. Prin's Coll. pt. 1, p. 26. In *Anno* 1213, 14 *Johan*, a Parliament was held at this Town of St. Albans, where *Jeoffery*, the Son of *Peter*, and the Bishop of Winchester, with the Archbishop, Bishops, and Nobles of the Kingdom were assembled; at which time the King's Peace was declared to all, and it was firmly commanded on the King's behalf, that the Laws of King *Henry* his Grandfather should be kept by all in the Kingdom, and all unjust Laws should be made void; moreover all Sheriffs, Foresters, and other the King's Officers were commanded, that as they loved their Lives and Members, they should not in any manner extort any thing violently, nor presume to wrong any, nor make Scotals any where in the Kingdom, as they were wont to do.

This Abbot did many works of Piety; and when he had governed this Church eighteen Years, in *Anno* 1214, 15 *Johan*. he exchanged this Life for a better.

XXII. *William de Trumpington*, on the Day of St. *Edmond* the King and Martyr, was elected and installed, and on St. *Andrew's* Day was blest by *Eustace*, Bishop of Ely, and received the Reward of his Blessing as the manner was before the great Altar: When the Pope suspended *Stephen*, Archbishop of Canterbury, for holding Correspondence with the Barons, and endeavoring to dethrone the King; upon Notice thereof, he came to this Monastery, caused the Suspension to be published here, and sent it from hence to be published in all Cathedral and Coventual Churches thro' England.

William Earl of Salisbury and *Falcatius de Brent*, with the Forces left under their Command at this Town, put very strong Garrisons into the Castles of Windsor, Hertford, and Berkhamsted, to observe the Barons in the City of London, and to hinder People from going and carrying Victuals thither; then marched into the Counties of Essex, Middlesex, Hertford, Cambridge, and Huntingdon, where they made the like Waste upon the Barons' Estates, as the King did Northward, and farther destroy'd the Parks and Warrens and cut down their Hortgrounds.

In *Anno* 1217, 1 *H.* III. Prince *Lewis* took the Castles of Hertford and Berkhamsted, then ravished this Country, and plunder'd the Inhabitants that resided in the way until he came to this Town, and requir'd the Abbot to do Homage to him; which he refused unless he was released from his Homage to the King of England; *Lewis* inraged at this Answer swore he would burn both the Abby and the Town, unless he would do it; whereupon the Abbot, by the Mediation of *Saher* Earl of Winton, made a Composition with him for himself and the Town, till the Candlemas following, and gave him fourscore Marks of Silver, to spare the Abby and Town so long, and then he returned to London.

The 22nd of *January* following, *Falcatius de Brent*, having gathered a Number of Ruffians out of the Castles of Oxford, Northampton, Bedford, and Windsor, came to the Abby of St. *Albans* in the Evening, spoiled the Town, took Men, Women, and Children, bound them, and slew some, so that the Abbot to save the Abby, and Town from burning, was forc'd to give *Falcatius* one hundred Pounds of Silver.

'Tis reported of this *Falcatius*, that after he had plunder'd this Town, slain divers of the Inhabitants, carried away others as Prisoners, and extorted a great Sum of Money from the Abbot and Townsmen, he came hither accidentally, to speak with *Pandulph*, Bishop of Norwich; and the Bishop asking him in the Presence of the Abbot, and others, if he had ever offended St. *Alban*, he answered, no; the Bishop reply'd, I asked thee this Question, because as I lay asleep in my Bed one Night, I dreamed, that I was in the Church of St. *Alban*, where standing before the High Altar, and praying, I looked behind me, and saw thee standing in the Quire; and casting mine Eyes upward, I saw a mighty Stone fall out of the Steeple, with such a Force, that it crushed thy Head and Body together, so that thou didst thereupon vanish, as if thou hadst been drowned; wherefore my Advice to thee is, that if thou canst call to mind, that thou hast in any sort offended that blessed Martyr, that thou wilt make full Satisfaction to him and

Hund. of Caishoe.

Brady's Hist. fol. 504.

Ibid. fol. 528.

Stow's Annals, fol. 176.
Matt. Paris, vol. 2, fol. 199

Dugd. Bar. vol. 1, fol. 745, 746.

all his, before the Stone doth fall upon thine Head; but this wretched Man, desiring Pardon from the Abbot and Convent, refused to give them any Satisfaction at all, for what he had extorted from them; and 'tis said, that his Death happen'd soon after, by Poison taken in a Fish, wherein it was put; and lying down after Supper, he was found dead, black, and noisome.

When the Solemnity of *Easter* was past, and the Castle of 𝔐ount 𝔖oril was beseiged, Prince *Lewis*, at the Instigation of *Saher* Earl of 𝔚inchester, the Lord, or Owner of the Castle, sends out of 𝔏ondon six hundred Knights, and above twenty thousand armed Men, who all gaped after Plunder, whereof the Chief were the Earl of 𝔓erch, Marshal of 𝔉rance, *Saher* Earl of 𝔚inchester, *Robert Fitz-Walter*, and many others, who were judged very fit for that Expedition: They set forth the last of *April*, marched towards this Town, burning and robbing all the Towns and Churches in their Way, spoiling all Sorts of Men, and cruelly tormenting them, that they might force excessive Ransoms from them, neither did they spare this Abby, tho' the Abbot a little before had satisfied *Lewis:* Then they proceeded to 𝔕edburne, where they spoiled the Church, and from thence marched to 𝔇unstable, where they did much mischief to that Church and from thence went forward to the North, with Intent to remove the Siege before the Castle of 𝔐ount 𝔖oril.

This Abbot was summon'd to appear among all the great Prelates of Christendom, at the Council of 𝔏ateran, which was called by Pope *Innocent* III.; from hence he went at great Charge, carrying with him two Monks, *Alexander de Appleton*, a very learned Man, and of good Behaviour, and *Roger Poretane*, who were well acquainted at the Court of 𝔕ome; and when this Abbot appeared in Council, he behaved himself with that Learning and Discretion, that the Pope and all the Prelates greatly applauded him.

On the 16th of the Calends of *January, Anno* 1232, 16 *H.* III. a great Consistory of Abbots, Priors, Arch-deacons, with almost all the Nobility of the Kingdom, Masters, and Clerks, met here by the Command of the Pope, that they might celebrate the Divorce between the Countess of 𝔈ssex and her Husband; but on the Morrow, the Consistory was discharged, and every one returned to their Homes.

This Abbot appointed a melodious and most sweet noted Bell, called by the Name of St. *Mary*, to be tolled thrice every Day at seasonable times, to call six Monks, with the chief at the Altar, and other faithful People of Christ and St. *Mary* humbly and devoutly administering to them, and praying for the Prosperity of this Church and their own.

He also rebuilt St. *Cuthbert's* Chappel, being as then

ruinous and ready to fall down, which he made to the Honour of St. *Cuthbert*, St. *John* the Baptist, and St. *Agnes* the Virgin; and when he had govern'd this Church twenty Years and almost three Months, he died on the Feast of St. *Matthew, An.* 1235, 19 *H.* III. and was buried on the 3d of the Calends of *March* following, by the Abbot of **Wantam**.

Hund. of Caishoe.

Matt. Paris fol. 125.

XXIII. *John* of **Hertford**, born at that Town, from whence he received his Name, and Prior of the Cell there, was created and install'd Abbot of this Church; he gave a Cap well embroider'd, with a bushy Robe to wear in the Quire, and a Cup guilded with Silver, very precious in Work and Substance, which he assign'd for the Refectory: He built a most noble Hall for the Use of Strangers, and added very many Bedchambers to the same, with an inner Parlour, and a Chimney, and a most noble Picture, and an Entry, and a small Hall; also a most noble Entry, with a Porch or Gallery, and very many fair Bedchambers, with their inner Chambers, and Chimneys, to receive Strangers honourably; for the Hall which was there was become ruinous, and very unsightly, but the new Hall was cover'd with Lead.

Ibid. fol. 133.

King *Hen.* III. by his Charter dated at **Woodstock**, 17 *May, Anno* 1248, 32 *Regni sui*, granted Free-warren to this Abbot and his Successors, in all their Demesne Lands whatsoever in **England**, and that no Person should hawk or hunt there without his License, upon the Pain of 10*l.*

Anno 1250, 34 *H.* III. upon St. *Lucies* Day, there was a great Earthquake in this Town and the Parts thereabouts, with a Noise under Ground as tho' it thundred, which was the more strange, for that the Ground is chalky and sound, nor hollow or loose as those are where Earthquakes often happen; and this Noise did so fright the Dawes, Rooks, and other Birds, which sat upon Houses or Trees, that they flew to and fro, as if they had been frighted by a Goss-hawk. *Augustine Galestius*, in his Book of Earthquakes, says, that the Cause of them proceeds from the Wind when it gets into the Bowels of the Earth, and being rarified by the Sun or Stars beginneth to swell, and seeking Passage to get forth, is pent up by the Solidness of the Earth, of which he setteth forth three Kinds;

Holl. vol. 2, fol. 243.

1. *Chasmatius*, when the Ground gapeth or sinketh down, like that which happen'd *Anno* 1175, 26 *H.* II. at **Oxenhall** near **Darlington**, in the Bishoprick of **Durham**, the Earth lifted up itself like an high Tower, and so stood from Morning till Night, then it fell down with a terrible Noise, leaving a hugh deep Pit, which *Leland* saith he saw, and is now called **Hell Kettle**.

2. Another Kind is *Brasta* or *Brasmatius*, as when the Earth riseth up like an Hill, and so moveth as **Markle**

Hund. of Caishoe. Hill in 𝕳erefordshire, *Anno* 1571, which for three Days together raised itself to a great Height, and so moved in a frightful Sort, with a roaring Noise, it overthrew 𝕽ownaston Chappel, Sheepcoat, and Trees, and at length rested, being now of the Height of 12 Fathoms.

3. The last Kind is *Epichienta*, as when the Earth trembleth and shaketh, like that great Earthquake in 1165, 12 *H.* II. in the Isle of 𝔈ly, 𝕹orfolk, and 𝕾uffolk, that overthrew them that stood on their Feet, and made Bells to ring in the Steeple.

Inspeximus. King *Henry*, by his Charter dated 13th of *October*, *An.* 1254, 38 *Regni sui*, discharged the Abbot of an Amercement of 100*l.* assess'd upon this Town and Liberty; because the Inhabitants came not before *Henry de Mare* and *William de Wilton* at 𝕮hesbunt, which is out of the Liberty, to enquire of Trespasses; and he released to this Abbot two Marks and an Half, which *Nicholas de Espiter*, *Alexander Stoile*, *William de Saurige*, and *Reginald* the Goldsmith, Tenants of the Abbot, were amerced out of the Liberty, for that Trespass, and the King confirmed this Priviledge because the Tenants of this Abbot ought not by their Charters to be summon'd out of this Liberty before any Justice or Inquisitors for any Cause whatsoever.

Anno 1247, 31 *H.* III. *John* and *Alexander*, two Friars Minors, Englishmen by Birth, were sent by the Pope to collect Money in 𝔈ngland, by his Authority, and under the Pretence of Charity; they obtained the King's License for it, then came to this Monastery, where they demanded of this Abbot 400 Marks to be paid to them for the Pope's Use: Who answer'd, that such Exactions were never known before, and very unjust, for that it was impossible to answer them, and in the Beginning of Lent following, they demanded again of the Abbot other 400 Marks, and then cited the Abbot to appear at 𝕷ondon within three Days, to satisfie the Pope's Demand; upon which the Abbot sent his Archdeacon to appear for him at the Place appointed, who after Demand made, obtain'd with some Difficulty a Copy of the Brief, and answer'd that the Abbot design'd to send special Messengers to 𝕽ome, to acquaint the Pope with these Grievances, and for Remedy appeal'd to him; but when the Messengers of the Abbot came to 𝕷yons, (where the Pope then resided) they were coldly received, and met with great Difficulties, and some Checks; but when they saw their Entertainment, and no Remedy, they compounded for 200 Marks, and their Expence amounted to a hundred Marks more.

Matt. Paris, pl. 2, fol. 255. *Anno* 1257, 41 *H.* III. the Archbishop of 𝕸essina came as Legate from the Pope with a great Train of Servants and Horses, and Letters of Procuration, and Authority to demand, receive, and punish such as should resist, and sent *Hund. of* Caishoc. his Commands in Writing to every Prelate to provide him Money by Way of Proxy, so that he received 21 Marks of this Church, and the Cells belonging to it, and when the Monks gave him a Visit in his House, and brought no Money with them, he asked them why they were such Beggars, and advised them to send to some Merchant that would lend them the Money, and detained them there as Prisoners untill such time that they had satisfied his covetous Demands.

This Abbot and Convent on *Palm-sunday, Anno* 1257, Brady's *Hist. of Engl.* fol. 619. received Letters from the Pope to let them know that they must pay five hundred Marks to certain Merchants, to whom they were bound in that Sum within a Month, otherwise they were to understand, that after that time they should be suspended; tho' they did not know that they were bound to any Man.

The Exactors or Usurers being severe upon this Church about the Feast of *Simon* and *Jude*, it was under Interdict Ibid. fol. 620. fifteen Days, not that it wanted great Priviledges, but that the detestable Addition of *Non Obstante* annull'd the pious Concessions and Authority of all the holy Fathers; therefore the Convent rather chose to comply with an unjust and violent Sentence, than be guilty of a Contempt.

Anno 1258, 42 *H.* III. King *H.* came to this Monastery; Matt. Paris, fol. 980. he continued three Days, caused them to carry the Martyr solemnly in Procession thro' the Cloyster of St. *Katharine*, where he perform'd his devout Oblations; and whilst he staid there, Messengers brought News that *Walter Cumin*, the most potent Earl of Scotland, was killed by a Fall from his Horse; and he also heard that *J——* Son of *Geoffrey*, not far from Guilford, was dead, for whom the King caused Mass to be solemnly celebrated in the Convent; and he was farther informed that *Brancaley*, a Senator of Rome, was dead, which was no small Detriment, and his Unkle was substituted in his Place.

Anno 1265, 49 *Hen.* III. this Town was fortified with a Ibid. fol. 909. Wall, and so close shut up with Locks and Bars on the Gates on the inside and outside for Fear of War, that Travellers desirous to pass, especially Horsemen, were denied Passage thro' the Town; at which time *Gregory* of Stock, Constable of Hertford, envying the Courage of the *Albanesses*, boasted that he would enter the Town with three Youths and four of the best Villains he had at Hertford, and in Order to it, enter'd the Town, and looking up and down as though he had done a great Act, making every where some foolish Discourse, he at length said to his Youths, See which Way the Wind stands; by and by an Executioner thinking that he would burn the Town, I will teach thee, saith he, which Way the Wind stands, and pre-

Hund. of Caishoe.

sently gave him a Blow on the Cheek with such Force, that he laid him on the Ground at his Feet, and thereupon he with his Youths were encompassed in, and secured with Iron Rings and Fetters, and presently their Heads were cut off by the Executioner, and fixed upon long Poles, placed at the four Ends of the Town; but when the King heard all this, he amerced the Town at a hundred Marks, who presently paid the Money.

This Abbot did appropriate the Churches of Norton, Edlingham, Hertburne, and St. Michael; and bought a House in Church-street, very fit for Strangers, because 'twas a corner House, and open to the Street on the East, and to the other Street right over against the Abby Gate.

Weav. *Acts and Mon.* fol. 561.

XXIV. *Roger* in the time of *Edw.* I. succeeded, he was a very pious and religious Man, and wondrously loved the Beauty of this Church, he laid out great Costs and Charges upon the Repair thereof, and adorning it, gave three tunable Bells to the Steeple, whereof two were dedicated to the Honour of St. *Alban*, and the third to the Honour of St. *Amphibalus*, which he appointed to be rung at nine of the Clock every Night; whereupon it was called *Corfeu*, or cover Fire-bell, for that every one was bound to cover their Fire when the Bell was rung.

Ibid.

XXV. *John* of Berkhamsted was the next that was promoted to the pastoral Staff, who apply'd his Mind wholly to Works of Piety, and to Prayers for the Health of his Soul.

Inspeximus.

King *Edw.* I. by his Charter dated at Westminster, 23 *Jan.* 4 *Regni sui*, granted, that since the Abby was immediately subject to the Court of Rome, and exempt from all ecclesiastical and secular Authority, the Abbot shall certify all Excommunications into the Chancery, which shall be as effectual as the Certificate of any Bishop; and farther granted, that the Abbots should have episcopal Power over all Persons within their Jurisdiction.

Holl. vol 2. Norden, p. 22.

Anno 1290, 18 *Edw.* I. Queen *Elianor* died on the 28th of *November*, of a grievous Sickness at Herdby, a Town near Lincoln, as the King was on his Journey to Scotland, whereupon he returned to convey her Corps to London, and in every Town and Place, where her Body staid in her Passage from thence to Westminster, the King caused a stately Cross to be erected, whereupon one was built in this Town, garnish'd with the Image of the Queen, and his and her Arms fixt upon it in Commemoration of her; he lamented her Death, and bewailed the Loss of her all the Days of his Life, for she was a vertuous Lady, modest, pitiful, a Lover of the English Nation, and as it were, a Pillar of Defence to the whole Realm; her Bowels were buried in the Lady Church at Lincolne, where a Tomb was erected with the Arms of Castile, but her Body was buried at Westminster.

XXVI. *John Marines* was the next Abbot in Succession, and gave a Censor of great Price, and many other Necessaries to this Church.

Anno 1302, 30 *Edw.* I. King *Edward*, by his Charter dated at Caldestreame, 20 *July*, granted to the Abbot and Convent, that the Prior and Convent in all times of Vacation after the Death of any Abbot, shall have the Custody of the Abby, and of all their Lands and Goods, and shall dispose of them at their Pleasure; saving to the King and his Heirs, all Knights' Fees and Advowson of Churches, which shall happen in the times of any such Vacation, and one thousand Marks *per Annum*, to be paid by two equal Payments for so long time as the Vacancy shall continue; and that no Sheriff, Escheator, Bailiff, or other Officer shall intromit into any of their Lands, during any Vacation; only the Escheator shall enter the Ally Gate in the Vacation, and make a Seisure for the King, and that being taken, shall presently depart from thence without taking or carrying any thing away; nor that the Prior or the Convent in the time of Vacation, shall be disturbed for their own Knights' Fees.

XXVII. *Hugh* enlarged the Revenues of this Church, for he purchased the Mannor of Caldecot, and divers other fair Possessions, and obtained from King *Edward* divers great Gifts, with a Crucifix of Gold beset with precious Stones; a Cup of Silver Guilt of great Value, and divers Scotish Reliques, and Timber to repair the Quire, and one hundred Pounds in Money.

The Burgesses held this Town of the King in Chief, and they (as the Burgesses in other Boroughs in this Kingdom) of Right, did send to the King's Parliaments two Burgesses, when they happen'd to be summon'd, as they were used to do in all past times, for all Services which they ought to perform to the King, these Burgesses and their Predecessors performed in the time of King *Edward* late Father of the King, and his Progenitors, and in the time of the present King.

A Catalogue of the BURGESSES which this Borough heretofore sent to Parliament.

EDWARD I.

| 28 | At Westm. Ball. Libtat. nullum dederunt Responsum. |
| 35 | At Carl. Simon de Trewyck, Adam Ettestile. |

EDWARD II.

1	At North. Lucas Nedeham, Steph. d' Mulborn.
2	At Westm. The Return is torn off.
5	At Lond. Radus Picot, Petrus Picot.
5	At Westm. Petrus le Plomer, Pet. Picot.

Anno 1315, 8 *Edw.* II. the Burgesses of this Borough complained to the King by Petition, that the Sheriff of this County, by the Procurement of the Abbot, refused to warn

Hund. of
Caishos.   the Burgesses for this Borough, or retorn their Names according to his Duty, that they might do their Service, which was to the Prejudice of the Burgesses, and manifest Danger of disinheriting them: To which the King answered, That the Rolls of *Chancery* should be searched, if in the time of the King's Progenitors, the Burgesses used to come or not? and then they should have Justice done in this Matter, and such as have been called should be called, if there was Occasion; and afterwards they sent two Burgesses again to Parliament, as appears by this Catalogue.

EDWARD III.

Prin's Par.
Brev. pt. 4,
p. 900.

Ibid.

Ibid.

2	At York. *Roger Raison, John Sterthop.*
2	At North. *Rob. d'atte Hall, Will. d' Mareschal.*
4	At Winchest. *Thomas Son of John le Taillour, Roger Alleyn.*
4	At Westm. *Roger Rayson, Robert d' Morgan.*
5	At Nottingh. *Rog. Rayson, Will. Tidenhangre.*

All which Burgesses were made by the Commonalty of the Borough, as is manifest by the Records and Writs for their Election, who were the governing Burgesses of this Borough; But from the fifth Year of *Edw.* III. I cannot find that this Borough sent any more Burgesses to Parliament, supposing the Abbot prevailed with the King to discharge them from this Service: But when this Monastery was dissolved, King *Edw.* VI. restored this Priviledge to them by Charter dated 7 *Regni sui*, which I shall shew in the proper Place.

Weav. fol.
561.   XXVIII. *Richard de Wallingford* the next Abbot, was a Person endew'd with all Kind of Learning, both moral and divine, and pass'd thro' many Troubles in Defence of the Rights of this Church; he gave a Clock to the same which far exceeded all the Clocks that were at that time in England, and he repaired the Mills of the Park, the Moor, Codycot, and Luton, and made a Mill at this Town, and another at Stankfeild.

Dugd. Bar.
vol. 1, fol.391.   *Anno* 1321, 14 *Edw.* II. *Thomas* Earl of Lancaster, the Earl of Hereford, and divers other Noblemen incited others to their Party, and with one Accord, met at Sherburne in Elmede, and thence with Banners displaid, came to this Town, whence they sent the Bishop of Salisbury, Hereford, and Chichester to the King, requiring him to banish the *D'Spencers*, in Regard of their excessive Charge and Covetousness, and that they sway'd him which Way they pleas'd, and to grant his Pardon to all those who were in Arms against them: To which the King gave a sharp Answer, which so exasperated these great Lords, that they forthwith marched to London: When the King discerning his own Danger, he assented to their Demands, at the Instance of the Queen; whereupon the Barons called a Parliament by Writ, in which both the *D'Spencers* were banish'd, and the

Sentence was proclaimed at **Westminster**; and this Abbot died *Anno Dom.* 1334.

Hund. of *Caishoe.*

XXIX. *Michael de Mentemore* well deserved the Name of an Angel (saith my Author) for the Works which he did do testify what he was; and that all the time that he govern'd this Church, he was so pious and mild to his Brethren, that he was accounted as an Angel among them. He died in the Year 1342, and was buried in this Church, with this Superscription upon his Stone.

Weav Mon. fol. 561.

Hic jacet Dominus Michael, quondam Abbas hujus Monasterii Bacchalaureus in Theologia, qui obiit pridie Ious Aprilis, An 1342.

XXX. *Thomas de la More* Prior of **Tinmouth** in the County of **Northumberland**, was advanced to the Government of this Church.

Ibid.

Anno 1347, 21 *Edw.* III. the King granted to him and his Convent, that they might improve their Wasts, and let them to Tenants for Years, Life, or otherwise, for the true Value; and by Deed dated *Anno* 1350, 24 *Edw.* III. in Consideration that the Abbot and Convent had granted to the King the Advowson of **Datchet**, he released to them one Pension of five Pounds *per Annum,* which they paid to the King's Chaplains, till he was preferred, because the King's Progenitors were Founders of the Abby; and *Anno* 1357, 31 *Edw.* III. the King granted Leave to the Abbot and Convent, to inclose the Abby with a stone Wall, and that they should hold two Fairs in the Town of **Watford**, every Year, the one to continue for three Days, the other for two Days.

Ibin.

Ibid.

Anno 1381, 4 *R.* II. *Wat Tyler* and *Jack Straw* raised great Commotions in several Counties, which brought much Disturbance and Trouble upon this Abbot, for the Rebels came hither, demanded of him and the Monks all the Charters that concerned their Liberties, and to take such new ones as might serve their Purpose; the Abbot and Monks fearing every Hour that they would burn their House because they had them not; the Prior, certain Monks, and Laymen, Servants to the Abbot, fled for Fear of the Rabble, knowing their Hatred to them; but when they understood that their Captain *Wat Tyler* was slain, they began to be more moderate, and the rather, for that a Knight brought the King's Letters of Protection in Behalf of the Abbot and his House, yet they continued their Demands, that the Abbot would discharge them of all Services and accustomed Labours, so that they intended to be freed from all such Works and Customs, as heretofore they had usually done for their Landlords.

Holl. vol. 2, fol. 434.]

When the King had quieted the Commotions in **Essex**, he came with a great Number of armed Men and Archers to this Town, where he caused the Malefactors to be brought from 𝕳𝖊𝖗𝖙𝖋𝖔𝖗𝖉 Gaol to this Place, in Order to be tried for their several Treasons before Sir *Robert Tresilian,* Chief Justice of the *King's Bench;* whereupon *John Ball,* a wicked Priest, brought from 𝕮𝖔𝖛𝖊𝖓𝖙𝖗𝖞, was tryed by the King's Order, on *Saturday* the 13th Day of *July,* Anno 5 *R.* II. for High Treason, and the same Day, was condemned to be drawn, hang'd, and quartered; but thro' the Intercession of *William* Bishop of 𝕷𝖔𝖓𝖉𝖔𝖓, his Execution was respited, that he might obtain Repentance for the Health of his Soul, until *Monday* following, being the fifteenth Day of *July,* when his Body was quarter'd, and sent to four Cities of the Realm; then *William Greendecob, William Cadington, John Barbor,* and others of this Town and County, to the Number of fifteen Persons, were tryed, condemned, drawn, and hanged; also divers of the chief Men of this Town, as *Richard Wallingford, John Garleek, William Berewel, Thomas Putor,* and about eighty Persons of the Country, were committed to Prison, but afterwards were discharged upon the King's Pardon. The Townsmen possess'd with great Hatred and Malice against the Abbot and Convent,

tried many Ways to save those that were to be executed; and several of the Townsmen and Tenants of the Abbot and Convent having gotten Letters of Discharge from performing any bond Service to them, the King directed his Letters to *John Ludowick, John Westwicombe, John Kenting, Richard Perers, Walter Saunford, Richard Gifford, Thomas Eidon,* and *William Eccleshal,* to make Proclamation in all Towns and Places where 'twas necessary, through the Counties of 𝕭𝖚𝖈𝖐𝖎𝖓𝖌𝖍𝖆𝖒 and 𝕳𝖊𝖗𝖙𝖋𝖔𝖗𝖉; *That all and every Person and Persons that ought to do any Manner of Service or Duty, to the Abbot and Convent, whether they were Bondmen or Freemen, should do and perform the same in such Manner as they had used to do, before the late Troubles upon their Faith and Allegiance, to the King, upon the Forfeiture of all that they had to lose, and if any refused to do the same, that the Commissioners should commit them to Prison, till further Order for their Punishment.*

On St. *Margaret's* Day all the Commons of this County that were between fifteen and threescore Years of Age, a summoned to appear before the King in the great Court of this Abby, came hither, and took an Oath from henceforth to be faithful Subjects to him and never to rise, or make any Commotion to the Disturbance of his Peace, and rather die than consent to any rebellious Persons, whom they should to the uttermost of their Powers apprehend, and deliver to Prison, that they might be forth coming.

Soon after, the King came to 𝕰𝖆𝖘𝖙𝖍𝖆𝖒𝖘𝖙𝖊𝖉, to recreate himself with hunting, where he heard that the Bodies which

Hund. of
Caishoe.

Weav. fol.
338.

were hanged here were taken down from the Gallowes, and removed a great Way from the same; this so incensed the King, that he sent a Writ, tested the 3d of *August*, *Anno* 1381, to the Bailiffs of this Burrough, commanding them upon Sight thereof, to cause Chains to be made, and to hang the Bodies in them upon the same Gallowes, there to remain so long as one Piece might stick to another, according to the Judgment; but the Townsmen not daring to disobey the King's Command, hanged the dead Bodies of their Neighbours again, to their great Shame and Reproach, when they could not get any other for any Wages to come near the stinking Carcasses, but they themselves were compelled to do so vile an Office.

King *Richard* by his Charter, dated the 6 of *September* following, reciting, whereas King *Edward* I. had granted to the Abbot and Monks, that the Prior and Convent should receive the Profits of the Lands of the Abby, paying one thousand Marks *per Annum* to the King, granted to them all their Goods and Temporalities; and all that they should hereafter purchase for this Church to the Prior and Convent, as if it were *sede plena*; saving to the King the Knights' Fees, and Advowsons of the Churches, and Escheats, which should fall in the time of such Vacation; yeilding yearly to the King and his Heirs for ever, fifty Marks, and to be for ever discharged of the Payment of the thousand Marks in the time of any Vacation, and also to be excused from serving in his Wars, for the Lands they held of him; after this Abbot had waded through all his Troubles, he adorned this Church much more richly, than any of his Predecessors had done, appropriated the Church of Appleton, and covered the West Part of the Floor with Pavements, and the several Gifts which he gave to the same, cost him above four thousand Pounds; then he ended his Days very piously, *Anno* 1396, and was buried in this Church.

Weav. Mon.
fol. 561.

Inspex.

XXXI. *John Moot* was the next that was preferr'd to the Government of this Church, whom King *Richard* favoured; for he by his Charter dated at Westminster, *Feb. Anno* 1307, 20 *Regni sui*, reciting, whereas the Abby was immediately subject to the Pope of Rome, and by the Pope's Bull, they may elect their Abbot, paying twenty Marks yearly to the Pope's Collector in England; he confirmed this Bull, so as under the Seal of Convent they satisfied the King of the Death of every Abbot; and pray'd Leave to choose a new Abbot; he pardoned their Offence in procuring the Apostolical Letters without Leave, and granted the Rent of twenty Pounds *per Annum* to the Pope.

This Abbot erected a very fair House for himself and his Successors in the Mannor of Tittenhanger, where they

Mr. Cox.

s 2

might retire for their Ease and Pleasure, recreate themselves, and be merry with their Friends and Relations; but died before he had finisht the same, *Anno Christi* 1401, 1 *Henry* IIII.

XXXII. *William Hayworth* govern'd this Church, was admir'd much for his great Holiness and Devotion, beloved both of God and Man for the Strictness of his Life, and the Excellency of his Government, when he had performed many Acts of Piety, he died about the Year, 1434, 12 *Hen.* VI. and was buried in this Church.

XXXIII. *John de Whethamsted* was denominated from the Soil of his Place of Birth, a Village near this Town called 𝔚𝔥𝔢𝔱𝔥𝔞𝔪𝔰𝔱𝔢𝔡; but from his original Parents, *Bostock.* He was a Monk of the Priory of 𝔗𝔦𝔫𝔪𝔬𝔲𝔱𝔥 in 𝔑𝔬𝔯𝔱𝔥𝔲𝔪𝔟𝔢𝔯𝔩𝔞𝔫𝔡, to which he bequeathed a Challice of Gold, and from thence, was worthily promoted to the Government of this Church; where he was very famous for his great Learning, his Godly Life and Conversation, his pleasant Disposition, and his great Affection to the Beauty of the House of God; and he was so espoused and betrothed to it, that he raised great Sums of Money to adorn and enrich the same, and caused our Ladies Chappel to be trimmed and rarely painted, with Stories out of the Sacred History, and with Verses curiously drawn in Gold; he built a small Chappel on the South Part of the Church for his own burial Place, and caused new Windows to be made, and glaized in the North Part of his Church, which were somewhat dark, that it might appear more light and glorious, and several Hexameters were inscribed in the Glass under the Images of certain Heathen Philosophers, which had testified of the Incarnation of Jesus Christ, and caused a fair large Window to be made in the West End of the North Isle, to illuminate his Church.

He made a reverend kind of embroidered Vesture for himself and his Successors to use when they entered into the *Sanctum Sanctorum,* a new Mitre, and a Pastoral Staff, a Chalice of pure Gold, a Pair of Silver Censers, and a Pair of Silver Flagons Guilt, upon which the similitudes of a Lamb and an Eagle were engraved, for the Use of the Holy Altar; and upon the Pictures of Christ, the blessed Virgin, St. *Alban,* and the sacred Host, as they were to be carried into the Cloister or into the Town, and he caused diverse Verses to be written, to bring the People into a reverend Esteem of them.

He likewise trimmed up his Monastery with curious painted Imageries, and divers Inscriptions in Golden Letters, some in his own Lodgings, others in the Walk, betwixt the Hall and the Abbot's Chamber, others in the Chamber adjoyning to his Study, and others in the Windows of the Abbot's Study or Library; he gave a great Bason of Silver double Guilt to the Monastery, built a Chappel for the Convent, and in all his new Buildings or Repairings, he caused the Pictures of a Lamb and an Eagle to be drawn or painted thereupon with Verses, which might lately have been read upon the Roof or Top of the Quire of the Abby Church.

He also built much at his Mannor of Tittenhanger, greatly enlarged the Chappel there, and caused the Similitudes of all the Saints of his own Christian Name, *John*, with his own Picture to be painted upon the Walls; and this Prayer in a distick, *that the unworthy He might have a Place with his Namesakes in Heaven.* He rebuilt the Church of Redburn, and consecrated the Altar again; he erected a Library in the Monk's Colledge in Oxford, to which he gave many Books, also a Chappel adjoyning to the Library, and in the principal Windows the Pictures of the Crucifix, the Virgin *Mary*, and St. *John Baptist* were painted. Weav. Mon. fol. 566.

He bestow'd great charges upon the Abbot's House in London, and by his great Wisdom, perswaded *Humphry* Duke of Glocester, to give a Suit of Vestments worth 3000 Marks, with the Mannor of Pembrook in South Wales, that the Monks should pray for his Soul; chose this Church for the Place of his Burial; and when he had govern'd this Monastery about twenty Years, he resigned up his Staff. Ibid.

XXXIV. *John Stock*, Prior of Walingford, about *Ann.* 1455, 33 *Henry* VI. was elected from thence to govern this Church the same Year; the Duke of York accompanied with his choice Friends, the Earls of Salisbury and Warwick, the Lord *Cobham* and others, raised a potent Army, and marched towards London: The King levied another with Buckingham, *Humphry* his eldest Son, Earl of Stafford, *Edmund* Duke of Somerset, and divers others of the Nobility and Gentry, to the Number of two thousand Men of War, set forth from Westminster, the 21st Day of *May, Anno* 1445, 33 *Hen.* IV. and marching towards this Town to meet them, quartered that Night at Watford or Wateford, and the next Morning came early to this Town; about which time the Duke of York appeared in the Head of his Army, drawn up together in a Place called Keyfeild near this Borough, but the King pitched his Banner in a Place called Goselow some time Sandforth in St. Peter's Street, and commanded the Wards and Barriers of the Town should be strongly guarded. Stow's Annals fol. 398.

When the Duke of York had continued with his Army in the Feild from seven of the Clock in the Morning, till almost ten, the Duke by the advice of his Council, desired of the King in Writing, that his Majesty would be pleased Ibid. Holl. vol. 2, fol. 642.

to deliver such as they should accuse, that they might suffer as they had deserved.

So soon as the King received this Message, he commanded all People to avoid the Field, and threatened to punish every Mother's Son, according to Law, who should assist the Traitors, and rather than they should have any Lord to protect them, he would that Day live and die in the Quarrel.

But *Hollingshead* reports from this Abbot, that when the King first heard of the Duke's Approach, he sent the Duke of Buckingham and others, to know the Cause of his coming in that hostile Manner; the Duke answered, he and his Army were the King's faithful liege Subjects, and intended no Harm to his Majesty, only desired that he would deliver up into his Hands the Duke of Somerset, who had lost Normandp, taken no Care to preserve Gascoine, and had brought the Realm into this miserable Condition; then they would without Trouble or Breach of the Peace, return to their Countries, · otherwise they would rather die in the Field than suffer this Grievance.

The King resolving rather to try the Hazard of a Battle, than to deliver the Duke to his Enemies, the Duke of York made a Speech to encourage his Army to fight, and sounding their Trumpets to Battle, between eleven and twelve at Noon, broke in with his Soldiers in three several Places of the Town, during which time the King being at the House of *Edmond Westby*, Hundredor of that Liberty, and hearing the Duke was coming, commanded his Soldiers to kill all the Lords, Knights, Gentlemen, and others, that should be taken on his Part. This done, the Lord *Clifford* kept the Barriers of the Town so strongly, that the Duke of York could not enter into the Town with all his Power, the Earl knowing this, drew all his Men together, and broke into the Town, by the Garden Side, between the Sign of the *Key* and the *Exchequer* in Holliwell Street, and as soon as his Soldiers had entered the Town, they hollowed with an extraordinary Shout! crying a *Warwick*, a *Warwick!* and then the Duke of York entred the Town with a strong Hand, broke down the Barriers, and fought a fierce and cruel Battle, where there were slain on the King's Part, *Edmond* Duke of Somerset, *Henry* Earl of Northumberland, *Humphry* Earl of Stafford, Son to the Duke of Buckingham, *John* Lord *Clifford*, Sir *Robert Vere*, Sir *Barthram Entwisell*, Knight, (a *Norman* by Birth, who forsaking his native Country, to continue in his loyal Obedience to King *Henry*, came into England when Normandp was lost) Sir *William Chamberlain*, Sir *Richard Fortescue*, and Sir *Ralph Ferrers*, Kts. *William Zouch*, *John Boutreux*, *Ralph Babthorpe*, with

his Son *William Corwin*, *William Cotton*, *Gilbert Fald-
inger*, *Reginald Griffon*, *John Dawes*, *Elice Wood*, *John
Eith*, *Ralph Woodward*, *Gilbert Sherlock*, and *Ralph
Willoughby*, Esquires, with many others, as *Hall* saith
eight thousand, but certainly he meant eight hundred, which
is more agreeable to the Number of the King's whole
Army, which he brought with him to that Battle, for they
did not exceed two thousand, and of the other Part about
six hundred were slain, of all which Persons about forty
eight were buried in this Town, and at the Battle were divers wounded; of whom the King was shot in the Neck with
an Arrow, *Humphry* Duke of Buckingham, and the Lord
Sudley, in their Visages, and *Humphry* Earl of Stafford
in his right Hand with Arrows: The Earl of Dorset was
sore hurt that he could not go, but was carried Home in a
Cart, and Sir *John Wenlock* was so wounded, that he was
conveyed thence in a Chair, and divers Knights and Gentlemen were also wounded; *James Butler*, Earl of Ormond and Wiltshire, and *Thomas Thorpe*, Lord Chief
Baron of the *Exchequer*, with many others, fled away thro'
Gardens, Backsides, Shrubs, Hedges, and Woods, leaving
their Harness there, and seeking Places where to hide
themselves, until the Storm of that Battle were past; diverse of the King's House, who could better act the Part
of Courtiers than Soldiers, fled with the first, and the
speedy Flight of those of the Eastern Parts of this Realm,
did manifest their want of Courage; the King perceiving
his Men to have deserted him, retired into a poor Man's
Cottage, to save himself from the shot of Arrows, which
flew like Snow about him; the Battle ended; the Duke of
York, and the Earls of Warwick, and Salisbury, finding
the King there, humbled themselves before him on their
Knees, and begg'd his Majesty's Grace and Pardon, for
what they had done in his Presence; whereupon the King
desired, that they would require and charge their People,
to withold their Hands from doing any more Mischeif,
which Command they immediately obeyed; in the mean-
while the Soldiers that had obtained the Victory, stripped
not only those that had borne Armour against them, but
also the Inhabitants of the Town, and 'twas thought if the
King had lodged at his first coming in the Abby, as he did
in the Midst of the Town, to provide the better against his
Enemies, the Abby had been also spoiled.

Soon after the Queen obtained great Victories at Wakefield, and encouraged with the Success hereof, was desirous to recover the Company of her Husband the King,
and to repeal the Laws which had been made in the last
Parliament, to that intent she recruited her Army by the
Assistance of the Northern Lords who came with them

Stow's *Annals*,
fol. 413.

Hund. of
Caishoe.

hither, where she heard that the Dukes of Norfolk and Suffolk, the Earls of Warwick and Arundel, and the Lord *Bonvile*, and others, whom the Duke of York had left to govern the King in his Absence, had gather'd a great Army, which encamped near this Town.

Stow's Annals
fol. 413.
Holl. vol. 2,
fol. 660.
Bar. of Engl.

The Queen with these Lords on *Shrove-tuesday*, 17th of *Febr. Anno* 1461, 39 *Hen.* VI. marching forward with an Intent to pass through this Town that they might fight their Enemies, received in the Market-place a Storm of Arrows, which flew as thick as Hail, and quickly repulsed them, so that they were forc'd with Loss to retire to the West End of the Town, where by a Lane that leadeth Northwards up to St. Peter's Street they entered, and had a sharp Encounter with the King's Army; but after a great Slaughter on both Sides, they made their way through them, and upon the Heath at the North End of the Town, called by some Barnard Heath, by others No Mans Land, they had a far greater Conflict with four or five thousand of the King's Army, which made so fierce an Onset at the Beginning, that the Victory rested doubtful for some time, so that if the Eastern and Southern Men had continued as they began, they had obtained the Victory, but after the Fight had continued a long time, and none came to their Relief, Captain *Lovelace* with his Kentish Men, which was the Van of King *Henry's* Army, began to faint and soon after turning their Backs fled away, over Hedge and Ditch, through Woods and Bushes, seeking to escape the bloody Hands of their cruel Enemies, that followed them fiercely and killed many of them in the Flight, and more had been destroyed, if the Night had not approached.

The Earl of Warwick fled to the Earl of March, who was coming out of Wales towards London, and the Nobles that were about the King, perceiving that the Field was lost, and saw no Hopes of the King, who inclin'd to the contrary Part, withdrew, leaving the King accompanied only with the Lord *Bonnevile*, and Sir *Thomas Kiriell* of Kent, who would also have gone away, but the King assured them, that they should have no Hurt, and upon this Assurance, they tarried with him; nevertheless at the Instance of the Queen, the Duke of Exeter, and the Earl of Devonshire, both of them were beheaded.

Stow's Annals,
fol. 414.

In this Battle *Stow* saith 1916 Persons, but *Hollingshead* saith 230 Men, were slain, of whom no Nobleman is remembred, but Sir *John Gray*, who was the same Day knighted, in the Company of twelve others, in the Town of Colney.

Ibid.

When the King was in a Manner left alone without any Guard, *Thomas Hoo*, Esq. a Man well learned in Languages, and well read in the Law, advised the King to send a Messenger to the Northern Lords, and let them know, that he would gladly come to them, for he knew they were his Friends, and meant to serve him; the King approving it, appointed him to carry the Message, who first delivered it to the Earl of Northumberland, and returning back to the King, brought several Lords with him; they conveyed the King first to the Lord *Clifford's* Tent, that stood next to the Place, where the King's Army had encamped; then they brought the Queen, and her Son Prince *Edward* to him, whom he joyfully received; embracing and kissing them, and thanking God, who had restored his only Son to his Possession; and the Queen caused him to dubbe the Prince a Knight, with thirty other Persons, which the Day before had fought valiantly on her Part; then they went to the Abby, where the Abbot and Monks received them with Hymns and Songs, brought them to the High Altar, then to the Shrine, and thence conveyed them to the Chamber, in which the King was wont to lodge, the Abbot moved the King and Queen to restrain the Northern Men from spoiling the Town; and Proclamation was made to that Effect, but it availed nothing, for the Queen had covenanted with them, that they should have the Plunder and Spoil of their Enemies after they had past the River Trent, and they spared not any thing that they found, that was fit for them to carry away; after these Troubles were past this Abbot died in the Year of our Lord, 1452.

John of Whethamsted was elected again into this Place, and caused the Vallies once more to rejoice with Corn; He purchased the Mannors of Garston in the Parish of Watford, Apgnells in the Parish of Redburne, and built the beautiful Chappel at his own Charge on the North Side of St. Alban, which was solemnly consecrated to the Honour of St. *Andrew* the Apostle; He also purchased the Mannor of Radwell near Norton Burston near the Park of Cpwood, Boturwfke within the Vill of Sleepe, Newland and Squebillers in the Vill of Parke, Legates within the Vill of Walden, Amsells within the Vill of Pexton, the Messuage heretofore belonging to *Alan Brit* in London; also by way of Escheat the Mannor of Harpesfeild within the Lordship of Parksoken, the Mannor of Biggin in Rickmersworth, [the Land and Pasture formerly belonging to *Simon Pekesihill* in Bernet, of the yearly Value of five Marks, one Messuage near the Church in Norton, and many other Places.

He obtained also of the Lord *Grey* of Ruthin, a Release of the Advowson of the Priory of Belloloco, and by his great Merit he procured the Grant thereof from Pope *Eugenius* IV. for the Union of that Place. King *Edw.*

Per Inspex.

Ibid.

IV. by his Charter dated at 𝕎estminster, the 3d of *Nov.*
2 *Regni sui,* 1462, granted to him that the Abbot according to the Charter of *Hen.* II. should have the Retorne
and Execution of all theKing's Writs, all Goods and Chattles of all their Men, Tenants, and Inhabitants within their
Lands, Tenements, or Fees, outlaw'd for High Treason,
Felony, Contempt, Trespass, Debt, Accompt, or any Cause
whatsoever, Felons of themselves, and other Felonies whatsoever, of Fugitives, and condemned Persons, or of any
other Persons, that for any Felony or other Occasion
whatsoever, ought to lose their Life or Member, or shall fly
and refuse to receive Judgment, or shall be outlawed, or for
any Fault or Offence, or any other thing they shall do, for
which their Goods and Chattles ought to be lost, wheresoever
Justice ought to be done thereupon, and that the Servants of
the Abbot may Seize all such Goods and Chattels without
the Hindrance of the King's Officers, and keep the same for
the Use of the Abbot and Convent, though those Persons held
of the King: And that the Abbot shall have all Fines and
Amerceaments, for all Trespasses and other Offences
committed by their Tenants and Inhabitants within or upon
their Lands or Fees, and all Deodands, Treasure, Trove,
Wreck of Sea, and all things which ought or may belong to
the King, arising within the Vills or Hundreds of or in any
of their Lands or Fees, in any of the King's Courts.

The Abbot shall have Jurisdiction of all Manner of
Pleas, Lands, and Tenements arising within their Towns
of 𝔖t. 𝔄lbans, 𝔅ernet, the Hundred of 𝔠aisho, and Liberty of 𝔖t. 𝔄lban, and Assizes of Novell disiezin, Mor-
dauncester, Certificates, and Attaints of the same Lands
and Tenements before the King, or any of his Justices, &c.
or before themselves, and their Stewards, who may hear
and determine the same, and that none of the Justices or
Ministers of the King shall intromit.

The Abbot and Convent, and their Successors, shall appoint within their Liberty, their Justices to keep the
Peace, and to hear and determine all Manner of Felonies,
and Trespasses; and the Justices of the Peace for the
County shall not intromit: And they shall have a Goal for
their Liberty within the Town of 𝔖t. 𝔄lban to keep safe
Felons, and other Malefactors, which shall be taken within
their Vills, Hundreds, and Liberties, until they shall be
discharged according to Law: And the Steward of the
Abbot shall associate one or two learned Men of the Law
(whereof the Steward shall be one) who shall be Justices
to deliver the Goal of the Prisoners committed there for
what cause soever; and no other Justice shall enter into
the Liberty to deliver the Goal.

The Bailiff of the Abbot shall retorn all Juries, Pannels, Inquisitions Attachments, and Process, to Justices

and Steward, or to two of them appointed to deliver the Goal, and shall return and execute all Precepts, Warrants, and Judgments of the Justice and Steward, as is usual for the Sheriff to do.

The Abbot shall have the Assize and Assay of Bread, Wine, Ale, Meat, and Drink, and all other Victual, Measures, and Weights whatsoever, and of all other things pertaining to the Clerk of the Market of the King's Household, and to punish and correct so often and when it shall be expedient, and shall have all Fines, Redemptions, Amerceaments, and other Profits issuing from thence, and the Clerk of the King's Household shall not intromit.

The Abbot and Convent, and all their Tenants and Inhabitants whatsoever, of the Vills, Hundred, and Liberty, shall be free and quit from all Prizes, and from the taking of Horses, Carts, and other Carriages; also of Wheat, Barley, Winter-corn, Oats, Beans, Steers, Oxen, Cows, Heifers, Hogs, Porkers, Goats, Sheep, Lambs, Calves, Geese, Pullets, Capons, Hens, Chickens, Pidgeons, Fish, Eels, flying Fowls, Conies, and wild Beasts, Salt, Wood, Underwood, Coal, and other Utensils whatsoever, so that no Purveyor shall enter into the said Vills, Hundred, or Liberty, to take away any such Victual or Premises for the King's Household, without License of the Abbot.

This Abbot did stoutly defend the Lands and Liberties of his Church, adorn'd Duke *Humphry's* Tomb, gave Money by his Will to make a new Bell, which was called *John* after his own Name, and to new glaze the Windows in the Cloysters; and that which is most memorable and commendable of him was, that after so many great Charges and Expences, he left this Church free from Debt, and dyed the 20th of *Jan.* 1464, 4 *Edw.* IV. and was buried the 25th of *Feb.* then next following.

XXXVI. *William Alban*, Dr. of Law, born in this Town, whence he derived his Sirname, was first chosen Deacon of this Place, then raised to be Prior of this Church, after that was elected to the pastoral Staff on the last Day of *January*, 1464, in whose time the Art or noble Science of Printing was brought into 𝔈𝔫𝔤𝔩𝔞𝔫𝔡. The rude and savage People of 𝔊𝔯𝔢𝔢𝔠𝔢, ascribed the Invention of Letters to *Cadmus*, because he brought them thither, and instructed them therein, when they were as ancient as *Seth* or *Enoch*, for they left Letters written on Pillars of Stone and Brick long before the Flood, which *Josephus* affirms. *Jude* proves the Prophecies of *Enoch*, and some Part of his Books, which contained the Course of the Stars, and *Origen* saith their Names and Motions, were afterwards found in 𝔄𝔯𝔞𝔟𝔦𝔞 𝔉𝔢𝔩𝔦𝔵 in the Dominion of the Queen of 𝔖𝔥𝔢𝔟𝔞. *Tertullian* affirms he had seen and

Ral. *Hist. of the World,* cap. 7, sect. 4, fol. 115. Jude *Epist.* 21. Origen *Hom.* in Numb. 14.

read some whole Passages of it: and *Tertullian*, *Origen*, *Bede*, *Procopius*, *Gaseus*, and others, cite them in their Writings.

The *Chineses* had Letters and the Art of Printing long before the *Ægyptians* or the *Phenicians*, when the *Greeks* had not any civil Knowledge or Letters among them; but *Jo. Curthenberge*, a German Knight, brought the Device of Printing from the Eastern Parts of the World to 𝔐𝔞𝔤𝔲𝔫𝔠𝔢 in 𝔊𝔢𝔯𝔪𝔞𝔫𝔶; and *Conradus* and *Almaine* being taught by him, brought the Practice thereof to 𝔑𝔬𝔪𝔢; after which *Nicholas Gerson*, a Frenchman, improved the Letters and the Invention; and about the Year 1471, *William Caxton*, Mercer of 𝔏𝔬𝔫𝔡𝔬𝔫, brought this noble Art of Printing into 𝔈𝔫𝔤𝔩𝔞𝔫𝔡, which was first practised in the Abby of St. *Peter* at 𝔚𝔢𝔰𝔱𝔪𝔦𝔫𝔰𝔱𝔢𝔯; then *John Insomuch*, a Monk and School-master in this Town, erected a Printing Press in this Monastery, where several Books were printed; one intituled the *Fruit of Time*, another, *The Gentleman's Recreation*, or the Book of St. *Albans*, so termed, because printed here in a thin Folio, *Anno* 1481, and compiled by *Julian Barns*, the Abbess of 𝔖𝔬𝔭𝔴𝔢𝔩𝔩; and another Book intituled *The Rules of Honest Life*, written by *Martin* Bishop of ————, to

Holl. Chron.
2, fol. 648.
Stow's Annals
fol. 404.

which is added the *Inchiridion of a Spiritual Life*, written at 𝔖𝔱. 𝔄𝔩𝔟𝔞𝔫𝔰 in *Octavo* by *John Hereford* for Mr. *Richard Stevenage*, *Anno* 1558. Soon after Printing was used here, it was practised in the Abbies of St. *Augustine* at 𝔠𝔞𝔫𝔱𝔢𝔯-𝔟𝔲𝔯𝔭, and other Monasteries in 𝔈𝔫𝔤𝔩𝔞𝔫𝔡: This Abbot govern'd this Church with great Wisdom and Satisfaction, and exchanged this Life for a better on the first of *July*, 1476, 16 *Edw.* IV.

XXXVII. *William Wallingford* was first Archdeacon of 𝔖𝔱. 𝔄𝔩𝔟𝔞𝔫𝔰, then made Prior, after that advanced to the Pastoral Staff on the 5th of *August*, 1476, 16 *Edw.* IV. when he took this following OATH.

𝔍 shall faithful be and true, and 𝔣aith and 𝔠ruth shall here to you my 𝔖obereigne 𝔏ord, and to your 𝔥eires, 𝔎ing of England, of 𝔏yfe and 𝔏yme and of erthly 𝔚orship fer to lif and dye agenst alle pepell, and diligently 𝔍 shall be attendant unto your nedis and businesse after my wyt and power, and your 𝔠ouncell 𝔍 shall keepe and layne, and truly 𝔍 shall knowlach and due the serbices due of the temperaltees of my 𝔄bby of St. Albone, which 𝔍 claime to hold of you soberen 𝔏ord, and the which ye aebe and yeld me and to you and to your commandements in that, that to me appertepneth and belongeth for my temperaltees 𝔍 shall be obeyed;

So God helpe me and all his Saints.

This Abbot was abundantly charitable to the Poor, very noble to this Church, built that rich and costly Front of the High Altar, which dazzled the Eyes of all those that beheld it, and cost him a 1100 Marks; he paid one hundred Pound Sterling for his Chapel and a Tomb in the South Part of the Church near the High Altar, and the Iron-work Stone, and the Engraving of his Effigies in Marble, with the Rest of the Ornaments of his Chappel.

Hund. of Caishoe.

King *Edw.* IV. by his Charter dated the 2d of *May, An.* 21 *Regni sui*, 1481, granted to this Abbot, the Monks, and their Successors, the Advowson of the Priory of **Tinmouth**, the County of **Northumberland**.

Inspeximus.

This Abbot diligently defended the Liberties and Priviledges of this Church against the Archbishop of **Canterbury**, and the great Chancellor of **England**; he sent two of his Monks, *John* and *Thornton*, to **Rome**, appeal'd there, and cited the Archbishop and the Dean of the **Arches** thither, and those Monks solicited his Right until he obtain'd a just Victory, and preserv'd the Priviledges which had been violated against God and St. *Alban*; he laid out much Money in Repairs and Purchases, all which he concluded very piously on the eighth Day of *August, Anno* 1484, 1 *R.* III. and was buried in this Church under a Stone with this Inscription upon it.

> Gulielmus *quartus opus hoc laudabile cujus*
> *Extitit, hic pausat, Christus sibi præmia reddat*

XXXVIII. *Thomas Ramrige*, who had formerly been Prior of this Monastery, *Anno* 1492, 7 *H.* VII. was promoted to the Government of this Church; he was a pious and religious Man, beloved both of God and Man, and his Name was celebrated among them for his good Works to Posterity.

Weav. Mon. p. 556.

XXXIX. *Thomas Woolsey* born of mean Parentage in **Ipswich** in the County of **Suffolk**, and very industrious at School, was removed early from thence to **Oxford**, where he commenced Batchelour of Arts at fifteen Years of Age, and within short Space, made Fellow of St. *Mary Magdalen* Colledge, and Master of **Maudlin** School, at which time, the Marquis of **Dorset** committed three Sons to his Tuition, and when he found the great Improvement of them, he rewarded him with a Benefice at **Limington**: After the Death of this Marquess, Sir *John Naphant*, Treasurer of **Calais**, introduced him to the King, who made him one of his Chaplains, in which Station he was always very observant to those who had the greatest Influence upon the King: He obtained the Honour to serve his Majesty in the Quality of an Ambassador to the Emperor, which Business he performed with so great Speed, that upon his Return the King blamed him that he was not gone, not knowing he had been there, for his Expedition seemed incredible; he produced his Letters of Credence from the Emperor, and declared his Business to the King and Council with that Gravity and Eloquence that he obtained the greatest Applause of the King and Council; this inclined the King to bestow upon

Stow's *Annals*, fol. 497. Holl. vol. 2, fol. 921.

Hund. of
Caishoe.
him the Deanery of **Lincoln**, which was then one of the best
Promotions under the Office of a Bishoprick, and increasing
dayly in Favour with the King, he was promoted to be his
Almoner.

When King *Henry* VII. died, and the Crown came to
*H.*VIII. he behaved himself with that Policy at Court, that
he was advanced to be one of the Privy Council and made
Lord Chancellor of **England,** *An.* 1516, 7 *H.*VIII. after
that Bishop of **Turney** in **France;** when the King return'd
thence he was prefer'd to the Bishoprick of **Lincolne,** and
the same Year translated to the Archbishoprick of **York;** but
Canterbury claiming Superiority over him, the Pope sent
him a Cardinal's Cap, made him his Legate and General
Overseer of this exempt Monastery, *An.* 1524, 15 *H.*VIII.
was elected Abbot of this Church on the 30th of *Novemb.*
in the Year 1526, 17 *Regni sui,* and held this Office in
Commendam.

He was twice sent on Embasseys to the Emperor *Charles*
V. upon very great Importance between the King and the
Emperor, and was furnish'd with all things suitable to a
great Prince.

This Cardinal, saith *Campian* in his History of **Ireland,**
was exceeding wise, fair spoken, high-minded, full of Revenge, vicious of his Body, lofty to his Enemies, courteous
to his Friends, a ripe Schoolman, allured with Flattery,
insatiable to get, and more princely in his Benefactions, but
whosoever will know the Splendor of his Chappel, the Nobleness of his Tables, the Order of his daily Attendance in
Term-time to **Westminster,** and the Glory of his State and
Grandeur, may read the same in *Stow* and *Hollingshead,* to
whom I refer the Reader. But when he fell under the
King's Displeasure touching the Matter of Divorce between
the King and Queen *Katharine,* thro' Despair of recovering his Favour, a deep Melancholly seiz'd him, and he died
on St. *Andrew's* Eve at **Leicester,** *Anno* 1530, 21 *H.*VIII.
in his Passage from **York** to **London,** and was buried in the
great Church there, of whom *Hollingshead* gives this Dis-
cription, That he was of a great Stomach, counted himself
equal with Princes, obtained a vast Treasure by crafty Suggestion, forced little on Simony, was not pittiful, conceited
in his own Opinion, would say in publick that which was
false, was double in Speech and Meaning, would promise
much and perform little, was an ill Pastor to the Clergy,
sorely hated, and he feared the City of **London.**

Rot. Cur.
Man. de
Brantfeild,
Anno 1538.
XL. *Robert Catton* succeeded, and governed this Mon-
astery about eight Years, of whom I read no more than that
he died *Anno* 29 *H.*VIII.

Ibid. anno
1539.
XLI. *Richard Boreman* alias *Stevenache,* Prior of **Norwich,** was the last that was advanced to the Government of

this Church, *An. Christi* 1538, but enjoyed it a short time; for on the fifth of *December,* the next ensuing Year, the Abbot and Convent of this Monastery, through Fear, surrender'd to the King all their rich Monastery, with all the Revenues belonging to it, by delivering the Seal of the Convent into the Hands of *Thomas Pope,* Dr. *Peter,* Mr. *Cavendish,* and others, the King's Visitors, which Act afforded Matter of Example to many others; few enjoying that Security of Conscience, that they dared to claim their own. *Hund. of*
Caishor.
Stow, fol.577.
Herb fol.
442, 445.

And in Consideration hereof, the King, by his Charter, dated the 14th Day of the same Month, gave to the same Abbot the yearly Pension of 266*l*. 13*s*. 4*d*. for the Term of his Life, or to present him to one or more Benefices, or other Promotions of the clear yearly Value of 266*l*. 13*s*. 4*d*. And to *Thomas Kingsbury,* a Monk there, 33*l*. 6*s*. 8*d*. *per An.* To *John Alban* another Monk 13*s*. 6*s*. 8*d*. *per An.* To *Thomas Island* another Monk 8*l*. *per An.* To *William Hemingford* 8*l*. *per An.* To *William Estridge* 8*l*. *per An.* To *William Ashwell* 10*l*. *per An.* To *John Wendovor* 7*l*. *per An.* To *Thomas Newnham* 10*l*. *per An.* To *William Wyach* 6*l*. 13*s*. 4*d*. *per An.* To *Ralph Bary* 8*l*. 13*s*. 4*d*. *per An.* To *William Albon* 12*l*. *per An.* To *Geoffery Sterling* 8*l*. *per An.* To *Thomas Merchant* 8*l*. *per An.* To *Edward Hills* 8*l*. *per An.* To *John Whethamsted* 6*l*. 13*s*. 4*d*. *per An.* To *Ralph Campyon* 6*l*. 13*s*. 4*d*. *per An.* To *Robert Bury* 6*l*. 13*s*. 4*d*. *per An.* To *Robert Moreton* 8*l*. *per An.* To *Henry Bestney* 8*l*. *per An.* To *John Brightwise* 6*l*. *per An.* To *Stephen Baily* 13*l*. 6*s*. 8*d*. *per An.* To *Will. Este* 12*l*. *per An.* To *Ralph Rickmansworth* 8*l*. *per An.* To *John Salter* 13*l*. 6*s*. 8*d*. To *Edward Sibley* 8*l*. *per An.* To *Thomas Curtis* 6*l*. *per An..* To *Thomas Bartlin* 6*l*. *per An.* To *Richard Bennet* 8*l*. *per An.* To *William Leonard* 8*l*. *per An.* To *Robert Gregory* 6*l*. *per An.* To *Robert Gyles* 6*l*. 13*s*. 4*d*. *per An.* To *Peter Calton* 6*l*. *per An.* To *Thomas Albon* 8*l*. *per An.* To *Thomas Byngham* 100*s*. *per An.* To *Royer Mighell* 100*s*. *per An.* To *William Alen* 100*s*. *per An.* To *William Adam* 6*l*. 13*s*. 4*d*. *per An.* To *Richard Bever* 6*l*. 13*s*. 4*d*. *per An.* And to *Richard Milmars* 6*l*. 13*s*. 4*d*. *per An.* all of them Monks of this Monastery. CurAugment.

When this Monastery was dissolved, all the royal Concessions and Grants which the former Prince had made to this Church, were reserved in the Crown; but for the Preservation of the Government of this Town, King *Edw.* VI. by his Charter dated 12 *Maij,* 7 *Regni sui,* 1554, granted that this Town shall be incorporated by the Name of Mayor and Burgesses of the Burrough of St. Albans, and shall have perpetual Succession; and the Bounds of the Burrough shall include all the four Wards; whereof the East Ward shall extend to the Bars in Sopwell-lane, the West Ward to Cart. 7 Ed.
VI.

Hund. of Caishoe.

The Burrough shall be incorporated by the Name of the Mayor and Burgesses of the Burrough of St. Alban.

The Common Seal.

𝕶ingsburp-lane, the North Ward to 𝕹ewberrps, and the South Ward to the Bars near the Dwelling-house of Sir *Ralph Rowlet*, called the 𝕹ewberries, and all the Messuages, Parcel of the Burrough incorporate: And the Mayor and Burgesses shall implead and be impleaded by the Name of the Mayor and Burgesses of the Burrough of 𝖘t. 𝕬lbans; and shall have a Common Seal which they may alter at their Pleasure; and by that Name may purchase Lands, not exceeding 50*l. per Annum.*

The Common Council.

There shall be ten Chief Burgesses, who shall assist the Mayor, be the Common Council of the Burrough, may make other Burgesses at their Discretion, and Laws and Ordinances for the Government of the Burrough.

Justices of the Peace shall not intromit.

All such Persons who shall dwell in the Burrough, and be Justices of the Peace, and shall not exercise any Art, Mystery, or Occupation there; shall not be free of the Burrough, nor intromit in any Matters of the Burrough farther than they are inabled by the Commission of the Peace; but in all other Respects, shall be as Foreigners to the Burrough.

Steward and Chamberlain.

There shall be a Steward and a Chamberlain, who shall perform those Offices within the Burrough.

Clerk of the Market.

There shall be a Clerk of the Market, who shall do all such things as shall belong to that Office in the Burrough, as the Clerk of the Market of the King's House may do; and no other Clerk of the Market shall intromit within the Burrough.

Election of Burgesses for Parliament.

The Mayor and Burgesses of this Burrough, so often as any Parliament shall be summon'd, shall choose two discreet and honest Men to be Burgesses of Parliament for this Burrough, and shall send them to Parliament at their Charge, who shall be satisfy'd in such Manner and Form, as is used in other Burroughs, and those Burgesses shall sit in Council, and shall have Voices so long as the Parliament shall continue, and shall do all other things which any other Burgesses may or ought to do in Parliament for any other Burrough.

John Lockey shall be the present Mayor, and being sworn, shall execute the Office until the Feast of St. *Michael* the Archangel, when another shall be elected.

Chief Burgesses.

Thomas Johnson, Henry Gape, John Nonney, Robert Wanton, Thomas Moningham, James Ashford, Richard Sharpe, John Sibly, Ralph Dowe, and *John Spencer,* shall be the ten Chief Burgesses and Common Council of the Burrough.

First Chamberlain. Steward.

William Hudson shall be Chamberlain, *John Mainard,* Esq. shall be Steward for his Life; the Major shall be Clerk of the Market.

Justices of the Burrough

The Mayor and Steward, with others assign'd by Commission, shall be Justices of the Peace of this Burrough, and

shall enquire, hear, and determine all things, in as large a *Hund. of* *Caishoe.*
Manner as the Justices of the Peace in any County may or
ought to do; and no other Justice of the Peace may intromit.

The Charnel House or the Town House shall be the com- *The Common*
mon Hall, or House of the Mayor and Burgesses, where *Hall.*
their Conventions may be appointed, their Courts held, and
their necessary Business of the Burrough be performed.

The Burgesses, or the greater Part of them, shall every *The Election*
Year, on the Feast of St. *Matthew* the Apostle, between *of the Mayor.*
the Hours of nine and twelve in the Forenoon, meet in this
Hall, or other convenient Place within this Burrough, and
shall there nominate two of the Chief Burgesses before the
Inhabitants of this Burrough, to the Intent that they, or
the greatest Part of them, shall choose one of these two
Burgesses to be Mayor for the Year following, who shall
take his Oath to execute the Office ; and if any Person, after Notice of his Election, shall refuse the Office without
reasonable Cause, the Mayor and ten Chief Burgesses, or
the greater Part of them, shall commit him to the Goal,
there to remain until he shall execute the Office, or shall
impose a competent Fine upon him, and detain him in Prison until he shall pay the same ; and every Mayor elect
shall be sworn before the last Mayor, if he shall be living
and present, but if dead or absent, before the Steward and
the Burgesses there present: And if any Mayor shall die,
or be removed from his Place, the Burgesses shall within
eight Days, meet at the Town Hall, or some other convenient Place within the Burrough, and choose two Chief Burgesses before the Inhabitants there; to the Intent that they
shall elect one of those two Chief Burgesses to be Mayor
for the remainder Part of the Year, and he shall be sworn
as aforesaid.

If the Chamberlain shall die, or be removed, the Mayor *The Election*
and Chief Burgesses, or the greater Part of them, shall *of the Cham-*
within four Days after such Death or Removal, choose an- *berlain.*
other of the Burgesses to be Chamberlain, who shall be
sworn before the Mayor and Steward of the Burrough.

If any of the Chief Burgesses shall die, or live out of the *The Election*
Burrough, or be removed from his Office, the Mayor and *of the Chief*
Chief Burgesses, or the greater Part of them, shall within *Burgesses.*
eight Days after such Death or Removal, choose one or
more of the Inhabitants to be Chief Burgess for their Lives,
who shall be sworn before the Mayor.

If the Steward shall die or be removed, the Mayor and *The Election*
Chief Burgesses, or the greater Part of them, shall within *of the Stew-*
eight Days choose another fit Person, well learned in the *ard.*
Laws of **England**, to be Steward for his Life, who shall be
sworn before the Mayor.

The Clerk of the Market shall be sworn before the Chief *Clerk of the* *Market.*

Hund. of Caisboe.

Burgesses, or the greater Part of them, that he will well and faithfully execute his Office, without any Fear, Gift, Reward, or Favour.

Serjeant of the Mace.

The Mayor shall choose two honest, fit Persons to be Serjeants at the Mace, to continue so long as the Mayor shall please, and they shall execute all Proclamations, Arrests, Processes, Executions, and other things which belong to their Office within the Burrough, in like Manner, as the Serjeants of the Mace in the City of London may do: And either of them may carry a Mace with the King's Arms, engraved upon it, before the Mayor, within the Burrough, and every such Serjeant of the Mace shall be sworn before the Mayor.

Court of Record.

The Mayor and Chief Burgesses shall hold a Court of Record before the Steward within the Burrough, on Wednesday in every Week, except the Weeks of *Easter*, *Pentecost*, and *Christmas*, and so from Week to Week for ever; And the Steward may hear and determine by Plaint to be levied there, all Pleas, Plaints, and Actions of all Manner of Debts, Accounts, Agreements, Contracts, Trespasses by Force and Arms, or other things and Actions, personal and mixt, whatsoever, which shall arise within the Burrough; so that the same do not exceed the Sum of 38*l.* And the Mayor and Burgesses upon such Quarrels, Pleas, Plaints, and Actions, may summon, attach, and distrain all Defects, against whom any Plaints, Pleas, or Actions shall be brought in the said Court, by their Goods according to the Custom of the City of London; and for Want of Goods, may attach or take their Bodies, according to the Custom used in London; and may hear and determine all such Actions, Plaints, and Pleas, in such Manner as in London; and the Executions, Processes, and Judgments shall be made by the Serjeants, or either of them; and the Mayor and Burgesses shall receive all the Fines and Amercements which shall arise in the Court, to the Use of the Burrough, as they are levied in London; and the Mayor and Burgesses shall have Jurisdiction of all Manner of Pleas, Plaints, and Actions of Debt, Trespasses, and Agreements, Detinue, Deceipt, and whatsoever other Pleas and Plaints, personal or mixed at common Law, or by Statute for any Cause, arising within the Burrough; (except Informations and Actions popular upon any Statute) so that the Declaration exceed not the Sum of 38*l.* And the Steward shall hear and determine the same according to the Laws, Statutes, and Constitutions of this Kingdom; so that none of the King's Justices, Barons of the *Exchequer*, Steward or Marshal, Clerk of the Market of the King's Household, Sheriff or other Officer, shall by any Means intromit, nor shall hold any Pleas there, nor Juries, or Pannels concerning any Causes whatsoever, arising within the

Burrough, not exceeding 38*l.* shall retorn, nor any other, but only the Steward and Officers of the Burrough shall determine and perform the same. ^{Hund. of Caishoe.}

The Mayor and Burgesses shall have a Goal within the Burrough, to keep safe all Felons and Malefactors taken there, until they shall be delivered according to Law. ^{The Goal.}

· The Mayor and Steward shall be put in every Commission with others assigned to deliver Prisoners in the Goal; and no Custos or Justice of the Peace shall intromit: And the Serjeants of the Mace, and other Officers of this Burrough shall retorne all Juries, Pannels, Inquisitions, and Attachments to the Justices assigned to deliver the Goal, and shall execute all Precepts, Mandates, Warrants, and Judgments of the same Justices, in all things, as the Sheriff of any County may retorne and execute. ^{Commission to deliver Prisoners.}

The Mayor and Burgesses shall have the Assay and Assize of Bread, Wine, and Ale, and other Victuals within the Burrough; of the Measures and Weights, and the Emendation and Correction of them; and of all other Officers belonging to the Clerk of the Market of the King's Household, with the Punishment of them, and to execute whatsoever doth belong to that Office, they shall think necessary, and shall have all Fines, Redemptions, Amercements, and other Profits arising thereupon, to the Use of the Burrough. ^{Assize of Bread, Wine, and Beer.}

The Mayor and Burgesses shall have the View of Francpledge of all the Inhabitants and Resciants within the Burrough, in the Month after the Feast of St. *Michael,* and in the Month next after the Feast of *Easter,* which Courts shall be always held before the Mayor and Steward, or before the Steward alone. ^{The View of Franc-pledge.}

The Mayor and Burgesses shall have one Market on every *Wednesday* and *Saturday,* in every Week except *Christmas,* and shall hold three Fairs yearly, one at the Noon of the Vigils of the Feast of the Annunciation of the blessed *Mary* the Virgin, to continue until the Noon of the Morrow of the said Feast then next following; another Fair at the Noon of the Vigils of St. *Alban,* and to continue until the Noon of the Morrow after the Feast, and the third Fair to begin at the Noon of the Vigil of St. *Michael* the Archangle, and to continue until the Noon of the Morrow after the Feast, with a Pipowder Court, Stallage, Picage, Fines, Amercements, and all other Profits whatsoever, with all Liberties and free Customs belonging to the same, to be taken for the Use of the Mayor, Burgesses, and Commonalty of the Burrough. ^{Two Markets. Three Fairs.}

The Mayor and Burgesses shall have the Retorne of Assizes, and of all Manner of Writs, Precepts, Bills, Mandates, and Warrants, and of all Summons, Extracts, and ^{Retorne of Writs.}

T 2

Hund. of
Caishoe. Precepts of the *Exchequer;* and Extracts and Precepts of
the Justices Itinerants, as well at the Pleas of the Forrest,
as at the Common Pleas, or of other Justices whatsoever,
and Attachments of Pleas of the Crown, and of others in this
Burrough, and the full Execution of them; so that no Sheriff, Bailiff, or other Officer shall intromit within the Burrough, unless in Default of the Mayor and Burgesses.

Waifes, Chat-
tels of Felons
and Fugitives,
Deodands,
Estraies, &c. The Mayor and Burgesses shall have all Waifes, Goods,
and Chattels of Felons and Fugitives, of Felons of themselves, and outlawed Persons, or otherwise, in any Manner
condemned and convicted, Deodands, and Estraies whatsoever within the Burrough.

The Burgesses
shall not be
retorned upon
Juries in mat-
ters arising
out of the
Burrough. The Mayor and Burgesses, or any of the Inhabitants within the Burrough shall not be put or impannelled upon any
Inquisitions, Juries, Assizes, or Attaints to be brought of
any Matter, arising out of the Burrough, but only of such
Causes as shall arise within the Burrough.

In Consideration that the Inhabitants of this Burrough
have paid to the King the Sum of 400*l.* the King did grant
to the Mayor and Burgesses, that the late Monastery of St.
Alban, shall be called the Parish Church of the Burrough
for all the Inhabitants within the late Parish or Chapelry of
St. Andrews; and all the Messuages, Houses, Buildings,
Lands, Tenements, wast Ground and Soil whatsoever with-
The Parish of
St. Alban. in the late Parish of St. Andrew, shall be reputed Part of
the Parish of the Burrough of St. Albans; and also granted
to them, all the Walls, Structures, Buildings, Roofes, Lead,
Iron, Glass, and Bells of the Church, and the Land and
Soil thereof, and all the Chappels, Vestries, and Sumpter
Yard there, and Scite of the late Parish Church of St. An-
drew, and the Church-yard; and that in the Church of St.
Alban there shall be a Rector, who shall have the Care of
the Souls of the Parishoners, administer the Sacrament
there, and perform all other things, which shall belong to the
Office of the Rector of any Parish of this Kingdom, and
the King doth constitute *George Witherhall*, Clerk, the
Rector of the
same Parish
Church. first Rector of the Church of St. *Alban* for the Term of his
Life; and granted that *George Witherall*, and his Successors, shall have in Right of the Church, all Manner of Tythes,
Oblations, and all other ecclesiastical Rights and Profits
within the Parish of St. Alban yearly for ever; which
Tythes, Oblations, Rights, and ecclesiatical Profits did then
extend to the clear yearly Value of 10*l.* and shall be rated at
the Value of 10*l.* to the Payment of First-fruits, and at 20*s.*
yearly for the Tenths; and the King did grant the Advowson and Right of Patronage of the Rectory and Parish
Church of St. Albans, to the Mayor and Burgesses to hold
of the King by Fealty in free Burgage of the Burrough of
St. Alban; for all Services and Demands, and not *in Ca-*

pite, rendring yearly to the King 10*l.* in the Name of Fee- *Hund. of* **Caishoe.**
farm, to be paid at the Court of Augmentation at the Feast
of St. *Michael* the Archangel every Year, in Lieu of all
Rents, Services, and Demands whatsoever.

Provided that the Justice of the Peace for the Liberty The Goal.
of 𝔖t. 𝔄lban, shall have a Goal within the Burrough for
the keeping safe of Felons and other Malefactors taken
within the Liberty, and out of the Burrough, until they
shall be delivered according to Law; and may hold their
Sessions of the Peace and Goal Delivery for the Liberty
within this Burrough.

The Mayor and Burgesses may erect a Grammar School The Grammar
within the Burrough; and make Statutes and Ordinances School.
in Writing, touching the Government of the School, and
shall do all other things touching the School; so that the
same Statutes and Ordinances shall not be to the Prejudice
of the King, nor contrary to the Laws of the Realm; which
Statutes shall be inviolably kept, and observed for ever;
and that the Mayor and Burgesses may the better bear the
Charges of the Burrough and the School, and of the Master and the Usher, the King grants them Leave to purchase Lands, Tenements, and Hereditaments, not exceeding the yearly Value of forty Pounds.

By Vertue of this Charter, the Mayor and Burgesses of
this Burrough were enabled to choose Burgesses again to
serve this Burrough in Parliament, of whom I have collected these Names, out of the Records of the Rolls with
great Exactness.

MARY.

| 1 | Oct. | 5 | John Maynard,——— |
| 1 | Apr. | 2 | Thomas Wendy, Oliver Sterky |

Oxford.

PHILIP and MARY.

| 2,3 | 12 Nov. | John Ashley, Robert Stepney |
| 4,5 | 20 Jan. | ——— ——— Southwell, Esq. |

ELIZABETH.

1	23 Jan.	Christopher Smith, Esq. John Dodmer
14	8 May	Henry Cock, Charles Smith
28		Hen. Maynard, Humph. Cuningsby, Esquires
30		Hen. Maynard, Humph. Cuningsby, Esquires
39	24 Oct.	Hen. Maynard, Humph. Cuningsby, Esquires
43	27 Oct.	Hen. Frowike, Esq. in the Place of F. Bacon

JAMES 1.

| 1 | 19 Mar. | Francis Cotton, Adulph Carey, Esquires |
| 21 | 12 Feb. | Arthur Capel, John Luke, Esquires |

CAR. I.

1	17 May	Sir Charles Morison, Kt. and Bar. Sir Jo. Luke, Kt. both whom were chosen only by Burgesses according to the Charter, as appears by the Retorn
15	6 Mar.	Sir Jo. Jenings, Kt. of the Bath, Thomas Cuningsby, Esq.
16	3 Nov.	Sir J. Jenings, Kt. of the Bath, Edw. Wingate, Esq.

Hund. of
Caishoe.

CAR. II.

12	25 *Apr.*	*Rich. Jenings, Esq. Tho. Arris*, M. D.
13	8 *May*	*Rich. Jenings, Esq. Tho. Arris*, M. D.
30	6 *Mar.*	*Th. Pope Blount, John Gape*, Esquires
31	6 *Mar.*	*Sam. Grimstone, Th. Pope Blount*, Esquires.

JAC. II.

1 | 19 *May* | *George Churchil, Tho. Docwra*, Esquires

WILL. and MARY.

Convention.

1 | 23 *Feb.* | Sir *Sam. Grimstone*, Bar. *Geo. Churchil*, Esquires
2 | 20 *Mar,* | Sir *Sam. Grimstone*, Bar. *Geo. Churchil*, Esquires

WILL. III.

7 | *Nov.* | Sir *Sam. Grimstone*, Bar. *Geo. Churchil*, Esquires
   | *Aug.* | Sir *Sam. Grimstone*, Bar. *Geo. Churchil*, Esquires.

Upon the Passing of this Charter, a Coat of Arms was granted to this Burrough, wherein they bear *Azure, a Saltier Or.*

Queen *Mary* by her Charter dated 18th *December*, 1554, 1 *Regni sui*, did confirm the Charter of *Edw.* VI *in ipsissimis verbis.*

In the 3 and 4 Years of the Reign of *P.* and *M.* Sir *Richard Lee*, Kt. bargain'd and sold to *Richard Bourman*, of *London*, Clerk, late Abbot of St. *Albans*, the Scite of that Monastery which he the said *Richard Bourman* by his Deed dated 29th *December*, 3 and 4 *P.* and *M.* granted to Queen *Mary* for diverse Uses, which was done with Intent to restore that Abby again.

Queen *Elizabeth* by her Charter dated 7th *Feb. Anno* 1560, 2 *Regni sui*, confirmed both the former Charters of *Edw.* VI. and Queen *Mary*, and upon the Petition of Sir *Nicholas Bacon*, Kt. Lord Keeper of the Broad Seal, by her Charter dated at *Gorham Bury*, 24th *Mar. Anno* 1570, 12 *Regni sui*, reciting the Grant of the School made by *Edw.* VI. for the farther Relief and Maintenance of the Master and School, granted that the Mayor and Burgesses may appoint two discreet and honest Inhabitants within the Burrough, to sell there all Manner of Wine, and may discharge them, or either of them, from such selling, and appoint other discreet Persons in the Place of one or either of them, so often as the Mayor and Burgesses shall think fit, to sell Wine, and shall grant them

Licences to sell Wine.

License by themselves, or Assigns in their Inns or Messuages within the Burrough, to keep two Wine Taverns, so long as they shall please to sell all sorts of Wine, by any

Measures and at any Price, to the greatest Profit of either of them without any Forfeiture; and no other Person shall sell any Wine within the Burrough upon the Penalty of 20*l.* so often as he shall do the same; provided if the Mayor and Burgesses shall not pay to the Master of the School the yearly Annuity of 20*l.* for his Maintenance at the Feast of St. *Michael,* the Archangel, the Birth of our Lord, the Annunciation of the blessed Virgin *Mary,* and Nativity of St. *John* Baptist by equal Portions, or within one Month next after any of the Feasts, that then this Faculty shall be supended and cease, until the Master of the School shall be fully satisfied of such Annuity of twenty Pounds, and all the Arrearages thereof.

King *James* I. by his Charter dated at Westminster, 10 *Cart. 3 Jac. I.* Maii *Anno* 1605, 3 *Regni sui,* Ang. & Scot. 43, reciting the several Grants touching the School made by *Edward* VI. and Queen *Eliz.* and also reciting another Grant, whereas he by Letters Patents dated at Westminster, 18th *December,* 1606, 4 *Regni sui,* Ang. & Scot. 44. had granted free Liberty to *Robert Wooley* of this Town, *Leonard Wooley* his Son, and *Robert Wooley* the younger, another of his Sons, and their Assigns, that *Robert Wooley* the elder during his natural Life, *Leonard Wooley* after the Death of *Robert* his Father during his natural Life, and *Robert Wooley* the younger after the Death of *Robert Wooley* the elder, and *Leonard Wooley* his Son during the Life of *Robert Wooley* the younger, shall have one Tavern or Cellar of Wine within the Burrough of St. Alban in the Dwelling House wherein *Robert Wooley* the elder, *Leonard* and *Robert* his Sons, now dwell, or they or their Assigns shall dwell within the Town, and in it may sell and drink by Retail, by the Gallon, Pottle, Quart, or less or greater Measure, all Manner of wholesome Wines at their Pleasure, and for such Prices as the Wine with reasonable Profit may be sold without any Forfeiture, paying yearly to the Mayor and Burgesses to the Use of the Free Grammar School, for an Augmentation of the Stipend yearly paid to the Master, four Marks at the Anunciation of the blessed Lady the Virgin *Mary,* the Nativity of St. *John* Baptist, of St. *Michael,* the Archangel, and the Birth of our Lord, by equal Portions, during the natural Lives of *Robert Wooley* the elder, *Leonard Wooley,* and *Robert Wooley* the younger, and the longer Liver of them, and to the Intent that the several Rents of 20*l.* and four Marks shall continue hereafter to the Mayor and Burgesses, the King Grants to them, that within the Burrough and two Miles thereof, there shall be no more than three Wine Taverns for the future; and that after the Death of *Robert Wooley* the elder and his two Sons, and the Surrender or

Hund. of
Caisbot.

Forfeiture of their Interest, the Mayor and Burgesses may appoint one discreet and honest Person, (besides the two Persons appointed as aforesaid,) to sell all Manner of Wines within the Burrough, and to remove him, and to appoint another in his Place, so often as they shall think fit; and that no other Person shall sell Wine within the Burrough, or two Miles thereof, upon the Penalty of 20*l.* and the Mayor and Burgesses may search any Cellar, House, or Place within the Burrough or two Miles thereof, and if any Wine shall be found there to sell contrary to this Grant, they may seize the same to the Use of the King, and imprison the Offender, till he shall be bound to the Mayor and Burgesses, that he will not hereafter sell any Wine within the Burrough or two Miles thereof.

Provided that if the Mayor and Burgesses shall not yearly pay to the Master of the School the yearly Rent or Annuity of four Marks as aforesaid, this Faculty shall cease until the Master shall be fully satisfied of the four Marks and all the Arrearages thereof.

Charles I. by his Charter dated at 𝕎estminster, 17th Day of *December*, 8 *Regni sui*, *Anno* 1632, reciting the ancient Bounds of the Burrough in the time of the Abbot did extend from 𝔊onnerston to 𝕂ingsbury, and from thence to the Corner of 𝔇unheg, and from thence to the Corner of 𝔗onmanditch, from thence to the Grange of 𝔖t. 𝔓eter, from thence to 𝔅ernet 𝔚ood, from thence to 𝔖tone 𝔠ross, from thence to the Corner of the Church-yard of St. *Peters*, on the East, from thence to the Grange or Barn of *John*, the Son of *Richard Baldwin*, from thence by 𝔗onmanditch to 𝔖optwel 𝕃ane, from thence to the Croft of *John de Hampton*, from thence to 𝔊reen 𝕃ane 𝔈nd, from thence to 𝔗ptwood 𝕃ane, from thence to 𝔥olliwall 𝔅ridge, and from thence to the River of 𝔊unmerston; and to ascertain these Meets and Bounds, did grant that the Mayor and Burgesses by the Oaths of twelve honest and lawful Men of the Burrough, should walk round the same, and set out all the Meets, Bounds, and Divisions so often as they should find it necessary.

There shall be twenty four Assistants to be chosen by the Mayor and Chief Burgesses, which Assistants shall aid and assist the Mayor and Cheif Burgesses, so often as they shall require them, in the Management of the Affairs and Business of the Burrough, and they shall hold the Offices for their respective Lives, with a Clause to confirm all things contained in the former Charters.

King *Charles* II. by his Charter, dated at 𝕎estminster, the 27th of *July*, *Anno* 1664, 16 *Regni sui*, granted that the Mayor and Burgesses of this Burrough, shall be incorporated by the Name of Mayor, Aldermen, and Burgesses, of St. Albans in the County of Hertford; and by that Name shall have perpetual Succession, plead and be impleaded, and purchase Lands and Tenements, Goods or Chattels, without Limitation.

There shall be a Mayor and twelve Aldermen of the Burrough, who shall be the Common Council of the Burrough, and *Robert New* shall be the Mayor, until the Feast of St. *Michael* the Archangel, and from thence until another of the Aldermen shall be chosen, and sworn to hold this Office; and *Robert Ivory, Edward Eames, Gawen Crosfeild, Thomas Oxen, Thomas Cowley* the elder, *William Marston, John Gape, John New, Thomas Cowley* the younger, *Ralph Pollard, William Wiseman,* and *William Raunce,* shall be the present Aldermen to continue for their Lives, unless any of them for their ill Government, or other reasonable Cause shall be discharged.

There shall be twenty four Assistants, who shall be chosen by the Mayor and Aldermen, or the greater Part of them, who shall assist the Mayor and Aldermen, when requested, in Matters touching the Government of the Burrough, to continue, during their natural Lives, unless any of them, for some just Cause, shall be removed.

There shall be an High Steward, to advise and direct the Mayor and Aldermen in Business touching the Burrough; and a Recorder to do and execute all things in the Burrough, which belong to any Recorder in any other Burrough, and a Coroner, who shall perform all things in the Burrough; which belongs to the Office of a Coroner; and a Common Clerk to make and write all the Recognizances taken before the Mayor, and other Justices of the Peace in the Presence of the Mayor, and to ingross the same in Parchment, and to enter all Actions, Plaints, and Pleas, and other original and judicial Writs, and Process, and Judgments thereupon in the Court of Record, which any Common Clerk within any Burrough incorporate, may do by his Office, and he shall have all the Fees, Rewards, and Profits belonging to the Office of a Common Clerk; and there shall be three or four Attornies to prosecute, defend, and execute all things necessary, in Suits, Plaints, Causes, and Matters, which shall happen in the Court of Record.

Sir *Harbottle Grimstone,* Bart. Master of the Rolls, shall be high Steward, and shall continue during his Life; *John Simpson,* Esq. shall be Recorder for his Life; the Mayor and Aldermen shall choose a Coroner who shall continue during their Pleasure; *Thomas Richard* shall be Common Clerk, who shall continue during their Pleasure; and they shall choose three or four Attornies of the Court

Hund. of Caisbot. of Record, who shall personally attend there; and the Recorder, Common Clerk, Coroner, Attornies, and Assistants, shall be sworn before the Mayor and Aldermen before they execute their Offices.

The Mayor and Aldermen may choose inferior Officers within the Burrough, and ordain and administer to them a fit Oath.

The Markets and Fairs mentioned in the former Charter are confirmed; and the Mayor and Aldermen shall hold the Fair in the Vigils, and in the Day, and the Morrow of the Feast of the Purification of the blessed *Mary* the Virgin, in the waste and void Places of the Soil in the Burrough, to continue as in the former Charter, with Pipowder Court.

No Forreigner, except in open Markets or Fairs, may buy or sell any Merchandise, beside Victuals, within the Burrough by Parcels or Retail, nor shall use any Mistery, Occupation, or manual Art within the Burrough, or Liberties thereof.

The Mayor nor any Person, who have been Mayor, shall be compelled to carry Arms in proper Person at any Muster before the Lord Lieutenants or Deputy Lieutenants in any County, but shall be for ever quit thereof; yet they shall find some other fit Person to serve in their Arms, when it shall be necessary.

The Mayor and Aldermen, upon every Market day, or other Day in the Week, may search in every House, Granary, Cellar, Chamber, Shop, and other Places within the Burrough, where there shall be just Cause of Suspition, that any Grain or Corn shall be hid or laid up, to advance the Price of such Grain; and if any such Corn shall be found, the same shall be brought into the open Market to be sold, at a reasonable Price for the publick Good of the Inhabitants within the Burrough.

Every Mayor shall be a Justice of the Peace for the Burrough for the Year next after his Mayoralty, if he shall live so long, and if he shall die, the eldest Alderman shall be sworn a Justice of the Peace in his Room, for the Remainder of his Year to come; and every Mayor during the Year next after his Mayoralty, shall have Precedency of all the Aldermen and Burgesses of the Burrough.

There shall be a Court of Record held before the Mayor, Aldermen, and Recorder, or any of them, (whereof the Mayor or Recorder shall be one) and in the Absence of the Mayor and the Recorder, before two or more of the elder Aldermen in the Common Hall, or some other convenient Place, on *Friday* in every Week, except the Weeks of *Easter, Pentecost,* and *Christmas,* and so from Week to Week for ever. And the Mayor, Aldermen, and Recorder, and every of them, may hear and determine there all the Plaints, Pleas, and Actions, and other things contained in the Charter of *Edw.* VI. so that in the Declaration of any such Causes, Pleas, Plaints, or Actions, they do not exceed the Sum of fifty Pounds.

The Mayor and Aldermen shall have all Manner of Fines, Forfeitures, and Amerciaments, which shall be imposed at the Quarter Sessions to be held for the Burrough for any Cause whatsoever.

If any Person shall be chosen an Assistant, and shall refuse to take his Oath to execute the Office, the Mayor and Aldermen may set such reasonable Fine upon him as they shall think fit to be levied by Distress or Action of Debt, for the Use of the Burrough.

John Simpson, Esq. the present Recorder, may make a Deputy, who shall be sworn before the Mayor, and in the Absence of the Recorder shall have full Power to do all things belonging to the Office to all Intents and Purposes, as the Recorder might have done, and the Recorder shall be a Justice of the Peace of the *Quorum* within the Burrough.

All former Grants are confirmed with such Additions and Alterations as are herein mentioned : And all Officers shall take the Oaths of Allegiance and Supremacy; and every High Steward, Recorder, and Town Clerk, upon their Election, shall be approved by the King before they shall be admitted to execute their Office.

King *James* II. by his Charter dated at 𝔚𝔢𝔰𝔱𝔪𝔦𝔫𝔰𝔱𝔢𝔯, 16th of *March, Anno* 1685, 1 *Regni sui,* granted that one of the most honest and discreet Men within the Burrough or elsewhere in the County of 𝔥𝔢𝔯𝔱𝔣𝔬𝔯𝔡, shall be Mayor of this Burrough, and eighteen of the most discreet Men in the Burrough or County, who shall be Aldermen and Common Council of this Burrough ; and *John Selioke* shall be Mayor, to continue until the Feast of St. *Michael* the Archangel; Sir *Francis Leigh,* Sir *Benjamin Titchborne,* Sir *William Parkins,* Sir *Thomas Fotherly,* Sir *Charles Cleaver,* Sir *Robert Marsham,* Kts. *Henry Guy, Thomas Halsey, James Willimot, Edward Seymour, John Withered,* Esquires, *John Gape, Thomas Cowley, Ralph Pollard, Thomas Eccleston, William Marston, Stephen Adams,* and *Edward Seabrooke,* Gentlemen, shall be the present Aldermen of the Burrough.

John Viscount *Churchill* of 𝔄𝔭𝔪𝔬𝔲𝔱𝔥 shall be High Steward, *Anthony Farringdon,* Recorder, and *Thomas Richards,* Common Clerk of the Burrough.

Every Alderman who shall hereafter be chosen Mayor, and shall not be resident in the Burrough, may make any Aldermen residing in the Burrough his Deputy, and such

Deputy shall have full Power to act in all things touching the Burrough as the Mayor ought to do.

The Mayor shall be a Justice of the Peace for the County of 𝕳𝖊𝖗𝖙𝖋𝖔𝖗𝖉, and the Justices of the Peace for the County shall hold the General Quarter Sessions of the Peace for the County, which shall hereafter be yearly held after the Feast of St. *Michael* the Archangel and the *Epiphany*, within the Burrough of 𝕾𝖙. 𝕬𝖑𝖇𝖆𝖓𝖘, and not elsewhere.

The Recorder and eldest Alderman residing within the Burrough, shall be Justices of the Peace within the Burrough; provided always that in all Cases concerning the Nomination, Election, removing any Officer, or the Government of the Burrough, any nine Aldermen, whereof the Mayor shall be one, may do all things which the Mayor and Aldermen have been used to do, (except the Court of Record) shall be held as heretofore hath been used; provided the King may remove at his Pleasure the Mayor, High Steward, Recorder, Common Clerk, or any of the Aldermen, declared under the Seal of the Privy Council; and he confirmed all former Gifts and Grants, with such Additions and Alterations as are herein mentioned,

Note, That this Charter as all others made by King *James* II. for the Government of other Corporations are now made void. The same King by his Charter dated at 𝕾𝖊𝖘𝖙𝖒𝖎𝖓𝖘𝖙𝖊𝖗, 25th *Febr.* 1687, 3 *Regni sui*, granted unto *John* Lord *Churchill*, *George Churchill*, and *Thomas Docwra*, Esquires, and to their Heirs and Assigns for ever, all those the Advowsons and Right of Patronage, of, in, and to the Rectories and Parish Churches of 𝕾𝖙. 𝕸𝖆𝖗𝖞 𝕹𝖔𝖗𝖙𝖍𝖈𝖍𝖚𝖗𝖈𝖍 *alias* 𝕹𝖔𝖗𝖙𝖍 𝕭𝖊𝖗𝖐𝖍𝖆𝖒𝖘𝖙𝖊𝖉, and 𝕸𝖚𝖈𝖍 𝕸𝖚𝖓𝖉𝖔𝖓 in the County of 𝕳𝖊𝖗𝖙𝖋𝖔𝖗𝖉, with their and either of their Rights, Members, and Appurtenances upon Trust to present the Rector of 𝕾𝖙 𝕬𝖑𝖇𝖆𝖓𝖘, to such of the Rectories or Parsonages as shall first become void, towards his better Support. Provided always that when and so soon as one of the Churches of 𝕾𝖙. 𝕸𝖆𝖗𝖞 𝕹𝖔𝖗𝖙𝖍𝖈𝖍𝖚𝖗𝖈𝖍 *alias* 𝕹𝖔𝖗𝖙𝖍 𝕭𝖊𝖗𝖐𝖍𝖆𝖒𝖘𝖙𝖊𝖉, and 𝕸𝖚𝖈𝖍 𝕸𝖚𝖓𝖉𝖔𝖓, which are now both full, shall by the Death of the present Incumbent, or otherwise, become void, that then this Grant as to the other of them shall cease and become void; and the same shall remain in the free Dispose of the King, his Heirs, and Successors.

The Names of the MAYORS, &c. of 𝕾𝖙. 𝕬𝖑𝖇𝖆𝖓𝖘.

1552	*John Lockey*	1560	*William Hudson*
1553	*John Johnson*	1561	*Robert Woolley*
1554	*Henry Gape*	1562	*Richard Grubb*
1555	*Thomas Monningham*	1563	*Richard Seale*
1556	*Richard Sharpe*	1564	*John Gape*
1557	*John Sibly*	1565	*Thomas Johnson*
1558	*Randolph Done*	1566	*John Lockey*
1559	*Gilbert Comport*	1567	*John Lawrence*

1568 *William West*	1633 *Henry Gape*	Hund. of
1569 *John Sibley*	1634 *Gawin Crosfeild*	Caishoe.
1570 *William Hudson*	1635 *William Humphry*	
1571 *Robert Woolley*	1636 *Thomas Oxton*	
1572 *John Gape*	1637 *Ralph Pollard*	
1573 *William Rolfe*	1638 *Ralph Pemberton*	
1574 *John Grace*	1639 *Thomas Cowley*	
1575 *John Lawrence*	1640 *Richard Ruth*	
1576 *William West*	1641 *William Newe*	
1577 *John Clarke*	1642 *Robert Ivory*	
1578 { *John Sibly*	1643 *Edward Eames*	
{ *Robert Woolley*	1644 *Thomas Oxton*	
1579 *John Gape*	1645 *Gawin Crosfeild*	
1580 *John Goodridge*	1646 *William Humphry*	
1581 *John Arnold*	1647 *Ralph Pollard*	
1582 *Thomas Woolley*	1648 *John Simpson*	
1583 *Francis Babb*	1649 *William Newe*	
1584 *William Warren*	1650 *Thomas Cowley*	
1585 *James Carter*	1651 *William Marston*	
1586 *William Rolfe*	1652 *Ralph Gladman*	
1587 *Robert Gostwick*	1653 *Robert Ivory*	
1588 *Robert Shrimpton*	1654 *Edward Eames*	
1589 *Richard Lockey*	1655 *Gawine Crosfeild*	
1590 *Thomas Rockit*	1656 *Thomas Oxton*	
1591 *William Fisher*	1657 *William Humphry*	
1592 *John Clerk*	1658 *John Gape*	
1593 *Francis Babb*	1659 *John Newe*	
1594 *Ralph Gape*	1660 *Thomas Cowley, Jun.*	
1595 *John Moseley*	1661 *Thomas Cowley, Sen.*	
1596 *Robert Shrimpton*	1662 *William Marston*	
1597 *John Saunders*	1663 *Robert Newe*	
1598 *Thomas Woolley*	1664 *Robert Ivory*	
1599 *Thomas Rockit*	1665 *Ralph Pollard*	
1600 *William Antrobus*	1666 *William Rance*	
1601 *Robert Woolley*	1667 *Thomas Oxton*	
1602 *John Oxton*	1668 *John Gape*	
1603 *John Moseley*	1669 *William Oxton*	
1604 *William Spencer*	1670 *John Newe*	
1605 *Robert Shrimpton*	1671 *William Rugg*	
1606 *Francis Babb*	1672 *Thomas Cowley, Jun.*	
1607 *Richard Gilmet*	1673 *Thomas Haward*	
1608 *Robert Woolley*	1674 *William Marston, Sen.*	
1609 *John Clerke, Jun.*	1675 *John Dogget*	
1610 *John Saunders*	1676 *Ralph Pollard*	
1611 *Robert Skelton*	1677 *Thomas Eccleston*	
1612 *Robert Gilmet*	1768 *William Marston*	
1613 *Thomas Goodridge*	1679 *John Gape*	
1614 *John Oxton*	1680 *John Newe, Jun.*	
1615 *Thomas Rockit*	1681 *Stephen Adams*	
1616 *Thomas Wells*	1682 *John Newe, Sen.*	
1617 *Michael Dixon*	1683 *Thomas Crosfeild*	
1618 *Richard Wilmet*	1684 *John Selioke*	
1619 *John Clarke*	1685 *Henry Guy, Esq.*	
1620 *John Saunders*	1686 *Sir Francis Leigh, Kt.*	
1621 *Robert Skelton*	1687 *Edward Seabrooke*	
1622 *Thomas Woodridge*	1688 *Thomas Cowley*	
1623 *John Oxton*	1689 *Thomas Haywood*	
1624 *William Humphry*	1690 *Edward Horsell*	
1625 *Thomas Rockit*	1691 *Henry Dobyns*	
1626 *Ralph Pollard*	1692 *Samuel Loft*	
1627 *Ralph Pemberton*	1693 *John Tisdell*	
1628 *Richard Ruth*	1694 *Stephen Adams*	
1629 *Michael Dixon*	1695 *John New, Gent.*	
1630 *William Newe*	1696 *Nicholas Sparling*	
1631 *Robert Ivory*	1697 *Stephen Adams*	
1632 *Edward Eames*	1698 *John Sparling*	

Hund. of Caishoe.

Names of the CHIEF STEWARDS of the Burrough.

1559 Sir *Nicholas Bacon*, Kt. Lord Keeper of the Great Seal of England, of whom you may read in Gorham-Bury.

1596 Sir *Thomas Egerton*, Kt. Lord Keeper of the Great Seal of England, of whom you may read in Little Gabesden.

1616 Sir *Francis Bacon*, Kt. Lord Keeper of the Great Seal of England, of whom you may read in the Mannor of Gorham.

1625 Sir *Thomas Coventry*, Kt. who was constituted Solicitor General, Anno 14 *Jac.* I. and Reader of the *Inner Temple*, Attorney General Anno 18 *Jac.* I. and Keeper of the Great Seal Anno 1 *Car.* I.

1660 Sir *Harbottle Grimston*, Bar. Master of the Rolls in the Court of Chancery, of whom you may read in the Mannor of Gorham-Bury.

1685 John Viscount *Churchil*, of Aymouth in Scotland, was created Baron of Saundridge, 14 *May*, 1685, Earl of Marlborough, 9th of *May*, 1689, *Will.* and *Mary*.

STEWARDS of the Burrough of St. Albans.

1554 *John Maynard*, Esq. *Nicholas Kempe*, Esq.

1589 *Henry Frowick* of *Lincoln's Inn*, Esq.

1617 *Henry Ewre* of the *Middle Temple*, Esq.

1619 *John Howland* of the *Middle Temple.* Esq. who was discharged from this Office Anno 1644, by Reason of his Loyalty to King *Charles* I.

RECORDERS.

1644 *William Foxwist*, Esq. one of the Benchers and Governors of *Lincoln's Inn*, from Anno 12 *Car.* II. to Anno 22 *ejusdem Regis*

1661 *John Sympson*, Esq. one of the Benchers of the *Inner Temple*, afterwards advanced to the State and Degree of Serjeant at Law, one of the Judges of the *Sheriff's Court* in London, and was knighted.

1681 *Anthony Farringdon*, Esq. another of the Benchers of the *Inner Temple*, who received a Writ to be a Serjeant at Law, Anno 1683 and afterwards was constituted one of his Majesty's Justices for the Counties of Cardigan. Pembroke, and Carmarthen, in the Principality of Wales, also a Justice of the Peace for this County, and for this Liberty of St. Albans.

The Names of the CHIEF BURGESSES of the Burrough of St Albans.

1553 *John Lockey*
Thomas Johnson
Henry Gape
John Nonney
Robert Wanton
Thomas Moningham
James Ashford
Richard Sharpe
John Sibley
Ralph Dowa and *John Spencer*, the first Burgesses by Charter
Randolf Done
Gilbert Comport
William Hudson
Robert Woolley
Richard Grubb
Richard Seale
John Gape
John Lawrence
William West
William Rolfe
John Grace
John Clarke
John Goodridge
John Arnold
Thomas Woolley
Francis Babb
William Warren

James Carter
Robert Gostwick
Robert Shrimpton
Thomas Rockit
Richard Lockey
1590 *William Fisher*
1591 *John Porter* elected, and refusing to hold was committed till he paid his Fine
W. Antrobus chosen, and refusing to hold was committed till he paid his Fine
J. Halfhide chosen, but afterwards excused by reason of his Poverty
1594 *John Moseley*
Ralph Gape
Robert Woolley
John Saunders
1596 *William Wilson*
1597 *William Antrobus*
John Oxton
1598 *William Spencer*
1601 *John Clarke*
1606 *Richard Gilmet*
1609 *Robert Gilmet*
1610 *Robert Skelton*

1611 *Thomas Goddridge*	1632 *Thomas Oxton*
1612 *Anthony Jackson*	*Thomas Crawley*
Thomas Wells	1645 *John King*, Dr. in Phi.
1614 *Michael Dixon*	*John Simpson*
1621 *Simon Beckit*	1648 *William Marston*
William Humphry	1649 *Ralph Gladman*
1624 *Ralph Pollard*	1654 *John Gape*
Ralph Pemberton	1655 *John New*
1626 *Richard Ruth*	1657 *Thomas Crawley*, Jun.
1627 *William New*	1659 *Robert New*
Robert Ivory	1662 *Ralph Pollard*
1628 *Henry Gape*	1663 *William Rance*
1629 *Edward Eames*	*William Wiseman.*
1631 *Gawin Crosfeild*	

Hund. of
Caishoe.

ALDERMEN by the Charter dated 27th of *July* 1664 16 *Car.* II.

Robert New, Mayor	*William Rance*
Robert Ivory	1665 *William Oxton*
Edward Eames	*Thomas Rotherham*, Jun.
Gawen Crosfeild	*William Rugge*
Thomas Oxton	1668 *Thomas Haward*
Thomas Cowley, Sen.	1669 *John Docket*
William Marston	1673 *Thomas Ecclestone*
John Gape	*John New*, Jun.
John New	*Stephen Adams*
Thomas Cowley, Jun.	*Thomas Crosfeild*
Ralph Pollard	*John Selioke.*
William Wiseman	

ALDERMEN by the Charter dated the 16th of *March, Anno* 1 *Jac.* II.

John Selioke, Mayor	*John Gape*
Sir *Francis Leigh*	*Thomas Cowley*
Sir *Benjamin Tichbourn*	*Ralph Pollard*
Sir *William Parkins*	*Thomas Ecclestone*
Sir *Thomas Fotherley*	*William Marston*
Sir *Charles Cleaver*	*Stephen Adams* and
Sir *Robert Marsham*	*Edward Seabroke*, Gent.
Henry Guy	1687 *Thomas Crosfeild*
Thomas Halsey	1689 *Henry Dobbyns*
James Willimot	*Edward Horsel*
Edward Seymour	*Samuel Loft*
John Withered, Esq.	*John Tisdel*

CHAMBERLAINS and CLERKS of the Papers.

Gilbert Stoughton	*Conon Rawlin*
1589 *Thomas Randoll*	

TOWN CLERKS by Charter dated the 17th of *Sept.* 8 *Car.* I.

Conon Rawlin	1677 *Thomas Richards*
1648 *Thomas Richards*	

ASSISTANTS of the Burrough of St. Albans.

1686 *Thomas Cross*	*John Davis*
John Kilbie	*William Marston*
Thomas Facy	*William Fisher*
Richard Gray	*John Clarke*
Thomas Gilmet	*Thomas Robinson*
Willam Spencer	*John Harding*
John Smith	*Thomas Camfeild*
John Porter	*Hugh Gilbert*
John Casterton	*William Antrobus*
Richard Chadesty	*Hugh Eliot*
James Lockey	*John Oxton*
Richard Collet	*Thomas Brown*
Thomas Whitefeild	*Richard Studesbury*

Hund. of Caishoe.

John Moseley
John Saunders
John Halfhide
William Pharoe
1589 Gilbert Wells
1590 Robert Palmer
Robert Wooley
1591 John Skinner
Robert Skelton
Ralph Gape
1594 Edward Potton
Ferdinand Fretheren
Barnaby Lawrence
John Taylour
Thomas Webster
John Long
Michael Collet
William Rolfe, Jnn.
1597 Thomas Webster
Richard Gilmet
1598 Matthew Davy
Thoms Cole
Thomas Stoughton
John Munck
Hugh Spencer
1599 Richard Denton
John Lee
1601 Walter Antrobus
1604 Anthony Jackson
William Heathcock
Thomas Wells
Thomas Harris
Andrew Coltman
Richard Winstanley
1606 Thomas Gooddridge
1607 George Crawley
1608 John Binder
1610 Canon Rawlin
John Arnold
1612 Leonard Wilkes
John Street
William Humphry
Tristram Nash
Ralph Pollard
1613 Robert Bridges
George Shrimpton
1614 Richard Ruth
Henry Gape
James Clarke
John Wells
William Hale
1618 Anthony Selioke
Pierce Thompson
1619 William New
1621 Elizeus Axtel
Roger Hunt
Andrew Cock
1622 Nicholas Cotchet
Thomas Laurence
John Gape
Blastus Goldey
Ralph Gladman
1624 William Hinxman
Edward Eames
1625 Williamson Arnold

Gawine Croasfeild
Anthony Jackson
1626 Thomas Cowley
John Shad
1627 Jeremy Fitch
Edward Ruth, Jun.
Thomas Hale
Richard Streete
1628 Christopher Arlan
John Ruth
1629 William Marston
Fromabove Done
1630 Lionel Campion
1631 Walter Crawley
1632 John Medley
1634 Leonard Howe
John New
William Walker
1635 John Mease
William Redwood
Gilbert Selioke
1637 Ralph Pollard, Jun.
Thomas Tanner
1640 Jonathan Parker
Henry Godley
Nathaniel Ewre
1642 William Henchman
1645 Robert Newe
1647 John Browne
John Crofts
1648 Thomas Haward
Robert Fletcher
1649 William Stone
Thomas Woodward
Ralph Gladman
1650 Ralph Loft
1651 Richard Millard
1653 Thomas Richards
William Moore
1654 Soloman Smith
1656 Godfrey Schoolfeild
Nicholas Cotchet
1673 Thomas Crosfeild
1676 Walter Cowley
William Morris
1677 John Seliock
Henry Dobyns
Edward Horsel
John Tisdal
Edward Seabrock
John Cowley
Thomas Holdham
John Burton, Jun.
Joseph Marsham
William Stephens
Thomas Jones
John Halfhide
Richard Neal
Walter Beach
Thomas King
Samuel Loft
Thomas Grub
William Williamson
Robert Swainton
1679 Ralph Gladman

Josiah Russel	*James Bradbury*
John Streete	1686 *Robert Hazles*
1680 *John Edmonds*	*John Wilkinson*
1681 *Henry Stephens*	*William Prentice*
1682 *Ralph Marston*	*Robert Romford*
Abel Rumford	*John Sparling*
Francis Halford	1689 *Robert Scot,* Jun.
John Sheppeth	*Edward Wilson*
James Tristram	*John Edmonds*
William Butler	*John Halsey*
1684 *Nicholas Sparling*	*William James*
1685 *Zacheriah Reeve*	*William Howe*

The Hospital of ST. JULIAN

JEOFFERY, the sixteenth Abbot of the Monastery of St. Albans, founded and erected the Hospital of St. *Julian*, by the Advice and Consent of the same Convent, near the Way that leads to London; and called divers miserable poor People together, provided for them, and gave a Maintenance to support them, which you may read among the Acts of that Abbot.

Matt. Paris *de Vitis Abbat.* fol. 57.

Upon the Dissolution of this Monastery this Hospital came to the Crown, from whence it was conveyed to *Thomas Lee*, whose Pedigree follows.

Robert Lee.— Daughter and Heir of Wallis.

John Lee of Titleworth,— ———— Daughter of Sir
in the County of Sussex. | Roger Lewknor, Kt.

John Lee of— Elizabeth, Daughter of Ralph Sherley,
——— Anno | Secretary to the Earl of Arundel.
10 H. VII.

Richard Lee.— Elizabeth, Daughter of Robert Hall of
More, by the Sister of Edmond Dudley.

Daughter of— Thomas Lee of— Alice, Daughter of Tho.   Sir Richard Lee— ——— Daugh. of
| St. Julians. | Cocks of Beamont in   of Sopwell in | ——— Green-
  this County.   this County. | feild.

1	2	3					
Wife of Finch.	Joane, Wife of String.	Mary, w. of Robert Burton.	Eliz. mar. Griffith Williams of Wales.	Mary, 1 mar. J. Luxford. 2 Paul Belamy. 3 W. Ticknel.	Ann, Wife of Tickenal of Ireland.	Ann, Da. & Cohe. Wife of Edwin Sadler.	Maud, w. of Sir Hum. Coninsby, Kt. 2. of Pemberton. died without Issue.

From which Family this Monastery came to *Everard Digby*, who was possest hereof, married *Alice* Daughter of ——— *Fulbraham*, by whom he had Issue two Sons, *John Digby*, marryed to *Mary Zinzam* and *Thomas Digby*; and I suppose it was sold from one of this Family to

John Ellis, Esq. who was a Draper in London, fined for Alderman of that City, built a fair House here, and gave it to *Thomas* his second Son, who sold it to

Henry Killigrew, Esq. one of the Admirals of the Navy, An. 1693, and is the present Possessor hereof.

Hund. of
Caishoe.

The Hospital of ST. MARY DE PREE, or
in the Meadow.

Matt. Paris,
fol. 97.
Mon. Angl.
vol.1, fol.347.

GARINE, the twentieth Abbot of the Church of St. *Alban* and his Convent, in the Reign of *R.* I. gave to the sick Women of St. *Mary de Pree*, the Place wherein the Church was built, and divers other things, which you may read before among the Acts of that Abbot.

King *John*, by Charter dated the first of *May*, 5 *Regni sui*, for the Health of his Soul and the Souls of his Ancestors, and his Heirs, gave to God and the Church of St. *Mary de Pree*, and to the leprous and diseased Women, thirty Acres of the Essart in the Wood of **Esbroc**; to wit, twelve Acres near the Essart of *William* Son of *Alan*, on one Side of the Way which leads from **Hamelsted** to **St. Alban**; and twelve Acres on the other Side of that Way near the Essart of *Robert* Son of *Alan*, to have and to hold in free, pure, and perpetual Alms; who enjoyed it till the Dissolution of this Monastery, when it came to the Crown.

King *H.* VIII. by his Charter dated the 12th of *May*, *An.* 32 *Regni sui*, granted the Scite of this Priory to *Ralph Rowlet* the elder of **St. Albans**, Esq. who was constituted Sheriff of this County and **Essex** the next succeeding Year: He was shortly after knighted, and dyed leaving Issue

Ralph Rowlet, who was his Heir, was knighted afterwards, dyed seized hereof without Issue, whereupon it past to his two Sisters *Mary* and ———— who were his Coheirs; of whom I intend to treat in the Parish of **Sandridge**.

The Chappel of ST. GERMANS.

Camd. *Brit.*
tit. Herts.
fol. 410.
Weav *Mon.*
fol. 583.

THE Pelagian Heresie, by the Means of *Agricola*, Son to the Bishop of **Severianus**, prevailing much in this Island, and polluting the British Churches, *German* Bishop of **Auxerre**, and *Lupus* Bishop of **Trois**, were sent for hither out of **France** about the Year 429, to maintain the Truth; and they, especially *German* gained a reverend Esteem among the *Britains*, by refuting this Heresie; which induced them

Matt. Paris,
fol. 39.

to dedicate many Churches to *German*; among whom *Ulpho* Prior of the Church of St. *Alban*, a Man of great Holiness, by the Permission of *Eadfrith* the fifth Abbot, built a famous Chappel near the ruin'd Walls of the City of **Verulam**, to the Honour of this Saint, in which Place he had openly preached God's Word out of the Pulpit, as the ancient Records of St. *Alban's* Church do testifie; which *German*,

Camd. *Brit.*
tit. Herts.
fol. 410.

saith *Camden*, flourished in the time of *Constantine*, and commanded the Sepulcher of St. *Alban* to be opened, and laid certain Reliques of Saints in it, that whom one Heaven had received, should also be lodged together in one Sepulcher; which he notes by the Way, that you may observe and consider the Fashions of that Age ; and the Ruins of that Chappel were lately to be seen, when it was expos'd to a prophane Use; but Sir *Thomas Cotton* bought it about the Year 1687, and sold it to *Henry Killigrew*, Esq. who was one of the Admirals in the Fleet, 1693, and has since demolisht it.

The Mannor of NEWLAND SQUILLERS

WAS Parcel of the Revenue of the Church of St. Albans: Upon the Dissolution of that Monastery, it came to King *H.*VIII. who granted it to Sir *Richard at Lea*; he held it of the King by the yearly Rent of 5*l.* 4*s. ob.* in the time of *Edw.* VI. it was conveyed to —— *Grace*, a Citizen and Goldsmith of London, whose Daughter and Heir married

John Robotham the Son of *Robert Robotham*, by whom he had Issue, *John, Elizabeth, Grace,* and *Ann.*

John Robotham was his Heir, married, and had Issue, *Robert, William,* and *Elizabeth ;* whereof

Robert Robotham succeeded, was a Justice of the Peace for this County and the Liberty of St. Albans divers Years, during the Reign of King *Charles* II. King *James* II. King *William,* and Queen *Mary,* and is now the present Possessor hereof.

The Mannor of BUTTERWICK in the Parish of ST. PETERS

WAS Parcel of the Possessions of the Monastery of St. Albans, which came to the Crown on the Dissolution of that Church; from thence it was convey'd to *Anthony Denny,* Esq. who sold it to Sir *Richard Cox,* Master of the Houshold under Queen *Eliz.* King *James,* and King *Charles* I. from whom it descended to *John Cox,* his younger Brother, and from him it past to *Alban* the third Brother, who had Issue *John* and *Alban,* both whom died without Issue, *Thomas, John, Mary, Mary,* and *Anne,* which three Daughters died Virgins.

Thomas marryed *Elizabeth,* one of the Daughters and Coheirs of *Thomas Cowley,* by whom he had Issue, three Sons, *Alban, John,* and *Thomas,* and six Daughters, *Ann, Elizabeth, Mary, Susan, Martha,* and ——. Upon his Death, this Mannor came to *Alban,* who is his Heir, and the present Possessor hereof.

The Mannor of BEECH,

SO termed from *Godfride de Beech,* who obtained it by the Gift of *William* the Conqueror, afterwards it was given to the Church of St. Albans, came to the Crown upon the Dissolution, from whence it was granted to *Anthony Denny,* Esq. one of the Gentlemen of the Privy Chamber, in which

Hund. of Caishoe. Name it remained until it was sold to *John Dell*, who gave it to *Anne* his Wife for her Life, the Remainder to *Joseph Dell*, who conveyed it to *John Dell* his elder Brother, and the present Possessor hereof.

The Mannor of SOPWELL.

Mon. Angl.
vol. 1, fol. 341. IN the time of *Jeoffery*, Abbot of the Church of St. Albans, and in the Year of the Incarnation of our Lord 1140, or thereabouts, two religious Women made a poor House by wradling of the Boughs of Trees with Rods, and covering it with Bark, near the Wood called Eiwood, not far from the River; where they began to live with Fasting and Prayer, under a wonderful Abstinence, and happily continued their new Religion with irreproveable Chastity, afflicting their Bodies with Bread and Water: And when their laudable and unchangeable Behaviour for many Years was made known to Abbot *Jeoffery*, he, perswaded by the Matt. Paris,
fol. 58. Oracle of God, built a Cell here, and commanded that convenient Houses should be erected for the Women, and appointed that they should be clothed with Vests after the Manner of Nuns, and should live there under the Order of St. *Benedict;* and he undertook by the Grace of God to build Houses for their Spirituals and Temporals; and by the Assistance of *Mary* the blessed Mother of God, to whom it was dedicated, he illustrated the neighbouring Parts with the sweet smell of their good Report: And the Abbot who was the Founder of this House gave certain Possessions and Rents to support their honest, though exiled Life. This memorable House was called Sopwell from a neighbouring Well near that Place, whence the former Women were wont to fetch Water to dress their Meat; moreover, the Abbot tender of the Credit and Safety of his Nuns, ordained that they should be inclosed in their House under Locks and Bolts, and the Seal of the Abbot for the time being; and that none should be taken into their Colledge, but a select and limited Number of Virgins: He gave to them a Churchyard, which he caused to be dedicated, and appointed that none but those of the Nunnery should be buryed there.

Mon. Angl.
vol. 1, fol. 384. *Henry* of Albin, and the Lady *Cicely* his Wife, gave two Hides of Land in the Mannor of Cotes to St. *Mary*, and the House near St. Alban, which *Roger* his solitary Brother formerly repaired for the Use of that Church, and those Handmaids and Servants of God, and their Successors, who devoutly worshipped him there; and ordained that they should take from the Wood of the said Mannor, Necessaries for their House, their Fire, and their Enclosure. This Gift was made for the Soul of King *William*, who subdued England, and his Sons; and for our Fathers and Mothers, and their Sons and Daughters, and for their own Sons, which God now hath, and shall give to them.

When *Robert* of 𝕬𝖑𝖇𝖎𝖓 and *Cicely* his Mother placed *Amy*, a little Maid, Sister of *Robert*, and Daughter of *Cicely*, in this Cell, to serve God continually there, they gave with her to God, and the Holy *Mary*, and the Maidens of *Christ* in this Cell, one Virgate of Land in 𝕮𝖔𝖙𝖊𝖘, which *Salid* held.

Hund. of 𝕮𝖆𝖎𝖘𝖍𝖔𝖊.

Mon. Angl. vol. 1, fol. 384

Richard de Tany granted to St. *Mary*, and the Nuns of 𝕾𝖔𝖕𝖜𝖊𝖑𝖑, all his Land, which *Robert Niger* held in the Soke of 𝕿𝖎𝖙𝖊𝖍𝖆𝖓𝖌 called 𝕭𝖑𝖆𝖈𝖐𝖍𝖎𝖉𝖊, in pure, perpetual, and free Alms, to hold quit from all Services, Customs, and Exactions.

Ibid.

At the Suppression of this House, *Weaver* saith it was valued at no more than 68*l*. 8*s*. *per Annum;* but Sir *William Dugdale* says, no more than 40*l*. 7*s*. 10*d*. *per Annum.*

Weav. *Mon.* fol. 583. *Mon. Angl.* vol. 1, fol. 1041.

Upon the Dissolution King *Henry* VIII. granted it to Sir *Richard a Leigh*, Knight, who married the Daughter of ———*Greenfield*, by whom he had Issue, two Daughters, *Anne* and *Mary*, who were his Coheirs: He bore *Per Cheveron Or and Gules, in Chief two Lyons combatant Sable*.

This Monastery came to *Anne Leigh* the eldest Sister, who married *Edward Sadler*, the second Son of Sir *Ralph Sadler* of 𝕾𝖙𝖆𝖓𝖉𝖔𝖓 in this County, Kt. and Bart. by whom he had Issue four Sons, *Leigh, Richard, Edward*, and *Thomas;* he died the 4th of *April, Anno* 25 of *Elizabeth;* but this Seat with all the Land belonging to it was settled on

Richard the second Son, who married *Joyce* Daughter of *Robert Honiwood* of 𝕮𝖍𝖆𝖗𝖎𝖓𝖌 in the County of 𝕶𝖊𝖓𝖙, Esq. by whom he had Issue several Children, *Robert, Mary, Raphaell, Richard, Dorothy, Margaret, Thomas, Edward, Blount*, and *Henry*.

Robert Sadler succeeded, was a Captain in the Militia for this County, and a Justice of the Peace for the Liberty of 𝕾𝖙. 𝕬𝖑𝖇𝖆𝖓𝖘; he died seized hereof, and left

Helen, who was his sole Daughter and Heir, and married *Thomas Saunders* of 𝕭𝖊𝖊𝖈𝖍-𝖜𝖔𝖔𝖉 in the Parish of 𝕱𝖑𝖆𝖒𝖘𝖙𝖊𝖉 in this County, Esq. by whom he had Issue, *Thomas, Robert, Helen, John, Anne*, and *Helen;* all of them, saving *Anne*, dyed in their Infancy: He sold this Monastery to

Sir *Harbottle Grimston*, Baronet, Master of the Rolls in *Chancery*, and upon his Decease, it descended to Sir *Samuel Grimstone*, Bart. who was his Heir, and is the present Possessor hereof.

The Mannors of WELDRANDOLFES and NEWBERRIES.

THE Mannor-house is ancient, well scituated, compassed with a Mote, having a Park adjoyning to it, at the Centre of four Parishes, 𝕾𝖙. 𝕻𝖊𝖙𝖊𝖗𝖘 in 𝕾𝖙. 𝕬𝖑𝖇𝖆𝖓𝖘, 𝕾𝖙. 𝕾𝖙𝖊𝖕𝖍𝖊𝖓𝖘, 𝕬𝖑𝖉𝖊𝖓𝖍𝖆𝖒, and 𝕽𝖎𝖉𝖌𝖊, and some of the Demeasne Lands lie in 𝕾𝖍𝖊𝖓𝖑𝖊𝖕; which Parish Church lying nearest to 𝖂𝖊𝖑𝖚-𝖍𝖆𝖑𝖑, the Family usually resorts thither to pay their Devotions to God in Respect of their Distance from 𝕾t. 𝕻𝖊𝖙𝖊𝖗𝖘, which is their proper Parish; therefore I have placed these Mannors here.

John Somersham of 𝕬𝖘𝖍𝖆𝖒, Lord of 𝕮𝖔𝖗𝖓𝖊𝖗𝖚 in the County of 𝕾𝖚𝖋𝖋𝖔𝖑𝖐, possest them in the seventh Year of *Edw.* III. For I find that *John Fally* was his Bailiff at that time, and *Walter Attehac, An.* 18th of the same King; and that both these Bailiffs accounted to him for the Profits of these Mannors in those Years: He had Issue only Daughters, whereof

Margaret married *William Ash*, who thereby became possest of these Mannors in her Right. He had by her only one Daughter called

Elizabeth, who was his Heir, and married *Thomas Frowick* of 𝕺𝖑𝖚𝖋𝖔𝖑𝖚; he enjoyed them in the time of *H.V.* and he had Issue by her

Henry Frowick, who was their Heir, and married *Ellenor* Daughter of *Thomas Throckmorton* of 𝕮𝖔𝖚𝖌𝖍𝖙𝖔𝖓 in the County of 𝖂𝖆𝖗𝖜𝖎𝖈𝖐, by whom he had Issue

Thomas Frowick of the 𝖋𝖔𝖑𝖚, to whom these Mannors descended: He married *Joan* the Daughter and Coheir of Sir *Thomas Leuknor* in 𝕾𝖚𝖘𝖘𝖊𝖝, by whom he had

Henry Frowick, who succeeded his Father, and married *Anne* one of the Daughters and Coheirs of *Robert Knowles* Lord of the Mannor of 𝕹𝖔𝖗𝖙𝖍𝖒𝖎𝖒𝖘; from whom these, with the Mannors of 𝕹𝖔𝖗𝖙𝖍𝖒𝖎𝖒𝖘, descended to

Elizabeth their sole Daughter and Heir, who married *John Coningsby*, the third Son of Sir *Humphry Coningsby*, who was Lord Chief Justice of the *King's Bench*, in the Reign of King *H.*VIII. He possessed these Mannors, and was constituted Sheriff of this County and 𝕰𝖘𝖘𝖊𝖝, the 38th of the same King; upon his Death

Henry Coningsby was his Heir, succeeded him, and was constituted Sheriff of this County, 1569, 11 *Eliz.* and in the Year 1582, 24 *Eliz.* was knighted, and married *Elizabeth*, Daughter of Sir *John Boteler* of 𝖂𝖆𝖙𝖙𝖔𝖓 𝖂𝖔𝖔𝖚𝖍𝖆𝖑𝖑 in this County, Kt. by whom he had Issue, *Ralph, Philip,* and *Henry*, and died seized of these Mannors, leaving

Ralph Coningsby his Heir, who was constituted Sheriff of this County *Anno* 1596, 38 *Eliz.* afterwards knighted, and married *Margery* Daughter of *Whetle* alias *Whethill,* of the Town of 𝕮𝖆𝖑𝖆𝖎𝖘, by whom he had Issue *Francis* and *Thomas;* and after her Decease, he married *Jane* Daughter of Sir *John Lamme,* and Relict of *William Button* of 𝕬𝖑𝖙𝖔𝖓 in the County of 𝖂𝖎𝖑𝖙𝖘, Esq. by whom he had Issue *Robert.*

Francis Coningsby was his Heir, succeeded him, was knighted, and married the Daughter of the Lord *North;* but dying without Issue these Mannors came to

Thomas Coningsby, who was his second Brother and Heir; married *Martha,* Daughter of *William Button* of Alton in the County of Wilts. Esq. by whom he had Issue, *Henry, Jane, Jane* married to *Ellis Hicks,* Esq. *Martha, Elizabeth, Bridget, Mary, Margery, Theophania, Susannah, Dorothy :* He was elected Sheriff of this County, *Anno* 1637, 13 *Car.* I. shortly after great Dissentions arising between the King and his Parliament, which put the Nation into a great Ferment, the King being then at Reading in Berkshire, sent a Commission to him to be High Sheriff again of this County, with the Letter here inserted.

Charles *Rex,*

TRUSTY and well-beloved, we greet you well, and do hereby give you our assurance, that although we have at present made choice of you to be our High Sheriff of our County of Hertford, we have done it out of no other respect than as a mark and testimony of our Favour and Confidence of the utmost of your Service in these times, wherein we intend to employ Persons of the greatest integrity, and known affection to us, and the good of our Kingdom ; of which you have formerly given sufficient testimony : And although it may bring upon you great expence and trouble, yet we are confident you will not value it in regard of our Service, and the good of that our County, which shall not be forgotten by us on all occasions. So we bid you heartily Farewell.

From our Court at Reading,
this 11th of *November,* 1642.

Soon after this Letter, Mr. *Coningsby* received a Writ and Proclamation from Oxford, which declared the Earl of Essex and his Adherents Traytors, and authorized him to array the County for the King's Service : He executed his Writ at St. Albans, where *Oliver Cromwell* took him Prisoner for executing the Commission of Array, plundered his House, seized his Estate, carryed him to the *Tower,* and kept him a Prisoner there for many Years.

Harry Coningsby succeeded him, and married *Hester,* Daughter of Sir *James Cambell,* by whom he had Issue *Marthagnes,* who married Sir *William Hicks* of Rookholes in the County of Essex ; *Theophania* the Wife of *Edward Briscoe* of Rocks Bushes in this County, Esq. and *Geneveiva,* who espoused *Thomas Aram* of *Grays Inn,* Esq. to whom he conveyed these Mannors, and made him the present Lord of them.

PEDIGREE OF THE CONINGSBYS AND FROWICKS.

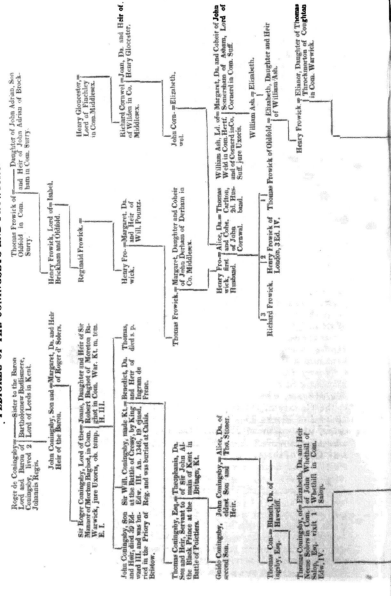

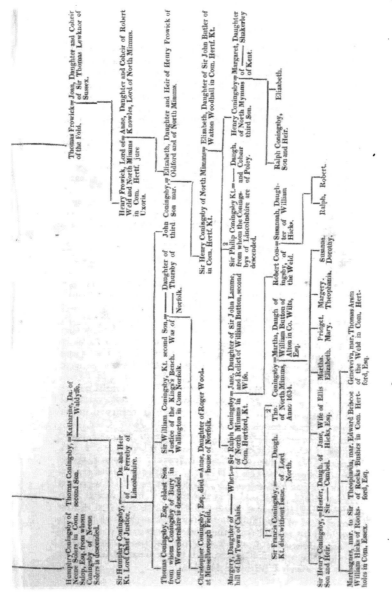

The Mannor of KINGSBERY.

SO termed from the Saxon Kings, who were the ancient Possessors hereof, and often resided and kept their Court there, among whom *Bertulph*, King of the *Mertians*, celebrated a parliamentary Council there on *Friday* after *Easter*, in the Year of *Christ* 851, where King *Bertulph* himself, *Ceolnoth* Archbishop of Canterbury, *Swithulph* Bishop of London, *Swithen* Bishop of Winchester, *Easten* Bishop of Shireburn, *Orkenwald* Bishop of Lichfield, *Rethum* Bishop of Leicester, *Goodwin* Bishop of Rochester, *Wulfard* Abbot of Evesham, *Libing* Abbot of Winchelcomb, *Hedda* Abbot of Medehamsted, Duke *Ernulph*, Duke *Ofrith*, Earl *Serto*, Earl *Elber*, Earl *Huda*, and *Oflat*. Cupbearer to King *Ethelwolph* and Legate to the Pope, were present, and treated as well of the great and public Affairs of the Kingdom, as of the Bounds and Marshes belonging to the Monastery of Cropland, which King *Bertulph* granted and solemnly confirmed there.

There was a stately Pallace that belonged to the Castle of Kingsberry, scituated at the West End of the Town of St. Albans, where the Saxon Kings delighted much, and their Nobles and Officers so often resorted thither that they became a great Burden and Charge to the Abbot and Monks of St. Albans, which induced them to purchase it; and after they had made many Addresses to the King for it, *Alfric*, who had been Chancellor to King *Etheldred*, whilst he was a Secular, prevailed with the King to sell to them all the royal Mannor of Kingsberry, with the Parks and Woods belonging to it, excepting one small Fortress near the Monastery, which the King would not suffer to be demolisht, that the Marks of his royal House might not be forgotten; and the Abbot and Monks bought and enjoyed it till the time of the Dissolution, when it returned to the Crown; from thence it was conveyed to *John Cox*, from him it descended to *Thomas Cox*, his Son, who had Issue *Richard Cox*, who was knighted: His Arms were *Or, three Barrs Azure on a Canton Argent, a Lyon's Head coupé Gules; Crest on a Wreath, a Goat's Head erazed Sable attired and eared Or, struck through with a broken Arrow Gold.* He sold it in the time of King *James* I. to

Sir *Francis Bacon*, Viscount Verulam, Keeper of the Broad Seal of England; but when the Seal was taken from him, and he retired from the Court, he conveyed it to Sir *Thomas Meautys*, from whom it past in the same Manner as the Mannor of Gorham did to Sir *Samuel Grimston*, Bart. to which I refer the Reader.

The Mannor of GORHAM BURY.

THIS Mannor was Parcel of the ancient Revenue of the
Church of St. Albans, and in all Probability was so termed
from *Robert de Gorham*, who was elected Abbot of this
Monastery *Anno* 1151, 16 *Sept.* and the Abbots held it until
the Dissolution of that Church, when it came to the Crown.

King *Henry* VIII. by Charter dated the 12th of *May*,
32 *Regni sui*, granted the Mannors of Gorham, Sandridge,
Newham, Caldecot, Radwell, Westwic, Apsa, and the
Priory of the Prey to

Ralph Rowlet, Esq. who was afterwards knighted: His
Arms were *Gules, on a Cheveron between two Couple of
Dases Argent three Lyons rampant of the Field*; and I
guess he conveyed it to

Sir *Nicholas Bacon*, Kt. who was descended from an an-
cient Family in the County of Suffolk, educated in *Corpus
Christi Colledge* in Cambridge, removed thence to *Gray's
Inn*, where he apply'd himself to the Study of the Common
Law, was made Attorney of the Court of Wards *Anno* 38
*H.*VIII. and his Patent for that Office was renew'd 1 *Edw.*
VI. He was constituted Treasurer of *Gray's Inn, Anno* 6
Edw. VI. and was thence advanced to be Keeper of the
great Seal in the Year 1558, 1 *Eliz.* He married ———
the Daughter of——— ———, by whom he had Issue three
Sons, Sir *Edmund Bacon* of Redgrave in the County of
Suffolk, Bart. who was his Heir——— ——— And after her
Decease, he married *Anne*, second Daughter to Sir *Anthony
Cook* of Giddy-hall in the County of Essex, Governess to
King *Edw.* VI. a choice Lady, eminent for Piety, Vertue,
and Learning, exquisitely skilled for a Woman, in the Greek
and Latin Tongues; by whom he had Issue two Sons, *An-
thony* and *Francis:* He was a Man of great Learning, rare
Wit, and deep Experience; continued Lord Keeper about
twenty Years, during which time this Office was made equal
in Authority with the Chancellor; but towards his latter
End he grew so corpulent in Body that it was very troublesome to him to walk from *Westminster-hall* to the *Star
Chamber*, insomuch that when he sat down in his Place, it
was not usual in those Days for any Lawyer to speak in that
Court till the Lord Keeper gave the Signal with his Staff:
He was a good Man, and a grave Statesman, one who preferred true Honesty before an Estate ill-gotten, and delighted in a House suitable to his Estate; for when Queen *Eliz.*
came hither and told him, my Lord, your House is too little
for you: He wittily reply'd, No Madam, but 'tis your Highness hath made me too great for my House. He chose for

Hund. of
Caishoe. his Motto *Mediocria firma,* and made it the Rule of his
Practice, and died on the 20th of *February,* 1579, 21 *Eliz.*
and was buried in the Quire of St. *Paul,* London.

This pleasant Seat he conveyed to *Anthony* his eldest
Son, by his second Venter, who was very eminent for his
Wit; but dying in the Prime of his Years without Issue,
it descended to

Francis his Brother, whom he entirely loved, they two
being all the male Issue of their Mother; this *Francis* was
the Glory of his Age and Nation, whose primary Years past
not away without some Mark of Eminency, and the Preg-
nancy of his Wit presaged that deep and universal Apprehension, which made him known to several Persons of great
Honour and Place, especially to the Queen, who, saith my
Author, delighted much to confer with him, to prove him
with Questions; and asking him, then a Youth, how old he
was? He answered with much Discretion, that he was two
Years younger than her Majesty's happy Reign; when he
was grown fit for the University, his Father placed him in
Trinity Colledge in Cambridge, under the Tuition of Dr.
John Whitgift, then Master of the Colledge, and afterwards
Archbishop of Canterbury, where he greatly improved his
time in the Study of Philosophy and the liberal Arts, then
he was sent into France with Sir *Amyas Paulet* her Majesty's Legier Embassador, who entrusted him with a Message
to the Queen, which he performed with great Approbation;
after that returned again with an Intention to continue there
for some Years, but the Lord Keeper dying in the mean-
while, and his Maintenance growing very short, he return'd
home and apply'd himself to the Study of the Common Law
in *Gray's Inn,* where he was highly valued for his great
Abilities, chosen Reader at his Age of twenty eight, *Anno*

Origin. Jurid.
fol. 295. 1588, 30 *Eliz.* which he performed with much Applause;
made one of the Clerks of the Privy Council *Anno* 1590,

Pat. 32 Eliz.
Origin. Jurid.
fol 295. 32 *Eliz.* was double Reader in the same Society *Anno* 1600,
42 *Eliz.* was knighted at *Whitehall, July* 23, 1603, 1 *Jac.*

MS. in Offic.
Armor. I. was made one of the King's Council learned in the Law

Pat. 2 Jac. I. extraordinary by Patent dated 1604, 2 *James* I. in which an
annual Fee of 40*l.* was granted to him, a Favour not known
before; was constituted his Majesty's Solicitor General

Pat. 5 Jac. I. *Anno* 1607, 5 *James* I. was joyned in Commission with Sir
Pat. 9 Jac. I. *Thomas Vavasor,* 1611, 9 *James* I. then Knight-Marshal
of the Knight-Marshall's Court, newly erected within the
Virge of the King's House; was made Attorney General

Bar. of Engl.
vol. 2, fol. 438. and sworn of the Privy Council, 27 *October* 1613, 11 *James*
I. and when he attained to the Age of fifty-four Years, was
advanced to be Lord Keeper of the Great Seal on the 7th
of *March,* 1616, 14 *James* I. when the King admonished
him that he should seal nothing rashly, judge uprightly, and

not extend the royal Prerogative too high: He was made *Hand of* Caishor. Lord Chancellor of England on the fourth of *Jan.* 1618, 16 *James* I. created Lord Verulam on the 11th of *June* follow- Pat. 16 Jac. I. ing, and advanced to the Dignity of Viscount St. Alban, on the 27th of *January*, 1620, 18 *James* I. his solemn In- Pat. 18 Jac. I.
Bar. of Engl.
vol. 2, fol. 436. vestiture being then performed at Theobalds in this County, where the Lord *Carew* carried his Robe before him, and the Lord *Wentworth* his Coronet. But soon after he was charged with Corruption in the Performance of that great Office of Chancellor, when it was generally believed that his Servants were most guilty, and his Fault was only Negligence in not examining the Extortion of his Servants; this caused him to say when he saw his Servants rise from their Seats as he once passed thro' the Hall when they were at Dinner, *Sit you down, my Masters, Sit you down, your Rise is my Fall*; and soon after the Great Seal was taken *Origin. Jurid.*
fol. 102. from him, in *Lent*, 18 *James* I. and delivered to the Custody of *Henry* Viscount *Mandevile*, then President of the Council, and other Lords Commissioners. He married *Alice* one of the Daughters and Coheirs to *Benedict Barham*, Alderman of London, with whom he had a fair Fortune, but no Children to perpetuate his Memory; however his learned Works being composed for the most Part in the five last Years of his Life, will preserve it to Prosterity. He visited the Earl of Arundel at his House in Highgate near London, and died there about a Week after, on *Easter* Day, being the ninth of *April, Anno* 1626, 2 *Car.* I. in the sixty sixth Year of his Age, and was buried in the North Side of the Chancel in St. *Michael's* Church in St. Albans, according to the Directions of his Will, because the Body of his Mother lay interred there, and that it was the only Church remaining in the Precinct of Old Verulam, where he hath a Monument of white Marble representing his full Body in a contemplative Posture sitting in a Chair, erected by Sir *Thomas Meautys*, Kt. who was formerly his Lordship's Secretary, afterwards Clerk of the Privy Council under two Kings, succeeded his noble Lord and Patron in this Mannorhouse of Gorhambury, and held it sometime, then it past to

Sir *Thomas Meautys*, who was his Cousin and next Heir, married *Anne* Daughter of Sir *Nathaniel Bacon* of Culford Hall in the County of Suffolk, Knight, and gave this Mannor to her for Life, the Remainder to his Heirs, and died leaving his Wife surviving. She married Sir *Harbottle Grimston*, Baronet, and shortly after *Jane* her Daughter dying about the Age of ten or eleven Years, the Reversion of it descended (as I have been informed) to *Hercules Meautys*, the Son of the Brother of Sir *Thomas Meautys*, who sold all his Right and Estate herein to

Sir *Harbottle Grimston*, Baronet, Son and Heir of Sir

Hund. of Caishoe. *Harbottle Grimston* of 𝔅𝔯𝔞𝔡𝔣𝔢𝔦𝔩𝔡 in the County of 𝔈𝔰𝔰𝔢𝔵, Knight, created Baronet by Patent dated the 25th Day of *November, Anno* 1612, 10 *James* I. He studied sometime the Common Law, became a learned Man in that Profes, sion, then married ——— Daughter of Sir *George Croke,* Kt. one of the Justices of the Court of *Common Pleas,* whose Reports he published; and by her he had Issue *George,* who married *Sarah,* Daughter and Coheir of Sir *Edward Alston* of 𝔏𝔬𝔫𝔡𝔬𝔫, Kt. Dr. in Physick, and died without Issue, and *Samuel*; and two Daughters, *Mary* married to Sir *Capell Lucking* of 𝔏𝔦𝔱𝔱𝔩𝔢 𝔚𝔞𝔩𝔱𝔥𝔞𝔪 in the County of 𝔈𝔰𝔰𝔢𝔵, Baronet, and *Elizabeth* to Sir *George Grubham How* of 𝔅𝔞𝔯𝔴𝔦𝔠𝔨 in the County of 𝔚𝔦𝔩𝔱𝔰. Bart. And after her Decease, this Sir *Harbottle* married *Anne,* the Relict of Sir *Thomas Meautys,* by whom he had Issue *Anne,* who died in her Minority. He served in several Parliaments for the Borough of 𝔆𝔬𝔩𝔠𝔥𝔢𝔰𝔱𝔢𝔯, and in that Healing Parliament held *An.* 1660, 12 *Car.* II. was chosen Speaker there, where he was very active and instrumental to restore that King to his Throne, and for his great Merits was worthily advanced on the third Day of *November* in the same Year, to be Master of the Rolls of the Court of *Chancery,* which Office he executed with great Justice and Equity, to the great Satisfaction of his Prince and all good People, for the Space of six and twenty Years: He had a nimble Fancy, a quick Apprehension, a rare Memory, an eloquent Tongue, and a sound Judgment, which Parts he maintained to the last; he was a Person of free Access, sociable in Company, sincere to his Friend, hospitable in his House, charitable to the Poor, and an excellent Master to his Servants; and died in a good old Age on the — Day of *January, Anno* 1683, leaving an honourable Name behind him, and a plentiful Estate to

Sir *Samuel Grimston,* Baronet, his only surviving Son and Heir, who married *Elizabeth,* Daughter of *Heneage Finch,* Earl of 𝔑𝔬𝔱𝔱𝔦𝔫𝔤𝔥𝔞𝔪, by whom he had Issue one Daughter, married to *William* Marquess of 𝔥𝔞𝔩𝔩𝔦𝔣𝔞𝔵, and after the Decease of his first Lady he married ——— Daughter of ——— Earl of 𝔗𝔥𝔞𝔫𝔢𝔱: He is a Justice of the Peace, and Deputy Lieutenant for 'his County, also a Justice of the Peace for the Liberty of 𝔖𝔱. 𝔄𝔩𝔟𝔞𝔫𝔰, and hath served the Borough of 𝔖𝔱. 𝔄𝔩𝔟𝔞𝔫𝔰 in five several Parliaments, and is the present Lord hereof.

The Mannor of CHILDWICK.

WAS granted by *Ailwin* the Black, and *Ailfled* his Wife, to the Church of 𝔖𝔱. 𝔄𝔩𝔟𝔞𝔫, and upon the Dissolution it came to the Crown, from whence, I am informed, it was conveyed to the *Prestons,* in whose Name it continued until it was sold to *Joshua Lomax*, Esq. from whom it descended to *Joshua Lomax*, who was his Heir, and is the present Lord hereof.

The Mannor of *WINDERIDGE*.

WAS in the Possession of *Godfride de Bech* in the time of *William* the Conqueror, whereof he held part of the Abbot of St. Albans, and the other Part, I suppose, in his own Right, as it appears by *Domesdei Book*, where 'tis recorded in these Words:

In Danais Hundred. in Wenrige ten. Godfridus de Bech un. hid. et dimid. de Abbate Terr est duo car. in Dominio una et quinq; Villi cum duobus Bord. habentibus unam carucatum, Pastura ad pec. Silva trecent porcis, valet quadragint. sol. Quando recepit quadragint. sol. tempore Regis Edwardi quinquagint. sol. Hanc terram tenuit Osbertus Monachus et Goding homo ejus, non potuerunt separare ab Ecclesia, ut Hundred. testatur.

Domesd. Lib. fol.135, nu.10.

In Danais Hundred. Godfridus de Bech in Wenriga et Radulph, de eo tenuit unam hidam et dimid. Terra est duo car. ibi est una, et altera potest fieri, ibi tres Bord. Silva trecent porc. pastura ad pec. haec terra valet et valuit vigint. sol. tempore Regis Edwardi quinquagint. sol. hanc terram tenuit Ailmer homo Com. Levini et vendere potuit.

Domesd. Lib. fol.139, nu.34.

Godfry de Bech held one Hide and an half of the Abbot of St. Albans in Wenrige in Danais Hundred. The arable is two ploughed Lands, in Demeasne one, and five Villains with two Bordars having one ploughed Land; Common of Pasture for the Cattle, Wood to feed three hundred Hogs; 'tis worth forty Shillings by the Year, when he received it forty Shillings a Year, in the time of King *Edward* (the Confessor) fifty Shillings a Year. *Osbert* a Monk, and *Goding* a Man (under his Protection) held this Land, and they could not separate it from the Church, as the Hundred can witness.

Godfry de Bech and *Ralph* held of him one Hide and an half in Wenrige in Danais Hundred. The arable is two ploughed Lands, there is one, and another may be made, there are three Bordars, Wood to feed three Hundred Hogs, Common of Pasture for the Cattle, this Land is worth, and was worth twenty Shillings by the Year, in the time of King *Edward* (the Confessor) fifty Shillings by the Year. *Ailmer*, a Man (under the Protection) of Earl *Lewin* held this Land and might sell it.

This Hamlet was denominated from the Ridge of the Hill whereon it is scituated, and at the time of making this Record was part of Danais Hundred, now called Dacorum Hundred; but I guess it was laid to the Hundred of Caisho when it was made a Liberty, and Jurisdiction was granted to the Abbot over the same.

Anno 30 *Edw.* III. I find this Mannor was in the Possession of *Joane Pyrrat*, and after her Decease it past to *John Peacock*, who held it on the ninth of *December*, An. 15 *Edw.* III.

In the time of *H.* VI. it was in the Possession of *John Fortescue*, from whom it descended to

Henry Fortescue, Esq. who was his Son and Heir, and of full Age at the Death of his Father; he sold it to

Henry Cock, Esq. who enjoyed it *Anno* 3 *H.*VIII. and it descended from him to

Fin. 29 H. VIII. Bag of old Deeds of Hertford, in cur. recept. Scac.

Philippa, who was his Daughter and Heir, married Sir

Hund. of
Caishoe.

Francis Bryan, who held it in her Right for the Term of her Life, and after her Decease it past to

Thomas Law, Gent. from whose Family I guess it came to the Crown, where it remained till King *James* I. conveyed it *An.* 12 *Regni sui,* to

John Crosby, Esq. who married *Mary* Daughter of *Robert Halsey* of *Great Gadesden,* Esq. He conveyed it to *Mary* his Wife, for her Life, but dying without Issue, and she surviving, held it, and married *Robert Bertie,* one of the younger Sons of *Robert* Earl of *Lindsey,* and upon her Decease it came to

Edward Crosby, who was Brother and Heir to *John Crosby:* He enjoyed it a small time and then sold it to

Sir *Harbottle Grimston,* Bart. and Master of the Rolls in *Chancery,* from whom it descended to

Sir *Samuel Grimston,* Bart. who was his only Son and Heir, and is the present Lord hereof.

John Churchil, Earl of *Marlborough,* has built for his own Habitation a fair House at the West End of this Burrough, near the River, where he has a fair Garden, through which passeth a Stream in which he keeps Trouts and other *Dale's Cat. of* Fish for the Convenience of his Table: He was created *Nob. p. 82, 83.* Baron *Churchil* of *Aumouth* in *Scotland,* by Letters Patent dated *Dec.* 1682, 34 *Car.* II. Baron *Churchil* of *Sandridge* in this County by Letters Patent dated 14 *May,* 1685, 1 *Jac.* II. and Earl of *Marlborough* the 9th of *April,* 1689, 1 *William* and *Mary.* He bears *Sable, a Lion rampant Argent, on a Canton of the second St.* George's *Cross;* which *Canton* is an Augmentation.

The Names of those Noble Persons that have derived their Honours from this Town.

FRANCIS Bacon, Lord *Verulam,* and Lord Chancellor of *England,* was created Viscount *St. Albans,* on the 18th Day of *January,* 1620. He gave for his Arms *Gules, on a Chief Argent two Mullets Sable, a Crescent for Difference.*

2 *Richard de Burgh,* Earl of *Clanrichard* in the Kingdom of *Ireland,* was created Earl of *St. Albans,* 23rd *Aug.* 1628. He gave for his Arms *Or, a Cross Gules, in the dexter Canton a Lyon rampant Sable.*

3 *Ulick de Burgh,* Earl of *St. Albans* and *Clanrichard,* dyed 1657, without Issue, and gave the same Arms.

4 *Henry Jermin,* Baron of *St. Edmunds Bury,* Lord Chamberlain to his Majesty's Houshold, was created Earl of *St. Albans* by Patent dated the 11th of *May,* 1671. He gave for his Arms *Sable, a Crescent between two Mullets in Pale Argent.*

Ibid. p. 20.   5 *Charles Beauclaire* was created 27th *Dec.* 1676, 38 *Car.* II. Baron of *Heddington,* Earl of *Burford,* and Duke

𝕾t. 𝕬lbans, by Patent dated the 10th of *Jan.* 1683, 35
Car. II. He gave for his Arms, *The Royal Arms of
England, Scotland,* and *Ireland, with a Baston Sinister
Gules, charged with three Roses Argent, seeded and
barbed Proper.*

This Town was famous for the Birth of three eminent
Persons.

1 Sir *John Mandeville,* born here to a fair Estate, attained
to a great Perfection in the Study of Physick, then travell'd
for thirty-four Years together, till at last returning Home,
he, like *Ulisses,* was quite grown out of the Knowledge of
his Friends. He wrote his own Itinerary through 𝕬frica,
the East and North Part of 𝕬sia; and the Variety of Wonders caused some Suspition of the Truth of his Relations;
but all things that seem improbable are not impossible, and
the Ignorance of the Reader does oftentimes weaken the
Truth of the Author; but his Writings have proved of that
great Value in foreign Parts, that they contend as well for
his Burial as his Birth, and say he died 1372, and was buried
in the Convent of the *Williamites* at 𝕷eige in 𝕲ermany, but
others affirm he was buried in this Town.

To him I shall add two others, famous for their Learning
in this last Age.

Sir *John King* descended by the Father's Side from
Monsieur *du Roy* alias *King,* the French Resident in 𝕰ngland, about the Beginning of the Reign of King *James* I.
and by his Mother from the ancient Family of the *Roberts*
at 𝖂illden in 𝕸iddlesex; from whom he derived the Prin-
ciples of Ingenuity and Goodness. He was admitted into
Queen's Colledge in 𝕮ambridge, in the Year 1655, where Mr.
Samuel Jacomb was his Tutor; Dr. *Zachary Cradock,* Dr.
Simon Patrick, (two eminent Divines) and Dr. *Walter
Needham* (a learned Physitian) were his most intimate Acquaintance; by whose Conversation, and indefatigable Industry in searching the Depths of ancient and modern Learning, he improved his admirable Parts and rare Endowments
of Nature into a *Prodigy* of Learning. When he commenc't Batcholor of Art, his Parents obliged him to study
the Law, though his Inclination was for Divinity; yet like
a dutiful Son, he followed the Advice of his Parents, and
was admitted in *November,* 1660, into the *Inner Temple,*
where he spent seven Years in the Study of the Common
Law; and within short time after was called to the Bar:
He became a great Practitioner there, was made Sollicitor
General to the Duke of 𝕯ork, constituted Council in Ordinary to King *Charles* II. who knighted him *Decemb.* 10,
1674, and delighted (as he was wont to say) to hear Sir *John
King* plead at the Council-board; which King was esteem'd

by all that knew him, to be a great Judge of English Wit
and Sense. As to the Conduct and Care of his Clients, the
great Lord Chancellor *Finch* declared, he had hardly ever
known his Equal: And the Lord Chancellor *Shaftsbury,*
designing a Regulation of the *Chancery,* chose him out of
a select Number of learned Men in the Law for that Purpose, who met at his House, and made a great Progress
therein, though time allowed them not the Liberty to effect
the same. He continued his learned and eloquent Plead-
ings (which were the instructive Entertainment, as well as
Admiration of all that heard him) till a Fever seized on him
at the *Chancery* Bar. He ordered his Clerks to return all
his Breviates and Fees to his Clients, and so retired to his
House in Salisbury Court, where he took his Bed, and in
full Strength of Mind, made his last Will, and declared that
he died in the Communion of the Church of England, pro-
fessing the Christian Faith, as it is set forth in her Articles
and Homilies; after this he resign'd his Soul to his Maker
with all Quietness and Patience, on the 29th of *June,* 1677,
whilst he was in the Arms of his near Kinsman and dear
Friend Mr. *Robert Wolley,* a Merchant in London, who marryed his only Sister of the whole Blood, and had the Honour
of a great and intimate Acquaintance with him. He lived
thirty eight Years, four Months, and twenty four Days;
and his Body was interred on the fourth of *July,* in the *Tem-*
ple Church; where the Right Honourable *Heneage Finch,*
Lord Dabentry, Lord High Chancellor of England, Sir *Har-*
bottle Grimstone, Baronet, Master of the Rolls, the Judges
and Barons of the King's Courts at Westminster, the Serjeants at Law, the Benchers, Barresters, and Students of
the *Inner Temple* attended his Corps to the Vault. Dr.
Cradock was desired to make his funeral Oration, which he
declined at the first in Regard of his extraordinary Respect
and Friendship with him: however he accepted the Office
afterwards and demonstrated to his Auditory, that as he
neither could nor would be guilty of Flattery in the Praise
of his Friend, so Sir *John King* deserved the Tongue of an
Angel to describe his true and real Worth.

St. Albans had the Honour of his Birth, Eaton laid the
Foundation of his School Learning, *Queen's Colledge* advanced him in the University Studies, and the *Inner Tem-*
ple compleated him in those of the Law: The *Temple* Church
is the Repository of what is left of him that is mortal, and is
grac'd with an Epitaph, which tho' much to his Honor, yet
comes far short of his Merit.

M. S.
Elogium ut in Æde Templorum Marmore albo insculpit.

Hic juxta jacet
Johannes King, *Miles.*
Serenissimo Carolo II. *Regi in Legibus* Angliæ *Consultus.*
Illustrissimo Jacobo Duci Eboracenci *Solicitator Generalis,*
Et Interioris Templi *Secius.*

Qualis Quantusve sis Lector
Profundum obstupesce
Labia digitis comprime,
Oculos lachrymis suffunde,
En! ad pedes tuos.
Artis et Naturæ suprema conamina,
Fatorum ludibria
non ita pridem.
Erat iste pulvis, omnifariam Doctus
Musarium Gazophylacium
Eloquentium calluit claram, puram, innocuam
Legibus suæ patriæ instructissimus
Suis charus, Principibus gratus, omnibus urbanus
Amicus verus
Seculi ornamentum illustre, desiderium irreparabile
Hinc disce Lector
Quantillum Mortalis Gloriæ animæ
Splendidissimus decoratæ dotibus, obtingit
Dulcem soporem agite
Dilecti, eruditi, beati cineres.

Obiit xxix. Junii *Anno Domini* MDCLXXVII. *Annoq;* Ætatis suæ xxxviii.

$\left\{ \begin{array}{c} Sic \\ transit \\ Gloria \\ Mundi \end{array} \right\}$

His Soul was great, which seemed as it were mismatcht
with too slender a Constitution of Body, his sublime Facul-
ties were two brisk and operative to be long confined within
so brittle a Tenement, therefore we may think they made
earlier Preparations for a Flight to more lasting Habitations.
His Memory was wonderful, also his Reading (besides that
of his Profession) in History, Philosophy, Poetry, and the
Languages, ancient and modern ; but especially in the sacred Writings, and among these the Gospels, and Epistles
of St. *John ;* insomuch that some judicious Persons believed,
that if he had lived, the Followers of *Socinus* might have
expected the severest Confutation from his Pen. In a Word,
as to his Intellectuals, he was Master of all useful and po-
lite Learning ; as to his Morals, he was assiduous in his Devotion to his Maker, and in a more eminent Manner obedient
to his Parents ; for which we may presume that God conferr'd upon him the Blessing promis'd unto those who observed the fifth Commandment : For tho' he seem'd to die
young, yet, as his learned Orator observed, by a pertinent
Application to that Text in *Wisdom: Honourable Age is*   *Wisdom* iv.
not that which standeth in Length of time, nor that is mea-   8, 9.
sured by Number of Years, but Wisdom is the grey Hair
unto Men, aud an unspotted Life is old Age.

x 2

The other was Sir *Francis Pemberton*, whose Ancestors were originally extracted out of the ancient Family of *Pemberton*, denominated from 𝔓𝔢𝔪𝔟𝔢𝔯𝔱𝔬𝔫 in the County Palatine of 𝔏𝔞𝔫𝔠𝔞𝔰𝔱𝔢𝔯, from whom Sir *Goddard Pemberton*, Kt. descended ; who purchased a fair Estate, settled in this Burrough, and was constituted Sheriff for this County, *Anno* 1615, 13 *James* I. but dying within the Year, *Lewis Pemberton* of this Town, Esq. was his Heir, succeeded him in his Shrievalty, and held it the last Part of the Year ; afterwards *Roger Pemberton*, of this Place, Esq. inherited his Estate, was likewise elected Sheriff for this County, in the Year 1620, 18 *James* I. from whom issued *Ralph Pemberton*, twice Mayor of this Burrough, *Anno* 1627, 3 *Car.* I. and 1638, the 14th of the same King. He was the Father of this eminent Lawyer, who received his first Breath here, and was educated at the School in this Town, where he gave early Testimonies of his future Perfection in Learning ; from thence he was transplanted to the University of 𝔠𝔞𝔪𝔟𝔯𝔦𝔡𝔤𝔢, where he was admitted in *Emanuel Colledge*, on the 12th of *August*, 1640, under the Tuition of the late pious and learned Dr. *Benjamin Whichcote*, where he continued until the 22d of *Feb.* 1644, after which he was entred in the *Inner Temple*, on the 14th of *Oct.* 1645, where he perform'd his Exercises with great Applause, and was call'd to the Bar, the 17th of *November*, 1654. He was made one of the Council of the Court of the *Marshalsea*, and drew the Patent granted by King *Charles* II. for the Enlargement and Confirmation of the Priviledges of that Court. He studied the old Records at 𝔚𝔢𝔰𝔱𝔪𝔦𝔫𝔰𝔱𝔢𝔯, the Rolls, the *Tower*, and made Collections of them, from whence he learn'd the original Reasons and Grounds of the Common Law, and became thereby Master of his Profession. He read learnedly in the *Inner Temple*, in the *Quadragesimes* in the Year 1674, and kept a noble Table there. He received a Writ to be Serjeant at Law, retornable the 29th of *January* following, was made King's Serjeant 11th of *Aug.* 1675 ; knighted at *Whitehall*, on the sixth of *October* next ensuing ; created one of the Justices of the Court of *King's Bench* on the 30th of *April*, 1679 ; advanced to be Chief Justice of the same Court in *Easter* Term, 1681 ; removed thence to be Chief Justice of the *Common Pleas* in *Hilary* Term, 1682, and about the same time sworn of his Majesty's Privy Council. He would not suffer any Lawyers upon Trials before him, to interrupt or banter Witnesses in their Evidence, a Practice too frequently used by some Council in bad Causes, to stifle Truth and obstruct Justice ; but allowed every Person to recollect his Thoughts, and to speak without Fear, that the Truth might be the better discovered ; neither would he permit Council to ask impertinent Questions, nor make long Speeches, nor Harangues in Court, to mislead Juries; but heard all Persons with great Deliberation, Patience, Indifferency, and Impartiality, distinguishing clearly between Truth and Falsehood in his Directions to the Jury, that they might not err; and delivered his Judgment in all Causes depending before him, with great Justice and Solemnity, which much awed the Spectators, and advanced the Reputation of the Court; during all which time no Temptations of Profit or Preferment, no Threats, no Menaces of Deprivation, nor Loss of Place nor Honour, could move him to act any thing against Law; and when he was dismist from the Bench, he disdained not the Attendance at the Bar again, where his Practice made ample Satisfaction for his Removal from the Bench to the Bar, notwithstanding his great Generosity to his Friends and his Charity to the Distressed. He was endowed with a ready Wit and a quick Apprehension, which were attended with a rare Memory and excellent Parts, by the Help of which, and his own indefatigable Industry, he attained to a great Perfection of Judgment in the Laws of the Land. His Notions were curious, his Distinctions nice, and his Reasons weighty; which render'd him very skilful in the Form of good Pleading, the Foundation and Basis of the Common Law, and very learn'd in the Laws of Conveyancing, wherein he was choice in his Method, abandon'd all Tautologies and impertinent Expressions, and confin'd himself to the most apt, neat, significant, and pertinent Words for his Purpose. He married *Anne* the eldest Daughter of Sir *Jeremy Whichcote* of Hendon in the County of Middlesex, Bart. by whom he had Issue three Sons, *Francis, Jeremy,* and *Ralph,* and four Daughters, *Anne* married to *George Scot* of Scots-hall in the County of Kent, Esq. *Mary* to *William Stanley,* D. D. &c. *Elizabeth* to *Nathaniel Stephens,* the present High Sheriff of the County of Gloucester, and *Jane* unmarried. He built a large House at Highgate in the County of Middlesex, where he resided, and died the 10th Day of *June,* in the Year of our Lord, 1697, aged seventy two Years, and was buried in the Parish Church of Highgate, where his Executors erected a fair Monument with this Inscription engrav'd upon it.

M. S.
Venerabilis admodum viri
D. Francisci Pemberton. *Equitis aurati,*
Servientis ad Legem,
E Sociis Interioris Templi
Nec non sub Serenissimo Principe
Carolo II.
Banci Regii *ac* Communis *Capitalis Justiciarii,*
Sacræ Majestati a Secretioribus Conciliis.
Vir planè Egregius,
Ad Reipublicæ, Pariter ac Suorum,
Dulce Decus et Præsidium, fœliciter natus.

Patre Radulpho *in agro* Hertford: *Gen:*
Ex antiquâ Pembertonorum *Prosapiâ;*
In Com. Palat. Lancastriæ *oriundo.*
Charissimam sibi adscivit Conjugem,
Annam
Domini Jeremiæ Whichcote *Baronetti,*
Filiam natu maximam;
Ex quâ liberos undecim suscepit,
Quorum septem superstites reliquit;
E viris placide ac pie excessit
10. *Die* Junii *Anno Domini* MDCXCVIImo.
Ætatis suæ LXXII.

He bore *Argent a Cheveron between three Buckets Sable,
the Bail and Hoops Or, impaling the Arms of* Whichcote
*Ermine, two Boars passant in pale Gules, their Brisles
tusk'd and membred Or.*

In this Burrough are three Parish Churches; one dedicated to the Honour of St. *Alban* the Martyr, another to St.
Peter the Apostle, and the other to St. *Michael* the Archangel.

THE Parish Church was formerly called St. *Andrews,* for it was dedicated to the Honour of St. *Andrew* the Apostle, but demolish'd since the
Reign of King *Edward* VI. who sold the Cathedral Church, which belonged to the late Monastery *Anno* 7 *Regni sui* in Consideration of 400*l.*
to the Mayor and Burgesses of this Borough, and made it a Parish
Church, and nam'd it St. *Albans;* it was then valued in the King's Books
at the rate of 10*l. per Annum,* and the Mayor, Aldermen, and their Successors were constituted Patrons hereof.

The RECTORS.

7 *Edw.* VI. *George Witherall,* Clerk
Edward Carter, Arch-Deacon of St. Albans, in whose time the Grant
of the Rectory of Much Mondon was annexed to it.
John Cole, Arch-Deacon, the present Rector.

This Church is situated upon an Hill about the Middle of the Town,
and is a very large Building, with a square Tower in the midst of it, (in
which is a Ring of five Bells,) covered with lead, having a short Spire
erected upon it, and within the Church are several Monuments and
Gravestones which shew the following Inscriptions.

The Picture of *Offa* in his Throne placed on the North Side at the entrance into the Church. Under the Effigies is this Subscription.

Fundator Ecclesiæ circa annum Christi 793
Quem male depictum et restdentem cernitis alte
Sublimen Solio Mercius Offa fuit.

Where the Shrine stood is this Inscribed.

S. Albanus Verolamensis Anglorum Protomartyr
xvii *Junii* CCXCIII.

On the Wall under the East Window.

In Memory of St. Alban *first Martyr of Great Britain.*
Renowned *Alban* Knight first Martyr of this Land,
By *Dioclesian* lost his life through bloody hand.
Who made him Soveraign, Lord High Steward of this Isle,
And Prince of Britains Knights to dignifie his stile;
He verity embrac't, and *Verulam* forsooke,
And in this very place his Martyrdom he took;
Here *Offa* Mertians King, did *Albans* bones enshrine,
So all things were disposed by Providence Divine.

At the East End of the South Isle near Duke *Humphry's* Tomb.

Piæ Memoriæ V. Opt.
Sacrum
Serotinum

Hic jacet Humphredus, *Dux ille* Glocestrius *olim,*
Henrici *sexti Protector, fraudis ineptæ*
Detector, dum ficta notat miracula cæci:
Lumen erat Patriæ, Columen venerabile regni,
Pacis amans, Musisq; favens melioribus, unde
Gratum opus Oronio, *quæ nunc Schola sacra refulget:*
Invida sed mulier Regno Regi, sibi nequam,
Abstulit hunc humili, vix hoc dignata sepulchro;
Invidiâ rumpente tamen, post Funera vivit.
Deo Gloria.

Five Epitaphs over the Altar Tomb of Mr. *Maynard.*

Hoc exangue jacet Clausum sub marmore Corpus
Radulphi Mainard, *Generoso stemate nati;*
Nomina Johannes *et* Margeria *Parentum:*
Inclytus armigeri titulo dignoscitur ille,
Hæc Germana Soror Radulphi Rowlat *Equestris*
Ordinis, ac fratri fuit ex hæredibus una.
Hisce Deus summe clemens peccata remisit.
Inq; Solo sedes concessit non Scrituras.
Ætat. sua 77. Die Mort. 14 Jan. 1613.

To the Memory of Ralph Mainard, *Esq.* 1613.

The Man that's buried in this Tomb
In heavenly Canaan hath a room.
A Gentleman of ancient name
Who had to wife a vertuous Dame.
They liv'd together in godly sort
Forty five years with good report.
When Seventy and seven years he'd spent
His Soul to his Redeemer went.
His Body by Will here under lies
Still hearkening for the great Assize.
When Christ the Judge of Quick and Dead
Shall raise him from this earthly bed,
And give him Heavens eternal bliss
To live and Reign with Saints of his.
Ærumnarum requies Mors.

To the Memory of Margery Rowlet, *late Wife to* John Maynard, *Esq.* 1541.

Here lies intomb'd a Woman worthy Fame,
Whose Vertuous Life gives Honour to her Name.
Few were her years, she died in her Prime,
Yet in the World fulfilled she much time,
Which vertuously she spent providing still
The hungry Bellies of the Poor to fill.
Unto the God of Heaven thrice every Day,
With great Devotion Saint-like did she Pray.
Her Prayers were heard, God knew her hearts desire,
And gave her Heaven for her eternal Hire:
Where now she doth enjoy that endless bliss,
Which her Redeemer purchased for his.
Virtus in æternum vivit.

To the Memory of Margery Seal, *Wife to* Ralph Maynard, *Esq.* 1619.

Lo here intombed lies a Widdow worthy praise,
Who in the fear of God devoutly spent her days.
With Charitable Alms relieving still the poor,
For empty handed none departed from her Door.
A Mirror in her time for Vertues of her mind,
A Matron for her years the like is hard to find.

Belov'd, bewail'd of all, in life and death was she,
An Honour to her sex as any of her degree.
Her Body into dust returned, here doth sleep,
Her sanctified Soul in Heaven the Angels keep.
Her worthy name still lives, by fame, who sounds her praise,
With Trumpet clear, till Christ appear, her hence to raise.

Virtus Post Funera vivit.

Robert Maynard *the sorrowful Son of his most dear and worthy Parents,*
in his Duty to their Memory erected this Monument.

Near to this place lies the Body of *Charles Maynard,* Esq; with the Body
of Mrs. *Mary Maynard* his dear Sister; He died the 3d. of *June* 1665. in
the 31th. Year of his Age. She died the 20th of *Jan.* 1663. in the 20th
Year of her Age; who were Son and Daughter to Auditor *Charles*
Maynard of Walthamstow in the County of Essex, Esq; who died the
19th of *November.* 1665. in the 67th Year of his Age, who lies interred
at Eiston with his Brother the Right Honourable *William* Lord *Maynard*
Baron of Eiston in Essex.

Under the East Window.

Here under lies interred the Bodies of *Robert Nicoll,* late of this Burrough, Gent. and *Mary* his Wife, second Daughter of *John Gape* of the
same Burrough, Esq; she departed this Life *Decemb.* the 1st 1685. and
he the 9th of *March* 1689. They left Issue *Ann, Ellen* and *William.*

Terra tenet Cineres Animas sed summus Olympus.
In Memoriam defunctorum erectum fuit hoc Monumentum 4to die Julii. *An.*
Dom. 1694.

On the Wall near the South Door.

Sacred to the Memory of Mrs. *Barbara Griffith,* late Wife of *Edward*
Griffith, Esq; Daughter of *Rich. Jenyns,* late of St. Albans, Esq; who
died in London the 22d day of *March* 1678. in the 27th Year of her
Age; having left one only Daughter named *Barbara.*

Youth, Beauty, Vertue here intomb'd doth lie,
O Death, luxurious in Cruelty,
Glutted with Age and Vice, thy common prey,
How greedily this life thou'st snach'd away,
Which Vertue and Good Manners did so grace,
Whose Death doth sweeten and adorn this place. }
And cheers the Ashes of her Ancient Race.
Thus Vertue disappoints Deaths cruel skill,
They only die untimely, who die ill.
Whose early steps the sacred hight do clime,
'Tis just their happiness should begin betime.

Barbara only Daughter of the said Mrs *Griffith* died the 22d. day of
July 1679. and lies here likewise buried.

In the Chancel round a Gravestone of a Mitred Abbot.

Vir Crucis et Christi tumulo jacet insitus isti
Carcere de tristi salvetur Sanguine Christi
Arma Crucis sumpsit intrando Religionem
Mundum contempsit propter celi Regionem
Hic Studuit Clauatro pondus sufferre laboris
In Studii stadio bravium percepit honoris
Flatus Fortuna grandes patiens tolerabat
Gaudia tristitias æquali Lance librabat
Nil adversa timens nec multum prospera curans
Se medio tenuit per ferrea tempora durans
Omni gestura constans nil triste timebat
Omni pressura laudes Christo referebat
Armis justicia cinctus Deitatis amore
   Hostibus Ecclesiæ restitit in facie
Ad Tumulum proceres mors impia transferet omnes
   Et puerilis Amor defluit omnis Honor.

Upon the Stone is his Effigies engraved, and three Labels about his Head.

Celica Regna bone animi denter quæso patronæ
Penas Compesse requiem da virg la Jesse
Me precor Amphibole solvens ad sidera sume.

Under the Lamb and Eagle on the high Arch in the Chancel.

Sic ubicunq; vides sit pictus ut agnus et ales
Effigies operis Sexti patris ista Jonannis.
Esse vel in toto juvisse vel infaciendo
Est opus hoc unum vausavit eum fuciendum.

In the Chancel.

Ecce Sacerdos eram, jam factus vile Candaver.
Et cito pulvis erit: quæso, memento mei
Siste gradum, qui me terris hic, et funde precatur,
Me Deus ut levet, hinc ducat ad usq; polum.
Richardus Stondon *obiit* ———— *die* ————
Anno MV.

Round the Monument of a Mitred Abbot in the Chancel.

Hic jacet Dominus Thomas *quondam Abbas hujus Monasterii.*

In the Chancel.

Hic jacet frater Robertus Bonner, *quondam hujus Monasterii Monachus:*
qui Quadraginta sex Annis continuis et ultra ministrabat in diversis officiis
majoribus et minoribus Convent. Monasterii præscripti: videlicet, in Of-
ficiis Vergi prioris, Coquarii, Refectorarii, et Infirmarii; Et in Officiis
Subrefectorarii Superium Convent. Pro cujus anima fratres Charissimi
fundere preces dignemini ad judicem altissimum piissimum Dom. Jesu
Christum, ut concedat sibi suores veniam peccator. Amen.

Round the Monument of a Mitred Abbot on the South Side.

Benedicta sit Sancta Trinitatis atq; indivisa unitas, Benedicamus, ei Quia
nobiscum fecit misericordiam, Amen.

Written in Stone Letters about the Tomb of Abbot *Ramryg*
in the Chancel.

Sancti Spiritus assit nobis gratia: Veni Sancto Spiritus Repte tuorum
corde fidelium, et tui amoris in ejis ignem accende. Amen.

Designed for Abbot *Ramryg's* Tomb.

Hic jacet, aut certe jacuit Ramrygius: *Abbas*
Ille olim fani maximus hujus erat.
Quid sibi vult Aries cum Ryge hint inde sepulchro?
Sic nomen signat scilicet ipse suum.

Upon the fourth Pillar in the Body of the Church

H. S. E.
Johannes Jones Wallus,
Scholæ Albanensis *Hypodidasculus literatissimus,*
Qui
Dum Ecclesia hæc Anno 1684 *publius impensis*
Instauraretur
Exsculpsit sibi quoq; Monumentum
Quod inscripsit.
FANUM. St. Albani.
Poema Carmine Heroico
Hoc lapide, hoc etiam æde, ævoq; perennius omni
Obiit Anno 1696.

On the second Pillar in the North Isle from the West Door.

Siste gradum properans requiescit Mandevil *urnâ*
Hic humili: Norunt et Monumenta mori

Lo in this Inn, of Travellers doth lie
One rich in nothing but a Memory:
His Name was Sir *John Mandevil*, content
Having seen much with a small Continent,
Towards which he travell'd ever since his Birth,
And at last pawn'd his Body for the Earth,
Which by a Statute must in mortgage be,
Till a Redeemer come to set it free.

Over the West Door.

Propter vicinii situm et amplum hujus Templi spatium, ad magnum confluentium multitudinem excipiendam, opportunum temporibus. Hen. VIII. *R.
et denuo R.* Elizabethæ *peste* Londini *serviente Conventus juridicus hic
agebatur.*

Under this.

*Princeps Dei Imago, lex principis opus
Finis legis justitia.*

In the Chancel upon a Tombstone.

*Hic quidam terra tegitur, peccati solvens debitum;
Cui nomen non imponitur, in libro vitæ sit conscriptum.*

Over the South Door entering the Chancel.

*Non procul hinc dormit, procul hinc Hylocomius ortus,
  Quem peperit, pepulit patria silva ducis,
  Per Varios casus hic sedem denique fixit
  Albana moderans rector in urbe Scholam.
Hunc* Galli, Hiberni, *Belgæ coluere Magistrum,
  Inclyta Grammatices quæis documenta dedit.
Hunc colit, et longum recolet de gente* Britanna,
  *Tam generosa cohors, quam numerosa cohors.
Ad bona Cuncta fuit promptissimus, almus Egeris,
  A quo nemo petens tristis abire solet.
Religione, Fide, Pandore notabilis, atqui
  Omnibus exutis hic levis umbra jaces.
Nec Moreris totus, Cæli pars optima Civis
  Infima pars facta est, sed rediviva, cinis.
Te quia defunctum sine honore queruntur alumni,
  Huc tibi sera dedit Carmina * Vestra Manus.*
                   * Joh. Westerman.

In Memoriam venerabilis viri Johannis Thomæ Hylocomii Buscroducensis
apud Belgas, *hujus Oppidi olim Civis munifici, Scholarchæ celeberrimi.*

On the right Hand of the former, over the Abbot of Whethamsted's Tomb.

Johannes
De loco frumentario.
Quis jacet hic? pater ille Johannes, *nomina magna
Cui* Whethamstedio *parvula Villa dedit.
Triticeæ in tumulo signant quoque nomen aristæ
Vitam res claræ, non Monumenta, notant.*

Round about the Tomb are bunches of Wheat Ears, and written about
them, *Valles abundabunt.*

On the left hand of the great South Door.

Vir domini verus jacet hic Heremita Rogerus,
Et sub eo clarus meritis Heremita Sigarus

Under a South Window in the Body of the Church where was all painted Glass with St. Alban beheaded, and his Executioner weeping out his Eyes which he holds in his Hand.

MDCXXIII.

This Image of our frailty, painted Glass
Shews where the life and death of *Alban* was.
A Knight beheads the Martyr, but so soon
His Eyes dropt out to see what he had done,
And leaving their own head, seem'd with a Tear
To wail the other Head lay mangled there:
Because before his eyes no tears would shed.
His Eyes themselves like tears fell from his head
O Bloody fact that whilst St. *Alban* dies
The Murderer himself weeps out his Eyes.

In Zeal to Heaven, where holy *Albans* bones
Were buried, *Offa* raised this heap of Stones,
Which after by devouring time abused,
Into the dying parts had life infused
By *James* the first of **England** to become
The glory of *Alban's* Protomartyrdom.

Near the Font.

Quin terram leviter premis sacra est amice:
Sub hoc marmore Componitur
Exemplar ævi fugacis non prætereundum,
Martha Brown,
Matthæi Crutchfeild *civis et salar.* **Lond.** *Janæq;*
Obsequentissima filia,
Uxor autem charissima.
Johannis Brown *Med. Doctoris de* **Lond.**
Hoc in Oppido nati, et hac in æde renati.
At qualis fœmina,
Divinis animi corporisq; ditata bonis,
Suavissimis moribus, Ingenio peracuto,
Piam, probam, jucundam cogites, ipsissima est mea.
Uni placere studuit, et Deo placuit, et omnibus.
Quæ Marthæ *primogenitæ superstes*
Hic juxta consepultæ.
Anno post Nuptias altero ferè exacto
Anno Salutis MDCLXVIII. *Ætat.* xxix *incunte*
Dominus pariundis Cum incubuisset fortiter.
Nono post die Feb. viii. *(pro dolor) occubuit:*
Ex quibus binos (faxit Deus) vitales cura pignora
Desiderio sui leniendo post se reliquit.
Abi, lector, Vitæ sic institue si pennas præcideris,
Virtus tua celari nec possit, vel lapides loquentur.
Chara fugis, nec te lachrymæ flexere parentis,
Nec dulces nati, nec pia Cura viri.
Quippe Vocat Christus, proles tibi bina preivit,
Nos sumus haud longè turba futura Comes.
Hæc justa defunctæ persolvit Maritus mœrens. J. B.

ST. PETER'S CHURCH.

VICAR. John Rochford.

THE Church of St. *Peter's* is situated on the North Part of the Borough *Anno* 26 *H.* VIII. was valued in the King's Books at 9*l.* 8*d. per Annum*, and is a fair Church covered with Lead, with a Chancel at the East End covered with Tyle, and at the West End hath a square Tower covered with Lead, wherein hang six Bells, with a short Spire upon it; and in the Church and Chancel are several Gravestones with these Inscriptions.

This Church and Church-yard was filled with the Bodies of those that were slain in the two Battles fought in this Town, among whom Sir *Bertin Entwysel* fighting on the King's Part died of a Wound received in the first Battle, upon whose Tomb this Inscription inlaid in Brass is yet to be read.

Here lyeth Sir Bertin Entwysel, Kt. which was born in Lancashire, and was Uicount and Baron of Brykbeke in Normandy, and Bailiff of Constantine, who died the 28. of May 1455. on whose Soul Jesu have mercy.

These *Entwysels* were Gentlemen of good account in Lancashire, whose Mansion-house retains the Name of *Entwyse'*, and the last Heir of that House was one *Wilfred Entwysel*, who sold his Estate and served as a Lance at Musselburrow Feild, *Anno* 2 *Edw.* VI. after that he served the *Guyes* in defence of Meth, and he was one of the four Captains of the Fort of Newhaven, where being infected with the Plague and shipped for England landed at Portsmouth, and uncertain of any House in *Sept.* 1549. died under an Hedge.

Ralph Babthorpe the Father and *Ralph* the Son of *Babthorpe* in the East Riding in the County of Yorke, fighting in this Town for King Hen. VI. were both slain and lye buried together with this Epitaph.

Cum Patre Radulpho Babthorp jacet, ecce Radulphus
Filius, hoc duro marmore pressus humo.
Henrici serti Dapifer. Pater armiger ejus,
Mors satis it docuit sidus uterque fuit.
C. Domini quater M. semel L. semel D. semel Anno
Nos necat haud solos mors truculenta duos.
Lux hiis postrema Maii bicena secunda,
Det Deus his lucem, det sini fine diem.

Behold wheer two Ralph Babthorpes, both the Son and Father lie
Under a Stone of marble hard, interr'd in this mould drie :
To Henry sixth the Father Squire, the Son he Sewer was,
Both true to Prince and for his sake, then both their Life did passe
The year one thousand and four hundred fifty five,
Grim Death, yet not alone, did them of breath depribe
The last day of their light was the twentieth two of May :
God granted them light in Heaven, and without end, a Day.

In the yere of Christ on thowsand four hundryd full trew with fowr and
Richard Skipwith Gentylman in birth, late fellow of New Inne   [sixteen
In my age twenti on my Soul partyd from the body in August the sixteenth
And now I ly her abiding. Gods mercy under this ston in clay,   [day.
Desyring you that this sal see, unto the Mayden prey for mee
That dare doth God and Man
Like as ye wold that oder for yee-shod,
When ye ne may nor can.

Hic duo consortes Skipwith que Joanna Joannes
Compausant una, generosus et unus, et alter :
At pariter pausant in pace procare quiescant
Tu qui metra legis, sic quod requiescere possis
Hic jacet Georgius Skipwith, Ar. &c.

On the Wall on the South Isle in *St. Peters.*

Hic inter patrios cineres requiescit,
Johannes Radston, L. L. D.
Ex antiqua et honesta admodum Familiâ,
Hoc in oppido natus ;
Studiis liberalioribus Oxoniæ innutritus ;
In Accademiæ Curia Assessor,
Ad altiora in jure civili numera promovendus,
Nisi amicorum votis obstitisset invida Mors
Aug. 5. 1691. *Ætatis suæ* 35
Vir egregiis Animi dotibus præditus,
Ad maxima quæq; capessenda idoneus :

Leniores virtutes,
Quæ virum bonum propius attingunt,
Præcipue coluit; his ornatus
Summorum familiaritate optatissime usus est
Et æqualium suavissime.

In amicis juvandis,
Studio, concilio, opera constans, sincerus indefessus;
Cæteris satisfecit omnibus, sibi ipsi nunquam.
Quæ tam eximia merita,
Ut alias exemplo essent,
Monumentum hoc inscribi curavit
Johannes Michell. *Armig.*
Familiæ Rudstonianæ
Ex utroq; parente consanguineus.

In the Body of the Church.

Here lies the Body of *John Cox*, Esq; late of Beamonds, one of the Marshalls of the Hall to Queen *Elizabeth*, King *James*, and King *Charles*, who departed this Life the 12th of *September, Anno Domini* 1630. at the Age of 77 years; and left *Alban Cox* his Nephew sole Executor, who was at the Charge of this Monument.
Hic requiesco in spe Resurrectionis.

In the Chancel.

Here lieth the Body of *John Robotham*, Esq; who died the 11th of *Sep.* 1615.

In the Chancel.

Hoc sub lapide in sepulchro condito per Richardum Lee *de* Sopwell, *in commitatu* Hertford *Miles jaciunt corpora predicti* Richardi *et* Margarettæ *uxoris ejus, et duarum filiarum eorundem* Richardi *et* Margarettæ *nunc dormitorium est Familiæ* Sadlierorum *de* Sopwell *predict. per conjugium factum et celebratum inter* Edwardum Sadlier *arm. filium secundum* Rodolphi Sadlier *de* Standon *Comitatu predict* Bannereti *et* Ann. *filiam secundam et unam cohærundum predicti* Richardi Lee. *Resurgemus.*

In the Chancel.

Here lyeth the Body of *Robert Robotham*, Esq; sometime Steward and Secretary to the right Honourable *Henry* Lord *Clifford* Earl of Cumberland, and in Commission for the Peace for the County of Stafford. He gave five pounds *per annum* to the Vicar of this Parish, and his Successors for ever; and four pounds *per annum* to be given to Eighty poor People of this said Parish. He died the 6th of *March* in the year of our Lord God 1672. in the 75th year of his Age, left *Robert Robotham* of this Parish, Esq; and *Arthur Smithson* Citizen of London his Executors, to whose pious Memory they dedicated this,

Junior ense rui fueram tunc Ensifer uni
De Borea Comiti, dicto cognomine Percy,
Ut Perii periit sibi proh Dolorensis ademit.
Transcursum stadii, pax sit eiq; mihi,
Ipse Thomas *dictus,* Pakinton *eramq; vocatus.*

Hic jacet Edwardus Beulled, Ar. quondam Magister Ludi henatici infra Libertatem Abbatis de Sancto Albano et Alicia uxor ejus, qui Edwardus Obiit, 8 Jan. 1475.

William Wittor and his Wapfte Grase
Under this Ston ben burped her
In Hevyn good Lord grant them plase,
As thow them boght with thy Blood so der,
Which William as her hii doth apper
The ninth dey of March past this present Iyst
On Thowsand four Hundryd and six yer
Of Crist; whos grase be ther preserbatyst.

Hund. of
Caishoe.

𝕳𝖎𝖈 𝖏𝖆𝖈𝖊𝖙 Edmundus Westby quondam 𝕳𝖚𝖓𝖉𝖗𝖊𝖉𝖆𝖗𝖎𝖚𝖘 Sancti Albani et Joanna uxor ejus filia et 𝖍𝖊𝖗𝖊𝖘 Ade Stonham et 𝕮𝖔𝖓𝖘𝖆𝖓𝖌𝖚𝖎𝖓𝖊𝖆, et 𝕳𝖊𝖗𝖊𝖘 Alicie Attehall..... ob ultimo 𝖉𝖎𝖊 Julii, 1447.

𝕳𝖎𝖈 𝖏𝖆𝖈𝖊𝖙 Cecilia Westby uxor Bartholomei Westby, quæ obiit 2. Julii, anno 1495.

𝕳𝖎𝖈 𝖏𝖆𝖈𝖊𝖙 Willelmus Westby quondam 𝕳𝖚𝖓𝖉𝖗𝖊𝖉𝖆𝖗𝖎𝖚𝖘 et 𝕭𝖆𝖑𝖑𝖎𝖇𝖚𝖘 liber=tatis. ——

𝕳𝖎𝖈 𝖏𝖆𝖈𝖊𝖙 Edmundus Westby, 𝕬𝖗𝖒. 𝕵𝖚𝖘𝖙𝖎𝖈𝖎𝖆𝖗𝖎𝖚𝖘 pacis 𝕮𝖔𝖒. Hertford. et 𝕳𝖚𝖓𝖉𝖗𝖊𝖉𝖆𝖗𝖎𝖚𝖘 ac 𝕭𝖆𝖑𝖑𝖎𝖇𝖚𝖘 𝖉𝖊 𝕱𝖗𝖆𝖓𝖈𝖍𝖊𝖘𝖎𝖆 Sancti Albani et Margaretta uxor ejus, qui Edwardus obiit, 18 Sept. 1475.

Henry VI. was in this *Edmond's* House, then Hundredor of 𝕾t. 𝕬lbans' during the time of the first Battle in the Town.

𝕳𝖎𝖈 𝖏𝖆𝖈𝖊𝖙 Thomas Astry 𝕲𝖊𝖓. filius Radulphi Astri 𝖒𝖎𝖑𝖎𝖙𝖎𝖘, et Elizabetha uxor ejus filia Willielmi Skipwith, 𝖆𝖗𝖒𝖎𝖌𝖊𝖗𝖎, qui quidem Willielmus, obiit, 1507.

> 𝕯e Studely 𝕯omina natus John Lind que bocatus;
> 𝕸orte ruit stratus hic armiger intumulatus
> 𝕬ula 𝕸areschallum quem 𝕽egia 𝕹obilitabit
> 𝕰rga lues rapuet, raptum cineri sociabit
> 𝕾upplico qui graberis, seu in marmore lumina figis,
>   𝕺ra cum superis sit sibi pausa piis
>   ob. 3 Sep. anno 1464.

Under a Marble Stone in the Quire, a religious Man lieth interred, whose Name is worn or stolen out with the Brass; only the Form of a Rose remaineth, and in the turning of the Leaves this Inscription.

> 𝕷o all that 'ere 𝕴 spent, somtym had 𝕴.
> 𝕬l that 𝕴 gau to good intent, that now han 𝕴.
> 𝕮hat which 𝕴 neither gau nor lent, that now abu 𝕴.
> 𝕮hat 𝕴 kept. till 𝕴 went, that lost 𝕴.

An old Translation from these Latine Couplets following.

> 𝕼uod expendi. habui.
> 𝕼uod donabi, habeo.
> 𝕼uod negabi, punior.
> 𝕼uod serbabi, perdidi.

In the South Isle.

Memoriæ et virtutis Sacrum.

Here lies *Roger Pemberton*, Esq; sometime High Sheriff of this County, who by his last Will ordain'd six Alms houses to be built near this Church, for six poor Widows, and hath given out of his Mannor of 𝕾helton in the County of 𝕭edford 30l. *per annum* for ever, for their Maintenance. To whose pious Memory *Elizabeth* his loving Wife, and *Ralph Pemberton* their dutiful Son, Mayor of this Town, Executors of his last Will, have dedicated this Remembrance. He lived well, and departed this life the 13. of *November* 1627. the 72 year of his Age.
Here now his Body rests in expectation of a joyful Resurrection.

  Filii dicti Rogeri *et* Elizabethæ   *Fil. dicti* Rog. *et* Eliz.
  Ralph, Robert, John.   Eliz. Eliz. *et Tecta.*

ST. MICHAEL'S CHURCH.

VICAR, John Cole.

THE Church of St. *Michael* is situated in the North West Part of this Town, and cover'd with Lead; at the West End thereof is a square Tower, wherein hang four Bells; and *Anno* 26 *H.* VIII. it was valued in the King's Books at 10l. 1s. 2d. *per Annum*, and within this Church are several Monuments and Marbles which have these Inscriptions.

John Pecock et Mawd sa femme gisant icy,
E Dieu de sont almes eit mercy, Amen.

Hic jacet Thomas Wolvey (or Wolven) atomus in arte, nec non Armiger illustrissimi Principis Ricardi secundi. quondam Regis Angliæ: qui obiit an. Dom. 1430 in bigilia Sancti Thomæ Martyris. Cujus animæ propitietur Deus, Amen.

It seems by this Inscription, that this Man was the Master Mason or Surveyor of the King's Stone Works, as also Esquire to the King's Person.

Hic jacet Richardus Wolvey (or Wolven) Lathonius filius Johannis Wolven cum Uxoribus suis Agnete et Agnete et cum octo filiis et decem filiabus suis, qui Richardus ob. an. 1494. quorum animabus.

Vertitur in cineres isto sub marmor corpus
Willielmi Lili spiritus astra petit.
Quisquis es, hoc facies supplex pia numina poscas
Ut sibi concedat regna beata poli.

Here is my Lord *Bacon's* Effigies in Alablaster sitting in an Elbow Chair, leaning on his Elbow in a musing posture, in a Nitch in the Wall on the North Side the Chancel, and his Feet on a Pedestal on a Marble Altar. Tomb invironed with an Iron Rail.

H. P.

Francisc. Bacon, *Baro de Verulam. Sanct.* Albani *Viceco'*
Seu notioribus Titulis
Scientiarum Lumen, Facundiæ Lex,
Sic sedebat:
Qui post quam omnia naturalis sapientiæ
Et civilis Arcana evolvisset,
Natura Decretum explevit.
Composita solvantur
Anno Dom MDCXXVI.
Ætat. LXVI.

Tanti viri
Mem.
Thomas Meautys
Superstitis Cultor
Defuncti Admirator.

In the Body of the Church on the Floor.

Here lieth the Body of *George Grimston*, Esq; Son and Heir apparent of the Honourable Sir *Harbottle Grimston*, Bar. Master of the Rolls. A Gentleman full of piety and humility, dutiful to his Parents, loving and beloved, his Person and Comportment both worthy observation, of a comely Shape, and most perswasive behaviour, but death put a period to his growing hopes in the 23d year of his age.

In the Body of the Church on the Floor.

Here lieth *Henry Gape* and *Florence* his Wife,
Who out of this World changed this life
In the Month of *September* the seventh day,
The year of Salvation 1558 the truth to say.
Whose Soul we wish as Love doth bind
In Heaven with Christ a place to find.

In the South Isle in the Wall, in Memorial of John Maynard, *Esq.*

(The two first lines so raced they are not legible.)

In Faith most firm to God, most loyal to the Crown,
Learned in the Law, first Steward of St. *Albans* Town,
Him fairer Arms in Heaven Gods Angels have emblaz'd
Never shall his Christian name out of God's Books be raz'd
He died *October* the 20th. 1556, *anno* 3 *et* 4
Regis Phil. *et Reginæ* Mariæ.

In the Body of the Church on the Floor.

Exuviæ
Gratissimæ Cælis Animæ,
Margarettæ Lowe
Quæ
Primo Rowlando Knight, Mercatori **Londonensi**
Sui vincam peperit Filiam:
Dein Georgio Lowe, *Hospitii* **Lincolniensis,** *Armig'*
Honoratissimo Domino Harbottello Grimston, *Baronet.*
Sacrorum Magistro a Secretis,
Castissimo juncta est Connubio;
Conjugium tam congrue annexum,
Ut crederetur existis Vinculis
Firmior nasci Libertas.
Adeo in illius vultu illuxit Sinceritas, in verbis Fides
Solita in moribus undequaque Symetria,
Intra Alacritatem severa,
Intra severitatem alacris,
Odia subegit Innocentia.
Innocentiam prudentia præmunivit.
Constans virtutum Cultrix, ac Ornamentum,
De Fortuna ultra Sexum triumphavit infractus Animus
Ite viri imitemini.
Hoc in perennem Memoriam G. Lowe *Conjux mæstissimus*
P. D. C.
Obiit Martii 29. *an. Dom.* MDCLXXIII.

ABBOTS LANGLEY.

ABOUT three Miles distant from St. Albans this Vill

appears upon an Hill among the Woods towards the South: *Egelwine* the Black, and *Winefled* his Wife, gave it to the Abbots of St Albans, from whence it had the Adjunct of Abbot, to distinguish it from the neighbouring Vill, and was denominated Langley from the Length of the Vill, for the Name signifies a long Land; and King *Edward* the Confessor, and Queen *Editha* his Wife, at the Instance and Procurement of *Leofstan* the Abbot, and their Confessor, confirmed the Grant hereof, and they held it in the time of the Conqueror, when it was thus recorded:

In Danais Hundred. Abbas *ten.* Langelai *pro quinque hidis se defendebat et dimid tempore Regis* Edwardi, *et modo pro tribus hidis. Terra est quindecim car. in Dom. duo hide et dimid. et ibi sunt quatuor car. et quinta potest fieri. Ibi est Presbiter et un. Francig. cum decem Vill. habentibus decem car. Ibi quinque Bord. et duo servi, et duo mold. de vigint. sol. pratum quinque car. pastura ad pec. Silva trecent porc. de hac terra habet unus Miles dimid. hid. In totis valent. valet decem lib. Quando recepit duodecem lib. tempore Regis* Edwardi *quindecem lib. Hoc Manerium jacuit et jacet in Ecclesia Sancti* Albani. *De hoc Manerio tulit et occupavit* Herbertus *filius* Ivonis *unam hidam inter boscum et planum Tpr.* Bajocensis Episc. *Ipsa hida jacebat in Ecclesia Sanct.* Albani *die qua Rex* Edwardus *fuit vivus et mortuus. Modo tenet Comes* Moritonus.

The Abbot of St. *Alban* held Langley in Danais Hundred, it was rated for five Hides and half an Hide in the time of King *Edward* (the Confessor) and now for three Hides. The arable is fifteen Carucates, in Demeasne two Hides and an half, and there are four Carucates, and a fifth may be made. There is a Presbiter or Priest and one Frenchman born, with ten Villains having ten Carucates. There are five Bordars and two Servants, and two Mills of twenty Shillings Rent by the Year,

Meadow five Carucates, Common of Pasture for the Cattle, Wood to feed three hundred Hogs; one Knight had half an Hide of this Land. In the whole Value it is worth ten Pounds by the Year, when he received it twelve Pounds by the Year, in the time of King *Edw.* (the Confessor) fifteen Pounds by the Year. This Mannor did lie, and doth lie in the Church of St. *Alban.* *Herbert,* the Son of *Ivo* enjoyed and occupied one Hide of this Mannor, lying between the Wood and the Plain of the then Father of the Bishop of 𝔅𝔞𝔶𝔢𝔲𝔯 this Hide did lie in the Church of St. *Alban* on the Day in which King *Edward* (the Confessor) was alive and dead, now Earl *Moreton* holds it.

Hund. of *Caishor.*

In or about the time of *Henry* I. *Nicholas* surnamed *Breakspear,* denominated from a House of that Name in 𝔐𝔦𝔡𝔡𝔩𝔢𝔰𝔢𝔵, was born in this Village, and Son to a Servant in the Abby of 𝔖t. 𝔄𝔩𝔟𝔞𝔫𝔰, where he was put to School, but neglecting his time was afterwards denied the Cloath upon his Request, for that he was not qualified for it, whereupon he went to 𝔓𝔞𝔯𝔦𝔰, improv'd his time much better there; so that at Length he was advanced to be a Cardinal, and afterwards elected Pope by the Name of *Adrian* IV. and continued in that Station four Years, eight Months and eight and twenty Days, during which time he depress'd the Citizens of 𝔕𝔬𝔪𝔢, when they aspir'd to their ancient Freedom; caused *Frederick,* Emperor of 𝔕𝔬𝔪𝔢, to hold his Stirrup when he alighted from his Horse, gave large Priviledges to the Church of St. *Alban,* and as he was drinking *Anno* 1158, was choaked with a Fly.

Camd. *Brit.* tit. Herts. fol. 419. Fuller's *Worthies,* tit. Herts. fol. 20.

Camd. *Brit.* fol 415. Fuller's *Worthies,* fol. 20.

Anno 1 *Johannes* that King confirmed the Grant of this Mannor for the clothing of the Monks of the said Monastery; and it was found *Anno* 6 *Edw.* I. the Abbot of that Church held the Mannors of 𝔖𝔞𝔫𝔡𝔯𝔦𝔠𝔥𝔢, 𝔎𝔞𝔭𝔰𝔥𝔬, 𝔏𝔞𝔫𝔤𝔢𝔩𝔢𝔭, 𝔠𝔥𝔦𝔩𝔡𝔴𝔦𝔠𝔨, 𝔒𝔨𝔢𝔫𝔢𝔭, 𝔠𝔯𝔢𝔨𝔢𝔰𝔥𝔬, and 𝔗𝔦𝔡𝔢𝔯𝔦𝔫𝔤 *in Capite* of the King by the Service of four Knight's Fees and an half.

Quo Warr 6 Ed. 1. Rot.56, in cur. recept. Scac.

The Abbots of this Church held this Mannor until the time of the Dissolution, when it came to the Crown, where it remained until Prince *Charles* held a Court here in *October,* 22 *Jac.* I. shortly after it was conveyed to

Thomas Combe, Esq. who married *Anne,* Daughter of *Thomas Greenhill,* Gent. and dying on the 21st Day of *May,* 1641, without Issue, devised this Mannor with certain Lands, and most of his Library, to *Sidney College* in 𝔠𝔞𝔪𝔟𝔯𝔦𝔡𝔤𝔢, and *Trinity College* in 𝔒𝔵𝔣𝔬𝔯𝔡, for the educating in Piety and Learning the Descendants of his own and his Wife's Kindred for ever.

The President, Fellows, and Scholars of the Colledge of the Lady *Frances Sidney Sussex,* within the University of 𝔠𝔞𝔪𝔟𝔯𝔦𝔡𝔤𝔢, by Lease under their Common Seal, dated the 10th of *June,* 1675, demised to *Thomas Greenhill* and *William Greenhill* their Moyety or half Part of the capital Messuage, Mannor, and Premises for the Term of one and twenty Years, to commence from the Feast of St. *Michael* then last past, under the Rents and Covenants therein contained.

Hund. of
Caishoe.

The President, Fellows, and Scholars of the Colledge of the holy and undivided *Trinity* in the University of 𝔒𝔵-𝔣𝔬𝔯𝔡, by their Indenture of Lease under their Common Seal, dated 15th Day of *Sept.* 1680, demised to *T. Greenhill* and *W. Greenhill* their Moyety and half Part of their capital Messuage in 𝔞𝔟𝔟𝔬𝔱𝔰 𝔏𝔞𝔫𝔤𝔩𝔢𝔭 in this County, and all the Rents for the Term of one and twenty Years, to commence from the Feast of St. *Michael* the Archangel, then last past, under the Rents and Covenants therein compriz'd, and by Vertue of these Leases *Thomas Greenhill* and *William Greenhill* held Courts for this Mannor, and received the Rents and Profits hereof, till such time that *Thomas Greenhill* convey'd his Moyety or half Part of these Leases and Mannor to his Son *Henry Greenhill*, by Reason whereof this *Henry* and *William Greenhill* held this Mannor jointly of the said Colledge, and now hold Courts in their Names: And they give *Vert, two Barrs Argent, in Chief a Leopard proper.*

The Mannor of the HIDE.

W AS derived, as I suppose, from the last Mannor, and denominated from some Possessor thereof, and was heretofore sold to *Henry Greenhill* of 𝔊𝔯𝔢𝔢𝔫𝔥𝔦𝔩𝔩 in 𝔥𝔞𝔯𝔯𝔬𝔴 in the County of 𝔐𝔦𝔡𝔡𝔩𝔢𝔰𝔢𝔵, who died seized hereof about the Year of our Lord 1655, and it descended to

E Relatione
H. Greenhill,
Clerici.

William Greenhill, who enjoyed it about twenty Years, then devised it by his Will to

William Greenhill, who married *Elizabeth* Daughter and Coheir of *William White* of 𝔏𝔬𝔫𝔡𝔬𝔫, by whom he had Issue, *William, John, Henry, Thomas,* and *Elizabeth, Catharine,* and *Anne.*

William Greenhill married *Mary,* the sole Daughter and Heir of *Thomas Sheriff* of 𝔓𝔞𝔤𝔯𝔞𝔳𝔢 in the County of 𝔖𝔲𝔣-𝔣𝔬𝔩𝔨, by whom he had Issue *William, John, Mary, Katharine, Susan,* and *Elizabeth;* and upon the Death or Alienation of any customary Tenant, the Heir or the Purchaser shall pay for a Fine 6*d. per* Acre, and 10*s.* for a Heriot.

T HE Church is situated in the Middle of the Vill, in the Deanery of 𝔖t. 𝔞𝔩𝔟𝔞𝔫𝔰, in the Diocess of 𝔏𝔬𝔫𝔡𝔬𝔫, and the Vicaridge was rated *Anno* 26 *Hen.* VIII. in the King's Books at 10*l. per Annum,* and *Henry Child* is Patron thereof.
. This Church is covered with Lead, has a fair Tower annexed to the West End thereof, wherein is a Ring of five Bells, and a short Spire upon it.

In the Chancel.

A small Monument is erected in the Wall, which has the Effigies of a Woman, with this Inscription.

This Monument of Mrs. *Anne Combe* Daughter of *Thomas Greenhill,* Gentleman, and Wife of *Francis Combe,* Esq; who died without Issue the 21st of *May* 1641. and lies intombed in 𝔥𝔢𝔪𝔰𝔩𝔥𝔢𝔪𝔭𝔰𝔱𝔢𝔡 amongst his

Ancestors; and by his Will gave much out of his Lands to Pions and Charitable uses to the maintenance of several Lectures in 𝔥emel= hempsted, Barkhamsted and 𝔖t. Albans, and also for several Schools in 𝔥emelhempsted, Watford, and Abbots Langley, and allowances to the poor of several Parishes for ever; and also gave the Mannor of Abbots Langley, with certain Lands and most of his Library, himself being Learned, to 𝔖idney=Colledge in Cambridge, and Trinity=Colledge in Orford, for the Educating in Piety and Learning the Descendants of his own and his Wives Kindred for ever; and also by his Will ordered this Monument to be here erected in memory of his forementioned Wife Mrs. *Anne Combe*, being the place of her Nativity, who having led a pious life, died *November* 6 1640. aged 24 years, and lyeth buried in the Chancel.

Hic jacet Nicholaus Martin *armig. qui obiit* 2 *die* Decembris *anno Dom.* 1669.

The Bodies of the Reverend Minister of this Parish, near 53 years of Age, who departed this Life the 16th of *September* 1679. Aged 89 Years, and *Elizabeth* his Wife who departed this Life the 22d. of *May* 1672 aged 66 Years.

Here lieth *Robert Nevil* and *Elizabeth* his Wife, which *Robert* deceased the 28th of *April*, in the year of our Lord God 1475. This World is but a Vanity, to Day a Man, to Morrow none.

Mors mihi transitus in vitam æternam, et Resurgam Georgius Stringer, *filius et heres* Georgii Stringer *de* Abbots Langley *generosi, vixit annos* 6. *obiit* 5 *die* Octobris 1641.

In a Chapel erected on the North Side of the Chancel, which belongs to the Family of Mr. *Child*.

A Table containing this Inscription hangs on the Wall.

Christo S. S.
Johannes Lewes, *Brito* Caermarboniensis,
In parochiâ de Melvern *natus Collegii*
Jesu *Academiæ* Cantabrigiensis *quondam*
Alumnus, Divini verbi Concinator,
Qui per annos 54 *hujusce Ecclesiæ,*
Fuit Pastor fidelis et Vicarius: Post
Vitam pie gestam, pacifice requiescit
In Dominio, et hic tumulatus,
Patri suo omni pietatis officio imprimis
Colendo, Radulfus Lewes, *illius primogenitus,*
Hoc Monumentum possuit non sine Lacrymis.
Obiit 29 *die Augusti anno a Christo nato* 1626.
Vixit annos 80.
Memento juris tui: mihi heri, et tibi hodie:
Sola mihi virtus superest, post fata beatam
Æterno vitam ducere posse Deo.

In a Press there is a small Library of Books. There is a fair Stone without Subscription in this Chappel.

In the Body of the Church.

𝔥ere lyeth buried the Body of Robert Child and his Wife, which Robert died the 6th Day of ——— in the year of our Lord God 1601.

In the Churchyard is a Tomb which has these Inscriptions.

Here lyeth the Body of *John Brewer*, Junior, Yeoman, eldest Son of *Thomas Brewer* of Westwood, Yeoman; which was interred the 26th of *April* 1654.

Here also lyeth the Body of *John Brewer*, Senior, Yeoman, whch was interred the 21st. Day of *August* 1664.

Here also lyeth the Body of *Mary Waters*, Daughter of *John Brewer*, Sen. Yeoman, which was interred the 26th of *August* 1664.

Hund. of
Caishoe.

Here also lyeth the Body of *William Brewer* Yeoman, third Son of *John Brewer* of 𝔚𝔢𝔰𝔱𝔴𝔬𝔬𝔟, Yeoman; which was interred the 25th day of *May* 1666.

Here also lyeth the body of *Elizabeth Brewer*, the Relict of *John Brewer*, Sen. Yeoman abovesaid; which was interred the 13th day of *July* 1682.

Here also lyeth the body of *Thomas Brewer*, Gent. second Son of *John Brewer*, Sen. of 𝔚𝔢𝔰𝔱𝔴𝔬𝔬𝔟 abovesaid, who departed this Life when he was Principal of 𝔊𝔥𝔞𝔟𝔦𝔰 𝔍𝔫𝔫, 𝔏𝔬𝔫𝔟𝔬𝔫: and was interred the 19th day of *November* 1691.

SYRET now called SARRET.

Mon. Angl.
vol.1, fol. 178.
Lib MS. Mr.
Cox.

THIS Vill lies about four Miles distant from 𝔄𝔟𝔟𝔬𝔱𝔰 𝔏𝔞𝔫𝔤𝔩𝔢𝔭, towards the South West, which *Offa* King of the *Mertians*, granted to the Monastery of 𝔖𝔱. 𝔄𝔩𝔟𝔞𝔫𝔰, *Anno* 796, 33 *Regni sui*, so called from *Syret*, a *Saxon*, who, I suppose, was an ancient Possessor of it, and King *Etheldred* confirm'd the Gift by that Name, but no Mention is made of it in *Domesdei Book*, however I find King *Henry* I. and King *John* confirm'd it again by the same Name to that Church.

MS. in Bibl.
Cottoni.
fol. 263.

King *Edw.* I. gave all his Lands called 𝔏𝔞 𝔗𝔯𝔬𝔭, in this Vill of 𝔖𝔭𝔯𝔢𝔱, with the Messuages, Rents, Woods, Meadows, Pastures, and Commons to

Oliver de Burdegans, who by his Deed dated at 𝔖𝔱. 𝔄𝔩𝔟𝔞𝔫𝔰, the 16th Day of *July*, *Anno* 8 *Edw.* II. granted all his Land called 𝔏𝔞 𝔗𝔯𝔬𝔭 in this Vill, with the Messuages, &c. and also the Lands and Tenements which *Geoffrey Turkeyld*, and *Alexander* the Fool, his Bond-tenants, held of him in 𝔙𝔦𝔩𝔩𝔢𝔫𝔞𝔤𝔢, with their Bodies, Chattels, and Sequels, and all other things belonging to the said Lands, which he had of the Gift of King *Edward*, to the Abbot and Convent of the Monastery of St. *Alban* and their Successors for ever, to hold by the Services due, and of Right accustom'd to be paid to the chief Lords of the Fee, which Deed was attested by Sir *John Aignel*, Sir *Richard Chamberlain*, Sir *Stephen de Cheyndut*, *John de Lattin* then Steward of the Liberty of 𝔖𝔱. 𝔄𝔩𝔟𝔞𝔫𝔰, *Roger de Meridene*, *John Gregory*, and many others.

The same King by his Charter dated at 𝔚𝔞𝔩𝔱𝔬𝔫, the 4th Day of *July*, *An.* 12 *Regni sui*, confirm'd the former Grant, and the Abbots of this Church held this Mannor until the Dissolution of that Monastery, when it came to the Crown, from whence it was granted to

Fin. 4 & 5 P.
and M. in re-
cept. Scac.

William Ibgrave, who held it of the King in the time of *Edw.* VI. by the yearly Rent of 12*s.* 7*d.* but he soon parted from it, for I find that in *Michaelmas* Term, 4 & 5 *P. & M.* a Fine was levied of this Mannor by the Name of *Rose-hall* in 𝔖𝔞𝔯𝔯𝔢𝔱 between *William Luddington*, Plaintiff, and *Tho-*

mas Wanford, Deforceant; since which it was in the Possession of one *Cockshut*, who lived here, but whether he was Owner of it I do not certainly know; his Arms were *Gules, three Guts Argent on a Chief of the second, a Griffin passant Sable; Crest on a Wreath, a demi Griffin Argent collard Gules thereon, three Drops Silver*, after whom this Mannor came to

Francis Kingsley, who married *Abigail* Daughter of ———— *Staines*, by whom he had Issue

William Kingsley, who married *Dorothy* Daughter of Sir *Edward Botiler* of 𝕯𝖆𝖓𝖇𝖚𝖗𝖞 in the County of 𝕰𝖘𝖘𝖊𝖝, who lived here Anno 1634, and had Issue

William Kingsley, who was his Son and Heir; his Arms were *Vert, a Cross ingrail'd Argent; Crest on a Wreath, a Goat's Head coupé*—— and I guess he sold it about the Year 1655, to

Thomas Child, who enjoyed it during his Life; his Arms were *Azure, a Fess embattled Ermins between three Eaglets close, Or; Crest on a Wreath, a Dove volant Ermin, with a Trefoile in her Bill vert;* and when he died, it came to

Henry Child, who was his Son and Heir, and sold it to *Robert Child*, he granted it to *Robert Gilbert*, who convey'd it to *John Duncomb*, the present Lord hereof.

THIS Rectory *Anno* 26 *H.* VIII. was valued in the King's Books at 9*l.* per *Annum*, and the Lords of this Maunor have been Patrons hereof.

The RECTORS.

Mr. *Cowheard*	Mr. *Chinciek*
Mr. *Clerke*	Mr. *Joell.*
Mr. *Clerke*	

This Church is erected in the Middle of the Vill, in the Deanery of 𝕾t. 𝕬lbans, in the Diocess of 𝕷ondon, after the Form of a Cross, and at the West End is a little Tower of Brick, in which are three small Bells, and within the Chancel is

A Monument erected in the South Side where are the Effigies of a Man and his Wife, with their three Sons behind the Man, and one Daughter behind the Woman.

In piam memoriam viri Ornatissimi Guliel Kingesley, Armigeri, mariti sui longe clarissimi, Katharina Uxor ejus multum dilecta, hoc Monumentum pietatis ergo dedit dedicatq;

> *Vilis inanis homo, meditaris inania, discas*
> *Quam cito vita fugit more fluentis aquæ*
> *Armiger hic* Kingesley *obiit sic omnia currant.*
> *Terra taget terris, quicquid honoris erit.*

𝕺f your 𝕮haritie pray for the 𝕾ouls of John Hedon and Lettice his 𝖂ife, whyche John dyed the 15th day of February, Anno Dom. 1553. for whose 𝕾oules 𝕵esu habe mercy. Amen.

𝕻ray for the 𝕾oules of James Hedon and Johanna his 𝖂ife, the which James Deceased the 29th day of March, in the year of our 𝕷ord 1503. on whose 𝕾oules 𝕵esu habe mercy. Amen.

RICKMERESWORTH.

IN old Records this Town was called 𝕽𝖎𝖈𝖐𝖒𝖊𝖗𝖊𝖘𝖜𝖊𝖆𝖗𝖙𝖍, or
𝕽𝖎𝖈𝖐𝖒𝖊𝖗𝖊𝖘𝖜𝖊𝖆𝖗𝖉, from the Scituation hereof in a Nook of
Land, where the River coming from 𝕮𝖍𝖊𝖘𝖍𝖆𝖒 in 𝕭𝖚𝖈𝖐𝖎𝖓𝖌-
𝖍𝖆𝖒𝖘𝖍𝖎𝖗𝖊 falls into the 𝕮𝖔𝖑𝖓𝖊, and made here a rich Pool of
Water; for *Ric* in the Saxon Language signifies Rich, and
Mear a Lake or Pool, and *Wearth* or *Weard* a Place scitu-
ated between two Rivers, or the Nook of Land where two
Waters passing by the two Sides thereof, do enter the one
into the other; all which is agreeable to the Scituation of
this Place which is about three Miles distant from 𝕭𝖆𝖗𝖗𝖊𝖙.

Verst. *Restit.*
of *Decayed*
*Intelligence.*p.
228, 200, 207.

MS. Mr. Cox.

Offa, the great King of the *Mertians*, gave the Mannor
of 𝕽𝖞𝖐𝖊𝖒𝖊𝖗𝖘𝖜𝖔𝖗𝖙𝖍, 𝕮𝖗𝖔𝖘𝖘𝖊𝖑𝖊𝖞, 𝕯𝖆𝖈𝖍𝖊𝖘𝖜𝖔𝖗𝖙𝖍, and 𝕸𝖎𝖈𝖍𝖊𝖑𝖋𝖊𝖑𝖉,
with their Appurtenances, to his great Abby of 𝕾𝖙. 𝕬𝖑𝖇𝖆𝖓𝖘;
and after his Decease *Egfride* his Son, who succeeded him
in his Throne, gave the Mannor of 𝕻𝖞𝖓𝖊𝖘𝖋𝖊𝖑𝖉 to the same
Monastery, and King *Etheldred* confirm'd all these Grants
to the Abbot of this Church, who held this Mannor in the
time of the Conquest, when it was recorded,

Domesd. Lib.
fol. 136, n. 10.

*In 𝕬𝖑𝖇𝖆𝖓𝖊𝖘𝖙𝖔𝖓 Hundred. Abbas tenuit 𝕽𝖎𝖈𝖍𝖊𝖒𝖆𝖗𝖊𝖜𝖔𝖗𝖉 pro quindecim
hidis se defendebat. Terra est vigint. car. in Dom. quinq; hidæ, et ibi sunt
tres car. et adhuc duo possunt fieri, ibi quatuor Francig. et duo vigint. Vill.
cum novem Bordis habentibus quatuor decem car et adhuc un. potest fieri ibi
quinque Cotar. et quinque Servi, et un. molend. de quinque sol. et quatuor
denar. pratum quatuor car. De piscibus quatuor sol. pastura ad pecud. Silva
mille et ducent. porc. in totis valent. valet vigint. lib. et decem sol. Quando
recepit duodecem lib. tempore Regis Edwardi vigint. lib. Hoc Manerium
tenuit et tenet in Dom. 𝕾𝖆𝖓𝖈𝖙. 𝕬𝖑𝖇𝖆𝖓𝖎.*

The Abbot of St. *Alban* held 𝕽𝖞𝖈𝖍𝖊𝖒𝖆𝖗𝖊𝖜𝖔𝖗𝖉𝖊 in 𝕬𝖑𝖇𝖆𝖓𝖊𝖘𝖙𝖔𝖓 Hundred,
it was rated for fifteen Hides. The arable is twenty Carucates, in Demeasne five Hides, and there are three Carucates and now two more may
be made, there are four Frenchmen born, and two and twenty Villains
with nine Bordars, having fourteen Carucates, and now one more may
be made, there are five Cottagers, and five Servants, and one Mill of five
Shillings and four Pence Rent, Meadow four Carucates, in Fish four
Shillings by the Year, Common of Pasture for the Cattle, Wood to feed
one thousand and two hundred Hogs; in the whole Value it is worth
twenty Pound and ten Shillings by the Year, when he received it twelve
Pounds, in the time of King *Edward* (the Confessor) twenty Pounds.
He held and doth hold this Mannor in the Demeasne of 𝕾𝖙. 𝕬𝖑𝖇𝖆𝖓𝖘.

MS. in Bibl.
Cottoni.

Inq. 6 Ed. I.
cur. recept.
Scac.

Since this time King *Hen.* I. and King *John* confirmed
the Grants of this Mannor and those of 𝕯𝖆𝖈𝖍𝖊𝖘𝖜𝖔𝖗𝖙𝖍, 𝕮𝖗𝖔𝖘-
𝖘𝖊𝖑𝖊𝖞, and 𝕸𝖎𝖈𝖍𝖊𝖑𝖋𝖊𝖑𝖉 to the Church of St. *Alban;* and
King *H.* III. granted to the Abbot and Monks hereof, a
Market to be held on Wednesday in every Week, in the
Vill of 𝕽𝖞𝖐𝖊𝖒𝖊𝖗𝖊𝖘𝖜𝖔𝖗𝖙𝖍; and upon an Inquisition it was
found *Anno 6 Edw.* I. that this Mannor was ancient De-
measne, and time out of Mind, before the Conquest, in the
Hands of the Predecessors of the Abbot and Convent of 𝕾𝖙.
𝕬𝖑𝖇𝖆𝖓𝖘, and the Abbot acknowledged the same; shortly

after *Jeoffrey*, one of the Abbots of this Church, gave to the Sacrist hereof this Church of St. *Mary*, Rpckmeareswearth, and *John de Whethamsted*, another famous Abbot of the same Monastery, having the Mannor of Wigging in this Parish by Escheat, gave it to the same Abby, and the Abbots enjoy'd all these Mannors until the time of the Dissolution of that Church, which happen'd *Anno* 31 *Hen*. VIII. then they fell to the Crown.

King *Edw*. VI. by Charter dated the 22d *April*, 4 *Regni sui*, granted to *Nicholas Ridley*, then Bishop of London, the Mannor, Rectory, and Church of Rickmansworth, with the Rights, Members, and Appurtenances belonging to the late dissolved Monastery of St. Albans, and also the Advowson and Right of Presentation to the Vicaridge of the Church of Rickmansworth, late belonging to the Monastery, with divers other Mannors to hold of the King in free, pure, and perpetual Alms, rendring therefore yearly one hundred Pounds payable at the Feast of the Nativity of Christ.

But when Queen *Mary* came to the Crown she deprived him of the Bishoprick, restored *Edmond Bonner* to it, and by Letters Patents dated the third Day of *March*, 1 *Mary*, granted to this Mannor, Rectory, Church, Advowson, and Right of Presentation to the said Vicaridge in the Words mentioned in the former Grant to *Edmond* Bishop of London, and his Successors for ever; but afterwards this Mannor returned to the Crown, and King *Charles* I. by Letters Patents dated 3 *Regni sui*, granted it to the six Clerks in *Chancery*, for the Security of the Payment of a Sum of Money; at length that King and the six Clerks convey'd it to *Hewet*, who sold it to

Sir *Thomas Fotherley*, Kt. who had Issue *John, Thomas*, and *Lucy*, and upon his Death, it descended to

John Fotherley, Esq. who was constituted Sheriff of this County in the Year of Christ 1652, and the fourth Year of King *Charles* II. is a Justice of Peace for the County and Liberty of St. Albans, aud the present Lord of this Mannor; his Arms are *Gules, a Fess dancette Or*; *Crest on a Wreath, a broken Lance in Saltire Or, headed Argent insigned with a Penoncell slit Silver, charged with a Cross Gules:* He had Issue

Thomas, married to *Frances* Daughter to *Edw. Seymour* of Woodlands in the County of Dorset, Esq. knighted at Windsor, on the 29th of *July*, 1681, and since deceased without Issue.

John, who was swallowed up with his Daughter his only Child in the Earthquake at Jamaica, and *Dorothy* who married *Robert Wankford* of Topsfield in the County of Essex, Gent. but since died without Issue.

Hund. of
Caishot.

The Mannor of CROSSELY

WAS Parcel of the Revenue of the Abby of St. Albans, and upon the Dissolution of that Church, came to the Crown. Queen *Eliz.* granted it to Dr. *Caius,* who was her Physitian in Ordinary; he built a fair Addition to *Gonvile-hall* in Cambridge, converted it from a Hall to a Colledge, and added this Mannor to the Revenue thereof, and *Robert Brady,* M. D. the Custos, and the Fellows and Scholars of that Society are the present Lords hereof.

This Colledge bears the Arms of the Founders, *Edward Gonvile* and *John Caius, in Pale within a Bordure gobonee Silver and Sables,* viz. *For* Gonvile *Argent, on a Cheveron Sable between two Couples-close Dancette of the same three escallop Shells Or;* and for Caius, *Gold, semyed with Floure gentyl in the Middle of the Cheif Seagreen over the Heads of two whole Serpents in Pale, their Tails knit together, all in proper Colour, resting upon a square Marble Stone Vert, between their Breasts a Book Sable garnish'd Gules, Buckles Gold.*

The Mannor of the MORE.

Pat. 4 H. VI.
p. 2, m. 10. IN 4 *Henry* VI. that King granted License to inclose 600 Acres of Land in Rykemeresworth and Watford, to make a Park, and to imbattle the Scite of the Mannor of Moor in Rykemeresworth. It was Part of the Possession of *George Nevil,* the youngest Son of *Richard* Earl of Warwick and Salisbury, who was consecrated Bishop of Exeter, *Anno* 1455, 33 *H.* VI. constituted Chancellor of England in the Year 1460, 38 *H.* VI. and consecrated Archbishop of York, 1466, 5 *Edw.* IV. but afterwards this Mannor came to the Crown, and King *H.* VII. by Letters Patents dated 1 *Regni sui,* in Consideration of the memorable Services which *John Vere* Earl of Oxford had performed at Bosworth-feild, where he commanded the Vaunt-guard for that Army, and was the chief Instrument in the obtaining that Victory, granted this Mannor by the Name of De la More, to the said *John* Earl of Oxford and *Margaret* his Wife, and to the Heirs of *Margaret,* who was the Daughter of *Richard Nevil* Earl of Salisbury, but afterwards it past to the Crown, and King *James* I. at the Request of the Earl of Bedford, by Patent dated *An.* 1617, 15th of the same King, granted it to —— *Woodward* and —— *Lucy,* Esqrs. and their Heirs, who levied a Fine thereof, and declared the Use to the said Earl for Life, the Remainder to *Lucy* his Wife and her Heirs, who by Deed dated *Anno* 1626, 2 *Car.* I. sold it to

William Earl of Pembrook, in Trust for him and his Heirs: He conveyed it by another Deed dated *Anno* 1631, 7 *Car.* I. to Sir *Charles Harbord* and others in Trust for him, who in the Year 1655, past it to

Sir *Richard Franklin*, who was created Baronet by Letters Patents dated 26th *Oct.* 1660, 12 *Car.* II. and served for this County in Parliament the Year following. His Arms *Argent, on a Bend Azure three Dolphins of the Field.* *The Crest on a Wreath, a Dolphin embowed Argent, struck thro' the Middle with two harping Irons saltier-wise purple, headed Argent.* He sold it in the Year 1672, 24 *Car.* II. to

Sir *William Bucknal* who was knighted the 20th Day *September, An.* 1670, and upon his Decease it descended to

Sir *John Bucknal*, who received the Honour of Knighthood on the 23d Day of *February*, in the Year 1685; served the County of **Middlesex**, in the Parliament held *Anno* 9 & 10 *William* III. and is the present Lord hereof. His Arms are *Or, two Chevernels Gules, between three Buck's Heads caboched Sable.*

MORE PARK

WAS anciently Parcel of the Estate of Cardinal *Woolsey* and the House being a Lodge in the Park, devolv'd to the Crown.

King *James* convey'd it to *Francis* Earl of **Bedford**, for his Life, the Remainder to *Bridget* his Wife and her Heirs; she survived him, and granted it to

William Earl of **Pembrook**, from whom it past to

Robert Cary third Son of *Henry* Lord *Hunsdon*, was knighted, made Warden of the Marshes towards **Scotland**, *Anno* 40 *Eliz.* created Lord *Cary* of **Lepington** in the County of **York**, by Patent dated 6th of *Feb.* 19 *Jac.* I. Earl of **Monmouth** on the 5th of *Feb.* 1 *Car.* I. and died at **More Park**, 12th of *Apr.* 1639, 15 *Car.* I. leaving Issue by *Elizabeth* his Wife, the Daughter of Sir *Hugh Travanian* of **Corihrigh** in the County of **Cornwal**, Kt. two Sons, *Henry Cary*, made Kt. of the Bath, *Anno* 1616, at the Creation of *Charles* Prince of **Wales**, and *Thomas*, and one Daughter called *Philadelphia*, married to Sir *Thomas Wharton*, Kt. Son and Heir to this Lord *Wharton*.

Sir *Henry* succeeded, married *Martha* eldest Daughter to *Leonel* Earl of **Middlesex**, by whom he had Issue two Sons, *Leonel* and *Henry*, both whom died in the Life-time of their Father without Issue; and eight Daughters, *Ann* married to *James Hamildon*, Viscount **Claneboy**, and Earl of **Clanbrazel**, *Philadelphia* died unmarried, *Elizabeth*, *Mary* married to *William* Earl of **Desmond**, *Treviana* died unmarried, *Martha* to *John* Earl of **Middleton** in **Scotland**, *Theophila* and *Magdalen* both died unmarried, and he died the 13th of *June*, 1661, and was buried at **Rickmansworth**.

Shortly after this Seat was sold to Sir *John Francklin*, Kt. who had Issue four Sons, *Richard, John, George*, and —— and died seized hereof, it descended to

Hund. of
Caishoe.

Richard Francklin, who was his Son and Heir, whom I mentioned before; he sold it to

Sir *Charles Harbord,* Kt. from whom it came to

Sir *Richard Franklin,* who aliened it to

James Duke of 𝔒rmond.

Thomas Earl of 𝔒ssory, the eldest Son of the Duke of 𝔒rmond, whose Family descended paternally from *Henry*

Dale's *Catal.*
of Nob.

Walter, a great Baron of this Realm in the time of King *H.* II. whose Son *Theobald* assumed the Sirname of *Boteler* by Reason of his Office, which was Butler of Ireland, he was honoured with the Title of Earl of 𝔒rmond, by the most victorious *Edw.* III. King of England, on the 2d of *Novemb. Anno 2 Regni sui;* and *James Butler* or *Boteler,* the present Duke's Grandfather, was created Marquess the 30th of *Aug.* 18 *Car.* I. Earl of Brecknock, and Lord *Butler* of Lanthony in Wales the 20th of *July,* 12 *Car.* II. Duke of 𝔒rmond in Ireland the 13th of *March,* the 13th of King *Charles* II. and a Duke of England, by the Name and Stile also of Duke of 𝔒rmond the 9th of *November,* 1682, 34 *Car.* II. *Thomas* his eldest Son, (who died before him, and was Father to the present Duke) was by the King's Writ of Summons, dated the 14th Day of *Septemb.* 18 *Car.* II. 1666, called to the Parliament then sitting at Westminster, by the Title of Lord *Butler* of Moore Park, and took his Place there accordingly as youngest Baron, and upon the 18th Day of the same Month was elected Knight of the most noble Order of the Garter. In the Month of *Sept.* 1672, made Rere Admiral of the blew Squadron of his Majesty's Fleet, and commanded in that great Sea Fight against the *Dutch.* He married the Lady *Amelea* of Nassau, Daughter to *Lewis de Nassau* Lord of Beberwaert, Son to the illustrious *Maurice,* late Prince of 𝔒range, and Count of Nassau, by whom he had Issue three Sons, *James* and *Charles,* another *James* dying young, and four Daughters, *Elizabeth* married to *William* Earl of Derby, *Amelia, Henrietta,* and *Katharine,* and two others, *Mary* and *Henrietta,* who deceased in their Childhood: He bears *Or, a Chief indented Azure;* but shortly after this valiant Lord sold this Seat and Park to

James Fitz Roy, one of the natural Sons of King *Charles* II. who by Letters Patents dated at Westminster, the 14th Day of *Feb.* in the 15th Year of *Car.* II. was created Baron of Tinedale, in the County of Northumberland, Viscount Doncaster, and Duke of Monmouth, installed Knight of the most noble Order of the Garter, and constituted Master of the Horse; but upon the Accession of King *James* II. to the Crown, this Duke withdrew himself into Holland, where he raised an hundred Men, which he landed on the eleventh of *June, Anno* 1685, at Lime, in the County of

Hund. of Caishoe.

Dorset, there he rested them about a Week, then marched with them to **Taunton** in **Somersetshire,** a great Clothing Town, where he augmented his Army with divers Journeymen and Apprentices, thence he removed to **Bridgwater,** another great Clothing Town, which increased his Army with great Numbers of raw undisciplin'd Men; from thence he removed forward towards **Bristol,** summon'd that City to surrender; but upon their Refusal he marched with the Lord *Grey* to **Keynsham,** where some Part of his Army pass'd over the River in Order for **Glocester,** but the Country People failing their Expectation, and he hearing that great Forces were coming from **London** towards them, returned back again to **Bridgwater,** where he was proclaim'd King, and the Lord *Grey* made General of the Horse; but soon after the Earl of **Feversham,** who commanded the King's Army followed them and encamped at **Sedgemore,** where the Duke of **Monmouth** viewed his Army by a Prospective Glass from off a Steeple of a Church in **Bridgwater,** and observing the Number of Men and Manner of their Encampment, marched with his Army very silently in the next Night to **Sedgemore,** designing to have past by the King's Army in the Night undiscover'd, and to have surpriz'd the General in his Quarters, but being unexpectedly discover'd by some of the King's Scouts was soon engaged with the whole Army, and mistaking his own Men in the Dark, for the King's, charged upon his own Party, and by Reason hereof was routed on the sixth Day of *July* following; the Duke fled to the **New Forest,** was pursued, found in a Ditch on the eighth of *July*, and brought to **Whitehal,** where he was examin'd, sent thence to the Tower, and being attainted by Act of Parliament, was without any Trial executed upon a Scaffold on **Tower-hill,** on the fifteenth Day of *July*, where his Head was sever'd from his Body, and his Body was privately interr'd in the Chappel in the Tower: He married the Lady *Anne* Daughter and sole Heir of *Francis* Earl of **Buccleugh** in **Scotland,** by whom he had Issue two Sons, *Charles* who died *An.* 11 *Ætat. suæ, James, Anne,*——— and after the Decease of this Duke, this Seat came to

Anne his Dutchess, who married *Charles* Lord *Cornwallis*, Baron of **Cornwallis** of **Eye,** in the County of **Suffolk,** and Baronet, who in her Right, is Possessor hereof. His Arms are *Sable, gutté argent, on a Fess of the second three Cornish Choughs proper.*

Dale's Catal. of Nob. p.150.

The Mannor of MICHELFELD

WAS Part of the Revenue of the Saxon Kings, and King *Offa* gave the same with divers other Mannors to the Church of **St. Albans** in the Year 795, 35 *Regni sui*, and the Abbots held it to the time of the Dissolution of their Monas-

Hund. of Caishoe. tery, when it came to the Crown, and since to the Family of the *Robinsons* in Suffolk, whereof *John Robinson*, Esq. is the present Owner hereof.

The Mannor of WOODOAKES

WAS the ancient Seat of the *Colts*, whereof Sir *John Colt* had Issue *John*, who held it some time, from him issued *Gentillis*, who was his Daughter and Heir, and married Sir *Benjamin Titchburne*, who received the Honour of Knighthood on the 20th Day of *January*, in the Year of Christ 1669. His Arms, *Vary Chief, Or; Crest on a Wreath, a Hind's Head coupé proper between two Wings Gules;* he was the Son of *Francis Titchborne* of the Parish of Aldershot in the County of Southampton, Esq. Son of Sir *Walter Titchborne*, and in Right of his Lady, is the present Owner hereof. His Arms are *Vary Argent and Azure a Chief Or*.

F. Relatione Ben. Titchborne, Mil. Above this Mannor-house upon the Warren Hill is an Eccho, which will repeat to a Trumpet twelve times together.

Stow's Survey of London, fol. 584. *Fuller's Worthies, tit. Herts.* This Town was honoured with the Birth of Sir *Thomas White*, who was a Merchant Taylour of London, and Lord Mayor of the same City, *Anno* 1553. He built Gloucesterhall, and afterwards erected and endowed St. *John's* Colledge in Oxford, and gave great Sums of Mony to several Corporations to be employed circularly for the Benefit of the poor Freemen who resided there.

THIS Vicaridge *Anno* 26 *H.* VIII. was rated in the King's Books at the yearly Value of 16*l. per Annum* and ———— ———— is Patron hereof.

The VICARS.

William Edmonds, D. D.	*Robert Brewse*
Samuel Packer	*John James.*

This Church is erected in the Deanery of St. Alban, in the Diocess of London, is a fair Church covered with Lead, with a square Tower at the West End of it, wherein is a Ring of five Bells, and a Spire upon the Tower covered also with Lead; and within the Chancel and Church are several Monuments and Gravestones, which have these Inscriptions.

A Monument in the Chancel raised about five Foot.

Here lies interred (in hopes of a joyful Resurrection) the Body of the Right Honourable *Henry Cary* Baron of Lepington Earl of Monmouth, and *Elizabeth Trevanian* his Wife, which *Robert* was the tenth Son to *Henry Cary* Baron of Hunsdon, he died the 13. of *June Anno Domini* 1661. aged 65 years. He was married 41 years to the Lady *Martha Cranfeild* eldest Daughter to *Lionel* Earl of Middlesex, and had by her ten Children, two Sons and eight Daughters, *videlicet*, *Lyonel*, the eldest never married, was slain *anno Domini* 1644. at Marston Moor fight in his Majesties service, and *Henry* who died of the Small Pox, *anno Domini* 1649. and lies interred at the Savoy. He left no issue but one Son since deceased, also the last Heir male of this Earls Family, the Daughters were as followeth *Anne*, *Philadelphia*, *Elizabeth*, *Mary*, *Trevania*, *Martha*, *Theophila*, and *Magdalen*.

Within this place lies also Buried the Bodies of the abovenamed *Robert* Earl of Monmouth, *Elizabeth*, Countess of Monmouth his Wife, and the Ladies *Philadelphia*, *Trevania*, *Theophila*, and *Magdeline Cary;* and

the Bodies of *James* Lord *Clenoboy* and the Lady *Jane Hambleton* his Sister, being the Children of the aforesaid Lady *Anne Cary*, which she had by *James Hambleton* Viscount Clenoby Earl of Clanbrasill of the Kingdom of Ireland.

Sacred to the Memory

Of the Right Honourable the Lady *Elizabeth Cary* one of the Daughters and Coheirs of the Right Honourable *Henry* Lord *Cary* Baron of Lepington and Earl of Monmouth, she died the 14. of *December* in the year of our Lord 1676. and in the 46. year of her Age, having lived all her time Unmarried, but now expecting a joyful Resurrection, and to be joyned to her only Spouse and Saviour Jesus Christ, lies here interred near the said Earl her Father.

Here lies interred the Body of *James Hambleton* Lord Clenoby, eldest Son to *James* Earl of Clanbrasill, born *September* the 7th. 1642. Deceased *May* the 8th. 1658.

Here lies buried the Bodies of *Thomas Fotherley*, Gent. and *Tabitha* his Wife, one of the Daughters of *Giles Howse*, Gent. which *Tabitha* departed this Life the 19th. day of *June* in the year of our Lord God 1584. being about 36. years old, the said *Thomas Fotherley* departed also this Life the 23. day of *April* 1624. being aged 80. years or there abouts; they had issue between them *Thomas* their only Son, *Mary* and *Martha* their Daughters; *Thomas* in testimony of his Duty and Love towards his said Parents caused this Stone to be made.

Here lieth the Body of *Timothy Neal*, Esq; Son of *John Neal* late of Deale in the County of Bedford, who died the 27. day of *January* in the year 1679.

Here lieth interred the Body of Mrs. *Anne Neal*, the Daughter of *John Neal*, of Neitherbane in the County of Bedford, Esq; She departed the 17. day of *January* 1672.

Here lieth the Body of *Gidion Awnsham*, Esq; Son of *Nicholas Awnsham* of Heston in the County of Middlesex, Gent. who departed this Life on the 17. of *September* 1648.

He first took to Wife, *Margaret* Daughter and Coheir of *Gidion Awnsham* of Heston aforesaid, Esq; and after *Margaret* Daughter of *Mathew Nicholas* of Pillinton in Middlesex, Gent. Aged 46. years.

Francisca Horne *mater* Johannis Colt, *Militis, hic jacet quæ Sepulta fuit* 29. *die* Decemb. 1630.

In confidentia beatæ resurrectionis restat.

As Nature yeilds us breath and life, so death draws on by kind.
By death again the only Faith in Christ eternal life we find.
A Proof behold by one that did enjoy my vital breath
Near twenty and nine years and she gave place to death.
An Esquire, a Justice of the Peace, I *Roger Coult* by name,
I was like you, and now am Earth, as you shall be the same.
Of one Son and one Daughter eke the Lord me Father made.
And in my youthful years of Life bereft here under laid.
He died the first of *December* 1575.

A Monument in the Wall.

Memoriæ Sacrum.

Here under lieth the Body of *John Colt* late of Rickmersworth in the County of Hertford, Esq; Son and Heir of *Roger Colt*, Esq; which *John* married *Frances* one of the Daughters of *Ralph Woodcock*, late of London Alderman, by whom he had issue three Sons, *viz. John, Rowland,* and *Thomas,* and four Daughters, *viz. Mary, Ursula, Mary,* and *Elizabeth,* and he departed this Life the 20. of *April, anno Domini* 1610. being about 32. years of age.

To whose Memory the said *Frances* his most loving Wife hath caused this Monument to be erected.

Here lieth Buried under this stone
The Body of *Thomas Day*
And his two Wives *Alice* and *Joane*

Alice ⎫   ⎧ the 10th. of *June* 1585.
Joane ⎬ deceased ⎨ the 6th. of *August* 1598.
Thomas ⎭   ⎩ the 10th. of *July* 1613.

The times here see you may
These three no doubt had Faith in Christ
Their sins for to forgive
And they can tell that knew them well
The Poor they did relieve.

In the Chapple or Burial Place of the *Ashbies*.

Here lieth Anne Ashby 𝔚ife of John Ashby of Herfeild, 𝔈sq; 𝔇aughter
of Thomas Peyton of Iselbam, 𝔈squire; who died the 22. of October
1503. on whose Soul Jesu habe merry. Amen.

Here ly byrid undyr this stone
Thomas Davy and his two 𝔚yfs Alice and Joan.

WATFORD

IS scituated upon the River Colne, about three Miles distant from Rickmersworth, towards the North-west, and
was denominated from Wet Ford, at the South End of
the Town; it was anciently Parcel of that large Revenue,
which that great and magnificent King *Offa* so generously
gave to the Monastery of St. *Alban*, and divers of his royal
Successors confirmed this noble Gift, with the Additions of
many large Immunities and Priviledges; among whom
King *Hen*. I. granted that the Abbots and their Successors
should have a Market in this Town; and King *Edw*. IV.
by Letters Patent dated at Dodington, 1 *November*, 1469,
9 *Edw*. IV. granted to them two Fairs to be held in this
Town for Victuals, and other Things, to continue for five
Days, to wit, one to be held on *Monday* in the Morrow of
the Holy Trinity, and to continue for two Days then next
following, and the other to be held on the Day and the
Morrow of the Decollation of St. *John* Baptist, with all the
Liberties and Freedom belonging to Fairs; and these Abbots and Monks successively possest and enjoyed this Mannor until the Dissolution of their Monastery, which happened on the fifth Day of *Dec. Anno* 1549, 38 *Hen*. VIII.
when they surrendred it to the King's Visitors; and it
came to the Crown, where it remained until King *James* I.
by Letters Patent dated at Westminster, the 24th Day of
July, 1609, 7 *Regni sui*, freely granted to *Thomas Marbury*
and *Richard Cartwright* of London, Gent. and their Heirs,
all the Mannor of Watford, in this County, with all and
every the Rights, Members, and Appurtenances, all the
Rents of the Freeholders amounting to 11*l*. 16*s*. 03*d*. per
ann. all the Rents of Assize of customary Tenants amounting to 6*l*. 8*s*. 2*d*. *ob. per Annum*, all moveable Rents being
1*s*. 6*d*. *per Annum*, of the Price of one Quarter of Oats for

certain Lands late in the Possession of *Thomas Woodward,*
that Messuage or Tenement called 𝕳𝖆𝖗𝖜𝖆𝖗𝖉𝖘 in 𝖂𝖆𝖙𝖋𝖔𝖗𝖉,
and the House built thereon, all those Lands, Meadows,
and Pasture belonging to it of the yearly Rent of 8*l.*
13*s.* 4*d.* all that Piece of waste Ground in 𝕹𝖊𝖜 𝕾𝖙𝖗𝖊𝖊𝖙,
which *Robert Bateman* had by Copy of Court Roll, two
Acres of Land in 𝕮𝖔𝖗𝖘𝖊𝖓-𝖍𝖊𝖉𝖌𝖊, also all the Toll of the
Market of the Vill of 𝖂𝖆𝖙𝖋𝖔𝖗𝖉, and the Toll of the
two Fairs there, with all the Perquisites and Profits of
Court valued one Year with another at 117*l.* 08*d. ob.* and
all Court Leets, Views of Franc-pledge, and Law-days,
Assize and Assay of Bread, Wine, and Ale, Waifes, Estraies, Chattels of Felons and Fugitives, of Felons of themselves, put in Exigent, Condemned, Outlawed, Deodands,
Knight's Fees, Wards, Marriages, Releifes, Heriots, Escheats, Fines, Amerceaments, Free-warrens, and all other
Rights, Jurisdictions, and Profits, in as large and ample
Manner as any Abbots of the late Monastery of 𝕾𝖙. 𝕬𝖑𝖇𝖆𝖓𝖘
enjoyed the same, excepting the Advowson and Right of
Patronage of all the Churches, Vicaridges, Chappels, and
other ecclesiastical Benefits whatsoever belonging to the
same, all which Mannor and Premises were granted to the
said *Thomas Marbury* and *Richard Cartwright* in Trust for
the Right Honourable *Thomas* Lord *Egerton,* Baron of
𝕰𝖑𝖊𝖘𝖒𝖊𝖗𝖊, Lord Chancellor of 𝕰𝖓𝖌𝖑𝖆𝖓𝖉, in Consideration of
the great Services which he hath done for the Crown: from
this great Lord this Mannor is descended to

John Earl of 𝕭𝖗𝖎𝖉𝖌𝖊𝖜𝖆𝖙𝖊𝖗, his rightful Descendant, and
the present Lord hereof, whom I intend to treat of when I
shall come to 𝕬𝖘𝖍𝖊𝖗𝖎𝖉𝖌𝖊, that noble Seat where his Lordship
now resides.

The Mannor of CAISHOBURY.

WHEN the *Romans* invaded this Island the Inhabitants
hereof were called *Casii* or *Cassians,* as some think in Respect of their martial Prowess: They were governed at that
time by *Cassivelaunus,* or rather *Cassibelinus,* for *Belinus*
then signified the chief King, Prince, or Ruler, as *Ceno-
belinus,* Prince of the 𝕴𝖈𝖊𝖓𝖎𝖆𝖓𝖘, and was the common Name
which the Inhabitants of this Isle gave at that time to their
cheif King: He was without Doubt the most Potent Prince
among them, for all the other Kings of this Land chose
him to lead their Armies against the *Romans,* and when the
Enemy approacht near 𝖁𝖊𝖗𝖚𝖑𝖆𝖒, he commanded *Cingetorix,
Carvillius, Taximagulus,* and *Segonax,* four Kings in 𝕶𝖊𝖓𝖙,
to set upon the Roman Camp, where their Navy was kept,
with all the Power they could make, that by this Means
they might give *Cæsar* a Diversion, and oblige him to call
back his Army. There is a Tradition that this was the

Camd. *Brit.*
fol. 391.
Brady's *Hist.*
of Engl. fol.9.

Ibid.
Cæsar's *Com.*
fol. 99.

Hund. of
Caisbor.
royal Seat of *Cassibeline*, and 'tis very probable, for the
Name of this Place in the British Language imports the
Dwelling-place or Habitation of *Cassi*, and is scituated
very conveniently for his chief City of Verulam.

When the *Saxons* subdued this Realm by Conquest, and
divided the Government hereof into an Heptarchy, this
Mannor was made a Seat of the Mertian Kings, and continued in their Possession until King *Offa* gave it *Anno*
33rd of his Reign to enlarge the Revenue of the Monastery
of St. *Alban*, and the Abbots of that Church held it in the
time of the Conqueror, when it was recorded that

Domesd. Lib.
fol. 135, n. 10.
*In Albaneston Hundred. ten. Caissou pro viginti hidis se defendebat de his
ten. Abbas novemdecim. Terra vigint. duo car. in Dominio sex hidæ, et ibi
sunt quinq; car. et sexta potest fieri, ibi tres Francig. et 36 Vill. cum octo.
Hordis habentibus quindecim car. et adhuc una potest fieri, ibi tres Bordi
adhuc et duo servi, et quatuor molend. de sex vigint. sol et octo denar. pratum
duo vigint. car. pastura ad pec Silva mille porc. in totis valent valet octo
vigint. lib. Quando recepit quatuor vigint. lib. tempore Regis Edwardi trigint. lib Hoc Manerium tenuit et tenet Sanctus Albanus in Dominio.*

Ibid. fol. 139,
n. 33.
In Albaneston in Caisson ten. Turoldus de Goisfrido de Manevile *unam
hidam. Terra est un. car. sed non est ibi, pratum un. car. Silva trigint. porc.
valet et valuit quinq; sol. tempore Regis Edwardi vigint. sol hanc terram
tenuit Aluvinus Venator homo Eddid. Reginæ et vendere potuit hanc apposuit* Goisfridus *in Cassei ubi non fuit in tempore Regis* Edwardi.

The Abbot of St. *Albans* held *Caisho* in *Albaneston* Hundred, it was
rated at twenty Hides, the Abbot held nineteen of them. The arable is
two and twenty Carucates, in Demeasne six Hides, and there are five
Carucates, and a sixth may be made, there are three Frenchmen born,
and thirty six Villains with eight Bordars having fifteen Carucates, and
now one other may be made, there are now three Bordars, and two Servants, and four Mills of six and twenty Shillings and eight Pence Rent
by the Year, Meadow two and twenty Carucates, Common of Pasture
for the Cattle, Wood to feed one thousand Hogs; in the whole Value it is
worth eight and twenty Pounds by the Year, when he received it four
and twenty Pounds, in the time of King *Edward* (the Confessor) thirty
Pounds; St. *Alban* did hold and doth hold this Mannor in his Jurisdiction.

Turold held one Hide of *Goisfride de Manerile* in *Caisho* in *Albaneston*
Hundred. The arable is one Carucate, but now there is not so much,
Meadow one Carucate, Wood to feed thirty Hogs; it is worth and was
worth five Shillings by the Year, in the time of King *Edward* (the Confessor) twenty Shillings; *Alwine* a Huntsman to Queen *Editha* held this
Land and might sell it, *Goisfride* laid this Land to Bushei where it was
not in the time of King *Edward* (the Confessor.)

By the great Quantity of Land contained here in Caisbor,
it seems all the Land mentioned before in Watford is comprehended within it; since which time several Princes of
this Realm have confirmed the Gift of these Mannors to
Mon. Angl.
vol. I.
the Church of St. Albans; and upon an Inquisition *Anno*
Inq. 6 Ed. I.
Rot. 33, cur.
recept. Scac.
6 *Edw.* I. the Jury found that the Mannors of Caisboe,
Rykemeresworth, and Saundertoge were ancient Demeasne,
held of the King time out of Mind before the Conquest of
England, in the Hands of the Predecessors of the Abbots
of St. *Albans*, and the Abbot acknowledged it; and he held
Ibid. Rot. 56.
the Mannors of Sandrigg, Rapsboe, Langley, Childwyck,
Oxenep, Crekesboe, and Tyverning *in Capite* of the King,
of the Service of four Knight's Fees, and an Half; and the

Abbots and Monks of that Church successively enjoyed it in their Turns until the time that their Monastery was dissolved, when it came to

King *H.* VIII. who by Letters Patents dated the 20th of *Aug.* in the 37th Year of his Reign, conveyed to *Richard Morisin,* Esq. this Mannor of Caíshœburp, Court Leet, View of Franc-pledge, Goods, and Chattels, waifed Goods, and Chattels of Felons and Fugitives, Felons of themselves, Deodands, Estraies, Liberties, Emoluments, and Hereditaments whatsoever, in as large and ample Manner as the Abbots held the same.

This *Richard Morisin* was in the time of his Youth, bred up in the University, where he studied Philosophy ; and when he had attained to some Perfection of Knowledge in the Latin and Greek Tongues, and the liberal Arts, he removed thence to the Inns of Court, where he became well skilled in the Common and Civil Law, and by Reason of his great Learning, obtained much Esteem and Favour with King *H..*VIII. and *Edw.* VI. so that they often employed him upon several Ambassages to the Emperor *Charles* V. and the mightiest Princes in their times ; he proving both honest and able in the Performance of all these Negotiations : He married *Bridget,* Daughter of *John* Lord Hussep of Sleforð in the County of Lincoln, by whom he had Issue *Charles,* who was his Heir, and two Daughters, *Jana Sibella* married to *Edward* Lord *Russel,* eldest Son to the Earl of Beðforð, and after his Decease to *Arthur* Lord *Grey* of Wilton ; and *Elizabeth* married to *William Norris,* Esq. Son and Heir apparent to *Henry* Lord *Norris :* he began a fair and large House in this Place, scituated upon a dry Hill not far from a pleasant River in a fair Park ; and had prepared Materials for the finishing hereof, but before the same could be half built, he was forced to fly beyond the Seas, and returning out of Italp died at Strasburgþ, on the 17th Day of *March, Anno* 1556, 2d and 3d of *Philip* and *Mary,* to the great Grief of all good Men: After his Decease this Mannor came to the Possession of

Bridget his Widow, who enjoyed it; and *An.* 1561, 3 *Eliz.* married *Henry* Earl of Rutlanð, who was made Lord President of the Council for the Northern Parts of this Realm in the same Year, and installed Knight of the most noble Order of the Garter, during whose Intermarriage, Courts were held in both their Names for this Mannor: He died without Issue by her upon the 17th of *Sept.* 1563, 5 *Eliz.* after his Decease she married *Francis* Earl of Beðforð, who died without any Issue by her, on the 28th of *July, Anno* 1585, 27 *Eliz.* in the 58th Year of his Age: Afterwards she died the 12th of *Jan. Anno* 1600, 43 *Eliz.* and in the 75th Year of her Age.

Hund. of Caíshœ.

Bar. of Engl vol. 2, fol 297

Ibid. fol. 280.

Hund. of
Caishot.

Eliz. Pip. 21
Rot.

Sir *Charles Morisin*, Knight, Son and Heir of Sir
Richard Morisin and *Bridget* his Wife, succeeded, was
constituted Sheriff for this County, *Anno* 1579, 21 *Eliz.*
and married *Dorothy*, the Daughter of *Nicholas Clerk*,
Esq. by whom he had two Children, *Charles* his only Son,
and *Bridget* his sole Daughter, married to *Robert* Earl of
Sussex: He compleatly finished the House which his Fa-
ther begun, and died the Day before the Calends of *April*,
Anno 1599, 41 *Eliz.* in the 51st Year of his Age: After his
Death this Mannor came to the Lady

Dorothy Morisin his Relict, who held Courts here from
the second Year of King *James* I. in her own Name, to
the fourth Year of the same King inclusive: Upon her
Decease this Mannor descended to

Sir *Charles Morisin*, Knight, Son and Heir of Sir
Charles, who was made a Baronet by Letters Patents
Pat. 9 *Jac.* I.
dated 22nd *May*, 1611, *Anno* 9 *Jac.* I. invested with the
honourable Order of the Bath at the Coronation of King
Charles I. in the year 1625, 1 *Car.* I. He served for the
Borough of St. Albans in the Parliament held at Westminster, 17th of *May*, 1 *Car.* I. For the Borough of Hertford,
in the Parliament held 1628, 4 *Car.* I. And for this County
in the Parliament held 21 *Jac.* I. He married *Mary* the
second Daughter of Sir *Baptist Hicks*, Viscount Cambden: He gave *Or, on a Chief Gules, three Chaplets of the
first*; and died on the 20th of *August*, leaving only *Elizabeth*, his sole Daughter and Heir.

William Moryson of Chardwell in the County of York.

William Moryson. = Elizabeth, Da. to Roger Lee of Preston in Yorkshire.

Thomas Moryson = ——— Daughter to Tho. Merrey of
of Hertfordshire. Hatfeild in Hertfordshire

Sir Richard Moryson, = Bridget, Daughter to John Lord Hussey, after his decease she mar-
Kt. of Caishobury. ried Henry Earl of Rutland, after him Francis Earl of Bedford, by
   which two last Husbands, she had no Issue.

Jana Sibilla = Edw. Ld. Russel, eldest   Sir Charles = Dorothy, Da.   Eliz. = Will. Norris,
   Son to the Earl of Bed-   Moryson.   of Nicholas   Heir apparent
   ford, Arthur Lord Grey   Clark, Esq.   of H. L. Nor-
   of Wilton.   ris.

Sir Charles Moryson, = Mary, youngest Daughter and   Bridget. = Robert Earl of Sussex
Kt. and Bar. Coheir to Sir Baptist Hicks,
   Viscount Cambden.

Elizabeth Moryson, sole Da. and Heir, mar. Arthur Lord Capel, Baron of Hadham.

From whom this Mannor is come by Right of Inheritance
to *Algernoon* Earl of Essex; of whose noble Family I have
already treated in the Parish of Little Hadham, to which I
refer the Reader.

The Mannor of the GROVE

WAS the ancient Seat of the *Heydons*, whereof *John Heydon* died seized, on the first of *March*, 1408, leaving Issue

William, who was his Heir, and married the Daughter of *Robert Awbury* of the County of 𝔅uck𝔰, by whom he had

William, who married *Alice* Daughter of *Alexander Newton*, whose Heir was

Henry Heydon: He married *Anne* Daughter and Heir of *Edward Twyhoe* of 𝔠𝔥ipton in the County of 𝔊loucester.

Francis was his Heir, constituted Sheriff for this County *Anno* 25 *Eliz.* and married *Frances* the Daughter of *Arthur Lonquille*, Esq.

Edward Heydon succeeded, and gave for his Arms, *Quarterly Argent and Azure, a Cross ingrailed, quarterly counterchanged; Crest on a Wreath, a Talbot passant Argent, spotted Sable.*

This pleasant Seat was alienated from this Family to the Ancestors of Sir *Dennis Hampton* of 𝔅uckingham𝔰𝔥ire, who sold it to

Robert Ashton, Esq. who was the eldest Bencher of *Lincolns Inn* for divers Years together, and upon his Decease it descended to

William Ashton, Esq. his Son and Heir, and the present Possessor hereof.

The Mannor of GARSTON.

JOHN de Frumentarius, otherwise called *John* of 𝔚𝔥ethamsted, the thirty third Abbot of the Monastery of 𝔖t. 𝔄lbans, about the latter End of the Reign of King *Edw.* IV. purchased this Mannor for the Use of that Church, and the Abbots enjoyed it till their Dissolution, when it came to the Crown; from whence it was granted to *Richard* and *John Randoll,* who held it in the time of *Edward* VI. by the yearly Rent of 1*l.* 8*s.* from whom it came to *Robert Carle,* who married *Petronel* Daughter of *William Curete,* by whom he had Issue *William Carter,* whose Arms were *Argent, a Cheveron Sable betwen three Catharine Wheels Vert; Crest upon a Wreath, on a Mount proper a Talbot sejant, reposing his dexter Foot on an Escocheon Argent, charged with a Catharine Wheel Vert:* and he sold it to *John Marsh,* Esq. who died seized hereof; from whom it descended to *Joseph Marsh,* who was his Son and Heir, and is the present Owner hereof.

The Mannor of MERIDEN

WAS another Parcel of the Revenue of the Church of 𝔖t. 𝔄lbans, which the Abbots enjoyed till the time of their Dissolution, when it came to the Crown; from whence it was granted to *Anthony Denny,* Esq. one of the Gentlemen of the Privy Chamber, and Groom of the Stool. He held it of the King by the yearly Rent of 1*l.* 4*s.* 6*d.* from whom it descended to Sir *Henry Denny* his Son; and from him it

Hund. of
Caishor.

descended to *Edward Denny* his Son, who was knighted *An.* 1589, 31 *Eliz.* and summon'd to Parliament by the Title of Lord *Denny* of 𝔚altham 𝔥oly 𝔠ross, *Anno* 3 *Jac.* I. and he sold this Mannor *Anno* 5 *Jacob.* I. to *Robert Briscoe* of 𝔄ldenham in this County, Esq. whose Ancestors descended from the second House from *Westward* in 𝔠umberland: His Arms are *Argent, three Grey-hounds current in pale Sable; Crest on a Wreath, a Grey-hound in full Course Sable with a Hare in his Mouth proper:* This *Robert* aliened it to *Thomas Ewre* of the 𝔏ea, who sprung from the second Branch descended from ———— *Ewre* of 𝔥untonbridge in 𝔄bbots 𝔏angley: His Arms were *Or, a Tyger passant Sable, on a Chief Gules, three Crosses formee Argent; Crest on a Wreath, a Pheon's Head with a Piece of the Shaft therein Or, enwrapt by a Snake Vert:* and he is the present Possessor hereof.

The Mannor of CAROLAND

WAS a small Mannor, another Parcel of the Possessions of the Church of 𝔖t. 𝔄lbans, and falling to the Crown upon the Dissolution was afterwards conveyed to the Warden and Fellows of *Merton Colledge* in 𝔒xford, who are the present Possessors hereof.

The Mannor of BYRSTON

WAS Parcel of the Revenue of King *Offa*, which he gave to the Monastery of 𝔖t. 𝔄lbans, *Anno* 795, 35 *Regni sui*, and the Abbots held it till the fatal Year of their Dissolution, when it came to the Crown, and King *H.*VIII. conveyed it to *Anthony Denny*, Esq. from whom it passed as the Mannor of 𝔐eriden did, until it came to the *Kentishes*, and ———— *Kentish* died seiz'd hereof, leaving two Daughters, who were his Coheirs; whereof one married *Godman Jenkings* of 𝔥arpenden, Esq. the other *Thomas Nicholl* of 𝔅usby, Gent. who in Right of their Wives, are the present Owners.

The Mannor of OXEY

WAS denominated from Sir *Richard de Oxey*, Kt. who granted to God and the Church of 𝔖t. 𝔄lbans, all his Land which *Osbert West* sometime held in the Vill of 𝔒xey, with the Meadow belonging to the same Land, and the Pasture in all his Woods and Lands in the same Vill, which lies between the Land of *Richard Pinnore* of the one Part, and the Land late *Henry Boinards* of the other Part; to have and to hold to them and their Successors the aforesaid Lands, with the Houses, Gardens, Woods, Meadows, Pastures, Ways, Waters, Rents, Homages, Releases, Services, Wards, Escheates, and all other things whatsoever belonging to the

Land, in pure and perpetual Alms: The Witnesses were Sir *William Aete*, Kt. then Steward of the Liberty of St. Albans, Sir *Roger de Dachworth*, Sir *William de Gorham*, Kts. *Edward Aynelle*, *John Kenelone*, *Gregory Halegod*, *William de Okerlee*, *William de Bolum*, Clerk, *Roger de Wymandeham*, and others; and the Abbots held it to the Dissolution of their Church, when it came to the Crown; from whence, I suppose, it was conveyed to —— *Heydon*, and one of that Name sold it to

Sir *James Altham*, Knight of the Bath, Lord Chief Baron of the *Exchequer*, whom I have mentioned before in the Parish of Buckland; he died, and lies interred with his Lady in the Chappel belonging to this Place; and left Issue only one Daughter and Heir, who marryed

John Lord *Vaughan*, Earl of Carberry, and being possest hereof in her Right, sold it to

John Heydon, Esq. who was knighted, but having Issue only one Daughter, upon her Marriage with Sir *Edward Boughton*, whose Ancestor was created Baronet by Letters Patents dated the 4th of *Aug. Anno* 1641, 17 *Car.* I. he gave her a considerable Portion, and sold this Mannor to

Sir *William Bucknal*, who was knighted on the 20th of *Sept.* 1670, made Alderman of the City of London, built a fair House here, and died leaving Issue

John Bucknal, who was his Son and Heir, knighted on the 23rd of *Feb.* 1685, and marryed *Mary* Daughter of Sir *John Read* of Brocket Hall in the Parish of Hatfield, in this County, Bart. and is the present Possessor hereof.

The Rectory was granted to *John* Lord *Russel*, who held it in the time of King *Henry* VI. by the yearly Rent of 2s. 4d. from whom it passed to the *Morisins*, and from them to *Arthur* Lord *Capel*, by the Marriage of *Elizabeth*, the Daughter and Heir of Sir *Charles Morisin* of Caishoe Bury, from whom it descended to *Arthur* Earl of *Essex*, and from him to *Algernoon*, the present Earl and Owner thereof.

THIS Vicaridge, *Anno* 26 *H.* VIII. was valued in the King's Books at 21l. 12s. *per Ann.* of which the Abbots of St. Albans were anciently Patrons; but since, the Advowson past with the Mannor, and *Algernoon* Earl of Essex is the present Patron hereof.

VICARS.

	Anthony Watson.	1659	*William Davenant.*
1629	*Cornel Burges*, D.D.	1661	*John Goodman*, D.D.
	John Smith.	1675	*John Berrow*, the present
	Philip Goodwin.		Vicar.

This Church is situated near the Middle of the Town, and contains three large Isles, with a fair Chancel at the East End, and two Chappels on either Side of the Chancel, whereof the largest was built by Sir *Charles Morisin*, where the Lords of Caishoburp are interred: The Church, Chancel, and Chappels are covered with Lead; at the West End of the Church adjoyns a square Tower, in which hang a Ring of six Bells, with a short Shaft or Spire erected thereupon.

In the first Chappel, which belongs to **Caishobury**, you may behold a fair and costly Monument erected on the North Side hereof, whereon the Effigies of a noble Lady standing in an Arch, defended with two Marble Columns on either Side, kneeling upon a Cushion, having a short Cloak over her Shoulders, and a Gown girt round her, with a Surcingle, a Boograce, and a Hood tyed behind her, and an Hour Glass plac't before her; with the Words underneath her contained in 1 *John cap.* ii. *ver.* 17.

Then a Table plac't before her with a Book upon it, and divers Texts in Scripture engrav'd upon it in Words at Length, *Job cap.* xix, *ver.* 25—27, then follows *John cap.* ii, *ver.* 25, 26, 1 *Thes. cap.* iv, *ver.* 14. On the Top of the Tomb three Coats of Arms are engrav'd, in the Middle is a Woman's Coat of Arms, with a black Table of Marble underneath ; and at the Foot of this Monument lies a Marble with this Inscription.

> Seventy two Years of Goodness lies inhum'd
> Under this Stone her Bones may be consum'd
> By Time, but Memory
> Shall with her Soul live to Eternity,
> To rich and poor, her Children and her Friends,
> Her Life was dedicated, she had no End
> But Love and Charity, and her good Mind
> God grant to us which here are left behind.

A little Space below follows these Words.

To the Memory of the vertuous Lady *Katherine Rotheram,* late Wife to Sir *John Rotheram* ; first espoused to Sir *Robert Hampson,* Kt. and Alderman of **London,** by whom she left two Sons and two Daughters ; she departed this Life the 22d of *Feb. Anno Dom.* 1625, *Ætatis sui* 72.

On the same Side of the Chancel, a very fair and large Monument is erected of Marble, with four large Pillars and a Roof of Marble double hatcht, with a Coat of Arms of the *Morisius,* and his Lady impaled ; and a Table within the Arch which shews this Inscription.

Splendidissimo et Clarissimo Viro Domino Carolo Morysono, *celeberimi Ordinis* Balnearii *Equiti Aurato, et Baronetto, eximiam ejus erga Deum Pietatem, erga Homines virtutem, Generis Splendores Ingenii acumen, egregiam in Publicis Provinciæ in quâ florebat negotiis administrandis prudentiam, et dexteritatem, Corporis, venustatem, Morum Suavitatem, et Elegantiam, Humanitatem, et Beneficentiam, bonis omnibus charissimo, et omni Laude cumulando : Florente adhuc ætate postquam viginti et alterum annos, cum amantissimâ Conjugæ concordissimè, et conjunctissimé sine Querelâ, seu Nebulâ ullâ, (utroque eorum mutuo amore in Vicem, ita contendentæ, ut dubium reliquerent uter in amore superior fuerit) vixisset ; immaturâ morte præcepto, dulcissimo et desiderantissimo Conjugi, et Baptistæ et Hickso Morisonis suavissimis Filiolis, in ipso Blandissimo Pucritiæ flore extinctis* Mariæ *Prænobilis Viri Domini* Baptisti *Vice Comitis* **Cambden** *et Baronis de* **Elmingdon,** *Filiarum altera, uxor dessolatissima, et mæstissima mater, tot Domesticis funeribus contra Votum superstes ; hoc Mortale Monumentum Immortalis Amoris et Pictatis, in spem beatæ reparationis, et ad gratissimam dilectissimi Conjugis et virtutum suarum Memoriam perpetuò colendam et celebrandam, Hic majorum suorum Conditorio cum Luctu et Lachrymis posuit et consecravit.*

A little beneath lies the Portraiture of Sir *Charles Morison* in Armor on one Side, leaning upon his right Shoulder with a Death's Head under his Hand ; and a little beneath him lies the Effigies of his Lady in her Habit, and under a black Table, whereon is written,

Natus est decimo octavo die Aprilis, *Anno Salutis humanæ millessimo quingentessimo octogessimo septimo denatus vicessimo die sextilis Anno Millessimo sexcentessimo vicessimo octavo unicâ tantum Filiâ superstite* Elizabethâ *illustri viro Domino* Arthuro Capel *amplissimi viri Domini* Arthuri Capell, *Equitis Aurati et Primogenito Filio Nepoti enuptâ.*

The Effigies of two Sons of Sir *Charles Morisin* are erected at his Feet and his Daughter standing at his Head.

*In the Middle of the Chappel another Monument is erected with the Effigies
of a Countess in her Robes edged with Ermine, having a Coronet upon her
Head, and a Hart standing by her, with a Collar and a Chain about the Neck
of the Hart, and a Cherry-tree between the Hart and her Feet ; and the Portraiture of two Gentlemen on each Side of her kneeling upon a Cushion, and
this Inscription at the End of the Monument.*

The Monument of the Lady *Bridget* Countess Dowager of Bedford, a Woman of singular Sincerity in Religion, in civil Conversation and Integrity, in Hospitality bountiful and provident, in all her Actions, discreet
and honourable, in great Favour with her Prince, and generally reputed
one of the noblest Matrons of England, for her Wisdom and Judgment.
She was Daughter to *John* Lord *Hussey,* and she was thrice married,
first to Sir *Richard Morryson,* Kt. then to *Edward Manners,* Earl of Rutland, thirdly to *Francis Russel* Earl of Bedford, and she had Issue only
by her first Husband, one Son Sir *Charles Morryson,* Kt. and two Daughters, the one named *Jana Sibilla,* first married to *Edward* Lord *Russel,*
eldest Son to her late Husband the Earl of Bedford, afterwards married
to *Arthur* Lord *Grey :* the other Daughter named *Elizabeth,* was married
to *William Norrys,* Esq. Son and Heir apparent to *Henry* Lord *Norrys,*
and Father to *Francis* the now Lord *Norrys,* at whose Charges this
Monument was here erected, being her sole Executor and Nephew, who
hath married the Lady *Bridget Vere,* Daughter to *Edward* Earl of Oxford, after *Elizabeth* the second Daughter married *Henry Clinton* Earl of
Lincoln.

This noble Countess of Bedford living 75 years in most honourable
Reputation died most quietly answerable to her Life, in perfect Sense
and Memory, the 12th of *January* 1600, in the 43. year of our most
Gracious Soveraign Queen *Elizabeth.*

*Another Monument below it in the middle Isle supported by six Marble
Pillars, on which lies the Effigies of a Baroness in her Robes with a Coronet
at her Feet, and a Lyon issuing out of the Coronet, and at the West End is a
Table of Marble with this Inscription.*

To the Virtue, Honour, and Memory of the Right Honourable Lady Dame
Elizabeth Russel, Daughter and sole Heir of *Henry Long* of Skingay in
the County of Cambridge, Esq. Wife of the Right Honourable Sir *William Russel,* Kt. Lord *Russel* of Thornhaugh late under the Reign of the
most excellent Princess of renowned and most worthy Memory Queen
Elizabeth, Lord Governour of Vlushing, and since Lord Deputy of the
Kingdom of Ireland, and one of the Sons of the Right Noble Lord *Francis* late Earl of Bedford ; this Lady, besides many commendable Gifts
of Nature, wherewith she was liberally indued, for Religion, true Godli-
ness, Chastity, Wisdom, Temperance, virtuous and honourable Conversation, and for many other Respects most worthy to be honoured, and
to be reputed and numbered among the principal Matrons of her time.
Dame *Dorothy Morryson* a most loving and affectionate Mother, surviving,
contrary to the ordinary Course of Nature, and her own Heart's Desire,
her most dear and most dearly loving and beloved Daughter hath for
the last Office, and for an eternal Pledge of her motherly Love and Affection in the Hope of a glorious and joyful Resurrection consecrated this
Monument.

*At the East End of this Monument is a Table of Marble which
has this Inscription on it.*

This noble Lady passing the few and evil Days of her Pilgrimage here in
this Vale of Tears, in the often Meditations of Death, and thereby having
learned to number her Days did apply her Heart to Wisdom, as ap-
peareth by many holy Meditations and religious Observations, which
she, in the Course of hearing and private reading of the Holy Scriptures had conceived, and for her own Use and Comfort, under her own
Hand had committed to Writing, and being now grown weary of the
Vanity and Vexation of this present Life, by the Instinct of God's good
Spirit, whereby she was fully assured of his Love and Promises in Jesus,
desired to be dissolved, and to be with Christ, and she having lived Re-

ligiously, Virtuously, and honourably forty three Years, and of them seven and twenty in holy and unspotted Wedlock, having Issue only Sir *Francis Russell*, Kt. in the Invocation of God's holy Name, quietly and sweetly slept in the Lord the twelfth Day of *June*, 164—.

On the South Side of this Chappel stands a Monument with the Arms of the *Morrysins*, and two Angels on either Side with two Trumpets in their Hands, and a double Arch underneath in which were five Cherubims with this Inscription.

Non humili serpit alata virtus.

And the outsides of these Arches are supported by two Marble Pillars, and between the Pillars are two Tables of black Marble, and this Inscription is engraved in the first Table.

Virtuti Honori et æternæ Memoriæ

Clarissimi et Ornatissimi viri Domini Caroli Morisoni Equitis Aurati, istius Ecclesiæ Patroni hereditarii; et hujus Sacelli Fundatoris; Patris optimo et longé charissimi, Carolus Morisonns Eques Auratus et Baronellus, pietissimus Filius hanc aram sepulchralem (supremum Amoris et Pietatis Officium parenti bene merenti exolvendo) in spem certissimorum gloriosæ et beatæ Resurrectionis pienter et officiose consecravit.

In the other Table is this Subscription.

Qui sumptâ in Uxorem Dorothea, Nicholai Clark, Armigeri, Filiâ, liberos ex eâ duos suscepit adhuc superstites; eundem Carolum Filium unicum; et Filiam itidem unicam Dominam Brigittam, Nobilissimo viro Roberto Comiti Sussexiæ elocatum.
Obiit pridie calendos Aprilis Anno a partu deipara Millessimo quingentessimo nonagessimo nono Ætatis suæ quinquagessimo primo.

Underneath these two Tables his Portraiture lies drawn in Armour leaning upon his left Elbow, with his Hand upon the Hilt of his Sword; and under that are two small Tables in Marble with this Inscription upon the first Table.

Patrem habuit amplissimum virum, Dominum Richardum Morisonum, Equitem Auratum, omni nobiliori literaturâ instructissimum, et multis apud Cæsarem aliosque orbis Christiani Principes legationibus magnâ cum laude defunctum.

In the other Table is this Inscription.

Matrem, illustrem heroniam, Dominam Brigidiam, Johannis Baronis Hussey Filiam, Rutlandiæ, et deinde Bedfordiæ dotali Jure Commitissam.

At the End of this Monument stands the Portraiture of Sir *Charles Moryson* in Armour, who was his Son, kneeling on his Knee with a Canopy over his Head, and at the West End stands the Effigies of his Daughter *Bridget* Countess of Sussex, with a Canopy over her Head.

In the West End of the Chapple lies a Stone with the Portraiture of three Men cut out in Brass in their Cloaks, with this Inscription underneath.

Here lieth buried the Bodies of *Henry Dixon George Miller*, and *Anthony Cooper*, who were late Servants to Sir *Charles Morryson*, Kt. and after retained in Service with *Dorothy* Lady *Morryson* his Wife, and Sir *Charles Morryson*, Kt. and Bart. their Son, by the space of forty Years, in Memory of them the said *Dorothy* Lady *Morryson* hath vouchsafed this Stone and Inscription over their Heads; *Henry Dixon* deceased the 25. *June*, 1610, *George Miller* deceased the 5th of *April*, 1613. *Anthony Cooper*........

In the Chancel.

Here lieth in Hope of a joyful Resurrection, the Body of *Henry Baldwin* of Rich Heath in this Parish Son of *Henry Baldwin* a young Man of especial Meekness and Plainness of Heart, who gave his Soul to God, in the Flower of his Youth, viz. in *Anno* 1601, *January* the last; He marryed

Alice Daughter of *Henry Martin* of **Ibor**, and had by her three Children, *Henry, John,* and *Alice, John* an Infant died, the other lives to God's good will and pleasure.

> Behold a Pattern plain of Nature's frail Estate
> When neither Youth, nor Strength, nor Wealth,
> One jot or moment of a time can ought prolong his Date.

Here lieth the Body of *Henry Ewre,* Gent. the only Son of *Henry Ewre* of the **Lea** of this Parish, Esq; who departed this Life the 31. of *January anno Domini* 1653.

Here lieth interred the Body of *Henry Ewre* eldest Son of *Henry Ewre* Esq; of this Parish, who was born the 21. of *June* 1643. and departed this Life the 22. of *December* 1664.

Here lieth interred the Body of *Humphry Ewre* second Son of *Henry Ewre,* Esq; of this Parish, who was born the 24th. day of *August* 1646. and departed this Life the 3d. of *Feb.* 1666.

Here lieth the Body of *Henry Ewre* the Elder, Esq; who departed this Life the 24th. day of *Octob.* 1657. *Ætatis suæ* 77.

Here lieth the Body of *Elizabeth Ewre* the only Daughter of *Henry Ewre* the younger, Esq; who lived to the Age of five years and upwards, and deceased the 28th. day of *August, Anno Dom.* 1647.

Here lieth the Body of *James Ewre* the Son of *Henry Ewre* in the County of **Hertford,** Gent. who died the first of *August, anno Domini* 1650.

A Monument in the Wall hath this Inscription.

In Memory of *Henry* of the **Lea,** Esq; and *Elizabeth* his Wife, and *Henry Ewre* his only Son, who married *Jane* Daughter of *Humphry Rogers,* Esq; and had issue *Elizabeth, Henry, Humphry, James, Thomas* and *David Ewre.*

This Monument was erected by the said Jane, 10 *of* April 1667. *and these following lie here interred, viz.*

> *Elizabeth* the Grandchild died the 28. of *August* 1647.
> *Elizabeth* the Grandmother died the 10. of *April* 1649.
> *James Ewre* died the 1st. of *August* 1650.
> *Henry* the Son died the 31st. of *Jan.* 1653.
> *Henry* the Father died the 24th. of *October* 1657.
> *Henry* the Grandchild died the 21st. of *Decemb.* 1664.
> *Humphry* died the 3d. of *February* 1666.

Here resteth under this Marble the Body of *John Marsh* of **Garston,** Esq; who departed this Life the 9th. of *Sept. an.* 1681, Aged 78 years.

In the little Chapple on the South Side.

Here lyeth John Heydon of the Grove **Esq; who died** ———— 1400.

Here lieth William Heydon of Newstreet in Watford, **Esq; and** Joane **his Mother, who built the South Isle of this Church, and died** anno 1505.

———— William Heydon of Newstreet in Watford, **Esq; and** Elizabeth **his Wife, Daughter** of Robert Aubery of Dalley, **Esq; and** of Christian **his Wife, the which** William **deceased the tenth day** of Aug. an. Dom. 1515. **whose Bodies lie in the Abby Church** at Westminster, **the which** William **with** Johanna **his Mother newly builded or finished this Isle or Chapple** of St. Katharine.

Hic jacet Hugo de Holes **Miles,** quondam **Justiciarius** Banci Regis tempore ———— obiit an. 1415.

Hic jacet Margaretta, quæ fuit **Uxor** Hugonis de ———— obiit 1416. 5. die Martii.

Here lieth buried the Body of *Elizabeth* Wife of *John White,* Esq; who departed this Life the 33. of *Novemb.* 1655. *Ætat.* 18.

Hund. of
Caishoe.

This Stone was laid to continue the Memory of *Nicholas Colborne*, Gent. who lieth hereunder buried, he had to Wife *Elizabeth* the Daughter of *John Finch*, with whom he lived in Wedlock 50 years, 4 months, and 14 days, who never had any Children of their own, yet were the means to bring up and Educate many Children; He lived years 81 and departed this Life the 6th. of *April* 1630. his Dear Wife *Elizabeth* surviving hath laid this Stone and lieth hereunder buried. She departed the 8th. day of *July* 1641.

Here lieth the Body of *Elizabeth* Wife of Mr. *Richard Roberts* of 𝔉𝔢𝔢𝔰𝔡𝔬𝔫 Family in 𝔐𝔦𝔡𝔡𝔩𝔢𝔰𝔢𝔵. sometime Minister of the Parish of 𝔒𝔬𝔲𝔩𝔰𝔡𝔬𝔫 in 𝔖𝔲𝔯𝔯𝔶, the Daughter of Dr. *William Gouge* of 𝔅𝔩𝔞𝔠𝔨 𝔉𝔯𝔶𝔢𝔯𝔰, 𝔏𝔬𝔫𝔡𝔬𝔫, who died the ninth of *May* 1676. in the 52 year of her Age.

Here lieth also Mr. *Richard Roberts* Husband to the said *Elizabeth*, who departed this Life the 3d. of *March an. Dom.* 1676. in the 71 year of his Age.

𝔥𝔢𝔯𝔢 𝔲𝔫𝔡𝔢𝔯 𝔱𝔥𝔦𝔰 𝔖𝔱𝔬𝔫𝔢 𝔩𝔦𝔢𝔱𝔥 𝔟𝔲𝔯𝔦𝔢𝔡 𝔱𝔥𝔢 𝔅𝔬𝔡𝔶 of James Pavyor, 𝔊𝔢𝔯𝔫𝔱. 𝔴𝔥𝔬 𝔡𝔢𝔠𝔢𝔞𝔰𝔢𝔡 𝔱𝔥𝔢 9th. 𝔡𝔞𝔶 𝔬𝔣 February 𝔦𝔫 𝔱𝔥𝔢 𝔶𝔢𝔞𝔯 𝔬𝔣 𝔬𝔲𝔯 𝔏𝔬𝔯𝔡 1515.

𝔥𝔦𝔠 𝔧𝔞𝔠𝔢𝔱 Johannes Attewelle, qui obiit —— —— mensis an. Dom. 14. —— et Alicia uxor ejus, quæ obiit 16 𝔡𝔦𝔢 Septembris an. Dom. 1450. quibus animabus ——

Here lieth the Body of *Thomas Carpender*, Gent. son of *William Carpender* of 𝔒𝔬𝔩𝔣𝔬𝔯𝔡 in the County of 𝔊𝔩𝔬𝔠𝔢𝔰𝔱𝔢𝔯, who took to Wife *Elizabeth* the Daughter of *John Major* of 𝔅𝔩𝔞𝔫𝔡𝔣𝔬𝔯𝔡 in the County of 𝔅𝔬𝔯𝔰𝔢𝔱, Gent. and had issue by her five Sons and three Daughters, whereof *John*, and *Mary* lie buried near this Place, he departed this Life the 10th. of *January* in the year of our Lord 1677. in the 61. year of his Age.

Sub hoc Marmore requiescit corpus Mariæ nuper uxoris Gulielmi Carpender, *armigeri, quæ obiit 13 die* Decembris *an.* Dom. 1683.
Ætatis suæ 27.

Hunc tumulum in perpetuam Charissimæ Conjugis memoriam mœrens Maritus posuit dicavitque.

Hic etiam jacet Anna *uxor* Gulielmi *predicti secunda.*

A Monument erected in the Wall.

M. S.
Hic juxta reconditur Anna,
Uxor Gulielmi Carpender, *armigeri, nuper secunda;*
Fœmina Gratis ac Virtutibus nudique ornata;
Erga Deum Pia;
Homines, justa et benefica, comes et modesta:
Exemplar illustre Seculo præbuit,
Et tandem, multum desiderata et deplorata,
Ex hâc vitâ in Beatorum Regiones transmigravit,
30 *die* Martii Ann. Dom. 1689,
Ætatis 32.
Hoc Monumentum perpetuæ Dilectissimæ
Conjugis Memoriæ mœstissimus
Maritus consecravit.

M. S.
Hic situs est Edmundus Bagshawe, Edmundi *in agro* 𝔅𝔢𝔡𝔣𝔬𝔯𝔡𝔦𝔢𝔫𝔰𝔦 *Generosis, Filius unigenitus, Collegii* S. S. 𝔗𝔯𝔦𝔫𝔦𝔱𝔞𝔱𝔦𝔰 *in Academiâ* 𝔒𝔞𝔫𝔱𝔞-𝔟𝔯𝔦𝔤𝔦𝔞 *Socius, Parochiæ de* 𝔒𝔩𝔬𝔭𝔥𝔦𝔩 *in Dioces.* 𝔏𝔦𝔫𝔠𝔬𝔩𝔫𝔦 *Rector natus* Apr. 29. 1636. *Denatus* Septemb. 1664.
Vir (siquis alius) fœlicis et acerrimi ingenii, morum integerimus, majoris quam pro ætate par erat in omni gena literaturâ profectus: cui cum in tempestivâ sedulitate incumberet, Tabe elanguit quâ ingravescente huc commigravit, ut in Sinum amici efferet animam: exuvias deponi coluit ubi maximum reliquerat Desiderium
Opt. amico P.
J. G.

. Here lieth the Body of *Mary* Daughter of *Samuel Blackwell* of this
Town, Esq; and Wife of *William Paine*, Esq; son of Sir *Robert Paine*
of 𝕭arton 𝕾tacy in the County of 𝕾outhampton, Knight, She died the
27th. day of *July* 1669. after She was delivered of two Sons at a Birth
Ætatis suæ 21 years.

> Two buds with the Flower are cropt whilst all bemoan
> His unkind Fate who has lost three in one
> And in that Losse his Paradise is gone
>
> *Multis illa bonis Flebilis occidit ;*
> *Nulli Flebilior quam mihi,*
> Wilielmo Payne, *mæstissimo Marito.*

Acts of PIETY and CHARITY.

*M*ICHAEL *Heydon*, Esq. granted to Dame *Dorothy Morison*, the
Widow of Sir *Charles Morison* the elder of 𝕮aishobury in the Parish of
𝔚atford, by Deed dated 18th *Oct.* *Anno* 11 *Jac. prim.* a Lease of one
capital Messuage in 𝔚atford called *Watford-place*, with all Barns,
Stables, Rooms, Gardens, Orchards and Appurtenances to the same belonging, for one hundred years, under a yearly Rent; and the Lady
placed *Thomas Valentine*, M.A. Preacher of God's Word, and four poor
Widow Women, or Alms Women in the several Rooms, Parcel of the
said Messuage, to continue, during their Lives and good Behaviour, and
intended that after their Departures thence, other like learned Preachers
and poor Widows should be placed in their Steads during the Lease; afterwards Sir *Charles Morison*, Kt. and Bar. her Son and Executor, for the
Accomplishment of this charitable Act, by Indenture dated the 10th
March, 8 *Carol. primi* assigned over the Lease to twelve of the then chief
Inhabitants of 𝔚atford, to be Trustees for this Charity, and for the Accomplishment of the charitable Intention, and a sufficient Maintenance
for the Preacher and four Alms Women for ever. Sir *Charles Morison*
and Sir *Baptist Hicks*, Kt. and Bar. afterwards Viscount *Cambden* by the
same Indenture granted to the Trustees and their Heirs one Annuity of
fifty Pounds, to be yearly issuing out of 𝕶ing's 𝕷angley 𝕻ark in this
County, to be paid on Lady-day, and Michaelmas Day, yearly, upon
Trust to be employed to the Uses aforesaid, and by the Deed it is appointed, that when such a number of the Trustees are dead or removed
out of the Parish, the Residue shall choose so many other of the Inhabitants of the Parish as shall make up the Number of twelve; and
Sir *Charles Morison* by Indenture dated the 8th of *August*, in 2 *Car.* I.
purchased the Reversion and Inheritance of the capital Messuage of
Richard Bellamy and *William Rolfe*, Esquires, and granted it to Trustees
Inhabitants of the Parish of 𝔚atford, to be used and imployed for this
charitable Purpose for ever.

The Lady *Morison*, or Sir *Charles* her Son. also granted to the several
Trustees a Water Corn Mill and Lands belonging to it in *Essex* now let
at 30*l. per annum*, for the Maintenance of a Preacher for ever, who is
bound to preach a Sermon in 𝔚atford Church on every *Tuesday* in the
Forenoon before the Market Bell rings, from whence this capital Messuage is now call'd the *Lecture House*, and the Preacher the Lecturer,
who is nominated and chosen by the present Trustees, Sir *Charles Gerard*
of 𝕳arrow on the 𝕳ill, Bar. *Silius Titus* of 𝕭ushy, Esq. and *John Conyers*
of the *Middle Temple*, Esq. one of his Majesties Council, learn'd in the
Law, who lately elected *Nicholas Farmborow*, Clerke, the present
Lecturer.

The Family of the *Morisons* have also erected eight Alms-houses for
eight poor Widows in 𝔚atford, made a handsome Yard before and
Gardens behind the Houses, and for their Maintenance given each of
them two Shillings a Week, two hundred of Faggots, Cloath sufficient to
make them a Gown and new Hats every Year, which the said Earl of
Essex, the lineal descendant of that Family, doth constantly pay and
allow.

Dame *Mary Cowper*, first Widow of Sir *Charles Morison* the younger,
afterwards of Sir *John Cowper*, and one of the Daughters and Coheirs of
Baptist late Viscount *Cambden*, by her Deed dated the eighth Year of

Hund. of Caishoe.

King *Charles* I. granted to several Trustees a Rent Charge of twenty Pounds *per Annum* for ever, payable out of her Lands in **Tewksbury** and other Places in **Glocestershire**, to the Churchwardens of **Watford** and **King's Langley** in **Hertfordshire**, on the Feast Day of the Circumcision of our Saviour called New-years-day, in the several Parish Churches of **Watford** and **King's Langley**, to wit, ten Pounds yearly to each Parish; from whence it is called by the Name of the New-years Gift paid by the Earl of **Essex**, and usually distributed yearly on that Day to the poor Inhabitants of each Parish.

Dame *Mary Cowper* by one other Indenture dated in *Novemb.* the same Year, granted to several Trustees a Rent Charge of fifty Pounds *per Annum* issuing out of certain Lands in **Ilmington** and elsewhere in the County of **Warwick**, to be paid half yearly on Michaelmas and Lady-day for ever, to the Vicar of **Watford**.

Dame *Dorothy Morison* also granted to several Trustees, Inhabitants of **Watford** aforesaid, an Annuity of 52*l. per Annum*, to be issuing out of a Farm and Lands in **Watford**, fifty Pounds thereof to be yearly imployed by the Trustees for the putting forth of poor Children of the Parish of **Watford** to be Apprentices, and forty Shillings Residue to be yearly expended by the Trustees at their Meetings to put forth such Children.

Francis Combs, Esq. of **Hemelhempsted** in this County, by his Will dated the 1st of *May*, 1641, gave out of all his Messuages, Lands, and Tenements in **Hemelhempsted** aforesaid, ten Pounds *per* ever to a Free-school for teaching poor Children in **Watford** to cast Accompts, to read English, and to write.

He also gave by his Will for the Benefit of the Poor of **Watford** for ever, two Cottages and three Acres of Land, lying at a Place called **Bricket Wood**, and several other yearly Payments for ever, for a Free-school at **Hemelhempsted**, a weekly Sermon or Lecture in the Church of **Hemelhempsted**, the Abby Church of St. *Albans*, and the Parish Church of **Berkhampsted St. Peters** in this County, and charged all his Lands and Tenements in **Hemelhempsted** with the Payment thereof, and several other Gifts given to charitable Uses by his said Will.

Thomas Baldwin of the Parish of **St. Martin's** in the Fields in the County of **Middlesex**, Esq. a younger Brother of the *Baldwins* of **Kedheath** in the Parish of **Watford**, by his last Will, dated in *September*, 1639, did give his Part of the Springs and Waters near **Hyde-Park** in the County of **Middlesex**, and brought to serve the City of **Westminster** with Water, to the Poor of **Watford** where he was born, to the Poor of **Berkhampsted St. Peter's** where he was a Scholar, and to the Poor of **St. Martin's** where he then dwelt, to be equally divided amongst the Poor of these several Parishes aforesaid, being let altogether at one hundred and twenty Pounds *per Annum*, each Parish received forty Pounds *per Annum* for their Dividend.

ALDENHAM.

MS. Mr. Cox. Norden, p. 9.

OFFA, King of the *Mertians*, gave this Vill to his Monastery, which he dedicated to St. *Alban*, by the Name of **Eldenham**, which signifies an ancient Vill or Seat; and in the time of *William* the Conqueror 'tis recorded, that

Domesd. Lib. fol. 134.

In **Eldenham** *ten. Abbas novam hidas. Terra est sex car. in dominio quatuor hid. et ibi est uno carucata, et altera potest fieri, Prepositus cum octo Vill habentibus tres car. et quarta potest fieri, ibi quinq; cotar. et duo servi, et un molin. de quinq; sol pratum un. car. pastura ad pec. Silva octingent. porc. valet et valuit tres libr. tempore Regis Edwardi octo lib. Hoc Manerium jacuit et jacet in dominio Ecclesiæ Sancti Petri de* **Westmonast.**

Ibid fol. 135.

In **Eldenham** *ten. Goisfridus de Bech sub Abbat un. hid. Terra est un. car. sed deest car. ibi duo cotar. Silva centum porc. valet et valuit duodecim sol. tempore Regis Edwardi quindecim sol. hunc terram ten.* Blache *homo Sancti Albani non potuit vendere.*

The Abbot of St. *Albans* held nine Hides in **Aldenham**. The arable is six Carucates, in Demeasne four Hides; and there is one Carucate, and another may be made; a Reeve, or a Bayliff with eight Villains, having three Carucates, and four may be made; there are five Cottagers and two Servants, and one Mill of five Shillings Rent, Meadow one Carucate, Common of Pasture for the Cattle, Wood to feed eight hundred Hogs; 'tis worth and was worth three Pounds by the Year, in the time of King *Edward* (the Confessor) eight Pounds. This Mannor did lie and doth lie in the Jurisdiction of the Church of St. *Peter* **Westminster**.

Goisfride de Bech held one Hide in **Aldenham** under the Abbot of St. *Albans*. The arable is one Carucate, but the Carucate is wanting; there are two Cottagers, Wood to feed one hundred Hogs; it is worth and was worth twelve Shillings by the Year, in the time of King *Edward* (the Confessor) fifteen Shillings. *Blacke* a Man (under the Protection) of the Church of St. *Alban* held this Land, he could not sell it.

But *Frederick*, the Abbot of the Church of **St. Alban**, in the time of the Conquest, well weighing the great Loss which Travellers sustain'd in their Passage by these Woods from and to **London**, he demised this Mannor to the Abbot of **Westminster** for the Term of twenty Years, reserving every Year one hundred Shillings, with four fat Oxen, which Term being elapsed, the Mannor should return to the Hands of Abbot *Frederick*, notwithstanding upon this Condition, that the Abbot of **Westminster**, should keep those Ways safe, and should answer the Damage there sustained and if Default should be made therein he should forfeit the same; but that Abbot of **Westminster**, being great at Court, and a Favourite to *William* the Conqueror, loading him with Presents at his Coronation at **Westminster**, he was so elevated that he would not perform his Agreement; but desired to have more, especially the Wood which was not far distant from **Aldenham**; and for its Pleasantness was call'd *Bruteite quase Prudeitte*, or Pritty in English; and puft up with Pride, he quarrelled with Abbot *Frederick*, saying that it did belong and ought to be laid to the Mannor; complaining of this to the King, he caused Commotion and Difference, whereupon Abbot *Frederick* was much damnified; and when the twenty years expired, the Abbot of **Westminster** would not restore the Mannor to the Abbot of **St. Albans**, saying that Abbot *Frederick* had wrong'd him by detaining the Wood from him, which never belonged to that Mannor; and by crafty Insinuations, and continual Clamours, wherein he was supported by the King's Favour, notwithstanding all that *Frederick* could possibly do, did hold it in his Possession for divers Years; upon which *Frederick* ceased to contend any longer.

This Mannor coming to the Crown upon the Dissolution, King *H.* VIII. granted it with the Advowson, to *Henry Stepney*, who died leaving Issue,

Ralph Stepney, who held it in the Reign of King *Edw.* VI. of the King *in Capite:* He gave *Gules, a Fess compone, counter-compone Or and Azure, between three Owles*

(margin notes:) Hund. of Caishoe. — Matt. Paris, fol. 46.

*Argent; Crest on a Wreath, a Talbot's Head erazed
Gules, eared Or, collard compone, counter-compone, Gold
and Azure with an Attire of a Buck in his Mouth Or:* He
conveyed this Mannor with the Advowson to

Sir *Edward Cary*, Kt. and his Heirs; he married *Catharine* the Daughter of Sir *Henry Knivet*, Kt. and Widow
of *Henry* Lord *Paget*, by whom he had Issue

Henry afterwards created Viscount *Falkland*, who succeeded, was a most accomplisht Gentleman and complete
Courtier, whom King *James* constituted Deputy of Ireland,
here he discharged his Trust very well, but some rebellious *Irish* complained of hard Usage because he kept them
in Subjection, though with much Lenity; for some beginning to counterfeit his Hand, he used to incorporate the
Year of his Age in a Knot flourished beneath his Name,
concealing the Day of his Birth to himself, and by compa-
ring the Date of the Month with his own Birthday, (unknown to the Forgers) he not only discovered many false
Writings that were passed, but also deterred others from
attempting the like for the future; And when he return'd to
England, he lived here honourably until by a sad Casualty
he broke his Leg on a Stand in Theobalds Park, of which
Wound he died seiz'd of this Mannor, *Anno* 1633, 9 *Car.*
I. leaving Issue by *Elizabeth* his Wife, Daughter and
Heir to Sir *Lawrence Tanfield*, Kt. Lord Chief Baron of
the *Exchequer.*

Lucius his Son and Heir, who married *Lettice*, the
Daughter and Heir of *Richard Moryson* of Tooly Park in
the County of Leicester; and being a Person eminently
learned, and of exquisite Parts, King *Charles* I. made him
one of his principal Secretaries of State; afterwards out of
his great Zeal for his Majesty's Service in the rebellious
times, he sold this Mannor in the Year 1641, to

Sir *Job Herby*, Knight, one of the Commissioners under
that King in his *Custom-house*, and by Patent dated 17th
of *July*, *Anno* 12 *Car.* II. was created Baronet for the
good Services which he had done in the late time of Rebellion, and he died seized hereof, leaving

Sir *Erasmus Herbey* his Son and Heir, but for the Satisfaction of the Debts which his Father had contracted upon
the Account of King *Charles* I. in the time of that unhappy
Rebellion, was compelled to sell it to

Densil Lord *Hollis*, who was sent into France on the 7th
of *July*, 1663, as Ambassador extraordinary, where he
continually kept a noble Table furnished with Dishes of
Meat after the English Fashion for the Honour of his
Country, and in Contempt of the French Mode; and he
returned thence the 24th Day of *May*, *Anno* 1666. After
that he was sent to Breda as Plenipotentiary to the Treaty

Hund. of
Caishoe.

there with the Ambassadors of France, Denmark, and the States of the United Probinces: He married *Dorothy* the sole Daughter and Heir to Sir *Francis Ashley* of Dorchester in the County of Dorset, Knight, Serjeant at Law to King *Charles* I. by whom he had Issue four Sons, Sir *Francis Holles* of Winterburn St. Martin in the County of Dorset, Baronet, 2 *Denzil*, 3 *John*, 4 *Denzil*, which three last died in their Infancies; and after the Decease of this *Dorothy* his Wife, he married *Jane* the Daughter and Coheir of Sir *John Sherley* of Isbilt in the County of Sussex, Knight, Widow of Sir *Walter Covert*, Knight; and after her Decease he married *Hester* the second Daughter and Coheir of *Gideon de Low*, Lord of the Mannor of Columbiers in Normandy, Widow of *James Richer*, Lord of the Mannor of Chambernon in the same Province: but neither of these had any Issue: He died seiz'd hereof leaving

Sir *Francis*, who was his Heir, held it a while, then died leaving

Denzil his only surviving Son and Heir, who dying without Issue, this Mannor came to

John Hollis, (whose Ancestor was created Baron Houghton of Houghton, by Patent dated on the 9th of *July*, 1616, 14 *Jac*. I. Earl of Clare the 2nd of *Nov*. 1624, 22 *Jac*. I. advanc'd to be Marquiss of Clare and Duke of Newcastle upon Tine 14 *May* 1694, 6 *W. & M.* and installed Knight of the most honourable Order of the Garter, *Anno* 1698. He gives *Ermin, two Piles, (their Points meeting in Base) Sable*. He is Lord Lieutenant and *Custos Rotulorum* for the County of Nottingham, as also for the Town and County of Nottingham, and High Steward for the Borough of Retford in the County of Nottingham.

Dale's Exact
Catal. of Nob.
p. 28.

A Duke was so termed from the French Word *Duc à Ducendo*, from leading an Army, therefore the *Romans* called them *Duces*; *Otho* and *Charles* the Great about the Year 970, made this Name Duke a Title of Honour, and to oblige the Politick and Martial Men the more firmly to him, endowed them with Regalities and Royalties, which were either Dignities, as Dukes, Marquisses, Earls, Captaines, Valvasers, Valvasines, or otherwise, Lands in Fee. When the French Kings had chased the *Romans* out of Galia, and found some of the Provinces thereof governed under the Emperors by certain martial Commanders term'd *Duces*, they gave the same Title (a little curtail'd *à la Francoise*) to their own principal Captains, which they plac'd in their Rooms; but those French Dukes were only Officers and Vassals, and their Functions and Fiefs revocable at the Pleasure of the Prince; afterwards they held them for their Lives; and many such Dukes were here in the time of the *Saxons*, but had no Addition of Place, for

Hund. of
Caishoe.
they only assisted their Kings in the leading their Armies,
and with their Advice in their great Councils; which was
the Reason that their Names with the Title of Duke were
only annex'd to divers Charters made in those Councils
where they were present: And it is observable, where
there was a Duke and a Count in one and the same Province and Town, the Title of Duke was conferred on him
who was the more warlike, and commanded the Souldiers,
and the Title of Count or Earl upon him who was the civil
Officer and governed the People.   The Coronets of the
Seld. Tit of
Hon. pt. 2,
cap. 3, p. 496.
ancient Dukes of Bretange, Burgundy, Normandy, Aberg-
ne, Bourborne, and such, were not only Circles of Gold enrich'd with Stones, but also *Fleurie* with Flowers evenly
and highly raised, or *à hautes Fleurons touts de une
hauteur;* which kind of Coronet was imposed at the first
Creation; also when the Dutchy descended, like the Crowns
of Kings, by the greatest Prelate of the Dutchy: But
when *William* the Conqueror came to the Crown he reserved the Power of these Offices in himself, that they might
not grow too great and potent for him; and to please his
Normans, who had obliged him by their Assistance in that
Conquest, he dignified them with the Titles of all these
Offices, (except Duke,) and made them Hereditary to
their Children; but the King and his Successors having
the Name of no other Title than Duke to Normandy,
thought it some Diminution to themselves to adorn any of
their Subjects with the Title of Duke, till the time that
Edward III. created his Son Duke of Cornwall, by putting
a Wreath upon his Head, a Ring upon his Finger, and by
giving him a Silver Verge or Rod, in Imitation of the
Dukes of Normandy, who were created in old time by the
Delivery of a Sword and a Banner to them; but afterwards
these Dukes were created by girding of the Sword of the
Dutchy, and a Circle of Gold garnished with little golden
Roses on the Top.   And the same King created his two
Sons in Parliament, *Lionel* Duke of Clarence, and *John*
Duke of Lancaster, by girding of a Sword, and setting
upon their Heads a furr'd *Chapeau*, or a Cap with a Cir-
clet or Coronet of Gold, Pearl, and a Charter delivered
unto them; but of late Days, when a Duke is created, he
must have his Surcoat and Hood upon him, and shall be lead
between two Dukes, if there be any present, if not, a Marquis or Earl; and the Earl shall carry the Cap of Estate
with the Coronet on it, somewhat on the right Hand, and
another Earl shall carry the golden Rod on the other Side;
and a Marquis shall bear the Sword before the Duke that is
to be created, and an Earl shall bear the Mantle or Robe of
Estate lying on his Arms before the last Earl; and all these
Nobles that do serve must be in their Robes of Estate; and

when they come to the King sitting in State, they are created with these or the like Words in their Charter, *We give and grant the Name, Title, State, Stile, Place, Seat, Preeminence, Honour, Authority, and Dignity of a Duke, to I——— and by the Cincture of a Sword, and Imposition of a Cap, and a Coronet of Gold upon his Head, and also by delivering unto him a Verge of Gold, We do really invest———*

These Dukes are usually styled by the King, *Our Right Trusty and Right Entirely beloved Cousin;* but when of his Majesties Privy Council, they have this Addition, and *Counsellors.*

In Letters, they are stiled, *The High, Puissant, and most Noble Prince;* and the Title of *Grace.*

These Dukes precede all Marquisses, Earls, &c. and they and their Dutchesses may have in all Places, out of the King's or Princess's Presence, a Cloth of Estate hanging down within Half a Yard of the Ground; and a Dutchess may have her Train born up by a Baroness; and all Dukes' eldest Sons, by the Courtesie of England are styled Marquisses, and have Precedency of Earls; and their younger Sons have the Addition of Lord to their Christian Names, and precede all Viscounts: But to proceed.

PENS PLACE

IS a small Mannor scituated upon the Common where *Henry Coghill,* Esq. built a fair House of Brick: He was constituted Sheriff for this County, *Anno* 1632, 8 *Car.* I. Upon his Decease it descended to *Henry,* who was his Son and Heir, and also Sheriff for this County, *Anno* 1673, 25 *Car.* II. and is the present Possessor hereof.

PICKETS or NEWBERRY

IS another small Mannor which *William Briscoe,* one of the Yeomen of the Guard, held in this Vill: Upon his Death it came to *Edward Briscoe,* who was his Son and Heir, and is the present Possessor hereof.

THIS Church was valued in the King's Books *Anno* 26 *Henry* VIII. at 24*l.* per *Annum* and ——— is Patron hereof.

'Tis situated about the Middle of the Vill, upon an Hill in the Diocess of London near Berry Grove, which, I suppose, was the Wood that the Abbots of St. Albans and Westminster contended for, and does extend from thence towards the River: This Church contains three fair Isles, with two Chancels covered with Lead, and a square Tower at the West End, where hang a Ring of six Bells with a Spire upon the Tower, and within the Church and Chancels are several Monuments and Gravestones, which have the Inscriptions following.

M. S.

Domini Edwardi Cary *Militis ex* Catherina *Domina* Paget *filia, nobilis virtuosa et lectissima Fæmina* 15 *die Maij obiit* 1600.

In cujus Memoriam laudabilem et dignissimam Thomas Crompton *Junior, tam optimæ Consortis mortem intempestivam maxime lugens, hoc Monumentum amorissui pignus mæstissimus posuit.*

Another Stone has this Inscription.

Here under this Stone lyeth, in hope of a joyful and glorious Resurrection, the Body of *Edward Brisko* of **Orgar Hall** in this Parish, Gent. Son and Heir of *Edward Brisko*, Gent. descended of the Family of the *Brisko's* of **Brisko** and **Crofton** in the County of **Cumberland**, Esq; which first mentioned *Edward Brisko* having issue by *Helen* his first Wife, *Edward Brisko* his only Son and Heir; who in the invocation of God's holy Name, and full assurance of his Mercy, ended this Life the 16th day of *April An.* 1608.

Edwardus Brisko *patri optimo et carissimo pietatis et observantiæ erga M. P.*

*On the North Side of the Wall next the Middle Chancel
a Monument of Marble is fixt which says,*

To the Pious Memory of *Catharine Cade*, descended from the Ancient Family of the *Throckmortons* of **Corton** in **Warwickshire**, deceased the 25th of *May Anno* 1615.

> Made generous by Birth, she kept that fount,
>   From Times pollution, striving still to rise
> Above her Earth high in the World's account,
>   For outward Grace and inbred Courtesie
> Her Actions, Alms, her Life, Faith, Hope, and Love,
>   A suffering Spirit rendring right for wrong,
> Her Heart a Sphere where all good thoughts did move
>   Whose Influence was dispersed by the Tongue.
> Religion was her Companion, Truth her Slave
>   In surging Seas of World's Adversity
> Malice her Enemy, Flesh and Blood her War,
>   Yet Wisdom made this Discord Harmony.
> Then Marble keep to all posterity
>   Her Lives dear Memory (upon whose Urne)
> And to her Obsequies, (obsequiously)
>   In loves sweet odorous Hearts shall ever burn
> And let each Christian Heart joyn with my Pen
>   To embalm her Virtues in the minds of Men.

William Cade *her most entirely affected Husband in remembrance of her Vertuous Life and Godly Death, erected this Monument.*

> Thou Bed of rest reserve for him a Room
>   Who lives a Man divorct from his dear Wife;
> That as they were one Head, so this one Tomb
>   May hold them both in Death as linkt in Life.
> She's gone before, and after comes her Head
>   To sleep with her among the Blessed Dead.

Another Stone has this Inscription.

Here lieth interred the Body of Mrs. *Faith Coghill*, Wife to *Henry Coghill*, Esq; and Daughter and Coheir of *John Sutton*, Esq; who departed this Life upon the 31st. of *May Anno Dom.* 1670. at 75 Years of Age. She left issue behind her, two Sons, *Henry* and *John*, and one Daughter named *Elizabeth.* By her Son *John*, who married *Deborah Dudley* of **Bilestres**, Esq; she had two Grandchildren *John* and *Lucy*, both which are buried under this Stone.

This Inscription is engraved upon the same Stone.

Henry Coghill, Esq; deceased the 22d. of *August* 1672. aged 83.

On another Stone this Inscription is engraved.

Here lies the Body of the Pious and truly Religious Gentlewoman Mrs. *Lucy Dudly*, Relict of *William Dudly*, Esq; who lived to the 80th. year of her Age, and departed this Life the first of *March Anno Dom.* 1684. She left issue only one Daughter, *Deborah*, the Wife of *John Coghill* of **Bently**, Gent. In the same Grave lies buried three Children of the said *Coghills*, viz. one Daughter and two Sons, who died young.

Inscriptions upon Stones lying in the North Isle.

In Memoriam.

Antonii Yardly, *forma præstantissimi, summi ingenii, optimæ indolis, maximeq; spei* Adolescentuli, *filii* Antonii Yardly, *Generosi primogeniti : qui cum Apoplexiâ tribus plus minus diebus detentus fuisset, diem suum clausit quarto nonas* Maii *An. Dom.* MDCLXX. *et Ætatis suæ fere nono. Saxum hoc (quod et cineres illius teget) parentum curâ ac impensis positum est.*

> Reader a while contemplate on,
> What lies beneath this Marble stone,
> And if thou canst but spare a Tear,
> Thou mayst do well to shed it here,
> Here lies in years a Child, a Man
> In Humor, Wit, Discretion.
> His outward shape was very rare,
> But that within beyond compare;
> This is indeed by Death defac't,
> But that is only higher plac't
> He acted well, away is gone,
> Spectators thought he went too soon.
> His Parents Joy whilst he had breath:
> His Parents Grief since ta'n by Death.
> Till they this Mortal come to see
> Clothed with Immortality.

On another Stone in the same Isle you may read this Inscription.

Here lieth the Body of *John Robinson* the only Son of *John Robinson* of Aldenham Wood, who departed this Life *May* 3d. 1674. and in the four and twentieth year of his Age.

> Death parts the dearest Lovers for a while
> And makes them mourn, who only used to smile;
> But after Death our unmixt loves shall tie,
> Eternal Knots betwixt my dear and I.
> *J. R.*
>
> I *Sarah Smith* whom thou didst love alone
> For thy Dear love have laid this Marble Stone.

Another Inscription.

Here lyeth buried the Body of John Long, Salter Citizen, and Alderman of London, and Dame Margery his Wife: which John died the 6 day of July MVCXXXVI. whose Soul Jesus pardon.

Weav. Fun. Acts, p. 591.

This Man was Sheriff of *London* in the Year 1528, born at Berkhamsted in this County, the Son of *William Long,* Gent. anciently descended from the *Longs* in Wiltshire, and Father to *John Long* of Holms Hall in the County of Derby, Gent. who was Father to *George Long,* Esq. Clerk of the Office of *Pleas* in his Majesty's Court of *Exchequer,* and one of the Justices of the Peace in the County of Middlesex. He lived after he was made free of London (which was in *An.* 11 *Henry* VII.) 43 Years.

Another.

> Augusti, ter quingenti, si dempseris unum
> Et ter, tres, decies, ut erat verbum caro factum
> Crux tur undena; miser is subtraxit Asylum.
> Patronum patriæ; decus orbis, laurpade morum
> Quem decorant Latria. Sapientia, Spesq: Fidesq:
> Scilicet Edmond Brook: Solbetur ut ipse precemur.

Mr. *Weaver* makes this Construction of this intricate Epitaph, that this Man (here so much commended) died the 11th Day of *August,* 1490.

Another.

> Here lyeth John Pen, who in his lusty Age,
> Our Lord list call to hys Mercy and Grace
> Benign and curteys free without yn rage

Ibid.

A a 2

Hund. of
Caishoe.

And Sqwire with the Duc of Clarence he was,
The eyghtenth dep of Jun, doth did him embras,
The yer from Christs incarnatioon
A Thowsand four Hundred sebenty and oon.

Hic jacent Johánnes Dentwel ——— et Christiana uxor. ——— 1388.

Here lyeth William Warner and Joan his Wiif, Which William died ———
1531. and Joan 1588. on whose Souls.

Here under this Marble Ston
Lyeth Lucas Goodyer departed and gon,
It pleased the Lord God in October the tenth day
The being in Childbed deceasyd without yn nay;
And Edmond her liffe Sonne lyeth her by,
On whos Sowlys Jesu habe mercy.
1547.

Weav. p 592. Here lyeth Ralph Stepny, Esq: the first Lord of the Lordship of this Town
of Aldenham, and Patron of this Church, who dyed 3. Decemb. 1544.
on whose Sowl Jesu habe Mercy. Amen.

In the South Wall of this Church, the Proportion of two Women lie cut
in Stone, who (as I have it by Relation) were two Sisters here intombed,
the Founders of this Church, and Coheirs to this Lordship, which at their
Deaths gave the said Lordship to the Abby and Convent of Westminster.

EAGLESTREE, IDLESTREE
now ELSTREE.

Norden, p. 16. OFFA, that great and noble Founder of the Church of St·
Albans, gave among other things to God and St. *Alban*, by
the Name of Eaglestree, Nemus Aquilium, a Grove, where
'tis thought Eagles usually bred in times past; for though
it is now hilly and heathy, yet formerly this Place did greatly
abound with stately Trees, where such Fowls delighted to
resort and harbour: And at the time of the Conquest, it
was a waste Piece of Ground overgrown with Wood, which
is the Reason no mention is made of it in *Domesdei Book*,
and Parcel of the Mannor of Park, which belonged to the
Monastery of St. Albans; Upon the Dissolution of that
Church, it came to the Crown, and thence by the Statute
made at the Parliament held *Anno* 33 *H.*VIII. to
Anthony Denny, Esq. from him it descended to
Sir *Henry Denny*, who was his Son and Heir, and married *Honora*, Daughter to *William* Lord *Grey*, of Wilton,
by whom he had Issue
Edward Denny, Esq. who sold the Mannor of Parkbury,
Anno 5 *Jacob.* I. to
Robert Briscoe of Aldenham; and he granted it with the
View of Franc-pledge and Court Baron to
Sir *Baptist Hicks*, reserving among some other things,
so much of the Court Baron as lies within this Parish to
himself and his Heirs; since which time the Inhabitants of
this Vill paid to Sir *Baptist Hicks*, and the successive Lords
of the Mannor of Park, one Shilling at every Court Leet,

due there for a common Fine, by the ancient Custom of that Mannor. But *Robert Briscoe* enjoyed the Court Baron for this Vill, and hath ever since held Courts there by the Name of the Mannor of 𝕰𝖑𝖘𝖙𝖗𝖊𝖊, after which he conveyed it to his Nephew

Edward Brisco of the Parish of 𝖆𝖑𝖉𝖊𝖓𝖍𝖆𝖒, who granted it to

Edward Brisco his eldest Son, the present Possessor hereof.

THIS Rectory *Anno 26 Henry* VIII. was valued in the King's Books at the Rate of 8*l. per Annum*, of which the Kings and Queens of this Realm have been Patrons from the time of the Dissolution of the Monastery of St. *Albans.*

The RECTORS.

John Boyle	*Abraham Spencer*, sequestred
John Foster	for his Loyalty
John Blake	*Arnold Spencer.*
William Flyer	

This Church is situated near the Street, upon a great Hill in a small Churchyard, in the Deanery of 𝖘𝖙. 𝖆𝖑𝖇𝖆𝖓, in the Diocess of 𝕷𝖔𝖓𝖉𝖔𝖓, and has one Isle divided from the Body with a Wooden Building at the West End thereof, in which hang three small Bells.

In the Wall on the North Side of the Chancel, is a small Monument which has this Inscription.

Summæ Trinitati Sacrum.

Behold and know how Heaven is repossest
Of her sweet Soul whose Corps interr'd doth rest
Near to this place; for silence would be wrong
If that my Muse had not addrest this Song
Of sacred Trophies in her vertuous praise,
Which cannot die but must survive always.
A fruitful peaceful *Olive* was her Name,
So was her Life, her Death, her Faith the same;
Emblem'd by Dove with Olive Leaf in bill,
Which shew'd glad *Noah* God had done his will,
And forc'd the swelling Deluge Flood resort
To Channels low, in bank, in bounds their port;
This *Olive* liv'd much more content with me,
Than did this Dove, good *Noah*, in Ark with thee;
And brought me Olive branch to glad my heart,
As Dove rejoic'd, the ceasing floating part,
And then with Ghost to penetrate the skies
More high than Dove, beyond object of Eyes:
Her Heart, her Mind, her Soul, and Faith most pure
Were linkt in Christ so stedfast and so sure,
As helpt her Soul more high than Dove can flie,
Now therefore *Noah*, thy Dove I must pass by.
Mounting the Heavens by wings of Faith,
Her Souls aspect discharged of sin and pain;
Where hope assures and puts me out of doubt
That this late *Olive* mine is round about,
Beset with Gods favour and mercy seat,
And with his love of all his Joys for meat,
Which power shall adamantine wise restore
Her Corps to sent which clad her Soul before.
Dignified, Glorified, Eternized;
Sanctified at last, as first Baptiz'd. .

Hund. of
Caisfor.

Underneath the same Monument follows.

Obiit 11 Nov. 1603. *Ætatis suæ* 20. *habens superstites sex liberos, Harmanum, Johannem, Thomam, Jocobum, Joannam et Susannam, per Nicolaum Atwood de* Sandristed *in Comitatu* Surr. Gen. *Cui prius nupta fuit.*

Septimumq; Superstitem, Olivum filium unicum per Johannem Buck de Alborham. Gen. qui hanc virtutum energiam Mastissimam, Uxoris suæ præcharissimæ Olivæ, filiæ et heredis Jacobi Harman, fratris Edmundi de Burford Caniton et Watford in Comitatu Oxonii, Arm. Pietatis ergo Memoriæ dicavit.*

Henreux *le corpe qui pour l' ame laboroit ;*
Henreuse *le ame qu' en tel corps demouroit.*

Atwood's Arms, Gules, with a Lion rampant, three Grapes on either Side Or.

A Gravestone in the Middle is thus engraved.

Here lieth the Body of *John Blake* late Minister of Elstre, who was about 55 years of Age, and died the 30th of *September* Anno 1638. who had to Wife *Annis Aylward,* and had issue by her two Daughters, the elder buried in this place, *June* 1621. the younger named *Anne* baptiz'd *March* 14. 1623.

SULLONICA.

Norden, p.23. NEAR this Vill of Elstre, in old time stood a most famous City, which *Antonine* mentions in his Itinerary, and placeth twelve Miles distant from London, and nine from Verolam; some, in Regard only of this Distance have thought it was scituated about Chipping Bernet: Mr. *Cambden* supposes it stood upon Brocklep-hills, but Mr. *Norden* having the Opportunity of making a more curious Inquiry in his Travells there, discovered by some decayed Foundations, and sundry Pieces of Romish Coin that have been found there, and the Distance of the said Places mention'd by *Antonine,* that this City stood among the said Hills near Watling-street extending from this Vill to the neighbouring Hill on the South in Middlesex, where a fair Seat is now erected; and the Inhabitants there have confirmed this Opinion to me.

BERGNET, HIGH BERNET, or CHIPPING BERNET.

IN the time of the *Saxons,* this Place was a great Wood, granted to the Church of St. Albans, by the Name of the Woods of Suthaw, Worham, and Husehege, the former was called Suthaw, to distinguish it from the great Wood term'd Northaw, where the Vill of Northall is now seated; but since divers Kings of this Realm have confirmed the ancient Grant hereof by the Name of Bergnet, from the high Scituation hereof, for the Word Bergnet in the Saxon Language, signifies *Monticulus,* a little Hill; and afterwards it had the Adjunct of Chipping Bernet from the Market, which King *Hen.* II. granted to the Abbots of St. Albans to be kept in this Town, it was famous for Cattle, and held on every *Monday* in the Week.

Mon. Angl. vol. 1, fol 178.

Norden, p. 14. Quo Warr. 6 Ed. 1 Rot. 36, cur. recept. Scac.

Anno 18 *Edw.* I. the Abbot of St. Albans impleaded several Persons for prostrating his Ditch, and burning his Hedges and Fences in the Night at Bernet; *Richard Tykering* one of the Defendants said, that because the Abbot inclosed his Pasture with Hedge and Ditch, so that he and the Tenants there, could not have their Common, as their Ancestors were wont to have, they did lay open the same: The Abbot answered that they ought not to have Common there; but 'twas found by the Jury that the Tenants ought to have Common; and Judgment was given against the said *Richard Tickering* only for that he burnt the Hedge.

Hund. of Caishos.
Plac. Oct.
Trin. anno 18
Ed. I. cur. re-
cept. 8cac.

A bloody Battle was fought on the 5th Day of *April*, being *Easter-day, Anno* 8 *Edward* IV. upon Gladmore Common near this Town, between the two Houses of York and Lancaster, with variable Success for five or six Hours, but at length a thick Mist covering the Face of the Ground, divers Spectators could not discern which Side Fortune favoured, so that some Horsemen galloping to London, reported that King *Edward* was overthrown, whilst others hastning thither, affirmed that the Earl of Warwick was routed, and thus in a few Hours many Men related what they desired; but in the End the Victory fell to King *Edw.* IV. by Reason some of *Warwick's* Men mistook their own Party in the Fog, and destroyed their Friends, which was the Cause of his Death, and made King *Edward* Master of the Field.

Upon the Dissolution of this Monastery, this Mannor came to the Crown, where it remained until 1 *Mary,* when that Queen granted it to *Anthony Butler,* Esq. who held a Court Leet and Court Baron here the same Year; he had Issue, *Charles* and *Anthony.*

Rot. cur.
Man. 1 Mary.

Charles succeeded, had Issue *William* by *Douglas* his Wife, who dying in the Life-time of his Father,

This Mannor came, upon the Decease of *Anthony* the Grandfather, to

William the Grandson, who being within Age at that time, the Guardianship of *William* was granted to *Douglas* his Mother, who held Court for this Mannor *An.* 8 *Jac.* I. but this *William Butler,* Esq. attaining the Age of twenty one, *An.* 10 *Jac.* 1. held a Court there in the same Year in his own Name; but in short time after died, for this Mannor was in the Possession of

Ibid. 8 Jac. I.
Ibid. 10 Jac.I.

Anthony Butler, Gent. *An.* 11 *Jac.* I. who being at that time under Age, the Guardianship of the said *Anthony* was granted to *Robert Tirwhit,* Esq. who, by Reason hereof, held a Court here the same Year.

Ibid. 11 Jac.I.

Not long after this *Anthony Butler* attained to his full Age, and conveyed this Mannor *Anno* 17 *Jac.* I. to

Sir *John Weld,* Kt. who demised it to

Sir *James Stonehouse*, Kt. *John Weld, William Whit-more*, and *George Whitmore*, Esqrs. after the Death of Sir *John Weld*, it came to the Possession of

Humphry Weld, Esq. *Anno* 17 *Car.* I. who soon after died, for

Frances Weld, the Widow of the said *Humphry*, held the same *Anno* 18 *Car.* I. from whom it was conveyed to

William Small and *Thomas Urmstone*, Gent, *Anno* 21 *Car.* I. who by Deed dated *Apr.* 30, 1658, aliened it to

Thomas Munday, Esq. he granted it *An.* 17 *Car.* II. to *John Elsome*, Gent. who conveyed it in the 17th Year of *Charles* II. to

John Latten, Esq. and it was sold *Anno* 3 *Jac.* II. to *Richard Haleys*, Esq. and *Thomas Mariot*, Gent. in Trust for *John Nichols* of **Hendon-place** in the County of **Mid-dlesex**, Esq.

THE PEDIGREE OF JOHN NICOLL, ESQ.

1 H. V. 1412.
John Nicoll and Agnes his Wife.

William Nicoll.　　　John Nicoll of Wavys, 26 H. VI. 1448.

Allan Nicoll of Ridgeway, 16 H. VII. 1501.

Allan Nicoll.

Richard Nicoll, 26 Eliz. 1584.

Thomas Nicoll and Mary his Wife, 41 Eliz. 1602.

William Nicoll and Ann his Wife.

Paul Nicoll, Esq. and Anne his Wife.

John Nicoll, Esq. and Sarah his Wife.

John Nicoll, Esq.

John Nicols, Esq. who sold this Mannor *An.* 1695 to

Sir *Thomas Cooke*, Kt. late Sheriff of **London**, and one of the Aldermen there, and the present Lord hereof.

THE Church is situated in the Middle of the Town, which contains three Allies divided with four Arches on either Side of the Middle Isle, covered with Lead, with a Chancel at the East End hereof, and a small Chappel or Vestry House built by *Thomas Ravenscroft*, Esq. a square Tower is erected at the South End of the Church, wherein hang a Ring of five Bells covered with Lead, and a short Spire erected upon it; but 'tis no more then a Chappel of Ease to **East Bernet**, and hath the same Minister, who finds a Curate to serve the Cure, and is the Patron of both.

A fair Monument of white Marble in the Wall on the South Side of the Chancel railed in with Iron Bars, and supported with three Pillars of Grey Marble on an Altar Tomb, where lies the Portraiture of an old Man in a Gown set with Buttons and Loops, and a Ruff, with his Hands in a Praying posture, a Canopy over it, and this Inscription over him.

Thomæ Ravenscroft, *Armigero illibatæ integritatis Viro Ingenio felice, Magnitudine Anima perquam cœlebri inter suos ; propter constantem Amicitiam caro apud omnes, propter Justitiam colendo ; Cui fortuna plus debuit quam attulit Respublica plus gratiæ quam retulit.* Jacobus *heres et filius verè pius, nè tanti meriti Memoria et Virtutis adeò exemiæ, aut longo mortis silentio, aut Posteritatis ingratitudine contabescerent; propriis sumptibus redivin. hoc Monumentum Æternæ Pietatis et gratitudinis testimonium excitarit, An. Dom.* 1632.

Natus Hatwarden *in Comitat.* Flint *genitus ex antiqua* Ravenscroftorum *prosapiâ. Uxoris, si vultis, duas habuit;* Thomasinam Smith, *et* Brigettam Powel; *ex quarum primâ filios habuit* Jacobum, Thomam, Johannem, *et* Georgium, *Filias,* Elizabetham *et* Thomasinam : *Vixit annos sexaginet.* Septemb. *obiit* 12 *die* Febr. *anno salutis,* 1630.

Under his Portraiture in one Column is writ.

Jacobus *primogenitus Patre superstite uxorum ducit* Mariam, *Filiam* Gulielmi Peck *Armigeri; cujus memori hoc summam fuit* Solamen *et oblectamentum, quod vitam vixit et gratum Patri et ad optatum.*

In the second Column.

Thomas *filius natu secundus, optimæ sæpei summæq; suavitatis puer, annos natus* 5. *immatura morte occubuit.*

In the third Column.

Johannes *filius natu tertius; cujus vitæ studium et mores sicut grata et jucunda fueri Patri; Ita Charissimi Parentis mors et amissimo, filio pientissimo ingentes luctus atq; dolores attullere.*

In the fourth Column.

Georgius *filius natu minimus, bonarum Literarum et vere Virtutis studiosissimus, magnæ spei adolescens; in medio studiorum cursu, florentibus annis, immatura morte abreptus. Vixit annos* 17. *obiit* 27 Maii 1628.

In the fifth Column.

Elizabetha *et Filia et Fæmina, Religione in Deum, Pietate erga Parentes, Charitate in suos, Comitate in omnes insignis; cui conjugi vita brevis, et mors fælicior successit* 31 Maii 1630. *Ætatis suæ* 28.

In the sixth Column.

Thomasina *nupta* Godfrido Copley *de* Skelbrooke Ebor. *Filia Patri Charissima et Superstes. hoc ipso suis usq; charior, quod fæcundior.*

*A Monument in the Wall on the East End in the North Corner
of the Chancel.*

In Memory of *Tomasin Ravenscroft*, the Wife of *Thomas Ravenscroft*,
Esq ; she died the 12th of *December* 1611.

Whom Nature made a lovely modest Maid,
And Marriage made a loving Virtnous Wife,
Her Death hath made a Corps, and here hath laid
A Goddess-Saint in everlasting life.

Blest in her Choice, a Husband true and kind ;
Blest with three Sons, two Daughters left behind :
Blest in her Life, whilst lov'd of each degree ;
Blest now most blest in Souls Felicity.

Then weep not you (her Friends) for her,
For she among the Saints doth Sing
And pray to Jesus Christ, that he
Will you to her in Heaven bring.

Another Gravestone has this Inscription.

*Hic
Juxta Avum suum sepultus jacet*
Georgius Ravenscroft,
Filius secundo Genitus
Jacobi Ravenscroft, *Armigeri,
Obiit* 7. Julii *An. Dom.* 1683.
Ætatis *suæ* 51.

Superstite uxore Dominâ Hellenâ ——— ——— *nec non* Jacobo *filio,* Maria
et Elizabetha *filiabus; reliquis liberis ante Obitum suum morte sublatis.*
R. J. P.

Another Stone below the former has this Inscription.

Here lieth interred the Body of *William Noell* of 𝕶𝖎𝖗𝖐𝖇𝖞 𝕸𝖆𝖑𝖔𝖗𝖞 in the County of 𝕷𝖊𝖎𝖈𝖊𝖘𝖙𝖊𝖗. Esq; He married *Frances* the Eldest Daughter, and one of the Coheirs of *Richard Creshel* late one of the Justices of the Commonpleas, and departed this life the first of *March*, *Anno Dom.* 1645. aged about 55 years.

Another Gravestone below the Rails in the Chancel.

Here lieth the Body of *George Proctor*, Vintner and Citizen of 𝕷𝖔𝖓𝖉𝖔𝖓, he departed this Life, *September* the 8th. 1656. leaving three Sons by *Sarah* his Wife surviving, one of the Daughters of *Henry Owin* of this Town.

Sarah the Relict of *George Proctor* died the Wife of *Walter York, Octob.* 3d. 1661. who had issue by him two Daughters, *Sarah* and *Bridget ;* here she sleepeth expecting a joyful Resurrection.

Another Stone below the Rails in the Chancel.

Here lieth interred the Body of *Isabella,* late Wife of Mr. *Edw. Bellew* Citizen and Vintner of 𝕷𝖔𝖓𝖉𝖔𝖓, who departed this Life *Decemb.* 20th. 1666.

Epitaphum.

Faithful to God, to Strangers kind, to Husband dear,
To her Children sweet, to all, yea to herself, severe.
Fruitful in Progeny, in Life and Death devout,
Poor Soul!
Long tired with lingering pain, at last marched out
Into a purer air, there to remain
Until her Soul and Body shall meet again.

Decessit ex hac vita tanquam ex hospitio non tanquam ex Domo commorandi enim natura diversorium et non habitandi dedit.

Another Marble.

Here lieth the Body of *John Marsh* late of the 𝕸𝖎𝖉𝖉𝖑𝖊-𝕿𝖊𝖒𝖕𝖑𝖊, Gent. Son of *William Marsh* of this Parish, Gent. he died the 10th. day of *August* 1685. *Ætat. suæ* 22.

Here also lieth the Body of *Matthew Marsh* Son of *William Marsh* the younger of this Parish, Gent. He died the eighth day of *Septemb.* *Anno Dom.* 1685 : *Ætat. suæ* 24. weeks.

Nomen idem, Domus una fuit, nunc una duobus.
Hic sunt fœlices terq; quaterq ; duo.

Hic scitus est.

Jacobus Ravenscroft, *Armig. ex antiquâ Familiâ* Ravenscroftorum *de* Bretton, *in Com.* 𝕮𝖊𝖘𝖙𝖗𝖎𝖆 *oriundus. Natus* 𝕷𝖔𝖓𝖉𝖎𝖓𝖎, Thoma Ravenscroft, *Armig. Patre.* Tomasinâ, *uxore ejus, Matre.*

Consortem habuit Mariam, *Filiam*
Gulielmi Peck de 𝕾𝖕𝖎𝖈𝖐𝖜𝖔𝖗𝖙𝖍 *in Comitatu*
𝕹𝖔𝖗𝖋𝖔𝖑𝖈𝖎𝖆 *Armigeri, superstitem;*

Filios, Thomam, Georgium, Jacobum,
Johannem, Robertum, Franciscum,
Edwardum; *Filias* Thomasinam.
Elizabetham, Mariam, Catherinam.
Vixit annos 85.
Obiit X. Decembris 1680.
Cum generis humani et Patriæ suæ
Mutationes Longum vidisset.
In memoriam Patris Charissimi
Posuit Georgius *Filius.*

Two fair Marbles on the Ground have these Inscriptions.
Jacobus Ravenscroft, *Armig.*
Vixit annos 65
Obiit X Decemb. 1680.

Upon the other Stone.

D. O. M.

Et Memoriæ

Johannis Ravenscroft *Filii Thomæ, Armig. cujus Pietati ac Religioni maxime obstricta est Tota hæc* Ravenscroftorum *Familia, Obiit Cælebs* 24 Nov. *Anno Dom.* 1681. *Postquam vixisset annos fere* 75.

R. J. P.

A Monument erected in the Wall, on the North Side of the Chancel.

Here lieth *Eleanor Palmer*, Wife of *Edward Taylor* and after of *John Palmer*, Esq. of 𝕶entish 𝕿own. one of the Daughters of *Edward Chesemar*, who was Cofferer to King *H.* VII. which *Eleanor* did give —— Acres of Meadow Ground in 𝕶entish 𝕿own holden of the Prebend of 𝕻ancras 𝕮antelouns unto the Use of the Poor of this Town and of 𝕶entish 𝕿own for ever; which said *Eleanor* deceased 29 *Feb. Anno Dom.* 1558.

In the Middle Isle facing the North Door a Stone has this Inscription.

𝕺ra pro anima Johannis Beauchamp hujus 𝕺peris 𝕱undatoris.

The CHARITIES.

The Almeshouses.

D. O. M.

Maneat posteris intemperatum
Hoc Zenodochiolum,
Gratitudinis in Deum.
Perenne Monumentum.
Fundavit Jacobus Ravenscroft, *Armiger.*
Et Maria Uxor ejus,
Anno Salutis Humanæ 1672.
Benedictus Benedicat.
Benedictus Benedicatur.

This House is a Rainge of Brick Building scituated in 𝖂ood-street in 𝕳igh 𝕭ernet, with a Court-yard inclosed from the Street with a Brick Wall covered with Free-stone, and contains six poor Women, each furnish'd with a Table, a Bedstead, and a Chair; and this *James Ravenscroft* gave Houses and Lands in 𝖀hereditch, to the Value of almost forty Pound *per Annum*, whereof he allowed ten Pounds to the Repair of the Chappel in 𝕭ernet, forty Shillings to entertain the Governors at a Meeting once in two Years; and appointed nine Governors, whereof the Church-wardens of the Parish of 𝕳igh 𝕭ernet, and the two oldest Aldermen in Years of the Borough of 𝕾t. 𝕬lbans, to be four, and the other five to be elected out of the Gentry of this Country, (none of them living in this Parish) and one of these Governors to be Treasurer, who shall receive the Rents and pay the Charity; and five of the Governors to make a Court to elect the poor Women, and to let the Houses to Tenants.

The Free School.

Queen *Elizabeth* erected a Free School in the same Street, a fair Pile of Building of Brick for the Master and Usher, and endowed it with a House of 7*l. per Annum;* and Alderman *Owen* gave about 8*l. per Annum* towards the Maintenance hereof, to be paid by the Company of Fishmongers in 𝕷ondon; and appointed twenty-four Governors, whereof thirteen make a Court, and they choose the Master and Usher, who are bound to teach nine *gratis*, and the Rest of the Children in the Parish at a Crown by the Quarter.

EAST BERNET, BERGNET

THIS Vill was Part of 𝕮hipping 𝕭ernet, in the time of *William* the Conqueror, for no Mention is made of it in *Domesdei Book*; and it was since distinguish'd from the

Hund. of
Caishoe.

last Vill by the Addition of **East Bernet**, denominated from the Scituation thereof, about a Mile toward the East near the Chace among the Hills, and is now Parcel of the former Mannor, and has always past with it : Therefore I shall only take Notice of two fair Seats erected within this Vill, one by *George Hadley*, Esq. who was constituted Sheriff of this County *Anno* 3d *William* and *Mary*, the other (call'd by the Name of *Prickitts*) by Sir *John Wolf*, who was elected one of the Sheriffs of **London** and **Middlesex**, *An.* 1696, 8 *William* III.

THIS Church is situated in the Middle of this Vill, in the Deanery of **St. Albans**, in the Diocess of **London**, and was rated *Anno* 26 *H.*VIII. at the yearly Value of 22*l.* 2*s.* 7. whereof ———— is Patron.

Rectors of **High Bernet** and **East Bernet**.

Matthias Milward, D. D.	*Robert Taylor*, D. D. the
John Goddwin, D. D.	present Incumbent.
John Goodwin, M.A.	

The Church is ceiled within and covered with Tyle, to which joyns an Erection of Wood at the West End thereof, wherein are three small Bells and a short Spire upon it, and the Chancel was rebuilt *Anno* 1663, by Sir *Robert Bartlet*, and others of the same Parish.

Here lies the Body of *William Green*, Esq. who died quietly and christianly the 6th of *June* in the 68th Year of his Age, lamented by his Widdow and three Daughters, and missed by all who conversed with him, especially by his poor Neighbours.

Here is also interred the Body of Mrs. *Grace Green*, Wife of the above named *William Green*, Esq. she lived beloved, and died bewailed of all that knew her, especially the Poor, and on the 4th Day of *Jan.* 1685, departed this Life in the 87th Year of her Age, and the 41st of her Widowhood.

Another Stone hath this Inscription.

In Memory of

The religious and vertuous Mrs. *Isabel Conyers*, Widow, who after more than 75 Years in this mortal Life, departed to an immortal upon the 14th Day of *March*, 1644.

This is engraved on another Stone.

Here lieth the Body of *Richard Baldwin*, Esq. who died the 12th Day of *July*, 1677. Aged 66 Years.

On this Stone you may read.

Here lieth the Body of *Elizabeth Wickham*, late Wife of *Henry Wickham*, Doctor of Divinity, who died *April* 21. 1659.

Another Stone sheweth this Inscription.

Here lieth the Body of *Jane*, the dearly beloved Wife of *Matthew Thwaites* Gent. who was married unto her said Husband 41. Years and 6. Months Aged 63. Years, and 3. Months, and was buried *Novemb.* 26. 1650.

> A Virtuous Pattern of a pious Mind
> To Heaven is gone, her Body here behind
> Is left intombed to follow her most sure;
> Her Spotless Body of a Soul most pure
> Through Christ in this for ever to endure.

NORTHALL, NORTHAWE.

THIS Vill was waste Ground in the time of the Conquest, for there is no Mention of it in *Domesdei Book*, and I find in ancient Authors, that this Place was a Wood which belonged to the Monastery of St. *Alban*, and *Paul*, Abbot of that Monastery in the time of *William* the Conqueror, granted it to *Peter de Valoines* the elder, and his Son *Roger*, for so long time as the said Abbot should live, upon Condition that when the Abbot should die, it should return again to the said Monastery, for if it should continue to the Son, the Grandson and the great Grandson in Succession, it would be thought they had the Right of Inheritance, and by the Custome of the Realm, might hold the same for ever.

Matt. Paris *de Vitis. Abbat.* fol. 82, 83. *Mon. Angl.* vol. 1, fol. 178

But when this Abbot died, which was the third of the Ides of *November, An. Christi,* 1093, 5 *W.* II. the Church of St. Alban was vacant for four Years following, and this *Peter* unwilling to part with so fair an Estate, took that Opportunity to hold the Possession ; and afterwards to gain the Consent of *Richard* the succeeding Abbot, that he might still hold the said Wood ; he and *Albreda* his Wife, Sister to *Eudo Dapifer* (who was Steward to King) *H.* I. for the Health of the Soul of King *William* the Conqueror, and *Maud* his Queen, and for the good Estate of King *Hen.* I. founded the Priory of Binham in Norfolke, for Monks of the Order of St. *Benedict*, and made it a Cell to this Abby, amply endowing it with Lands and Revenues.

Ibid. fol. 343. *Bar. of Engl.* vol. 1, fol 441.

Upon the Death of this *Peter, Roger,* who was his Son and Heir, detained the Possession hereof, and married *Gundred de Warren*, by whom he had Issue *Peter* and *Robert de Valoines.*

Matt. Paris *de Vitis Abbat.* fol. 82. *Bar. of Engl.* vol. 1, fol. 441.

Which *Peter* possest this Wood many Years, till at length falling sick, kept his Bed and began to languish, *Robert* then Abbot of St. Albans, hearing the same, made no Delay, but sent two Monks to admonish him earnestly before he died, that he would restore the Wood of Northawe to the Monastery again, according to the Agreement, but when they came, they were not suffer'd to see him, which things being imparted to him, he confest, that he and his Ancestors did not hold the Wood by Right of Inheritance, but by the meer good Will of the Convent of St. Albans, however the Day following at Night, he died before he had delivered the Wood to their Pleasure.

Matt. Paris, fol. 83.

When *Robert* the Abbot heard of his Death, he sent Officers who took Possession of this Wood, whereupon *Robert de Valoines*, Brother and Heir to the said *Peter,* (for he had not any Children) did grieve very much that he was depriv'd

Ibid.

Hund. of
Caishoe. of so much Land, and often requested the said Abbot by some of the chiefest of the Nobility, that he would give him Possession of the Wood, which the other in no Wise would grant; whereupon *Robert de Valoines, An.* 1162, 8 *H.* II. repaired to the King, who was then in **France**, and did earnestly move him that he would command the Abbot to grant him the Wood; the King wearied with his Importunities, and busied then at the Siege of the City of **Tholouse**, by the Advice of his Nobles, did grant his Desires, and by Letters sent into **England**, by the same *Robert*, commanded the Abbot to give him the Wood, which Letters were immediately delivered to the Abbot, who caused them to be publicly read in the Audience of him and his Monks; this done, *Robert de Valoines* demanded Restitution of the Wood according to the King's Command, inasmuch as he ought to hold the same by Right of Inheritance of the Church of **St. Alban**, but the Abbot in no wise inclining to answer his Demand, said that he ought not at any Hand to have brought those Letters to any of them, when he knew well, that none of his Predecessors held any Lands of them by Right of Inheritance, whereupon *Robert de Valoines* departing in an Anger applied himself to *Robert* Earl of **Leicester**, then Cheif Justice of **England**, and delivered the Letters to him in which this Clause was contained, *Et nisi feceritis* Robertus *Comes Legriæ faciat: Ne oporteat eum inde amplius vexari, pro penuria Recti;* From whom he easily obtained a Summons directed to the Sheriff of **Hertford**, by which he should summon *Robert* the Abbot, that he being instructed of the said Wood should shew his Right, and should give him a full Answer, but unwilling to stand to the Judgment of the Earl, came not tho' he was summon'd, but appointed *Hugh*, a wise and discreet Monk, to appear there on his Behalf.

The said Earl not bearing with the Absence of the Abbot, caused him to be summoned again, and he himself not appearing, the Earl did condemn him, and in the King's-Court did adjudge the aforesaid Wood to *Robert de Valoines*, and on the King's Behalf commanded the Sheriff of the Province of **Hertford**, that he should put him into Possession, who obeyed the Writ, and did execute the same.

Robert de Valoines having obtained the Possession during the short time he enjoyed it (as one who unjustly possest it) often wasted the same, causing it to be cut beyond Measure, which was not lawful for his Ancestors according to the Tenor of their Deeds.

When the Abbot heard these things, he sent Officers to view the Waste, who found that the Damage committed there could not be repaired; then he hastened to Earl *Robert*, and obtained his Letters that he would restrain the injurious Acts of *Robert de Valoines;* but he slighting the Commands of the Earl did twice the Damage he did before, which the Abbot hearing, did address himself to Queen *Eleanor,* then in 𝔈𝔫𝔤𝔩𝔞𝔫𝔡, requesting her Letters to *Robert de Valoines,* to reprove his bold, rash, and unjust Doings, whose Admonitions he obeyed for a time, but soon after committed double Damage again; then the Abbot complained of these Wrongs to the Pope, who sent his Letters to *Theobald* Archbishop of 𝔠𝔞𝔫𝔱𝔢𝔯𝔟𝔲𝔯𝔭, and *Hillary* Bishop of 𝔠𝔥𝔦𝔠𝔥𝔢𝔰𝔱𝔢𝔯, that they cause the said *Robert* within thirty Days to restore the Possession of the Wood to the Abbot, and upon his Contempt to declare Sentence of Excommunication against him.

The Bishop having read the Letters, feared to publish the Excommunication against him, for that the King had prohibited them from excommunicating any of the Nobility in the time of his Absence, in the mean while the Abbot sent one of the Monks, to sollicite the King remaining then near 𝔗𝔥𝔬𝔩𝔬𝔲𝔰𝔢 with his Army, that he would command *Robert* Earl of 𝔩𝔢𝔦𝔠𝔢𝔰𝔱𝔢𝔯, that he would hear Judgment in his Court between himself and *Robert de Valoines* concerning the Wood of 𝔑𝔬𝔯𝔱𝔥𝔞𝔴, according to the Tenor of the Charters by which the Monastery of 𝔖t. 𝔞𝔩𝔟𝔞𝔫 did possess the same, but the King denying his Petition till at length overcome with his importunate Prayers, writ to the said Earl of 𝔩𝔢𝔦𝔠𝔢𝔰𝔱𝔢𝔯, commanding him that he should not by any Means suffer the said *Robert de Valoines* to cut, give, or sell, any of the said Wood before his Return into 𝔈𝔫𝔤𝔩𝔞𝔫𝔡, which Commands the Earl laid upon him, and he tho' unwilling, yet observ'd them; moreover the Abbot taking it very heavily that himself and the Church should be unjustly bereaved of the Wood, called a Council of the Monks and went to the King, return'd from the Siege of 𝔗𝔥𝔬𝔩𝔬𝔲𝔰𝔢, still remaining in 𝔑𝔬𝔯𝔪𝔞𝔫𝔡𝔭, and one hundred Pounds being given, obtained a Writing to Earl *Robert,* wherein he was required, that both Parties being called before him and the Allegations thereupon being heard, he should decide the Cause of the Right of Propriety according to the Tenor of the Deed of the Lord Archbishop of 𝔠𝔞𝔫𝔱𝔢𝔯𝔟𝔲𝔯𝔭, and other Deeds, and give definitive Sentence therein, which things acted so successively, and having the King's License to depart, he returned Home, and delivered the King's Letter to Earl *Robert;* thereupon *Robert de Valoines* was summoned before the said Earl, and forty Days were granted to him to appear; in the meantime the Abbot desired Leave to visit the Monks at the Cell of 𝔗𝔥𝔭𝔫𝔢𝔪𝔲𝔢.

When the Day came that the Abbot and *Robert de Valoines* ought to try the Matter in Difference between them at Law, *Symon* the Prior of the Church of 𝔖t. 𝔞𝔩𝔟𝔞𝔫𝔰, made his Claim at 𝔩𝔬𝔫𝔡𝔬𝔫 according to his Mandate, but

Hund. of *Robert de Valoines* never appeared; the Earl displeased at
Caistor. the Absence of the Abbot admonish'd the Prior that he
should direct a speedy Messenger to his Abbot, that he
should not be absent at the second Summons at **Leicester.**

Robert the Abbot stayed about fifteen Days at **Thynemue,**
and then took a Journey towards **Scotland,** and passing over
the Sea, came to the Abby of **Dumfirmelin,** where having
washt his Hands, he intended to lie down to Sleep, and behold a certain Boy in Hast, and out of Wind, came to him,
and brought him Letters from *Symon* the Prior, which having viewed, he lost no time, but refresht himself and mounting on horseback, commanded his Servants that they should
immediately follow him, whose Command being fulfilled,
he crossing the Sea, came the same Day to his Inn fasting,
but the Day breaking, he hastned his Journey towards **Lei-**
cester so fast as he could, yet he could not be there at the
prefixt Day, by Reason of the Distance of the Place, and
the high Waters of the Rivers; however he came near **Lei-**
cester, where he rested at a certain Street all Night, and
humbly excused himself to the Earl; but notwithstanding,
Symon the Prior came thither by the Command of the Abbot, at the Day appointed, and *Robert de Valoines* would
not appear before the Judge, yet Judgment was deferr'd
the second time notwithstanding the Diligence of the Abbot was declared to all.

Robert de Valoines is summoned the third time by the
Earl to appear at the same Place, and forty Days are given
to him again to be at the Tryal: but on the Day appointed
the Abbot appearing and *Robert de Valoines* absenting himself, the Earl seized the Wood which he had forfeited to
the King for his Contempt, then he caused him the said
Robert to be summoned the fourth time, and granted
him six Weeks for his Appearance, but the Day coming
and the said Abbot making his Claim at **Leicester,** and *Ro-*
bert de Valoines not appearing, nor sending his Answer,
nor Counsel as before, he did adjudge the Wood of **Nor-**
thaw to the Abbot by the Judgment of the Court, and
thereupon put him into Possession by the Bough of a Tree
and did compel *Robert de Valoines* to make Restitution for
the Damage and Injury he had done.

Afterwards King *John* did confirm the Grant of this
Wood, among many other things, to that Monastery, and
the Abbot and Monks did quietly enjoy the same until the
5th Day of *Dec.* 1539, 31 *Hen.* VIII. when that Monastery
was dissolved, and came to the Crown, from whence the
Mannor of **Northaw, Nynne,** and **Cuffely** was granted to

William Cavendish, who held it of the King in the time
of *Edw.* VI. by the yearly Rent of 3*l.* 12*s.* 2*d. ob.* conveyed
it to Sir *Ambrose Dudley,* who in 3 *Edw.* VI. served under
the Command of his Father, General of those Forces sent

to suppress the Rebels in 𝕹𝖔𝖗𝖋𝖔𝖑𝖐. In 1 *Mary* he was
attainted of High Treason, but in 3 & 4 *P.* and *M.* through
the special Favour of that Queen was restored in Blood,
and was shortly after at the Siege of 𝕾. 𝕼𝖚𝖎𝖓𝖙𝖎𝖚𝖘 in 𝕻𝖎𝖈𝖆𝖗𝖉𝖞.
In 1 *Eliz.* obtained a Grant of the Mannor of 𝕶𝖎𝖇𝖜𝖔𝖗𝖙𝖍 *Bar. of Engl. vol.2, fol. 220.*
𝕭𝖊𝖆𝖚𝖈𝖍𝖆𝖒𝖕 in the County of 𝕷𝖊𝖎𝖈𝖊𝖘𝖙𝖊𝖗, to be held by the
Service of Pantler to the Kings and Queens of this Realm
at their Coronations; In 2 *Eliz.* was advanced to the Office *Pat. 2 Eliz.*
of Master of the Ordinance for Life; in 4 *Eliz.* upon *Pat. 4 Eliz.*
Christmas-day, to the Title of Baron 𝕷𝖎𝖘𝖑𝖊, and the next
Day to the Dignity of Earl of 𝖂𝖆𝖗𝖜𝖎𝖈𝖐; 6th of *April* he *Inscript. Tumu.*
had a Grant of the Castle, Mannor, and Borough of 𝖂𝖆𝖗-
𝖜𝖎𝖈𝖐, and divers other Lordships in that County, which his
Father had forfeited to the Crown by his Attainder. He *Ibid.*
was made Captain General of all her Forces in 𝕹𝖔𝖗𝖒𝖆𝖓𝖉𝖞,
and during his Continuance there, was elected Knight of
the most noble Order of the Garter, in 13 *Eliz.* He was
constituted Cheif Butler of 𝕰𝖓𝖌𝖑𝖆𝖓𝖉, and in 15 *Eliz.* was
sworn of her Privy Council; he raised here a stately House
from the Ground, and contrived it in very beautiful Order,
gracing it with delightful Gardens and Walks, and sundry
other Pleasant and necessary Devices.

He married three Wives, first *Anne* Daughter and Co- *Bar. of Engl.*
heir to *William Whorewood,* Esq. Attorny General to *vol.2, fol. 220.*
King *H.* VIII. second *Elizabeth* Daughter to Sir *Gilbert
Tailboys,* Kt. Sister and sole Heir of *George* Lord *Tailboys,* and the third *Anne* Daughter to *Francis* Earl of 𝕭𝖊𝖉𝖋𝖔𝖗𝖉; he died at 𝕭𝖊𝖉𝖋𝖔𝖗𝖉-𝖍𝖔𝖚𝖘𝖊 without Issue, 21 *Feb.* 1589,
32 *Eliz.* and was buried in that beautiful Chapel at 𝖂𝖆𝖗𝖜𝖎𝖈𝖐 adjoining to the Collegiate Church, where his Monument is still to be seen.

But I have heard, shortly after this Mannor came to the
Possession of Lord *Russel* of 𝕿𝖍𝖔𝖗𝖓𝖍𝖆𝖚𝖌𝖍𝖘, and after him
to *Richard Sidley,* Esq. who in *Anno* 1624, 22 *Jac.* I. was
constituted Sheriff of this County.

William, who was his Heir, as I have shewed before in
𝕯𝖎𝖌𝖘𝖜𝖊𝖑𝖑, sold this Mannor to

William Leman, Esq. who in *Anno* 1634, 10 *Car.* I.
was constituted Sheriff of this County, and on the 17th of
November in *Anno* 1645, 21 *Car.* I. was elected a Burgess
to serve for the Burrough of 𝕳𝖊𝖗𝖙𝖋𝖔𝖗𝖉 in Parliament, in the
Place of Sir *Thomas Fanshaw,* Kt. of the Bath; he gave an
hundred Pounds to discharge the Debts of that Burrough,
and upon his Decease this Mannor came to

William, who was his eldest Son and Heir, which *William* was created Baronet by Letters Patents dated the 3d
of *March* 1665, 17 *Car.* II. in *Anno* 1676, 28 *Car.* II.
was constituted Sheriff for this County, in *Anno* 1690, 2
W. & M. was elected one of the Burgesses of Parliament

for the Burrough of 𝔥𝔢𝔯𝔱𝔣𝔬𝔯𝔡, and is the present Lord hereof.

THIS Church is a Donative, and the Lord of this Mannor is Patron hereof.

The VICARS.

—— Tompson	William Pyke
—— Starebrace	John Pinchback.
Robert Gery	

This Church is erected in the Deanery of St. Alban in the Diocess of London, the Body of the Church is celled, and Sir *William Leman* hath added a fair Chappel to it; there is a Tower at the West End of the Church, whereof the lower Part is built with Stone, the upper Part with Wood, wherein is one Bell, and in the Church are some Monuments and Gravestones thus inscribed.

Mrs. *Frauncis Russell* Daughter to Sr. *Frauncis Russell* of Northall, Kt. and *Catharine* his Wife about the age of fifteen months, deceased the 29th. of *August* 1612.

> Virginity, Beauty, Honour, all in One
> If these could turn Marble into pretious Stone.
> Stone thou art pretious who entombed lie
> In one all Honour, Beauty, Virginity.

Here lyeth the Body of *Cony Hayward*, Gent. who dyed the 28th. day of *April* ann. 1671.

> *Cubat hic inhumatus*
> Patritius Cary, *Arm.*
> *Clausit ille diem extremum*
> *Decimo octavo* Junii
> *Ann. Orbis Redempti* 1669.

Another.

Here lyeth the Body of *Helen Robins*, the Wife of *Elisha Robins*, Mercer, Daughter of *William Boulton*, Esq; who departed this life the 31 of *March* 1647. aged 32.

Here lye the Bodies of *Anne* and *Margaret* the Daughters of *Robert Masters*, of this Parish, Gent. *Anne* deceased the 24th. of *July* 1679. *Margaret* deceased the 15th. of *May* 1680.

Here lyeth *George Southaik*, Citizen and Grocer of London, who married *Elizabeth* one of the Daughters of *Philip Gunter* of London, Alderman, he had issue by her five Sons and five Daughters, and deceased the ninth day of *March* 1606. Ætat. suæ 86. his Son *Thomas Southaik* of London, Grocer, caused this Monument at his Charge to be erected.
> He lyeth not here, here is but his Dust,
> His Soul is living with the Just.

Here lyeth the Body of Mrs. *Margaret Tythan*, the Daughter of Mr. *Thomas Tythan* of this Parish, Gent. who died the 25th. of *September* 1686.

Here lyeth the Body of *Peter Southaike* the Son of *Peter Southaike* of London, he died the 15th. day of *January* 1678-9 aged 5 Months.

CHARITIES.

King *James* I. gave 40*l.* per *Annum* to this Town, in lieu of the Ground that he inclosed out of the Common and laid to his Park, whereof 20 Marks is employed to the Use of the Schoolmaster, and the Rest is distributed among the Commoners or Housekeepers there at 5*s.* a piece.

Richard Colter gave 50*l.* to the Poor of this Parish, the Interest thereof to be imployed yearly to their Use, and 10*s.* to the Parson for a Sermon.

Rachel Braggate, Spinster, gave 50*l.* the Interest thereof to be imployed in the same manner as the last is directed.

Babbington Stanely gave 50*l.* the Interest thereof to be yearly imployed to the Use of the Poor.

Sir *William Leman,* Lord of this Mannor, of his own free good will, allows the Rent of the Wells which is 10*l. per Annum* to the Poor of this Parish, and 'tis hoped will settle the same upon them, but that is at his Pleasure.

RIDGE.

'TIS very propable that this Vill was waste Ground at the time of the Conquest, belonging to some of the Neighbouring Vills, for I find no Mention of 𝔯𝔦𝔡𝔤𝔢 in those Days, which doubtless was since denominated from the Ridge of the Hill, whereon the Church is since erected; it belonged to the Monastery of 𝔖t. 𝔄lban, and *John Moot,* the sixth Abbot of that Chrstian Name, began a fair Mansion at 𝔗ittenhanger within this Vill, where he and his Successors might retire for their Ease and Pleasure, and recreate themselves with their Friends and Relations, but died before he could finish the same.

John of 𝔚hethamsted succeeded him, who did not only finish what his Predecessor had begun, but also made a fair Addition to it: He enlarged the Chappel, and caused the Similitude of all the Saints of his own Christian Name of *John* to be painted on the Wall, with his own Picture, which seemingly thus pray'd

Cum fero per Nomen per ferre precor simul omen ;
Tum paribusque pari licet impar luce locari

The Abbots held this Mannor till the fatal Year of their Dissolution, when it came to the Crown, and King *Henry* VIII. granted it to

Sir *Hugh Paulet,* who had Issue *Elizabeth,* who was his Second Daughter, and one of his Coheirs; she married Sir *Thomas Pope,* Kt. both whom levy'd a Fine of the Mannor of 𝔅lackhide *alias* 𝔠orsers, four Messuages, and certain Lands in 𝔠olewood *alias* 𝔠elwood, 𝔠orsers, and 𝔯udge, to the Use of them and his Heirs: They held it of King *Edward* by the yearly Rent of 5*l.* 11*s.* 3*d. ob.* and he was constituted Sheriff of this County and 𝔈ssex, *Anno 6 ejusdem Regis,* and he served again in the same Office for the same Counties in the 5th and 6th Years of *P. & M.* and soon after he died, leaving one Daughter, who was his sole Heir, and married

Thomas Blount, Esq. a second Branch from 𝔅lounts-hall in the County of 𝔖tafford, and I guess was bound by his marriage Agreement to bear the Name of *Pope,* to preserve it to Posterity, for from that time he annext it to his Sirname ; and he was constituted Sheriff for this County *An.* 40 *Eliz.*

De Fin. Mich.
1 Ed. VI.
Rot. 355.

Rot. Pip. 6
Ed. VI.
Rot. Pip. 5 &
6 P. and M.

Rot. Pip. 40.
Elis.

Hund. of Caishoe.

Rot. Pip. 13 *Car.* II.

Henry Pope Blount succeeded, travelled into 𝔗𝔲𝔯𝔨𝔢𝔶, and the Eastern Parts of the World; upon his Return into 𝔈𝔫𝔤𝔩𝔞𝔫𝔡 was knighted, constituted Sheriff for this County, *Anno* 1661, 13 *Car.* II. built here a fair Structure of Brick, made fair Walks and Gardens to it, and died seiz'd hereof.

Thomas Pope Blunt was his eldest Son, resided here, married *Anne* the only Daughter of Sir *Henry Cæsar* of 𝔅𝔢𝔫𝔦𝔫𝔤𝔱𝔬𝔫 𝔓𝔩𝔞𝔠𝔢, in this County, Kt. was created Baronet by Letters Patents, dated the 27th. of *Jan. Anno* 1679, 31 *Car.* II. He served for the Burrough of 𝔖𝔱. 𝔄𝔩𝔟𝔞𝔫𝔰 in two Parliaments, one held 7 *Feb. Anno* 30 *Car.* II. the other held in the 13th of *August, Anno* 31 *Car.* II. He served for this County in three other Parliaments, one held 1 *W. & M.* another in the second Year of the same King and Queen, and the third held *Anno* 7 *W.* III. and he died on the 9th of *June* 1697, leaving Sir *Thomas* his Son and Heir, the present Lord hereof; His Arms are *Barry nebulee of six Or and Sable, within a Bordure, Gobonee Argent and Azure; Crest out of a ducal Coronet, two Hornes issuant Or.*

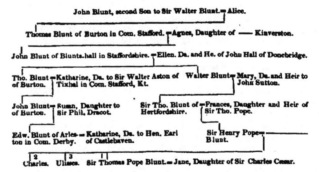

This Sir *Thomas Pope Blunt* being a Baronet, I think necessary to give some Account of this Honour, which was instituted *Anno Dom.* 1611, 9 *Jac.* I. to raise Money to propagate a Plantation in the Province of 𝔘𝔩𝔰𝔱𝔢𝔯 in the Kingdom of 𝔍𝔯𝔢𝔩𝔞𝔫𝔡, or to maintain thirty Soldiers a piece in 𝔍𝔯𝔢𝔩𝔞𝔫𝔡 for three Years, after the Rate of eight Pence Farthing per Day, which was paid in a Sum into the *Exchequer* upon the sealing of their Patent, which is the Reason they bear the Arms of 𝔘𝔩𝔰𝔱𝔢𝔯 in a Cantone, or in an Escochen, *viz, in a Field Argent, a sinister Hand couped at the Wrist Gules:* They are created by Patent under the Broad Seal, to them and the Heirs of their Body lawfully begotten, and sometimes with a Remainder to another, and the Heirs Males of his Body, a Copy of which is at large in the Titles of Heraldry.

By their Patent they have the Addition of Sir to themselves, and the Title of Madam and Lady to their Wives, with Precedency before all Knights, except Knights of the Garter, Privy Counsellors, Master of the Court of *Wards* and *Liveries*, Chancellor and Under-treasurer of the *Exchequer*, Chancellor of the Dutchy, the Chief Justices of the King's Bench, the Master of the Rolles, the Chief Justice of the *Common Pleas*, the Chief Baron of the *Exchequer*, and all other the Judges and Barons of the Degree of the Coif, the younger Sons of Viscounts, and Barons and Banerets made by the King under his Standard display'd in an Army Royal, in open War in the Presence of the King; they have also Place in the Gross, near the King's Standard in his Royal Army; their eldest Sons attaining the Age of one and twenty Years may receive Knighthood, they and all their other Sons and Daughters and their Wives, shall have Place respectively before the eldest Sons and other Sons, Daughters, and Wives, and all others whom their Fathers precede.

THIS Church was valued *Anno* 26 *Hen.* VIII. in the King's Books at the rate of 6*l.* 13*s.* 4*d. per Annum,* whereof ———— ———— is Patron hereof.

In the Church are these Inscriptions.

Here lie the Bodies of *William Blunt* the Father, and Sir *Thomas Pope Blunt,* Knight, his Son, with the Lady *Frances Blunt* his Wife, who had issue four Sons, Sir *Thomas Pope Blunt*, Knight, *Charles, Henry,* and *Charles Blunt* 1633.

We praise God for all his Mercies.

Here lies the Lady *Busby,* Wife of Sir *John Busby* of Addington in the County of Bucks, Daughter to the Lady *Blunt* by her first Husband Sir *William Mainwairing,* who was slain in the defence of Chester for the King; she died the 28th. *Decemb.* 1667. in the Nineteenth year of her Age in Childbed of her second Child, a Daughter which survives to succeed her in those admirable perfections which made her memory dear to all that knew her.

Here lies the Body of *Charles Chamberlain* Citizen and Merchant of London, deceased the 10th of *October* 1663. *Ætatis* 59.

Here I shall conclude the Division of this High Constable with this Parish, and proceed to the next, which contains the Vills, Hamlets, and Wards of St. Stephens, Parkward, Sleep, Smalford, Tittingbanger, Windridge-ward, St. Michaels, Sedburn, and Sandridge.

The second Part of the fourth Division.

ST. STEPHENS PARISH.

THIS Vill borrowed its Name from the Saint to whom the Church is dedicated, and the magnificent *Offa* gave it

Hund. of Caishot. among other things, by other Names, which is the Reason that neither this Vill nor Mannor is mentioned by these new Names in *Domesdei Book*, only known there in general under the Title of *Terra Abbatas Sancti Albani*, and the Abbots held it until the time of their Dissolution when it came to the Crown; then King *H.* VIII. held a Court Leet and Court Baron in the five and thirtieth Year of his Reign, in his own Name, for this Mannor.

But at a Parliament begun at Westminster, 16th. of *Jan.* *Anno* 33 *ejusdem Regis,* it was enacted that *Anthony Denny,* Esq. one of the Gentlemen of the Privy Chamber, should have to him and his Heirs, all the Mannor or Lordship of the King in Parkbury, in the County of Hertford, and all the Lands, Tenements, and Hereditaments, with the Appurtenances in Park, called Boreham, Spirth, and Grimesgate-field, late in the Occupation of *John Coningsby,* the first Crop of a Meadow in Park, called Mapenham-mead, seven Acres of Land called Cleypits next Eiwood, one annual Pension or yearly Rent of 26s. 8d. accustomed to be paid yearly out of the Vicaridge of St. Stephen, all the Tythes of Hey in Sleep, Smalford, Thread, Busses, and Beach, the two Water-mills called the Park-mill and the Moor-mill, with all Water-courses and Profits belonging to them, the Grange, or Farm called the Beach, and the Grange or Messuage called Butterwick, in the Parish of St. Peters; the Views of Franc-pledge, Courts, Profits, of Views of Franc-pledge and Courts, Heriots, Relieves, Escheates, Waifes, Estraies, Wards, Marriages, Liberties, and all other Hereditaments, with their Appurtenances, in the Parishes of St. Stephens, Park, Sleep, Smalford, Thread, Busses, and Beach, Boreham, Folestre, British, and Nasthoe, belonging to the Mannor of Parkbury, also Stordwood, Beach-grove, Walls-grove, Mead-grove, Butterwick-copice, Hailp-grove, and Park-grove, except Cowlep-mill, Stanford-mill, Sopwell-mill; and the Advowsons and Patronages of Churches, Chappels, and Chauntries, to hold of the King, his Heirs, and Successors, in Chief by Knight's Service, to wit by the 20th Part of one whole Knight's Fee, at the yearly Rent of 1l. 10d. Sterling, payable at the Feast of St. *Michael* the Archangel.

Which *Anthony Denny, Anno* 34 *H.* VIII. was one of the Gentlemen of the Privy Chamber, Groom of the Stool, one of the Privy Council, and married *Joan* Daughter of Sir *Philip Champernon* in the County of Devon, by whom he had Issue *Henry, Edward, Arthur, Douglas* married to *John Dive,* Esq. *Mary* to *Thomas Astley,* sworn of the Privy Chamber to Queen *Elizabeth,* and *Honora* to *Thomas Wingfield,* Esq. But this *Anthony* surrender'd his Office of Gentleman of the Privy Chamber, and conveyed this Mannor of Park to *Henry Denny* his Son, who held a Court

Leet and Court Baron the same Year for this Mannor: He married *Elizabeth* Daughter of *John* Lord *Grey* of 𝔓𝔦𝔯𝔤𝔬, and after her Decease, *Honora* Daughter to *William* Lord *Grey* of 𝔚𝔦𝔩𝔱𝔬𝔫, by whom he had Issue two Sons, *Henry* and *Edward*, and four Daughters, *Anne* married to *George Goring* of 𝔥𝔲𝔯𝔰𝔱 𝔓𝔦𝔢𝔯𝔭𝔬𝔦𝔫𝔱 in the County of 𝔖𝔲𝔰𝔰𝔢𝔵, Esq. *Dorothy* to *William Purvy* of——— in the County of 𝔥𝔢𝔯𝔱𝔣𝔬𝔯𝔡, Esq. *Katharine* to Sir *George Fleetwood* in the County of 𝔅𝔲𝔠𝔨𝔰, Kt. and *Elizabeth* who died unmarried: He died about the 17 Year of Queen *Elizabeth*, leaving *Edward* his Heir, who was very young at that time, with *Arthur* Lord *Grey* of 𝔚𝔦𝔩𝔱𝔬𝔫, Knight of the Garter, and *Francis Walsingham*, Principal Secretary of State, and one of the Privy Council, Executors of his last Will and Testament, who by Virtue thereof held a Court Leet and Baron in their Names on the 10th of *May*, in the same Year; and I find that from that time all the Courts for this Mannor were held in their Names until the 30th Year of the Queen, who held a Court here in her Name in that Year, but I suppose he attained to the Age of 21 Years in the Year 1589, 31 *Eliz.* for then the Queen conferred the Honour of Knighthood upon him, and in the last Year of her Reign, he was constituted Sheriff for this County, and attended King *James* with 140 Men, suitably apparell'd and well mounted, and presented his Majesty with a gallant Horse, and rich Saddle and Furniture, when he came from 𝔖𝔠𝔬𝔱𝔩𝔞𝔫𝔡 thro' this County to 𝔏𝔬𝔫𝔡𝔬𝔫; but before the Year of his Shrievalty expired, he was summoned by Writ to Parliament by the Title of Lord *Denny* of 𝔚𝔞𝔩𝔱𝔥𝔞𝔪 𝔥𝔬𝔩𝔶 ℭ𝔯𝔬𝔰𝔰; and afterwards by Letters Patents dated the 24th of *October*, 2 *Car.* I. was advanced to the Dignity of an Earl, by the Title of Earl of 𝔑𝔬𝔯𝔴𝔦𝔠𝔥: He married *Mary* Daughter to *Thomas* Earl of 𝔈𝔵𝔢𝔱𝔢𝔯, by *Dorothy* his Wife, Daughter and Coheir to *John Nevel*, Lord 𝔏𝔞𝔱𝔦𝔪𝔢𝔯, by whom he had Issue *Honora*, who was his Daughter and Heir: but this *Edward* Lord *Denny*, 5 *Jacob.* I. levied a Fine of this Mannor and conveyed it to

Robert Briscoe, Esq. who sold it about the 14th Day of *August*, 1607. to

Sir *Baptist Hicks*, Kt. and *William Topperly*, and the Heirs of Sir *Baptist Hicks*, who being a wealthy Mercer in 𝔏𝔬𝔫𝔡𝔬𝔫, and a Justice of the Peace for the County of 𝔐𝔦𝔡𝔡𝔩𝔢𝔰𝔢𝔵, built a fair House in the Street called 𝔖𝔞𝔦𝔫𝔱 𝔍𝔬𝔥𝔫𝔰 𝔖𝔱𝔯𝔢𝔢𝔱 in the Suburbs of 𝔏𝔬𝔫𝔡𝔬𝔫, in the Year 1612, 10 *Jac.* I. Part thereof for a Court, where the Justices of the Peace for that County might hold their Sessions of the Peace, and the other Part for a Prison or House of Correction, from whence it was called *Hick's Hall*; and he founded an Hospital for six poor Men and six poor Women at 𝔠𝔞𝔪𝔟-

ten in the County of **Glocester**, in which every of them have
two Rooms and a little Garden with two Shillings weekly
for their Maintenance; he was created a Baronet by Letters Patents dated the first of *July*, 1620, 18 *Jac.* I. and
advanced to the Honour of a Baron of this Realm by the
Title of Lord *Hicks* of **Ilmington** in the County of **War-**
wick, also of Viscount *Cambden* of **Cambden** in the County
of **Glocester**, with Remainder for Default of Issue Male of
his Body to *Edward* Lord *Noel*, and the Heirs Males of his
Body: He married *Elizabeth* Daughter to *Richard May*
of **London**, Sister to Sir *Humphry May*, Vice Chamberlain
to the King, by whom he had Issue three Sons, *Arthur*,
Arthur, and *Baptist*, all whom died young, and two Daughters, *Julian* married to *Edward* Lord *Noell*, and *Mary* to
Sir *Charles Morison* of **Caishoburp** in this County, Kt. and
after his Decease to Sir *John Cowper* of **Winbourne St.**
Giles in the County of **Dorset**, Bart. and upon the Marriage of his Daughter *Mary* to Sir *Charles Morison*, he
conveyed this Mannor to

   Sir *Charles Morison* and *Mary* his Wife, for the Term of
their natural Lives and the Life of the longer Liver of them,
the Remainder to the Heirs Males of the Body of Sir
Charles begotten on the Body of *Mary*, the Remainder to
the right Heirs of Sir *Charles* for ever, of whom I have
treated in **Caishoburp**; he died *Anno 4 Car.* I. leaving

   Elizabeth his sole Daughter and Heir, who married *Ar-*
thur Lord *Capel* of **Hadham**, of whom I have discoursed
in that Parish, from whom this Mannor is come by lineal
Descent to *Algernon* Earl of **Essex**, the present Lord hereof.

Customs of this Mannor.

ALL Surrenders of Copihold Estates holden of this Mannor, must be taken by the Lord or the Steward of this Court,
unless the Copiholder making such Surrender lye in *ex-*
tremis, then two Tenants sworn to take such Surrenders in
extremis may take it, but if such Copihold Tenant that
made such Surrender shall recover and go abroad, such Surrender shall be void.

   The Wife of a Copihold Tenant shall be endowed of the
Thirds in his customary Estate.

   The Husband of a Copiholder shall be Tenant by the
Courtesie.

   Copiholders may demise their customary Lands without
License for three Years, but no longer.

   Copihold Tenants may fell Timber without License.

   If a Copiholder die seized of any customary Lands leaving no Issue male, only Daughters, the eldest Daughter only shall inherit, and in Case of no Daughters, but two or
three Sisters, the eldest Sister shall be sole Heir by the Custom; the like Customs are in the Mannor of **Caishoburp**.

ABSA now APESBURY.

IN the time of *William* the Conqueror, I find that the Abbot of St. Albans was possest of this Mannor, for 'tis recorded in *Domesdei Book*, that

Abbas St. Albani tenuit Absa pro quatuor hidis se defendebat, tempore Regis Edwardi, et modo pro dim. hidæ. Terra est iv car. In dominio duo hidæ et dimid. et ibi sunt duo car. et duo Vill. cum iv Bord. habent. ii car. ibi ii Servi et i Molend. de x sol. pratum un. car. pastura ad pec. Silva ccc. porc. Val. hoc Manerium xl. sol. quando recepit xx. sol. tempore Regis Edwardi quatuor lib. Hoc Manerium tenuit Godric homo Stig. Arch. non potuit mittere extra Ecclesiam St. Albani.

The Abbot of St. *Albans* held Absa, it was rated for four Hides in the time of King *Edward* (the Confessor,) and now for half an Hide. The arable is four Carucates, in Demeasne two Hides and an half, and there are two Carucates and two Villains, with four Bordars having two Carucates, there are two Servants, and one Mill of ten Shillings Rent, Meadow one Carucate, Common of Pasture for the Cattle, Wood to feed three hundred Hogs in Pannage time. This Mannor is worth forty Shillings, when he received it twenty Shillings, in the time of King *Edward* (the Confessor) four Pounds; *Godric* a Man (under the Protection) of *Stigan* the Archbishop held this Mannor, he could not put it out of the Jurisdiction of St. Alban.

The Abbots and Monks of St. Albans held this Mannor until the time of their Dissolution, and the Inhabitants hereof paid to the Abbots, who were Lords of the Leet for the Mannor of Parke, one Shilling for a common Fine, and when it came to the Crown, King *H.*VIII. granted it by Charter dated 12th of *May, Anno 32 Regni sui* to *Ralph Rowlet* the elder and his Heirs, which *Ralph, Anno* 1542, was constituted Sheriff of this County, and soon after was knighted, and he died seiz'd hereof without Issue, leaving two Sisters, who were his Coheirs, from whom I guess it might come to——— *Marston*, who was Lord hereof. His Arms are ——— *a Fess dancette Ermin between three Fleurs de Liz.* Afterwards it came to the *Briscoes*, and then it descended to *William Brisco* of London Conp, Esq. a Justice of the Peace for this County, and the present Possessor hereof.

THIS Church was erected upon an Hill by *Ulsin* or *Ulsig*, one of the Abbots of St. *Alban* in the Reign of King *Ethelred*, about *Anno Christi* 950, in the Deanery of St. Alban in the Diocess of London, and in *Anno* 26 *Henry* VIII. it was rated in the King's Books at the yearly Value of 15*l.* whereof *Henry Killigrew*, Esq. is the present Patron.

The Church is covered with Tyle and hath a small Tower at the West End thereof, with a short Spire upon it; in the Church are some Gravestones with these Inscriptions.

Hic jacet Willielmus Robins, armiger nuper Clericus Signeti Edwardi quarti nuper Regis Angliæ; et Katharina Uxor ejusdem Willielmi: qui quidem Willielmus obiit 4. die mensis Novembris an. Dom. 1489. quorum animabus———

Clericus Signeti or *Signetti*, is an Officer continually attendant on his Majesty's Principal Secretary, who always hath the Custody of the Privy Signet as well for sealing of his Majesty's private Letters, as also such

Grants as pass his Majesty's Hand by Bill signed; of these there are
four that attend in their Course, and were wont to have their Diet at the
Secretaries Table, whose Office is set forth at large in the Stat. of 27
Hen. VIII. ca. 11.

Another Stone has this.

Here lyeth Robert Turbervile and Dorothy his Wife, which Robert dyed
the 26. of Feb. 1529. and Dorothy the 7. of October 1521.
Sancta Crinitas, unus Deus, miserere nobis.

Here lyeth John Turbervile Vicar of this Church who died —— 1536 ——

Quos tegit hæc Petra, junxit Chorus, et Domus una.
Jam pulbis factus, Willus Davis nomine dictus,
Cum Margaretá Sponsali fœdore juncta:
Cum prece debota, qui transis, sta, præcor, ora.

Hic jacet Johannes Gril, quondam Magister
Sancti Juliani, et Vicarius istius Ecclesiæ,
Qui obiit sexto die Decembris 1449.
Cujus animæ propitietur altissimus.

In the Chancel of St. Stephens.

Here lies interr'd the Body of *Edmund Coles*, late of Park-berry. Gent.
who deceased the 17th. day of *August* 1679. aged 71.
Honestè Vixit,
Neminem læsit,
Suum cuiq; tribuit.
Many of the same Family are buried here.

On the South Wall of the Church.

Memoriæ Sacrum.
Under this Marble lies the Body of *James Rolfe*, Esq; Official of the
Archdeaconry of St. Albans, Commissary of the Archdeaconry of
Huntingdon. and one of the Masters of *Chancery*, who lived 65. years
and died the 27. of *Octob. Anno Domini* 1630.

Epitaphium.

James art thou here? and must this Church of *Stephen*
Inshrine thy body now thy Soul's in Heaven?
Had not thy Monument been better fixt
Nearer that of Abbot *John* the sixth,
By *Albans* Shrine, where thy religious care
Redeem'd those sacred relicks from despair.
No, thou wast wise, and sure thou thought it better
To make each Protomartyr's Church thy debtor
That glories kept by thee from ruins rust
And this may glory that it keeps thy Dust.

Mrs. *Grace Rolfe* in a pious love to the worthy Memory of her deceased
Husband erected this Monument.

In the South Isle.

Here lies the Body of Captain *Simon Gordan* of Bornhill in Hertfordshire,
who died the 18th. day of *October* 1669. aged 68. years, was married
to *Sarah Hoste* 18. years, 3. quarters, by whom he had issue two Sons
and three Daughters.
Of honest birth, of Merchant trade
A man of Worthy fame,
A Captain of St. Christophers,
Simon Gordan by name,
From burning Sun to frozen Sun
His youthful years he spent;
The Wonders of the Lord he saw
To his Souls great content.

Religious was his life to God,
To men his dealings just,
The Poor and Strangers they can tell
That Wealth was not his trust.
His Soul to God he did commend,
His body to the dust,
Where he sings continual Praise
In glory with the just.

Here lieth *James Ellis* Son of *John Ellis*, Esquire, of St. Julians, born the 15 of *March* 1643. and died the 29. of *June* 1668.

PARKEWARD

WAS denominated from the Mannor of Parke, rated severally by itself from any other Place, and is Part of the said Mannor.

SLEEPE and SMALLFORD,

ANOTHER Hamlet, Parcel of the Mannor of Parke, which lie in the Parish of St. Peters in the Town of St. Albans, but is rated severally by itself from any other Part of the Parish, and is chargeable by the High Constable of this Division.

TITTENHANGER

IS a small Hamlet within the Parish of Ridge, but chargeable by itself in all Rates and Taxes from the Rest of that Parish, and laid to this Division.

ST. MICHAELLS

IS one of three Parishes in St. Albans, of which I have treated already, because the Church is situated there, but the Parish extending out of the Town, is chargeable in all publick Taxes to this Division.

WINDRIDGEWARD

COMPREHENDS the Mannor of Windridge, of which I have treated in the Town of St. Albans, because it is Parcel of the Parish of St. Michaels, where the Church is erected, however is ratable distinctly by itself from the Parish, and charged in this Division.

REDBURNE.

EGELWINE the Black, and *Wincelfled* his Wife, by and with the Consent of King *Edward* the Confessor and *Editha* his Wife, gave this Mannor to the Monastery of St. Albans, by the Name of Redburne, so termed from the River near which 'tis seated, and the Road which leads from St. Albans through the River there to Dunstable; for *Red* or *Road* signifies in our old *English* a Passage where People ride or travel, and *Burne* a petty Rivulet;

Matt. Paris *de
Vita Abbatis,*
fol. 45.
Mon. Angl
vol. 1, fol.178.
Dugd. *Warw.*
fol. 219.

Hund. of
Cais̄hoe.

others say, that *Redburne* signifies red Water, yet the Water in the River is no more red, than the Water in the red Sea; and others say, that it was so called *ab arundine*, from a Place overgrown with Reeds.

Camd. Brit.
tit Herts. fol.
341.
Matt. Paris de
Vita Pauli
Abbat. fol. 50.

When *William* the Conqueror had obtained that great Victory in the Battle of 𝕷𝖊𝖜𝖎𝖘, where he slew King *Harold*, he marched with his Army through 𝕶𝖊𝖓𝖙, 𝕾𝖚𝖗𝖗𝖞, and 𝕭𝖊𝖗𝖐=𝖘𝖍𝖎𝖗𝖊 to 𝖂𝖆𝖑𝖑𝖎𝖓𝖌𝖋𝖔𝖗𝖉, where he passed over the 𝕿𝖍𝖆𝖒𝖊𝖘, there rested his Army a while, them came from thence through 𝕺𝖝𝖋𝖔𝖗𝖉𝖘𝖍𝖎𝖗𝖊 and 𝕭𝖚𝖈𝖐𝖎𝖓𝖌𝖍𝖆𝖒𝖘𝖍𝖎𝖗𝖊, to 𝕭𝖊𝖗𝖐𝖍𝖆𝖒𝖘𝖙𝖊𝖉 in this County, where finding many Trees laid across the Way so that he could not pass with his Army, and learning that *Frederick* the Abbot of 𝕾t. 𝕬𝖑𝖇𝖆𝖓𝖘 had done the same, sent for him, and demanded the Reason of it; he boldly answered that he had done nothing, but what the Duty of his Birth and Profession required, and if others of his Rank had performed the like (as they well might and ought) it had not been in his Power to have marcht so far into the Land; but this and his other bold Answers so offended the King, that he took this Town from the Abby, with all the Lands and Revenues belonging to that Monastery which lay between 𝕭𝖊𝖗𝖓𝖊𝖙 and 𝕷𝖔𝖓𝖉𝖔𝖓 𝕾𝖙𝖔𝖓𝖊, and the Abbot to avoid the Danger of his Wrath, went to 𝕰𝖑𝖞, where he desisted not from his Contrivances against the Conqueror, till he ended his Days in great Grief of Mind, but upon the Death of this Abbot, *Paul*, a Monk of 𝕮𝖆𝖓𝖊, succeeded, and he by the Aid and Assistance of *Lanfranc* Archbishop of 𝕮𝖆𝖓𝖙𝖊𝖗𝖇𝖚𝖗𝖞, obtained from the Conqueror the Restoration of this Town, and all other Lands and Revenues back again; and when that great Survey was made, it was recorded that

Domesd. Lib.
fol. 135, n. 10.

In 𝕽𝖊𝖉burne ten. Abbas St. Albani septem hid. et un. virgat. Terra est sexdecem car. in Dominio tres hidæ et un. virgat. et ibi quatuor car. ibi sexdecem Vill habentes duodecim car. ibi unus Servus. et duo Molend. de vigint. sex so'id. pratum un. car. et dimid. pastura ad pec. Silva trecent. porc. in totis valent. valet trigint. lib. quando recepit quindecim lib. tempore Regis Edwardi sexdecim lib. Hoc Manerium jacuit et jacet in Ecclesia St. Albani, Stigan Archiepiscopus tenebat die mortis Regis Edwardi, sed ab Ecclesia separare non poterat.

In 𝕽𝖊𝖉burne ten. Amelger de Abbate tres virgat. et dimid. Terra est duo car. et ibi sunt. cum duobus Vill. et duobus cotar. Silva ducent porc. valet trigint. sol. quando recepit trigint. sol. tempore Regis Edwardi quadragint. sol. Hanc terram tenet et tenuit St. Albanus.

The Abbot of St. *Albans* held seven Hides and one Virgate in 𝕽𝖊𝖉=burne. The arable is sixteen Carucates, in Demeasne three Hides and one Virgate, and there are four Carucates, there are sixteen Villains having twelve Carucates, there is one Servant and two Mills of six and twenty Shillings Rent by the Year, Meadow one Carucate and an half, Common of Pasture for the Cattle, Wood to feed three hundred Hogs; in the whole Value, it is worth thirty Pounds by the year, when he received it fifteen Pounds, in the time of King *Edward* (the Confessor) sixteen Pounds. This Mannor did lye and doth lye in the Jurisdiction of the Church of 𝕾t. 𝕬𝖑𝖇𝖆𝖓. *Stigan* the Archbishop held it on the Day of the death of King *Edward* (the Confessor,) but he could not sever it from the Church.

Hund. of
Caishoe.

Ameiger held three Virgates and an half of the Abbot of St. *Alban* in **Redburne.** The arable is two Carucates, and they are there, with two Villains and two Cottagers, Wood to feed two hundred Hogs; it is worth thirty Shillings by the Year, when he received It twenty Shillings, in the time of King *Edward* (the Confessor) forty Shillings. St. *Alban* held and doth hold this Land.

King *H.* I. confirmed the Grant of this Vill in the first MS. Mr. Cox. Year of his Reign, amongst divers other things, to the Monastery of **St. Albans,** and moreover gave this Church to the clothing of the Monks, and King *John* in the first Year Mon. Angl. vol. 1, fol. 178. of his Reign, confirmed the said Grants to the Monastery again.

But about *Easter* 1 *H.* III. *William Marshall* the elder, *Ranulph* Earl of **Chester,** *William* Earl of **Albemarle,** *William* Earl **Ferrers,** *Robert de Vetereponti, Brienus de Insula, William de Entelope,* alias *Lentelupe, Philip de More, Robert de Gangis, Falcatius de Brent,* and others, having gathered together great Forces to besiege the Castle of **Mount Sorrill** in **Leicestershire,** *Henry de Braybrook* the Governor of that Castle, sent to *Sayer de Quincy,* Earl of **Winchester,** then at **London,** with the Frenchmen to aid him against them, whereupon Earl *Patricius* the Marshal of **France,** *Sayer de Quincy, Robert Fitzwalter,* and others, marching thither towards his Relief, in their Way, spoiled and defaced this Church as they past thro' the Town.

This Place has been very famous, and many People have Weav. Acts and Mon p. 585. Norden, p. 21 resorted hither in Respect of the Bones and Relicts of a certain Clerk, called by some *Amphibalus,* which have been found here, who is reported to have lodged at the House of St. *Alban* in the City of **Verulam,** to avoid the Persecution which then happened to the Christians under the Government of *Dioclesian,* during which time he had the Opportunity to instruct *Alban,* and to convert him to the Christian Faith; He was a Man, saith *Bale,* unmatchable for Learning and good Life, and had great Success in preaching the Gospel throughout all Parts of **Britain.** He fled from **Verulam** with a great Number of his Converts into **Scotland** to escape the Execution of the Edict made by *Dioclesian* against all those who profest the Christian Religion; from thence he went into the Isle of **Anglesy** in **Wales,** where he was made Bishop of that Place, and preacht the Word of God in all Places there, and disputed against the worshiping of Idols and false Gods, but being afterwards apprehended, he was brought to the same Place where *Alban* suffered Martyrdom, was whipt about a Stake to which his Entrails were tied, and so winding his Bowels out of his Body, he was stoned to Death like another *Stephen;* and some of the persecuted Christians stole his Body and buried it privately here, from whence it was removed and enshrin'd by the Relicts of St. *Alban* on the 25th Day of *June,* 1178.

Hund. of
Caisbor.

Nullum unquam tam jucundum tam salutarem diem vidit
Verulamium, saith Harpesfeild, *occurrebat enim Martyr*
Martyri, Magistri Discipulus, Hospes Hospiti, & Cœles-
tis Civis concivi Cælesti.

The Convent of St. Albans was so careful that his Reliques should be devoutly preserved, that *Thomas* then Abbot, made a Decree that a Prior and three Monks should
be appointed for so sacred an Office, for which they allow'd
them a Sallary of *20l. per Annum.* He was a rare Linguist
and a great Divine for those times, he wrote a Book against
the Errors of the Gentiles, and certain Homilies upon the
four Evangelists, with other learned Works mentioned by
Bale.

This Town is seated upon that common and military Highway which is called Watling-street, and hath near it a certain Brook called Wenmer, otherwise Womer, which
never breaketh forth and riseth, but it foretelleth Dearth
and Scarcity of Corn, or else some Extremity of dangerous
times, as the common People observe : since this time this
Mannor has continued in the Possession of the Abbots of
St. Albans, until the Dissolution of that Monastery when
it came to the Crown.

The Mannor of AIGNELL

BORROWED its Name from *John de Aignell,* who was
Lord hereof in the time of King *Edw.* II. but he residing
at Tring, I shall treat of him there, to which I shall refer the
Reader. *John* of Whethamsted, a famous Abbot, purchas'd this Mannor in the Reign of King *Edward* IV. for
the Use of the Church of St. Albans, in whose Possession
it continued until the Dissolution thereof, when it came to
the Crown, from whence it was conveyed to *John Cocks,*
who held it in the time of King *Edw.* VI. by the yearly Rent
of *10s. ob.* from which Family it was conveyed to —— *Be-*
south, in whose Name it continued till it past to *Francis*
King, Gent. by the Marriage of *Mary,* one of the Daughters and Coheirs of *John Besouth,* by whom he had Issue
Francis and *Mary.*

Francis succeeded, and married *Sarah* Daughter of ——
Cotton of Turners-hall, in the Parish of Harding, Gent. by
whom he had Issue *Francis* married to *Anne* Daughter of
William Cotton of Lincolns Inn, Esq. *Thomas* married to
Sarah, Widow of *Charles Day* in the Town of Cambridge,
John, and three Daughters ; and *Francis King* the elder is
the present Possessor hereof.

In the time of King *H.* VI. *John* of Whethamsted, that
famous Abbot of St. Albans, rebuilt this Church and consecrated the Altar there : it is scituated near the Vill in the
Deanery of St. Albans, in the Diocess of London, and *An.*

36 *H.* VIII. was rated in the King's Books at the yearly Value of 16*l.* 5*s.* whereof ——— is Patron hereof.

SANDRUAGE, now SANDRIDGE.

THIS Vill being Part of the Revenue of the Mertian Kings, King *Egfrid* Son of *Offa*, gave it *An.* 796, 1 *Regni sui* to the Church of St. Albans, by the Name of Sandruage, so denominated by the *Saxons*, from the Soil of the Place, and the Service by which the Inhabitants held their Lands, for the Soil is sandy, and *Age* signifies the Service of Bond-tenants, and the Abbot of this Church held it in the time of the Conqueror, when it was recorded that

MS. Mr. Cox.

In Albaneston *Hundred. Abbas Sancti Albani ten:* Sandridge *pro decem hidis se defendebat. Terra est tresdecim car. in Diminio tres hidæ, et ibi sunt duo car. et tertia potest fieri, ibi vigint. sex Vill. habentes decem car. ibi duo cotar. et un. Servus, et un. Molend. de decem sol. pratum duo car. pastura ad pec. Silva trigint. porc. in totis valentiis valet octodecim lib. quando recipit duodecim lib. et consuetud. tempore Regis* Edwardi. *Hoc Manerium jacuit et jacet in Dominio Ecclesiæ* Sancti Albani.

Domsd. Lib. fol. 135.

The Abbot of St. *Albans* held Sandridge in Albaneston Hundred, it was rated for ten Hides. The arable is thirteen Carucates, in Demeasne three Hides, and there are two Carucates, and a third may be made, there are twenty six Villains having ten Carucates, there are two Cottagers, and one Servant, and one Mill of ten Shillings Rent, Meadow two Carucates, Common of Pasture for the Cattle, Wood to feed thirty Hogs; in the whole Value it is worth eighteen Pounds by the Year, when he received it twelve Pounds, the Rent in the time of King *Edward* (the Confessor.) This Mannor did lye and doth lye in the Jurisdiction of the Church of St. Albans.

King *Henry* and King *John*, in their several Reigns, confirmed the Grants of this Mannor to the said Monastery; and upon an Inquisition *Anno* 6 *Edw.* I. it was found that the Predecessors of the Abbots of St. Albans held the Mannors of Raisho, Rickmeresworth, and Sandridge, that they were ancient Demeasne time out of Mind before the Conquest of England, and the Abbots acknowledged the same; these Abbots held this Mannor until the Year of their Dissolution, when it came to the Crown; from whence it was conveyed by Charter dated the 12th of *May, An.* 32 *Hen.* VIII. to

Ralph Rowlet, Esq. Father of Sir *Ralph Rowlet*, Kt. who died seiz'd hereof, leaving two Sisters, who were his Coheirs, *Mary* married to *John Maynard* of St. Albans, Esq. the other to *Ralph Jennings* of Church, in the County of Somerset; and upon the Partition, this Mannor fell to the Wife of *Ralph Jennings*, who had Issue *Thomas* and *John.*

Thomas Jennings succeeded, but dying without Issue, it descended to

John Jennings, who was his Brother and Heir, and married *Anne* Daughter of Sir *William Bronker*, by whom he had Issue *John* and *Thomas* married to *Veere* Daughter to

Hund. of
Caisboe.

Sir *James Palmer*, Knight, and Lord of the Mannor of
Sapes in the County of 𝕸𝖎𝖉𝖉𝖑𝖊𝖘𝖊𝖝, but this Mannor of
𝕾𝖆𝖓𝖉𝖗𝖎𝖉𝖌𝖊 came to

John Jennings, who was his Son and Heir, and married
Alice the third Daughter of Sir *Richard Spencer*, by whom
he had Issue *Richard*, *Anne*, who died unmarried, *Elizabeth* wedded to ———— *Hill*, a Turkey Merchant, ——
married to ———— *Grove*, he was invested Knight of the
Honourable Order of the Bath at the Creation of *Charles*
Prince of 𝖂𝖆𝖑𝖊𝖘, constituted Sheriff of this County *Anno*
1626, 2 *Car.* I. served for the Burrough of 𝕾t. 𝕬𝖑𝖇𝖆𝖓𝖘 in
two several Parliaments, one held *Anno* 15 *Car.* I. the
other in the Year following, and he died seiz'd hereof, leaving Issue

Richard, who was his Heir, succeeded him, and married
Frances Daughter and Heir to Sir *Giffard Thornhurst* of
𝕬𝖌𝖓𝖊𝖘 𝕮𝖔𝖚𝖗𝖙 in 𝕶𝖊𝖓𝖙, Bar. by whom he had Issue, *John,
Ralph, Francis* married to Sir *George Hambleton*, Knight,
in the Kingdom of 𝕾𝖈𝖔𝖙𝖑𝖆𝖓𝖉, after him to *Richard Talbot*
Duke of 𝕿𝖞𝖗𝖈𝖔𝖓𝖊𝖑, *Barbara* married to *Edward Griffith,*
Esq. and *Sarah* married to *John Churchill*, Earl of 𝕸𝖆𝖗𝖑-
𝖇𝖔𝖗𝖔𝖚𝖌𝖍, Baron *Churchill*, of 𝕾𝖆𝖓𝖉𝖗𝖎𝖉𝖌𝖊, &c. whose Titles
I have set forth in 𝕾t. 𝕬𝖑𝖇𝖆𝖓𝖘.

John succeeded his Father, but dying without Issue this
Mannor came to

Ralph Jennings, his Brother, who enjoyed it a short time,
and dying without Issue it descended to his three Sisters
and Coheirs, *Frances* Dutchess of 𝕿𝖞𝖗𝖈𝖔𝖓𝖊𝖑, *Barbara*
Wife of *Edward Griffith* Esq. and *Sarah* Countess of
𝕸𝖆𝖗𝖑𝖇𝖔𝖗𝖔𝖚𝖌𝖍; and upon the Partition the two elder Sisters
sold their Part to *John* Earl of 𝕸𝖆𝖗𝖑𝖇𝖔𝖗𝖔𝖚𝖌𝖍, who is thereby become possest of the entire Mannor, and is the present
Lord hereof.

This Vicaridge is situated near the Vill, in the Deanery of 𝕾t. 𝕬𝖑𝖇𝖆𝖓
in the Diocess of 𝕷𝖔𝖓𝖉𝖔𝖓, and *Anno* 26 *Henry* VIII. was rated in the
King's Books at the yearly Value of 8*l*. whereof the Lord of this Mannor
is Patron.

VICAR, Mr. *Edmund Wood.*

Here I shall conclude this Part of this Division, and proceed to the next, which contains the several Vills and Parishes of 𝕻𝖆𝖚𝖑𝖘 𝖂𝖆𝖑𝖉𝖊𝖓, 𝕮𝖔𝖉𝖎𝖈𝖔𝖙𝖊, 𝕭𝖗𝖆𝖓𝖋𝖎𝖊𝖑𝖉, 𝕾𝖍𝖊𝖕𝖍𝖆𝖑𝖊,
𝕳𝖊𝖝𝖙𝖔𝖓, 𝕹𝖔𝖗𝖙𝖔𝖓, and 𝕹𝖊𝖜𝖍𝖆𝖒.

The third Part of the fourth Division.

WALDEN.

THE magnificent *Offa*, King of the *Mercians*, gave this
Vill to the great Abby which he founded, and was dedicated to the Honour of *St. Alban*, the Protomartyr of 𝕭𝖗𝖎𝖙𝖆𝖎𝖓,

Hund. of
Caishoe.

by the Name of **Walden**, so called from the Springs which
rise in the Vale; for *Wall* in the Saxon Language signifies
Springs boyling out of the Earth, and *Den*, a Vale; all
which agrees with the Scituation of this Vill; and the Abbots of this Church held it in the time of the Conquest,
when it was recorded under the title of *Terra Abbatis
Sancti Albani.*

Domesd. Lib.
fol. 136, n. 10.

*In Albaneston Hundred. Abbas Sancti Albani ten. Waldene, pro decem
hidis se defendebat. Terra est quatuor decem car. in Dominio tres hidæ, et
ibi sunt duo car. et tertia potest fieri. Ibi septemdecem Vill. cum uno francig.
habent decem car. et adhuc un. potest fieri, ibi novem Bord. et tres Servi, et
un. Molend. de quindecem sol. pratum un. car. pastura ad pec. Nemus ad
sepes et domos in totis valent. valet et valuit octodecim lib. et decem sol.
tempore Regis Edwardi vigint. lib. et decem sol. Hoc Manerium jacuit et
jacet in dominio Ecclesiæ Sancti Albani.*

The Abbot of St. *Alban* held **Walden** in **Albaneston** Hundred, it was
rated for ten Hides. The arable is fourteen Carucates, in Demeasne
three Hides, and there are two Carucates and a third may be made;
there are seventeen Villains and a Frenchman born, having ten Carucates,
and now other may be made; there are nine Bordars and three Servants,
and one Mill of fifteen Shillings Rent, Meadow one Carucate, Common
of Pasture for the Cattle, Wood for Hedges and Houses; in the whole
Value it is worth and was worth eighteen Pounds and ten Shillings by
the Year, in the time of King *Edward* (the Confessor) twenty Pounds
and ten Shillings by the Year. This Mannor did lye and now doth lye
in the Jurisdiction of the Church of **St. Alban**.

This Vill was called **Abbots-Walden**, because the Abbots
were the Lords hereof, and kept Courts here, which were
called *Hallmotes*, until the tenth Year of *H.* VIII. and
then these Courts were called Views of Franc-Pledge, and
and by that Name were held until the fatal Year of the
great Dissolution of Abbies, when this Mannor came to the
Possession of King *H.* VIII. and a Court Leet and Court
Baron was held here in his Name on the ninth Day of *May*,
Anno 32 of his Reign; but it did not continue long in his
Possession, for about the 36th Year of his Reign he granted the same to the Dean and Chapter of **St. Paul, London**, who held a Court Leet and Court Baron for this
Mannor in their Name on the 7th of *July*, in the same Year
of that King, and from that time this Parish has been
known by the Adjunct of **Pauls Walden**, and has ever
since continued in the Church of *St. Paul,* **London;** the
Dean and Chapter of that Church having been the Lords
hereof.

Rot Cur.
Man 32 H.
VIII.
Ibid. 36 H.
VIII.

By the Custom of this Mannor all Surrenders of Coppihold Estates must be taken by the Lord of the Mannor,
or their Stewards, unless a Coppiholder lie *in extremis* and
then he may surrender the same by the Hands of a Coppiholder, sworn in some Court to take Surrenders of Tenants,
who lie *in extremis*, but if such Tenant, who has made such
Surrender, shall happen to recover and go abroad, the Surrender so made to become void.

Hund. of
Caishoe.

There is another Custom, That if any Coppiholder die seiz'd of any customary Land, held of this Mannor, his Wife (if surviving) shall have Dowre.

The Mannor of HOO.

WAS derived from the Mannor of 𝕸𝖆𝖑𝖉𝖊𝖓, and received its Name from *Hough*, which in the Saxon Language signifies high, and gave Name to *Hoo* an ancient Saxon, who was Lord hereof, in whose Family it has continued for many Ages, till of late Days when the Name expired by an Heir Female, who married Sir *Jonathan Keate*, Bart. who in Right of her became Lord of this Mannor, therefore I think it necessary to give what Account I have seen of this Family.

Robert Hoo 'tis said, possessed this Mannor in the time of King *Canutus* the *Dane*, and was a great Man in those Days, for he married *Anne* the Daughter of *Iden* or *Guido*, Descent. Rot. Lord *Griffith* of 𝕸𝖆𝖑𝖊𝖘, who died the 26th of *Oct. Anno* ———— She was Mother to Sir *Thomas Hoo*, and lieth buried in the Parish Church of 𝕷𝖊𝖜𝖙𝖔𝖓, where his Arms were depicted with his Wives.

Sir *Thomas Hoo* married *Amy* Daughter of Sir *William Walton*, by whom he had Issue, *Robert*, and he died 19th of *Oct. Anno* 1018, and lieth buried in the Church of 𝕷𝖊𝖜𝖙𝖔𝖓, in the County of 𝕭𝖊𝖉𝖋𝖔𝖗𝖉.

Rot. memb. 1. Sir *Robert Hoo*, Knight, married *Wylmote* Daughter of *John Malmaynes*, but in an ancient Roll, called *Malmanes* of 𝕹𝖔𝖗𝖒𝖆𝖓𝖉𝖞, he died the 23rd of *February* 1129, and she died the 24th of *January* 1148, leaving Issue *Robert*.

Sir *Robert Hoo*, Knight, married *Rosamond* Daughter of *Thomas* Lord *Chelteron*, by whom he had Issue *Alexander*, he died the first of *August*, 1166, and she the 23rd. of *July* 1191, in *Anno* 2 *Rich.* I.

Rot. memb. 2. Sir *Alexander Hoo*, married *Dernelle*, in the old Descent *Darmagnel* Daughter of *Alexander*, King of 𝕾𝖈𝖔𝖙𝖑𝖆𝖓𝖉, by whom he had Issue, *Robert*, he died the eighth of *March*, *A. D.* ——— and lieth buried in the Island of 𝕽𝖍𝖔𝖉𝖊𝖘, and she died the 15th. of *March A. D.* ———

Sir *Robert Hoo* died the 12th. of *Jan. A. D.* ——— and was buried in the Church of 𝕬𝖑𝖑𝖘𝖔𝖚𝖑𝖘 at 𝕮𝖔𝖘𝖊𝖑 𝖘𝖚𝖕𝖊𝖗 𝕳𝖚𝖒𝖇𝖊𝖗.

Sir *Robert Hoo*, Brother to the last *Robert* married *Beatrice* Daughter of *Alexander*, Earl of 𝕬𝖓𝖉𝖎𝖇𝖊𝖑 in 𝕹𝖔𝖗𝖒𝖆𝖓𝖉𝖞, by whom he had Issue *Robert* he was elected Knight of the Shire in the Parliament held *Anno* 26 *Edw.* I. and died the ninth of *May*, 1310, lieth buried at 𝕷𝖊𝖜𝖙𝖔𝖓, Prin's *Parl.* *Brev.* pt 3. she died the 28th of *May*, 1314, and was buried at 𝕶𝖓𝖊𝖇𝖜𝖔𝖗𝖙𝖍, in this County.

Sir *Robert Hoo* was installed Knight of the noble

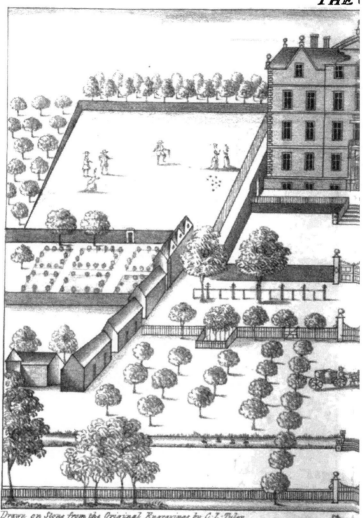

Drawn on Stone from the Original Engravings by C. L. Tyler.

To Gilbert Hoo

This Draught is

Pub.d by I.M.Mullinger

Keate Esq.ʳ

humbly presented by

J. Drapentier.

Bps Stortford. 1826.

Order of the Garter, and married *Hawise* Daughter of
Fulk, Lord *Fitzwaren* by whom he had Issue *Thomas*,
he died the 1st. of *November*, *Anno* 1311, and was buried
in the Church of 𝔄𝔩𝔩𝔰𝔬𝔲𝔩𝔰 at 𝔠𝔬𝔴𝔰𝔢𝔩 upon 𝔥𝔲𝔪𝔟𝔢𝔯, she
died the 2nd. of *September Anno* 1344, and was buried in
the Church of the Grey Friars at 𝔇𝔲𝔫𝔰𝔱𝔞𝔟𝔩𝔢.

Hund. of
Caishoe.
Rot. memb. 2.

Sir *Thomas Hoo* married *Isabel*, the Daughter and next
Heir to *John St. Legier*, by whom he had Issue, *William*,
died on the 28th Day of *Sept. An.* 1380, and was buried in
the Church of 𝔖t. 𝔄𝔩𝔟𝔞𝔫𝔰, *Isabel* his Wife died on the 22d
of *July*, *An.* 1393, and was also buried in the same Church.

Esc. 9 Ed.
III. no. 21,
North.

Sir *William Hoo* was knighted, and married *Alice*, the
eldest Daughter and Coheir of *Thomas de Sto Omero*, and
of *Petronella* her Mother, one of the Daughters and Coheirs of *Nicholas de Malemaynes*, by whom he had Issue
Thomas, he died on the 22nd of *Novemb.* 1410, and *Alice*
died the 10th of *Oct. An.* 1456, and was buried at 𝔐𝔬𝔫𝔨-
𝔟𝔲𝔱𝔬𝔫 or 𝔐𝔲𝔩𝔟𝔞𝔯𝔱𝔬𝔫 in Norfolk.

Esc. 40 Ed
III. no. 36,
Norf.

Sir *Thomas Hoo* married *Almore*, one of the Heirs of
Sir *Thomas Felton* Kt. and though in the Roll of his Descent, the Words *Comitis* 𝔥𝔲𝔫𝔱𝔦𝔫𝔤𝔬𝔫 be added, and so
was called there Earl of 𝔥𝔲𝔫𝔱𝔦𝔫𝔤𝔬𝔫, yet certainly that was
a great Mistake, for it seems in the old Latin Copy of this
Descent, the Words are written Com. 𝔥𝔲𝔫𝔱𝔦𝔫𝔡. which signified *Comitatus* 𝔥𝔲𝔫𝔱𝔦𝔫𝔤𝔬𝔫; and he had Issue by her
Thomas, and died on the 23rd Day of *August*, *An.* 1420,
Almore his Wife on the 8th Day of *August*, *Anno* 1400,
and after her Decease, *Thomas* married *Elizabeth* Daughter of *William de Eckingham*, and had Issue

Thomas Hoo, Esq. who was created a Baron of this
Realm by the Title of Lord *Hoo* and *Hastings*, in the time
of King *H.* VI. was installed Knight of the noble Order
of the Garter, he first married *Elizabeth* Daughter and
Heir to Sir *Thomas Felton*, Kt. by whom he had Issue
Thomas, who dyed in his Life-time without Issue, after her
Decease he married *Elizabeth* the Daughter of Sir *Richard
Wychingham*, Kt. by whom he had only Issue one Daughter *Anne*, who married *Geoffery Boleyn*, Kt. Citizen and
Mayor of 𝔏𝔬𝔫𝔡𝔬𝔫, from whom Queen *Elizabeth* and the
Lord of 𝔥𝔲𝔫𝔰𝔡𝔬𝔫 descended, and after her Decease he mar-
ryed *Eleanor* Daughter and one of the Heirs of *Leo* Lord
𝔚𝔢𝔩𝔩𝔢𝔰, by whom he had Issue *Jane* married to *Roger Cop-
ley*, Citizen and Mercer of 𝔏𝔬𝔫𝔡𝔬𝔫, *Eleanor* married to *Tho-
mas Eckingham*, Esq. Son of Sir *Thomas Eckingham*, Kt.
by whom she had no Issue, and after his Decease she married *James Carew* of 𝔅𝔢𝔡𝔦𝔫𝔤𝔱𝔬𝔫 in the County of 𝔖𝔲𝔯𝔯𝔶,
Esq. the second Son, but at length Heir male to *Nicholas
Carew* of 𝔅𝔢𝔡𝔦𝔫𝔤𝔱𝔬𝔫 aforesaid, Esq. *Elizabeth* the youngest
Daughter of *Thomas* Lord *Hoo* and *Hastings* married

Hund. of
Caishoe.

Esc. 33 H.VI.
n. 11, Norf.

Thomas Massingberg, Citizen and Mercer of 𝕷𝖔𝖓𝖉𝖔𝖓, and after his Decease, Sir *John Devenish*, and this *Thomas* Lord *Hoo* and *Hastings* died on the 13th Day of *Feb. An.* 33 *H.*VI.

After his Decease, this Mannor came to *Thomas Hoo*, Esq. who married the Daughter and Heir of *Norwood*, by whom he had Issue, *Thomas;* he died *Anno* 1480, and was buried in the Parish of 𝕽𝖞𝖒𝖕𝖙𝖔𝖓.

Thomas Hoo, Esq. succeeded, married the Daughter of *Edmund Bardolfe*, Esq. by whom he had Issue *Thomas*, died on the 20th Day of *March*, 1516, and lyeth buried in this Parish Church.

Thomas Hoo, Esq. was his Heir, married the Daughter and Heir of *John Newman* of 𝕳𝖆𝖙𝖋𝖊𝖑𝖉, by whom he had Issue *Thomas*, *Anne* married to *Thomas Read* of 𝖂𝖆𝖗𝖙𝖔𝖓, Esq. *Dorothy* married to ———*Cater*, and *Margaret* to *Nicholas Brocket*, Esq. he died on the 11th day of *June*, *Anno* 1551, leaving Issue

Thomas, who held a Court for this Mannor on the 9th Day of *Jan. Anno* 31 *Eliz.* and married *Hellen*, the Daughter of *William Purient*, by whom he had Issue *William*, *Thomas*, and *Elizabeth*.

William succeeded, and married *Mary*, the Daughter of Sir *Francis Bickley* of 𝕭𝖆𝖗𝖑𝖊𝖘𝖙𝖔𝖓 in 𝕳𝖆𝖈𝖐𝖓𝖞 in the County of 𝕸𝖎𝖉𝖉𝖑𝖊𝖘𝖊𝖝, by whom he had Issue *Thomas* and *Susan;* he was constituted Sheriff of this County *Anno* 1629, 5 *Car.* I. and died the 14th of *March*, 1636.

Thomas succeeded, but dying without Issue,

Susan was his sole Heir, and married Sir *Jonathan Keate*, who was created Baronet by Patent dated the 12th of *June*, 1660, 12 *Car.* II. was constituted Sheriff of this County *Anno* 17 *Car.* II. served this County in Parliament *Anno* 30 *Car.* II. He had Issue by her *Hoo*, *Mary*, *Susanna*, *Elizabeth*, and *Jonathan*, whereof, the two last are dead, and *Susan* the Mother died on the 11th of *Jan. Anno* 1673, and was buried in the Chapple of 𝕽𝖎𝖒𝖕𝖙𝖔𝖓. After her Decease he married *Susanna Orlibear* the Daughter of *Richard Orlibear* of the City of 𝕷𝖔𝖓𝖉𝖔𝖓, Woollen Draper: By the Marriage of his first Lady, he became Lord hereof.

The Descent of the ancient and noble Family of *Hoo*, was transcribed out of an old Copy remaining in the Possession of *Thomas Hoo* of 𝕳𝖔𝖔𝖇𝖚𝖗𝖞 in 𝕬𝖇𝖇𝖔𝖙𝖘 𝕸𝖆𝖑𝖉𝖊𝖓 in this County; the Original was either written in a Ledger Book or Register belonging to some Abby, or in some ancient Roll or MSS. pertaining to the Family of *Hoo*, which upon the Division was allotted to one of the Coheirs, or remained still in the Custody of *Thomas Hoo*, Esq. Brother and Heir male of *Thomas* Lord *Hoo* and *Hastings*, as appears by several original Deeds and other Writings found in the Custody of

Sir *Francis Carew* of 𝔅𝔢𝔡𝔦𝔫𝔤𝔱𝔬𝔫 in the County of 𝔖𝔲𝔯𝔯𝔭, Kt. of the Bath, who had all or the greater Part of the original Deeds, and other Minuments and Writings in his Possession, after the Decease of *Thomas* Lord *Hoo* and *Hastings* his Brother. The Coat Armour of *Hoo* being *Quarterly Sable and Argent* is impaled in the before-mention'd Descent or Roll, with the several Coat Armours as followeth.

Hund. of Caishoe.

 Hoo and *Griffith, Azure, a Griffin Rampant with Wings displayed Or. Hoo* and *Wanton, Argent a Cheveron Sable. Hoo* and *Malmaines, Azure, three Sinister Hands two, one Argent. Hoo* and *Chiveron, Gules, two Chiverons Ermine. Hoo* and the Daughter of *Alexander* King of *Scots, Or, a Lyon Rampant within a double Tressure fleurette Gules. Hoo* and the Daughter of the Earl of 𝔄𝔫𝔡𝔢𝔟𝔦𝔩𝔢 𝔦𝔫 𝔑𝔬𝔯𝔪𝔞𝔫𝔡𝔭, *Or, a Fess Azure.*

Ibid. memb.1. MS. penes Dom. Jonathan Keate, Bar. Ibid. memb.2.

 This Coat is doubtless one of those five which is seen upon the Seals hanging to the original Deeds of Sir *William de Hoo*, Kt. the great Grandchild to that Lady whose Name was *Beatrix*.

 The other four Coats are *Hoo's* own paternal Coats, *in the middle of St. Legiers, on the upper Sinister Corner, St. Omers in the lower dexter Corner,* and *Malmaynes in the lower Sinister Corner.* For whereas Sir *William de Hoo* should have borne his own Coat Armour *Quarterly* in the first and fourth Place, with *Andevile* in the second, and *St. Legier* in the third, and so have impaled the Arms of *St. Omer* and *Malmaines quarterly*, he only caused these several Coates to be engraved on his Seals in Manner and Form as is above expressed, as being Arms which his Posterity might bear and enquarter with their own.

MS. penes Dom. Jonathan Keate, Bar.

 Hoo and *Fitzwarin, Argent and Gules quarterly per Fess indented. Hoo* and *St. Legier, Azure, a Fret Argent, a Chief Gules. Hoo and St. Legier, quarterly impaling St. Omers,* the first Wife and *Malmaynes quarterly, viz. Azure a Fess between six Crosse Croslets Or, in the first and fourth Place,* and *Azure three dexter Hands two, one Argent;* the Hands should be sinister, and yet they are dexter Hands, also in the Coat of *Malmaynes* found in the Seals of Sir *William de Hoo;* but that it seems happened by the Error of the Workman who engrav'd or insculped them left Hands on the Seal, which was right, not considering that they would prove dexter Hands in the Impression. *Hoo* quarterly in the first and fourth Places, with St. *Omer* in the second, and St. *Legier in the third*, impaling *Wingfield, Argent, on a bend Gules three Hawks lures of the first between two Cotizes Sable;* this was the second Wife of Sir *William de Hoo*, Kt. *Hoo* and *Felton, Gules, two Leopards passant Ermine;* first Wife, *Hoo* and *Echingham, Azure frette Argent.* This was the second Wife of Sir *Thomas*

Ibid memb.3.

Hoo, Kt. *Hoo and St. Omers quarterly, with St. Legier in*
an Escocheon of Pretence, which was the usual Bearing of
the Lord *Hoo* and *Hastings* in his Seals, and was on his
Plate at **Windsor**, being a Kt. of the Garter, empaling
Wichingham the first Wife, *Ermine, on a Chief Sable three*
Crosses formee pattee Argent.   *Hoo, viz.* with the same
Bearing impaling **Wells**, *Or, a Lyon rampant Sable ;* this
was the Lord *Hoo's* second Wife, but the Coat is mistaken,
for the Lyon should be with a double Tayl.

THIS Rectory is appropriated to the perpetual Use of the Dean and
Chapter of St. *Paul* in **London**, and the Vicaridge in *Anno* 26 *Hen.* VIII.
was rated in the King's Books at 10*l. per Annum.* The Dean and Chapter of St. *Pauls* are Patrons hereof.

The VICARS.

Mr. *Loker.*   Mr. *Bentham*, the present Vicar.

The Church is erected in the Deanery of **St. Albans** in the Diocess of
London. it contains the Body, and one Isle on the North Side covered
with Lead, and the Chancel with Tyle, and a little Chappel erected by
the *Hoo's* covered with Lead ; at the West End of the Church adjoyns a
low square Tower, wherein hang a Ring of five good Bells, with a Spire
Staff of Wood and a Weather Cock upon it; in the Chancel and Church
are these Inscriptions.

Here lieth interred the Body of Dame *Elizabeth Hale*, late Relict of Sr.
John Hale of **Stagenhoe**, Kt. who departed this life *August* the fifth
1675. in the 63d. year of her Age, who left one only Daughter, *Rose*
married to Sr. *John Austen* of **Hall Place** in the County of **Kent**, Bar.

Nigh to this place lie interred the Bodies of *Henry Stapleford*, Gentleman,
and *Dorothy* his Wife, the said *Henry* was Servant to Queen *Elizabeth*,
King *James*, and King *Charles*, till the time of his Death. He departed this life the 31st. of *May ann. Dom.* 1631. and aged 76. years,
Dorothy his Wife died the 2d. day of *Febr. ann. Dom.* 1620. aged 72.
years, the said *Henry* and *Dorothy* having issue then, and yet living,
Dorothy married to *Henry Henn*, Esq; who had issue *Mary* who died
at the age of six Months and lieth here interred by her Grandmother.
This Monument was erected at the Charge of the said *Henry Henn*.

Here lieth interred the Body of *William Hoo* of the **Hoo** in **Pauls Walden**, Esq; who deceased the 14th. of *March ann. Dom.* 1636. leaving
Susan his Wife, by whom he left issue *Thomas* his Son and *Elizabeth*
his Daughter. *Ætat. suæ* 56.
In Mundo moritur in Æterno obitur.

Here lieth the Body of *Thomas Hoo* the ⸻ Son of *Thomas Hoo*, Esq ;
and *Hellen* his Wife lately deceased the 14th. of ⸻ also here lieth
George Hoo, Gentleman, who died in his ⸻

Here lieth the Body of Mrs. *Hellen Hoo*, the Wife of *Thomas Hoo*, Esq ;
and Daughter of *William Puryent*, Esq; who deceased the ⸻

In the North Window next the Pulpit is the Effigies of St. *John*, with
his Fan in his Hand, and the Virgin *Mary* with a Child in her Arms.

CHARITY.

Mr. *Smith* gave 14*l. per Annum*, issuing out of Lands in **Colson Darcey**
in **Essex**, to bind out one or more Children in **Pauls Walden** Apprentices, upon the Request of Sir *Henry Henn* one of his Trustees.

Hund. of Caishoe.

CUDICOTE, CODICOTE.

THIS Vill was Parcel of the ancient Possessions of the Monastery of St. Albans, and belonged to the same at the time of the Conquest, when it was recorded under the Title of *Terra Ecclesiæ* St. Albani. *Mon. Angl. vol. 1, fol. 178.*

In Bradewater *Hundred.* Codicote *et* Oxewich *duo Manerii fuerunt tempore Regis* Edwardi, *et modo est unum, pro octo hidis se defendebat. Terra est duodecim car. in dominio tres hidæ et un. virgat et ibi quatuor car. ibi sexdecim Vill. habentes septem car. et octava potest fieri. Ibi unus Francig. et tres cotar. et quatuor servi et duo molend. de duodecim sol. pratum duo car. pastura ad pec. Silva ducent. porc. in totis valentiis valet sex lib. quando recepit quinq; lib tempore Regis* Edwardi *duodecim lib. Hæc duo manerii jacuerunt in Ecclesia* St. Albani *tempore Regis* Edwardi, *ibi* Alavinus Gotone *ten. tres hidas sub Abbate, non potuit ad Ecclesia separare, de hac terra quindecim acras invaserunt homines Comitis* Moreton *super Abbatem ut Homines de Hundred. testantur.* *Domesd. Lib. fol. 135.*

Codecote and Oxewich in Bradewater Hundred were two Mannors in the time of King *Edward* (the Confessor) and now it is one, it was rated for eight Hides. The arable is twelve Carucates, in Demeasne three Hides and one Virgate, and there are four Carucates, there are sixteen Villains having seven Carucates, and eight may be made, there is one Frenchman born and three Cottagers, and four Servants, and two Mills of twelve Shillings Rent, Meadow two Carucates, Common of Pasture for the Cattle, Wood to feed two hundred Hogs; in the whole Value it is worth six Pounds by the Year, when he received it five Pounds, in the time of King *Edward* (the Confessor) twelve Pounds. These two Mannors did lye within the Jurisdiction of the Church of St. Alban in the time of King *Edward* (the Confessor) there *Alwine Gotone* held three Hides under the Abbot, he could not separate them from the Church; Men (under the Protection) of Earl *Moreton* entered upon the Abbot and wrongfully detains fifteen Acres of this Land, as the Men of the Hundred can witness.

'Tis observable by this Record that this Vill lay in the Hundred of Bradewater, in the time of *Edward* the Confessor and *William* the Conqueror, and the Name hereof signifies a Cottage, a small House or a Place for Sheep; they did also confirm to them the Grants of the Lands of all those Knights who were bound by their Tenures to defend all Scutages, and all other foreign Services, among whom *Alexander* the Son of *Thurold, An.* 1 *John,* held the Mannor of Sissebernes.

King *H.* I. and King *John* confirmed the Grant of this Mannor to the Church of St. Albans, and King *Hen.* III. granted a Fair to the Abbot to be held there, every Year on the Feast of St. *James* at Codicote, and a Market on every Friday in the Week. MS. in Bibl. Cottoni.

The Abbot claimed by the Grant of King *H.* III. a Fair in this Town, and 'twas allowed; and since the last, *Iter* the Abbot held a Market in this Vill, on Friday in every Week for ten Years then last past, which was to the great Damage of the King and his Borough of Hertford. *Quo War* 6 *Ed.* I. Rot. 36 and 48, cur. recept. Scac.

The Mannor of SISSEVERNE.

IN the Reign of *Edw.* I. *Henry Chevall* was possest of this Mannor, he had Issue two Sons *Robert* and *Nicholas,* and after his Death great Strife and Debate arose between these Brethren, touching the Propriety of their Father's Estate in 𝕮𝖚𝖉𝖎𝖈𝖔𝖙𝖊 and elsewhere, till some Friends accommodated the Difference, and then it was agreed and concluded between them by Indenture dated the 11th *Edw.* II. that these Lands should be entailed upon this *Robert,* and the Heirs of his Body, and he died seized of them, leaving Issue

John Chevall, who was possest of his Father's Estate, and made a Feofment thereof to *John Whiteham,* Vicar of 𝕮𝖚-𝖉𝖎𝖈𝖔𝖙𝖊 and his Heirs, who in short Space by Indenture dated on the *Monday* on the Morrow of St. *Michael* the Archangel, *Anno* 15 *Edw.* III. reconveyed the same to the said *John Chevall* and *Luce* his Wife, and the Heirs Males of the Body of *John Chevall,* who left Issue

Robert Chevall, who was his Heir, and had one Son call'd *John Chevall,* who enjoy'd it to his Death, when

Edmond Chevall who was his Heir succeeded, and had Issue two Sons, *Edmond* and *Edward,* and he dying seized

Edmond Chevall was his Heir, and upon his Decease it descended to

Luce who was his Daughter and Heir, and in the time of King *Hen.* VIII. married *John Penn,* Groom of the Privy Chamber, Porter and Barber to that King, and upon the Dissolution of Monasteries, he gave to him the Mannor of 𝕮𝖔𝖉𝖎𝖈𝖔𝖙𝖊 for his good Services, and he had Issue *Thomas, Robert, John, Eleanor* married to —— *Barr, Elizabeth,* and *Dorothy,* and upon his Decease,

Thomas Penn succeeded and married *Margery* Daughter of *Thomas Saunders* of 𝕬𝖌𝖒𝖔𝖓𝖉𝖊𝖘𝖍𝖆𝖒, in the County of 𝕭𝖚𝖈𝖐𝖘, by whom he had Issue *John, Susan, Mary,* and *Luce,* but *John* and *Thomas* both dying in the Life-time of their Father, this Mannor upon his Death, came to

Thomas Penn, the Son and Heir of *John,* who had Issue two Sons *John* and *Thomas,* but in the Year 1625, he sold both Mannors to

Thomas Penn his younger Brother, who enjoyed them until the Year 1659, about which time he conveyed them to

George Poyner, Citizen and Merchant of 𝕷𝖔𝖓𝖉𝖔𝖓, he built a fair House in the Mannor of 𝕮𝖔𝖉𝖎𝖈𝖔𝖙𝖊, with convenient Stables and Out-houses, and died about the Year 1670, leaving Issue *George, John, Mary* married to —— *Hemsworth* of 𝕷𝖔𝖓𝖉𝖔𝖓, Merchant, *Elizabeth* married to *Samuel Garret* of 𝕷𝖔𝖓𝖉𝖔𝖓, Grocer, second Son of Sir *John Garret* of 𝕷𝖆𝖓𝖒𝖊𝖗, Bart.

George Poyner was his Heir, who lived sometime as a Factor at Smirna, afterwards returned to England, and married *Anne* the Daughter of———by whom he had Issue one Daughter called *Anne*, but his Wife dying, he espoused——— and settled this Mannor of Codicote upon himself and his Wife for Life, in Lieu of her Jointure, by whom he had Issue *George* who died in his Infancy; and *George* the Father died on the 15th Day of *March*, 1681, upon whose Decease, the Mannor of Codicote came to his Widow, who married *Godding Barrington*, Gent. who was a Captain of a Foot Company in the Militia for this County; but in the Year 1694, she died, and upon her Death, the Mannor of Codicote descended to *Ann* the Daughter and sole Heir of *George Poyner*, but the Mannor of Sissebernes, as I am informed, past to *John* Brother of *George*, and his Heirs.

The Custom for taking Surrenders in this Mannor, is the same as in the Parke Mannor.

THE Rectory was appropriated to the Use of the Monastery of St. Albans by Pope *Honorius* in the Year 1218, and the Abbots were Patrons until the time of the Dissolution of that Monastery, when King *Hen.* VIII. granted the Advowson of the Vicaridge to the Bishops of Ely and their Successors, and it was rated 26 *Hen.* VIII. in the King's Books at the yearly Value of 7*l.* 5*s.* 8*d.*

Mon. Angl. vol. 1, fol 179.

The VICARS.

1342 16 *Edw.* III.	*John Whiteham*
1558 5 *Mary*	*John Darling*
1611 9 *Jac.* I.	*Thomas Rookes*
1663 15 *Car.* II.	*Thomas Loker*
1674 26 *Car.* II.	*William Swalden.*

This Church is situated upon a dry Hill near the Mannor House in the Deanery of St. Albans, in the Diocess of London, covered with Lead, and at the West End is a square Tower wherein is a Ring of five Bells, and within the Church lye several Gravestones which have the following Inscriptions.

In the Chappel belonging to Sissebernes.

Here lyeth interred the Body of *George Poyner*, Sen. Esq; and Merchant of London, who departed this life in the threescore year of his age, on the 24th. of *December* 1668.
In the Top of the Stone his Coat of Arms is engraved, which is a *Field, Or, a Parrot proper.*

Here lieth *Jeremiah Burwell* late Minister of St. *Andrews* Hertford, who departed this life *Febr.* 11. Ann. 1668. *Ætatis suæ* 44.

Here lieth the Body of *Elizabeth* the Wife of *Samuel Garrard*, second Son of Sr. *John Garrard*, Bar. Daughter of *George Poyner*, Esq; She died in the 20th. year of her age on the eleventh of *April.*
MDCLXXVII.

Here lieth interred the Body of *George Poyner*, Esq; Son of *George Poyner*, Esq; who departed this life in the 30th. year of his Age on the 15th. day of *March* 1681. who left issue one Son, and one Daughter *George*, and *Anne.*
His Arms are engraved on the upper Part of the Stone.

Here lieth the Body of *Anne* the Wife of *George Poyner*, Esq; by whom She had issue one Daughter, who departed this life in the 20th. year of her Age the 17. day of *Octob.* Ann. *Dom.* 1678.

Hund. of
Caisbos.

　　　　　　The Arms of the *Poyners* are on the Wall.

Mantled *Azure, doubled Gules with the Helmet according to his Degree. In a Torse Or and Gules, a Stag issuant holding a Brench of Laurel between his Feet.*

Here also lieth one *Chivall,* an ancient Owner of **Bisseberues,** the Inscriptions in Brass are gone, but his Coat of Arms remain thereon, which is *Or, three Horses' heads couped at the Neck Sable, crested and bridled Argent;* 'tis also in the Glass Window.

In the same Window the same Arms are quartered with the Arms of the *Penns,* who were the last Owners of **Bisseberues** by the marriage of the Heir of the *Chivalls,* the Arms of *Penn* is, *Argent, on a Fess Gules between three Peacocks (close) Azure, a Lion passant gardant Or, between two Combs silver; the Crest on a Wreath, a Demi Lyon rampant Gules supporting a Comb Argent.*

　　　　　　Upon the Wall is written,

Here under are interred the Bodys of *Anne Poyner Daughter, and of Charles Hemsworth Grandson of George Poyner, Sen. Esq;*

　　　　　On the Wall in the Communion Chancel.

By stealing Steps of Time from Day to Month and Year
My earthly race is run, my Body's buried here.
Samuell Michell was my name, I make it known to Thee
One Wife, and Children five, the Lord hath lent to me,
My Soul is now with God to which my Corps shall come,
And both shall Sentence have from Christ in day of Doome.
When by his bloody Death, who is my Saviour just,
I shall have life for Aye, among his Saints I trust.
Now of my earthly race, if you the date will know
The Day, the Month, and Year are all exprest below.
　　　6 *June Anno Domini* 1605.

Here lied the Body of *Mary Michell,* the Wife of *Richard Michell,* Gentleman, Daughter of *John Brocket* of **Betthamsted.** Esq; and had by the same *Richard* four Sons, and was buried the two and twentieth of *February* 1661.

Edward Wingate, *Esq. one of the Justices of the Peace for this County, did Certifie under his Hand, Ann.* 1627, *that there was a great Walnut Tree, grew on* **Scissebernes Greene,** *in this Parish, which was of that great extent that the Branches thereof cover'd* 76. *Poles of Ground: it fell with Age, and the weight of the Boughs cleft the Body of the Tree in the Middle to the Ground. Mr. Penn (who was Lord of the Mannor) sold so much of it to a Gunstock-maker of* **London,** *as he would carry thither for ten pounds which he paid, and sawed out in Planks of two inches thick, and half as much as filled nineteen Carts and Waggons. Mr. Penn had thirty Loads more which the Man left with the roots and branches; with the end of one root he wainscoted a fair Room, made a Portall and many Chairs and Stools of the remainder; and Mr. Penn averred to my self and others, that he had divers times been offered fifty pounds for this Tree.*
　　　　　　　　　　　　　　Edward Wingate.

Jasper Docwra born in **Hallwoods** in **Cobirote,** doth averre that in the year 1622. *He measured the circumference of Mr. Penns Walnut Tree, he being then* 15. *years old, and it was eight of his Fathomes of both arms in compasse round the Body.*
　　　　　　　　　　　　　　Jasper Docwra.

BRANDEFELLE, BRANTFIELD

IN the time of *William* the Conqueror that King gave this Mannor to *Hardwin de Escalers,* a great *Norman* that assisted him in the Battle near **Hastings;** for 'tis recorded of him in *Domesdei Book,* That

In **Hertford** *Hundred.* Hardvinus de Scalers *tenuit* **Brandefelle** *pro quinq; hidis se defendebat. Terra est sex car. in dominio quatuor hidæ, et ibi est un carucat. et dimid. et dimid. potest fieri. ibi decem Vill. habentes duo car. et dimid et adhuc un. car. et dimid. potest fieri, ibi unus Servus, pratum un. car. pastura ad pecud. Silva centum porcis, et duodecim denar de ea. In totis valentiis valet quatuor lib. quando recepit quadragint. sol. tempore Regis* Edwardi *centum sol. Hoc Manerium tenuit* Achi *Teignus Comitis* Heraldi *et vendere potuit.*

Hardwin de Scalers held **Brandefelle** in the Hundred of **Hertford**; it was rated for five Hides. The arable is six Carucates, in Demeasne four Hides, and there is one Carucate and an half, and half another may be made, there are ten Villains having two Carucates and an half, and now another Carucate and half may be made, there is one Servant, Meadow one Carucate, Common of Pasture for the Cattle, Wood to feed one hundred Hogs, and twelve Pence Rent by the Year for Water. In the whole it is worth four Pounds a Year, when he received it, forty Shillings, in the time of King *Edward* (the Confessor) one hundred Shillings; *Achi* a Thane of Earl *Harold* held this Mannor and might sell it.

About the latter End of this King's Reign *Hardewine de Scalers* and *Odel* his Wife, gave this Mannor to the Abbots and Monks of the Monastery of **St. Albans**, that they might pray for their Souls, and King *H.* I. confirmed the Grant hereof.

In *An.* 6 *Edw.* I. 'twas found upon a *Quo Warranto,* that *John* the Abbot of **St. Alban,** within seventeen Years before that time had withdrawn the Service of this Vill, which was wont to answer before the Justices of that Hundred, and he had there Gallows, View of Franc Pledge, Tumbrell, Pillory and Retorn of Writs, &c. And the Abbots and Monks of that Church have been Lords of this Mannor and enjoyed the Profits hereof until the time of the Dissolution when it came to the Crown.

But in short Space this Mannor came to *George Dacres,* Esq. who in *An.* 3 & 4 *P. & M.* held a Court here, and sold it to

John Foster, who held another Court, *An.* 4 & 5 *P. & M.* but afterwards he granted it to

Edward Skegg, Esq. who also held a Court, after which conveyed it to

James Smith, Esq. who held a Court for this Mannor, the 20th of *May, An.* 13 *Eliz.* and died seiz'd hereof, leaving Issue

James, who was his Heir, and kept a Court here the 3d. of *Sept. An.* 37 *Eliz.* He sold it to

Sir *Henry Boteler,* who was knighted and married *Katharine* Daughter of *Robert Waller,* of **Badley,** by whom he had Issue, *John, Edward, George,* and *Ralph,* and three Daughters, *Katharine* married to Sir *John Brown* of **Essex,** *Elizabeth* married to Sir *Anthony Chester,* of **Bucks,** Bart. and *Mary* married to *John Lynn,* and upon his Death

John, who was his eldest Son succeeded him, and in 1 *Jac.* I. was knighted, and in the same Year was constituted Sheriff of this County; He married *Elizabeth* the Daughter of *George Villers* of Brocksby, in the County of Leicester, and eldest Sister to *George* Duke of Buckingham; and by Letters Patents dated 12 *April, A. D.* 1620, 18 *Jac.* I. he was created Baronet, and by Letters Patents dated 20 *Sept.* 4 *Car.* I. he was advanced to the Dignity of a Baron of this Realm by the Title of Lord *Boteler* of Branfield; he had Issue by *Elizabeth* his Wife, six Sons, *John, Henry, Philip, Francis,* another *John,* and *William,* all whom died without Issue, and six Daughters, *Audry* married to Sir *Francis Anderson,* Kt. afterwards to Sir *Francis Leigh* Lord of Dunsmore, afterwards Earl of Chichester, *Hellen* married to Sir *John Drake* of Ash in the County of Devon, Kt. *Jane* married to *James Ley* Earl of Marlborough, Lord Treasurer of England, and after his Decease to —— *Ashburnham,* one of the Grooms of the Bed-chamber to King *Charles* I. *Olive* married to *Endimion Porter,* another of the Grooms of the Bed-chamber to the same King, *Mary* married to *Edward* Lord *Howard* of Escrick, and *Anne* married to *Mountjoy Blount,* Earl of Newport, and Master of the Ordinance, and after him to *Thomas* Earl of Portland; and departing this Life at his Lodgings at St. Martins in the Feilds within the Liberties of Westminster, the 27th of *May* 1637, 13 *Car.* I. was buried at Bigham Gobion in the County of Bedford, leaving *William* his only Son, who did survive him.

Which Lord *William* dying unmarried, this Mannor came to his said six Sisters, *Audry, Hellen, Jane, Olive, Mary,* and *Ann. Frances* Lord Dunsmore and Earl of Chichester having by *Audry* his Wife, the eldest Sister of *William* Lord *Boteler* of Braqfield, *George* who died without Issue, *Audry, Elizabeth* married to *Thomas* Earl of Southampton, and *Mary* to *George Villers* Viscount Grandison in the Kingdom of Ireland: This *George* Lord Grandison purchased the Interest of *Hellen, Jane, Olive, Mary* and *Anne,* Sisters of the said *William* Lord *Boteler,* in this Mannor, and the Interest of *Audry* and *Elizabeth* Countess of Southampton, who were Sisters to his own Lady and Coheirs with the sixth Part of *Audry* their Mother, whereby he became sole Possessof of this Mannor, and is the present Lord hereof.

THIS Rectory was a Donative, and the Abbot and Convent of St. Albans received the Profit thereof, and were bound to find a Curate to serve the Cure at their Charge: But since the Dissolution of that Church, the Lords of this Mannor have been Patrons.

The RECTORS.

Mr. *Bird.*   Mr. *Bolton.*   Mr. *Gouge.*

This Church is erected in the Middle of this Vill, in the Deanery of St. Albans in the Diocess of London, consists only of the Body with a small

Chancel at the East End of it, and at the West End thereof is an erection of Timber covered with Boards, wherein are three small Bells, of which the two greatest are broke; and within this Chancel lies a fair Marble which has this Inscription.

Here lieth the truly Religious
Lady *Mary*
Wife to *George* Lord Viscount
Grandison,
Who died here the 7th of *July*
in the year of our Lord
1671.

SHEEPHALL, SCEAPHALE, SHEEPESHALE.

THIS Vill was termed 𝔖𝔥𝔢𝔢𝔭𝔥𝔞𝔩𝔩 from the wholsome Food of Sheep, which produc'd Wooll, the great Manufacture of this Kingdom, and was Parcel of the ancient Possessions of that great Monastery of 𝔖t. 𝔄𝔩𝔟𝔞𝔫, yet in the time of *William* the Conqueror, *Stigand,* the Archbishop of 𝔠𝔞𝔫𝔱𝔢𝔯𝔟𝔲𝔯𝔶, held some Land here under the Abbot, but the Abbot himself held the Mannor as appears by *Domesdei Book,* where it is thus recorded that

Norden, p.23.
Mon. Angl. vol. 1, fol. 178.

In 𝔅𝔯𝔞𝔡𝔢𝔴𝔞𝔱𝔢𝔯 *Hundred. in* 𝔈𝔰𝔠𝔢𝔭𝔢𝔥𝔞𝔩𝔢 *tenuit* Anschitillus *de Archiepiscopo duo hid. Terra est quinq; car. in dominio est una, et alia potest fieri, et tres Vill. habentes duo car. et tertia potest fieri, pratum dim. car. Silva vigint. porc. valet tres lib. quando recepit sexagint. sol. tempore Regis Edwardi quatuor lib. Hanc terram tenuit* Aluric *homo* Stigandi Archiep. *de dominio Ecclesiæ* 𝔖𝔞𝔫𝔠𝔱𝔦 𝔄𝔩𝔟𝔞𝔫𝔦 *fuit tempore Regis* Edwardi, *nec potuit vendere, nec separare ab Ecclesia.*

Abbas 𝔖𝔞𝔫𝔠𝔱𝔦 𝔄𝔩𝔟𝔞𝔫𝔦 *tenuit* 𝔈𝔰𝔠𝔢𝔭𝔢𝔥𝔞𝔩𝔢 *tres hidas. Terra est quinq; car. in dominio un. hid. et dimid. et ibi est una. car. et altera potest fieri, ibi octo Vill. habentes tres car. ibi duo cotarii, et un. servus, pratum un. car. pastura ad pecud. silva decem porc. In totum valet quatuor lib. Quando recepit tres lib. tempore Regis* Edwardi *quatuor lib. Hoc Manerium jacuit et jacet in dominio Ecclesiæ* 𝔖𝔞𝔫𝔠𝔱𝔦 𝔄𝔩𝔟𝔞𝔫𝔦.

Domesd. Lib. fol. 134, n. 10.

Anschitil held two Hides of the Archbishop of 𝔠𝔞𝔫𝔱𝔢𝔯𝔟𝔲𝔯𝔶 in 𝔈𝔰𝔠𝔢𝔭𝔢𝔥𝔞𝔩𝔢 in 𝔅𝔯𝔞𝔡𝔢𝔴𝔞𝔱𝔢𝔯 Hundred. The arable is five Carucates, in Demeasne is one, and another may be made, and three Villains having two Carucates, and a third may be made; Meadow half a Carucate, Wood to feed twenty Hogs; it is worth three Pounds a Year, when he received it sixty Shillings, in the time of King *Edward* (the Confessor) four Pounds; *Aluric* a Man (under the Protection) of *Stigan,* the Archbishop, held this Land; it was in the time of King *Edward* (the Confessor) in the Demeasne of the Church of 𝔖t. 𝔄𝔩𝔟𝔞𝔫; neither might he sell nor separate it from the Church.

The Abbot of 𝔖t. 𝔄𝔩𝔟𝔞𝔫𝔰 held three Hides in 𝔈𝔰𝔠𝔢𝔭𝔢𝔥𝔞𝔩𝔢. The arable is five Carucates, in Demeasne one Hide and an half, and there is one Carucate and another may be made; there are eight Villains having three Carucates, there are two Cottagers and one Servant, Meadow one Carucate, Common of Pasture for the Cattle, Wood to feed ten Hogs in Pannage time; in the whole it is worth four Pounds a Year, when he received it three Pounds, in the time of King *Edward* (the Confessor four Pounds. This Mannor did lie and does lie in the Demeasne ot the Church of 𝔖t. 𝔄𝔩𝔟𝔞𝔫.

In the latter End of the Reign of King *William* the Conqueror, *Paul,* Abbot of the Church of 𝔖t. 𝔄𝔩𝔟𝔞𝔫𝔰, obtained the Restoration of two Hides of Land in this Vill, which *Asketill de Ros,* had held of *Lanfranc* the Archbishop, and since of the Church of St. Alban.

In *anno* 1 *Johan.* that King did confirm the Grant of this Mannor, by the Name of Scrpeale, to the same, Church but Mr. *Norden* calls it Sherpeshale in Regard that this Place has been accounted a wholsome Walk for Sheep.

Wimer de Ardes, and *Alice* his Wife gave seventy and six Acres of arable Land with one Marsh in Scrpehale, and *Robert de Tailbois* and *Ralph* his Son, gave all their Land lying between the Highway which leads from Stevenage to Hertford, and is divided from Scrpehale; these Abbots ever since enjoy'd this Mannor until the fatal Year of their Dissolution when it came to the Crown by the Statue of 32 *H.* VIII.

But shortly after, it was conveyed from the Crown to *George Nodes,* who formerly was Tenant to the same under the Abbot: He held it in the time of King *Edw.* VI. by the yearly Rent of 1l. 16s. 1d. was Serjeant of the Buckhounds to King *H.* VIII. King *Edward,* Queen *Mary,* and Queen *Elizabeth,* he married *Margaret* Daughter of *Thomas Grimston,* but dyed without Issue, whereupon this Mannor came to

John, who was his Brother and Heir, also a Servant to King *H.* VIII. and died seiz'd hereof, leaving Issue

Charles who lived here, and married *Elizabeth* the Daughter of *Thomas Mitchel* of Cobicote in this County, by whom he had Issue

George, who married *Hellen* the Daughter and Heir of *Edward Dowcra* of the Brother-house in Hitchin, by whom he had Issue *Charles, George, John* married to *Margaret* Daughter of *Thomas Crump,* and *Hellen* married to *William Boteler* of Bygrenham in the County of Bedford; he died the 24th Day of *July,* 1643, and the said *Hellen* died the first of *April,* 1658.

Which *Charles* married *Jane* Daughter of *Simeon Brograve* of Hamels, by whom he had Issue *George,* who died in his Infancy, and one Daughter; and after the Decease of *Jane* his Wife, he married *Frances* the Daughter of *William Pert* of Arnolds in the County of Essex, by whom he had Issue eight Children, whereof *George, Edmond, Elizabeth,* and *John* survived him, and he died on the 15th of *October,* 1651, leaving Issue *George,* the present Possessor hereof.

THIS Rectory *Anno* 26 *Henry* VIII. was valued in the King's Books at 9l. 5s. 8d. *per Annum,* and the Lord of this Mannor is Patron hereof.

The VICARS..

John Rudd	*Peter Fisher,* D. D.
Thomas Knight	*William Milner.*
Richard Shoard	

Here lieth the Body of George Nodes, Gentylman, Sergeant of the Buck-
hounds to King Henry the 8th, King Edward the 6th, Queen Mary and
Queen Elizabeth, which dyed the 14th day of May, anno 1564. and Margaret his Wife died the —— day of —— anno 1——.

There is this Inscription on the South Side of the Chancel on a
Marble Stone in a Brass Plate.

Here under lies the Body of Margaret Nodes, Wife of George Nodes,
late of Shephal-Bury, Sergeant of the Buck-hounds to King Henry, King
Edward, Queen Mary and Queen Elizabeth, which Margaret deceased
the 6th day of June, 1682.

Here resteth the Body of *George Nodes* of Shephal in the County of
Hertford. Esq; who had to Wife *Hellen* the eldest Daughter of *Edward
Docwra* of Hitchin in the same County, Esq; and had issue by her six
Sons and two Daughters. He departed this life the 24th. of *July* 1643.
Ætat. 70.

Here lies the Body of *Hellen Nodes* Wife of *George Nodes* of this Parish,
Esq; and Daughter of *Edw Docwra* of Hitchin in the County of Hertford, Esq; She departed this life the 1st. of *April* 1658. *Ætat.* 78.

This Inscription is in the Middle of the Chancel on a Brass Plate as the other.

Here lies the Body of *Charles Nodes* of Shephal, Esq; who first married
the Daughter of *Simeon Brograve* of Hamells in the County of Hertford. Esq; who had issue by her one Son that died and one Daughter
surviving. Also he married *Frances* the Daughter of *William Pert* of
Arnolds in the County of Essex, Esq; who had issue by her eight
Children, whereof four living, *George, Edmond, Elizabeth, John;* he
departed this life the 15th of *Octob.* 1651. in the 48th. year of his age.

Here lies the Body of *George Nodes,* eldest Son of *Charles Nodes,* late of
Shephal. Esq; by *Frances* his last Wife: He departed this life *Apr.* 9.
1654. being 14 years of age on the 5th of *March* 1653.

Here lies the Body of *John Nodes,* youngest Son of *Charles Nodes,* Esq;
who departed this life the 3d of *December* 1652. aged about 14 Months.

Edmundi Nodes, *Armigeri*
Hic conditur Cinis:
Qui *Patris* Caroli Nodes, *Armig.* (è tribus quæ reliquit) filius unicus;
Spes Matris olim, nunc Desiderium (nec plus amatus quam amabilis) efflo-
rescente Ætate, supremum obiit diem,
Decimo sexto Kalendas Martii
An. Dom. 1603. Ætat. 19.
Discite Mortales, claves uteri et Mortis
Ejusdem esse potestatis Dominus dedit et
Dominus abstulit. Sit nomen Domini benedictum.

Here lies the Body of *George Nodes* of London, Esq. who left issue by
his only Wife *Susanna, George, John* and *Charles,* and three Daughters, *Sarah, Susanna* and *Jane.* He departed this life the 7th of *Sept.*
1664. *Ætat.* 60.

*These Inscriptions are all on Marble Stones on the Floor in the Chancel.
This next is in the Body of the Church, and the only one there.*

Here lies the Body of
John Nodes, Gent.
Second Son of *George Nodes,*
of London, Esq;
and *Susanna* his Wife
Who departed this life the 20th
of *May* 1688. *Ætat.* 33.

Hund. of
Caishoe.

Hic jacet
Quod mori potuit
Edmundi Field *de Harden, Armig.*
Hominis, si pietatem spectas, severi, si litteras Eruditi, si mores, prudentis
et placidi. Melior pars in Cœlum rapta Æternæ Fœlicitatis portum
attigit. Uxorem habuit sibi dilectissimam Franciscam, Willielmi Pert
de Arnolds in Com. Essexiæ. Armig. Filiam tertiam; Quæ indulgenti
Patri peperit amores Pignora Annum, quæ infans moritur; Thomam et
Edmundum *Patri Superstites, obiit 3. Junii 1676. Ætat. 56.*
Vivit post Funera Vertus.

Reliquiæ Thomæ Knight, *D. B. Pastoris Fidelis:*
Qui octodecimum muneris persolutus annum
Curà Animarum maximâ, subsidium
Moriens constituit pauperibus annuam:
Quantum si quæris, refectos consule;
Pietati silicet locavit, non ambitioni.
Abi tu et fac simile
Talia voluit memoriæ ergo
Relicta lugens effari marmora.

Here lies interr'd in hope of the Resurrection, the Body of *Richard Sheard,*
Vicar of Shephal and Rector of Stebrnage; who married *Lettice* Daughter of *Eustace Needham* of Wimondley, Esq; and Widow of Mr. *William Langhorn.* He dy'd the 17th of *Novemb.* 1679. *Ætat.* 41.

These two are in the Chancel on the Floor, on Marble Stones.

Near this place lies buried the Body of *John Rudd* the faithful Pastor of
this Parish 45 years, who died a Bachelor the 13th of *July,* 1640. *Ætat.*
72.

Son of Thunder, Son of the Dove,
Full of hot Zeal, full of true Love.
In preaching truth, in living right,
A burning Lamp, a shining Light.

This is against the North Side of the Chancel under the Window on a
small Marble Monument, upon which is the Effigies of Mr. Rudd *(in a*
Shield) with a short Cloak and a Shepherds Crook in his Hand, and bearing
a Sheep on his Neck.

ANTIQUITIES IN HEXTON

Collected by *Francis Taverner,* Esq. and set up by him in
a Table in St. *Nicholas's* Chapel in Hexton.

NEAR unto the Roman military Way called Icknild or
Ikenild-street, which passeth by this Parish upon a very high
Hill is to be seen a warlike Fort of great Strength, and ancient Works, which seemeth to have been a Summer standing Camp of the *Romans:* And near it on the Top of another Hill call'd Wapting-hill, a Hillock was raised up,
such as the *Romans* were wont to rear for Souldiers slain,
wherein many Bones have been found. The *Saxons* call'd
this Fort Ravensburgh, from a City in Germany, whereof
the Duke of Saxony beareth the Title of Lord at this Day.
And this Town, which the *Britains* perhaps call'd Hesk of
Reed, which doth abound much in this Place; the *Saxons*
call'd Heckstanes-tune, that is the Town of Reed and

Stones, if not rather **Hockstanes-tune**, that is, the Town of
Mire and Stones, for old *Englishmen* call deep Mire, Hocks:
Or may be from Grates set in Rivers or Waters before
Floodgates, which are call'd Hecks; neither is it unlikely
but that the *Danes* made some Use of this Fort, for a Parcel of Ground near thereunto is called **Dane-furlong** to this
Day. Some of these Conjectures may be true, but this is
certain, that *Offa*, a Saxon King, of the *Mertians* about
795, founded the Monastery of **St. Albans**, in Memory of
St. *Alban*, and that *Sexi* an honourable and devout *Dane*
(as it is in the Chartulary of the Abby) about *Anno Dom.*
1030, gave to the said Monastery the Town of **Hockstane-
tune**, and the Abbot of **St. Albans** held this Mannor in the
time of King *William* the Conqueror, for it was then recorded in *Domesdei Book*, that

In Dimidio Hundred de **Hit**, *in* **Hegastanestone** *tenuit Abbas* **Sancti Al-**
bani octo hidas, et tres virgat. Terra est duodecim car. in Dominio quatuor
hida et ibi quatuor car. et quinta potest fieri, ibi tresdecim Vill. cum tribus
Bordis habentibus tres car. et adhuc quatuor possunt fieri, ibi tres cotar. et
quatuor servi, et Gosfridus de Bech *tenuit ibi dim. hid. sub Abbate, ibi duo*
molend. de tribus sol; et quatuor denar, pratum duo car. pastura ad pecud. in
totis valentiis valet septemdecim lib. et decem sol. quando recepit duodecem
lib. tempore Regis Edwardi sexdecem lib. Hoc Manerium jacuit et jacet in
Dominio Ecclesiæ **Sancti Albani.** *De hac terra tenuit unus Anglicus tres*
hidas sub Abbate.

Domesd. Lib.
fol. 135, n. 11.

The Abbot of **St. Albans** held eight Hides and three Virgates in **Hegastanestone** in the half Hundred of **Hit**. The arable is twelve Carucates,
in Demeasne four Hides, and there are four Carucates, and a fifth may be
made, there are thirteen Villains with three Bordars, having three Carucates, and now four more may be made, there are three Cottagers and
four Servants, and *Goisfride de Bech* held there half an Hide under the
Abbot, there are two Mills of three Shillings and four Pence Rent by the
Year, Meadow two Carucates, Common of Pasture for the Cattle ; in the
whole Value it is worth seventeen Pounds and ten Shillings, when he received it twelve Pounds, in the time of King *Edward* (the Confessor)
sixteen Pounds. This Mannor did lye and does lye in the Demeasne of
the Church of **St. Alban**. An Englishman held three Hides of this Land
under the Abbot.

This Vill at that time did lie in the Half-hundred of **Hit**,
and from that time during the Space of 510 Years, the Abbots of **St. Albans** were Lords of the Mannors now call'd
Hexton. They were also Patrons of this Church (dedicated
to St. *Faith*, which Saint had her Statue erected over a
Fountain near this Church Yard, call'd *St. Faith's Well*)
for *John de Hertford*, the 23d Abbot, did appropriate this
Church of **Hexstoneston** to the said Monastery. The Cel-
larers of which Monastery kept the Court Leet and the
Court Baron, and received the Rents of the Demeasnes and
Customary Tenants of this Mannor; and the Sacrists had
the disposing of the Profits of the Rectory. After the Dissolution of the said Monastery, King *H.* VIII. in the 36th
Year of his Reign, granted this Mannor to

Sir *Richard a Lee*, Kt. who dying in the Year 1575, left the same to

Anne, one of his Daughters and Coheirs, the Wife of *Edward Sadlier*, Esq. who *Anno Dom.* 1579, alienated the same to his Brother

Henry Sadlier, Esq. who sold it in 1593, to

Peter Taverner, Son of *Richard Taverner* of Wood-Eaton in the County of Oxford, Esq. who seated himself in Hexton Burystead, and dying the 6th of *April*, 1601, was interr'd in this Chappel peculiar to the said Burystead.

The said Fort, which the common People call Ravensborough Castle, is cast up in the Form of an Oval, and containeth sixteen Acres, one Rood, and fifteen Poles of Ground, and is naturally strengthened with mighty deep and very steep Combs, which the Inhabitants called *Lyn*.

The Town of Hexton is seated at the Foot of the Mountains, whence issue many Springs of Water; the Mountains are a continued Rock of Stone.

Warin le Taverner, had Land there about the latter end of King Edw. I. Anno 1300. See the Deed.

Sir Nicholas le Taverner.

William le Taverner of Denwich in Suff. who had a Corrodie in the Abby of Sibton in Suff. Anno 10 Edw. II.

John Taverner, had Lands in Norf. 36 Edw. III. and in North Elmham, 16 R. II. 1393. See a Record and a Deed thereof.—Cecilie Gelham, Wife of John Taverner.

Henry Taverner, Counsellor at Law in H. V. and H. VI. he had Lands in North Elmham, died 6 Edward IV. | John Taverner, a Soldier at the Battle of Agin-Court, and in the Wars of France, | William Taverner, Freeman of London, obiit 1454.

Nicholas Taverner, lived in the time of King Edw. IV. and H. VII. and died 1492.—Margaret, Daughter of Thomas Dethick of Warmegay, alias Wrongey | Henry Taverner, second Son. | Thomas, third Son.

Ann, second Wife of John, Daugh. of Crow of Bilney in Norfolk, Gent. = John Taverner, held Lands in North Elmham, 3 H. VII. he died 37 H. VIII. 1545, and lies buried in Brisly Church. = Alice, the sole Daughter and Heir of Robert Silvester of Brisley in Norfolk, Gent. first Wife of John Taverner. | Robert, second Son of Nicholas, a Canon in the Monastery of Walsingham in Norfolk.

James Taverner, Prosor of North Elmham, eldest Son; Da. of Room... of Wigton in Norfolk, the Relict of Edm. Bedingfield, Esq; by his Mother, the sole Da. of Gogge of Wigton, which James was Father of Tho. who held Land in North Elmham

Tho. Taverner, Lord of the Manont of Kettshum in Norf. mar. Da. of —Not... folk, whose Son Robert, mar. Da. of Grimston, and had Issue one Da. Wife of T. Shouldham of Sudim, Alderman of Norwich.

Margaret, Wife of New-gate in Norfolk, whose Da. Margaret, via Wife of Rich. Harris of Harrie, Clerk, Fath. of Dr. Nath. Harris and Jo. Harris Warden of Winchester 1636, Aunt. second Da. of Jo. Wife of Shouldham in Norwich.

Margaret, the Da. of Walter Lambert, Esq; of Cognham in Surry by his Wife, Da. of Sir John Guldford of Craribunt in Surry, Kt. = Rich. Taverner of Wood Eaton in Com. Oxon, Clerk of the Signet to King H. VIII. Justice of the Peace and High Sheriff of Oxon, obiit 1575. = Mary, Da. of Sir Jo. Harcourt of Stanton-Harcourt in Com. Oxon, Kt.

Roger Taverner of Upmaster in Ess. Esq; Surveyor-General of the King's Woods beyond Trent, had Issue Jo. Taverner, Esq; Surveyor of the King's Woods, Fath. of Rose Taverner of Upminster, living 1634.

Silvester Taverner of Maston in Bedf. Father of Silvester, the John and Richard, &c.

Robert Taverner of Arnolls in Lamborn in Ess. Surveyor-General of the King's Woods beyond Trent, mar. Da. of Charles Newcomen by whom a Da. in Lincolnshire, Feb. of Th. Taverner of Arnolls, Fath. of Robert of Arnolls, and of Tho. of London, Merchant.

Martha, Wife of Geo. Colfield, Esq; Record. of Oxon and Judge of Assize in Wales Fath. to Sir Wil. Colfeild, Kt. Lord Colfeild in Ireland.

Harcourt Taverner and a Da. Penelope, mar. to Mr. Petit, Capt. of the Traunk in Oxon.

Richard Taverner of Wood-Eaton, Esq; Just. of Peace, 26 Eliz. mar. Elinor, Da. of Fra. Wyton of Greenwich, Esq.

John Taverner, M. A. a Divine, died without Issue.

Jane, Wife of Tho. Wentman of Witting Perkin, Oxon, Esq. | Edm. Taverner of Soundmess in Oxon, Esq; Justice of Peace, 3 Jac. mar. Lucy, Da. of Charles Hales, by his Wife, Sister to Sir Thomas Lucy, Kt. obiit. | Margar. mar. to Tales of Witney, Gen 2. to E. Freer of Wat. Eaton.

Peter Taverner of Hexton, mar. Frauncy, Da. of Tho. Docwra of Putteridge in Com. Hertford, Esq. | John, one of Professors in Gresham Coll. and Rector of Stoke Newing-ton, obiit 1653. | Mary, Wife of Edward Wingate, Esq. | Richard Taverner, the Combatant, Servant to King James and Natha-niel a Barreste of Grays Inn, both dead. | Edm. Taverner, Secretary to Fet. Earl of Pembr. Col. of J. Smith of Wrington in Somerset. | John Taverner, of Soundmess, m. Judith, Da. and Coh. of J. Smith of Wrington in Somerset.

Francis of Hexton, mar. Joan, Da. of Geo. Needham of Wymondly Priory in Hertfordshire, Esq.

John, the Soldier, served in the Wars in Ireland, under the Ld. Lambert, and died in the Wars between Sweden and Denmark, and Richard his Brother of Yeung in Surry.

Richard, mar. Martha, Da. of Matthew Bedoll, who lived for Alderman of London 1656.

Frank, 1637. | Richard, 1638. | Jon, 1639. | Edward, 1640. | Mildrew, 1641. | Peter, 1644. | Thomas, 1645. | John, 1647. | Henry, 1648. | Granado, 1650. | Jeremy, 1651. | Robert, 1652.

Hund. of
Caishoe.

THIS Church *Anno 26 Henry* VIII. was rated in the King's Books at the yearly Value of 7*l.* 13*s.* 4*d.* and the Lord of the Mannor is Patron.

The Church contains three Isles covered with Lead, and a Chancel covered with Tyle; at the West End is a square Tower wherein hang four Bells, and upon the Tower stands a Spire about twenty Foot high covered with Lead.

In this Church are two Monuments.

In the one is this Inscription.

Beati
Mortui qui
in Domino moriuntur.

Under which are two Coats of Arms ; and under them this Inscription.

Here lieth buried the Body of *Peter Taverner* Lord of this Town of 𝕭erton, who married *Frances* the Daughter of *Thomas Decwra* of 𝕭ut-teritge in the County of 𝕭ertford, Esq; which two had Issue *Thomas* who died a youth, *Francis, John,* and *Margaret* married to *Edward Wingate,* Gent. the said *Peter* died the sixth of *April, Anno Dom.* 1601.

And at the lower End of the Monument is this Inscription.

Frances the Wife of *Peter* was a Grave, Prudent, Provident, above her Sex Learned, and Religious Matron, who after she had lived a Widow 35 years, to the good Example of others, and to the comfort and benefit of her Children, meekly and Christianly rendered her Soul to God 21 *June, Anno Dom.* 1631. Ætat. 79. and was here under interred.

In the other Monument is this Inscription, with a Coat of Arms at the Head of it.

Johannes Taverner, Natus in Comitat. 𝕭ertford. *Familiâ honestâ, parentibus piis et probis, à primâ Infantiâ literis operam dedit, primo sub private Magistro, denuo Westmonasterii institut.* 𝕮antabrigiæ, *studuit pro an.* 8. *ubi item Magisterii gradum suscepit. dein* 𝕺xonii *pro an.* 5. *posteaq ; Johanni King Episcopo* 𝕷ondon. *a Libellis pro An.* 9. *et unus prelectorum in Collegio* 𝕮ressam, 𝕷ondon. *pro an.* 28. *deniq; sacris Ordinibus susceptis, Vicarius de Tillingham in Com.* 𝕮ssex *an* 5. *postremo Rector hujus Ecclesiæ pro an* 9. *hic subtus expleto curriculo sepultus*
Fœlicem Resurrectionem sperat natus 1584. *Denatus an.* 1638.

Vitam vixit in cælibatu.

Vixi, nec quicquam vel vitæ nomine dignum
  Sensi, vel quare vita petenda foret.
Hic situs est, quires Divinas calluit, Artes
  Omnes, cui lingua et plurima et una fuit :
Qui bene Judicio purum Solidavit acumen :
  Famam, Ultra pondens, ac sine teste pius :
Qui potuit citus quam quærere munus, obire;
  Seu quod Civilis, seu toga, Docta regit.
Mens humilis fuit, in sublimi corpore pectus
  Sincerum, donans dextera, penna volans.
Pulcher erat primo, cum vir virtute venustus
  In æne ; mors vixit, dormit is, illa fuit.

NORTON.

THIS Vill was another Parcel of the Revenue of the Monastery of 𝕾t. 𝕬lbans, which the Abbot possest at the time of the Conquest, for 'tis recorded in *Domesdei Book* under the Title of

Terra Ecclesiæ 𝕾ancti 𝕬lbani.

Domesd. Lib.
fol. 134.

In 𝕭radewater *Hundred. Abbas* 𝕾ancti 𝕬lbani *ten.* Nortone *pro quatuor hidis se defendebat. Terra est decem car. in Dominio duo hidæ, et ibi sunt*

tres car. Ibi Presbiter et quædam Francigena cum quatuordecem Vill. haben- Hund. of
tibus septem car. ibi quinq; Cotarii, et unus Servus, et duo Molend. de sex Caishoe.
decim sol, pratum duo car. pastura ad pec. In totis valent. valet et valuit
sexdecim lib. tempore Regis Edwardi *septemdecim lib. Hoc Manerium ten.*
et tenuit Sanctus Albanus *in Dominio.*

The Abbot of St. Albans held Norton in Bradewater Hundred, it was
rated for four Hides, in Demesne two Hides, and there are three Carucates, there is a Presbiter or Priest, and a certain Frenchwoman born,
with fourteen Villains having seven Carucates, there are five Cottagers
and one Servant, and two Mills of sixteen Shillings Rent by the Year,
Meadow two Carucates, Common of Pasture for the Cattle. In the
whole Value it is worth and was worth sixteen Pounds by the Year, in
the time of King *Edward* (the Confessor) seventeen Pounds, St. *Alban*
doth hold, and did hold this Mannor in his Jurisdiction.

At the time of the making this Survey, this Mannor did
lie in the Hundred of Bradewater: and King *H.* I. by his Mon. Angl.
Charter dated at Wallingford, 1 *Regni sui*, confirmed the vol. 1, fol. 178.
Grant hereof to that Church by the Name of Norton, which
was very proper in Regard that it was situated in the North MS. in Bibl.
Part of the County; and *Simon* the Abbot granted in the Cottoni.
Reign of King *H.* II. this Vill of Norton and Part of the
Tith of Cundale to *Ralph* the Son of *Aldrick* and his Heir
in Fee-farm; reserving three Marks to be yearly paid to the
Abbot and Monks; and also that the said *Ralph* shall pro-
vide as well for the Abbot and Monks as the Men of St.
Albans, and Tine-men, honourable Entertainment, and
what things are necessary for Strangers in their Journey to
Northumberland, and in their Return again; afterwards,
King *John* by his Charter dated 1 *Regni sui*, confirmed the
Grant of this Vill to this Church; and *John Whethamsted,*
alias *Bostock*, a famous Abbot of the said Monastery, in the
Reign of King *H.* VI. gave one Messuage scituated near
the Church in this Vill, and appropriated it to the Use of
the Church of St. Albans, who enjoyed it till the Dissolution of that Convent.

John Boles of Wallington purchased it from the Crown,
held it in the time of *Edw.* VI. by the yearly Rent of 5*l.* 10*s.*
6*d.* and it continued in this Family, which I have treated
of in the Parish of Wallington, until it came to *Lewis Boles,*
who sold it 1 *Car.* I. to

Richard Cleaver, Gent. who had Issue *Richard* and *Catharine*, who married *Thomas Cole* of Radwell, Gent. upon
his Decease, *Richard* the Father surviving his Son, it came to

Philadelphia the Wife of *John Sayer* of the *Inner Temple*, Esq. and *Ann* married to *Courteen*, Daughters and Coheirs of *Richard Cleaver* the Son deceased, who sold it to
William Pym, Esq. the present Lord hereof.

THE Vicaridge was rated *Anno* 26 *Hen.* VIII. in the King's Books at
the yearly Value of 5*l.* 6*s.* 8*d.* and is now situated in the Deanery of St.
Alban in the Diocess of London, and *William Haslefoot* is Patron hereof.

The VICARS.

———— *Saunders.*   *Samuel Sparrowhauke.*

Hund. of
Caisho.

This Church consists only of the Body which is covered with Lead, the Chancel with Tyle, and there are three Bells in the square Tower, and these Inscriptions in the Chancel and Church.

Here lieth interred *Benjamin Hasleden*, Gent. He was born at Radwell in the County of Hertford. the 19th of *April* 1651. and died the 25th of the same Month, being six days old.

Here lieth *Anne Bury* Daughter of *Haseldon Bury*, Gent. of the Age of two years, who died the 2d. of *May* 1607.

In the Church.

Guy Son of *William Pym*, Esq; and *Elizabeth* his Wife, was born the 17th of *February* 1685. And died the 30. of *April* following.

CHARITY.

Ralph Skinner of Hitchin, Gent. gave 5*l.* to the Poor of this Parish.

NEWHAM, NEWNHAM.

THIS Vill was also Part of the Possessions that belonged at the Monastery of St. Albans, which the Abbots enjoyed to the time of the Conquest, as appears by *Domesdei Book*, where it is found under the Title of *Terra Ecclesiæ Sancti Albani*.

Domesd. Lib.
fol. 135.

In Ovesei Hundred. Abbas Sancti Albani ten. Newham pro tribus hidis se defendebat. Terra est octo car. in Dominio un. hida et tres virgat. et ibi sunt duo car. ibi decem Vill. cum octo Bord. habentibus quatuor car. et adhuc duo fieri possunt, ibi tres Cotarii pratum un. car. pastura ad pec. in totis valentiis valet et valuit novem lib. tempore Regis Edwardi decem lib. Hoc Manerium jacuit et jacet in Dominio Ecclesiæ Sancti Albani.

The Abbot of St. Albans held Newham in the Hundred of Ovesey, it was rated for three Hides and three Virgates. The arable is eight Carucates, in Demeasne one Hide and three Virgates, and there two Carucates, there are ten Villains with eight Bordars having four Carucates, and now two more may be made, there are three Cottagers, Meadow one Carucate, Common of Pasture for the Cattle; in the whole Value it is worth and was worth nine Pounds by the Year, in the time of King *Edward* (the Confessor) ten Pounds. This Mannor did lye and doth lye in the Jurisdiction of the Church of St. Albans.

When this Record was made, this Vill did lie in the Hundred of Ovesey, but when King *Edw.* IV. granted that the Abbot and Convent should have the Jurisdiction and Government of all their Lands, and that they should be laid within their Liberty, this Vill I suppose was made Parcel of the Hundred of Caisho.

King *H.* I confirmed the Grant hereof to this Church about 1 *Regni sui* by the Name of Newham, which signifies a new Place of Shelter, or more properly, Habitation; King *John* confirmed all the Grants hereof by his Charter dated 1 *Regni sui* to the same Church, and the Abbots received the Profits hereof until the time of their Dissolution, then King *H.* VIII. by Charter dated the 12th of *May*,

Capella Rot.
in Chanc.

granted this Mannor of Newnham with the Scite of the Priory of the Pree, Sandridge, Caldecot, Radwell, Westwick, Gorham, and Apsa to

Ralph Rowlet the elder, Esq. and his Heirs: He was Sheriff of this County *Anno* 1542, 33 *H.* VIII. and died leaving Issue *Ralph* and two Daughters; after his Decease it descended to

Ralph Rowlet, who was knighted and died seiz'd hereof without Issue, leaving two Sisters his Heirs, who I suppos might sell it to

Richard Hale, Grocer and Citizen of London in the time of Queen *Elizabeth,* who afterwards disposed of it to

Richard Hale his younger Son, who enjoyed, and afterwards gave it to

Robert Hale his younger Son, who held it some time, then sold it about the Year 1678, to

Sir *William Dyer* of Tottenham in the County of Middlesex, who was created Baronet by Letters Patents dated the sixth Day of *July A.D.* 1678, 30 *Car.* II. and he died on the 27th of *Jan.* 1680, when he gave it to

William Dyer his second Son, who married *Mary Howard,* and after her Decease *Anne* Sister to Sir *Hele Hook* Bar. He has lately built a very fair House upon the same, was constituted Sheriff for this County *An.* 1694, 6 *Will.* III. and is the present Lord hereof.

THE Rectory was appropriated to the Use of the Monastery of St. *Alban,* and the Vicaridge was rated *Anno 26 Hen.* VIII. in the King's Books at the yearly Value of 5*l.* and *William Dyer* is the present Patron hereof.

This Church is situated about the Middle of this Vill, in the Hundred of Caisho, in the Deanery of St. Alban, in the Diocess of London; the Body of the Church and Chancel are covered with Lead, and a square Tower adjoyns the West End of the Church, in which are three Bells, and these Inscriptions engraved upon Marbles there.

Here lieth *Joan Dowman* the Wife of *James Dowman* who was the Daughter and Heir of *Henry Gowshull,* Esq; Son and Heir of *Robert Gowshull* of Bedford in Hamldurness in the County of York, Esq; which *Joan* died the 10th of *Nov.* 1607. in the 61 year of her Age, leaving seven Children living, *viz.* One Son and six Daughters

    Edward, Margaret, Elizabeth, Jane, Anne, Constance, Mary, Susan and *Susan.*

Here lieth the Body of Sir *William Dyer,* Bar. who departed this life the 27th of *January* 1680. he married the Granddaughter and sole Heiress to Sir *John Swinnerton* once Lord Mayor of the City of London, had issue by her four Sons and three Daughters, whereof four is now living, *viz.* two Sons and two Daughters; he was a true Christian, an upright Liver, a faithful Husband, a tender Father, and Lord of this Mannor of Newnham.

    Here under lies now buried in the Dust
    The Man whose life was sober, pure, and just,

  His Coat of Arms, *Or, a chief indented Gules.*

There is another Stone, the Inscription whereof was taken away in the late time of Rebellion.

Having now concluded this Hundred of Caishoe, I shall proceed to the Hundred of Dacorum, which is the fifth and last Division of this County.

THE FIFTH DIVISION OF THIS COUNTY.

CONTAINING

THE HUNDRED

OF

DACORUM.

Hund. of
Dacorum.

IN the time of *William* the Conqueror, it was sever'd by the Names of **Danais** and **Treung** Hundreds, but about the Reign of *Edw*. III. they were consolidated into one Hundred, now called **Dacorum** from the *Danes* that were in old times Inhabitants here. It was Parcel of the Kings Revenue, and the Sheriffs were wont to hold Courts for every Hundred, for the registring of Mortgages and Sales of Land, inroling of Deeds, Tryals of Titles of

Dugd. *Orig.*
Jurid. fol. 25.
Brady's *Hist.*
of Engl. fol.
114, 145.
Old Nat. Bre.
fol. 2.
Glan. lib. 12,
cap. 6, 7, 8.
Glan. lib. 9,
cap. 8, 9, 10.
Bract. lib. 3.
Tract. 2, cap.
32, fol. 150.
and cap 28,
fol. 147.
Spelm. *Gloss.*
tit. *Serviens,*
fol. 513.
Dugd. *Origin.*
Jurid. fol. 27,
28, 31, 93. 94.
Brady's *Hist.*
of Engl. fol.
146.

Land, levying of Fines within the Jurisdiction of the Hundred before the Steward, who was styled *Serviens Regis ad Legem*, the Kings Serjeant at Law, because the County and Hundred Courts, were the King's Courts, and he was the King's Officer, and to distinguish him from those Serjeants who were Stewards to the Lords of Mannors in their Court Barons : hence I conceive this Distinction among the Serjeants was originally derived, and no Persons in those Days were held qualified to exercise the Office of Steward in any of these Courts, unless he had taken the Degree of Serjeant, because Fines were levied, and Titles of Land heard and determined here, which none but a learned Man in the Law was capable to perform, but when the Profits of these Courts were farmed out to inferior Persons, and Mannors were broke into Pieces, or divided into Parcels, either by Coparcinary or Sale, and by such Means derived unto Men under the Degree of Barons, it seems they constituted Stewards who were not skilled in the Law to hold these Offices, insomuch that the People complained of this Grievance in the time of King *John*, who thereupon granted by his Charter dated 17 *Regni sui* that the Common-pleas should not follow the Court, but should be held in some certain Place, to the End all People might have free Liberty to resort thither for Justice, for before that time no Person, under the Rank of Barons, unless allowed by the King's Patent, could sue or bring any Action before the King, or his Chief Justice of England, or his Justices in his Palace, but were bound to bring all their Actions in their Lord's Court, or the Hundred or County Court, and after this Liberty and Priviledge was confirmed to the People, by the Statute of *Magna Charter* granted 9 *H.* III. the Court of Common Pleas was established in *Westminster-Hall*, and all these Serjeants at Law who have been Stewards as well of Court Barons as of the Hundred, and County Courts, where they had usually taken Fines, were bound by Oath always to attend at the Court of Common-Pleas, and have always since taken Fines upon any *Dedi-mus potestatem* after such Manner as the Justices of the Bench may do, and the Election of the Justices and Judges of the Courts in *Westminster-Hall*, have been always restrained to these Serjeants; but to proceed, the Sheriffs for this County have from time to time, accounted in the *Exchequer* for the Profits hereof with the Rest of the County, and the Justices of the Peace, and the Commisioners for the King's Taxes do generally appoint their Privy Sessions, and keep their Publick Meetings at 𝕳𝖊𝖒𝖊𝖑 𝕳𝖊𝖒𝖕-𝖘𝖙𝖊𝖉, to manage the Business of this Hundred: it is bounded on the North and East Part with the Hundred of 𝕮𝖆𝖎𝖘𝖍𝖔, and 𝕭𝖗𝖆𝖉𝖊𝖜𝖆𝖙𝖊𝖗, on the South with 𝕸𝖎𝖉𝖉𝖑𝖊𝖘𝖊𝖝, and on the West with 𝕭𝖚𝖈𝖐𝖎𝖓𝖌𝖍𝖆𝖒𝖘𝖍𝖎𝖗𝖊, and contains several Parishes and Hamlets which are divided between three Chief Constables; the first has in his Division the Parishes and Hamlets of 𝖂𝖍𝖊𝖙𝖍𝖆𝖒𝖘𝖙𝖊𝖉, 𝕳𝖆𝖗𝖕𝖊𝖉𝖔𝖓, 𝕹𝖔𝖗𝖙𝖍 𝕸𝖞𝖒𝖒𝖘, 𝕾𝖍𝖊𝖓𝖑𝖞, 𝕿𝖍𝖊𝖔𝖇𝖆𝖑𝖉𝖘𝖙𝖗𝖊𝖊𝖙, 𝕷𝖊𝖇𝖊𝖘𝖉𝖊𝖓, and 𝕭𝖚𝖘𝖍𝖊𝖞, which lie dispersedly from the Rest. Another Chief Constable has the Parishes and Hamlets of 𝕶𝖎𝖓𝖌'𝖘 𝕷𝖆𝖓𝖌𝖑𝖊𝖞, 𝕳𝖊𝖒𝖊𝖑 𝕳𝖊𝖒𝖕𝖘𝖙𝖊𝖉, 𝕭𝖔𝖛𝖎𝖓𝖌𝖉𝖔𝖓, 𝕱𝖑𝖆𝖚𝖓𝖉𝖊𝖓, 𝕷𝖎𝖙𝖙𝖑𝖊 𝕲𝖆𝖉𝖊𝖘𝖉𝖊𝖓, 𝕱𝖗𝖎𝖘𝖉𝖊𝖓, 𝕲𝖗𝖊𝖆𝖙 𝕲𝖆𝖉𝖊𝖘𝖉𝖊𝖓, 𝕾𝖙𝖚𝖉𝖍𝖆𝖒, 𝕶𝖊𝖓𝖘𝖜𝖔𝖗𝖙𝖍, 𝕮𝖆𝖉𝖎𝖓𝖌𝖙𝖔𝖓, and 𝕱𝖑𝖆𝖒-𝖘𝖙𝖊𝖉; and the other Chief Constable has in his Division the Parishes and Hamlets of 𝕭𝖊𝖗𝖐𝖍𝖆𝖒𝖘𝖙𝖊𝖉, 𝕹𝖔𝖗𝖙𝖍 𝕮𝖍𝖚𝖗𝖈𝖍, 𝕬𝖑-𝖉𝖊𝖇𝖚𝖗𝖞, 𝕿𝖗𝖎𝖓𝖌, 𝖂𝖎𝖌𝖎𝖓𝖌𝖙𝖔𝖓, 𝕷𝖔𝖓𝖌 𝕸𝖆𝖗𝖘𝖙𝖔𝖓, 𝖂𝖎𝖑𝖘𝖙𝖊𝖗𝖓𝖊, 𝕻𝖚𝖙𝖙𝖊𝖓𝖍𝖆𝖒, and 𝕮𝖔𝖑𝖊𝖘𝖍𝖎𝖑𝖑, after which Order I shall proceed.

WHETHAMSTED,

SO called from the great Plenty of excellent Wheat which that Place afforded; the chief Mannor was Parcel of the

[margin notes: Hund. of Bacorum. / Matt. Paris, fol. 255, n. 50. MSS. in Bibl. Coll. Corp. Christi Cant. / Stat. Magna Charta, cap. 11, 9 H. III. / Coke, 2 Inst. fol. 214, 512. Vet. N. B. fol. 103. Bro. tit. Fines 120.]

Possessions of King *Edward* the Confessor, which he imployed towards the Provision of his Table, until such time that he gave it to the Abbot and Convent of 𝔚estminster, who held it in the time of *William* the Conqueror, when it was recorded in that memorable Survey of *Domesdei Book*, under the Title of *Terra Abbatis* 𝔚estmonaster.

Domesd. Lib.
fol. 135, n. 9.

In 𝔅anais *Hundred. Abbas de* 𝔚estmonaster, *St. Petri tenet* 𝔚atamestede *pro decem hidas se defendebat. Terra est decem car. in Dominio quinq; hidæ, et ibi sunt tres car. et udhuc duo possunt fieri. Ibi Presbiter cum quindecem Vill. habentibus quinq; car. Ibi duodecem Bord. et novem Coterii, et quatuor molin. de quadragint. sol. pratum quatuor car. pastura ad pec. Silva centum porc. in totis valent. valet et valuit sexdecem lib. tempore Regis Edwardi trigint. lib. Hoc Manerium jacuit et jacet in Dominio Ecclesiæ St. Petri.*

The Abbot of St. *Peter* of 𝔚estminster held 𝔚hethamsted in 𝔅anais Hundred, it was rated for ten Hides. The arable is ten Carucates, in Demeasne five Hides, and there are three Carucates, and now two others may be made, there is a Presbiter or Priest with fifteen Villains having five Carucates, there are twelve Bordars, and nine Cottagers, and four Mills of forty Shillings Rent by the Year, Meadow four Carucates, Common of Pasture for the Cattle, Wood to feed one hundred Hogs; in the whole Value it is worth and was worth sixteen Pounds by the Year, in the time of King *Edward* (the Confessor) thirty Pounds by the Year. This Mannor did lye and doth lye in the Demeasne of the Church of St. *Peter.*

Quo War. 6
Ed. 1. Rot.35,
cur. recept.
in Scac.

The Jury found *An.* 6 *Edw.* I. that 𝔚hethamsted was ancient Demesne of the King, which the Abbot and Convent of 𝔚estminster held of the Gift of St. *Edward* the Confessor, and was worth 50*l.* by the Year, and that Master *John* of 𝔏eicester the Parson, claimed as belonging to his Church of 𝔚achamstede, View of Franc-pledge, and free Court to hold from three Weeks to three Weeks, and Assize of Bread and Ale, with divers other Liberties, from that time the Dean and Chapter of the same Church held this Mannor, are the present Lords hereof, and have now Jurisdiction of Court Leet and Baron.

The Mannor of *LAMERE.*

IS scituated upon a dry Hill in the same Parish, and was so denominated from *Pontius Lamere*, who was Lord hereof in the Reign of *H.* III to whom that King granted the Wardship of the Lands of *William de Say* in 𝔖abridgeworth, during his Minority. But in Process of time it came to the Possession of Sir *William Roch*, Alderman of 𝔏ondon, Son to *John Roch* of 𝔚ixley in 𝔜orkshire; He was Lord Mayor of the same City, and committed to the Fleet, *An.* 1545, 36 *H.*VIII. for speaking Words against the Benevolence, which displeased the King's Council,

Stow's *Annals*
fol. 388.

where he remained until Passion Sunday following; in the time of his Mayoralty, the English Bible was used in every Parish Church, and he died seized hereof, leaving only Issue one Daughter

Grizill, who was his Heir, and married Sir *John Boteler* of 𝔚𝔬𝔬𝔡𝔥𝔞𝔩𝔩 in this County, Kt. they levied a Fine of this Mannor in *Michaelmas* Term, *Anno* 3 *Edw.* VI. by the Name of Lands in the Parish of 𝔚𝔥𝔢𝔱𝔥𝔞𝔪𝔰𝔱𝔢𝔡, otherwise called the 𝔥𝔬𝔢-𝔤𝔯𝔬𝔲𝔫𝔡, to the Use of the said Sir *John Boteler* and *Grizill* his Wife, and his Heirs, from whom it descended to

Philip Boteler his Son and Heir, who sold it as I guess to Sir *William Garret* or *Garrard*, Son of *William Garrard* of 𝔖𝔦𝔱𝔱𝔦𝔫𝔤𝔟𝔲𝔯𝔫𝔢 in the County of 𝔎𝔢𝔫𝔱, Esq. He was an Haberdasher, and Lord Mayor of 𝔏𝔬𝔫𝔡𝔬𝔫 in the third Year of *Philip* and *Mary;* He had Issue Sir *William*, *George*, and *John*, who was his third Son, Sheriff of 𝔏𝔬𝔫𝔡𝔬𝔫 *Anno* 1592, and Lord Mayor there *An.* 1601. He died the 7th of *May*, 1625, and was buried in St. *Magnus* Church in 𝔏𝔬𝔫𝔡𝔬𝔫, leaving Issue

John Garrat, who was his Son and Heir, created Baronet by Letters Patents dated the 16th of *Feb. An.* 1621, 19 *Jac.* I. he married *Elizabeth* one of the Daughters of Sir *Edward Barkham*, Kt. who was Lord Mayor of 𝔏𝔬𝔫𝔡𝔬𝔫 the same Year, and was Sheriff of this County, *Annis* 19, 20 *primo medio Anni* 21 *Car.* I. and he died leaving Issue

John, who succeeded his Father in his Honours and Estate, and married *Jane* the youngest Daughter and Coheir of Sir *James Enyon*, Bart. the Widow of Sir *George Boswell*, Bart. by whom he had only Issue *Jane*, who is his Daughter and Heir, married to Sir —— *Drake*, and this Sir *John* is the present Lord hereof.

Hund. of 𝔇𝔞𝔠𝔬𝔯𝔲𝔪.

Fin. levat.
Mich. 3 Ed.
VI. Rot. 62,
cur. recept.
in Scac.

THE Rectory is a Messualty derived out of the Mannor of 𝔚𝔥𝔢𝔱𝔥𝔞𝔪𝔰𝔱𝔢𝔡, and is situated in the Deanery of 𝔅𝔢𝔯𝔨𝔥𝔞𝔪𝔰𝔱𝔢𝔡 in the Diocess of 𝔏𝔦𝔫𝔠𝔬𝔩𝔫, and this Rectory with the Chappel of 𝔥𝔞𝔯𝔭𝔦𝔫𝔤𝔡𝔬𝔫, *Anno* 26 *Hen.* VIII. was rated in the King's Books at the yearly Value of 42*l.* 1*s.* 10*d.* and the King is Patron hereof.

The RECTORS.

Henry Killegrew, D. D.   *John Lamb*, D. D. Dean of 𝔈𝔩𝔶.

This Church is situated on the West Side of the Vill, erected after the Manner of a Cathedral, having a Cross and a Tower in the Middle thereof, with a Spire and a Balcony round the Middle of the Spire, all covered with Lead, in which are five Bells, and in the Chancel and Church are these Inscriptions.

A Marble under the Altar is thus engraved.

Here *William Bristowe* Gentleman,
  And *Agnis* late his Wife,
Do rest themselves till Judgment Day:
  He passed from this Life
Aprilis Seventeenth one Thousand and
  Five Hundred ninety nine;
And in *September* ninety God
  Cut off her vital Line.
Three Daughters they, Coheirs did leave
  Luce, *Martha*, *Margaret*,
Who in regard of Parents Love,
  This Monument hath set.

——— Domini Willielmi Grettewelle, quondam Rectoris istius Ecclesiæ de Whethamstede, ac Canonici in Ecclesia Cathedralis Lincoln. Qui obiit 4. Ibus Febr. Anno Dom. Milessimo CCCC primo.

Uxori Charissimæ.
Dominæ Janæ Leventhorpe,
Filiæ Domini Richardi Mickell *nuper hujus Parochiæ*
Quæ secundo fatu pregnans, febre correpta.
Immatura prolem, cum anima maturâ, reddidit,
       June 28. *A. D.* 1661 *Ætat.* 27.
            Ob.

   Pietatem, in Deum singularem ;
    Mores erga omnes suavissimos ;
   Amorem in virum supra muliebrem.

   Hoc voluit extare miremosynon
   Staffordus Leventhorpe,
   Pastor Ecclesiæ de Shephall.

Heic unicum reliquit Pignus charissimum
     Thomam Leventhorpe,
Patris solatium amicorum Delectamentum,
    Qui quarta post mense
Huc Matrem (proh Dolor) sequutus est.
   Ætatis suæ mensæ duodecimo.

Here lyeth the Body of *John Hunsdon,* Gent
    Aged Seventy one Years.
     Obiit Aprilis 26.
      An. Dom. 1676.

Here resteth the Body of *Alice,* late Wife of *Jonas Baily* of Makarpend in this Parish, Gent. the sole Daughter of *William Hodson* of Bourton in the County of Bucks, Gent. who deceased the 26th of *Feb. Anno Dom.* 1642. in the 27th Year of her Age, and had issue two Sons and one Daughter; whereof the youngest, a Son deceased, lyeth buried by her.

In Memory of whose Piety towards God, Charity to her Neighbours, Loving Deportment to her Husband, Motherly Affection to her Children, the said *James Baily* hath caused this Stone to be laid.

Directly underneath this Place lyeth buried *John Heyworth* of Mackerynend, Esq. and *Joan* his Wife. They had three Children buryed in their Infancy, wherefore they both did adopt *Margaret Hoo* their sole Heir : Her first Husband was *Jerram Reynold,* by whom he had no Issue: Her second Husband was *Nicholas Brocket,* Esq. who lieth buried next to Mr. *Heyworth,* they had Issue *John,* who at the Commandment of the said *Margaret,* erected this Monument; the said *John Heyworth* deceased 25th Day of *Decemb. Anno Dom.* 1558.

Here lieth interred the Body of *Mary Brocket* Wife of *John Brocket* of Whethamsted in the County of Hertford, Esq. and Daughter of *George Banister* of Braydon in the County of Middlesex, Gent. and had Issue by him six Sons and two Daughters, *viz. George, Thomas, Mary, John, William, Elizabeth, Banister,* and *Henry.* She departed this Life the —— day of ——— *Anno Dom.* 1669, Aged 73. Years.

Here lieth *Edward Brocket,* second Son to Sir *John Brocket,* and Dame *Mary* his Wife; the said *Edward Brocket,* married Dame *Ethel* ——— *Chall* ———, Widow, one of the Daughters of *Frad. Sham* of Elton in Cheshire, by whom he had a Son and two Daughters, who were living at the time of his Death, which was in *Anno* 1599, the 3d of *September.*

Here lieth the Body of *Edward Brocket,* Gent. eldest Son of *John Brocket,* late of Whethamsted in the County of Hertford, Esq. and late Husband of *Mary* the Daughter of *Henry Tooke,* late of Bishops Hatfield, in the County of Hertford, Gent. and had Issue by her one Son and four Daughters *John, Mary, Elizabeth, Frances,* and *Anne* : He departed this Life the ninth day of *January, Anno Dom.* 1669. Aged 64 Years.

Heic juxta
Thomas Stubbing
Civis et Mercator Londinensis
in Ordinem Senatorium ascitus
F. Marci
(hujus Ecclesiæ per Lustra Rectoris)
ex Elizabetha, F. George Rotheram
De Farley *in Com.* Bed. *Armig.*
Anno fœlicissimi redditus Carolina III
propter Parentes requiescit
post ibi
lapsis 15 *Annis*
Illum excipit Anna *mœstissima Conjux*
Liberis 5 *Superstitibus.*

M. S.
Hic situs est
P. Nathan Vereard *apud* Cantabrigiæ A. M.
Vir Pius, Prudens, Probus, et Doctus,
Noxius nemini, singulis Benevolus,
In Vita Religiosus ad exemplum,
In tædio morbi, ac morte patiens ad miraculum,
Ille magno suorum et omnium mœrori,
Anno } *Christi* MDCLXXXV.
      } *Ætatis suæ* xxxvii
Improles (proh Dolor) et vivis excessit,
Et heic Servatoris sui expectat adventum,
Abi, Lector, Ora,
Et
Imitare

This is engraved on a Monument in the Wall.

Here lieth the Body of
The Vertuous Lady, Dame *Elizabeth Garrard*, late Wife of Sir *John Gar-*
rard, Kt. and Baronet, one of the Deputy Lieutenants of this County,
Son of Sir *John Garrard*, and Grandchild of Sir *William Garrard*,
Knights, both of them sometime Lord Mayors of the City of London,
whose Ancestors lie buried in the Parish Church of Sittingburn in Kent,
but themselves in the Parish Church of St. Magnus in London: she
was the eldest Daughter of Sir *Edward Barkham*, Knight, sometime
Lord Mayor of the City of London, married in the year of our Lord
1611. called by God out of this Life the 17th day of *April*, in the year
of our Lord 1632. being then in the 39th year of her Age, Mother of 14
Children, six Sons and eight Daughters (whereof two, a Son and a
Daughter, went before her to Heaven, the rest she left behind her upon Earth; first commending by devout Prayers unto God, and then
delivering them over with hearty desires to her beloved Husband, to
be farther instructed in the fear of God;) towards God a most Faithful
Child, towards her Husband a Loyal Spouse, towards her Children a
most loving Mother, towards the Poor a most Charitable Neighbour;
in Health praising God, in Sickness bearing patiently, she lived most
Godly, and died most Comfortably, bequeathing her Body unto Earth
in assured hope of blessed Resurrection, and her Soul unto God in confidence of her Salvation.
Here resteth the virtuous Body of *Isabella Garrard*, youngest Daughter
of Sir *John Garrard*, Kt. and Baronet, and by his Wife the Lady *Jane*
Garrard, who left this Life for a better in the ——— of her Age, 10th
Day of *August, Anno Dom.* 1677.
Virtus sepuleri ignara est.
Underneath lies the Effigies of the said Knight and his Lady.

HARPEDON

IS scituated about three Miles distant from Whethamsted, upon an Hill towards the South, from whence it de-

Hund. of
Barorum.
Cart. 20 Ed.t.
Bar. of Engl.
vol.2. fol. 233.
rives its Name; 'tis a Hamlet belonging to that Parish, and I suppose was waste Ground in the time of *William* the Conqueror, for there is no Mention made of it in *Domesdei Book;* but when the Lands were improved, the *Hoo's,* an ancient Family in this County, possest them, for *Robert Hoo* was Lord hereof *Anno* 1292, 20 *Edw.* I. when he obtained the King's Charter for Free-warren within this Lordship: He was elected Knight of the Shire in the Parliament held *Anno* 26 *Edw.* I. and died the 9th of *May*, 1310.

Sir *Thomas Hoo* held it *Anno* 11 *Edw.* III. obtained a Grant for Free-warren in all his Lordships of **Hoo,** **Stopesley,** and **Wbethamsted** in this County.

T. Walsingh.
anno 1387, p.
363.
Sir *William Hoo*, Kt. was his Son and Heir, succeeded him, and upon the Flight of *Michael de la Poole*, Earl of **Suffolk,** *Anno* 1387, 10 *Rich.* II. helpt him away to **Calais,** that he might avoid the Danger that attended him at that time, and served in that Garison under *John* Earl of
Rot. Franc.
8 H. IV.
Somerset, *Anno* 1407, 8 *H.* IV. then Captain there: He married *Alice* the Daughter and Heir to Sir *Thomas St. Maur* by *Jane* his Wife, Daughter and Heir to *Nicholas Malmaines*, by whom he had Issue

Holl. fol. 612.
Thomas, who was sent to suppress the *Normans* upon a new Rebellion made about **Caux,** *Anno* 1436, 14 *H.* VI. where he slew many of them, and made great Waste in the Country: The King imployed him again in the Wars of
Rot. Franc.
24 H. VI.
France, *Anno* 1446, 24 *H.* VI. where he merited so well that the King by Letters Patents dated the 2d of *June,*
Pat. 26 H.VI.
Bar. of Engl.
vol. 2, fol 234
1448, 26 *H.* VI. advanced him to the Dignity of a Baron of this Realm by the Title of Lord *Hov* and *Hastings*, to hold to the Heirs Males of his Body; and he was elected into the honourable Society of Knights of the Most Noble
Claus de iisd.
ann. indorso.
Order of the Garter; he was summon'd to Parliament from the 27th to 31st of *H.* VI. inclusive, and he married three Wives, first *Elizabeth* Daughter and Heir to Sir *Thomas Felton*, Kt. by whom he had Issue one Son called *Thomas*, who died in his Life-time without Issue; and after her Decease, he married *Elizabeth* Daughter and Heir to Sir *Ni-*
Bar. of Engl.
vol. 2, fol. 234
cholas Wichingham, by whom he had Issue only one Daughter named *Anne*, married to Sir *Geoffery Bullen*, Kt. sometime Lord Mayor of **London;** and after the Decease of *Elizabeth*, he married *Eleanor* Daughter to *Leo* Lord **Wells,** Sister and Coheir to *Richard* Lord **Wells** her Brother, by whom he had Issue, three Daughters who became his Coheirs; *Eleanor* married to Sir *James Carew* of **Beddington,** in the County of **Surry,** Kt. *June* to Sir *Roger Copely*, Kt. and *Elizabeth* to Sir *John Devenish*, Knight, shortly after this Mannor was sold to

Matthew Cressy, who held it in the Reign of King *Edw.* IV. and married *Joan* the Daughter of *Edmond Perient* of

Bigswell in this County, Esq. and *Ann* his Wife, Daughter of *Thomas Vernon*, Esq. it was at that time called Wrackhamsted, and continued in that Name and Family, for many Descents, until it came to *William Cressy*, who died seiz'd hereof on the 24th Day of *October*, 1558, 1 *Eliz.* from whom it came to

Edmond Cressy, who left only Issue

Elizabeth, who was his Daughter and Heir; his Arms were *Argent, a Lyon rampant queve four che azur;* she married *Edmond Bardolfe*, by whom she had Issue

Edmond, who married *Elizabeth* Daughter to *Robert Dartnold* of Penshunt, in Kent: by whom he had

Richard Bardolfe who was his Son and Heir, and succeeded him; from whom descended

Richard Bardolfe, who gave *Azure, a Cheveron between three cinquefoils Or; Crest out of a Ducal Coronet, a Dragon's Head issuant Or.* He sold it to

Sir *John Witherong*, who was created Baronet by Letters Patents dated the 2d of *May*, 1662, *Anno* 14 *Car.* II. and he gave it to

James Witherong his second Son, who is an Utterbarister of *Lincoln's Inn*, Recorder of the Burrough of St. Albans, and the present Lord hereof.

But since this Gentleman is an Utter Barister, it may not be unfit to make some Remarks upon the Antiquity of that Degree: When the Court of *Common Pleas* was fixed in a certain Place by the Statute of *Magna Charta*, doubtless the Students of the Law, and the Officers of the Court settled themselves in some Places near it, most proper for their Studies, and convenient for their Practice, their Conference, and their Business; and for their more regular Government, King *Edward* I. *Anno* 20 *Regni sui*, commanded *John de Metingham*, then Lord Chief Justice of the Court of *Common Pleas*, and the other Justices there, that they should provide and ordain at their Discretion, a certain Number of Attornies and Apprentices at Law, of the better, lawful, and most learned Men in every County, who might best serve, and be most profitable to his Court and People, and that only those and no other should follow his Court, and solicite Business there; and it seemed meet to the King and his Counsel, that sevenscore were a sufficient Number for that Imployment; notwithstanding the Justices were allowed to appoint a greater or lesser Number, and ordered to dispose of the Residue of them according to their Discretion. Tho' there is no Memorial left of the direct time and Place where these Attornies and Lawyers then resided; yet in all Probability they were settled in Hostels or Inns near the Court, where they might with the greater Conveniency attend the Courts of Justice, serve their Country, and learn to dance,

Hund. of Bacorum.

Mag. Charta, 9 H. 1ll. cap. 11.

Pl. in Parl. 20 Ed. I. Rot. 5, indorso. Seld. Notes on Fortiscuede Laudibus Legum Angl. cap. 5, co. 9, Rep. in Proemio. Origin. Jurid. fol. 141.

Hund. of Bacorum.

Inter Com. Plac. in Hustings, Lond. die Lunæ in Festo 5. Clem. Papæ, 23 Ed. III. Origin. Jurid. fol. 271. Seld. Notes upon Fortescue, cap. 8.

sing, and play upon Instruments on their Days of Vacancy, study Divinity on the Lord's Day, and practice such Exercises as were most modish in the King's Court on Festival Days; from whence they derived the Name of Inns of Court: Some judicious Men believe that divers of them were settled at a House in *Fleet-street*, now called *Clifford's Inn*, from the Lord *Clifford*, who demised it in the time of *Edw.* III. *Apprenticiis de Banco* to the Lawyers; and that others resided at *Thavies Inn* in *Holburn*, for *John Tavy* the Owner of that House, had this Expression in his Will, made in the Reign of *Edw.* III. *Totum illud Hospicium in quo Apprenticii ad Legem habitare solebant:* All that Inn in which the Apprentices at Law were wont to dwell: They were called Apprentices from the French Word *Apprendre*, to learn, for every one was learning here to fit and qualifie himself for the Station he designed; but the Number of these Lawyers encreasing, and the House probably growing too streight for their Company, they removed hence (as we have it by Tradition) to the *New Temple* scituated over against the South End of *New-street*, now called *Chancery-lane*, containing all that Space of Ground extending from the *White Fryars* on the East, to *Essex-house* in the West; including Part of that House without *Temple Bar*, which they held in the time of King *Edw.* III. upon a Demise from the Knights Hospitallers, under the yearly Rent of 10*l.* where they were at that time formed into a Society, chose all necessary Officers, and were distinguished after the Method of the Universities by these Degrees.

1. Students attired in Gowns, like those which the Undergraduates wear in *Cambridge*; and when they had spent four Years in the Study of the Law, they were termed Mootesmen for Distinction from the Puisny Students, so denominated from their Mootes and Exercises, which they performed there; but certainly this was no more a Degree than that of Sophisters in the University; and when they had studied seven or eight Years, performed all Duties and Exercises, and fitted themselves for Business, they were preferred to the Bar in the Parliament, Council, or Pension held for their Society, and called

2. Utter Baristers, for that the Readers and Masters of the Bench in their Society had qualified them to argue Cases, and manage Causes for their Clyents without the Bar, and adorn'd them with a noble Robe, faced down before, guarded with two Welts of Velvet on the Sleeves, extending from the Shoulder to the Elbow, and another on the Bordar of it, like the Gards which the *Romans* used to distinguish the different Degrees of Men among them: these Robes were great Ornaments, which the Reverend Judges

maintained in the Height of the late Rebellion, to the Glory of the Profession, when others laid aside their proper Habit, through Fear of the Souldiery, or to please the Faction of that Age; but 'tis great Pity, and it seems very ominous, that these learned Men should now decline this noble Robe, and wear a scandalous Livery, which resemble those that Bearers usually wear at Funerals, as though the Law lay a dying: However, 'tis greatly hoped, that that worthy Patron of the Law, Sir *John Holt,* the present Lord Chief Justice, will thoroughly reform this ill Practice, and that none of the reverend Sages of the Law will suffer those Gentlemen to share in the Profit and Advantage of that Profession which they scandalize by devesting it of that ancient Robe, and introducing an ignominious Habit in the Room of it. When these Lawyers had practised at the Bar by the Space of twelve Years or more, they were advanced to the Degree of

3 Readers, who were wont to read upon some peculiar Statute in the open Hall within their Society three Days in every Week, for the Space of three Weeks together, entertaining the Gentlemen and their Friends with Exceedings all the other Days, till these Readings were shortened to a Week, in Regard of their extraordinary Expense, which discouraged many learned Men from this Exercise: and they were distinguish'd from the Utterbaristers by a black Cloth Gown, garded with a broad Welt of Velvet cross their Backs: These Readers and Utterbaristers were the Pleaders men tioned in the Statutes of **Westminster** the first, and *Edw.* III. and out of the Number of the Readers the King usually selected by Writ,

4 Serjeants at Law, of whom I have treated before in the Vill of **Risden,** to which I refer the Reader.

These Societies were excellent Seminaries and Nurseries for the Education of Youth, some for the Bar, others for the Seats of Judicature, others for Government, and others for the Affairs of State; but *Walsingham* tells us that the Rebels did do much Mischief to these Lawyers in 4 *R.* II. where he saith, *Locum qui vocatur* **Temple Barre** *in quo Apprenticii Juris morabantur Nobiliores irruerant:* and Mr. *Stow* confirms it, saying, the Rebels of **Essex** and **Kent,** *An.* 1381, destroyed the House and Lodgings in the *Temple,* took the Books and Records of the Apprentices at Law out of their Hutches in their Church, and burnt them in the Streets: but notwithstanding this great Damage done to their Society, they increased much in the time of *H.* VI. when 'tis reported, that a great Dissension and Quarrel happening then among them, touching the Houses of **York** and **Lancaster,** and increasing to a great height, they parted with much Wrath and divided into two Societies:

Stow's Survey of London, fol 443.

*Hund. of
Bacorum.*
whereof one Party built a new Hall in the back Yard, where the Stables and Hosteries of the Knight's Templers stood, erected Chambers near it, assuming the *Pegasus* for their Arms, termed it the *Inner Temple* in Respect it was seated between the *Old Temple* and 𝕷𝕺𝕹𝕯𝕺𝕹, and appropriated the South Side of the Church for their Part, whilst the other kept Possession of the Hall of their old Society, scituated between 𝕻𝖚𝖒𝖕 and 𝕰𝖑𝖒 𝕮𝖔𝖚𝖗𝖙, after the Form of the Round Walk in the *Temple Church*, and pull'd down in the Year 1639; claim'd the *Holy Lamb*, the Arms of the old House to themselves, as their ancient Right, and reserved the North Side of the Church for their peculiar Use, which in those Days was held the upper Side, for that the Gospel was always read at the North End of the Altar; and these Members dividing according to their Affections for the several Houses of 𝖄𝖔𝖗𝖐 and 𝕷𝖆𝖓𝖈𝖆𝖘𝖙𝖊𝖗, is the Reason why the Chambers of these Societies, are at this Day intermixt with each other House. In short time after this Division, Sir *John Fortescue*, then Lord Chief Justice of the *King's Bench*, a Member of *Lincoln's Inn*, saith, there were then four Houses of Court, which are now, *Origin. Jurid.*
fol. 320.
Ord. 6 Car I.
nu. 5.
Ibid fol. 321.
Ord. 16 Car.II
nu. 5.
Origin. Jurid.
fol. 142. each containing two hundred Persons; and ten Inns of Chancery, every one consisting of an hundred Men; which he called the Lawyers' University, whereof the four Houses of Court were appropriated wholly for the Use of the Sons of the Nobility and Gentry, who studied the Law and learned the Accomplishments of a Gentleman, for the vulgar Sort could not bear the Expense of a Student there; which required eighty Scutes *per Annum*, *Ferne's Glory
of Generosity,*
p. 24. that is twenty Marks: And Sir *John Ferne*, sometime a Student in the *Inner Temple*, confirms the same, where he saith, That nobleness of Blood joyned with Vertue, compteth the Persons as most meet to the enterprizing of any publick Service: And for that Cause it was, not for nought, that our ancient Governours in this Land, did with a special foresight and Wisdom provide, that none should be admitted into the Houses of Court, being Seminaries, sending forth Men apt to the Government of Justice, except he was a Gentleman of Blood. And that this may seem a Truth, I my self, saith he, have seen a Kalendar of all those, who were together in the Society of one of the same Houses about the last Year of King *H.* V. with the Arms of their House and Family, marshalled by their Names; and moreover, saith he, I assure you the self same Monument doth both approve them all to be Gentlemen of perfect Descents, and also the Number of them much less than now it is, being at that time scarcely threescore in one House.

'Twas the great Policy and Wisdom of the ancient Kings and Princes, not only of this Realm, but also of 𝕱𝖗𝖆𝖓𝖈𝖊 and other neighbouring Kingdoms in this Part of the World, to **Hund. of** ordain that their Nobility and Gentry should be exercised **Bacorum.** in military Discipline, and instructed in the liberal Arts and Sciences, to the End they might be qualified to be Commanders in their Armies, and Judges in their Courts of Judicature; for these were Officers of great Trust, and nearly concerned the Crown; which was the Reason that none but the Nobility and Gentry were permitted to hold Lands by the Tenure of Knight's Service; by which Tenure they were bound to teach their Children the Feats of Arms, and to learn them the liberal Arts and Sciences in the University and Inns of Court; therefore Nurseries were appointed for these Purposes, where their Sons were fitted for Business, and qualified by Law and Experience to dispence Justice, and govern the People, which made them great in the Eye of the inferior Sort, who were ordain'd for Husbandry, Trade, manual Arts and Occupations, Labour, and Service; but now these Mechanics, ambitious of Rule and Government, often educate their Sons in these Seminaries of Law, whereby they overstock the Profession, and so make it contemptible; whilst the Gentry, not sensible of the Mischief they draw upon themselves, but also upon the Nation, prefer them in their Business before their own Children, whom they bereave of their Imployment, formerly designed for their Support; qualifying their Servants by the Profit of this Profession to purchase their Estates, and by this Means make them their Lords and Masters, whilst they lessen the Trade of the Kingdom, and cause a Scarcity of Husbandmen, Workmen, Artificers, and Servants in the Nation.

These Motives might incline King *James* I. *Anno* 1 *Regni* Order, 1 J. 1. *sui*, to declare his royal Pleasure, by Sir *John Popham*, Kt. 1603. *Origin. Jurid* then Lord Chief Justice of the *Kings Bench*, and his other fol. 316. Judges, that none should be admitted into the Society of any House of Court who was not a Gentlemen by Descent; Order, n. 8, 6 and that those Gentlemen might be qualified to manage the Car. I. Business of their Clyents, the Judges ordered that none should *Origin. Jurid.* be called to the Bar, but at the Parliament, Council, or Pensi- Order, no. 8, on holden for their Society, and only those that had continued *Origin. Jurid.* seven Years in the House, performed all their Exercises, and fol. 323. frequented Commons there; and that none should plead in any 1594. Court at **Westminster**, nor sign any Bill, Answer, Replica- fol. 313, 314. tion, or other Pleading in Chancery, nor any Action, Bill, 1574. or Plea in any Court of Record, under five Years standing *Origin Jurid.* at the Bar; nor might plead before the Justices of the As- Stat. 21 J. 1. size; nor be Steward or Recorder of any Court of Record Clapham's in any Borough or Town Corporate, unless they were three Case. Years standing at the Bar, in one of the Inns of Court; and it is worth the Consideration of a Parliament to extend these Laws to all Court Barons, and Conveyances of Land for the general Good and Benefits of the People, that all Stewards of Court Barons may be qualified by Law to avoid and prevent those Doubts and Mischiefs which often arise there, as well upon Surrenders and Admissions to Copiholds, as Grants and Conveyances for the passing of Land and Estates; for the Mistakes made in Surrenders and Admissions to Copiholds, and in the Grants and Conveyances of other Lands, made without Advice of Council have multiplied great Suits at Law in the several Courts at Westminster, caused great Expence of Mony, and indangered the Loss of several Estates, whilst 'tis impossible that unlearned Men in the Law can prevent them.

The Mannor of ANABULL

WAS denominated from *William Anabull*, who held it and was Lord hereof in the time of King *H.* VI. but having observed little of it in my Reading, I shall take Notice only that *Christopher Smith* held it in the Reign of Queen *Elizabeth*, and married *Margaret*, Daughter of *John Hide* of Albury, by whom he had Issue

Nicolas Smith, who lived at Westminster, in the Year of our Lord 1602, and married *Katharine*, the Daughter of *William Gardiner* of Southwarke, by whom he had two Sons, *Edmund* and *Nicolas*, late Vicar of Braughing, and one Daughter, *Frances* married to *William Tucker*.

Edmond Smith was his Son and Heir, sometime one of the Clerks of his Majesty's Council in Ireland, where he married *Grace* Daughter of *John Percival* of Kingsale, on whom he begat five Sons, *Edmund, Christopher, Nicolas, John, James*; and five Daughters, *Mary* married to *James Reding, Margaret* to *Robert Morris, Alice* to *Matthew Louk*, *Frances*, and *Grace*.

THIS Church is situated not far from the Vill, which is a fair Building covered with Lead, and a square Tower adjoyns the West End hereof, wherein is a Ring of five Bells; it is also leaded, and a short Spire is erected upon it: 'Tis a Chappel of ease to Hethamsted, and hath some Gravestones with these Inscriptions.

Hic jacet Willielmus Seabrooke, qui obiit 2 April. 1462. et Joanna uxor ejus —— quorum ——

Orate pro animabus Mathei Cressey et Johannæ uxoris ejus quondam, filiæ Edmundi Peryent, Armig. et Annæ dicti Mathei uxoris, quondam filiæ Thomæ Vernon, Armigeri, quæ Johanna obiit 29. Novemb. 1478.

Hic jacent Willielmus Anabul et Isabella uxor ejus, qui quidem Willielmus obiit 4 die mensis Octobris 1457.

Hic jacent Nathan et Maria liberi Guilielmi Cotton de Curnory Hall, Armigeri, et Elizabethæ uxoris ejus, filiæ senioris Godmanni Jenkins, Gener. Anno Dom. 1661.

Here under lies the body of *William Cressy*, who deceased the 24th day of *October* in the first year of Queen *Elizabeth*; *Grace Johnson* his Wife died the 14 of *May* 1571. and was one of the Daughters of *Robert Dartnold* of Penhurst in the County of Kent.

Hic jacet Nathan Cotton *de* Curnors Hall *generosus, Servus domesticus* Hund. *of*
Jacobi, Caroli I. *et* Caroli II. *Regum* Angliæ *obiit octavo die* Novembris Bacorum.
anno Dom. 1661. *Ætatis suæ* 74.

Beatam in Christi Adventu Resurrectionem præstolans Corpus Godmanni
Jenkins, *Generosi, qui duorum Regum illustrium* Jacobi *et* Caroli *primi
Servus fuit domesticus, obiit autem* Novembris *die tertio anno* 1670.
Hic etiam quiescit corpus Elizabethæ *uxoris ejus, quæ è vita migravit die*
17. Junii 1666.

NORTHMYMMES.

THE *Saxons* added this Adjunct to the Name of this Vill.
to distinguish it from the next Town of the same Denomination in Middlesex; it lies about eight Miles distant from
Whethamsted, dispersedly among other Towns in Caisho
Huudred; and *William* the Conqueror granted it to *Robert*
Bishop of Chester, for I find it recorded in *Domesdei Book*
under the Title of *Terra Episc.* Cestrensis.

In Danais Hundred. Robertus Episc. *de* Cestre *tenet* Mimmine *pro octo* Domesd. Lib.
hidis et un. virgat. se defendebat tempore Regis Edwardi*, et modo pro octo* fol. 134. n. 7.
*hidis. Terra est tresdecem car. in Dominio quatuor hidæ. et ibi sunt duo car.
et tertia potest fieri, ibi septemdecim Vill. cum octo Bord. habentibus decem
car. ibi tres Cotarii, et unus Servus, pastura ad pec. Silva quatuor centum
porc. in totis valent. valet et valuit octo lib. tempore Regis* Edwardi *decem
lib. Hoc Manerium tenuerunt tres Teigni homines Reginæ* Eddid. *et vendere
potuerunt. Hoc Manerium non est de Episcopatu sed fuit* Rainerii *Patris*
Roberti Episc.

Robert Bishop of Chester held Mimmes in Danais Hundred, it was
rated for eight Hides and one Virgate, in the time of King *Edward* (the
Confessor,) and now for eight Hides. The arable is thirteen Carucates,
in Demeasne four Hides, and there are two Carucates, and a third may be
made, there are seventeen Villains with eight Bordars having ten Carucates, there are three Cottagers, and one Servant, Common of Pasture
for the Cattle, Wood to feed four hundred Hogs; in the whole Value it is
worth and was worth eight Pounds by the Year, in the time of King *Edward* (the Confessor) ten Pounds. Three Thanes, Men (under the Protection) of Queen *Edditha*, held this Mannor and might sell it. This
Mannor was not held in right of the Bishoprick, but of *Rainer* Father of
Robert the Bishop.

In short time after, this Mannor came to the Possession Mon. Angl.
of *Jeoffery de Magnivile*, descended from a noble Family of vol. 1, fol. 449
the *Normans*, which I have treated of in the Parish of Sabridgeworth and Gedleston, to which I refer the Reader; he
erected this Church and gave the Tyths hereof to support
the great Abby, which he founded at Walden in Essex, and
he died on the 16th Calends of *Oct. Anno* 1144, 9 *Steph.*

This Mannor pass'd as those of Sabridgeworth and Gedleston did, until the Name extinguish'd, when it came to

Beatrix the Wife of *William Say,* who was the next Heir
general of this Line; she had Issue two Sons, *William* and
Jeoffry Say.

William Say dying in the time of his Father, left Issue
two Daughters, who were his Heirs, *Beatrix* and *Maud.*

Beatrix married *Jeoffry Fitzpiers,* from whom those of

Hund. of
Dacorum.

Quo Warr. 6
Ed. 1 cur.
recept. Scac

that Line, who afterwards assum'd the Sirname of *Mande-vile*, and were Earls of Essex, descended. *Maud*, the other Sister, married *William de Buckland*.

'Twas found *Anno* 6 *Edw.* I. that *Peter Pycote*, *Roger de Bachesworth*, *Arnulph de Monte Caviso*, and *Ralph* of the same, claimed to hold in the Vill of Northmymmes of the Honour of *Mandevile* and Glocester, the View of Franc-pledge, the Correction of the Assize of Bread and Ale, Gallows, Waife, Free-warren, Easements from the Sheriff's Torns, and of all his Men, for Half a Mark to be given for all Services.

About fifty or sixty Years after, I find Sir *Robert Knolles* possess this Mannor, who had advanc'd himself from a low Fortune by a military Course of Life to a fair Estate; for he obtained so great Wealth by the Troubles in Normandy and Britany, that he became an eminent Commander in those Parts, *Anno* 32 *Edw.* III. and was made General, *Anno* 44 *Edw.* III. of all those Forces which King *Edward* sent at that time into France: He was Governor of the Castle at Brest in Britany, *Anno* 1 *R.* II. assisted the Duke of Britany against the *French*, *An* 3 *R.* II. and landing then at Calaice, march'd quite through France without Resistance: He led on the Citizens of London, 4 *R.* II. against *Jack Straw* and his Followers, in that dangerous Insurrection against the King; and besides all these military Acts which made him famous in those Days, he built that stately Bridge over the River Medway near Rochester in Kent, founded a Collegiate Church in the Town of Pontefract, dedicated to the Honour of the *Holy Trinity*, and plac'd a Master and six or seven Priests there, and erected an Hospital by it for the Relief of thirteen poor Men and Women; he enlarged the House of Fryars Carmelites, commonly called the *White Fryars* in London, and died at his Mannor-house of Scene Thorpe now Sculthorp in the County of Norfolk, about the Feast of the Assumption of the blessed Virgin, *Anno* 1407, and was buried with the Lady *Constance* his Wife in the Body of the Church at the *White Fryars* London, which he had so lately repaired, leaving Issue

Thomas Knowles, who married *Margaret* the Widow of *John Chichley*, Chamberlain of London, from whom descended

Robert Knowles, who was his Heir, and married *Elizabeth* the Daughter and Heir of *William Troutbeck* of Cheshire, by whom he had Issue

Anne, who was his Daughter and Heir, and married *Henry Frowyck* of Weley, by whom he begat *Thomas*, *Isabel* married to *Thomas Bedlow*, and *Elizabeth* wedded to *John Coningsby*.

Thomas Frowick died without Issue, leaving *Isabel* and

Elizabeth his Sisters and Coheirs, and upon the Partition, this Mannor came to

Elizabeth, the Wife of *John Coningsby*, who was constituted Sheriff for this County, *Anno* 38 *Henry* VIII. from whom this Mannor pass'd, as I have shew'd before, as the Mannors of 𝔚𝔢𝔩𝔡, 𝔚𝔞𝔫𝔡𝔬𝔩𝔣𝔢𝔰, and 𝔑𝔢𝔴𝔟𝔢𝔯𝔯𝔦𝔢𝔰, past in the Parish of 𝔖𝔱. 𝔓𝔢𝔱𝔢𝔯𝔰, to

Thomas Coningsby, Esq. of whom I have treated there; he sold this Mannor to

Sir *Nicholas Hide*, who married *Bridget* the Daughter of *Michael Sandis* of 𝔏𝔞𝔱𝔦𝔪𝔢𝔯𝔰 in the County of 𝔅𝔲𝔠𝔨𝔰, Esq. was knighted *An.* 1 *Jac.* I. constituted Sheriff of this County in the 17th Year of the same King, and created Baronet by Letters Patents dated the 8th of *Novemb.* 1621, 19 *Regni sui*, and died leaving Issue

Sir *Thomas* who was his only Son and Heir, and married *Mary* the Daughter of *John Whitchurch* of 𝔚𝔞𝔩𝔱𝔬𝔫 near 𝔄𝔩𝔢𝔰𝔟𝔲𝔯𝔭, in the County of 𝔅𝔲𝔠𝔨𝔦𝔫𝔤𝔥𝔞𝔪, Gent. on whose Body he begat

Bridget, who was his sole Heir, and married *Peregrine Osborne*, Lord *Osborne* of 𝔎𝔦𝔟𝔢𝔱𝔬𝔫, commonly called Marqueus of 𝔠𝔞𝔯𝔪𝔞𝔯𝔱𝔥𝔢𝔫, Viscount 𝔇𝔲𝔫𝔟𝔩𝔞𝔦𝔫 of the Kingdom of 𝔖𝔠𝔬𝔱𝔩𝔞𝔫𝔡, the only surviving Son and Heir apparent to his Grace *Thomas* Duke of 𝔏𝔢𝔢𝔡𝔰, &c. summon'd to Parliament 14 *Mar.* 1690, 2 *W.* and *M.* and had his Place according to the Antiquity of his Father's Barony, whose Title of Marquess gives me Occasion to discourse this Honour.

Those Counts or Graves, whom the Emperor employed, in the Government of Provinces near the Frontiers of the Empire had the Title of *Marchio* and *Margravius* in Latin, and *Markgrave* in Dutch, and in Italian *Marchese*, whence the later *Greeks* have their Μάρχεσις Μάρχεσινη for a Marquess and Marchioness, because those Frontiers were known by the Name of *Marken* or *Marks*, or Limits of the Empire, in the same Sense as the Marshes of 𝔖𝔠𝔬𝔱𝔩𝔞𝔫𝔡, or 𝔚𝔞𝔩𝔢𝔰, for the Word *Mark* or *March* signifies a Limit, Bound, or Frontier in the Dutch, or rather in the Language of the *Goths* or *Vandals*.

This Title, it seems, was distinguish'd when Duke and Count were made a third Dignity, different from both of them, inferior to the one, and superior to the other: But Mr. *Selden* saith this Word *Marchio* occurred not in the Empire before *Charles* the Great appointed Governors by that Name in 𝔊𝔞𝔰𝔠𝔬𝔫𝔭, yet this Title was then only officiary, not feudal till the time of the Emperor *H.* I. nor in 𝔈𝔫𝔤𝔩𝔞𝔫𝔡 till the Reign of *William* the Conqueror, when he granted fair Possessions and large Territories to some valiant *Normans*, upon the Confines or Borders of the *British* or *Welch*, which were not then reduced to Obedience, to

Marginal notes:

Hund. of Dacorum.

Dale's Catal. of Nobility.

Seld. tit. Hon. pt. 2, cap. 1. p. 420.

Ibid. cap. 3, p. 528.

Hund. of
Dacorum.

the End that they might defend them from the Inroads and Invasions of those Enemies, and enlarge their Dominions by the Recovery of their Country from them, which was the Service by which they held their Honours and Possessions, and these were commonly called Marchers, whereof one had the Care of the North Border of Wales, who was created Earl of Chester, and his Territory was made a County Palatine; and the Lord Marchers of the middle Part, and of the South Wales, had also a Palatine Jurisdiction, for they had a Court of *Chancery*, and Writs only among themselves pleadable, to the Intent that they might not have Occasion to draw them from their Charge or Employment; but the other Part of South Wales, was sufficiently fenc'd with the River of Severn and the Sea.

This Title of Marquess was not known with us before *R.* II. who created *Robert Vere* Marquess of Dublin, in the 9th Year of his Reign. Marquesses are now created like other Dignities by Letters Patents, and at the time of Creation, a Marquess must have his Surcoat and Hood, and shall be led by a Duke or Marquess, and the Sword and Cap shall be born by two Earls.

As their Dignity is between a Duke and a Count, so their Coronets set over their Arms are mix'd of those of a Duke and Count, but have four Flowers of less Height than the Duke's Coronets, and between them three such pearled Points as are in the Coronets of Counts, and his Mantle is

Dale's Catal. of Nobility.

double Ermine, which is of three Doublings and an Half: He hath the Title of, and in all Letters ought to be stiled, most noble and puissant Prince: and the King terms them *Our right trusty and well beloved Cousin*, and if they be Privy Counsellors, they have this Addition, *and Counsellors;* and may have his Cloath of Estate reaching within a Yard of the Ground, the King or a Duke not being present; and a Marchioness may have her Train born up by a Knight's Lady in her own House, but not in a Dutchess's Presence; and their younger Sons shall be called Lords by the Courtesie of England.

The Mannor of BROOKMANS

WAS anciently derived from the Mannor of North-mpmms, for it is holden of it by Fealty and certain Rent; 'tis a fair Mannor, and has a large Rental which shews a great Number of Tenants that belong to it, but wanting Information, Sir *Paul Pindar* is the first Lord hereof that I have met with, and after his Decease, it was sold to

Sir *William Dudley*, who enjoy'd it sometime, then convey'd it about the Year 1666, to

Andrew Fountain of Saul in the County of Norfolk, Esq. He married *Theophila* Daughter of Dr. *Stubs* of

Elmham in the same County, and the Widow of *William Wells* of **Halbegate**, Gent. by whom he had no Issue, and after her Decease he wedded *Sarah Chichley*, Daughter of Sir *Thomas Chichley*, Kt. Master of the Ordnance and Chancellor of the Dutchy of **Lancaster** in the Reigns of King *Charles* II. and King *James* II. by whom he had Issue *Andrew*, *John*, *Brig*, *Elizabeth*, and one Daughter, whereof *Andrew*, *Brig*, and *Elizabeth* are now living; he built a very fair House upon this Mannor in the Year 1682, from whence you have a pleasant Prospect from the Front thereof towards the East over **Essex**, and from the Back thereof toward the West into **Bedfordshire**; it has Jurisdiction only of Court Baron, and lies within the Leet of **Northmymms**.

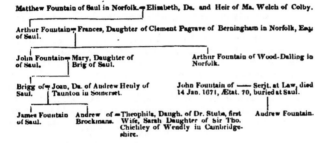

The Mannor of POTTERELS.

WAS doubtless denominated from some Owner of that Name, and is a Mannor of itself, or Parcel of the Demesne of some adjacent Mannor, for I cannot learn that it pays any Duty or Service, or depends upon any other Mannor. It came, as I am inform'd, by the Purchase of a Lady, who married into this Family, and had Issue

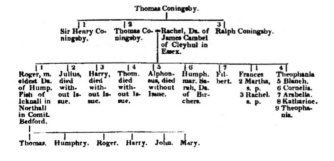

Within this Mannor is a Place called 𝕭𝖆𝖑𝖊, in a Cops
Wood surrounded with Trees, and when any Rains fall, a
great Flux of Water flows from the Hills to a Place call'd
𝕶𝖎𝖙𝖊𝖘𝖇𝖔𝖚𝖗𝖓𝖊, and thence runs in a Channel through the
Woods to this Bottom, where the Water drains into the
Ground through small Holes in the Bottom, where is no
Grass, and makes a Noise in the Earth as it passes away;
and 'tis supposed runs by certain Wells near the Church,
about half a Mile distant from this Swallow, for the Waters
there upon any such Floods turn white, but none could inform me of any Place where they break forth again.

The Mannor of GOBIONS.

SO termed from the *Gobions*, who were Lords hereof,
whom I have mentioned in the Vill of 𝕾𝖙𝖆𝖕𝖑𝖊𝖋𝖔𝖗𝖉, where
they held a Mannor call'd by their own Name, and another
in the County of 𝕭𝖊𝖉𝖋𝖔𝖗𝖉, which retains the Name of 𝕳𝖎𝖌-
𝖍𝖆𝖒 𝕲𝖔𝖇𝖎𝖔𝖓 to this Day.

Origin. Jurid.
Chron. Series,
fol. 80.
This Mannor was Parcel of the ancient Revenue of the
Mores, and I find that Sir *John More* possessed it in the
time of *H.* VII. He studied the Laws of this Realm in
Lincoln's Inn, where he read in Autumn 9 *H.* VII. was
call'd to the State and Degree of a Serjeant at Law, by
Writ retornable *Tres Michaelis,* 20 *H.*VII. constituted one
of the Justices of the Common-Bench 9 *H.* VIII. and removed thence to the Court of *King's Bench,* as appears by
his Will dated 26th of *Feb.* 1526, 18 *H.* VIII. He married ———— Daughter of ————*Hancombe* of 𝕳𝖔𝖑𝖕𝖜𝖊𝖑𝖑, in
the County of 𝕭𝖊𝖉𝖋𝖔𝖗𝖉, by whom he had Issue *Thomas,*
Jane married to *Richard Saffreton,* and *Elizabeth* to *John
Rastal* Father of Judge *Rastal;* after her Decease he
married *Alice* Daughter of one of the *Mores* in 𝕾𝖚𝖗𝖗𝖕,
Great Aunt to Sir *William More,* to whom he gave this
Mannor in Jointure; and she survived Sir *Thomas* about
ten Years, died, and lieth buried at 𝕹𝖔𝖗𝖙𝖍𝖆𝖑 in this County:
He was sweet and pleasant in Conversation, innocent and
harmless, meek and gentle, merciful and pittiful, just, and
free from Corruption.

Thomas More his only Son, was born in 𝕸𝖎𝖑𝖐-𝖘𝖙𝖗𝖊𝖊𝖙,
𝕷𝖔𝖓𝖉𝖔𝖓, *Anno* 1480, 20 *Edw.* IV. educated there at a Free
School, called St. *Anthonies,* under *Nicholas Holt,* a famous
and learned Man, removed thence to the House of Cardinal
Moreton, Archbishop of 𝕮𝖆𝖓𝖙𝖊𝖗𝖇𝖚𝖗𝖕, and Lord High Chan-
cellor of 𝕰𝖓𝖌𝖑𝖆𝖓𝖉, who would often try his Parts and ex-
ercise his pregnant Wit, from whence he sent him to
Christ Church in 𝕺𝖝𝖋𝖔𝖗𝖉, where in two Years' time he
greatly improved his Studies in Rhetorick, Logick, and
Philosophy: He married *Jane,* the Daughter of Mr. *John
Colt* of 𝕹𝖊𝖜𝖍𝖆𝖑 in 𝕰𝖘𝖘𝖊𝖝, by whom he had Issue *John,*

Margaret, a Woman of singular Wit, great Wisdom, rare
Piety, and extraordinary Learning, married to *William
Roper* of Tenham and Eltham in the County of Kent, Esq.
Elizabeth wedded to the Son and Heir of Sir *John Dancy*,
Kt. and *Cicily* espoused to *Giles Heron* of Shackletoell in
the County of Middlesex, Esq. He was admitted in *Lincoln's Inn*, read in Autumn 3 *H*.VIII. and the King taking
Notice of his great Parts, Learning, and Diligence, sent him
into France to claim certain Debts due to him, which Employ
he perform'd to the great Satisfaction of both Kings; after
that he went upon an Ambassage into Flanders, where he
confirmed the League betweed England and Burgundy, for
which Service the King offer'd him an yearly Pension upon
his Return, but he refused it. He wrote his famous Book
of *Utopia, Anno* 1516, when he was about 36 Years of Age,
the History of *Richard* III. and divers other learned Pieces.
He was created a Councellor of State, dubb'd a Knight,
made Master of the Requests, Treasurer of the *Exchequer*,
one of the Prince's Council, Speaker of the House of Commons, *Anno* 14 *H*. VIII. Chancellor of the Dutchy of Lancaster, and at length Lord Chancellor of England, 25 *Oct*.
in the 25th Year of *H*.VIII. He managed that Office for
the Space of two Years and an Half, with that Justice and
Wisdom, that none ever exceeded him; but he foreseeing
the Incertainty of the King's Favour, and greatly sensible
of the Misfortune and Danger that attended the Fall of great
Officers, prevailed with his Majesty to receive the Seal, and
to discharge him from the high Office of Chancellor, which
the King granted with a large Encomium of his great Service; he had a convenient House not subject to Envy, yet
magnificent enough, where he pleas'd himself with the Enjoyment of his Wife and Children; it was a School or University of Christian Religion, where no Quarrelling or in-
temperate Words were heard, no Strife or Envying was allowed, but every one learned the Method of Complaisance,
and studied quietly the liberal Sciences; this Discipline he
exercised, not by proud and lofty Words, but with all kind
and courteous Benevolence, great Alacrity, and sober Mirth;
his first Wife was young, instructed in Learning and all
Kind of Musick: His second Wife he chose for a Governess to his Family, and tho' she was somewhat harsh and covetous by Nature, yet she performed her Task every Day
upon the Lute, Viol, or some other Instrument. He would
not suffer any of his Servants to be idle, but assign'd to
every one his Task, some to labour in his Garden, others to
sing, others to play on the Organ, but allow'd none to use
Cards or Dice; he constantly said certain Prayers with
them every Night, and required every of them to be at Mass
on Sundays or Holidays: They watch'd the Eves all the

Hund. of
Bacorum.

time of Mattins upon great Feasts; and he read the holy
Passion to them upon Fridays, oftentimes interposing something of his own to move them to Compassion, Compunc-
tion, or such pious Affections, allowing none to reside there,
who was touch'd with the least Aspersion of evil Fame. 'Tis
observable that all the Revenues and Pensions which he received from his Father, or by Marriage, or his own Purchase (except his Mannors of **Duckington**, **Frinckford**, and
Warly Park in **Oxfordshire**, which the King freely bestow'd
upon him by Patent) exceeded not the yearly Value of 50*l.*
for his Mother in Law, who survived him, held this Mannor for her Jointure; and though he lived very prudently
all the time he managed those great Offices which he enjoy'd, Mr. *Roper*, the Husband of his beloved Daughter
Margaret, attested upon his own Knowledg, that when he
resigned the Office of Chancellor of **England**, he had not
one hundred Pounds in Gold and Silver, his Debts paid, and
Chain excepted; which was a great Demonstration of his
Honesty and Uprightness whilst he executed all those great
Offices, shew'd his Contempt to all worldly Riches, and
manifested his Bounty to the Church, and his Charity to
the Poor; and when the Bishops of **England** considered he
was not rich, nor advanced according to his Worth in yearly
Revenue, they raised four thousand Pounds in their Convocation, and presented it to him towards a Gratification of
his Pains in writing many learned Books in Defence of the
Catholick Faith.   He acknowledged that their Present was
indeed very honourable, yet he set so much by his Pleasure,
and so little by his Profit, that he would not for much more
Mony have lost the Rest of so many Night's Sleep as he
spent upon the same, yet wish'd that, upon Condition all
Heresies were supprest, all his Works were burnt, and his
Labour utterly lost; this was a strong Evidence that the
Pains he took, was only the Respect he had for the Honour of God, and not for vain Glory or worldly Profit. And
when he called all his Children together, asked their Advice how he might (now his Ability was impaired by the
Surrender of his Office) maintain them as he had, and gladly
would do, and all were silent; he answered, his Revenue
was one hundred Pound *per Annum*, if they lived together,
they must be content to contribute together, and live at the
Rate he did at *Lincoln's Inn*, if they could not maintain it,
then according to **Oxford** Fare, and if their Purses would
not answer that, then they would beg together with Basket
and Wallet, hoping some good People would afford them
their Charity, and at every Man's Door they would sing a
Salve Regina, whereby they should keep Company, and be
merry together; thus he exprest his Love towards his Children, but more towards God, taking patiently whatsoever

should befall him, and provided for the worst, that he might be better prepared to endure lesser Crosses.

But afterwards Sir *Thomas More* refusing to take the Oath whereby all Subjects were required to renounce the Pope's Authority, and to maintain the Succession of Queen *Ann's* Children, was arraigned before Sir *Thomas Audley*, Kt. Lord Chancellor of England, Sir *John Fitz James*, Lord Chief Justice, Sir *John Baldwin*, Sir *Richard Leicester*, Sir *John Port*, Sir *John Spilman*, Sir *Walter Luke*, and Sir *Anthony Fitzherbert*, at the *King's Bench* Bar, on the 7th of *May*, 1535, for refusing to renounce the Pope's Authority, and maintain the Succession of Queen *Ann's* Children, contrary to the Statute made in the Parliament *Anno* 1534. To which Indictment Sir *Thomas* pleaded, Not guilty; and thereupon Sir *Thomas Palmer*, Sir *Thomas Peirt*, *George Lovel*, *Thomas Burbage*, Esquires, *Jeoffry Chamber*, *Edward Stockmore*, *William Browne*, *Jasper Leak*, *Thomas Billington*, *John Parnel*, *Richard Bellame*, and *George Stokes*, Gentlemen, were sworn upon the Jury, and when Sir *Thomas More* had alleged what he could say in his own Defence, the Jury withdrew for a small time, and upon their Return found him Guilty; and after Sir *Thomas More* had taken Exceptions to the Indictment and they were overul'd, the Lord Chancellor pronounced upon him the usual Sentence given in Cases of High Treason, which afterwards was changed only to beheading, because he had been Lord Chancellor, and when he heard what Favour the King had granted to him, he answer'd merrily, *God forbid, the King should use any more such Mercy to any of his Friends*: He was led from thence by Sir *William Kingston*, a tall comely Gentleman, Constable of the Tower, and his very good Friend; the Axe carried before him, and the Edge turned towards him; in the Way his Son threw himself at his Feet, humbly craving his Blessing with Tears, which he gave him and most affectionately seal'd it with a Kiss, commending greatly his Behaviour; a rare Pattern and Example for those young Men who in this Age have forgot their Duty to God and their Parents; then Mrs. *Roper* his beloved Daughter attended his Return at Tower Wharfe, where she receiv'd his Blessing and kiss'd him; then he advised that she should submit her Will to the Pleasure of Almighty God, and be patient for her Loss, for whatsoever he should suffer was not without the Will of God: When Sir *Thomas Pope* gave him Notice of his Execution, and taking his Leave wept bitterly, he advised him to quiet himself, for he hoped to see him again in Eternal Bliss, and to divert his Melancholy, Sir *Thomas More* took his Urinal in his Hand, and casting his Water, merrily said, *I see no Danger but this Man may live longer if it shall please the King;* when he was gone, Sir *Thomas More* preparing for his Execution, like one invited to a solemn Banquet, put on his Silk Chamblet Gown, but the Lieutenant perswading him to change it for a worse, that the Executioner might not have it for his Perquisites, he answer'd, *He should think it well bestowed on him if it was Cloath of Gold, for St.* Ciprian, *that famous Bishop of* Carthage, *gave thirty Pieces of Gold to his Executioner because he should be the Instrument that should transfer him thence to Heaven.* Yet the Lieutenant at length prevailed with him to put on a Gown of Frieze; then he attended him from the Tower to the Place of Execution about nine of the Clock, whilst Sir *Thomas* walked thither with a long Beard, contrary to his wonted Fashion, and a red Cross in his Hands, often fixing his Eyes upon Heaven, refused a Cup of Wine presented to him in his Passage, because Christ at his Passion drank only Gall and Vinegar: When he mounted the Scaffold which seem'd so weak that 'twas ready to fall, he said merrily to the Lieutenant, *I pray, Sir, see me safe up, and for my coming down let me shift for myself;* The Sheriff interrupting him when he would have spoke to the People, he desired their Prayers and that they would testify that he died a faithful Servant to God and the King, in and for the Faith of the Holy Catholick Church, then he kneeling down pronounced the Psalm of Mercy with great Devotion, and chearfully rising again kist the Executioner, saying, *Thou will do me this Day a greater Benefit, than any mortal Man can give me, pluck up thy Spirit, Man, be not afraid to do thy Office, my Neck is very short, take heed therefore that thou strike not awry, for saving thy Honesty*; then fitting his Head to the Block, he bad the Executioner stay until he had removed aside his Beard, saying, *That that had never committed any Treason;* after which he received the fatal Blow of the Ax with great Alacrity and spiritual Comfort; he was of mean Stature, well proportioned, his Complexion tending to Phlegmitick, his Colour white and pale, his Hair between black and yellow, his Eyes gray, his Countenance lovely and chearful, his Voice plain and distinct, his Body reasonable healthful, complain'd only towards his End of a Pain in his Breast by using much Writing. He chiefly drank Water in his Youth, and only tasted Wines when he pledged others; he affected salt Meats, especially powder'd Beef, Milk, Cheese, Eggs, and Fruit; and usually eat of coarse brown Bread, which some supposed was rather for Mortification than any Love he had for it; he was quallified with such a mild Behaviour and excellent Temper that none could move him to Anger or Passion, and would always esteem that beneficial to him which he could not prevent; he was endew'd with a ready Wit, a rare Tongue, and great Elocution, always blending his grave Discourses with his witty Jokes, and was never known to smile or take Notice when a Jest fell from him, which render'd his Company the more acceptable, and his Discourses the more pleasant, he was admirable in all Kind of Learning, Latin, Greek, prophane and divine; he was wise in Council, would declare the Truth to his Prince without Fear, manage an Ambassage with great Prudence, and delivered his Judgment with an extraordinary Grace: 'Tis observable, that when he was at the Height of his Prosperity, he would always shew his Duty to his Parents, and in his Passage to the *Chancery Court* every Morning usually waited upon his Father, one of the Justices of the Court of *King's Bench*, an Office much inferior to that of Chancellor, begged his Benediction there, and then proceeded to his high Seat of Judicature: an admirable Instance to reprimand the young Men of this Age, who contemn their Parents, and covet their Death that they may gain their Estates before the time God hath appointed.

John More was his only Son and Heir, but enjoy'd his Estate a small time, for two Acts of Parliament were immediately past after the Attainder of his Father, the one to deprive him of the King's Royal Bounty to his Father, the other to defeat him of the Paternal Estate settled upon him before the Statute was made upon which he was attainted, and then attainted this *John* upon the same Law; but when he had lost all, 'tis very remarkable that the Blessing of his Parents rested upon his Head, for the King granted him his Pardon and his Liberty, and. though this Mannor was settled upon Queen *Elizabeth* for her Life, which was the Reason Queen *Mary* could not restore it in her Life time, yet it return'd to the Family upon the Death of Queen *Elizabeth*. This *John* married *Anne*, the sole Daughter and Heir of *Edward Cressacre* of Baronburgh, in the County of York, who brought a fair Estate to him, and a goodly Offspring, *Thomas, Augustine, Thomas* the younger, *Edward, Bartholomew*, who died in his Youth, *Margaret, Elizabeth*, and *Cicely*, the two first Sons dying without Issue

Thomas More, the third Son, was the Heir of this Family, born at Chelsey, 8th of *August, An.* 23 *H.*VIII. and married *Margaret* Daughter of *John Scrope* of Hambledon, in the County of Bucks, Esq. second Son of *Henry* Lord *Scrope*, from whom descended

Cressacre More of More Hall, alias Gubbins, in the Parish of Northmpmns, who was born at Baronburgh, 3d of *July*, 1572; he obtained this Mannor upon the Death of Queen *Elizabeth*, and married *Elizabeth* Daughter of *Thomas Gage* of Furles in the County of Sussex, by whom he

Hund. of Dacorum. had Issue *Thomas, Hellen,* and *Bridget*; she died the 15th of *July,* 1618, but he was living *Anno* 1638.   Afterwards

Thomas More succeeded, lived here, and married *Mary,* Daughter of Sir *Basil Brook* of *Madeley* in the County of *Salop,* Kt. by whom he had Issue

Basil More, who married *Anne* Daughter of Sir *William Humble,* who was created Bar. by Letters Patents dated the 21st day of *June,* in the Year of our Lord 1660, 12 *Car.* II.

Sir John More, Kt. one of the Justices of the Kings Bench, 1526.	— Da. of —— Hancomb of Holywell in the County of Bedford.

Jane, mar Rich. Sa-freton.	Sir Thom. More, Kt. Lord Chancellor of England.	Jane, Daughter of Jo. Colt of Newhal in Essex, Gent. first Wife, Alice, Daughter of —— Relict of —— Middleton, second Wife.	Elizabeth, mar. Joh. Rastal.

Margaret, m. W. Roper.	Elizabeth, mar. Son and Heir of Sir Jo. Dancy, Kt.	John More	Anne, Daughter and Heir of Edward Creswell of Baron Burgh.	Cicely, mar. Giles Heron of ——

1 Thomas More, died without Issue.	2 Augustine, died without Issue.	3 Thomas, the younger.	Margaret, Da. of Jo. Scrope.	4 Edward.	5 Bartholomew, died in his youth.	1 Margaret 2 Elizah. 3 Cicely.

Cresacre More. — Elizabeth, Da. of Tho. Gage of   Helen. Bridget.
Furles in Sussex.

Thomas — Mary, Daughter of Sir Basil Brook of Madeley in the
More.   County of Salop. Kt.

Basil More — Anne, Da. of Sir William Humble, Bar.

The great Losses which this *Basil* sustain'd by reason of his Loyalty to his Prince, caused him to sell this Mannor to

Sir *Edward Desbovery* of *London,* Merchant, who died seiz'd hereof, *Anno* 1694, leaving Issue two Sons, *William* and *Jacob,* who lived a while here, and it was sold to —— *Bitckcraft,* Packer at *Blackwel-hall, London,* in the Year 1697, who is the present Possessor hereof.

THIS Vicaridge *Anno* 26 *Hen.* VIII. was rated in the King's Books at the yearly Value of 10*l.* —— is Patron hereof.

The VICARS.
John Clarke.   Samuel Pyke.

This Church is situated in the Middle of the Vill, in the Deanery of *Berkhamsted* in the Diocess of *Lincoln,* covered with Lead, to which adjoyns a square Tower, wherein is a Ring of five Bells, with a fair Spire of Lead erected upon it, and within the Church are Gravestones which are inscribed as follows.

Hic jacet Robertus Knolles, *Armig.* qui *obiit* —— *die Mensis,* anno *Dom.* 14 —— *et* Elizabetha *Uxor ejus,* quæ *obiit bicessimo octabo die Mensis* Novembris, *Anno* 1458. *ac pueri eorundem* ——.

Here lieth the Body of *Thomas Hewes,* late of *Uxbridge* in the County of *Middlesex,* Esq; who departed this life the 27th of *March, anno* 1587. and also the Body of *Elizabeth* his Wife, sole Daughter and Heir of Sir *Griffith Dunne,* Kt. deceased the 2d. day of *December* 1590.

𝔒𝔣 𝔭𝔬𝔲𝔯 𝔠𝔥𝔞𝔯𝔦𝔱𝔦𝔢 𝔭𝔯𝔞𝔶 𝔣𝔬𝔯 𝔱𝔥𝔢 𝔖𝔬𝔲𝔩𝔢 𝔬𝔣 Thomas Leucas, 𝔖𝔬𝔫 𝔞𝔫𝔡 𝔥𝔢𝔦𝔯𝔢 𝔞𝔭⸗ parant 𝔬𝔣 John Leucas, 𝔬𝔣 𝔱𝔥𝔢 ——— 𝔬𝔣 Kent, 𝔱𝔥𝔢 𝔴𝔬𝔯𝔱𝔥𝔦𝔢 Thomas 𝔦𝔫 𝔠𝔥𝔦𝔩𝔡𝔥𝔬𝔬𝔡 𝔡𝔢𝔭𝔞𝔯𝔱𝔢𝔡 𝔦𝔫 𝔊𝔬𝔡 𝔦𝔫 𝔱𝔥𝔢 ——— 𝔬𝔣 August, 𝔦𝔫 𝔱𝔥𝔢 𝔶𝔢𝔞𝔯 𝔬𝔣 𝔬𝔲𝔯 𝔏𝔬𝔯𝔡 𝔊𝔬𝔡 1531. 𝔬𝔫 𝔴𝔥𝔬𝔰𝔢 𝔖𝔬𝔲𝔩𝔢 𝔞𝔫𝔡 𝔬𝔫 𝔞𝔩𝔩 𝔠𝔥𝔯𝔦𝔰𝔱𝔦𝔞𝔫 𝔖𝔬𝔲𝔩𝔢𝔰 𝔍𝔢𝔰𝔲 𝔥𝔞𝔳𝔢 𝔪𝔢𝔯𝔠𝔶.

𝔥𝔦𝔠 𝔧𝔞𝔠𝔢𝔱 Henricus Covert 𝔭𝔯𝔦𝔪𝔬𝔤𝔢𝔫𝔦𝔱𝔲𝔰 Williel. Covert, 𝔖𝔢𝔫𝔦𝔬𝔯, 𝔡𝔢 ———, 𝔄𝔯𝔪𝔦𝔤. 𝔮𝔲𝔦 𝔬𝔟𝔦𝔦𝔱 𝔦𝔫 𝔣𝔢𝔰𝔱𝔬 𝔖𝔱𝔦. Edri. 𝔦𝔢𝔤𝔦𝔰, 𝔦𝔫 𝔄𝔫𝔫𝔬 𝔇𝔬𝔪. 1488. 𝔠𝔲𝔧𝔲𝔰 𝔞𝔫𝔦𝔪æ 𝔭𝔯𝔬𝔭𝔦𝔱𝔦𝔢𝔱𝔲𝔯 𝔇𝔢𝔲𝔰.

William de Bathane 𝔧𝔞𝔳𝔦𝔰 𝔅𝔬𝔱𝔦𝔩𝔢𝔯 l' 𝔭𝔯𝔦𝔫𝔠𝔢 𝔤𝔦𝔰𝔱 𝔦𝔠𝔶 𝔇𝔦𝔢𝔲 𝔡𝔢 𝔰𝔞𝔩𝔪𝔢 𝔢𝔦𝔱 𝔪𝔬𝔯𝔲𝔰𝔱.

Here is a Chappel or Burying-place which the Coningsby's reserved to themselves upon the sale of this Mannor, wherein is a large Monument erected four Foot high without Inscription upon it.

In the Church-yard stands a Monument there three Foot high with this Inscription.

Here lieth interr'd the Body of *Henry Grigg* (the Son of *Thomas Grigg*) late of this Parish, Citizen and Brewer of *London*, who gave to the Poor of this Parish 20*l.* to be bestowed in Land to their use yearly to the Worlds end, who departed this life the 24th of *August* 16—

> Thus Youth, and Age, and all things pass away,
> Thy turn is now, as his was yesterday,
> To morrow shall another take thy room,
> The next day he a prey for Worms become:
> And on your dusty bones shall others tread,
> As you now walk and trample on the dead,
> Till neither Sign nor Memory appear,
> That you had ever Birth or Being here.

SENLEY, SHENLEY.

WHICH Names this Vill might take from some Owner hereof; 'tis about four Miles distant from 𝔖𝔱. 𝔄𝔩𝔟𝔞𝔫𝔰 to the South, and in the time of the Conqueror, the Church of 𝔖𝔱. 𝔄𝔩𝔟𝔞𝔫𝔰, and *Geoffry de Mandevile*, a great *Norman*, held the same, for 'tis recorded in *Domesdei Book*, That

Domesd. Lib. fol. 135, n 9.

In 𝔄𝔩𝔟𝔞𝔫𝔢𝔰𝔱𝔬𝔫 *Hundred. Abbas* 𝔖𝔞𝔫𝔠𝔱𝔦 𝔄𝔩𝔟𝔞𝔫𝔦 *tenuit* 𝔖𝔠𝔢𝔫𝔩𝔞𝔦 *pro sex hidis se defendebat. Terra est octo car. in dominio duæ hidæ, et ibi sunt duo car. ibi undecim Vill. cum uno Francig. habentes quinque car. et sexta potest fieri, ibi tres cotar. pratum dimid. car. pastura ad pecud. Silva cccc porc. in totis valentiis valet duodecem lib. quando recepit sex lib. et consuetud. tempore Regis Edwardi: Hoc Manerium jacuit et jacet in Dom. Ecclesiæ* 𝔖𝔞𝔫𝔠𝔱𝔦 𝔄𝔩𝔟𝔞𝔫𝔦.

Ibid. fol. 139.

Goisfridus de Manevile tenuit 𝔖𝔢𝔫𝔩𝔞𝔦 *pro octo hid. et tribus virgat. se defendebat. Terra est novem car. in dominio tres hidæ, et ibi sunt duo car. ibi duodecem Vill. habentes septem car. et adhuc tres possunt fieri, pratum. un. car. pastura ad pecud. Silva sexcentis porcis, in totis valentiis valet quatuor lib. quando recepit quinq; lib. tempore Regis Edwardi octo lib. hoc Manerium tenuit* Asgar, *et ibi duo Soch. homines ejus habuerunt un. hid. et tres virgat. et vendere potuit.*

The Abbot of 𝔖𝔱. 𝔄𝔩𝔟𝔞𝔫 held 𝔖𝔢𝔫𝔩𝔢𝔶 in 𝔄𝔩𝔟𝔞𝔫𝔢𝔰𝔱𝔬𝔫 Hundred, it was rated for six Hides. The arable is eight Carucates, in Demeasne two Hides, and there are two Carucates, there are eleven Villains with one Frenchman born, having five Carucates and a sixth may be made; there are three Cottagers, Meadow half a Carucate, Common of Pasture for the Cattle, Wood to feed four hundred Hogs; in the whole Value it is worth twelve Pounds a Year, when he received it six Pounds and Rent; in the time of King *Edward* (the Confessor) this Mannor did lye and doth lye in the Demeasne of the Church of 𝔖𝔱. 𝔄𝔩𝔟𝔞𝔫𝔰.

Jeoffery de Manevi'e held 𝔖𝔢𝔫𝔩𝔢𝔶, it was rated for eight Hides and three Virgates. The arable is nine Carucates, in Demeasne three Hides, and there are two Carucates, there are twelve Villains having seven Ca-

Hund. of Bacorum. rucates, and now three more may be made, Meadow one Carucate, Common of Pasture for the Cattle, Wood to feed six hundred Hogs; in the whole Value it is worth four Pounds a Year, when he received it five Pounds, in the time of King *Edward* (the Confessor) eight Pounds: *Asgar* held this Mannor, and two Sochmen, Men under his Protection had one Hide and three Virgates there and they might sell it.

Bar. vol 1, fol. 203.

The one Mannor remain'd in the Church of St. Albans, and the other remain'd in the Family of the *Mandeviles*, who had also the Church of this Vill. This *Jeoffery de Mandevile* was Earl of Essex, *Anno* 1 *Steph.* and gave the Tyths belonging to it, to the great Abby of Walden in Essex, which was of his own Foundation, of whom I have treated in Sabridgeworth, to which I refer the Reader. After his Death it came to *Jeoffery* his Son and Heir, but did not continue long in his Name, for I find that his Son *William* died without Issue, and it was found *An,* 6 *Edw.* I. that *Adam de Stratton*, Chief Baron of the *Exchequer,* and *Walter de Mereden* were Lords of this Mannor, and held View of Franc-pledge here: This *Adam de Stratton* was attainted 18 *Edw.* I. his Estate forfeited, his Body imprison'd; he was fined 35000 Marks, and this Mannor came to the Crown, where it remained till the time of *Edw.* III. when it was conveyed by the Name of the Mannor of Shenley to

Rot. 56, cur. recept. Scac.

John Poultney, who was Citizen and Lord Mayor of London, *Anno* 1331, who paid yearly for it and the Mannor of Ditton in the County of Cambridge, 3*s.* 4*d.* for an old Rent to the Crown *Anno* 1330, 1331, 4 and 5 *Edw.* III. His Family continued at Misterton in Leicestershire, of which I have seen this PEDIGREE.

Stow's Survey of London, fol. 550.

Adam de Poultney.

Sir John Poultney, Kt. four times Mayor of = Margaret. = Sir Nicholas Lovel, Kt. second London, obiit 1349. | Husband.

William, died without Issue. | Sir John Poultney of Misterton, Kt. in Com. Leicester, second Son

Thomas Poultney, 8 H. V. | Sir John Poultney, Kt. 8 H. V. 26 H. VI.

Margaret, mar. William Purefey of Draiton, Com. Leicester, 8 H. V. | John Poultney of = Margaret. Misterton.

T. Poultney. = Roise. | Margaret.

Sir Th. Poultney, Kt. = Ann, Da. of Sir Ralph Sherley of Stanton, Herald in Com. Leicester.

Sir F. Poultney, Kt. = Margaret, Daughter of Nicholas Ld. Vaux of Harowden.

Gabriel Poultney of Misterton, died 1597. = Dorothy, Daughter and Coheir of Thomas Spencer of Everton in Com. Northampton.

Sir John Poultney, Kt. = Margery, Da. of Sir John Fortescue, Kt.

John Poultney, Esq. died s. p. | Magdalen, Sister and Coheir, mar. Sir Tho. Aston of Aston in Cheshire, Bar. she died without Issue. | Jane, Sister and Coheir mar. Sir Clipsby Crew of Crew in Cheshire.

John Crew of Crew, Esq. sold this Mannor of Shenly and other Lands belonging to it, to

Stephen Ewre and *Joshuah Lomax*, Gentlemen, Attorneys at Law, who dealt much in buying and selling of Lands, by which this *Joshuah Lomax* obtained a fair Estate, and was constituted Sheriff of this County in the Year 1674, 26 *Car.* II. They were termed Attorneys at Law from the French Word *Tourner*, in Latine *Vertere*, and signified One appointed to act other Men's Business at Common Law, and was the same which was called in the Civil Law, Procurator, *Responsalis, Nuntius,* or *Missus*, and is an Officer of great Antiquity, for *Josias Berault*, in his Comment upon the Grand *Custumarier* of Normandy, saith, *Nos Procureurs d'anjour d'huy sont semblables, a ceux qui olim a Dominis in judicio constituebantur qu'on appelle on* Normandie *passes Attournies, ou ausquells, ou baille procuration qu'on appelle ad lites desquels de pauvoir cessoit en la presence de la parte qui les avoit constitues,* &c. But neither the *Romans*, nor yet the *French* after them, allowed any Person to sue or act by their Procurator or Attorny without the King's Writ. These Attornies came from Normandy about the time of the Conquest, and the Norman Order and Usage was observed here, for no Attorny was allowed to appear or sollicite in any Court for his Clyent without the King's Writ, as is manifest by the Register of Writs; afterwards the Kings of this Realm left it to the Discretion of the Judges of the Court where the Suit was commenc'd, whether the Clyent should have an Attorny, as is evident by the Writ of *Dedimus potestatem de Attornato faciendo vel recipiendo*, which requires the Steward or Judge of the Court to grant and allow them Attornies; but since the 20th Year of *H.* III. divers Laws have been made, that any Person may make their Attorny, which general Liberty encouraged many ignorant and unskilful Men in the Law, to take upon them this Office, which introduced great Damage and Mischief to the People; this was the Reason of the Statute of *H.* IV. was made to restrain the Number of them, by which it was ordain'd that all Attornies should be examin'd by the Justices, and by their Discretions, their Names should be recorded in the Roll, and they that be good and vertuous, and of good Fame, should be received and sworn well and truely to serve in their Offices, and especially that they make no Suit in a forreign County; and the other Attornies should be put out at the Discretion of the Justices, and that their Masters for whom they were Attornies should be warned to take others in their Places, so that no Damage or Prejudice should come to their said Masters in the meantime, and if any of the said Attornies died or ceased, the Justices for the time being by their Discretion should make another vertuous and learned Man in his Place, and swear him in Manner aforesaid: and to pre-

Hund. of Dacorum.

Rot. Pip. in Scac. 26 C. II. Spelm. Gloss. tit. verb. Attornat. fol. 49.

Fitzherb. N B. p. 156.

Stat. 20 H. III cap. 10, 6 E. I. cap 8, 12 E. II. cap. 1, 15. E. II. 7 R. II cap. 14.

Stat. H. IV. cap. 18.

Hund. of
Bacorum.

Stat. 3 Jac. 1.
cap. 7.

serve the Learning and Reputation of these Officers, a Law was made in the Reign of King *James* I. that none should be admitted Attornies in any of the King's Courts of Record but such as have been well brought up in the same Courts, or otherwise have been well practiced in soliciting Causes, and been found skilful and honest Men in their Dealings, and that no Attorney shall admit any other Person to practice in his Name; which Laws have rendered these Officers very useful, necessary, and beneficial to the People, and qualified them with so great a Reputation in the World, that many Gentlemen of considerable Families have not disdain'd to breed up their Sons, under the Government of these Attornies in one of the Inns of Chancery, where they may

Fortescue de
Laud. Leg.
Angl. cap. 49.

learn the first Elements of the Law, according to the old Method of England, and when grown good Proficients therein may be transplanted to some Inns of Court, where Part of the usual Fine taxed upon the Admission of others should be abated to them, and two Years time allowed for their Encouragement upon their Call to the Bar; and 'tis observed that divers eminent Judges in this Kingdom have had their Rise and Beginning from this Method: But to return to

Joshuah Lomax, he died leaving Issue two Sons, *Joshuah* and *Thomas*, whom he educated at the Inns of Court, and took their Degree of Barresters at Law, whereof *Thomas* the younger Son is the present Possessor hereof; and this Mannor is Parcel of the Dutchy of Lancaster.

PORTERS

HERE is an old Seat called Porters, which lately was possest by *Cox*, a second Branch from *Cox* of Beamonts, his Arms are described in vol. 2, p. 314. He sold it to ———— *Oxey*, who past it to Sir *Edmond Anderson*, who was created Baronet by Patent dated the 11th of *December*, 1660, 12 *Car*. II.

Trin. 7 Joh.
Rot.8, in dors.
recept. Scac.

'TWAS found *Anno 7 Johan* that *Roger de Sumery* presented *John* his on to the Church of Shenley, whose Advowson *Ralph de Chesueduit* claimed against the Abbot of Waleden, and they found that *Miles de Sumery* was his Heir, and that the same *Miles* did quit claim to *Henry* Son of *Reiner*, all his Right and Claim which he had in that Advowson by the Deed made between them, and *Henry* had a Writ to the Bishop, &c.

Stephen Ewre and *Joshua Lomax* sold the Rectory or Impropriation about the Year 1682, from the Mannor to *Thomas Laundre*, Vicar, the present Possessor of it: This Vicaridge *Anno 26 Henry* VIII. was rated in the King's Books at the yearly Value of 16*l*. 8*s*.

The VICARS.

John Elliot.   Thomas Launder.

This Church is erected in the Deanery of Berkhamsted in the Diocess of Lincoln, and there are these following Inscriptions.

In Memory of *Edmond Anderson*, Son of Sir *Edmond Anderson* of this Parish, Bar. who married *Carr*, Daughter and Heir of *John Shaw* of 𝕷𝕚𝕟=colnshire ——— the Marble is broke.
Edmundus Anderson, *Armig* obiit 17. die Sept. 1685.

Hic jacet spe beatæ Resurrectionis corpora Gulielmi et Mariæ Anderson, ille primogenitus illa unica filia Edmundi et Margaretæ Anderson de 𝔓𝔬𝔯𝔱𝔢𝔯𝔰 *in Agro* 𝔥𝔢𝔯𝔱𝔣𝔬𝔯𝔡. *Armig. qui prematuro fato vitam cum more commutarunt Gulielmus nondum peracto undecimo ætatis anno obiit 7. die Martii 1673 Maria vix septimanam in terris morata 23. Augusti 1664. Iterum in Cælum Rediit.*

Εισ γμας οϕεθν ενοεβησ ησα *Via longa vita brevis,*

Via quidem longa est Dicat mortale sed Audi Nostros preme Gradus, tum via brevis erat.

Here lieth the Body of *William Cox* of 𝔓𝔬𝔯𝔱𝔢𝔯𝔰, who departed this Life at 𝔓𝔬𝔯𝔱𝔢𝔯𝔰, the 24th of *October* 1649. being the 42. year of his age.

Here lieth also the Body of Mrs. *Mary Jessop*, who was formerly the Wife of Mr. *William Cox*; she departed this Life at 𝔅𝔢𝔯𝔨𝔥𝔞𝔪𝔰𝔱𝔢𝔡 16. *Novemb.* 1660. being the 48th year of her age.

Here lieth the Body of Mrs. *Elizabeth Cox* their youngest Daughter, who departed this Life at 𝔓𝔬𝔯𝔱𝔢𝔯𝔰 1651. in the 5th. year of her age.

Hic jacet Richardus Cole *de* 𝔖𝔥𝔢𝔫𝔩𝔢𝔶𝔥𝔞𝔩𝔩 *alias* 𝔖𝔞𝔩𝔰𝔟𝔲𝔯𝔦𝔢𝔰 *in Com.* 𝔥𝔢𝔯𝔱=𝔣𝔬𝔯𝔡, *Armig. unacum Uxore ejus* Dorothea *filia* ——— Scargil *de* 𝔎𝔫𝔞𝔭=𝔴𝔢𝔩𝔩 *in Com.* 𝔠𝔞𝔫𝔱𝔞𝔟𝔯. *octogenar. uterque obierunt.* Hic 27. Sept. 1653. *Hæc* 26. Febr. 1662. *Filios habuerunt* quinq; *Filiam* unicam.

> Under this Marble Stone here lies
> A Jewel of rich prize;
> Whom Nature in the Worlds disdain,
> But shew'd, and then put up again. '

Here lies *Elizabeth* Daughter of *Ralph Alway*, who died the 19th of *January* 1610 : being of six years and upwards.

Here lies the Body of a zealous and religious Gentleman Mr. *Ralph Alway* of 𝔠𝔞𝔫𝔫𝔬𝔫𝔰, who departed this Life the 22th day of *March* 1621. As also the Body of *Dorothy Alway*, who departed the —— of —— *An. Dom.* —— they had issue Daughters, *Mary*, *Ann*, *Dorothy* and *Elizabeth*.

Here lies the Body of the Vertuous and Religious *Rebecca Palmer*, Relict of *Robert Palmer*, Minister, formerly Wife to *Robert Snow* her first Husband; she was the beloved Niece of Sir *Jeremy Snow*, and Dame *Rebecca* his Wife, and Daughter of *Richard* and *Mary Goulty*; she departed the 3d. of *January* 1694. anno *Ætat.* 28.

Here lieth the Body of *Robert Snow*, Gent. (Nephew of Sir *Jeremiah Snow*, Kt. and Bar.) Lord of this Mannor of 𝔖𝔥𝔢𝔫𝔩𝔢𝔶, who died *October* the —— 1684. aged 32. and also *Jeremy* and *Rebecca Snow* his Children, Twins.

THEOBALD STREET

CALLED 𝔗𝔦𝔱𝔱𝔢𝔟𝔲𝔯𝔰𝔱 in *Domesdei Book*, where 'tis recorded, that

In 𝔗𝔦𝔱𝔱𝔢𝔟𝔢𝔯𝔰𝔱 *ten. Abbas de* 𝔚𝔞𝔯𝔰𝔱𝔪𝔬𝔫𝔞𝔰𝔱𝔢𝔯. *Sanct.* Petri *un. hid. Terra est dim. car. Silva* xl *porc. val. et valuit* x *sol. tempore Regis* Edwardi xiii *sol.* iv *denar.*

Domesd. Lib. fol. 134.

In eadem Villa ten. Goisfridus de Magnavile *tres virgat. de Abbate. Terra est dim. car. Silva* xii *porc. val. et valuit* vi *sol. et* viii *denar. tempore Regis* Edwardi x *sol.*

In 𝔗𝔦𝔱𝔱𝔢𝔟𝔢𝔯𝔰𝔱 *ten.* Goisfridus de Abbate 𝔖𝔱. 𝔄𝔩𝔟𝔞𝔫𝔦 *dim. hid. valet et valuit semper* vi *sol. Quidem Sochmannus ten. tempore Regis* Edwardi, *homo Abbatis* 𝔖𝔱. 𝔄𝔩𝔟𝔞𝔫𝔦 *non potuit vendere extra Ecclesiam.*

Ibid. fol. 139.

Hund. of
Darorum.

In **Banais** *Hund.* Goisfrid. de Maneville *et* Radus *de eo ten. in* **Titteberst** lii *virg.* Terra est dim. car. ibi un. Vill. et un. Bord. Silva xii porc. valet et valuit v sol. tempore Regis Edwardi x sol. hanc terram tenuerunt tres Soch. Duo eorum homines Asgari Stalri, et tertius, homo **St.** **Albani** non potuit vendere sed alii duo potuerunt.

In **Titteberst** *ten.* Lovet de Goisfrido de Bech *dim. hid. Terra est* vi bobus, et ibi est unus Vill. Silva xxiv porc. valet et valuit semper v sol. hanc terram ten. quidem. Sochmannus homo Abbatis **St.** **Albani** et vendere potuit.

The Abbot of St. *Peters,* **Westminster,** held in **Titteberst** one Hide. The arable is half a Carucate, Wood to feed forty Hogs; it is worth and was worth ten Shillings by the Year, in the time of King *Edward* (the Confessor) thirteen Shillings and four Pence.

Goisfride de **Maneville** held three Virgates of the Abbot in the same Vill. The arable is half a Carucate, Wood to feed twelve Hogs; it is worth and was worth six Shillings and eight Pence by the Year, in the time of King *Edward* (the Confessor) ten Shillings.

Goisfride held of the Abbot of **St.** **Albans** half an Hide in **Titteberst.** it is worth and always was worth six Shillings by the Year; a certain Sochman, a Man (under the Protection) of the Abbot of **St.** **Albans** held it in the time of King *Edward* (the Confessor,) he could not sell it from the Church.

Goisfride de **Maneville** and *Ralph* held of him three Virgates in **Titteberst** in **Banais** Hundred. The arable is half a Carucate, there is a Villain and a Bordar, Wood to feed twelve Hogs; it is worth and was worth five Shillings by the Year, in the time of King *Edward* (the Confessor) ten Shillings. Three Sochmen held this Land, two of them Men (under the Protection) of *Asgar Stalri,* and a third, a Man (under the Protection) of **St.** **Alban.** he could not sell, the other two might sell.

Lovet held half an Hide of *Goisfride de Bech* in **Titteberst.** The arable is six Oxgangs, and there is one Villain, Wood to feed four and twenty Hogs; it is worth and always was worth five Shillings by the Year, a certain Sochman, a Man (under the Protection) of the Abbot of **St.** **Albans** held this Land and he might sell it.

Matt Paris de
Vila Abbat.

In the time of King *Will.* II. *Hugh de Titteberst* gave all his Land in **Titteberst** to the Church of **St.** **Albans,** and *William* the Son of *Racon* in the Reign of King *H.* I. gave 431 Acres of Land in **Titteburst** to the same Church.

Pas. 15 Ed. 1.
Rot. 45, cur.
recept. Scac.

Thomas de Wanz, in Pas. Anno 15 *Edw.* I. gave by Deed to *Ade de Stratton,* Clerk, the yearly Rent of *6s.* 8*d.* which *Walter de Blund* and his Ancestors were wont to pay to the same *Thomas* for *William Noel* and his Ancestors, for one Virgate of Land which *Walter* held of *William* in **Titteburst,** and also granted to *Ade* the Homage of the said *William,* &c. to hold to him and his Heirs.

LEVESDEN

IS an Hamlet charged by itself to the King's Taxes, and is Parcel of this Hundred, though Part of the Parish and Mannor of **Watford,** most of which lies in the Hundred of **Caishoe,** where I have treated of it.

BUSHEY.

Norden, p. 14 THIS Vill was aptly called by this Name **de** **Dumis** from the Bushes and Woods which heretofore did abound in this Place, and was one of the Mannors which *William* the Con-

Drawn on Stone from the Original Engravings by C.L.Tyler.

To ye Right Worpll Sr Robert Marsham,

This Draught is humbly

Published by J.M.Mullinger.

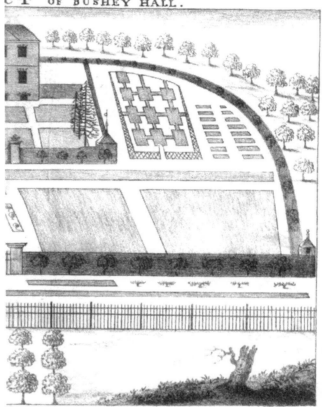

Knight & Baronet.

presented by

J. Drapentier.

Bishops Stortford 1826.

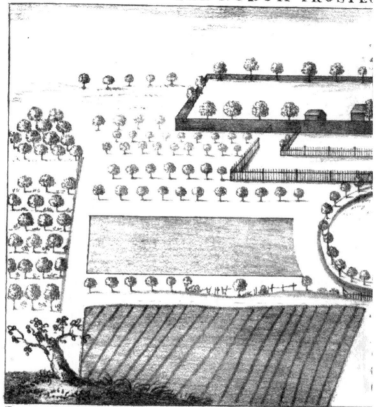

Drawn on Stone from the Original Engravings by C.I. Tyler.

To y.ᵉ Right Worp.ᵘ S.ʳ Robert Marsham,

This Draught is humbly

Pub.ᵈ by I.M. Mullinger

Knight & Baronet.

presented by

J. Drapentier.

Bps. Storeford. 1826.

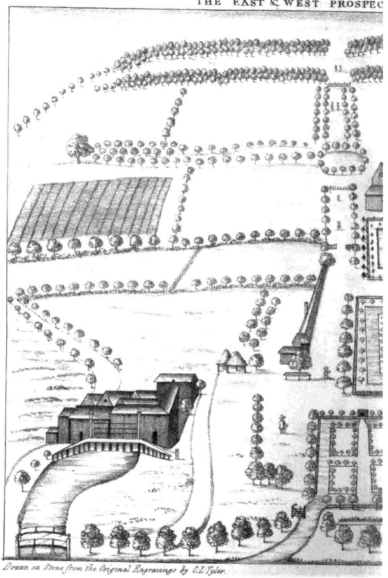

Drawn on Stone from the Original Engravings by C.L.Tyler.

Published by J.M.Mullinger, Bis...

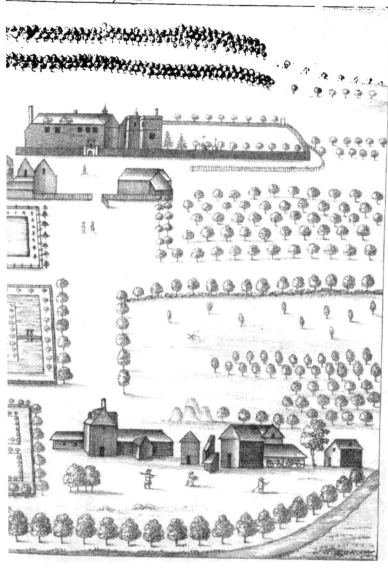

queror gave to *Jeoffery de Magnaville*, a valiant *Norman*, who assisted him in the Conquest of this Kingdom; for it is recorded in *Domesdei Book*, that

Hund. of
Dacorum.

> *Goisfridus de Mandevile in* Danais *Hundred. tenuit* Bissei *pro quindecim hidis se defendebat. Terra est decem car. in dominio quing; hidæ ibi sunt duo car. et tertia potest fieri; ibi decem Vill. cum uno Francig. et octo Bord. habentibus quinq; car. et sexta potest fieri. ibi duo molin. de octo solidis pastura ad pecud. Silva mille porc. in totis valentiis valet et valuit decem lib. tempore Regis* Edwardi, *quindecem lib. Hoc Manerium tenuit Leuuinus Teignus Regis* Edwardi. *ibi est unus Sochmanus qui non fuit ibi tempore Regis* Edwardi, *unam hidam habet; homo Reginæ* Eddid *fuit tempore Regis* Edwardi, *et vendere potuit.*

Jeoffery de Mandevile held Bushey in Danais Hundred, it was rated for fifteen Hides. The arable is ten Carucates, in Demeasne five Hides, and there are two Carucates, and a third may be made, there are ten Villains with one Frenchman born, and eight Bordars, having five Carucates, and a sixth may be made; there are two Mills of eight Shillings Rent by the Year, Common of Pasture for Cattle, Wood to feed a thousand Hogs: In the whole Value it is worth and was worth ten Pounds by the Year, in the time of King *Edward* (the Confessor) fifteen Pounds. *Lewine* a Thane of King *Edward* (the Confessor) held this Mannor: There is one Sochman who was not there in the time of King *Edward* (the Confessor) he had one Hide; he was a Man (under the Protection) of Queen *Edditha* in the time of King *Edward* (the Confessor) and he might sell it.

But in the time of King *H*. III. this Mannor was in the Possession of *David de Jarpenvil*, who claimed by a Grant of *H*. III. *Anno* 3 *Edw*. I to have View of Franc-pledge, and a Park and Free-warren in this Vill, and a Fair on the Vigils, Day, and Morrow of St. *James* every Year, and one Market on Thursday in every Week, and Warren in his Demeasne Lands, and upon the View of this Grant, all these Priviledges were allowed; but shortly after it came to the Crown; and King *Edw*. III. by several Charters dated the 26th and 27th of *February, Anno* 1 *Regni sui*, granted unto *Edmond* of Woodstock, this Mannor of Bushey in this County, and to the Heirs of his Body.

Quo Warr. 6
Ed 1. *Rot.* 54,
cur. recept.
in Scac.

This *Edmond* was his third Brother by *Margaret* the second Wife of *Edw*. II. and was created Earl of Kent, *An*. 15 of the same King. He was in that Expedition made 1 *Edw*. III. into Scotland. But was attained 4th of the same King, because he desired his Brother King *Edw*. II. should have been restored; and at the time of his Execution he staid till Evening, because an Executioner could not be gotten, until a Ribauld out of the *Marshalsey*, (to save his own Life) beheaded him upon Monday the Eve of St. *Cuthbert*, 4 *Edw*. III. And by Reason of his Attainder this Mannor came to the Possession of the King, who in the same Year granted it to

Rot. Scot. 1
Ed. III. m. 6.

Dugd Bar.
vol. 2, *fol.* 93.
Claus. 4 *Ed.*
III. m. 38.
Rot. Fin. 4 E.
III. m. 22.
Dugd. Bar.
vol 2, *fol.* 34.

Bartholomew de Burghersh for the Term of his Life, in Recompence of his Services. He went upon several Expeditions into France, was there when the famous Battle of Cressy was fought, where the *English* had so great a Victory; and for his good Service in those Wars, obtained in [l.]

Rot. Franc. 19
Ed. III. m. 5.
30 *Ed.* III. p.

Hund. of
Dacorum.

Pat. 21 Ed.
III. p. 2. m 5.
Pat. 29 Ed.
III. p.2, m.22.
Esc 29 Ed.
III.
Dugd. Bar.
vol. 2, fol. 35
Rot. Fin. 30
Ed. III. m 15.

Claus de iisd.
Annis indorso

Rot. Franc. 34
Ed. III. m 5.
Claus. 35 Ed.
III. m. 34.

Esc. 20 R. II.
n. 30.

Dugd Har.
vol. 2, fol. 76.

Ibid. vol 2,
fol. 292.

the Year following a Grant from the King of the Marriage
of *Isabel*, one of the Sisters and Heirs of *Edward de Saint
John*, Son and Heir of *Hugh de St. John*, deceased. He
was made Constable of the *Tower* of **London**, 29 *Edw*. III.
and having been summon'd to Parliament from 1 *Edw*. III.
till 28 inclusive, departed this Life beforethe End of that
Year, upon Sunday next after the Feast of St. *Peter ad
Vincula*. In 30 *Edw*. III. this Mannor came to the Possession of

Thomas Holland Earl of **Kent**, in Right of *Joan* his Wife,
who was Daughter and Heir of *Edmond* of **Woodstock**,
Earl of **Kent**, and he had Summons to Parliament from 27
Edw. III. to 31 *Edw*. III. inclusive. He assumed the
Title of Earl of **Kent**, *Anno* 34 *Edw*. III. And he was
constituted the King's Lieutenant and Captain General in
France and **Normandy**, the same Year; but he died upon
the 28th of *December* following, seized then of divers Mannors, among which this was one, and he left Issue

Thomas Earl of **Kent**, who was his Son and Heir; but
this Mannor came to

Joan his Mother, who married *Edward* Prince of **Wales**,
and held it for her Life, and after her Decease, which happened on *Monday* next after the Feast of St. *Lawrence*,
being the 7th of *Aug*. in the same Year,

Thomas Earl of **Kent** doing his Homage obtained a special Livery hereof, and also of **Ware** in this County, among
divers Mannors in other Counties. He declared upon
Easter-day, *Anno* 20 *Rich*. II. his Testament by the Title
of Earl of **Kent**, and Lord of **Ware**, whereby he appointed
his Body to be buried in the Abby of **Brune**: He bequeathed
to *Alice* his Wife, the Daughter of *Richard* Earl of **Arundel**, and to *Thomas* his Son, all his Goods and Chattels, and
died the 25th of *April* next ensuing, seized, among other
Lordships, of this Mannor and of **Ware**, in this County,
leaving *Thomas* his Son and Heir, twenty three Years of
Age, and he had also *Edmund* another Son, and five Daughters, *Alianore, Joane, Margaret*, another *Alianore*, and
Elizabeth: And this

Thomas shortly after doing Homage, had Livery of his
Lands, from whom this Mannor passed, by the same Persons
as the Mannor of **Ware** did, (to which Parish I refer the
Reader) until it came to

Margaret, the Wife of Sir *Richard Poole*, Knight, and
Daughter to *George* Duke of *Clarence*, by whom she had
Issue four Sons, *Henry, Geoffery, Arthur, Reginald*, and
one Daughter called *Ursula*, married to *Henry* Lord **Staf-
ford**: But 'twas her hard Fate to be attainted of Treason,
Anno 31 *H*. VIII. under Colour of Compliance with the
Marquess of **Exeter**, (then also attainted) and was executed

on the 27th. of *May*, 1541, 33 *H.* VIII. at which time she
was seized of this Mannor, which was then valued at 25*l.*
12*s.* 10*d.* and by this Attainder it came to the Crown, and
King *H.* VIII. by Letters Patents dated in the Year 35
Regni sui, granted the Mannor-house and most Part of the
Demeasne Lands belonging to it, to

William Alexander alias *Milward*, and his Heirs, also a
Lease for Years of the Mannor, Rents, Services and Copiholders, which said Demeasne Lands were afterwards sold
to divers Persons. But Queen *Mary* by her Letters Patents dated at 𝕲𝖚𝖕𝖑𝖋𝖔𝖗𝖉, 22 *June*, 1 *Regni sui*, granted this
Mannor to

Sir *Thomas Hastings*, Knight, and the Lady *Winifred*
his Wife, one of the Couzins and Heirs of the said Dame
Margaret, Countess of 𝖘𝖆𝖑𝖎𝖘𝖇𝖚𝖗𝖕, *viz.* one of the Daughters of *Henry* Lord *Montague*, eldest Son of the said
Margaret Countess of 𝖘𝖆𝖑𝖎𝖘𝖇𝖚𝖗𝖕, and to the Heirs of the
Body of the said *Winifride*, with divers Remainders over :
and soon after the said Sir *Thomas Hastings* dying, the
said *Winifride* married Sir *Thomas Barrington* of 𝕳𝖆𝖙𝖋𝖎𝖊𝖑𝖉 𝕭𝖗𝖔𝖆𝖉 𝕺𝖆𝖐𝖊 alias 𝕶𝖎𝖓𝖌'𝖘 𝕳𝖆𝖙𝖋𝖎𝖊𝖑𝖉 in the County of
𝕰𝖘𝖘𝖊𝖝, to whom Queen *Elizabeth* by her Letters Patents
dated at 𝖂𝖊𝖘𝖙𝖒𝖎𝖓𝖘𝖙𝖊𝖗, 22 *November, Anno Regni sui Octavo*, granted the Reversion of the said Mannor, &c. to hold
to him and his Heirs as heretofore they were holden before
the Attainder of the said Countess of 𝖘𝖆𝖑𝖎𝖘𝖇𝖚𝖗𝖕. This Sir
Thomas Barrington and Dame *Winifride Hastings* his
Wife, on 25th *Nov.* 8 *Eliz.* levied a Fine and suffered a Recovery of this Mannor to the Use of *Andrew Jenour*, Esq.
of 𝕸𝖚𝖈𝖍 𝕯𝖔𝖓𝖒𝖔𝖜 in the County of 𝕰𝖘𝖘𝖊𝖝, and his Heirs,
who conveyed it by Deed dated 28 *April*, 15 *Eliz.* to

Robert Blackwell of 𝕭𝖚𝖘𝖍𝖊𝖕, Gent. and his Heirs: He
had Issue by *Joan* his Wife, three Sons, *George, Robert* and
Richard, and by his Will dated the 4th Day of *April, Anno* 1580, gave this Mannor (*inter alia*) to *Joan* his Wife
for her Life, the Remainder to *Robert* his second Son, of
Gray's Inn in the County of 𝕸𝖎𝖉𝖉𝖑𝖊𝖘𝖊𝖝, Esq. and the
Heirs of his Body lawfully begotten, and the greatest Part
of his Land holden in Socage to

George, his eldest Son, and the Heirs Males of his Body
lawfully begotten, paying yearly four Pence to the Mannor
of 𝕭𝖚𝖘𝖍𝖊𝖕, on Condition that if he the said *George* do not
molest or trouble any other of his Sons, but if he do, then he
that is so troubled shall have the said Lands held in Socage
bequeathed as aforesaid to the said *George:* He gave to
Richard his third Son other Lands in 𝕭𝖚𝖘𝖍𝖊𝖕, to good Value holden in Socage, and by Copy of Court Roll. After
whose Death *George* his eldest Son exasperated against
Robert his younger Brother, for that his Father had given

Hund. of
Bacorum.

this Mannor, and made him Tenant to him, took Advantage of the Statute which enacts, That a third Part of Lands holden by Knight's Service shall descend to the Heir notwithstanding any Devise; and not regarding the Condition annexed to the Lands given to him, entred on the third Part of the said Mannor in the Life-time of *Joan* his Mother; whereupon *Robert Blackwell* the second Son entred upon the Lands bequeathed to the said *George*, and divers Suits in Law and Equity were commenced between them; upon all which the two Brothers at length submitted themselves to the Award of *Francis Heydon* and *Robert Wilbraham*, Esquires, and *George Boucher*, Gent. who awarded that the said *Robert Blackwell* should pay a certain Sum of Mony to the said *George Blackwell* his elder Brother, in Consideration whereof he should convey the said third Part of the said Mannor to the said *Rob. Blackwell*, and his Heirs Males: but before the Conveyances were perfected, *George* the elder Brother, still envying his younger Brother, about the 26th of *February*, 1583, sold this third Part to *Charles Morisin* of Caishoburp in this County, Esq. who joyned with the said *Robert Blackwell*, Esq. Owner of the other two Parts of this Mannor, and in *Hillary Term*, 15 *Jac.* I. conveyed by Fine to the King, all his Estate in this Mannor: Then King *James* I. by Letters Patents dated at Westminster, 21st of *May*, *Anno* 16 *Regni sui*, granted the Mannor of Bushep, Messuages, Lands, Tenements, Meadows, Feedings, Pastures, Demesne Lands, Court-leets, Views of Franc-pledge, Law-daies, Assizes and Assay of Bread, Wine, and Ale, and all Manner of other Victuals whatsoever, Goods and Chattels, Debts and Credits of Felons and Fugitives, Felons of themselves, attainted, convicted, condemned, and outlaw'd, and the Goods and Chattels, Credits and Debts of all such and every of them which will not stand to Judgment, Fines and Amercements of the Men, and Tenements, Chattels, Waifs, Estraies, Treasure-trove, Deodands, Free-warren, and all things that belong to Freewarren, hawking and hunting, Foldage, Turbage, Commons, Ways, Wast-grounds, and all other Rights, Jurisdictions, Franchises, Liberties, Priviledges, Profits, Commodities, Advantages, Emoluments, and Hereditaments whatsoever, and the Right of Advowson to the Church of Bushep, with the Appurtenances to *Ellis Wynne* and *Francis King* and their Heirs, in as large a Manner as they were formerly granted to the Duke of Lancaster, and as fully as the Countess of Salisbury held the same, and the said Trustees conveyed this Mannor to the several Persons again, according to their several Interests as aforesaid. Afterwards Sir *Charles Morison*, Kt. and Bart. died seized of this third Part of this Mannor, leaving Issue

Elizabeth, who married *Arthur Capel,* Esq. in whose Right he held this Mannor, from whom it descended to

Arthur, late Earl of **Essex,** who was the Son and Heir of the said *Arthur* Lord *Capel,* and the said Lady *Elizabeth* his Wife, and upon the Death of the said Earl, it descended to *Algernon* Earl of **Essex,** who is the present Lord hereof.

Robert Blackwel, Esq. by Deed dated 14th of *April,* 1638, conveyed the two other Parts to the Use of himself and *Eleanor* his Wife, who was the Daughter of *John Kitchin* of *Grayes Inn,* Esq. for their Lives, the Remainder to *Richard Blackwel,* who was the only Son of *Robert Blackwel,* Esq. the eldest Son of the said *Robert* the elder, and one of the three chief Clerks of the Pettibagg in *Chancery,* and of *Mary* his Wife, Daughter of *Francis Heyton* of **East Greenwich** in the County of **Kent,** Esq. and the Heirs of the Body of the same *Richard,* and for Want of such Issue to *Thomas Blackwell,* Gent. second Son of the said *Robert* and his Heirs; *Robert* the Father died on the 14th of *May,* 1630. *Robert* the Grandfather survived him, and by his Will confirmed the former Settlement, and died the third of *April,* 1645.

Richard Blackwel the Grandson succeeded, to whom the said two Parts descended by Virtue of the said Settlement, and married *Winifride* the Daughter of *John White* of the *Middle Temple,* **London,** Esq. and had Issue by her three Sons, *Robert* who died in his Infancy, *Robert* and *Richard,* and two Daughters, *Winifrid* and *Mary;* the second *Robert* died also: And *Richard* the Father died seiz'd hereof on the 6th Day of *April,* 1655, leaving

Richard who was his Heir, and married *Susan* the Daughter of *Charles Evans* of **Beech-hill** in the County of **Berks,** Gent. and died in the Year 1677, without Issue, upon whose Death the said two Parts by Virtue of the said Deed of Intail came to

Susan and *Anne,* Daughters of *Thomas Blackwel* (Brother to the aforesaid *Robert)* by *Susanna* his Wife, Daughter of *Stephen Sedgewick* of **Hackney** in the County of **Middlesex.**

Susan married *William Parkins* of **Marston Jabit** in the County of **Warwick,** Esq. who was one of the six Clerks in *Chancery,* on whom King *Charles* II. conferred the Honour of Knighthood the 10th Day of *June,* 1681, and in her Right he became possest of one Moyety of the said two Parts of this Mannor; and *Anne* the other Sister married *Rowland Pitt,* Gent. in whose Right he became possest of the other Moyety of these two Parts of this Mannor, and the said *Rowland* and *Anne* his Wife, An. 1684, sold their Moiety of these two Parts to

Hund. of
Dacorum.

Sir *William Parkyns*, by Reason whereof he became possest of the whole two third Parts of this Mannor, and sued out a Writ of Partition at Common Law, *Anno* 1686, and by Virtue thereof his two Parts of this Mannor were divided from the other third Part which belonged to the Earl of *Essex*; but this Sir *William Parkyns* and *Susan* his Wife mortgaged her third Part to ———— *Parkyns*, Gent. who was Uncle to the said Sir *William*, and the other third Part which Sir *William* bought of *Rowlaud Pitt* and *Anne* his Wife, Sir *William* mortgaged to *Richard Parkyns* of *Drapton* in the *Mould*, Gent. after which Sir *William* was attainted of High Treason *Anno* 1696, for attempting to assacinate King *William*, and to raise Men to assist the late King *James* in the Recovery of the Crown, and upon that Attainder he was executed, and both the Mortgagers to secure their Mony, got into Possession of these two third Parts of this Mannor, and are the present Lords of them.

The Mannor of BOURNE HALL

Mich. 10 Ed.
II. Rot. 115,
cur. recept.
Scac.

WAS in the Possession of Sir *Thomas Barnard*, Kt. *An.* 10 *Edw.* II. and in *Michaelmas* Term released all his Right herein to *John de Wengrave* Citizen of *London*, and *Christian* his Wife, and *John* their Son, and the Heirs of the said *John*; and in *Hill.* 10 *Edw.* II. *Edward de Chibere* released also all his Right in the same Mannor to the said *Christian* and *John* her Son.

10 Ed. II.

Holl. Chron.
fol. 562, n. 30.
Rot. Franc.
7 H. V. m. 4.
Pat. Norm. 9
H. V. p. 1,
m. 2.

Reginald de West was seiz'd of this Mannor in the time of *H. V.* he was made Governour of *St. Lo*, *An.* 4 *H. V.* Captain of the Castle *de la Moet* in *Normandy*, 7 *H. V.* serv'd again in the French Wars, *An.* 9 *H. V.* and upon the Death of *Thomas* Lord *la Ware* had Livery of the Lands of his Mother's Inheritance, who was Heir to the said *Thomas*. He was summon'd to Parliament by the Title of Lord *la Ware* from 5 *H.* VI. to 28th of the same King inclusive, during which time I find his Name return'd *Anno* 12 *H.* VI. among the Gentlemen in this County that could dispend 10*l.* *per Annum*, which induces me to believe that this was the Place of his Residence, and he dyed seiz'd of this and *Hertesborn* in this County, among divers other Mannors, on the 27th of *August*, 29 of *H.* VI. leaving

Rot. Fin. 5 H.
VI. m. 4.
Claus. de iisd.
an. in dorso.

Esc. 29 H VI.
21.

Richard de West his Son and Heir, a stout Assertor of the Lancastrian Interest : and in Consideration of his good Services, King *H.* VI. granted him forty Pounds *per Annum*, issuing out of the Profits of the Mannor of *Old Wutton* in the County of *Wilts*, for his Life, but the Scene changing soon after, and taking no Pleasure to live under the Government of those whom he had so vigorously opposed, obtained Leave *Anno* 3 *Edw.* IV. to take with him, twelve Servants, and as many Horse, not exceeding the

Pat. 38 H VI.
p. 2, m. 22.

Rot. Franc. 3
Ed. IV. m. 12
Claus. de iisd.
annis in dorso.

Value of forty Shillings a piece, and to continue beyond the Seas; he was summon'd to Parliament from 38 *H.* VI. to the 12 of *Edw.* IV. inclusive, and died upon the 10th of *March*, 16 *Edw.* IV. seiz'd of this Mannor of 𝔥𝔢𝔯𝔱𝔢𝔰𝔟𝔬𝔯𝔫, and several others.

Hund. of *Dacorum.*

Esc. 16 E. IV. p. 2, m. 6.

Thomas de West was his Son and Heir, and though he was no more than nineteen Years of Age at the Death of his Father, yet obtained a special Livery of his Lands upon the first of *September* following; he stood in such Favour with King *H.* VII. that he obtained a Grant in the first Year of his Reign, of the Castle, Barony, Honor, and Borough of 𝔅𝔯𝔢𝔪𝔟𝔯𝔢 in 𝔖𝔲𝔰𝔰𝔢𝔵, the Mannors of 𝔎𝔦𝔫𝔤'𝔰 𝔅𝔢𝔯𝔫𝔢𝔰, 𝔚𝔢𝔰𝔱 𝔊𝔯𝔦𝔫𝔰𝔱𝔢𝔡, 𝔎𝔫𝔞𝔭, and 𝔚𝔞𝔰𝔥𝔦𝔫𝔤𝔱𝔬𝔫, the Towns and Borough of 𝔖𝔥𝔬𝔯𝔥𝔞𝔪 and 𝔥𝔬𝔯𝔰𝔥𝔞𝔪, the Forest of 𝔖𝔱. 𝔏𝔢𝔬𝔫𝔞𝔯𝔡, the Parks of 𝔅𝔢𝔞𝔫𝔟𝔲𝔰𝔥 and 𝔎𝔫𝔞𝔭, and six or seven Hundreds which came to the Crown by the Attainder of *John* Duke of 𝔑𝔬𝔯𝔣𝔬𝔩𝔨, slain at 𝔅𝔬𝔰𝔴𝔬𝔯𝔱𝔥 𝔣𝔢𝔦𝔩𝔡; he was a great Commander in the Army, sent the 7 *H.* VII. into 𝔣𝔩𝔞𝔫𝔡𝔢𝔯𝔰, in Aid of *Maximilian* the Emperor, and commanded the Forces raised 12 *H.* VII. to suppress the Insurrection of the Cornish Men, and he died about 12th of *Feb.* 17 *H.* VIII. leaving four Sons *Thomas*, *Owen*, *George*, and *Leonard*; and three Daughters, ——— Wife of Sir *Anthony S. Amaud*, Kt. *Katharine*, and *Barbara*.

Pat. 16 E. IV. p. 2, m. 6.

Pat. 1 H. VII. p. 4.

Polyd Virgil, p. 584, n. 30.

Ibid p. 600, n. 30.

Thomas succeeded, and joyned with the Peers, 22 *H.* VIII. in the Declaration sent to Pope *Clement* VII. advertizing him that his Supremacy would be rejected, if he did not comply with *H.* VIII. in the Divorce of Queen *Katharine*; this Lord having no Issue of his Body, bred up *William* his Brother's Son, in the House, with an Intent to make him his Heir; but he impatient to wait his Uncle's Death, prepared Poison to dispatch him quickly, and the Discovery so highly incensed the good old Lord, that upon Complaint made thereof in Parliament, *Anno* 2 *Edw.* VI. he procur'd a special Act to attaint him, and disable him to hold his Lands or Honours, and departed this Life at 𝔒𝔣-𝔣𝔦𝔫𝔤𝔱𝔬𝔫, on Tuesday, the 9th of *Oct.* 1554, 1 & 2 *P.* and *M.*

n. 1, in Offic. Arm. fol. 35.

William succeeded, because he was his next Heir, bore the Title of Lord *la Ware*, served in the English Army 4 *Mary*, at the Siege of 𝔖𝔱. 𝔔𝔲𝔦𝔫𝔱𝔦𝔲𝔰 in 𝔭𝔦𝔠𝔞𝔯𝔡𝔶, and obtained an Act in the Parliament held 5 *Eliz.* for his Restoration in Blood, and a new Creation to the Title of Lord *la Ware*; he married *Elizabeth* Daughter to *Thomas Strange* of 𝔠𝔥𝔢𝔰-𝔱𝔢𝔯𝔱𝔬𝔫, by whom he had Issue *Thomas*, and dyed in the Year, 1595, 38 *Eliz.*

Holl. fol. 133. Rot. Parl. de eodem anno.

Thomas was his Heir, inherited his Honor and Estate, exhibited his Petition to the Queen in Parliament held 39 *Eliz.* to be restored to the Place and Precedency of his Ancestors, obtained his Desire, and married *Anne* Daughter

Journ. of Parl. de eodem anno.

Hund. of
Bacorum.
MSS. in Offic.
Arm.

of Sir *Frances Knolles*, Knight of the Garter, and Treasurer of the House to Queen *Elizabeth*, by whom he had Issue two Sons, *Robert* and *Thomas*, and six Daughters, *Lucie* married to *Henry Ludlow*, Esq. *Katharine* who died unmarried, *Elianor* married to *William Savage*, *Anne* to *John*, Son and Heir to Sir *Bryan Pellet*, Kt. *Penelope*, and *Elizabeth*.

Robert was the eldest Son, married *Elizabeth* one of the Daughters and Coheirs of Sir *Henry Cock*, Kt. but died in the Life-time of his Father without Issue.

The next Lord that I meet with, was an *Hickman*, and from one of that Name it was sold to

James Mayne of 𝕭𝖔𝖇𝖎𝖓𝖌𝖉𝖔𝖓, Esq. of whose Family I intend to treat in the Vill of 𝕭𝖔𝖇𝖎𝖓𝖌𝖉𝖔𝖓, where he lived, to which I refer the Reader; he had Issue one Son, who died in his Minority, and two Daughters who were his Coheirs, whereof

Sarah his youngest Daughter married Sir *William Glascock*, Knight one of the Masters of the Requests to King *Charles* II. to whom this Mannor and the Lands belonging to it, came in Right of his Wife, as Part of her Share, which descended to her from her Father, and he and she sold it to

George Hadley of 𝕰𝖆𝖘𝖙 𝕭𝖊𝖗𝖓𝖊𝖙 in this County, Esq. the present Lord hereof.

In this Vill Sir *George Walker*, Kt. Dr. of the Civil Law, erected a fair House upon the River 𝕮𝖔𝖑𝖓𝖊, and dying seized hereof, it came to *George*, who was created Bart. by Patent dated the 28th Day of *January*, *An.* 1679, 31 *Car.* II. and afterwards he sold this Seat to *Robert Marsham*, Esq. one of the six Clerks in *Chancery*, who was the 2d Son of Sir *John Marsham* of 𝕮𝖚𝖝𝖙𝖔𝖓 in 𝕶𝖊𝖓𝖙, created Baronet by Patent dated 12 *Aug.* 1663. This *Robert* was knighted on the —— Day of *July*, *Anno* 1681, upon the Death of Sir *John Marsham* his eldest Brother, and his Son, their Honour descended to him, he is the present Possessor hereof.

This Rectory was rated *Anno* 26 *Henry* VIII. in the King's Books at 18*l.* 2*s.* and Mr. *Smith* is Patron hereof.

The RECTORS.

Dr. *Seaton*	Mr. *Smith*
Mr. *Ward*	1694 Mr. *Smith*.

This Church is erected in the Middle of this Vill, in the Deanery of St. Albans in the Diocess of London, is cover'd with Tile, and at the West End thereof is a square Tower wherein are three tunable Bells. Within the Chancel lye several Gravestones, which have these Inscriptions.

M. S.
Silius Titus *Armig.*
Unacum Constancia
Conjuge suâ
II. S. E.

Ille vicessimo quarto Novembris 1637.
Illa vicessimo secundo Octobris 1667.
Animam Deo reddidit
Requiescant in pace.
Stephanus *tertius Filius eorum*
Tertius nuper Castri quod
Dolæ est in agro Cantiano
Pro Defectus in eodem tumulo
Cum parentibus servitus est
Obiit Mar. 30. 1671.

Here in hope of happy Resurrection through Christ, lies the Body of *John Gale*, Esq; who was Father to *Mary Gale* by his second Wife *Jane*, and Sister to Mrs. *Elizabeth Terry*, both which are here interr'd next unto him: He lived to the age of 70. years, and peaceably departed this life, *Jan.* 5. 1655.

The next Stone has this Inscription cut in the Border thereof.

Here lieth the Body of *Mary Gale*, Daughter and sole Heir of *John Gale*, Gent. and *Jane* his Wife, who departed this Life the 13th day of *May* 1642, aged 5 years.

Under this Stone lieth the Body of *Elizabeth Terry*, Widow, late Wife of *John Terry* of London, Esq; aged 85 years, who departed this life the 7th day of *Feb.* in the year of our Lord God 1654.

On the same Stone.

Here lies the Body of Mrs. *Mary*, Grandchild of the said *Elizabeth*, Wife of *George Blackwell* of this Parish, Gent. she died the 15th of *January* 1665. aged 34.

Here lieth the Body of *Thomas Hobson* of the Inner Temple, London Esq; the Kings Clerk of the Office of the Pettibag in his Majesties high Court of Chancery: He was eldest Son to *Thomas Hobson* of this Parish, Gent. and was born in this Parish, and died the 30th of *August* 1679, at his House call'd Watford Place in the Parish of Watford in the County of Hertford, aged 49 years.
Mors mihi Lucrum.

He married *Elizabeth* the only Daughter of *John Comyn*, alias *Chilcot* of London, Merchant, by whom he had one Son, who died before he was a year old, and was buried in this Church. *Pulvis et anima fumus.*

Here lieth the Body of *Richard Ward*, 37 years Rector of this Parish, a constant Preacher, and a constant Practicer of what he preach'd, Learned, Charitable, Peaceable, Pious, a Contemner of this World because he knew it and expected a better; Thou who dost read this imitate.
Obiit Julii 25. 1684.
Ætat. suæ 82.

Here lyeth interr'd the Body of *Richard Blackwel*, Esq; the Son of *Robert Blackwel*, who deceased *Apr.* the 6th. 1649. leaving behind him three Children, one Son and two Daughters.
This Tomb his Body,
This Stone his name;
Heaven doth his Soul in endless bliss retain.

Round this Stone on a Bordar.

Subsit, Resurrectionis jacet hic Robertus Blackman, *Armig. nuper unus Clericorum parcæ Bagæ Curiæ Cancellariæ qui obiit decimo quarto die* Maii, *Anno. Dom.* 1630.

Hund. of
Dacorum.

Hic jacet Depositum Thomæ Hobson *natalibus probi* Merringtonii *in Agro Dunelmensi, qui scribatum in Officio Parcæ·Bagæ* 32 *annos cum laude gessit et spe letæ Resurrectionis anno Salutis* 1651. *Ætat.* 59. 6. Jan. *obdormivit, qui dum vixit fuit pietate insignis amicis, charius omnibus sincerius re mediocri cumulatus pauperibus bonus, moribus casta, beatus Uxore nomine* Barbara, Roberti Blakewell *de* Bushei, *Armig. filia ex qua susceperat liberos novem quatuor Fœminas et quinque Mares quorum unus cui* Robertus *erat nomen in Curiæ Banci Regis Clericus, quo Officia honeste fangebatur, et anno Dom.* 1661. *Ætat.* 28. 8. Jan. *hanc vitam cum immortalitate mutavit.*

On the verge of the next Stone.

Here lieth the Body of *Robert Blakewel*, Son of *Richard Blakewel*, Gent. who died the 11th of *Decemb.* 1643.

In the Middle of the Stone.

Here's two in one, and yet not two but one,
Two Sons, one Tomb; two heirs one name alone.

In the entrance to the Church.

Sub spe orta Resurrectionis.

In Christo requiescunt hic corpora Thomæ Blakwell *et* Roberti *filii sui, et* Johannæ *Uxoris dicti* Roberti; *idem* Thomas *obiit Mense* Octobris 1541. *dictus* Robertus *obiit Mense* Aprilis 1580. *et predicta* Johanna *obiit Mense* Decembris 1607. Georgio, Roberto *et* Rich. *Filiis dictorum* Roberti *et* Johannæ *extunc viven.*

Orimur.   *Morimur.*

In the Church-yard a Tomb.

Johannis Ewre *indolis optimæ*
Juvenis Monumentum hoc
Mæsti parentes
Pie.

Stay Passenger and lend a Tear,
Youth and Vertue both resteth here,
He that lives and rests, how mild, how good,
How toward he was, how much he understood;
All but sixteen may think that Fate did wrong
To trust such Vertue in a Mind so young,
Or else that finding so much goodness there,
She thought Time old, mistook and tomb'd him here.
Deceased *Octob.* the 2d. 1624.

The CHARITY.

John Gale gave by his Will to twenty Widows, twenty Pecks of Pease, twenty Fishes, and twenty great Loaves, and if there were not so many Widows, then the poorest in this Parish.

And now I shall conclude the Division of this High Constable, and proceed to the next, which contains the Vills and Parishes of 𝕶ings 𝕷angley, 𝕳emelhempsted, 𝕭obingdon, 𝕱launden, 𝕷ittle 𝕲adesden, 𝕱rithsden, 𝕲reat 𝕲adesden, 𝕾tudham, 𝕽ensworth, 𝕮adington, and 𝕱lamsted, and I shall pass from one to the other after this Order.

The second Part of the fifth Division.

KINGS LANGLEY.

WHEN King *William* the Conqueror had subdued this Realm, he gratified Earl *Moreton* a valiant *Normau* with divers large Possessions for his great Services, among which was this Vill, as it is recorded in *Domesdei Book*, under the Title of *Terra Comitis* Moretoniensis.

Radulphus tenet 𝕷𝖆𝖓𝖌𝖊𝖑𝖊𝖎 *de Comite pro una hida et dimid. se defendebat. Terra est sexdecem car. in Dom. nulla est, sed duo possunt fieri ibi unus Francig. cum quatuor Vill. et quinque Bord. habentibus duo car. et duodecem car. possunt fieri, ibi duo Molini de sexdecem sol. et duo Servi, pratum tres car. pastura ad pecud. Silva ducent porc. et quadragint. in totis valent. valet quadragint. sol. quando recepit quatuor lib. tempore Regis Edwardi octo lib. hoc Manerium tenuerunt duo homines Com.* Leuvini, Tburi *et* Seric.

Ralph held 𝕷𝖆𝖓𝖌𝖑𝖊𝖞 of Earl *Moreton*, it was rated for one Hide and an half. The arable is sixteen Carucates, in Demeasne there is none, but two may be made, there is one Frenchman born, with four Villains and five Bordars having two Carucates, and twelve Carucates may be made, there are two Mills of sixteen Shillings a Year Rent, and two Servants, Meadow three Carucates, Common of Pasture for the Cattle, Wood to feed two hundred and forty Hogs; in the whole Value it is worth forty Shillings by the Year, when he received it four Pounds, in the time of King *Edward* (the Confessor) eight Pounds, *Thurie* and *Seric* two Men (under the Protection) of Earl *Lewin* held this Manuor.

This Earl married *Maud*, Daughter to *Roger de Montgomery*, by whom he had Issue

William, who raised a Rebellion against King *H.* I. upon which he forfeited this Mannor to the Crown, where King *H.* III. erected a royal Seat, from whence it received this Adjunct to its Name; and *Roger* the Son of *Robert Helle,* an English Baron, founded a religious House for preaching Fryars near his Pallace, consisting of a Prior and Convent; to which Fraternity, King *Edw.* I. gave by his Patent dated at this Pallace, 20 *Dec. Anno* 2 *Regni sui,* 1274, all that their House belonging to the Parish Church of the same Vill, forty one Pearches of Land, and also twenty seven Pearches of other Land, to hold in free and pure Almes; and the same King by his Letters Patents dated at 𝖂𝖊𝖘𝖙𝖒𝖎𝖓𝖘𝖙𝖊𝖗, 3 *July, Anno* 8 *Regni sui,* 1280, gave the Mannor of 𝕷𝖆𝖓𝖌𝖑𝖊𝖞, with the Close adjoyning the Priory, and the Vesture of the Wood called 𝕮𝖍𝖎𝖕𝖕𝖊𝖗𝖇𝖎𝖑𝖊 Wood, to the Prior and Convent and their Brethren, to hold in free and pure Almes, to have and take at their Pleasure for Fewel and other Necessaries for ever.

Edmund the fifth Son of King *Edw.* III. was born at this Mannor-house *Anno* 1344, 15 *Edw.* III. baptized by *Michael*, then Abbot of 𝕾t. 𝕬𝖑𝖇𝖆𝖓𝖘, and took his Sirname from this Place, by Reason of his Birth: The King his Father granted *Anno* 1347, 21 *Edw.* III. to him in special Tail, all the Castles, Mannors, and Lands beyond 𝕿𝖗𝖊𝖓𝖙, which were formerly *John Warrens*, Earl of 𝕾𝖚𝖗𝖗𝖞, but in Regard of his Minority, Queen *Philippa* his Mother received the Profits of them for the Maintenance and Education of him and other her younger Children. The same King by Patent dated 13 *Novemb. Anno* 36 *Regni sui,* 1362, created him Earl of 𝕮𝖆𝖒𝖇𝖗𝖎𝖉𝖌𝖊 whilst he was in 𝕴𝖗𝖊𝖑𝖆𝖓𝖉. And for his

Weav. Fun. Mon p. 588.

Pat 2 Ed. I.

Pat. 8 Ed I.

Dugd. Bar of Engl. vol 2, fol 134.

Hund. of
Bacorum.
Pat. 9 R. II.
great Services and Merits, King *R.* II. advanced him to the
Dignity and Title of Duke of York by Patent dated the
6th of *August*, 1386, 9 *R.* II. and the yearly Rent of 100*l.*
out of the Profits of the County of York, 40*l. per Annum*
out of the Customs of Wools, Skins, and Felts in Kingston
upon Hull, 500*l. per Annum* out of the Port of London
until 1000*l.* yearly in Lands and Rents should be settled
upon him; and he was created by the Ceremony of the Cincture with a Sword, and putting a Cap on his Head with a
Circle of Gold.

He married *Isabel*, the younger Daughter of *Don Pedro*
King of Castile, by whom he had Issue *Edward* Earl of
Dugd. Bar.
vol. 2, fol. 155
Rutland, *Richard* Earl of Cambridge, and *Constance* married to *Thomas Spencer*, Earl of Gloucester; this *Isabel*, by
his Consent devised by her Will dated 9 *Decemb. An.* 1382,
6 *R.* II. that her Body should be buried wherever her Husband the King should appoint; ordaining that upon the Day
of her Death an hundred Trentals and an hundred Sauters
should be said for her Soul; likewise four Priests, or one at
least, should sing for her, by the Space of four Years; moreover that upon the Day of her Burial, her best Horse should
be delivered for her Mortuary: She also bequeathed to the
King her Heart of Pearls, to the Duke of Lancaster, her
Tablet of Jasper, which the King of Armorie gave her: To
Edward Earl of Rutland, (her Son) her Crown to remain
to his Heirs; to *Constance le Dispencer* (her Daughter) a
Fret of Pearls; and to the Dutchess of Gloucester, her Tablet of Gold with Images, as also her Sauter with the Arms
of Northampton; and to King *Richard* (after her other Le-
gacies paid) all the Remainder of her Goods, with Trust
that he should allow unto *Richard* her younger Son (his
Godson) five hundred Marks *per Annum* for his Life: And
'tis said that this great Lady having been somewhat wanton
in her younger Years, became an hearty Penitent, and departed this Life *Anno* 1394, 17 *R.* II. and was buried in
this Church.

After her Decease this great Duke married *Joan* Daughter of *Thomas*, and Sister and Coheir to *Edmond Holland*,
Earl of Kent, and when he drew near his Death, by his
Will dated the 25th of *November, An.* 1400, 1 *Hen.* IV.
wherein he stiles himself Duke of York, Earl of Cambridge,
and Lord Tibedale, bequeathed his Body to be buried in this
Church near to the Grave of *Isabel* his first Wife, appoint-
ing that two Priests should be ordained by his Executors to
perform Divine Service there every Day for his Soul, and
the Souls of all his Kindred, departed this Life 1st of *Aug.*
Anno 1403, 3 *H.* IV. and was buried here accordingly in
this Church, where his Monument remains at this Day.

Stow, fol. 306.
Anno 1392, 15 *R.* II. King *Richard* with Queen *Anne*

his Wife, four Bishops, as many Earls, the Duke of York, many Lords, and fifteen Ladies, held a royal Christmas at this Town. *Hund. of Bacorum.*

When King *Richard* II. was barbarously murder'd in the Castle of Pontefrac, by Sir *Piers Exton* and eight other Assassinates, his Body was imbalm'd and seer'd, and covered with Lead, saving the Face, to the Intent that all that desired it might see him, that they might be assured that he was dead; and as the Corps was thence convey'd to London, a Dirge was sung in the Evening, and Mass of *Requiem* in the Morning, in all the Towns and Places where the Corps did stay all Night, and as well after the one Service as the other, his Face was shew'd to all that coveted to see it; from the *Tower* it was conveyed thro' the City to the Cathedral Church of St. *Paul*, with the Face open, where it lay three Days together that all Men might behold it, and there was a solemn Obsequie performed for him, first at *Pauls*, and afterwards at Westminster, where the King and the Citizens of London were present: From thence the Corps was conveyed hither, and buried here in the Church of the Fryars Preachers, where the Bishop of Chester and the Abbots of St. Albans and Waltham celebrated the Exequies for the Funeral; but none of the Nobles nor other Persons of Quality were present there. Afterwards King *H*.V. removed the Body from hence to Westminster, where it was honourably intombed by Queen *Ann* his Wife. *Holl. fol. 517.*

King *Edw*. IV. by his Letters Patents dated at Westminster, the 14th of *July*, *Anno* 1466, 6 *Regni sui*, gave to *Thomas Betts*, Prior of the Priory of Langley, and his Successors for ever, a certain Park called Homeparke, the Fryars Wood, with the same Park, a Wood called Chipperbile Wood, one Meadow called Fryars Meadow, and the Toll of the Grain at the King's Mill, to hold in pure and perpetual Alms. *Cart. 6 E IV.*

King *H*.VII. by his Letters Patents dated *Anno* 1505, 20 *Regni sui*, gave all the Mannor and Park of Kings Langley, with the Appurtenances, to Queen *Katharine* his Consort, for the Term of her natural Life. *Cart. 20 H. VII.*

King *H*.VIII. by Letters Patents dated *Anno* 1534, 25 *Regni sui*, granted to Queen *Anne* his Consort this Mannor of Langley, with the Park and all the Appurtenances, for the Term of her Life. *Pat 25 H. VIII.*

The Prior and Convent of the Priory of Langley, *Anno* 1538, 30 *H*.VIII. surrendered all their Mannors, Lands, and Tenements belonging to their Priory into the Hands of the King, which was then valued at 127*l*. 14*s*. ½*d*. but *Anno* 26 *H*. VIII. Sir *William Dugdale* says, in his Catalogue of Monasteries, it was then valued at no more than 122*l*. 4*s*. *Cart. penes Hen. Smith.*

G g 2

Hund. of Bacorum.

Pat. 3 & 4 P. and M.

King *Philip* and Queen *Mary* by their Letters Patents dated the 25th Day of *June, Anno* 1557, 3 & 4 *Regni suorum*, gave and restored to this Priory all the Houses and Scite of this Priory with the Appurtenances; but *An.* 1559, 1 *Eliz.* this Priory with the Appurtenances reverted again to the Crown.

Cart. 42 Eliz.

Queen *Elizabeth* by Letters Patents dated the 27th of *June, Anno* 1600, 42 *Regni sui*, gave to the Bishop of 𝔈𝔩𝔶, all that the Rectory of 𝔎𝔦𝔫𝔤𝔰 𝔏𝔞𝔫𝔤𝔩𝔢𝔭 with the Rights, Members, and Appurtenances, Lands, Meadows, Pastures, and all the Tith of Grain, Corn, and Hay arising in the Vills and Fields of 𝔏𝔞𝔫𝔤𝔩𝔢𝔭, which was Parcel of the Estate of the late Priory, and valued at 40*l.* 0*s.* 8*d. per Ann.*

Cart. 4 Jac. I

King *James* I. by his Letters Patents dated at 𝔚𝔢𝔰𝔱minster, 22d *December, Anno* 1606, 4 *Regni sui*, gave to *Edward Newport* and *John Compton* their Heirs and Assigns, upon the Petition of *William Razon Mounteagle*, all that the Scite of the late House or Priory of the Fryars of 𝔎𝔦𝔫𝔤𝔰 𝔏𝔞𝔫𝔤𝔩𝔢𝔭, and all other the Houses belonging to the same, also all that their Orchard and Dove-house, and other Buildings whatsoever, within the Circuit and Precinct of the same House, containing seven Acres, late in the Tenure and Occupation of *Thomas Ewre* and *Thomas Edlin* reserving to the King, his Heirs, and Successors, the yearly Rent of twenty Pence.

Which *Edward Newport* and *John Compton* granted the Scite of the late House or Priory of the Fryars to *Robert Dixon* and his Heirs, from whom it came to *Theodosia* his Daughter and Heir, who married Sir *Richard Braughin*, and after his Decease she sold the same to *Joseph Edmonds*, Esq. who conveyed it to *William Houlker*, Gent. he granted it to Sir *Richard Combes*, Kt. who held it a while, then reconveyed it to the said *William Houlker*, and his Heirs, who demolish'd the House and Buildings belonging to the same.

Cart. 7 Jac. I.

The same King by his Letters Patents dated at 𝔚𝔢𝔰𝔱minster, the 19th of *May, Anno* 1609, 7 *Regni sui*, gave to *Edward Furras* and *Francis Phillips*, Gent. their Heirs and Assigns, all those his two Mills, with their Appurtenances, in 𝔎𝔦𝔫𝔤𝔰 𝔏𝔞𝔫𝔤𝔩𝔢𝔭, with all Stock and Suit of the Mills, to hold in Fee-farm, reserving the yearly Rent of 68*l.* and 4*d.*

Cart. 8 Jac. I.

The same King by his Letters Patents dated at 𝔚𝔢𝔰𝔱minster, the 1st of *Sept. Anno* 1610, 8 *Regni sui*, granted his Lordship or Mannor, Park, and Chase of 𝔎𝔦𝔫𝔤𝔰 𝔏𝔞𝔫𝔤𝔩𝔢𝔭, with the Appurtenances, to his most dear and eldest Son *Henry*, Prince of 𝔚𝔞𝔩𝔢𝔰, Duke of 𝔠𝔬𝔯𝔫𝔴𝔞𝔩 and 𝔜𝔬𝔯𝔨, and Earl of 𝔠𝔥𝔢𝔰𝔱𝔢𝔯, who was a hopeful Prince, but dying without Issue, this Lordship reverted again to the Crown:

And King *James* by his Letters Patents dated at 𝔚est-minster, in the same Year, conveyed all this Lordship, Mannor, Park, and Chase of 𝔎ings 𝔏angley, unto his most dear Son *Charles,* Prince of 𝔚ales, Duke of 𝔠ornwal and 𝔜ork, and Earl of 𝔠hester.

King *Charles* I. by his Letters Patents dated at 𝔚est-minster, the 18th of *Dec. Anno* 1626, 2 *Regni sui,* gave and granted, and did Farm-let to Sir *Charles Morisin,* all his Park of 𝔎ings 𝔏angley, and all the Lands, Tenements, and Hereditaments, inclos'd and called by the Name of 𝔎ings 𝔏angley 𝔓ark, and all the Deer, Marsh, Grass, Wood, and all Trees whatsoever, with all and every their Appurtenances, to hold the same Premises for the Term of 99 Years then next following, paying to the King 37*l.* 6*s.* 8*d.* Cart. 2 Car. I.

But afterwards, upon the Petition of Sir *Charles Morisin,* King *Charles* by his Letters Patents dated at 𝔚est-minster, the 28th Day of *Dec.* following, granted all the said Premises to Sir *Baptist Hicks,* his Heirs and Assigns for ever, to commence from and after the said Term of Years granted to Sir *Charles Morisin,* reserving to the King 7*l.* 6*s.* 8*d. per Annum.* Cart. 2 Car. I.

The same King by his Letters Patents dated at 𝔚est-minster, the 25th Day of *Sept. Anno* 1628, 4 *Regni sui,* gave to *Edward Pitchfield, John Highlord, Humphry Clarke,* and *Francis Moses,* their Heirs and Assigns, all that his Lordship or Mannor of 𝔎ings 𝔏angley, with the Rents of Assize, Free-warren, Fishings, Rights, Members, and Appurtenances, Court Leet and Court Baron, and all other Priviledges in as full and ample Manner as the King enjoy'd it. Cart. 4 Car. I.

Sir *John Walter,* Sir *James Fullerton,* and Sir *Thomas Trever,* by Indenture dated 19th of *July, Anno* 4 *Car.* I. granted to Sir *William Williams, Robert Mitchell, Walter Marks,* and *Robert Marsh,* and their Heirs, the Mannor and Lordship of 𝔎ings 𝔏angley aforesaid, with all and every their Appurtenances, for the Term of 99 Years; and afterwards the said Sir *William Williams,* and the other Trustees, by their Indenture dated the 20th of *Feb. Anno* 1630, 6 *Regni Car.* I. conveyed the same Mannor and Lordship of 𝔎ings 𝔏angley to *Thomas Houlker* of 𝔏ondon, Gent. and his Heirs and Assigns for ever. Cart. 4 Car. I.
Cart. 6 Car. I.

Which *Thomas Houlker* had Issue *Thomas,* who sold the same to *Henry Smith,* Gent, the present Possessor hereof.

THE Rectory is appropriated to the perpetual Use of the Bishop of 𝔈ly and his Successors; and *Anno* 26 *Henry* VIII. this Vicaridge was valued in the King's Books at 8*l. per Annum,* of which the Bishops of 𝔈ly have been Patrons since the time of the Reformation; and *Benjamin Laney,* late Bishop of that Diocess, granted to the Vicar of that Church and his Successors, an Augmentation of 36*l.* 10*s. per Annum* for their better Support and Livelihood.

Hund. of
Bacorum.

1631 Mr. *John Southen*   1671 Mr. *Edward Carter*
1635 Mr. *Thomas Juice*   1688 Mr. *Thomas Evans.*

This Church is situated upon a side Hill not far from the River, in the Deanery of **Berkhamsted** in the Diocese of **Lincoln.** The Chancel is cover'd with Tyle, but the Church and Tower at the West End hereof is cover'd with Lead, and in the Tower hang four small Bells.

On the North Side of the Chancel there is a Monument raised about five Foot, with the Arms of **France** and **England,** with three Labels upon it, also the Arms of *Peter,* King of **Castile** and **Leons,** by which Coats it seems to be the Tomb where *Edmond de Langley,* the fifth Son of *Edward* III. and *Isabel* his Wife, one of the Daughters of *Don Pedro* King of **Castile,** was interr'd.

On the South Side of the Chancel a Monument is erected in the Wall which has this Inscription.

Underneath lieth interred the Body of the Honourable Sir *William Glascocke* of **Alvanhowe** in the County of **Essex,** Kt. Master of Requests, and Judge of the Admiralty in the Kingdom of **Ireland,** under King *Charles* the Second, Son of *William Glascock,* of **Alvanhowe** aforesaid, Esq; He married *Sarah* Daughter and Coheir to *James Mayne* of **Bobingdon** in the County of **Hertford,** Esq; by whom he had issue *Sarah* his Daughter and only Heir, he departed this Life the 14th day of *July* 1688. *Ætatis suæ* 73.

Another Stone shews this Inscription.

Here lieth interred the Body of *Elizabeth Cheyney,* late Wife of the Worshipful *Francis Cheyney,* Esq; who departed this life the 20th of *March, an. Dom.* 1620. and in the 30th year of her age.

The next Stone tells you

Here lieth interr'd the Body of *Nicholas Sprague* of **Chipperfield,** within this Parish, Gent. who departed this life the 30th day of *November* in the 23rd year of his age, *Annoq; Domini* 1679.
Non diu vixit sed multum.

Another shews you

Here lieth the Body of *Thomas Hemington* one of the Yeomen Ushers of his Majesties Guard, who departed this life 25th of *November* 1637. and *Margaret Hemington* his beloved Wife.

This is inscrib'd upon another Stone.

Here lieth the Body of *Dorothy Over,* Daughter of *Richard Over* of **London,** Gent. who departed this life the 16th day of *January* 1627.

Another Stone has this Inscription.

To the Memory of *Richard Over,* Gent. who being divested of his mortality the 19th day of *December* 1642. expects the second coming of our Saviour.

Upon another Stone you may read

Here lies interr'd the Body of *Mary Dixon,* who departed this life the 10th of *July* 1622. being then but three years of age, to whose sweet remembrance *I. B.* for the love she bore her here dedicates her self, and this;

> This well may serve to set my Passion forth,
> But greater Piles must character thy worth;
> Affection only consecrates this Stone,
> That it should melt when I forbear to mourn.
> I see no cause why either yet should blame.
> Sun never Sets, but 'tis to Rise again.

Another Marble hath these Characters.

Mors mihi transitus in vitam æternam et resurgat Robertus Dixon, *Filius et Hæres* Roberti Dixon de **Langley Regis,** *Armig.*

On the next is inscribed,

Here lies interr'd the Body of *Lucia Dixon,* one of the Daughters of *Robert Dixon* of **Kings Langley,** Esq; who deceased the 6th day of *September* 1643. to whose precious memory *J. B.* dedicates this, and her self.

> Loe, Reader, here a Virgin lies,
> Whose well spent life the Gospel justifies,
> In that she wisely trim'd her Lamp with Oyl
> To meet the Bridegroom freed from him by foil
> Of Earth's Corruption; thus prepar'd to be
> Seated with him in Immortality,
> Whilst here below, the memory of her Name
> Becomes a sacred Story of her Fame;
> Whose sweet Demeanour, they who knew can tell,
> Others in Grace and Virtue to excell.
> Let after times her Piety compare, .
> None merits now with her an equal share.
> Thus by her death in Characters of Stone
> We read her happy Resurrection.

These Characters are engraved on another Marble.

Here lieth interr'd the Body of *John Cheyney,* Gent. who departed this life in the true Faith of Christ Jesus the first day of *February Anno Dom.* 1597.

You may view these letters on another Stone.

—— William Carter and Alice **his Wife, which** William **departed this life on the 2d. day** of August 1528. ——

These Words are engrav'd on another Stone.

Here lieth the Body of *John Carter,* late of **Giffres,** who had two Wives; by the first he had issue four Sons and five Daughters, by the second he had issue five Sons and four Daughters, and he was buried the 9th of *August* 1588.

On another Marble these lines are ingraved.

> Loe, here's interr'd a Wife of worthy Fame,
> Whose Virtues great, and honest Life deserve the same :
> *Margaret* was her name, by marriage *Cheyney* hight,
> Late Wife of *Cheyney* Son to *Chesham Boys* by right
> Her due Descent from *Skipwiths* Line, late of **St. Albans** Town ;
> And married to that *Cheyneys* Heir, a House of old renown.
> Full ten years she in marriage spent, five Children was her share,
> The Heavens have two of the five, three left to Fathers care.
> Her life so good, her death not ill, I hope shall not deny
> But that her Soul in Jesus Christ shall live eternally.

30. January 1578. *secundem computationem Ecclesiæ Anglicanæ.*

CHARITABLE GIFTS.

The Lady *Cooper* gave 10*l. per Annum,* issuing out of the Towns of **Cowbury, Bedington,** and **Ashchurch** in the County of **Glocester,** to be paid on the first day of *January* to the Poor of this Parish.

William Knight gave to the Poor of this Parish 3*l. per Annum,* issuing out of certain Lands call'd **Oatlands,** lying in this Parish.

Mr. *Smith* gave 5*l. per Annum* to the Poor of this Parish, to be paid by Sir *Henry Hen,* Feoffee in trust for the payment hereof.

The Lady *Morison* gave forty Shillings *per Annum* to the Poor of this Parish, issuing out of the House situated in this Parish where Mr *Buckock* lived.

HEANHAMSTED, HEMSTED.

OFFA, that great and magnificent Prince, King of the *Mertians*, gave six Mansions in 𝕳𝖊𝖆𝖓𝖍𝖆𝖒𝖘𝖙𝖊𝖉, scituated about three Miles distant from 𝕶𝖎𝖓𝖌𝖘 𝕷𝖆𝖓𝖌𝖑𝖊𝖞 Northward, to the Monastery of 𝕾𝖙. 𝕬𝖑𝖇𝖆𝖓𝖘, which was of his own
Foundation; and King *Etheldred* confirmed the Grant hereof to the same Church; but the other Part of this Vill continued Parcel of the Revenue that belonged to the Saxon Kings, until the time that King *William* the Conqueror gave it to Earl *Moreton*; for 'tis recorded in *Domesdei Book*, that the Abbot of 𝕾𝖙. 𝕬𝖑𝖇𝖆𝖓𝖘, and Earl *Moreton* held this Vill.

In 𝔄𝔩𝔟𝔞𝔫𝔢𝔰𝔱𝔬𝔫 Hundred. Abbas 𝔖𝔞𝔫𝔠𝔱𝔦 𝔄𝔩𝔟𝔞𝔫𝔦 tenuit 𝔥𝔞𝔪𝔢𝔩𝔥𝔞𝔪𝔰𝔱𝔯𝔡 pro riginta hidis, se defendebat. Terra est viginti cur. In dominio sex hidæ et ibi sunt tres car. et quarta potest fieri, ibi viginti sex Villani cum quatuor Francig. habentibus tresdecem cur. et adhuc tres possunt fieri, ibi tres Bord. et unus Servus, et duo Mol. de vigint. sol. pratum tres car. et tresdecem sol. pastura ad pec. Silva mille porc. in totis valentiis valet et valuit duodecim lib. et decem sol. tempore Regis Edwardi viginti quinq; libras hoc Manerium jacuit et jacet in dominio Ecclesiæ 𝔖𝔞𝔫𝔠𝔱𝔦 𝔄𝔩𝔟𝔞𝔫𝔦.

In 𝔈𝔯𝔯𝔲𝔫𝔤 Hundred. Comes Moritonus tenuit 𝔥𝔞𝔪𝔢𝔩𝔞𝔪𝔰𝔱𝔢𝔡𝔢 pro decem hidis se defendebat. Terra est trigint car. in Dominio tres hid. et ibi quatuor car. et adhuc duo car. possunt fieri, ibi duo Francig. cum tresdecem Bord. habentibus vigint. car. et adhuc quatuor possunt fieri, ibi octo Servi, et quatuor Mold. de trigint. sept. sol. et quatuor denar. et trescent. anguillis vigint. quinq. minus pratum quatuor car. pastura ad pec et duo sol. Silva mille et ducent. porc. in totis valentiis valet vigint. duo lib. quando recepit vigint. et quinq; lib. et consuetud. tempore Regis Edwardi. Hoc Manerium tenuerunt duo fratres homines Comitis Lenvini fuerunt.

The Abbot of 𝕾𝖙. 𝕬𝖑𝖇𝖆𝖓 held 𝕳𝖆𝖒𝖊𝖑𝖍𝖆𝖒𝖘𝖙𝖊𝖉𝖊 in 𝕬𝖑𝖇𝖆𝖓𝖊𝖘𝖙𝖔𝖓 Hundred, it was rated at twenty Hides. The arable is twenty Carcates, in Demeasne six Hides, and there are three Carucates, and a fourth may be made, there are six and twenty Villains with four Frenchmen born, having thirteen Carncates, and now three others may be made, there are three Bordars, and one Servant, and two Mills of twenty Shillings Rent by the Year, Meadow three Carucates, and thirteen Shillings Rent by the Year, Common of Pasture for the Cattle, Wood to feed one thousand Hogs; in the whole Value it is worth and was worth twelve Pounds and ten Shillings, in the time of King *Edward* (the Confessor) five and twenty Pounds. This Mannor did lye and doth lye in the Demeasne of the Church of 𝕾𝖙. 𝕬𝖑𝖇𝖆𝖓.

Earl *Moreton* held 𝕱𝖆𝖒𝖊𝖑𝖍𝖆𝖒𝖘𝖙𝖊𝖉𝖊 in 𝕰𝖗𝖗𝖚𝖓𝖌 Hundred, it was rated for ten Hides. The arable is thirty Carucates, in Demeasne three Hides, and there are four Carucates, and now two Carucates may be made, there are two Frenchmen born, with thirteen Bordars, having twenty Carucates, and now four more may be made, there are eight Servants, and four Mills of seven and thirty Shillings and four Pence Rent by the Year, and three hundred Eels wanting five and twenty, Meadow four Carucates, Common of Pasture for the Cattle, and two Shillings Rent by the Year, Wood to feed one thousand and two hundred Hogs; in the whole Value it is worth two and twenty Pounds, when he received it five and twenty Pounds, and Rent in the time of King *Edward* (the Confessor.) Two were Brethren, Men (under the Protection) of Earl *Lewin*, they held this Mannor.

The Abbots of 𝔖t. 𝔄lbans held the former, till the time of the Dissolution of their Church, and Earl *Moreton*, who was half Brother to King *William* the Conqueror, held the last Mannor in their Name and Family, till it came to the Crown, in such Sort as is set forth in the Parish of 𝔅erk- hamsteb; and King *H.* III. gave it to *Richard* his Brother, who was afterwards King of 𝔄lmain and Earl of 𝔠ornwal, from whom it came to *Edmond* his Son, who in the fifth of *Edw.* III. granted it to the Church of 𝔈sserugg, which was of his own Foundation, with all and singular their Appurte- nances (except the Advowson of the Church and his War- ren there,) and all the Rights, Liberties, and free Customs which he had in this Mannor: Moreover he granted that the Tenants thereof should be quit of all Suits of Courts, Hundreds, and Views of Franc-pledge.

Hund. of Dacorum.

Mon. Angl. vol. 3, fol. 67.

Cart. 5 E III.

Mon. Angl. vol. 3, fol. 68.

This Vill, says *Norden*, was denominated from an high Hemp-land, which, in all Probability, might at that time be planted upon the high Hill on the East Side of the Town, for 𝔥eanhamsteb imports as much.

Norden, p. 18. Camd. Brit. tit. Herts. fol. 415.

John Waterhouse, Esq. Auditor to King *H.*VIII. gave that King a great Entertainment at his House, which, I sup- pose, was 𝔥empsteb 𝔅urp, the Seat of his Ancestors; and upon his Request, the said King, by his Letters Patents dated at 𝔚estminster, the 29th of *Decem. Anno* 21 *Regni sui*, did incorporate this Vill by the Name of Bayliff and In- habitants, granting to them perpetual Succession, and that from thenceforth one Person should be chosen Bayliff by the Inhabitants every Year to govern this Vill; and ap- pointed *William Stephens*, one of the Inhabitants within this Vill, to be Bayliff for that Year, to continue until the Feast of St. *Michael* the Archangel, then next ensuing, and that they may plead and be impleaded by the Name of Bay- liff and Inhabitants, and shall have a Common Seal; that the Bayliff and Inhabitants, and their Successors for ever, shall have a Market every Week, to be held on every Thursday in this Vill, and a Fair every Year to be held on the Feast of *Corpus Christi*, to continue one Day, with Pi- powder Court during the said Market and Fair, together with all the Issues, Profits, and Amercements arising out of the same Market, Fair, and Court; which Market is now become one of the greatest for Wheat in this County.

Fuller's Wor- thies, fol 21.

Pat. 21 H. VIII.

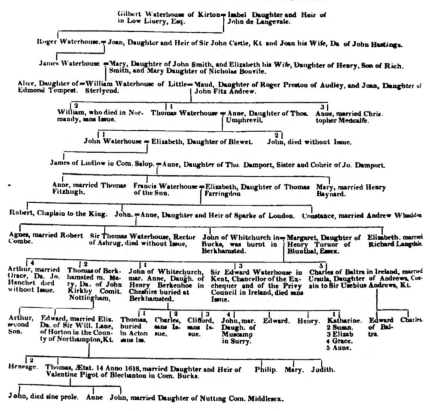

Gilbert Waterhouse of Kirton in Low Linery, Esq. = Isabel Daughter and Heir of John de Langevale.

Roger Waterhouse. = Joan, Daughter and Heir of Sir John Castle, Kt. and Joan his Wife, Da. of John Hastings.

James Waterhouse = Mary, Daughter of John Smith, and Elizabeth his Wife, Daughter of Henry, Son of Rich. Smith, and Mary Daughter of Nicholas Bouvile.

Alice, Daughter of = William Waterhouse of Little = Maud, Daughter of Roger Preston of Audley, and Joan, Daughter of Edmond Tempest. Sterlyend. John Fitz Andrew.

2 | William, who died in Normandy, sans Issue.   1 | Thomas Waterhouse = Anne, Daughter of Thos. Umphrevil.   3 | Anne, married Christopher Medcalfe.

1 | John Waterhouse = Elizabeth, Daughter of Blewet.   2 | John, died without Issue.

James of Ludlow in Com. Salop. = Anne, Daughter of Tho. Damport, Sister and Coheir of Jo. Damport.

Anne, married Thomas Fitzhugh.   Francis Waterhouse of the Sun. = Elizabeth, Daughter of Thomas Farringdon   Mary, married Henry Baynard.

Robert, Chaplain to the King.   John. = Anne, Daughter and Heir of Sparke of London.   Constance, married Andrew Whaddon

Agnes, married Robert Combe.   Sir Thomas Waterhouse, Rector of Ashrug, died without Issue,   John of Whitchurch in Bucks, was burnt in Berkhamsted. = Margaret, Daughter of Henry Turuor of Blunthal, Essex.   Elizabeth, married Richard Langdale.

4 | Arthur, married Grace, Da. Jo. Hanchet died without Issue.   2 | Thomas of Berkhamsted m. Mary, Da. of John Kirkby Comit. Nottingham,   1 | John of Whitechurch, mar. Anne, Daugh. of Henry Berkenhoe in Cheshire buried at Berkhamsted.   3 | Sir Edward Waterhouse in Kent, Chancellor of the Exchequer and of the Privy Council in Ireland, died sans Issue.   5 | Charles of Baltra in Ireland, married Ursula, Daughter of Andrews, Cousin to Sir Usebius Andrews, Kt.

2 | Arthur, second Son.   Edward, married Eliz. Da. of Sir Will. Lane, of Horton in the County of Northampton, Kt.   1 | Thomas, buried in Acton sans Issue.   2 | Charles, sans Issue.   3 | Clifford, sans Issue.   4 | John, mar. Daugh. of Muscamp in Surry.   Edward.   Henry.   1 | Katharine. 2 Susan. 3 Elizab 4 Grace. 5 Anne.   Edward of Baltra.   Charles

2 | Heneage.   Thomas, Ætat. 14 Anno 1618, married Daughter and Heir of Valentine Pigot of Blechanton in Com. Bucks.   Philip.   Mary.   Judith.

John, died sine prole.   Anne   John, married Daughter of Nutting Com. Middlesex.

THIS Vicaridge is in the Deanery of Berkhamsted in the Diocess of Lincoln, and in *Anno* 26 *Henry* VIII. was rated at the yearly Value of 16*l.* 1*s.* 10*d.* and upon every Avoidance, the Bishop of Lincoln nominates, and the Dean and Chapter of St. *Paul*, London, presents the new Vicar.

The VICARS.

———— *Scriven*, A.M.   *Joel Jones*, A.M.   *Robert Brabant.*

This Church is erected near the Town, 'tis covered with Lead, to which a square Tower is annexed, wherein is a good Ring of six Bells, and a very fair and tall Spire covered with Lead erected upon it, which is a great Ornament to the Town.

Upon a fair Tomb of Marble and Tuch, inlaid with Brass, with the Pourtraiture of a Man armed, of goodly Lineaments, together with his Wife, is this French Inscription.

Robert Albyn gist icy Et Margereta sa femme oubike luy Dieu de ley Almesept mercy.

BOVINGDON.

IN the time of *William* the Conqueror, I suppose this Manor was that Part of this Vill which that King gave to Earl *Moreton*, and afterwards return'd it to the Crown again, from whence it might come to

John de Arcy, who held it in the time of *Edw.* III. when it was known by the Name of the Manner of *Westbrook*.

This *John de Arcy* descended from that *Norman de Arcy*, a great Baron, to whom King *William* the Conqueror gave no less than thirty three Lordships in *Lincolnshire* for his Services. He was summon'd among the Barons of this Realm from the 22nd until the 28th of *Edw.* III. He married *Elizabeth* the Daughter and Heir of *Nicholas Menil*, by whom he had Issue *John* and *Philip*, and died at *Retton*, upon *Saturday* next after the Feast of *St. Chad*, *Anno* 30 *Edw.* III. seiz'd of this Manner Claus 31. Ed III.
Bor fol. 37.3.

John was his Heir, about five Years old at the Death of his Father, but died in his Minority on the 26th of *August*, *Anno* 36 *Edw.* III. without Issue , whereupon it came to

Philip, who was his Brother and Heir, then eleven Years of Age, who proving his Age *An.* 47 *Edw.* III. did his Homage and had Livery of his Lands. He was an active Man in the Wars of *France*, where he commanded divers Men at Arms and Archers, for the Recovery of the King's Rights there, and was constituted Admiral of all the King's Fleet from the *Thames* Northward, 9 *R.* II. took many Prizes there, which he brought into the Port of *Sandwich*, and in Lieu of his great Services the King commanded that they should be redelivered to him for his own Use; but I read no more of this Manner till the Reign of *H.* VII. when it came to the Possession of Rot. Franc.
3 R. II.

Claus. 9 R. II.

John Mayne of *Ascot* in the County of *Bucks*, who gave it to

Robert Mayne his second Son ; he married the Daughter of ———— *Bradshaw*, enjoy'd it some time, then died seized hereof, leaving Issue

Henry, who succeeded him and married *Ann* the Daughter and Heir of ———— *Randolf* in the County of *Bucks*, by whom he had Issue Offic. Armor.

James, who succeeded, married *Mary* Daughter and Heir to *John Andrews* of *Hitchin* in this County, by whom he had Issue

James, who married *Dorothy* the Daughter and Heir of *John Hawes* of *London*, Merchant, by whom he had Issue one Son, who died in his Minority, and two Daughters who were his Coheirs, whereof

Sarah married Sir *William Glascock*, one of the Masters of the Court of Requests, and they sold this Mannor to

Joshuah Lomax, Esq. who gave it to

Thomas his younger Son, who has built a very fair Mansion House of Brick there, and is the present Owner hereof.

The Mannor of MARTIALLS.

DENOMINATED from some Owner hereof, and has passed with the former Mannor to the same Persons, till it came to *Thomas Lomax*, Esq. the present Lord hereof.

This Vill is scituated upon an Hill, from whence it might derive its Name, whereof the top is a level Piece of Ground containing three Miles over every Way, famous for broad Greens and pleasant High-ways, Apples and Black Cherries which grow in every Hedge, and proves a very wholsome Air.

THE Church is erected in the Middle of the Vill in the Deanery of Berkhamsted, in the Diocess of Lincoln, cover'd with Lead, and has a square Tower at the West End thereof, wherein are four Bells and a short Spire upon it, they have Churchwardens and all other Parochial Officers of their own.

FLAUNDEN.

THIS Vill, I suppose, was waste Ground in the time of *William* the Conqueror, that belonged to the Mannor of Hemel Hemsted, and was afterwards granted to *Thomas Flaunden*, and when he had improved it, it was called after his Name, and became a Vill like Bobingdon, but still remain'd a Parcel of the same Mannor, for he held it of that Mannor by Homage and other Services, and erected a small Church in the Vale near the River, for the Ease of himself and the Conveniency of his Tenants, with a small Erection of Timber and Boards made at the West End thereof, wherein are three very small Bells; Here are Church Wardens, and all other parochial Officers, and it seems the Vicar of Hemsted, finds a Curate at Bobingdon and this Vill, who christens, buries, and performs all other Ecclesiastical Rights and Duties, as appears by this ensuing Record.

Admissio Bernardi *de* Graveleigh *ad Vicarium de* Hemelhemsted *cum Capellis de* Flaunden *et* Bobingdon, 1235.

Exhibit ex parte Thomæ Walker *et* Johannis Turner, *Gard. de* Hemelhemsted, con' Thomam Gould *de* Bobingdon.

UNIVERSIS *et singulis Christi fidelibus ad quos presentes Literæ, testimonial' pervenerint seu quos infra script. tangunt seu tangere poterint quomodolet in futur.* Christoferus Nevil *Legum Doctor reverendi in Christo Patris ac Dom.* Georgii *providen' Divina* Lincoln' Episcop' *Vicarius spiritualibus generalis et Officialis princ' in et per totum Diocess* Lincoln' *legitim' constitut. salutem authores salutis. Ad universitatis vestr' noticiam deducim' et de volunt' per presentes Quod scrutato Registr' Episc' Lincoln' in quodam Rot. antiquo institutionum tempore Dom' Roberti Grosthed olim Episc. Lincoln. qui cepit preesse Ecclesiæ Lincoln' Anno Dom. Millesimo Ducent^mo. Trice^mo. Quinto Annoq; Pontific' sui tertio decimo penes Johannem Pregion Notar' Public' Registr' princ' Dom. reverendi in Christo Patris Dom. Episc. Lincoln' fideliter custodit' et remanend' inter alia ibid' regrata comprimus, et invenimus prout sequit' viz. Huntingdon Arch' Hemelhemsted Bernardus de Graveleigh cap' presentat' pro Hug' de Niceto procuratorem Domini Phil' de Scaban, Rector' Ecclesiæ de Hemelhemsted per literas datum et admissum ud Vicar' de Eccles. de Hemelhemsted in perpetuo dict' Rectoris facta prius inquisit' pro L. Areham' Hunt' per quam, &c. ad eandem admissus est et in ea Vicarius institut' et in perpetuum dict' Rectoris dictus autem Vicarius habebit nomine Vicariæ suæ totum alteragium tam matricis Eccl' quam capellarum, videl. de Flaunden et de Bobingdon et persol' dict' Matrici Ecclesiæ deserveret dict' Capellas per duos idoneos Capellos faciet deservire ad sustentationem vero Capelli in Capella de Bobingdon invenient Parochiani dictæ Capelle xx sol' dict' Vicar' solvend. idem etiam Vicar' omnia onera Archidiac' et ordin' sustinebit siliter libros et ornamenta tam in matrice Eccles' quod in diis Capellis et Chancell' Eccl' et Capellarum in bono Statu sustinebit valet ut dict' Vicar' sic taxata xxx Marc' et mand' est eidem Archinato ut ips' &c. In quorum omn' et singulor' premissor' fidem has literas nostras testimonial' exinde fieri, ac eas Sigilli noctri appentione quo in hac parte utimur communicari et coroborari fecimus Dat' Lincoln' vicessimo octavo die Mensis Julii, Anno Dom' millesimo Sexentesimo decimo nono, 1619.*

Christopher Nevil, John Pregion.

Concordat' cum originali Ita testor
Guil' Rolfe Notor' publicus.

Tract' e Registr' Dom' Arch. Hunt' Com' Hertford.
Ita testor Tho. Woodward Notar' publicus.

From hence it seems that the Vicar of **Hemel Hemsted**, and his Successors have the Nomination of the Several Curates of **Bobingdon** and **Flaunden,** who have usually held those Curacies under him without any Disturbance or Molestation so long as they behaved themselves well, and 'tis Pitty they have no better Stipend for their Encouragement. But in those Days 20s. did answer the Value of fifty Pounds.

GATESDEN or *GADESDEN PARVA.*

THIS Vill was denominated from the Vale where the River **Gade** rises, is distant three Miles from **Hemelhemsted** towards the North, and was held of Earl *Moreton* in the time of *William* the Conqueror, for 'tis recorded in *Domesdei Book,* that

Humfridus tenuit de Comite Gadesdene pro quing; hid. se defendebat. Terra est tres car. in Dominio est una et quinque Vill. cum duobus Bord. habentibus duo car. ibi un. Servus, pastura ad pec. Silva quinquagint. porc. in totis valent. valet quadragint. sol. quando recepit sexagint. sol. tempore Regis Edwardi quatuor lib. Hoc Manerium tenuit Edmer Attile, et fuit Berewich. in Berchamstede.

Humphry held of Earl *Moreton* **Gadesden** (in **Treunge** Hundred,) it was rated for five Hides. The arable is three Carucates, In Demeasne is one, and five Villains, with two Bordars, having two Carucates, there is one Servant, Common of Pasture for the Cattle, Wood to feed fifty Hogs in

Pannage time; in the whole Value it is worth forty Shillings a Year, when he received it sixty Shillings, in the time of King *Edward* (the Confessor) four Pounds. *Edmer Attile* held this Mannor, and it was a Berewick in **Berkhamsted**.

I shall treat of Earl *Moreton* in the Parish of **Great Berk-hamsted**, to which I refer the Reader, for that this Mannor passed in the same Manner with that to the Crown, where it continued till King *H.* III. gave it to *Richard* Earl of **Cornwal**, who was his youngest Son, and afterwards King of the *Romans*, from whom it descended to

Edmond Earl of **Cornwal** who was his Son, and Heir to his Honours and large Possessions, and by his Charter dated at **Langet**, the 17th Day of *April, Anno* 14 *Edw.* I. gave to God and the blessed *Mary*, and the Parson and Frater-nity of *Bonhomes*, founded there in Honour of the precious Blood of Christ, and for the Sustentation of twenty Breth-ren, whereof thirteen shall be Priests, his Mannor of **Ash-ridge** with **Pitstone**, and all other the Appurtenances, which he had of the Gift and Grant of one *Ulion Chendit*, and the Close of the Park of the Mannor of **Ashridge**, within the Parish Churches of the blessed St. *Peter* of **Berkhamsted** and **Pitstone**, and also this Mannor of **Little Gadesden** with all the Appurtenances, as well to the Lands and Tenements which the Lord *Jeoffrey Lucy* held there, as the Lands and Tenements which he had of the Gift and Grant of *Thomas Viatestone*, belonging to the Mannor, and also his Mannor of **Hemelhemsted** with all the Appurtenances, except the Advowson of the Church and his Warren, with the Returns of the King's Writs, Pleas of Withernam, Pleas of the Crown, the Goods of Felons and Fugitives, the View of Franc-pledge, and all that doth belong to the said View, the Assize of Bread and Ale, and with Hue and Cry to be made, and Pleas of Bloodshed, and all the Homage and Ser-vice of the Lord *Jeoffry Lucy*, for all the Lands and Tene-ments which he held in the Vill of **Gadesden**, and the Hom-age and Service of the Heirs of *Thomas Flaunden*, for all the Lands and Tenements which he held in **Hemelhemsted**, with the Homage and Service of *Luce Lovel*, for all the Lands and Tenements which he held of him in this Vill, and all the Rights, Liberties, and free Customs, and the Hom-ages, Fealties, Wards, Reliefs, Hereditaments, Foreign Suits, Escheates, Rents, Services, Suits of Courts, the Fines imposed upon any of their Servants that shall trespass in his Warren in **Hemelhemsted**, and also Common of Pas-ture in his Wood of **Barkhamsted**, called the **Frith**, for all their Cattle, and shall feed all their Hogs in his Wood in the time of Pannage, and Houseboot and Hayboot, shall be free from Toll in the Burrough of **Berkhamsted**, and all Ex-actions and Payment of Tolls, making of Bridges, Stallages, Passages, and Customs, as his Men of **Berkhamsted** and

𝕸allingford every where shall be; and that all the Lands, *Hund. of Barorum.*
Tenements, and Rents of the said Brethren, shall remain
in their Hands during the Vacation of any Rector there,
and when they shall elect any Rector, the Bishop of the
same Place shall confirm him, tho' he was not presented by
the Patron; and they shall have all Return of Writs, and all
Pleas and Summons of the Mannor of 𝕬shridge, 𝕻itstone,
𝕳emelhemsted, and 𝕲addesden, and of the Men belonging
to the said Mannors, and shall hold the same as his free,
pure, and perpetual Arms.

This Earl *Edmond* brought these *Bonhomes* into 𝕰ngland, who professed the Rule of *St. Augustine*, and were,
according to the Manner of the Eremitans, clad in sky colour'd Garments, and they consisted of twenty Clerks,
whereof thirteen were Presbiters, and King *Edw.* I. by his
Charter dated 22nd of *March, Anno 5 Regni sui*, confirmed
all these Priviledges to the Rector and Brethren of the
Church of 𝕬shridge.

This Monastery was a Place of Receipt in the time of *Inter Placita de Parl. apud Ashridge, an. 19 Ed. I. Rot. 12. Coke, Inst. 2, fol. 511.*
King *Edw.* I. for that King held a Parliament here *A. D.*
1291, and *Regni sui* 19, where there was a great Debate in
the Case of *Margery*, late the Wife of *Thomas Weyland*,
about the original Institution of Fines, and the necessary
Use of them, upon which it was recorded in a Roll of that
Parliament. *Nec in Regno isto provideatur vel sic aliqua
Securitas major vel solemnior, per quam aliquis statum
certiorum habere possit, vel ad statum suum verificandum
aliquod solemnius testimonium producere, quam finem in
Curia Domini Regis levatum, qui quidem fieris sic vocatur
eo quod finis & consummatio, omnium placitorum esse debet.*
And tho' Mr. *Pulton* takes no Notice of this Parliament
because it was of short Continuance, and no Act pass'd at
that Sessions, yet several Judgments were given there, as
appears by the Record which made it a Parliament.

These *Bonhomes* held this Monastery until 26 *H.* VIII.
when they made their Recognition of the King's Supremacy in this following Form.

*QUUM ea sit non Solum Christianæ Religionis et Pietatis ratio sed nostre
etiam obedientie regula Dom. Regi nostro Henrico ejus Nominis octavo (cui
Unio et soli post Christum Jhesum servatorem nostrum debemus universa non
modo omnimodam in Christo et eandum synceram integram perpetuamq; animi
devotionem fidem observantiam Honorem cultum reverentiam prestemus sed
etiam de eadem fide et observantia nostra rationem (quotiens cunque postu-
labitur) reddamus et palam omnibus si repostulat libenti sime testemur:
Noverint Universi ad quos presens scriptum pervenerit quod nos Thomas
Rector et Conventus Domus sive Collegii de 𝕬shrug 𝕷incoln. Dioces. uno
ore et voce atque unanimo consensu et assensu hoc scripto nostro sub Sigillo
nostro communi in Domo Capitulari Dato pro nobis et successoribus nostris
omnibus et singulis imperpetuum profitemur testamur ac fideliter promittimus
et spondemus. Nos dict. Rectorem et Conventum et Successores nostros
omnes et singulos integram inviolatam sinceram perpetuamq; fidem obser-*

Hund. of
Dacorum.

vantiam et obedientiam semper prestituram erga Dom. Regem nostrum Henricum octavum et erga Annam Reginam Uxorem ejusdem et erga sobolem ejus ex eadem Anna legitime tam progenitam quam pro generand. et quod hæc eadem populo notificabimus prædicabimus et suadebimus ubicunq; dabitur locus et occasio. Item quod confirmatum ratum quæ habemus semper quæ et perpetuo habitur' (unus quod predict. Rex noster Henricus est caput Ecclesiæ Anglicanæ. Ita quod Episc. Romanus qui in suis Bullis Papæ nomen Usurpat' et summi Pontificis principatum sibi arrogat' non habet majorem aliquam jurisdictionem collatam sibi a Deo in sacrâ Scripturâ in hoc Regno Angliæ quam aliquis alius externus Episcopus. Item quod nullus nostrum in ullâ sacrâ concione privatim vel publice habendâ eundum Episc. Romanum appellabit nostri Papa aut summi Pontificis sed nostri Episc. Romani vel Ecclesiæ Romanæ. Et quod nullus nostrum orabit pro eo tanquam Papa sed tanquam Episcopo Romano. Item quod soli dicto Dom. Regi et successoribus suis adherebimus et ejus Leges ac decreta manutebimus. Episc. Romani Legibus et decretis et Canonibus qui contra Legem Divinam et sacram Scripturam aut contra jura hujus regni esse invenientur imperpetuum renunciantes. Item quod nullus nostrum omnium in ullâ vel privata vel publicâ concione quacunq; ex sacris litteris desumptum ad alienum sensum detorquere presumet. Sed quisque Christum ejus quæ verba et facta simpliciter aperte sincere ad normam seu Regulam Sacrarum Scripturarum et veré Catholicarum atq; Orthodoxorum Doctorum predicabit Catholice et Orthodoxe. Item quod unusquisqe nostrum in suis orationibus et comprecationibus de more faciendis primum omnem Regem tanquam supremum caput Ecclesiæ Anglicanæ Deo et populi precibus commendabit. Deinde Reginam Annam cum suâ sobole cum dicti Archiepiscopis Cantuar. et Ebor. cum ceteris Clerico ordinibus prout Videbitur. Item quod omnes et singuli predict. et Conventus et Successores nostri conscientiæ et jurisjurand. Sacramento quantum de jure possuimus nosmet firmiter obligamus quod omnia singula prædicta fideliter imperpetuum observabimus. In cujus rei Testimonium huic Scripto nostro commune Sigillum nostrum appendimus et nostra nomina propria quisq; manu Subscripsimus Dat. in Domo nostra Capitular. 14 die Mensis Septembris Anno Dom. Millessimo quingentesimo 34.

Thomas Waterhouse, *Rector.* Thomas Hyll, Elias Bernard, Michael Draper, Johannis Hatfelde, Robert. Hitchinham, Richard. Gardyner, Willielmus Knighton, Richardus Bedford, Roger. Byrchley, Willielm. Downham, Richardus Lawnders, Johan. Axstyl, Willielmus Brook, Joseph Stepneth, Richardus Canaan, Williel. Young.

In the same Office I found above a hundred and seventy more made to the same effect.

And the Rector and Convent held and enjoy'd this Mannor until the time of the Dissolution of the Priory, when it came to the Crown, where it continued until

Pat 17. Eliz. Queen *Elizabeth* by Letters Patents dated the 29th Day of *January,* 17 *Regni sui,* granted the Mannor of Ashridge to *John Dudley,* and *John Aiscough* and their Heirs.

Cart. 17 Eliz.
penes Com.
Bridgewater. Which *John Dudley* and *John Aiscough* by their Indenture dated the 12th of *Feb.* 17 *Regni sui,* granted it to *Henry* Lord *Cheyney* and *Jane* Lady *Cheyney* his Wife, and to the Heirs of the Lord *Cheyney.*

This *Henry* Lord *Cheyney* did by his Indenture, grant it to Sir *Robert Newdigate* and others, to the Use of *Jane* Lady *Cheyney,* and the Heirs of her Body, and in Default of such Issue, to the Use of the Lady and her Heirs, and the Lord *Cheyney* died without Issue of his Body, by which Means this Mannor came to the Lady *Cheyney* and her Heirs.

The Mannors of ASHRIDGE, GADESDEN PARVA, and FRISDEN.

QUEEN *Elizabeth*, by Letters Patents dated the 21st of *July*, 32 *Regni sui*, granted the Mannors of Gadesden Parba and Frithsden, with their Appurtenances, to *Jane* Lady *Cheyney* and her Heirs. Pat. 32 Eliz.

The Lady *Cheyney*, Sir *John Crofts*, and Dame *Mary* his Wife, by Indenture dated the 27th of *Novemb.* 44 *Eliz.* bargain'd and sold these Mannors of Ashridge, Gadesden Parba, and Frisden, to *Ralph Marshal* and his Heirs. Cart. 44 Eliz.
penes Com.
Bridgewater.

Which *Ralph Marshal*, by Indenture inrolled, dated the 7th of *March*, 45 *Eliz.* conveyed them to *Randolfe Crew*, *Thomas Chamberlain*, and their Heirs; and in Easter Term, 1 *Jac.* I. levied a Fine of them to the Use of the Parties; and in the same Term, the Lady *Cheyney*, Sir *John Crofts*, and Dame *Mary* his Wife levied another Fine of the Mannors of Ibingoe, Ashridge, Gadesden Parba, Frithsden, and Northwood, to the Use of the same Parties and their Heirs. Ibid. 45 Eliz.

Randolfe Crew, *Thomas Chamberlain*, and *Richard Cartwright*, by their Indenture dated the 21st Day of *October*, 2 *Jac.* I. granted the Mannors of Ashridge, Gadesden Parba, and Frithsden, to *Thomas* Lord Ellesmere, and Sir *John Egerton*, and the Heirs Males of the Body of the said Lord Ellesmere, and for Default of such Heirs Males, to the Use of the right Heirs of the said Lord Ellesmere for ever.

The Mannor of LUCYES

WAS denominated from Sir *Jeoffery de Lucy*, or some of his Ancestors, who were Lords hereof: one of them conveyed it to *Edmond* Earl of Cornwal, and he disposed of it to the Support of the religious House which he founded at Esserug.

In *Easter* Term *Anno* 26 & 27 *H.*VIII. *Henry* Earl of Essex, and others obtained a Recovery against *Thomas Butler* and *William Kent* of this Mannor, who vouched over Sir *Thomas Vats*, Kt. Lord Harrowden, who vouched over the common Vouchee.

Sir *Robert Dormer* was possest of this Mannor, and by Indenture dated the 5th of *November*, *An.* 43 *Eliz.* granted it to *John Eames* and *Robert Eames* and their Heirs, and the said Sir *Robert Dormer* and Dame *Elizabeth* his Wife, in *Michaelmas* Term, 44 *Eliz.* levied a Fine of the same to *John Eames* and *Robert Eames*, and their Heirs, from whom it was conveyed to

Thomas Lord Ellesmere, who descended from an ancient Family of that Name in Cheshire, and studying the Laws in *Lincolns Inn*, for divers Years, at length became famous

Hund. of
Bacorum.

for his Knowledge therein, insomuch that Queen *Elizabeth* made him her Sollicitor General on the 28th of *June*, 1581, 23rd of her Reign, and within the Revolution of one Year, he read in the *Quadragesimes* in that Honourable Society; afterwards was knighted, and was constituted Attorny General on the 2nd of *June*, in the Year 1592, 34 *Regni sui*; was made Master of the Rolls, 10th *April*, 1594 *An.* 36 *Eliz.* and advanced to be Lord Keeper of the Great Seal, *A. C.* 1596, 38th of her Reign, which eminent Office he held during the Remainder of her happy Life; he was raised to the Degree of a Baron of this Realm, 21st *July*, 1603, 1 *Jac.* I. by the Title of Lord Ellesmere, preferred to be Lord High Chancellor of England upon the 24th Day of the same Month, and advanced to the Honour of Viscount Brackley in Northamptonshire on the 7th Day of *Novemb.* 1616, in the 4th Year of the same King's Reign; during which time he married *Elizabeth* Daughter of *Thomas Ravenscroft* of Bretton in the County of Flint, Esq. by whom he had Issue *Thomas, John,* and *Mary* married to Sir *Francis Leigh* of Newnham Regis in *Com.* Warwick, Knight of the Bath, and after her Decease he espoused *Elizabeth* Daughter of Sir *George Moore,* Widow of Sir *John Woolley,* Kt. Chancellor of the Garter, and after her Death *Alice* Daughter to Sir *John Spencer* of Althorp in the County of Northampton, Kt. Widow of *Ferdinando* Earl of Derby, but he had not any Issue by either of these Ladies: He died on the 27th of *May, Anno* 1617, 15 *Jac.* I. being at that time seventy Years of Age, and his Corps was sent to Dodleston in Cheshire, and privately interr'd there.

He was a Person of quick Apprehension, profound Judgment, and of a most venerable Gravity, having (as my Author says) been seldom seen to smile: But to proceed to *Thomas* his eldest Son; he married *Elizabeth* Daughter of *Thomas Venables* of Kinderton in the County of Chester, Esq. by whom he had Issue only three Daughters, *Elizabeth* married to *John Dutton,* Son and Heir apparent to *Thomas Dutton* of Dutton in the County of Chester, Esq. *Vere* married to *William Booth,* Son and Heir apparent to Sir *George Booth* of Dunham in the County of Chester, Bar. and *Mary* married to *Thomas Leigh,* eldest Son of Sir *John Leigh,* Kt. at that time Son and Heir apparent to Sir *Thomas Leigh* of Stonely in the County of Warwick, Kt. and Bar. But this Sir *Thomas Egerton,* traveling into Ireland, *Anno* 1599, 41 *Eliz.* died there in the Life-time of *Thomas* Viscount Brackley his Father, who survived him, and lived until the 15th of *March, Anno* 1617, 15 *Jac.* I. when he was seventy Years of Age, and then died, and was privately buried at Dodleston in Cheshire.

John his second Son succeeded in his Honour, to whom this Mannor descended; He was advanced to the Dignity of an Earl on the 27th Day of *May, Anno* 1627, 15 *Jac.* I. by the Title of Earl of Bridgewater, and married the Lady *Frances*, one of the Daughters and Coheirs to *Ferdinando* Earl of Derby, by whom he had Issue four Sons, *James* and *Charles*, both whom died young, *John* and *Thomas*, who survived him, and eleven Daughters, *Frances* married to Sir *John Hobart* of Blickling in the County of Norfolk, Kt. and Bar. Son and Heir to Sir *Henry Hobart* Kt. and Bar. late Lord Chief Justice of the Court of *Common Pleas*; *Arabella* married to *Oliver* Lord *St. John*, Son and Heir apparent to *Oliver* Earl of Bulingbrook; *Elizabeth* to *David Cecil*, Son of Sir *Richard Cecil*, Kt. second Brother to *William* Earl of Exeter, and afterwards Earl of Exeter; *Cecilie* who died unmarried; *Mary* wedded to *Richard Herbert*, Son and Heir to *Edward* Lord *Herbert* of Chirbury; *Penelope* to Sir *Robert Napier* of Luton Hoo in the County of Bedford, Kt. and Bart. *Alice* who died young; *Katharine* to *William Curtein*, Son and Heir apparent to Sir *William Curtein*, Kt. a great Merchant in London; *Magdalen* to Sir *Gervase Cutler* of Stainburgh in the County of York, Kt. *Anne* who died young; and *Alice* to *Richard* Lord *Vaughan*, Earl of Carberry in Ireland: and he died the 4th of *Decemb. An.* 1649, 1 *Car.* II. and was buried in this Parish Church.

John was his Son and Heir, inherited his Honours and Estate, and married *Elizabeth* Daughter to *William* Duke of Newcastle, by whom he had Issue five Sons, *John* Lord Brackley and Sir *William Egerton*, both made Knights of the Bath at the Coronation of King *Charles* II. whereof Sir *William* married *Honora*, Sister to *Thomas* Lord *Leigh* of Stoneley, by whom he had *John* and *Honora*, and died at *Christmas*, 1691, and was buried at Hemelhempsted; *Thomas* espoused *Esther* Daughter of Sir *John Busby* of Arrington in the County of Bucks, Kt. by whom he had Issue *John, Thomas, William*, and *Elizabeth*; *Charles* took for his Wife *Elizabeth* the Relict of *Randolfe Egerton* of Betley in the County of Stafford, Esq. and Daughter of *Henry Murry*, Esq. one of the Grooms of the Bedchamber to King *Charles* I. and *Jane* his Wife, since Viscountess *Banning* and *Stewart*; and *Elizabeth* married *Robert Sidney*, Viscount Lisle, eldest Son to *Robert* now Earl of Leicester; this *John* Earl of Bridgewater was sworn of the Privy Council, 13th of *February*, 1666, constituted Lord Lieutenant and *Custos Rotulorum* of the County of Buckingham, and afterwards the same Offices were confirmed on him in this County of Hertford, in the Reign of King *Charles* II. and King *James* II. He was a Person of middling Stature,

somewhat corpulent, had black Hair, a round Visage adorn'd
with a modest and grave Aspect, a sweet and pleasant Countenance, a comely Presence, and allowed free Access to all
Persons who had any Concerns with him; he was a learned
Man, delighted much in his Library, and was endewed with
all the rare Accomplishments of Virtue and Goodness; very
temperate in eating or drinking, complaisant in Company,
spoke sparingly but always very pertinently; he was very
pious to his God, most devout in his Acts of Religion, and
firm to the Church of England; he was very loyal to his
Prince, wary in Council, most affectionate to his Lady, very
tender to his Children, remarkable for Hospitality to his
Neighbours, his Charity to the Poor, his Liberality to Strangers, true to his Word, faithful to his Friend, strict in his
Justice, and punctual in all his Actions; which noble, good,
and vertuous Lord died on the 26th Day of *October, Anno
Dom.* 1686, *Ætat. suæ* 64, to the great Grief of the Author and all good Men that knew him, and was interred in
this Parish Church of Gaddesden in this County.

John Lord Brackley succeeded this good Earl in his Honours and Estate, having first married *Elizabeth* eldest Daughter and Coheir to *James* Earl of Middlesex, by whom he had
Issue *John* who died in his Infancy: after her Decease he
wedded *Jane* eldest Daughter to *Charles* now Duke of Bolton, by whom he had *Charles* Viscount Brackley, and *Thomas*, both whom were unfortunately burnt in their Beds at
Bridgewater-house in Barbican; *Scrope* now Viscount
Brackley, *William, Henry,* and *John,* and —— *Mary* and
Elizabeth; he is one of the Lords of the Privy Council, the
first Commissioner of Trade, and Lord Lieutenant of the
County of Buckingham: He bears *Argent, a Lion rampant
Gules, between three Pheons sable, with a Bordure in-
grailed of the last,* which Bordure has of late been disused.

The *Saxons* termed these Earls *Erligs* or *Ethlings;* the
Germans, Graves, as *Lantgrave, Palsgrave, Cheingrave,*
or the like; and the *Danes, Eorles;* but the *Normans, Comites, Counts;* and for Gravity in Council they were term'd
Comites illustris a Comitando Principem: His Head is
adorn'd with a Cap of Honour, and a Coronet of Gold,
which is pyramidal pointed, and pearled between each Pyramid, a Flower much shorter than the Pyramid; and his
Body is robed with a Hood, Surcoat, and Mantle of State,
with three Guards of Fur upon the Shoulders, and begirt
with a Sword.

Selden's *Tit.
of Hon.* pt. 2,
cap. 5, p. 679.
This Crownet or *Circulus aureus* (as it is termed in the
Charters of Creation) is very ancient; for *John* of Eltham,
Brother to King *Edw.* III. Earl of Cornwal lies buried in
St. *Edmonds* Chappel at Westminster, with a Crownet on
his Head, the Form whereof is Fleury, as a Duke's Crownet

is at this Day; but he died almost two Years before any Duke was made in 𝔈𝔫𝔤𝔩𝔞𝔫𝔡, from whence some conceive the Crownets of some Earls were of the like Mode to those of the Dukes before the Creation of Dukes; so *Aymer de Valence* Earl of 𝔓𝔢𝔪𝔟𝔯𝔬𝔬𝔨, who died *An.* 16 *Edw.* II. had a golden Crownet; and *Richard* Earl of 𝔄𝔯𝔲𝔫𝔡𝔢𝔩 had three Crownets of several Sorts and Worth, which he disposed of by his Will dated at 𝔄𝔯𝔲𝔫𝔡𝔢𝔩 Castle the 5th of *December*, 1375, 49 *Edw.* III. wherein he gave the best Crownet to the Lord *Richard* his Son and Heir, afterwards Earl of 𝔄𝔯𝔲𝔫𝔡𝔢𝔩, to remain to him and the Heirs of his Dignity; the second Crownet to the Lady *Joan* his Daughter, and the Heirs of her Body; and the third to the Lady *Alice* and the Heirs of her Body.

An Earl hath the Title of Prince, and is stiled the most Noble and Puissant Lord, but having treated of the Antiquity of this Honour in fol. 37, vol. 1, I refer the Reader thither.

THIS Rectory is in the Deanery of 𝔅𝔢𝔯𝔨𝔥𝔞𝔪𝔰𝔱𝔢𝔡 in the Diocess of 𝔏𝔦𝔫-𝔠𝔬𝔩𝔫, and was rated in the King's Books *Anno* 26 *Henry* VIII. at the yearly Value of 11*l.* 12*s.* 8*d.* and these Earls have been successively Patrons hereof.

RECTOR, *George Burghope*

The Church hath a square Tower at the West End thereof, wherein are four small Bells, with a short Spire upon it; and both the Church and Chancel have fair Ceilings, are kept very neat, and are adorn'd with several curious and fair Monuments, which gives me Occasion to take notice of the original Cause of erecting Monuments in Churches.

These Monuments were denominated *a Muriendo*, because they were at the first erected to defend the Bodies of the dead from the savage Brutishness of wild Beasts, which otherwise might have destroyed the Bodies in their Graves, for in those Days all were buried in the Fields near some Way, or at the Feet or Top of Mountains, as now in 𝔗𝔲𝔯-𝔨𝔢𝔭, and the Eastern Parts of the World; about which time 'twas the Usage in 𝔈𝔫𝔤𝔩𝔞𝔫𝔡 to inter their Dead upon the Ridges of Hills or spacious Plains, fortified or-fenced about with pointed Stones, Pyramids, Pillars or such like Monuments, as 𝔖𝔱𝔬𝔫𝔢𝔥𝔢𝔫𝔤𝔢 on 𝔖𝔞𝔩𝔦𝔰𝔟𝔲𝔯𝔶-𝔭𝔩𝔞𝔦𝔫, those near 𝔄𝔦𝔩𝔢-𝔣𝔬𝔯𝔡 in 𝔎𝔢𝔫𝔱, 𝔅𝔞𝔯𝔱𝔩𝔬𝔢 in 𝔆𝔞𝔪𝔟𝔯𝔦𝔡𝔤𝔢𝔰𝔥𝔦𝔯𝔢, and 𝔖𝔱𝔢𝔟𝔢𝔫𝔞𝔤𝔢 in this County, to put Passengers in Mind of their Mortality; and though the British Cities had Churches from the Be- ginning of Christianity, yet the Christians always buried their Dead without the Walls of Towns and Cities, until the time of *Gregory* the Great, who was Bishop of 𝔯𝔬𝔪𝔢, *Anno* 590, when the Monks, Fryars, and Priests began to offer Sacrifices for the Souls departed; at length they obtained Church-yards for Places to bury their Dead for the Advantage of their Profit; and in Process of time License to bury in Churches, that so often as their Relations came

Hund. of
Dacorum.
Wear. p 8.
to those holy Places and beheld their Sepulture, they might remember and earnestly pray to the Lord for them; for which Reason *Constantine* was buried in the Porch of the Apostles in *Constantinople*, *Honorus* in the Porch of St. *Peter* at *Rome*, and the Empress in the Church: and in *England*, *Augustine* the Monk, Bishop of *Canterbury*, was buried in the Porch of the Church of St. *Peter* and St. *Paul* near *Canterbury*, a religious House of his own Foundation without the City, and the six next succeeding Bishops of the same Province were interred near him.

Lamb. Peram.
of Kent, p. 87.

Chron. MSS.
Stilling. Anttq
of the British
Churches,
fol. 30.
Cuthbert, the eleventh Archbishop of *Canterbury*, consecrated *Anno* 341, obtained a Dispensation about the Year 758, from the Pope to make Cementories and Church-yards in *England*, for the Burial of their Dead; for before his time the Bodies of the Kings and Archbishops in *England* were not buried in Cities, for in those Days they followed the Example of our Saviour, who was buried without the Gate, and this Archbishop was the first that was interred in Christ's Church. Shortly after Gravestones were made, and Tombs erected with Inscriptions ingraved upon them, declaring briefly, with a Kind of Commiseration, the Name, Age, Merit, Dignity, State, Praise, Fortune, Time, and Manner of the Death of the Party interred; which was called an Epitaph, and have always been accounted the greatest Mark of Respect, because they express a great Love to the deceased Person, and preserves his Memory to Posterity, which was a Comfort to his Friends and Relations, and put them in Mind of his Mortality.

Camd. Rom.
p. 306.

The Invention of these Epitaphs proceeded from the Presage or Sense of Immortality implanted naturally in all Men, and is attributed to the Schollars of *Linus*, the *Theban* Poet, (who flourished about the Year of the World 2700,) for they first bewailing this *Linus* their Master in doleful Verses when he was slain, those Verses were called from him *Ælinum*, afterwards *Epitaphia*, because they were first sung at Burials, and after engraved upon the Sepulchers; which may be called Monuments, *a Memoria*, for that they are Memorials to put Men in Mind of their frail Condition, and their deceased Friends; or *a Monendo*, to warn Men of their Mortality, and to excite their inward Thoughts by the Sight of Death to a better Life; and these Monuments were accounted so sacred, that such as violated them were heretofore punished with Death, Banishment, Condemnation to the Mines, or Loss of Members, according to the Circumstance of Fact and Person.

Coke, Inst. 3,
fol. 303.
These Monuments serve for four Uses or Ends: They are Evidences to prove Descents and Pedigrees. 2. To shew the time when the Party deceased. 3. They are Examples to follow the Good, and eschew the Evil. 4. Memorials to

put the living in Mind of their Mortality; for these Reasons any Person may erect a Tomb, Sepulcher, or Monument for the deceased in any Church, Chancel, Chapel, or Church-yard, so that it be not to the Hindrance of the Celebration of Divine Service; the defacing of them is punishable at Common Law; and the Party that built it shall have his Action at Common Law during his Life, and the Heir of the deceased after his Death, but now to return to these Monuments here.

Hund. of Bacorum.

9 Ed. IV. 14.
Lady Wyches
Case, Mich.
10 Jac. I. Cor-
ven and Pym.
Coke. 3 Inst.
fol. 202.

A fair Monument in the Chancel hath these two Inscriptions.

M. S.
Hear rests
(Till the last Trump awakens his Dust)

The Right Honourable and truly Noble Sir *John Egerton*, Kt. of the Honourable Order of the Bath, Earl of Bridgewater, Viscount Brackley. and Baron of Elesmere, &c.

He was Son to the renowned Patriot, Sir *Thomas Egerton*, Baron of Elesmere, Viscount Brackley and Lord Chancellor of England, and was sole Heir both of his Estate and Virtues. He married the Right Honourable the Lady *Frances Stanley*, Second Daughter and one of the Coheirs of *Ferdinando* Earl of Derby, &c. a Wife worthy such a Husband, by whom he was blest with a numerous and vertuous Off-spring; four Sons and eleven Daughters; three of his Sons died before him, viz. *James* Viscount Brackley his eldest, and *Charles* Viscount Brackley his second Son, who both died in their Infancy, and Mr. *Thomas Egerton* his fourth Son, who lies here interred, dying unmarried in the three and twentieth year of his age, and three of his Daughters, viz. the Lady *Cecilia Egerton*, Mrs. *Alice Egerton*, and the Lady *Anne Egerton*; his third and only surviving Son and Heir *John* Viscount Brackley he saw happily married to the Right Honourable the Lady *Elizabeth Cavendish*, the second Daughter to the Right Honourable *William* Marquess of Newcastle, &c. Seven of his Daughters he likewise saw well and honourably married, viz. the Lady *Frances*, the Lady *Arabella*, the Lady *Elizabeth*, the Lady *Mary*, the Lady *Penelope*, the Lady *Katharine*, and the Lady *Magdalen*; and left only his eleventh Daughter the Lady *Alice Egerton* unmarried.

He was endewed with incomparable Parts, both Natural and Acquired, so that both Art and Nature did seem to strive which should contribute the most towards the making him a most accomplish'd Gentleman, he had an active Body and a vigorous Soul, his Deportment was graceful, his Discourse excellent, whether extemporary or premeditated, serious or jocular, so that he seldom spake but he did either instruct or delight those that heard him; he was a profound Scholar, an able Statesman and a good Christian; he was the dutiful Son to his Mother the Church of England in her Persecution, as well as in her great Splendor, a loyal Subject to his Sovereign in those worst of times, when it was accounted Treason not to be a Traytor

As he lived 70 years a pattern of Vertue, so he died an example of Patience and Piety, the fourth of *December* in the year of our Lord 1649.

Prov. *the* 10th *and* 7th.
The Memory of the Just is blessed.

M. S.
In hope of a happy Resurrection

Here lieth the Right Honourable and most noble Lady *Frances* Countess of Bridgewater.

She was second Daughter and one of the Coheirs of the Right Honourable *Ferdinando* Earl of Derby, &c. Wife to the Right Honourable Sir *John Egerton*, Kt. of the Honourable Order of the Bath, Earl of Bridgewater, Viscount Brackley, Baron of Elesmere and Lord President of

Males and the Marshes thereof, by whom she was a happy Mother of fifteen Children, four Sons and eleven Daughters, five of which she buried young, viz. the Lord *James* Viscount Brackley her eldest, the Lord *Charles* who succeeded him in Birth and Honour second Son, the Lady *Cicilia Egerton*, Mrs. *Alice Egerton* her eighth, and the Lady *Anne Egerton* her tenth Daughter, who lies here interred, dying in the eighth year of her age, seven Daughters she married richly and honourably, viz. the Lady *Frances* her eldest, the Lady *Arabella* her second, the Lady *Elizabeth* her third, the Lady *Mary* her fifth, the Lady *Penelope* her sixth, the Lady *Katharine* her seventh, and the Lady *Magdalen* her ninth, one of her Daughters, viz. the Lady *Alice* her eleventh she left unmarried, as she likewise did two of her Sons, the Lord *John* Viscount Brackley her third, and Sir *Thomas Egerton* her fourth Son; she was unparralleld in the Gifts of Nature and Grace, being strong of Constitution, admirable for Beauty, generous in Carriage, of a sweet and noble Disposition, Wise in her Affairs, Chearful in her Discourse, Liberal to the Poor, Pious towards God, and Good to All.

She lived vertuously 52 years; she died religiously the 11th day of *March* in the year of our Lord 1635. and she reigns triumphantly for ever.

Psal. 116. 15.
Pretious in the sight of the Lord is the Death of his Saints.

Here lies interred
John Earl of Bridgwater Viscount Brackley, Baron of Elesmerr, and one of the Lords of the Privy Council, and Lientenant of the County of Bucks and Hertford, and *Custos Rotulorum* of both, to King *Charles* the second and King *James* the second. Who desired no other Memorial of him but only This,

That having (in the 19th year of his age) married the Lady *Elizabeth Cavendish*, Daughter to the then Earl since Marquess, and after that Duke of Newcastle, he did enjoy (almost 22 years) all the happiness that a man could receive in the sweet society of the Best of Wives, till it pleased God in the 44th year of his age to change his great Felicity into as great Misery, by depriving him of his truly loving and intirely beloved Wife, who was all his worldly Bliss; after which time humbly submitting to, and waiting on the Will and Pleasure of the Almighty, he did sorrowfully wear out 23 years, 4 Months and twelve days, and then on the 16th day of *October*, in the year of Lord 1686. and in the 64th year of his own age, yeilded up his Soul into the merciful hand of God who gave it.

Job 13. 15.
Though he slay me, yet will I trust in him.

Another fair Monument hath this Inscription.

D. D.
To the sacred memory of the late transcendently virtuous Lady, now glorious Saint, the Right Honourable *Elizabeth* Countess of Bridgwater.

She was second Daughter to the Right Honourable *William* Marquiss of Newcastle, and Wife to the Right Honourable *John* Earl of Bridgwater, and whose Family she had enriched with a hopeful issue, six Sons; viz. *John* Viscount Brackley her eldest, Sir *William Egerton* second Son, both Knights of the Honourable Order of the Bath, Mr. *Thomas Egerton* a third, Mr. *Charles Egerton* her fourth, Mr. *Henry Egerton* her fifth, Mr. *Steward Egerton* her sixth Son, and three Daughters, viz. Mrs. *Frances Egerton* her Eldest, the Lady *Elizabeth* her second, and the *Katherine Egerton* her third Daughter, all of which Children three, viz. Mr. *Henry Egerton* her fifth Son, Mrs. *Frances* her eldest, the Lady *Katherine Egerton* her third Daughter lye here interred, dying in their Infancy, the rest are still living Pictures of their deceased Mother, and the only remaining Comforts of their disconsolate Father.

She was a Lady in whom all the accomplishments both in Body and Mind did concur to make her the Glory of the present, and Example of

future Ages, her Beauty was so unparalleld that 'tis as much beyond the Art of the most elegant Pen, as it surpasseth the skill of several the most exquisite pensils (that attempted it); to describe and not to disparage it; she had a winning and an attractive Behaviour, a charming Discourse, a most obliging Conversation; she was so courteous and affable to all persons that she gained their Love, yet not so familiar to expose herself to contempt; she was of a Noble and Generous Soul, yet of so meek and humble a Disposition that never any Woman of her Quality was greater in the Worlds opinion, and less in her own, the rich at her Table daily tasted her Hospitality, the poor at her Gate her Charity; her Devotion most Exemplary if not Inimitable, (witness) besides several other occasional Meditations and Prayers full of the holy transports and rapture of a sanctified Soul) her Divine Meditations upon every particular Chapter in the Bible, written with her own hand, and never (till since her death) seen by any eye but her own, and her then Dear but now sorrowful Husbands, to the admiration both of her eminent Piety in Composing, and of her Modesty in Concealing, then she was a most affectionate and observing Wife to her Husband, a most tender and indulgent Mother to her Children, a most kind and bountiful Mistress to her Family; in a word she was so Superlatively good, that Language is too narrow to express her deserved Character; her Death was as religious as her Life was vertuous, on the 14th day of *June* in the year of our Lord 1663. of her own age 37. she exchanged her earthly Coronet for an heavenly Crown.

Pro. 31. 28. 29.

Her Children rise up and call her Blessed, her Husband also and he praiseth her: Many Daughters have done vertuously but thou excellest them all.

Another Monument shews this Inscription.

To the Memory of

The late no less truly vertuous than Right Honourable the Lady *Elizabeth* Vicountess Brackley, eldest Daughter and Heir of the Right Honourable *James* Earl of Middlesex, Wife to the Right Honourable Sir *John Egerton*, Kt. of the Honourable Order of the Bath, Viscount Brackley, eldest Son and Heir apparent to the Right Honourable *John* Earl of Bridgewater; She had issue one Son *John Egerton*, who died in the second year of his age, and one Daughter, who died as soon as she was born and both lye interred together with their excellent Mother.

She was a Lady of a noble Extraction, and adorned with a temperate Mind equal to her Birth, her Person was lovely, Nature having better provided for her than Art for others, her Wit was quick and innocently free without affectation, her Speech whether in the English or French tongue, was modestly grave, and gracefully delightful; she was an exact observer of whatsoever was noble or vertuous, discreet or pious, civil and obliging, her Closet, the private Chapple, and publick Church, did witness her devout, decent, and daily discharge of her Duty to Almighty God, her constant and passionate affection to her dear Husband (who sorrowfully undergoes the great affliction of her Love) placed her among the best of Wives, and her meek and affable Conversation (whereby she was still most esteemed by those that knew her best) among the best of Women.

In the Morning of her age (too bright to last long,) she found (even before her noon) her Evening, for after a short but sharp Sickness on *Thursday* 3d of *March* (in her 22. year) in the year of our Lord God 1669. she exchanged this Mortal Life for Immortality.

Pro. 31. 30. *A Woman that feareth the Lord, she shall be praised.*

On the right Hand of the Altar, on the Ground over the Vault at the Foot of the great Monument lies a black Marble Stone, with this Inscription.

In assurance of a happy and Joyful Resurrection
here lyeth interred
The Lady *Ann Egerton*,
Who died the 27th of *December* 1625.
In the 8th year of her age,

**And was
One of the Daughters of the Right Honourable**
John Lord *Ellesmere*, Viscount **Brackley**.
Earl of **Bridgwater**, by the right
Honourable the Lady *Frances*, Viscountess,
Daughter, and one of the Coheirs of
The Right Honourable *Fardinand* Earl
of **Derby**.

On the left Hand of the Altar stands Dr. *Fowler's* Monument in white
Marble with this Inscription.

Spe Resurgendi
Exuvias hîc deposuit Mortale, Vir verè Reverendus,
ac omnibus (quibus notus erat) amore dignissimus,
Thomas Fowler *Sacræ Theolog. Professor;*
Ortus Generosâ Familiâ in comitatu **Stafford**;
Prænobili Comiti de **Bridgwater**, τῳ μαρκαῆιτη, *à Sacris*
domesticis; Et filii ejus (Honoratissimo illo titulo nunc
gaudentis) non sine magno fructu fidelis Tutor;
Albi Monasterii in Agro **Salopiensi** *Rector:*
Vir de Republicâ literarum optimè meritus;
Piêtatis, Probitatis, Comitatis, et Candoris vivum exemplar,
Subditus fidelis;
Ecclesiæ Anglicanæ obsequentissimus filius;
Theologus insignis;
Concionator eloquens et assiduus;
Omni denique virtutum genere clarus:
Qui varius motuum superorum casibus huc illuc agitatus,
Cum tandem patriam suam à prædonibus spoliatam, Regum
Optimum â Perduellibus sceleratissimus securi traditum, et
Ecclesiam Anglicanam tantum non Extinctam, videsset,
Vitam pertæsus, ad superos migravit,
27. die Febr. *An. Dom. Millessimo sexentesimo quinquagesimo*
secundo, Ætatis suæ 52.
Et sui desiderium amicis omnibus reliquit.
Optime Patri;
Johnnnes *et* Thomas Fowler, *Filii amatissimi*
(Benigno concessu et candore Prænobilis Dom. Johannis
Comitis de **Bridgwater**) *Hoc Monumentum*
M. S.
Piè posuerunt.
Marmore non opus est Tibi (sed Nati hoc posuere
Ne si aliter jaceas, vitior umbra fores)
Nam tibi qui similis vicit moriturq; sepulchrum
Ipsâ sibi vivax, et sibi marmor erit.

On the Stone under this Monument.

Thomas Fowler, *S.S. Theologiæ Professor, Albi Monasterii in Comitatu*
Salopiensi *Rector: Hic situs est.*

Another Monument hath this.

Spe Resurgendi,
Hîc requiescit pars Mortalis
Marthæ Eddowes,
Filiæ Reverendi Jacobi Betton *Sacræ Theologiæ Professoris, et* Johannis
Eddowes, *Armig. nuper Conjugis amantissimæ:*
Quæ, dum vixit, Piêtatis, Constitatis, Comitatis, Amoris Conjugalis, erga
propinquos benignitatis et Cordatæ ad Amicos Constantiæ, Sexus deniq;
sui extitit laudabile Exemplar. Ætatis suæ Ann. quadragessimo octavo
placidè obdormivit in Domino, die sexto Junii, An. Æræ Christianæ,
1678.

Johannes Eddowes in *defunctæ Conjugis memoriam*
Amoris ergô hoc Monumentum posuit.

A Monument in the Wall on the North Side of the Church
sets forth this Inscription.

Henricum Stanley,
Medicinæ Doctorem,
Celiberrimi utriusq; Collegii
Novi, primum in Universitate Oxon.
Medicorum deinde in Civitate London.
Socium et Ornamentum:
Unàcum tribus suis suavissimis Liberis
Henrico, Thoma *et* Francisca;
Et charissimâ Conjuge Margaritâ,
Thomæ Panton, *Equitis aurati*
Belgisq; in re militari notissimi filiâ,
Voluit
Resurrectionem in hoc sacrario præstolarier
Johannis, Comitis Bridgwater
Supremus Favor;
Ut
Quem vivum in sinu receperit,
Defunctum etiam daret
(*Nulli cessurâ fato benignitate*
Sibi suisq; quam proxime recumbere
Obiit } Anno { Domini 1671.
{ Ætatis 67.
Mense Feb. *die*
Vicessimo quarto.

This Inscription is engraved on another Monument.

Heus
Alibi Sistende, tantum
Huc etiam advocandæ
Viator,
Ad Lugubris pariter et letabundi funeris
Dubiam pompam:
Henrico Stanley.
Patris Henrici Filio primogenito
Ceteris orbatis liberis mox etiam unico,
Cumulatioris Spei adolescentulo:
(*Heu!*)
Artium messem ⎫ ⎧ *Herbâ Gramaticali;*
Virtutum Autumnum ⎬ in ⎨ *Vernâ innocentiâ;*
Gratiarum triumphum ⎪ ⎪ *Tyrocinio morum;*
Virum perfectum ⎭ ⎩ *Germine Tenello;*
Mors prævocavit invida:
Poterat ornatior si diuturnior superesset.
Abi, et mecùm plora.
Quin eidem
(*Vah!*)
⎧ *Artibus, cognitionem intuitivum;*
⎪ *Virtutibus, beatam Sanctimoniam;*
Pro ⎨ *Gratiis; gloriam;*
⎩ *Longivitate, eviternium*
Mors præstitit invidenda:
Poterat desideratior, haut Auspicatior mori.
Adi et mecum exulta.
Utroque pathemate divisus pater posuit
⎧ Anno { Dom. 1670.
⎪ { Ætat. 14.
Obeunti ⎨ *Mense* Aprilis
⎩ *Die* 14.

A Stone at the Foot of this Monument has this Inscription.

Francisca Stanley, Hen. *et* Margarettæ *filiola biennis, vixit patri Curarum*
levamen Suave ———— *matris Mortuæ Corpusculum hic pulveri, animula*
cælitum Choro Miscetur. Obiit Novemb. 26. 1661. *non amissa, sed*
præmissa.

Another Inscription.

Thomæ Stanley *Suavissimo filiolo* 16. *Mensium spaciolo.*
Nᵗᵒ. *et* Dᵗᵒ.
Mæstissimus pater Henricus **Londinensis** *medicus hæc*
parentavit veniola.

Tibi, gnate, Uso	*Breve et Cordeale*
Lucis, brevi fuso	*Carmen Tripedale,*
Citoque hic concluso	*Curto non siet male :*
(Misero me deluso)	*Longum Nihil*
Hoc memoriale.	*Nisi Vale.*

D. D.
Obiit Sept. 24. 1658.
Christâ Senechdochiâ tibi parte revertor in istâ,
Exige me totum, cum libet, absque Tropo.

Another Stone hath this.

Henrici Stanly *Filii, Igniculi animæ in muto lucent corpusculi favilla, heic latent.*

On the same Stone.

Henrici Stanly, *Patris et* Margaritæ *Uxoris, etiam Cineres si requiras, heic sunt.*

A Monument at the lower End of the Church, on the right Hand
of the Belfrey, has this Inscription.

M. S.
Richardi Blower, *Generosi,*
Christopheri Blower *de* **Kuleston** *in Comitatu* **Oxoniensi**
Armigeri filii ;
Secundum Jesu Christi adventum expectans hic jacet
pars Terrestris.
7. Nov. *die An. Christi,* 1681. *Et Ætatis suæ*
quadragessimo nono, mortem obiit:
Sed non prius quàm erga Deum, Regem, Patriam,
Et Johannem *Comitem de* **Bridgwater** *Dominum suum*
uc herum optimum bene se gesserat :

In cujus memoriam Elizabetha (Johannis Oliver, *Generosi de* **Killington**
in Comitatu **Derbiensi** *Filia) hujus vero Uxor dolore multum gravata, cui*
duos filios nec filias pauciores (hos etiam omnes morte beatos) enixa est,
Monumentum hoc posuit, ut quibus vivus optimè innotuit.
Mortuus non omnino è memoriâ excidat.

Underneath this Monument, a Stone has this Inscription.

In hopes of a Blessed Resurrection, here lieth the Body of *Richard Blower,* Gen. who exchanged this mortal life for immortality, *Nov.* 1681, *Ætat.* 49.

GATESDEN, GADESDEN.

IN the time of *William* the Conqueror, *Edward de Saresbury,* Sheriff of the County, held this Vill, above a Mile distant from **Little Gadesden** towards the East, for it was then recorded in *Domesdei Book,* That

Domesd. Lib.
fol. 139.

In **Danais** *Hundred.* Edwardus de Saresburie *tenuit* **Gatesdene** *pro sex hid. se defendebat. tempore Regis* Edwardi, *et modo pro quatuor hidis, sed un. existis se defendebat in* **Treunge** *Hundred. et hic æpprecianda est. Terra est duodecim car. in Dominio duo hidæ et ibi sunt quatuor car. et quindecim Vill. cum Presbiter. habente sex car. et adhuc duo possunt fieri, ibi duo Bord. et un. cotar. et octo Servi et un. Molin. de quinque sol. pratum un. car. et dimid pastura ad pec. Ville Silva quingent. porc. in totis valentiis valet* *vigint. et duo lib. quando recepit vigint. lib. tempore Regis Edwardi vigint. et quinque lib. Hoc Manerium tenuit Ualuuen die qua Rex Edwardus fuit vivus et mortuus de Abbate Sancti Albani, non potuit mittere extra Ecclesiam sed post mortem suam redire debebat ad Ecclesiam ut Hundred. testatur.*

Edward de Saresburie held Gabesbene in Banais Hundred, it was rated for six Hides in the time of King *Edward* (the Confessor) and now for four Hides, but one of these is rated in Creunge Hundred and is·here appraised. The arable is twelve Carucates, in Deamesne two Hides, and there are four Carucates, and fifteen Villains with a Presbiter or Priest, having six Carucates, and now two others may be made, there are two Bordars, and one Cottager, and eight Servants and one Mill, of five Shillings Rent by the Year, Meadow one Carucate and an half, Common of Pasture for the Cattle of the Vill, Wood to feed five hundred Hogs in Pannage time; in the whole Value it is worth two and twenty Pounds by the Year, when he received it twenty Pounds, in the time of King *Edward* (the Confessor) five and twenty Pounds; *Wulwen* held this Mannor of the Abbot of St. Albans on the day wherein King *Edward* was alive and dead, he could not take it away from the Church, but after his Death he ought to return it to the Church as the Hundred can witness.

This *Edward de Saresbury* was the younger Son of *Walter de Ewrus,* Earl of Rosmar, one of the puissant *Normans,* who accompanied Duke *William* in that Expedition for the Conquest of this Realm, to whom he gave the Lordships of Saresburie and Ambrusberie, in Consideration of his Valour and good Service in that signal Battle, where the Duke obtained the Victory; after which this *Edward* was born in England, sirnamed *Saresburie* from the Lordship Saresburp where he then dwelt, and was the Progenitor of the ancient Lords of Saresburp; and for the eminent Merits of his Father, *William* the Conqueror, bestowed on him two Lordships in Dorsetshire, three in Somersetshire, three and thirty in Wiltshire, two in Hantshire, one in Surrp, one in Middlesex, two in Buckinghamshire, and two in this County, all which he possest at the time when that memorable Survey was made. He was a Standard Bearer to King *H.* I. *Anno* 20 of his Reign, in that famous Battle at Brenebile in Normandp, where he behaved himself with singular Courage and Military Skill in the Presence of the King, who was victorious; he left Issue *Walter* and *Maud* married by the Appointment of *William Rufus* to *Humphry de Bohun.*

Walter wedded *Sibilla de Caworth,* by whom he had Issue *Patrick,* and surviving his Wife, took the Habit of a Cannon in the Priory of Bradenstoke in the County of Wilts, which was of his own Foundation. He died there, and was buried with her in one Grave near the Quire.

Patric was his Heir, and Steward of the Household to Queen *Maud,* who advanced him to the Title and Dignity of Earl of Salisburp: He married *Maud,* and after her Decease *Ela* one of which Wives was Daughter of the Earl of Ponthieu by whom he had Issue *William;* but in his Attendance upon Queen *Eleanor* Wife to Queen *H.* II. he was slain by *Guy de Lezinian* upon his Return from a Pil-

Hund. of
Dacorum.
grimage, which he made to *St. James* in 𝔊𝔞𝔩𝔦𝔱𝔦𝔞, and was
buried at 𝔖t. 𝔥𝔦𝔩𝔩𝔞𝔯𝔦𝔢𝔯.

William succeeded him in the Earldom of 𝔖𝔞𝔩𝔦𝔰𝔟𝔲𝔯𝔭, and
at the Coronation of King *R.* I. bore the Golden Sceptre
with the Dove on the Head of it; he married *Eleanor de
Vitrei*, and died *Anno* 1196, 8 *R.* I. leaving Issue.

Ela, who was his sole Daughter and Heir, from whom I
guess this Mannor might come to *Roger Zouch*, who was a
Branch of the Earls of 𝔅𝔯𝔦𝔱𝔞𝔫𝔭, for he held it in the time
of King *John*, who gratifi'd him with the Grant of several
Mannors for his Loyalty, and upon his Death it descended
to

Alan, who was his Son and Heir, and married *Elene* one
of the Daughters and Heirs of *Roger de Quincy*, Earl of
𝔚𝔦𝔫𝔠𝔥𝔢𝔰𝔱𝔢𝔯 : Some say that *John* Earl *Warren* killed this
Alan upon a Quarrel at *Westminster Hall*, touching some
Title of Land, but he was only wounded, for it appears by
the Inquisition taken after his Death, that he died in the
54th Year of *H.* III. which was about two Years after,
leaving Issue

Roger la Zouch, who was then twenty eight Years old,
and *Eudo* his younger Son. He claimed *An.* 6 *Edw.* I. before *John de Rygate* and others Justices, Itinerants at 𝔥𝔢𝔯𝔱𝔣𝔬𝔯𝔡, to have in this Mannor the View of Franc-Pledge,
the Correction of Assize of Bread and Ale, Tumbrel, Gallows, Waife, and Free-Warren, with divers other Liberties, and they were allowed, and leaving Issue

Quo Warr. 6
Ed. I. Rot.34,
cur. recept.
Scac.

Alan de Zouch, who was his Son and Heir, and succeeded
him; he was a Person of a warlike Spirit, for he was several times in the Wars of 𝔊𝔞𝔰𝔠𝔬𝔦𝔫𝔢, 𝔅𝔬𝔲𝔯𝔡𝔢𝔞𝔲𝔵, and 𝔖𝔠𝔬𝔱𝔩𝔞𝔫𝔡, and *Anno* 7 *Edward* II. died seiz'd of this Mannor,
and the Advowson of this Parish Church, leaving *Ellen*,
the Wife of *Nicholas St Maur*, at that time 26 Years of
Age; *Maud* the Wife of *Robert de Holland* 24 Years of Age;
and *Elizabeth* then a Nun at 𝔅𝔯𝔢𝔴𝔬𝔬𝔡 in the County of
𝔖𝔱𝔞𝔣𝔣𝔬𝔯𝔡, 20 Years of Age, his Daughters and Heirs. Between whom Partition was made in 8 *Edward* II. of all
the Land descended to them from their Father, and this
Mannor was equally divided between the said *Ellen*, and
the said *Maud*.

Esc. 13 Ed. I.
n. 30.
Rot. Vasc. 22
Ed. I. 24 Ed.
I.
Rot. Scac.
16 Ed. I.

Dugd. Bar
vol. 1, fol.690.

Nicholas St. Maur, the Husband of *Ellen*, was in several
Expeditions made into 𝔖𝔠𝔬𝔱𝔩𝔞𝔫𝔡, summon'd to the Parliament held 8 *Ed.* II. and died 10th of that King's Reign,
seized of the Moyety of this Mannor in her Right, leaving
by her *Thomas*, his Son and Heir, nine Years of Age, after
his Decease she married *Alan de Cherleton*, who left Issue
by her, from whom the *Cherletons* of 𝔄𝔭𝔭𝔢𝔩𝔱𝔬𝔫, descended.

Rot. Scac. 27
Ed. I. m. 17.
29 Ed. I. m 5.
31 Ed. I. m.
12. Rot. Esc.
10 Ed. II. n.
59.
Dugd. Bar.
vol. 2, fol. 89.
Cart. 2 Ed. II.
n. 46.
Claus 12 Ed.
II. m. 23.
Claus. 15 Ed.
II. m. 2.

But to return to *Maud* the Wife of *Robert Holland*, to
whom the other Moyety of this Church was allotted. He

was summoned to Parliament among the Barons of this
Realm from 8 *Edw.* II. to the 14th of the same King.

But upon that Insurrection made by *Thomas* Earl of **Lancaster**, *Anno* 15 *Edw.* II. he promised to bring all the Power
he could raise to his Assistance, but he failing, that Earl (being then at his Castle of **Tutbury** in *Com.* **Stafford**) fled
Northwards, was taken at **Boroughbridge** in the County of
York, and when this *Robert* had Notice thereof, he rendered himself to the King at **Derby**, and was sent Prisoner to
Dover Castle, which unfaithful Act to his Lord (who had
raised him from nothing) drew such a general Hatred upon
him from the People, that they taking him into a Wood
near **Hemly Parke** towards **Windsor**, beheaded him on the
Nones of *October*, and Sir *Thomas Wyther*, Kt. and some
other Private Friends sent his Head to *Henry* Earl of
Lancaster, then at **Waltham-Cross** in this County. He
left Issue by this *Maud* four Sons, *Robert* 16 Years of
Age at his Fathers Death, *Thomas* who became a great
Man, *Alan* who had the Mannors of **Dalbury** and **Werks-
worth** in the County of **Derby**, and *Otho* who was elected
into the Society of the most noble Order of the Garter by
King *E.* III. at the time of its Foundation, but afterwards
accompaning his Brother *Thomas* into **Britany**, 29 *Edw.*
III. was taken Prisoner at **Graunsors** in **France**, and died
in those Parts, 33 *Edw.* III. leaving

Sir *Robert Holland*, Kt. his elder Brother, his next
Heir, who was forty Years of Age, was engaged in seve-
ral Expeditions into **France**, and having been summon'd to
Parliament from 16 *Edw.* III. until the 46th of that King's
Reign dyed 16 *March*, 47 *Edw.* III. leaving Issue

Maud, his sole Daughter and Heir, married to Sir *John
Lovel*, Kt. seventeen Years of Age, but afterwards all this
Mannor of **Gadesden** came to the Possession of

John Holland, Earl of **Huntindon**, who married *Anne*
the Widow of *Edmond Martin* Earl of **Marsh**, Daughter
of *Edmond* Earl of **Stafford**, in the 8th Year of *H.*VI. was
joyned in Commission with the Earl of **Northumberland** in
the 14th Year of the same King's Reign, for guarding the
East and West Marshes towards **Scotland**, and also constituted Admiral of **England**, **Acquitain**, and advanced by Letters Patents dated 6th of *January*, 21 *H.*VI. at **Windsor**,
to the Title of Duke of **Exeter**, (which Dignity his Father
lost by Attainder 1 *Hen.* IV.) with this special Priviledge,
That he and his Heirs Males should have Place and Seat
in all Parliaments and Councils next to the Duke of **York**
and his Heirs Males, and was constituted *Anno* 24 *H.* VI.
Lord High Admiral of **England**, **Ireland**, and **Acquitain**
for his Life, his Son *Henry* being also joyned with him in
the Grant for his Life : and made in the same Manner, Constable of the *Tower* with his Son, on the 25th of *H.*VI.

Hund. of
Bacorum.

Weav. Mon.
p. 425.
But in the ensuing Year he died, leaving Issue by *Anne* his first Wife, only *Henry*, who was his Son and Heir, and by *Anne* his last Wife, *Anne* a Daughter, first married to *John* Lord *Nevil* the Son and Heir of *Ralph Nevil*, the second Earl of 𝕸estmorelanꝺ of that Family, by whom having no Issue, she took to Husband Sir *John Nevil*, Kt. Uncle to her former Husband; but

Pat. 28 H.VI.
p. 2, m 17.
Dugd. Bar.
vol. 2, fol. 82.
Henry was Heir to his Father, and tho' he had not at that time accomplisht his full Age, yet in Consideration of his Father's Services, he obtained Livery of all his Castles, Mannors, and Lands in 𝕰nglanꝺ and 𝕸ales, in the 28th Year of King *H*.VI.

Stow's Annals,
Ibid.
And the same King in Recompence of his Services, *An*. 38th of his Reign, granted to him the Office of Constable of 𝕱otheringay Castle for Life, which by Forfeiture of *Richard* Duke of 𝕐ork came to the Crown.

Ibid.
But soon after the Lancastrians being totally routed at 𝕿owton 𝕱ielꝺ, he escaped thence, and fled with the Duke of 𝕾omerset and some others to 𝕐ork, where the King and Queen then were, and went thence with them into 𝕾cot-lanꝺ, whereupon King *Henry* was deposed, and he with many others were attainted in the ensuing Parliament be-

Rot. Parl.
1 Ed.1V.
gun at 𝕸estminster, 1 *Edw*. IV.

Stow's Annals
After which he appeared again in Arms with the Lancastrians at 𝕭ernaꝺe-fielꝺ, where he fought manfully till he was sore wounded, and left for dead from seven of the Clock in the Morning till four in the Afternoon, and then being brought to the House of one of his Servants called *Ruthland*, he had a Chyrurgeon, and was afterwards conveyed

Ibid.
to the Sanctuary at 𝕸estminster; but in 13th *Edw*. IV. was found dead in the Sea betwixt 𝕯over and 𝕮alais, tho' not known how he came thither. He married *Anne* Daughter

Esc. 15 Ed
IV. n. 36.
Claus. 16 Ed.
IV. m. 10.
Dugd. Bar.
vol. 2, fol. 82.
of *Richard* Duke of 𝕐ork, and Sister to King *Edw*. IV. but having no Issue by her, she the 12th of *Novemb*. 1472, (12 *Edw*. IV.) was at her own Suit divorced from him. After his Decease this Mannor came to the Crown, and King

Pat 1 H.VII.
Henry VII. by Letters Patents dated 27th of *October*, 1 *Regni sui*, created

Thomas Lord *Stanley* (who was married to the King's Mother) Earl of 𝕯erby, by the Cincture of the Sword, to hold the said Title to him and the Heirs Males of his Body, with the annual Fee of 20*l*. and for the Support of his Honour gave unto him the Mannors of 𝕲reat 𝕲aꝺesꝺen and 𝕾tagnow near 𝕾t. 𝕬lbans, with their Appurtenances in this County: And this Mannor coutinued in this Name and Family until the Lady *Anne Stanley*, Lady *Strainge*, and and the Ladies *Frances* and *Elizabeth Stanley* Daughters and Coheirs of *Ferdinando* Earl of 𝕯erby, by Indenture

Cart. 43 Eliz.
penes Com.
Bridgewater.
dated the 4th of *Jannary*, 43 *Eliz*. suffered a Recovery of this Mannor, and conveyed it to the Use of

Sir *Robert Cecil*, Kt. Principal Secretary of State, one *Hund. of Barorum.* of her Majesty's most honourable Privy Council, and Master of her Highnesses Court of Wards and Liveries, and his Heirs, who by Deed dated the 8th of *Feb. 44 Eliz.* Cart. 44 Eliz. granted it to penes Com. Bridgewater.

Adolph Cary of Berkhamsted in this County, Esq. who was knighted at Whitehall, 3 *Jac.* I. and by Indenture dated the 7th of *March*, 4 *Jac.* I. conveyed it to *Richard* Cart. 4 Jac. I. *Speed* of Berkhamsted, and his Heirs, declaiming the Use ibid. of himself and the Heirs of his Body, and for Default of such Issue to the Use of Sir *Philip Cary* his Brother, and the Heirs of his Body, and for Want of such Issue, to the right Heirs of the said *Adolph* for ever; but this Sir *Adolph* dying without Heirs of his Body, this Mannor came to

Sir *Philip Carey* of Cadington in this County, Kt. who with Sir *Henry Carey* of Berkhamsted in this County, Kt. by Indenture dated the 20th of *May*, 9 *Jac.* I. granted this Cart. 9 Jac I. Mannor to ibid.

Sir *Thomas Egerton*, Kt. Lord Elesmere, Lord Chancellor of England, and Sir *John Egerton*, Kt. Son and Heir apparent of the said Lord Elesmere, to the Use of the said Lord Elesmere, and Sir *John Egerton*, and the Heirs of the Body of the said Lord Elesmere, and for Default of such Issue, to the right Heirs of the said Lord Elesmere for ever, with a Covenant that the said Sir *Henry Carey* and his Wife should levy a Fine of this Mannor to the Use of this Deed.

From which Lord Elesmere this Mannor came to

The right Honourable *John* Earl of Bridgewater, who is the true Descendant of that noble Family, and the present Lord hereof.

The Mannor of SOUTHAL

IS another Lordship in the same Parish, which was heretofore Parcel, of the Possessions of the Family of the *Clerks*, and *Anno* 13 *Jac.* I. *Henry Clerk* the elder was Cart. 13 Jac. Lord hereof, he conveyed it to II. ibid.

Henry Clerk of Tring, and *Elizabeth* his Wife, who by their Indenture dated the 16th Day of *October*, 14 *Car.* I. Cart. 14 Car. granted the same to I. ibid.

Henry Lake of Buckland in the County of Bucks, and to his Heirs and Assignes for ever, who by Indenture dated the 20th of *May*, 1658, granted this Mannor to

John Halsey of Gaddesden, Esq. and *Thomas Bamptford* of Asheridge, Gent. and their Heirs; they by their Indenture dated the 4th Day of *October*, 16 *Car.* II. granted it. Cart. 16 Car.

To the Right Honourable *John* Earl of Bridgewater, from II. ibid. whence it came to *John* Earl of Bridgewater, who was his Son, and is now the present Lord hereof.

THIS Rectory is appropriated to the perpetual Use of *John Halsey,* Esq. and it lyes in the Deanery of **Berkhamsted,** in the Diocess of **Lincoln,** and *Anno* 26 *Henry* VIII. this Vicaridge was valued in the King's Books at the yearly Rate of 10*l.* 1*s.* 10*d.* and *John Halsey,* Esq. is Patron hereof.

This Church is situated about the Middle of this Vill, and is cover'd with Lead, having a square Tower annexed to the West End thereof, wherein are four Bells, and a short Spire erected upon it.

A glorious Monument of white Marble erected on the South Side near the East Window in the Chancel, in Memory of Sir *John Halsey,* bearing the lively Portraiture of his Person on the Top, and hath this Inscription.

H. S. E.
Johannes Halsey, *Eq. Aur.*
Vir miri Candoris et multiplicis Scientiæ.
Nec minoris Modestiæ
In Quo
Religio Literæ, et Virtutes,
Tanquam in Collegio sororiantes coaluêre
Præside vel ipsâ Juris prudentiâ
Quippe

Quum **Oxoniæ** *Juventam expolierit*   *Quum ex Hospitio* **Lincoln:** *Jura* *Societate et Sanguine* Wiccha-   *percalluere Spectatæ Probitatis* micus.   *et Peritiæ I C:*

Æquitatem denuò excoluit Cancellariæ Magister,
Bono publico magis quàm sibi Notus.
Denatus est Anno { *Æræ Christianæ* 1670
                { *Ætatis suæ L V.*
Ite Viri
Habetis vel abhinc quo amissam Lugeatis
Boni Justitiam et Egeni Charitatem.
Sed
Immortale sui desiderium reliquit
Qua Maritus qua Pater.

Underneath a fair Marble Stone with the Coat of Arms proper to the Family covering the Body, with this Inscription.

Johannes Halsey *Miles.*
Obiit xxix. *Junii*
Anno Domini MDCLXX.
Ætat. L V.

A comely Marble Monument on the East End of the Chancel, next the Window on the right Hand, fixed in the Wall, with this Inscription.

Judithæ Halsey
Uxori Johannis merito Charissimæ
Filias inter et Cohæred. Jacobi Necton, *Arm. natu max.*
Post Filios quinq; juxta hic reconditos.
Anno Ætat. xxxi. *Conjugis* xvi.
In Puerperio xi. *febre vihiculo in Patriam redeunti*
Aprilis xxv. MDCLVIII.
Epibaterium.
Cui fas sic Accinere
       { *Fam. Christianâ Charitatem*
In { *Matre familiâs Prudentiam*
       { *Conjuge Suavitatem*
Majorem (absit Invidia) voveat forte an Quisquam
Experietur Nemo
Ista sciens Præsens avum Credensq. futurum
Beatam utrumq; prædicet.

On the Floor underneath a fair Marble covering her Body with the Coat of Arms, and the Inscription thus.

Judith Halsey
Wife of *John Halsey,* Esq;
April xxv. MDCLVIII.

On the North Side of the Chancel a fair Marble with a Coat of Arms, and this Inscription.

Necton Halsey, *Armiger*
Fil. Joh: Halsey, *Mil.*
Sextus
Maximus Tamen Natu
Obiit xii. *Dec.*
Anno Domini MDCLXX.
Ætat. Plus quam
XIX.

On the same Side a comely Marble Monument fixed in the Wall, with this Inscription.

P M S

Hic	*Hi*
Communi Pulveris Lecto	*Primogenitum Filium Lugerunt*
Requiescunt Conjuges notæ fidei	Robertum
Gulielmus *et* ⎱ Halsey.	*Ætat.* 21. *præreptum*
Læticea. ⎰	*Filiam unicam reliquerunt*
Utriusq; Voto juxta positi Occubue-	Dorotheam
runt circiter sexagenarii	Georg. Franklin, *Ar. Nuptam*
Ille Novem. 27. *An.* 1637.	*Filiumq; unicum et Hæredem*
Hæc Junii 23. *An.* 1649.	Johannem
Ambo desideratissimi.	*Qui Hæc Mærens posuit.*

Anno Salut. MDCL
Lector ab hinc æternitatem cogita.

At the Lower End of the Chancel, going into the Church, a handsome Marble, covering the Body, with this Inscription.

Here lyeth the Body of *Lætitia Halsey* second Daughter of Sr. *John Halsey,* Kt. Decd. who dyed the 26. Day of *December* MDCLXXIX. in the 30. Year of her Age.

Near the Middle on the Chancel Floor lies a fair Marble covering the Body, with the Coat of Arms, underneath this Inscription.

M. S.
Spe Resurgendi
Hic jacet
Christopherus Abdy, *Armiger.*
Christopherus Abdy *de* Uxbridge.
Equitis Aurati, Filius
Qui
Aug. xxi. *An. Sal.* MDCLXIV.
Ætat. suæ xxxi
Corpus Telluri Animam Deo reddidit
Cui
Mæstissima Uxor Dorothea
Johannes Halsey, *Armigeri,*
Filia natu maximâ
Hoc
Amoris pariter sui ac Doloris
Monumentum
D. D.

Adjacent to a fair Marble as aforesaid, with Coat of Arms, and beneath inscribed thus.

M. S.

Here lyeth the Body of *Dorothy Abdy* eldest Daughter of Sr. *John Halsey* of Great *Gaddesden,* Kt. 21. Years and upwards the faithful Widow of *Christopher Abdy,* Esq; Son and Heir of *Christoph. Abdy* of *Uxbridge,* Kt. a true example of Piety, Charity, and Chastity, dyed 16 *April, An. Salutis* MDCLXXXVI. *Ætatis suæ* XLI. *Eximiis braris est ætas et rara senectus.*

Hund. of
Dacorum.

At the lower End of the Church on the North Side Wall, a decent
Marble is fixed with this Inscription

Here lieth *Stephen Munn* born in this Parish, bred up in the Parsonage
house in the place of a Cook, where he lived all this time a Pattern of
a most faithful and desired Servant, and there dying he divided the
£100. *Goods that God had given him, equally betwen the Vicar and the
Poor of this Parish to continue for ever. And now expects that joyful
Eloge.

Euge bone serve et fidelis.
He died Aged 51. 1656.

There are besides two Marble Stones, very large, with Inscriptions there-
on; but by their long date are much worn and made dim, that I can give no
perfect Account.

In the Middle Isle towards the West End there's a fair Marble plain
on the Floor, with this Inscription.

Depositum
Thomæ Wells
Filii natu maximi Thomæ Wells *nuper*
Parochiæ hujus, Generosi, In Uxorem duxit Aliciam *Residuam* Roberti
Baldwin *nuper de* Chesham *in Comitatu* Buckingens. *Generosi, qui e vi-*
vis excessit nono die October, Anno Dom. 1605.
Ætatis suæ 59.

Acts of CHARITY.

Sir *John Halsey* gave to the Vicar of this Parish Church, by his last
Will and Testament, a considerable Portion of the great Tythes for the
Augmentatioh of his Revenue.
Also he gave 20*l.* to be lent to poor Tradesmen of this Parish by 5*l.* a
piece, for their Help and Encouragement, giving Security for the Principal, without payment of any Interest, to continue as their Occasion
requires.
Mrs. *Lettice Halsey*, second Daughter of Sir *John Halsey*, gave 20*l.* to
be lent to poor Tradesmen of this Parish, in the manner as aforesaid.
Mrs. *Dorothy Abdy*, the eldest Daughter of Sir *John Halsey*, gave 20*s.*
to be distributed every Year at Christmas for her Life, among eight
poor old Widows of this Parish, and at her Death she continued the
payment of the same Annuity for ever.
Stephen Munne gave all his Goods, which were valued at 100*l.* to be
divided equally between the Vicar, and the Poor of this Parish.

STUDHAM.

The Mannor of BARWITH.

IS Parcel of the Vill of Studham, scituated about three
Miles Distance from Great Gadesden towards the North in
the County of Bucks, whereof this Mannor lies in the
County of Hertford, and anciently belonged to the Crown,
Mon. Angl. till such time that King *H.* I. gave it to the Church or
vol. 1.
Camd. Brit. Priory of Dunstable, which he founded by the Authority
Cattieuchlam, of Pope *Eugenius* the third, where he placed regular Can-
Bedforda. fol.
402. nons, and it continued in that Church till the Dissolution
Stow's Annals, thereof, when it came to the Crown.
fol. 136.
    In the time of Queen *Elizabeth* it was in the Possession
of *Will. Belfeild*, Citizen of London, who marryed the
Daughter of *Pigot* in *Com.* Cambridge, by whom he had
Issue,

William Belfeild, who was his Heir, and married *Effam*
Daughter to ——— *Morley*, by whom he had Issue, *John*,
Frances married to *James Ward*, *Dorothy* to *Richard Lo-
vet*, *Elizabeth* to ——— *Web*, *Ellen* to *Edward Brocket*,
Mary to *John Alway* of 𝔖𝔱𝔯𝔢𝔱𝔩𝔶 in 𝔅𝔢𝔡𝔣𝔬𝔯𝔡𝔰𝔥𝔦𝔯𝔢, *Margaret*
to *John Squire* of 𝔅𝔞𝔩𝔡𝔬𝔠𝔨, *Amy* to ——— *Rochford* of
𝔅𝔞𝔩𝔡𝔬𝔠𝔨, and *Alice* to *Tho. Bugg.*

John succeeded his Father in this Mannor, and married
Elizabeth Daughter of *Richard Para* of 𝔊𝔯𝔢𝔞𝔱 𝔊𝔞𝔡𝔢𝔰𝔡𝔢𝔫,
by whom he had Issue, *William*, *Richard*, *Ann* wedded to
George Wingate, *Jane*, *Mary*, and *Elizabeth*.

This *William* married ——— Daughter of ——— by
whom he had Issue *Henry Belfeild*, who is the present
Possessor hereof.

KENSWORTH.

THIS Vill was denominated in all Probability from some
Possessor hereof, whose Habitation was here. 'Tis scituated about a Mile distant from 𝔖𝔱𝔲𝔡𝔥𝔞𝔪 towards the East,
belongeth to the Church of *St. Paul*, 𝔏𝔬𝔫𝔡𝔬𝔫, and King
Edward the Confessor was Lord hereof, and gave it to the
same Church, which Church held it in the time of the Conquest, as appears by *Domesdei Book*, where 'tis recorded
that

*In 𝔅𝔞𝔫𝔞𝔦𝔰 Hundred. Canonici 𝔏𝔲𝔫𝔡𝔬𝔫𝔦𝔢𝔫𝔰𝔦𝔰 tenuerunt 𝔎𝔞𝔫𝔢𝔰𝔴𝔬𝔯𝔡𝔢 pro
decem hidis se defendebat. Terra est decem Carucat. in dominio quinq;
hidæ, et ibi sunt duo car. et adhuc tres possunt fieri, ibi octo Vill. cum tribus
Bordis habentibus duo car. et adhuc tres possunt fieri, ibi quatuor Servi,
pastura ad pec. Silva centum porc. et de reddita Silvæ duo sol. in totis
valentiis valent septuagint. sol. Quando recepit centum sol. et consuetudine
tempore regis Edwardi. Hoc Manerium tenuit Lewinus Cilt de Rege Edwardo.*

The Cannons of 𝔏𝔬𝔫𝔡𝔬𝔫 held 𝔎𝔢𝔫𝔰𝔴𝔬𝔯𝔱𝔥 in 𝔅𝔞𝔫𝔞𝔦𝔰 Hundred, it was
rated for ten Hides. The arable is ten Carucates, in Demeasne five
Hides, and there are two Carucates, and now three more may be made,
there are eight Villains with three Bordars having two Carucates, and
now three others may be made, there are four Servants, Common of
Pasture for the Cattle, Wood to feed an hundred Hogs in Pannage time,
and for the Rent of the Wood two Shillings a Year; in the whole Value
it is worth seventy Shillings, when he received it an hundred Shillings,
and Rent in the time of King *Edward* (the Confessor;) *Lewin Cilt* held
this Mannor of King *Edward* (the Confessor.)

The Dean of *St. Paul*, in 𝔏𝔬𝔫𝔡𝔬𝔫, *Anno 6 Edward I.*
held in 𝔎𝔞𝔱𝔦𝔫𝔤𝔡𝔬𝔫, and 𝔎𝔢𝔫𝔰𝔴𝔬𝔯𝔱𝔥, the Jurisdiction of
Court-Leet, and View of Franc-Pledge, and Gallowes,
Tumbrel, and Assize of Bread and Ale.

*Quo Warr. 6
Ed. I. Rot.56,
cur. recept.
Scac.*

Since which time the Dean and Chapter of that Church,
have been possest of this Mannor, and have from time to time
held Courts here, where there is a Custom that every Tenant upon Admission to his Coppihold, pays as well, upon
Descent as Purchase, a Fine certain of one Penny and no

Hund. of
Bacorum.

more, tho' the Value of the Land be great or small; and there is the like Custom for a Relief for their free Lands.

THIS Rectory is appropriated to the perpetual Use of the Dean and Chapter of St. *Paul's,* London; and lyes in the Deanery of Berkhamsted, in the Diocess of Lincoln, and this Vicaridge *Anno 26 Henry* VIII. was rated in the King's Books at the yearly Value of 9*l.* 13*s.* 4*d.* and the Dean and Chapter of St. *Paul's,* London, are the Patrons hereof.

CADINGDONE

Dugd. of St Paul, fol. 4, 18, 19 4.
Mon. Angl vol. 3, fol. 307.

IS a Mile distant from Kensworth North East, which Mannor King *Athelstan* gave among others to the Cannons of the Church of St. Paul, London, takes its Name from the Hill or Down on which 'tis scituated, and when William the Conqueror made that memorable Survey of *Domesdei,* it was recorded that

Domesd. Lib. fol. 136, n 83.

In Banais *Hundred. Canonici* Lundoniensis *tenuerunt* Cavendone *pro decem hidis se defendebat. Terra est decem car. in dominio quatuor hidæ, et ibi est una car. et adhuc tres possunt ee. ibi vigint. et duo Vill. habentes sex car. ibi quinque Bord. et duo Servi, pastura ad pec. Silva centum porcis, et duo solid. in totis valent. valet centum et decem sol. quando recepit sex lib. et consuetud. tempore Regis Edwardi. Hoc Maner. tenuit* Leuinus *de Rege Edwardi.*

The Cannons of London held Cavendon in Banais Hundred, it was rated for ten Hides. The arable is ten Carucates, in Demeasne four Hides, and there is one Carucate, and now three more may be made, there are two and twenty Villains having six Carucates, there are five Bordars, and two Servants, Common of Pasture for the Cattle, Wood to feed an hundred Hogs in Pannage time, and two Shillings Rent by the Year; in the whole Value it is worth one hundred and ten Shillings by the time when he received it six Pounds, and Rent in the time of King *Edward* (the Confessor,) *Lewine Cilt* held this Mannor of King *Edward* (the Confessor.)

Plac. 8 Johan. Rot. 11, in dorso recept. Scac.

'Twas agreed betwen *Roger de Tony, William, Thomas,* and *Richard* Archdeacon of Essex, *Robert* the Clerk, *Roger, Robert* the Son of *Roger, Abel* the Son of *Edwic, Robert Forestar, William* the Son of *William,* and *Baldwin Pulein,* touching the Common of Pasture between Katendon and Flamsted, to wit, that all the Wood which is between Wikesland to Bebeford shall remain to the Treasurer and Cannons of St. *Paul,* and all the Plain that is out of that Wood towards the North, shall remain to *Roger,* and from Bebeford to Papiate, all the Wood remaining to the Cannons of St. *Paul* according to the Bounds set there, and the Residue of the Wood, with the Plane towards the North, shall remain to *Roger,* according to the said Bounds, &c. yet neither Party shall cut off *Walter de Luton,* for that he came and claimed Common in the Portion of either Part.

Quo Warr. 6 Ed. 1. Rot. 59, in dorso recept Scac.

The Dean of St. *Paul's* Church in London held Jurisdiction here of a Court of View of Franc-pledge in Katen.

ɗon and **Kensworth**, and had all things belonging to it, and had Gallows, Tumbrel, and Assize of Bread and Ale, &c.

Hund. of Bacorum.

Since which time the Dean and Chapter of that Church have been Lords of this Mannor, and have continually held Court Leetes, and View of Franc-pledge, and Court Barons there, and have enjoyed the Profits hereof to this Day; and you may read the Priviledges which several Kings have granted to the Church of *Pauls* in this Mannor, in the Parish of **Ardleage**.

The Priory of ST. TRINITY in the WOOD.

NEAR **Merkgat**, *Geoffrey*, Abbot of **St. Albans**, built the Church of the *Holy Trinity* of the **Wood**, and the other Buildings, twice from the Foundation, at the Costs and Charges of that Church, and granted without the Consent of the Convent, all their Tyths of **Caisho**, and two Parts of their Tyth Corn of all the Parish of **Watford** to the same Church.

Mon. Angl. vol. 1, fol. 350

Ralph, the Dean and Chapter of *St. Paul*, **London**, in the Year of our Lord 1145, granted of their Charity for ever, all that their Ground and Scite whereon their Monastery of the *Holy Trinity* is built, in their Territory of **Cadendone**, as the Ditch contained, and the Wood which was between the Ditch and **Watlingstreet**, otherwise **Watlingstreet**, which contained in Length three Roods and thirty Perches, to *Christina* and her Successors, in the said Monastery, so that every Year she should pay three Shillings to the Chapter of *St. Paul*, for the Acknowledgement of the Ground; but the Wood should remain undestroyed for the Benefit of the Monastery; and that whosoever should succeed her, should be chosen by the Nuns residing there, and ordained by the said Chapter, that she and the succeeding Prioress should swear Fealty to the Chapter for their Tenure, and also that the then Nuns should swear Fealty to the Chapter, and that they should not receive any succeeding Prioress without the said Oath of Fealty to the said Chapter, and that the succeeding Nuns should be sworn to their Prioress in their Chapter.

Ibid vol. 2, fol. 872.

*The Petition of three poor Nuns of **Mergate**.*

**We three pore Nuns of Mergate
Pytiously compleyneth to your gud estate
Of one Sr John of Whipesuade,
Who hath stopped our watergate.
Wlyth too stons and a stake
Helpe us Lord for Christ his sake.**

Wlav. Fun. Mon. fol 583.

But upon the Dissolution of small Monasteries, this Priory came to the Crown.

FLAMSTED.

THIS Vill is seated upon an Hill, about two Miles distant towards the South from **Cadington**, and was anciently termed **Verlamsted** from the River **Verlam** which riseth here; and the Word *Verlamsted* proving tedious in Pronunciation, was by Contraction called **Flamsted**; but others hold it was denominated from a Seat which the Flamines held in the time of the *Britains*, a common Name given to all the Priests in the Roman Cities; and the *Flamen Divorum omnium* was the Chief Priest among them; they were called Flamines from a Thred or String (as *Varo* saith) with which they bound their Heads, some Pileamines from a Cap they wore; and from sacrificing they were termed Priests; and every one of them performed the proper Offices and Duties that belonged to their particular Gods; at first they were only three. 1. *Jupiter* had his *Flamen Dialis*. 2. *Mars* his *Flamen Martialis*. 3. *Romulus* his *Flamen Quirinalis*; and afterwards every God had his *Flamen*. But to proceed to this Vill: *Leofstane* the Abbot of **St. Albans,** gave this Mannor unto three Knights, *Turnot, Waldese,* and *Turman*, to defend and secure this Country against Thieves in the time of King *Edward* the Confessor.

But when *William* the Conqueror had subdued this Realm, he took it from them and gave it to *Roger de Todeny* or *Torry*, a noble *Norman* (saith *Camden,*) others say to *Ralph de Tony*, who was the Son of *Roger* and Standard Bearer to *William* the Conqueror in that great Battle against *Harold* whereby he obtained the Crown of this Realm, as appears by *Domesdei*, where 'tis recorded under the Title of *Terra Radulfi Todeni.*

Stilling f. An.
of the British
Churches,
fol. 79
Sam's Antiq.
of Brit. fol.
264.

In **Danais** *Hundred.* Radulphus de Todeny *tenuit* **Flamstede** *pro quatuor hidis se defendebat tempore Regis* Edwardi, *et modo pro duabus. Terra est duodecem car. in dominio duo hidæ, et ibi sunt duo car. et viginti et duo Vill. habentes octo car. et adhuc duo possunt ee. ibi septem cotarii; et quatuor Servi. Silva mille porcis, in totis valentiis undecem lib. tempore regis* Edwardi *duodecem lib. Hoc Manerium tenuit* Achi Teignus *Regis* Edwardi.

Ralph de Todeny held **Flamsted** in **Danais** Hundred, it was rated for four Hides in the time of King *Edward* (the Confessor) and now for two Hides. The arable is twelve Carucates in Demeasne two Hides, and there are two Carucates, and two and twenty Villains having eight Carucates, and now two others may be made, there are seven Cottagers, and four Servants, Wood to feed a thousand Hogs in Pannage time; in the whole Value it is worth eleven Pounds by the Year, when he received it nine Pounds, and in the time of King *Edward* (the Confessor) twelve Pounds, *Achina* a Thane of King *Edward* (the Confessor) held this Mannor.

This *Ralph de Todeny* did afterwards make this Place his chief Residence, and married *Elizabeth*, or as others say, *Isabel* the Daughter of *Simon de Montford*, by whom he had

Issue *Roger*, who died in the Life-time of his Father, *Ralph* who succeeded him, and *Godechild*, first married to *Robert* Earl of **Mellent** and afterwards to *Baldwin* Son of *Eustace* Earl of **Bolein**; and he died the 9th *Kal. Apr. An.* 1102, 2 *H.* I. and was buried with his Ancestors in the Abby of **Conches** in **Normandy**.

Hund. of **Dacorum**.

Dugd. Bar. vol. 1, fol. 469.

This *Ralph* married *Judith* one of the Daughters of *Walthe* Earl of **Huntingdon** and **Northumberland**, by whom he had Issue *Roger* and *Hugh*, and divers Daughters, then died

W. Gemet, fol. 312. Ord. *Vit.* fol. 813.

Roger, was his Heir, married the Daughter of the Earl of **Henault**, and died *Anno* 1162, 8 *H.* II. leaving Issue only

Dugd. Bar. vol. 1, fol. 470.

Roger, who was very young at the time of his Father's Death, whom the Jury found *Pas.* 7 & 8 of King *John*, that he despoiled *William de Ely*, *Robert de Alfay*, and others, of the Common of Pasture belonging to his Free Tenants of **Flamsted**.

Fin. 7 & 8 Joh.

Bar. vol. 1.

Ralph succeeded, who was in Armes against King *John*, with the Rest of the rebellious Barons of that time, for which in the 18th of his Reign that King granted unto *Walleray Teys*, this Mannor of **Flamsted** towards the Charge of defending the Castle of **Berkhamsted**; but it seems that in the time of *H.* III. he was received into Favour among the other Barons; and being signed with the Cross, among divers other Nobles in the Year 1239, 23 *H.* III. he took a Journey to the Holy Land, and about *Michaelmas* following, died on the Sea; and the Wardship of

Claus. 18 J. m. 2.

Matt. Paris, fol 489. Pat. 23 H. III. m. 7.

Roger his Son and Heir by Reason of his Minority, was granted to *Humphry de Bohun* Earl of **Essex** and **Hereford**, adhered firmly to the King *Anno* 48 *H.* III. when the rebellious Barons gave him Battle at **Lewis**, and took him Prisoner, for which they seized his Castle at **Kirthling**, and committed it to the Custody of *Henry de Hastings*, one of the most active Men of their Party; and died 5 *Edw.* I. leaving

Esc. 5 Ed. I. n. 30.

Ralph his Son and Heir, twenty two Years of Age, who claimed upon a *Quo Warranto*, brought *Anno* 6 *Edw.* I. in this his Mannor of **Flamsted**, View of Franc-pledge, Correction of the Assize of Bread and Ale, Infangtheife and Gallowes, Free-warren, Easement from Suites, &c. in the County, and from all Pleas and Plaints which belonged to the Sheriff in the Hundred Court, and from the Plea of Murder and Theft, and they were allowed. He was in that Expedition made into **Gascoin**, *Anno* 22 *Edw.* I and died there, for which good Service his Executors obtained all the Profits of his Lands from the time of his Death until they were seized into the King's Hands; and he left Issue

Quo Warr. 6 Ed. 1. Rot. 36, cur. recept. in Scac.

Rot. Vasc. 22 Ed. I. m. 1. Rot. Fin. 21 Ed. I. m. 6. Claus. 25 Ed. I. m. 11.

Robert his Son and Heir, who did his Homage had Livery of his Inheritance *Anno* 25 *Edw.* I. and was the same Year in that Expedition made into **Gascoin**, and that of

Rot. Vasc. 25 Ed. I. m. 5. Rot. Scac. 26 Ed. I. m. 7.

Hund. of Barorum.

Rot. Cart. 27 Ed. I. n. 13.

Esc. 3 Ed. II. n. 33.

Dugd. *Bar.* vol 1, fol 471.
Rot. J. Rous.
Dugd *Bar.*
vol. 1, fol. 231.

Ibid.

Ibid. fol 232.

Esc. 43 Ed. III. n. 19.

Esc. 32 Ed. III n. 27.
Esc. 43 Ed. III
Claus. 44 Ed. III. m. 21.

T. Walsingh. fol. 243, n 30.

Ibid. fol. 304.

Cons. de anno 17 R. II. penes Archer.

Scotland made the Year following; he obtained a Charter from the King for a weekly Market on every *Thursday* in this Mannor, dated the 27 *Edw*, I. and a Fair yearly on the Eve, Day, and Morrow after the Feast of *St. Leonard*, and five Days following; and he died seiz'd of this Mannor without Issue, 3 *Edw*. II. and

Alice the Widow of *Thomas Leyborn* was found to be his Sister and Heir, and at that time twenty six Years of Age, who soon after married *Guy de Beauchamp* Earl of **Warwick**, by whom he had Issue *Thomas* who succeeded his Father in his Honour, and *John* a martial Knight; and *Maud* married to *Geoffry* Lord *Say; Emme* to *Rowland Odingsells; Isabel* to ——— *Clinton; Elizabeth* to *Thomas* Lord *Asteley;* and *Lucia* to *Robert de Napton.*

Thomas succeeded, and was very young at the time of his Father's Death, but when he arrived at the Years of Action, he gave large Testimonies of his great Courage and Valour, for he was seldom out of some great and memorable Employment; and in the War near **Calice** fell sick of the Pestilence, and died the 13 *Nov. Anno* 43 *Edw.* III. leaving divers Children, *Guy, Thomas, Reynburn, William,* and *Roger,* and nine Daughters.

Guy his eldest Son received the Honour of Knighthood, in 29 *Edw.* III. married *Philippa* Daughter to *Henry* Lord *Ferrers* of **Trey**, and had Issue *Katharine, Elizabeth,* and *Margaret.* He was a stout Soldier, but in 32 *Edw.* III. died at **Vendosme** in **France**, and leaving *Katharine* and *Elizabeth* his Heirs, but his Father surviving

Thomas the second Son succeeded, being then 24 Years of Age, did his Homage and had Livery of his Lands; he was also a great Souldier, and the Commons in Parliament chose him, being a Man most just and prudent, *Anno* 3 *R.* II. Governour of the King, who was then very young; but before he arrived to Man's Estate he took the Reigns of Government into his own Hands, or suffered them to be guided by those Favorites, whose Miscarriages were the Cause of his Ruin; and about a Year following, the King assembling his Nobles, told them he was now of Age to govern himself and the Kingdom, and changed some of his great Officers whereof this Earl was one, who thenceforth retiring himself built that strong and stately Tower standing in the North-end corner of *Warwick Castle,* which cost 395*l.* 5*s.* 2*d.* and the whole Body of the Collegiate Church in **Warwick**; But from that time he could never regain the King's Favour; for afterwards the King inviting him to a Feast, who suspecting no Danger came thither, but soon found it otherwise, for there he was arrested and carried away Prisoner; and putting himself upon the Parliament for Justice, had Judgment of Death passed upon him; which hard Sentence, the King

at the Instance of the Earl of 𝕾𝖆𝖑𝖎𝖘𝖇𝖚𝖗𝖕 suspended, and
instead thereof he was banish'd to the 𝕴𝖘𝖑𝖊 𝖔𝖋 𝕸𝖆𝖓, and
the King gave his Castle and Mannor of 𝖂𝖆𝖗𝖜𝖎𝖈𝖐, and
divers of his Mannors and Lordships unto *Thomas Holland*,
Earl of 𝕶𝖊𝖓𝖙, and to the Heirs Males of his Body, but in
1 *H*. IV. all that had been in the Parliament of 21 *R*. II.
was made void, and this Earl *Thomas* was then restored to
his full Liberty, Honour, and Possessions, and he died on 8th
April, 1401, 2 *H*. IV. leaving Issue *Richard*, and was buried in the South Part of the Collegiate Church at 𝖂𝖆𝖗𝖜𝖎𝖈𝖐, under a fair Monument of Marble, with *Margaret* his
Wife, Daughter to *William* Lord *Ferrers* of 𝕲𝖗𝖔𝖇𝖞, who
also died 22 *Jan*. 1406, 6 *H*. IV.

Earl *Richard* her Son being then 25 Years of Age, was
made Knight of the Bath at the Coronation of King *H*. IV.
did his Homage, and had Livery of his Lands; the fourth
Year of the same King he gave Evidence of his Valour
against that great Rebel *Owen Glendours*, whose Banner he
took, put him to Flight; performed the like Service against
the *Percies* in that memorable Battle of 𝕾𝖍𝖗𝖊𝖜𝖘𝖇𝖚𝖗𝖞, and
soon after was made Knight of the most noble Order of the
Garter; he was in great Esteem with King *H*. V. at whose
Coronation he was constituted High Steward of 𝕰𝖓𝖌𝖑𝖆𝖓𝖉
for that Solemnity; and made a Commissioner to treat
with others from the King of 𝕱𝖗𝖆𝖓𝖈𝖊, touching a firm
Peace between both Crowns, and a Marriage betwixt
King *Henry* and *Katharine* Daughter to the King of
𝕱𝖗𝖆𝖓𝖈𝖊, for the better Security thereof. When King *H*.
V. died, he appointed by his Will, that this Earl should
have the Government of his Son, then an Infant, until
the 16th Year of his Age, and the Parliament approv'd
thereof; in 9 *H*.VI. he founded that Chantry of *Guy's* Cliff
in that very Place whereunto the famous *Guy* of 𝖂𝖆𝖗𝖜𝖎𝖈𝖐,
after his many renowned Exploits, retired and led an Hermit's Life; and before this Foundation a small Chappel and
a Cottage, whereon an Hermit dwelt only stayed there; to
which Chantry he gave the Mannor of 𝕬𝖘𝖍𝖇𝖔𝖗𝖓 *in Com*.
𝖂𝖆𝖗𝖜𝖎𝖈𝖐, with one Messuage and one Carucate of Land,
and 5*l*. 17*s*. 10½*d*. yearly Rent, lying in 𝖂𝖍𝖎𝖙𝖓𝖆𝖑𝖍 and
𝖂𝖊𝖑𝖎𝖘𝖇𝖚𝖗𝖓, for the Maintenance of two Priests, who were
obliged daily to sing Mass in the Chappel for the good Estate of himself and his Wife during their Lives, and afterwards for the Health of their Souls, and the Souls of all
their Parents and Friends, and all the faithful deceased, and
he caused a large and goodly Statue of the famous *Guy* to
be placed there. He married *Elizabeth* Daughter and Heir
of *Thomas* Lord *Berkley*, by whom he had three Daughters,
Margaret born at 𝕲𝖔𝖔𝖉𝖗𝖊𝖘𝖙 in 𝖂𝖊𝖉𝖌𝖓𝖔𝖈𝖐-𝖕𝖆𝖗𝖐 near 𝖂𝖆𝖗𝖜𝖎𝖈𝖐, the next Year after the Battle of 𝕾𝖍𝖗𝖊𝖜𝖘𝖇𝖚𝖗𝖞, second

Hund. of
Dacorum.

Froissart, vol.
2, fol. 292.

Pat. 20 R. II.
p. 3, m. 8.
Rot. Pat. 1
H. VI. n. 112.

Esc. 2 H. IV.
n. 50.

Dugd. *Bar.*
vol. 1, fol.
245.

Pat. 1 H. V.
p. 1, m 36.

Pat. 9 H. VI.
p. 1, m. 23.

Ex Rot. J.
Rous.

Wife to the famous *John Talbot*, Earl of 𝔖𝔥𝔯𝔢𝔴𝔰𝔟𝔲𝔯𝔭; *Eleanor* born at 𝔚𝔞𝔩𝔨𝔦𝔫𝔰𝔱𝔬𝔫 in 𝔈𝔰𝔰𝔢𝔵, shortly after the Feast of our Ladies Nativity, 9 *H.* IV. first married to the Lord *Roos*, afterwards to *Edmond Beaufort*, Marquess of 𝔇𝔬𝔯𝔰𝔢𝔱 and Duke of 𝔖𝔬𝔪𝔢𝔯𝔰𝔢𝔱; and *Elizabeth* born in 𝔚𝔞𝔯𝔴𝔦𝔠𝔨-𝔠𝔞𝔰𝔱𝔩𝔢, Wife to *George Nevil*, Lord *Latimer*; and after the Decease of *Elizabeth*, he married *Isabel* Daughter of *Thomas le Spencer* Earl of 𝔊𝔩𝔬𝔠𝔢𝔰𝔱𝔢𝔯, who by the Death of her Brother *Richard* and elder Sister *Elizabeth*, without Issue, became Heir to all their Lands: He had Issue by her *Henry* and *Anne*, and died on the 29th of *April*, 1439, 17th of *H.*VI. at the Castle of 𝔔𝔬𝔞𝔫 in 𝔑𝔬𝔯-𝔪𝔞𝔫𝔡𝔭.

Henry at the time of his Father's Death, was about the Age of fourteen Years, and before he accomplish'd the Age of nineteen he tendred his Service for Defence of the Dutchy of 𝔄𝔮𝔲𝔦𝔱𝔞𝔦𝔫, in Consideration whereof, the King by his Charter dated 2d of *April*, 22 *Regni sui*, created him *premier* Earl of 𝔈𝔫𝔤𝔩𝔞𝔫𝔡, and for a Distinction between him and the other Earls, granted to him and the Heir Male of his Body, Leave to wear a golden Coronet about his Head, as well in his own Presence as elsewhere, upon great Festivals, when Coronets used to be worn, and within three Days following, in Consideration of the high Deserts of his noble Father, advanced him to the Title of Duke of 𝔚𝔞𝔯-𝔴𝔦𝔠𝔨, granting him Place in Parliament, and in all other Meetings next to the Duke of 𝔑𝔬𝔯𝔣𝔬𝔩𝔨, and before the Duke of 𝔅𝔲𝔠𝔨𝔦𝔫𝔤𝔥𝔞𝔪, and 40*l. per Annum*, to be paid by the Sheriff of 𝔚𝔞𝔯𝔴𝔦𝔠𝔨𝔰𝔥𝔦𝔯𝔢 and 𝔏𝔢𝔦𝔠𝔢𝔰𝔱𝔢𝔯𝔰𝔥𝔦𝔯𝔢, out of the Revenue of those Counties toward the better Support of that Honour; this done he granted further to him the Reversion of

Dugd. Bar.
vol. i. fol.
248.

the Isle of 𝔊𝔢𝔯𝔫𝔰𝔭, 𝔍𝔢𝔯𝔰𝔭, 𝔖𝔢𝔯𝔨, 𝔈𝔯𝔪, and 𝔥𝔞𝔯𝔢𝔟𝔢𝔭, after the Death of *Humphry* Duke of 𝔊𝔩𝔬𝔠𝔢𝔰𝔱𝔢𝔯, reserving the yearly Rent of a Rose to be paid at the Feast of the Nativity of St. *John* Baptist, the Mannor and Hundred of 𝔅𝔯𝔦𝔰𝔱𝔬𝔩 *in Com.* 𝔊𝔩𝔬𝔠𝔢𝔰𝔱𝔢𝔯, reserving the yearly Rent of 60*l.* and all the King's Castles and Mannors within the Forrest of 𝔇𝔢𝔞𝔫, reserving the Rent of 100*l. per Annum*. To all which Honours this was added, to be crowned King of the Isle of 𝔚𝔦𝔤𝔥𝔱 by the King's own Hand: he married *Cecilie* Daughter to *Richard Nevil*, Earl of 𝔖𝔞𝔩𝔦𝔰𝔟𝔲𝔯𝔭, by whom he had *Anne* his only Daughter, born at 𝔠𝔞𝔢𝔯𝔡𝔦𝔣𝔣𝔢, in the Month of *February*, 1439. But this hopeful Earl was cropt off in the Flower of his Youth, for he died at 𝔥𝔞𝔫𝔩𝔢𝔭 the Place of his Birth upon the Feast of St. *Barnabas*, being the 11th of *June*, 1445, 23 *H.*VI. when he was twenty two Years of Age, and was buried in the Abby of 𝔗𝔢𝔴𝔨𝔰-𝔟𝔲𝔯𝔭, about the Middle of the Quire, at the Head of Prince *Edward*, Son and Heir to King *Henry* VI. and committed

his Daughter to the Tutelage of Queen *Margaret*, and afterwards of *William de la Pool*, Duke of 𝔖𝔲𝔣𝔣𝔬𝔩𝔨, and she had the Title of Countess of 𝔚𝔞𝔯𝔴𝔦𝔠𝔨, but did not long survive, for the 3d of *January*, 1449, 27 *H.*VI. she died at 𝔑𝔢𝔴𝔢𝔩𝔦𝔫𝔢 in 𝔒𝔵𝔣𝔬𝔯𝔡𝔰𝔥𝔦𝔯𝔢, a Mannor of that Duke's, and was buried in the Abby of 𝔕𝔢𝔞𝔡𝔦𝔫𝔤, next to the Grave of *Constance* Lady *Dispenser*, her great Grandmother, Daughter to *Edmond* of 𝔏𝔞𝔫𝔤𝔩𝔢𝔶, Duke of 𝔜𝔬𝔯𝔨, whereupon

Anne her Aunt, Sister of the whole Blood to the late Duke of 𝔚𝔞𝔯𝔴𝔦𝔠𝔨, became Heir to this Earldom, then the Wife of *Richard Nevil* Earl of 𝔖𝔞𝔩𝔦𝔰𝔟𝔲𝔯𝔶, who by Reason of that Marriage, and his special Services about the King's Person, and in the Wars of 𝔖𝔠𝔬𝔱𝔩𝔞𝔫𝔡, obtained a Patent of the Dignity and Title of Earl of 𝔚𝔞𝔯𝔴𝔦𝔠𝔨, confirm'd and declared to him, and his Wife, and to her Heirs. Shortly after by Fine levied *Quin. Trin.* 28 *Hen.*VI. the Castle of 𝔚𝔞𝔯𝔴𝔦𝔠𝔨, with divers Lordships in that, and sixteen other Counties were intail'd upon the Issue of their two Bodies lawfully begotten, and in Default thereof, upon the Issue of her the said *Anne*, with Remainder to *Margaret* eldest Daughter to the same *Richard Beauchamp*, late Earl of 𝔚𝔞𝔯𝔴𝔦𝔠𝔨, and her Heirs. This is that *Richard Nevil* who was commonly called, the stout Earl of 𝔚𝔞𝔯𝔴𝔦𝔠𝔨, and an eminent Actor in those tragick Broiles between the Houses of 𝔏𝔞𝔫𝔠𝔞𝔰𝔱𝔢𝔯 and 𝔜𝔬𝔯𝔨; for he put himself in Arms with an Intent to advance *Richard* Duke of 𝔜𝔬𝔯𝔨 to the Crown, for which he and his Adherents were attainted of High-Treason at a Parliament held at 𝔈𝔬𝔟𝔢𝔫𝔱𝔯𝔶, *Anno* 38 *H.*VI. But after *Richard* Duke of 𝔜𝔬𝔯𝔨 was slain at 𝔚𝔞𝔨𝔢𝔣𝔦𝔢𝔩𝔡, 39 *H.* VI. this Earl with the Earl of 𝔐𝔞𝔯𝔰𝔥 escaped by Flight to 𝔏𝔬𝔫𝔡𝔬𝔫; they raised a mighty Power on the Behalf of *Edward* Duke of 𝔜𝔬𝔯𝔨, who took upon him the Title, and was proclaim'd King by the Name of *Edw.* IV. then hastned Northward against those Forces which King *Hen.* had raised there, and at 𝔗𝔞𝔲𝔫𝔱𝔬𝔫 obtained a mighty Victory. After which there was nothing of Honour, Authority, or Profit that he desired but King *Edward* granted, for that he had been the great Instrument to gain the Crown for him, therefore he was soon made Captain of 𝔈𝔞𝔩𝔞𝔦𝔰, the Tower of 𝔕𝔦𝔰𝔢𝔟𝔞𝔫𝔨, Lieutenant of the Marshes there, and Governour of the Castle of 𝔊𝔲𝔦𝔫𝔢𝔰, also General Warden of the East Marshes towards 𝔖𝔠𝔬𝔱𝔩𝔞𝔫𝔡, and Lord Great Chamberlain of 𝔈𝔫𝔤𝔩𝔞𝔫𝔡 for Life, and Constable of 𝔇𝔬𝔟𝔢𝔯-𝔠𝔞𝔰𝔱𝔩𝔢, and Lord High Steward of 𝔈𝔫𝔤𝔩𝔞𝔫𝔡.

But 'tis said by some, that after King *Edward* had obtained the Crown thro' the Power of this Earl, suspecting Danger by his Greatness, he endeavoured to lessen him all that he could, the Earl discerning it, he sought all Occasions to work the King's Ruin, but concealed the Effects

Hund. of
𝔅𝔞𝔠𝔬𝔯𝔲𝔪

Dugd. Bar.
vol. 1, fol.
304.

Hund. of
Dacorum. of his Discontents till the 7th of *Edw*. IV. when-being in *Warwickshire*, he sent for his Brothers *George Nevil*, Archbishop of *York*, and *John* Marquess *Mountague*, and communicated his Mind to them with divers Reasons for the Restoration of King *Henry*, and obliging them to him, he allured *George* Duke of *Clarence*, the King's Brother, by Reason of some Discontents which he had harbour'd ; and to fix him the firmer to him, gave him *Isabel* his eldest Daughter in Marriage 8. *Edw*. IV. in our Lady's Church at *Calais*, with Half the Lands of her Mother's Inheritance, and by their Assistance raised so great a Power, that in *October* he entred *London*, delivered King *Henry* out of the *Tower*, and set him again on his Throne, whereupon he was

Dugd. Bar.
vol. 1, fol.306. made Lord High Admiral of *England*. But within a Year after, King *Edward* landing here again, and encreasing his Strength very much, it so daunted the Duke of *Clarence*, that he made his Peace with him, and offered to do the like for this Earl his Father in Law, had not his Stomach been too great; so that then there was no other Way to determine the Matter, but by the Sword, and it was decided on *Easter* Day at *Barnet-field*, in which Battle this stout Earl lost his Life with many others, to a great Number; upon which the Bodies of him and the Marquess *Mountague* his Brother were brought to *London*, exposed to public View in *Pauls*, conveyed from thence to *Bysham* in *Com*. *Berks*. and interred in that Monastery with his Ancestors the *Mountacutes*, by whom it had been founded.

Rot. Parl. 14
Ed. IV. But after his Death his Countess was driven to great Want, for all her vast Inheritance was taken from her by Parliament, and settled upon *Isabel* and *Anne* her two Daughters and Heirs, the eldest married to *George* Duke of *Clarence*, the other to *Richard* Duke of *Gloucster*, as if she herself had been naturally dead, and was witheld from her till the third of *H*.VII. when both the Daughters being dead, that King procured a new Act of Parliament to repeal the former, and in Consideration of the true faithful Service and Allegiance which she had born to King *H*.VI. was restored to her Estate again, with Power to alien the same or any Part thereof; and by a special Feofment dated the 13th of *December*, and a Fine levied thereupon, she conveyed it to

The King, entailing it upon the Issue Male of his Body, with Remainder to herself and her Heirs, and among the Names of the particular Lordships contain'd in that Grant, this Mannor of *Flamsted* is express'd, which remain'd in the Crown till the 27th Year of *H*. VIII. about which time that King granted this Mannor to

George Ferrars and his Heirs, in whose Line it continued until it came to

Knighton Ferrars, who had Issue

Katharine, who was his sole Heir, and married *Thomas* Lord Viscount *Fanshaw* of **Drummore** in the Kingdom of **Ireland**: She joyn'd with him to convey it to

Edward Peck, Serjeant at Law, who had Issue *William,* who was his Son and Heir, and the present Possessor hereof.

This Mannor has Court Leet and Baron, consists of about six or seven hundred Acres of Demeasne, and divers Coppiholds, finable at the Will of the Lord, and upon the Demeasne is an ancient Farm House.

The Priory of ST. GILES in the WOOD.

ROGER de Tony founded a Religious House in this Parish, which was dedicated to *St. Gyles in the Wood,* and did consist of a Prioress and ten Nuns, to be ordered or visited by him and his Heirs, and were bound to pray for their Souls &c. and they were independent of any other Religious House or Order, and he endowed the same with large Demesnes. This Place was then called **Wood-church,** after *St. Gyles in the Wood,* and of late **Beach-wood** from the Abundance of Beach growing there, the Soil being very natural for that Plant, where it grows and thrives exceedingly. *Mon. Angl. vol. 1, fol. 545, n. 40. Dugd. Bar. vol. 1, fol. 470.*

By the Accession of new Grants of some of the Family of the *Tonies,* and of *Agatha* the Wife of *William* of **Gades-den,** who gave all the Land which she had in **Hamelam-estede,** and of *Isabel* Daughter of *Bernard* Son of *Nicholas,* who gave all the Lands to the said Priory which she had in the Vill of **Edelesbure,** and of others, the same became a Mannor of pretty large Extent, but coming to the Crown by the Statute of 27 *H.* VIII. of the Dissolution of the lesser Religious Houses, was granted by *H.* VIII. to Sir *Richard Page,* Kt. and his Heirs, then Lieutenant of the Band of Pensioners. *Mon. Angl. vol. 1, fol. 503.*

This Sir *Richard Page* had Issue only one Daughter, who inherited this Mannor, she married Sir ——— *Skipwith* of **Lincolnshire,** and soon after ——— *Skipwith* and his Wife conveyed the same to ——— *Saunders,* then resident at **Puttenham** in **Hertfordshire,** by the Marriage of the Daughter and Heir of ——— *Puttenham,* but formerly of the County of **Buckingham,** and the same is now come by Descent to *Thomas Saunders,* Esq. a Member of the Society of *Lincolns Inn,* who claims his Descent by his Grandmother from the *Coningsby's* of **Northmimmes,** and by his Great Grandmother from the *Botelers* of **Watton Wood-hall,** both ancient Families in the County of **Hertford,** and has made this Mannor an excellent Seat, and the Place of his Residence: But he died *An.* 1693, leaving Issue only *Anne* his Daughter and Heir, married to Sir *Edward Seabright,*

whose Ancestor was created Baronet, 20 *Dec.* **Anno** 1626, 2
Car. I. and is now in Right of his Wife the present Possessor hereof.

Upon enquiry into the Foundation of the said **Religious**
House of 𝔅eech𝔴oo𝔡, I received Information from the said
Mr. *Saunders* that he had the original Grant of the Foundation under the Hand of *Roger de Tony*, and all farther
Endowments thereof, and divers Grants of Priviledges from
several Popes by their Bulls to the Prioress and Nuns,
besides a fair Legier Book containing all Grants, &c. and
believes there is not wanting one Deed, Grant, or Patent
under Seal, or any Court Roll concerning the said Mannor
or Estate, from the time of the Conquest and first Foundation thereof, but he hath the same in his Custody; however
for same Reasons was unwilling to expose them to publick
View.

The RECTORY or PARSONAGE

OF this Parish is appropriated, and time out of mind was in the Crown,
and farm'd for some Term of Years, the Farmer usually hired a Curate to
officiate for such small Sallary as they could agree, sometimes 20*l. per
Annum*, seldom more until King *James* I. by Letters Patents dated ——
Regni sui granted the Reversion to *Morice* and *Philips*, Trustees, who
conveyed it to Mr. *Gunsly*, then present Incumbent *Anno* 1618, and the
Reversion (after the expiration of a Lease then in being from the Crown
for 42 Years) was devised in this manner, *viz.* Part of the Tyths to his
next Heir at Law, of whom the said *Thomas Saunders*, Esq. purchased
them; and the Rectory and the other Part of the Tyths to the Master
and Fellows of University Colledge in 𝔒rfor𝔡, and their Successors,
ordaining by his Will that for the future the Curate shall have 60*l. per
Annum* Sallary, and the Master and Fellows shall always appoint the Curate; the present Rector or Curate is *Edward Ferrars*, Senior Fellow of
the said Colledge, who receives the Sallary of 60*l.*

The Church is in the Deanery of 𝔅erk𝔥amste𝔡 in the Diocess of 𝔏incoln,
dedicated to the Honour of St. *Leonard*, and situated upon a Hill. *Anno*
26 *Henry* VIII. it was rated in the King's Books at the yearly Value of
41*l.* 6*s.* 8*d.* and this Church contains three fair Isles, the Roof of the
Church is covered with Lead, but the Chancel with Tyle, and to the
West End adjoyns a square Tower, wherein is a Ring of five Bells, and a
Shaft or Spire about twenty Foot high, erected upon the Tower cover'd
with Lead.

In the Chancel lay a Stone with this Inscription.

𝔥ic jacet Johannes Oundeley 𝔐ector istius 𝔈cclesiæ et 𝔡e Barugby Lincoln. 𝔇ioces. et 𝔆anon in 𝔈ccles. 𝔆ollrg. beatæ Mariæ 𝔡e Warwick, et
𝔆amerarius ex parte 𝔆omitatis War. in 𝔖cacario 𝔇omini 𝔐egis, qui
obiit 7 Maii 1414.
          𝔐isere miserator, quia bere sum peccator,
          𝔔u𝔡e precor licet reus miserrre mei 𝔇eus.

In the Wall at the East End of the Communion Table.

Here lies He dead deprived of Breath by Death
    Whose Fame shall out live death, *B. F.*
Here lieth the Body of Sir *Bartholomew Fouke*, Kt. who served King *Edward*, Queen *Mary*, and was Master of the Houshold to Queen *Elizabeth* for many years, and to King *James* that now is, in memory, of
whose vertuous life (worthy eternal Remembrance) *Edward Fouke*,
Gent. his Brother hath erected this Monument.
                        Obiit 19 Julii 1604. *Ætat. suæ* 69.

At the upper End of the Middle Isle lieth interred the Body of *George* *Cordal*, Esq; who served Queen *Elizabeth*, and was Serjeant of the Ewry to King *James* and the late King *Charles*, in all sixty years, who married *Dorothy* the only Daughter and Heir of *Francis Pryor* of this Parish, with whom he lived 57 years, and deceased the 25th of *May* 1653, he being aged 84 years.

Mortale quiescat.

Dom. Mariæ Luke *quæ filia quinta* Henrici Coningsby de ſ҉ipmms *Boreali Equitis Aurati, et* Eliz. *claræ Familiæ* Botelorum *de* ꏠ҉oothal *in Com.* ꜧertford, *Conjux olim fuit* Johannis Saunders *de* ꟷutternham, *Armig. (et ibid. sepulti) in dict. Com. Tandem* Johi. Luke *de* ꜰlamstev, *Milit. nupta et viduata conservit et obiit.*

Filius et Heres Tho. Saunders, *Armig. (juxta illam sepeliri cupiens) charissimæ, amantissima, et pientissimæ Matris.* L. M. P.

Emigravit 22 Augusti 1664 *Admodum chara Mors sanctorum in conspectu Domini.*

And of late there is erected in the Corner of the South Isle of this Church a very rich and stately Monument, all of pure Italian Marble of several hundred Pounds Value, with a large square before the same raised a Foot high, paved with black and white coarse Marble, railed in with an Iron Rail or Grate.

The Tomb is framed Altarwise, the lower Part of it most of Black Marble curiously wrought and polished with cringed Cherubs of white Marble on each Side.

On the Altar are five Images or Effigies of Children, kneeling, all of pure white Marble, and by the Side thereof, one other Image in a mournful posture kneeling and pointing to the other five.

By the Sides are two large Pillars of white Marble supporting an Arch above of curious wrought work fruitage, and other, and over the same the Coat of Arms of the Family of the *Saunders* carved and gilded in the mantling; he beareth *Party per Cheveron Sable* and *Argent, three Elephants Heads counterchanged*, with this Motto, *Magnis Amoris Amor*.

In the Middle over the Altar there is a very fair large flat Stone of white Marble polished, and encompass'd about with Stones of black Marble, and upon the white Stone in large fair black Capital Letters is this Inscription.

Thomas Saunders, *peccatorum maximus, credent, in unum Deum Divina sua providentia, terrena quæcunque gubernantem et sapientissima disponentem, et in Jesum Christum ejus Filium die ultimo futurum judicem. Cum ex* Helena *Filia et Hærede* Roberti Sadlier, *claræ et antiquæ in hoc agro Familiæ, sex liberos susceperit*

Thomam,	Johannem,
Robertum,	Annam *et*
Helenam,	Helenam.

Quorum quinq; ante parentes decesserunt, et Anna *tantum parvula superstes existit: In eorum piam memoriam, quibus nihil amplius dari possit, hoc Monumentum lugens posuit, spe certa confidens se futurum hæredem Regni cælorum et licet e corpore hæredem in terris non relinquet. hanc tamen Consolationem Assecutus Quodex se*
Additur Regno Cælorum.

Below the Altar on a large Stone of Black Marble, curiously mantled and finely wrought and polished, is this Inscription in Gold Letters.

Who so looketh hereon may consider how fleeting all worldly comforts are, and how great a vanity it is to place his affection thereon; such things there are as worldly comforts 'tis true; but they ought to be look'd on as little streams, and whoever delights in them more than in the Fountain from whence they proceed, may soon find them dry and vanished. The truth of which he that wrote this hath sensibly found, and wills others to place their affections chiefly on that object of love which is unchangable, and is the center of all true Joy and Felicity.

Under the Pedestal of the Altar the Images of five Children cut in Marble
are placed, and underneath them is wrote

Talium est Regnum Cælorum.

Without the Gate or Rail, and some good distance from the Tomb, lies
a Gravestone (under which there is said to be Stairs leading to a fair
Vault beneath the said Pavement) on which this Latine Distich is engraved.

Ipse tuos cineres si notis amice moveri
Post mortem, hunc vivus ne moveas Lapidem.

This Inscription on a Marble near the Passage into the Vault.

M. S. E.

Thomas Saunders *Filius natu maximus* Gulielmi Saunders *de Ledburn.
Generosi, Fratris* Thomæ Saunders *de Beechwood in hac Parochia Armigeri, Et* Abigalis *Uxoris ejus Filiæ* Thomæ Saunders de Habham *in
Com Bucks, Armig. Obiit* 15. Feb. *Anno Dom.* 1691. *Ætat. suæ undecimo. Indolis optimæac maximæ spei Luctus nunc, olim Deliciæ parentem,
Hic juxta reconditur* Gulielmus, *Vix Bimestris filius natu minor* Gulielmi *suprædicti.*

In this Isle is buried the Body of *Anne Poure,* 2d. Daughter to *Francis
Poure* of *Blechington* in the County of *Oxon.* Esq; and of *Anne* his
second Wife, the third Daughter to *Julius Ferrers* of *Market* in the
County of *Hertford,* Esq; who died the 13. day of *June* 1631. and in the
14th year of her age.
Poure, Rich was in the Spirit
Anne Poure, Rich *Poure* by Christs merit.

This Parish is of large Extent, containing six thousand
Acres, or more, of Land inclosed, the greatest Part thereof
lies upon high Ground with a Vale in the Middle, through
which runs a small Rivulet from a Place called Row Beech
in the Highway of Watlingstreet, and passes from thence
through the Midst of Flamsted near the said Road, and
sometimes crosseth the Road towards Redburne, and from
thence to St. Albans. The Air is clear and very wholesome, and the Place well wooded; especially that Part
thereof which lyeth on the South-side of the River, and
Watling-street leading to Dunstable, being the higher Hill,
on which Side is that ancient Religious House of *St. Gyles*
alias Beech-wood: near whereto was a Woman of late, one
Ann Prior, Widow, who lived to the Age of sixscore
Years compleat. Which, (upon some Controversie about a
Rate or Tax between the two Hundreds of Caisho and
Dacorum) Sir *Henry Blount* an Inhabitant of Caisho did
allege in a joking Way, "That therefore the Hundred of
Dacorum ought to pay somewhat more for their excellent
Air." To whom was reply'd, "That if Sir *Henry* would
take Care that the Distress upon Default of Payment should
be only taken in that Element so profitable to them only,
without touching upon any other, they were content."

There is a Tradition, that in the Infancy of *Edw.* VI.
he was removed thither by the Advice of his Physitians
for some time, and did reside in the said Religious House,
granted to Sir *Richard Page* as aforesaid. There are no

Remains of the old House, Cloysters, Chappel, &c. but the Mannor-house is a fair Brick House, of the Figure of a Roman H, wherein is yet Part of a curious wrought Bedstead inlaid, and Curtains of green Velvet richly embroidered, said to be the Repository of the said *Edw*. VI. and in some Windows of the House are the Arms of 𝔉rance and 𝔈ngland, quarter'd with a Label of three, said to be taken out of the Glass of the old religious House.

This Parish consists most of arable Land, being a Clay mixed with Flint, and in most Places, Chalk is to be found within a Fathom of the Superficies, in some Places within a Foot, but in other Places 'tis exceeding stony, insomuch that after any great Shower of Rain (by which that little Earth or Clay which is turned up by the Plow is washed below the Stones) not any thing appears, save as it were, a Heap of large rugged broken Flints, so as a Man cannot foul a Glove by rubbing on the said Soil in the dirtiest time of Winter, and yet very good Corn often grows on such Places in a dry Summer; and the Reason given for it is, because the Warmth of the Flint (having a Seed of Fire in it) preserves the Corn from the Cold in Winter, and the Closeness of the Body prevents the scorching and the parching Heat of the Sun in Summer (for those Grounds never chop nor crack) so as stringy Fibers of the Root reaching to the Clay below, fail not to send up Moisture to the Blade and Stalk.

'Tis said, that these stony Parts are never without Hares, but 'tis a very bad Place to course in; and 'tis affirmed, that their veriest Curs bred there, and used to those Grounds, will beat the best Grey-hounds brought from elsewhere.

And now I shall conclude the Division of this High Constable, and proceed to the next, which contains the Vills, Parishes, and Hamlets of 𝔅erkhamsted, 𝔑orthchurch, 𝔄lbury, 𝔗ring, 𝔚illesethorn, 𝔚igington 𝔏ong 𝔐erston, 𝔓uttenham, and 𝔠olshil.

The third Part of the fifth Division.

BERKHAMSTED ST. PETERS.

Norden, p. 13.

THE *Saxons* in old time, saith *Norden*, called this Town 𝔅erghamstedt, because it was seated among the Hills, for *Berg* signified a Hill, *Ham* a Town, and *Stedt* a Seat, all which was very proper for the Scituation hereof. In this Place the Kings of 𝔐ercia often resided and kept their Court, among whom *Whithred*, King of 𝔎ent and 𝔐ercia, *Anno Christi* 697, 5 *Regni sui*, held a Parliament or great Council at this Town, where *Birtwald*, Archbishop of 𝔠an-

K k 2

Hund. of
Doccorum.

terbury, one of the King's Privy Council, presided, *Gybmund* Bishop of Rochester, all the Prelates and military Men were assembled, mildly treated, and by the common Assent of all decreed;

Sprim. Con.
fol. 194.

PRAYERS shall be made for the King; and his Commands shall be freely obey'd; that the Church may be free and enjoy its Laws and Possessions.

2. Whosoever shall violate the peace of the Church shall forfeit fifty Shillings.

3. Adulterers shall be reduc'd from their Sins to a honest life, or be excommunicated from the Church.

4. But Strangers who shall be defiled with this uncleanness, and will not reform, shal be banish'd; carrying away their Sins with their Wealth, even as they are driven from the Communion of the Church in other Countries.

5. If a military Man shall happen to be taken in Adultery, and contemn the Law of the King, the Bishops, and the Judgment of this Court, he shall pay a hundred Shillings.

6. If a Farmer or an Husbandman shall commit this Offence; he shall pay fifty Shillings.

7. If a Priest shall forsake Adultery, and shall not wickedly relinquish his Baptisme, nor be addicted to Drunkenness, he shall hold his Office and the priviledge of his Habit.

8. If a Tonsure shall be irregular, he shall go to another House, if any will receive him; but this shall not be done unless License shall be granted to keep him a long time there.

9. If any shall enfranchise his Servant at the Altar, he shall be free and capable to inherit, and shall be manumised without limit.

Sam's Antiq.
of Brit. fol.
418.

* This shall
be extended
only to the
part of Satur-
day after Sun
set.

10. If the Servant by the Command of the Master shall do any servile Work after the Sun shall be set on Saturday or on Sunday, the Master shall pay eighty Shillings for the fact.

*11. *If a Servant shall travel on either of those Days, he shall pay six Shillings or be whipt.*

12. If a Freeman shall travel on a Day forbidden, he shall stand in the Pillory, and the Informer shall have half, as well as the Mulct as the Wirgil.

13. If a Husbandman without the knowledge of his Wife shall offer any thing to the Devil, he shall forfeit his Estate, and stand in the Pillory, but if both of them shall offend, she also shall lose all her Goods and stand in the Pillory.

14. If a Servant shall offer any thing to the Devil, he shall lose six Shillings or be whip'd.

15. If any Person shall give Flesh to his Servant to be eaten on a Fast Day, his Servant shall be free.

16. If any Servant shall voluntarily eat it, he shall either pay six Shillings or be whip'd.

17. The Word or Affirmation of the King or the Bishop without Oath shall be irrefragible, or shall purge them.

18. The Chief Officer or Governour shall make profession as a Priest to the Monastery; but the Priest shall say before the Altar after this manner: I speak the truth in Christ, I lie not; in the same manner shall Deacons be purged.

19. An inferior Clerk with four Compurgators shall purge himself, bowing his head; and one Hand shall be extended to the Altar, the other to the Oath.

20. The Stranger swearing only upon the Altar shall be purged, so shall a Thane or a Nobleman.

21. The Farmer or Husbandman with four Compurgators, his Head bowed down to the Altar, shall be discharged; and after this manner all their Oaths shall be administered.

22. If any Person shall accuse the Servant of a Bishop, this shall belong to the Jurisdiction of the Church, or he shall be turned over to the Jurisdiction of the King, or the Governour of the Town or Place, who shall purge him, or cause him to be beaten.

23. *If any Prisoner of God shall be accused in an Assembly, his Master shall purge him by his simple Oath, if he has taken the Eucharist, but if he never came to the Eucharist, he shall find a good surety for his Oath, or he shall pay or be delivered to be whipt.*

24. *If the Servant of a Laic shall accuse the Servant of an Ecclesiastic, or the Servant of an Ecclesiastic shall accuse the Servant of a Laic, the Master shall purge him by his single Oath.*

25. *If a secular Man shall kill a Thief, no Composition shall be made by the Kinsman of him that is slain.*

26. *If any Freeman shall take a Thief carrying away any thing that is stolen, the King shall choose any one of these three Punishments, either that the Thief shall be slain, or banished beyond the Seas, or rather his Wirgild, (which was the Value of his Head or Life) and he who apprehended him shall have half his Goods, but if he shall kill him he shall pay seventy Shillings.*

27. *If any Servant shall be robbed and shall suffer the Thief to escape, he shall pay seventy Shillings, or ———— which the King pleases; but if any one shall slay him, his Master shall have half his Goods.*

28. *If any Stranger shall wander privately thro' the Country, and shall neither cry aloud nor sound his Horn, he shall be taken for a Thief, and shall either be slain or banisht.*

From which time this Mannor remained in the Crown, until *William* the Conqueror invaded this Island, and after he obtained that signal Victory at 𝕭attle 𝕬bby, he passed thence with his Army over the 𝕿hames at 𝖂allingford, and thence marched with his Forces to this Town in Order to go forward to 𝕷ondon; where he was forced to make some Stay at this Place, for *Frederick*, that bold Abbot of 𝕾t. 𝕬lbans, had caused the Timber Trees growing near this Road, which belonged to his Church to be felled, and laid cross the Way to obstruct his Passage, and during the time of his Continuance here, the great Lords and Nobles of 𝕰ngland, consulting how they might free themselves from the Slavery of the Norman Yoke, met the Conqueror, by the Advice and Perswasion of that couragious Abbot, at this Town, where after great Debate of Matters in the Presence of Archbishop *Lanfranc*, the King fearing if he should not comply with them, he should lose with Shame the Kingdom which he had got by the Effusion of so much Blood, yielded so far that he laid his Hand upon the holy Gospel, and swore upon all the Relicts of 𝕾t. 𝕬lbans Church, before Abbot *Frederic*, who administered the Oath, that he would observe and keep inviolably the good and approved ancient Laws of the Kingdom, which the holy and devout Kings of 𝕰ngland his Predecessors, especially King *Edward* had ordained; this done, they submitted themselves to his Governance, and swore Fealty to him; who with many fair Words received them immediately into his Protection, and promised to give his Daughter in Marriage to Earl *Edwine*; and all of them were present at his Coronation: however through the deceitful Counsel of the *Normans,* nothing of this was performed, but soon after be evilly intreated most of those Peers and Nobles, carried them with him into 𝕹ormandy, under Pretence they should assist him against the

Hund. of Bacorum.

Camd. Brit. tit Herts, fol. 414.

Hund. of
Dacorum.

Rebels there, but in Truth that they might not provide for their own Safety in his Absence: then he seized all their Estates, and disposed of them to his *Normans*, among whom he gave this Town to *Robert* Earl of 𝔐oreton, his half Brother by the Mother's Side, who fortified this Castle with a double Trench and Rampier; and in *Domesdei Book* 'tis recorded, under the Title of *Terra Comitis* Moreton, That

Domesd. Lib.
fol. 136, n. 15.

In 𝔈reunge *Hundred. Comes* Moreton *tenuit* 𝔅ercljeljamstelie *pro tresdecem hidis ne defendebat. Terra est sex et vigint. car. in Dom. sex hid. et ibi sunt tres car. et aliæ tres possunt fieri, ibi Presbiter cum quatuordecim Vill. et quindecim Bord. habent. duodecem car. et adhuc octo possunt fieri, ibi sex Servi, et quidam Fossarius habet dimid. hid. et Ranulphus un. virgat. servien. Comit.*

In Burbio hujus Ville quinquagint. et duo Burgienses qui reddunt de Tholoneo quatuor lib. et habent. dimid. hid. et duo Molin. de vigint. sol. ibi duo arpend. vineæ. pratum octo car. pastura. ad pecud. Vill. Silva mille porcis et quinque sol. in totis valentiis valet sexdecem lib. quando recepit viginti lib. tempore Regis Edwardi *quatuor vigint lib. hoc Manerium tenuit* Edmarus Teignus Heraldi *Comitis.*

Earl *Moreton* held 𝔅ercljeljamstelie in 𝔈reung Hundred, it was rated for thirteen Hides. The arable is six and twenty Carucates, in Demeasne six Hides, and there are three Carucates, and three others may be made, here is a Presbyter; or Priest with fourteen Villains, and fifteen Bordars having twelve Carucates, and now eight more may be made, there are six Servants, and a certain Ditcher had half an Hide, and *Ralph*, a Servant of the Earl, one Virgate.

In the Borough of this Vill are two and fifty Burgesses, who pay four Pounds a Year for Toll, and they have half an Hide, and two Mills of twenty Shillings Rent by the Year, there are two Arpends of Vineyard, Meadow eight Carucates, Common of Pasture for the Cattle of the Vill, Wood to feed a thousand Hogs, and five Shillings Rent by the Year; in the whole Value it is worth sixteen Pounds, when he received it twenty Pounds, in the time of King *Edward* (the Confessor) four and twenty Pounds, *Edmar* a Thane of Earl *Harold* held this Mannor.

Dugd. Bar.
vol. 1, fol. 25.

This Earl *Moreton* married *Maud* Daughter to *Roger de Montgomery*, by whom he had Issue *William*, who succeeded him in these Earldoms of 𝔐oreton and 𝔒ornfoal, and three Daughters whose Christian Names are not exprest, whereof the first married *Andrew de Detrei*, the second *Guy de Val*, and the third the Earl of 𝔗ljoulouse, Brother to *Raymond*, Count of 𝔖t. 𝔈giles, who behaved himself valiantly in that Expedition to 𝔍erusalem.

Dugd. Bar.
vol. 1, fol. 24.
Matt. Paris,
fol. 54.

When King *William Rufus* had the Misfortune to lose his Life by the Glance of an Arrow from a Tree in the 𝔑eto 𝔉orrest shot by *Walter Terril*; this Earl or his Son *William*, then hunting in the Woods near the Place where the King was slain, his Attendance having left him alone in the same Hour, and knowing not any thing of the King's Death, accidentally met a great black Goat bearing the Body of the King all black, naked, wounded through the Midst of his Breast, and besmeared with Blood, upon Sight thereof, he adjured the Goat by the Holy Trinity, to tell what that was he so carried? To which he answered, *I am carrying your King to Judgment; yea that Tyrant* William Rufus, *for*

*I am an evil Spirit, and the Revenger of the Malice which
he bore to the Church of God: It was I that caused this
his Slaughter; for the Protomartyr of England commanded
me so to do, who complained to God of him for his grievous
Oppressions in this Isle of Britain, which he first hallowed.*
All which the Earl related soon after to his Followers.

This Earl *William* was a Person of a malicious and arro-
gant Spirit from his Childhood; and envying the Glory of
King *Henry* I. raised a Rebellion against him in Normandy; Whereupon all his Estate in England was seized, his
Castle rac'd to the Ground, and he was banish'd this Realm;
by this Means this Town and Mannor came to the Crown.

Henry II. granted that all the Men and Merchants of
the Honour of Wallingford and Berkhamsted St. Peters,
should have firm Peace through all his Land of England
and Normandy, wheresoever they shall be; and he did give
and grant to them for ever, all the Laws, Liberties, and
free Customs as they enjoyed them honourably in the time
of King *Edward*, (which was *Edward* the Confessor) King
William, Great Grandfather to the said King *Henry*, and
that they should remain with their Merchandize to be
bought or sold through England, Normandy, Acquitain,
and Anjou, by Water, by Land, by Wood, and by Strand,
Quit of Tallage, Pontage, Lastage, Passage, and all Customs and Exactions, upon the Forfeiture of 10*l.* And this
he prohibited and commanded upon the same Forfeiture.

And the King granted to the Men and Merchants of
Wallingford and Berkhamsted for ever, all Laws and Customs like as they had in the time of King *Edward*, and
King *Henry* his Grandfather: And he also granted to them
wheresoever they should go with their Merchandizes, to buy
or sell thro' all England, Normandy, and Spain, by Water
and by Strand, by Wood and by Land, they should be quit
of all Toll, and Passage of Bridges and Piccage, Paviage,
and Stallage, and Shires and Hundreds, of Aids, Viscoun-
tels, and Service of Guilds, and Daneguilds, of Hidage,
Bloodewite, Fredewite, Murders, Assart Guard, and Le-
guard, and of Works of Castle Walls, Ditches, Bridges,
Streams, and of all Customs and Exactions secular, and of
all servile Works, and they should not be disquieted by any
Man upon the Forfeiture of 10*l.* and that no Man should
vex or disturb them; and to enlarge their Liberties, the
King further granted that no Summons, Attachments, Distress, Inquisition, or Execution should be executed by any
of the King's Officers within the Liberties of Wallingford
and Berkhamsted; but by the High Steward, Escheator,
Coroner, and their Bayliffs and Ministers, of the same Honour and Liberty; and should have the Return of all Writs,
and Execution of the same, and the Law day, and what be-

Hund. of
Bacorum. longs to the same; and that no Surveyor or other the King's
Officer shall make any Price within the said Honour, and
Liberty of the Goods of the King's Liege Men and Mer-
chants, their Heirs and Successors, against their Wills.

No Sheriff, Escheator, Marshal, or Clerk of the Market
of the King's House, or his Heirs, shall sit or do his Office
within this Honour and Liberty, nor shall take any Men or
Merchants of this Honour, out of this Liberty for any thing
done within this Honour; and none of the King's Officers
or Purveyors shall buy or sell any thing within this Honour and Liberty touching this Office; and the King farther
granted, that the Liege Men and Merchants residing within
this Honour and Liberty, and their Successors, and their
Goods thro' all 𝕰𝖓𝖌𝖑𝖆𝖓𝖉, and Ports of the Sea, shall be quit
of all Tolls, Passage, Laystage, Carriage, Paunage, Picage,
Murdridge, Pannage of Scot and Lot, Brasel, Child, Vice-
geresgrind, Scotal, Terrage, Pasage, Silver, Anchory, Bo-
rowbreach, Boroughbote, Teipgild, Forestal, Horngild,
Danegild, Hormsoken, House-breach, Wren-white, Mis-
kuming, Sacasoken, Sock de Sheronge, Toll, Them, Wa-
pentake, Wardwite, Utlage, and of all other Customs; and
they may have Infangtheif, and Outfangtheife, Treasure
Trove, Waife, Estray, Goods and Chattels, and Year, Day,
and Waste. No Market shall be held within seven Miles
of this Town, neither shall the Men or Merchants attend at
the Assizes or Sessions. King *H.* 11. kept his Court in this
Mon. Angl.
vol. 2, fol.
420. Town, where he granted the Church of 𝕳𝖆𝖇𝖊𝖗𝖎𝖓𝖌 to the
Monastery of St. *Bernade de Monte Jovis,* to make Fires
for the poor People there, and it continued in the Crown
until *Anno* 1206, 7 *Johannis,* when that King granted this
Castle and Honour of 𝕭𝖊𝖗𝖐𝖍𝖆𝖒𝖘𝖙𝖊𝖉 to

Jeoffery Fitzpiers Earl of 𝕰𝖘𝖘𝖊𝖝, with the Knight's Fee
thereto belonging, in Feefarm for an hundred Pounds *per*
Ibid. fol 411,
437
Dugd Bar.
vol. 1, fol. 705 *Annum,* to hold to him and the Heirs of his Body by *Ave-*
line then his Wife; and as for his Works of Piety, he gave
to the Brethren of the Hospital of St. *Thomas* of 𝕬𝖈𝖗𝖊𝖘, in
the City of 𝕷𝖔𝖓𝖉𝖔𝖓, the Guardianship of St. *John Baptist*
in 𝕭𝖊𝖗𝖐𝖍𝖆𝖒𝖘𝖙𝖊𝖉, and also the Hospital of St. *John* the
Evangelist of Lepers.

But before the 14th Year of King *John* he died, and was
buried at 𝕾𝖍𝖔𝖚𝖑𝖉𝖍𝖆𝖒, of whom our Historian gives this
Character, that he was a Person of great Power and Authority, and died on the second Day of *October,* to the general Loss of the whole Realm, being a firm Pillar thereof,
generous, skilful in the Laws, rich in Money and of every
thing else, and allied to all the great Men of 𝕰𝖓𝖌𝖑𝖆𝖓𝖉,
either in Blood or Friendship, so that the King feared him
above all Mortals, for 'twas he that held the Reines of Government, and after his Death the Realm was like a Ship

tost in a Tempest without a Pilot. He married *Beatrix* the *Hund. of* *Bacorum.* eldest Daughter of *William Say*, by whom he had Issue three Sons, 1. *Jeoffrey* his immediate Successor. 2. *William* Successor to him. 3. *Henry* then Dean of 𝔚oolberhampton, and *Maud* married to *Henry de Bohun* Earl of ℌertford: and by *Aveline* his second Wife, *John Fitzpiers*, who was Lord of 𝔅erkhamsted and Justice of Ireland.

But *Anno* 1215, 16 *Johan.* this Castle and Town of 𝔅erkhamsted was in the Crown, for when the Barons lay still, *Brady's Hist. of Engl.* fol. 505. King *John* possest himself of the Castle, and appointed *Rainulph* the *German* to have the Custody thereof.

Anno 1216, 17 *Johan.* Prince *Lewis* eldest Son to the *Matt. Paris,* fol. 290. *Stow's Annals* fol. 176. King of 𝔉rance, laid Siege to this Castle, and invested the same with his Army on the Feast of St. *Nicholas,* and whilst the Barons which *Lewis* commanded, pitched their Tents on the North Side thereof, and their Officers and Souldiers were careless in their several Stations, the Knights and Souldiers issued out of the Castle with a great Force, seized the Chariots, and Provisions of the Barons, took the Banner of *William* Earl of 𝔐andeuile, and returned with all the Chariots and Provisions unto the Castle; and whilst the Barons were sitting at Table the same Day, the Knights issued out of the Castle again, and carrying the Banner, which a little before they had taken away to the great Con- *Dugd. Bar.* vol 1, fol. 762. fusion of the Barons, disarmed them, and hasteued again into the Castle; but after a long Siege, the King commanded them to yield the Castle to Prince *Lewis.*

Anno 2 *H.* III. 7 *die Maii*, the Market at 𝔅erkhamsted was changed from *Sunday* to *Monday*, *M.* 61. *pars* 2. and

King *H.* III. on the third Day of Pentecost, being the third Day of the Calends of *June, Anno,* 1227, 11 *H.* III. advanced *Richard* his younger Brother, for his good Services at the Siege of the Castle of 𝔅iole in 𝔉rance, to the Title and Dignity of Earl 𝔠ornwal at 𝔚estminster with great Solemnity; he gave this Honour and Castle to him, but soon after much Difference happened between the King and him, touching the Lordship of 𝔗ies, which King *John* gave to *Walera Teutonic*, for he alleged that it was Parcel *Ibid.* fol. 211. *Matt. Paris,* fol. 337. of the Earldom of 𝔠ornwal, and caused Possession of it to be taken for himself, which Breach proved so great, that the King did injuriously take from him this Castle of 𝔅erkhamsted; upon which this Earl communicated all his Grievances to his trusty Friend *William Marshall* Earl of ℌembrook, who immediately repaired to the Earl of 𝔠hester, and thro' the Power and Interest of their Friends, raised a potent Army and randevouzed at 𝔖tamford, from whence they sent a minatory Message to the King, imputing all the Fault to *Hubert de Burgh*, then Justice of England, and advising the King to secure him, required also the Confirmation of that Charter of the Forest, which had been cancelled at Oxford.

The King discerning this Cloud, appointed a Meeting at Northampton, on the third of the Nones of *August* next following, assuring them that he would there do full Right unto all; where he met accordingly, and among other his Condescentions, he gave this Earl *Richard* his Mother's Dowry, with all the Lands of England which did belong to the Earl of Britany, and all those Lands which did belong to the Earl of Boloin then deceased, upon which he had Livery of the whole County of Rutland, and he was restored again to this Castle of Berkhamsted.

Anno 1231, 15 *H.* III. in the Month of *April*, when the Feast of *Easter* was solemnized, he married *Isabel* Countess of Glocester, Widow of *Gilbert de Clare* Earl of Glocester, and Sister to *William Marshall* then Earl of Pembrook, and in the same Year he obtained a Grant of the Mannor, Castle, and Honour of Knaresburgh in the County of York to himself and the Heirs of his Body by the same *Isabel*, to hold by the Service of two Knight's Fees.

Anno 1236, 20 *H.* III. this Earl with *Gilbert Marshal* then Earl of Pembrook, and divers other great Men, took upon him the Cross for a Journey to the Holy Land, and for the better furnishing himself with Money, sold many of his Woods, until the latter End of *An.* 23 *H.* III. 1239, and 18 Calends of *February*, the same Year *Isabel* his Wife died in Child Bed at his Mannor of Berkhamsted, and was buried in the Abby of Beaulieu; but after this Funeral was passed, divers of the Nobility met together at Northampton, where they did by Oath oblige themselves to go forthwith into the Holy Land for the Service of God and the Church, and he having prepared all things ready for his Journey, came to the Abby of St. Albans, where in full Chapter he desir'd the Prayers of the whole Convent, for his good Success, then took his Leave of the King, the Legate and Nobles at London, and so hasted to Dover, whence passing thro' France, he came to the Holy Land, *Anno* 1241, 25 *H.* III. where he accepted of a Truce of the Soldan of Babylon, upon Condition that the *French* who were Prisoners there should be released, and that Jerusalem, with all the Parts adjacent should be free from any Molestation, as also upon divers other Articles honourable to the Christians, and the next Year following *Anno* 1242, 26 *H.* III. he returned, and the King having Notice of it, with the Queen, met him at Dover.

This Earl with *William Longespe* Earl of Salisbury, took another Journey to the Holy Land, and returned thence in *Anno* 1243, 27 *H.* III. After this he attended the King into Gascoine in Aid of *Hugh de Brun*, Earl of March, (who

had married the King's Mother) and was with him in that
Battle near *Xanct* against the King of *France*.

In the next ensuing Year this Earl *Richard* married
Senchia Daughter of *Raymond* Earl of *Probince*, Sister to
the Queen; the Wedding was kept at *Westminster* with
great Pomp, and he endowed her at the Church Door with
a third Part of all his Lands of which he was then possest,
or should afterwards acquire, whereof this Castle and Mannor of *Berkhamsted* was Part.

Anno 29 *H*. III. that King granted that *Richard* Earl
of *Cornwal* and his Heirs should have one Fair at his Mannor of *Berkhamsted* every Year, to continue by the Space
of eight Days; viz. on the Day of the Invention of the Holy
Cross, and for seven Days next following.

Anno 1257, 41 *H*. III. this Earl being a Person of
high Repute for his heroick and noble Endowments, certain Nobles of *Almain* arriving here, represented to the
whole Baronage of *England*, then met in Parliament, that
this Earl was elected King of the *Romans* by unanimous
Consent of the Princes of the Empire, and showed the Letters Testimonial that did manifest the same, and soon after
the Bishop of *Colen* and divers of the Nobles of that Country came hither and did Homage to him, upon which he
gave them 500 Marks towards their travelling Expences,
and a rich Mitre adorn'd with pretious Stones, which pleased the Archbishop so well, that he said, *As he has put this*
Mitre on my Head, I will put the Crown of Almain *on his.*

In Order hereto, this Earl committed himself to the
Prayers of the Religious, took his Leave of his Friends,
and began his Journey on the third Day in Easter Week.
He took Shipping at *Yarmouth*, and arriving in short time
at *Aguisgrabe*, was there crowned King upon Ascention
Day.

Having received this great Honour he return'd thence
the next Year after, and landed at *Dover* upon the Day of
St. *Julian*, where the King met him with much Joy; after
this during his Stay here, he made great Preparation for
his Journey back to receive the Crown of the Empire,
which the Pope under Hand endeavoured to obtain for him.

Anno 1264, 48 *H*. III. he marched with the King to
Northampton, against those proud and high spirited Barons,
headed by *Mountford* Earl of *Leicester*, and *Clare* Earl of
Glocester, assisted the King in the Siege and taking of that
Town, and then pursued their dissipated Forces into *Sus-*
sex (where the Londoners with all their Power recruited
them,) and there he commanded the Body of the King's
Army in the Battle of *Lewes*, where the King and he were
taken Prisoners.

Hund. of
Dacorum.

Dugd. Bar.
vol. 1, fol.
764.

Anno 1267, 51 *H.* III. this Earl went again into Germany, where he married *Beatrix* Neice to the Archbishop of Bolen.

Anno, 1271, 55 *H.* III. he was made Governour of Rockingham Castle in the County of Northampton, and Warden of the Forrest, and when he had acted a long Part

Matt. Paris,
fol. 1097.
Mon. Angl.
vol. 1, fol. 934

on the Theatre of this World with great Honour, he had a tedious Sickness at this Mannor of Berkhamsted, died upon the fourth of the Nones of *April, Anno* 1272, 56 *H.* III. His Heart was buried at the *Gray Fryars* in Oxford, under a costly Pyramid, and his Body in the Abby of Hales, which was of his own Foundation.

He had no Issue by *Rose de Dover* his first Wife, but by *Isabel* his second Wife he begat *John, Henry, Rickard,* and *Nicholas,* of whom *John* and *Rickard* died in their Infancy, and *Nicholas* with his Mother in Child-bed, and a Daughter who died in her Cradle, but *Henry* survived them for divers Years, however he died in the Life-time of his Father. He had Issue by *Senchia* his third Wife, *Richard* who died young, and *Edmond* who succeeded him in this Earldom of Cornwal, but by *Beatrix* his fourth Wife he had no Issue.

At the time of his Death he held of the King *in Capite,* by Knight's Service the Mannors of Berkhamsted and Hemelhamsted, and at Berkhamsted there were 400 Acres of Arable Land, 4 Acres of Pasture, 16 Acres of Meadow, 200 Acres of Wood, a Park, three Watermills, 10*l.* Rents of Assize, and 9*l.* Rents of Assize, and in the Borough of Berkhamsted were 11*l.* of Rents of Assize, and there were two Watermills, which were yearly worth 6*l.* 13*s.* 4*d.* the Toll of the Borough was yearly worth 4*l.* and the Perquisites of the Portmoot were worth 40*s.* a Year.

This Epitaph is recorded of him.

Hic jacet in Tumulo Richardus Teutonicorum
Rex vivens, propria contentus sorte bonorum
Anglorum Regis Germanus Pictaviensis
Ante Comes dictus; sed tandem Cornubiensis.
Demum Teutonicis tribuens amplissima dona
Insignitus erat, Caroli rutilante Coronâ.
Hinc Aquilam gessit clypeo, sprevitq; Leonem
Regibus omnigenis præcellens per rationem.
Dives opum Mundi; sapiens, conviva modestus;
Alloquio, gestu, dum vixit, semper Honestus.
Jam Regnum Regno commutans pro meliore,
Regni cælorum summo conregnat honore.

Dugd. Bar.
vol. 1, fol.
765.

Esc. 26 H.III.

Edmond Plantagenet succeeded his Father in the Earldom of Cornwal, and *Anno* 1271, 25 *H.* III. he accomplish'd his full Age of 21 Years, then received the Honour of Knighthood upon St. *Edwards* Day, and soon after was invested with the Title of Earl of Cornwal by Cincture

Hund. of
Bacorum.

with the Sword, and before the End of the Year he married *Margaret*, the Sister of *Gilbert de Clare* Earl of Glocester, and shortly after had Livery of the Castles of Knaresburgh, Wallingford, Ockham, and Berkhamsted, of his Inheritance.

Anno 1287, 15 *Edw.* I. he had a Grant of the Castle of Ockham, to hold in Fee with the Shrievalty of this County of Rutland, and *Anno* 1288. 16 *Edw.* I. he was made Warden of England during the King's Absence in the Wars of Scotland, and during that time he laid Siege to Droselan Castle and demolished the Walls thereof, and *Anno* 1289, 17 *Edw.* I. he was constituted Sheriff for the County of Cornwal in Fee.

Rot. Pip. 15
& 19 Ed' I.
T Walsing.
anno 1288.

Rot. Pip. 17
Ed. I.

In an Inquisition upon a Writ of *Ad quod Dampnum* brought *Anno* 18 *Edw.* I. the Jury found that the Earl of Cornwal and his Ancestors had, 1. A Court of View of Franc-pledge, and all things belonging to it. 2. Full Return of all Writs of the King. 3. Power to hold all Pleas in his Court which the Sheriffs hold in their County Courts, except Appeals and Outlaries. 4. Power to attach all Trespassors against the King's Peace found within the Liberty, and to keep them in Berkhamsted Goal until the next Goal Delivery to be made by the King's Justices. 5. Authority to institute a particular Coronet for that Liberty. 6. All Justices assigned by the King were obliged to execute their Office within the Liberty touching all Matters that related to the Liberty. 7. All the Justices Itinerants were bound to hear and determine all Offences and Matters in the Liberty which did arise there. 8. The Earl shall have all the Fines and Amerceaments of all his Tenants of the Honour of Berkhamsted, before all Justices, and levy them by his own Ministers. 9. Also the Goods of Felons and Fugitives, the Year, Day, and Wast. 10. The Earl and all his Tenants were free of Common Fines and Amerceaments of the whole County.

It was also found by Inquisition, taken at Berkhamsted, *Anno* 28 *Edw.* I. that there were four Knights' Fees held of *Edmond* Earl of Cornwal as of his Honour of Berkhamsted, of which *Nicholas de Bosco*, held the Mannor of Northcote by one Knights' Fee worth 40s. *per Annum*; *Jeoffrey de Lucy* held Aspenton and Wetlam by another Knights' Fee worth 40s. *per Annum*, and Gadsden Parba by another Knights' Fee worth 40s. *per Annum*, and *Ralph de Wedon* held Wedon, Agmondesham, and Swaneburn in the County of Bucks by another Knight's Fee, and the Jury found by the same Inquisition, that

Esc. 28 Ed. I.

Edmond Earl of Cornwal, held of the King *in Capite*, in his Demeasne as of Fee the Castle of Berkhamsted, together with the Vill of Berkhamsted, and the same Halimot

with the other Appurtenances, the Services by two Knights'
Fees, excepting two Messuages together with the Goal,
the Pleas of the Crown, and other the Appurtenances,
which the Rector of 𝔄𝔰𝔥𝔢𝔯𝔲𝔤, and Convent of the same
Place, held in the same Vill, which they had of the Gift of
the said *Edmond* Earl of 𝔠𝔬𝔯𝔫𝔴𝔞𝔩, and by the Confirmation
of the King, to them and their Successors, so that the said
Rector and Convent, with all their Tenants, are quit in the
said Vill from all Mannor of Tolls.

Also they say that there are 12 Burgesses in the Borough
of 𝔅𝔢𝔯𝔨𝔥𝔞𝔪𝔰𝔱𝔢𝔡, of which the Abbot of 𝔐𝔢𝔰𝔰𝔢𝔡𝔬𝔫 held one
Burgage, and ought Suit of Portmoot from 15 Days to 15
Days, the Abbot of 𝔕𝔢𝔞𝔡𝔦𝔫𝔤 held another Burgage, and
ought Suit as the aforesaid Abbot, and there are also 62
Free Tenants in the said Borough, and 22 Free Tenants
of Serjeanty.

And there is a certain Wood called the 𝔉𝔯𝔦𝔱𝔥, which
contains in itself 763 Acres and one Rood, and a Common
as well for the Freemen as the Villaines of 𝔅𝔢𝔯𝔨𝔥𝔞𝔪𝔰𝔱𝔢𝔡 by
the Year, excepting the time of Pannage, that is between
the Feast of St. *Michael*, and the Feast of St. *Martin*, and
Common for the Rector of 𝔄𝔰𝔥𝔢𝔯𝔲𝔤 and all his Tenants for
the whole Year, as well in the time of Pannage as at
other times, and the said Rector shall have House-boot
and Hey-boot out of the said Wood.

Also they say that the Master of the House of St. *Thomas*, the Martyr of 𝔄𝔠𝔬𝔫, holds to him one Free Messuage
and one Virgate of Land in 𝔅𝔢𝔯𝔨𝔥𝔞𝔪𝔰𝔱𝔢𝔡, and ought Suit
of Court from three Weeks to three Weeks, and once Attendance at the Court of the View of Franc-Pledge for all
Services; also they say that *Bartholomew Cryol* Lord of
𝔄𝔩𝔡𝔢𝔯𝔟𝔲𝔯𝔭 and the same Vill, had free Ingress and Regress
from the Wood of the 𝔉𝔯𝔦𝔱𝔥, and ought to mow in one of
the Parks with 16 Men, for Meat for the Lord one Day,
and the Work of every Man was worth one Penny, and he
himself or his Servant shall ride or go to view the Workmen, and he shall have Meat of the Lord twice in the Day;
they also say that there was 33*s*. 6*d*. a Year paid for the common Fine at the great Court, of which the Vill of 𝔚𝔭𝔤𝔦𝔫𝔱𝔬𝔫
paid 2*s*. a Year, the Vill of 𝔊𝔬𝔟𝔩𝔦𝔫𝔠𝔬𝔱𝔢, 2*s. per An.* the Vill
of 𝔅𝔢𝔱𝔩𝔞𝔴, 2*s. per An.* the Vill of 𝔏𝔢𝔢 and 𝔑𝔬𝔯𝔱𝔥𝔠𝔬𝔱𝔢, 2*s.*
per An. the Vill of 𝔐𝔞𝔯𝔰𝔱𝔬𝔫, 2*s. per An.* the Vill of 𝔇𝔯𝔢𝔭-
𝔱𝔬𝔫, 2*s. per An.* the Vill of 𝔄𝔩𝔟𝔲𝔯𝔭, 10*s. per An.* the Vills
of 𝔚𝔬𝔟𝔢𝔱𝔬𝔫, 𝔚𝔢𝔰𝔱𝔬𝔫, and 𝔏𝔬𝔠𝔥𝔱𝔬𝔫, 2*s. per An.* the Vill of
𝔥𝔦𝔩𝔡𝔢𝔰𝔡𝔢𝔫, 12*d. per An.* the Vill of 𝔚𝔞𝔟𝔦𝔫𝔤𝔡𝔬𝔫, 12*d. per
An.* the Vill of 𝔄𝔤𝔪𝔬𝔫𝔡𝔢𝔰𝔥𝔞𝔪, 12*d. per An.* the Vill of
𝔖𝔴𝔞𝔫𝔟𝔲𝔯𝔫, 2*s. per An.* the Vill of 𝔏𝔶𝔪𝔣𝔬𝔯𝔡, 1*s. per An.*
the Vill of 𝔖𝔞𝔩𝔡𝔢𝔫, 2*s. per An.* the Vill of 𝔥𝔭𝔡𝔢 in 𝔐𝔲𝔯-
𝔰𝔩𝔢, 1*s. per An.* the Vill of 𝔚𝔢𝔫𝔤𝔯𝔞𝔳𝔢, 1*s. per An.* the Vill
of 𝔚𝔩𝔢𝔡𝔬𝔫, 12*d. per An.*

This Earl *Edmond* founded a Colledge at Asherugg in the County of Bucks, in Honour of the Blood of our Saviour, for certain Brethren called *Bonhomes*, and for the Soul of *Richard* King of Almain his Father; he gave to the Monks of Rewley in the Suburbs of Oxford, all his Lands in North Osny, also his Mannor of Erdington and Mills at Earsington in that County; also one Acre of Land in Bell near Roslin, with the Advowson of the Church of Wendrove in the Hundred of Rerier in the County of Cornwal; also all his Woods at Nettlebed, and divers Houses in London, scituate in the Parish of St. *Thomas* the Apostle, with certain Lands in Wnplanston, and sixty Shillings yearly Rent payable to the Monks of Thame out of the Mannor of Stocke Talmach; and he died without Issue at Asherugg on the Calends of *October*, *Anno* 1300, 28 *H.* I. being at that time seized of this Mannor among divers others.

Then this Honour and Castle of Berkhamsted reverted to the Crown; and *Anno* 1308, 1 *Edw.* II. *Piers Gaveston* having married *Margaret*, the second Sister and Coheir to *Gilbert de Clare* Earl of Gloccster, Daughter to *Joan* of Acres the King's Sister, at this Castle where the King was present, he procured a Grant of the Earldom of Cornwal, and this Castle to himself and this *Margaret* in Tail, with Remainder to the King and his Heirs, and soon after he obtained a Grant of the whole Earldom of Cornwal with this Castle, and the Mannor and Lands thereunto belonging, and of the Shrievalty of that County; but his Advancement with these rich Possessions made him insolent, that he despised the best of the Nobles, which exasperated them and inrag'd the People in general against him to that Height, that he was forced to fly to Scarborough Castle for Security, where they besieged him, and wearied out the Guards within with frequent Alarms, that *Piers* seeing no Remedy, yielded himself, promising to stand to the Judgment of the Barons, so that he might have Liberty to speak with the King; but as they were conveying him thither, a sober Person standing by, told them, that it would be a great Folly, having been at such a Charge and Trouble to take him, to hazard the losing of him again, saying, *That it would be much better that he should suffer Death, than that the Realm should be disturbed by a War*; Upon which they brought him out of the Prison to an Ascent called Blacklow, about a Mile North East from Wartwick, where by the Hands of a Welch Man he was beheaded as a publick Traytor, which fulfilled the Prophecy, *That he should feel the sharp Teeth of the black Dog of* Arden; for so he used to call the Earl of Wartwick.

Anno 1329, 2 *Edw.* III. *John*, born at Eltham in Rent, second Son to King *Edw.* II. was advanced to the Earl-

Hund. of Dacorum.

Mon. Angl. vol. 1, fol. 934.
Ibid. vol. 2, fol. 344.

Esc. 28 H. I.

Dugd. *Car.* fol. 43.

dom of Cornwal in that Parliament, which began at Salisburp, after the *Quindesm.* of St. *Michael,* and *Anno* 1331, 4 *Edw.* III. the King granted this Castle, Town, and Honour, with divers other Mannors valued at 2000 Marks *per Annum,* to him in Tail general; and *Anno* 1332, 5 *Edw.* III. upon the King's Expedition into Scotland, this Earl was made Lieutenant here during the King's Absence.

Anno 1336, 10 *Edw.* III. the King having Intelligence that the *French* had promised to aid the *Scots,* he marched himself into that Realm with a great Army, and fortified the Castle of Stribeling with a deep Ditch, as also the Town of St. Johnstones, at which Place this *John* Earl of Cornwal falling sick, died without Wife or Issue, and was afterwards honourably buried in St. *Edmond's* Chappel within the Abby Church of Westminster, where his Monument still remaineth.

Anno 1346, 20 *Edw.* III. this King advanced *Edward* his eldest Son, called the Black Prince, to the Title and Dignity of Duke of Cornwal, and gave him the Castle, Mannor, and Vill of Berkhamsted, with the Park and the Honour of Berkhamsted, to hold to him and the Heirs of him, and the eldest Sons of the Heirs of the Kings of England, and the Dukes of the said Place, together with the Knights' Fees, Advowsons of Churches, Abbies, Priories, Hospitals, Chappels, Hundreds, Pischaries, Forrests, Chaces, Parks, Woods, Warens, Fairs, Markets, Liberties, Free Customs, Wards, Reliefs, Escheates, and Services, as well of Free as Bond Tenants, and all other things that belonged to the Castles, Vills, Mannors, Honours, &c. And this Duke attended the King in that great Expedition into France, where he tho' no more than sixteen Years of Age, commanded the Van of that great Battle of Cressey, and laid on so fiercely with Spear and Shield, whilst the Battle continued three Parts of the Night; in which time the *French* gave five great Assaults against the *English,* till at last they being conquered, ran away.

The next Day four Armies of fresh Souldiers came to the Assistance of the *French,* and gave the *English* Battle again, who withstanding them very stoutly, after a sharp Conflict, forced the *French* to fly, and in the Pursuit three thousand Men were slain on both Days, among whom were the Kings of Bohemia and Majorica, the Archbishop of Zanximus, the Bishop of Noyon, the Dukes of Lorain and Burbone, the Earls of Alanson, Harecourt, Aumarl, Saboy, Nois, Mountbiliard, Nibers, and of Flanders, with the Grand Prior of the Hospital of France; and four hundred Men at Arms, besides common Souldiers without Number.

The Black Prince granted a Warrant dated *An.* 22 *Edw.*

III. to distrain the Bailiff of **Alesbury** by all his Goods Hund. of Bacorum. found within the Honours of **Wallingford** and **Berkham- steb**; and to detain them there, till he satisfie the Prince for his Contempt in distraining the Prince's Tenants to pay Toll, and until he recompense the said Tenants.

Anno 1356, 30 *Edw.* III. this valiant Prince fought that famous Battle of **Poitiers** in **France**, where King *Philip*, his Son, and a great Number of their Nobility were taken and brought into **England** on the 5th of *May*, and on the four and twentieth Day of the same Month, came to **London**, where the Citizens received the Prince with great Honour, then conveyed him to **Westminster**, where the King sitting in great State in the great Hall, received him and all his Prisoners, whence the French King was carried to a Lodging, where he lay awhile, and then was removed to the **Savoy**, which was at that time the House of the Duke of **Lancaster**, and a very pleasant Place.

But the 8th of *June*, *Anno* 1376, 50 *Edw.* III. this noble Stow's Annals fol. 271. and valiant Prince died in the Archbishop's Pallace at **Canterbury**, who was in his time the Flower of Chivalry, and on the Feast of St. *Michael* the Archangel, buried with great Solemnity at *Christ Church* in **Canterbury**; after which King *Edward* created *Richard* his Son, Earl of **Chester**, Duke of **Cornwal**, and Prince of **Wales**.

Anno 1388, 11 *Richard* II. when *Robert de Veer* was advanced to the Title and Dignity of Marquess of **Dublin**, and afterwards Duke of **Ireland**; this King gave him Liberty to reside at this Castle, which was one of his own royal Pallaces, allowing him Wood and Fuel, to be taken out of his Woods and Park for his Firing.

Anno 1400, 1 *H.* IV. *Henry* of **Monmouth** eldest Son to King *H.* IV. was created Duke of **Cornwal**, and possest of this Castle, Honour, and Town of **Berkhamsted**.

Anno 1422, *Henry* of **Windsor** eldest Son to King *H.* V. was advanc'd to the Dukedom of **Cornwal**, and enjoy'd this Castle, Honour, and Town of **Berkhamsted**.

Anno 1454, this Castle and Town was granted to *Edward* of **Westminster**, eldest Son to *H.* VI. but when Dugd. Bar. vol. 2, fol. 264. that King was deposed, they came to the Possession of King *Edw.* IV. who granted the Stewardship of this Castle and Lordship, *Anno* 1461, 1 *Regni sui*, to *John* Lord *Wenlock*, who was preferr'd to the Dignity and Degree of a Baron, and made one of the King's Privy Council.

Cicely Daughter of *Ralph Nevil*, Earl of **Westmorland**, Norden, p.13. Wife to *Richard* Duke of **York**, and Mother to this King, *Anno* 1496, 11 *H.* VII. died in this Place, after she had seen the deserv'd Fall of usurping *Richard*, who some say Stow's Annals fol. 480. was born in this Castle, and since that time this Castle and

Hund. of
Dacorum.
Pat. 2 Eliz.

Honour has been annexed to the Dukedom of **Cornwal**, and appropriated to the Princes of **Wales** successively.

Anno 1560, 2 *Eliz.* that Queen demised the Scite, Circuit and Precinct hereof to *Edward Cary* for a Term of Years, under the Yearly Rent of a Red Rose, payable to the Queen at the Feast of St. *John Baptist*, and by other Letters Patents demised to him two Water Mills in this Town and Lordship, under the Yearly Rent of 7*l.* 8*s.* and the same Queen did grant by her Letters Patents the Mansion House, with this Lodge and Park, to this Sir *Edward Carey* and the Lady *Paget* his Wife, and to the Heirs Males of their Bodies for ever, to hold of the Queen, her Heirs and Successors, as of this Lordship, by Fealty only in free Socage, and not *in Capite*, rendring a Fee Farm Rent of 8*l.* 6*s.* 8*d.*

And the same Queen by Letters Patents dated *Anno* 2 *Regni sui* constituted this Sir *Edward Carey* High Steward of this Honour and Mannor. This Sir *Edward Carey* obtained a Lease of this Castle and Mannor, and from him this Mannor and Castle came to Sir *Adolph Carey* who dying the 10th of *April,* 1609, it descended to Sir *Edward Carey,* who succeeded him, and two third Parts of the Mannor-house being burnt down, about 30 Years since he repaired the House, but not above a third Part or a little more remains now standing, and yet is a very fair large Building, but since he sold the same to *John Sayer,* Esq. who held it sometime, and died possest hereof on the 11th of *February,* 1682, leaving Issue three Sons, *John, Edward,* and *Joseph,* whereof *John* and *Joseph* are dead, and *Edward* is now the present Possessor hereof.

Customs of the Honour and Mannor of BERKHAMSTED.

THE Court Leets for the Honour of **Berkhamsted** shall be kept at five several Places, viz. the Halimoot of **Berkhamsted** shall be kept every Year at an House built on the Ground where the old Castle stood, on *Monday* in *Witson* Week, and *Monday* next after the Feast of *St. Michael* the Archangel. The Court for the Honour, and Mannor or Burrough of **Berkhamsted,** shall be yearly held in the *Church House* or *Loft* in the Town of **Berkhamsted,** on every *Tuesday* in *Witson* Week, and on every *Tuesday* next after the Feast of *St. Michael* the Archangel.

The Mannor of **Aldbury,** part of the said Honour and Mannor, shall be held in the Town of **Aldbury** (where several other Towns and Hamlets appear as Members thereof) and two more, one in **Buckinghamshire,** and the other in

BARKHAMSTED

Drawn on Stone from the Original Engraving by C. L. Tyler.

To the Worp.ll Edward Sayer,

This Plate of the Mannor House

Pub.d by I. M. Mullinger.

MANNOR HOUSE .

of Barkhamsted Place Esq.ʳ

is humbly dedicated by

John Oliver.

Bps: Stortford, 1826.

Northamptonshire, shall be held sometimes in one Town, and sometimes in another, at Discretion.

The Towns, Hamlets, &c. which appear and choose Constables, &c. at Albury Leet are, 1 Albury, 2 Wigginton, 3 Northcot *cum* Lee, 4 Dunsley *cum* Grove, 5 Pendley, 6 Drayton Beaucham, 7 Cheddingdon, 8 Gubblecote, 9 Long Marston, 10 Pelstrap, Grounds belonging to the Lord *Cheiny*, 11 Betlow, Grounds belonging to the Lord Marquis Caermarthen and Earl of Danby, which were formerly a Village.

The Towns and Hamlets, &c. in Buckinghamshire, which are Parts and Members of the Honour and Mannor of Berkhamsted and Part of the Dutchy of Cornwal, and do elect Constables, &c. at such of the same Town, as shall be appointed for the keeping the Leet of that County are, 1 Agmondesham *alias* Amersham, 2 Weedon on the Hill, 3 Wingrave, 4 Weston, 5 Burston House, 6 Weedon in the Vale, 7 Cheyne Fee in Swanburn Village, 8 Hillesdon *alias* Hildesden, 9 The Village of Hyde in Mursly now only an House, 10 Salden House anciently a Village, 11 Lamford, 12 Lowton *alias* Lothton, 13 Wafton *alias* Wobeton, 14 Wabingdon *alias* Waundon, 15 Weston, under Wood.

The Towns, Hamlets, &c. in Northamptonshire are, 1 Old Stratford, 2 Fortho *cum* Cosgrabe, 3 Gaston *cum* Hulcot now Sir *William Farmer's* House, 4 Foxleys, a House and Grounds, 5 Bloxley, 6 Middleton Cheyne, 7 Charlton, 8 Charwelton, 9 Westfarnden, 10 Snoscumbe, 11 Preston on the Hills, 12 Forsley an House, 13 Thornix Dabentry, 14 Welton, 15 Haselbeech, 16 Harleston, 17 Crowlton, 18 Thornby, 19 East Farndon, 20 Bowdon Parba, 21 Oxenden Parba, now only some Grounds that lie within a Mile from Bowden, 22 Dingly now Sir *Edward Griffins* House, 23 Barleton, 24 Arthingworth, 25 Old Thorpe and Harleston, the first is the Lord *Sunderland's* House, 26 Thorpe near Dabentry, 27 Hanging Houghton.

These Towns and Hamlets, &c. in Northamptonshire and Bucks, I suppose, used anciently to appear at the great Court where all the Rest of the Tenants met, and were but one united Court kept in the Castle of Berkhamsted whilst it was standing; but now each County hath its several Court Leets, besides the *Certum Lete*, or Head Silver, and the said Towns or most of them pay certain Sums of Money for Relaxation of Court.

The whole Number of Towns belonging to the said Honour and Mannor of Berkhamsted and Northchurch are 55; besides that two Hamlets are sometimes put together for one, as Norcot *cum* Lee, Dunsley *cum* Grove.

The Court Barons are kept in two Places, viz: in the said Castle and in the *Loft* at Berkhamsted.

One customary Tenant may in the Presence of another take Surrenders out of Court.

The Lord upon the Admission of any Tenant, either upon Descent or Purchase, shall have a certain Fine to the yearly Value of one Year's Quit Rent.

Copihold Lands may be entailed by the Custome.

Copiholder may be Tenant by the Courtesie.

Fem Copiholder may have Dower of the third Part of the Copihold Lands that her Husband was seiz'd of.

Customary Tenant may devise his Copihold Lands for three Years without License, but no longer without Forfeiture.

The Lord's Bailiff receives all Waifs, Estraies, Felons' Goods, Treasure Trove, and such like Profits arising out of the Burrough.

The Bailiffs of the Burrough receive all Waifs &c. arising within the Burrough to their own Use, paying yearly to the King's High Steward for them and the Profits of the Fair, twenty Shillings.

On *Monday* in every Week a Market shall be kept within this Burrough, and on the Feast Day of St. *James* the Apostle, a Fair shall be held there every Year; and the Church Wardens of the Parish Church by ancient Usage have received the Profits thereof for the Repair of the Church and Relief of the Poor.

18 *Decemb.* 1584, 27 *Eliz.*

An AGREEMENT made between the Bailiff of the Honour and the Bailiff of the Burrough and Inhabitants of 𝕭𝕖𝕣𝕜𝕙𝕒𝕞𝕤𝕥𝕖𝕕.

Whereas there have been divers Controversies between the Bailiff of the Honour of 𝕭𝕖𝕣𝕜𝕙𝕒𝕞𝕤𝕥𝕖𝕕, and the Bailiff of the Town or Burrough, and the Inhabitants there, for the Pacifying of all Strifes, they have concluded as follows.

Imprim. *THE Bailiff of the Town shall collect all the Amercements and Estreats in the Burrough, and for non payment shall destrain, and account at the next Court Leet, and pay the one half to the Bailiff of the Honour; and they shall not pardon any Fine or Amercement without order from the High Steward, or can shew sufficient cause to the Bailiff of the Honour, and such as they shall pardon or release to be forgiven notwithstanding the Estreats.*

Item, *The Bailiffs of the Town or Burrough shall yield a true Account or pay to the Bailiff of the Honour, the one half of the Waifs, Estraies, Fugitives, or Felons Goods whatsoever at the End of their Year; and if any such Goods be not equally valued, than if the Bailiff of the Honour will give to the Bailiff of the Burrough more than they will pay or give to him for the other half, then he to have and take such Goods as will give the other most in recompence, provided if the Bailiff of the Burrough deny such Payment or Accompt, then the Bailiff of the Honour shall destrain for such things so denied.*

Item, *It is agreed that the Bailiff of the Honour or his Deputy may distrain any within the Town that come to them, which have been amerced in any of her Majesties Courts abroad in other Places, within the Honour.*

Item, *If the Bailiff of the Honour at any time come to the Town to make any privy search, or to redress any Disorders or disorder'd Persons, the Bailiff of the Town and other Officers shall accompany him, and help to reform any thing that shall be amiss.*

Item, It is fully agreed, as well by the Bailiff of the Honour as the Bailiffs and other Inhabitants of the Town or Burrough aforesaid, that if any manner of Controversie arise, or grow from any manner or such Cause between them as they cannot agree, they shall refer the matter, and stand to the Judgment of the High Steward for the ending of the same.

In witness whereof as well the Bailiff of the Honour, as the Bailiffs and other Inhabitants of the Town or Burrough, hereunto have set their Hands.

Will. Saltmarsh	*Th. Waterhouse*	*Rich. Adkins*
Francis Witherid	*Ri. Chapel* } Bailiffs of the Burrough,	*Step. White*
	Tho. Aston }	*Mich. Clark*
Thomas Reynolds	*Robert Burton*	*Ch. Cramwel*
Robert Atwell	*Richard Pinfold*	*Hen. Field*
	John Hudnal	*Joh. Blunt*
	John Grover	*Rom. Clarke.*

Brief Notes of the LIBERTIES and PRIVILEDGES of Berkhamsted, collected out of the Charters granted by the Kings of this Realm to the Prince, by Mr. Auditor *Huckmore.*

$\mathcal{N}$O *Sheriff, Escheator, Commissioner, Coroner, or Clerk of the Market of the King's, shall enter into his Highness's Liberties for execution of any Writs or Precepts.*

2. *No Sheriff or other Officer aforesaid shall Attach, Distrein, or Arrest any of his Highness's Tenants, although they find them out of his Highness's Liberties, but send their Process to the Prince's Ministers.*

3. *Recognizances and Fines for Regrating and Forestalling.*

4. *No Sheriff, Escheator, nor other Officer of the King shall intermeddle in the collection of Tithingpence, Headsilver, Hundredsilver, Aid, Vicountell, Fines for Suit or Ward, or Fines for the Sheriff, within his Highness's Liberties.*

5. *His Highness's Tenants shall be free and quit from all Tolls, Pontage, Pannage, Stallage, and Customes whatsoever within the Kingdom of England.*

6. *His Highness's Tenants shall be free from Purveyance.*

7. *Neither the Steward, Marshall, Coroner, nor other Officer of the King's Househould, shall enter into his Highness's Liberties for the execution of their Office.*

8. *All Liberties granted in as ample manner as Prince Edward Son of Edward III. or any other Prince of Wales, Duke of Cornwal, and Earl of Chester, had, or enjoyed the same by Vertue of any former Grant.*

BERKHAMSTED BURROUGH.

PARLIAMENT at Westminster, 14 *Edw.* III. *John Bartlet* and *John Hammond* were elected to serve as Burgesses for this Burrough in this Parliament.

Prin's Parl,
Brev. pt. 4.
p 917

Mr. *Prin* takes Notice of no more Burgesses of Parliament retorned for this Burrough; but Dr. *Brady* that learned Gentleman, and sometime Keeper of the Records in the Tower, affirmed to me, that he had seen another Retorn there from this Burrough.

When the Charter of this Corporation was first obtain'd from the Crown, most of the Inhabitants of Berkhamsted were sensible that their Priviledges by their ancient Charters were very great, and opposed the Grant of this Charter thro' Fear that it should destroy or weaken any of their former Grants, Freedoms, or Priviledges.

Hund. of
Dacorum.

Pat. 16 Jac. I.

King *James* I. by his Charter under the Great Seal of England dated the 18th Day of *July*, *Anno* 16 *Regni sui*, incorporated the Inhabitants of this Burrough into one Body corporate and politick, by the Name of Bailiff and Burgesses of the Burrough of 𝔅𝔢𝔯𝔨𝔥𝔞𝔪𝔰𝔱𝔢𝔡 𝔖𝔱. 𝔓𝔢𝔱𝔢𝔯 in the County of ℌ𝔢𝔯𝔱𝔣𝔬𝔯𝔡, and by the same Name, to have perpetual Succession to buy Goods and Chattels, and to purchase Lands and Tenements, and also to grant and devise the same, and by the same Name to implead and answer.

Power to pur-
chase.

CommonSeal.

Their Bailiff and Burgesses may have a common Seal, and may break and renew the same at Pleasure.

Bailiff.

There shall be one Bailiff in the Burrough for the future, who shall be chosen out of the Burgesses, and *Francis Barker* the elder, Gent. an Inhabitant, and one of the Burgesses of the Burrough is constituted the first Bailiff of the Burrough, to continue in this Office from the Date of the Charter till *Michaelmas* then next following, and from thence till another Burgess should be chosen and sworn to the said Office, if the said *Francis Barker* shall so long live; the said *Francis Barker* to be sworn before the twelve capital Burgesses, or the major Part of them.

Chief Bur-
gesses.

There shall be twelve Men in the Burrough of the best and most honest Burgesses, who shall be called Capital Burgesses of the Burrough, and the said Bailiff or Capital Burgesses shall be the Common Council of the Burrough, and Assistant to the Bailiff for the time being in all Causes and Matters concerning the Burrough; and *James Mayne*, Esq. *Thomas Newnham*, Batchelour of Divinity and Rector of the Church of 𝔅𝔢𝔯𝔨𝔥𝔞𝔪𝔰𝔱𝔢𝔡, *Thomas Hunt*, M. A. *Francis Withred*, Gent. *Arthur Blunt*, Gent. *Francis Spring*, Gent. *George Dover*, Gent. *Richard Speed*, Gent. *Oliver Haynes*, Gent. *William Pitkin*, Gent. *Henry Field* the younger, and *Stephen Besouth*, Inhabitants of this Burrough were constituted the first twelve Capital Burgesses of this Burrough, to continue in their Offices so long as they well behaved themselves, taking their Oaths before the Bailiff, who is required to administer the same.

Guildhall.

The Bailiff and Burgesses might purchase a Council House or Guild Hall within the Burrough, where they, or the major Part of them, (whereof the Bailiff for the time being shall be one) might at their Pleasure hold a Court or Convocation to make Statues, Laws, and Ordinances for the Burrough, and to consult the good Government thereof, and to impose Pains, Fines, Penalties, and Imprisonments upon Offenders, and to levy them to their own Use, without any Account for the same, so that such Laws and Ordinances shall not be repugnant to the Laws and Statutes of the Realm.

Some honest and discreet Man, learned in the Laws, *Hund. of Dacorum.* shall be elected Recorder by the Bailiff and Burgesses, or the major Part of them, (of whom the Bailiff shall be one) *Recorder.* who shall be sworn before the Bailiff and Chief Burgesses for the time being, or four of them at the least, and shall execute the said Office at their Pleasure.

There shall be a Common Clerk chosen yearly in the like *Common Clerk.* Manner on the Monday before *Michaelmas,* who shall be sworn before the Bailiff and Capital Burgesses, or any four or three of them, and if he dies or shall be removed, the Bailiff and Chief Burgesses shall choose and swear another in like Manner within eight Days then next following, to exercise the Office during the rest of the Year,

When any of the Chief Burgesses shall die or be removed from his Place by the Bailiff or Chief Burgesses, or major Part of them, for any reasonable Cause, then the Bailiff and the remaining Part of the Chief Burgesses shall choose one or more of the Burgesses or Inhabitants of the Burrough in their Rooms who shall be sworn before the Bailiff.

The Bailiff and Chief Burgesses, or major Part of them, *Election of the Principal Burgess.* shall yearly choose on the Monday next before *Michaelmas* one of the Chief Burgesses to be principal Burgess or Bailiff designed for the ensuing Year; and shall take his Oath before the Bailiff and Chief Burgesses there present; and he honestly behaving himself for that Year shall be chosen Bailiff the next Year, and shall be sworn before the last Bailiff his Predecessor on *Michaelmas* day, or if he be absent, before any other who hath been Bailiff in the presence of *Election of Bailiff.* the Capital Burgesses, or the major Part of them, or any four of them at the least, and if he happen to die or be removed from his Office within the Year, then another of the Chief Burgesses shall be chosen in his Room by the Capital Burgesses or major Part of them, for the Residue of the Year, and shall be sworn as aforesaid.

The Bailiff, Recorder, and principal Burgess, or Bailiff *Justices of the Peace.* designed, shall be Justices of the Peace in the Burrough, and they and every of them may do whatsoever, one, two of three Justices of the Peace for the County of Hertford, or elsewhere within this Realm, may do, so that they proceed not to the Determination of any Fault touching Life or Loss of Member, without a special Warrant from the King, his Heirs and Successors.

The Bailiff shall be sworn before the Capital Burgesses, *Swearing of Justices.* or four of them at the Least, well and truly to execute the Office of Justice of the Peace within the said Burrough and Liberty thereof, and the Recorder and Principal Burgess shall be sworn to execute the said Office of Justice of the Peace within the said Burrough and Liberty before the

Hund. of Bacorum.

Bailiff of the said Burrough, and afterwards every Bailiff shall be elected, and sworn to execute the said Office before his Predecessor,

Serjeants at Mace.

There shall be two Serjeants at the Mace elected yearly on Monday next before *Michaelmas* out of the Burgesses inhabiting within the said Burrough, to hold the said Office for one whole Year, by the Bailiff and Capital Burgesses, or the major Part of them, (whereof the Bailiff shall be one) to execute Process, Mandates, and other Businesses in the Burrough, and to attend from time to time on the Bailiff; and they shall be sworn before the Bailiff and Burgesses or the major Part of them, (of whom the Bailiff shall be one) and they shall bear a Silver Mace engraven'd and adorned with the Arms of the most illustrious Prince *Charles,* most dear Son to King *James* I. before the Bailiff of the Burrough for the time being and his Successors, every where within this Burrough, Liberties and Precincts hereof, and if any Bailiff, capital Burgess, or other inferior Officer of this Burrough (except the Recorder or Common Clerk) shall after such Choice or Notice thereof, and three Days following, refuse the said Office, then the Capital Burgesses or major Part of them, may impose such Fines or Amercements as they shall think fit to levy by Distress of the Goods and Chattels of the Refusers, or commit them to Goal, till they shall pay them to the Use of this Burrough.

Court of Record.

The Bailiff and Burgesses, and their Successors, shall hold within this Burrough one Court of Record on Tuesday, once in every Month, before the Bailiff, or in his Absence, before the Principal Burgess and Capital Burgesses, or any three of them, and the Recorder for the time being, and therein shall have Cognizance by Plaint of all and all Manner of Pleas, Actions, Suits, and Demands whatsoever, Trespasses, Force and Arms, Threatnings, burning of Houses, and Loss of Men, or otherwise, done or which shall be done in Contempt of the King, his Heirs and Successors, or against the Form of any Statute for the keeping of the Peace, or Security of the People, of Thieves, and of whatsoever other Transgressions, Faults and Offences perpetrated within the Burrough, Liberties, and Precincts of the same; and of all and all Manner of Debts, Accompts, Covenants, Deceipts, and Detentions of Charters, Writings, and Miniments, and Goods, Chattels, and Cattle taken and detained, and other Contracts whatsoever, for whatsoever Causes or Things (not touching Life or Loss of Member as aforesaid) arising within this Burrough, Liberty or Precinct hereof, so as the same Trespasses, Debts, Accompts, Covenants, Deceipts, and Detentions, or other Contracts do not exceed the Sum of ten Pounds; and that such Pleas, Complaints, &c. shall be heard and determined before the Bailiff and Principal Burgesses, or either of them, and the Capital Burgesses for the time being, or before three of them, and the Recorder by such and like Manners and Ways, and ac-according to the Law and Custome of England, and in as ample Manner and Form as is used and accustomed in any Court of Record, in any City, Burrough, or Town corporate within England; and all Fines, Amerciaments, and other Profits of this Court shall be to their proper Use, without any Account or other Thing to be paid to the Crown for the same. *Hund. of Bacorum.*

The Bailiff and Chief Burgesses shall have a Prison or Goal within this Burrough, and the Bailiff shall be Keeper thereof. *Goal.*

The Bailiff and Burgesses, and their Successors, may hold a Market on every *Thursday* within this Burrough, besides the ancient Market held there on every *Monday* in the Week, with all Tolls, Stallage, Shops, and other Emoluments thereof arising there, to be paid to the Bailiff and Chief Burgesses, and their Successors, to their own proper Use, without any Accompt to be made to the King, his Heirs or Successors. *Market.*

They shall also hold two Fairs more, one on *Shrove-Tues-day*, the other on *Whitson-Monday*, in every Year, besides the ancient Fair on St. *James's* Day, with a Court of Pypowder, and shall have all Commodities, Stalls, Stallage, Shops, Emoluments, and Advantages whatsoever arising by the said Fairs, without any Accompt. *Fair.*

They shall also hold and quietly enjoy all the Customes, Liberties, Priviledges, Franchises, Immunities, Exemptions, Exonerations, Quietances, Rights, and Jurisdictions, heretofore granted by any of the Kings or Queens of England, or by Prince *Charles*, to them or their Predecessors. *Customs and Usage.*

That the Bailiff and Chief Burgesses of this Burrough might the better sustain and support the Burden and Charges within this Burrough, the King granted License to them to buy and possess as well of the King as any other his leige People or Persons whatsoever, Mannors, Messuages, Lands, Tenements, Rectories, Tenths, Rents, Revenues, Services, Hereditaments whatsoever, to them and their Successors, so as they were not held of the King, his Heirs or Successors, *in Capite*, or by Knight's Service, without any special License of the King or Lord of the Mannor, and so as the said Mannors, Messuages, &c. shall not exceed the yearly Sum of forty Marks; and that the said Bailiff and Burgesses might have these Letters Patents made and sealed under the Great Seal of England, without Fine or Fee to the King in his Hanaper or else where. *License to purchase.*

William Camden, Clarencieux King of Arms, by his Grant dated the 25th of *September, Anno* 16 *Jac.* I. reciting

Hund. of Dacorum. the said Grant that the King had incorporated the Burrough of 𝕭erkhamsted 𝕾t. 𝕻eters in the County of 𝕳ertford, by the Name of Bailiff and Burgesses of the Burrough of 𝕭erkhamsted 𝕾t. 𝕻eters in the said County of 𝕳ertford, and withal had granted to them a Mace adorned with the Arms of his most dear Son Prince *Charles,* and a peculiar Seal for the Administration of their Affairs, assigned to them these Arms: *In a Shield Or, a triple tow'd Castle Azure, with a Bordar of* 𝕮ornwal, *viz. Sables besanted.*

Prince's Lease. *Charles* Prince of 𝖂ales, Duke of 𝕮ornwal and 𝕵ork, and Earl of 𝕮hester, by Indenture made the 16th Day of *June,* in the 17th Year of King *James* I. over 𝕰ngland, in the 52nd Year over 𝕾cotland, &c. granted to the Bailiff and Burgesses of 𝕭erkhamsted 𝕾t. 𝕻eters, then incorporate,

Coroner. Clerk of the Market. That the Bailiff should be Coroner and Clerk of the Market to his Highness within the Burrough of 𝕭erkhamsted 𝕾t. 𝕻eters, and Halimot thereunto adjoyning, and within the several Parishes of 𝕭erkhamsted 𝕾t. 𝕻eter, and 𝕭erkhamsted 𝕾t. 𝕸ary *alias* Northchurch, and to take lawful Fees for the same to the Use of the Corporation.

Bailiff for the retorn of Writs. That the Bailiff shall be the Prince's Bailiff for the Execution and Retorn of all Writs and Process of the King within the Burrough, Halimote, and said Parishes by himself or his Deputies, taking due Fees for the same to the Use of the Corporation; and also the Prince demised to the Bailiff and Burgesses all Fines and Amerceaments assess'd in any of his Highness's Courts within the Burrough of *Fines and Amercem. ments.* 𝕭erkhamsted 𝕾t. 𝕻eter, and 𝕭erkhamsted 𝕾t. 𝕸ary *alias* 𝕹orthchurch; and the High Steward shall deliver the Extracts, and give Warrant to the Bailiff and Burgesses to levy the Fines and Amerceaments by their own Ministers to the Uses aforesaid, and also all Waifs and Estraies, and all Goods and Chattels of Felons, Fugitives, and Outlawes, and all other Profits whatsoever belonging to a View of Franc-pledge, and all Deodands and Waifs in the Burrough and Parishes, and the Profit of all Recognizances forfeited by any Person within the Burrough or Limits aforesaid, and also the Toll and Profit of the ancient Fair and Market there, to the Uses aforesaid.

Tolls, Stallage That all his Highness's Tenants, and all the Inhabitants within the Burrough shall be free and exempted from all Tolls, Stallage, and other Customes, whatsoever within 𝕰ngland, (except it be for Pontage or Highways,) to have and to hold the same Liberties, Priviledges, Profits, and Commodities, and all and singular the Premises with their Appurtenances to the Bailiff and Burgesses aforesaid, and their Successors, from the Feast of St. *Michael* last past, for the Term of one and thirty Years, paying twenty Shillings a Year to his Highness's particular Farmer for his

Highness's Use, at *Lady-day* and *Michaelmas* by equal Portions; and if the Rent should be behind for twenty-eight Days after any of the said Feasts, then the Grant shall cease and be void.

The Names of the BAILIFFS, RECORDERS, CAPITAL BURGES-SES, and other Officers of the Burrough of 𝔅𝔢𝔯𝔨𝔥𝔞𝔪𝔰𝔱𝔢𝔡.

BAILIFFS.

⌐ 1628	*William Lake*	1649	*William Hill*
1635	*Oliver Hains*	1650	*Francis Pitkin*
1636	*William Pitkin*	1651	*Robert Rennold*
1637	*Stephen Besouth*	1652	*Robert Newman*
1638	*Samuel Dagnal*	1653	*Ralph Benning*
1639 {	*William Halsey*	1654	*John Hore*
	Robert Blunt	1655	*Thomas Aldridge*
1640	*William Hill*	1656 {	*Robert Benning*
1641	*Robert Reynold*		*William Hill*
1642	*Ralph Benning*	1657	*Maurice Kellet*
1643	*John Benning*	1658	*Francis Nixon*
1644	*John Tey*	1659	*Thomas Newman*
1645	*Robert Benning*	1660	*Christop. Woodhouse*
1646	*John Barker*	1661	*William Hill*
1647	*William Barker*	1662	*Robert Rennold*
1648	*George Dover*	1663	*Robert Newman*

RECORDERS.

1639	*Henry Guy*, Esq.	1644	*Henry Exre*, Esq.
1640	*John Duncomb*, Esq.	1650	*John Norbury*, Esq.
1643	*John Howland*, Esq.	1656	*William Cotton*, Esq.

CHIEF BURGESSES.

⌐ 1628	*William Lake*		*William Parker*
	William Hill		*Maurice Kellet*
	George Dover		*Francis Pitkin*
	Francis Barker		*William Pitkin*
	William Pitkin		*Stephen Besouth*
	Thomas Newman		*Robert Blount*
	Francis Withered	1648	*John Baily*
	Edward Kellet		*William Theede*
	Thomas Hunt	1649	*Robert Newman*
	Oliver Hains		*John Hore*
	Stephen Besouth		*Francis Nixon*
	Samuel Dagnal	1651	*Thomas Aldridge*
	William Axtel	1652	*Thomas Newman*
1638	*Ralph Benning*	1656	*Christoph. Woodhouse*
	Robert Darvol, elected		*Mordecay Herne*
	but fined	1657	*Francis Withered*
	John Benning	1659	*John Nash*
	Robert Rennold	1662	*Francis Clerk*
	Robert Benning		*William Hill*
1640	*John Tey*		*John Child*
1641	*Robert Benning*		*Thomas Topping*
1643	*William Lake*		*William Babb.*
1645	*John Barker*		

COMMON CLERKS.

1637	*Robert Blunt*, Gent.	1645	*Richard Dover*, Gent.
1639	*William Axtel*, Gent.	1653	*George Dover*, Gent.
1640	*John Dover*, Gent.	1659	*Francis Clerke*, Gent.
1642	*Forster Rainsford*, Gent.	1663	*Daniel Clerke*, Gent.
1643	*Robert Blount*, Gent.		

Hund. of
Dacorum.

SERJEANTS at MACE.

1638 *John Varney, Thomas Hudnol,*	1644 *George Geary, James Eames*
William Cock, elected in the place	1646 *William Bulley, John Wray*
of *Thomas Hudnol.*	1656 *John Wray, James Eames*
1639 *William Cock, John Varney*	1658 *James Eames, William Bulley*
1640 *John Cock, William Keeper*	1659 *William Bulley, John Addams*
1641 *John Cock, Thomas Hudnol*	1660 *Will. Bulley, Will. Hawes.*

A *Quo Warranto* was brought in —— — Term, *Anno* 16—— against the Bailiff and Burgesses of this Corporation, who pleaded their Charter, upon which I was informed there was no farther Proceeding, but the Corporation growing very poor in the time of the late War, let their Government fall, however four of the Chief Burgesses are still living in the Town, who by the Charter may choose a Bayliff, and may still fill up the Number of Burgesses.

THIS Church is a Rectory and a rural Deanery, scituated in the Deanery of Berkhamsted, in the Diocess of Lincoln, and *Anno* 26 *H.*VIII. was rated in the King's Books at the yearly Value of 20l. and the King is Patron hereof.

RECTORS.

Thomas Newman	*Robert Brabant,* A.M. and Chaplain to
John Napper	King *William* and Queen *Mary*

This Church is dedicated to the Honour of St. *Peter* the Apostle, and is erected near the Middle of the Town by *Richard Torrington* (as the Inhabitants have a Tradition) a Man who was in great Favour with *Edmond Plantagenet* Duke of Cornwal, the Son of *Richard Plantagenet* second Son of King *John* Earl of Cornwal, and King of the *Romans;* and the Tower at the West End of the Church was rebuilt *An.* 27 *Hen.* VIII. as is supposed by *John Philip:* 'Tis well leaded and adorned, in very good Repair; and there is in it a Ring of five Bells, but not very tuneable; and at the upper End of the Body of the Church is their present Majesties' Arms, with the Garter, Mantlings, Doubling, Helmet, Crest, Supporters, Motto's, Inscriptions, &c. well and largely painted, and laid with Gold over the same, a rich Cap of State, and over all, their Majesties' Names, *William* and *Mary* in Characters upheld by two Cherubs; on the right Side of the Arms stands Justice with a Sword in her right Hand, and a Ballance in her Left, looking towards the Effigies of Mercy, which stands on the left Side of the Arms, with a Pardon sealed in her right Hand, and her golden Scepter in her left, both of them depicted at large, standing upon two Pedestals of Stone between two Pillars of the like firmly carved on the Top; Justice having writ on her Head in Letters of Gold, *Fear God and honour the King.* And upon the Pedestal, *To do Justice is more acceptable to the Lord than Sacrifice,* Prov. cap. xxi, v. 3. *Whosoever resisteth the Power receive to themselves Damnation.* And upon her Pedestal, *Mercy and Truth preserveth the King.* Prov. xx, 28. And on each Side the whole are two Pillars marbled.

Underneath their present Majesties, is Queen *Elizabeth's* Arms newly painted again, which remained all the late civil Laws untouched or blemish'd; so did also the Arms of King *James* I. which were lately changed into King *Williams* and Queen *Mary,* nor the Arms of King *Edward* VI. in the Chapel of St. *John* suffered any Injury in the Heat of all those Troubles.

Under the Arms of Queen *Elizabeth* is writ.

This mighty Queen is dead, and lives,   ·
And leaves the World to wonder,
How she a Maiden Queen did rule,
Few Kings have gone beyond her.

On both Sides the Arms of Queen *Elizabeth,* are the ten Commandments, and on each Side the Commandments stand *Moses* with his budedd

Rod in his right Hand, and the Tables with the ten Commandments characterized after the Manner of the Eastern Languages, and Letters in his left Hand in the Habit of a Prince, and *Aaron* standing on the left Hand clothed in his priestly Vestiments, and having the Censor burning in his left Hand.

The Pillars of the whole Church are marbled; the Creeds and the various Sentences of Scripture are incirculed and adorned with Paintings.

At the lower End of the Body of the Church a very good Marble Font is erected between two Pillars, by *Francis Withered*, Esq. Controller of the Works of his Majesty King *Charles* II. *Anno* 1667, with a guilt Crown thereon and a guilt Dove over it, and has a decent Cover which with Pullies rise and falls as the same is covered or uncovered.

The Pulpit is adorn'd in proportion to the rest of the Church. The Communion Table is decently railed in, the Seats are uniform to each other, and the Walls of the whole Church are beautified and kept in good Repair.

In the Chancel.

In the Isle on the East Side of the Altar, Sir *Adolph Cary*, Kt. was buried on the 10th Day of *April*, 1609. *Anno* 7 *Ja.* I. his Banners were taken down not long since; having hung as long as they could, but the Helmet, Sword and Crest, which is on a *Wreath Argent and Sable, a Swan proper, on its Breast a Cressent Sable* are still remaining on the Side of a Pillar: in the Isle his Paternal Coat is in a *Field Argent, on a Bend Sable three Roses of the second, Barbed proper, with a Crescent for the difference of his Family;* which is impaled with another Coat thus, *In a Feild Argent, a Bend Sable within a Bordure engrailed of the second.* Under them in a Compartment is subscribed for a Motto *Non Antiquitas sed Virtus Honor.*

In the same Isle near the former is an ancient Tomb, the Brass Inscription whereof is gone, but by the Atchievement, which is curiously inlaid thereon with Brass, Iron, &c. compared with the Register Book of the Parish for Burials, 'twas in memory of Sir *John Cornwallis*, Kt. who was one of the Council to Prince *Edward*, afterwards King *Edward* VI. he died at **Asheridge**, and was buried here, 1 of *May*, 1543, 35 *Henry* VIII.

The Atchievement on his Tomb is as follows.

Party per pale Baron and Fem, his five Coates marshalled viz. the first, *Sable Guttee de Eaw, on a Fess Argent three Cornish Choughs proper, by the name of* Cornwallis. The second, *a Cross Floree.* The third, *a Bend Dexter between six Croscroslets fitchet in Base.* The fourth, *Barry of fourteen pieces, a Dexter quarter.* The fifth, *a Cheveron between three Storkes (as I believe) proper; here is a Cheveron between three Phæons, the whole insigned with an Helmet answerable to his Degree, mantled and doubled, and on a Turf a Cornish Chough proper with the Wings expansed, and holding in his Mouth two blades of Grass, one of Cinquefoyle the other of Troyfoyle.*

In the Chancel going into the Church by the Belfry, one Tomb in the Wall has this Inscription on the Gravestone before it.

Hic jacet Johannes Waterhouse *et* Margaretta *uxor ejus.*

Upon the Tomb on the Wall is an Atchievement containing twelve Coats of Arms: The first a Paternal Coat whereof is, *Or a Pile engrailed Sable,* ———— and under the Atchievements are these Verses

Ecce sub hoc Tumulo Conjux Uxorque jacemus
Æternam Pacem donet Utriq; Deus.
Nil unquam abstulimus, si quid benefecimus ulli,
Est qui pro Meritis præmia digna dabit.
Est tamen una salus Christi, Miseratio, quam qui
Transis, Ambobus sæpe precare precor.

Upon the Marble on the Wall over the Tomb is written

John *Waterhouse*, Gent. deceased died the 11th day of *August* an. 1666. and *Margaret* his Wife deceased the 10th day of *January* in the same year, which *John* and *Margaret* had issue, viz. *John, Thomas, William, Edward, Arthur,* and *Charles.*

Not far from the former Monument is another thus,

Here under lyeth interred the Body of the worthy Lady Dame *Margaret Waterhouse* deceased, Daughter of *Thomas Spilman of Chart* in the County of Kent, Esq; in the Memory of whose virtues and Dearest Love Sir *Edward Waterhouse,* Kt. her Husband hath caused this Monument to be erected; She died the 6th day of *July* 1587. *ætatis suæ* 16. and he 30th of *October ætatis suæ* 55. and lyeth buried with his last wife Dame *Deborah,* at the Mannor of Woodchurch in Kent.

Over this Inscription is the beforementioned Paternal Coat of *Waterhouse* impaled with hers, which is, in *a Feild sable, two Bars Argent, between two Mullets in Cheif Or, and a Besant Base;* and under the Coat, of Arms, and over her Effigies, which is kneeling, is thus written.

Blessed are they that die in the Lord.

There is another that has this Inscription.

Hereunder lie the Bodies of *Thomas Waterhouse,* Gent. deceased, and *Mary* his Wife, who lived together in Marriage 32 Years, and had Issue between them six Sons and five Daughters; he died the 7th Day of *September, Anno* 1600, in the 68th Year of his Age, and she died the 4th Day of *December, Anno* 1598. in the 54th Year of her Age, both of them in the Love and Favour of God and Man.

And over this Inscription is the paternal Coat of *Waterhouse* impaled with hers, which is, in *a Field Argent, two Bars Or, Dexter Canton Gules:* and by the Parish Register, it appears that many more of this Name have been buried here.

Here is another Gravestone with an Effigies of Brass at full Length let into it, and this Inscription upon it in Brass.

Hic jacet Edwardus De la hay, Armiger qui obiit in decimo quinto Mensis Junii, Anno Dom. MVCX. Cujus Animæ propitietur Deus. Amen.

At the Entrance into the Body of the Church is a Burial Place enclosed with very good Work and well beautified, wherein is a very stately Monnment of black and white Marble, with two black Marble Doors standing open, supported on both Sides by two large Effigies in white Marble; on the upper Part of the Monument is the Coat of Mr. *Baldwin,* which is, *an Escocheon quarterly quartered, in the first six Blades of Wheat 2 2 and 2, and a Canton, in the second a Fesse Checque, the third as the second, the fourth as the first, mantled and doubled; and Helmet according to his Degree, and for Crest, on a Wreath, a Squirrel sejant.*

Under the former, and on the other Side of the Table of Inscription, is the same quartered Coat of *Baldwin,* impaled with his Wives, viz. *a Bar Dancet, and in the Cheif three Leopards' Heads Barwise,* and on the left Side of the Table is his own again; Under all the forementioned is this Inscripton,

Bonæ Memoriæ
Thomæ Baldvini *armigeri*
Hertfordiensis
Qui natus est in hoc ipso agro Hertford.
2do Maii Anno Salut Reparat CIɔICLXVIII.
Vitam cum morte commutavit XX Junii Anno
CIɔICC.XLI: et ætatis suæ LXXIIIY.
Pia et Mæsti Conjux Katherin. quæ cum illo per 44 Annos
Conjunctissime vixit XLIIII hoc in Loco ex Testamento
Monument ac. C.
Semina non nisi corrupta vvrirescunt
1 *Cor.* xv. 36.

In St. JOHN'S CHAPEL are several Gravestones thus inscribed.

Hic jacet Johannes Incent *Generosus*, (here some of the Brasses are wanting, and then follows) *Dom.* Ceciliæ *Ducissæ* Ebor. *Matris Serenissimorum Regum Angliæ* Edwardi *quarti et* Richardi *tertii atque Proavæ excellentissimi Regis* Henerici *octavi, qui quidem* Robertus Incent *obiit* xxviii *die* Septembris, *Anno Dom. Millessimo* CCCC. this is cut in Brass round the Stone.

Upon the same Stone is also inscribed in Brass.

Here lieth buried under this Stone, the Body of Robert Incent, Gentleman; Servant unto the noble Princess Lady Cecily Dutchess of York, and Mother unto the worthy King Edward the fourth, and Richard the third, which Robert Incent died of the Great Sweating Sickness the first Year of the Reign of King Henry the seventh, upon whose Soulys Jesu have Mercy, Amen

He was her Secretary as I am informed. Under the Inscription is his Coat of Armes. *In a Shield on a Bend dexter, a Rose, and in the Honour point a Dove.* Above the Inscription is his Effigies at Length in Brass let into the Stone.

The second is written round the Stone in old Romish false Latin, which is the Reason my Friend translated it to me in English.

Here lyeth *Katharine* the wife of *Robert Incent*, Gent. the Mother of that venerable Man *John Incent*, Dr. of the Laws, who at his own cost Reedified the Chappel, and conferred his own proper Goods upon this other of St. *John*, which said *Katharine* died the 11th day of *March* in the year of our Lords Incarnation, *M. Quingentesimo Vicesimo, et anno Regni Regis* Henrici *octavi duodecimo.*

Upon the same Stone is this engraved.

Here lyeth buried under this Stone the Body of Katherine sometime the wife of Robert Incent, Gent. Father and Mother unto John Incent, Dr. of the Law, who hath done many benefits and ornaments given unto this Chappel of St. John; which said Katharine died the 11th day of March the 12th year of the Reign of King Henry the eight.————

Underneath is the same Coat of Armes of *Incent*, and over the Inscription is her Effigies as her Husbands at large in Brass.

Another Gravestone has this Inscription.

———— ———— Edmundi Cook, qui obiit 24 die mensis Junii Anne Dom. 1409. The Head of the Effigies is broke off, but a Label has this Inscription, Jesu filii Die miserere mei.

Another Stone sets forth this Inscription.

Hic jacet Johannes Raven, Armiger, qui obiit 15 die Martii Anno Domini 1395.————

In the Window of this Chappel are two Coates of Arms impaled; the first is the Arms of *France* and *England, quarterly quartered; the other is Gules a Saltire Or, over all is a Ducal Crown;* and without side of the Tower fronting the Highstreet is an Escotcheon engraved with the same two Coats impaled without a Crest, and on the sinister Part thereof is cut in Stone *John Philip* and *Alice* his Wife; and the Inhabitants believe that he might reedyfie or build this Tower, for that the Sheild, Arms, and Sculpture are wrought in the solid work of the Tower itself.

In the Middle of the Body of the Church there is a stately Tomb of an ancient rich Fabrick strangely depicted, whereon the Portraiture of a Man in knightly Habiliments, with his Wife lying by him, are cut in Alablaster; and about the Verge of a large Marble thereunto adjoyning is this Inscription in Brass.

Hic jacet Richardus Torrington et Margaretta uxor ejus, qui quidem Richardus obiit die Martii anno 1356. et Margaretta obiit 20 die Mensis Maii 1349.

Hund. of
Bacorum.

On his Monument is the same Coat of Arms born by the *Incents*, and several Coats placed round the Monument, and on the Gravestone near the Monument in the Dexter Corner the same Coat born by the *Incents*, and in the sinister Corner is another Shield bearing a St. George's *Cross, in the Dexter Chief thereof, a Saltier engrailed, and in the Sinister Chief a Cross doubly crossed.* Their Effigies are broken.

The same Coats of *Torrington* and *Incent* are round the Church on every Pillar, and on the Woodwork on the Side of the Church, and is thus blazoned.

He beareth *Or, on a Bend Gules a Rose of the First, in the Honour point a Dore Sable* and on the Gravestones are the Portraictures of him and his Wife in Brass and very full and large.

There is a Tradition that this *Torrington* was the Founder of this Church, a Man of special Favour with *Edward Plantagenet* Duke of *Cornwal*, who was Son of *Richard Plantagenet* the second Son of King *John*, Earl of *Cornwal* and King of the *Romans*, which *Richard*, full of Honours and Years ended his life here at his Castle of **Berkhamsted**, but was buried at his Abby of **Hales**.

In the Isle on the East from the Chancel lyes a Gravestone, on the Top whereof is this Coat of Arms.

In a Field Sable a Cheveron Argent, between three Cinque Foyles Ermines, Guttee de Sangue with Mantling, Doubling, Helmet, and for Crest *over a Torse Argent an Hercules issuant.*

Under the Coat of Arms is this Inscription.

M. S.
Hoc Tumulo Conditur
Christopherus Woodhouse
Berkhamstadiæ *in Comitatu*
Hertfordiensis
Incola
Ubi
Percontinua quinque Lustra ———
Et binos in super annos
Mortalitat. decurrit Stadium
In ipsa Meta
Æternitatem animæ
Perpetuitatem famæ
Quam Deus et Lucubratio illi consecrarant, Spartam traditurus
Sedulo excoluit
Medicinæ Cultor, omnis generis morborum Curator
Indefessus fælix,
Charitate erga egenos stupenda,
Ostentatione Nulla
Probitate summa
Ita
. *Candelæ instar*
Dum aliis prodest ;
Sibi consumitur ;
Die 26 Julii A. S. 1682.
Ætatis 61.
Suspende Gradum Lector
et Lugenti suæ Patriæ Condoleas
ut sacro Quæ huic Busto
bene preceris
Obtestatur.

Another Gravestone in the same Isle tells you,

Here lyeth the Body of Dame *Frances Fotherly* Daughter of *Edward Seymour*, Esq; of **Mosoulands** in the County of **Dorset**, who departed this life the 16th of *June* 1691.

Another Stone shews.

Hic jacet Richardus Westbrook, qui obiit 29 September, 1485. **supplicans bobis ex charitate bestra pro Anima sua biscere pater nostre et Abe——**
And his Effigies are at length in Brass.

There seems to have been two quartered Coats in two several Escotcheons; the first in the Escotcheon on the dexter Corner of the Stone is a *Flower de Luce*, the second a *Fess Dancet*, the third as the second, the fourth as the first. In the Escotcheon on the sinister Corner of the Stone, the first Bearing has no Impression, and cannot be discerned, the second is some Sort of *Fish Naiant*, the third as the second, the fourth not to be discerned.

A fourth Part of the same Isle is very handsomely enclosed, and in the Middle thereof stands a very good Tomb of black and white Marble to the Memory of *John Sayer*, Esq. deceased, whereon his Coat of Arms is engraved, which is *In a Field Party per pale Gules and Azure, on a Cheveron Or, between three Seapie proper, a Rose and Crown of the first*, and on the West Side thereof is this Inscription.

Johannes Sayer, *Armig. Serenissimi Dom. Regis Caroli secundi Archimagirus, cui temporibus defficilimis tam foras quam domi in regnis suis Angliæ et Scotiæ constanter adhæsit; singularem erga Deum Pietatem, erga proximos egenos precipue Charitatem semper exercuit, et mille Libras Testamento legavit ad inopem hujus Burgi de Berkhamstediæ sustentationem prudentia Dilectissimæ Conjugis Mariæ disponend. per quam tres Optimæ indolis filios reliquit; Johannem, Edwardum et Josephum. Obiit undecimo die Februarii MDCLXXXII. Ætatis suæ LXIII.*

In the Communion Chappel, over the Vestry Door, is a good Monument of white Marble variously carved, guilt and adorned with two Pillars of black Marble, on the Side between which are the Effigies of two young Youths, under them a Piece of black Marble inscribed thus,

Josephum *et* Jacobum Moravias
Adolescentes indole Suavissimos,
Fratres Charitate propinos
Filios Obsequio piissimos
Infælix mater.
Pepetuæ securitati, et
Memoriæ æternæ,
Fato cedens Commendavit.

These *Morays* were an ancient Family in **Scotland**, and **Mrs.** *Moray*, who lived here in the time of King *James* I. was Nurse to King *Charles* I. and her Husband was also his Secretary as I have been informed.

On a Gravestone near the same Monument is this Inscription.

Hic jacet in spe Resurrectionis Jacobus Moravius *septimus Masculus* Thomæ Moravii, *Armigeri defuncti Caroli Principi ab epistolis.*

In the Parish Register of Burials several others of this Name are buried here.

Another Stone.
Hic jacet Robertus Spalding ————

Another Stone this

In spe beati Resurrectionis
Hic jacet Edwardus Kellet, *Armiger.*
qui obiit decimo septimo die Septembris.
Anno Dom. 1635.

Another Stone.

Here lies the Body of *Ellen Rodway* late one of the Daughters and Coheirs of *Richard Rodway*, late Citizen and Merchant Taylor of **London.** *Obiit* 4. Decemb. *Anno Dom.* 1636.
Ætatisq; suæ 20.

Hund. of
Dacorum.

On the said *Rodways* Gravestone is a Coat of Arms, *Quarterly quar-tered, viz.* In the first, *on a Bar between three Bugle Horns stringed three Roses ;* In the second, *three Bucks Tripping, and a Cheif;* the third as the second, the fourth as the first.

By the Register Book of Burials in this Parish it is recorded, that

Sir *William Thomas,* Kt. was buried here on the 29th *Jan.* 1545, 36 *Hen.* VIII.
Sir *Raufe Verney,* Kt. was buried here on the 26th *Apr.* 1545, 36 *Hen.* VIII.
Sir *John Maddox,* Clerk, was buried here on the 6th *June,* 1571. 13 *Eliz.*
Elizabeth, the Daughter of Sir *John Cowper,* Clerk, 8 *Dec.* 1573, 16 *Eliz.*
Ursula, the Daughter of Sir *Adrian Scroop,* 29 *October,* 1610, 8 *Jac.* I.

To the Memory of all or some of whom, 'tis very probable the Grave-stones whose Brasses are gone, might be laid.

The Foundation of the FREE-SCHOOL.

ANNO 15 H. VIII. all the Inhabitants of the Town of Berkhamsted consulted together, and agreed that the Lands of their Brotherhood (who then were known by the Name of the President, Wardens, and Brethren of the Guild or Fraternity of St. *John* the Baptist in Berkhamsted St. Peter) should be employed towards the building of a School, and the maintaining of a Schoolmaster to teach their Children there, and Dr. *Incent* Dean of St. *Pauls* Church in London, being born here, and at that time President and Cheif of the said Fraternity, gave all the Lands which he had here, for the said Use, and sent a Schoolmaster who taught their Children in the Brotherhood House, and they were always after ac-counted and reputed as Part of the Brotherhood Lands; which Course was continually observed until *Anno* 33 *H.* VIII. when the Dean fearing the Lands being in the Name of a Brotherhood, might not be so secure, for the better Establishment of the same, obtained of the King a License to purchase 40*l. per Annum,* to found a School with an Incorporation at Berkhamsted, whereof the Kings of this Realm should be always Found-

2 & 3 Ed. VI.   ers, and should name and place the Schoolmaster there as often as the Place should happen to be void, which thing was settled by Act of Parliament.

Then the Dean with the Assistance of the Inhabitants in the Town, and his Friends, erected a Fair large School of Brick and Freestone, with a Lodging for the Schoolmaster adjoyning to the West End thereof, where the Dean himself did lye and kept House divers times before his Death; and at the East End of the School were two other Lodgings erected, one for the Usher, and the other for the Chaplain or Chantry Priest, which building remains at this Day, very fair and strong.

When the School was finisht, the Dean sent for the cheif Men in this Town, and gave thanks with them upon their Knees to Almighty God, for having given him Life to see the Perfection of that Work, which both he, the Town, and Country had been performing about the space of twenty Years, then he called Mr. *Reeve,* and placed him in the Seat there made for the Schoolmaster, and so did ordain, make, and pro-nounce him the first Master of the School; then gave to him and his Successors for ever, Possession of the Lodgings appertaining to that Of-fice, also he constituted Mr. *John Audley* Usher, and Mr. *John East* Chaplain.

This done he gave Possession by his Deed dated 23d of *March, Anno* 26 *H.* VIII. to *Richard Reeve, John Audley,* and *John East,* and their Successors for ever, of all the Lands granted to the School, which are

3 & 4 Ed. VI.   particularly expressed in the said Act of Parliament.

Then the Dean began *Te Deum Laudamus,* then which being finished with certain other Prayers and Ceremonies, the whole Company drank to-gether and departed.

The Occasion of the second Foundation of the School.

The Dean dying the next Year after the Erection of the School, some evil Persons informed the King, that the Dean had granted to the School a larger Revenue than his License did allow.

Whereupon the King appointed *Henry Haydon* and *John Waterhouse,* Gentlemen, to survey the Lands on the 11th Day of *Jan. Anno* 38 *H.* VIII. who found the whole Rents of the Lands, did not exceed the yearly Value of 30*l.* 13*s.* and 8*d.* as appears by the said Survey.

Anno 1 *Ed.* VI. the Schoolmaster was required to shew the Foundation of the School to such Persons as the King's Council had appointed, and upon View thereof they demanded an Incorporation besides the License and other Writings, which Incorporation, and the Dean's Will, were supposed to be imbezelled by one *Forster,* who pretended to be Heir to the Dean, and after his Death had gotten the same out of his Study, so that the Schoolmaster could not produce them, therefore it was feared that the Foundation of the School was imperfect, and he disturbing the School about fourteen Years together, the Schoolmaster upon Advice, petitioned Parliament to confirm the Erection and Foundation of the School, which was accordingly done, and the Schoolmaster compounding with the right Heir of the said Dean *Incent* and paying 50*l.* to him and some other of his Relations, he was licensed to sell 36*l.* and 8*d.* of the said Revenues belonging to the School to pay fifty Marks to the Heirs; and the Grant was exemplify'd under the Great Seal of England, *in pepetuam rei memoriam.*

The Master, Usher, and Chaplain, were incorporated by the Name of Master, Chaplain, and Usher of the Free-school and Chantry of Dean *Incent* of Berkhamsted, and by this Name do implead and are impleaded, and have one Common Seal, with Dean *Incent's* Coat of Arms, and are inabled to purchase Lands and Tenements in Fee simple, to hold to them and their Successors in free and perpetual Almes to the clear yearly Value of ————— *pro ut* in the Act of Parliament made for the said School; the Warden of the Colledge of *All Souls* in Oxford is constituted Visitor, and may visit once in three Years, and at every such Visitation the Master and Usher shall pay to him 13*s.* 4*d.* out of the Revenues of the School.

The Motto of the School Seal.

Sigillum Commune Liberæ Scholæ de Berkhamsted.

These Mottoes in the Windows of the School.

Virtus laudata crescit.
Innocens Innocentium testimonio comprobatur.

The Names of the Schoolmasters.

1. *Richard Reeve,* M. A.
2. *William Barker.*
3. *William Saltmarsh,* buried 9 *Jan.* 1599, 42 *Eliz.*
4. *Thomas Hunt,* buried 3d *Febr.* 1635, 11 *Car.* I.
5. *Henry Hunt,* buried 19 *July,* 1636, 12 *Car.* I.
6. *William Pitkin,* buried at St. *Dunstans* in Fleetstreet.
7. *Timothy Taylor,* who died of the Plague in 1648.
8. *Archibald Oagle.*
9. *Thomas Hawes,* buried 13 *Jan.* 1661, 13 *Car.* II.
10. ———— *Burgenhead.*
11. *Thomas Fossau.*
12. *Edmund Newboult,* now Rector of Cheddington in Com. Bucks.
13. *Thomas Wren,* now Rector of Kelshall in this County.
14. *John Theed,* M. A. of *Oriel* Colledge in Oxford, present Master.

Here were two Hospitals one called St. *Leonards,* situated at the South-East End of the Highstreet, and the other called St. *James* from St. *James's* Well, at the other End of the same Street, and there were formerly several religious Houses, as appears by some old Writings, but now 'tis not known where they stood.

The last Will and Testament of *Edward de la Hay,* Esq. dated the 20th of *May,* 1510, by which he first bequeathed his Soul to Almighty God, and his blessed Moder and Virgin our Lady St. *Mary,* and to all the Holy Company of Heaven; and ordered his Body to be buried in this Church of Berkhamsted, in the Chappel of St. *Katharine,* at the South End of the

Altar of St. *Katharine* (which is the Chancel where the *Waterhouses* were buried;) he gave to the Altar of the said Church 6s. 8d. to the Use of the Light of our Lady of Grace in the Church 6s. 8d. to the Use of the Rood Lights, where they sing Mass, at the South Door of the same Church 6s. 8d. to the Churchworks of the Church of Berkhamsted 20s. to the Reparation of the Bells 13s. 4d. to the Reparation and Maintenance of the Torches in the same Church 3s. 4d. to ten Priests which should be required to be at his Obsequies 6d. a piece; also he gave to the Churchworks of Great Gadesden 10s. of Hemelhempsted 20s. to the Reparations of the Chappel of Bobingdon 10s. to the Reparation of the Parish Churches of Marsworth, Chesham, and Bulberton in Buckinghamshire 10s. to each of them. To the *Black Fryers*, *London*, called Dominick, for three Trentals 30s. to the Prior and his Brother of King's Langley for one Trental 10s. to the Prior of the Fryars of Dunstable, and his Brother, for one Trental 10s. to the Prior and his Brother of *Black Fryers of* *Northampton* for one Trental 10s. He gave 10l. to his Brother Sir *William Delahay*; and an House in Berkhamsted, formerly Bourbanks, and another there formerly Curnours, and then used as a Stable to the former, to Sir *Raufe Verney*, Kt. and a Close lying thereto, paying 20l. in full contentation to the Performance of his said last Will; and the Rest of his real Estate (which was very great) he gave to his Daughters, *Luce, Mary,* and *Joan,* and if either of them, or any for them, should make any Strife or Debate against the Will, her Portion was to be sold by his Executors to the best Value, and to be distributed in good Works for the said *Edward Delahays* Soul, and all Christain Souls; he made the said Sir *Raufe Verney*, *Raufe Verney* of Pendley, Esq. Mr. *John Stepneth*, and Mr. *Richard Goodere*, his Executors, and gave to the said Sir *Raufe Verney*, 3l. and to the said Mr. *Raufe Verney*, Mr. *Stepneth*, and Mr. *Gooderre*, 40s. a piece, for their Labour and Diligence in fulfilling his Will, which he directed them to fulfil as they should think best, and most necessary, as they would answer before Almighty God, if it should be needful for him the said *Delahay*, to ask accompt of his Testament and last Will, in as much as he left sufficient Goods and Substance to perform the same, after the good Provision of his Executors, as it should be most expedient for the health of his Soul, and his Faders and Moders, and all his Friends Souls, with all Christian Souls.

CHARITIES.

King *James* I. gave an 100l.

Prince *Charles* gave an 100l. to employ the Poor of this Town at work in Jersey, which was accordingly perform'd till the Undertakers broke.

King *Charles* I. *Anno* 1626, gave 100l. more to supply the Poor with Wood, for Firing ; and for Security of the Money, *Edward Kellet,* and *Francis Withered*, Esqs. *William Pitkin* and *Stephen Bevouth*, Gents. were bound to the King in the *Exchequer*, but since all (save *Pitkin*) have, in discharge of their Bonds, respectively charged some Part of their Estates in Proportion for Security thereof.

William Saltmarsh, gave 42l.	The Lady *Barret*, 3l.
Mr. *Young*, 50l.	*Thomas Turnour*, 10l.
Sir *Richard Goddard*, 20l.	Mr. *Norwood*, 8l.
Sir *Adolph Carey*, 10l.	*John Grover*, 5l.
John Haines, 4l.	Mrs. *Sterne*, 10l.
Sir *Edward Carey*, 10l.	Sir *Edward Bacsh*, 10l.

With a great Part of this Money, the Churchwardens and Overseers of the Poor have purchased some small Tenements, situated at the West End of the Town, for the Habitations of poor People, and a 100l. more of the said Money was laid out in purchase of certain Lands called Cunridge, in the Parish of Little Chesham in the County of Bucks, to wit one Close of arable Land and Wood Ground, containing seven Acres, three Roods, and thirty nine Pole, and one Coppice Grove, or Parcel of Wood Ground called Horselrps and Coppice, containing three Acres three Roods, and thirty one Pole, and one other Close of Land called Horselrps Close, containing five Acres, three Roods, and ten Poles, which amounts to the Value of 5l. per *Annum*, to be distributed among the Poor.

Henry Clerk of the Parish of **St Giles** without **Cripplegate**, **London**, in the County of **Middlesex**, Esq. by his Will dated 13th *Nov.* 7 *Ja.* I. charged his House in **Whitecross Street**, with the yearly payment of 10*l.* to the Relief and Sustenation of five of the honest and poorest Householders of the Borrough of **Berkhamsted**.

William Hay of **Berkhamsted St. Peter**, Gent. gave 15*l.* to provide six Penny Loaves, to be given to six poor People every Sabbath Day for ever.

Robert Partridge of **Berkhamsted**, Clothier, gave three Acres of arable Land in **Greenwayfeild** in **Berkhamsted**, to the Use of the Poor, which the Churchwardens and Overseers of the Poor of this Town, by Consent of the Parishioners at a Vestry sold for 20*l.* and the said *William Halsey* and the other Parishioners, with the 100*l.* given by King *James* I. the 15*l.* given by Mr. *Halsey*, and the 20*l.* raised upon the Sale of *Partridges* Land, did purchase with 90*l.* thereof, one Close called **Williams Hill** situated in the Hamlet of **Ashley Green**, in the Parish of **Chesham**, in the County of **Bucks**, containing twelve Acres, more or less, now divided into three Closes; and with 15*l.* more, they bought a Messuage or Tenement with an Orchard called **Pages House**, situated in **Berkhamsted**, and with 20*l.* more, they bought certain Lands of one *John Surman*; and the Closes called **Williams Hill** are employ'd to find a Manufactory to set the Poor on Work, according to the direction of King *James*; and **Pages House** is employ'd to provide six Penny Loaves for six poor People according to the Intent of Mr. *William Halsey*.

Sir *Henry Atkins* of the Parish of **Christchurch**, **London**, Kt. gave 200*l.* and therewith purchased a Wood or Coppice, called **Stubbings Coppice**, with an Edgerow, and a Close of arable and Wood Ground called **Stubbings Bottom**, and a Close of arable called **Stubbings Close** of the yearly Value of 10*l.* and settled the same in Trustees for the Poor of **Berkhamsted**, the Profits thereof to be paid to them, at the Feast of the Nativity of our Saviour Christ, or within twenty two Days next after the Feast of St. *Andrew* the Apostle, to be given to twenty poor People by equal Distribution. Twelve of whom are to be yearly nominated by the Churchwardens and Overseers, and so many of the Feoffees residing in the Town as shall be present, or the greater Number of them, and these other eight are to be yearly nominated and appointed by the Heirs of the said *Henry*; and if the Churchwardens, Overseers, and Feoffees, for the time being shall not yearly choose twelve, and distribute as aforesaid, then the said Sir *Henry Atkins* and his Heirs shall choose and distribute to so many as they neglect to choose and distribute to; and if the said Sir *Henry Atkins* and his Heirs, shall not within the said time choose the said Number every year, of eight poor Persons dwelling in the said Parish, to receive the said Alms according to the Proportion aforesaid, then the Churchwardens, Overseers, and Feoffees, or the greater Number of them, shall appoint so many as shall not be nominated by the said Sir *Henry Atkins* or his Heirs, within the time aforesaid.

Henry Atkins gave 40*l.* to the Stock of the Poor for ever.

Thomas Baldwin, Esq. who was born at **Watford**, educated at **Berkhamsted**, and lived at **St. Martins** in the Feilds, by his Will gave the Profits of his moyety of Waterworks, running into, and by **Hyde Park**, to the Parishes of **St. Martins Watford**, and **Berkhamsted**, for 80 Years or thereabouts, after his Wives Decease, whereof one third Part was given to **Berkhamsted**.

John Sayer, Esq. by his last Will dated the 2d of *July*, 1681, gave Sir *Stephen Fox*, Sir *Robert Sayer*, Kts. and *Joseph Sayer*, Clerk, Rector of **Berkhamsted St. Mary**, 100*l.* for the building of an Almshouse, and the purchasing of Lands for the Relief of the Poor in **Berkhamsted St. Peter**.

John Sayer dying, *Mary* his Executrix caused an Almshouse to be built consisting of twelve Rooms, placed six poor Widdows there, allotted two Rooms to each Widdow; and adding 300*l.* to the 1000*l.* by Deed dated the 12th of *June* 1688, hath since purchased certain Land in **Chilton** in *Com.* **Bucks**, to the yearly Value of 75*l.* 5*s.* in the Name of the said Trustees, and charged them with an Annuity of 36*l.* *per Annum* to the Poor of **Berkhamsted**, and hath provided to purchase a Close called **Woodclose**, adjoyning to the Almshouses in the name of the Trustees, for the same

Purpose, the Widdows to be placed and displaced by Mrs. *Mary Sayer* at her Pleasure, and after her Decease, when any of them shall die or be displaced, the Heir of the said *John Sayer*, the Rectors of 𝕭𝔢𝔯𝔨𝔥𝔞𝔪𝔰𝔱𝔢𝔟 𝔖𝔱. 𝔐𝔞𝔯𝔶 and of 𝕭𝔢𝔯𝔨𝔥𝔞𝔪𝔰𝔱𝔢𝔟 𝔖𝔱. 𝔓𝔢𝔱𝔢𝔯, for the time being, or any two of them, whom the said *Mary* doth appoint Governors of the Almeshouses, shall choose at the Feast of the Annunciation of the Blessed Virgin *Mary*, others in their Rooms, who have inhabited ten Years at least in the Parish of 𝕭𝔢𝔯𝔨𝔥𝔞𝔪𝔰𝔱𝔢𝔟, being of good Fame, constant Frequenters of Divine Service, as by Law is now Established in the Church of 𝔈𝔫𝔤𝔩𝔞𝔫𝔟, aged 55 Years at the least, and of them, such to be preferred whose Husbands, Parents, or Children, or who themselves have been Tenants of the Demeasne Lands in 𝕭𝔢𝔯𝔨𝔥𝔞𝔪𝔰𝔱𝔢𝔟 or any Part of them, every poor Widdow to have 8*s.* the Month (reckoning twenty eight Days to the Month) paid her on the Tombstone in the Church of 𝕭𝔢𝔯𝔨𝔥𝔞𝔪𝔰𝔱𝔢𝔟, near the Monument lately erected for *John Sayer*, on the *Sunday* after Evening Service, and a Cloath Gown once in two Years at the Feast of our Saviours Nativity, of 20*s.* Value at the least; and the Profits of the Garden or Orchard adjoyning to the Almshouse to be equally divided among them, the Almshouses to be kept in good Repair by the Monthly Stipend or Stipends, which by any Vacancy shall remain unpaid till the Election Days. The said *Mary* hath also allow'd to the Governours out of the Revenue so settled on the said Almshouse s, 10*s.* yearly to be spent in a Collation at the Anniversary Feast of the Blessed Virgin St. *Mary*, at such time as they meet together to elect into any Vacancy, and to consider of the good Rule and Government of the said House, and hath made several other good Rules and Orders for the better Government thereof.

BERKHAMSTED ST· MARYES,
otherwise NORTHCHURCH.

THIS Vill is about a Mile distant from 𝕭𝔢𝔯𝔨𝔥𝔞𝔪𝔰𝔱𝔢𝔟 𝔖𝔱. 𝔓𝔢𝔱𝔢𝔯 to the North, and 'tis propable was waste Ground belonging to the former Vill of 𝔖𝔱. 𝔓𝔢𝔱𝔢𝔯 of 𝕭𝔢𝔯𝔨𝔥𝔞𝔪𝔰𝔱𝔢𝔟, for 'tis omitted out of that memorable Record of *Domesdei* made in the time of *William* the Conqueror, but since has been improved to a Vill, and denominated from the Saint to whom the Church was dedicated, to distinguish it from the other Vill, but of late Days it has been commonly called 𝔑𝔬𝔯𝔱𝔥𝔠𝔥𝔲𝔯𝔠𝔥, from the Scituation of the Church, for that it stands North to the other Parish, and there were several Mesnalties here, whereof 𝔑𝔬𝔯𝔥𝔠𝔬𝔱𝔢 is the cheif, which *An.* 28 *Edw.* I. was in the Possession of *Nicholas de Bosco*, who was Lord hereof, and held it of the Honour of 𝕭𝔢𝔯𝔨𝔥𝔞𝔪𝔰𝔱𝔢𝔟 by one Knight's Fee; after him it came to *Ralph de Marshall* who held it of the Prince of 𝔚𝔞𝔩𝔢𝔰 in the time of *Edw.* II. and as his Honour of 𝕭𝔢𝔯𝔨𝔥𝔞𝔪𝔰𝔱𝔢𝔟 by several Services, and the third Part of a Knight's Fee, from whom it came to *Thomas Luton* by the Marriage of *Margaret* his Daughter, for she surviving her Husband held the same for her Life; and upon her Death it was found by Inquisition *Anno* 13 *R.* II. that it descended to *William de Luton*, who was the Heir.

Robert de Luton succeeded him, was knighted, and he and *Katharine* his Wife held this Mannor of 𝔑𝔬𝔯𝔱𝔥𝔠𝔬𝔱𝔢, joyntly together with the Appurtenances of the Honour of

Berkhamsted in Socage by a yearly Rent, and the Performance of divers Works in Harvest in Lieu of all Services ; and 'tis observable in those Days, that when Men deserved well of their Prince, the King would often change the Tenure of such Tenants from Knight Service to Socage, to ease their Charge.

After some Limit of time, *Jeremy Hamden* possest this Mannor, and held it of the Honour of Berkhamsted by Fealty and a certain annual Rent which he paid in Lieu of all Services, and died seized hereof *Anno* 33 *H.*VIII.

Upon his Death, *Michael Hamden* succeeded, for it was found, that he held this Mannor of Northcote of the Honour of Berkhamsted by Fealty and a certain annual Rent, that he died seiz'd hereof *Anno* 13 *Eliz.* and

Alexander was his Son and Heir, who enjoyed it some time, then conveyed it to *William Edlyn*, Gentleman, who died seized hereof, *Anno* 4 *Jacobi*, after his Decease it descended to *John Edlin*, Gent. who gave it by his Will to

Sarah Edlyn his eldest Daughter, who married *Thomas Emerton*, Gent. who with his Wife, are now Lords hereof.

Here were two other Mesnalties in this Vill, as Maudleins and Durrants, which were held of the Honour and Mannor of Berkhamsted, were long since dismembered and sold in several Parcels, to divers Men, who now pay Rent, and perform their Services for the same at every Court held for the Honour and Mannor of Berkhamsted.

The Kings, Queens, Dukes, and Earls of Cornwal, have been Patrons, and have had the Advowson and Gift of the Parsonage of Northchurch, until *Anno* 2 *Eliz.* when that King granted the same by Letters Patents to Sir *Thomas Bemor*, who granted it to Sir *Edward Carey*, Kt. but now the Advowson is return'd to the Crown again.

THIS Rectory *Anno* 26 *Henry* VIII. was rated in the King's Books at the yearly Value of 21*l.* 1*s.* 2*d.* but by a Survey of the Mannor it was presented there to be worth 21*l.* 10*s. per Annum*, which, I suppose, might be a Mistake.

The RECTORS.

Joseph Sayer, Archdeacon of Lewes.　　*John Smolte*, D. D. 1698.

In this Church is one Gravestone on which are two Coats of Arms impaled, *Per Baron et Feme*, *viz.* the first is *a Cheveron ingrailed between three Boars Heads erased ;* the second is *a Cheveron Ermines between three Milroynes.*

The same Stone is thus inscribed.

Here lyeth in assurance of a joyful Resurrection the Body of Mrs. *Mary Agar*, the truly virtuous and loving Wife of *Thomas Agar*, of Barnes, in the County of Surry, Esq; Daughter and Heir of Mr. *Jonas Turnour* of Chesham in the County of Bucks, she resigned her Soul into the hands of him that gave it, on the fourth day of *August* in the year of our Lord 1652. and in the beginning of the 21st year of her age.
Non diu vixit sed Multum.

On *Ascension* Day, 1555, 3d *Mariæ Reginæ* Mr. *Thomas Waterhouse*,
Clerk, was buried here; he was Rector of *Asbridge* at the Dissolution by
King *Henry* VIII.

Henry Axtil, a rich Man starved himself, and was buried here *April*
12, 1625, 1 *Car.* I.

There were several Chappels of Ease in this Parish, but they are now
demolished and converted into Barns.

ALBURY

IS another Vill scituated about two Miles distant from
Northchurch towards the North East, which King *William*
the Conqueror gave to Earl *Moreton*, for 'tis recorded in
Domesdei Book, under the Title of *Terra Comitis Morito-
niensis.*

Comes Moriton *tenuit* **Albebetie** *pro decem hidis se defendebat. Terra est
septem Car. in dominio sex hid. et ibi sunt tres Car. et octo vill. cum uno
Sochman. et uno Francig. habent. quatuor Car. ibi unus Bord. et quatuor
servi. pratum dimid. hid. Silva quingent. Porcis, in totis valentiis valet cent-
tum et decem sol. Quando recepit octo lib. et consuetud. tempore Regis* Edwardi. *Hoc Manerium tenuit* Aluvinus *Teignus Regis* Edwardi.

Earl *Moreton* held **Albeberrie**, it was rated for ten Hides. The arable
is seven Carucates, in Demeasne six Hides, and there are three Carucates and eight Villains, and one Sochman, and one Frenchman born,
having four Carucates, there is one Bordar, and four Servants, Meadow
half a Hide, Wood to feed five hundred Hogs in Pannage time; in the
whole Value it is worth an hundred and ten Shillings by the Year, when
he received it eight Pounds, and Rent in the time of King *Edward* (the
Confessor;) *Alwin* a Thane of King *Edward* (the Confessor) held this
Mannor.

Having treated before of this Earl *Moreton* in the Parish
of **Great Berkhamsted**, I shall proceed to the next Lord of
this Mannor whom I meet with, who was *Bartholomew de
Criol*, he was made *Custos* of this County for the last fourth
Part of that 33d Year of *H.* III. Sheriff of the Counties of
Essex and **Hertford**, for the Year following, and died leaving Issue *Bertram* and *John.*

John succeeded in this Mannor, and was summon'd among
others to attend *Anno* 41 *H.* III. at **Bristol**, with Horse
and Arms well accoutred, on the Octaves of St. *Peter*, to
oppose the Incursions of *Lewellin ap Griffith*, Prince of
Wales, and died in 48 *H.* III. leaving

Bertram his Son and Heir, who married *Alianor*, one of
the Daughters and Heirs of *Hamon de Crevequer* by *Maud*
his Wife, Sister and Heir to *William de Abrincis* or *Ave-
ronches*, and had in her Right Part of the Barony of **Fol-
keston**, which was of the Inheritance of *William de Averon-
ches*; and it was found *Anno* 28 *Edw.* I. that he held this
Mannor, and had free Ingress and Egress from the Wood
called the **Frith**, ought to mow with sixteen Men in one of
the Parks once a Day for Meat for the Lord's Horses; and
the Work of every Man was valued at a Penny, and he or

his Servants shall view the Workmen twice every Day;
and he died leaving Issue

John, who was his Son and Heir, and 30 Years of Age,
Anno 30 *Edw*. I. and died seized hereof *Anno* 34 *Edw*. I.
leaving *Joan* the Wife of *Richard de Rokesle*, Kt. his Sister and Heir, from whom I guess it came to the *Hides*, who
held it for some Generations in their Name, which it seems
was suspended awhile by *Joan* the Daughter and Heir of
Hide, who married Sir *Thomas Denham*, Kt. for this Mannor was in his Name, *An*. 10 *H*.VI. but he dying without
Heirs of her Body, she married again to *William Fitzwil-*
liams, who held another Court here in her Right, *Anno* 21
of the same King, and he dying without Issue of her Body,
she held a Court Baron *Anno* 27 *H*. VI. in her own Name,
which was in the time of her Widdowhood, but she having
a great Respect for the Name of the *Hides*, because it was
not only her paternal Name, but also very ancient, she prudently settled this Mannor in the Name of the *Hides* again,
from whom it came to *Thomas Hide*, Gent. who held a
Court Baron here *Anno* 1 *Edw*. VI. and a Court held here
Anno 12 *Eliz*. where he is styled Esq. and upon his Death
it seems that he conveyed this Mannor to his Wife for Life,
the Remainder to *George* who was his Heir, and she held a
Court here *Anno* 13 *Eliz*. in the Name of *Frances Hide*,
Widdow; after her Decease, *George Hide* held another
Court here for this Mannor *Anno* 16 *Eliz*. in his Name,
and upon his Death it came to

Robert Hide, Esq. who was his Heir, and held a Court
here *Anno* 23 *Eliz*. and at the time of his Death this Mannor descended to *Nicholas*, who was his Son and Heir.

This *Nicholas* was knighted *Anno* 17 *Jac*. I. constituted
Sheriff for this County, created Baronet by Letters Patents
dated 8th of *November*, 1621, 19 *Jac*. I. held a Court here
in his own Name by this Title *Anno* 22 *Jac*. I. and he died
leaving Issue

Thomas, who was Sheriff for this County *Anno* 3 *Car*. I.
and held a Court Baron for this Mannor *Anno* 7 *Car*. I.
married the Daughter of *Emerton*, Gent. by whom he had
Issue only one Daughter *Bridget* who was his Heir; his
Arms were *Or, a Cheveron between three Lozenges Azure,*
on a Chief Gules an Eagle displayed Gold.

This *Bridget* married *Peregrine* Viscount **Dunblane**, in
the Kingdom of **Scotland**, the Son and Heir of *Thomas* now
Duke of **Leedes**, Marquess of **Carmarthen**, Earl of **Danby**,
Viscount *Latimer*, and Baron *Osborn* of **Kiveton** *vulgo*
Keelton *Anno* 21 *Car*. II. and they held a Court Baron
in both their Names on the 21 *Car*. II. and are the present Lords hereof.

THIS Rectory is in the Deanery of Berkhamstd in the Diocese of Lincoln, and Anno 26 Hen. VIII. was rated in the King's Books at the yearly
Value of 20l. 8s. 6d. whereof the Marquess in Right of his Marchioness is
Patron; and the Church is situated about the Middle of the Vill, cover'd
with Lead, hath a large old fashion'd Stone Font therein, and a square
Tower at the West End thereof, where are four Bells, and a short Spire
erected upon it, within which Church lye divers Gravestones which have
the following Inscriptions and Coats of Arms engraved upon them.

Behind the Pulpit is a Chancel and Vault, being the Burial-place belonging to Pendley.

Therein is a Stone Tomb wherein lyes one of the *Verneys*, who were
ancient Owners of Pendley, and his Lady; and he lyes armed with an
Helmet, a Cheveron, a Phenix in her inflamed Nest, which is his Crest
under his Head, and a Savage with a Staff raguled and trunked in his
Hand, under his Feet; and she hath two square Pillows under her Head,
and a Faun at her Feet; round the same Stone are several Coats of
Arms cut, (*viz.*) first, *in a Field Azure, on a Cross Argent five Mullets ;*
the second, *Azure, two Cheverronnels Or, in a Dexter Canton an Holy
Lamb, Staff, Cross, and Bar Gules;* the. third, *Or, a Lyon Rampant
Gules, a Cheif Or ;* the fourth, *a Garter buckled and nowed between three
Buckles.*

In the said Chancel lyes *Henry Anderson*, Esq. *Richard Anderson*, Esq.
the two Sons of Sir *Richard Anderson* of Pendley, Baronet, whose Banner with their Paternal Coats are put up there; their Paternal Coat being *Argent, a Cheveron between three Cross Molines Sable, mantled Argent,
doubled Sable, on a Wreath and Sable, a Ducal Crown Argent therein; a
Deers Head peirced through with a Dart Argent, entering in at the fore
Part of the Neck.*

The said *Henry Anderson*, Esq. died a Batchelor, his younger Brother
Richard Anderson, Esq. was married, and his Coat is there impaled with
his Lady's, which is *In a Feild —— Fess Ermine between three Griffins
Heads erased Argent, by the name of Spencer.*

Mr. *Henry's* Motto is ——————— *in Cœlo Quies*
Mr. *Richard's* Motto is ——————— *in Morte Quies*

Elizabeth, the only Daughter of the said Sir *Richard Anderson*, and
Wife of *Simon Harcourt*, Esq. was lately buried there, whose Arms being in a *Field Gules, two Bars Or*, are impaled with hers.

They were the only three Children of the said Sir *Richard Anderson* by
Dame *Elizabeth* his Wife, who was Sister and one of the Coheirs of
George Lord Viscount *Hewet*, lately deceased, and all of them died
young, but Mrs. *Harcourt* hath left behind her three Sons and three
Daughters by *Simon Harcourt*, Esq.

*In the Communion Chancel is also a Gravestone lately laid down, which was
the Cover of a Tomb.*

Thereon at each Corner are the *Verneys* three first mentioned Coats,
and the fourth as the first impaled with hers, which are two Coates
Quarterly and an Inescotcheon of Pretence; the first whereof is, *a Cheveron
between three Eagles Legs erased Alaquise ;* the second is, *Varry, three
Bendlets ;* the third as the second, the fourth as the first : the *Inescotcheon of
Pretence hath four Coats Quarterly, viz.* first, *On a Bend three Goats Passant ;* the second, *a Cheveron engrailed between three Bulls Heads Caboss-
ed ;* the third, *a Fess between six Crosses Patee*, and the fourth *hath two
Bends.*

In the next Chancel to the Communion Chancel is fixt against the
Wall westerly, a very fine ancient Marble Monument of various Colours,
towards the Top whereof are thus written.

*Omnia Mors sternit,
Quod natum est, Occidit,
Una fine caret Virtus
et Benefacta manent.*

In the Middle round two Deaths Heads are written, on the right Side ———— *Despice Formam.* On the left Side ———— *Respice finem.* At the Bottom is written thus,

Humanitur hic infra sub illo Marmore cadavera Thomæ Hidæ *Armigeri, et* Georgii *filii, et Hæredis sui quorum illo Decimo sexto die* Octobris *An. à Christo Nato* 1570 *naturam satisfecit, hac vero decimo Nono die* Januarii *Anno Salutis Humanæ* 1580 *extremum spiritum effudit.*

On the same are three Coats of Arms, (*viz.*) the first is the Paternal Coat, *Or, a Cheveron between three Lozenges Azure, on a Cheif Gules, an Eagle displayed of the first.* The second is, *Azure, a Cheveron between three Cups with Covers Or, a Mullet for Difference.* The third is, *Azure, a Bar Wavy between three Goats Heads erased Or, mantled Argent, doubled Gules on a Wreath Or, and Locks Gules; a Head erazed Azure crested and Jollopped proper,* this is on the Paternal Coat on the Top of all.

In the same Chancel on the Wall next to the Communion Chancel is a fair Marble Monument, in Memory of Sir *Thomas Hyde,* thus inscribed.

Siste Viator et hoc Sacro Marmore Exemplar potius quam Epitaphium Lege: Hic enim exuviæ Nobiles Thomæ Hidæ *de* Alburia *in agro* Hertfordiensi *filii* Nicholai Hidæ *Militis et Baronetti ex* Bridgitta *filia* Michaelis San-dis *de* Latymer *in Agro* Buckinghamsi, *Armig. adavitos Cineres, habent reconditos; Vir erat tam Animi quam Corporis elegatis Ornatissimus, Hoc tantum ambiens ut sibi quippe et imprimis placeret, fidelitatis erga Regiam Majestatem, Tenax, ut ab afflictissima æque et justissima* Caroli *Primi Regis Septimi contra perduelles causa, nec — injuriæ inimicorum scelus (Heu minus prosperam) Dominus poterant; qua itidem periculosa procella post plures sustentatos Labores et toleratas plurimas afflictiones hinc inde jact. solatium in Matrimonio quæsicit; Uxorem ducens* Mariam *Filiam* Johan-nis Whitchurch *de* Walton juxta Alesbury *in agro* Buckinghaminsi, *Gener. ex qua unicam suscepit per Aviæ de nomine* Bridgittam, *natam in Manerio suo de* Mims Boreali *in Comitatu* Hertfordiensi *xviii die* Maii CIƆI *ubi post conjugium Quinquemale feliciter peractum ut dictarum Villarum pauperes effusa alens Charitate et Amicis undiquaque larga benignitate; a Naufragio fidei et Conscientiæ bone Tutus, ærumnis suis eliberatus, et in Sinum* Abrahæ *appulsus Dives ibi feliciter suisque Carus extitit cæliti-bus, Nobis vero triste mansit desiderium, a die* xviii Maii

Anno { *partis virginei* CIƆIƆCLXV
{ *ætatis suæ* ——— LXXI.

Hunc Tabulam erigi curavit superdicta Maria *post Nuptias suas secundas habitas cum* Roberto Vyner *Milite et Baroneito* Londinensis *Senatore et* Aldermanio.

The said *Thomas Hyde* gave 100*l.* to the Poor of Alburbury with which a Close of Land was bought in the Parish of Berkhamsted St. Peter, and settled for their Uses.

There is a Marble Tomb also in the Wall of the Communion Chancel, and several other ancient Gravestones about the Church, but the Brasses are all gone.

In the Church Window over the Font are two Coats of Arms, on the right is *Azure, two Cheverons,* and that on the left is *Argent, a Cross Gules.*

TREUNG, TRING.

THIS Vill stands in a Bottom, two Miles from Alburp to the West, and was a Place of great Antiquity, for when King *Alfred* divided this County into Hundreds, this Hundred was then denominated Treung from this Vill, which Name it bore when the Conqueror subdued this Realm, who then gave it to *Robert* Earl of Ewe, one of his Chief Coun-

Hund. of
Dacorum.

sellors at that time, and his Services were rewarded with great Honours and large Revenues, among which 'tis recorded in *Domesdei Book*, that

Domesd. Lib.
fol. 137.

Comes Eustachius tenuit **Treunge** *pro novem trigint. hidas se defendebat tempore Regis Edwardi et modo pro quinque hidis et una virgat. Terra est Vigint. car. in dominio duodecem hid et ibi sunt tres Car. et adhuc possunt fieri, duo, ibi un et vigint Vill. cum sex bordis, et sexdecem cotariis, et tribus Sochiis habentibus novem car. et adhuc possunt sex fieri, ibi octo Servi, et duo molin. de novem Sol. pratum decem Car. pastura ad pec. ville, et tres Sol. Silva milli porcis, in hac villa est Berewicha ubi sedent octo villi habentes duo car. et tertia potest fieri.*

In totis valentiis valet duo et vigint. lib de albo denar. ad pensum hujus Comitis, quando recepit vigint. lib. tempore Regis Edwardi quinq. et vigint. lib. hoc Manerium tenuit Engelri tempore Regis Edwardi, et ibi fuerunt duo Sochm. homines Ulsuli filii Frani duo hid. tenuerunt et vendere potuerunt, hoc Sochman apposuit iisdem Engelricus huic Manerio post Adventum R. W. ut Homines de Hundred. testantur et unus homo Abbis de **Ramsyg.** *quinq. hid. de hoc Manerio habuit adeundem modum. Ipse non potuit dare vel vendere terram suam extra Ecclesiam* **Sancti Benedicti,** *quem Engelri apposuit huic Manerio post adventum Regis Will. qui non fuit ibi tempore Regis Edwardi, ut Hundred. testatur. Illi prædicti tres Sochman. qui adhuc ibi sunt un. hid. habentes homines Engelrici fuerunt et terram suam vendere potuerunt.*

Earl *Eustace* held **Treung,** it was rated for nine and thirty Hides in the time of King *Edward* (the Confessor,) and now for five Hides and one Virgate. The arable is twenty Carucates in Demeasne twelve Hides, and there are three Carucates, now two more may be made, there is one and twenty Villains with six Borders and sixteen Cottagers, and three Sochmen having nine Carucates, and now six more may be made, there are eight Servants, and two Mills of nine Shillings Rent by the Year, Meadow ten Carucates, Common of Pasture for the Cattle of the Vill, and three Shillings Rent by the Year, Wood to feed one thousand Hogs in Pannage time. In this Vill is a Berewick (now I think called the **Berry**) where eight Villains sat, having two Carucates, and a third may be made.

In the whole it was valued at two and twenty Pounds of white Money by the weight of this Earl, when he received it twenty Pounds in the time of King *Edward* (the Confessor) five and twenty Pounds; *Elgeric* held this Mannor in the time of King *Edward* (the Confessor) and there were two Sochmen, Men (under the Protection) of *Usulf* Son of *Frane,* held two Hides and might sell them, the same *Engelric* laid these Sochmen to this Mannor after the coming of King *William* as the Men of the Hundred can witness; and one Man (under the Protection of the Abbot of **Ramsey** had five Hides of this Mannor after the same manner. He could not give nor sell this Land from the Church of **St. Benedict,** which *Engelric* had laid to this Mannor after the coming of King *William* the Conqueror which was not there in the time of King *Edward* (the Confessor) as the Hundred can witness. Those aforesaid three Sochmen who are now there having one Hide, were Men (under the Protection) of *Engelric,* and might sell their Land.

Mon. Angl.
vol. 1, fol. 688.

Shortly after this Mannor returned to the Crown again and *Anno* 1148 King *Stephen* founded the Church of **Febersham** in **Kent,** and gave to the Abbot and Monks, this Mannor of **Tring** with all the Appurtenances, in perpetual Alms for the Health of the Souls of *Maud* his Queen and all faithful People. And Queen *Maud* gave all this Mannor of **Treung** with all its Appurtenances to the Abbot and Monks of **St. Saviours** of **Febersham,** in free, pure, and perpetual Alms. To have and to hold well and in Peace with all its Appurtenances, and with all other Liberties and

Free Customs for ever, quit and free from all secular Exactions, Suits, and Demands.

William Earl of 𝕭olon, 𝖂arfoic, and 𝕸oreton, Son of King *Stephen* and Queen *Maud*, confirmed this Grant of this Mannor of 𝕿reung, with all its Appurtenances, and the Service of Stoches which belonged to this Mannor of 𝕿reung, and was the fourth Part of a Knight's Fee, in free and perpetual Alms, to pray for the Souls of his Father King *Stephen*, and Queen *Maud* his Mother, and *Eustace* his Brother, for his own Soul, and the Souls of all his Ancestors.

And King *Henry* II. confirmed the Grant which Queen *Maud* had given to them, and the Lands which she bought of *Fulke de Newenham*, and gave to them.

King *H.* III. also confirmed these Grants of this Mannor to the Church of 𝕱ebersham, govern'd according to the Order of the *Cluniacensis*. To have and hold with Soc, Sac, Toll, Theam, Infangthef, and with all Liberties and Free Customs, as freely as the Church of 𝕱ebersham might hold them by the Grant of King *Henry* his Grandfather, and King *John* his Father, and the Grants of the said Donors. *Mon. Angl.* vol. 1, fol.686.

The Abbot of 𝕱ebersham, upon a *Quo Warranto*, brought before *John Rygate*, and others, Justices Itinerants at 𝕳ertford, on the Morrow of the Feast of *All Souls, Anno 6 Edw.* I. claimed by the Grant of King *Stephen*, to hold this Mannor which was ancient Demeasne, and was then worth by the Year 30*l*. King *Edw.* II. in the ninth of his Reign, granted to the Abbot of 𝕱ebersham, and the Monks in the Mannor of 𝕿ring, one Market to be held on *Friday* on every Week, and two Fairs. King *Edw.* III. 14th of his Reign, granted to the Archbishop of 𝕮anterbury, the Return of all Writs, Summons, Attachments, also Chattels of Felons, Fugitives, Amerceaments, Issues, Forfeitures, Year, Day, and Waste, which shall at any time happen in this Mannor. *Quo Warr.* 6 Ed. I. Rot.56. in dorso cur. recept Scac.

Cart. 9 Ed. II. fol. 53, m. 48, 14 Ed. III. n. 19.

The Abbots of this Church held this Mannor to the time of the Dissolution of their Monastery, when it came to

The Crown, and from thence it was conveyed to the Archbishop of 𝕮anterbury, who *Anno 37 Hen.* VIII. granted it and the Advowson and Patronage of the Parsonage and Rectory of the Church of 𝕿ring, with all their Rights, Members, and Appurtenances in this County. To have and to hold the same to the King, his Heirs and Successors for ever. *Stat.* 37 H. VIII. cap. 16.

But the same Archbishop by another Grant dated the same Year, conveyed it as Parcel of his Possessions to

Sir *Edward North*, Kt. who was then Treasurer of the Court of Augmentations, and Chancellor of that Court, grew at length so far into the Favour of that King, that he was constituted one of his Executors; but shortly after this Sir *Edward* granted this Mannor with the Appurtenances to *Cart.* 14 Ed. III. n. 10.

Sir *Richard Lee* of 𝔚lunts, who *Anno* 1 *Edw.* VI. exchanged it with the King for Lands in the Town of St. Albans, from whence *Edw.* VI. *secundo Regni sui,* regranted
it to the Archbishop of Canterbury, from whom it was reconveyed to the Crown, after which King *Philip* and Queen
Mary by their Charter dated at Westminster, *secundo Die
Julii, Annis* 1 and 2 *P.* & *M.* in Consideration of the acceptable Service which *Henry Peckham,* Esq. had done for
that Queen in those Rebellions of *John* Duke of Northumberland, and afterwards of Sir *Thomas Wyat,* granted to

Henry Peckham and *Elizabeth* his Wife, all that their
Lordship or Mannor of Tring, late Parcel of the Possessions
of *Richard Lee,* with all the Rights, Members, and Appurtenances, and the Advowson, and the Rights of Patronage
of the Church, the Court Leet, View of Franc-pledge, and
all things belonging to it, Chattels, Waifes, Estraies, Fairs,
Markets, Tolls, Free-warren, and all other Rights, Jurisdictions, Franchises, Priviledges, Profits, and Hereditaments whatsoever. To have and to hold the said Mannor
and Premises to *Henry Peckham* and *Elizabeth* his Wife,
and the Heirs and Assigns of him the said *Henry Peckham*
for ever, of the Queen *in Capite,* by the Service of the for-
tieth Part of a Knight's Fee, for all Rents, Services, and
Demands whatsoever; who had the hard Fate to be attainted of High Treason, *tempore Elizabethæ,* by Reason whereof this Mannor return'd again to the Crown, and King *James*
I. granted it *Anno Regni sui,* to Trustees, for the Use of
the Prince of Wales for 99 Years; but King *Charles* I.
settled it in Trustees, for the Maintenance of Queen *Mary,*
after her Decease, it remained to the Crown until it came to

Henry Guy, Esq. who was one of the Grooms of the
Bedchamber, and after that Clerk of the Treasury in the time
of King *Charles* II. King *James* II. and *William* and *Mary;*
and has served as a Member of Parliament in all the Parliaments held under the three last Kings for the Borough of
———— in the County of York, and is now the present Lord
hereof.

By the Custom of this Mannor, every Tenant shall, upon
his Admission to any Copihold Land, pay to the Lord the
Value of two Years Quit Rent for a Fine.

MASCEWEL, MISSEWEL.

KING *William* the Conqueror gave this Hamlet to *Robert de Todeni,* another of his great *Normans,* for his good
Services in the Conquest of this Kingdom, for 'tis recorded
in *Domesdei Book,* that

In Treung *Hundred Robt. de* Todeni *et* Radus de eo tenuit Mascewell
*pro quatuor decem hidis se defendebat tempore Regis Edwardi, et modo pro
tribus hidis et duobus virgat. et dimid. tamen sunt semper quatuor decem hidis.
Terra est septem car. in dominio sunt duo, et quindecem Vill. cum quatuor*

Drawn on Stone from the Original Engravings by G. H. Tyler.

To the Honourable

House. Esq.ʳ this Plate

Humbly dedicated,

Pub.ᵈ by J.N. Mullenger.

Henry Guy of Tring
of yᵉ Mannor House is
by John Oliver.

Bps. Stortford, 1826.

Bord. habentibus quinque carucat. pratum septem Car. pastura ad pec. et duo Hund. of
sol. Silva quingint Porcis, in totis valentiis valet centum sol. et unam unicam Dacorum.
auri quando recepit septem lib. tempore Regis Edwardi *octo lib. Hoc Manerium tenuit* Osulfus *filius* Franc. *Teignus Regis* Edwardi *antecessor* Roberti
Todeniensis.

Robert de Todeni and *Ralph* held of him ᴹᵃˢᶜʳᵘᵉˡ in Ʈreung Hundred,
it was rated for fourteen Hides in the time of King *Edward* (the Confessor)
and now for three Hides and two Virgates, and half an Hide, notwithstanding they are always accounted fourteen Hides. The arable is
seven Carucates, in Demeasne are two, and fifteen Villains, with four
Bordars having five Carucates, Meadow seven Carcates, Common of Pasture for the Cattle, and two Shillings Rent by the Year, Wood to feed five hundred Hogs, in the whole Value it is worth one hundred Shillings, and
one Ounce of Gold, when he received it seven Pounds, in the time of
King *Edward* (the Confessor) eight Pounds, *Osulfe* the Son of *Franc,* a
Thane of King *Edward* (the Confessor) Ancestor of *Robert Todeni* held
this Mannor.

But in short time this Mannor came to *Robert de Belun,* Mon. Angl.
fol. 689.
a *Frenchman,* born in the Province of Artois, who granted
it to the Abbot and Monks of St. *Saviours* of Ƒebersham
at Fee-farm, and they held it to the time of the Dissolution
of their Monastery, when it came to the Crown.

The Mannor of BUNSTRUX & RYCARDYNGS

WAS also Parcel of the Revenue of the Church of Ƒebersham, and the Abbot and Monks there granted this Mannor-house or Chief Messuage, &c. with Houseboot, Hayboot, and Fireboot in their Wood in Ʈring, called West-wood, from time to time, when it was necessary to take it,
and also yearly Pasture for the Feed of two Horses, and six
Oxen for the Draught of the Plough in the several Pastures of this Mannor of Ʈring, with the yearly Feed of such
Beasts in the same Mannor, and for all other Animals *sans*
Number, together with the Lords of Ʈring's Cattle in all
the commonable Places of Ʈring whatsoever; by which
Means the Mannor came to the Possession of *Robert de
Whittyngham,* who was knighted, constituted Sheriff of
this County and Essex, *Anno* 17 H. VI. and he died seiz'd Rot. Pip.
17 H. VI.
hereof, leaving *Margaret* who was his Daughter and Heir;
but upon his Death, this Mannor came to *Agnes* his Wife,
the Daughter and Heir to *Richard Buckland,* who survived him and held it during her Life, and upon her Decease it descended to his Daughter *Margaret,* from whom
it passed by the same Persons as the Mannor of Pendly to Rot. Cur. 14
and 15 H.VII.
Sir *Richard Anderson* and his Heirs, who held Court here
Anno 1490, and is the present Lord hereof.

The Mannor of PENDLEY or PENTLAI.

KING *William* the Conqueror gave this Mannor of
Pentlai to Earl *Moreton,* of whom it is recorded in *Domesdei Book,* that

In Pentlai *tenuit* Comes Moritonus *duo hid. Terra est duo Car. ibi un.* Domesd. Lib.
Vill. cum sex Bord. habentibus un. Car. et alia potest fieri, pratum un Car. fol. 136, n. 1o.

Hund. of Dacorum.

et dimid. valet trigint. sol. quando recepit vigint. sol. tempore Regis Edwardi quadragint. sol. hanc terram tenuit Eddeva Monial. de Ingelric non potuit dare, hæ duo hid. sunt de septem hid. quas sumpsit Comes Moritonus in Treung.

Earl *Moreton* held two Hides in **Pendleg.** The Arable is two Carucates; there is one Villain with six Bordars having one Carucate and another may be made, meadow one Carucate and an half; it is worth thirty Shillings a Year, when he received it twenty Shillings, in the time of King *Edward* (the Confessor) forty Shillings. *Eddeva* a Nun held this Land, she could not give it away from **Ingelric**: These are two Hides which Earl *Moreton* took away from the seven Hides in **Tring.**

Having treated of this Earl *Moreton,* in the Parish of **Berkhamsted St. Peters,** I shall proceed to the next Lord of this Place that I find, who is *John de Aygnel,* and he held this Mannor *Anno* 10 *Edward* II. He is writ *Tenens de* **Pendele,** in Regard he held it of the Honour of **Berkhamsted,** but without Question is Lord hereof, and the Son and Heir of *John de Aygnel,* who served for this County with

Prin's *Parl. Brev.* pt. 3, p. 115.

Robert de Hoo in the Parliament held *Anno* 26 *Edw.* I. and *Ralph de Munchansey* in the Parliament held *Anno* 30th of the same King, and *Gerard de Braybrocks* in the Parliament held *Anno* 1 *Edw.* II. and *Ralph de Monte Caviso* in the Parliament held *Anno* 2nd of the same King. He held

Rot. Cur. 19 Ed. I. Prin.

another Court in this Mannor in the 19th Year of the same King, and several other Courts from *An.* 2nd until the 24th Year of *Edw.* III. he served in this County in the first Parliament held 12 *Edw.* III. and conveyed this Mannor to

Rot. Cur. 27 Ed III.

Andrew de Dures, who held Court here in the 27th Year of the same King; but afterwards sold it to

Rot Cur. 49 Ed. III.

Sir *John de la Hay,* who held Court here *Anno* 49 *Edw.* III. and was the Son of *John de la Hay,* who served for this County in four several Parliaments, whereof two were held *Annis* 12 *Edw.* II. and 15 *Edw.* II. and the other

Priu.

two *Annis* 5 and 6 *Edward* III. and was Sheriff for this County and **Essex,** the last Half of the sixth Year, and the first Half of the seventh Year of *Edward* III. I guess he had Issue only two Daughters, *Alice* married *Robert Whittyngham,* and *Joan* married to *Walter Pain,* who were his Coheirs, for a Court was held for this Mannor, *An.* 3 *Hen.* IV. in their Names, and doubtless *Walter Paine* and *Joan* his Wife conveyed their Moyety of it to *Robert Whittingham,* or otherwise they dying without Issue, their Moiety might come to *Alice* the Wife of *Robert Whittingham,* who had Issue

Rot Cur. 1 H. V. 24 H. VI.

Robert, who held Court for this Mannor *Anno* 1 *Hen.* V. and other Courts continually here, until 24 *Hen.* VI. during which time he was knighted; and that King in the 18th Year of his Reign granted License to this *Robert* to inclose a Park for Deer, and Free-warren in **Tring** and **Albury.** He was afterwards attainted of High Treason in the time of *Edw.* IV. for adhering to King *H.* VI. upon which this Mannor came to *Edw.* IV. who 7 *Regni sui,* granted it to

Drawn on Stone from the Original Engravings by C.L. Tyler.

To the Honourable S.ʳ

This Plate of the Manner

humbly

Pub.ᵈ by J.B. Mulinger

Richard Anderson Bar.ᵗ

House of Penley is

dedicated by

John Oliver.

Bps. Stortford 1826.

Humphry Bourchier, Lord *Cromwel*, the third Son to *Henry* the first Earl of **Essex** of that Family, who married *Joan* the Daughter of *Richard Stanhope*, Niece and Coheir of *Richard* Lord *Cromwel* of **Tatshal**, and was summoned to Parliament by the Title of Lord *Cromwel*; but on the 11th of *Edw*. IV. fighting valiantly on the Part of King *Edward* at **Barnet-field** was slain, and dying without Issue, I guess, upon some Agreement, this Mannor was restored again to

Sir *Robert Whittingham*, who died leaving Issue *Margaret*, who was his Daughter and Heir. His Arms were *Per Fess Argent and Or, a Fess Vert, over all a Lyon rampant Gules*.

Margaret succeeded, married *John Varney*, held Court here in the 14th and 15th Years of *Edward* IV. in their Names, and from thence to the third Year of King *H.*VII. when he died; he left Issue Rot. 14 & 15 Ed. IV. 3 H. VII. Rot. Pip. 15 H. VII.

John, who was knighted, constituted Sheriff of this County and **Essex**, *Anno* 14 *H.* VII. and after his Decease

Sir *Ralph Varney* was his Heir, succeeded him in this Mannor, and held a Court here *Anno* 8 *H.*VIII. He made his Will, and left Sir *Richard Weston* and other Feoffees in Trust for the Performance thereof, and died leaving Issue Rot. Cur. 8 H. VIII.

Edmond his Heir; but the next Court was held *Anno* 23 *H.* VIII. in the Names of Sir *Richard Weston*, and the other Feoffees appointed for the Performance of the last Will and Testament of Sir *Ralph Varney*, Kt. Rot. Cur. 23 H. VIII.

Afterwards the Courts for this Mannor were held *Anno* 38 *Eliz.* in the Name of *Edmond Varney*, Esq. who was Sheriff for this County *Anno* 19 *Eliz.* and held this Mannor until such time that he sold it to Rot. Cur. 38 Eliz.

Richard Anderson, Esq. who held a Court here *Anno* 5 *Jac.* I. was knighted 7 *Jac.* I. and died leaving Issue *Henry*, who held a Court for this Mannor *An.* 1637, 13 *Car.* I. was created Baronet by Letters Patents dated the 3d of *July*, 1643, and died leaving Issue Rot. Cur. 5 & 7 J. I. 13 C. I. Pat. 17 Car. I.

Sir *Richard*, who was his Son and Heir, married to *Elizabeth* the eldest Daughter of Sir *Thomas Hewyt* of **Pishoburÿ** in this County, Kt. and Baronet, by *Margaret* his second Wife, the eldest Daughter of Sir *William Lytton* of **Knebworth-place** in this County, Kt. and is the present Lord hereof.

BUBLECOAT

IS an ancient Hamlet which one *Fulke* held of Earl *Moreton* in the time of *William* the Conqueror, when 'twas recorded in *Domesdei Book*, that

Fulkoldus tenuit **Bublecote**, *de Comite Moriton pro una hid. et dimid. se defendebat. Terra est un. car. et dimid. in Dominio est car. et tres Vill.* Domesd. Lib. fol. 136, n. 15.

Hund. of
Bacorum.

habentes dimid. ibi duo Bord. et un. molin. de duodecem sol. et quatuor denar. pratum duo car. valet et valuit trigint. sol. tempore Regis Edwardi quadragint. sol. Hanc terram tenuit Eddeva de Ingelrico, *non potuit mittere extra* Tredung. *Hæc terra est de septem hidis quas sumpsit Comes* Moritomus de Tredung.

Fulke held Bublecoate of Earl *Moreton*, it was rated for one Hide and an half. The arable is one Carucate and an half, in Demeasne is a Carucate, three Villains, having half a Carucate, there are two Bordars, and one Mill of twelve Shillings and four Pence Rent by the Year, Meadow two Carucates; it is worth and was worth thirty Shillings a Year, in the time of King *Edward* (the Confessor) forty Shillings. *Eddeva* held this Land, she could not take it out of Tring from *Egelric*. This Land is Part of seven Hides which Earl *Moreton* took from Tring.

DANESLAI.

Domesd. Lib.
fol. 16.

'TIS recorded in *Domesdei Book*, that

In Daneslai *tenuit quædam Vidua de Comes* Moreton *tertiam partem dimid. hidæ. Terra est un. bovi, valet et valuit semper duodecem denar. hanc terram tenuit* Ingelricus *de terra septem hid. de* Tredung *quam sumpsit* Comes.

A certain Widdow held of Earl *Moreton* the third Part of half an Hide in Danesley. The arable is an Oxgange; it is worth and always was worth twelve Pence. *Ingelric* held this Land, 'twas Part of the Land of seven Hides which Earl *Moreton* took away from Tring.

But this also I pretermit because it is no Mannor as I can learn, but I suppose the Place is very ancient, and might give the Name to Danais Hundred.

WILLESTON, or WILLESTHORNE

IS a Hamlet and Mannor which did anciently belong to the Family of the *Lakes*, as is evident by their Coat of Arms in ancient Glass in the North Window in Tring Church, which are *Quarterly four Crescents Or and Azure, counterchanged*, thus

This Mannor is now in the Possession of *William Lake*, Gent. descended from *Jeoffery de Lake*, who was Sheriff of this County for the first Half of the 14th Year of *Edw.* II. and it has continued in that Name till it came to *Thomas Luke*, who married *Anne* Daughter of ———— *Badham*, by whom he had Issue *William*, who married *Faith* Daughter of *Thomas Duncombe* of Ibingo, by whom he had Issue *William*, *Lydia*, the Wife of *John Duncombe*, *Elizabeth*, and *Faith*.

Which *William* married *Rebecca*, Daughter of *Henry Reeves*, and after her Decease, he married *Martha* Daughter of *John Kidgel*, by whom he had Issue *William*, *Anne*, and *Elizabeth:* There was a Chappel of Ease in this Hamlet, which was lately demolished.

THIS Rectory of **Cring** is appropriated to the Use of the Dean and Chapter of *Christ Church* in **Oxford**. who are obliged by Reason hereof to find a Curate to officiate at **Cring**, **Wigington**, and **Long Marston**, and they have demised the Parsonage and the Tythes of these three Parishes to *Henry Guy*, Esq. the Vicaridge is rated in the King's Books at the yearly Value of 77*l.* 13*s.* 4*d.*

This Church is erected about the Middle of the Vill, in the Deanery of **Berkhamsted** in the Diocess of **Lincoln**, 'tis a large pile of Building with a fair Chancel annexed to the East End, and a Tower at the West End thereof, cover'd with Lead, and in the same is a good Ring of six Bells, with a short Spire upon it, the Chancel is fair and large, and about eight Foot in height, and was well wainscoated at the sole Charges of Sir *Richard Anderson* of **Pendley**. Baronet. And there is a fair Monument which is thus Inscribed.

Mane parumper Hospes, quisquis es,
Hic Mortalitatem deposuit
Immortalitate donandus, Henricus Andersonus de **Pendley** *Baronettus, qui cum, sub Christi vexillo, 45 Annos meruisset, (ut Cœlum quod diu Anhelasset opportune arriperet.)*
Lubens fato Cessit
filium interim filiamq; superstites
reliquit utriusq; Sexus Ornamentum.
Ut et Viduam Virtute Pietate
et armore conjugali insignem.
Quam licet secundis Nuptiis
ductam nulli tamen
Secundam Invenit.
Obiit Julii 1653.
Vir amicis Charus, quos intimè
Dilexit, Regi dilectus, quem
Non (vel desertum) deseruit.

His Paternal Coat, and the Arms of Ulster as Baronet is at the Bottom.

A large black Marble also, whereon are Coates of Arms twice *(viz.)* On the right is impaled, *two Coats Quarterly Quartered* (viz.) in the first Escotcheon, *a Cheveron between three Crosses flowered, and a Flower de Luce for Difference, by the Name of* Anderson. The second is *Sable, two single Shack Bolts and one double Argent, by the Name of* Anderson. *The third as the second, the fourth as the first.*

The second Escotcheon is Quartered three Coates, *(viz.)* First, *three Roses, two and one, and in Chief three more.* The second is *Barry of six Pieces, in Cheif three Fowles.* The third, *three Crescents; and the fourth as the first:* Which three Coates quartered are the Arms of the *Cæsar's* of **Hertfordshire**, and were impaled by Sir *Henry Anderson* in Right of his Wife. The Atchievement on the left is the said *Cæsars* alone.

Underneath is written as follows.

Mortalitatis reliquias sub hoc Marmore servari voluit, Jacomina Anderson Henrico Anderson, *Armig. (ut Connubio sic Amore) junctissima, cujus Animam viginti tres annos Corpori Mancipatum in Cœlum transtulit, qui e Cœlo dimisit Deus nec tota abiit Maritum, enim prolebis Gemina ditavit; quam inter Cœlum terramq; portita est duas filiolas (Cœlo Inhians) ad Cœlum præmisit Filium autem Filiamq; Morito superstiti, superstites reliquit, hanc vitam finivit ut æternam Inchoaret.*
Pridie ID. Octob. *anno* S. 1639.

Before the two former is another Gravestone with the Paternal Coat of *Anderson*, and the *Flower de Luce* Difference, thus inscribed.

En Lector,
Annam *et* Mariam Anderson *filiolas ut in eadem. Natura cum Matri charissimæ, ita etiam Morte cum Consortes, quarum Corpora, ut idem uterus conclusit viva sic idem Tumulus continet Mortuas.*

There is also an old Stone, wants Brasses, lyes on the left of the former.

Within the Rail of the Communion Chancel are the rest, (viz.) a large black Marble with the Arms of the *Andersons*, and Difference as aforesaid, on the Dexter Corner and on the Sinister Corner is the same, and another impaled (viz.) the Armes of the *Spencer's*, which is *Quarterly Argent and Gules, the second as the third charged with a Fret Or, over all on a Bend Sable three Escalops of the first.*

Underneath is writtten thus,

Hic placide in Christo obdormiscit in eodem
Christo demum evigilaturus Richardus Anderson
de Pendley*. Eques Auratus, cujus Anima in Cœlos*
Ministerio Angelorum delata Depositi etiam
hujus Cooptationem in consortium ejusdem
Gloriæ per Archangeli imperium expectat.
ob 2° Augusti
A. R. 8.
1632.

Then are the same impaled Arms again.

On the right of the former is another large black Marble, on the Top thereof of the former Arms of *Anderson* and *Anderson* Quartered.

Thus inscribed.

Hic jacet Matrona prestantissima Maria Anderson, Richardi Andersoni *de* Pendley*, Militis, Relicta,* Roberti Spencer *de* Stormelrighton *Baronis filia, Quæ post Maritum Cœlis premissum, post 5 Filios Redditibus satis amplis ditatos; et 10 Filias feliciter elocatas (suis pene omnibus Superstes) ex hac vita Migravit* Julii 14. 1658.

Breve hoc Testimonium (Amoris et Officii ergò posuit) Richardus Anderson Baronettus defunctæ (ex primogenito) Nepos.

Underneath is the Atchievement of the Lord *Spencer* her Father; which is thus blazoned, viz. He bears eight Coats Marshalled in one Shield, as followeth, viz. First, *Quarterly Pearl and Ruby, the second and third charged with a Fret Topaz, over all on a Bend Diamond, three Escallops of the first, being the ancient Coat belonging to this noble Family, as a Branch* descended from the Spencers, Earls of Glocester and Winchester. The second is *Saphire, a Fess Ermine between six Seamews Heads erased Pearl,* born also by the Name of *Spencer.* The third is *Ruby, three Stirrops Leathered in pale Topaz,* bp the Name of *Deverel.* The fourth is *Topaz, on a Cross Ruby five Stars Pearl,* by the Name of *Lincolne.* The fifth is *Pearl, a Cheveron between three Cinquefoils pierced, Ruby,* by the Name of *Warsteed.* The sixth is *Ermine, on a Cheveron Ruby five Beazants, a Crescent in chief of the second,* by the Name of *Graunt.* The seventh is *Pearl on a Bend between two Lyons rampant Diamond, a Wieorne, with the Wings Overt of the first,* by the Name of *Rudings.* The eighth and last is *Party per Cheveron Saphire and Topaz, three Lyoncels passant guardant counterchanged, a Chief Pearl,* by the Name of *Catlyn.* All within the Escocheon.

On the left of Sir *Richard Andersons* lies a large white Marble Stone, which has the Paternal Coat of the *Andersons* with the Difference as before, and thereon is written thus,

Maria Richardi Anderson, *Equit. Aurat. filia secunda, quæ obiit* 21 Maii, *Anno Dom.* 1638.

At the Foot of the former, and next to the Communion Table is a small black Marble, on the top thereof two Coats impaled, viz. The first, *within a Border charged with some sort of Rundles, a Field Checque, on a dexter Canton three Coronets, flores.* The second is the Paternal Coat of the *Andersons;* there under is written.

Here reateth the Body of Richard *Warren,* the Son of *Thomas Warren* and of *Frances* his Wife, who soon hasted from the Cradle to the Grave, and died a quiet Innocent, to live a joyful Saint, the ninth month of his age, being *April, Anno Dom.* 1640.

On the Wall on the North Side of the Communion Chancel within the Rail is a white Marble Table thus inscribed.

Hic cælo rapta Pallam post se reliquit.
Non jam constantior quam olim superstes
Templi Incola, Templi Diva,
Nobilis virgo Maria Anderson,
Digna haud simplici Marmore, sed Legum tabulis condi;
Quæ aliis preceptorum huic vitæ Historiam exhibeant,
Ita quippe cum Deo versata est,
(Hei quam immani pietate)
Ut raro seculi Morbo Tabuerit Cæli desiderio,
Et pro Phthisi exederit Domus sacra Zelum :
Ita cum hominibus versata,
(Quantâ alii instante Morte, aut urgente Morbo Religione)
perinde quasi in Templo, aut sanctorum
Communione ageret
Tertii cujusdam sexus reddidit Sanctitas.
Qualem Angeli jactant, et beatorum cælitum Incolæ
Et quotquot, cælo nupti, terrenis Consortiis repudium
Miserunt.
Hæc illa,
Quæ in vivis, tanquam extra vivorum numerum
In carne Quasi extra Carnem vixerat,
Non jam primum Mortua
Sed mortem confessa est.
Anno ætat. 28. Salutis 1638.

On the South Side of the Communion Chancel, and within the Rail, is a large black Marble, on the Top thereof are the arms of Mr. *Guy,* and hers by the Name of *Wethered,* impaled, *viz.* his being *Gules, seven Lozenges Vareè,* and hers being *Gules, a Cheveron between three Flesh Pots, Or.* Underneath is thus written.

H. S. E.
Venerabilis Matrona,
Domina Elizabetha Guy
Francisci Wethered de Ashlings in Com. Hertf.
Armig. filia, Henrici Guy
de Cring, *Armig. quondam Uxor ;*
Quinquaginta Annorum Vidua,
Qua nec Graviorem, nec Sanctiorem vidit omnis Antiquitas,
nec ætas nostra comitiorem aut jucundiorem.
Vitam suavissimam honestissime Actam,
Cunctis Matronalium virtutum Laudibus insignivit ;
Pietate primævâ in Deum,
Candidissimis Moribus in omnes
Liberalitate Generosâ invicinos,
Beneficentia singulari in egenos,
Authoritate mitissima in famulos
Indulgentiâ prudentissimâ in filium filiamque,
Henricum et Elizabetham,
Filium Obsequentissimum filiam sui quam simillimam,
Ad præclaras has virtutes exercendas,
Quibus erat omnibus exemplo, omnibus in deliciis,
Amplissimum vitæ spacium indulsit Deus.
Quippe quæ, regnante Elizabethâ, *Nata,*
In Gulielmi *et* Maria *Regnum duravit,*
Beatissimis seculis, orta et extincta.
Viridem vegetamque senectam,
Fælici corporis habitudine consecuta,
Eandem presigni temperantia firmavit,
Equanimitate mirâ et Lenissimo ingenio ornavit ;
Nihil erat in illa senectute, quod ipsa incusaret,
Nihil quod Amici non diligerent, simul et Colerent,
Placidissimam hanc vitam
Pari tandem exitu finivit,

Cumque Nonagenaria jam decessisset,
Tanto suorum, bonorumque omnium
Mærore et desiderio elata est,
Ut prematurâ morte abrepta videretur,
Anno Dom. MDCXC.
Matri optimæ et charissimæ
Henricus *filius,* P. P.

Over the last Monument are two Pennons with the Arms of *Guy* and *Wethered* impaled as aforesaid.

There are four more ancient Gravestones in *Tring* Church, whose. Brasses are gone, and had Effigies on them, whereof one is very large, and seems to have been armed Capape, and hath eight Plates on it, where Coats of Arms have been inlayed.

In one of the North Windows are Mr. *Lakes* Arms twice, and *W. L* between them.

In one of the South Windows is, *In a Field Argent, two Bars Nebule Azure, over all on a Bend Gules, a Lyon passant regardant, Or*, by the Name of *Elliot*, who was buried there.

This Parish of *Tring* lieth partly in the *Chiltern* and partly in the Vale of *Alesbury*, the chief place whereof is *Tring*, a Market Town, having one Market weekly on *Friday*, and two Fairs, one on the Feast of St. *Peter*, the other on the Feast of St. *Michael* the Archangel.

LONG MARSTON

IS an Hamlet which was waste Ground in the time of *William* the Conqueror, for there is no Mention of it in *Domesdei Book*; but since it has been improved, it hath been made Part of the Parish of *Tring*, and heretofore was a very fair Seat in the time of *Edw.* III.

Robert Stratford, Parson, &c. granted by Deed to *Christine Bardolfe* the Mannor of *Long Marston* for his Life, the Remainder to Sir *Roger de Puttenham*, Kt. and *Margery* his Wife, and the Heirs of their Bodies begotten, and for Want of such Issue, the Remainder to the Heirs of the said *Roger*. Afterwards it was Parcel of the Possession of the *Wilmots*, who were Ancestors to the late Earls of *Rochester*; then was conveyed to the *Clerks*, who enjoyed it in their Name till it passed to *Thomas Saunders*, by the Marriage of *Jane* the Daughter and Heir of *Clerk*, and remained in that Name as is hereafter set forth in *Puttenham*, to which I refer the Reader; it continued some time in that Name till *Thomas Saunders*, Esq. a Barrister at Law, sold it to *Thomas Bromley*, Citizen of *London*, who died seized hereof, leaving Issue *Nathaniel Bromley*, the present Possessor hereof.

In this Hamlet there is a Church or fair Chappel, where the Dean and Chapter of *Christchurch* in *Oxford*, who have the Impropriation of the Tith of this Place, ought to find a Curate to officiate there for the Ease of the Inhabitants.

CHARITIES.

John Wing gave twenty Nobles to the Chappelwardens to be let out by them, and the Interest to be disposed of among the Poor.
John Cock gave three Pounds in the same manner, and the Interest to be disposed yearly among the Poor.

WIGENTONE, WIGINTON.

WHEN *William* the Conqueror made a Conquest of this Realm and disposed of the Lands of this County, he bestowed this Mannor upon Earl *Moreton*, as appears by *Domesdei Book*, where 'tis recorded, that

Humfridus tenuit de Comes Moreton Wigentone pro septem hidis et dim. **Domesd. Lib. fol. 136. n. 15.** *et tertia parte dimid. hidæ se defendebat. Terra est quinque car. in Dominio est una, et alia potest fieri. Ibi quinque Vill. habentes duo car. et tertia potest fieri, ibi sex cotar. et un. Servus, et un. Molin. de quing; sol. pratum un. car. Silva centum porc. in totis valentiis valet quatuor lib. quando recepit quadragint. sol. tempore Regis Edwardi sex lib. De hoc Manerio Brictric tres hid. et dimid. homo Eddid Reginæ, et Godvin homo Engelrici habuit tres hid et tertia part. dimid. hid. non potuit dare nec vendere extra Creuunga, et hæ sunt pars de septem hid. quas sumpsit Comes Moritonus de Creuunga, et Leuricus homo Osulfi tenuit dimid. hid. et potuit vendere et alia dim. hid. jacuit in Berchamstede.*

Humphry held of Earl *Moreton* Wigentone, it was rated for seven Hides and an half, and the third Part of half an Hide. The arable is five Carucates, in Demeasne is one, and another may be made, there are five Villains having two Carucates, and a third may be made; there are six Cottagers, and one Servant, and one Mill of five Shillings Rent by the Year, Meadow one Carucate, Wood to feed one hundred Hogs; in the whole Value it is worth four Pounds a Year, when he received it forty Shillings, in the time of King *Edward* (the Confessor) six Pounds. *Brictric* a Man (under the Protection) of Queen *Edditha* held three Hides and an half of this Mannor, and *Goewide* a Man (under the Protection) of *Engelric* had three Hides, and the third Part of half an Hide, he could not give nor sell it from *Creung*, and these are Part of seven Hides which Earl *Moreton* took away from *Creung*; and *Leuric* a Man (under the Protection) of *Osulfe* held half an Hide and might sell it, and the other half Hide lay in Berckhamsted.

I have treated before of this Earl *Moreton*, in whose Name this Mannor remained till the time of King *John*, when it came to the Possession of *Eve Brock* and *Margaret* of Apgeton, who levied a Fine of four Hides of Land in this Vill to the Use of *Eve*, but *Gilbert Gernet*, Brother of *Margaret*, forfeited the Land for Felony to the Lord of the Fee, and *Margaret* held it by the Will of *Walter de Keisnow* and *Eve* his Wife; and I find that *Jeoffery de Lucy*, the Lord of the Mannor of Gatesden, was Lord hereof, in whose Name they continued till it came to
Sir *Reginald de Lucy*, who was possest of both of them 2 *H.*VI. from whom it descended to Sir *Jeoffery de Lucy*, who I suppose conveyed it to
Sir *Henry Corbet*, who held it *Anno* 21 *Hen.*VII. and died leaving Issue

(margin notes: Fin. 30 Joh. Mich. Rot. 2, in recept. Scac. / Plit. Hil. 28 Ed. I. Rot in recept. Scac.)

Hund. of
Dacorum.

Rot. Cur. 9 H
VIII. Rot. I
E. VI.

Roger, his Son and Heir within Age, upon which his Guardianship was granted to Sir *Andrew Winsor*, Kt. who by Reason hereof, held a Court for this Mannor in his Name, *Anno* 9 *H*.VIII. but this *Roger Corbet* coming of Age *An*. 1 *Edw*. VI. he then held a Court here in his own Name; and some time after

Rot Cur. 24
Eliz.

John Churchil, Gent. purchased this Mannor, and held a Court here *Anno* 24 *Eliz*. soon after he granted it to

Rot. Cur 30
Eliz.

James Williams, Gent. who held another Court here on the 30th of *Eliz*. in his Name; but in short Space after it was sold again to

Rot Cur. 35
Eliz.

William Palmer, Esq. who held his Court for this Mannor in his Name, in the 35th Year of Queen *Elizabeth*; within some Space following it was conveyed to

Rot. Cur. 40
Eliz.

Thomas Palmer, Esq. who held a Court here *Anno* 40 *Eliz*. from whom it came to

Rot. Cur. 6
J. I.

Edmond Palmer, Citizen and Mercer of **London**, and *Richard Palmer*, Citizen and an Apothecary of **London**, who held a Court here *Anno* 6 *Jac*. I. and they conveyed this Mannor to

Sir *Francis Cheiny*, who held it of the Honour of **Berkhamsted**, and dying seized hereof, it was found that *Francis Cheiny*, was his Cozen and next Heir; which *Francis* sold it to

Rot. Cur. 21
J. I.

Sir *Richard Anderson*, Kt. who held a Court here *Anno* 21 *Jac*. I. and died seized hereof, leaving Issue

Henry Anderson, who was afterwards created Baronet, from whom it is descended to Sir *Richard Anderson*, Bar. who was his Heir, and is the present Lord hereof.

Here is a small Church, and in a Chancel divided from it lyeth a large Gravestone of black Marble thus inscribed.

Here lyeth the Body of *Thomas Weedon* of **Aldiginton** in the County of **Hertford**, Esq; who departed this Life the 14th of *February* 1672. in the 47th year of his age.

On the Wall is this Inscription.

In Memoriam desiderandi usq; Amici Tho. Weedon.

Effare marmor, terra quem virum tegit,
Non mentiente (Quæ soles) Panegyri;
Huic Jura tribuus Mortuo, quicquid bonum est,
Natura quem sic dotibus compleverat
Ut semper esset omnibus Charum Caput:
Pietate constans (Hoc tacenda seculo) .
Animi pusilli nempe Grandis.

There are the Arms of the *Weedons* impaled with the *Crooks*, viz. *Argent, two Bars Gules, three Martlets in cheif Sable*, by the Name of *Weedon*. Second, *Gules, a Fess between six Martlets Argent*, by the Name of *Crook*; there is also the Atchievement of the *Crooks* as is supposed; for the said *Thomas Weedon* married the Daughter of Sir *Henry Crook*.

Here lyeth the Body of *Lucy Weedon*, second Daughter of *Thomas Weedon* the Elder, Esq; who dyed the 28th day of *October*, in the 16th year of her age 1676.

Another Gravestone full of Inscriptions, but only this to be read.

Here lyeth the Body of *Frances* late Wife to *John Spark*, Citizen of London, and Daughter to *William Young* of Bristol, Esq;

PUTEHAM.

LEOFWIN, who was an Earl and Brother to *Harold* and *Gurth*, was possessed of this Vill before the time of the Conquest, and when *William* the Conqueror obtained the Crown, he gave it to the Bishop of Bapeux in France, as appears by *Domesdei Book*, where 'tis recorded, under the Title of *Terra Episcopi Bajocensis*, that

In Creunga *Hundred. Episcopus* Bajocensis *tenuit* Puteham *pro quatuor hidis se defendebat* Rogerius *tenuit de Episcopo. Terra est quatuor car. in Dominio est una et alia potest fieri, ibi quatuor Vill. cum duobus Bordis habentibus duo car. ibi quatuor cotarii, et duo Servi, et duo Molini de decem sol. et octo denar. pratum quatuor car. et quatuor solid. pastura ad pecud. Valet sexagint. sol. quando recepit quadragint. sol. tempore Regis Edw. quatuor lib. hoc Manerium tenuit* Lenvinus *Comes.*

Domesd. Lib. fol. 134.

The Land of the Bishop of Bapeux.

The Bishop of Bapeux, in France, held Puteham in Creung Hundred, it was rated for four Hides, *Roger* held it of the Bishop. The arable is four Carucates, in Demeasne is one and another may be made, there are four Villains with two Bordars having two Carucates, there are four Cottagers, and two Servants, and two Mills of ten Shillings and eight Pence Rent by the Year, Meadow four Carucates, and four Shillings Rent, Common of Pasture for the Cattle; it is worth sixty Shillings a Year, when he received it forty Shillings, in the time of King *Edward* (the Confessor) four Pounds; Earl *Lewin* held this Mannor.

This Vill with the Mannor of Astrop, was Parcel of the Possessions of the *Cheynies*, who descended from *Ralph de Caine*, i. e. *Cheyney*, who came into England with *William* the Conqueror; but I am not able to set forth the particular Lords hereof who were of that Name, for I am a Stranger to that ancient Family, but I find it came from them to the Name of Puttenham, who, I suppose was denominated from this Vill, in whom it continued till it came to *Edmond Puttenham*, the younger Brother of Sir *George Puttenham*, who died without Issue Male, leaving only

Elizabeth, who was his Daughter and Heir, married —— *Skipwith* of Lincolnshire, who was possest of this Mannor in her Right, and shortly after sold it to *John Saunders*, who had

Thomas Saunders, and *Richard Saunders* of Dinton in the County of Bucks, *Thomas* married *Jane* the Daughter and Heir of —— *Clerk* the Owner of Long Marston, which he held in her Right, lived there, and had Issue

John Saunders of Long Marston, who married *Mary* Daughter of Sir *Henry Conisby*, by whom he had Issue

Thomas Saunders of 𝔅𝔢𝔢𝔠𝔥𝔴𝔬𝔬𝔡, who I guess, sold it to *Francis Duncomb* of 𝕴𝖇𝖎𝖓𝖌𝖔 in the County of 𝔅𝔲𝔠𝔨𝔰, Gent. the present Owner hereof.

This Mannor lies within the Leet of 𝖂𝖊𝖘𝖙𝖔𝖓 in the County of 𝔅𝔲𝔠𝔨𝔰, but the Court Baron belongs to *Francis Duncomb*, Gent. Several of the Lands in this Parish with the Quit-rents, (as 'tis supposed) have been formerly sold from the Mannor, which may be the Reason they pay no Rents nor Services at this Day.

THIS Rectory is in the Deanery of 𝔅𝔢𝔯𝔨𝔥𝔞𝔪𝔰𝔱𝔢𝔡, in the Diocess of 𝔏𝔦𝔫𝔠𝔬𝔩𝔫, *Anno* 26 *Hen.* VIII. was rated in the King's Books at the yearly Value of 10*l.* 1*s.* and the Bishop of 𝔏𝔦𝔫𝔠𝔬𝔩𝔫 is the Patron hereof.

RECTOR, *Edward Sculthorp*, M.A.

The Church is small but the Tower is large and beautiful, built with square Stones, and Flints laid in Squares; the Chancel, and a great Part of the House, has been lately erected by Mr. *Sculthorp*, the present Rector.

The Arms of Queen *Eliz.* and King *James* I. are fixed in the Church, and in the Top thereof is very good carved Work, among which a Coat of Arms, bearing a *Field Argent*, a *Cheveron Sable*, *voided between three Chaplets Gules*, which are supposed to be the Arms of the Founder.

CHARITIES.

An Headland given to the Church, which the Churchwardens hold of the Lord of the Mannor for the Benefit of the Church.
Richard Sare gave 5*l.* to the Poor of this Parish.
Henry Stonnel gave 5*l.* to the Poor.
———————— gave 2*l.* 1*s.* to the Poor, which is lost.

COLESHIL, *alias* OULD STOCK,
or STOCK PLACE.

THIS was an ancient and fair Seat, belonging to a small Mannor called 𝔠𝔬𝔩𝔢𝔰𝔥𝔦𝔩, from its Scituation on a Hill of that Name, but heretofore called 𝖔𝖚𝖑𝖉 𝖘𝖙𝖔𝖈𝖐, otherwise 𝖘𝖙𝖔𝖈𝖐-𝖕𝖑𝖆𝖈𝖊, which in the Saxon signifies a Place of Habitation; 'tis an Hamlet belonging partly to 𝔄𝔤𝔪𝔲𝔫𝔡𝔢𝔰𝔥𝔞𝔪 an ancient Saxon Town and Borough in the 𝔠𝔥𝔦𝔩𝔱𝔢𝔯𝔫 Part of 𝔅𝔲𝔠𝔨𝔦𝔫𝔤𝔥𝔞𝔪𝔰𝔥𝔦𝔯𝔢, and partly to 𝔅𝔢𝔞𝔠𝔬𝔫𝔰𝔣𝔢𝔩𝔡, another pretty Town and Thorowfare in that County, so as about two third Parts lie in 𝔅𝔢𝔞𝔠𝔬𝔫𝔰𝔣𝔢𝔩𝔡, the Rest in 𝔄𝔪𝔢𝔯𝔰𝔥𝔞𝔪 Parish. It is a Member of this County of 𝔥𝔢𝔯𝔱𝔣𝔬𝔯𝔡, but dissevered from the Body thereof by the Interposition of its own Parish 𝔄𝔪𝔢𝔯𝔰𝔥𝔞𝔪; and time has well nigh worn out the Remembrance of the Way that joyned this Hamlet to 𝔥𝔢𝔯𝔱𝔣𝔬𝔯𝔡𝔰𝔥𝔦𝔯𝔢: and the Reason why Lands lying in one County, were sometimes laid to the adjacent County was, where the Sheriff of the one County, had Mannors or Lands in his neighbouring County, he would by Composition or Grant from the King, procure his Mannors or Lands to be annexed to his own Jurisdiction, and by Reason hereof, made it Part of his own County, and incorporated it with the same. But others conjecture, that in the time of the Saxon Heptarchy, when continual Encroachments and Invasions were made by those Kings upon their bordering Neighbours, they would incroach Lands which did often lye of Right in anothers County, and under anothers Authority, and having usurped and gotten them, would keep them by Force, and incorporate them with their own County, to which they were adjacent. In Form it is almost quadrangular, the Diameter being somewhat more than a Mile; the Scite is healthy, as lying high and dry; the Soil stony and not very fertile; and perhaps not less than a fourth Part may be Woodland.

This Seat did anciently belong to that great Family of the *Bohun,* Earls of **Hereford** and **Essex,** and was Parcel of the Revenue of *Humphry de Bohun, Anno* 21 *Edw.* I. in whose time *Walter de Agmundesham,* did acknowledge one Messuage, one Carue of Land, twenty Acres of Wood, 30*s.* 1*d. ob.* Rent in the Stock which *William de Cotten* held of *Walter,* for Term of Life to be the Right of *Humphry de Bohun,* Earl of **Hereford** and **Essex,** and his Heirs for ever.

After them the Family of the *Brudenels* succeeded, and lived here successively above two hundred Years ago, and in the time of *H.* VII. *Robert Brudenel* was possest hereof; he was an eminent Lawyer, and received a Writ to be a Serjeant at Law, returnable *tres Mich. An.* 20 *Hen.* VII. and the same Term was constituted by Patent one of the King's Serjeants; he was preferred to be one of the Justices of the *King's Bench* by Patent dated 28th of *April,* 22 *H.* VII. and afterwards was advanced by another Patent dated at **Westminster,** 13th of *April,* 12 *H.* VIII. to be Chief Justice of the Court of *Common Pleas.*

This *Thomas Brudenel* conveyed this Mannor *Anno* 20 *H.*VII. by Fine and Recovery to *William Counser,* who held it sometime in that Family, but at length it came to the Possession of *Edmond Waller,* Gent. who lived in this Seat, and had Issue

Ann, who married *Peter Saltonstall,* the fourth Son of Sir *Richard Saltonstall,* Kt. one of the Aldermen of the City of **London,** 42 *Eliz.* both whom soon after conveyed it to

Sir *Basil Brook* of **Madeley Court** in the County of **Salop,** Kt. but in Consideration of 1860*l.* he sold it to *George Coleshil* of **Ibinghoo Aston** in the County of **Bucks,** Gent. by Deed of Feoffment dated *Anno* 13 *Jac.* I. 1615, in which he conveyed with all Fishing, Free-warrens, Park, Villains with their Sequels, Court Leets, Views of Franc-pledge, and the Perquisites and Profits of Courts, Franchises, Li-

berties, Goods and Chattels of Felons and Fugitives, outlawed Persons, Waifes, Estraies, Fees, Wards, Marriages,
Reliefs, Escheates, Heriots, Fines, &c. and forty three
Shillings and three Pence Chief-rents, for Land holden of
this Mannor.

This *George Coleshil* was an Attorny at Law, who demolished a great Part of this House, and with the Materials thereof built several Tenements, and then sold what he
had left of the Mannor-house and Lands to

James Perrot of 𝔄mersham, who conveyed it to *Henry
Child* of 𝔠oleshil, Yeoman. He soon after granted it to

Henry Child of 𝔄mersham, Yeoman, who had Issue
Henry, and dying seized thereof it came to

Henry the Son, who is the present Possessor of this Mannor, and enjoys the Quit Rent of 43*s.* 3*d.* but the House is
reduced to a Farm House, and the remaining Part of the
Lands doth not now exceed 30*l.* a Year.

The Inhabitants have a Tradition that within this Hamlet stood an ancient Chappel, and there are some Circumstances to confirm it, for the Foundation of an old Building hath been lately ploughed up in a certain Field in this
Vill, and the Farm to which that Field belongs, bears the
Name of *Chappel Farm;* without Doubt this little Spot of
Land hath in some Ages past been a Place of some Note,
for besides those above mentioned, other great Piles of
Building have stood here, but those demolished so long since,
that no Man here can tell what or whose they were, nor
should this Age have known that any such at all had been,
did not the Rubbish and Foundations remaining yet within
the Ground bespeak it. Of these the most considerable is
found within a Wood called 𝔅rainford Wood, at the Entrance into the Hamlet on 𝔄mersham Side; and not far
from that in a ploughed Field stood another smaller Pile,
the Foundation of which being of late Years digged up, discovered very curious paving Work in Manner of Dice
Work. The common Opinion is, that this was a Chappel or
Oratory belonging to the adjacent greater Structure. And
my Author tells me that he was well acquainted with the
Man who some Years since plowed up a Weathercock in
that Place, which was suposed to have stood upon the Chappel; and he farther related to me that he once saw a Piece
of Brass come (about the Bigness of Half a Crown) which
was also ploughed up there, but thro' the Carelessness of
him that had it, 'tis now lost.

HAVING treated of the several Titles of Honour, Degrees, and Ranks of Men as they fell in my Way, I thought
it would be a great Satisfaction in general to shew their Pre-

cedency, which first proceeded from Priority of Birth or of Choice, or Creation among Men of equal Rank or Quality; but in after Ages 'twas given to several Men in Respect of their Honours or of the Eminency of their Offices or Places in the Commonwealth; which Order was observed among the *Jews, Grecians, Romans,* and in most Parts of the more civilized World; among others 'twas settled in England by the Statute of *H.*VIII. which directs the Order of the Nobility, the greater Clergy, and some of the greatest Officers of State; and also by the Patent for the Creation of Baronets, and the Decrees made for the Precedency of them and other Dignities; from which Laws and the Customs of England all Men and Women take their Precedency after this Manner.

Stat. 21 H VIII. cap. 10. Decree Rot. Pat. 10 J. I. pt. 10, nu. 8. Decree Rot. Pat. 14 J. I. pt. 2, nu. 24. 13 Martii. Seld. *Tit. of Hon.* cap. 9, pt. 2, fol. 748.

1 The King and Queen
2 The Prince and Princess of Wales
3 Dukes and Princesses of the royal Blood, who are the Sons, Brothers, Uncles, and Nephews of the King
4 Dutchesses and Princesses of the same royal Blood
5 The Vicegerent
6 The Archbishop of Canterbury
7 The Lord High Chancellor or Lord Keeper of the great Seal
8 The Archbishop of York
9 The Lord High Treasurer of England
10 The Lord President of his Majesty's Privy Council
11 The Lord Privy Seal
12 Other great Officers of Estate after this Order; 1 The Lord Great Chamberlain of England. 2 The Lord High Constable of England. 3 The Lord High Admiral 4 The Lord Steward of the King's Household. 5 The Lord Chamberlain of the King's Household, being of or above the Degree of Barons precede all other Persons of the same Estate and Degree with them
13 Dukes and Dutchesses
14 The eldest Sons of Dukes of the royal Blood and their Ladies
15 Marquisses and Marchionesses
16 Dukes' eldest Sons and their Ladies
17 Earls and Countesses
18 Marquesses' eldest Sons and their Ladies
19 Dukes' younger Sons of the royal Blood and their Ladies
20 Dukes' younger Sons and their Ladies
21 Viscounts and Viscountesses
22 Eldest Sons of Earls and their Ladies
23 Bishops after this Order: 1 The Lord Bishop of London. 2 The Lord Bishop of Durham. 3 The Lord Bishop of Winchester. And 4 All other Bishops after their Ancienties
24 Barons and Baronesses
25 The King's Chief Secretary, being a Bishop or a Baron, shall precede all others of the same Estate and Degree with him
26 Eldest Sons of Viscounts and their Ladies
27 Younger Sons of Earls and their Ladies
28 Eldest Sons of Barons and their Ladies
29 Knights of the most noble Order of the Garter being under the Degree of Barons
30 Knights Bannerets made by the King under his Standard displayed in an Army royal in open War, and their Ladies
31 Knights Privy Councellors
32 The Chancellor of the *Exchequer*
33 The Under Treasurer of the *Exchequer*
34 The Chancellor of the Dutchy
35 The Lord Chief Justice of the Court of *King's Bench.*

36 The Master of the Rolls
37 The Lord Chief Justice of the Court of the *Common Bench*
38 The Lord Chief Baron of the *Exchequer*
39 All the other Justices and Barons of the said Courts being of the De-
    gree of the Coife, according to their Ancienty in their respective
    Courts
40 Baronets and their Ladies
41 Knights Bannerets made by the General in the Absence of the King
    under his Banner in open War, and their Ladies
42 Knights of the Bath and their Ladies
43 Knights Batchelors and their Ladies
44 Serjeants at Law
45 Eldest Sons of the younger Sons of those Gentlemen who are of the
    Degree of, or above, Barons, and their Wives.
46 Eldest Sons of Barouets and their Wives
47 Eldest Sons of Knights of the Bath and their Wives
48 Eldest Sons of Knights Bachelors and their Wives
49 Esquires by Office, as Justices of the Peace, and Sheriffs of Counties,
    &c.
50 The younger Sons of Baronets and their Wives
51 The younger Sons of Knights of the Bath and their Wives
52 The younger Sons of Knights Batchelors and their Wives
53 Gentlemen and Gentlewomen
54 Citizens and Burgesses and their Wives
55 Labourers and Servants.

INDEX

OF THE

NAMES OF THE PLACES, AND MATTERS RELATIVE THERETO, CONTAINED IN THIS BOOK.

The Letters *a* and *b* refer to the first and second Volume. The Mannors are arranged under the Parishes to which they belong.

INDEX

GENERAL SUBJECTS, CONTAINED IN THIS BOOK.

The Letters *a* and *b* refer to the first and second Volumes.

INDEX

OF THE

NAMES OF PERSONS CONTAINED IN THIS BOOK:

DISTINGUISHING ALL THE OLD NAMES TAKEN OUT OF DOMESDEI BOOK,
AND THE FORMER HISTORIES BEFORE THAT TIME, BY ITALICKS.

The Letters *a* and *b* refer to the first and second Volumes.

SIR H. CHAUNCY'S PROPOSALS

FOR THE

PRINTING OF THE HISTORY AND ANTIQUITIES OF HERTFORDSHIRE.

This Treatise having been approved and recommended by several Antiquaries who have had the perusal of it, as a Work that will be both acceptable and useful to the Nobility and Gentry, and give great satisfaction and information to those who have any Estates and Concerns in the said County, and the Publishing of it being very much desired by some Gentlemen; it is now going to be put to the Press, to be printed in as fair a Character, and in [on] as large and as good Paper as this Proposal and Specimen is printed on: but by reason of the Dearness of Paper and Chargeableness of Print, the Book making a great many Sheets, cannot be afforded under Twenty Shillings a Book in Quires to the Subscribers, there being to be printed but 500 Books, which will not be sold after it is printed, to any but to those Gentlemen who subscribe for it, under Twenty-five Shillings a Book. It will make about 140 or 150 Sheets beside the Maps, which will make 38 Sheets more, so that it will be near 170 or 180 Sheets in all, or thereabout. There will be in it a very large Map of the County in two Sheets, a Map of St. Albans, a Map of Hertford, and a Map of Hitching, with 35 Maps of the particular Sheets [Seats] and Monuments of several Gentlemen. It is therefore desired by the Undertakers, that such Gentlemen who are willing to encourage the Bringing of the said Treatise into public Light, do subscribe their Names for such Book or Books as they shall think fit underneath, no Money being expected for them till they are printed and ready to be delivered to them.

J. M. Mullinger, Printer, Bishops Stortford, Herts.

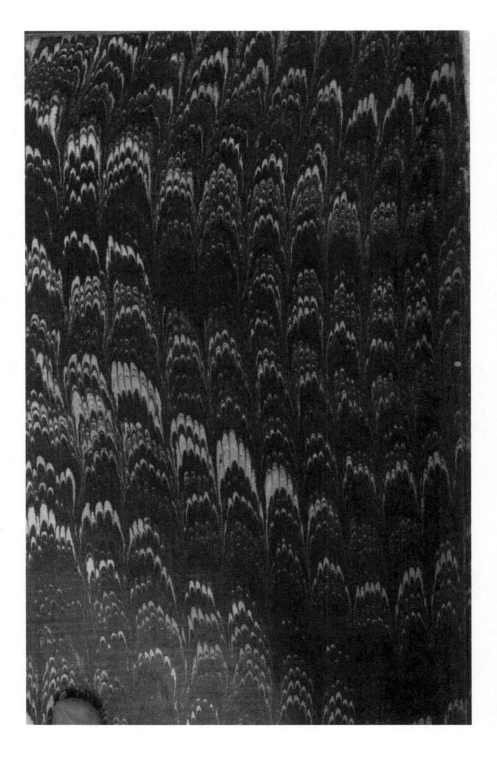

Lightning Source UK Ltd.
Milton Keynes UK
UKHW020306100223
416720UK00002B/379